한국의 토익 수험자 여러분께,

토익 시험은 세계적인 직무 영어능력 평가 시험으로, 지난 40여 년간 비즈니스 현장에서 필요한 영어능력 평가의 기준을 제시해 왔습니다. 토익 시험 및 토익스피킹, 토익라이팅 시험은 세계에서 가장 널리 통용되는 영어능력 검증 시험으로, 160여 개국 14,000여 기관이 토익 성적을 의사결정에 활용하고 있습니다.

YBM은 한국의 토익 시험을 주관하는 ETS 독점 계약사입니다.

ETS는 한국 수험자들의 효과적인 토익 학습을 돕고자 YBM을 통하여 'ETS 토익 공식 교재'를 독점 출간하고 있습니다. 또한 'ETS 토익 공식 교재' 시리즈에 기출문항을 제공해 한국의 다른 교재들에 수록된 기출을 복제하거나 변형한 문항으로 인하여 발생할 수 있는 수험자들의 혼동을 방지하고 있습니다.

복제 및 변형 문항들은 토익 시험의 출제의도를 벗어날 수 있기 때문에 기출문항을 수록한 'ETS 토익 공식 교재'만큼 시험에 잘 대비할 수 없습니다.

'ETS 토익 공식 교재'를 통하여 수험자 여러분의 영어 소통을 위한 노력에 큰 성취가 있기를 바랍니다.

감사합니다.

Dear TOEIC Test Takers in Korea,

The TOEIC program is the global leader in English-language assessment for the workplace. It has set the standard for assessing English-language skills needed in the workplace for more than 40 years. The TOEIC tests are the most widely used English language assessments around the world, with 14,000+ organizations across more than 160 countries trusting TOEIC scores to make decisions.

YBM is the ETS Country Master Distributor for the TOEIC program in Korea and so is the exclusive distributor for TOEIC Korea.

To support effective learning for TOEIC test-takers in Korea, ETS has authorized YBM to publish the only Official TOEIC prep books in Korea. These books contain actual TOEIC items to help prevent confusion among Korean test-takers that might be caused by other prep book publishers' use of reproduced or paraphrased items.

Reproduced or paraphrased items may fail to reflect the intent of actual TOEIC items and so will not prepare test-takers as well as the actual items contained in the ETS TOEIC Official prep books published by YBM.

We hope that these ETS TOEIC Official prep books enable you, as test-takers, to achieve great success in your efforts to communicate effectively in English.

Thank you.

입문부터 실전까지 수준별 학습을 통해 최단기 목표점수 달성!

ETS TOEIC® 공식수험서
스마트 학습 지원

www.ybmbooks.com에서도 무료 MP3를 다운로드 받을 수 있습니다.

ETS 토익 모바일 학습 플랫폼!
ETS 토익기출 수험서 <u>어플</u>

구글플레이   앱스토어

교재 학습 지원	• 교재 해설 강의 • LC 음원 MP3 • 교재/부록 모의고사 채점 분석 • 단어 암기장
부가 서비스	• 데일리 학습(토익 기출문제 풀이) • 토익 최신 경향 무료 특강 • 토익 타이머
모의고사 결과 분석	• 파트별/문항별 정답률 • 파트별/유형별 취약점 리포트 • 전체 응시자 점수 분포도

ETS 토익 학습 전용 온라인 커뮤니티!
ETS TOEIC® Book <u>공식카페</u>

etstoeicbook.co.kr

강사진의 학습 지원	토익 대표강사들의 학습 지원과 멘토링
교재 학습관 운영	교재별 학습게시판을 통해 무료 동영상 강의 등 학습 지원
학습 콘텐츠 제공	토익 학습 콘텐츠와 정기시험 예비특강 업데이트

*toeic.

토익˚ 단기공략

850⁺

LC **RC**

ETS 토익
단기공략 850+

발행인   허문호
발행처   YBM

편집   윤경림, 이혜진, 박효민, 오유진
디자인   DOTS, 이현숙
마케팅   정연철, 박천산, 고영노, 김동진, 박찬경, 김윤하

초판발행   2022년 7월 1일
6쇄발행   2024년 12월 5일

신고일자   1964년 3월 28일
신고번호   제 1964-000003호
주소   서울시 종로구 종로 104
전화   (02) 2000-0515 [구입문의] / (02) 2000-0563 [내용문의]
팩스   (02) 2285-1523
홈페이지   www.ybmbooks.com

ISBN   978-89-17-23795-5

*toeic®

ETS 기출 한국 독점출간

토익® 단기공략 850⁺

LC RC

PREFACE

Dear test taker,

The purpose of this book is to help you prepare for success on the TOEIC Listening and Reading Test. A good TOEIC score is a helpful tool to use when you need to demonstrate your proficiency in communicating in English to colleagues and clients in Korea and around the world. Now more than ever, English proficiency is a tool that can yield great professional rewards.

This book provides practical steps that you can use right now, in a two-week or four-week program of study, to prepare for the TOEIC test. Use your TOEIC test score as a respected professional credential and a sign that you are ready to take your career to the next level. Your TOEIC score is recognized globally as evidence of your English-language proficiency.

With <ETS 토익 단기공략 850+>, you can make sure you have the best and most thorough preparation for the TOEIC test. This book contains key study points that will familiarize you with the test format and content, and you will be able to practice at your own pace. The test questions are created by the same test specialists who develop the TOEIC test itself, and the book contains questions taken from actual TOEIC tests.

Here are some features of <ETS 토익 단기공략 850+>.

- · This book contains carefully selected questions taken from actual TOEIC tests that were chosen specifically for their advanced level of difficulty.
- · The content contained in this book is suitable for two-week or four-week short-term study plans.
- · You will hear the same voice actors that are used for the actual TOEIC Test.
- · Key study points are provided to help you achieve your target score with the least amount of time and effort.

In preparing for the TOEIC test with <ETS 토익 단기공략 850+>, you can be confident that you have a solid resource at hand and are taking the best approach to maximizing your TOEIC test score. Use <ETS 토익 단기공략 850+> to become familiar with the test, including actual test tasks, content, and format. You will be well prepared to show the world what you know by taking the test and receiving your score report.

We hope that you will find this high-quality resource to be of the utmost use, and we wish you all the very best success.

출제기관이 만든
점수대별
단기 완성 전략서!

고난도 최신 기출 문항으로 완성된 단기 완성 시리즈
고난도 기출 문항뿐만 아니라 토익 출제기관인 ETS가 정기시험과 동일한 유형 및 난이도로
개발한 문제들로 구성된 고품질의 전략서이다.

단기 목표 달성에 최적화된 구성
LC와 RC를 한권으로 구성하고, 목표 점수 달성에 필요한 핵심 내용만 수록하여 학습 부담
을 최소화 하였다.

정기시험과 동일한 성우 음원
토익 정기시험 성우가 실제 시험과 동일한 속도와 발음으로 직접 녹음하였으므로 실전에 완
벽하게 대비할 수 있다.

ETS만이 제시할 수 있는 체계적인 공략법
토익 각 파트에 대한 이해를 높이고 원하는 점수를 달성하기 위한 체계적인 공략법을 제시
하고 있다.

토익 최신 경향을 반영한 명쾌한 분석과 해설
이 책의 모든 토익 문항은 최신 출제 경향을 완벽하게 분석하고 반영하여 고득점을 달성하
게 해줄 해법을 낱낱이 제시하고 있다.

CONTENTS

LC

PART 1

INTRO — 018
UNIT 1 인물 중심 사진 — 020
UNIT 2 사물·풍경 중심 사진 — 024
PART 1 만점 빈출 표현 — 028

PART 2

INTRO — 034
UNIT 3 Who / What · Which 의문문 — 036
UNIT 4 When / Where 의문문 — 040
UNIT 5 Why / How 의문문 — 044
UNIT 6 일반 / 선택 의문문 — 048
UNIT 7 부정 / 부가 의문문 — 052
UNIT 8 요청 · 제안문 / 평서문 — 056
PART 2 만점 빈출 표현 — 060

PART 3

INTRO — 066
UNIT 9 주제 · 목적 / 화자 · 장소 문제 — 068
UNIT 10 세부 사항 / 문제점 · 걱정거리 문제 — 074
UNIT 11 요청 · 제안 / 다음에 할 일 문제 — 080
UNIT 12 의도 파악 / 시각 정보 연계 문제 — 086
PART 3 만점 빈출 표현 — 093

PART 4

INTRO — 098
UNIT 13 전화 메시지 — 100
UNIT 14 공지 / 회의 — 104
UNIT 15 설명 / 소개 — 108
UNIT 16 광고 / 방송 — 112
PART 4 만점 빈출 표현 — 116

RC

PART 5

INTRO		122
UNIT 1	명사	124
UNIT 2	대명사	130
UNIT 3	형용사＆부사	138
UNIT 4	전치사	148
UNIT 5	자·타동사/수 일치/태/시제	154
UNIT 6	to부정사＆동명사	166
UNIT 7	분사＆분사구문	174
UNIT 8	부사절 접속사＆등위·상관접속사	180
UNIT 9	관계사	186
UNIT 10	명사절 접속사	192
UNIT 11	ETS 기출 어휘	198

PART 6

INTRO		220
UNIT 12	문법 문제	222
UNIT 13	어휘 문제	228
UNIT 14	접속부사 문제	234
UNIT 15	문장 고르기 문제	240

PART 7

INTRO		248
UNIT 16	주제/목적 문제	250
UNIT 17	세부 사항 문제	254
UNIT 18	Not/True 문제	258
UNIT 19	추론/암시 문제	262
UNIT 20	동의어 문제	266
UNIT 21	의도 파악 문제	270
UNIT 22	문장 삽입 문제	274
UNIT 23	연계 문제	278

TOEIC 소개

TOEIC

Test of English for international Communication(국제적 의사소통을 위한 영어 시험)의 약자로, 영어가 모국어가 아닌 사람들이 일상생활 또는 비즈니스 현장에서 꼭 필요한 실용적 영어 구사 능력을 갖추었는가를 평가하는 시험이다.

시험 구성

구성	PART	유형		문항 수	시간	배점
Listening	Part 1	사진 묘사		6	45분	495점
	Part 2	질의 응답		25		
	Part 3	짧은 대화		39		
	Part 4	짧은 담화		30		
Reading	Part 5	단문 빈칸 채우기		30	75분	495점
	Part 6	장문 빈칸 채우기		16		
	Part 7	독해	단일 지문	29		
			이중 지문	10		
			삼중 지문	15		
Total	7 Parts			200문항	120분	990점

평가 항목

LC	RC
단문을 듣고 이해하는 능력	읽은 글을 통해 추론해 생각할 수 있는 능력
짧은 대화체 문장을 듣고 이해하는 능력	장문에서 특정한 정보를 찾을 수 있는 능력
비교적 긴 대화체에서 주고받은 내용을 파악할 수 있는 능력	글의 목적, 주제, 의도 등을 파악하는 능력
장문에서 핵심이 되는 정보를 파악할 수 있는 능력	뜻이 유사한 단어들의 정확한 용례를 파악하는 능력
구나 문장에서 화자의 목적이나 함축된 의미를 이해하는 능력	문장 구조를 제대로 파악하는지, 문장에서 필요한 품사, 어구 등을 찾는 능력

※ 성적표에는 전체 수험자의 평균과 해당 수험자가 받은 성적이 백분율로 표기되어 있다.

수험 정보

시험 접수 방법

한국 토익 위원회 사이트(www.toeic.co.kr)에서 시험일 약 2개월 전부터
온라인으로 접수 가능

시험장 준비물

신분증	규정 신분증만 가능 (주민등록증, 운전면허증, 기간 만료 전의 여권, 공무원증)
필기구	연필, 지우개 (볼펜이나 사인펜은 사용 금지)

시험 진행 시간

09:20	입실 (9:50 이후 입실 불가)
09:30 ~ 09:45	답안지 작성에 관한 오리엔테이션
09:45 ~ 09:50	휴식
09:50 ~ 10:05	신분증 확인
10:05 ~ 10:10	문제지 배부 및 파본 확인
10:10 ~ 10:55	듣기 평가 (LISTENING TEST)
10:55 ~ 12:10	독해 평가 (READING TEST)

TOEIC 성적 확인

시험일로부터 10~11일 후,
오전 6시부터 인터넷과 ARS(060-800-0515)로 성적 확인 가능
성적표는 우편이나 온라인으로 발급 받을 수 있다. 우편으로 발급 받을 경우 성적 발표 후 대략
일주일이 소요되며, 온라인 발급을 선택하면 유효기간 내에 홈페이지에서 본인이 직접 1회에 한해
무료 출력할 수 있다. TOEIC 성적은 시험일로부터 2년간 유효하다.

토익 점수

TOEIC 점수는 듣기 영역(LC)과 읽기 영역(RC)을 합계한 점수로 5점 단위로 구성되며 총점은
990점이다. TOEIC 성적은 각 문제 유형의 난이도에 따른 점수 환산표에 의해 결정된다.

LC 출제 경향 분석

PART 1

문제 유형 및 출제 비율 (평균 문항 수)

사람을 주어로 하는 사람 묘사 문제가 가장 많은 비중을 차지하며 사람 / 사물 혼합 문제, 사물 / 풍경 묘사 문제가 각각 그 다음을 이룬다.

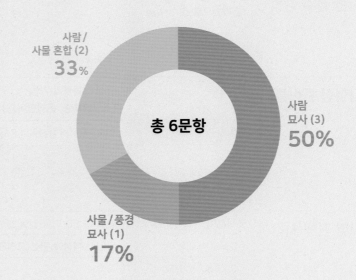

사람/
사물 혼합 (2)
33%

사람
묘사 (3)
50%

총 6문항

사물 / 풍경
묘사 (1)
17%

PART 2

문제 유형 및 출제 비율 (평균 문항 수)

의문사 의문문이 거의 절반가량을 차지하며 일반 의문문과 평서문이 그 다음을 이룬다. 부가 / 부정 / 선택 의문문은 평균 2문항씩 출제되며 간접 의문문은 간혹 1문제 출제된다.

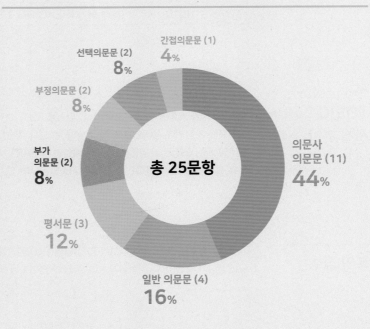

선택의문문 (2)
8%

간접의문문 (1)
4%

부정의문문 (2)
8%

부가
의문문 (2)
8%

총 25문항

의문사
의문문 (11)
44%

평서문 (3)
12%

일반 의문문 (4)
16%

PART 3

문제 유형 및 출제 비율
(평균 문항 수)

세부 사항을 묻는 문제가 가장 많은 비중을 차지하며 주제, 목적, 화자, 장소 문제, 다음에 할 일, 미래 정보 문제가 그 다음을 차지한다. 문제점 및 걱정거리 문제는 출제 빈도가 다소 낮다. 의도 파악 문제와 시각 정보 연계 문제는 각각 2문항, 3문항 고정 비율로 출제된다.

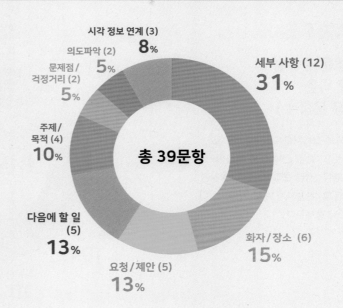

시각 정보 연계 (3) 8%
의도파악 (2) 5%
문제점 / 걱정거리 (2) 5%
세부 사항 (12) 31%
주제 / 목적 (4) 10%
총 39문항
다음에 할 일 (5) 13%
요청 / 제안 (5) 13%
화자 / 장소 (6) 15%

PART 4

지문 유형 및 출제 비율
(평균 지문 수)

전화 메시지와 공지, 안내, 회의 발췌록이 가장 많이 출제된다. 광고, 방송, 보도가 그 다음을 차지하며 여행, 견학, 관람, 인물, 강연, 설명은 출제 빈도가 다소 낮다.

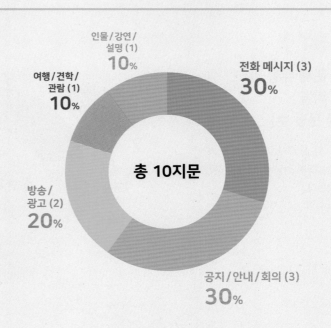

인물 / 강연 / 설명 (1) 10%
여행 / 견학 / 관람 (1) 10%
전화 메시지 (3) 30%
총 10지문
방송 / 광고 (2) 20%
공지 / 안내 / 회의 (3) 30%

RC 출제 경향 분석

PART 5

문법 문제 유형 및 출제 비율 (평균 문항 수)

전치사와 접속사를 구분하는 문제와 동사 문제, 품사 문제 출제 비중이 가장 높다. 기타 문법에서는 준동사가 1~2문항, 관계사가 매회 거의 1문항씩 출제된다.

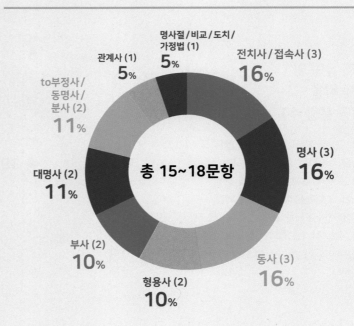

관계사 (1)
5%

명사절 / 비교 / 도치 / 가정법 (1)
5%

전치사 / 접속사 (3)
16%

to부정사 / 동명사 / 분사 (2)
11%

명사 (3)
16%

대명사 (2)
11%

총 15~18문항

동사 (3)
16%

부사 (2)
10%

형용사 (2)
10%

PART 5

어휘 문제 유형 및 출제 비율 (평균 문항 수)

전치사, 명사, 부사 어휘 문제가 가장 많이 출제되며 형용사, 동사 어휘가 그 뒤를 잇는다.

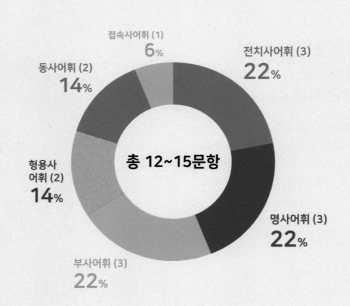

접속사어휘 (1)
6%

동사어휘 (2)
14%

전치사어휘 (3)
22%

형용사어휘 (2)
14%

총 12~15문항

명사어휘 (3)
22%

부사어휘 (3)
22%

PART 6

문제 유형 및
출제 비율
(평균 문항 수)

문법과 어휘 비중이 비슷하게 출제되며
접속부사는 1~2문항 출제된다. 문장
삽입 문제는 4문항 고정 비율로
출제된다.

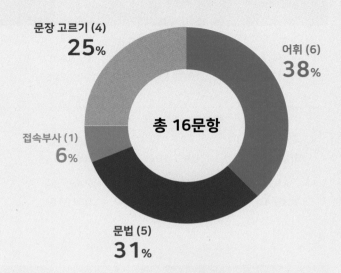

문장 고르기 (4)
25%

어휘 (6)
38%

접속부사 (1)
6%

총 16문항

문법 (5)
31%

PART 7

문제 유형 및
출제 비율
(평균 문항 수)

세부 사항 문제가 가장 높은 비율을
차지하며 추론/암시 문제와 (NOT)
mention/true 문제가 그 다음으로
출제율이 높다. 주어진 문장 넣기와
의도 파악 문제는 각각 2문항씩
고정 비율로 출제된다. 이중, 삼중
지문에서는 연계 문제가 8문항 정도
출제된다.

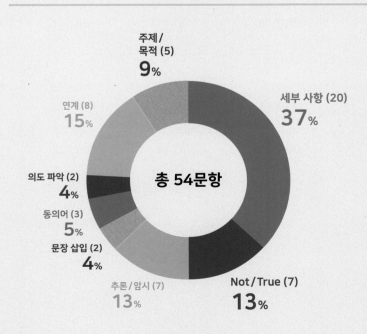

주제 /
목적 (5)
9%

연계 (8)
15%

세부 사항 (20)
37%

의도 파악 (2)
4%

동의어 (3)
5%

문장 삽입 (2)
4%

총 54문항

추론/암시 (7)
13%

Not/True (7)
13%

2주 완성 플랜

초단기에 고득점을 달성하고자 하는 중·고급 수험생을 위한 2주 완성 플랜

	DAY 1	DAY 2	DAY 3	DAY 4	DAY 5
LC	PART 1 UNIT 1&2	PART 2 UNIT 3&4	PART 2 UNIT 5&6	PART 2 UNIT 7&8	PART 3 UNIT 9
RC	PART 5 UNIT 1&2	PART 5 UNIT 3&4	PART 5 UNIT 5&6	PART 5 UNIT 7&8	PART 5 UNIT 9&10
	PART 7 UNIT 16	PART 7 UNIT 17	PART 7 UNIT 18	PART 7 UNIT 19	PART 7 UNIT 20

	DAY 6	DAY 7	DAY 8	DAY 9	DAY 10
LC	PART 3 UNIT 10	PART 3 UNIT 11	PART 3 UNIT 12	PART 4 UNIT 13&14	PART 4 UNIT 15&16
RC	PART 5 UNIT 11	PART 6 UNIT 12	PART 6 UNIT 13	PART 6 UNIT 14	PART 6 UNIT 15
	PART 7 UNIT 21	PART 7 UNIT 22	PART 7 UNIT 23	PART 7 UNIT 23	PART 7 UNIT 23

4주 완성 플랜

짧은 기간 차근차근 고득점을 달성하고자 하는 중·고급 수험생을 위한 4주 완성 플랜

	DAY 1	DAY 2	DAY 3	DAY 4	DAY 5
LC	PART 1 UNIT 1	PART 1 UNIT 2	PART 1 REVIEW	PART 2 UNIT 3	PART 2 UNIT 4
RC	PART 5 UNIT 1	PART 5 UNIT 2	PART 5 UNIT 3	PART 5 UNIT 4	PART 5 UNIT 5

	DAY 6	DAY 7	DAY 8	DAY 9	DAY 10
LC	PART 2 UNIT 5	PART 2 UNIT 6	PART 2 UNIT 7	PART 2 UNIT 8	PART 2 REVIEW
RC	PART 5 UNIT 6	PART 5 UNIT 7	PART 5 UNIT 8	PART 5 UNIT 9	PART 5 UNIT 10

	DAY 11	DAY 12	DAY 13	DAY 14	DAY 15
LC	PART 3 UNIT 9	PART 3 UNIT 10	PART 3 UNIT 11	PART 3 UNIT 12	PART 3 REVIEW
RC	PART 5 UNIT 11	PART 6 UNIT 12	PART 6 UNIT 13	PART 6 UNIT 14	PART 6 UNIT 15

	DAY 16	DAY 17	DAY 18	DAY 19	DAY 20
LC	PART 4 UNIT 13	PART 4 UNIT 14	PART 4 UNIT 15	PART 4 UNIT 16	PART 4 REVIEW
RC	PART 7 UNIT 16&17	PART 7 UNIT 18&19	PART 7 UNIT 20&21	PART 7 UNIT 22&23	PART 7 UNIT 23

PART 1
사진 묘사

INTRO

UNIT 1 | 인물 중심 사진

UNIT 2 | 사물·풍경 중심 사진

PART 1 만점 빈출 표현

PART 1 사진 묘사

총 6문항

주어진 사진을 가장 잘 설명한 것을 고르는 문제 유형으로, 사람이나 사물의 동작이나 상태, 풍경 등을 묘사하는 문장이 사진 당 4개씩 나온다.

◆ 기본 풀이 전략

📋 문제지

🔊 음원

Number 1. Look at the picture marked number 1 in your test book.

(A) They're carrying some buckets.
(B) They're locking a cabinet.
(C) They're holding a box.
(D) They're using a copy machine.

STEP 1 문제 듣기 전 사진 파악하기

등장 인물: 여자 2명
동작 / 자세 / 상태: holding, carrying, wearing a skirt, wearing glasses
주변 / 사물: door, containers, boxes
장소 / 배경: indoors, office

STEP 2 오답 소거하며 정답 찾기

(A) X 양동이를 나르고 있는 모습이 아니다.
(B) X 캐비닛을 잠그고 있는 모습이 아니다.
(C) O 상자를 들고 있는 모습이다.
(D) X 복사기를 사용하고 있는 모습이 아니다.

◆ 최신 출제 경향

❶ 사진 유형	인물 등장 사진이 주를 이루며, 사물 / 풍경 사진은 보통 후반에 1~2문항 정도 출제된다.
❷ 사진 장소	실내 업무 및 실외 작업 장소의 비중이 높고, 상점, 거리, 공원 등 다양한 장소도 등장한다.
❸ 정답의 시제와 태	현재 진행 시제(be + -ing)가 가장 많이 사용되며, 현재 완료 수동태(have + been + p.p.)와 단순 현재 수동태(be + p.p.)도 자주 나온다.
❹ 보기의 구성	인물 묘사 보기만 있는 문제 〉 인물 묘사, 사물 묘사 보기가 섞인 문제 〉 사물 / 풍경 묘사 보기만 있는 문제 순으로 많이 출제된다.

◆ 오답 유형

1. 사진에 없는 사람/사물을 언급하는 경우

사진에 없는 사물이나 사람 어휘에 주의한다.

오답 She's looking at a **menu**.
여자가 메뉴를 보고 있다.

정답 She's having a meal in a restaurant.
여자가 식당에서 식사하고 있다.

2. 잘못된 동작/상태를 묘사하는 경우

인물 묘사에서 자주 등장하는 오답 유형으로, 동작이나 상태를 혼동시키거나 잘못 묘사한 동사 어휘가 나온다.

오답 They're **removing** their aprons.
사람들이 앞치마를 벗고 있다.

정답 One of the people is holding a cart handle.
한 사람이 카트 손잡이를 잡고 있다.

3. 잘못된 위치를 묘사하는 경우

위치만 틀리게 묘사하여 오답을 유도하는 경우가 있으므로, 끝까지 확실하게 듣는다.

오답 A lamp is **in the middle of a room**.
램프가 방 한가운데에 있다.

정답 A wall is decorated with a patterned design.
벽이 무늬가 있는 디자인으로 장식되어 있다.

4. 혼동 어휘를 사용하는 경우

유사 발음, 다의어 등을 이용해 순간적인 혼동을 유도하는 오답이 등장한다.

오답 She's **working** on a road.
여자가 도로에서 작업을 하고 있다.

정답 She's pushing a bicycle.
여자가 자전거를 밀고 있다.

UNIT 1 인물 중심 사진

인물 사진은 출제 비중이 높으며, 사람의 동작이나 상태를 be + -ing 형태로 묘사하는 경우가 대부분이다.

| 고득점 | 전략 | 1인 등장 사진 | ● 출제비율 2~3문항 / 6문항 |

1. **사람의 동작을 설명하는 수식어구가 늘어나는 추세이다. 동사 하나만으로는 섣불리 판단 금지!**
   - 이어지는 목적어나 수식어구 때문에 혼동되는 경우가 있으니 끝까지 잘 듣도록 한다.

2. **사진에 없는 사물을 언급하면 바로 오답 소거한다.**

(A) The man is reading <u>a sign</u> on the building. → 없는 사물
(B) The man is **walking past some newspaper racks**. → 정답
(C) The man is <u>stacking</u> newspapers on the walkway. → 동작 오류
(D) The man is <u>tying a string</u> around a box. → 동작 오류

🎧 850_P1_01

(A) 남자가 건물 간판을 읽고 있다.
(B) 남자가 신문 선반을 지나가고 있다.
(C) 남자가 보도 위에 신문을 쌓고 있다.
(D) 남자가 상자를 끈으로 묶고 있다.

만점 TIP 동작과 상태 표현을 혼동하지 말자!

wearing vs. **putting[trying] on**
입은 상태   입는 동작

wearing an apron (O)
putting on an apron (X)

riding vs. **getting on**
탄 상태   타려는 동작

riding a bicycle (O)
getting on a bicycle (X)

| **ETS 유형 연습** | 음원을 듣고 적절한 응답을 고르세요. | 🎧 850_P1_02 정답 및 해설 p.002 |

1.

(A) (B) (C) (D)

2.

(A) (B) (C) (D)

3.

(A) (B) (C) (D)

| 고득점 | 전략 | **2인 이상 등장 사진** | ● 출제비율 2~3문항/6문항 |

1. **사람들의 공통 동작과 개별 동작에 주의한다.**
   - 공통/상호 동작이나 한 명의 두드러지는 개별 동작을 묘사하는 경우가 많다.
2. **보기에 서로 다른 주어가 제시되므로 주어를 듣고 해당 인물에 주목한다.**
   - 1인 주어, 복수 주어, 사물 주어 등이 모두 등장할 수 있다.

 850_P1_03

(A) The people are <u>setting</u> the table. → 동작 오류
(B) The people **are gathered in a lobby**. → 정답
(C) One of the people is pointing at <u>some framed artwork</u>. → 목적어 오류
(D) One of the people is <u>folding up a newspaper</u>. → 동작 오류

(A) 사람들이 식탁을 차리고 있다.
(B) 사람들이 로비에 모여 있다.
(C) 사람들 중 한 명이 미술품 액자를 가리키고 있다.
(D) 사람들 중 한 명이 신문을 접고 있다.

| 만점 TIP | 〈사물 주어 + 현재 진행 수동태(be + being + p.p.)〉가 사람의 행동을 묘사하는 구문이 점점 더 많이 등장하고 있다. |

<u>A bicycle</u> **is being worked** on. 자전거가 손보아지고 있다.
<u>They</u> are working on a bicycle. 사람들이 자전거를 손보고 있다.

| **ETS 유형 연습** | 음원을 듣고 적절한 응답을 고르세요. | 850_P1_04 정답 및 해설 p.002 |

1.

(A) (B) (C) (D)

2.

(A) (B) (C) (D)

3.

(A) (B) (C) (D)

ETS 고득점 실전 문제

1.

(A)　(B)　(C)　(D)

2.

(A)　(B)　(C)　(D)

3.

(A)　(B)　(C)　(D)

4.

(A)　(B)　(C)　(D)

5.

(A)　(B)　(C)　(D)

6.

(A)　(B)　(C)　(D)

7.

(A)   (B)   (C)   (D)

8.

(A)   (B)   (C)   (D)

9.

(A)   (B)   (C)   (D)

10.

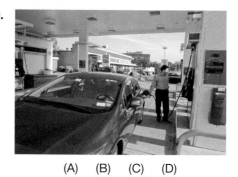

(A)   (B)   (C)   (D)

11.

(A)   (B)   (C)   (D)

12.

(A)   (B)   (C)   (D)

사물·풍경 중심 사진

사물·풍경 사진은 보기에 다양한 주어와 동사 형태가 등장하여 난이도가 높은 편이다. 사물의 위치 및 상태 또는 풍경을 묘사하는 경우가 대부분이지만 인물 묘사가 포함되는 경우도 많다.

고득점 전략 | 사물·풍경 중심 사진 🔵 출제비율 1~2문항/6문항

1. ⟨be + p.p.⟩, ⟨have been + p.p.⟩ 구문이 주로 나오며, 위치를 표현할 때는 **There is / are** 구문도 등장한다.
2. ⟨be + being + p.p.⟩는 사람의 동작을 묘사하는 표현이므로 사람이 없는 사진에서는 대부분 오답이다.

(A) A printer has been put on a chair. → 위치 오류
(B) Computer monitors are lined up in a row. → 모니터는 한 대만 있음
(C) Notices have been posted on a bulletin board. → 정답
(D) Documents have been left on top of a desk. → 없는 사물

🎧 850_P1_06

(A) 프린터가 의자 위에 놓여 있다.
(B) 컴퓨터 모니터들이 일렬로 정렬되어 있다.
(C) 게시판에 공지들이 붙어 있다.
(D) 서류들이 책상 위에 놓여져 있다.

만점 TIP | 풍경 사진 묘사에는 다음과 같은 어휘가 단순 현재형으로 주로 나온다.

① 도로, 길, 다리 등 표현 동사
run/extend: 길이 나 있다/뻗어 있다
lead to/wind: ~로 이어지다/굽이치다
cross/divide[separate]: 가로지르다/나누다

A path leads to the ocean. 길이 바다로 이어진다.

② 건물 및 주변 풍경과 관련된 동사
overlook/face: 내려다보다/마주 보다[향하다]
surround: 둘러싸다

Some benches face a garden. 벤치가 정원을 향해 있다.

ETS 유형 연습 | 음원을 듣고 적절한 응답을 고르세요. 🎧 850_P1_07 정답 및 해설 p.006

1.

(A) (B) (C) (D)

2.

(A) (B) (C) (D)

3.

(A) (B) (C) (D)

| 고득점 | 전략 | 사람/사물·풍경 혼합 사진 | ● 출제비율 1~2문항/6문항 |

1. 사람 묘사 보기와 사물·풍경 묘사 보기가 함께 제시되는 경우가 많다.
2. 사물 주어지만 사람의 동작을 묘사하는 표현에 주의한다.
   - be being p.p는 대부분 사람이 사물에 어떤 동작을 하고 있다는 의미이다.

(A) Some workers are raking the soil. → 정답
(B) A lawn is being mowed. → 동작 오류(잔디가 보이지도 않음)
(C) Some gardeners are trimming bushes. → 동작 오류
(D) The windows of a building are being cleaned. → 동작 오류

🎧 850_P1_08

(A) 작업자들이 흙을 갈퀴로 긁어 모으고 있다.
(B) 잔디가 깎이고 있다.
(C) 정원사 몇 명이 덤불을 다듬고 있다.
(D) 건물의 창문이 청소되고 있다.

만점
TIP 사람의 동작을 묘사하는 〈be + being + p.p.〉 vs. 사물의 상태를 나타내는 〈be + being + p.p.〉

A document is being photocopied.
서류가 복사되고 있다.

Fruit is being displayed in a market.
과일이 시장에 진열되어 있다.

→ be being displayed(진열되어 있다), be being grown(재배되고 있다) 등은 사람의 동작을 묘사하는 것이 아니라 사물의 상태를 설명하는 것이므로 혼동하지 않도록 주의하자.

ETS 유형 연습 | 음원을 듣고 적절한 응답을 고르세요. 🎧 850_P1_09 정답 및 해설 p.007

1.

(A) (B) (C) (D)

2.

(A) (B) (C) (D)

3.

(A) (B) (C) (D)

1.

(A)　(B)　(C)　(D)

2.

(A)　(B)　(C)　(D)

3.

(A)　(B)　(C)　(D)

4.

(A)　(B)　(C)　(D)

5.

(A)　(B)　(C)　(D)

6.

(A)　(B)　(C)　(D)

7.

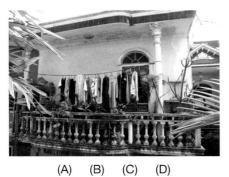

(A)   (B)   (C)   (D)

8.

(A)   (B)   (C)   (D)

9.

(A)   (B)   (C)   (D)

10.

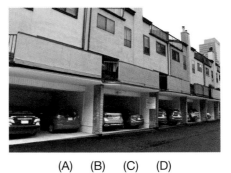

(A)   (B)   (C)   (D)

11.

(A)   (B)   (C)   (D)

12.

(A)   (B)   (C)   (D)

만점 빈출 표현

◆ 손 동작

securing some equipment to a post
기둥에 장비를 고정하고 있다

wiping off a telephone
전화기를 닦고 있다

rolling up a poster 포스터를 둘둘 말고 있다

holding an oar 노를 잡고 있다

rearranging some furniture
가구를 재배치하고 있다

adjusting the glasses
안경을 고쳐 쓰고 있다

setting a plastic bin on a shelf
선반에 플라스틱 통을 놓고 있다

taking an item out of a refrigerator
냉장고에서 물건을 꺼내고 있다

grabbing a handful of carrots
당근을 한 움큼 움켜쥐고 있다

putting some items in a bag
가방에 물건들을 넣고 있다

reaching for a light switch
전등 스위치를 향해 손을 뻗고 있다

pointing at a location on a map
지도 위의 지점을 가리키고 있다

loading a cart 카트에 짐을 싣고 있다

unloading a truck 트럭에서 짐을 내리고 있다

◆ 발 동작

walking under an archway
아치형 입구 아래로 걸어가고 있다

entering a storeroom
창고로 들어가고 있다

stepping down from a train
열차에서 내리고 있다

strolling on a beach 해변을 거닐고 있다

approaching an entrance
입구 쪽으로 다가가고 있다

◆ 착용하는 동작 vs. 착용한 상태

putting on a jacket
재킷을 입고 있는 중이다 (동작)

tying an apron 앞치마를 매고 있다 (동작)

untying a cloth apron
천 앞치마를 풀고 있다 (동작)

wearing long-sleeved shirts
긴 소매 셔츠를 입고 있다 (상태)

buttoning his coat 외투 단추를 채우고 있다 (동작)

removing[taking off] a safety vest
안전 조끼를 벗고 있다 (동작)

◆ 시선

staring out a window 창밖을 보고 있다

studying the menu 메뉴를 살펴보고 있다

facing a fireplace 벽난로를 마주보고 있다

looking into a cabinet
캐비닛 안을 들여다보고 있다

inspecting the tires on a vending cart
가판 수레의 타이어를 점검하고 있다

examining some safety glasses
보안경을 검사하고 있다

◆ 자세

standing by a podium
연단 옆에 서 있다

bending over a bicycle
자전거 위로 몸을 굽히고 있다

resting her hand on a bench
손을 벤치 위에 얹고 있다

leaning against the trunk of a tree
나무 몸통에 기대어 있다.

lying on the grass
잔디에 누워 있다

holding onto a railing 난간을 잡고 있다

kneeling down 무릎을 꿇고 있다

◆ 사무실 / 회의실 / 강의실 / 강당

arranging some papers
서류를 정리하고 있다

sorting papers 서류를 분류하고 있다

filing a document 문서를 파일로 철하고 있다

reaching for a telephone
전화기에 손을 뻗고 있다

refilling a copy machine with paper
복사기에 종이를 다시 채우고 있다

placing a binder on a table
바인더를 테이블 위에 놓고 있다

passing out pens 펜을 나누어 주고 있다

be seated in a circle 둥그렇게 둘러앉아 있다

standing next to an entrance
입구 옆에 서 있다

adjusting a microphone
마이크를 조절하고 있다

Some chairs are occupied.
의자 몇 개가 사용되고 있는 중이다.

Some chairs are stacked in a corner.
의자 몇 개가 모퉁이에 쌓여 있다.

A drawer has been left open.
서랍이 열려 있다.

A desk is covered with papers.
책상이 서류로 덮여 있다.

Two computers are set up next to each other. 컴퓨터 두 대가 나란히 설치되어 있다.

Some notices have been posted to a bulletin board.
공고문들이 게시판에 붙어 있다.

Some folders have been placed on top of a file cabinet.
폴더들이 파일 캐비닛 위에 놓여 있다.

◆ 작업실 / 실험실

plugging in a fan 선풍기 플러그를 꽂고 있다

putting some tools in a toolbox
공구 상자에 공구를 넣고 있다

packing up some equipment
장비를 챙기고 있다

organizing boxes of materials
자재 상자를 정리하고 있다

picking up a test tube
시험관을 집어 들고 있다

putting away a microscope
현미경을 치우고 있다

◆ 서점 / 도서관 / 병원 / 은행

installing a bookshelf 책장을 설치하고 있다

standing on a stool 의자 위에 서 있다

posting a sign on the wall
벽에 팻말을 붙이고 있다

examining a patient 환자를 진찰하고 있다

counting money from a machine
기계로 돈을 세고 있다

be seated in a waiting area
대기실에 앉아 있다

filling out a form
양식을 작성하고 있다

There are papers piled on a chair.
의자 위에 서류가 쌓여 있다.

Some books are spread out on a counter.
책 몇 권이 카운터 위에 흩어져 있다.

Some books are being placed on a cart.
책들이 카트에 실리고 있다.

Some reading materials have fallen on the floor. 읽을거리들이 바닥에 떨어져 있다.

◆ 여가 / 취미

putting up a tent 텐트를 세우고 있다

watering some flowers
꽃에 물을 주고 있다

boarding an airplane
비행기에 탑승하고 있다

framing a piece of art
미술 작품을 액자에 넣고 있다

unpacking a picnic lunch near a tree
나무 근처에서 소풍 도시락을 풀고 있다

A concert hall is unoccupied.
공연장이 비어 있다.

A stage has been set up indoors.
무대가 실내에 설치되어 있다.

Some suitcases are being loaded onto a bus. 여행 가방 몇 개가 버스에 실리고 있다.

상점

lifting a box onto a cart
박스를 들어 올려 카트에 싣고 있다

stocking shelves with merchandise
선반에 상품을 채우고 있다

opening a cash register
금전 등록기를 열고 있다

paying for a purchase
물건값을 지불하고 있다

be stored on a rack
선반에 보관되어 있다

browsing in a store
상점 안을 둘러보고 있다

holding some merchandise
상품을 들고 있다

facing a refrigerated display case
냉장 진열장을 마주보고 있다

pushing a shopping cart
쇼핑 카트를 밀고 있다

weighing an item on a scale
저울에 물품의 무게를 재고 있다

waiting to make a purchase
구매하려고 기다리고 있다

organizing a display of fruit
과일을 진열하고 있다

be on opposite sides of a counter
카운터의 반대편에 있다

removing an item from a shelf
선반에서 물건을 꺼내고 있다

An assortment of food is displayed.
다양한 음식이 진열되어 있다.

Some baskets are lined up on the floor.
바구니 몇 개가 바닥에 일렬로 놓여 있다.

Items have been left in a shopping cart.
물품들이 쇼핑 카트 안에 놓여 있다.

Some merchandise is arranged on shelves.
상품이 선반에 정리되어 있다.

A glass counter is being wiped off.
유리 카운터가 닦이고 있다.

Some vegetables are on display in a store.
채소들이 상점 안에 진열되어 있다.

 식당

cutting a piece of bread
빵을 자르고 있다

spreading out a tablecloth
식탁보를 펼치고 있다

sipping from a coffee mug
머그잔으로 커피를 마시고 있다

stirring a pot
냄비를 젓고 있다

stacking some dishes
접시를 쌓아 올리고 있다

carrying trays of food
음식 쟁반을 나르고 있다

hanging an apron on a hook
앞치마를 고리에 걸고 있다

walking with an empty tray
빈 쟁반을 들고 걸어가고 있다

putting some groceries in a drawer
식료품을 서랍에 넣고 있다

using a knife to slice some food
칼을 사용하여 음식을 썰고 있다

standing behind a cash register
금전 등록기 뒤에 서 있다

getting some food from a cafeteria
구내식당에서 음식을 가져가고 있다

A server is taking an order.
종업원이 주문을 받고 있다.

A tablecloth is being removed.
식탁보가 치워지고 있다.

A customer is handing a worker some cash.
고객이 직원에게 현금을 건네고 있다.

Some pots are being filled with water.
냄비들에 물이 채워지고 있다.

Sets of utensils have been arranged on napkins.
식사 도구 세트들이 냅킨 위에 놓여 있다.

Some tables are covered with tablecloths.
탁자들이 식탁보로 덮여 있다.

Eating utensils are piled on a plate.
식사 도구들이 접시 위에 쌓여 있다.

◆ 실외 작업

twisting some wires 전선을 꼬고 있다

erecting scaffolding 비계를 세우고 있다

pushing a wheelbarrow 손수레를 밀고 있다

trimming some bushes 관목을 다듬고 있다

mowing the lawn 잔디를 (기계로) 깎고 있다

raking leaves 나뭇잎을 갈퀴로 모으고 있다

paving a walkway 보도를 포장하고 있다

climbing a ladder 사다리를 오르고 있다

shoveling some soil 삽으로 흙을 퍼내고 있다

sweeping the street 길을 쓸고 있다

replacing broken tiles
깨진 타일을 교체하고 있다

putting away some rope
밧줄을 치우고 있다

spreading cement with a shovel
삽으로 시멘트를 펴 바르고 있다

installing a roof on a house
집에 지붕을 설치하고 있다

pruning a bush next to a building
건물 옆에 있는 관목 가지를 치고 있다

A streetlamp is being repaired.
가로등이 수리되고 있다.

A building is being painted.
건물에 페인트가 칠해지고 있다.

A box is being loaded onto a truck.
상자가 트럭에 실리고 있다.

A bench is being moved into a corner.
벤치 하나가 구석으로 옮겨지고 있다.

◆ 교통 / 차량 관련 작업

crossing at an intersection
교차로를 건너고 있다

be docked in a harbor 항구에 정박되어 있다

A vehicle is stopped at the traffic signal.
교통 신호에 차량 한 대가 멈춰 있다.

Light bulbs are being replaced in streetlamps.
가로등 전구들이 교체되고 있다.

A car is parked on the side of a road.
차 한 대가 도로 한쪽에 주차되어 있다.

Some trees are being planted on a street.
나무 몇 그루가 거리에 심어지고 있다.

Some people are lined up at the side of a road. 몇 사람이 길가에 줄지어 있다.

Tree branches are being cleared off a walkway.
나뭇가지들이 보도에서 깨끗이 치워지고 있다.

A garage door has been opened.
차고 문이 열려 있다.

◆ 사물 / 풍경

Trees are lining a walkway.
나무들이 보도를 따라 늘어서 있다.

Some plants have been arranged in a row.
식물들이 일렬로 배열되어 있다.

A flower basket is hanging from the ceiling.
꽃바구니가 천장에 매달려 있다.

Some vehicles are facing a low wall.
차량 몇 대가 낮은 담을 향해 있다.

Some curtains have been closed.
커튼 일부가 닫혀 있다.

There's a deck overlooking a lake.
호수가 내려다보이는 데크가 있다.

There's a sign posted on a fence.
울타리에 붙여진 팻말이 있다.

A wheel has been propped against a stack of bricks. 바퀴가 벽돌 더미에 기대어 놓여 있다.

Refreshments have been left on a table.
다과가 테이블 위에 남아 있다.

A fruit basket has been emptied.
과일 바구니가 비어 있다.

A motorboat is passing under a bridge.
모터보트가 다리 아래를 지나고 있다.

An umbrella has fallen on the ground.
우산이 땅에 떨어져 있다.

Some light fixtures are mounted on the walls. 조명 기구들이 벽면에 설치되어 있다.

A seating area is decorated with plants.
좌석 구역은 식물들로 장식되어 있다.

An armchair has been placed under a window. 안락의자가 창문 아래에 놓여 있다.

Some papers are scattered on the ground.
서류가 땅에 흩어져 있다.

PART 2
질의 응답

INTRO

UNIT 3 | Who/What·Which 의문문

UNIT 4 | When/Where 의문문

UNIT 5 | Why/How 의문문

UNIT 6 | 일반/선택 의문문

UNIT 7 | 부정/부가 의문문

UNIT 8 | 요청·제안문/평서문

PART 2 만점 빈출 표현

PART 2 질의 응답   총 25문항

질문 또는 서술문을 듣고 주어진 보기 3개 중 가장 알맞은 응답을 고르는 유형으로, 다양한 종류의 의문문이 등장한다.

◆ 기본 풀이 전략

📋 문제지

7. Mark your answer on your answer sheet.

🔊 음원

Number 7.

M How many interviews do we have on the schedule?
W (A) Yes, two o'clock works.
   (B) Just five more.
   (C) In the conference room.

다른 파트와 달리 파트 2에서는 문제지에 아무 것도 주어지지 않는다.

STEP 1 질문 파악하기

질문 유형 : 의문사 vs. 비의문사 확인
키워드 : 의문사, 주어, 동사에 집중

STEP 2 오답 소거하며 정답 찾기

(A) X 의문사 의문문에 Yes/No로 응답할 수 없다.
(B) O 인터뷰 일정 개수를 답한 정답이다.
(C) X Where 의문문에 적합한 응답이다.

◆ 최신 출제 경향

❶ 의문사 의문문 출제 비율		과거에는 의문사 의문문이 평균 50퍼센트 이상을 차지하였으나, 최근에는 그 이하로 출제된다.
❷ 비의문사 의문문 및 평서문 출제 비율		제안·요청 의문문, 부가 의문문, 평서문의 출제 비중이 높아지고 있다. 응답을 예측하기 어려운 평서문이 예전보다 많이 출제되므로 난이도가 높아졌다고 할 수 있다.
❸ 다양해진 응답 패턴		질문에 직접적인 답변을 주지 않고 우회적으로 답하는 경우가 많아지고 있다. 따라서 다양한 응답 패턴을 미리 익혀두는 것이 좋다.

질문	Where should I put these product samples?	이 제품 샘플들을 어디에 놓을까요?
직접적 응답	On the desk over there.	저쪽에 있는 책상 위에요.
간접 응답	Let me make some space in the cabinet.	제가 캐비닛에 공간을 좀 만들어 볼게요.
'모른다' 응답	Try asking Ms. Diaz.	디아즈 씨에게 물어보세요.
제3의 응답	Oh, I thought we handed them all out earlier.	아, 전 우리가 아까 전부 나누어 줬다고 생각했는데요.
역질문 응답	How many of them are there?	몇 개 있나요?

◆ 오답 유형

파트 2에서는 기본적으로 질문의 키워드를 정확히 파악하고 가장 적절한 응답을 선택하는 것이 중요하다. 다만 아래와 같은 대표적인 오답 유형을 알아두면 소거하는 데 도움이 될 수 있다.

1. 유사 발음 / 다의어 / 반복 어휘 / 파생어 활용 답변

질문에서 들린 단어와 발음이 동일하거나 유사한 단어, 다른 의미의 같은 어휘, 혹은 파생어를 포함한 오답이 종종 등장한다. 하지만 이러한 보기가 간혹 정답이 될 수도 있으니 무조건 소거하는 일은 없도록 한다.

Where did you **park** your car?
차를 어디에 주차하셨어요?

오답 : He often walks in the **park**.
그는 종종 공원을 산책해요.

정답 : Next to the office building.
사옥 옆에요.

2. 연상 어휘 답변

질문에 쓰인 특정 단어에서 연상되는 어휘가 오답 보기에 활용되기도 한다. 다만 응답 패턴이 다양해진 만큼 정답에도 쓰일 가능성이 충분히 있기 때문에, 응답을 듣기 전에 질문을 정확히 파악하는 데 중점을 두도록 한다.

What **theater** are we going to?
우리 무슨 극장에 가나요?

오답 : Wasn't that a great **show**?
정말 멋진 쇼였죠?

정답 : The one on Second Street.
2번 가에 있는 거요.

3. 의문사 의문문에 Yes / No 답변

Who, What, When 등으로 시작해 특정 정보를 묻는 의문사 의문문에는 Yes, Okay와 같은 긍정 응답이나 No, Not at all과 같은 부정 응답을 할 수 없다.

Who's attending the company picnic?
회사 야유회에 누가 참석하나요?

오답 : **No**, you can choose it.
아니요, 당신이 선택하셔도 돼요.

정답 : The whole office.
전 직원이요.

4. 의문사를 혼동하는 답변

질문에 사용된 의문사 대신 다른 의문사가 들어갔다면 정답이 될 수 있는 보기가 오답으로 나오기도 한다. 질문의 키워드를 명확히 기억하고 있어야 이러한 오답을 피해 갈 수 있다.

When are we leaving for dinner?
우리 저녁 먹으러 언제 나가나요?

오답 : **In the large dining room**.
큰 식당에서요.

정답 : At six thirty P.M.
오후 6시 30분이에요.

UNIT 3 — Who/What·Which 의문문

1 Who 의문문

●출제비율 1~2문항/25문항

Who 의문문은 사람 이름, 직위, 직업과 같은 직접적인 답변이 주를 이루지만, 다양한 우회적 응답 표현도 등장한다.

고득점 전략 빈출 답변 유형 익히기 🎧 850_P2_01

◆ 직접적으로 답하기

Q **Who** was the last person to use the fax machine? | | 팩스를 마지막으로 사용한 사람이 누구죠?
A1 I think it was **Sarah**. | 사람 이름 | 사라 같아요.
A2 **No one** in my department. | 부정대명사 | 우리 부서에는 없어요.
A3 One of the **interns**, I think. | 직책 | 인턴 중 한 명인 것 같아요.

Q **Who** edits the company newsletter now? | | 사보는 지금 누가 편집하나요?
A1 **Bill Sharma** took over that job. | 사람 이름 | 빌 샤르마 씨가 그 일을 맡았어요.
A2 **Someone** from marketing is supposed to do it. | 부정대명사 | 마케팅 부서의 누군가가 하기로 했어요.

◆ 우회적으로 답하기

Q **Who** wants to attend the annual convention? | | 누가 연례 회의에 참석하고 싶어 하나요?
A1 I'll see who's interested. | 제3의 답변 | 누가 관심이 있는지 알아봐야겠어요.
A2 Our supervisor will know. | 모른다 답변 | 부서장님이 알 거예요.
A3 It's already been decided. | 간접 답변 | 이미 결정되었어요.

Q **Who**'s installing the new equipment? | | 새 장비는 누가 설치하나요?
A1 Didn't you get my e-mail? | 역질문 답변 | 내 이메일 못 받았나요?
A2 I have the schedule here. | 간접 답변 | 여기 일정이 있어요. → 보고 확인하라는 의미

Q **Who** was selected to work on the advertising project? | | 광고 프로젝트 작업에 누가 선정되었나요?
A1 I haven't heard. | 모른다 답변 | 못 들었어요.
A2 I thought you are in charge of that. | 모른다 답변 | 당신이 담당하고 있다고 생각했어요.

ETS 유형 연습 | 음원을 듣고 적절한 응답을 고르세요. 🎧 850_P2_02 정답 및 해설 p.011

1. (A) (B) (C)　　　　　**4.** (A) (B) (C)

2. (A) (B) (C)　　　　　**5.** (A) (B) (C)

3. (A) (B) (C)　　　　　**6.** (A) (B) (C)

❷ What · Which 의문문

What · Which 의문문은 시간, 종류, 이유, 상황, 의견 등 질문의 내용이나 형태가 다양하므로 의문사 뒤에 오는 부분에 특히 집중해서 들어야 한다.

고득점 전략 빈출 답변 유형 익히기

🎧 850_P2_03

◆ 직접적으로 답하기

Q	**What**'s causing the delay in the shipping department?	이유	발송 부서에서 지연되는 이유가 뭔가요?
A1	They've been very busy.		그들이 바빴어요.
A2	They ran out of packing materials.		포장 재료가 다 떨어졌어요.
A3	There are still a few issues to resolve.		아직 해결해야 할 몇 가지 문제가 있어요.
Q	**Which supplier** did we decide on?	종류	어느 공급업체로 결정했죠?
A1	We're staying with our current one.		기존 업체와 계속 하기로 했어요.
A2	The one on Hastings Street.		헤이스팅스 가에 있는 업체요.
A3	The one that Kathy recommended.		캐시가 추천한 곳이요.

◆ 우회적으로 답하기

Q	**What**'s the status of the recording contract?	상황	녹음 계약 건은 어떻게 되어 가고 있나요?
A1	I'm still waiting to hear.	모른다 답변	아직 소식을 기다리고 있어요.
A2	Ms. Alvarez takes care of it.	모른다 답변	알바레즈 씨가 처리해요.
A3	We need to meet again tomorrow.	간접 답변	내일 다시 만나야 해요.
Q	**What**'s included in next year's product line?	종류	내년 제품군에는 무엇이 포함되나요?
A1	Didn't Jane give you the list?	역질문 답변	제인이 목록을 주지 않았나요?
A2	It still hasn't been decided.	모른다 답변	아직 결정되지 않았어요.
Q	**What time**'s the flight supposed to arrive?	시간	비행기가 몇 시에 도착하기로 되어 있나요?
A1	I sent you the itinerary.	간접 답변	제가 여행일정표를 보냈어요.
A2	Matthew has the schedule.	모른다 답변	매튜가 일정을 갖고 있어요.

ETS 유형 연습 | 음원을 듣고 적절한 응답을 고르세요.

🎧 850_P2_04 정답 및 해설 p.012

1. (A) (B) (C)   **4.** (A) (B) (C)

2. (A) (B) (C)   **5.** (A) (B) (C)

3. (A) (B) (C)   **6.** (A) (B) (C)

1. Mark your answer.   (A)   (B)   (C)

2. Mark your answer.   (A)   (B)   (C)

3. Mark your answer.   (A)   (B)   (C)

4. Mark your answer.   (A)   (B)   (C)

5. Mark your answer.   (A)   (B)   (C)

6. Mark your answer.   (A)   (B)   (C)

7. Mark your answer.   (A)   (B)   (C)

8. Mark your answer.   (A)   (B)   (C)

9. Mark your answer.   (A)   (B)   (C)

10. Mark your answer.   (A)   (B)   (C)

11. Mark your answer.   (A)   (B)   (C)

12. Mark your answer.   (A)   (B)   (C)

13. Mark your answer.   (A)   (B)   (C)

14. Mark your answer.   (A)   (B)   (C)

15. Mark your answer.   (A)   (B)   (C)

16. Mark your answer.   (A)   (B)   (C)

17. Mark your answer.   (A)   (B)   (C)

18. Mark your answer.   (A)   (B)   (C)

19. Mark your answer.   (A)   (B)   (C)

20. Mark your answer.   (A)   (B)   (C)

PART 2

UNIT 3

When / Where 의문문

① When 의문문

🔴 출제비율 1~3문항/25문항

When 의문문은 특정 시점이 들어간 표현이 정답으로 많이 나오지만 불확실하거나 비약적인 답변에 주의해야 한다.

고득점 전략 빈출 답변 유형 익히기

🎧 850_P2_06

◆ 직접적으로 답하기

Q	**When** will the shipment leave the warehouse?		배송품은 창고에서 언제 출발하나요?
A1	On March 5th.	구체적 시점	3월 5일에요.
A2	Not before next week.	모호한 시점	다음 주 전에는 안돼요.
A3	As soon as I finish this paperwork.	부사절 표현	내가 이 서류작업을 끝내는 대로요.

Q	**When** can I call Mr. Freeman back?		프리먼 씨에게 언제 다시 전화하면 되나요?
A1	Anytime tomorrow morning.	모호한 시점	내일 오전 아무 때나요.
A2	As soon as you can.	부사절 표현	되도록 빨리요.

◆ 우회적으로 답하기

Q	**When** are you available for an interview?		언제 인터뷰 가능하신가요?
A1	I'm going out of town this week.	간접 답변	제가 이번 주에는 여기 없을 거예요.
A2	The schedule is still being arranged.	모른다 답변	아직 일정 조정 중입니다.
A3	Didn't you get the e-mail this morning?	역질문	오늘 아침에 이메일 못 받으셨나요?

Q	**When** will the software updates be released?		소프트웨어 업데이트는 언제 출시됩니까?
A1	Sorry, I don't work here.	모른다 답변	죄송하지만, 저는 여기서 일하지 않아요.
A2	William might know.	모른다 답변	윌리엄이 알지도 몰라요.

Q	**When** was the budget report last updated?		예산 보고서가 언제 마지막으로 업데이트됐죠?
A1	I forgot when it was.	모른다 답변	언제였는지 잊어버렸어요.
A2	You'd have to ask the supervisor.	모른다 답변	상사에게 물어보셔야 할 것 같아요.

ETS 유형 연습 | 음원을 듣고 적절한 응답을 고르세요. 🎧 850_P2_07 정답 및 해설 p.017

1. (A) (B) (C)   **4.** (A) (B) (C)

2. (A) (B) (C)   **5.** (A) (B) (C)

3. (A) (B) (C)   **6.** (A) (B) (C)

② Where 의문문

출제비율 1~2문항 / 25문항

Where 의문문은 답변이 장소로만 나오지는 않는다. 출처나 사람을 언급하는 경우도 있으며, When 질문과 혼동되도록 유도된 오답이 자주 나오므로 주의한다.

고득점 전략 | 빈출 답변 유형 익히기

🎧 850_P2_08

◆ 직접적으로 답하기

Q	**Where**'s the book you and Pierre were talking about?		당신과 피에르가 얘기했던 책은 어디에 있나요?
A1	At the reception desk.	장소	안내데스크에요.
A2	Over there on the table.	위치	저기 테이블 위에요.
A3	Anthony borrowed it.	사람	앤소니가 빌려갔어요.
Q	**Where** should I send the package?		소포를 어디로 보내면 되나요?
A1	Directly to the hotel.	장소	호텔로 바로요.
A2	To the same place as before.	장소	예전과 같은 장소로요.

◆ 우회적으로 답하기

Q	**Where** should I put this new monitor?		이 새 모니터를 어디에 두어야 하죠?
A1	You'd better ask Ms. Barry.	모른다 답변	배리 씨에게 물어보는 게 좋겠어요.
A2	Jansen organizes all the supplies.	모른다 답변	얀센이 모든 물품들을 정리합니다.
A3	There's no space in this room.	간접 답변	이 방에는 공간이 없습니다.
Q	**Where** can I find the women's clothing section?		여성복 매장은 어디에 있나요?
A1	The building directory is behind you.	모른다 답변	건물 안내도가 당신 뒤에 있네요.
A2	I'm not the best person to ask.	모른다 답변	저 말고 다른 사람에게 물어보는 게 낫겠어요.
A3	I'll take you there.	간접 답변	제가 모셔다 드릴게요.
Q	**Where** is the annual conference being held?		연례 총회는 어디서 열리나요?
A1	Check with Angela.	모른다 답변	안젤라에게 확인해 보세요.
A2	Didn't you receive the e-mail?	역질문 답변	이메일을 받지 못했나요?
A3	We won't know until March.	제3의 답변	3월은 되어야 알 수 있어요.

ETS 유형 연습 | 음원을 듣고 적절한 응답을 고르세요.

🎧 850_P2_09 정답 및 해설 p.018

1. (A) (B) (C)

2. (A) (B) (C)

3. (A) (B) (C)

4. (A) (B) (C)

5. (A) (B) (C)

6. (A) (B) (C)

PART 2   UNIT 4

1. Mark your answer.   (A)   (B)   (C)

2. Mark your answer.   (A)   (B)   (C)

3. Mark your answer.   (A)   (B)   (C)

4. Mark your answer.   (A)   (B)   (C)

5. Mark your answer.   (A)   (B)   (C)

6. Mark your answer.   (A)   (B)   (C)

7. Mark your answer.   (A)   (B)   (C)

8. Mark your answer.   (A)   (B)   (C)

9. Mark your answer.   (A)   (B)   (C)

10. Mark your answer.   (A)   (B)   (C)

11. Mark your answer.   (A)   (B)   (C)

12. Mark your answer.   (A)   (B)   (C)

13. Mark your answer.   (A)   (B)   (C)

14. Mark your answer.   (A)   (B)   (C)

15. Mark your answer.   (A)   (B)   (C)

16. Mark your answer.   (A)   (B)   (C)

17. Mark your answer.   (A)   (B)   (C)

18. Mark your answer.   (A)   (B)   (C)

19. Mark your answer.   (A)   (B)   (C)

20. Mark your answer.   (A)   (B)   (C)

① Why 의문문

🔵 출제비율 1~2문항 / 25문항

Why 의문문에 대한 대답은 주로 because를 사용하지만 because를 생략하거나 다른 방식으로 답변하는 경우도 많다.

고득점 **전략** 빈출 답변 유형 익히기

🎧 850_P2_11

◆ 직접적으로 답하기

Q	**Why** is Ms. Thompson taking another job?	톰슨 씨는 왜 다른 직장을 잡은 거죠?
A1	Because the salary's better.	급여가 더 나아서요.
A2	She has found a more interesting position.	더 흥미로운 자리를 발견했대요.
Q	**Why** aren't you going to tonight's dinner party?	오늘 저녁 만찬에 왜 안 가세요?
A1	I've already made plans.	선약이 있어서요.
A2	Because I need to finish a report.	보고서를 끝내야 해서요.

◆ 우회적으로 답하기

Q	**Why** have the renovations to the third-floor lobby been delayed?		3층 로비의 개조가 왜 늦어졌나요?
A1	You'll have to ask the project manager.	모른다 답변	프로젝트 매니저에게 물어봐야 할 거예요.
A2	Didn't you get the memo from Sandra?	역질문 답변	산드라에게서 회람을 못 받았어요?
Q	**Why** can't I take Wellspoint Road all the way to Parkview Plaza?		왜 웰스포인트 로를 타고 파크뷰 플라자까지 갈 수 없는 거죠?
A1	There's a detour because of the road construction.	간접 답변	도로 공사 때문에 우회로가 있어요.
A2	Sorry, I'm new around here.	모른다 답변	미안해요, 제가 이 근처가 처음이라서요.
Q	**Why** hasn't the architect for the new building been announced yet?		왜 아직 새 건물의 건축가가 발표되지 않았죠?
A1	The contract hasn't been finalized.	간접 답변	계약이 아직 확정되지 않았어요.
A2	I don't know what's wrong with it.	모른다 답변	뭐가 문제인지 모르겠어요.

ETS 유형 연습 | 음원을 듣고 적절한 응답을 고르세요.

🎧 850_P2_12   정답 및 해설 p.023

1. (A)   (B)   (C)   **4.** (A)   (B)   (C)

2. (A)   (B)   (C)   **5.** (A)   (B)   (C)

3. (A)   (B)   (C)   **6.** (A)   (B)   (C)

❷ How 의문문

How가 단독으로 쓰일 때는 방법이나 상태, 의견 등을 묻는 질문이, How 뒤에 형용사/부사가 같이 오는 경우는 수량, 가격, 기간, 빈도 등을 묻는 질문이 주로 나온다.

고득점 전략 | 빈출 답변 유형 익히기

🎧 850_P2_13

◆ 직접적으로 답하기

Q **How** did you decide where to go on holiday? 방법 휴가 때 어디로 갈지 어떻게 결정했나요?
A I researched places on the Internet. 인터넷으로 장소들을 조사했어요.

Q **How many** people have signed up for the online seminar? 수량 온라인 세미나에 몇 명이나 참가 신청을 했나요?
A About a dozen. 약 12명이요.

Q **How often** are paychecks mailed from this branch? 빈도 이 지점은 급여를 얼마나 자주 지급하죠?
A They're sent out bi-weekly. 격주로 나가요.

◆ 우회적으로 답하기

Q **How** do we predict monthly sales? 방법 월별 매출을 어떻게 예측하나요?
A1 Insook can show you. 모른다 답변 인숙 씨가 알려 줄 수 있어요.
A2 I sent you an e-mail. 간접 답변 이메일 보내드렸어요.
A3 I don't work in this department. 모른다 답변 저는 이 부서에서 일하지 않아요.

Q **How many** job interviews are we conducting this week? 수량 이번 주에 면접을 몇 개나 하나요?
A1 Here's the schedule. 간접 답변 일정표 여기 있어요.
A2 Didn't you get the e-mail? 역질문 답변 이메일 못 받았어요?
A3 It hasn't been announced. 모른다 답변 공지되지 않았어요.

Q **How long** will it take you to replace the tires? 기간 타이어를 교체하는 데 시간이 얼마나 걸리나요?
A1 I'll be done tomorrow. 간접 답변 내일이면 끝납니다.
A2 Let me check the schedule. 제3의 답변 스케줄을 확인해 보겠습니다.

ETS 유형 연습 | 음원을 듣고 적절한 응답을 고르세요.

🎧 850_P2_14 정답 및 해설 p.024

1. (A) (B) (C)   **4.** (A) (B) (C)

2. (A) (B) (C)   **5.** (A) (B) (C)

3. (A) (B) (C)   **6.** (A) (B) (C)

PART 2   UNIT 5

1. Mark your answer.   (A)   (B)   (C)

2. Mark your answer.   (A)   (B)   (C)

3. Mark your answer.   (A)   (B)   (C)

4. Mark your answer.   (A)   (B)   (C)

5. Mark your answer.   (A)   (B)   (C)

6. Mark your answer.   (A)   (B)   (C)

7. Mark your answer.   (A)   (B)   (C)

8. Mark your answer.   (A)   (B)   (C)

9. Mark your answer.   (A)   (B)   (C)

10. Mark your answer.   (A)   (B)   (C)

11. Mark your answer.   (A)   (B)   (C)

12. Mark your answer.   (A)   (B)   (C)

13. Mark your answer.   (A)   (B)   (C)

14. Mark your answer.   (A)   (B)   (C)

15. Mark your answer.   (A)   (B)   (C)

16. Mark your answer.   (A)   (B)   (C)

17. Mark your answer.   (A)   (B)   (C)

18. Mark your answer.   (A)   (B)   (C)

19. Mark your answer.   (A)   (B)   (C)

20. Mark your answer.   (A)   (B)   (C)

PART 2

UNIT 5

UNIT 6 일반 / 선택 의문문

❶ 일반 의문문

🕐 출제비율 2~4문항 / 25문항

Be/Do/Have 또는 조동사로 시작하는 일반 의문문은 시제와 주어를 잘 듣는 것이 중요하다. 의문사 의문문과 달리 Yes/No 대답이 가능하나, Yes/No를 사용하지 않는 함축적 또는 회피성 답변도 등장한다.

고득점 전략 빈출 답변 유형 익히기

🎧 850_P2_16

◆ 직접적으로 답하기

Q	**Have** you paid the caterer for the award ceremony yet?		시상식 출장요리 업체에 돈을 지불했나요?
A1	Yes, with the company card.	Yes/No 답변	네, 회사 카드로요.
A2	Not yet.	Yes/No 대체 답변	아직이요.

◆ 우회적으로 답하기

Q	**Did** you go to the seminar last night?		어젯밤에 세미나에 갔었나요?
A1	It was canceled.	간접 답변	취소되었어요.
A2	I was on vacation.	간접 답변	전 휴가 중이었어요.
A3	It will be held tonight.	제3의 답변	오늘 밤 개최돼요.
A4	Was I supposed to?	역질문 답변	그래야 했나요?

만점 TIP

의문사 의문문이 일반 의문문 안에 포함된 구조인 간접 의문문도 가끔 등장한다. 주로 〈**Do you know/ Can you tell me** + 의문사 + 주어 + 동사?〉의 형태가 많이 나온다.

Q. **Do you know** what's in that box?   저 상자 안에 뭐가 있는지 아세요?
A. Yes, some client files.   네, 고객 파일이요.

→ What's in that box?라고 직접 의문문의 형태로 물었다면 Yes/No 답변은 오답이 되지만, Do you know를 이용하여 간접 의문문으로 물었기에 Yes/No 답변이 정답이 될 수 있다.

ETS 유형 연습 | 음원을 듣고 적절한 응답을 고르세요.

🎧 850_P2_17   정답 및 해설 p.029

1. (A) (B) (C)   4. (A) (B) (C)

2. (A) (B) (C)   5. (A) (B) (C)

3. (A) (B) (C)   6. (A) (B) (C)

② 선택 의문문

〈A or B〉 형태의 선택 의문문은 둘 중 하나를 답하는 경우가 가장 흔하나, 선택 사항을 우회적으로 돌려 말하는 경우도 있고 둘 다 선택하지 않는 제3의 답변이 등장하기도 한다.

고득점 전략 빈출 답변 유형 익히기

🎧 850_P2_18

◆ 직접적으로 답하기

Q Do you want to create **a radio commercial** or **a print advertisement**?

라디오 광고를 제작하고 싶어요, 아니면 인쇄 광고를 제작하고 싶어요?

A1 We'd prefer a commercial.　　　　하나 선택　　　라디오 광고가 더 좋겠어요.

A2 We need both.　　　　둘 다 선택　　　둘 다 필요해요.

Q Is the new furniture arriving **today** or **tomorrow**?

새 가구가 오늘 도착하나요, 아니면 내일 도착하나요?

A1 Neither. It's going to arrive next week.　　둘 다 아님　　둘 다 아니에요. 다음 주에 도착할 거예요.

A2 Either is fine.　　　　상관 없음　　　어느 쪽이든 좋아요.

◆ 우회적으로 답하기

Q Should we **walk** or **take a taxi** to the theater?

극장에 걸어서 갈까요, 아니면 택시를 타고 갈까요?

A1 Whichever is convenient for you.　　제3의 답변　　편한 대로 하세요.

A2 Isn't it supposed to rain?　　　역질문 답변　　비가 온다고 하지 않았나요?

A3 The movie starts in thirty minutes.　　간접 답변　　영화는 30분 후에 시작해요.

→ 영화가 30분 후에 시작하므로 시간이 별로 없으니 택시를 타자는 말로 볼 수 있다.

Q Would you prefer **a morning** or **afternoon appointment**?

오전과 오후 예약 중 어느 쪽이 좋으신가요?

A1 I need to look at my calendar.　　제3의 답변　　달력을 좀 봐야겠어요.

A2 I like getting up early.　　　간접 답변　　나는 일찍 일어나는 것을 좋아해요.

A3 How long do you think it'll take?　　역질문 답변　　얼마나 걸릴 것 같아요?

Q Shall I contact you **by e-mail** or **by phone**?

이메일로 연락드릴까요, 아니면 전화로 연락드릴까요?

A1 Actually, I'll be seeing you tomorrow.　　제3의 답변　　사실, 내일 직접 뵈려고 하는데요.

A2 Which is more convenient for you?　　역질문 답변　　어떤 게 더 편하세요?

ETS 유형 연습 | 음원을 듣고 적절한 응답을 고르세요.

🎧 850_P2_19　정답 및 해설 p.030

1. (A)　(B)　(C)　　　　**4.** (A)　(B)　(C)

2. (A)　(B)　(C)　　　　**5.** (A)　(B)　(C)

3. (A)　(B)　(C)　　　　**6.** (A)　(B)　(C)

1. Mark your answer.   (A)   (B)   (C)

2. Mark your answer.   (A)   (B)   (C)

3. Mark your answer.   (A)   (B)   (C)

4. Mark your answer.   (A)   (B)   (C)

5. Mark your answer.   (A)   (B)   (C)

6. Mark your answer.   (A)   (B)   (C)

7. Mark your answer.   (A)   (B)   (C)

8. Mark your answer.   (A)   (B)   (C)

9. Mark your answer.   (A)   (B)   (C)

10. Mark your answer.   (A)   (B)   (C)

11. Mark your answer.   (A)   (B)   (C)

12. Mark your answer.   (A)   (B)   (C)

13. Mark your answer.   (A)   (B)   (C)

14. Mark your answer.   (A)   (B)   (C)

15. Mark your answer.   (A)   (B)   (C)

16. Mark your answer.   (A)   (B)   (C)

17. Mark your answer.   (A)   (B)   (C)

18. Mark your answer.   (A)   (B)   (C)

19. Mark your answer.   (A)   (B)   (C)

20. Mark your answer.   (A)   (B)   (C)

PART 2

UNIT 6

UNIT 7 부정/부가 의문문

❶ 부정 의문문

🔊 출제비율 1~3문항/25문항

부정 의문문은 주로 사실 확인 또는 동의를 구하거나 제안할 때 사용된다. 부정어에 구애받지 말고 긍정 의문문과 똑같이 긍정 답변이면 Yes, 부정 답변이면 No로 생각하도록 한다.

고득점 전략 빈출 답변 유형 익히기

🎧 850_P2_21

◆ 직접적으로 답하기

Q **Aren't** security passes needed to enter the research lab?

연구실에 들어가려면 보안 출입증이 필요하지 않나요?

A1 Yes, we'll have to get you one. `Yes/No 답변`

네, 하나 드려야죠.

A2 Of course, I have mine here. `Yes/No 대체 답변`

물론이죠, 여기 제 것이 있어요.

Q **Doesn't** the train to New York leave from track one?

뉴욕행 열차는 1번 승강장에서 출발하지 않나요?

A1 No, it has changed to track five. `Yes/No 답변`

아니요, 5번 승강장으로 바뀌었어요.

A2 Usually, but today it's boarding on track three. `Yes/No 대체 답변`

보통은요, 하지만 오늘은 3번 승강장에서 탑승해요.

◆ 우회적으로 답하기

Q **Aren't** you quality testing that new software program?

그 새로운 소프트웨어 프로그램의 품질을 테스트하고 있지 않나요?

A1 That project was canceled. `제3의 답변`

그 프로젝트는 취소되었어요.

A2 Didn't you see my notes? `역질문 답변`

내 메모 못 봤어요?

A3 Kurt is responsible for that. `모른다 답변`

그건 커트가 책임져요.

Q **Shouldn't** the caterers be arriving soon?

출장 요리가 곧 도착하지 않을까요?

A1 They're supposed to be here by five o'clock. `간접 답변`

5시까지 여기 오기로 되어 있어요.

A2 Thanks for reminding me. `제3의 답변`

상기시켜 줘서 고마워요.

Q **Don't** you want to go out for lunch?

점심 먹으러 나가지 않을래요?

A1 I'll be ready in a few minutes. `간접 답변`

몇 분 후면 준비가 될 거예요.

A2 I brought my lunch today. `간접 답변`

오늘 점심을 싸왔어요.

ETS 유형 연습 | 음원을 듣고 적절한 응답을 고르세요.

🎧 850_P2_22 정답 및 해설 p.036

1. (A) (B) (C)

2. (A) (B) (C)

3. (A) (B) (C)

4. (A) (B) (C)

5. (A) (B) (C)

6. (A) (B) (C)

❷ 부가 의문문

● 출제비율 2∼3문항 / 25문항

부가 의문문은 평서문 뒤에 〈동사 + 주어?〉 형태의 의문문이 붙은 형태로, 부정 의문문과 마찬가지로 주로 사실 여부를 확인하거나 동의를 구하는 의문문이다. 의문문 대신 right, correct, don't you think 등이 붙기도 한다.

고득점 전략 빈출 답변 유형 익히기
🎧 850_P2_23

◆ 직접적으로 답하기

Q Ms. Asghar organized tonight's celebration, **didn't she?**
아스가르 씨가 오늘 밤 축하 행사를 준비했죠, 그렇지 않나요?

A1 Yes, I'm looking forward to it. `Yes/No 답변`
네, 기대가 됩니다.

A2 That's right. She's been working on it for more than a month. `Yes/No 대체 답변`
맞아요. 한 달 넘게 그 일을 맡아 해왔어요.

Q That photocopy machine is broken, **isn't it?**
저 복사기는 고장 났죠, 그렇지 않나요?

A1 No, give it a try again. `Yes/No 답변`
아니에요, 다시 해보세요.

A2 You're right—it needs to be replaced. `Yes/No 대체 답변`
맞아요. 교체해야 돼요.

◆ 우회적으로 답하기

Q You're going to manage the branch in Istanbul, **aren't you?**
당신이 이스탄불 지사를 관리하실 거죠, 그렇지 않나요?

A1 Actually, Mr. Grant is taking on that assignment. `간접 답변`
사실, 그랜트 씨가 그 임무를 맡을 거예요.

A2 They're still deciding. `모른다 답변`
아직 결정 못했어요.

Q You've already chosen a menu for the banquet, **haven't you?**
연회를 위한 메뉴를 이미 골랐죠, 그렇지 않나요?

A1 Yes, haven't you seen it? `역질문 답변`
네, 못 보셨어요?

A2 It hasn't been decided yet. `모른다 답변`
아직 결정되지 않았어요.

Q Jake bought the house about a year ago, **right?**
제이크가 약 1년 전에 그 집을 샀죠, 그렇죠?

A1 Has it been that long? `역질문 답변`
그렇게 오래됐나요?

A2 I thought he just leased it. `제3의 답변`
나는 그가 임대한 줄 알았어요.

ETS 유형 연습 | 음원을 듣고 적절한 응답을 고르세요.
🎧 850_P2_24 정답 및 해설 p.037

1. (A)　(B)　(C)　　　　**4.** (A)　(B)　(C)

2. (A)　(B)　(C)　　　　**5.** (A)　(B)　(C)

3. (A)　(B)　(C)　　　　**6.** (A)　(B)　(C)

1. Mark your answer.   (A)   (B)   (C)

2. Mark your answer.   (A)   (B)   (C)

3. Mark your answer.   (A)   (B)   (C)

4. Mark your answer.   (A)   (B)   (C)

5. Mark your answer.   (A)   (B)   (C)

6. Mark your answer.   (A)   (B)   (C)

7. Mark your answer.   (A)   (B)   (C)

8. Mark your answer.   (A)   (B)   (C)

9. Mark your answer.   (A)   (B)   (C)

10. Mark your answer.   (A)   (B)   (C)

11. Mark your answer. (A) (B) (C)

12. Mark your answer. (A) (B) (C)

13. Mark your answer. (A) (B) (C)

14. Mark your answer. (A) (B) (C)

15. Mark your answer. (A) (B) (C)

16. Mark your answer. (A) (B) (C)

17. Mark your answer. (A) (B) (C)

18. Mark your answer. (A) (B) (C)

19. Mark your answer. (A) (B) (C)

20. Mark your answer. (A) (B) (C)

PART 2

UNIT 7

UNIT 8 요청·제안문 / 평서문

❶ 요청·제안문

출제비율 2∼3문항 / 25문항

Can[Could] you, Would you mind, Please 등의 표현을 사용하는 요청문과 Would you like, Why don't you[we], How about, Let's 등으로 시작하는 제안문이 주로 출제된다.

고득점 전략 빈출 답변 유형 익히기

🎧 850_P2_26

◆ 직접적으로 답하기

Q	**Could you** look over these budget figures?	요청	이 예산 수치를 검토해 주시겠어요?
A1	Sure, I'll have time tomorrow.	수락	네, 내일 시간이 있어요.
A2	I wish I could, but I'm very busy.	거절	그러고 싶지만, 너무 바빠요.
Q	**Why don't you** type up the meeting report and e-mail it to the team?	제안	회의 보고서를 타이핑해서 팀원들에게 이메일로 보내는 게 어때요?
A1	OK, I'll do it immediately.	수락	네, 바로 하겠습니다.
A2	Sorry, I don't have time right now.	거절	죄송하지만, 지금은 시간이 없어요.

◆ 우회적으로 답하기

Q	**Can you** pick up the shipment for me?	요청	택배 좀 갖다 줄 수 있나요?
A1	I have to go to a meeting.	간접 답변	저는 회의에 참석해야 돼요.
A2	I'm free after lunch.	간접 답변	저는 점심 이후에 시간이 돼요.
Q	**Let's** ask the legal department about the new policy.	제안	새 방침에 대해 법률 부서에 물어봅시다.
A1	I tried to call them earlier.	제3의 답변	아까 전화하려고 했어요.
A2	Do you think that's necessary?	역질문 답변	꼭 그렇게 해야 한다고 생각하세요?
Q	**Would you like** a free sample of shampoo?	제안	샴푸 무료 샘플을 드릴까요?
A1	I got one already.	간접 답변	이미 하나 받았어요.
A2	I was just about to ask.	간접 답변	막 물어보려던 참이었어요.

ETS 유형 연습 | 음원을 듣고 적절한 응답을 고르세요.

🎧 850_P2_27   정답 및 해설 p.042

1. (A) (B) (C)

2. (A) (B) (C)

3. (A) (B) (C)

4. (A) (B) (C)

5. (A) (B) (C)

6. (A) (B) (C)

② 평서문

● 출제비율 2~3문항 / 25문항

평서문은 정보나 상황 전달, 의견/바람, 문제 제기, 요청, 제안/명령 등 다양한 의도를 내포하여 진술하는 문장으로 다양한 답변이 가능하므로 빠른 상황 판단이 중요하다.

고득점 전략 빈출 답변 유형 익히기

🎧 850_P2_28

◆ 직접적으로 답하기

Q Our flight's been delayed an hour.　상황 전달　우리 비행기가 한 시간 연착됐어요.

A I'm worried we'll miss our connection.　환승할 비행기를 놓칠까 봐 걱정이에요.

Q I think you should try a shorter haircut this time.　의견/바람　이번에는 머리를 좀 더 짧게 깎는 게 좋을 것 같아요.

A Yes, I have been considering that.　네, 그럴까 생각하고 있어요.

Q I'm calling to confirm your dentist appointment tomorrow.　요청　내일 치과 예약 확인차 전화드렸습니다.

A Yes, I'll be there.　네, 갈게요.

◆ 우회적으로 답하기

Q The proposal is due by Friday.　요청　제안서는 금요일까지예요.

A1 It can be turned in next week.　제3의 답변　다음 주에 제출해도 돼요.

A2 I've already submitted it.　간접 답변　이미 제출했어요.

Q You'll receive your next paycheck a week from Friday.　정보 전달　다음 급여는 금요일로부터 일주일 후에 받게 될 거예요.

A1 Will it be mailed to us?　역질문 답변　우편으로 보내주시나요?

A2 I got an e-mail about that.　간접 답변　그것에 관한 이메일을 받았어요.

Q You should leave at four p.m., before there's traffic.　제안　차가 막히기 전, 오후 4시에 출발해야 해요.

A1 Is that when you leave?　역질문 답변　그때 떠나시는 건가요?

A2 I'll be in meetings all day.　간접 답변　하루 종일 회의를 할 거예요.

ETS 유형 연습 | 음원을 듣고 적절한 응답을 고르세요.

🎧 850_P2_29　정답 및 해설 p.043

1. (A)　(B)　(C)

2. (A)　(B)　(C)

3. (A)　(B)　(C)

4. (A)　(B)　(C)

5. (A)　(B)　(C)

6. (A)　(B)　(C)

1. Mark your answer.   (A)   (B)   (C)

2. Mark your answer.   (A)   (B)   (C)

3. Mark your answer.   (A)   (B)   (C)

4. Mark your answer.   (A)   (B)   (C)

5. Mark your answer.   (A)   (B)   (C)

6. Mark your answer.   (A)   (B)   (C)

7. Mark your answer.   (A)   (B)   (C)

8. Mark your answer.   (A)   (B)   (C)

9. Mark your answer.   (A)   (B)   (C)

10. Mark your answer.   (A)   (B)   (C)

11. Mark your answer.   (A)   (B)   (C)

12. Mark your answer.   (A)   (B)   (C)

13. Mark your answer.   (A)   (B)   (C)

14. Mark your answer.   (A)   (B)   (C)

15. Mark your answer.   (A)   (B)   (C)

16. Mark your answer.   (A)   (B)   (C)

17. Mark your answer.   (A)   (B)   (C)

18. Mark your answer.   (A)   (B)   (C)

19. Mark your answer.   (A)   (B)   (C)

20. Mark your answer.   (A)   (B)   (C)

PART 2

UNIT 8

만점 빈출 표현

🎧 850_P2_31

◆ 신분 / 직업 / 직책

company 동료, 일행

accountant 회계사

new-hire 신입 사원

mechanic 정비사

receptionist 접수 담당자

job candidate 입사 지원자

department manager 부서장

section head 부장

mail carrier 집배원

trainee 수습 직원

technician 기사, 기술자

economist 경제학자

wholesaler 도매상

senior director 상무

assistant director 차장

overnight worker 야간 근무자

editorial assistant 편집 보조

technology consultant 기술 고문

senior account manager 선임 회계부장

director of public relations 홍보부 이사

security guard 보안 요원

potential client 잠재 고객

insurance agent 보험회사 직원

copyright attorney 저작권 전문 변호사

project manager 프로젝트 책임자

loading dock supervisor 하역장 관리자

safety inspector 안전 검사관

tenant 세입자

landlord 집주인

real estate agent 부동산 중개인

property manager 관리소장, 부동산 관리인

◆ 시간 / 시점

lately 최근에

half-hour 30분

an hour ahead 1시간 빠른

starting Wednesday 수요일부터

this time of day 하루 중 이맘때

in about an hour 약 1시간 후에

two hours at most 기껏해야 2시간

right after lunch 점심 식사 직후에

probably in late April 아마 4월 말쯤

Monday after next 다다음 주 월요일에

just a couple of days ago 불과 며칠 전에

not until the end of April 4월 말 이후에야

by Monday at the latest 늦어도 월요일까지

by seven thirty in the morning
아침 7시 30분까지

on the first Tuesday of every month
매달 첫째 주 화요일에

◆ 장소 / 위치

in my briefcase 내 서류 가방 안에

in the break room 휴게실에서

in the empty office down the hall
복도를 따라가면 있는 빈 사무실에

at the airline counter 항공사 카운터에서

at either of the appliance stores in town
시내에 있는 가전제품 매장 두 곳 중 아무 데서나

to the south entrance 남문 쪽으로

near the city convention center
시립 컨벤션 센터 근처에

third row on your right
오른쪽 세 번째 줄에

by the register 계산대 옆에

from the warehouse 창고에서

◆ 이유 / 목적

for a summer vacation
여름 휴가를 위해서

for personal business
개인적인 용무 때문에

for an upcoming project
곧 있을 프로젝트를 위해

to lead a seminar
세미나를 진행하기 위해

to renew a contract
계약을 갱신하기 위해

to expand our customer base
고객층을 넓히기 위해

due to inclement weather 악천후 때문에

because it's being repaired
수리 중이기 때문에

because the oven's being replaced
오븐이 교체되고 있기 때문에

Because team members have been out on vacation.
팀원들이 휴가를 갔기 때문이에요.

Because they need more production space.
더 많은 생산 공간이 필요하기 때문이에요.

so that more people can attend
더 많은 사람들이 참석할 수 있도록

There's a construction project on Route 23.
23번 도로에서 공사가 있어요.

I have a decade of experience in the industry. 그 업계에서 10년 경험이 있습니다.

◆ 방법 / 수단

by courier 택배로

by regular mail 보통 우편으로

by alphabetical order 알파벳 순으로

by using social media
소셜 미디어를 활용해서

The list was in an e-mail.
이메일에 목록이 있었어요.

We should make the font smaller.
글씨체를 작게 해야 해요.

Repair requests must be submitted online.
수리 요청은 온라인으로 제출해야 합니다.

◆ 상태 / 의견

It just left. 방금 떠났어요.

It was very informative. 매우 유익했어요.

It couldn't have been better.
정말 최고였어요.

It's not available in red.
빨간색 제품은 없어요.

The audience seemed to like it.
청중이 좋아하는 것 같았어요.

I think earlier would be better.
이를수록 좋은 것 같아요.

She seems really competent.
그녀는 정말 유능해 보여요.

I just got back from there.
방금 거기서 돌아왔어요.

I'm surprised it received so many awards.
그게 그렇게 많은 상을 받다니 놀랍네요.

It was a very productive discussion.
매우 생산적인 토론이었어요.

◆ 기간 / 빈도 / 가격 / 수량

once in a while 가끔

more than six months 6개월 이상

for a while 잠시, 당분간

up to three thousands 3000까지

biweekly 격주로(= every two weeks)

about a dozen 열두 명[개] 정도

It varies from month to month.
그것은 달마다 다릅니다.

every three months 3개월마다

every other week[month] 격주[월]로

Monday through Friday
월요일부터 금요일까지

50 dollars extra 50달러 추가

by twenty percent 20퍼센트만큼

It's almost doubled. 거의 두 배가 되었습니다.

a three-hour time difference
3시간의 시차

30 euros each 각각 30유로

◆ 잘 모른다 / 듣지 못했다

He might know. 그가 알 거에요.

He hasn't called yet.
그가 아직 전화를 하지 않았어요.

Not that I know of. 내가 알기로는 아니에요.

I'm not in charge of that.
제 담당이 아니어서요.

Jane has the schedule.
제인에게 일정표가 있어요.

I was out of the office.
전 사무실에 없었어요.

I just started working here.
여기서 일 시작한 지 얼마 안 됐어요.

I'm not the best person to ask.
저 말고 다른 사람에게 물어보는 게 낫겠어요.

That's news to me.
처음 듣는 이야기인데요.

I haven't been informed[notified].
통지받지 못했어요.

I can't remember the person's name.
이름이 기억나지 않아요.

We won't know until next week.
다음 주나 되어야 알 거예요.

I just moved to this neighborhood.
이 동네로 이사 온 지 얼마 안 됐어요.

I've never gone to that stop.
그 정류장에 가 본 적이 없어요.

Managers will be sharing information at today's meeting.
매니저가 오늘 회의에서 정보를 공유할 거예요.

Diego has the guest list.
디에고가 손님 명단을 가지고 있어요.

Mateo is responsible for that.
마테오가 그 일을 맡고 있어요.

You'd better ask Selena.
셀레나에게 물어보시는 게 나아요.

◆ 결정되지 않았다

It requires management approval.
관리자 승인이 필요해요.

The list isn't available yet.
목록이 아직 준비되지 않았어요.

It hasn't been announced.
공지되지 않았어요.

The company hasn't posted any details yet.
회사가 아직 자세한 내용을 발표하지 않았어요.

The position is still open.
그 자리는 아직 비어 있어요.

He'll let us know tomorrow.
그가 우리에게 내일 알려줄 거에요.

The board is reviewing it.
이사회에서 검토 중이에요.

We're still deciding.
아직 결정 중이에요.

It's still up in the air.
아직 결정 난 게 아니에요.

I haven't made up my mind.
아직 결정하지 못했어요.

I'm still looking into that.
아직 알아보는 중이에요.

It hasn't been decided[finalized] yet.
아직 결정[확정]되지 않았어요.

It hasn't been discussed yet.
아직 논의되지 않았어요.

It depends on the design.
그건 디자인에 따라 달라요.

Peter knows better than I do.
피터가 저보다 더 잘 알아요.

◆ 확인해 보다 / 문의해 보다 / 참고하다

Let me check that for you.
확인해 볼게요.

I'll check with Mr. Dubinsky.
두빈스키 씨에게 확인해 볼게요.

Let me figure it out. 알아볼게요.

I'll call ~ and find out.
~에 전화해서 알아볼게요.

I'll let you know later. 나중에 알려 줄게요.

It's on the corporate calendar.
회사 달력에 나와 있어요.

Let me show you the menu.
메뉴 보여 드릴게요.

Refer to your manual.
설명서를 참고해 주세요.

◆ 역질문

Didn't you get the e-mail this morning?
오늘 아침 이메일 못 받으셨어요?

Do you think that's necessary?
그게 필요하다고 생각하세요?

Oh, are you interested in helping out?
도와주시려고요?

Which is more convenient for you?
어느 쪽이 더 편하세요?

Haven't you seen the schedule?
일정표 못 보셨어요?

Why don't you ask the manager about that? 부장님께 여쭤보지 그래요?

Doesn't Maria have some good photographs?
마리아가 좋은 사진을 몇 장 가지고 있지 않나요?

◆ 하나 선택

I'd prefer eight. 8시가 더 좋아요.

One should be fine. 한 명이면 괜찮을 거예요.

I prefer the one on leadership skills.
리더십 능력에 관한 것이 더 좋아요.

I'd rather leave early.
일찍 출발하는 게 좋겠어요.

Please send me a paper copy.
종이 서류를 보내 주세요.

Lease payments are generally lower.
임대료가 일반적으로 더 낮습니다.

The afternoon would be best.
오후가 가장 좋겠어요.

For the earlier one, please.
더 빠른 것으로 부탁드립니다.

I never carry cash with me.
저는 현금을 절대 가지고 다니지 않아요.

I'd like to talk to someone face-to-face.
저는 대면으로 이야기하는 것이 좋아요.

It'll be nice to have some snacks.
간식을 먹는 게 좋겠네요.

I'm going on vacation first.
우선 휴가를 갈 거예요.

I'll go with the red one.
붉은 것으로 할게요.

◆ 모두 선택 / 상관없음

I'm OK with either. 어느 쪽이든 괜찮아요.

We can afford to do both. 둘 다 할 수 있어요.

Either (one) is fine (with me).
저는 어느 쪽이든 괜찮아요.

I'll leave it to you. 당신에게 맡길게요.

I'm considering both. 둘 다 고려 중이에요.

I don't have any preference. 아무거나 괜찮아요.

About the same of both. 둘 다 비슷해요.

◆ 모두 반대

I don't like either of them. 둘 다 싫어요.

That's all right; I don't want any.
괜찮습니다. 필요 없습니다.

Actually, neither of them.
사실 둘 다 아니에요.

None of the others were.
나머지 사람들 중 아무도 그렇지 않았어요.

◆ 수락 / 동의

Yes, that'd be great. 네, 좋아요.

Tomorrow should work. 내일 괜찮습니다.

Yes—thanks for the invitation!
네, 초대해 주셔서 감사해요!

OK, I'll work on that. 알았어요, 제가 할게요.

Yes, let's do that now. 네, 지금 그렇게 해요.

Sure, it'll be just a few minutes.
네, 몇 분이면 됩니다.

◆ 거절 / 반대

Sorry, but I'm busy at that time.
죄송하지만, 그 시간에 바빠요.

I already signed up. 저는 이미 가입했어요.

We've already ordered our meal.
식사를 이미 주문했어요.

I have a mandatory training that day.
저는 그날 의무 교육이 있어요.

I don't think they'll need to use it.
저는 그들이 그것을 사용할 필요가 있다고 생각하지 않아요.

That color's only sold online.
그 색은 온라인에서만 판매해요.

PART 3
짧은 대화

INTRO

UNIT 9 | 주제·목적 / 화자·장소 문제

UNIT 10 | 세부 사항 / 문제점·걱정거리 문제

UNIT 11 | 요청·제안 / 다음에 할 일 문제

UNIT 12 | 의도 파악 / 시각 정보 연계 문제

PART 3 만점 빈출 표현

PART 3 짧은 대화

총 13세트 39문항

두 사람, 혹은 세 사람의 대화를 듣고 이와 관련된 세 개의 문제를 푸는 유형으로, 업무와 일상 생활 관련 대화문이 출제된다.
매회 3인 대화가 2세트씩 포함된다.

◆ 고득점 풀이 전략

STEP 1	① 대화 듣기 전에 문제와 보기 읽기
문제 파악하기	② 의문사, 주어, 동사를 중심으로 키워드 파악하기(화자의 성별 구분 필수)

STEP 2	① 키워드 관련 내용이 나오면 답 체크하기
대화 들으면서	② 놓친 문제는 과감히 포기하고 다음 문제로 넘어가기
정답 찾기	③ 대화 종료 후 다음 대화의 문제와 보기 읽기

◆ ETS 예제

1. What department does **the man** most likely work in?

(A) Accounting
(B) Research and Development
(C) Customer Service
(D) Sales

2. Why does **the man** say he feels optimistic?

(A) Engine parts are easy to obtain.
(B) A color is popular with customers.
(C) A seat design is compact.
(D) A battery charger is fast.

3. According to **the woman**, what benefit can customers expect?

(A) A tax credit from the government
(B) Low-interest financing from a bank
(C) Low maintenance costs
(D) A discount on accessories

W **1.** Min-Soo, how is your research coming along? Has your team developed anything to improve our EXB model electric car?

M Well, **2.** we're feeling cautiously optimistic because we're working on a battery charger that works at twice the speed of standard chargers. Unfortunately, the cost may be higher than many customers are willing to spend.

W Let's not worry about that now. Besides, **3.** the tax credit on electric cars will still make the EXB attractive to customers. They can expect to get 5,000 dollars back from the government when they buy the EXB.

단서
1. 남자가 일하는 부서: 전기차 연구 개발 부서
2. 남자가 낙관적인 이유: 충전기 속도가 2배 빨라서
3. 여자가 혜택이라고 말하는 것: 정부의 세금 공제

정답
1. (B) Research and Development
2. (D) A battery charger is fast.
3. (A) A tax credit from the government

◆ 최신 출제 경향

① 주로 업무, 사무기기, 인사, 사내 행사와 같은 회사 생활과 관련된 대화가 출제되며, 교통, 쇼핑, 부동산 등 일상 생활 관련 내용도 등장한다.

② 구체적인 정보를 물어보는 세부 사항 문제가 가장 자주 출제되고, 주제/목적 및 장소/직업을 묻는 문제가 20퍼센트 이상 꾸준히 출제되고 있다. 시각 정보 연계 문제는 3개, 화자의 의도 파악 문제는 2개씩 고정적으로 출제된다.

◆ 패러프레이징[Paraphrasing]

패러프레이징이란 앞서 언급된 것을 뜻이 통하는 다른 말로 바꾸어 표현하는 것이다. 대화문에서 들리는 단어가 보기에 그대로 등장하는 경우도 있지만 패러프레이징 되어 나오는 경우가 많다.

1. 포괄적 개념을 지닌 상위어 활용

W That's a good idea. I'll call some other paper companies to see whether we can get a better deal.

여 좋은 생각이에요. 제가 **다른 제지업체들에** 전화해서 더 싸게 살 수 있는지 알아볼게요.

Q What does the woman say she will do?
A Contact some suppliers

질문 여자는 무엇을 하겠다고 말하는가?
정답 몇몇 공급업체에 연락하기

2. 동의어, 유사 표현

M We're having a sale later this month. Lots of computers will be discounted then.

남 저희는 이달 말에 세일을 할 예정입니다. 그때 많은 컴퓨터가 할인될 것입니다.

Q What will happen later this month?
A A sales event will be held.

질문 이달 말에 무슨 일이 있겠는가?
정답 세일 행사가 열릴 것이다.

3. 내용 축약

W I'm not a member here, but I'm interested in taking some dance classes, like jazz or hip-hop.

여 저는 여기 회원은 아니지만, **재즈나 힙합 같은 댄스 수업을** 듣는 데 관심이 있어요.

Q What kind of class is the woman interested in?
A Dance

질문 여자는 어떤 수업에 관심이 있는가?
정답 춤

4. 품사 변경

M I'm sorry, but the truck that's delivering the windows got stuck in the mud at a different work site.

남 죄송하지만, 창문을 **배달하던** 트럭이 다른 작업장의 진흙탕에 빠졌어요.

Q Why does the man apologize?
A A delivery is delayed.

질문 남자가 사과하는 이유는?
정답 배달이 지연되었다.

UNIT 9 주제·목적 / 화자·장소 문제

① 주제 · 목적 문제
출제비율 3~4문항 / 39문항

대화의 주제나 전화/방문의 목적을 묻는 문제로, 보통 첫 번째나 두 번째 문제로 출제된다. 주로 화자가 바라는 바를 이야기하는 부분이나 소식을 전하는 초반부에서 주제나 목적이 드러난다.

고득점 | 전략 단서 포착하기 🎧 850_P3_01 정답 및 해설 p.048

첫 화자가 화두를 꺼내면서 그와 관련된 내용이 이어지므로, 인사말 이후 처음 2~3문장에 집중하자.

W Hi, Wataru. **I'm preparing the quarterly report for management.** **M** So **you'd like to know about customer satisfaction?** → 초반부에 목적을 나타내는 단서 표현(you'd like to ~) 등장 **W** Right. As the head of customer service, have you identified a feature of our computers that people consistently praise?...	**Q.** **What** is the **purpose** of the woman's visit? (A) To congratulate a colleague (B) To explain a new procedure (C) To collect some information (D) To submit a complaint 정답 **(C) To collect some information** 패러프레이징 대화의 know about customer satisfaction → 정답의 collect some information

---

빈출 문제 유형 & 정답 단서 패턴

화자의 바람/희망, 필요 사항 등을 나타내는 표현을 파악해 둔다.

	문제	대화 속 정답 단서
주제	**What** are the speakers mainly **discussing**?	[필요/요청] **We need** some documents about this project before the meeting.
	What is the conversation mainly **about**?	[상황 설명] I placed an order last week, but it hasn't arrived yet.
목적	**What** is the **purpose** of the call?	[전화 목적] **I'm calling to** buy two tickets to the museum fund-raiser next week.
	Why is the woman **calling** the man?	[바람/희망] **I'd like to** take the next plane to Beijing this evening.

068

주제

1. **What** are the speakers **discussing**?
   (A) A trade show
   (B) An art exhibit
   (C) A storewide sale
   (D) A building renovation

2. What does the man recommend?
   (A) Scheduling more time
   (B) Increasing the budget
   (C) Reserving a larger space
   (D) Improving product quality

3. What does the woman give to the man?
   (A) An application form
   (B) An order receipt
   (C) A price list
   (D) A product description

4. What type of business does the man work for?
   (A) A dental office
   (B) A restaurant
   (C) A bank
   (D) A fitness center

목적

5. **Why** is the man **calling** the woman?
   (A) To register for a conference
   (B) To discuss an investment plan
   (C) To arrange a job interview
   (D) To confirm some business hours

6. What document does the man mention?
   (A) An invoice
   (B) A survey form
   (C) A professional certificate
   (D) A bank statement

주제

7. **What** is the conversation mainly **about**?
   (A) Leasing some retail space
   (B) Contracting new manufacturers
   (C) Traveling internationally
   (D) Entering new markets

8. Who most likely is the man?
   (A) A real estate agent
   (B) An investor
   (C) A lawyer
   (D) A marketing specialist

9. What does the woman's company sell?
   (A) Construction equipment
   (B) Electronic devices
   (C) Automotive parts
   (D) Sporting goods

PART 3　　UNIT 9

069

② 화자 · 장소 문제

🎧 출제비율 6~7문항 / 39문항

화자의 근무지/부서/직업 혹은 대화를 나누고 있는 장소 등을 묻는 문제이다. 대화 초반에 장소 및 직업이 직접적으로 언급되거나, 특정 업계 관련 어휘가 대화 곳곳에 등장하기도 한다.

| 고득점 | 전략 | **단서 포착하기** |

🎧 850_P3_03   정답 및 해설 p.050

여자의 직업을 묻는 질문이라도 상대 남자의 대사에도 주목해야 한다. 상대방이 직업을 알려 주는 경우도 있기 때문에, 반드시 전체 대사를 듣고 직업에 대한 정답 단서를 찾도록 한다.

M1 Thanks for making time to meet with us today, Isabel. We know **you're quite busy rehearsing for your TV show**.
→ 업계/근무지 관련 어휘 등장: 리허설, TV 쇼 → 배우
→ 여자의 직업을 묻고 있지만, 단서는 남자의 대사에 있음

W Luckily, I finished practicing my lines early today, since I'm not in many scenes in this particular episode. Anyhow, I'm excited to discuss representing your brand.

M2 Your endorsement of our product means a lot...

Q. **Who** most likely is the **woman**?
(A) An actor
(B) A caterer
(C) A makeup artist
(D) A clothing designer

정답 **(A) An actor**

| 빈출 문제 유형 & 정답 단서 패턴 |

화자·장소 문제의 단서가 제시되는 대표적인 방식을 파악하여 정답을 유추해내자.

문제	대화 속 정답 단서
[화자] **Who** (most likely) is **the man**?	[직업/장소 관련 어휘] Excuse me. I'm calling from **room 408**. Is there a place **near the hotel** where I can buy an umbrella?
[장소] **Where** do the speakers (most likely) **work**?	I wanted to ask you about the new **advertising campaign** for the Miller Company's coffee maker.
[화자] **What industry[field, department]** do the speakers **work in**?	So, from your résumé I can see you have a lot of experience with **local radio stations** in many different regions.
[장소] **Where** is the conversation **taking place**?	[첫 인사] **Welcome to** Martin's Car World. Are you looking for a new vehicle or a used one?
[화자] **What** most likely is the man's **job[profession]**?	[본인 소개] Hi, Marina. **This is** Jeffrey from the marketing department.

1. **Where** do the speakers most likely **work**?
   (A) At a landscaping company
   (B) At a garden center
   (C) At a farm
   (D) At a government office

2. What does the woman want to do?
   (A) Change a growing process
   (B) Apply for a bank loan
   (C) Purchase more equipment
   (D) Hire seasonal workers

3. What does the man say he will do today?
   (A) Submit a business proposal
   (B) Schedule some maintenance
   (C) Consult with an industry expert
   (D) Compile a list of potential clients

4. Why is the man calling?
   (A) His Internet connection is slow.
   (B) He wants to cancel a subscription.
   (C) He cannot read articles on a Web site.
   (D) His printer is not working.

5. What does the woman say can be found in an e-mail?
   (A) An invoice
   (B) An error code
   (C) A shipping date
   (D) An identification number

6. **What** most likely is the man's **job**?
   (A) Accountant
   (B) Researcher
   (C) Newspaper editor
   (D) Web designer

7. **What field** do the women **work in**?
   (A) Law
   (B) Accounting
   (C) Real estate
   (D) Education

8. What does the man ask about?
   (A) The criteria for intern selection
   (B) The process for evaluation
   (C) The kind of projects assigned
   (D) The compensation for interns

9. What will the man most likely do next?
   (A) Set up a workspace
   (B) Meet other team members
   (C) Complete some paperwork
   (D) Get an identification badge

1. Why is the woman calling?
   (A) To reschedule an appointment
   (B) To inquire about an apartment
   (C) To sell some products
   (D) To make a job offer

2. What will the woman send to the man?
   (A) A company directory
   (B) A contract
   (C) Some photographs
   (D) A price list

3. What does the woman remind the man about?
   (A) Where to park
   (B) Who to contact
   (C) When to arrive
   (D) What to wear

4. Who most likely are the speakers?
   (A) Reporters
   (B) Architects
   (C) City officials
   (D) Job recruiters

5. What does the man say about a new building?
   (A) It is leasing office space.
   (B) It will include an art gallery.
   (C) It will have a rooftop restaurant.
   (D) It will be the tallest structure in the city.

6. What does the woman suggest the man do?
   (A) Tour a facility
   (B) Revise a timeline
   (C) Conduct an interview
   (D) Update a Web site

7. Where does the man most likely work?
   (A) At a graphic design studio
   (B) At an eye doctor's office
   (C) At a pharmacy
   (D) At a computer store

8. What does the man recommend doing to fix a problem?
   (A) Adjusting a chair height
   (B) Replacing a battery
   (C) Refilling a prescription
   (D) Enlarging some text

9. What will the woman do next?
   (A) Complete a survey
   (B) Order some equipment
   (C) Read online reviews
   (D) Go out for lunch

10. Why is the man calling?
    (A) To ask about a payment plan
    (B) To complain about an incorrect delivery
    (C) To request a catalog
    (D) To arrange to have merchandise picked up

11. What does the woman say was entered incorrectly?
    (A) An item code
    (B) An e-mail address
    (C) An apartment number
    (D) A delivery date

12. What does the woman say she will do?
    (A) Issue a refund
    (B) Speak to an employee
    (C) Rush a delivery
    (D) Send a confirmation

13. What type of event are the speakers discussing?
(A) A workshop
(B) A craft fair
(C) An election
(D) A concert

14. What industry do the speakers most likely work in?
(A) Hospitality
(B) Journalism
(C) Music
(D) Fashion

15. What problem does the woman mention?
(A) An order has not arrived.
(B) More seating is needed.
(C) A presenter is unavailable.
(D) Some equipment is broken.

16. What are the speakers mainly discussing?
(A) Managing an office move
(B) Promoting a new product
(C) Planning a budget
(D) Organizing a workshop

17. What does the man like about a suggestion?
(A) It will attract new clients.
(B) It will save time.
(C) It will motivate employees.
(D) It will reduce costs.

18. What does Priyanka say her team will do first?
(A) Build a Web site
(B) Collect feedback
(C) Create some publicity materials
(D) Purchase supplies

19. Where do the speakers most likely work?
(A) In a travel agency
(B) In a car factory
(C) In a shipping company
(D) In an electronics store

20. According to the woman, what may have caused a problem?
(A) A worker is absent today.
(B) Some instructions are unclear.
(C) A machine was adjusted incorrectly.
(D) Some equipment is missing.

21. What does the man say he will do?
(A) Reallocate some work
(B) Restart a project
(C) Check a document
(D) Find some tools

22. Who is the woman?
(A) A city official
(B) An accountant
(C) An architect
(D) A sales director

23. What does the man ask about?
(A) A service agreement
(B) A hiring plan
(C) Some funding
(D) Some policy changes

24. What does the woman say she is excited about?
(A) Some cost savings
(B) A newspaper article
(C) A local festival
(D) Some artwork

PART 3

UNIT 9

UNIT 10 세부 사항 / 문제점·걱정거리 문제

❶ 세부 사항 문제

● 출제비율 12~13문항 / 39문항

파트 3에서 가장 많이 출제되는 유형으로, What, How 등 다양한 의문사를 사용하여 특정 정보를 묻거나 화자가 언급한 내용을 묻는 문제이다. 문제 및 보기의 키워드가 그대로, 혹은 패러프레이징 되어 등장한다.

| 고득점 | 전략 | **단서 포착하기** | 🎧 850_P3_06 정답 및 해설 p.057 |

문제와 보기를 먼저 읽고 키워드를 파악한 후, 해당 부분을 노려 듣는다. 인물, 사물, 시간, 장소, 숫자가 패러프레이징 되어 핵심어로 등장할 가능성이 높다.

W **This past week has been pretty chaotic with the move here to our new office building.**
→ 시간 키워드 패러프레이징: this past week
→ the last week

M I agree. Have you seen my desk calendar by any chance? The one with the pictures of European cities? I thought for sure I packed it, but it wasn't in any of the boxes that were delivered here.

W I haven't seen it. And, actually, I'm missing a few things, too…

Q. **What did** the speakers' company **do** within **the last week**?
(A) It hired an assistant director.
(B) It moved to a new office space.
(C) It acquired additional clients.
(D) It changed a logo design.

정답 **(B) It moved to a new office space.**

패러프레이징 대화의 the move here to our new office building → 정답의 moved to a new office space

핵심 포인트: 패러프레이징

각 문제에서 요구하는 세부 사항이 무엇인지 키워드를 체크하여 노려 듣기 하자.

문제	대화 속 정답 단서	정답
What does the woman **say about** the book?	I got this Chinese cookbook for my birthday yesterday, and it seems to be missing several pages in the middle.	It has a defect.
According to the speakers, what will the news article help to do?	That kind of positive media coverage will help with our recruitment campaign for new employees.	Increase job applications
What does the man notify the woman about?	Keep in mind that the Winter Orchid closes at nine o'clock tonight.	A closing time

074

1. **Why** does the man **select the woman** for an assignment?
(A) She has a light workload this week.
(B) She was recommended by a coworker.
(C) She has relevant experience.
(D) She expressed interest in fitness.

2. What does the woman say she will do?
(A) Form a planning committee
(B) Interview some vendors
(C) Research some event spaces
(D) Check an instructor's availability

3. What type of activity does the man suggest?
(A) A dance class
(B) A bicycle race
(C) A volleyball tournament
(D) A swimming lesson

4. **What** does the woman **say** is **causing a problem**?
(A) A staffing shortage
(B) A scheduling mistake
(C) Road construction
(D) Poor weather conditions

5. What is the man concerned about?
(A) Going over budget
(B) Missing a project deadline
(C) Being late to a meeting
(D) Passing an inspection

6. What does the woman suggest some clients do?
(A) Cancel a trip
(B) Visit a cafeteria
(C) Speak with a supervisor
(D) Review some documents

7. Who most likely is the woman?
(A) A reporter
(B) A salesperson
(C) An artist
(D) A tailor

8. **According to the man,** **what change** is expected?
(A) Manufacturing costs will decrease.
(B) More colors will be used in clothing designs.
(C) Merchandise will only be available online.
(D) Employees will begin to dress casually at work.

9. What does the woman ask to do?
(A) Take a private tour
(B) Meet the company president
(C) Take photographs
(D) Visit a warehouse

PART 3

UNIT 10

❷ 문제점 · 걱정거리 문제

● 출제비율 2~3문항/39문항

화자가 언급한 문제점이나 걱정거리를 묻는 문제가 출제되며, 주로 대화의 초·중반에 단서가 제시된다. 기기 고장, 계산 착오, 비용/매출 문제, 배송 및 일정 문제, 시간 제약 등 다양한 소재가 등장한다.

고득점 전략 단서 포착하기

🎧 850_P3_08 정답 및 해설 p.059

문제를 통해 누구의 대사에서 정답이 나올지 예상하고, 부정적인 표현에 집중하자.

W **Alexi**, I heard that someone from Xavier Solar Energy was here on Monday to evaluate our office buildings for solar panels. How did it go?

M1 Most of the buildings are ideal candidates, **but a few on the east side get too much shade from nearby trees to make solar panels productive**.
→ Alexi의 대사 주목, 부정어(but) 등장

M2 I see what you mean. I suppose we could cut a few trees down. What do you think, Karen?...

Q. **What problem** does **Alexi mention**?
(A) Some buildings get too much shade.
(B) Some generators use too much energy.
(C) An evaluation report has not arrived.
(D) A project is over budget.

정답 **(A) Some buildings get too much shade.**

빈출 문제 유형 & 정답 단서 패턴

문제점이나 걱정을 제시할 때는 반전이나 역접, 걱정을 나타내는 표현이 등장한다.

	문제	대화 속 정답 단서
문제점	**What problem** does the woman **mention**?	[부정적 의미의 어휘] Travelers using the airport **complain** that it needs to expand the parking lot. [부정어] It looks like we **don't** have any more in stock at the moment.
	What is the **problem**?	[대조/반전] It actually just arrived, **but** one of the items I ordered was missing.
걱정거리	**What** is the man **concerned about**?	[걱정] **I'm worried that** we might not be able to produce enough shirts to fill the Anderson Brothers order. **We're concerned that** another company just opened nearby.

1. Where does the woman work?
   (A) At a government office
   (B) At a paint shop
   (C) At a parking garage
   (D) At an apartment complex

문제점

2. **What problem** does the woman **discuss**?
   (A) Some prices have increased.
   (B) Some entrances are blocked.
   (C) Some signs are difficult to read.
   (D) Some lights are not working.

3. What does the man ask the woman to do?
   (A) Reschedule some appointments
   (B) Send some photos
   (C) Submit a form
   (D) Visit a building

4. What do the speakers do professionally?
   (A) Cook
   (B) Dance
   (C) Design clothing
   (D) Plan events

5. What is being discussed?
   (A) A professional-development workshop
   (B) A new marketing strategy
   (C) A series of competitions
   (D) A corporate banquet

걱정거리

6. **What** are the women **concerned about**?
   (A) Making sure that everyone can participate
   (B) Implementing a policy change
   (C) Raising funds for a charity event
   (D) Taking a disciplinary action

문제점

7. What event are the speakers most likely preparing for?
   (A) A community festival
   (B) A restaurant opening
   (C) A company picnic
   (D) A cooking class

8. **What problem** does the man **mention**?
   (A) Bad weather is expected.
   (B) An appliance is broken.
   (C) A guest list has not been approved.
   (D) A delivery has not arrived.

9. How does the woman say she will help?
   (A) By picking up some items
   (B) By researching some vendors
   (C) By hiring an additional worker
   (D) By changing an event time

ETS 고득점 실전 문제

1. What most likely is the man's area of expertise?
   (A) Computer programming
   (B) Accounting
   (C) Human resources
   (D) Architecture

2. Why is the man worried?
   (A) He does not know what to wear.
   (B) He may not have enough experience.
   (C) He thinks a process is inefficient.
   (D) He may need to renew a certification.

3. What does the woman ask the man about?
   (A) Whether his work location will change
   (B) Whether he needs a recommendation letter
   (C) Whether an interview will be recorded
   (D) Whether a company has other job openings

4. Who most likely is the woman?
   (A) A sports reporter
   (B) A physician
   (C) A fitness trainer
   (D) An event planner

5. What did Anjali Krishnan do this year?
   (A) She ran a race.
   (B) She applied for a new job.
   (C) She earned a scholarship.
   (D) She started a successful business.

6. What does the woman recommend the men do?
   (A) Keep daily records
   (B) Increase the size of their team
   (C) Talk to additional experts
   (D) Maintain a consistent schedule

7. Why is the woman visiting this particular store?
   (A) Her neighbor recommended it.
   (B) She saw an item in a display window.
   (C) She saw a newspaper advertisement.
   (D) She has a discount coupon.

8. What does the man say about a product?
   (A) It is stitched by hand.
   (B) It does not stain easily.
   (C) It is part of a limited edition.
   (D) It is available in many colors.

9. What does the man say is included in a price?
   (A) A discount
   (B) A warranty
   (C) Express delivery
   (D) Installation

10. Who most likely is the man?
    (A) A construction contractor
    (B) An architect
    (C) A property manager
    (D) An interior designer

11. What problem is the woman reporting?
    (A) An address is not correct.
    (B) An appliance is not working.
    (C) A delivery truck was late.
    (D) An appointment was missed.

12. What does the man say he will do?
    (A) Contact a worker
    (B) Process a payment
    (C) Postpone a deadline
    (D) Review a contract

13. Where most likely are the speakers?
(A) At a hair salon
(B) At a fitness center
(C) At a medical clinic
(D) At an automobile repair shop

14. What must the man do before his appointment?
(A) Change his clothes
(B) Move his car
(C) Make a payment
(D) Complete some forms

15. What does the woman suggest doing?
(A) Checking a bus schedule
(B) Downloading a mobile application
(C) Reading an article
(D) Waiting in the lobby

16. What are the speakers discussing?
(A) Meeting weekly sales goals
(B) Keeping employees informed
(C) Allowing employees to work from home
(D) Opening another branch office

17. What is the woman concerned about?
(A) Negative customer feedback
(B) Rising prices of real estate
(C) Finding a meeting time
(D) A decrease in productivity

18. What does the woman ask the man to do?
(A) Print an agenda
(B) Unlock a conference room
(C) Prepare for an inspection
(D) Order food for an event

19. Where do the speakers most likely work?
(A) At a repair shop
(B) At a department store
(C) At a sports facility
(D) At a factory

20. What problem does the man mention?
(A) A machine broke down.
(B) An order was canceled.
(C) An employee has not arrived.
(D) A shipment was delayed.

21. What will the woman most likely do next?
(A) Update a supply list
(B) Join a telephone call
(C) Write an e-mail
(D) Check a manual

22. What did the speakers apply for?
(A) A grant
(B) A loan
(C) A contract
(D) A permit

23. What does the man mean when he says, "I submitted it right before the deadline"?
(A) A process needs improving.
(B) A colleague was not available.
(C) A change cannot be made.
(D) A late fee has been avoided.

24. What technology do the speakers hope to use?
(A) Solar panels
(B) Electric vehicles
(C) Contactless payment systems
(D) High-capacity metro cars

PART 3

UNIT 10

요청·제안/다음에 할 일 문제

❶ 요청 · 제안 문제

● 출제비율 4~5문항/39문항

화자가 요청하거나 제안하는 문제는 주로 두 번째, 세 번째 문제로 출제되며, 대화의 중·후반부에 단서가 언급된다.

고득점 **전략** **단서 포착하기**

🎧 850_P3_11　정답 및 해설 p.067

요청한 것을 묻는지 아니면 요청받은 사항을 묻는지 문제의 요지를 확실히 파악한다.

M　Hi, Mary and Nikolay. I wanted to see how we're coming along with the project to add a bus route that makes several stops in the historic district. As you know, the town wants it to be in operation by the summer tourist season.	**Q. What was** the woman **asked to do**? (A) Apply for a permit (B) Update a Web site (C) Request some signs (D) Order refreshments
W　Yes. **You asked me to take care of getting the signs for the stops along the new route.** I've already put in a work order. 　→ 여자가 요청 받은 상황. 요청의 표현(You asked me to ~) 등장	정답 **(C) Request some signs** 패러프레이징　대화의 take care of getting the signs → 정답의 Request some signs
M　Great. And what about hiring more drivers to handle the route? Nikolay, have you reviewed the applications we've received so far?…	

빈출 문제 유형 & 정답 단서 패턴

요청이나 제안과 관련된 Can you ~?/I can/I suggest 등의 표현을 익혀 두자.

	문제	대화 속 정답 단서
요청	**What** does the man **ask** the woman **to do**? **What information** does the man **request**?	[요청] **Can you** give me a ride home after dinner today? **Would you** be able to forward the price list of the services?
제안	**What** does the man **offer to do**?	[도움 제안] **I can** have someone bring one up to your room, if you'd like.
	What does the man **recommend doing**?	[방법 제안] **You might** be able to find a better price there.
	What does the man **suggest** the woman do?	**I suggest** taking the subway because of the traffic congestion.

ETS 유형 연습

1. Why is the woman calling?
   (A) To make a suggestion
   (B) To order a product
   (C) To confirm a delivery
   (D) To ask for assistance

2. **What** does the man **ask** the woman **to do**?
   (A) Arrange a photo shoot
   (B) Send a photograph
   (C) Submit an invoice
   (D) Provide contact information

3. What does the woman say about the coworker in her department?
   (A) He is very busy.
   (B) He has been promoted.
   (C) He recommended an artist.
   (D) He deleted a message.

4. What does the woman want to do?
   (A) Travel with a pet
   (B) Transport a bicycle
   (C) Arrange for a group trip
   (D) Take an express route

5. **What** does the man **suggest** the woman do?
   (A) Transfer to a bus
   (B) Pay by credit card
   (C) Buy a special carrier
   (D) Travel during a specific time

6. Why does the man apologize?
   (A) A storage space cannot be reserved.
   (B) Some trains have been delayed.
   (C) Tickets cannot be exchanged.
   (D) A station is under construction.

7. What is the purpose of the meeting?
   (A) To plan a fund-raising event
   (B) To review survey results
   (C) To introduce a new client
   (D) To discuss marketing ideas

8. What is Mei Na concerned about?
   (A) Costs
   (B) Staffing
   (C) Deadlines
   (D) Transportation

9. **What** does the man **offer to do**?
   (A) Research design trends
   (B) Send some e-mails
   (C) Confirm a location
   (D) Draft a contract

PART 3

UNIT 11

❷ 다음에 할 일 문제

● 출제비율 4~5문항/39문항

화자가 다음에 할 일이나 미래의 특정 시점/불특정한 미래에 있을 행사 등을 묻는 문제이다. 주로 세 번째 문제로 출제되며, 마지막 대사에서 단서가 주어지는 경우가 많다.

고득점 전략 단서 포착하기

🎧 850_P3_13 정답 및 해설 p.069

미래를 나타내는 다양한 시제뿐 아니라 화자의 의지/결심이 드러나는 표현에도 주목해야 한다.

W Good morning, Sato Recycling Center.

M Hi, I'm interested in purchasing some materials from your company—recycled plastic from milk jugs and juice bottles.

W Oh, unfortunately we've stopped processing plastics. Well, I do know of another recycling company that may have what you need. **I'm sure I have their phone number here on my desk. Hold on a second.**

→ 의지/결심이 드러나는 표현(I'm sure) 등장

Q. What will the woman most likely **do next**?
  (A) See if her manager is available
  (B) Check a production schedule
  (C) Look for some contact information
  (D) Calculate a delivery cost

정답 **(C) Look for some contact information**

패러프레이징 대화의 phone number → 정답의 contact information

빈출 문제 유형 & 정답 단서 패턴

미래 시제/계획을 나타내는 표현이나 제안/요청의 표현이 등장하는 구간에서 정답을 찾는다.

문제	대화 속 정답 단서
What does the man say **will happen next**?	[미래/계획–will] **I'll** make sure the announcer will give an update right away with information about the new venue.
What does the man say he **will do** in the morning?	[미래/계획–be going to] Tomorrow morning **I'm going to** get a few estimates from some contractors.
What will take place next Wednesday?	[예정된 가까운 미래–be + ing] Stephen announced that **she's moving** to Boston for a new job next Wednesday.
What will the man probably **do next**?	[제안] **Let me** check the schedule with the manager. **I can** come take a look now.
What will the man most likely **do next**?	[상대방의 제안/요청] **Let's** take our lunch break now and revise the drawing after we eat. **Could you** get me a printout of this information right away?

1. What is the conversation mainly about?
(A) Paving a parking area
(B) Constructing a bridge
(C) Reopening a train station
(D) Renovating a building

2. What problem does the woman mention?
(A) A project will be too expensive.
(B) A deadline will not be met.
(C) Some staff members are unavailable.
(D) Some materials did not arrive.

다음에 할 일

3. **What** does the man say he **will do**?
(A) Organize a training session
(B) Contact a manager
(C) Review job applications
(D) Attend a workshop

4. Who most likely is the woman?
(A) A food caterer
(B) A musician
(C) A travel agent
(D) A lawyer

5. What problem does the woman mention?
(A) A flight has been delayed.
(B) An event must be canceled.
(C) Some contracts were not delivered.
(D) Some expenses are not covered.

다음에 할 일

6. **What will** the man most likely **do next**?
(A) Consult with a manager
(B) Book a hotel room
(C) Request some receipts
(D) Hire some additional staff

7. What does the woman ask the man to do?
(A) Update a procedure
(B) Restock some supplies
(C) Sample a new product
(D) Rearrange a cabinet

8. Why is the man unable to help?
(A) Not enough information has been collected.
(B) Some equipment is out of order.
(C) A researcher is currently unavailable.
(D) A shipment is late.

다음에 할 일

9. **What will happen at 1:30?**
(A) The woman's colleagues will arrive.
(B) The man will go to a store.
(C) The laboratory will close for the day.
(D) The maintenance team will make repairs.

1. Who most likely are the speakers?
   (A) Airport security guards
   (B) Customs officers
   (C) Airline pilots
   (D) Ticket agents

2. What is causing a delay?
   (A) Staff shortages
   (B) A maintenance issue
   (C) Traffic congestion
   (D) Poor weather conditions

3. What will the man do next?
   (A) Make an announcement
   (B) Contact an airport official
   (C) Check identification
   (D) Consult a manual

4. Where does the conversation most likely take place?
   (A) In a park
   (B) In a taxi
   (C) On a train
   (D) On an airplane

5. What does the man suggest the women do?
   (A) Ask a driver to turn around
   (B) Cancel a meeting
   (C) Request a refund
   (D) Get off at a different stop

6. What will Nadia ask a client to do?
   (A) Make a payment online
   (B) Meet at a restaurant
   (C) Save some seats at a lecture
   (D) Sample some products

7. What most likely is the woman's job?
   (A) Plumber
   (B) Safety inspector
   (C) Landscaper
   (D) Office manager

8. What does the man say about a hotel during a renovation?
   (A) It will be cleaned daily.
   (B) It will reduce its prices.
   (C) It will remain open.
   (D) It will stop hiring new employees.

9. What does the woman offer to do?
   (A) Make an appointment
   (B) Check some rooms
   (C) Buy some supplies
   (D) Calculate a cost

10. What are the speakers mainly discussing?
    (A) Developing some software
    (B) Training new employees
    (C) Ordering some equipment
    (D) Responding to a complaint

11. What does the man imply when he says, "Have you seen the budget for this year"?
    (A) He thinks a decision was necessary.
    (B) He is missing some data.
    (C) He has doubts about a suggestion.
    (D) He wants to know when some work will be finished.

12. What will the man do this afternoon?
    (A) Send out a survey
    (B) Buy a new computer
    (C) Change a work schedule
    (D) Research some companies

13. What does the speakers' company produce?
(A) Curtains
(B) Clothing
(C) Furniture
(D) Luggage

14. What does the woman ask the man to do?
(A) Visit a manufacturing facility
(B) Complete an inventory report
(C) Submit a maintenance request
(D) Find some fabric suppliers

15. Why will the woman be out of the office on Wednesday afternoon?
(A) She will be at a medical appointment.
(B) She will be meeting with an accountant.
(C) She will be moving to a new office space.
(D) She will be attending a family event.

16. What most likely is the man's job?
(A) Interior designer
(B) Electrician
(C) Restaurant chef
(D) Research scientist

17. What information does the man ask the women for?
(A) A mailing address
(B) An opening date
(C) An order number
(D) A product cost

18. What does the man say he plans to do?
(A) Visit a library
(B) Conduct a study
(C) Interview some experts
(D) Research online

19. What service does the speakers' business provide?
(A) Guided tours
(B) Photography
(C) Event planning
(D) Bike rentals

20. What resource do the speakers consult?
(A) A road map
(B) A calendar
(C) A company Web site
(D) A training manual

21. What does the man suggest doing?
(A) Offering special discounts
(B) Asking customers for feedback
(C) Taking some pictures
(D) Testing some options

22. Where do the speakers most likely work?
(A) At a software company
(B) At an advertising agency
(C) At a research laboratory
(D) At an architecture firm

23. What does the woman imply when she says, "Almost everybody from our office is going"?
(A) She hopes the man reserved a large bus.
(B) She thinks the man should reschedule his plans.
(C) She is concerned about exceeding a budget.
(D) She did not realize a conference was so popular.

24. What does the man say he will do?
(A) Print an e-mail
(B) Sign a card
(C) Make a telephone call
(D) Prepare a presentation

UNIT 12 의도 파악 / 시각 정보 연계 문제

❶ 의도 파악 문제

🔊 출제비율 2문항/39문항

제시된 문장의 숨은 의도를 묻는 문제로, 매회 고정으로 2문항씩 출제된다. 같은 표현이라도 문맥에 따라 의미가 달라질 수 있으므로 맥락을 잘 이해하는 것이 중요하다.

고득점 전략 **단서 포착하기** 🎧 850_P3_16 정답 및 해설 p.076

특정 단어를 노려 듣는 것이 아니라 제시 문구가 나올 때까지의 상황, 특히 앞뒤 문장을 잘 듣고 정답을 찾자.

M Simone, do you know anything about copy machines? I'm trying to copy the handout for this afternoon's meeting, but **it's only printing blank pages.** → 초반부에서 문제 언급: 복사기에서 빈 페이지만 인쇄 **W** Oh. **I'm not sure how to fix that.** You know our technical support team is very good. → 제시문 앞: 고치는 방법 모름 → 기술 지원팀에게 물어볼 것을 추천 **M** OK. But first, I think I'll try one more time to get it working…	**Q.** Why does the woman say, "**our technical support team is very good**"? (A) To complain about a decision (B) To express surprise (C) To refuse an offer (D) To make a recommendation 정답 **(D) To make a recommendation**

화자의 숨은 의도 파악하기

의도를 묻는 문장의 주변 대사를 반드시 이해해야 한다.

W You're driving to the company banquet on Saturday, right? Can I go with you? **M** I'm getting my car fixed.	의도 He is unable to provide a ride. → 회사 연회에 운전해서 갈 것인지 물으며 같이 가는 제안에 대해 차가 수리 중이라 태워 줄 수 없음을 표현
W And afterwards, perhaps you would like to have something to eat? There's a wonderful restaurant nearby. **M** Umm… my train leaves at noon.	의도 To decline an invitation → 근처에 근사한 식당이 있다고 하며 식사하자는 권유에 대해 기차가 정오에 출발해서 식사하러 갈 수 없음을 표현
M I looked up bakeries near here, and City Bakery is the closest. Are they any good? **W** Well, I've used The Cake Corner on a few occasions. They made my wedding cake last year.	의도 To suggest an alternative → 시티 베이커리가 맛있냐는 질문에 대해 다른 빵집인 케이크 코너를 몇 번 이용한 적이 있고 작년에 결혼 케이크도 주문했다고 하며 대안을 제시

1. What is the woman waiting for?
(A) A menu
(B) A phone call
(C) A server
(D) A friend

의도 파악

2. Why does the woman say, **"that's a lot of food"**?
(A) To decline an offer
(B) To correct a misunderstanding
(C) To complain about a policy
(D) To ask for assistance

3. What does the woman ask about?
(A) A chef's name
(B) A recipe
(C) A payment method
(D) A closing time

4. What problem does the man have?
(A) He missed his flight.
(B) He does not know his gate number.
(C) He lost his boarding pass.
(D) He wants to change his seat.

의도 파악

5. Why does the woman say, **"the airline has a mobile phone application"**?
(A) To request customer feedback
(B) To explain a delay
(C) To make a suggestion
(D) To correct an error

6. What will the man most likely do next?
(A) File an official complaint
(B) Reschedule his flight
(C) Call a gate agent
(D) Take a shuttle

7. How did the woman hear about a company?
(A) From a coworker
(B) From a Web site
(C) From a radio advertisement
(D) From a neighbor

의도 파악

8. What does the man mean when he says, **"I've done three projects like that this month"**?
(A) His schedule is full.
(B) He has a lot of experience.
(C) A new style is popular.
(D) Some work will not take long.

9. What does the man offer to send?
(A) Some photos
(B) Some references
(C) Some seeds
(D) Some instructions

PART 3

UNIT 12

❷ 시각 정보 연계 문제

🔵 출제비율 3문항/39문항

리스트, 지도, 그래프 등의 시각 정보와 대화 내용을 연계해서 풀어야 하는 문제로, 매회 고정으로 3문항씩 출제된다. 시각 정보에서 보기와 상응하는 부분, 혹은 질문의 일부가 대화 내에 단서로 등장할 수 있다.

고득점 전략 단서 포착하기

🎧 850_P3_18   정답 및 해설 p.078

보기가 직접 대화에 언급되기보다는 보기를 제외한 다른 주변 정보가 언급되는 경우가 많다. 따라서 시각 정보에서 보기를 제외한 나머지 항목에 유의해서 대화를 듣는다.

W Hello, welcome to the Landston Museum. Would you like to buy a ticket?

M No. I'm Anil Prasad, and I'm here for a photo shoot today. I'm going to be the featured artist in your museum's magazine in February.

W Ah, I see. Let me call the publicity director to let her know you're here.

M Great. Thanks. Actually, I'd like to get a cup of coffee. **Can you ask the director to meet me in the café when she's ready?**

→ 보기와 상응하는 정보인 'café'가 키워드로 등장

Floor 1: Permanent Collection
Floor 2: Café
Floor 3: Gift Shop
Floor 4: Featured Exhibit

Q. **Look at the graphic. Which floor** will the man most likely **go to next**?
(A) Floor 1
(B) Floor 2
(C) Floor 3
(D) Floor 4

정답 **(B) Floor 2**

시각 정보 유형별 필수 어휘

자주 출제되고 난이도가 높은 평면도와 그래프 관련 필수 어휘를 익혀 둔다.

마을, 산책로, 도로 등의 지도나 회사, 사업장 등의 다양한 평면도가 출제된다. **위치나 방향**에 관련된 표현들을 익혀 둔다.

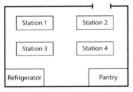

Floor plan(평면도)

right next to	~의 바로 옆에
on the other side of the aisle	통로 반대편에
on the corner of A and B	A와 B가 만나는 모퉁이에
on the back wall of the store	가게의 뒷벽에
closest to the main entrance	정문과 가장 가까운

수익이나 매출, 시장 점유율 등이 막대그래프, 원그래프 등의 형태로 출제된다. **최고점이나 최저점**에 관련된 표현들을 익혀 둔다.

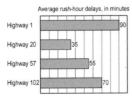

Chart(그래프)

the largest number	가장 큰 수치
the least amount	가장 적은 양
no more than $200	200달러 이하
the second most popular	두 번째로 인기 있는
the biggest portion	가장 큰 부분

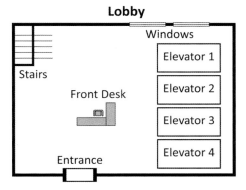

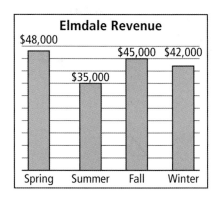

1. Why is the man visiting RKE Consulting?
   (A) To give a marketing presentation
   (B) To interview for a job
   (C) To meet a new client
   (D) To inspect a machine

2. **Look at the graphic. Which elevator**
   should the man **avoid**?
   (A) Elevator 1
   (B) Elevator 2
   (C) Elevator 3
   (D) Elevator 4

3. What will the man most likely do next?
   (A) Return to his car
   (B) Provide an e-mail address
   (C) Submit an application
   (D) Show his identification

4. What industry do the speakers most likely work in?
   (A) Manufacturing
   (B) Food service
   (C) Publishing
   (D) Retail

5. **Look at the graphic. Which amount**
   was **unexpected**?
   (A) $48,000
   (B) $35,000
   (C) $45,000
   (D) $42,000

6. According to the woman, how were some estimates made?
   (A) By considering sales from other locations
   (B) By speaking with contacts in the industry
   (C) By using statistics from a Web site
   (D) By hiring an outside consultant

PART 3 | UNIT 12

ETS 고득점 실전 문제

1. Where is the conversation most likely taking place?
   (A) In a fitness center
   (B) In a university classroom
   (C) In a dental clinic
   (D) In a pharmacy

2. What does the woman imply when she says, "we're not as busy here as you would think"?
   (A) She would like to move to a different location.
   (B) She is able to work with new customers.
   (C) She is worried about her business.
   (D) She is not interested in a product.

3. What does the man say he will do?
   (A) Show a video
   (B) E-mail a price list
   (C) Leave some equipment
   (D) Provide an information packet

4. What are the speakers discussing?
   (A) Following farming regulations
   (B) Using new harvesting equipment
   (C) Collaborating with other farmers
   (D) Monitoring nutrient levels in soil

5. What does the woman imply when she says, "I've been doing it the same way for years"?
   (A) She is an expert in her field.
   (B) She is frustrated with a process.
   (C) She considers farming to be rewarding.
   (D) She is hesitant to make a change.

6. What does the man offer to do?
   (A) Lower a fee
   (B) Send some photographs
   (C) Provide a consultation
   (D) Form an organization

7. What does the woman imply when she says, "I wasn't at yesterday's meeting"?
   (A) She is not a member of the project team.
   (B) She should not be blamed for a decision.
   (C) She needs help managing her current workload.
   (D) She is unaware of some information.

8. Where do the speakers most likely work?
   (A) At a law office
   (B) At a software company
   (C) At a computer repair shop
   (D) At a film studio

9. What does the woman say she is worried about?
   (A) Fixing a flawed product
   (B) Losing a major client
   (C) Exceeding a budget
   (D) Recruiting skilled employees

10. What did the man do last week?
    (A) He attended a national convention.
    (B) He processed a large shipment.
    (C) He participated in a staff retreat.
    (D) He met with potential clients.

11. What kind of business do the speakers most likely work for?
    (A) An architecture firm
    (B) A law firm
    (C) A graphic design company
    (D) An insurance agency

12. Why does the man say, "I've never filed a travel expense report"?
    (A) To disagree with a policy
    (B) To explain a mistake
    (C) To ask for assistance
    (D) To complain about a project

Shelf 1: Drinking glasses	
Shelf 2: Dinner plates	
Shelf 3: Dinner napkins	
Shelf 4: Dessert plates	

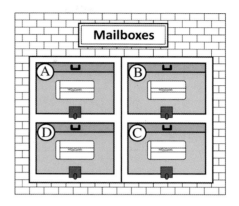

13. Where does the conversation take place?
(A) At a manufacturing plant
(B) At a banquet hall
(C) At a coffee shop
(D) At a department store

14. According to the woman, what has her team done?
(A) Prepared a reception
(B) Purchased new uniforms
(C) Completed an inspection
(D) Signed up for classes

15. Look at the graphic. Where will the dessert plates be moved to?
(A) To shelf 1
(B) To shelf 2
(C) To shelf 3
(D) To shelf 4

16. Why did the man visit the city?
(A) To see his family
(B) To go sightseeing
(C) To go to a job interview
(D) To attend a trade show

17. Look at the graphic. Where will the man put the key?
(A) In mailbox A
(B) In mailbox B
(C) In mailbox C
(D) In mailbox D

18. What did the man like about the apartment?
(A) The view of the city
(B) The size of the rooms
(C) The decorations
(D) The lighting

PART 3

UNIT 12

Wednesday				
	1:00 P.M.	2:00 P.M.	3:00 P.M.	4:00 P.M.
Anna	✕			
David			✕	✕
Ibrahim	✕	✕		
Marisol				✕

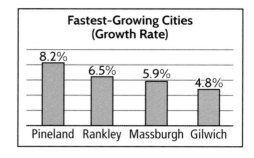

Fastest-Growing Cities (Growth Rate)

Pineland 8.2% Rankley 6.5% Massburgh 5.9% Gilwich 4.8%

19. What type of team do the speakers work on?
(A) Marketing
(B) Research
(C) Accounting
(D) Legal

20. Why does the man want to hold a team meeting?
(A) To collect feedback
(B) To clarify a policy
(C) To introduce a new team member
(D) To discuss a work space reorganization

21. Look at the graphic. At what time will the speakers hold the team meeting?
(A) 1:00 P.M.
(B) 2:00 P.M.
(C) 3:00 P.M.
(D) 4:00 P.M.

22. What did the mayor suggest at a city council meeting?
(A) Creating a new department
(B) Building a recreational facility
(C) Improving city parks
(D) Hiring university students

23. Look at the graphic. Which city are the speakers discussing?
(A) Pineland
(B) Rankley
(C) Massburgh
(D) Gilwich

24. What is the woman concerned about?
(A) Safety
(B) Staff training
(C) Funding
(D) Residents' complaints

만점 빈출 표현

 850_P3_21

◆ 회의 / 일정

board of directors 이사회

make some adjustments 조정하다

bring up the issue 문제를 제기하다

host a videoconference 화상회의를 열다

have a scheduling conflict 일정이 겹치다

set up a conference call 전화 회의를 열다

hard deadline 연장이 불가능한 마감 기한

move up the deadline 마감 기한을 앞당기다

keep ~ up to date ~에게 최신 정보를 제공하다

prepare for the management meeting
간부 회의를 준비하다

have a light workload 업무량이 적다

be on schedule 일정대로 하다

quarterly report 분기 보고서

apply for a grant 보조금을 신청하다

consult with a manager 관리자와 상의하다

have doubt about a suggestion
제안에 대해 의구심이 들다

consult a calendar 달력을 찾아보다

complete the blueprint
청사진을 완성하다

go forward with the next project
다음 프로젝트를 진행하다

clarify a policy 정책을 명시하다

reallocate some work 일부 업무를 재배정하다

allocate the funding 자금을 할당하다

ahead of the deadline 마감일 전에

follow up about the meeting
회의에 대해 더 알아보다

send out a reminder 독촉장을 보내다

make the production deadline
생산 마감 기한을 맞추다

revise some details on the application
신청 관련 세부 사항을 변경하다

There's a logistical concern.
업무 조직에 관한 우려가 있다.

◆ 출장 / 출근

fill in for ~을 대신하다

on business 업무로, 출장으로

be out sick 병가를 내다

keep the receipt 영수증을 보관하다

call in sick 아파서 결근하겠다고 전화하다

travel reimbursement request 출장비 환급 요청

get reimbursed for ~을 환급 받다

submit expense report 경비 보고서를 제출하다

make travel arrangements 출장 준비를 하다

come back from maternity leave
출산 휴가에서 돌아오다

file a travel expense report
출장 지출 품의서를 정리하다

◆ 인사 / 평가

associate 동료

replacement 후임

pool 이용 가능 인력

expected salary 예상 연봉

job description 직무 기술서

get[receive] a promotion 승진하다

open position 비어 있는 자리, 공석

take over the position 직책을 인계 받다

train new hires 신입 사원을 교육하다

come in for an interview 면접을 보러 오다

find qualified job applicants
자격을 갖춘 구직자를 찾다

performance evaluation[appraisal, review]
업무 평가, 인사 고과

recruit skilled employees
숙련된 직원을 채용하다

hire a seasonal worker
계절 노동자를 채용하다

the criteria for intern selection 인턴 선발 기준

employment agreement 고용계약서

◆ 계약/협상

win the bid 입찰을 따내다

send a quote 견적서를 보내다

reach an agreement 합의에 이르다

terminate the agreement 계약을 끝내다

receive a proposed contract 가계약서를 받다

terms and agreements of the contract
계약 조건

M&A(= merger and acquisition) 합병 및 인수

find a new supplier[vendor]
새로운 납품업체를 구하다

go over the budget 예산을 초과하다

confidentiality agreement 기밀 서약서

draft a contract 계약서 초안을 작성하다

provision for travel expenses 출장비 관련 조항

decline a suggestion 제안을 거절하다

meet prospective clients in person
잠재 고객을 직접 만나다

redirect funds from other areas
다른 영역에서 기금을 전용하다

navigate regulations 규정을 따르다

◆ 사내 행사/교육

keynote speaker 기조 연설자

company outing 회사 야유회

business function 비즈니스 행사

publicize the event 행사를 홍보하다

anniversary celebration 기념 축하 행사

event coordinator 행사 진행자, 책임자

extend an invitation 초대장을 보내다

reserve a banquet hall 연회장을 예약하다

grand-opening celebration 개업 축하 행사

workshop on skills development
역량 개발 워크숍

check an instructor's availability
강사가 시간이 되는지 확인하다

charitable fund-raiser 자선 모금 행사

participate in a staff retreat 사내 수련회에 참석하다

prepare a reception 환영회를 준비하다

oversee the training content 교육 내용을 감독하다

manage promotion and attendance
홍보와 참석률을 관리하다

◆ 사무기기/시설

interior renovation 내부 개조

instruction manual 사용 설명서

take inventory 재고 조사를 하다

maintenance worker 시설 관리 직원

mount a projector 프로젝터를 설치하다

issue a new computer 새 컴퓨터를 지급하다

arrive assembled 조립된 채 오다

report a malfunction 고장 신고하다

install new light fixtures 새 전등을 설치하다

storage rack 보관대, 보관 선반

restock some supplies 물품을 채워 넣다

replace the fixture 붙박이 시설을 교체하다

safety inspector 안전 감독관

retrieve data 데이터를 검색하다

adjust the screen resolution
화면 해상도를 조절하다

Some entrances are blocked.
입구가 봉쇄되었다.

◆ 마케팅/영업

put an ad in 광고를 내다

selling point 판매에 유리한 장점

product demonstration 제품 시연

broaden a market share 시장 점유율을 높이다

appeal to a younger demographic
젊은 층의 관심을 끌다

finalize a budget proposal 예산안을 마무리하다

work on a sales report 판매 보고서를 작성하다

focus on cost-cutting 비용 절감에 초점을 맞추다

acquire additional clients 추가 고객을 영입하다

increase our client base 고객층을 확대하다

file a complaint 항의를 제기하다

forward a proposal 제안서를 보내다

foot traffic 유동인구

speak with contacts in the industry
업계 인맥과 이야기하다

leave the demo machine 시연 기계를 두고 가다

endorsement (유명인에 의한) 상품의 보증, 홍보

compile a list of potential clients
잠재 고객 목록을 만들다

◆ 거래 / 배송

distributor 유통업체

unloading zone 하역 장소

sign the delivery confirmation form
배송 확인 양식에 서명하다

send an invoice 송장을 발송하다

waive the shipping cost
배송비를 면제하다

keep up with the demand
수요를 따라가다

proof of purchase 구매 증거물

rush the order 주문을 빨리 처리하다

load[unload] a vehicle
차에 짐을 싣다[내리다]

in three working[business] days
영업일 기준 3일 후에

The shipment is behind schedule.
배송이 일정보다 늦다.

◆ 쇼핑

carry 취급하다

issue a refund 환불해 주다

offer advance sales 사전 판매를 제공하다

be discontinued 단종되다

promotional giveaway 판촉용 증정품

affordable product 저렴한 상품

custom-made 주문 제작한

cutting-edge product 최첨단 상품

clearance (sale) 재고 정리 (세일)

wholesale store 도매점

gift certificate 상품권

at half-off the full price
정상가의 반액으로

have in stock 재고가 있다

under warranty 보증기간 내의

inquire about a product
제품에 대해 문의하다

come with (제품에) ~이 함께 오다, 딸려오다

promotional flyer 광고 전단

storewide sale 전 매장 할인

fabric upholstery 천으로 된 덮개

◆ 여행 / 여가

travel agent 여행사 직원

apply for a visa 비자를 신청하다

send an itinerary 일정표를 보내다

book the accommodation
숙소를 예약하다

complimentary breakfast
무료 아침 식사

exposition 박람회, 전시회

see the artwork 작품을 보다

check out a book 책을 빌리다

complimentary admission 무료입장

major landmark 주요 지형지물

be included with regular admission
정규 입장료에 포함되다

customs officer 세관원

take the longer scenic route
더 길고 경치 좋은 노선으로 가다

automotive trade show
자동차 박람회

the skyline of the entire city
도시 전체의 스카이라인

◆ 교통

schedule display board 일정 전광판

conductor 승무원, 역무원

be suspended 일시 중단되다

be overbooked 초과 예약되다

show a commuter ticket
정기권을 보여주다

connecting flight 연결 항공편

take a detour 우회하다

driverless vehicle 자율 주행 차량

head over to the station 역으로 가다

suffer from jet lag 시차증으로 고생하다

residential parking permit
거주자 주차 허가증

reduce congestion 교통 혼잡을 줄이다

clear for takeoff 이륙 허가를 받다

get a (traffic) ticket (교통) 위반 딱지를 받다

air traffic control 항공 교통 관제소

lose a boarding pass 탑승권을 잃어버리다

◆ 식당

platter 모둠 요리, 큰 접시

flavorful 풍미 있는, 맛 좋은

assorted 여러 가지의, 갖은

nutritious substitute
영양가가 높은 대체품

gourmet 미식가; (음식이) 고급인

culinary 요리의, 음식의

frequent user credits
단골 고객 포인트

food stand 매점

entrée 주요리

verify a reservation
예약 사항을 확인하다

vegetarian dishes
채식주의자를 위한 요리

grab a bite (to eat)
요기하다, 끼니를 간단히 때우다

The kitchen is really backed up.
주방에 주문이 많이 밀렸다.

◆ 부동산

mortgage 담보 대출

lease 임대차 (계약); 임대하다

real estate agency[agent]
부동산 중개소[중개인]

fully furnished 가구를 모두 구비한

walking distance 걸어서 갈 수 있는 거리

landlord 집주인

tenant 세입자

loan requirements 대출 자격 요건

studio apartment 원룸 아파트

perspective tenant 미래 세입자

pay a utility bill 공과금을 내다

outskirts 교외

rent check 임대료

residential[commercial] area
주거[상업] 지역

no utilities included 공과금 별도

make a deposit 계약금을 치르다

set up a tour 집 보러 갈 약속을 잡다

lease some retail space 소매점을 임대하다

◆ 은행

ring up (금전 등록기에 가격을) 입력하다

account balance 계좌 잔고

wire some money 돈을 송금하다

deposit[withdrawl] slip 입금[출금] 전표

international transfer 해외 송금

endorse (수표에) 이서하다

bank statement 은행 입출금 내역서

savings account 보통 예금 계좌

do transactions online 온라인으로 거래하다

apply for a bank loan 은행 대출을 신청하다

◆ 병원

cause eyestrain 눈의 피로를 유발하다

release form 열람 동의서

physical examination 건강 검진

fill a prescription 처방대로 조제하다

medical history 병력

remedy 치료법

get some vaccinations 예방 접종하다

prescribe some medicine 약을 처방하다

act up (병이) 재발하다

work at a private practice 개인 병원에서 일하다

migrate patient records 환자 기록을 옮기다

drop off prescriptions 처방전을 맡기다

vision test 시력 검사

◆ 기타 장소

- 공장

fill a large order 대량 주문을 납품하다

halt production 생산을 중단하다

stop the assembly line 조립 라인을 중단하다

robotic welding machines 자동 용접 기계

calibrate the machine 기계를 조정하다

- 우체국

surface mail 보통 우편

express mail service 속달 우편 서비스

overnight delivery 익일 배송

by courier 택배로

postage fee 우편 요금

PART 4
짧은 담화

INTRO

UNIT 13 | 전화 메시지

UNIT 14 | 공지 / 회의

UNIT 15 | 설명 / 소개

UNIT 16 | 광고 / 방송

PART 4 만점 빈출 표현

LC

한 사람이 말하는 담화문을 듣고 이와 관련된 세 개의 문제를 푸는 유형으로, 전화 메시지, 회의 발췌, 안내 방송 등 다양한 담화문이 출제된다.

◆ 고득점 풀이 전략

STEP 1 문제 파악하기	❶ 담화 듣기 전에 문제와 보기 읽기
	❷ 의문사, 주어, 동사를 중심으로 키워드 파악하기 (화자/청자 구분 필수)
STEP 2 담화 들으면서 정답 찾기	❶ 키워드 관련 내용이 나오면 답 체크하기
	❷ 놓친 문제는 과감히 포기하고 다음 문제로 넘어가기
	❸ 담화 종료 후 다음 담화의 문제와 보기 읽기

◆ ETS 예제

1. What will the **listeners** be **attending**?

(A) A board meeting
(B) A training course
(C) An award ceremony
(D) A trade show

2. What does the **speaker** give to the listeners?

(A) An itinerary
(B) A booklet
(C) A photograph
(D) A contact list

3. What are the **listeners** reminded to do?

(A) Confirm their room numbers
(B) Check their passports
(C) Print out name tags
(D) Submit reimbursement forms

I hope **1.** you're all looking forward to going to the international trade show in November. This is the first time we'll showcase our products at such a big event, so it's important that we're well prepared. **2.** I'm passing around copies of our trip itinerary, which includes the details of our flights and hotels. Oh, and **3.** don't forget— look at your passport's expiration date. You need to make sure it's valid for the dates of this trip.

단서

1. 청자들이 참석할 곳: 국제 무역 박람회
2. 화자가 청자들에게 주는 것: 출장 일정표
3. 청자들에게 상기시키는 것: 여권 만료일 확인

정답

1. (D) A trade show
2. (A) An itinerary
3. (B) Check their passports

◆ 최신 출제 경향

① 공지/안내 및 회의 발췌록, 전화 메시지가 가장 많이 출제되고, 발표/연설, 관광/견학, 광고/방송 등 다양한 지문들이 등장한다.

② 구체적인 정보를 물어보는 세부 사항 문제가 가장 자주 출제되고, 주제/목적 및 장소/직업을 묻는 문제가 20퍼센트 이상 꾸준히 출제되고 있다. 시각 정보 연계 문제는 3개, 화자의 의도 파악 문제는 2개씩 고정적으로 출제된다.

◆ 패러프레이징[Paraphrasing]

파트 4에서도 파트 3처럼 정답의 단서가 패러프레이징 되어 문제 및 보기에 제시되는 경우가 많다. 파트 4는 한 사람이 말하는 담화문이므로 긴 문장이 등장하며, 패러프레이징 방식이 복잡한 양상을 띠는 경우가 있다.

1. 상위어 + 유사 표현

Just make sure you don't step on any of the protected wildflowers while you're exploring.

탐험하는 동안에는 **보호받는 야생화를 밟지** 않도록 조심해야 합니다.

Q What are listeners cautioned about?

A Walking on plants

질문 청자들은 무엇에 대해 주의해야 하는가?
정답 식물 위를 걷는 것

2. 내용 축약 + 유사 표현

I'd like to thank you all for the late nights and weekends you spent working to design such a great product.

이렇게 훌륭한 제품을 디자인하기 위해 늦은 밤과 주말을 보내주신 여러분 모두에게 감사드리고 싶어요.

Q Why does the speaker thank the listeners?

A For working long hours

질문 화자가 청자들에게 감사한 이유는?
정답 오랜 시간 일했기 때문에

3. 한 문장에 두 개의 단서가 등장하는 경우

The Thursday night special here at Mario's Seafood Restaurant has always been the fish stew, but tonight, because of a delivery problem, we will not be serving it.

마리오 씨푸드 레스토랑의 목요일 밤 특별 요리는 **생선 스튜**였지만, 오늘 밤은 배달 문제 때문에 **그것을 제공하지 못합니다.**

Q According to the speaker, why might customers be disappointed?

A An item is not available.

질문 화자에 따르면, 고객들은 왜 실망할 것인가?
정답 메뉴가 제공되지 않는다.

4. 두 문장에 있는 단서를 조합해야 하는 경우

I know your company is finishing up a big construction job right now, so you might have some materials you no longer need. If that's so, I'd like to pick them up from you.

귀사가 지금 큰 공사를 마무리하고 있다는 것을 알고 있어요. 더 이상 **필요하지 않은 자재들이** 있다면, 제가 그것들을 **수거해 오고** 싶습니다.

Q What does the speaker want to do?

A Collect discarded materials

질문 화자는 무엇을 하고 싶어 하는가?
정답 폐자재 수거

전화 메시지

부재중인 상대방에게 남기는 음성 메시지가 대부분이고, 가끔 자동 응답 메시지(ARS)도 출제된다. 화자의 직업이나 근무지, 전화 목적, 요청이나 제안 사항을 묻는 문제가 자주 출제된다.

| 고득점 | 전략 | **담화 흐름 파악하기** | 🎧 850_P4_01 정답 및 해설 p.086 |

전화 메시지의 주제나 목적은 대부분 지문의 초반에 거론되지만, 담화문의 중반까지 들어야 파악할 수 있는 경우도 있으니 전체 흐름을 파악하자.

인사 / 소개	Hi, Mr. Wallace. ❷ **This is Julie Osborne from customer service at Staunton Mobile.**	
목적 / 용건	I see that you sent us a message with your concerns about our upcoming merger with Parsons Phone Company. ❶❷ <u>I just want to assure you</u> that your **international calling plan will remain the same even after we consolidate with Parsons next month.** → 지문 중반부에 전화 메시지의 목적 등장	❷ 회사의 업종: 통신업체
		❶ 전화 목적: 국제전화 요금제의 변경을 우려하는 고객을 안심시키기 위해
세부 내용	In the meantime, ❸ **we'll be posting answers to frequently asked questions this week on our Web site.** I hope you'll have a chance to look at this.	❸ 이번 주에 할 일: 회사 웹사이트에 답변 달기
마무리 인사	Thank you for your call—we appreciate your business.	

주제 / 목적	**1. What** is the **purpose** of the message?	정답 **(B)** 고객의 우려를 해결해 주려고
	(A) To request a payment	
	(B) To address a customer's concerns	

화자 / 장소	**2. What kind of company** is Staunton?	정답 **(B)** 통신업체
	(A) A market research firm	
	(B) A telephone company	

다음에 할 일	**3.** According to the speaker, **what will** the Staunton company **do this week**?	정답 **(A)** 웹사이트에 정보 게시
	(A) Post information on a Web site	
	(B) Hold a press conference	

1. **Why** is the speaker **traveling**?
   (A) To inspect a branch office
   (B) To meet with a client
   (C) To attend a conference
   (D) To visit family members

2. **What did** the speaker **recently do**?
   (A) He registered for a company credit card.
   (B) He revised a security policy.
   (C) He requested some extra training.
   (D) He changed a flight reservation.

3. **What** does the speaker **invite** the listener **to attend**?
   (A) A reception
   (B) A historical tour
   (C) A music festival
   (D) A workshop

4. **Where** does the speaker **work**?
   (A) At an electronics shop
   (B) At a post office
   (C) At a furniture store
   (D) At a car rental agency

5. **What** is the **purpose** of the call?
   (A) To cancel an order
   (B) To ask about a payment
   (C) To confirm a delivery time
   (D) To resolve a customer complaint

6. **What will** the listener **receive by e-mail**?
   (A) A survey
   (B) A receipt
   (C) A full refund
   (D) A discount code

7. **What** is the speaker **helping** the listener do?
   (A) Schedule a conference call
   (B) Book a hotel
   (C) Make a dinner reservation
   (D) Write a speech

8. What does the speaker imply when he says, "**they're trying to cut costs**"?
   (A) The listener should pay with a credit card.
   (B) The listener should not choose an expensive option.
   (C) A calculation error has been made.
   (D) An event must be rescheduled.

9. **Why** does the speaker **request** to be **contacted by phone**?
   (A) His computer is not working.
   (B) He will be away from his desk.
   (C) He needs an answer immediately.
   (D) Some information is confidential.

ETS 고득점 실전 문제

1. Which field does the listener work in?
   (A) Finance
   (B) Journalism
   (C) Engineering
   (D) Medicine

2. What is the main purpose of the call?
   (A) To request information for an article
   (B) To inquire about job openings
   (C) To confirm the details of a work trip
   (D) To inform the listener that a project has been approved

3. What is the listener invited to do?
   (A) Attend a reception
   (B) Tour a facility
   (C) Join a committee
   (D) Give a donation

4. What does the speaker say he received from the listener?
   (A) A receipt
   (B) A wireless money transfer
   (C) A draft of an article
   (D) An order form

5. What impressed the listener about a product?
   (A) It is comfortable.
   (B) It is easy to assemble.
   (C) It is affordable.
   (D) It is lightweight.

6. Why does the speaker say, "The Executive Style has that feature"?
   (A) To correct a misunderstanding
   (B) To recommend a product
   (C) To refuse an offer
   (D) To give a compliment

7. What type of business has the caller reached?
   (A) A bank
   (B) An electronics store
   (C) A delivery service
   (D) A cable television company

8. What does the speaker apologize for?
   (A) Incorrect instructions
   (B) A damaged product
   (C) Interrupted service
   (D) An office closure

9. According to the speaker, why should listeners visit a Web site?
   (A) To check account information
   (B) To order new parts
   (C) To get schedule updates
   (D) To learn about new offers

10. Who most likely is the speaker?
    (A) A real estate agent
    (B) A recording studio engineer
    (C) An architect
    (D) A house cleaner

11. What requirement is mentioned?
    (A) A permit
    (B) A starting date
    (C) A type of material
    (D) A payment

12. What does the speaker mean when he says, "we have other people interested"?
    (A) A message is incorrect.
    (B) A request cannot be fulfilled.
    (C) The listener should act quickly.
    (D) The listener should offer more help.

13. Why is the speaker calling?
(A) To suggest a way of saving money
(B) To ask for details about a recent bill
(C) To recommend an employee pay increase
(D) To confirm that a purchase was made

14. What problem does the speaker mention about some machines?
(A) They are not in the correct location.
(B) They are difficult to operate.
(C) They need to be repaired.
(D) They are not energy efficient.

15. Why is the speaker going to contact an organization?
(A) To learn about a grant program
(B) To identify job candidates
(C) To offer a business service
(D) To complain about a fee

16. What is the topic of the message?
(A) A product test session
(B) A pet training class
(C) A job interview
(D) A staff workshop

17. What does the speaker imply when he says, "the list of interested participants is growing"?
(A) An event will last for several days.
(B) A staff member did not follow instructions.
(C) A response should be provided quickly.
(D) A registration process has improved.

18. What does the speaker say will be sent to participants?
(A) A sample
(B) An invoice
(C) A questionnaire
(D) Some driving directions

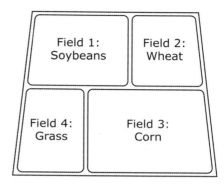

19. Look at the graphic. Where will the new crop be planted?
(A) Field 1
(B) Field 2
(C) Field 3
(D) Field 4

20. What does the speaker say he hopes to do next year?
(A) Renew a service contract
(B) Hire more employees
(C) Complete a certification course
(D) Purchase new equipment

21. What does the speaker say about the city farmers market?
(A) Table fees have increased.
(B) Additional space is available.
(C) The hours have been expanded.
(D) Parking is limited.

PART 4

UNIT 13

103

UNIT 14 공지 / 회의

출제비율 3~4세트 / 10세트

사내의 업무 관련 전달 사항, 요청 사항이나 고객을 대상으로 안내/당부하는 내용 혹은 직원 회의 등의 담화문에 해당한다. 최근에는 도입부의 인사말을 생략하고 바로 본론으로 시작하는 유형도 자주 등장한다.

고득점 전략 담화 흐름 파악하기

850_P4_04 정답 및 해설 p.092

후반부에 나오는 업무 전달 사항이나 요청 사항이 문제로 나올 수 있으니 끝까지 잘 들어야 한다. 요청 사항으로 자주 언급되는 단서 표현(Please / I'd like you to / Could you)에 주목한다.

회의 주제	We have only five minutes left, but ❶ **I'd like to touch on the last point on our agenda, a proposal to organize our storage rooms more efficiently**, which was submitted by our Somerville shop. I've made copies of the proposal—please take one.	❶ 회의 안건: 효율적인 창고 정리
주요 내용	❷ **The plan aims to save our auto mechanics time when looking for tools and replacement parts.** There are some interesting ideas here, but I'm not sure they apply to all our branches. Some of you are familiar with our other three locations.	❷ 근무지 암시: 자동차 정비 시간 단축
요청/당부	❸ <u>**Could you please e-mail me your thoughts about implementing these changes across the board?**</u> Thanks! → 후반부에 요청 사항 관련 표현(Could you please ~?) 등장	❸ 요청 사항: 변경 사항 실행에 대한 의견이 담긴 이메일 보내기

주제/목적

1. **What** does the speaker want to **discuss**?

   (A) A plan to reorganize storage spaces
   (B) Increases to Somerville staff salaries

   정답 **(A)** 보관 장소 재정리 계획

화자/장소

2. **What type of business** do the listeners most likely **work for**?

   (A) An auto repair service
   (B) An electronics store

   정답 **(A)** 자동차 수리 서비스

요청/제안

3. **What** does the speaker **ask** the listeners **to do**?

   (A) Revise a contract
   (B) E-mail some feedback

   정답 **(B)** 이메일로 의견 보내기

1. **Where** is the **announcement** most likely **being made**?
   (A) At a restaurant
   (B) At a theater
   (C) At a car dealership
   (D) At a department store

2. **What** are the listeners **encouraged** to **sign up for**?
   (A) A rewards program
   (B) A contest
   (C) A workshop
   (D) A focus group

3. **What** can the listeners **do on the second floor**?
   (A) Listen to some music
   (B) Meet a celebrity
   (C) Sample some food
   (D) Get photos taken

4. **Who** most likely are the **listeners**?
   (A) Repair technicians
   (B) Factory workers
   (C) Furniture salespeople
   (D) Construction workers

5. **What change** does the speaker announce?
   (A) Some new equipment will be installed.
   (B) Some shifts will end early.
   (C) A facility will be enlarged.
   (D) A new contract will be signed.

6. **What are** the listeners **asked to do**?
   (A) Read a manual
   (B) Fill out a questionnaire
   (C) Pick up a sample
   (D) Register for a training session

7. **What** were the listeners asked to **draft by today**?
   (A) Product reviews
   (B) Budget proposals
   (C) Job descriptions
   (D) User manuals

8. **What** does the speaker **say** she **will do** after the meeting?
   (A) Review some résumés
   (B) Send a list of names
   (C) Post a sign-up sheet
   (D) Create a project calendar

9. Why does the speaker say, "**several staff members are taking vacations this month**"?
   (A) To give an example of a job benefit
   (B) To request additional resources
   (C) To provide a reason for a delay
   (D) To encourage the listeners to complete a task quickly

PART 4

UNIT 14

105

ETS 고득점 실전 문제

1. What is the speaker mainly discussing?
   (A) A company merger
   (B) A relocation opportunity
   (C) A construction project
   (D) An upcoming workshop

2. What does the speaker ask the listeners to do?
   (A) Bring some extra chairs into the room
   (B) Consider alternate transportation options
   (C) Hold questions until the meeting ends
   (D) Work some additional hours

3. What does the speaker emphasize about an upcoming race?
   (A) It needs more publicity.
   (B) It will follow a different route this year.
   (C) The budget will not be increased.
   (D) The date of the event will not change.

4. Who is the speaker?
   (A) A quality-control inspector
   (B) A parts supplier
   (C) A company president
   (D) A hiring supervisor

5. What type of product is mentioned?
   (A) Office furniture
   (B) Computer software
   (C) Headphones
   (D) Motorcycles

6. Why does the speaker say, "we received some last-minute funding in the budget"?
   (A) To complain about a timeline
   (B) To explain the reason for a decision
   (C) To request that colleagues volunteer for a project
   (D) To suggest upgrading some equipment

7. Where most likely is the speaker?
   (A) At a craft shop
   (B) At a dry cleaning business
   (C) At a department store
   (D) At a clothing manufacturing plant

8. What problem does the speaker mention?
   (A) Sales numbers have declined.
   (B) Some deliveries were late.
   (C) Some products are defective.
   (D) Competition has increased.

9. What will the listeners have to do?
   (A) Work in a different area
   (B) Take a training course
   (C) Meet with a supervisor
   (D) Come in early

10. Why was the speaker unsure about a decision at first?
    (A) The company would be giving up some control.
    (B) The company would be making a large initial investment.
    (C) The company would have to research new markets.
    (D) The company would need to hire more staff.

11. What does the speaker say she did over the past week?
    (A) She presented a concept to investors.
    (B) She reevaluated a vacation policy.
    (C) She met with consultants.
    (D) She purchased new equipment.

12. Why did the company choose California?
    (A) It is close to the company's headquarters.
    (B) It has many potential customers.
    (C) It offers a variety of real estate options.
    (D) It is where many suppliers are based.

13. What is the main purpose of the announcement?
(A) To explain an increase in ticket prices
(B) To provide information about shows at the cinema
(C) To describe the food specials at the snack bar
(D) To request that the listeners silence their mobile phones

14. What does the speaker say about the 1:00 P.M. movie tomorrow?
(A) It is a movie premiere.
(B) It is part of a film festival.
(C) Ticket prices are reduced.
(D) A celebrity will sign autographs.

15. What will the listeners receive if they purchase tickets online?
(A) A complimentary snack
(B) A movie souvenir
(C) A contest entry
(D) A customer loyalty card

16. Where does the announcement most likely take place?
(A) At a hotel
(B) At a hair salon
(C) At a medical clinic
(D) At a conference center

17. Why does the speaker say, "There are two associates at the front desk"?
(A) To give the listeners instructions
(B) To request additional staff
(C) To complain that a process is slow
(D) To agree with a proposal to hire more staff

18. What does the speaker instruct some of the listeners to do online?
(A) Watch a video
(B) Sign up for a newsletter
(C) Give some feedback
(D) Complete some forms

Project List	Deadline
1. Radio advertisement	March 3
2. Web site	March 10
3. Promotional contest	March 26
4. Customer survey	April 5

19. Why does the speaker congratulate the team?
(A) Some work spaces are organized.
(B) Some clients are happy.
(C) A profit is larger than expected.
(D) An advertisement won an award.

20. Look at the graphic. Which project will the team focus on this week?
(A) Project 1
(B) Project 2
(C) Project 3
(D) Project 4

21. What does the speaker ask Adriana to do by tomorrow?
(A) Draw some logo designs
(B) Draft a project plan
(C) Prepare a list of questions
(D) Send a contract

설명 / 소개

직원 교육, 특정 인물 소개, 견학이나 대회 등 다양한 행사 안내, 혹은 제품에 대해 발표하는 내용의 담화가 주를 이룬다. 소개 대상에 관한 문제, 화자의 요청 사항이나 다음에 할 일 또는 일어날 일을 묻는 문제가 자주 출제된다.

고득점	전략	**담화 흐름 파악하기**	⌂ 850_P4_07　정답 및 해설 p.099

화자나 청자 정보는 담화의 초반부를 잘 듣는다. 도입부의 Welcome to / Thank you for attending[coming to]이나, 대명사 we, our, you, your에 집중하자.

인사/소개	Welcome, everyone. ❶ **I hope you've had a chance** **to say hello to each other and chat about your** **cooking backgrounds.** → 청자 정보를 나타내는 단서 표현(your) 등장	❶ 청자들의 신분: 요리 경력이 있는 요리사들
행사 개요	I know you're all excited to start cooking with the Fresh Café team.	
목적 설명	Over the coming weeks in this program, ❷ **you'll** **learn what you need to know to get started at** **one of our locations,** including how to prepare our innovative dishes and how to handle customers' special requests and dietary concerns.	❷ 프로그램의 목적: 매장에서 일을 시작하기 위해 알아야 할 것들을 배우는 것
할 일/ 일어날 일	❸ **On the final day, we'll head to a local farm,** **where we source seasonal vegetables.** It's always a day well spent!	❸ 마지막 날에 할 일: 재료를 공급받는 지역 농장 방문하기

청자	**1. Who** most likely are the **listeners**? (A) Community gardeners (B) Professional chefs	정답 **(B) 전문 요리사들**

주제/목적	**2. What** is the main **purpose** of the program? (A) To train new employees (B) To increase a customer base	정답 **(A) 신입사원 교육**

다음에 할 일	**3. What** does the speaker say the listeners **will do on** **the last day**? (A) Watch a demonstration (B) Visit a local supplier	정답 **(B) 지역 공급업체 방문하기**

1. **Where** is the speech most likely **being given**?
    (A) At a shareholder meeting
    (B) At a retirement celebration
    (C) At an awards ceremony
    (D) At a sales presentation

2. **What industry** does the speaker most likely **work in**?
    (A) Real estate
    (B) Finance
    (C) Health care
    (D) Agriculture

3. **What** does the speaker's company **pledge to do**?
    (A) Donate food to a summer festival
    (B) Create job programs for the region
    (C) Construct a new community center
    (D) Provide funding for educational programs

4. **What** is the talk mainly **about**?
    (A) Advertising on social media
    (B) Manufacturing in small quantities
    (C) Shipping products internationally
    (D) Investing in a franchise

5. **What benefit** does the speaker mention about a **business strategy**?
    (A) It is less expensive.
    (B) It is easier to regulate quality.
    (C) It can provide feedback faster.
    (D) It can reach a larger audience.

6. **According to** the speaker, **how** can the listeners find **more information**?
    (A) By touring a factory
    (B) By visiting a Web site
    (C) By attending a class
    (D) By reading a book

7. **What** does the speaker **give** the listeners?
    (A) Visitor badges
    (B) Audio headsets
    (C) Building maps
    (D) Tour tickets

8. **According to** the speaker, **what** is the **Bremington Estate known for**?
    (A) Winning awards for its landscaping
    (B) Having an extensive art collection
    (C) Being used as a film location
    (D) Being designed by a well-known architect

9. What does the speaker imply when she says, **"we are open until five o'clock"**?
    (A) Staff were given an incorrect schedule.
    (B) An informational brochure should be revised.
    (C) The listeners should wait for assistance.
    (D) The listeners will have time to see everything.

ETS 고득점 실전 문제

1. What is the topic of the workshop?
(A) Financial planning
(B) Book writing
(C) Leadership skills
(D) Digital marketing

2. What did Ming Yang recently do?
(A) He won an award.
(B) He published a book.
(C) He appeared on television.
(D) He took an international tour.

3. What does the speaker remind the listeners to do?
(A) Attend a reception
(B) Sign up for another workshop
(C) Leave some feedback
(D) Pick up some handouts

4. Who is the speaker?
(A) A mechanic
(B) A salesperson
(C) A news reporter
(D) A company president

5. What does the speaker imply when he says, "a national magazine published an article about us"?
(A) A business plan seems promising.
(B) A marketing campaign is unnecessary.
(C) A problem must be solved quickly.
(D) A decision has already been made.

6. What does the speaker say grant funds would be used for?
(A) Acquiring more products
(B) Paying off a loan
(C) Providing training opportunities
(D) Conducting environmental research

7. Who most likely is the speaker?
(A) An environmental scientist
(B) A restaurant owner
(C) A building inspector
(D) A sanitation engineer

8. What will be changing next month?
(A) A public transportation system
(B) A zoning law
(C) A waste-disposal process
(D) A utility fee

9. What will the speaker do next?
(A) Write an action plan
(B) Post a notice
(C) Give a demonstration
(D) Go to lunch

10. What will the listeners learn about at the museum?
(A) The history of art
(B) The history of films
(C) The history of science
(D) The history of flight

11. What does the speaker mean when she says, "there are museum employees in every room"?
(A) The museum is well funded.
(B) The artifacts are well protected.
(C) The listeners can ask questions.
(D) The museum is very busy today.

12. What does the speaker invite the listeners to do?
(A) Post photos on a Web site
(B) Visit a special exhibit
(C) Purchase souvenirs
(D) Become museum members

13. What most likely is the speaker's profession?
(A) Landscape designer
(B) Florist
(C) Event planner
(D) Park ranger

14. What does the speaker suggest doing first?
(A) Preparing a list
(B) Clearing some table space
(C) Taking measurements
(D) Locating a vendor

15. What does the speaker thank the audience for doing?
(A) Sharing recipes
(B) Sending photographs
(C) Recommending songs
(D) Asking questions

---

16. What kind of data does the speaker discuss?
(A) Records of work hours
(B) Annual sales reports
(C) Customer service call logs
(D) Employee survey results

17. Why does the speaker thank the Facilities Department employees?
(A) They installed some faster servers.
(B) They rearranged some work spaces.
(C) They completed a painting project.
(D) They repaired some furniture.

18. Why does the speaker say, "we all spend a lot of time staring at screens"?
(A) To explain why work hours have been changed
(B) To recognize the hard work of some employees
(C) To complain that a policy has not been followed
(D) To emphasize a professional recommendation

$83	$100	$129
Trekker Gloves		
$185	Multi-pocket Trousers	All-weather Jacket
Trailblazer Boots		

19. Why is the speaker meeting with the listeners?
(A) To ask for funding
(B) To introduce a company president
(C) To purchase materials
(D) To revise manufacturing regulations

20. Who most likely is the speaker?
(A) A product inspector
(B) A financial consultant
(C) A city official
(D) A company owner

21. Look at the graphic. Which product does the speaker use as an example?
(A) Trekker Gloves
(B) Trailblazer Boots
(C) Multi-pocket Trousers
(D) All-weather Jacket

광고/방송

광고에서는 제품, 서비스, 업체 광고가 주를 이루며, 방송은 다양한 분야와 지역 관련 소식을 전하는 뉴스 및 라디오 프로그램이 주로 출제된다. 광고 대상, 방송의 주제, 그리고 관련 세부 사항을 묻는 경우가 많다.

고득점 전략 담화 흐름 파악하기

🎧 850_P4_10   정답 및 해설 p.105

뉴스 담화문은 도입부에서 뉴스 주제를 언급한 후 세부 정보들이 계속 나오므로 체감 난이도가 비교적 높다. 초반에 등장하는 announced / revealed / reported 등에 집중하여 뉴스의 주제를 먼저 파악하자.

뉴스 주제	In today's business news, ① **the *Lancaster Morning Times* reported that its subscription numbers are continuing to go up.** → 뉴스의 주제를 나타내는 단서 표현 (reported) 등장	① **뉴스 주제:** 〈랭커스터 모닝타임즈〉의 구독자 수 증가
세부 내용	When the newspaper began publication one year ago, many considered it a risky financial venture, since most people now get their news on computers and mobile devices. ② **Mark Armstrong, the *Morning Times* editor in chief, attributed the newspaper's success to its focus on local news and events.** And, the *Morning Times* has plans to become further involved in the local community.	② **성공 이유:** 지역 뉴스와 행사에 초점을 둔 덕분
추가 내용	Mr. Armstrong said that ③ **in February, the newspaper will launch a weekly section written by high school students from the Lancaster region.**	③ **2월에 일어날 일:** 지역 고등학생들이 작성하는 주간 섹션 시작

세부 사항

1. What has **changed** recently at the *Lancaster Morning Times*?

(A) The Web site has been redesigned.
(B) The number of subscribers has increased.

정답 **(B) 구독자 수가 증가했다.**

세부 사항

2. According to Mark Armstrong, what has **helped** the newspaper achieve **success**?

(A) Implementing a detailed financial plan
(B) Focusing on local news

정답 **(B) 지역 뉴스에 초점**

다음에 할 일

3. What does Mark Armstrong **say** the newspaper **will do in February**?

(A) Publish a new weekly section
(B) Offer home delivery

정답 **(A) 새 주간 섹션 게재**

1. **What** has **Spellman Incorporated announced**?
   (A) A change in leadership
   (B) An increase in profits
   (C) A price reduction
   (D) A factory relocation

2. **What** is **special** about some **new products**?
   (A) They are inexpensive to produce.
   (B) They use organic ingredients.
   (C) They are advertised by a celebrity.
   (D) They are imported from abroad.

3. **Who** did **Maria Ortiz mention** in an **interview**?
   (A) Some longtime customers
   (B) Some retail business owners
   (C) Spellman Incorporated's marketing staff
   (D) Spellman Incorporated's sales Department

4. **What** is being **advertised**?
   (A) A toaster oven
   (B) A refrigerator
   (C) A vacuum cleaner
   (D) A washing machine

5. **What** is **unique** about the **500X model**?
   (A) It is fast.
   (B) It is small.
   (C) It is quiet.
   (D) It is energy efficient.

6. What does the speaker imply when he says, **"Inventory is limited"**?
   (A) Additional items will arrive soon.
   (B) A store will be crowded.
   (C) The listeners should act quickly.
   (D) The listeners can buy only one item.

7. **What** is the **topic** of today's broadcast?
   (A) Food trucks
   (B) Online meal ordering
   (C) The expansion of a farmers market
   (D) The grand opening of a café

8. **According to** the speaker, **why** is a type of business **popular**?
   (A) Its ingredients are locally produced.
   (B) It has affordable prices.
   (C) It provides free delivery.
   (D) It offers a wide selection.

9. **Who** is **Jerome Weber**?
   (A) A farmer
   (B) A journalist
   (C) A city official
   (D) A business owner

ETS 고득점 실전 문제

1. Who is the speaker?
    (A) A government official
    (B) A reporter
    (C) An architect
    (D) A general contractor

2. What construction project does the speaker discuss?
    (A) An office complex
    (B) A highway
    (C) A train station
    (D) A port facility

3. Why is the speaker pleased?
    (A) A budget was not exceeded.
    (B) New jobs will be created.
    (C) Profits will increase.
    (D) A delay has been resolved.

4. What is being advertised?
    (A) Equipment recycling
    (B) Commercial real estate
    (C) A school for technicians
    (D) Air conditioning maintenance

5. Why are listeners asked to call?
    (A) To set up an inspection
    (B) To arrange a pickup
    (C) To receive a demonstration video
    (D) To sign up for a workshop

6. What will happen at the end of the month?
    (A) Payments will be due.
    (B) A special discount will end.
    (C) Building construction will start.
    (D) A report will be published.

7. What is the television program about?
    (A) Tips for hosting a dinner party
    (B) A cooking competition
    (C) Recipes from around the world
    (D) Trends in the restaurant industry

8. Why does the speaker say, "they do see the dish before they taste it"?
    (A) To correct a misconception
    (B) To explain a delay
    (C) To compliment a chef
    (D) To suggest using a different plate

9. What did Anya Wilson recently do?
    (A) She opened a restaurant.
    (B) She traveled overseas.
    (C) She started a culinary school.
    (D) She designed a line of cookware.

10. What does the speaker say about Stefan Samir?
    (A) He is a famous architect.
    (B) He owns a hotel.
    (C) He will speak at a ceremony.
    (D) He has sold a property.

11. What is on the second floor of the hotel?
    (A) A fitness room
    (B) A business center
    (C) A swimming pool
    (D) A restaurant

12. Which hotel guests can receive a discount?
    (A) Retirees
    (B) Families with children
    (C) Returning customers
    (D) Businesspeople

13. What have some residents complained to city officials about?
(A) Traffic
(B) Rental costs
(C) Noise
(D) Lack of public transportation

14. What type of construction project is being discussed?
(A) Repairing a bridge
(B) Repaving a street
(C) Building a shopping center
(D) Restoring a historic building

15. What does the speaker imply when she says, "the city council has scheduled a special forum on Wednesday night"?
(A) A printed schedule contained an error.
(B) An opportunity to provide feedback will be available.
(C) A deadline extension has been accepted.
(D) Additional workers will be needed.

16. What is being advertised?
(A) An art exhibition
(B) A sporting event
(C) A musical performance
(D) A community festival

17. What does the speaker say the listeners can do on a Web site?
(A) Read biographies
(B) Make a reservation
(C) Download a map
(D) Submit reviews

18. What will happen at a reception?
(A) A video will be shown.
(B) A celebrity will sign autographs.
(C) A meal will be served.
(D) An award will be given.

Sunday Schedule	
11:30 A.M.	The Regents vs. the Mallards
1:45 P.M.	The Rovers vs. the Turtles
4:00 P.M.	The Diamonds vs. the Sailors
6:45 P.M.	The Stars vs. the Lightning

19. What sport is the speaker discussing?
(A) Softball
(B) Football
(C) Basketball
(D) Volleyball

20. Look at the graphic. What time does the recommended game start?
(A) 11:30 A.M.
(B) 1:45 P.M.
(C) 4:00 P.M.
(D) 6:45 P.M.

21. Who is Alexi Solokov?
(A) A writer
(B) An athlete
(C) A personal trainer
(D) A television producer

만점 빈출 표현

 850_P4_13

◆ 업무 관련 메시지

go over 검토하다

make it 가다, 참석하다

cut costs 비용을 줄이다

confidential information 기밀 정보

inspect a branch office 지점을 시찰하다

selection committee 선정 위원회

invite someone to a reception
축하 연회에 초대하다

conflicting schedule 겹치는 일정

set up a time 약속 시간을 잡다

schedule a conference call
화상 회의 일정을 잡다

award a grant 보조금을 주다

recommend a colleague for a task
직무에 적합한 동료를 추천하다

I'll call you with an update.
전화 드려서 소식 전할게요.

Let me know when you're available.
언제가 가능하신지 알려 주세요.

The schedule is flexible.
일정을 바꿀 수 있습니다.

add an e-mail address to the notification
list 참조 목록에 이메일 주소를 추가하다

leave a day after the conference ends
회의가 끝나고 하루 뒤에 출발하다

A formal invitation will be mailed.
정식 초청장이 우편으로 발송될 거예요.

can't afford to lose any profits
수익을 잃어도 될 만한 여유가 없다

approve the expense report
지출 보고서를 승인하다

meet at the medical convention
의학 총회에서 만나다

◆ 기업/기관 ARS 메시지

pound key (전화기) 우물 정자(#)

dial an extension number
내선번호를 누르다

latest offers and discounts
최근 혜택 및 할인

stay on the line 전화를 끊지 않고 기다리다

to be transferred to ~으로 연결되려면

You've reached ~. ~으로 전화하셨습니다

If your call is urgent, please leave a
message.
급한 용무가 있을 경우에는 메시지를 남겨 주시기 바랍니다.

We apologize for the interruption to the
service. 서비스 중단에 대해 사과의 말씀을 드립니다.

◆ 제품/서비스 문의 메시지

hotline 상담 전화

address a customer's concern
고객의 우려를 해결해 주다

sign up for the service 서비스를 신청하다

take a few days to process
처리하는 데 며칠이 걸리다

Please give me a call at your earliest
convenience. 가급적 빨리 전화 주세요.

in response to your inquiry 문의에 대한 회신

frequently asked questions
자주 묻는 질문(= FAQ)

We appreciate your business.
이용해 주셔서 감사합니다.

Refer you to page four of the instructions.
설명서 4쪽을 참조하세요.

receive lots of compliments
많은 칭찬을 받다

inventory check 재고 확인

◆ 사내 공지

outsource 외부에 위탁하다

in-house 사내의

refine a design 디자인을 개선하다

take a public transit
대중교통을 이용하다

time-reporting software program
시간 보고 소프트웨어 프로그램

fill in for ~을 대신하다

outage of Internet service 인터넷 작동 중단

before you begin your factory shifts today
오늘 공장 교대 근무를 시작하기 전에

pass around a sign-up sheet
등록 신청서를 돌리다

implement the change
변경 사항을 시행하다

accept a new position 새 직책을 수락하다

train a replacement 후임자를 교육하다

◆ 건물 내 안내 방송

patron 후원자, 고객

contest entry 경품 응모

customer loyalty card 고객 포인트 적립 카드

complimentary snack 무료 간식

give an instruction 설명하다, 지시하다

be committed to offering the lowest prices
최저 가격으로 제공하고자 노력하다

dairy product 유제품

stroll through 거닐다, 산책하다

offer delectable free samples
맛있는 무료 시식품을 제공하다

speed up the checkout process
계산 과정의 속도를 높이다

not function properly
제대로 작동하지 않는다

concession area 구내 매점

win free admission 무료 입장권을 얻다

Please consider that online alternative.
온라인으로 대체 가능한 점을 고려하세요.

◆ 회의

priority 우선 사항

order of business 업무 지시

sales fluctuation 매출 변동

review the proposal 제안서를 검토하다

need more publicity 더 많은 홍보가 필요하다

call the meeting 회의를 소집하다

with the understanding that
~이라는 조건 하에

wrap up the meeting 회의를 마무리하다

approve the permits for the renovation
개축 허가를 승인하다

an issue that is come to one's attention
알게 된 문제

receive some funding in the budget
예산의 일부를 지원받다

go over the project list
프로젝트 목록을 검토하다

share a job description
직무 기술서를 공유하다

touch on the point on the agenda
안건의 요점을 언급하다

be assigned a backup
지원 인력을 배정받다

take over responsibility
책임을 떠맡다

stop by the conference room
회의실에 들르다

discuss some alternatives
대안들을 논의하다

stick around after the meeting
회의가 끝나고 남다

approve the timeline
일정을 승인하다

surpass the production capability
생산량을 넘어서다

The deadline is further out.
마감일이 더 남았다.

sketch out a plan
대략적인 계획을 세우다

◆ 발표 / 연설

keynote speaker 기조 연설자

coordinator 책임 진행자

grand opening 개업식

testimonial 추천하는 글

publicize the event 행사를 홍보하다

on behalf of ~을 대표하여

in effect 시행 중인

secure a budget 예산을 확보하다

hands-on practice 실습

annual corporate retreat
연례 회사 야유회

compile the data 자료를 모으다

give a tutorial (사용법 등을) 설명하다

protocol 규정, 기준

information session 설명회

visiting consultant 객원 컨설턴트

fill out the questionnaire
설문지를 작성하다

feature in a publication
출판물에 등장하다

handle dietary concerns
식이 관련 사항을 처리하다

increase a customer base
고객층을 확대하다

make a pledge 서약하다

retirement celebration 은퇴 기념식

small-batch production 소량 생산

case study 사례 연구

reach a larger audience
더 많은 청중에게 도달하다

run an establishment
시설을 운영하다

use a composting system
비료화 처리 시스템을 사용하다

utility fee 공과금

shareholders' meeting 주주총회

emerging market 부상 중인 시장

◆ 소개

To honor his career
그의 경력을 기리기 위해

This workshop is intended to ~.
이 워크샵은 ~할 계획입니다.

leading expert on
~분야의 뛰어난 전문가

what sets ours apart
우리 제품이 돋보이는 점

proprietary 등록[전매] 상표가 붙은, 소유의

demonstrate the process
시범을 보이다

give a round of applause
박수를 보내다

come to the podium 연단으로 나오다

draw an entry 응모권을 추첨하다

find a replacement 후임자를 찾다

guest speaker 객원 연설자

◆ 관광 / 견학 / 관람

skilled artisan[craftsman] 숙련된 장인

magnificent city 멋진 도시

get the discounts and perks
할인 행사와 특전을 누리다

bring an identification card
신분증을 가져오다

state-of-the-art 최첨단의, 최고급의

excursion 소풍, (단체) 여행

wear protective gear 보호 장비를 착용하다

a large selection of 다양한

courtesy bus (손님용) 무료 버스

adjust the volume 볼륨을 조절하다

a mix-up in the schedule 일정상의 혼동

point out 언급하다

date back to ~으로 거슬러 올라가다

extensive art collection
광범위한 예술 소장품

permanent exhibit 상설 전시회

planetarium 천체 투영관

광고

exclusive 독점적인

be tired of ~에 싫증나다

look for volunteers 지원자를 모집하다

fill out an application 지원서를 작성하다

hit the shelves (서점·가게 등에) 나오다

sign up 등록하다, 가입하다

complimentary 무료의

trial period 무료 체험 기간

run a focus group 표적 집단을 운영하다

earn[redeem] points
포인트를 얻다[(다른 것으로) 교환하다]

create an account 회원가입을 하다

dependable company 믿을 만한 회사

top-of-the-line 최고급의, 최신식의

exceptional discount 이례적인 할인

completely adjustable
완전히 조절할 수 있는

be endorsed by a celebrity
유명인에 의해 홍보되다

create customized reports
맞춤형 보고서를 작성하다

take up space 공간을 차지하다

Inventory is limited. 재고가 한정되어 있다.

energy efficient 에너지 효율이 좋은

affordable prices 적당한 가격

energy audit (에너지 절감을 위한) 에너지 진단

culinary 요리의

design a line of cookware
조리도구 제품을 디자인하다

world-renowned 세계적으로 유명한

amenity 소모품, 편의 시설

as an added perk 추가 혜택으로

award-winning product 수상 제품

help business owners record
expenditures 사업주가 지출을 기록하도록 돕다

specialize in representing nonprofit
organizations
비영리단체를 대표하는 것을 전문으로 하다

 뉴스

initiative 계획

authority 당국

city mayor 시장

spokesperson 대변인

exclusive coverage 단독 보도

government official 정부 관계자

sign a petition 탄원서에 서명하다

implement a feature 기능을 시행하다

take an opinion poll 여론 조사를 하다

proceeds (자선 행사에서 나오는) 수익금

in the press release 기자회견에서

risky financial venture 재정적으로 위험한 벤처 사업

launch a weekly section
주간 섹션을 시작하다

announce a growth in profits
수익 증가를 발표하다

create well-paying jobs
고임금 일자리를 창출하다

general contractor 종합 건설업자

put forth a proposal 제안하다, 안을 제출하다

vote on a measure 법안에 대해 투표하다

top story this hour 이 시간의 주요 소식

라디오 방송

giveaway 증정품, 경품

commercial break 광고 시간

an important reminder
중요한 정보[알림]

message from our sponsor
광고주의 메시지[광고]

stay tuned to ~에 채널을 고정하다

call our hotline (방송 프로그램에) 전화하다

Great to have you on the show.
쇼에 출연해 주셔서 감사합니다.

This rivalry has been building all season.
시즌 내내 이런 경쟁 구도가 이뤄졌습니다

eagerly anticipated game
대망의 경기

PART 5
단문 채우기

INTRO

UNIT 1 | 명사

UNIT 2 | 대명사

UNIT 3 | 형용사 & 부사

UNIT 4 | 전치사

UNIT 5 | 자·타동사 / 수 일치 / 태 / 시제

UNIT 6 | to부정사 & 동명사

UNIT 7 | 분사 & 분사구문

UNIT 8 | 부사절 접속사 & 등위·상관접속사

UNIT 9 | 관계사

UNIT 10 | 명사절 접속사

UNIT 11 | ETS 기출 어휘

PART 5 단문 빈칸 채우기

총 30문항

파트 5는 총 30문항이 출제되며, 크게 문장 구조의 자리에 맞는 품사를 묻는 문법 문제와 문맥에 알맞거나 관용적인 표현을 요구하는 어휘 문제로 나뉜다. 토익이 업무, 조직 생활, 일상생활에서의 영어 활용 능력을 보는 실용영어 시험이라는 점을 유의하고, 자주 출제되는 소재와 상황, 빈출 유형을 익혀 두어야 한다.

문법편

◆ 최신 출제 경향

파트 5 한 문제당 20초를 넘지 않게 빠르게 풀어야 하며, 정확한 문장 구조와 문맥을 동시에 이해해야 한다.

→ 문장 구조에 맞는 명사, 형용사, 부사, 동사, 전치사, 접속사를 고르는 품사 자리 판단 문제와, 본동사와 준동사의 구별 문제, 종속절과 접속사의 활용을 묻는 문제가 출제된다.

◆ ETS 예제 및 풀이 전략

1. 보기가 문제의 힌트이다. 빈칸 주변과 보기를 확인하며 빈칸의 품사 자리를 판단한다.

101. The latest sedan by Hitato Motors is ------- more spacious than last year's model.

(A) notice   명사, 동사

(B) noticeable   형용사

(C) noticeably   부사

(D) noticing   준동사

① 빈칸 주변을 빠르게 보는 동시에 보기를 본다.

② 보기의 품사를 확인하며 빈칸이 어떤 품사의 자리인지 판단한다.

→ 빈칸 앞에는 be동사, 뒤에는 형용사가 있으므로 이를 수식하는 부사 자리이다.

③ 답이 될 수 있는 품사에 해당되는 보기가 2개 이상이면 해석으로 푼다.

2. 파트 5의 문제는 하나의 문장으로 구성되며, 문장 구조와 문맥 둘 다 완전해야 한다.

102. ------- is important to wear safety gear in the laboratory.

(A) It

(B) That

(C) There

(D) So

① 주어 자리에는 (A) It과 (B) That이 문법적으로 가능하지만, 문맥상 That(지시 대명사)은 대신하는 명사가 앞에 없다.

② 한 문장 안에서 문법 요소뿐 아니라 문맥 또한 완전해야 하는 파트 5 문제의 조건을 생각하면, That은 답이 될 수 없다.

③ 비인칭 주어 It은 뒤의 진주어(to wear)를 대신하는 가주어 역할이 가능하므로 답이 된다.

※ 정답뿐 아니라, 오답들의 이유 또한 중요하다. 함정으로 자주 출제되는 오답들의 유형도 익혀 두어야 한다.

어휘편

◆ 최신 출제 경향

파트 5 어휘 문제는 핵심 요소를 빠르게 해석하여 내용에 맞는 어휘를 찾는 단순 어휘 문제와 문법 요소가 들어간 어법 문제, 그리고 짝을 이루어 쓰는 연어(collocation) 문제가 출제된다.

◆ ETS 예제 및 풀이 전략

1. 어휘 문제 – 단순 어휘 문제는 최소한의 핵심 요소만 빠르게 해석하는 것이 중요하다.

103. The size of the staff at Ito Cement/ has almost -------,/so office space is shared.

(A) supported
(B) predicted
(C) controlled
(D) doubled

① 빈칸이 **동사 자리**이며 보기가 모두 **동사 어휘**임을 확인한다.
② 빈칸을 제외한 문장을 해석한다.
③ 주어(size 규모)와 호응되는 서술어(double 두 배가 되다)를 선택하고 전체 해석을 검토한다.
→ 이토 시멘트의 직원 규모가 거의 두 배가 되어 사무실 공간을 나누어 쓴다.

2. 어법 문제 – 어법 문제 풀이를 위해서는 동사의 자/타 구분, 함께 쓰이는 전치사 암기가 필수이다.

104. Please ------- all safety regulations when using the pool and fitness facilities.

(A) adhere   adhere to
(B) observe   타동사
(C) comply   comply with
(D) dedicate   dedicate A to B 또는 be dedicated to

① 빈칸이 동사 자리이며, 보기 구성이 자동사와 타동사가 섞여 있음을 확인한다.
② 빈칸 뒤에 목적어(all safety regulations)가 있으므로 타동사 observe를 선택하고 해석한다.
→ 수영장과 피트니스 시설 이용 시 모든 안전 수칙을 준수해 주세요.

3. 연어(collocation) 문제 – 빈출 collocation을 암기하면 어휘 문제가 3초 만에 풀린다.

105. For best results, ------- the instructions included with your new Franlea coffeemaker carefully.

(A) carry
(B) serve
(C) insert
(D) follow

① 목적어 instructions(지시 사항)와 **짝을 이루는 동사** follow(따르다)를 바로 선택한다.
② 빈칸에 follow를 넣고 전체 해석을 검토한다.
→ 최상의 결과를 위해 당신의 새 프랜리 커피메이커에 동봉된 지시 사항을 주의 깊게 따르세요.

UNIT 1 명사

전략포인트 1 명사는 주어, 목적어, 보어 역할을 한다.

주어	[An allowance / Allowed] is provided to employees on business trips in other cities. 다른 지역에서 출장 중인 직원에게 수당이 제공된다. → 주어와 동사의 수 일치에 항상 유의해야 한다.
타동사의 목적어	Please present the [receiving / receipt] from your purchase when leaving the store. 매장을 나가실 때 구입 영수증을 제시해 주세요.
전치사의 목적어	Upon [arrived / arrival], Mr. Lu will contact someone on our staff. 도착하자마자, 루 씨가 우리 담당 직원 중 한 분에게 연락을 드릴 거예요.
주격 보어	The reason why the client support program failed was a [short / shortage] of staff. 고객 지원 프로그램이 실패한 이유는 직원의 부족이었다.
목적격 보어	Reviewers are calling *The Northern Farm* the [book / booking] of the year. 비평가들은 더노던팜을 올해의 책으로 칭한다.

1. The ------- of employees is tested at the review and training sessions held every quarter.

(A) competent
(B) competence
(C) competently
(D) competences

2. Marked growth in sales enabled Galaxty Tools to move forward with plans for -------.

(A) expand
(B) expands
(C) expansive
(D) expansion

3. Because its grand opening sale was a huge -------, Earthrise Jewelers extended it through month's end.

(A) succeed
(B) successfully
(C) success
(D) successful

전략포인트 2 관사, 소유격, 형용사 뒤에는 명사가 온다.

관사 + 명사	The [direct / directory] of our staff is in the manual. 직원들의 명부는 설명서 안에 있다.
소유격 + 명사	Speak with one of our [represent / representatives] regarding the payment methods. 납부방식에 관해서는 우리 담당 직원 중 한 분과 얘기해 보세요.
형용사 + 명사	Everyone was sent a [comprehensive / comprehend] employee evaluation form. 모든 직원들이 포괄적인 직원 평가서 양식을 받았다.

1. The client's computer could not open the electronic document, so we will need to send it in a different -------.

(A) format
(B) formats
(C) is formatted
(D) formatted

2. The machine is functioning smoothly now that the necessary ------- has been done on it.

(A) maintain
(B) maintaining
(C) maintenance
(D) maintainable

3. Some of its usual ------- are unhappy about the changes in the payment process at Zanzibar Metals.

(A) supplied
(B) suppliers
(C) supplies
(D) supplying

전략포인트 3 가산명사와 불가산명사

■ **가산명사는 앞에 한정사가 붙거나 복수형 '-(e)s'이 되어야 한다.**

한정사

단수명사와 쓰이는 한정사
a
each 각각의
every 모두의
another (같은 종류의)
다른 하나

복수명사와 쓰이는 한정사
both 둘 다
all 모두
few 극소수의, 거의 없는
a few(=several/some)
몇몇의
other (같은 종류의) 다른

단·복수명사와 모두 가능
the
any 어느 ~든지

+

빈출 대표 가산명사

개체가 있는 사물(sample, item, product...), 사람(employee, consumer, resident...)
장소(city, store, building...), 단위(unit, liter, dollar...)는 주로 가산명사이다.

서류, 문서	document 서류	slip 전표	estimate 견적서	permit 허가증
	certificate 자격증	receipt 영수증	paper 문서, 신문, 논문	
돈, 가격	allowance 용돈, 수당		price 가격	rate 가격, 요금
	fee 수수료	cost 비용	expense 비용	fund 자금
	tax 세금	tariff 관세	proceed 수익금	
행사	opening 개장식	event 행사	meeting 회의	banquet 연회
가산 추상명사	discount 할인	refund 환불	order 주문	class 수업
	course 수업 과정	appointment 예약	plan 계획	profit 이익
	benefit 혜택	procedure 절차	process 과정	opinion 의견
형용사형 어미를 가진 가산명사	additive 첨가제	initiative 계획, 프로젝트	alternative 대안	
	objective 목표	representative 직원	executive 임원	
	perspective 관점	critic 비평가	professional 전문직 종사자	
	official 고위 공무원	individual 개인	periodical 정기 간행물	

■ **불가산명사는 복수형이 없으며 한정사 없이 단독으로 쓰일 수 있다.**

불가산명사와 쓰이는 한정사

a little(=some) 약간
little 거의 없는
much 많은
all 모든
other (같은 종류의) 다른

+

빈출 대표 불가산명사

access 접근	advice 조언	attendance 참석
baggage 수화물	clothing 의류	employment 고용
equipment 장비	furniture 가구	information 정보
manufacture 제조	merchandise 상품	misconduct 직권 남용
negligence 부주의	permission 허가	research 조사

H&J Chemical has <u>conducted</u> extensive [**research** / researches] about biodegradable plastic.
→ 불가산명사이므로 복수형이 없다.
H&J화학은 자연 분해되는 플라스틱에 대한 광범위한 연구를 실시해 왔다.

(만점팁) **소유격/any/the/most/some/all/other는 가산명사의 복수형 또는 불가산명사와 쓰인다**
<u>Other</u> [**merchandise** / products] <u>is</u> being displayed. 다른 상품들이 진열되고 있는 중이다.

---

1. Due to unforeseen circumstances, the salon is not scheduling ------- until next month.

(A) appointment
(B) appointments
(C) appointed
(D) appoints

2. ------- order on the company's Web site is filled within 12 hours and then mailed at once.

(A) Each
(B) Some
(C) Another
(D) All

3. We welcome any ------- from our customers regarding improvements to customer service.

(A) advice
(B) estimate
(C) alternative
(D) permit

명사는 사람명사와 사물/추상명사로 나뉜다.

- **사람명사와 추상명사의 의미 차이를 알고 있어야 한다.**

Interested [**participants** / participation] should contact Personnel by next Friday.
관심 있는 참가자들은 다음 주 금요일까지 인사부에 연락하셔야 합니다.

- **사람 / 사물 / 추상명사는 문맥에 따라 구분된다.**

an associate 직원, 동료	an association 협회	a subscriber 구독자	a subscription 구독
a patron 고객	patronage (고객의) 애용, 후원	a supplier 공급업자	supplies 물품
an attendee 참가자	attendance 참석	a recipient 수신인	a receipt 영수증
a consumer 소비자	consumption 소비	a participant 참가자	participation 참여
an authority 권위자	authorization 허가, 인증	a competitor 경쟁업체	competition 경쟁

[Attendee / **Attendance**] at the festival exceeded 1,000 people a day.
축제의 참석자 수가 하루 1,000명을 넘어섰다.

(만점팁) 사람명사는 가산명사이므로 한정사와 함께, 또는 복수형으로 써야 한다. 이에 해당이 안 되면 추상명사가 답일 수 있다.

1. We advise ------- of our magazine to take advantage of our convenient online billing system.

(A) subscribers
(B) subscription
(C) subscribing
(D) subscribed

2. If you encounter any problems while using this kiosk, please ask one of our sales ------- at the checkout.

(A) associate
(B) associated
(C) association
(D) associates

3. ------- on solar power is focused mostly on making solar cells more efficient.

(A) Research
(B) Researcher
(C) Researches
(D) Researched

'명사 + 명사'로 이루어진 복합명사

- **뒤에 오는 명사가 가산/불가산, 단/복수를 결정한다.**
  - 앞에 위치한 명사는 형용사와 비슷한 역할을 하며, 원칙적으로 복수형을 쓰지 않는다.

workplace safety 작업장 안전	worker productivity 직원 생산성	job responsibilities 직무, 책무
keynote speaker 기조 연설자	sales quota 판매 할당량	employee performance 직원 성과
maintenance work 정비 작업	work(ing) environment 근무 환경	press coverage 언론 보도
housing allowance 주거 보조금	price adjustment 가격 조정	living expenses 생활비
email confirmation 이메일 확인서	tourist attraction 관광 명소	salary freeze 연봉 동결
shipping charge 운송비	baggage allowance 수하물 허용 중량	building permit 공사 허가

Passengers are advised to check their baggage [**allowance** / permit] before packing.
승객들은 짐을 싸기 전에 수화물 허용 중량을 확인하셔야 합니다.

1. Prenzey Castle is the most visited tourist ------- in the Northern Lakes region.

(A) attract
(B) attraction
(C) attractive
(D) attractively

2. If you do not receive an e-mail ------- of your Hydrangea Hotel booking, please contact our customer service department.

(A) contribution
(B) guidance
(C) admission
(D) confirmation

3. All the employees were instructed that they needed to meet their ------- quota every month.

(A) sales
(B) sell
(C) sold
(D) salable

만점 공략 포인트

만점포인트 ① **복합명사에도 가산명사의 특징을 활용한다.**

Due to the recession, price ------ on our new line of cosmetics are necessary.

(A) adjust   (B) adjusted   (C) adjusting   (D) adjustments

■ 주어 자리의 단수명사 price는 앞에 한정사가 없으므로 복합명사의 일부로 판단해야 한다.

· 분사(adjusted/adjusting)가 price를 뒤에서 앞으로 수식하는 구조도 가능하지만, 가산 명사인 price 앞에 한정사가 없으므로 오답으로 소거할 수 있다.

만점포인트 ② **비슷한 의미의 혼동하기 쉬운 가산명사와 불가산명사**

Red ------ has been used for all holiday season deliveries.

(A) package   (B) packaged   (C) packaging   (D) packagings

■ 동명사처럼 보이는 packaging은 '포장재'의 뜻인 불가산명사이며 주어 자리에서 단수동사 has와 수 일치된다. 비슷한 모양의 package(소포)는 가산명사이므로 단수형으로 사용되면 앞에 한정사가 반드시 동반되어야 한다.

· 비슷한 의미의 혼동되는 가산·불가산명사

불가산	가산	불가산	가산
funding 재정 지원, 자금	funds 돈, 자금	advice 조언	a suggestion 제안
advertising 광고	an advertisement 광고	access 접근	an approach 접근
planning 계획 수립, 기획	a plan 계획	furniture 가구	furnishings 가구
housing 주택, 주택 공급	a house (단독) 주택	merchandise 상품	a product 상품
shopping 쇼핑	a shop 가게, 매장	mail 우편물	a letter 편지
seating 좌석 배치	a seat 자리	research 조사, 연구	a survey 설문조사
packaging 포장재	a package 소포, 우편물	permission 허가	a permit 허가
pricing 가격 책정	a price 가격	stationery 문구류	office supplies 사무용품

만점포인트 1 | 불황 때문에, 우리의 새 화장품 라인에 대한 가격 조정이 필요하다.   답 (D)
만점포인트 2 | 모든 명절 시즌 배송에 붉은 포장재가 쓰였다.   답 (C)

1. Mr. Chu's presentation on innovative sampling methods received very warm -------.

   (A) applaud
   (B) applauded
   (C) to applaud
   (D) applause

2. The chat feature on our Web site allows clients to speak directly with a financial -------.

   (A) represent
   (B) representing
   (C) representation
   (D) representative

3. With its new conference space, Stellway Hotel is now in ------- competition with the Brookwell Convention Center.

   (A) direction
   (B) direct
   (C) directly
   (D) directing

4. Chambers Brothers, Inc., is known for offering good ------- benefits.

   (A) to employ
   (B) employ
   (C) employee
   (D) employing

5. Mr. Pang was able to implement the new inventory management system with the ------- of the warehouse employees.

   (A) assist
   (B) assisted
   (C) assistant
   (D) assistance

6. A list of conference ------- can be found in the back of your programs.

   (A) attendance
   (B) attend
   (C) attendees
   (D) attending

7. ------- of interest in the program resulted in it being canceled by the director after one week.

   (A) Having lacked
   (B) Lacked
   (C) To lack
   (D) Lack

8. RGMA takes pride in providing effective solutions for clients' Internet security -------.

   (A) needing
   (B) will need
   (C) needs
   (D) needed

9. Frequent ------- can result in an individual spending too much money on personal items.

   (A) shops
   (B) shopping
   (C) shop
   (D) shopped

10. Vausas Filtration Systems provides online ------- in the use of its products.

   (A) variety
   (B) assembly
   (C) judgment
   (D) guidance

11. The logistics clerk is waiting for Treeland Toys to sign and return the contract before shipping any ------- for them.

(A) refunds
(B) trades
(C) transportation
(D) merchandise

12. Jellaville's Chamber of Commerce has initiated plans to develop the historic waterfront into a viable tourist -------.

(A) destination
(B) population
(C) method
(D) stage

13. The swimming pool at the community center is scheduled for ------- each weekend.

(A) clean
(B) cleaner
(C) cleaned
(D) cleaning

14. Within weeks, Mr. Sisneros had gone from being a consultant on the project to ------- it.

(A) manager
(B) managing
(C) be managing
(D) managed

15. Some research shows that too much vacation can reduce worker -------.

(A) production
(B) productivity
(C) productively
(D) producing

16. The latest ------- proposed by Mayor Marcon was perceived positively by most local residents.

(A) initiator
(B) initiation
(C) initiative
(D) initiating

17. Many interviewees commented on the work ------- at Felton Textiles as being a primary attraction.

(A) environment
(B) environmentally
(C) environmental
(D) environmentalist

18. J.D. Cooper stated that his restaurant's menu would feature an even larger ------- of dishes than before.

(A) source
(B) cover
(C) selection
(D) dimension

19. Hampton Logistics provides long-term ------- of goods for clients at several of its warehouses.

(A) to store
(B) store
(C) storage
(D) stored

20. ------- of travel visas will take longer than expected due to high demand during tourist season.

(A) Process
(B) Processing
(C) Procedure
(D) Proceed

UNIT 2 대명사

전략포인트 1 인칭대명사

- **인칭대명사는 격에 맞게 써야 하고, 문장에서의 자리가 정해져 있다.**

주격 주어 자리에 쓰이고 뒤에 반드시 본동사가 오며, 동사와 수 일치된다.

We are honored to receive this prestigious award. 우리는 이 명망 있는 상을 받게 되어 영광입니다.

목적격 타동사, 전치사 뒤의 목적어 자리에 쓰인다.

The manager assured the employees that he would let **them** know about any changes.
매니저는 직원들에게 변동사항에 대해 알려준다고 확언해주었다.

소유격 명사를 수식하는 자리에 쓰인다.

Please double-check **your** contact information on the application.
지원서의 연락처를 재확인해주세요.

(만점팁) 'he'나 'she' 또는 'they'와 같은 3인칭대명사는 지칭하는 명사가 앞에 있어야 하고 수, 인칭, 성별이 일치해야 한다.

1. Mr. Park, our advertising consultant, will submit ------- first report to us on Friday.

   (A) he
   (B) him
   (C) his
   (D) himself

2. Mr. Anderson spoke with Ms. Peebles and asked ------- to attend the trade fair in Boise.

   (A) him
   (B) her
   (C) them
   (D) it

3. Researchers at LIINT Electronics will discuss the wearable devices that ------- have been developing for a few years.

   (A) they
   (B) them
   (C) their
   (D) theirs

전략포인트 2 소유대명사와 소유격을 강조하는 one's own

- **소유대명사는 '소유격 + 명사' 역할을 하며 '~의 것'이라는 의미로, 모든 명사 자리에 사용 가능하다.**

The mobile phone on the table is red, but [you / **yours**] is black. → yours = your mobile phone
테이블 위에 있는 휴대전화는 빨간색이지만 당신의 것은 검정색이다.

- **소유격 강조 – one's own**

  one's own + 명사   명사 + of one's own

Mr. Park promoted **his own** short story on social media.
박 씨는 자신의 단편소설을 소셜 미디어에 홍보했다.

= Mr. Park promoted a short story of **his own** on social media.

1. The women who are picking up the rental vehicle should be told that ------- is the blue minivan.

   (A) their
   (B) theirs
   (C) they
   (D) themselves

2. The province of Manitoba imposes 7 percent sales tax on electronics, but ------- here is 10 percent.

   (A) we
   (B) ourselves
   (C) us
   (D) ours

3. Mr. Eagleson has enrolled in a business management program because he wishes to start a business of ------- sometime in the future.

   (A) him
   (B) himself
   (C) his own
   (D) his

전략포인트	3	재귀대명사는 '~자신, 직접'이라고 해석하며, 문장에서 목적어와 부사 자리에 쓰인다.

■ 재귀적 용법 – 타동사의 목적어 자리이고, 주어가 동사의 목적어일 때 쓴다.

Mr. Simson will introduce [him / himself] to you.
　　주어　　　　　　　　　　　　　타동사의 목적어 – 주어와 일치하는 목적어는 재귀대명사이다.
심슨 씨가 여러분들에게 자신을 소개하겠습니다.

We encourage **employees** to familiarize [themselves / ourselves] with the new regulations.
　　　　　　　　to부정사의 의미상의 주어
우리는 직원들이 새로운 규정을 숙지해 둘 것을 권장합니다.

(만점팁) 5형식 동사가 to부정사 등 준동사를 목적보어로 취할 때는 준동사의 의미상 주어가 문장 전체의 주어와 다르다는 점에 주의한다.

■ 강조적 용법 – 부사 자리이고, '직접'이라는 의미로 문장 끝이나 주어와 동사 사이에 위치하며 생략 가능하다.

The manager [himself / he] created the spreadsheet for everyone in the office.
매니저는 사무실 직원 모두를 위해 스프레드시트를 자신이 직접 만들었다.

Please ask for assistance instead of removing things from the top shelf [themselves / yourself].
맨 위 선반에서 물건을 직접 꺼내는 대신에 도움을 요청하세요.

■ 관용적 용법 – 전치사의 목적어 자리이고, 숙어로 암기해서 활용해야 한다.

> by oneself 혼자서, 스스로
> among themselves 저희들끼리, 자기들끼리
> in (and of) itself 그것 자체는
> between ourselves 우리끼리

During the workshop, the trainees do the layout for the flyer by [themselves / their own].
워크숍 동안에, 교육생들은 전단지 레이아웃을 스스로 만든다.

The policy is not a problem in [it / itself], but the application is.
정책 그 자체는 문제가 아니지만, 적용이 문제다.

---

1. Last week, Mr. Sarrafan completed all the assigned work -------.

(A) he
(B) him
(C) his
(D) himself

2. Mr. Henderson advised applicants to prepare ------- for the upcoming interviews at the job fair.

(A) itself
(B) himself
(C) themselves
(D) yourselves

3. The members of each team are asked to share ideas among ------- and develop a prototype for a motorbike during this quarter.

(A) themselves
(B) himself
(C) yourselves
(D) ourselves

■ '사람들'이라는 뜻의 'those'는 뒤에 수식어가 온다.

those who + 동사(~하는 사람들) – who는 주격 관계대명사이므로 뒤에 반드시 동사가 와야 한다.	
those + 분사구(V + -ing / V + -ed)	those + 전치사구

[~~They~~ / Those] who wish to participate in the event should apply before January 17.
행사에 참여를 바라는 사람들은 1월 17일 전에 지원해야 한다.

→ They는 뒤에 수식어가 붙을 수 없고, 앞에 They를 지칭하는 명사가 있어야 한다.

Access to the area will be granted to [those / ~~those who~~] with permission.
그 구역의 이용 권한은 승인을 받은 사람들에게 주어질 것이다.　　　전치사구

The outdoor activities are only for those [wearing / ~~wear~~] protective gear.
그 야외 활동들은 보호장비를 착용한 사람들만을 위한 것이다. 분사(V + -ing)

1. Mr. Nettles asked ------- who would like to work overtime tonight to let him know by 4:00 P.M.
   (A) these
   (B) those
   (C) them
   (D) they

2. All those ------- a career in the field of biomedicine should attend the seminar led by Dr. Holston.
   (A) considered
   (B) considering
   (C) consider
   (D) considers

3. Ms. Smith understands what to do better than ------- originally in charge of the project.
   (A) who
   (B) them
   (C) those who
   (D) those

■ 비교 상황에서 앞서 언급된 명사를 대신할 때 그 명사가 단수라면 that, 복수라면 those를 쓴다.

The (device) in the meeting room is more advanced than [that / ~~those~~] in the classroom.
　　　단수명사　　　　　　　　비교급　　　전치사
회의실에 있는 장비가 교실에 있는 것(장비)보다 더 좋다.

more/better/less … than ~보다 더/나은/덜 …한	comparable/similar to ~에 필적할 만한, 비슷한
the same as/identical to ~와 동일한	different from ~와 다른/differ from ~와 다르다
indistinguishable from ~와 구분이 안되는, 유사한	while/whereas 반면에/unlike ~와 달리

■ that과 those는 수식어구를 동반하지만 it과 them은 수식어구를 동반하지 못한다.

The (quality) of products in this store is comparable to [that / ~~it~~] of goods found in a department store. 이 매장에 있는 제품들의 품질은 백화점에서 파는 제품들의 그것(품질)에 필적할 만하다.

1. The number of shoppers at the store this holiday is similar to ------- of the previous holiday.
   (A) that
   (B) those
   (C) this
   (D) they

2. Because the actual color differed from ------- in the catalog description, Etoile Gowns returned two boxes of lace to the supplier.
   (A) that
   (B) including
   (C) except
   (D) only

3. Unlike the discontinued skincare products, ------- released this year are all in airless pump bottles.
   (A) it
   (B) them
   (C) that
   (D) those

전략포인트 6 수량을 나타내는 부정대명사

■ 앞에 언급된 명사의 수량을 반영하여 대명사로 쓰고, 주어 자리인 경우 동사와의 수 일치에 유의한다.

종류	의미	대명사	형용사	대명사일 때	형용사일 때
one	(막연한) 하나(의), ~것, ~사람	O	O	One is fine.	one suggestion
each	각각, 각각의	O	O	Each is fine.	each suggestion
another	다른 하나	O	O	Another is fine.	another suggestion
others	다른 것들	O	X	Others are fine.	X
the other	(특정 범위의) 나머지(의)	O	O	The other is fine.	the other choice(s)
some	몇몇의, 약간의	O	O	Some is/are fine.	some advice/suggestions
both	둘 다	O	O	Both are fine.	both suggestions
neither	둘 다 아닌 것	O	O	Neither is fine.	neither suggestion
either	둘 중 어느 하나	O	O	Either is fine.	either suggestion
most	대부분	O	O	Most is/are fine.	most advice/suggestions
all	전부	O	O	All is/are fine.	all advice/suggestions
none	전부 아닌 것	O	X	None is/are fine.	X
many	많은 사람들, 많은 ~것	O	O	Many are fine.	many suggestions
a few/few	몇몇의/거의 (아니다)	O	O	(A) Few are fine.	(a) few suggestions
a little/little	약간의/거의 (아니다)	O	O	(A) Little is fine.	(a) little advice
each other/ one another	서로서로(관용 표현)	O	X	They help each other. - 주어 자리에는 사용되지 않고 목적어 자리에만 쓰인다.	

만점팁 every와 other는 대명사 역할을 못 하고 형용사만 가능하므로 명사가 반드시 뒤따라야 한다.

•every employee (O) •every of the employees (X)   •other suggestions (O) •other of suggestions (X)

Mr. Chandler and Ms. Cook write in different genres, but [both / some] are highly regarded.
both가 가리키는 대상
챈들러 씨와 쿡 씨는 다른 장르를 집필하지만 둘 다 높이 평가받는다.

Out of three proposals, two have been dismissed, but [the other / one] will be considered.
세 가지 제안서 중에 두 개는 폐기되지만, 나머지 것은 고려될 것이다.
→ the other(s)는 일정한 수 중에서 나머지를 나타내기 때문에 앞에 out of three와 같이 주어진 수가 있어야 한다.

Personnel and marketing work closely with [one another / them].
인사부와 마케팅부는 서로 긴밀히 협력한다.

■ 부정(negative)의 의미를 가진 부정대명사가 주어일 때 동사와 함께 부정문으로 해석해야 한다.

few/little + 동사 거의 모두 ~ 아니다	none/neither + 동사 모두/둘 다 ~ 아니다

There are restaurants on the waterfront, but [others / none] are vegetarian.
none이 가리키는 대상   복수동사
해안가에 식당들이 있지만 채식 식당은 없다.

1. Our customer service survey was sent to one thousand people, but ------- did not respond.

(A) many
(B) amount
(C) much
(D) yet

2. It is ideal that employees motivate ------- to increase productivity.

(A) another one
(B) each other
(C) other
(D) their

3. While the audience members enjoyed the talk, ------- asked questions of the speaker when it concluded.

(A) none
(B) every
(C) little
(D) each other

■ 부분을 나타내는 부정대명사 뒤에는 'of the / 소유격 + 명사'가 자주 나오는데, 이때 수 일치에 주의해야 한다.

단수주어 취급	One, Each, Either, Neither	of the/소유격 <u>employees</u> 복수명사	is experienced. 단수동사
	(참고) Either와 Neither는 비격식 상황에서 복수동사와 쓰이기도 한다.		
복수주어 취급	(A) Few, Several, Many, Both	of the/소유격 <u>employees</u> 복수명사	are experienced. 복수동사
불가산주어 취급	(A) Little, Much	of the/소유격 <u>advice</u> 불가산명사	is helpful. 단수동사
복수/불가산주어 취급	Some, Most, Any, All, None, Half	of the/소유격 <u>employees</u> 복수명사	are experienced. 복수동사
		of the/소유격 <u>advice</u> 불가산명사	is helpful. 단수동사

[Every / **Each**] of the floors has a photocopier. 각 층에 복사기가 있다.

[Little / **Few**] of these companies participating in the job fair offer temporary positions.
이 취업 박람회에 참가하는 회사들 중 거의가 임시직을 제공하지 않는다.

[**Much** / Many] of the anticipation comes from the new economy policies.
많은 기대는 새로운 경제 정책에서 나온다.

The company has discontinued [**most of its** / most of] products from last year.
회사는 작년 제품들의 대부분을 단종시켰다.
→ '부정대명사 of' 뒤에 the나 소유격이 필요하다는 점도 유의해야 한다.

(만점팁) 'of the / 소유격'의 수식을 받지 않는 부정대명사

- thing - body - one	anything, something, nothing, anybody, somebody, nobody anyone, someone, no one	of the/소유격 + 명사 (X)	+	단수동사

If [anyone / **any**] of the participants do not respond to the call, the event will be canceled.
참가자들 중 어느 누구도 요청에 답변하지 않는다면, 그 행사는 취소될 것이다.
→ anyone은 전치사구의 수식을 받지 않는다.

1. Denise Cantor will keep working tonight until ------- her assignments for the week are finished.
(A) mostly
(B) most
(C) almost
(D) most of

2. ------- of the crates that arrived at the warehouse had been damaged in transit.
(A) That
(B) Anything
(C) Some
(D) Much

3. ------- of the five members of the team fulfilled their sales quota for the month of August.
(A) None
(B) No
(C) Nothing
(D) Nobody

만점 공략 포인트

만점포인트 ❶ '명사 + ＿＿＿ + 타동사(목적어 없음)'의 빈칸은 주격 인칭대명사 자리이다.

All new employees should submit the survey ------- were asked to complete by 4:00 P.M.

(A) they   (B) them   (C) themselves   (D) their

■ 빈칸이 주어(the survey)와 동사(were asked) 사이에 있어 재귀대명사가 정답처럼 보이지만, 주어인 the survey와 themselves 의 수가 일치하지 않는다. 목적격 관계대명사가 생략된 형용사절의 주어 자리이며, 뒤에는 목적어가 없는 타동사(to complete)가 온다.

· 명사 + (목적격 관계대명사) 주어 + 타동사(목적어 없음) 의 형태로 자주 출제된다.
                생략·   문제의 답
  ➔ 형용사절은 항상 선행사(명사)를 취한다.

만점포인트 ❷ those who는 복수동사, anyone who(=whoever)는 단수동사가 뒤따른다.

------- who have purchased the subscription this month will receive reward points.

(A) Those   (B) These   (C) Whoever   (D) Anyone

■ '~하는 사람들'의 those who는 뒤에 복수동사(have purchased)가 따라온다. 반면에 '~하는 누구나'의 의미인 anyone who (=whoever)는 단수동사와 짝을 이룬다.   ▶ Unit 10 명사절 참고

만점포인트 ❸ a와 소유격은 함께 쓸 수 없다. 대신, 'a + 명사 of 소유대명사'가 쓰인다.

Each student is allowed to bring a friend of ------- to the event.

(A) their   (B) theirs   (C) them   (D) themselves

■ 부정관사와 소유격은 둘 다 한정사인데, 한정사는 연속해서 쓸 수 없다. 대신에 'a + 명사 of 소유대명사'의 용법이 쓰인다.

· 전치사 of 뒤에 목적격을 오답으로 고르기 쉽다는 점에 유의한다. 친숙한 표현인 'a friend of mine'을 기억해 두면 좋다. 여기서 mine 은 my friends를 소유대명사로 표시한 것으로 'a my friend'와 같이 한정사를 중복해서 쓰지 않는다.

만점포인트 1 | 신입사원들은 작성하라고 요청 받은 설문지를 오후 4시까지 제출해야 합니다.   답 (A)
만점포인트 2 | 이번 달에 구독을 신청한 사람들은 보너스 포인트를 받게 됩니다.   답 (A)
만점포인트 3 | 학생들 각자는 행사에 자신들의 친구 한 명씩을 데려올 수 있습니다.   답 (B)

ETS 고득점 실전 문제

1. Ms. Reynolds and ------- team will make a presentation at the meeting tomorrow.

   (A) she
   (B) herself
   (C) her
   (D) hers

2. The manager asked Mr. Evans and Mr. Clark to present at the job fair, and instructed ------- to prepare the presentation in a very specific way.

   (A) it
   (B) him
   (C) her
   (D) them

3. ------- of the two proposals presented at the directors' meeting were approved.

   (A) Another
   (B) Neither
   (C) Whatever
   (D) Those

4. Large video screens will be set up on stage so ------- can see the presenters clearly.

   (A) everyone
   (B) nothing
   (C) each other
   (D) that

5. Angela Mercer was honored that a proposal of ------- was selected by the committee.

   (A) she
   (B) her
   (C) hers
   (D) herself

6. More than half of the complaints from our recent customer satisfaction survey ------- regarding the speed of service.

   (A) were
   (B) was
   (C) is
   (D) has been

7. Although the training sessions were quite difficult, the computer program ------- required little experience to use.

   (A) it
   (B) itself
   (C) themselves
   (D) them

8. The manager will inform Mark Walker that the job ------- applied for was filled by an internal candidate.

   (A) he
   (B) his
   (C) himself
   (D) him

9. Mark Kent insisted that he could translate all of the documents on -------.

   (A) him
   (B) himself
   (C) his own
   (D) his

10. Similar to the members of the marketing team, ------- in accounting mostly have advanced degrees.

    (A) them
    (B) their
    (C) this
    (D) those

11. While the special offer was sent to 300 customers, ------- ordered anything from the online store.

(A) few
(B) little
(C) much
(D) any

12. Repairs must be performed at once on ------- of the four assembly lines in the factory.

(A) which
(B) other
(C) every
(D) each

13. Most workers receive full benefits, but ------- working part time may not receive paid time off.

(A) them
(B) they
(C) those
(D) this

14. Ms. Dumont asked the CEO whether his startup could sustain ------- after one year of funding.

(A) herself
(B) himself
(C) itself
(D) themselves

15. The head of security spoke with the workers since ------- have requested new ID cards recently.

(A) such
(B) many
(C) another
(D) which

16. All wait staff, ------- those with seniority, are no more important than the cooks in the kitchen.

(A) even
(B) since
(C) without
(D) therefore

17. Sunny Shirts customers who wish to ------- their item for another will be charged the difference in price.

(A) exchange
(B) design
(C) wear
(D) display

18. Because ------- of the surveys have been returned yet, management is unsure how employees feel about the work conditions.

(A) no
(B) no one
(C) nothing
(D) none

19. Our committee will review all job descriptions next month and revise ------- that need changes.

(A) what
(B) any
(C) which
(D) somebody

20. ------- first request the complimentary tickets to the opera will be given them by the receptionist.

(A) Which
(B) Whoever
(C) Those who
(D) Someone

UNIT 3 · 형용사 & 부사

전략포인트 1 · 형용사는 명사 앞과 뒤에서 수식한다.

- (관사 / 소유격 / 한정사) + (부사) + 형용사 + 명사

It took a surprisingly **long** period of time to restore the bridge from the landslides.

산사태로부터 다리를 복구하는 데에 놀랄만큼 오랜 기간이 걸렸다.

- 명사 뒤에서 수식 – 형용사 뒤에 전치사구나 to부정사 등이 연결되면 명사 뒤에서 수식한다.

Please remove **information** irrelevant to the topic of the meeting. 회의와 연관 없는 정보는 삭제해 주세요.

(만점팁) -able / -ible로 끝나는 형용사는 명사 앞 / 뒤에서 수식이 가능하다.

Children enjoyed free boardgames **available** in the lobby. 어린이들이 로비에 마련된 무료 보드게임을 즐겼다.

1. With ------- contributions from staff, we bought flowers to celebrate Ms. Tanaka's promotion.

(A) generously
(B) generousness
(C) generosity
(D) generous

2. Mr. McKinney was the only individual ------- about attending the speech by Ms. Herbert.

(A) enthusiasm
(B) enthusiastic
(C) enthusiastically
(D) enthusing

3. It was determined that the prototypes ------- for the demonstration were in a warehouse in Dallas.

(A) suit
(B) suiting
(C) suitable
(D) suitably

전략포인트 2 · 형용사를 보어로 취하는 2형식 동사와 5형식 동사

- 2형식 동사

be동사 ~이다 / become ~되다	seem ~인 것 같다	go / come / get / grow ~하게 되다	
feel ~하게 느끼다	turn ~하게 변하다	look / appear ~하게 보이다	+ 형용사
remain / stay ~인 채로 있다	sound ~하게 들리다	prove ~이라고 판명되다	nice
smell / taste ~하게 맛이 나다 / 냄새가 나다			

Despite the recession, sales of local magazines have **remained** high.
불황에도 불구하고 지역 잡지의 매출은 높은 상태를 유지해 왔다.

- 5형식 동사

keep 유지하다	find 느끼다, 생각하다	consider 여기다	+ 목적어	+ 형용사
make 만들다	leave (~한 상태로) 놔두다		it	nice

Many employees **found** the workshop informative. 많은 직원들이 워크숍을 유익하게 생각했다.

(만점팁) 보어 자리의 형용사는 부사처럼 '~하게'로 해석되기도 하지만, 부사는 보어로 쓰일 수 없다.

1. Wyman Automotive has released a piece of software that is ------- to its braking system.

(A) essentialness (B) essentially
(C) essential (D) essentials

2. It sounds ------- that there will be a construction project which will help the local economy.

(A) promising (B) a promise
(C) promise (D) promises

3. Alice Steele finds working with the accounting program that was recently installed ------- pleasant.

(A) delighted (B) delight
(C) delightful (D) delightfully

전략포인트 3 수량 형용사는 수 일치에 유의한다.

- another / each / every / either / neither + 가산 단수명사
- many / (a) few / fewer / both / several / a number of / a majority of + 가산 복수명사
- much / (a) little / a large amount of / a great deal of + 불가산명사
- all / more / most / a lot of / lots of / plenty of / other / some + 가산 복수명사 / 불가산명사
- no / any + 가산 단·복수명사 / 불가산명사

Between the two options, <u>neither</u> one [is / are] affordable. 두 가지 선택 사항들 중, 어느 것도 저렴하진 않다.

(만점팁) every, another 뒤에 2 이상의 숫자가 오는 경우 복수명사를 쓴다.

The bus comes every <u>two</u> hour**s**. 버스가 2시간마다 온다.
It will take another <u>five</u> day**s**. 5일이 더 걸릴 것이다.

1. It is important to spread ------- flour on the surface before rolling out the dough for the crust.

(A) some
(B) many
(C) few
(D) any

2. Since the renovation last year, the representatives have dealt with fewer ------- regarding the parking.

(A) complains
(B) complaining
(C) complaint
(D) complaints

3. Every statistical analysis provided by Alterlab.com ------- developed and interpreted by industry professionals.

(A) is
(B) are
(C) to be
(D) have been

전략포인트 4 형태가 혼동되는 형용사

confident candidate	확신에 찬 후보자	confidential information	기밀 정보
considerate associate	사려 깊은 동료	considerable resource	상당한 자원
exhausted supplies	고갈된(다 쓴) 물자	exhaustive review	철저한 검토
extended deadline	연장된 기한	extensive research	광범위한 연구
qualified applicant	자격이 되는 지원자	qualifying exam / heat	자격 시험 / 예선 경기
successful project	성공적인 프로젝트	successive events	연속적인 사건

Due to the [extensive / extended] deadline, the next project was postponed.
연장된 마감 기한 때문에 다음 프로젝트가 연기되었다.

- '-ly'로 끝나는 형용사

timely 시기적절한	orderly 질서정연한	costly 비용이 드는	lively 활기찬	likely 유력한, ~일 것 같은

The employee completed the task in a [promptly / timely] fashion. 직원은 제때 일을 끝냈다.

(만점팁) 횟수를 나타내는 daily, weekly, monthly, yearly는 형용사와 부사 모두 쓰인다.

1. Quality control requires ------- reviews on the products.

(A) exhaust
(B) exhausted
(C) exhaustion
(D) exhaustive

2. Virtually all our apprentices passed the ------- exam for the data processing engineer license.

(A) qualifying
(B) qualified
(C) qualify
(D) to qualify

3. The ------- atmosphere of the fish market in downtown Cheonan is appealing to tourists.

(A) live
(B) lively
(C) lived
(D) living

■ 형용사 + 명사 빈출표현

regular/frequent/loyal customer 단골고객	primary concern 주요 관심사
prospective/potential customer 잠재 고객	substantial resources 상당한 자원
informative workshop 유익한(도움이 되는) 워크샵	resourceful leader 지략이 있는 지도자
instructive guidelines 유익한(도움이 되는) 지침서	challenging(=demanding) task 어려운 업무
temporary/permanent position 임시직/정규직	likely candidate 유력한 후보자
comprehensive insurance coverage 종합보험 보장범위	significant/substantial change 상당한 변화
competitive price 경쟁력 있는(저렴한) 가격	of the highest quality 최고급의

1. Anelli Motors is seeking an experienced and ------- leader to run the sales division.

(A) resourced
(B) resourceful
(C) resourcing
(D) resourcefully

2. Most residents believe that Zane Thomas will be the ------- winner of the upcoming election for mayor.

(A) like
(B) likely
(C) likeness
(D) liken

3. The primary ------- of the NGO is to monitor companies to ensure they are not releasing pollution.

(A) method
(B) appearance
(C) concern
(D) observation

■ be + 형용사 + to부정사

be eligible(=entitled) to부정사 ~할 자격이 되다	be hesitant to부정사 ~하는 것을 망설이다
be able to부정사(=be capable of) ~할 수 있다	be likely to부정사 ~할 가능성이 높다
be set/due to부정사 ~할 예정이다	be reluctant to부정사 ~하기를 꺼리다

■ be + 형용사 + 전치사 to + (동)명사

be beneficial to ~에 도움이 되다	be subject to ~될 수 있다, ~에 달려 있다
be comparable(=similar) to ~에 필적할 만하다, 비슷하다	be equivalent to ~와 동등하다
be relevant to ~와 관련 있다/irrelevant to ~와 관련 없다	be equal to ~와 같다
be accustomed to(=familiar with) ~에 익숙해지다	be vulnerable to ~에 취약하다
be accessible to ~에 접근이 가능하다, ~이 이용할 수 있다	be committed/dedicated to ~에 전념(헌신)하다

■ be + 형용사 + 기타 전치사 + (동)명사

be appropriate for(=suitable/suited for) ~에 적합하다	be critical of ~에 대해 비판적이다
be eligible for(=entitled to) ~에 자격이 되다	be aware of/conscious of ~을 알다
be compatible with ~와 호환이 되다	be known as/for ~으로/때문에 알려지다
be exempt from ~을 면제받다	be enthusiastic about ~에 대해 열성적이다
be compliant with ~을 따르다, 준수하다	be skeptical of ~에 대해 회의적이다

1. Ms. Sealey is ------- of reports that lack strong research components.

(A) critic
(B) critics
(C) critical
(D) criticize

2. Full-time employees are ------- to receive a mobile-phone allowance.

(A) profitable
(B) accurate
(C) careful
(D) eligible

3. Ms. Ross is the candidate best suited ------- the public relations position.

(A) for
(B) by
(C) with
(D) of

전략포인트 7 부사 자리 (1) – 동사, 형용사, 부사 수식

- **주어와 동사 사이, 조동사와 동사원형 사이, be -ing 사이, be p.p.사이, have p.p. 사이 모두 부사 자리이다.**

  Vittgor Internet <u>is</u> actively <u>promoting</u> its new plans. 비트고르 인터넷은 새로운 요금제를 활발히 홍보 중이다.

  The test result <u>has</u> finally <u>come</u> out. 테스트 결과가 마침내 나왔다.

- **완전한 문장 뒤**

  The photocopier <u>works</u> properly. 복사기가 제대로 작동한다.

- **형용사와 부사 앞**

  The measuring device is extremely <u>accurate</u>. 측정 장비가 상당히 정확하다.

- **일부 부사는 명사(구)를 수식할 수 있다.**

just, only, exclusively, simply 단지, ~만	mainly, largely, mostly 주로	especially, specifically 특히

  Only <u>the employees</u> with approval can access the R&D Department.
  승인을 받은 직원들만이 R&D센터 이용이 가능하다.

1. The Halifax Daily will no longer ------- free subscriptions as of next month.

(A) provide
(B) provided
(C) provision
(D) providing

2. To improve service quality, Raynar Activity Center requests client feedback -------.

(A) regular
(B) regularly
(C) regulars
(D) regularity

3. The recent increase in traffic to our Web site is ------- the result of our social media campaign.

(A) large
(B) larger
(C) largest
(D) largely

전략포인트 8 부사 자리 (2) – 준동사, 전치사, 부사절 접속사, 문장 전체 수식

- **준동사 수식**

  This survey is designed <u>to</u> thoroughly <u>evaluate</u> customer service satisfaction. → to부정사는 부사의 수식을 받는다.
  이 설문조사는 고객서비스 만족도를 자세히 평가하기 위해 만들어졌다.

  Manually <u>installing</u> the software is not easy for novice users. → 형용사의 수식을 받는 명사와 달리, 동명사는 부사의 수식을 받는다.
  소프트웨어를 수동으로 설치하는 것은 초보 사용자들에게 쉽지 않다.

- **전치사, 부사절 접속사 앞**

  Construction will begin immediately <u>after</u> the building permit is issued.

  건축 허가가 발부된 후 즉시 공사가 시작될 것이다.

- **주절 앞의 콤마 앞**

  Fortunately, <u>the deadline was extended</u>. 다행히, 마감 기한이 연장되었다. → 주절 앞에 콤마가 있다면 그 앞은 부사 자리이다.

1. Highlights of the weekend's soccer matches are posted online ------- after 10:00 P.M. on Sunday evening.

(A) short
(B) shorter
(C) shortly
(D) shorten

2. Thank you for so ------- reviewing the enrollment procedures with the new employees.

(A) being patient
(B) patiently
(C) patience
(D) patient

3. -------, Mr. Thomas arrived at the airport too late to catch his flight to Florence.

(A) Regrets
(B) Regretting
(C) Regrettably
(D) Regretted

■ 원급 강조 – 동사는 수식할 수 없다.

• 매우	very / so / highly	
• 꽤	fairly / quite	**+** 형용사의 원급
• 상당히	absolutely / extremely / excessively / exceedingly / exceptionally	부사의 원급

The event was <u>absolutely</u> [successful / succeed]. 행사는 상당히 성공적이었다.

The profits for this month dropped [significantly / fairly]. 이번 달 수익이 상당히 하락했다.

→ fairly는 '꽤, 매우'의 의미일 때 형용사와 부사의 상태를 강조하지만 동사는 수식할 수 없다.

• **too** 너무 (부정적인 의미를 지닌다)	• **too 형/부 to부정사** 너무 ~해서 …할 수 없다
• **enough** 충분히 (형용사와 부사를 뒤에서 수식한다 ⑩ good enough)	
• **so 형/부 that절** 매우 ~해서 …하다	• **such a 형/명 that절** 매우 ~한 (명사)여서 …하다

The plant was [so / very] short of workers <u>that</u> it had a hard time keeping the deadline.
공장은 직원들이 너무 부족해서 마감 기한을 지키는 데 어려움을 겪었다.

→ very는 that절과 사용할 수 없다.

■ 비교급 강조

• 훨씬 더/덜	a lot / much / even / far / still	• **형용사의 비교급**
• 상당히 더/덜	considerably / significantly / substantially / greatly	**+** quicker / less quick more / less important(+ than)
• 현저히 더	noticeably / remarkably	• **부사의 비교급** more quickly / less importantly

The new model is [very / far] more reliable than the existing ones.
새로운 모델이 기존 것들보다 훨씬 더 믿을 만하다.

■ 최상급 강조

		• **형용사의 최상급** the quickest / the most important
• 단연코 가장	simply / easily / by far	**+**
		• **부사의 최상급** the most quickly / the most importantly

• **the very best** 그야말로 최고인	• **the best possible** 가능한 한 최고로
• **the best ever / the best of all time** 그지금까지 봤을 때 최고인	

At Athens' Palace, you can enjoy the [good / best] Greek dining experience <u>possible</u>.
아테네 팰리스에서, 여러분은 가능한 한 최고의 그리스식 정찬의 경험을 누리실 수 있습니다.

---

1. We always run out of pens ------ quickly in our office that we have to order them in bulk.

(A) very
(B) so
(C) quite
(D) too

2. Ms. Blaire claimed that she was ------- happier working in the suburbs than she was in the urban center.

(A) much
(B) many
(C) so
(D) very

3. Jasmine Supermarket sells only the ------- largest strawberries that it can acquire from its suppliers.

(A) so
(B) highly
(C) very
(D) much

전략포인트 **10** 빈출 부사 (1)

■ 증감동사와 잘 어울리는 부사

증가하다	increase, rise, improve
향상하다	enhance, update, upgrade
하락하다	decrease, fall
변경하다	change, revise

+

considerably/substantially/significantly/greatly 상당히
sharply/dramatically/drastically 급격하게, 극적으로
noticeably/remarkably 눈에 띄게
steadily 꾸준히   gradually 점진적으로   slightly 약간

■ 특정 동사와 잘 어울리는 부사

arrive punctually 제시간에 도착하다
work collaboratively/cooperatively 협동하여 일하다
review thoroughly 자세히 검토하다
inspect regularly 정기적으로 점검하다
listen intently to 열심히, 열중하여 경청하다
rely heavily on(upon) ~에 매우 의존하다

fasten securely 단단히 매다, 잠그다
go smoothly 순조롭게 진행되다
evaluate/rate/appraise highly 높이 평가하다
function/work properly 제대로 작동하다
respond promptly to ~에게 즉시 답변해주다
speak highly of ~에 대해 칭찬하다

■ 특정 형용사와 잘 어울리는 부사

increasingly popular 점점 더 인기를 얻고 있는
readily available 손쉽게 구할 수 있는
temporarily unavailable 일시적으로 이용할 수 없는

highly likely ~할 가능성이 매우 높은
strictly confidential 극비의, 엄격히 기밀인
almost complete 거의 완료된

■ 특정 분사와 잘 어울리는 부사

reasonably priced 적정 가격이 매겨진
conveniently located 편리하게 위치한
recently appointed 최근에 임명된
unanimously approved 만장일치로 승인된
widely known 널리 알려진

highly recommended 매우 추천받는
highly regarded 높이 평가받는
mutually agreed 상호 간에 동의된
fully equipped 설비를 완전히 갖춘
deeply involved 깊이 연관된

Maria's Home sells [reasonable / **reasonably**] priced quality bedsheets and pillowcases.
마리아즈 홈은 적정 가격이 매겨진 품질 좋은 침대 시트와 베갯잇을 판매합니다. → 과거분사(가격이 책정된)

■ 전치사 & 부사절 접속사와 어울리는 부사

only when/only after 그제서야
soon/shortly/immediately/right + after/following 바로 직후에 + before 바로 직전에
mostly/largely/mainly + because/due to 주로 ~ 때문에
temporarily out of stock 일시적으로 재고가 없는

---

1. Mainstreet Books announced a merger with a software company, and its shares have ------- increased.

(A) exactly
(B) alternatively
(C) highly
(D) dramatically

2. The system server will be ------- unavailable due to an unexpected maintenance request.

(A) previously
(B) individually
(C) hardly
(D) temporarily

3. There will be a reception for the keynote speaker ------- following her talk in the auditorium.

(A) lately
(B) shortly
(C) quite
(D) justly

■ 숫자/수량을 수식하는 부사 및 전치사

approximately/roughly/almost/nearly/around/about 대략, 거의	
precisely/exactly 정확히	over/more than ~이상
under/below/less than ~이하	at least 적어도
merely/only/just/no more than 겨우	up to ~까지
almost/nearly/virtually + every/all 거의 모든	at most 기껏해야

The survey requires [roughly / highly] a thousand responses from various demographics.
그 설문조사는 다양한 인구 통계적 집단으로부터 대략 천 개의 답변을 필요로 한다.

■ **still + not vs. not + yet**

The planning was <u>not</u> done [yet / still], so the meeting was postponed.
기획이 아직 안 끝나서 회의가 미뤄졌다.　　　　→ still은 부정의 표현을 뒤에 취한다.

참고 yet은 부정문과 의문문에서 부사 '아직'으로 쓰인다. 그 외에는 but과 동의어인 등위접속사이다.
참고로 'have yet to부정사'는 not 없이 '아직 ~하지 않았다'의 관용 표현이므로 외워 두도록 한다.

■ 시제를 나타내는 부사

현재 시제 (빈도 부사)	always 항상	typically 전형적으로	generally 일반적으로	frequently 빈번히
	periodically/regularly 정기적으로		rarely/seldom 거의 ~하지 않다	
현재진행 시제	now 지금	currently 현재	presently 현재	

The new employees <u>are</u> [recently / currently] <u>taking</u> a tour of the facilities on these premises.
신입사원들은 현재 이 구역의 시설물들을 견학하고 있는 중이다.
→ recently는 과거와 현재완료에서 사용한다.

과거 시제	recently 최근에(과거 or 현재완료)	ago 전에	once 과거 한때

Mr. Kim, who <u>was</u> [yet / once] a famous actor, is now working for an advertising company.
과거 한때 유명한 배우였던 김 씨는 현재 광고회사에서 근무 중이다.
→ once가 '한때'의 뜻일 때 주로 문장 중간에 위치한다.

■ 접속부사: 두 개의 문장을 의미적으로는 연결하지만, 접속사와 달리 절과 절을 연결하지는 못한다.

however 그러나	therefore 그러므로	then 그러고 나서	likewise 마찬가지로
nevertheless/nonetheless/even so 그럼에도 불구하고		if so 그렇다면	if not 그렇지 않다면
otherwise 그렇지 않으면, 달리	meanwhile 그러는 동안에	afterwards 그 후에	besides 게다가

Please update your contact information; otherwise, you will not receive our newsletter.
연락처를 업데이트 해 주세요. 그렇지 않으면 소식지를 받으실 수 없을 거예요.
→ 세미콜론(;)이 두 문장을 연결시키는 접속사 역할을 한다.

---

1. There was ------- nobody in the theater five minutes before the performance was scheduled to begin.

(A) so
(B) such
(C) well
(D) still

2. The conference room is available on Monday beginning at ------- 10:00 A.M.

(A) extremely
(B) variously
(C) exceptionally
(D) approximately

3. The restaurant is ------- being renovated to accommodate double the number of customers that it used to accept.

(A) extremely
(B) currently
(C) once
(D) yet

만점 공략 포인트

만점포인트 ① 문장 구조에 따라 의미가 달라지는 조심해야 할 동사

It is widely believed that Dr. Madison's experiment proved ------- to the development of the new technology.

(A) instrument (B) instrumental (C) instruments (D) instrumenting

■ prove 다음에 형용사 보어가 오면 2형식 동사로 '~으로 드러나다, 판명(입증)되다'의 의미이다. '~을 증명하다'의 의미일 때는 3형식이므로 뒤에 목적어를 취해야 한다.

- 문장 구조에 따라 의미가 변하는 빈출 동사

appear useful 유용하게 보이다 / appear suddenly 갑자기 나타나다　　　go bad 상하다 / go smoothly 순조롭게 진행되다
find the question easy 문제를 쉽게 생각하다 / find the store easily 매장을 쉽게 찾다

만점포인트 ② highly와 well은 p.p.를 꾸민다.

The presentation was ------- received among the start-up businesses.

(A) very (B) well (C) quite (D) fairly

■ well은 p.p.(과거분사)를 강조하며 '잘, 많이 ~된'의 의미로 쓰인다. 일반적으로 동사를 수식하는 well은 주로 문장 맨 뒤에 위치하지만, 과거분사를 수식할 때는 중간에 위치한다.

- 강조 부사 highly도 과거분사를 수식하지만, very나 quite는 일반동사의 과거분사를 수식할 수 없다.
  [참고] very와 quite은 분사형 형용사인 감정동사의 p.p.는 수식할 수 있다.　예) very excited 매우 신이 난
- 자주 쓰이는 well + p.p.

well maintained 관리가 잘 된	well attended 참석률이 좋은	well prepared 준비가 잘 된
well deserved 자격이 충분한	well planned 계획이 잘 짜여진	well received 호응이 좋은

만점포인트 ③ '다양한'을 강조하는 형용사

Individuals who display a ------- variety of skills are more likely to be promoted to management positions.

(A) hopeful (B) vivid (C) severe (D) diverse

■ 'a range of'처럼 '다양한'을 의미하는 수량 한정사의 강조는 관용표현이므로 외워 두도록 한다.

- a **large** / **wide** / **broad** / **diverse** + range / selection / variety of 매우 다양한
- a **vast** majority of 대다수의

만점포인트 1 | 매디슨 박사의 실험이 새로운 기술의 발전에 도움이 되는 것으로 입증되었다고 널리 알려져 있다.　답 (B)
만점포인트 2 | 프레젠테이션은 창업 기업들 사이에서 호응을 많이 얻었다.　답 (B)
만점포인트 3 | 매우(갖가지) 다양한 기능을 발휘하는 사람은 관리직으로 승진할 가능성이 더 높다.　답 (D)

1. Pursuing software training with Kunishi Ltd. will lead to a ------- rewarding career.

   (A) financially
   (B) financial
   (C) finance
   (D) finances

2. For instructions on submitting your time sheets, please see the ------- document attached.

   (A) helps
   (B) helped
   (C) helpful
   (D) helpfully

3. For most businesses, keeping loyal customers is more ------- than attracting new ones.

   (A) profit
   (B) profitable
   (C) profits
   (D) profiting

4. Experts examine all of the raw materials to make sure they are of the ------- quality.

   (A) high
   (B) higher
   (C) highest
   (D) height

5. The ------- yet inexperienced employee is usually sent to headquarters to undergo more training.

   (A) observe
   (B) observant
   (C) observer
   (D) observation

6. Ms. Powers gave her presentation so ------- that she was able to acquire several new clients.

   (A) confidence
   (B) confident
   (C) confide
   (D) confidently

7. Given the praise for her debut novel, Nia Li is expected to ------- gain widespread fame.

   (A) ahead
   (B) soon
   (C) very
   (D) after

8. Although Phick T-shirts are also a cotton blend, they are ------- softer than other brands we have ordered.

   (A) highly
   (B) exactly
   (C) noticeably
   (D) closely

9. The renovation of the museum will be completed in ------- six weeks.

   (A) early
   (B) under
   (C) major
   (D) through

10. Despite the many differing opinions about how to approach the project, the meeting went ------- well.

    (A) surprise
    (B) surprised
    (C) surprising
    (D) surprisingly

11. Ms. Moss was ------- of the marketing campaign for her company's oatmeal, but the team convinced her of its potential.

(A) proud
(B) capable
(C) skeptical
(D) aware

12. Melanie practices hard and ------- expects to be selected when she auditions for performances.

(A) there
(B) often
(C) while
(D) before

13. The Melinsky Hotel's Web site can be accessed at all times, -------, through your mobile device.

(A) anywhere
(B) anyone
(C) everything
(D) everybody

14. Mr. Lazar was hired only last month but has ------- already saved the company a significant amount of money.

(A) moreover
(B) namely
(C) nevertheless
(D) similarly

15. Please run the errand fast ------- to do the next assignment on the list within the next hour.

(A) enough
(B) about
(C) around
(D) such

16. The landlord will fine any tenants who ------- shout or make other noises that bother residents.

(A) loud
(B) loudly
(C) louder
(D) loudness

17. The customer testimonials show ------- how powerful and easy it is to use our software.

(A) near
(B) alike
(C) just
(D) along

18. Watson Logistics makes deliveries for virtually ------- the factories located in the city's industrial park.

(A) all
(B) every
(C) some
(D) few

19. Everyone believed Dave Arnold was ------- the winner and should be selected by the judges.

(A) overly
(B) clearly
(C) successfully
(D) exactly

20. Leiffer Technology has made ------- updates to its latest generation of cell phones.

(A) favorite
(B) careful
(C) responsible
(D) substantial

UNIT 4 전치사

전략포인트 1 시간의 전치사는 시점과 기간을 구분해야 한다.

시점	기간

• at + 시각 / on + 요일, 날짜 / in + 월, 년도 ~에
• by (완료) / until (계속) ~까지
  - finish, complete, submit, pay + by
  - wait, remain, last, valid / not + until
• since (과거의 시점) + have + p.p. ~이래로
	• throughout / during / over + (행사, 기간) 명사 ~ 동안
	  for + (숫자) + 기간 ~ 동안
	• within + 기간 ~이내에
	• in + 기간 ~후에 (미래시제)

True Bank <u>remains</u> open [**until** / within] <u>6:00 P.M.</u> on weekdays. 트루 은행은 주중에 6시까지 문을 연다.

The client will be visiting the office [at / **in**] an hour. 고객이 한 시간 뒤에 방문할 거예요.

1. Items from Formal Clothes, Inc., may be returned for a full refund ------- 30 days of purchase.

(A) within
(B) including
(C) as soon as
(D) by

2. Ms. Lau from Vestino Bank was very helpful ------- the entire business loan process.

(A) throughout
(B) although
(C) later
(D) underneath

3. Managers at Sardis Industrial should complete the quarterly report ------- Thursday at 1 P.M.

(A) upon
(B) by
(C) until
(D) toward

전략포인트 2 장소/방향, 위치의 전치사

장소/방향	위치
• at + 장소, on + 층 / 거리, in + 도시, 나라 ~에서(는) • to / into / toward(s) ~에, ~으로, ~을 향하여 • from the top of the mountain 산 정상으로부터 • through the window 창문을 통하여, 통과하여 • along the path 길을 따라 • across the street 거리를 가로질러 • across / throughout the city 도시 전역에 걸쳐	• by / beside / next to ~옆에 • around / close to / adjacent to / near (by) ~근처에 • between + A and B / 복수명사 (둘) ~사이 • among + 복수명사 (셋 이상의) ~사이 = (out) of + 복수명사 ~중에서 (하나) • within + 범위(radius 반경 / distance 거리) ~내에 • across from = opposite 맞은편에 있는

[**Among** / At] <u>the options</u>, the first one seems promising. 선택 사항들 중에 첫 번째 것이 유망해 보인다.
= Of / Out of + 복수명사

The document was sent [along / **to**] the head office. 서류가 본사에 보내졌다.

1. Byrd Supermarket has over 50 locations ------- the northwest region.

(A) against
(B) off
(C) between
(D) across

2. There are several popular restaurants ------- walking distance of the Hastings Hotel.

(A) within
(B) during
(C) into
(D) for

3. Howard Construction is ------- the firms being considered for the building project.

(A) before
(B) among
(C) concerning
(D) over

전략포인트 3 양보/이유/추가/시간/제외/수단/목적의 전치사

양보	despite/in spite of/notwithstanding ~에도 불구하고	이유	due to/because of ~ 때문에 owing to/thanks to/on account of ~ 덕택에 given/considering ~을 고려하면, 감안하면
추가	besides/in addition to/on top of 게다가, ~에 더하여 as well as ~와 마찬가지로	시간	on/upon ~할 때, ~하자마자 after/following ~후에 before/prior to ~전에
제외	except (for)/apart from/other than ~을 제외하고 (all/every와 자주 쓰인다) without ~없이	수단	by/via + (교통·통신) 수단 ~에 의해서 with ~을 가지고 through ~을 통해서
		목적	for ~을 위해서

The museum is open everyday [except / without] Mondays. 박물관은 월요일만 제외하고 매일 문을 엽니다.

1. ------- inclement weather, the departure of Flight 675 has been delayed.

(A) Nevertheless
(B) In spite of
(C) Because of
(D) Whenever

2. The training session is mandatory for every department ------- the administration department.

(A) except
(B) down
(C) unless
(D) without

3. ------- the extensive marketing campaign, attendance at the annual film festival was low.

(A) Rather than
(B) As well as
(C) Despite
(D) Thus

전략포인트 4 기타 다양한 전치사

주제 연관성	about/on/over/regarding/concerning in[with] regard to/pertaining to ~에 관하여 as to/as for/in terms of ~관해 (말하자면) regardless of ~와 관련 없는	영향	under ~중에, 내에/~하에
		비교	like ~처럼
		분야	in ~에서
반대	against ~에 반대하여 contrary to/unlike ~와 달리	직책/자격	as ~으로서
포함	including/such as/like ~을 포함하여, ~와 같은	주변	around/about + 숫자, 시간, 장소 약 ~, 정도

[On / Unlike] the previous model, the new one prints double-sided.
이전 모델과 달리 새것은 양면 인쇄를 한다.

Please forward inquiries [as / regarding] interviews to the personnel department.
면접에 관한 문의는 인사부로 전달해 주세요.

1. Runners in tomorrow's race should expect poor weather, ------- rain and fog.

(A) according to
(B) meanwhile
(C) including
(D) provided that

2. The members of the hiring committee identified Ms. Jansen ------- the best candidate for the position.

(A) as
(B) since
(C) from
(D) like

3. Historians believe that the original manuscript was written ------- 1800.

(A) onto
(B) down
(C) at
(D) around

according to ~에 따르면	as of + 시점 ~부로, ~부터	ahead of ~보다 앞서
depending on ~에 따라	in accordance with ~에 따라서	in light of ~을 고려하여
in preparation for ~에 대비하여	in compliance with ~을 준수하여	in charge of ~을 담당하는
in response to ~에 응하여	in observance of ~을 준수하여	as a result of ~의 결과로
on behalf of ~을 대표하여	under the direction of ~의 감독하에	instead of/in place of ~대신에

SJ Co. has increased production at all of its facilities [as a result of / as of] high demand.
에스제이 사는 높은 수요의 결과로 모든 공장에서의 생산을 증가시켰다.

at one's disposal 마음대로 할 수 있는	in effect 시행 중인
at one's earliest convenience 가급적 빨리	in a timely manner(fashion) 시기적절하게, 제때에
on duty/at work 근무 중인	under(at) no circumstances 어떤 상황에서도 ~하지 않다

[Of / Under] no circumstances is vandalism allowed. 기물 파손은 어떠한 상황에서도 용납되지 않는다.

1. Each fall, firewood is gathered in preparation ------- the winter season.

(A) for
(B) on
(C) up
(D) over

2. Written articles should be completed ------- the agreed-upon schedule.

(A) except for
(B) such as
(C) according to
(D) so that

3. Please notify us of your availability for the conference ------- your earliest convenience.

(A) in
(B) by
(C) at
(D) with

look into (정보 등을) 알아보다	take apart 분해하다	carry out 수행하다	back up 지지하다
check through 면밀히 조사하다	make up for 보상하다	take over 인수하다	invest in 투자하다
switch on 스위치를 켜다	use up 다 써버리다	serve(sit) on ~의 일원으로서 역할을 하다	

Professor Kim was invited to serve [by / on] the jury. 김 교수는 배심원의 일원으로 역할을 해달라는 권유를 받았다.

rise/increase in ~의 증가	demand(need) for ~에 대한 수요, 요구	access to ~에 대한 이용, 접근
confidence in ~에 대한 자신감, 신뢰	impact(influence) on ~에 미치는 영향	response(reply) to ~에 대한 답변
inquiry about ~에 대한 문의	advantage/edge over ~보다 우위	comment on ~에 대한 견해, 언급

We welcome any comments [on / of] our products. 우리 제품에 대한 어떤 의견이라도 환영합니다.

1. Vance Moving Company confirmed that it will invest ------- hybrid vans for its fleet.

(A) of
(B) in
(C) at
(D) to

2. The technician will have to ------- your computer in order to determine what the problem is.

(A) take apart
(B) take place
(C) take up
(D) take of

3. The company survey revealed that the majority of employees have ------- in their managers.

(A) honesty
(B) strength
(C) motivation
(D) confidence

만점 공략 포인트

만점포인트 ❶ During은 동명사를 목적어로 취하지 않는다.

------- developing the floor plan, the architect realized that the measurement of the space was incorrect.

(A) During   (B) While   (C) At   (D) Of

- 전치사 'during'은 동명사를 목적어로 취하지 않는다. 반면에 부사절 접속사인 'while'은 '부사절 접속사 + 분사'인 분사구문을 이끌 수 있으므로 뒤에 현재분사인 '동사원형 + -ing'를 취할 수 있다. ▶ Unit 8 부사절 참고

- during + 사건/행사/기간 등을 나타내는 **명사**
  During this quarter, they reported record profits. 이번 분기 동안, 그들은 기록적인 수익을 냈다.

만점포인트 ❷ of는 위치에 따라 의미가 달라진다.

------- the presenters at the conference, Ms. Myers demonstrated the most confidence on stage.

(A) On   (B) As   (C) Of   (D) Up

- 'of'가 문장 맨 앞에 오면, 'among'의 의미로 뒤에 복수명사가 온다.

- 명사 + **of** + 명사 ~의   the amount of work 일의 양
- **of** + 복수명사 (=out of/among + 복수명사) ~ 중에서 (하나)   Of the three choices 세 가지 선택들 중에서

만점포인트 ❸ given, considering은 전치사, given that, considering (that)은 접속사이다.

------- the affordability of the production costs, we decided to work with Milton Material Co.

(A) Provided   (B) Given   (C) Considering that   (D) Regarding

- given/considering + 명사
  전치사
- given/considering that + 주어 + 동사 ~을 고려하여, 감안하여
  부사절 접속사

만점포인트 1 | 평면도를 만드는 동안에, 건축가는 공간의 측정이 잘못되었다는 점을 알았다. 답 (B)
만점포인트 2 | 학회 발표자 중 마이어스 씨가 무대에서 가장 자신감을 보였다. 답 (C)
만점포인트 3 | 생산 비용의 가격 적정성을 감안하여, 밀튼 재료사와 함께 일하기로 결정했다. 답 (B)

1. ------- the renovations, employees with firstfloor offices will work in the third-floor conference rooms.

   (A) Temporary
   (B) During
   (C) Recently
   (D) Whereas

2. *Swan Fountain*, the current production at Budbranch Theater, will close ------- two weeks.

   (A) now
   (B) just
   (C) in
   (D) as

3. Revenue ------- sales of imported lumber is 2 percent higher this month than in June.

   (A) up
   (B) out
   (C) into
   (D) from

4. ------- the survey results, we will need to increase our workflow capacity.

   (A) Whenever
   (B) As a consequence
   (C) According to
   (D) Because

5. ------- a free trial period, most people decide to purchase Norkirk's software.

   (A) After
   (B) Unless
   (C) Except
   (D) Beside

6. Workers must affix the required warning labels ------- sending products to the quality control department.

   (A) prior to
   (B) and
   (C) last
   (D) otherwise

7. ------- the information on the city's Web site, the swimming pool is now open until 9 P.M.

   (A) Provided that
   (B) Even though
   (C) As long as
   (D) Contrary to

8. You can deposit checks ------- our new banking app using your smartphone.

   (A) around
   (B) about
   (C) under
   (D) through

9. ------- each session with a job candidate, members of the recruitment team should take time to share their impressions.

   (A) Above
   (B) Following
   (C) Opposite
   (D) Without

10. ------- suffering some mechanical issues at the start of the journey, the train arrived on time.

    (A) Until
    (B) Despite
    (C) Upon
    (D) By

11. ------- the lack of interest in the professional development workshop, it was the right decision to cancel it.

(A) Given
(B) Since
(C) Like
(D) Within

12. ------- the receptionist, who will stay on-site, the entire staff will participate in the employee retreat.

(A) Likewise
(B) Except for
(C) Indeed
(D) Prior to

13. ------- the nominees for the prestigious software industry award is a startup firm called KW Tech.

(A) Among
(B) Without
(C) Except
(D) During

14. Quincy Heating customers must pay a delivery charge ------- the fee for the installation of the appliance.

(A) near to
(B) across from
(C) on top of
(D) in exchange

15. ------- the cold temperatures, the city's annual parade will be held on October 9 as scheduled.

(A) Regardless of
(B) Assuming that
(C) Consequently
(D) By the time

16. Owing to a failed safety inspection, the elevator will be off limits ------- further notice.

(A) before
(B) about
(C) until
(D) through

17. Sportsworld Monthly has experienced a steady increase in subscribers, ------- the general decline that the magazine industry is going through.

(A) notwithstanding
(B) furthermore
(C) while
(D) eventually

18. The HR team is still unsure ------- whether to hire one full-time bookkeeper or two part-time ones.

(A) ahead of
(B) as to
(C) out of
(D) back to

19. ------- the terms of the agreement, customers must give thirty days' notice to cancel the service.

(A) As a consequence
(B) On behalf of
(C) In accordance with
(D) In case of

20. ------- completing the online survey, customers are sent a discount code for fifteen percent off their next purchase.

(A) Over
(B) Near
(C) During
(D) Upon

자·타동사/수 일치/태/시제

🌙 출제비율 5~6문제/30문항

전략포인트 **1** **빈출 자동사 – 1형식 & 2형식 동사**

■ **1형식 자동사 – 부사나 전치사구가 자주 뒤따라온다.**

rise 오르다	behave 행동하다	work 일하다, 작동되다	function 작동되다	expire 만기가 되다
depart 출발하다	appear 나타나다	go(= proceed) 진행되다	commence 시작되다	diminish 줄어들다
vary 다양하다	differ 다르다	arise/happen 발생하다	emerge 떠오르다	fall 하락하다

The orientation will [**commence** / initiate] <u>at precisely 9:00 A.M.</u>
오리엔테이션은 정확히 오전 9시에 시작한다.　　　　　　　　전치사구

→ 'initiate'는 '~을 시작/착수시키다'라는 뜻의 타동사이다.

■ **2형식 자동사 – be, become을 제외한 일반 2형식 동사들은 주로 명사가 아닌 형용사를 보어로 취한다.**

remain 여전히 ~이다　seem/appear ~인 것 같다　prove 판명되다　**+** informative (O) / information (X)

The experiment appeared [success / **successful** / successfully]. 실험이 성공적인 것 같았다

---

1. Daringa Apparel's stock price ------- sharply after Tina Ness was chosen as CEO.

(A) maintained　(B) connected
(C) landed　(D) rose

2. Replacing faulty pipes is ------- easier than expected thanks to Mr. Smith's hard work.

(A) making　(B) resembling
(C) proving　(D) revealing

3. The merger went ------- since some contentious points had been resolved.

(A) smooth　(B) smoothly
(C) smooths　(D) smoothing

전략포인트 **2** **사람 목적어를 바로 취하는 타동사**

■ **4형식 동사**

give 주다　　offer 제공하다　　send 보내다　　grant 주다　　award 수여하다　　charge 부과하다

Ms. Han will **give** <u>the new hires</u> <u>a tour of the premises.</u> 한 씨가 신입사원들에게 회사 부지 견학을 시켜줄 것이다.
　　→ 4형식 동사 + '~에게'(간접 목적어) + '~을'(직접 목적어)

■ **사람 목적어를 취하고, 전치사구 또는 that절을 동반하는 동사**

inform/notify 알려주다 **remind** 상기시키다 **convince** 설득시키다	**+**	**사람 목적어** employees 직원들에게	**+**	**of/about** the new policy 새로운 정책에 대해/을 **that** the policy will be implemented soon. 정책이 곧 실시될 것이라는 점을

The manager [announced / **informed**] <u>staff</u> **of** the new policy. 관리자는 직원들에게 새 규정을 알려주었다.

→ announce도 '알려주다'라는 뜻이지만, 사람 목적어가 아닌 직접 목적어(~을)를 목적어로 바로 취하는 동사이다.

---

1. Springfield Library ------- patrons late fees for any materials borrowed but not returned by the due date.

(A) charges　(B) informs
(C) helps　(D) has

2. The manager ------- her employees of their deadlines for this month.

(A) observed　(B) considered
(C) reminded　(D) intended

3. Mr. Holiday wants his secretary to ------- him of any important calls while he is in a meeting.

(A) report　(B) notice
(C) announce　(D) inform

전략포인트 3 빈출 '자동사 + 전치사'와 주의해야 할 타동사

▪ 빈출 자동사 + 전치사

account for ~을 차지하다, 설명하다
coincide with ~와 일치하다, 동시에 일어나다
comment on ~에 대해 논평하다
concentrate/focus on ~에 집중하다
dispose of ~을 버리다
inquire about ~에 대해 문의하다
comply with/conform to/adhere to ~을 준수하다
apply for(to)/enroll in/register for ~에 등록/신청하다

invest in ~에 투자하다
proceed with ~을 진행하다
qualify for ~에 자격이 되다
refrain from ~을 삼가다
specialize in ~을 전문으로 하다
succeed in ~에 성공하다
benefit/profit from ~으로부터 혜택/수익을 얻다
work/cooperate with[on] ~와[~일에] 협력하다

▪ 같은 의미의 자동사와 타동사

자동사	타동사		
adhere to	observe/obey	the new regulations	새로운 규정을 따르다
appeal to	attract	tourists	관광객들을 끌어들이다
interfere with	interrupt	the progress	진행을 방해하다
participate in	attend	the meeting	회의에 참석하다
object to	oppose	his decision	그의 의견에 반대하다
respond/reply to	answer	the inquiries	문의 사항에 답해주다, 응답하다
speak with/to	contact	the candidates	지원자에게 연락하다
talk about	discuss	the issue	그 문제에 대해 논의하다

A lot of people [answered / responded] to the call for entries. 많은 사람들이 응모 요청에 응했다.

▪ 자·타동사 쓰임에 유의해야 하는 동사

lead to ~으로 이어지다
lead ~을 이끌다

lead to a shortage of resources 자원의 부족으로 이어지다
lead the workshop 워크숍을 이끌다

decline 하락하다
decline ~을 거절하다

decline sharply 급격히 하락하다
decline the offer 제안을 거절하다

operate/run 운영되다
operate/run ~을 운영하다

operate/run profitably 수익성 있게 운영되다
operate/run a business 사업을 운영하다

perform 수행하다
perform ~을 수행하다

perform productively 생산적으로 일을 수행하다
perform duties 직무를 수행하다

attend ~에 참가하다
attend to ~에 주의를 기울이다

attend the training 교육에 참가하다
attend to the surroundings 주변 환경에 주의하다

---

1. A client called and asked to ------- with Ms. Ramirez regarding an incoming shipment.

   (A) discuss
   (B) contact
   (C) say
   (D) speak

2. Because it is situated on the city's main avenue, Kari J's Cupcake Shop ------- from a high volume of customer traffic.

   (A) promotes
   (B) benefits
   (C) extends
   (D) explores

3. In order to operate -------, Devers International must run its assembly lines 14 hours a day.

   (A) profit
   (B) profitable
   (C) profitably
   (D) profitability

■ **단수주어 + 단수동사**

The supplier [have / **has**] informed us of its new pricing policy. 공급업자는 우리에게 새로운 가격정책을 알렸다.
단수명사 주어

Keeping personal information confidential [**is** / are] our priority. 개인정보를 기밀로 유지하는 것이 우선사항이다.
동명사 주어

It [**requires** / require] a lot of money to advertise on TV. TV에 광고하는 것은 많은 돈이 필요하다.
to부정사 주어 → 가주어 it이 대신하며, 단수동사와 쓴다.

What really helped [**was** / were] your dedication. 정말 도움이 되었던 것은 여러분의 헌신이었습니다.
명사절 주어

■ **복수주어 + 복수동사**

Workers [is / **are**] required to attend the safety workshop. 직원들은 안전교육에 참여해야 한다.

Usually, few of the customers [**answer** / answers] the survey. 대체로 거의 모든 고객들은 설문에 응하지 않는다.

Both inside and outside of the building [has / **have**] speakers set up.
건물 안과 밖 모두 스피커가 설치되어 있다.

1. Many of the items sold at the online store ------- ready to ship within 4 hours.

(A) is   (B) are
(C) being   (D) been

2. Approving new research projects ------- time because the relevant documents must be reviewed.

(A) takes   (B) take
(C) taking   (D) was taken

3. A courier is coming with the documents Mr. Hampton ------- to sign by this afternoon.

(A) need   (B) needing
(C) needs   (D) to need

전치사구 The villages on the south shore [**have** / has] attracted many tourists.

남쪽 해안가 마을들은 많은 관광객을 끌어들였다.

관계사절 The changes that **are** made to the policy [**represent** / represents] a more flexible

work environment. 정책에 반영되는 변경사항은 더 유연한 근무 환경을 나타낸다.

→ 관계대명사: 주격 관계대명사 뒤 동사(are)는 선행사(the changes)와 수 일치된다.

분사구 The idea proposed by the workers [are / **is**] a practical solution for cost reduction.

직원들에 의해 제안된 그 아이디어는 비용 절감을 위한 실질적인 해결책이다.

to부정사구 The team's ability to meet sales goals [depend / **depends**] on its member's commitment.

영업 목표를 달성하기 위한 그 팀의 능력은 직원들의 헌신에 달려 있다.

1. The winter sale at the West Hampton Shopping Center ------- to attract more than 25,000 customers per day.

(A) is expected
(B) are expected
(C) will expect
(D) have been expected

2. Government regulations covering workplace safety issues ------- by employees at all times.

(A) must be followed
(B) are following
(C) is followed
(D) has followed

3. The training the staffers must undergo before starting their employment ------- up to three weeks to complete.

(A) to require
(B) requires
(C) is required
(D) requiring

전략포인트 6 타동사 뒤에 목적어가 있으면 능동태, 없으면 수동태를 쓴다.

- **능동태** [Mr. Kim] [produced] [the documentary film]. 김 씨가 그 다큐멘터리 영화를 제작했다.
  주어　　　타동사　　　목적어

- **수동태** [The documentary film] [was produced] (by Mr. Kim). 그 다큐멘터리는 김 씨에 의해 제작되었다.

- **자동사는 목적어를 취하지 않으므로 수동태로 쓰지 않는다.**

  | 자동사 | function 작동하다　rise 오르다　originate 유래하다　become ~이 되다　differ 다르다, 다양하다 |

  This custom [originated / was originated] in the South East of Korea.
  이 관습은 한국의 동남부 지역에서 유래했다.

1. All printers in the accounting department ------- in December.

(A) have replaced
(B) were replacing
(C) will be replacing
(D) were replaced

2. Forms that require a doctor's signature should be sent to the office -------.

(A) directly
(B) directs
(C) direction
(D) directing

3. Opinions regarding whether to accept the proposal to merge with Maritime Shipping ------- greatly.

(A) will be differed
(B) has differed
(C) differed
(D) have been differed

전략포인트 7 4형식 & 5형식 동사의 수동태는 유의해야 한다.

- **4형식 동사의 수동태는 목적어를 취할 수 있으며, '~을 받다'라는 의미이다.**

  [Trenz Magazine] [sent] [the subscribers] [its latest issue]. 트렌즈 잡지사는 구독자들에게 최신 호를 보냈다.
  　　　　　　　　동사　　간접 목적어　　　직접 목적어

  [The subscribers] [were sent] [the latest issue] by Trenz Magazine.
  구독자들은 트렌즈 잡지사에 의해 최신 호를 받았다.

- **5형식 동사 (keep / find / consider / leave / name / appoint)의 수동태 뒤에는 명사, 형용사가 남는다.**

  [They] [named] [Ms. Evans] [the actor of the year]. 그들은 에반스 씨를 올해의 배우로 명명했다.
  주어　동사　　목적어　　　목적격 보어: 명사

  [Ms. Evans] [was named] [the actor of the year] (by them). 에반스 씨는 올해의 배우라고 명명되었다.

  Our security system is considered [reliable / reliably]. 우리 보안 시스템은 믿을 만하게 여겨진다.
  → 5형식 동사의 수동태 + 형용사 (O) / 부사 (X)

  (참고) 5형식 동사 수동태 뒤에 오는 형용사가 '~하게'처럼 해석되어 부사로 착각하기 쉬우므로 주의한다.

1. Ms. Anderson was ------- a medal for her performance in the contest last weekend.

(A) given
(B) won
(C) received
(D) acquired

2. A voucher for the next flight will be ------- to anyone who flies to Europe from Montreal.

(A) offered
(B) offering
(C) offer
(D) to offer

3. Mr. Martinez was appointed ------- for the outreach program.

(A) facilitate
(B) facilitated
(C) facilitating
(D) facilitator

recognize A for B A를 B에 대해 (공로를) 인정해주다	The university recognized Dr. Lee for his innovative research. 그 대학교는 혁신적인 연구에 대한 이 박사의 공로를 인정했다.
be recognized for ~에 대해 인정받다	He was recognized for his innovative research. 그는 혁신적인 연구에 대해 인정받았다.
involve/engage A in B A를 B에 관여/참여시키다	The company involved its employees in various social activities. 회사는 직원들을 다양한 사교 활동에 참여시켰다.
be involved/engaged in ~에 관여/참여하다	Students are engaged in the class activities. 학생들이 수업 활동에 (열심히) 참여한다.
allow/permit/let A in B(장소) A가 B에 입장하는 것을 허용하다	They did not let us in the reception. 그들은 우리가 환영회에 들어가지 못하게 했다.
be allowed/permitted in 장소 (장소 등에) 입장이 가능하다	No pets are allowed in the restaurant. 애완동물은 식당에 입장할 수 없다.
notify/inform A of B A에게 B를 알려주다	They informed employees of the new policy. 그들은 직원들에게 새 정책에 대해 알려주었다.
be notified/informed of ~에 대해(특정 상황, 정보 등을) 알다	The employees are informed of the new policy. 직원들은 새 정책에 대해 알고 있다.
assign A to B A를 B에 배정/배치하다	They assigned a staff member to the self-serve ticket kiosk. 그들은 직원 한 명을 무인 티켓 키오스크에 배치했다.
be assigned to ~에 배정/배치되다	I was assigned to the sales department. 나는 영업부에 배정되었다.
attribute A to B A를 B 덕택이라고 여기다	He attributed the high productivity to efficient management. 그는 높은 생산성이 효율적인 관리 덕택이라고 여겼다.
be attributed to ~ 덕택이다, 때문이다	The success was attributed to your hard work. 성공은 여러분의 노고 덕택입니다.
direct/forward A to B A를 B에게 전달하다	They forwarded inquiries about hiring to Personnel. 그들은 채용에 관한 문의 사항을 인사부에 전달했다.
be directed/forwarded to ~에게 전달되다	Any inquiries should be directed to Personnel. 어떤 문의 사항이든지 인사부에 전달되어야 한다.
limit/restrict A to B A를 B로만 제한시키다/가능하게 하다	They restricted parking to this area. 그들은 주차를 이 지역으로만 제한시켰다.
be limited/restricted to ~에게만 제한되다/가능하다	Parking is restricted to this area. 주차는 이 지역에만 가능하다.
prohibit/forbid/prevent/keep A from B(Ving) A가 B(하는 것)을 금지하다/못하게 하다	The museum forbids visitors from eating inside. 박물관은 관람객들에게 실내에서의 음식 섭취를 금지한다.
be prohibited/forbidden/prevented/kept from B(Ving) ~이 금지되다/못하다	Visitors are prohibited from eating inside. 관람객들은 실내에서 음식 섭취가 금지되어 있다.

1. Refrigerated trucks can keep fruits and vegetables ------- spoiling during the transportation process.

(A) on
(B) by
(C) from
(D) with

2. At our fund-raising gala, each volunteer will be ------- to a particular task.

(A) assigned
(B) influenced
(C) acquired
(D) corresponded

3. Visitors with guest passes are ------- in all areas shaded in green on the map.

(A) permitted
(B) responded
(C) approved
(D) promoted

전략포인트 9 단순 시제 – 과거/현재/미래 + 시간 부사 표현

- 현재 – 반복되는 일상, 직업, 습관과 사실, 지리적인 위치 등을 나타낸다.

frequently / often 자주	regularly 정기적으로	once in a while 때때로	every + 시점: every weekend 주말마다

Maintenance regularly [inspects / inspected] the elevators. 유지보수팀은 정기적으로 승강기를 점검한다.

- 과거 – 과거에 끝난 동작이나 상태를 나타낸다.

previously / formerly 이전에	ago 전에	once 한때	recently 최근에	last + 시점: last year 지난해에

The document [is / was] delivered to the recipient last Monday. 서류가 지난 월요일에 수신인에게 배송되었다.

- 미래 – 앞으로 발생할 일을 나타낸다.

shortly / soon 곧	the upcoming year 다음 해	in + 기간 ~ 후에	next + 시점: next quarter 다음 분기

The train [will leave / has left] shortly. 기차가 곧 떠날 것이다.

(만점팁) 현재 진행형은 가까운 미래도 나타낸다.
The meeting is starting in an hour. 회의는 한 시간 후에 시작한다.

1. Residents purchase memberships to Nitro Gym because it regularly ------- a wide range of group classes.

(A) to offer
(B) offered
(C) offering
(D) offers

2. Cassandra Veras, the new supervisor of the call center, ------- managed a team of twenty customer service agents.

(A) extremely
(B) ever
(C) previously
(D) always

3. Ms. Dietrich has not decided if the air conditioning system ------- repairs soon.

(A) undergo
(B) has undergone
(C) underwent
(D) will undergo

전략포인트 10 진행 시제 – 특정 시점에 진행되고 있는 일을 나타낼 때 쓴다.

- 현재진행 – am / are / is + 'V + -ing' + 현재의 한 시점
We are currently / presently / now seeking accountants. 우리는 현재 회계사를 찾고 있습니다.

- 과거진행 – was / were + 'V + -ing' + 과거의 한 시점
He was visiting London when he was invited to the talk. 강연회에 초대되었을 때 그는 런던을 방문 중이었다.

- 미래진행 – will be + 'V + -ing' + 미래의 한 시점
He will be meeting with his client at 10 A.M. tomorrow. 그는 내일 10시에 고객을 만나고 있을 것이다.

1. Mr. Cardwell ------- the résumés for the dental assistant position as they are received.

(A) screened
(B) is screening
(C) has been screened
(D) has screened

2. Ms. Kramer ------- a speech to the board members when the lights in the conference room went out.

(A) was delivered
(B) was delivering
(C) will be delivering
(D) is delivering

3. While the office is closed for renovations, team members ------- out their regular duties from home.

(A) had carried
(B) carries
(C) will be carrying
(D) have carried

■ **현재완료 – have + p.p.**

since 주어 + 과거동사 / since + 과거시점 ~ 이래로	in / for / during / over the last(past) + 기간 지난 ~ 동안

The work environment [has improved / had improved] [since] the new CEO joined the company.
새로운 CEO가 회사에 합류한 이래로 근무 환경이 향상되었다.　　　　　→ 현재완료와 쓰이는 since절의 시제는 과거이다.

■ **과거완료 – by the time + 주어 + 과거동사, 주어 had + p.p.**

by the time + 주어 + 과거동사 ~했을 즈음에는	before 주어 + 과거동사 ~하기 전에

By the time Mr. Park was offered the job, he already [had signed / signs] a contract with another company. 박 씨가 그 일자리를 제안받았을 즈음에는, 그는 이미 다른 회사와 계약을 맺었었다.

■ **미래완료 – by the time + 주어 + 현재시제 / by + 미래시점, 주어 will have + p.p.**

By the time the mall is ready to open, the construction of the station [is / will have been] completed. 쇼핑몰이 개장 준비가 되어 있을 즈음에는, 역사 공사가 완성되어 있을 것이다.

---

1. During the past few weeks, library patrons ------- out books at a much higher rate than usual.

(A) would have been checked
(B) have been checking
(C) will be checking
(D) are checked

2. By the time FC Household's new vacuum cleaner reaches stores, the team ------- the instructions in the user manual.

(A) will clarify
(B) is clarifying
(C) will have clarified
(D) had been clarifying

3. By the time the construction company completed the building's renovations, the owner ------- twenty percent more than expected.

(A) has spent
(B) will have spent
(C) would have spent
(D) had spent

■ **시간과 조건의 부사절에서는, 현재(완료)가 미래(완료)를 대신한다.**

시간 접속사 as / when / while / as soon as / by the time / once	조건 접속사 if / unless / as long as

If you [contact / will contact] us tomorrow, you will receive the file. 내일 연락 주시면, 문서를 받으실 거예요.

We can check the shipment when it [comes / will come] in tomorrow. 내일 도착할 때, 선적을 확인할 수 있다.

■ **주장 / 제안 / 요청의 동사와 당위성을 나타내는 형용사 뒤 that절에는 (should +) 동사원형이 온다.**

insist / urge / order / command 주장하다, 명령하다
request / ask / require / demand 요구하다, 요청하다
suggest / recommend / advise 제안하다, 권고하다
necessary / imperative / essential / vital / important / critical 필수적인, 중요한

[that절] 주어 **동사원형**
should 생략 가능

The mayor insisted that he [meets / meet] the residents in person.
시장은 주민들을 직접 만나야 한다고 주장했다.

It is important that the inquiry [is / be] answered promptly. 그 문의가 신속히 답변 되어져야 하는 것은 중요하다.

---

1. If you ------- in business courses anytime next week, the institute will give you a ten percent discount.

(A) enrolls　　　　(B) enrolled
(C) enroll　　　　(D) to enroll

2. Airline officials advise that the passenger ------- the bag prior to check-in to ensure it is small enough.

(A) measures　　　(B) to measure
(C) measure　　　(D) measuring

3. It is necessary that the label ------- removed from the cookware before use.

(A) is　　　　　(B) be
(C) has been　　(D) will be

전략포인트 13 동사 문제는 수 일치/태/시제가 섞인 형태로 자주 출제된다.

■ 동사 문제를 풀 때는 수 일치 → 태 → 시제의 순서로 따져서 정답을 가려낸다.

> Bryson Landscaping ------- residential and commercial gardens for the past fifteen years.
>
> (A) has designed　　(B) have designed　　(C) was designed　　(D) will design

① 수	고유명사 (단수) Bryson Landscaping에 수 일치해야 하므로 (B) have designed를 소거한다.
② 태	목적어 residential and commercial gardens가 있으므로 (C) was designed를 소거한다.
③ 시제	현재완료 시제의 단서 for the past fifteen years가 있으므로 (A) has designed를 정답으로 선택한다.

1. Staff members ------- to nominate deserving colleagues for the employee of the year award.

(A) reminded
(B) are reminded
(C) are reminding
(D) is reminded

2. The number of automobile designers ------- in recent years due to technological developments.

(A) increases
(B) has increased
(C) have increased
(D) is increased

3. The investigation of the project's viability under hostile climate conditions ------- in about a month.

(A) complete
(B) was completed
(C) will complete
(D) will be completed

전략포인트 14 가정법

■ **가정법 과거 – if 주어 + 과거동사, 주어 + would / could / might 동사원형(~이라면, …일텐데)**

If the machine <u>were</u> broken, I [would give / gave] up the project.
기계가 고장난다면, 일을 포기할 텐데.
→ 가정법 과거 if절의 be동사는 항상 'were'이다.

■ **가정법 과거완료 – if 주어 + 과거완료, 주어 + would / could / might have p.p.(~이었다면, …이었을 텐데)**

If I <u>had had</u> more time, I [could have / have] finished the job.
시간이 더 있었다면, 일을 끝낼 수 있었을 텐데.

■ **미래의 불확실한 상황을 가정할 때는 if절에 should를 쓴다.**

If you should have a question, feel free to contact me. 궁금한 사항이 있으시면, 언제든지 연락주세요.

(만점팁) 가정법 문장에서 if가 생략되면 '동사 + 주어' 순으로 도치된다.

If I (had) <u>had</u> more time, 시간이 더 있었다면,　　　If you (should) <u>have</u> a question, 궁금한 사항이 있으시면,
→ (Had) I <u>had</u> more time,　　　　　　　　　　　→ (Should) you <u>have</u> a question,
→ Had + 주어 + p.p.　　　　　　　　　　　　　　　　→ Should + 주어 + 동사원형

1. If the Internet were available, the representative ------- about the customer's payment record.

(A) finds out
(B) can find out
(C) could find out
(D) could have found out

2. If Mr. Jameson ------- the phone, he would have signed the contract.

(A) answered
(B) had answered
(C) has answered
(D) answers

3. ------- you have to report any violations of workplace safety regulations, please use extension 100.

(A) Had
(B) Will
(C) Should
(D) Might

만점포인트 ❶ 주어 자리의 '동명사 + 명사(목적어)' vs. '분사 + 명사'는 수 일치되는 동사가 정답 단서

Please observe that ------- building permits around this time of year usually takes a long time.

(A) issue   (B) issues   (C) issuing   (D) issued

- 동명사(issuing)는 building permits를 목적어로 취하고 단수동사(takes)와 수 일치되지만, 과거분사(issued)가 building permits를 수식한다면 permits는 복수주어가 되어 복수동사(take)와 수 일치되어야 한다.

만점포인트 ❷ 수동태 문장의 도치

------- are several carpet samples that were selected with your new office in mind.

(A) Include   (B) Including   (C) Included   (D) Inclusion

- 수동태 문장을 포함한 2형식 문장의 긴 주어는 보어와 자리를 바꿀 수 있다.

[**Conveniently** / Conveniences] located is the shopping center adjacent to an interstate highway exit.
    부사   + 형용사 / p.p. + be +   주어   +   수식어
고속도로 출구에 인접한 쇼핑센터는 편리하게 위치되어 있다. → 동사는 도치된 주어(the shopping center)와 수 일치된다.

만점포인트 ❸ 가정법과 어울리는 If not for

If not for the tax exemption, the company ------- its headquarters to Alberta.

(A) does not move   (B) is not moving
(C) will not have moved   (D) would not have moved

- 'If not for'는 '~이 없(었)다면, …할 텐데 / 했을 텐데'의 관용표현으로 가정법 시제와 주로 쓰인다.

· If it were not for your help, I **wouldn't be** able to succeed. 여러분의 도움이 없다면, 성공할 수 없을 거예요.

= If not for / Without your help,

· If it had not been for your help, I **couldn't have succeeded**.
여러분의 도움이 없었더라면, 성공할 수 없을 거예요.

만점포인트 1 │ 매년 이맘때 건축허가를 발급하는 것은 시간이 걸린다는 점에 유의해 주세요. 답 (C)
만점포인트 2 │ 당신의 새 사무실을 염두에 두고 선택된 몇 가지 카펫 샘플이 포함되어 있습니다. 답 (C)
만점포인트 3 │ 세금 면제가 없었더라면, 그 회사는 앨버타주로 본사를 이전하지는 않았을 것이다. 답 (D)

1. Members of the Featherbee's marketing team must work ------- on every advertising campaign.
   - (A) collaborate
   - (B) collaboratively
   - (C) collaborative
   - (D) collaboration

2. Every once in a while, Ms. Burke ------- a team meal so that staff members can socialize.
   - (A) to organize
   - (B) organizes
   - (C) organizing
   - (D) organize

3. Since the town of Greenville ------- the fares for local buses, it has observed an increase in passengers.
   - (A) lowers
   - (B) lowered
   - (C) lowering
   - (D) lower

4. The Q3 wireless headphone product manual ------- to the company Web site.
   - (A) was posting
   - (B) has been posted
   - (C) are posted
   - (D) will be posting

5. Once Ms. Madden ------- her department's spending habits, she was confident that the new copy machine was affordable.
   - (A) was reviewed
   - (B) reviews
   - (C) had reviewed
   - (D) be reviewed

6. Martin Bart, the CEO of Dobson, Inc., ------- how to enter Asian markets at his lecture tomorrow.
   - (A) discussing
   - (B) discussion
   - (C) will discuss
   - (D) will be discussed

7. Today's workshop ------- on using financial data to make better management decisions.
   - (A) catches
   - (B) belongs
   - (C) cooperates
   - (D) focuses

8. Mr. Fritz ------- some of the questions in the survey by the time his supervisor approved the file.
   - (A) was changed
   - (B) will have changed
   - (C) had changed
   - (D) to have changed

9. Ms. Foss ------- new samples of the material so that they could be inspected.
   - (A) implied
   - (B) reminded
   - (C) ordered
   - (D) notified

10. As soon as the loan application ------- submitted, bank employees will forward it to the appropriate department.
    - (A) was
    - (B) will be
    - (C) has been
    - (D) to be

11. Food critics ------- the combination of flavors in the seafood pasta since the taste is unique.

(A) to enjoy
(B) enjoying
(C) have enjoyed
(D) enjoy

12. Visitors are ------- from taking pictures of the exhibits in the museum at all times.

(A) prohibited
(B) disapproved
(C) refused
(D) vetoed

13. Unlike last year's models, those manufactured this year ------- for less than $5,000.

(A) is retailed
(B) retailing
(C) retails
(D) retail

14. Mr. Suarez would have found the building easily if he ------- a navigation system while driving.

(A) had used
(B) uses
(C) using
(D) will use

15. It is recommended that the laboratory be left ------- when the last person leaves the room.

(A) clean
(B) cleaning
(C) cleans
(D) is cleaning

16. This is a reminder that tenants ------- an additional charge on December 5 if the rent has not been paid.

(A) will incur
(B) incurred
(C) have been incurred
(D) were incurring

17. It is ------- that dishes be finalized with the caterer at least one week before the event.

(A) particular
(B) reliable
(C) imperative
(D) expectant

18. Highly ------- is John Haines College as a business school.

(A) regard
(B) regards
(C) regarded
(D) regarding

19. Individuals who register early for the seminar will be ------- the chance to meet Dr. Kingman in person.

(A) offers
(B) offering
(C) offer
(D) offered

20. Kevin Parker is ------- the most competent person working in the R&D Department.

(A) considered
(B) appeared
(C) regarded
(D) agreed

21. Eli Fry, CEO at Equidential, will ------- a seminar on investment strategies for novice investors.

(A) behave
(B) charge
(C) contact
(D) lead

22. This year's record profits at Carmine Manufacturing can be ------- to the hard work of its sales force.

(A) attributed
(B) blamed
(C) committed
(D) decided

23. Debated recruiting methods ------- offering signing bonuses and paying relocation fees to new employees.

(A) include
(B) includes
(C) has included
(D) including

24. The free-trade agreement that ------- three days ago has been temporarily suspended.

(A) to announce
(B) was announced
(C) announcing
(D) announces

25. ------- frozen meals have been a profitable item in the food industry.

(A) Process
(B) Processes
(C) Processing
(D) Processed

26. The supplier ------- that the goods were in stock but discovered certain items were missing from the inventory records.

(A) had confirmed
(B) confirm
(C) confirming
(D) will be confirmed

27. Sarah Stewart was appointed ------- of the team working on the new project.

(A) supervise
(B) supervision
(C) supervising
(D) supervisor

28. Cranson Valley Hospital requires that each visit from friends and family ------- to half an hour.

(A) limit
(B) are limited
(C) limited
(D) be limited

29. The interview committee will ------- applicants with transportation fees to enable them to visit Brisbane.

(A) provide
(B) offer
(C) give
(D) donate

30. Since chef Cristina Fedrizzi changed the restaurant's menu, diners ------- on the improved variety of options.

(A) have been commented
(B) have been commenting
(C) comment
(D) have to be commented

UNIT 6 to부정사 & 동명사

전략포인트 1 to부정사는 명사/형용사/부사 역할을 한다.

■ **명사적 용법**
'~하는 것'

Our mission is **to offer** people in isolated areas reading material.
우리의 사명은 외진 지역의 사람들에게 읽을거리를 제공하는 것이다.

■ **형용사적 용법**
명사 수식(~하기 위한)

We make every effort **to satisfy** our valued customers.
→ 명사 뒤에서 수식한다.
우리는 소중한 고객들을 만족시키기 위한 모든 노력을 다합니다.

■ **부사적 용법**
목적(~하기 위해)

To attract potential customers, the company advertised more aggressively.
= in order to 동사원형, so as to 동사원형
잠재고객을 유치하기 위해, 회사는 좀더 적극적으로 홍보를 했다.
→ 주절 앞 콤마와 함께 문장 맨 앞이나, 완전한 문장 뒤에 위치

이유(~해서 …하다)

Our theater is proud **to present** this award-winning performance.
우리 극장은 수상작인 이 공연을 상연하게 되어 자부심을 느낍니다.

■ **to부정사가 주어나 목적어일 때는 가주어, 가목적어 'it'이 대신하고 to부정사는 뒤에 보내진다.**

It is important for researchers **to communicate** ideas. 연구원들이 아이디어를 공유하는 것은 중요하다.

You will **find** it easy **to fix** furniture using this tool. 이 장비를 이용하면 가구 고치는 게 쉽다는 걸 알 거예요.

1. The objective of the event is ------- free health screenings to residents.

(A) to offer
(B) offered
(C) offers
(D) to offering

2. ------- the old factory to residential apartments, the building owner must get permission from city officials.

(A) Convert
(B) To convert
(C) To be converted
(D) Converted

3. The instructions for all Bellmead power tools are ------- and easy to follow.

(A) fresh
(B) smooth
(C) careful
(D) simple

전략포인트 2 to부정사를 목적어로 취하는 동사

■ **'소망/미래/의지/계획'의 의미를 지닌 동사**

wish to ~하기를 바라다	plan to ~할 계획이다	fail to ~하지 못하다
hope to ~하기를 바라다	agree to ~하는 데 동의하다	tend to ~하는 경향이 있다
hesitate to ~하기를 주저하다	decide to ~하기로 결정하다	try to ~ 하려고 노력하다
aim to ~하는 것을 목표로 하다	expect to ~하기를 기대하다	decline/refuse to ~하기를 거절하다
intend to ~하려고 의도하다	afford to ~할 여유가 있다	manage to 가까스로 ~하다

The government decided [**to reduce** / reducing] taxes on imported cars.
정부는 수입차량에 대한 세금을 낮추기로 결정했다.

1. The president decided ------- the business to Europe despite the differences in regulations.

(A) to promote
(B) promote
(C) promoting
(D) promotes

2. The city council ------- to make the city hall square available for the jazz festival.

(A) agreed
(B) suggested
(C) included
(D) placed

3. Aiming ------- its work force, Perquin Foods hopes to recruit 125 new assembly-line workers.

(A) expanded
(B) expanding
(C) to expand
(D) expansion

전략포인트 3 to부정사의 수식을 받는 명사

■ **to부정사와 함께 쓰이는 명사 (명사 뒤에서 수식)**

ability to ~할 능력	effort to ~하려는 노력	decision to ~하겠다는 결정
right to ~할 권리	chance/opportunity to ~할 기회	plan to ~할 계획
way to ~할 방법	attempt to ~하기 위한 시도	willingness to ~하려는 의향
tendency to ~하려는 경향	authority to ~할 수 있는 권한	reason to ~해야 하는 이유

There are plenty of <u>opportunities</u> [~~learning~~ / **to learn**] about new technology at the conference.
학술회에서는 새로운 기술에 대해 알게 될 기회가 많다.

1. An increase in vehicle traffic is another reason ------- in improving the roadways in the region.

(A) invest
(B) investing
(C) invests
(D) to invest

2. Ms. Lycett was praised for her ability ------- complex ideas to customers patiently and easily.

(A) is communicated
(B) to communicate
(C) will communicate
(D) be communicating

3. Unfinished wood surfaces have a ------- to change color unless treated properly.

(A) routine
(B) movement
(C) tendency
(D) trend

전략포인트 4 'to부정사'를 목적격 보어로 취하는 5형식 동사

■ **to부정사를 목적격 보어로 취하는 동사의 능동과 수동**

		목적어 (~이/에게)	to부정사 (~하도록/~하라고)
요청	ask/request 요청하다 require 요구하다 invite 청하다	employees	to attend the seminar.
허용	enable/allow/permit 가능하게 하다, ~하게 하다	직원들이/에게	세미나에 **참여하도록**
지시	urge 촉구하다 instruct 지시하다 remind 상기시키다		
권고	advise 권고하다 encourage 권장하다 convince 설득하다		
예정	expect 기대하다 schedule 일정을 잡다		

Employees 직원들은	are (be)	asked / requested / required / invited enabled / allowed / permitted urged / instructed / reminded / advised encouraged / convinced / expected / scheduled	to부정사 (~하도록/~하라고) to attend the seminar. 세미나에 **참여하도록**

All the staff members <u>are</u> [**instructed** / ~~instructing~~] <u>to leave</u> early for maintenance purposes.
유지보수를 위해 모든 직원들은 일찍 퇴근하도록 지시를 받았다.

→ 'be ------- to부정사'의 빈칸은 해당 동사의 과거분사(p.p) 자리이다.

1. The upgraded database will enable researchers ------- earlier studies more easily.

(A) search
(B) to search
(C) searching
(D) searches

2. The community center ------- the visitors not to use the elevator in the north end due to maintenance work.

(A) adjusted
(B) advised
(C) responded
(D) respected

3. All Delconom employees are ------- to attend a training session on the new e-mail system tomorrow.

(A) considered
(B) indicated
(C) required
(D) insisted

- 사역동사

| let/make/have ~하게 하다 | employees | <u>work</u> remotely 동사원형 | ▶목적어(employees)의 능동 |
| get/have ~되게 시키다 | the work | <u>done</u> on time 과거분사 | ▶목적어(the work)의 수동 |

He <u>had</u> the plumber [to inspect / inspect] the clogged pipes. 그는 배관공에게 막힌 파이프를 점검하게 했다.

He <u>had</u> the pipes [inspected / inspect]. 그는 파이프가 점검되게 했다.

- 준사역동사 **help**

help + (employees) (to improve) productivity   help + (to improve) work efficiency
         목적어   동사원형/to부정사   동사원형/to부정사

- help는 목적격 보어로 동사원형이나 to부정사를 취한다.   - 목적어를 생략할 수 있다.

The company retreat will focus on techniques that [encourage / help] (people) <u>think</u> more creatively. 회사 수련회는 (사람들이) 좀 더 창의적으로 생각할 수 있게 돕는 기법에 초점이 맞춰질 것이다.
→ 동사원형(think)이 help 뒤에 바로 올 수 있다.

1. Benson Airlines does not let passengers with a booking ------- their tickets to another person.

(A) transfer
(B) transferring
(C) to transfer
(D) transferred

2. The property manager had the air-conditioning units -------.

(A) install
(B) installed
(C) installing
(D) to install

3. Hiring a part-time worker during the busy tax season will ------- alleviate the pressure on senior staff members.

(A) make
(B) assure
(C) help
(D) advise

| 주어 | [Change / Changing] the battery every six months is recommended. |

6개월마다 배터리를 바꾸는 것이 권고됩니다.   → 동명사 주어는 단수동사와 수 일치된다.

타동사의 목적어 The renovation work includes [to fix / fixing] the floor and the furnace.
보수작업은 마루와 보일러 수리하는 것을 포함한다.

전치사의 목적어 Without [spending / spent] too much time, you can improve your photos using this app.
시간을 많이 들이지 않고도 이 앱을 이용하시면 사진을 보정할 수 있습니다.

1. ------- any necessary flights for employees is the responsibility of the administrative department.

(A) Arranged
(B) Arrangement
(C) Arranging
(D) Arrange

2. In order to reduce costs, Mr. Nelson considered ------- his business to a different neighborhood.

(A) relocated
(B) to relocate
(C) relocating
(D) relocates

3. The smartphone application by Theos Bank is a convenient way of ------- account activity while on the go.

(A) checked
(B) checking
(C) check
(D) being checked

전략포인트 7 동명사와 명사를 비교하는 유형이 출제된다.

■ **동명사 vs. 명사**

동명사 – 목적어 (O) / 부사(-ly)의 수식을 받는다. / 수량 형용사나 관사의 수식을 받지 못한다.

Temporarily deferring **the announcement** will allow us to check for any possible errors.
　　　부사　　　　동명사　　　　　목적어

일시적으로 발표를 연기시키는 것은 일어날 가능성이 있는 오류를 점검할 수 있게 해준다.

명사 – 목적어 (X) / 한정사와 형용사의 수식을 받는다. / 전치사가 종종 뒤에 온다.

A temporary deferral of the announcement will allow us to check for any possible errors.
한정사　형용사　　명사　　전치사

발표의 일시적인 연기는 일어날 가능성이 있는 오류를 점검할 수 있게 해준다.

1. The lightweight case is designed for ------- the delicate electronics of the laptop while it is in transit.

(A) protecting
(B) protection
(C) protects
(D) protected

2. The board members have yet to select a ------- for the current CEO, who is stepping down.

(A) replace
(B) replaced
(C) replacing
(D) replacement

3. The survey was conducted by ------- contacting managers at mid-sized companies in the area.

(A) directed
(B) direct
(C) direction
(D) directly

전략포인트 8 동명사를 목적어로 취하는 동사와 빈출표현

■ **동명사를 목적어로 취하는 동사**

keep 계속하다	finish 끝내다	quit, stop 그만두다	discontinue 중단하다
give up 포기하다	mind 꺼리다	avoid 피하다	include 포함하다
delay/postpone 미루다	consider 고려하다	enjoy 즐기다	recommend/suggest 제안하다

To avoid [paying / to pay] a late fee, you have to return the books on time.
연체료 내는 것을 피하시려면, 책을 제때에 반납하셔야 합니다.

■ **동명사의 빈출표현**

by -ing ~함으로써	be capable of -ing (= be able to부정사) ~할 수 있다	in -ing ~하는 데 있어서
upon -ing ~할 때, 하자마자	have difficulty -ing ~하는 데 어려움을 겪다	without -ing ~하는 거 없이
worth -ing ~할 가치(가 있는)	after/prior to (before) -ing ~한 후/~하기 전	despite -ing ~에도 불구하고

With this coupon, you can enjoy our luxurious hotel without [worry / worrying] too much about expenses. 이 쿠폰으로 비용에 대한 많은 걱정 없이 고품격의 우리 호텔을 경험해 보실 수 있습니다.

1. Factory workers should wear protective gear to help them avoid ------- themselves while operating the equipment.

(A) injured
(B) to injure
(C) injuring
(D) will injure

2. As the market was becoming more competitive, Ms. Gail ------- seeking alternative revenue streams.

(A) guaranteed
(B) recommended
(C) fulfilled
(D) committed

3. International travelers must secure the correct visa ------- departing for their destination.

(A) likewise
(B) except for
(C) unless
(D) prior to

■ **be + 형용사 + to부정사**

be supposed to ~하기로 되어 있다	be scheduled to ~할 예정이다	be due to ~할 예정이다
be eligible to ~할 자격이 되다	be entitled to ~할 자격이 되다	be ready to ~할 준비가 되다
be pleased / delighted to ~하게 되어 기뻐하다	be reluctant to ~하기를 꺼리다	be likely to ~할 것 같다
be honored to ~하게 되어 영광으로 여기다	be about to 막 ~하려고 하다	be hesitant to ~하기를 망설이다

We are delighted [to share / sharing] this moment with you, in which we demonstrate our one-of-a-kind recipe. 우리만의 독특한 요리법을 보여드리는 이 순간을 여러분들과 함께하게 되어 기쁩니다.

■ **전치사 to(~에) + (대)명사/동명사(-ing)**

be accustomed to ~에 익숙해지다	They are accustomed to dealing with emergencies. 비상상황에 대처하는 것에 익숙하다.
be applicable to ~에 적용되다	This rule is applicable to Sales. 이 규칙은 영업부에 적용된다.
be accessible to ~에 제공되다 / ~에 접근이 용이하다	This loan service is accessible to homeowners. 이 대출은 주택 보유자들에게 제공된다.
contribute to ~에 기여하다	Your opinion contributes to a better community. 당신의 의견이 더 나은 지역사회에 기여한다.
be committed to ~에 전념/헌신하다	The company is committed / devoted / dedicated to improving public relations. 회사는 홍보를 개선하는 데에 전념한다.
be vulnerable to ~에 취약하다	The security program is vulnerable to viruses. 그 보안 프로그램은 바이러스에 취약하다.
be entitled to ~에 자격이 되다 ~에 권리가 있다	All employees are entitled to sick leave. 모든 직원들은 병가에 대한 권리가 있다.
look forward to ~을 고대하다	I look forward to hearing from you soon. 곧 답변 듣기를 고대합니다.
be subject to ~될 수 있다	Reservations are subject to cancelation. 예약은 취소될 수 있습니다.

Our recruiters are committed [to providing / to provide] the best career opportunities.
우리 리쿠르터들은 경력을 쌓을 최고의 기회를 제공해 드리는 데에 전념합니다.

---

1. Greenway Supermarket is delighted ------- that it has reached its goal of reducing plastic waste by 30 percent.

(A) reported
(B) to report
(C) reporting
(D) reports

2. As the contract is poorly worded, some of the terms are subject to -------.

(A) interpreting
(B) interpret
(C) interpretation
(D) interprets

3. Delegation of tasks can contribute ------- your workload.

(A) to minimizing
(B) to have minimized
(C) to be minimized
(D) to minimize

만점 공략 포인트

만점포인트 ① 명사로도 쓰이는 동사

------- technical support is recommended if you run into any problems with this security program.

(A) Contact   (B) Contacting   (C) Contacted   (D) To contact

- 주의해야 할 명사와 동사의 형태가 같은 단어

access	명 have access to the data	동 access the data	자료에 접속하다
contact	명 make contact with the applicant	동 contact the applicant	지원자에게 연락하다
visit	명 pay a visit to the office	동 visit the office	사무실에 방문하다

빈칸 뒤에 전치사가 있으면 명사, 목적어가 있으면 동명사인 유형으로 출제된다. 동사의 경우 타동사이지만 '자동사 + 전치사'로 오해할 수 있으므로 유의한다.

[Access / Accessing] to the restricted area is provided only to the maintenance staff.
                전치사
제한 구역의 출입 권한은 관리직원에게만 주어진다.

만점포인트 ② by + 동명사 + 목적어 vs. by + 과거분사 + 명사

By ------- innovative designs, Loisy Sound Equipment established its presence in the portable device industry.

(A) create   (B) created   (C) creating   (D) creation

■ 문장 구조상 '전치사 + 동명사 + 목적어'도 가능하고 '전치사 + 과거분사 + 명사'의 조합도 가능하기 때문에 의미를 통해 정답을 고른다.

- 'by + 동명사'는 수단을 나타내는 '~을 함으로써'의 의미이고, 주절에는 'change (바꾸다) / improve (향상하다) / expand (확장하다) / secure (확보하다) / enter (진출하다) / establish (확고히 하다)' 등과 같이 긍정적인 효과를 나타내는 동사와 자주 출제된다.

만점포인트 1 | 이 보안 프로그램에 문제가 있을 시 기술지원팀에 연락하는 것이 권고됩니다. 답 (B)
만점포인트 2 | 혁신적인 디자인을 만들어냄으로써, 로이지 음향 기기는 휴대 장비 산업에서 자신의 입지를 확고히 했다. 답 (C)

1. ------- the deadline for the project is the best way to ensure the work is of high quality.

   (A) Extending
   (B) Extension
   (C) Extend
   (D) Extent

2. During the press conference, the spokesperson for Zhang Industrial ------- to discuss future plans at the Beijing site.

   (A) concealed
   (B) acquired
   (C) secured
   (D) declined

3. Ms. Kirkland had her living room ------- by the contractor to determine how much carpet to purchase.

   (A) that measures
   (B) measured
   (C) measuring
   (D) measure

4. In order for trainees ------- the course, they must pass an exam related to the company's policies.

   (A) completed
   (B) to complete
   (C) completing
   (D) complete

5. The new accounting software ------- employees to submit expense sheets very easily.

   (A) lets
   (B) allows
   (C) charges
   (D) approves

6. Guests who receive outstanding customer service at Nevis Hotel are more ------- to select the chain again.

   (A) likely
   (B) like
   (C) likelihood
   (D) likeness

7. The Manzi Biscuit Company's last board meeting was devoted ------- its food safety policies.

   (A) update
   (B) updated
   (C) to update
   (D) to updating

8. Inspectors are expected ------- potential safety issues in the facility that should be resolved.

   (A) identify
   (B) to identify
   (C) identifying
   (D) identifies

9. The new crystal vases from BC Home Furnishings are ------- fragile to ship with the standard packaging.

   (A) too
   (B) most
   (C) such
   (D) very

10. After ------- interrupting the presenter, audience members were asked to save their questions for the end.

   (A) frequencies
   (B) frequent
   (C) frequently
   (D) frequency

11. Employees should scan their ID badges for ------- to the laboratories on the second floor.

(A) accessed
(B) access
(C) accessible
(D) accessing

12. Management is considering ------- the new security measures until all employees have been briefed on them.

(A) postpone
(B) postponing
(C) to postpone
(D) having been postponed

13. ------- reinvesting its profits into further promoting the company, Slaton Enterprises hopes to build a solid customer base.

(A) Along
(B) As
(C) Near
(D) By

14. A business consultant was hired to evaluate the strengths and weaknesses of HG Financial -------.

(A) criticize
(B) critically
(C) critical
(D) critic

15. The founder of the museum has dedicated himself ------- historical artifacts that are significant to the region.

(A) preserves
(B) to preserve
(C) preserving
(D) to preserving

16. Thanks to its enormous popularity, director Alan Marino's latest film has the ------- to break box office records.

(A) authority
(B) confidence
(C) potential
(D) right

17. The backup battery is powerful ------- to run a refrigerator or other major kitchen appliances.

(A) quite
(B) more
(C) well
(D) enough

18. All rooms of the building need ------- by employees when the fire alarm sounds.

(A) to be vacated
(B) vacate
(C) have vacated
(D) be vacating

19. By ------- customized products and services, the company was able to secure its client base during the recession.

(A) provided
(B) providing
(C) provision
(D) provide

20. The new fitness app can ------- users track their progress in a variety of categories.

(A) allow
(B) expect
(C) remind
(D) help

분사 & 분사구문

출제비율 1~2문제/30문항

전략포인트 1 분사는 형용사 역할을 한다.

■ **명사를 앞이나 뒤에서 수식하고, 부사의 수식을 받는다.**

All clearly (marked) items should be stored in the designated boxes.

모든 명확히 표시된 제품들은 지정된 박스에 보관되어야 한다.

They released new materials (developed) for three years. 그들은 3년간 개발된 신소재를 출시했다.

■ **2형식/5형식 동사와 함께 보어 역할**

The picture frame remains [attached / attaching] to the door. 액자는 문에 붙여진 채로 있다.
　　　　　　　　　　2형식 동사

The museum kept the old books well [preserving / preserved]. 박물관은 그 고서들을 잘 보존되게 유지했다.
　　　　　　5형식 동사　　　　　　　　　→ 목적어와 목적격 보어의 능/수동 관계에 주목해야 한다.

---

1. As this is the company's first major award nomination, the staff members are quite -------.

(A) excite
(B) excites
(C) excited
(D) excitement

2. Mayor Suarez explained why she thinks the ------- city park will increase commerce in the downtown area.

(A) propose
(B) proposes
(C) proposed
(D) proposal

3. Many audience members reported that they found Dr. Lee's lecture very -------.

(A) fascinating
(B) fascinated
(C) fascinate
(D) fascinates

전략포인트 2 현재분사는 능동, 과거분사는 수동의 의미를 나타낸다.

■ **현재분사 + 명사 – 수식 받는 명사와의 관계가 능동일 때 사용하며, '~하는'으로 해석한다.**

Due to the [raising / rising] popularity of electric cars, more electric charging stations will be built.
상승하는 전기차의 인기 때문에, 더 많은 전기 충전소가 지어질 것이다.

■ **과거분사 + 명사 – 수식 받는 명사와의 관계가 수동일 때 사용하며, '~된, ~되는'으로 해석한다.**

There is a [limited / limiting] selection of products in the store. 그 매장은 제품 선택의 폭이 한정되어 있다.

---

1. Employees are reminded not to park in ------- spots, as these have been reserved for customers.

(A) designates
(B) designating
(C) designation
(D) designated

2. Volunteers will sort the ------- clothes by size so they can be sent to charities throughout the region.

(A) donate
(B) donates
(C) donating
(D) donated

3. Most visitors agree that the artwork in the hotel's lobby is arranged in a ------- way.

(A) please
(B) pleasure
(C) pleasing
(D) pleased

전략포인트 3 분사가 명사 뒤에서 수식할 때 목적어의 유무로 분사의 형태가 결정된다.

■ **목적어가 있으면 현재분사가 쓰인다.**

A written document [explained / explaining] office procedures has been distributed to the new hires.
　　　　　　　　　　　　　　　　　　　　　　　　　　목적어
일의 절차를 설명하는 서면 서류가 신입사원들에게 배포되었다.

■ **목적어가 없으면 과거분사가 쓰인다.**

We are not liable for items [misplacing / misplaced] by our patrons.
우리는 고객에 의해 분실된 물건에 대해 책임을 지지 않습니다.　　　　　　목적어(X)

■ **자동사는 현재분사만 가능하고 뒤에 부사나 전치사가 온다.**

The shipments [remaining / remained] in the warehouse will be moved to the back of the building.
창고에 남아 있는[남겨진] 적하물은 건물 뒤쪽으로 옮겨질 것이다.

1. Any straps ------- the containers to the truck should be double-checked before departure.

(A) securing
(B) secured
(C) secures
(D) secure

2. The two properties ------- by the metal fence belong to the same company, but one will be sold.

(A) separating
(B) to separate
(C) separated
(D) are separated

3. Due to inclement weather, the bus ------- from The South End bound for Hubley is out of service.

(A) depart
(B) departure
(C) departed
(D) departing

전략포인트 4 명사 앞에 쓰이는 분사

■ **현재분사 + 명사**

rewarding job 보람 있는 일	existing model 기존 모델	misleading information 오해의 소지가 있는 정보
outstanding payment 미지불 대금	qualifying exam 자격 시험	inviting atmosphere 매력 있는 분위기
lasting impression 지속되는 감동	emerging market 신흥 시장	impending storm 곧 닥칠, 임박한 폭풍우
promising opportunity 유망한 기회	challenging task 어려운 일	overwhelming number 압도적인 수

Due to the [impending / impended] storms, residents are advised to stay indoors.
곧 닥칠 폭풍우로 인해 주민들은 실내에 머물 것을 권고해 드립니다.

■ **과거분사 + 명사**

customized product 맞춤 상품	complicated situation 복잡한 상황	detailed account 자세한 상황 설명
established company 중견 기업	designated spot 지정 장소	accomplished artist 뛰어난 예술가
limited choice 한정된 선택	proposed initiative 제안된 계획	expired voucher 기한이 지난 바우처
varied selection 다양한 선집	desired result 바라던 결과	authorized dealership 공식 대리점

1. One team of researchers was assigned to each ------- market to identify the best sales strategies.

(A) to emerge
(B) emerge
(C) emerges
(D) emerging

2. An ------- number of complaints on the citizen's message board are about the city's public transit system.

(A) overwhelmingly
(B) overwhelming
(C) overwhelmed
(D) overwhelm

3. The manager prefers to hire an ------- company to carry out the tax accounting duties.

(A) establishment
(B) established
(C) establish
(D) establishing

■ 감정타동사의 현재분사와 과거분사

pleasing 기쁘게 하는	pleased 기뻐하는	exhausting 지치게 하는	exhausted 지친
frustrating 짜증나게 만드는	frustrated 짜증나는	overwhelming 압도하는	overwhelmed 압도된
distracting 산만하게 하는	distracted (마음이) 산만한	amusing 즐겁게 하는	amused 즐거워하는
encouraging 고무시키는	encouraged 고무된	surprising 놀라게 하는	surprised 놀란
disappointing 실망스러운	disappointed 실망한	satisfying 만족스러운	satisfied 만족하는
embarrassing 당황스러운	embarrassed 당황한	puzzling 당황스러운	puzzled 당황한

The sales figures for this quarter have been embarrassingly [disappointing / disappointed].
이번 분기의 판매 실적이 당황스러울 정도로 실망스러웠다.

The halftime show at the championship game left the viewers [amusing / amused].
결승전의 하프타임 쇼가 관객들을 즐겁게 했다.

1. The investors were ------- to discover that the construction project was three weeks ahead of schedule.

(A) pleasing
(B) please
(C) pleasure
(D) pleased

2. Ms. Devon announced the high sales along with other ------- news about the company's excellent performance.

(A) to encourage
(B) encouraging
(C) encouragingly
(D) encouraged

3. As soon as the deadline was met, the manager gave the ------- production team members a much-needed break.

(A) exhaustion
(B) exhaustive
(C) exhausted
(D) exhaust

■ 부사절과 주절의 주어가 같을 때, 접속사와 주어를 생략하고, 동사를 'V + -ing'나 'V + -ed'로 만든다.

Because [you] joined the premium service, [you] can access our large selection of movies.
　　　　　　　　　　　　　부사절　　　　프리미엄 서비스에 가입하셨기 때문에, 다양한 영화를 만나보실 수 있습니다.

→ [Joining] the premium service, [you] can access our large selection of movies.
　　　　　　목적어(O)　　콤마

After it was approved by management, the initiative was finally announced.
= [(Being) approved / having approved] by management, the initiative was finally announced.
→ 분사구문의 수동은 'being + p.p.', 'p.p.' 둘 다 가능하다.　목적어 (X)　그 계획은 경영진에 의해 승인된 후 마침내 발표되었다.

[Having organized / Organized] company retreats many times before, Mr. Kim knows what to prepare.
회사 야유회를 전에 여러 번 준비해 봤기 때문에 김 씨는 무엇을 준비해야 할 지를 안다.
→ 'Having p.p.'는 능동이며 주절의 시제보다 앞선 시제이다.

1. ------- in the second quarter last year, the Davenport Shopping Center is a popular destination for tourists.

(A) To complete
(B) Completed
(C) Having completed
(D) Completing

2. ------- the leader of the education association, Mr. Davis has been invited to offer lectures to new teachers.

(A) To be
(B) Be
(C) Being
(D) Been

3. ------- issues with his layover previously, Mr. Sloan booked a direct flight to Tokyo for his business trip.

(A) Experiences
(B) Being experienced
(C) Experienced
(D) Having experienced

전략포인트 7 분사구문의 다양한 형태

■ 완전한 문장 뒤에 오는 분사는 앞 문장의 내용을 받아 '그래서 ~하다'의 의미로도 연결된다.

The company's proposal to turn the vacant land into a park was well received, [making / made] it possible to win a bid. 비어 있는 땅을 공원으로 변경하자는 그 회사의 제안은 호응이 좋았고, 그래서 입찰을 따냈다.

■ 자동사는 뒤에 부사나 전치사가 올 수 있고, 능동인 'V + -ing'만 가능하다.

[Participated / Participating] in the seminar, Mr. Kim developed the topic of his dissertation.
= While Mr. Kim was participating in the seminar 세미나 참석 중에, 김 씨는 논문 주제를 발전시켰다.

1. ------- smoothly this season, the dance festival has the potential to become a more significant event.

(A) Having gone
(B) Gone
(C) Go
(D) Be gone

2. The supermarket adopted a no plastic policy, ------- positive responses from the community.

(A) having been received
(B) being received
(C) received
(D) receiving

3. The Graystone Corporation's manager canceled all business trips for April, ------- to use teleconferencing software for meetings instead.

(A) decided
(B) deciding
(C) decision
(D) decide

전략포인트 8 분사구문에서 명확한 의미를 위해 접속사는 생략하지 않을 수도 있다.

■ 주어와의 관계가 능동일 때

You must wear eye protection when [working / worked] with tools.
도구를 가지고 작업할 때는 보안경을 착용해야 한다. → 완전 자동사

■ 주어와의 관계가 수동일 때

Although [invited / inviting / invitation] to the awards ceremony, the recipient didn't show up.
→ 부사절 접속사 뒤 '주어 + 동사'의 구조가 아니면 분사구문 문제이다.   시상식에 초대되었지만 수상자는 오지 않았다.

[만점팁] 접속사 as는 과거분사와 함께 자주 쓰인다.

as stated 명시된 대로	as mentioned 언급된 대로	as advertised 광고된 대로
as stipulated 규정된 대로	as discussed 논의된 대로	as indicated 나와 있는 것처럼

As [discussed / discussion], you will receive a full refund. 논의된 대로, 전액 환불을 받으실 거예요.

[만점팁] 접속사와 분사 사이에는 부사가 올 수 있다.

부사절 접속사 + [부사] + 'V + -ing' (+ 목적어)   부사절 접속사 + [부사] + 'V + -ed' (+ 부사/전치사)

If [frequency / frequently] updated, the application will have very few problems.
자주 업데이트가 된다면 앱에는 거의 문제가 안 생길 것이다.
→ 접속사가 생략된 상태에서 'V + -ing' 또는, 'V + -ed'를 수식하는 부사 문제도 출제된다.

1. When ------- with new employees, ensure your instructions are clear and make time to answer questions.

(A) to interact
(B) interacted
(C) interact
(D) interacting

2. As ------- on the Web site, returns on custom-made items are usually not accepted.

(A) indicate
(B) indicating
(C) indicated
(D) indication

3. Once ------- dispatched from the warehouse, the merchandise will take approximately five days to arrive.

(A) success
(B) succeeding
(C) successful
(D) successfully

ETS 고득점 실전 문제

1. Fisherman's Cove is the most ------- tourist attraction in northeastern Canada because of its beautiful beaches and lobster farms.

   (A) visit
   (B) visited
   (C) visiting
   (D) to visit

2. Two similar studies conducted at Mr. Mehta's laboratory yielded ------- results.

   (A) conflict
   (B) conflicts
   (C) conflicting
   (D) to conflict

3. As ------- in the brochure, all rooms at Macon Resort have an ocean view, access to a private pool and many other amenities.

   (A) described
   (B) description
   (C) describes
   (D) describing

4. The meals and snacks ------- in the price of the conference registration are suitable for vegetarians.

   (A) include
   (B) will include
   (C) included
   (D) have included

5. The government grant helps ------- technologies reach their full potential.

   (A) to emerge
   (B) emerge
   (C) emerges
   (D) emerging

6. The graphic design department showed tremendous dedication while ------- the new visual campaign.

   (A) preparing
   (B) prepared
   (C) prepare
   (D) preparation

7. Although Ms. Bryant has management experience, handling teams across a number of branches has been -------.

   (A) challenging
   (B) challenges
   (C) challenged
   (D) to challenge

8. The majority of people who have seen director Brian Rubio's new film found the beach scene -------.

   (A) amusement
   (B) amusing
   (C) amused
   (D) amuse

9. To apply for the paralegal position, e-mail your résumé and the ------- job application to the Human Resources Department.

   (A) terminated
   (B) proficient
   (C) completed
   (D) immediate

10. Readers of the *Starkville Tribune* enjoyed the newspaper article ------- to highlight the personnel changes at Summit Investments.

    (A) published
    (B) was published
    (C) publishing
    (D) publisher

11. The landscaping firm will not visit the property again until every ------- payment has been settled.

(A) responsive
(B) timely
(C) dependable
(D) outstanding

12. The town of Asheville offers generous tax breaks and other incentives, ------- many small businesses to the area.

(A) attracting
(B) attracted
(C) being attracted
(D) attracts

13. Filing an insurance claim for vehicle damage can be a ------- experience for customers.

(A) frustrate
(B) frustration
(C) frustrating
(D) frustrated

14. ------- discussing safety in the community park, the residents agreed to install security cameras in the park.

(A) Despite
(B) While
(C) So
(D) In

15. Unless ------- stated in the agreement, there could be some confusion regarding the supplier's responsibilities.

(A) clearer
(B) clear
(C) clearly
(D) clarity

16. If left ------- for one week, the hotel room will be cleaned again to maintain its freshness.

(A) vacancy
(B) vacancies
(C) vacantly
(D) vacant

17. The negotiators ------- each party need to meet again to talk about their proposed changes to the contract.

(A) representing
(B) representative
(C) represented
(D) represent

18. ------- to work with the pharmaceutical company, the researcher submitted his résumé along with a list of publications.

(A) Hoping
(B) Hopes
(C) To hope
(D) Being hoped

19. The latest reports of pollution levels kept officials ------- of the need for tighter environmental regulations.

(A) to inform
(B) informed
(C) informing
(D) inform

20. ------- guaranteed to last for at least twenty years, the roofs installed by Joe Garrison are of high quality.

(A) Personally
(B) Personal
(C) Personalize
(D) Personality

UNIT 8 부사절 접속사 & 등위·상관접속사

전략포인트 1 시간/조건의 부사절 접속사

시간	when/as ~할 때 while ~ 동안	once/as soon as ~하자마자 by the time ~할 때 즈음에는, 까지는	until ~까지 before ~ 전에	since ~이래로 after ~후에

[**By the time** / Whether] we meet the clients next week, the planning will have been reviewed.
우리가 다음 주에 고객을 만날 때 즈음에는 기획안이 검토되어 있을 것이다.

조건	if ~하면 as long as ~하는 한, ~한다면 unless ~이 아니라면, ~하지 않는 한	providing (that)/provided (that) 만약 ~이라면 assuming (that)/supposing (that) ~이라고 가정하면 in case (that)/in the event (that) ~의 경우를 대비하여

The road will be inaccessible [**unless** / so] we clear the snow. 눈을 치우지 않으면 도로 이용이 힘들 것이다.

(만점팁) 시간과 조건의 부사절에서는 현재(완료)가 미래(완료)를 대신한다.

1. A memo will be sent out ------- the agenda for the board meeting has been finalized.

(A) once (B) owing to
(C) from (D) rather than

2. ------- Vice President Richter's schedule changes, we will move the strategy session to a later date.

(A) Ever (B) If
(C) In order that (D) So

3. The Evans Carpeting representative will begin calculating the estimate ------- all the measurements have been taken.

(A) along with (B) during
(C) as soon as (D) so

전략포인트 2 이유/양보/대조의 부사절 접속사

이유	because/as/since ~ 때문에 now that ~이므로, 때문에	considering that/given that ~을 고려하면, 감안하면 in that ~하다는 점에 있어서

[**Since** / When] the desk was all assembled, it is ready to use. 책상 조립이 다 끝나서, 사용하면 된다.
→ 주절의 시제가 'have + p.p.'가 아닌 다른 시제일 때 'since'는 '때문에'이다.

양보/대조	although/though ~에도 불구하고	even if/even though ~일지라도	while/whereas ~인 반면에

[As if / **Even if**] the sales increased, the overall profits declined.
판매가 늘어났을지라도 전체 수익은 내려갔다.

(만점팁) as if/as though + 가정법 시제: '마치 ~인 것처럼'

They will proceed with the project **as if** the agreement <u>were</u> made.
그들은 마치 합의가 된 것처럼 일을 진행할 것이다. → 가정법 과거의 be동사는 항상 'were'이다.

1. Some companies offer discounts to customers who like them on social media ------- it enhances their online presence.

(A) because (B) instead
(C) despite (D) moreover

2. ------- Mr. Ko has received the nation's Medal of Merit, he considers his contributions to be trivial.

(A) Even though (B) Given that
(C) Instead (D) In spite of

3. ------- that Ms. Woodall has three years of customer service experience, the suggested hourly rate is reasonable.

(A) Considering (B) Rather than
(C) In fact (D) Except

전략포인트 3 기타 다양한 빈출 부사절 접속사

so that / in order that ~ (can / may) ~하기 위해서	except that ~이라는 점을 제외하고
so + 형 / 부 + that절 너무 ~해서 …하다	such (a) 형 + 명 + that절 매우 ~한 (명사)여서 …하다

The location will be changed **so (that)** we **can** accommodate all the participants.
모든 참가자들을 수용하기 위해서 장소가 변경될 것이다. → 'that'은 생략 가능하다.

whether ~ or (not)	~든지에 상관없이, ~이든지 간에
복합관계대명사 whoever, whatever, whichever	누가(누구를) / 무엇이(을) / 어떤 것이(을) ~하든지 간에 / 상관없이
복합관계부사 whenever, wherever, however	언제든지 / 어디에서든지 / 어떻게, 얼마나 ~하든지 간에 / 상관없이

(참고) whether와 복합관계대명사는 부사절뿐만 아니라 명사절도 이끈다.

[**Whatever** / What] you buy, you will get a 10% discount. 무엇을 구입하시든지 간에, 10퍼센트 할인을 받게 됩니다.
→ what은 명사절만 이끈다.

Whether the management will agree or not, the event has to be postponed.
운영진이 동의하든지 안 하든지에 상관없이 행사는 미뤄져야 한다.

1. Samples of each of our perfumes are available ------- customers can try them before making a purchase.

(A) whereas
(B) anyhow
(C) in order that
(D) across from

2. ------- you are a new or returning buyer, Blauvelt Bank can give you a mortgage.

(A) As well as
(B) Whether
(C) According to
(D) Throughout

3. This week's special gives customers the opportunity to sample three menu items, ------- they prefer.

(A) both
(B) whichever
(C) enough
(D) anybody

전략포인트 4 부사절 축약 – 접속사 + 'V + -ing' / 'V + -ed' / 전치사구

■ 능동태의 분사구문 – 접속사 + 'V + -ing' + 목적어

[Of / **After**] getting the budget approved, we can start the project.
일단 예산이 승인된 후 그 일을 시작할 수 있다.

■ 수동태의 분사구문 – 접속사 + p.p.(+ 전치사 / 부사)

Although [**discontinued** / discontinuing] almost a decade ago, the cars are still popular.
거의 십년 전에 단종되었지만, 그 차들은 여전히 인기가 있다.

(만점팁) 부사절 접속사 + 전치사구

Please do not drink beverages, [**while** / at] in the lab. 실험실에 있는 동안 음료를 마시지 마세요.
→ 명령문의 주어 'you' = while you are in the lab

1. Employees are reminded to follow the guidelines carefully ------- editing manuscripts submitted by authors.

(A) either
(B) when
(C) even
(D) onto

2. Although ------- out early, the item you purchased is still going through the customs process.

(A) send
(B) sent
(C) sending
(D) having sent

3. Trash receptacles have been positioned outside, as food and beverages are not permitted ------- in the museum.

(A) while
(B) visiting
(C) always
(D) since

등위접속사는 앞뒤로 동일한 품사와 구조를 연결한다.

and 그리고	but/yet 그러나	or 또는, 그렇지 않으면	so 그래서

[단어 + 단어]   The short but [informative / information] workshop was very well-received.
짧지만 유익했던 워크숍은 호응이 매우 좋았다.

[구 + 구]   The bank attempted to contact the client [as / and] deliver the notification.
은행은 그 고객에게 연락해서 안내 사항을 전달하기 위해 애썼다.
→ 부사절 접속사 as 앞뒤에는 완전한 절이 온다.

[절 + 절]   The company offers good benefits, [because / so] it attracts many applicants.
그 회사는 좋은 복리후생 제도를 제공해서 많은 지원자들이 몰린다.
→ so는 앞뒤 완전한 절만 연결한다.

참고   [But / Although] the earphones received high ratings in performance, they didn't sell well.
성능 면에서 그 이어폰은 높은 평가를 받았지만, 잘 팔리지는 않았다.
→ 등위 접속사는 문장 맨 앞에 올 수 없다.

1. To view time sheets and ------- any changes, log in to the employee-portal section of the company Web site.

(A) making
(B) made
(C) make
(D) makes

2. Mr. Imura is out of the office, ------- Ms. Gunadi is available to meet with clients.

(A) for
(B) too
(C) but
(D) or

3. Seating at the music festival is on a first-come, first-served basis, ------- attendees should arrive early.

(A) until
(B) so
(C) yet
(D) unless

상관접속사는 짝을 찾는 문제가 출제된다.

both A and B A와 B 둘다	either A or B A나 B 둘 중 하나
not only A but also B/B as well as A A뿐만 아니라 B도	neither A nor B A도 B도 둘 다 아닌
rather A than B/A rather than B B보다 차라리 A	not A but B A가 아니라 B

Restructuring the old library is not only expensive [but / and] also time-consuming.
오래된 도서관을 개조하는 것은 비용이 비쌀 뿐만 아니라 많은 시간이 걸린다.

We would rather come back later [but / than] wait. 기다리느니 차라리 나중에 다시 오겠어요.
→ would rather + A(동사원형) than B(동사원형) 'B 하느니 차라리 A 하겠다'

1. Carry-on bags must be stowed either in the overhead bins ------- under the seat in front of you.

(A) so
(B) or
(C) both
(D) and

2. The laptop maintenance service includes ------- checking the device for virus activity and removing dust from the interior casing.

(A) both
(B) as well
(C) not only
(D) either

3. Due to the late start time, neither the watercolor class ------- the oil painting class was at capacity.

(A) but
(B) and
(C) nor
(D) for

만점 공략 포인트

만점포인트 ❶ unless otherwise + p.p. '달리 ~이 아니라면'

All farmers market events will be held on Saturdays from 9 A.M. to 4 P.M. ------- otherwise indicated.

(A) since　　　　　(B) neither　　　　　(C) unless　　　　　(D) toward

■ 'unless otherwise + p.p.'는 '달리 ~이 아니라면'이라는 뜻의 분사구문으로 빈출도가 높은 표현이다.

・unless otherwise stated / stipulated / noted / announced 달리 언급 / 명시된 것이 없다면 (평소대로 한다)

만점포인트 ❷ 부사절을 이끄는 복합관계부사와 복합관계대명사의 비교

Employees are required to record their hours in the online system ------- they work overtime.

(A) especially　　　　(B) whenever　　　　(C) as well as　　　　(D) whatever

■ 복합관계부사(whenever / wherever)와 복합관계대명사(whatever / who(m)ever / whichever)는 부사절을 이끈다. 복합관계대명사 뒤에는 불완전한 문장이 오고, 복합관계부사는 대체로 완전한 문장을 취한다.

・**whenever / wherever** + 완전한 문장
[Whichever / Wherever] you go, respect the local culture. 어디를 방문든지 간에 지역 문화를 존중하세요.

・**whatever / who(m)ever / whichever** + 불완전한 문장
[Whatever / Whenever] you suggest, we will listen.
당신이 무엇을 제안하는지 간에 우리는 경청할 것입니다.
→ 복합관계대명사는 명사절도 이끈다. ▶Unit 10 명사절 참고

만점포인트 ❸ since는 주절의 have + p.p.의 유무가 중요한 단서이다.

------- opening a bakery on Main Street two months ago, Mr. Simmons has created over thirty custom cakes.

(A) Rather　　　　(B) Since　　　　(C) That　　　　(D) During

■ 주절의 시제가 현재완료이므로 since는 부사절 접속사인 '~이래로'의 뜻이며 '접속사 + V-ing' 구조의 분사구문을 이끌 수 있다.

Since 2011 , the theater has presented musicals. 2011년 이래로, 그 극장은 뮤지컬을 선보여 왔다.
→ 전치사 '~ 이래로': 'since + 과거 시점'이면 주절에 'have + p.p.'가 있어야 한다.

Since she moved to Seoul , Ms. Pae has worked for a bank. 배 씨는 서울로 이사한 이래로 은행에서 근무를 해 왔다.
= Since moving to Seoul, → 접속사 '~ 이래로': 주절에 'have + p.p.'가 있으면, since절엔 과거시제가 온다.

Since the flight is delayed , we offer free drinks to our passengers. 비행기가 연착되어 승객들에게 무료 음료를 제공합니다.
→ 접속사 '때문에': 주절에 현재완료 이외의 다양한 시제가 올 수 있다.

만점포인트 1 | 모든 농산물 직판장 행사는 달리 언급이 없는 한 토요일 오전 9시부터 오후 4시까지 열릴 것이다.　답 (C)
만점포인트 2 | 직원들은 초과 근무를 할 때마다 온라인 시스템에 근무 시간을 기록해야 한다.　답 (B)
만점포인트 3 | 두 달 전 메인 스트리트에 빵집을 연 이래로, 시몬스 씨는 30개가 넘는 맞춤 케이크를 만들었다.　답 (B)

1. ------- a new energy-efficient air conditioner has been installed, the electricity usage at the site has significantly dropped.

   (A) About that
   (B) Now that
   (C) In order that
   (D) For that

2. ------- Harish Dalal's mystery novel won the Exceptional Book Award, he quickly wrote a sequel.

   (A) However
   (B) Furthermore
   (C) Naturally
   (D) After

3. The Stroud Chapel is the village's oldest and ------- popular structure for tourists to visit.

   (A) most
   (B) far
   (C) how
   (D) though

4. Employees may attend the 4:00 P.M. seminar ------- they have notified their supervisor in advance.

   (A) in case
   (B) at least
   (C) as long as
   (D) except that

5. Volunteers should wear their ID badges ------- visitors to the national park can easily identify them.

   (A) in case
   (B) just as
   (C) so that
   (D) that is

6. The online training session continued ------- some participants had lost their connection to the Web site.

   (A) even though
   (B) for one thing
   (C) similarly
   (D) lastly

7. ------- in the theater's auditorium, keep your phone turned off so that it does not disturb others.

   (A) Since
   (B) While
   (C) Through
   (D) Yet

8. Tickets for the exhibit may be purchased at the front desk, ------- museum members may also order them online.

   (A) for
   (B) how
   (C) unless
   (D) but

9. ------- the insulation is installed correctly, the building's heating bills will be reduced by approximately twenty percent.

   (A) Provided that
   (B) Instead of
   (C) After all
   (D) At least

10. Ms. Henderson urged her department to work overtime ------- extend the deadline for the budget review.

    (A) in summary
    (B) even if
    (C) rather than
    (D) in regard to

11. Interpreters have been hired for the summit ------- delegates can hear the talks in their native language.

(A) though
(B) once
(C) because
(D) so

12. Purchasing travel insurance is a good idea because a problem can arise ------- you least expect it.

(A) whichever
(B) what
(C) whenever
(D) therefore

13. ------- guests reserve a room online or by phone, they will receive an e-mail confirmation within fifteen minutes.

(A) Although
(B) Thus
(C) Either
(D) Whether

14. Any ladder exceeding six feet is to be used only ------- another employee can hold it at the bottom.

(A) should
(B) than
(C) when
(D) that

15. On Fridays, staff members who finish their assignments ------- the closing time are permitted to leave early.

(A) along
(B) with
(C) until
(D) before

16. ------- the cleaning product's packaging previously had to be discarded, it can now be fully recycled.

(A) However
(B) Whereas
(C) Unless
(D) Which

17. The ------- yet practical suggestions put forth by the committee will help the company to save money.

(A) creators
(B) creative
(C) created
(D) create

18. ------- the software still has defects, it will not be put on the market on the planned date.

(A) Despite
(B) As if
(C) Given that
(D) Moreover

19. ------- thoroughly mixed into regular paint, the powder will make each coat up to three times more durable.

(A) Which
(B) What
(C) That
(D) When

20. The main lobby in the hotel, ------- unpleasant to the eye, is more spacious than the other lobbies.

(A) though
(B) only if
(C) before
(D) despite

UNIT 9 관계사

전략포인트 1 관계대명사는 선행사를 대신하는 대명사인 동시에 접속사 역할을 한다.

■ 주격 – 선행사 + who/which/that + (부사) 동사

Politicians [who / whom] regularly speak with the public are reliable.
사람 선행사　　　　　　　　　　　　　　　　대중과 정기적으로 소통하는 정치인들은 믿을 만하다.

■ 목적격 – 선행사 + who/whom/which/that + 주어 + 타동사(목적어 없음)

The material [which / who] you requested is not available now.
사물 선행사　　　　　　　　　　당신이 요청하신 재료는 현재 구할 수 없습니다.

■ 소유격 – 선행사(사람/사물명사) + whose + 명사 + 동사

We promote projects whose goals are to help youths.　우리는 청년들을 돕는 데에 목표를 둔 일을 추진한다.

만점팁 that은 콤마나 전치사 뒤에는 올 수 없다.

- the program, [that / which] is easy to use　사용이 쉬운 프로그램

- the program with [that / which] designers create templates　디자이너들이 견본을 만들 때 쓰는 프로그램

1. A farewell party will be held on Friday for Ms. Zhou, ------- is retiring after 25 years at Greenford Technologies.

(A) that　　　(B) each
(C) hers　　　(D) who

2. The Renway Theater has installed a ramp at its front entrance, ------- was previously only accessible by stairs.

(A) since　　　(B) which
(C) and　　　(D) unless

3. Try our drawing tool ------- various functions can help you create drawings like professional artists.

(A) whom　　　(B) which
(C) whose　　　(D) that

전략포인트 2 관계대명사의 생략

■ '주격 관계대명사 + be동사'의 생략

The proposals (which were) [accepted / accepting] will be presented soon.
선행사　　　생략 가능　　　과거분사　　　　수락된 제안서들이 곧 발표될 것이다.

참고 '주격 관계대명사 + be동사'가 생략되면 명사를 뒤에서 수식하는 분사가 된다.

■ 목적격 관계대명사의 생략

We circulated the notice (which) [you / yourself] sent to us.　보내 주신 공지문을 공유했습니다.
　　　　　명사　　생략 가능　주격 대명사　　타동사(목적어 없음)

The journal (that) the center publishes has attracted a lot of attention.
　　　명사　생략 가능　명사(주어)　타동사(목적어 없음)　센터가 발행하는 학술지가 많은 관심을 끌었다.

1. Those convention attendees ------- to the venue late should sit at the back of the auditorium.

(A) arrive　　　(B) arriving
(C) have arrived　(D) will arrive

2. Employees ------- of the security issues should back up any important data before the maintenance work.

(A) who inform　(B) inform
(C) to inform　　(D) informed

3. Customers frequently praise our restaurant on social media because of the delicious dishes ------- offer.

(A) ours　　　(B) us
(C) we　　　(D) ourselves

전략포인트 3 선행사 + 전치사 + whom/which

■ 사람 선행사 + 전치사 + whom – 'whom' 자리에 사람 선행사를 대입시켜 해석한다.

We have experts with [whom / which] you can discuss your financial problems.
= the experts   완전한 문장
우리는 **전문가들**이 있습니다 / **그 전문가들** (과) 당신의 재정 문제를 논의할 수 있는

■ 사물 선행사 + 전치사 + which – 'which' 자리에 사물 선행사를 대입시켜 해석한다.

Keep the receipt on [which / whom] there is a raffle number.
= the receipt   완전한 문장
영수증을 간직하세요 / **그 영수증** (위에) 추첨 번호가 있는

(참고) 전치사 뒤의 목적격 관계대명사(whom/which)는 생략할 수 없다.

There will be a meeting during which they will discuss the plan. 계획을 논의할 회의가 있을 것이다.

---

1. The researcher to ------- the grant was given is developing his study on renewable energy.

(A) what
(B) which
(C) whom
(D) whose

2. This tour includes visiting a magic house inside ------- children can enjoy amusements.

(A) which
(B) whom
(C) until
(D) although

3. The orientation session, ------- which new employees learn about the company, will last approximately four hours.

(A) against
(B) while
(C) during
(D) until

전략포인트 4 선행사 + 수량표현 + of + whom/which

■ 선행사가 사람일 때 whom – 'whom' 자리에 사람 선행사를 대입시켜 해석한다.

We have applicants, all of [whom / which] have a medical background.
= the applicants
우리는 **지원자들**을 받았다 / **그 지원자들** (중의 모두가) 의료 학력을 가진

■ 선행사가 사물일 때 which – 'which' 자리에 사물 선행사를 대입시켜 해석한다.

They make huge profits, some of [which / what] are from video streaming.
= the profits
그들은 **큰 수익**을 낸다 / **그 수익** (의 일부가) 동영상 스트리밍으로부터 나오는

---

1. Matson Hotels operates ten sites in the northwest region, three of ------- are located on the beach.

(A) another
(B) either
(C) each
(D) which

2. Olivier Design's staff includes eight architects, ------- graduated from prestigious universities.

(A) most of whom
(B) some of whose
(C) the reason being
(D) due to them

3. The repair shop is well known for handling old watches, some of ------- have been discontinued.

(A) their
(B) whose
(C) whom
(D) which

관계부사 when/where/why/how + 완전한 문장

시간   Next May, **when** they have a reunion, alumni will raise funds for research grants.
시간 명사   = in which
그들이 동창회를 하는 다음 5월에 동문들은 연구 장학금을 위한 자금을 모을 것이다.

장소   The athlete visited the city **where** he won the gold medal.
장소 명사   = in which
그 운동선수는 금메달을 땄던 그 도시를 방문했다.

이유   A lack of marketing was the reason **why** the business failed.
홍보의 부재가 사업이 실패한 이유이다. 이유 명사   = for which

방법   They negotiated the way **how** the merger would take place.
그들은 합병이 이루어지는 방법에 대해 협상했다.
→ 선행사 the way와 관계부사 how는 동시에 쓸 수 없다.

(만점팁) 선행사 'the way'는 how와 함께 쓸 수 없지만 in which는 가능하다.
They suggested a few ways [in which / how] we can get through this financial crisis.
그들은 **몇 가지 방법**을 제시해 주었다 / **그 방법들로** 우리가 이번의 재정위기를 헤쳐나갈 수 있는

1. Summer is the season ------- the view of the flora and fauna of the region attracts a lot of tourists.

(A) when
(B) which
(C) whom
(D) how

2. Drivers should renew their licenses in person at City Hall, ------- an employee will take a new photo.

(A) where
(B) which
(C) whom
(D) that

3. In order to get your proposal approved, provide a justification ------- your project is necessary.

(A) which
(B) when
(C) what
(D) why

전략포인트 6   관계대명사 + 불완전 문장 vs. 관계부사 + 완전한 문장

- **that / who(m) / which + 불완전한 문장(주어나 목적어가 빠진 구조)**
They run a nursery [which / where] grows rare plants. 그들은 희귀 식물을 키우는 묘목장을 운영한다.

- **when / where / why / how + 완전한 문장**
They own a nursery [which / where] there are many rare plants.
= at the nursery (전치사구) + 완전한 문장
그들은 많은 희귀 식물이 있는 묘목장을 운영한다.

1. This year's trade expo will take place in Dallas, ------- attendees can find plenty of options for accommodations.

(A) that
(B) there
(C) where
(D) each

2. The items ------- have a yellow tag are an additional thirty percent off.

(A) they
(B) how
(C) among
(D) that

3. Tourists are urged to avoid public transportation during morning hours ------- commuters are going to work.

(A) or
(B) when
(C) each
(D) even

만점 공략 포인트

만점포인트 ① 목적격 관계대명사 vs. 소유격 관계대명사

Jessica Ward, ------- design for the logo was selected, has a lot of graphic design experience.

(A) which   (B) whom   (C) whose   (D) whoever

- 빈칸 뒤의 문장 구조가 '주어 + 수동태 동사(was selected)'인 완전한 문장이므로 목적격 관계대명사는 답이 될 수 없다. 목적격/소유격 관계대명사 모두 뒤에 명사가 오기 때문에 뒤따라오는 동사의 목적어 필요 여부가 중요한 단서가 된다.

This is the camera [which / whose] photographers must have. 이것이 사진가들이 꼭 가져야 하는 그 카메라이다.

→ 목적어가 없는 타동사일 때는 목적격 관계대명사

만점포인트 ② '자동사 + 전치사'의 전치사가 whom이나 which 앞으로 올 수 있다.

Mr. Martin invested in the robotic industry ------- which people with limited mobility can benefit.

(A) from   (B) to   (C) at   (D) during

- 관계대명사 뒤의 '자동사+전치사'나 'be + 형용사 + 전치사' 등의 구조에서 전치사는 목적격 관계대명사 whom이나 which 앞으로 이동 가능하다. 단, 관계대명사 that과 쓰일 때 전치사는 뒤에 남는다.

a lot of tasks for which I am responsible = a lot of tasks that I am responsible for 내가 맡은 많은 일들

the associate with whom I collaborate = the associate that I collaborate with 나와 협력하는 동료

만점포인트 ③ 전치사 뒤 which/whom과 what의 구분은 뒤따라오는 문장 구조로 판단할 수 있다.

This workshop will give you communication skills with ------- you can succeed in business settings.

(A) which   (B) whose   (C) that   (D) what

- '전치사 + which/whom'은 형용사절을 이끄는 관계대명사로, 선행사를 취하고 뒤에 완전한 문장이 온다. 명사절을 이끄는 관계대명사 what은 선행사를 취할 수 없으며 뒤에 주로 불완전한 문장이 온다.

- 전치사 + which/whom + 완전한 문장

the tool with which we can make a poster
선행사   완전한 문장
도구 / 그 도구를 가지고 우리가 포스터를 만들 수 있는

- 전치사 + what + 불완전한 문장   ▶unit 10 명사절 참고

Make anything out of what is available.
선행사 (X)   불완전한 문장(주어 없음)
있는 것을 이용하여 무엇이든지 만드세요.

만점포인트 1 | 로고 디자인으로 채택된 제시카 워드는 그래픽 디자인 경험이 풍부하다. 답 (C)
만점포인트 2 | 마틴 씨는 거동이 불편한 사람들이 혜택을 얻을 수 있는 로봇 산업에 투자했다. 답 (A)
만점포인트 3 | 이 워크샵은 비즈니스 환경에서 성공할 수 있는 의사소통 기술을 제공할 것입니다. 답 (A)

1. Pete McKeown is an experienced ------- who has helped countless residents with their plumbing projects.

   (A) contracting
   (B) contractor
   (C) contracts
   (D) contract

2. The pharmacist clearly explained the side effects that ------- accompany the medication.

   (A) any
   (B) everybody
   (C) sometimes
   (D) many

3. The taxi, which ------- promptly after the call, took the passengers to the airport.

   (A) arrived
   (B) arrives
   (C) arrive
   (D) arriving

4. The only ------- that can conceivably surpass Biltextur Ltd. in sales revenue this year is Remont Fabrics, Inc.

   (A) more
   (B) which
   (C) none
   (D) one

5. The journalist for ------- the award was named was known for investigating intriguing stories.

   (A) when
   (B) that
   (C) whom
   (D) whoever

6. The manager explained that exercise -------, which have been recently added to the hotel, are available daily.

   (A) facility
   (B) facilities
   (C) facilitating
   (D) facilitated

7. Residency in Glenville is required of those ------- want to serve on the City Council.

   (A) us
   (B) everyone
   (C) who
   (D) whichever

8. World Travel hires travel agents ------- genuine interest in the field is an asset to the company.

   (A) who
   (B) what
   (C) whose
   (D) when

9. This manual is for the mandatory training the cashiers ------- at Bremley Supermarket.

   (A) undergoing
   (B) undergo
   (C) undergoes
   (D) to undergo

10. The factory ------- the candy bars are made also produces a variety of breakfast cereals.

    (A) in it
    (B) where
    (C) which
    (D) in that

11. The fitness instructor demonstrated two ways ------- athletes can prevent sore muscles.

(A) in that
(B) however
(C) what
(D) in which

12. After the medication was given, few symptoms were found in ------- with seasonal allergies.

(A) whoever
(B) those
(C) those who
(D) anyone who

13. The magazine article shows a list of care ------- delicate fabric such as silk usually requires.

(A) who
(B) whose
(C) which
(D) of which

14. Customers should wait two weeks for the package to arrive, after ------- they can report it as missing.

(A) each
(B) which
(C) when
(D) those

15. The conference's technicians want to speak with any presenters ------- plan to show slides during their talks.

(A) who
(B) what
(C) whose
(D) whoever

16. Of the manuscripts ------- by the publisher, most are still kept on file for two years.

(A) are rejected
(B) reject
(C) who rejected
(D) rejected

17. The full-time sales position ------- which Ms. Reyes applied requires a lot of travel.

(A) onto
(B) for
(C) between
(D) around

18. Ms. Stoehr toured several office buildings, none of ------- seem suitable for her legal practice.

(A) where
(B) which
(C) that
(D) who

19. The workshops ------- rate the highest will be offered again next quarter.

(A) employ
(B) employed
(C) employees
(D) employment

20. Due to the budget, the interior decorator was unable to proceed with ------- the client requested.

(A) other
(B) everything
(C) many
(D) each

UNIT 10 명사절 접속사

전략포인트 1 **that은 '~라는 것'이라는 의미로 명사절을 이끈다.**

■ **문장의 주어/목적어/보어 자리에 쓰인다.**

[~~It~~ / That] is amazing **that** the research was finally completed. 연구가 드디어 끝났다는 것은 놀랍다.

→ 주어 자리의 that절은 주로 가주어 it이 대신한다.

I insist [~~on that~~ / that] we should modify the plan. 우리가 그 계획을 변경해야 한다는 것을 주장합니다.

→ 'that' 명사절은 원칙적으로 전치사의 목적어 역할을 할 수 없다.

(만점팁) 선행사가 없으면 명사절 접속사, 있으면 관계대명사 – that절 앞의 선행사 유무를 항상 확인한다.

·명사절 – 선행사 (X) + **that** 완전한 문장	·관계대명사 – 선행사 (O) + **that** 불완전 문장
Mr. Smith hopes that he will get a promotion next year.	The coffee that was sold out is now available.
타동사　　　　　　완전한 문장	선행사　　　불완전한 문장(주어 없음)
스미스 씨는 내년에 승진하기를 바란다.	품절되었던 커피가 이제 구입 가능하다.

1. The technician suggested ------- we purchase a new router to improve our Internet connectivity.

(A) that
(B) while
(C) either
(D) must

2. One feature of the Wessel-360 air purifier is ------- the user can set it to turn off automatically.

(A) at
(B) thus
(C) that
(D) whether

3. The article states ------- recognition is the key to helping employees feel motivated.

(A) unless
(B) that
(C) if
(D) who

전략포인트 2 **명사절 that을 취하는 빈출 동사 & 형용사**

■ **동사 + that절**

agree that ~에 동의하다	confirm that ~을 확인하다	make sure/ensure that ~을 확실하게 하다
announce that ~을 발표하다	indicate that ~을 나타내다	note/observe that ~을 유의하다
predict that ~을 예측하다	assume that ~이라고 추정하다	state/say that ~이라고 언급하다, 말하다
assure/convince/remind/inform + 사람 + that ~에게 …이라는 점을 보장해 주다/납득시키다/상기시키다/알려주다		

■ **형용사 + that절**

be aware/conscious that ~을 알고 있다	be certain/sure/confident/positive that ~을 확신하다
be likely that ~일 가능성이 높다	be hopeful/optimistic that ~을 희망[낙관]하다
be afraid/sorry that ~이라니 유감이다	be glad/happy/pleased/delighted that ~이라니 기쁘다

1. Ms. Pereira is ------- that the company's rebranding efforts will be successful.

(A) confident
(B) strategic
(C) responsible
(D) ambitious

2. Theater visitors should be ------- that cell phones must be turned off during the performance.

(A) awake
(B) aware
(C) allocated
(D) apparent

3. Museum volunteers are reminded ------- they must wear their ID badges while on duty.

(A) by
(B) what
(C) of
(D) that

전략포인트 3 whether/if는 '~인지/아닌지'라는 의미로 명사절을 이끈다.

■ 문장의 주어/목적어/보어 자리에 쓰이고, 완전한 문장이 뒤따라온다.

[Whether / If] the expenses will be compensated has not been decided.
　　　[주어]　　　　　　　　　　　　　　　　　　　　　비용이 보상될지는 결정이 안 났다.

→ 명사절 'If'는 타동사의 목적어 역할만 가능하다. 문장 맨 처음의 'If'는 부사절 접속사이다.

■ 미확정 사실을 암시하는 동사 + whether/if

| ask 물어보다 | wonder 궁금해하다 | not know 모른다 | decide 결정하다 | determine 결정하다 |

The committee asked [if / that] the project was viable. 위원회는 그 프로젝트가 실행 가능한지를 물어봤다.

비교) The customer asked [that / if] she get her money back. 고객은 환불을 받아야 한다고 요청했다.
　　　　　　　　　　요청하다　　　　should가 생략된 동사원형

■ 전치사의 목적어는 whether만 쓰인다.

A question arose as to [whether / if / that] the experiment followed the protocol.
그 실험이 실험 규정을 따랐는지에 대한 의문이 생겼다.

---

1. ------- the change to the tax rate will be approved depends on public support.

(A) If
(B) Whether
(C) Though
(D) Either

2. The new bookcase was put through several tests to determine ------- it could withstand enough weight.

(A) unless
(B) if
(C) than
(D) while

3. Regardless of ------- the applicant's résumé is impressive, it will not be accepted after the deadline.

(A) whether
(B) concerning
(C) that
(D) when

전략포인트 4 의문사는 명사절을 이끌수 있다.

■ 의문대명사 – who(m) 누가[누구를] ~하는지 / what 무엇이[을] ~하는지 / which 어떤 것이[을] ~하는지

[Who / That] will manage the funds is the main issue. 누가 자금을 관리할 것인지가 주요 쟁점이다.

→ 의문대명사 + 불완전한 문장: Who가 명사절의 주어

(만점팁) 주어 자리의 명사절은 단수동사와 수 일치한다.

■ 의문부사 – when 언제 ~하는지 / where 어디서 ~하는지 / why 왜 ~하는지 / how 어떻게 ~하는지

[When / What] we will open the branch has been publicized. 언제 우리가 그 지점을 열지가 홍보되었다.

→ 의문부사 + 완전한 문장

■ 의문형용사 – what[which] + 명사 무슨[어떤] ~이[을] ~인지 / whose + 명사 누구의 ~이[을] ~인지

The manager asked [where / which] promotional materials should be sent to our clients.
매니저는 어떤 홍보 자료가 우리 고객들에게 보내져야 할 지를 물었다.

→ '의문형용사 + 명사' + 불완전한 문장 – which는 material을 꾸미는 형용사인 동시에 의문사절을 이끈다.

---

1. The guide will explain to participants ------- is recommended for the hike.

(A) what
(B) how
(C) where
(D) but

2. The informational video outlines ------- the museum's staff prepare the artifacts for display.

(A) which
(B) what
(C) who
(D) how

3. On the award nomination form, please describe exactly ------- contribution the person has made to the company.

(A) several
(B) but
(C) what
(D) how

- **whether to부정사(or not) (= whether + 주어 + should + 동사) ~해야 할지(안 할지)**

The startup hasn't decided [if / whether] (to lease an office).
그 신규업체는 사무실을 임대할지를 결정하지 않았다. → whether + to 타동사 + 목적어 **완전한 구조(목적어 있음)**

(참고) that, if가 이끄는 명사절은 'to부정사'로 축약할 수 없다.

- **의문사 to부정사(= 의문사 + 주어 + should + 동사) 의문사 ~해야 할지**

I don't know [whether / what] (to make). 무엇을 만들어야 할지를 모르겠다.
→ 의문대명사 + to 타동사 **불완전한 구조(목적어 없음)** – what이 make의 목적어

I don't know [where / what] (to go). 어디로 가야 할지 모르겠다.
→ 의문부사 + to 자동사 **완전한 구조** – 완전 자동사 go

I don't know [how / which] option (to choose). 어떤 옵션을 선택해야 할지를 모르겠다.
→ 의문형용사 + 명사 + to 타동사 **불완전한 구조(목적어 없음)** – which option이 choose의 목적어

1. Ms. Miller is considering ------- to outsource bookkeeping tasks or hire a full-time accountant for her business.

(A) nor
(B) who
(C) if
(D) whether

2. The online user manual shows ------- to restore the factory settings of the phone.

(A) what
(B) except
(C) including
(D) how

3. Notes within the employee directory explain ------- to contact in a variety of different situations.

(A) where
(B) whom
(C) whether
(D) what

- **복합관계대명사 + 불완전 문장**

	명사절(~든지)	부사절(~든지 상관없이)
whoever	anyone who ~하는 사람은 누구든지	no matter who 누가 ~하든지(에 상관없이)
whatever	anything that ~하는 것은(을) 무엇이든지	no matter what 무엇이 ~하든지(에 상관없이)
whichever	anything that ~하는 것은(을) 어떤 것이든지	no matter which 어느 것이 ~하든지(에 상관없이)

명사절 [Those / Whoever] meets the requirements will be contacted for an interview.
요건을 충족하는 누구든지 면접을 위해 연락이 갈 것이다.
→ 'whoever'는 단수동사와 수 일치한다.

We take [whatever / whether] you say seriously.
우리는 당신이 하는 말은 무엇이든지 중요하게 여깁니다.

부사절 [Whichever / Which] you prefer, you should purchase one before the end of the month.
어떤 것을 선호하는지에 상관없이 이달 말까지 구입하셔야 합니다.

1. The various booths at the trade fair allow attendees to explore ------- catches their attention.

(A) whatever
(B) anyway
(C) whenever
(D) anything

2. ------- is selected to represent our company will serve as a public relations spokesperson.

(A) Who
(B) Anyone
(C) That
(D) Whoever

3. The architect will use Bronx Couriers or Hartfield Shipping to send the blueprints, ------- is less expensive.

(A) whichever
(B) when
(C) where
(D) however

만점 공략 포인트

만점포인트 ① 동격의 명사절 that

Those signing up for a library card must provide evidence ------- they live or work in Lexington.

(A) which   (B) that   (C) as   (D) what

- that 명사절과 동격인 명사가 that 앞에 올 수 있고 that 뒤에는 완전한 문장이 온다.

the fact that ~이라는 사실	the news that ~이라는 소식/뉴스	the rumor that ~이라는 소문
the verification that ~이라는 입증	the idea that ~이라는 생각[발상]	the opinion that ~이라는 의견

참고 위에 언급된 명사가 있더라도 that 뒤의 문장 구조가 불완전하다면 관계대명사 that이다.

The news **that** there will be a financial crisis made me worried. 금융위기가 있을 것이라는 뉴스가 나를 걱정시켰다.
└─────────────────────┘ 완전한 문장(which로 교체 불가능)

The news **that** made me worried was not true. 나를 걱정시킨 뉴스는 사실이 아니었다.
└─────────────────────┘ 주어가 없는 불완전한 문장(which로 교체 가능)

만점포인트 ② How/However + 형용사/부사

------- easy the instructions may seem, please read them thoroughly before assembling the furniture.

(A) How   (B) However   (C) What   (D) Whenever

- how와 however 뒤에는 부사나 형용사가 바로 나올 수 있다. how는 명사절, however는 부사절을 이끈다.

- how + 형/부 얼마나 ~하는지 → 명사절
Please let me know how long it will take.
얼마나 오래 걸릴지 알려주세요.

- however + 형/부 얼마나 ~하는지(에 상관없이) → 부사절
However quickly it is done, there will be an extra charge.
얼마나 빨리 처리되는지 상관없이, 추가 금액이 있을 거예요.

만점포인트 ③ whichever/whatever는 명사를 수식할 수 있다.

------- supplier we choose does not affect the fact that the material will be double the current price.

(A) Whose   (B) Now that   (C) Whichever   (D) Whenever

- whichever와 whatever는 뒤에 오는 명사를 수식하고, '어떤/무슨 ~이/을 하든지(에 상관없이)'의 의미로 명사절과 부사절을 이끈다.

만점포인트 1 | 도서관 카드를 신청하는 사람들은 렉싱턴에서 거주하거나 일한다는 증명서를 제공해야 한다. 답 (B)
만점포인트 2 | 설명서가 얼마나 쉬워 보이는지에 상관없이, 가구를 조립하기 전에 설명서를 자세히 읽어주세요. 답 (B)
만점포인트 3 | 어떤 공급업자를 선택하든지 재료가 현재 가격의 두 배가 될 것이라는 사실에 영향을 주지 않는다. 답 (C)

ETS 고득점 실전 문제

1. The city commission is analyzing mass transit patterns to determine ------- more downtown buses are needed.

   (A) another
   (B) into
   (C) whether
   (D) elsewhere

2. ------- works more than forty hours in a week will be entitled to receive overtime pay.

   (A) Those who
   (B) Whoever
   (C) Anybody
   (D) Everyone

3. The Web site informs users ------- the plants should be treated in order to promote growth.

   (A) which
   (B) who
   (C) what
   (D) how

4. The judging panel for the contest will decide ------- artwork best meets the requirements.

   (A) which
   (B) like
   (C) who
   (D) and

5. The product will be recalled ------- the company learns about a safety hazard that could affect the public.

   (A) if
   (B) that
   (C) yet
   (D) whether

6. Anyone who sets the security alarm at night should make sure ------- everyone else has left the building.

   (A) once
   (B) that
   (C) who
   (D) what

7. The managers are considering ------- bank employees should wear uniforms to project a more professional image.

   (A) who
   (B) and
   (C) whether
   (D) whoever

8. Mason Marketing's low turnover rate is attributed to the ------- that the company offers a generous compensation package.

   (A) concept
   (B) fact
   (C) degree
   (D) story

9. City council members will vote on ------- to cut the budget for local parks.

   (A) who
   (B) if
   (C) whether
   (D) what

10. The plumber was unable to determine specifically ------- had contributed to the leak.

    (A) when
    (B) these
    (C) that
    (D) what

11. Successful entrepreneurs realize that ------- they take risks, they will not be able to expand their business.

(A) these
(B) which
(C) what
(D) unless

12. ------- of the ten accountants finishes the task first will be allowed to go home early.

(A) Somebody
(B) Whichever
(C) Whatever
(D) Others

13. Medical personnel at the hospital must be able to handle ------- comes their way.

(A) anybody
(B) though
(C) whatever
(D) however

14. A number of acclaimed scholars will gather to discuss ------- developing alternative energy sources is important.

(A) what
(B) why
(C) whose
(D) in that

15. The planning committee still needs to choose ------- topics this year's conference should cover.

(A) that
(B) which
(C) then
(D) whether

16. Ms. Yi will review the documents to decide ------- need to be added to active client files.

(A) some such
(B) one another
(C) which ones
(D) even if

17. We need to decide which level of service ------- our organization best going forward.

(A) fitting
(B) fitter
(C) fitted
(D) fits

18. The mobile phone service provider is ------- that it will expand into new markets by the next quarter.

(A) positive
(B) responsive
(C) representative
(D) comprehensive

19. ------- much the technician charges, it will be worth it to have the computer operating again.

(A) However
(B) Whenever
(C) Whichever
(D) Whomever

20. Customers typically insist on test-driving several cars before deciding which one -------.

(A) buy
(B) to buy
(C) buying
(D) bought

197

❶ 기출 핵심 어휘 - 동사

resume	재개하다	commemorate	기념하다
coordinate	기획하다	attain	달성하다
designate	임명하다, 지명하다	allocate	할당하다
ensure	반드시 하게 하다	eliminate	제거하다
gauge	측정하다	evolve	진화하다, 발전하다
worsen	악화시키다	refrain	삼가다
administer	관리하다	withstand	견디다, 버티다
specify	명시하다	disregard	무시하다
offset	상쇄하다	facilitate	용이하게 하다
boast	자랑하다, 뽐내다	misplace	분실하다
explore	탐구[답사]하다	convey	전달하다
diminish	감소하다	attribute	탓으로 돌리다
call off	취소하다	patronize	후원하다, 단골로 삼다
access	이용[접근]하다; 이용	commute	통근하다
certify	증명하다	urge	강력히 권고[촉구]하다
accommodate	수용하다	anticipate	예상하다, 기대하다
yield	생산하다	surpass	능가하다, 뛰어넘다
abandon	버리다	minimize	최소화하다
initiate	시작하다, 착수시키다	devise	고안하다
clarify	분명히 하다	conform	따르다, 순응하다
aspire	열망하다	disclose	공개하다
compensate	보상하다	assure	확신시키다, 약속하다
amend	고치다, 개정하다	vary	다르다, 다양하다
utilize	활용[이용]하다	outline	개요를 설명하다
flourish	번성하다	classify	분류하다
forbid	금지하다	convert	개조하다, 변환하다
dispose	처리하다, 버리다	substitute	대체하다; 대체물[대체자]
interpret	해석하다	convince	설득하다
simplify	간소화하다	terminate	끝내다, 종료하다
thrive	번영하다	incorporate	통합하다, 포함시키다

❷ 기출 핵심 어휘 – 명사

amenity	편의시설	proficiency	숙달, 숙련도
element	요소	confirmation	확인
tendency	성향, 기질	compliance	준수
prescription	처방전	accommodation	숙박
patent	특허	commission	수수료, 위원회; 위탁하다
admission	인정, 입장	delegate	대표; 위임하다
drawback	결점	neglect	방치; 방치하다
recipient	수령인, 수상자	guidance	지도[안내]
contrast	대조	extension	연장, 확대, 내선 번호
setback	차질	entry	출품작, 입장
remainder	나머지	fame	명성
characteristic	특징	motivation	동기 부여
confidence	신뢰, 자신	accomplishment	업적
dimension	치수, 규모	perspective	관점
negligence	부주의, 태만	quota	할당량
proceeds	수익금	auction	경매
observance	준수	periodical	정기 간행물
morale	사기, 의욕	acquisition	인수
output	생산량	judgment	판단
privilege	특권	procedure	절차
persistence	끈기	patronage	후원
client base	고객층	occupancy	사용, 점유
nature	성질	scope	범위
audit	회계 감사; 감사하다	interval	간격
resignation	사직, 사임	delegation	대표단, 위임
congestion	혼잡	setting	환경, 배경
phase	단계, 국면	resolution	해결책, 해상도
antique	골동품	concentration	집중, 농축, 밀집
transaction	거래	specifics	세부사항
sequence	순서, 차례	component	부분, 부품, 구성요소

③ 기출 핵심 어휘 - 형용사

consecutive	연속하는	core	핵심적인
preferable	선호되는	spontaneous	자발적인
unforeseen	예상치 못한	distinguished	뛰어난
attentive	주의 깊은	designated	지정된
dense	밀집한	feasible	실행 가능한
profitable	수익성 있는	stringent	엄격한
controversial	논란이 많은	complicated	복잡한
consistent	꾸준한, 끊임없는	exempt	면제된
charitable	자선의	sizable	상당한
predictable	예측 가능한, 뻔한	unanimous	만장일치의
imperative	반드시 해야 하는	substantial	상당한
encouraging	고무적인	unprecedented	전례 없는
accountable	책임이 있는	proficient	능숙한
competent	유능한	adverse	불리한
certified	공인된	delicate	섬세한, 까다로운
permanent	영구적인	customary	관례적인
compulsory	의무적인	authentic	진짜의, 진품의
overdue	기한이 지난	diligent	근면한
internal	내부의	complimentary	무료의
fragile	부서지기 쉬운	distinct	뚜렷한
successive	연속적인	eminent	저명한
established	인정 받는, 기존의	accomplished	뛰어난
utmost	최고의	sturdy	견고한, 내구성 있는
exceptional	뛰어난, 이례적인	convincing	설득력 있는
enormous	엄청난	adequate	충분한, 적절한
considerable	상당한	committed	전념하는
excess	여분의; 초과	superior	우수한, 상급의
independent	독립된	accustomed	익숙한
customized	고객 맞춤형의	skeptical	회의적인
desirable	바람직한	prolonged	장기적인

④ 기출 핵심 어휘 - 부사

externally	외부적으로	regrettably	유감스럽게도
formerly	이전에	fondly	애정을 담아
collectively	총체적으로	ultimately	궁극적으로, 결국
patiently	참을성 있게	momentarily	일시적으로
likewise	마찬가지로	overly	지나치게, 몹시
loosely	느슨하게	extremely	극도로
instantly	즉시, 즉각	leisurely	한가하게, 여유롭게
remotely	원격으로	comfortably	편안하게
seemingly	겉보기에	consequently	결과적으로
strategically	전략적으로	seldom	좀처럼[거의] ~ 않는
accidentally	우연히, 실수로	marginally	약간
greatly	대단히	publicly	공개적으로
expertly	전문적으로	moderately	알맞게, 적당하게
domestically	국내에서	particularly	특히
barely	겨우	virtually	사실상, 거의
generously	관대하게	thereby	그렇게 함으로써
subsequently	그 다음에	intentionally	고의로, 의도적으로
sensitively	민감하게, 예민하게	apparently	외관상, 듣자 하니
dominantly	지배적으로	severely	심하게, 혹독하게
altogether	아예, 완전히	adequately	적절히
reportedly	보도에 따르면	customarily	통상적으로
markedly	눈에 띄게, 상당히	improperly	부적절하게
definitely	분명히	presumably	아마도
solely	오로지, 단독으로	occasionally	가끔
progressively	점점	professionally	전문적으로
overall	종합적으로; 종합적인	overwhelmingly	압도적으로
expressly	명백하게	preferably	되도록, 가급적
somewhat	다소	aggressively	적극적으로
swiftly	신속하게	eventually	결국
fairly	상당히, 꽤	entirely	전적으로, 완전히

❶ 기출 고득점 어휘 - 동사

acclaim	칭찬하다	overhaul	점검하다; 점검
deduct	공제하다	ascribe	탓으로 돌리다
outperform	능가하다	evacuate	비우다, 대피하다
transcribe	필기하다	consolidate	통합하다, 합병하다
derive	끌어내다, 유래하다	confiscate	압수하다
stipulate	규정[명시]하다	affiliate	제휴하다
compromise	타협하다, 위태롭게 하다	confer	상의하다, 수여하다
scrutinize	면밀히 조사하다	abbreviate	요약하다
foster	촉진하다	coincide	동시에 일어나다
commend	칭찬하다	defer	미루다, 연기하다
endorse	지지하다, 보증[홍보]하다	acquaint	익히다, 숙지하다
alleviate	완화시키다	forfeit	몰수당하다
render	~되게 하다, 주다	culminate	끝나다, 정점에 이르다
take down	분해하다, 해체하다	accuse	비난하다, 고소하다
adjourn	중단하다, 휴정하다	ascend	오르다
command	명령하다; 언어 구사력	attest	증명하다
accrue	누적하다, 누적되다	remit	송금하다
recite	낭독하다, 인용하다	evoke	불러일으키다
subsidize	보조금을 지급하다	deteriorate	악화시키다, 악화되다
adorn	장식하다	preside	주재하다, 사회 보다
convene	모이다	appraise	평가하다
contend	싸우다, 씨름하다	oblige	강요하다
rectify	바로잡다	entail	수반하다
entrust	맡기다	fluctuate	오르내리다, 변동하다
precede	앞서다	abolish	폐지하다
accelerate	가속화하다	formulate	만들어 내다
contrive	고안하다	mandate	명령하다
subside	가라앉다, 진정되다	advocate	지지하다; 지지자
commence	시작하다	engrave	새기다
deter	단념시키다	wear out	닳다

❷ 기출 고득점 어휘 - 명사

consent	동의; 동의하다	detergent	세제
endeavor	노력; 노력하다	upholstery	커버, 덮개
deficit	부족, 적자	accumulation	축적
oversight	간과, 실수	prototype	샘플, 시제품
correspondent	특파원	facilitator	진행자
discretion	재량(권)	vicinity	부근, 근접
annex	부속건물; 병합하다	outfit	의상
rebate	환불	prosperity	번영
alumni	졸업생	duplicate	사본
appraisal	평가	premises	구내, 부지
outbreak	발생	fraud	사기
consensus	합의	referral	추천
proprietor	소유자	sequel	속편
glitch	작은 실수	aptitude	적성
hygiene	위생	integrity	진실성, 온전함
intermission	중간 휴식	acquaintance	지인
installment	할부(금)	configuration	배열, 배치
lodging	숙박	disruption	혼란, 지장, 중단
correspondence	서신	mortgage	담보 대출(금), 융자
criteria	기준	precision	정밀함
credentials	자격(증)	bookkeeping	회계 장부
stretch	구간; 늘리다	testimony	증명, 증언
allowance	허용량, 수당	discrepancy	불일치, 모순
inauguration	취임, 준공식	particulars	세부사항
reassurance	안심, 재확신	paralegal	준법률가
apparel	의류, 의복	circulation	유통, 판매부수
garment	의복	proximity	근접성
adhesive	접착제; 들러붙는	conglomerate	대기업
flair	솜씨, 재주	commitment	약속, 전념
health screening	건강 검진	subsidiary	자회사

pertinent	적절한, 관련된	seasoned	노련한, 경험 많은
rigid	엄격한	deficient	부족한[결핍된]
sluggish	부진한	comprehensive	포괄적인
recurrent	되풀이되는	impulsive	충동적인
prestigious	명망 있는	classified	분류된, 기밀의
lenient	관대한	provisional	임시의
tech-savvy	최신 기술에 능통한	elaborate	정교한
compelling	흥미로운, 고무적인	consequential	결과로 일어나는
sanitary	위생의, 위생적인	preceding	앞서는, 이전의
tedious	지루한, 싫증 나는	sleek	세련된
pending	임박한; ~ 동안	impeccable	흠잡을 데 없는
reciprocal	상호간의, 서로의	viable	실행가능한
compatible	호환이 되는	accommodating	친절한
incidental	부수적인	eloquent	달변의
inviting	매력적인	perpetual	영구의, 끊임없는
perishable	상하기 쉬운	meticulous	꼼꼼한
cordial	진심 어린	measurable	눈에 띄는
contemporary	동시대의, 현대의, 당대의	commensurate	비례하는
impending	임박한	adjacent	근접한
obsolete	구식의	farthest	가장 먼
extravagant	사치스러운, 너무 비싼	thrifty	검소한, 절약하는
combustible	가연성의	emerging	신생의, 신흥의
contingent	~에 달려 있는	perceptive	인지하는
robust	원기 왕성한	abundant	풍부한
forthcoming	다가오는	formidable	엄청난
distinctive	독특한	anonymous	익명의
meteorological	기상의, 기상학의	interim	잠정적인, 임시의
probationary	견습의, 수습의	considerate	배려하는
ample	충분한	obscure	애매한
volatile	변덕스러운, 휘발성의	municipal	시의, 지방자치의

❹ 기출 고득점 어휘 – 부사

coincidentally	우연히, 동시 발생적으로	intriguingly	흥미롭게
sparsely	드문드문하게, 성기게	undeniably	명백하게, 틀림없이
convincingly	설득력 있게	identifiably	알아볼 수 있게
concurrently	동시에	concisely	간결하게
arguably	단언컨대	generically	일반적으로
inevitably	필연적으로	reluctantly	마지못해
imaginably	상상할 수 있게, 당연히	effortlessly	쉽게, 노력하지 않고
obediently	고분고분하게	magnificently	화려하게
meaningfully	의미 있게	intermittently	간헐적으로
ethically	윤리적으로	simultaneously	동시에
artificially	인위적으로, 인공적으로	excessively	지나치게
exceptionally	유난히, 특별히	unbearably	참을 수 없게
agreeably	기분 좋게	meticulously	꼼꼼하게
hastily	급히, 서둘러서	boldly	대담하게
abruptly	갑자기, 불쑥	cordially	진심으로
assertively	단호하게, 단정적으로	proportionately	비례하여
exponentially	기하급수적으로	vastly	대단히, 엄청나게
drastically	급격하게, 과감하게	illegibly	불명료하게
sensibly	분별 있게	indefinitely	무기한으로
forcefully	강력하게, 단호하게	inherently	본질적으로
vaguely	애매[모호]하게	explicitly	명백하게
legibly	읽기 쉽게	gracefully	우아하게
affirmatively	확정적으로, 긍정적으로	chronologically	연대순으로
rightfully	정당하게, 마땅히	unknowingly	모르고
rigidly	엄격하게	inadvertently	무심코, 부주의로
deliberately	고의로, 신중하게	decidedly	결정적으로, 명백하게
utterly	완전히, 전혀	intently	열심히, 골똘히
discreetly	신중하게	scarcely	거의 ~ 않다
leniently	관대하게	allegedly	주장하는 바에 따르면
conspicuously	눈에 띄게, 두드러지게	plentifully	풍부하게

기출 핵심 Collocation

implement a change	변화를 시행하다	follow guidelines	지침을 따르다
institute a system	시스템을 마련하다	assume responsibility	책임을 맡다
exemplary performance	모범적인 업무수행	operate properly	제대로 작동하다
exhaustive study	철저한 연구	fulfill a request	요청을 이행하다
work closely	긴밀히 협력하다	primarily due to	주로 ~ 때문에
unanimously approve	만장일치로 찬성하다	reach an agreement	합의에 도달하다
redeemable coupon	상품 교환 쿠폰	announce officially	공식적으로 발표하다
conveniently located	편리한 곳에 위치한	effective immediately	즉각 발효되는
build recognition	인지도를 쌓다	distribute evenly	고르게 배포하다
routine maintenance	정기 보수	take a precaution	예방 조치를 취하다
waive a fee	수수료를 면제하다	activate an account	계좌를 활성화하다
arrive punctually	제시간에 도착하다	partially covered	부분적으로 덮인
until further notice	추후 통지 시까지	extend one's gratitude	감사를 표하다
renew a subscription	구독을 갱신하다	shortly after	직후에
settle a disagreement	이견을 해소하다	outstanding balance	미지불 잔액
unusually high	유난히 높은	increase incrementally	점진적으로 증가하다
not necessarily	반드시 ~은 아닌	establish partnerships	협업 관계를 구축하다
disposable containers	일회용 용기	issue a statement	성명서를 발표하다
achieve a goal	목표를 달성하다	address a concern	문제를 다루다
environmentally friendly	친환경적인	optimal performance	최적의 성능
nearly double	거의 두 배가 되다	eagerly await	간절히 기다리다
fully operational	풀가동하는	exercise caution	주의하다
collaborative effort	공동의 노력	welcome addition	환영받는 신입[신규의 것]
slightly differ	약간 다르다	contribute financially	금전적으로 기여하다
prominently displayed	눈에 띄게 진열된	file a complaint	불만을 제기하다
comparable brand	유사 브랜드	tentatively scheduled	잠정적으로 예정된
equivalent experience	동등한 경험	compile information	정보를 수집하다
impose a fine	벌금을 부과하다	densely populated	인구가 밀집한
unless otherwise	달리 ~하지 않는다면	preferred means	선호되는 수단
preliminary research	예비 조사	readily available	쉽게 이용 가능한

take the initiative	솔선수범하다	speak highly of	~을 매우 칭찬하다
meet the standard	기준을 충족시키다	periodically monitor	정기적으로 확인[점검]하다
solicit donations	기부를 간청하다	competitive edge	경쟁 우위
skillfully written	솜씨 있게 작성된	adversely influence	부정적으로 영향을 미치다
determine the cause	원인을 알아내다	obtain permission	허가를 받다
generate interest	관심을 불러일으키다	direct questions to	질문을 ~로 보내다
introductory rate	출시 특가	plan accordingly	그에 따라 계획을 세우다
launch a new product	신상품을 출시하다	thorough review	철저한 검토
streamline a process	절차를 간소화하다	reliable service	믿을 수 있는 서비스
raise awareness	인식을 높이다	resolve an issue	문제를 해결하다
unexpected delays	예상치 못한 지연	progress smoothly	순조롭게 진행되다
issue a permit	허가증을 발급하다	rigorous inspection	엄격한 검수
currently in stock	현재 재고가 있는	successful candidate	합격자, 당선자
adhere strictly to	엄수하다	specifically designed	특별히 고안된
solidify a position	입장을 공고히 하다	win a bid	입찰을 따내다
highly regarded	높이 평가받는	deliver a speech	연설하다
reserve the right	권한을 보유하다	generous donation	후한 기부
concentrated effort	집중적인 노력	reasonably priced	합리적 가격의
display initiative	진취성을 보여주다	prior engagement	선약
critically acclaimed	비평가의 극찬을 받은	mutually beneficial	상호 이익이 되는
deal exclusively with	독점적으로 다루다	beyond expectations	기대 이상으로
rise substantially	상당히 증가하다	extensive knowledge	폭넓은 지식
strictly prohibited	엄격히 금지된	anticipated outcome	예상되는 결과
absolutely free	완전 무료인[무료로]	consistently positive	꾸준히 긍정적인
well received	호평을 받은	acknowledge receipt	수령을 확인하다
rate among	~중 하나로 평가되다	decline an invitation	초청을 거절하다
enhance efficiency	효율성을 향상시키다	commonly used	통용되는
increase productivity	생산성을 높이다	put emphasis on	~에 중점을 두다
conduct a survey	설문 조사를 실시하다	undergo an inspection	점검을 받다
widespread popularity	광범위한 인기	take a measure	조치를 취하다

1. Employee handbooks outline the basic ------- of the employer-employee relationship.

   (A) exercises
   (B) elements
   (C) similarities
   (D) recipes

2. The outside ------- is being conducted by an independent accounting firm that specializes in charitable foundations.

   (A) area
   (B) audit
   (C) purpose
   (D) product

3. The visit of the royal couple to the National Museum is likely to ------- affect traffic in the area.

   (A) previously
   (B) dramatically
   (C) punctually
   (D) sternly

4. Ms. Roh noted that Mr. Abdullahi is ------- late to a meeting.

   (A) little
   (B) far
   (C) seldom
   (D) well

5. With its added features, the Nardex N10 is ------- the most advanced smartphone on the market.

   (A) negatively
   (B) doubtfully
   (C) sincerely
   (D) arguably

6. Customer satisfaction is of ------- importance to a company aiming to increase its client base.

   (A) diminished
   (B) utmost
   (C) conditional
   (D) farthest

7. A well-known, ------- financier gave the keynote speech at a seminar series on investment strategies.

   (A) predicted
   (B) accomplished
   (C) categorized
   (D) apparent

8. Traffic is heavy around the construction project, so drivers are advised to avoid the area -------.

   (A) quite
   (B) absolutely
   (C) altogether
   (D) overall

9. To keep costs down, Matunis Fashion will outsource the ------- of its sportswear line.

   (A) practice
   (B) information
   (C) objective
   (D) production

10. The interim manager is so busy that she may be unable to ------- any additional responsibilities.

    (A) locate
    (B) deny
    (C) criticize
    (D) assume

정답 및 해설 p.160

1. The company rose to ------- when it broke all records for first-year growth.

   (A) rumor
   (B) level
   (C) neglect
   (D) fame

2. Mooring Accounting is highly regarded for serving the community with its ------- values of honesty and integrity.

   (A) final
   (B) annual
   (C) prompt
   (D) core

3. Dappled Perfection, Inc., will be opening twelve new ------- stores as part of its targeted expansion.

   (A) adverse
   (B) incidental
   (C) consequential
   (D) regional

4. Please save the data to the designated folder so that it can be ------- by all users.

   (A) accessed
   (B) tolerated
   (C) simplified
   (D) contributed

5. After looking ------- for the missing file and not finding it, the team believed it was accidentally discarded.

   (A) everywhere
   (B) straight
   (C) ahead
   (D) outward

6. The reopening of the renovated City Art Museum is scheduled to ------- with the annual arts festival.

   (A) coincide
   (B) advance
   (C) report
   (D) conduct

7. The company recently expanded its in-house recycling program to ensure ------- with environmental regulations.

   (A) settlement
   (B) relaxation
   (C) approval
   (D) compliance

8. When purchasing accounting software, it is important to confirm that it is ------- with your computer.

   (A) confident
   (B) compatible
   (C) determined
   (D) specialized

9. The hands-on training sessions are set to ------- after the classroom instruction has concluded.

   (A) withdraw
   (B) commence
   (C) anticipate
   (D) reveal

10. The vendor guarantees that orders for personalized T-shirts will take less than ten ------- business days to fulfill.

    (A) selective
    (B) calculated
    (C) consecutive
    (D) accumulated

1. Mr. Soto and his team will visit the office
    ------- this week.

    (A) almost
    (B) always
    (C) nearly
    (D) later

2. The Monville Town Council announced that
    Whitecrest Station will undergo routine
    ------- beginning next month.

    (A) maintenance
    (B) reassurance
    (C) management
    (D) resignation

3. The popularity of this game has helped
    EMJJ Gaming ------- its position as a
    leader in the industry.

    (A) revise
    (B) organize
    (C) insure
    (D) solidify

4. The cafeteria closes at 1:00 P.M., so staff
    should plan their lunch breaks -------.

    (A) accordingly
    (B) primarily
    (C) definitely
    (D) subsequently

5. The mayor's office is looking for volunteers
    to ------- the information desk at the annual
    festival.

    (A) employ
    (B) load
    (C) report
    (D) staff

6. Dr. Gu Yun was recognized locally
    for raising ------- of necessary health
    screenings.

    (A) output
    (B) awareness
    (C) resources
    (D) spaces

7. The negotiating teams are confident that
    the merger deal will offer a ------- outcome
    for both businesses.

    (A) comprehensive
    (B) pessimistic
    (C) desirable
    (D) personal

8. Increased concern for the environment
    has led local business leaders to -------
    eco-friendly products.

    (A) perform
    (B) endorse
    (C) disregard
    (D) project

9. Late ------- will neither be accepted nor
    reviewed by the panel of judges.

    (A) interviewers
    (B) awards
    (C) winners
    (D) entries

10. The position requires a Master's Degree in
    Business Administration, or four years of
    ------- experience in the workplace.

    (A) obligated
    (B) equivalent
    (C) substitute
    (D) unlimited

1. The ------- of cost savings generated by upgrading your computer systems far exceeds the initial investment.
   - (A) number
   - (B) statistic
   - (C) reason
   - (D) amount

2. Wendall Flooring promises that customer complaints will be responded to -------.
   - (A) abruptly
   - (B) lively
   - (C) promptly
   - (D) hardly

3. Waynetown Stores will ------- the official launch of Dentalize, the new dental hygiene product line.
   - (A) sign
   - (B) host
   - (C) sample
   - (D) charge

4. We ------- Burkham City regulators to update land-use laws.
   - (A) arise
   - (B) urge
   - (C) opt
   - (D) recite

5. We have a policy of ordering office supplies only when they are needed, ------- reducing waste.
   - (A) however
   - (B) thereby
   - (C) because
   - (D) otherwise

6. Employees transferring to US-based offices should note that it is ------- to tip moving crews there.
   - (A) customary
   - (B) reported
   - (C) optimistic
   - (D) accustomed

7. The City Library sponsors a book club to ------- interest in reading among young people.
   - (A) limit
   - (B) avoid
   - (C) replace
   - (D) generate

8. Marcell, Inc.'s annual revenue is ------- to that of its larger competitors.
   - (A) considerable
   - (B) promoted
   - (C) potential
   - (D) equivalent

9. The decrease in visits to the beach resort areas was ------- due to the unusually rainy weather.
   - (A) favorably
   - (B) fortunately
   - (C) primarily
   - (D) conditionally

10. Our store purchases ------- inventory from suppliers at reduced prices, and then passes the savings on to customers.
    - (A) compliant
    - (B) sold
    - (C) diminished
    - (D) excess

1. Filmmakers must hire traffic control workers to minimize disruption to ------- businesses.
   (A) ready
   (B) convenient
   (C) pleasant
   (D) nearby

2. To interest potential ------- in the medical research laboratory, Dr. Kalinya is preparing an informational session.
   (A) investors
   (B) supplies
   (C) guides
   (D) reasons

3. Phone conversations are ------- in designated quiet areas of the commuter train.
   (A) filled
   (B) chosen
   (C) forbidden
   (D) resumed

4. To ------- exceptional quality, Grayson's Goods' items are produced in limited numbers.
   (A) ensure
   (B) apply
   (C) confirm
   (D) arrange

5. All our consultants ------- monitor their e-mail activity outside the office and can respond to urgent inquiries.
   (A) periodically
   (B) principally
   (C) progressively
   (D) suitably

6. All suppliers wishing to sell their products to Riley's Supermarket must meet ------- criteria for quality and reliability.
   (A) transformed
   (B) probationary
   (C) nominated
   (D) rigorous

7. To protect their data, it is ------- that remote workers install antivirus software on their laptop devices.
   (A) expanded
   (B) imperative
   (C) discussed
   (D) convenient

8. Online recruiting sites can greatly ------- the process of hiring new staff for your business.
   (A) facilitate
   (B) obligate
   (C) approach
   (D) impress

9. Details on the building materials to be used must be written ------- in the work contract.
   (A) controllably
   (B) arguably
   (C) expressly
   (D) seriously

10. We have a team of professionals who can ------- statistical data and present the results in understandable terms.
    (A) know
    (B) express
    (C) interpret
    (D) announce

ETS 고득점 실전 문제 6

1. Most of the antiques for sale at this month's auction were in excellent -------.

(A) quality
(B) condition
(C) value
(D) result

2. Ms. Nomura will be ------- for a raise at the end of the fiscal year.

(A) eligible
(B) capable
(C) likely
(D) beneficial

3. The finance department approved the ------- to increase the budget for the annual picnic.

(A) request
(B) creation
(C) production
(D) permit

4. The final design for the digital piano app turned out to be quite different from the ------- idea.

(A) single
(B) similar
(C) frequent
(D) original

5. Mogensen Art Emporium offers a unique ------- of art prints from both emerging and established artists.

(A) selection
(B) commitment
(C) extension
(D) agreement

6. Employees are encouraged to attend our Healthy Living Workshop, which ------- on Monday.

(A) goes over
(B) takes place
(C) brings up
(D) occurs to

7. Entrepreneurs should be prepared to discuss the ------- of their business plan with a bank officer.

(A) particulars
(B) signatures
(C) climates
(D) closures

8. The restaurant's head chef has won several ------- culinary awards, including "Best Pastry Chef."

(A) imaginative
(B) disposable
(C) prestigious
(D) attractive

9. ------- exposure to loud noise can be harmful, so the production workers must wear protective headsets.

(A) Keen
(B) Attended
(C) Competitive
(D) Prolonged

10. Because of its ------- to downtown's large office buildings, the hotel is popular with business travelers.

(A) locale
(B) appearance
(C) proximity
(D) position

1. The construction of the community center is the ------- phase of the new housing project.
   (A) complete
   (B) final
   (C) strong
   (D) absolute

2. The Web site is updated ------- to show the latest weather forecasts.
   (A) eagerly
   (B) severely
   (C) frequently
   (D) indefinitely

3. Holiday decorations may be displayed this month, but they must be ------- next month.
   (A) used up
   (B) worn out
   (C) taken down
   (D) called off

4. Articles should be submitted two weeks before the date of publication to leave ------- time for review.
   (A) adequate
   (B) perpetual
   (C) impulsive
   (D) deficient

5. When members of the Hong Kong ------- arrive on Tuesday, Ms. Hart will give them a tour of the laboratory.
   (A) delegation
   (B) precision
   (C) intention
   (D) translation

6. City officials said they will broaden the ------- of the park improvement project.
   (A) variety
   (B) decision
   (C) report
   (D) scope

7. The automaker's management is ------- to proceed with developing a new electric van.
   (A) obvious
   (B) reluctant
   (C) considered
   (D) denied

8. This company is ------- the only place where fax machines are still heavily used.
   (A) revealingly
   (B) sincerely
   (C) reportedly
   (D) comparably

9. All members of the audience are asked to ------- from taking photos during the musical performance.
   (A) refrain
   (B) attempt
   (C) deter
   (D) stop

10. For a product to be labeled "100% natural," it must consist ------- of organic ingredients.
   (A) severely
   (B) apparently
   (C) solely
   (D) variously

1. Suggestions for the theme of the upcoming conference are ------- being considered.

   (A) currently
   (B) loudly
   (C) exactly
   (D) brightly

2. Walk-in patients are ------- at Springfield Health Clinic.

   (A) interested
   (B) welcome
   (C) relative
   (D) low

3. To the delight of its customers, Blingo is ------- expanding its mobile phone coverage areas.

   (A) strangely
   (B) formerly
   (C) rapidly
   (D) hardly

4. ------- inquiries should be sent to the Compliance Department.

   (A) Improved
   (B) Never
   (C) Preferable
   (D) Internal

5. The new software program for invoicing is expected to ------- the workflow of the billing department.

   (A) occupy
   (B) recall
   (C) borrow
   (D) streamline

6. Museum tour guides receive training but are expected to be generally ------- about art.

   (A) knowledgeable
   (B) predictable
   (C) distinctive
   (D) creative

7. Because trains are running late, some staff might not ------- the office until after 9:00 A.M.

   (A) prefer
   (B) travel
   (C) stay
   (D) reach

8. Subway trains on the Greenville inner-city loop arrive at each station at twenty-minute -------.

   (A) divisions
   (B) priorities
   (C) intervals
   (D) intersections

9. The new fabric cutting machines will take up a ------- portion of the factory floor.

   (A) sizable
   (B) plenty
   (C) consecutive
   (D) considerate

10. This construction site adheres to ------- safety standards, so workers must always wear protective clothing.

    (A) relaxed
    (B) differential
    (C) maintained
    (D) stringent

1. Ventura Bank welcomes Vin Singh, a ------- mortgage company vice president, to oversee its loan department.
   (A) former
   (B) best
   (C) final
   (D) clear

2. Food and beverages are ------- prohibited in all research laboratories.
   (A) scientifically
   (B) importantly
   (C) accurately
   (D) strictly

3. Based in Cape Town, Myrick Civils is one of the most ------- companies in the road-construction industry.
   (A) future
   (B) admired
   (C) operational
   (D) actual

4. Although sales were sluggish in the first quarter, Ocarus Ltd. has ------- the competition once again.
   (A) outperformed
   (B) displayed
   (C) relocated
   (D) delegated

5. The summer interns are ------- students majoring in business administration.
   (A) except
   (B) primarily
   (C) until
   (D) closely

6. Since the conference room is ------- used by our employees, perhaps it should be assigned to another department.
   (A) wisely
   (B) rarely
   (C) readily
   (D) publicly

7. Elmwood Printing has ------- from a local supplier to a well-known regional distributor.
   (A) determined
   (B) focused
   (C) evolved
   (D) permitted

8. Because Northom is a windy region, renewable wind energy can ------- as a source of electricity for residents.
   (A) substitute
   (B) manufacture
   (C) represent
   (D) apply

9. Before erecting scaffolding, be sure it was ------- inspected by the construction manager.
   (A) almost
   (B) already
   (C) very
   (D) ever

10. During the conference, each ------- speaker reinforced the important points made in the previous talk.
    (A) mentioned
    (B) selective
    (C) original
    (D) successive

1. A technician will visit the sales office to ------- the cause of the computer's slow operating speed.

   (A) determine
   (B) anticipate
   (C) exchange
   (D) remember

2. Central City's Health and Wellness Expo has experienced ------- levels of attendance in recent years.

   (A) professional
   (B) impressed
   (C) unprecedented
   (D) absolute

3. Baderson Ltd. is proud to ------- only the highest quality materials in manufacturing its furniture products.

   (A) standardize
   (B) utilize
   (C) merge
   (D) sell

4. This smartphone has been proven to ------- a drop of up to 2 meters onto a hard surface.

   (A) withstand
   (B) involve
   (C) last
   (D) affect

5. Research has shown that shorter meetings focused on only one topic can ------- significant results.

   (A) appeal
   (B) confirm
   (C) yield
   (D) predict

6. Social media advertising helps build ------- of a new brand among younger consumers.

   (A) replacement
   (B) motivation
   (C) recognition
   (D) confirmation

7. Bank employees are asked to complete all ------- with clients before 4:00 P.M. to allow time for processing.

   (A) suggestions
   (B) transactions
   (C) currencies
   (D) management

8. The report summarizes the results of an ------- study on leisure travelers' preferences for hotels and activities.

   (A) exhaustive
   (B) upcoming
   (C) influenced
   (D) invested

9. A training program for runners should start with shorter runs and then ------- increase the distance.

   (A) downwardly
   (B) economically
   (C) incrementally
   (D) invaluably

10. Past participants in the Learning Center's series of cooking workshops speak ------- of the program.

    (A) highly
    (B) expectedly
    (C) softly
    (D) carelessly

PART 6
장문 채우기

INTRO

UNIT 12 | 문법 문제

UNIT 13 | 어휘 문제

UNIT 14 | 접속부사 문제

UNIT 15 | 문장 고르기 문제

◆ **최신 출제 경향**

4문항으로 구성된 지문이 총 4세트 출제되며 파트 5와 마찬가지로 문법과 어휘 문제가 출제된다. 단, 파트 5와 달리 빈칸이 속한 문장뿐만 아니라 지문 속의 다른 문장들이 정답의 단서가 될 수 있다. 또한 지문의 흐름에 맞는 문장을 고르는 문제는 파트 6에서만 매 지문 한 문항씩 출제된다.

◆ **ETS 예제**

Questions 135-138 refer to the following memo.

To: All Severus Bank Employees
From: Sang-Hoon Park
Date: August 3
Subject: Good news

I -------- received an e-mail from Vivian Paris of *Cash and*
135.
Currency magazine. I am very pleased to inform you that
the magazine has rated us number one in customer service.
We have also made ------- top ten list of best banks in the
136.
nation! Well done, everyone. ------- . We will be updating the
137.
bank's advertising in newspapers and social media to reflect
this wonderful news. ------- , I encourage you to continue
138.
the good work you have all been doing.

수신: 세베루스 은행 전 직원
발신: 박상훈
날짜: 8월 3일
제목: 희소식

방금 〈캐쉬 앤 커런시〉 잡지사의 비비안 패리스로부터 이메일을 받았습니다. 해당 잡지가 우리를 고객 서비스 부문 1위로 평가했음을 여러분께 알려 드리게 되어 기쁩니다. 우리는 또한 **잡지사의** 국내 최우수 은행 10위 명단에 들었습니다. 모두들 수고하셨습니다. **해당 호를 읽고 싶으시면 월요일에 온라인으로 확인할 수 있습니다.** 이 멋진 소식을 반영하기 위해 신문과 소셜 미디어에 은행 광고를 업데이트할 예정입니다. **그동안에** 여러분 모두가 계속해서 수고해 주시기를 당부 드립니다.

어휘 문제

135 (A) just
(B) later
(C) soon
(D) next

문법 문제

136 (A) its
(B) my
(C) his
(D) our

문장 고르기 문제

137 (A) Make sure you have the correct contact information.
(B) If you would like to read the issue, it will be available online on Monday.
(C) It is very important to find the right bank for your needs.
(D) Our customer service department is now hiring.

접속부사 문제

138 (A) However (B) In contrast
(C) Nevertheless (D) In the meantime

정답 135 (A) **136** (A) **137** (B) **138** (D)

◆ 풀이 전략

135 어휘 문제

글의 주제와 앞뒤 문맥이 정답을 결정한다.

잡지사로부터 이메일을 받고 그 내용을 직원들에게 알리는 회람이므로 과거 시제 동사인 received와 어울려 '방금 이메일을 받았다'는 의미가 되는 부사 (A) just를 선택한다.

136 문법 문제

주변 문장에서 정답의 단서가 제공된다.

대명사 문제는 가리키는 대상을 지문 내에서 찾아야 하는데, '잡지사가 선정한 국내 최우수 10개 은행 목록에 들었다'는 내용이 되어야 하므로, 앞 문장에서 나온 '잡지사'를 가리킬 수 있는 대명사 it의 소유격인 (A) its를 선택한다.

137 문장 고르기 문제

주제, 문맥, 문법적 요소(대명사, 지시어 등)를 따져서 정답을 고른다.

빈칸 앞 문장에서 잡지사가 선정한 국내 최우수 은행 10위 명단에 들었다고 했고, 모두들 수고했다고 했으므로, 해당 잡지를 확인할 수 있는 요일과 방식을 알려주는 (B) 문장을 선택한다.

주제, 논리적 관계, 문법적 요소가 일치하지 않는 문장은 오답으로 소거할 수 있어야 한다.
(A) 정확한 연락처를 소지하지 하고 있는지 확인하세요. (✗) ➡ 주제 이탈
(B) 해당 호를 읽고 싶으시면 월요일에 온라인으로 확인할 수 있습니다. (○)
(C) 귀하의 요구 사항에 알맞은 은행을 찾는 것이 매우 중요합니다. (✗) ➡ 대상 불일치
(D) 우리 고객 서비스 부서가 현재 채용 중입니다. (✗) ➡ 주제 이탈

---

138 접속부사 문제

역접, 인과, 첨가, 대조 등 빈칸 앞뒤 문장의 논리적 관계를 따져서 정답을 고른다.

앞 – 이 멋진 소식을 반영하기 위해 신문과 소셜 미디어에 은행 광고를 업데이트할 예정입니다.
뒤 – 여러분 모두가 계속해서 수고해 주시기를 당부 드립니다.

빈칸 앞은 잡지에 실린 소식과 관련된 은행의 대외적 업무 계획에 대한 내용이며, 빈칸 뒤는 은행 내부 직원들에게 당부하는 사항을 나타내고 있으므로 두 가지 시점·사건들 사이에서 '그동안에'라는 의미로 동시에 일어나는 일을 나열할 수 있는 (D) In the meantime을 선택한다.

출제 공식

파트 6의 문법은 파트 5에 등장하는 문법이 다양하게 출제되나, 특히 문장 구조, 대명사, 시제 파트에서 자주 출제된다. 문법적인 요소뿐만 아니라 독해적인 요소, 즉 글의 목적과 대상, 전체 시제 등을 파악하면서 내용을 이해하는 것이 중요하다.

ETS 예제 **기사문**   번역 p.169

풀이 전략

The fundraising committee ------- various software options for tracking donations to our organization. **The goal is to gain a better understanding of trends in giving.** Over the past three months the committee has tested several alternatives. It is now ready to discuss its choice at the board of directors meeting scheduled for March 23. Please make every effort to attend.

(A) explore
(B) will explore
(C) has been exploring
(D) exploring

STEP 1 동사 자리 시제 문제임을 파악한다.

모금 위원회는 다양한 옵션을 [(A) 조사한다/(B) 조사할 것이다/(C) 조사해 오고 있다]

STEP 2 시제의 단서를 파악한다.

이후 문장에서 '지난 석 달간 몇 가지 옵션을 테스트해 왔다'라는 현재완료 시제를 쓰고 있으므로 '조사가 지금까지 진행되고 있다'를 뜻하는 현재완료진행 시제가 적합하다.

STEP 3 보기에서 알맞은 시제를 선택한다.

(C) (지금까지) 조사해 오고 있다.

만점 공략 노트

공략 1   주변 문장의 시제를 통해 빈칸 시제를 파악하자.

We **will be updating** our product line. We **will concentrate** on linens, uniforms, and towels. The new inventory [had been / **should be** / should have been] available in October.

신규 제품 라인이 업데이트될 예정으로 아직 일어나지 않은 미래의 일에 대해 논의하고 있으므로 추측을 나타내는 **should be(~일 것이다)**를 고른다.

As always, your expertise [will be appreciated / **was appreciated**]. Our technicians especially **benefited** from your demonstration of the updated imaging systems.

기술자들이 귀하의 시연으로부터 도움을 얻었다며, 이미 일어난 일에 대해 감사하고 있으므로 과거형인 **was appreciated(감사했다)**를 고른다.

공략 2   다양한 문장 구조에 익숙해지자.

Shreveport residents are invited [they attended / **to attend** / the attendance of] an open house from 1:30 P.M. to 3:30 P.M. on June 9.

보기는 모두 다양한 구의 형태로 구성되어 복잡해 보이지만, **be invited to(~하도록 요청된다)**를 덩어리 표현으로 알고 있으면 쉽게 풀 수 있다.

The system is [needed / **in need of** / a need for] some urgent work to accommodate the increasing demand for water use in Kenilworth.

'긴급한 작업을 필요로 한다'라는 의미가 되어야 하므로 '~을 필요로 하는'이라는 뜻의 덩어리 표현 **in need of**가 정답이다.

Only by maintaining a precise flow of inventory [is able to / **are we able to** / our ability to] minimize costs and ensure prompt shipments.

only 부사구가 문두에 오면 도치가 일어나므로, we are able to에서 주어와 동사가 자리를 바꾼 **are we able to**가 정답이다.

Questions 1-4 refer to the following press release.

FOR IMMEDIATE RELEASE

Contact: Jeff Baines, 504-555-0162

Bando Gets a Boost

NEW ORLEANS (June 1)—Bissett Renewables ------- a 30 percent interest in the Bando offshore
1.
wind farm project. This was a key step in the financing of Bando, which will be the largest

offshore wind farm in Japan. During the project's trial phase, two turbines were constructed.

------- . The total number of turbines in the Bando project will be enough to power a small city.
2.

"We are delighted to support the key players in a project of such importance," said Martha

Wiseman, the CEO of Bissett Renewables. "Not only will Bando be a powerful wind farm in Asia,

------- the involvement of foreign sponsors will also set a new precedent for projects of this type.
3.
We hope this encourages future ------- in the region."
4.

---

1. (A) was acquired
(B) has acquired
(C) is acquiring
(D) will acquire

3. (A) as
(B) or
(C) so
(D) but

2. (A) Bissett Renewables funds turbines on
farms in other countries, too.
(B) The wind farms will face some
challenges in the near future.
(C) Fifty more will be installed in the next
stage of the project.
(D) Several companies decided not to
finance additional turbines.

4. (A) travel
(B) events
(C) regulations
(D) investment

Questions 1-4 refer to the following article.

Curci Appointed CEO at Notley Leeds

Notley Leeds Partners, a national network of dental providers, has announced that industry executive Federico Curci will be its next CEO. "Mr. Curci shares our ------- to excellence and
1.
growth, and we are so pleased to have him take us forward," said Alan Fowle, a board member.

Mr. Curci brings 25 years of experience in growing medical practices. He previously held the CEO position at Randall Surgery Centers and oversaw its expansion into 30 states. ------- . "I -------
2.   **3.**
thrilled to move Notley Leeds into new markets and grow the organization," said Mr. Curci.

Based in El Paso, Notley Leeds partners with dentists ------- the country to provide management
4.
and support services.

---

1. (A) committed
    (B) commitment
    (C) commit
    (D) committee

2. (A) Smith-Cox Recruiting will be retained to
        handle the search.
    (B) The experience was available to all
        Notley Leeds executives.
    (C) Profits increased by 10 percent during
        his time there.
    (D) The merger was a surprise to many
        industry experts.

3. (A) am
    (B) was
    (C) had been
    (D) have been

4. (A) among
    (B) along
    (C) into
    (D) throughout

Questions 5-8 refer to the following e-mail.

To: <martin90@rapidonet.co.uk>
From: <careers@attacomma.co.uk>
Date: 16 April
Subject: Employment opportunities

Dear Mr. Martin,

Attacomma Industries is currently hiring in Sheffield. Full-time, part-time, and seasonal positions are available. Find the one that works ------- you by visiting www.attacomma.co.uk/jobs. Starting
5.
pay for warehouse workers is £18 an hour. -------, employees become eligible for merit-based
6.
raises after just six months of employment. ------- the high demand for labor, an additional £100
7.
sign-up bonus is being offered to successful applicants through the end of the year. ------- .
8.
Simply fill out our online application.

Sincerely,

Jenna Robinson, Talent Acquisition Specialist

---

5. (A) for
(B) on
(C) along
(D) near

6. (A) Finally
(B) However
(C) Regardless
(D) Consequently

7. (A) To meet
(B) Meet
(C) Being met
(D) Having met

8. (A) No résumé or prior work experience is needed.
(B) Attacomma Industries is expanding its business.
(C) The offer must be redeemed by May 11.
(D) Sheffield is the most populous city in the region.

PART 6

UNIT 12

Questions 9-12 refer to the following notice.

To register for tours or information sessions at the Kelwin Shoe factory, visit us at KelwinShoes.com. Note that tours fill up quickly. ------- . If a date that is suitable for you is not currently listed, **9.** we encourage you to routinely check the schedule page. New tour dates are posted ------- . If **10.** you would like to arrange a special group tour for your class or organization, you can submit a Special Tour Request form. An electronic copy of the form can be found on ------- Web site. **11.** Please note that special tours are available to groups only. ------- parties should make requests **12.** at least two weeks before the desired date.

---

9. (A) Advanced planning is thus encouraged.
   (B) Unfortunately, they have been canceled.
   (C) Drivers may park in one of our many lots.
   (D) Our Web site allows for easy product comparisons.

10. (A) separately
    (B) internally
    (C) regularly
    (D) favorably

11. (A) its
    (B) our
    (C) any
    (D) which

12. (A) Interested
    (B) Interesting
    (C) The interest of
    (D) To be interested

Questions 13-16 refer to the following e-mail.

To: Chris Pikula <cpikula@lmnmail.com>
From: Joanie Carlin <jcarlin@brighting.com>
Date: April 18
Subject: Vending Machine Stock

Hello Chris,

I would like to request some changes to the item selections in ------- vending machine. If
                                                                    13.
possible, I would like the changes ------- effect at your next restocking visit on Thursday.
                                    14.

Employees go through the pretzels, crackers, and candy bars quickly. Could we double the
quantity of each of these products in the machine? To make enough space, perhaps some of
the less popular products could be eliminated. As you noted during your last visit, certain snack
types are rarely purchased. ------- , we can get rid of them all together. ------- .
                            15.   **16.**

Thanks very much!

Joanie

---

13. (A) its
    (B) our
    (C) such
    (D) any

14. (A) will be taking
    (B) took
    (C) to take
    (D) will take

15. (A) Similarly
    (B) Likewise
    (C) Furthermore
    (D) Therefore

16. (A) The rest of the item inventory can remain
        unchanged.
    (B) The vending machine is conveniently
        located.
    (C) Our employees enjoy stopping by the
        cafeteria.
    (D) We look forward to the new machine.

UNIT 13 어휘 문제

출제 공식 어휘 문제는 글의 주제와 관련이 있다. 빈칸이 있는 문장뿐 아니라 주변 문장을 통해 글의 주제와 문맥을 파악해야 정답을 고를 수 있다.

ETS 예제 **회람**   번역 p.172

Subject: Office closing

To prepare for the end-of-year employee ------- on Saturday, December 20, the office will be closing at 3:00 P.M. on Friday, December 19. –중략– I will send an e-mail invitation this week regarding Saturday's affair. Please reply promptly so that I know how many people are planning to come to the party.

(A) evaluations
(B) reports
(C) training
(D) banquet

풀이 전략

STEP 1 빈칸에 보기 어휘를 대입해 본다.
① 연말 직원 평가 ② 연말 직원 보고
③ 연말 직원 교육 ④ 연말 직원 연회

STEP 2 정답의 단서를 포착한다.
마지막 문장에서 '파티 참석 여부를 알려 달라'고 했으므로 'the party'가 가리키는 어휘가 정답이다.

STEP 3 보기에서 알맞은 어휘를 선택한다.
(A) 평가 (B) 보고 (C) 교육 **(D) 연회**

만점 공략 노트

공략 1   지문의 전반적인 내용을 이해하자.

We will need to limit **the number of people** at this year's picnic. Starting this year, each employee will be allowed to **bring a maximum of five people**. They can be **family, friends, or anyone else you choose to invite**. Please reply to this message and include the names of your [clients / **guests**].

야유회 **인원** 제한과 관련하여, **최대 5명까지 데리고 올 수 있으며, 가족, 친구, 그 밖에 누구든지 초대가 가능**하다고 했으므로 야유회에 초대할 수 있는 사람을 나타내는 **guests(손님)**가 정답이다.

공략 2   지문 속의 관련 어휘를 포착하자.

An ecological nonprofit organization is **raising funds** to plant 2,000 trees in the city. All [returns / **proceeds**] will go toward this effort.

모금 활동을 통해 발생하는 돈을 '수익금'이라고 하므로 **funds(자금)**를 단서로 하여 **proceeds(수익금)**를 정답으로 고른다.
returns도 '수익'이라는 뜻이 있지만 투자 / 생산 활동을 통해 발생하는 수익을 뜻하므로 오답이다.

One area identified for drastic improvement is [financing / **shipping**]. Almost a quarter of the participants reported experiencing late or incorrect **deliveries**.

대폭적인 개선이 필요한 영역은 '배송'과 관련된 어휘여야 하므로 **deliveries(배송)**를 단서로 하여 **shipping(운송)**을 정답으로 고른다.

Thank you for your recent [review / **purchase**] of the Daqtex Mini-V camera. We are contacting everyone who has **recently bought** this product to inform them that certain models are being recalled for repair.

편지 수신 대상이 '최근에 카메라를 구입한 사람들'이므로 recently **bought(최근에 구입했다)**를 단서로 하여 **purchase(구매)**를 정답으로 고른다.

228

ETS 유형 연습

Questions 1-4 refer to the following product review.

I was ------- to try powdered milk because I didn't think it would taste the same as regular milk.
    1.
But last week, my local grocery store was sold out of regular milk, so I decided to give Jumi Milk
a try. I was ------- surprised.
    2.

------- . Then I tried using a high-speed blender and mixing a larger quantity. This method takes
3.
extra time, but the milk is smooth and tasty. I would definitely recommend ------- despite the
    4.
extra effort.

I will likely buy regular milk the next time I shop, but I will be sure to keep some Jumi Milk on
hand as well. Unlike regular milk, I can keep it on my shelf for years.

— Cynthia Cisneros

---

1. (A) hesitated
    (B) hesitant
    (C) hesitates
    (D) hesitation

2. (A) rarely
    (B) remotely
    (C) probably
    (D) pleasantly

3. (A) I will not make that mistake again.
    (B) A larger supermarket would have had
        more options.
    (C) Getting the right consistency was a
        challenge at first.
    (D) Jumi Milk can be used as a substitute in
        most recipes.

4. (A) it
    (B) several
    (C) them
    (D) some

ETS 고득점 실전 문제

Questions 1-4 refer to the following memo.

To: All staff
From: Vandana Tilakdhari, CEO, Genovic Laboratories
Subject: Merger with SWD
Date: August 23

If you have seen today's edition of *Biznotes*, our online daily newsletter, you already know that the merger negotiations between our company and Scotia Wholesale Distributors are in their final stages. The ------- will provide us with the means to be more competitive in the pharmaceutical market.
1.

I am certain that many of you are wondering about the impact the merger ------- on your current position. I assure you that all employees will retain their jobs. ------- . So, in this respect you have no reason whatsoever to be concerned.
2. **3.**

I will be happy to address any of your questions or concerns at Thursday's all-staff meeting. In the meantime, I want to thank you for the patience you have shown with the management team ------- the last six months.
4.

---

1. (A) studies
   (B) measures
   (C) partnership
   (D) information

2. (A) had
   (B) may have
   (C) would have had
   (D) to have

3. (A) In fact, we plan to hire additional staff soon.
   (B) Consequently, the staff meeting has been canceled.
   (C) Moreover, our distribution center ships orders quickly.
   (D) Of course, we do not underestimate our competitors.

4. (A) toward
   (B) among
   (C) upon
   (D) over

Questions 5-8 refer to the following e-mail.

To: All Members
From: Rajat Singhal
Date: Monday, 8 April
Subject: New conference location

Dear HNA Members,

Due to circumstances beyond our control, this year's annual conference of the Haryana Nurses Association (HNA) had to be relocated. Now, it ------- place at the Haryana Conservancy instead
5.
of the Municipal Conference Centre. While the workshops and presentations will undoubtedly consume much of your time, we hope you will also use the opportunity to ------- the venue
6.
grounds. ------- . You can stroll along lush green paths or enjoy bird-watching from a majestic
7.
overlook. And the lake on the premises is ------- for an early-morning or late-afternoon swim. We
8.
suggest, therefore, that you bring along comfortable clothing, walking shoes, swimwear, and, for the bird-watchers, binoculars.

We look forward to seeing you in June.

Sincerely,

Rajat Singhal, Conference Coordinator
The Haryana Nurses Association

5. (A) took
(B) will take
(C) has taken
(D) taking

6. (A) lease
(B) explore
(C) beautify
(D) promote

7. (A) They are truly breathtaking.
(B) They attract many economic activities.
(C) They are home to many sea creatures.
(D) They are sold to conference goers only.

8. (A) supposed
(B) operated
(C) perfect
(D) modest

Questions 9-12 refer to the following notice.

Traffic Advisory for October 2: Upcoming Road Closures

There will be a street closure today on Easton Terrace. The street will be closed between Homestead Avenue and Lake Place from 8:00 A.M. to 5:00 P.M. ------- for street resurfacing.
9.

Another closure will occur on Homestead Avenue in front of the Homestead Elementary School between West Fifth Street and West Sixth Street. This brief closing will accommodate a -------
10.
event at the school between 1:00 P.M. and 2:30 P.M.

West Elm Street between Sullivan Way and Spruce Avenue will be closed Friday, October 4, to prepare for the Fall Festival Parade. The closing will start at 2:00 P.M. The area will also be closed all day on Saturday, October 5, ------- the actual parade. ------- .
11.   **12.**

---

9. (A) allows
  (B) allowed
  (C) to allow
  (D) will allow

10. (A) special
  (B) numerous
  (C) cautious
  (D) flat

11. (A) for
  (B) to
  (C) beside
  (D) beyond

12. (A) Thank you for supplying the street-closure barriers.
  (B) You are invited to participate in the school's event.
  (C) The street will reopen Saturday, October 5, at 8:00 P.M.
  (D) We are thankful for your continued contributions.

Questions 13-16 refer to the following memo.

To: Behram Road Residents and Business Owners
From: Kotai Universal Group
Date: 3 September
Subject: Timetable update

Kotai Universal Group has released the following update to our construction timetable.

Construction of the twenty-story building on Behram Road is proceeding as planned. Although it will primarily serve as our Mumbai corporate office, the new building will ------- house television
                                                      13.
studios and other media spaces. Demolition of the existing structures began last summer and has been taking longer than we had hoped. ------- expected to be finished in two months.
                                                      14.
------- . The entire project should be completed in approximately two years. We appreciate your
15.
------- . We know that lengthy construction can be an inconvenience, but we are confident that
16.
the finished building will be a welcome and worthwhile asset to the neighborhood.

13. (A) ever
   (B) also
   (C) much
   (D) quite

14. (A) It is
   (B) Ours is
   (C) There are
   (D) Theirs are

15. (A) Construction codes have been updated in recent years.
   (B) Kotai employees may share company news on social media.
   (C) Two other broadcasting companies exist in the vicinity.
   (D) Nearby residents will continue to hear a moderate amount of noise.

16. (A) gift
   (B) efforts
   (C) patience
   (D) investment

UNIT 14 접속부사 문제

출제비율 1~3문제/16문항

출제 공식

접속부사는 문장과 문장을 논리적으로 연결하는 부사로, 빈칸 앞뒤 문장의 논리적 관계에 따라 역접, 인과, 첨가, 대조 등 알맞은 접속부사를 선택해야 한다.

ETS 예제 기사문
번역 p.175

풀이 전략

An upcoming report by the Agricultural Review Board predicts that ❶ soy production will decrease next year for the first time in 25 years. ------- , ❷ grain production will likely increase. – 중략 – Soy prices could skyrocket while grain supplies keep wheat, corn, and rice prices low.

(A) To summarize
(B) For example
(C) In contrast
(D) Likewise

STEP 1 앞뒤 문장을 해석한다.

❶ 내년 콩 생산량이 감소할 것이다.
❷ 곡물 생산은 증가할 것 같다.

STEP 2 두 문장의 논리적 관계를 파악한다.

'감소'와 '증가'는 내용은 서로 상반되므로 두 문장은 역접 관계이다.

STEP 3 보기에서 알맞은 접속부사를 선택한다.

(A) 요약하자면　　(B) 예를 들어
(C) 이와 대조적으로　(D) 마찬가지로

만점 공략 노트

공략 1　빈출 접속부사를 반드시 암기하자.

역접	However 그러나	Nevertheless 그럼에도 불구하고	Even so / Still 그럼에도 불구하고	On the other hand 반면에	In contrast 그와 대조적으로
인과	Therefore 따라서	Accordingly 그에 따라	Consequently 결과적으로	As a result 그 결과	Thus 그러므로
추가	In addition 게다가	Moreover 게다가	Furthermore 게다가	Besides 게다가	Plus 또한
기타	For example 예를 들어	For instance 예를 들어	Then 그 다음에	In fact / Indeed 사실	Otherwise 그렇지 않으면
	To that end 그 목적으로	In short 간단히 말해서	Instead 대신	Meanwhile 그동안에	In the meantime 그동안에
	In particular 특히	Likewise 마찬가지로	Alternatively 또는	If so 만약 그렇다면	Namely 즉, 다시 말해

공략 2　접속부사와 접속사/전치사를 구분하자.

접속부사 vs. 접속사	Items are free. [**However** / Although], there are shipping costs. 물품은 무료입니다. **그러나**, 배송비가 있습니다.
	[**Although** / However] items are free, there are shipping costs. 물품은 무료이나 배송비가 있습니다.
접속부사 vs. 전치사	Items are free. [**In addition** / ~~In addition to~~], free delivery will be offered. 물품은 무료입니다. **또한**, 무료 배송이 제공됩니다.
	[**In addition to** / ~~In addition~~] the free items, free delivery will be offered. 무료 물품뿐 아니라 무료 배송이 제공됩니다.

Questions 1-4 refer to the following e-mail.

To: Silomark employees
From: Davit Sabounjian
Subject: Employee survey
Date: 3 March

Hello, everyone,

I want to thank each of you for your time, care, and thoughtfulness in ------- the employee
1.
satisfaction survey. The leadership team has now had the chance to review all the responses,
and an executive team has been consulting with human resources to determine how best to
address your concerns. ------- , we have already been able to take steps toward expanding some
2.
of our employee benefits. ------- . I will have additional positive ------- to tell you about soon. For
3.   **4.**
now, thank you all again for your dedication to Silomark.

Sincerely,

Davit Sabounjian
Vice President of Corporate Development

---

1. (A) complete
    (B) completely
    (C) completion
    (D) completing

2. (A) As a result
    (B) On the contrary
    (C) By comparison
    (D) In that case

3. (A) Please be certain to sign these papers
        and return them promptly.
    (B) We are in the process of updating our
        Web site to address those problems.
    (C) A session on conducting workplace
        surveys will be offered next month.
    (D) Information about these changes will be
        sent to you next week.

4. (A) articles
    (B) performances
    (C) developments
    (D) regulations

Questions 1-4 refer to the following notice.

Hunter Classic Theater requests that all mobile devices, such as smartphones and tablets, be turned off and put away once the theater lights ------- . Merely setting devices to silent does not

1.

address other issues with their use during movies. The use of these devices can distract nearby

------- . The light from your small screen, ------- , makes it very difficult for others to concentrate

2.   **3.**

on the film on the big screen.

On occasion, you may need to make a phone call or check a text message. ------- . When you

4.

return to your seat, we request that you avoid disturbing those seated nearby.

---

1. (A) dims
   (B) to dim
   (C) dimming
   (D) have dimmed

2. (A) directors
   (B) performers
   (C) viewers
   (D) witnesses

3. (A) for example
   (B) as a result
   (C) therefore
   (D) nevertheless

4. (A) In this case, please exit the theater and go to the lobby.
   (B) Please inform a theater worker about any problems.
   (C) We hope that you have enjoyed the show.
   (D) Regrettably, we cannot issue a refund.

Questions 5-8 refer to the following e-mail.

From: Rebeccah Yifrah
Sent: October 29
To: Farhan Almontaser
Subject: A special thank you

Hello, Farhan,

Please convey my thanks to everyone who participated in the review of our Customer Welcome Kit, Ms. Ghansah in particular. She brought two important matters to my attention. First, she informed me early on in the review process that some ------- were missing. Somehow, obtaining
5.
those authorizations had completely escaped me. ------- , she had discovered a discrepancy
6.
involving the product details and, having informed me, took the initiative to fix it.

Ms. Ghansah showed great sensitivity to our marketing timelines and worked diligently -------
7.
us in getting the Welcome Kit completed. Her proactive efforts, flexibility, and responsiveness helped us to finish our project ahead of the deadline. ------- . Once again, my thanks to everyone.
8.

Regards,

Rebeccah Yifrah
Senior Manager
Customer Relations Specialist
Britenite Marketing

5. (A) pages
    (B) graphics
    (C) approvals
    (D) customers

6. (A) In addition
    (B) As a result
    (C) Nonetheless
    (D) All of a sudden

7. (A) assistance
    (B) to assist
    (C) assisted
    (D) assists

8. (A) It will therefore have to be revised.
    (B) The kit is sent to all new customers.
    (C) I have attached a copy of her review.
    (D) I look forward to working with her again.

Questions 9-12 refer to the following article.

WELLINGTON (3 April)—Sewing-machine manufacturer Rapsidy announced this week the start of its new Green Stitches (GS) Initiative. The GS Initiative seeks ------- the recycling of materials
9.
among Rapsidy's worldwide customer base. A new Web site will allow ------- to list fabric scraps
10.
they wish to donate. Clothing makers around the world can then browse the site for pieces they want. All items will be free of charge to members of the GS Initiative community. -------, they
11.
would still need to cover shipping costs. ------- .
12.

9. (A) encouraging
    (B) to encourage
    (C) encouragement
    (D) having encouraged

10. (A) using
    (B) used
    (C) uses
    (D) users

11. (A) However
    (B) Namely
    (C) As a result
    (D) For example

12. (A) Rapsidy's earnings have grown steadily over the last quarter.
    (B) Some materials can be quite expensive.
    (C) Repurposing fabric is not a new idea.
    (D) The fee will vary based on the weight of items ordered.

Questions 13-16 refer to the following e-mail.

To: Demitri Ladas, Contracting Manager
From: Lenore Velis
Date: 7 July
Subject: Need for new distributors

Dear Mr. Ladas,

I just learned that our current vendor, Tocatan Distribution Systems, will not be expanding into the American market next year after all. ------- , I will be looking for new distributors for our olive
13.
oil. As you know, our three-year expansion plan includes this as a key objective. ------- .
14.

Last year you found a new distributor for our imported cheeses. While conducting that search, did you come across any distributors that also offered a wide array of olive oils? ------- , I hope to
15.
find olive oils produced in Greece. If you have any leads, could you please send me the contact information?

I would ------- it if you could send any information you have by Wednesday.
16.

Thank you,
Lenore Velis

---

13. (A) During
(B) Therefore
(C) Otherwise
(D) However

14. (A) We would like to sign a contract by August 1.
(B) Our previous distributor is out of business.
(C) Please submit a copy of our distribution costs.
(D) We will complete our inventory by September.

15. (A) Specifically
(B) Unfortunately
(C) Surprisingly
(D) Continually

16. (A) appreciates
(B) appreciating
(C) appreciated
(D) appreciate

문장 고르기 문제

출제 공식 빈칸에 넣었을 때 자연스럽게 연결되는 문장을 고르는 문제로, 정관사, 대명사, 지시어, 접속부사, 주변 어휘 등을 활용하여 정오답을 판별하는 것이 핵심 풀이 방법이다.

ETS 예제 | **광고**

번역 p.178

풀이 전략

Feel Terrific Fitness App

Do you want to sweat with the best? Try the Feel Terrific Fitness app. –중략– ❶ We provide options for people at various levels of ability. ------- . ❷ You will find the difficulty level noted next to each workout routine. Try out our app now for free for 90 days. When the trial period ends, you can continue using the Feel Terrific Fitness app for only $14.99 per month.

(A) Accounts may be canceled at any time.
(B) Stretching before a workout is important.
(C) We recommend buying an exercise mat.
(D) You can choose from beginner to advanced.

STEP 1 앞뒤 문장을 해석한다.

❶ 저희는 다양한 능력 수준에 맞춘 옵션을 제공합니다.
❷ 난이도는 각 운동 루틴 옆에 적혀 있습니다.

STEP 2 주제와 흐름을 파악한다.

'능력 수준'을 주제로 하며, '난이도'로 연결된다.

STEP 3 오답을 소거하고 정답을 검토한다.

(A) 주제가 계정 취소이므로 오답
(B) 주제가 스트레칭이므로 오답
(C) 주제가 운동 매트이므로 오답
(D) '초보자부터 상급자까지'라는 능력 수준을 언급하므로 정답

만점 공략 노트

공략 1 관사, 지시어, 대명사를 활용하자.

The center has 28 medical examination rooms. In addition, it houses two laboratories, a pharmacy, and a physical therapy room. **The center will provide a wide range of services. -------.**

(A) These include pediatric, adult, primary, and urgent care.
(B) ~~They~~ have many years of medical experience.

의료 시설을 소개하고 있고, 해당 시설이 다양한 서비스를 제공한다고 했으므로 **services**를 (A)의 **지시어 these**로 받으면 내용이 자연스럽게 연결된다.

(B)의 They는 의료진을 가리키므로 대명사 활용이 맞지 않다.

공략 2 지문 내용과 상충되는 오답을 쳐내자.

The fitness club will hold its annual 5-kilometre run at 12 noon on Saturday, **15 November.** The cost of registration is £10, which should be brought to the front desk **by 10 November along with a participation form**. This year's race will benefit the local primary school. -------.

(A) Please complete registration ~~on the day of the race~~.
(B) It will begin at the village park gate and wind through the village.

달리기 시합 날짜는 **11월 15일**이고, 신청서는 **11월 10일**까지 제출해야 한다고 했으므로 신청서를 달리기 시합 날짜에 작성해 달라는 (A)는 지문 내용과 상충된다.

빈칸 바로 앞 문장에서 신청서와 관련된 내용을 다루고 있으므로 주제가 같은 (A)를 선택하기 쉬우나, 사실 관계가 지문 내용과 불일치하므로 오답이다. 이처럼 매력적인 오답을 피하려면 팩트 체크를 소홀히 해서는 안 된다.

ETS 유형 연습

Questions 1-4 refer to the following e-mail.

To: srafid@rafidfitness.co.uk
From: hlloyd@mugpro.co.uk
Date: 12 February
Subject: Fitness equipment

Dear Mr. Rafid,

As the owner of one of Manchester's largest fitness centres, you know how ------- high-quality
  1.
workout machines are. They are especially valued for their functionality and dependability.

------- , even the best equipment eventually breaks down. One of the biggest expenses in running
  2.
a fitness centre is the money spent on replacing equipment. If you are shopping for machines but

------- by the costs, Marino Used Gym Products has the brand-name used machines for you.
  3.

------- .
  4.

Call us at 0160 496 0063 for more information and a free quote from one of our experienced
sales associates.

Sincerely,

Haydon Lloyd

1. (A) committed
   (B) expensive
   (C) fragile
   (D) elevated

2. (A) Thus
   (B) Conversely
   (C) Nevertheless
   (D) Instead

3. (A) challenging
   (B) to challenge
   (C) had challenged
   (D) are challenged

4. (A) Thank you for applying to our service
       department.
   (B) Moreover, this will include a free ticket
       to the championship event.
   (C) As always, your public support of our
       company is much appreciated.
   (D) Best of all, we offer them for a fraction
       of their original prices.

Questions 1-4 refer to the following e-mail.

From: Falcetti, Matthew
Sent: May 17
To: Library Staff
Subject: Second floor Wi-Fi signal

Dear Staff:

Please note that a new wireless Internet access point was recently installed on the library's second floor. There is ------- a wireless signal in the public study area there. In the past, we had
1.
discouraged patrons ------- trying to access the Internet in that space because the signal was
2.
not very strong. ------- .
3.

This is the first of three new access points we will be installing. Soon we expect to improve the signal ------- in the art gallery and lobby as well.
4.

Matthew Falcetti

Head of Information Services

---

1. (A) still
   (B) never
   (C) now
   (D) unfortunately

2. (A) by
   (B) from
   (C) before
   (D) across

3. (A) This will no longer be necessary.
   (B) This area is off-limits to small children.
   (C) It will be featured in Friday's newspaper.
   (D) Many patrons bring their own computers.

4. (A) strength
   (B) is strong
   (C) strongest
   (D) strengthens

Questions 5-8 refer to the following invitation.

To Whom It May Concern:

All of us at Live Green Summit would like to invite your company to participate in our annual Green Cleanup Day at Higginston Park. Every year, we invite local businesses to send ------- to
5.
help make this event a success. Those volunteers participate in one day of our efforts to clean up one of our community's favorite green spaces. We ask that all participants plan to ------- in the
6.
park for at least three hours. ------- .
7.

Please respond by June 30. Once we have heard from all participating businesses, we will be in touch with more details. Cleanup schedules will be sent out on or ------- July 20. As always, we
8.
are grateful for your employees' time.

All best,

Maria Cuomo, Live Green Summit Team Coordinator

5. (A) supplies
   (B) equipment
   (C) representatives
   (D) capital

6. (A) work
   (B) run
   (C) play
   (D) drive

7. (A) Free Range Foods is one of the participants.
   (B) Our community has six public parks.
   (C) Higginston Park is named after Sir Daniel Higginston.
   (D) The cleanup can then be done in a day.

8. (A) perhaps
   (B) beside
   (C) before
   (D) also

Questions 9-12 refer to the following e-mail.

To: Mark Kootman
From: Batsheva Abadi
Date: April 23
Subject: Banquet

My string quartet and I are looking forward to playing at your outdoor banquet next month.
Please note that we have certain requirements when we perform outside. We need to set up our
------- in a shady area that is protected from sun and moisture. This is essential because our
    9.
violins, viola, and cello can be damaged in adverse weather conditions. ------- , if it is very windy
                                                            10.
outside, we may need to move to an alternate location. ------- . Finally, if the weather is very hot
                                            11.
or cold on the performance date, we will need to move indoors. It is difficult to play with cold or
sweaty fingers in ------- temperatures. Feel free to contact me with any questions or concerns.
            12.

Sincerely,

Batsheva Abadi

---

9. (A) instruments
   (B) easels
   (C) cameras
   (D) experiments

10. (A) After all
    (B) Despite this
    (C) At that time
    (D) In addition

11. (A) We do not want our music stands
        blowing over.
    (B) If the event starts late, we will charge an
        extra fee.
    (C) We usually prefer to play indoors at small
        events.
    (D) It is easy to find suitable locations on our
        Web site.

12. (A) extremes
    (B) extremity
    (C) extreme
    (D) extremely

To: All Administrative Staff
From: Hye-Jin Nam, Human Resources Manager
Date: May 15
Subject: New protocol for time sheet submissions

As of June 15, all administrative staff will be required to ------- two new time sheet submission
13.
procedures. First, all leave requests must now be made through our new online portal, Alpha

Time. ------- . The new online system should be much more efficient. Second, overtime hours
14.
must now be listed under the code OH. The code OT is no longer ------- in the system. Finally,
15.
please note that ------- regarding time sheets should now be directed to Karl Figaro.
16.

13. (A) design
(B) provide for
(C) comply with
(D) measure

15. (A) actual
(B) restricted
(C) valid
(D) confident

14. (A) These policies can be complicated to
understand.
(B) Monday is a vacation day for all staff.
(C) For instance, it can perform complicated
functions.
(D) We will be retiring our current software.

16. (A) question
(B) questions
(C) questioned
(D) to question

PART 7
독해

INTRO
UNIT 16 | 주제/목적 문제
UNIT 17 | 세부 사항 문제
UNIT 18 | Not/True 문제
UNIT 19 | 추론/암시 문제
UNIT 20 | 동의어 문제
UNIT 21 | 의도 파악 문제
UNIT 22 | 문장 삽입 문제
UNIT 23 | 연계 문제

◆ 최신 출제 경향

비즈니스와 관련된 이메일, 기사, 회람 및 주문서 초대장 등과 같은 각종 양식이 지문으로 등장한다. 약 54분의 제한된 시간 내에 빠르게 지문 정보를 파악하는 능력, 어휘력, 논리력 등 전반적인 독해 평가가 54문항 내에서 이루어진다.

◆ ETS 예제

Questions 164-167 refer to the following letter.

번역 p.181

Dear Client,

—[1]—. I am writing to inform you that Divine Chocolates will be relocating to a new city on September 1. The address is 2165 Forest Road, Worcester, MA 01602. Please make a note of it in your records. Our main contact number remains the same: (508) 555-0120.

Since our company was founded a decade ago, the loyal support of our customers has enabled us to grow steadily over the years. —[2]—. [164]**That growth has resulted in our current facility no longer meeting our needs and requirements for storage and work space.** —[3]—. **That is why we made arrangements to move to a more spacious location.** Please be assured that our commitment to our customers will not change. [166,167]**We will continue to** [165]**devote ourselves to providing you with the best chocolates from around the world.** —[4]—.

Sincerely,

Roberta Vogt, Manager

세부 사항 문제

164 Why is the company relocating?
(A) The rent was too expensive.
(B) The building has been sold.
(C) The current space is too small.
(D) There was not enough parking.

동의어 문제

165 The word "devote" in paragraph 2, line 6, is closest in meaning to
(A) worship
(B) dedicate
(C) give
(D) elect

추론/암시 문제

166 What is indicated about the company?
(A) It sells imported chocolates.
(B) It first relocated ten years ago.
(C) It was founded by the Vogt family.
(D) It is currently located in Worcester.

문장 삽입 문제

167 In which of the positions marked [1], [2], [3], and [4] does the following sentence best belong?

"Feel free to contact us with any questions you have concerning the new location."
(A) [1]　(B) [2]　(C) [3]　(D) [4]

정답 **164** (C)　**165** (B)　**166** (A)　**167** (D)

❶ 글의 주제나 목적을 묻는 **주제/목적 문제**
❷ 언제, 어디서, 어떻게, 왜 등과 같은 육하원칙을 묻는 **세부 사항 문제**
❸ 지문 내용 일치 여부를 묻는 **Not/True 문제**
❹ 지문 내용을 바탕으로 논리적으로 유추해야 하는 **추론/암시 문제**
❺ 지문의 단어와 동일한 뜻을 지닌 어휘를 찾는 **동의어 문제**
❻ 둘 이상이 주고받은 채팅이나 문자 메시지에서 특정 대화의 의도를 묻는 **의도 파악 문제**
❼ 지문에서 제시문이 들어갈 적절한 위치를 찾는 **문장 삽입 문제**
❽ 두 지문 또는 세 지문 간의 연관 관계를 파악해야 하는 **연계 문제**

◆ 풀이 전략

164 세부 사항 문제

육하원칙에 해당하는 의문사와 키워드를 바탕으로 정답을 구한다.

질문에서 'Why(왜)'와 'relocating(이전)'을 키워드로 잡고 이전의 이유에 대해 언급하는 문장이 나올 때까지 지문을 읽는다. 두 번째 단락 2행에서 '회사의 성장으로 인해 현재 시설이 더이상 조건에 맞지 않다'고 했고 '따라서 더 넓은 장소로 이전한다'고 이유를 밝혔으므로 (C)를 정답으로 고른다.

165 동의어 문제

동의어를 빈칸이라고 가정하자.

devote oneself to -ing = dedicate oneself to -ing ~에 전념하다
두 단어는 동일한 구조로 쓰이며, devote가 빈칸이라고 가정할 때, 해당 자리에 dedicate를 넣으면 동일한 의미가 유지되므로 (B) dedicate를 정답으로 고른다.

166 추론/암시 문제

지문에서 언급된 사실로 유추할 수 있는 내용을 정답으로 고른다.

마지막 문장에서 '계속해서 세계 각지에서 온 최상의 초콜릿을 제공하는 데 전념할 것이다'라고 했으므로 이 회사는 수입 초콜릿을 판매하는 회사임을 유추할 수 있다. 따라서 (A)를 정답으로 고른다.

167 문장 삽입 문제

제시문을 지문의 빈칸에 삽입하여 앞뒤 흐름이 자연스러운지 확인한다.

"Feel free to contact us with any questions you have concerning the new location."

'문의 사항이 있으면 언제든지 연락하라'는 내용은 주로 문장 끝에서 맺음말로 등장한다.
문장 끝에 들어갔을 때 앞 문장과 내용이 자연스럽게 연결되므로 (D) [4]를 정답으로 고른다.

UNIT 16 주제/목적 문제

● 출제비율 5~6문제/54문항

출제 공식

1. 출제빈도가 매우 높은 유형으로, 해당 지문의 첫 번째 문제로 출제된다. 주로 제목이나 지문의 초반부에 근거가 제시되는 편이나 주제가 지문 전반에 걸쳐 제시되는 경우도 있다.
2. 내용의 흐름을 바꿀 수 있는 반전 표현(however, but, unfortunately, actually) 뒤에 주제/목적이 나오는 경우가 많다.

문제 유형

■ What is the purpose of the e-mail? 이 이메일의 목적은 무엇인가?
■ What does the information mainly discuss? 이 안내문은 주로 무엇에 대해 다루는가?

ETS 예제 **이메일**　　　　　　　　번역 p.181　　**풀이 전략**

Q. Why did Mr. Kwan write the e-mail? ·······

(A) To point out a mistake in a service charge
(B) To request an adjustment to an agreement ·······
(C) To offer feedback on a service from Parbat Rentals
(D) To ask Ms. Caron to visit a construction site

Date: February 23
Subject Follow-up ·······

Hello, Jenna,

I am writing to follow up on the phone call we had earlier this week, in which I agreed to rent a crane from March 15 until April 10. **– 중략 –** We actually need the crane a week later, from March 22 until April 17. Is the crane available for those dates? Would there be any additional charges related to the date change? Please get back to me when you can.

Thanks,

David Kwan

STEP 1 질문을 파악한다.
이메일을 쓴 목적을 묻는 문제이다.

STEP 2 지문을 읽는다.
제목과 이메일의 초반부를 중심으로 근거문을 찾는다.

> 3월 15일에서 4월 10일까지 크레인을 대여하기로 했던 전화 통화에 이어 추가 문의를 드리고자 메일을 드립니다. –중략– 실상 크레인이 한 주 뒤인 3월 22일에서 4월 17일까지 필요하게 되었습니다. 해당 날짜에 크레인을 이용할 수 있을까요?

STEP 3 보기를 읽고 정답을 구한다.
(B) 합의 사항 변경을 요청하려고

정답으로 가는 PARAPHRASING

지문 속 주제/목적이 드러나는 정답의 단서	패러프레이징된 정답
This is to share an important change we made to **the event location.**	→ To **announce a new venue** 새로운 장소를 알리려고
Did you already e-mail me **the list of this week's invoices?**	→ To **determine** whether **information** has been **sent** 정보가 전송되었는지 확인하려고
We **need your assistance** in **checking the accuracy** of the records.	→ To **request verification** of some information 일부 정보의 확인을 요청하려고
I would like to offer my sincere thanks for your **generous gifts.**	→ **To express appreciation** for his **donation** 기부에 대해 감사를 표하려고

250

Questions 1-3 refer to the following report.

Technology Assistance Center
Status Report

Issue:	We are currently experiencing a phone outage in our offices in Westwood and Jaytown. Many staff members have reported that they have not been able to receive incoming calls or make outgoing calls since yesterday. A ticket was opened last night to address the problem.
Employees affected:	All Pearce Corporation employees working at offices in Westwood and Jaytown.
Ticket filed with Technology Assistance Center:	July 5, 6:30 P.M.
Estimated resolution:	July 7, 9:00 A.M.
Impact on Pearce Corporation:	Westwood and Jaytown employees will be unable to receive calls from outside organizations. Pearce Corporation employees located outside of Westwood and Jaytown will be unable to call in to those locations.
Recommendations:	Please use e-mail until the outage is resolved tomorrow.

1. What is the purpose of the report?

(A) To explain a telephone outage
(B) To notify users of a software update
(C) To alert users of an Internet disruption
(D) To announce a temporary office relocation

2. When did the Technology Assistance Center receive a ticket?

(A) On July 4
(B) On July 5
(C) On July 6
(D) On July 7

3. What does the Technology Assistance Center recommend that employees do?

(A) Communicate via instant messages
(B) Use personal mobile phones
(C) Cancel upcoming conference calls
(D) Contact Westwood and Jaytown staff by e-mail

Questions 1-3 refer to the following e-mail.

To:	d.marusik@seltermanhospital.org
From:	y.shaw@seltermanhospital.org
Subject:	Request for assistance
Date:	October 15

Dear Ms. Marusik:

I'm currently teaching a course on hospital management at Stillwater University. One of my goals is to give the students an insider's perspective on how a hospital such as ours is run. To this end, on November 5, I will be taking them on a tour of the most vital departments within our hospital. A 20-minute information session will be held at each department, during which a staff member of the department will briefly describe the daily duties and answer students' questions. The tour will begin at 10:00 A.M. and is expected to end by 3:00 P.M. Lunch will be provided during the break from noon to 1:00 P.M.

Please ask your staff members in the medical records department if one of them would be so kind as to participate in this activity. Then pass the person's name on to me at your earliest convenience, but no later than October 31.

Thank you for your assistance in this matter.

Sincerely,

Dr. Yuya Shaw
Executive Assistant, Administrative Services, Selterman Hospital

---

1. Why did Dr. Shaw send the e-mail?

(A) To promote a hospital management course

(B) To announce an updated room assignment

(C) To schedule a series of job interviews

(D) To recruit a volunteer

2. What is NOT indicated about the event on November 5 ?

(A) It will include descriptions of various job responsibilities.

(B) It will involve staff from different departments.

(C) It will last for two hours.

(D) It will include a meal.

3. What is indicated about Ms. Marusik?

(A) She works in the medical records department.

(B) She regularly gives presentations to hospital staff.

(C) She used to teach at Stillwater University.

(D) She is Dr. Shaw's assistant.

Questions 4-7 refer to the following article.

NEWBOLD (August 7)—In an era when many comic book stores are closing in favor of online stores, Kyle's Comic Life just opened its doors in Newbold. — [1] —. Destined to become a popular gathering spot for people of all ages, Kyle's Comic Life boasts a large collection of vintage and new comic books in addition to action figures and toys. Moreover, there is a lounge for entertainment and relaxation, and visitors are encouraged to bring their own refreshments to enjoy. — [2] —. The unique décor in the lounge resembles the setting of a popular science-fiction comic book.

A monthly open-microphone night will be held in the lounge for poets, musicians, comedians, and other artists to showcase their work. — [3] —. Saturday afternoons are for family activities, and there are meetings on Sunday evenings for board game enthusiasts. Furthermore, the store plans to offer a variety of themed events. — [4] —.

Kyle's Comic Life is located at 2204 South Street in Newbold.

---

4. What is the purpose of the article?

   (A) To review a comic book series
   (B) To introduce a new business
   (C) To announce a store relocation
   (D) To promote a Web site

5. What is stated about the lounge?

   (A) It is decorated like a setting from a book.
   (B) It has a schedule of events posted online.
   (C) It has snacks available for purchase.
   (D) It is owned by local artists.

6. What is NOT mentioned about Kyle's Comic Life?

   (A) It sells toys.
   (B) It hosts family events.
   (C) It is the most popular store in the neighborhood.
   (D) It is a place where people can play board games.

7. In which of the positions marked [1], [2], [3], and [4] does the following sentence best belong?

   "The first will be Superhero Weekend, scheduled for September 18 and 19."

   (A) [1]
   (B) [2]
   (C) [3]
   (D) [4]

출제비율 15~20문제/54문항

출제 공식

1. 파트 7에서 가장 높은 비율로 출제되며 언제, 어디서, 어떻게, 왜 등과 같은 구체적인 사실 정보를 묻는다.
2. 질문에는 날짜, 고유명사 등의 키워드가 존재하며, 키워드는 지문 속에서 패러프레이징되는 경우도 많다.

문제 유형

- Why is the company relocating? 회사는 왜 이전하는가?
- What option is available to customers? 소비자는 어떤 선택 사항을 이용할 수 있는가?

ETS 예제 공지   번역 p.184   풀이 전략

Q. What will happen on February 8 ?

(A) The Carlton location will stay open later than usual.
(B) A surprise party will be given for ACC employees.
(C) A private event will be held at ACC's Southbank location.
(D) Durham Road will be temporarily closed.

Temporary Closure

Thank you for joining us today at Arthur's Continental Cuisine (ACC) on Durham Road in Southbank. We hope that you will dine with us again, but please note that this location will be closed for a private party on Tuesday, 8 February, from 4:00 P.M. to closing. Our other locations will remain open to the public on that date. To make a reservation, call your location of choice or visit our Web site at www.arthurscc.com.au.

STEP 1 질문을 읽고 키워드를 파악한다.

키워드: February 8

STEP 2 지문을 읽는다.

내용을 파악하며 지문을 처음부터 읽어 오다가 키워드가 포함되어 있는 근거 문장을 정독한다.

> 이 지점은 **2월 8일** 화요일 **비공개 파티**를 위해 문을 닫을 예정입니다.

STEP 3 보기를 읽고 정답을 구한다.

(C) ACC 사우스뱅크 지점에서 비공개 행사가 열릴 예정이다.

정답으로 가는 PARAPHRASING

지문 속 세부 사항이 드러나는 정답의 단서	패러프레이징된 정답
Come to Becker Books to celebrate the opening of our new **rooftop cafe**!	**Q** 카페의 위치는? → **Above a bookstore**
We will send you **a coupon for 20 percent off the price of your next purchase**.	**Q** 편지 수신자가 받는 것은? → **A discount on a future purchase**
You will receive **company assistance in finding and purchasing a home**.	**Q** 회사가 제공하는 지원은? → **Finding a place to live**
The newspaper will publish a **special career section** devoted to **occupations in health care**.	**Q** 신문의 특별 코너가 다루는 것은? → **Jobs in medicine**

Questions 1-4 refer to the following press release.

FOR IMMEDIATE RELEASE   CONTACT: Felix Walter, fwalter@rbcorp.net

Raeburne Corporation to Announce Second-Quarter Financial Results

PARKDALE, OREGON (July 20)—Raeburne Corporation, a global leader in energy solutions, today announced that it will release its second-quarter financial report on August 1 during a conference call at 1:00 P.M. Pacific Time (4:00 P.M. Eastern Time). This event will offer a chance to discuss the corporation's most recent financial results and outlook. The first-quarter conference call and webcast on May 19 had more than 200 participants and was well received. More interest is expected in the upcoming conference call because of the recent success of the Eneral line of services. Investors and industry analysts are encouraged to join the conference call or webcast as follows.

Raeburne Corporation Second-Quarter Conference Call
Date: August 1
Time: 1:00 P.M. Pacific Time (4:00 P.M. Eastern Time)
U.S. Conference Call Number: 1–888–555–0181
International Conference Call Number: 1–206–555–0181
Conference ID: 3885650
Webcast: http://www.rbcorp.net/investor-relations

Please note that the webcast is for observational and informational purposes only. To participate in the discussion you must join the conference call live. A recorded version of both the webcast and conference call will be available on the company's Web site for 30 days following the broadcast.

---

1. What is the purpose of the press release?

   (A) To provide information about a financial report
   (B) To introduce a new product from Raeburne Corporation
   (C) To invite journalists to discuss the energy market
   (D) To explain how to use the new Eneral services

2. When will a conference call be made available for participants?

   (A) On May 19
   (B) On July 20
   (C) On August 1
   (D) On September 30

3. The word "chance" in paragraph 1, line 4, is closest in meaning to

   (A) ticket
   (B) risk
   (C) opportunity
   (D) probability

4. What is indicated about the upcoming event?

   (A) It will describe leadership changes at a corporation.
   (B) It will be recorded to meet legal requirements.
   (C) It will be summarized in a written report.
   (D) It will likely be better attended than a previous event.

ETS 고득점 실전 문제

Questions 1-3 refer to the following report.

Executive Summary

Overview
Costa Gusta, Inc., is seeking to obtain funds to develop a storefront business that will augment its import and wholesale activities. Further loan request information can be found starting on page 10.

Products and Services
The business to be developed by Costa Gusta, Inc., will generate revenue through the sale of beverages produced with the company's well-known imported coffee beans. The new business will also sell complementary items, such as pastries, as well as branded coffee mugs and other accessories with the company logo.

Sales Forecasts
Due to its established reputation in the trade, Costa Gusta predicts a strong rate of growth following the start of operations. Sales projections for the coming four years are shown in the table below.

Product Type	Year 1	Year 2	Year 3	Year 4
Beverages	$81,000	$122,000	$134,000	$140,000
Food Items	$22,000	$36,000	$41,000	$50,000
Branded Accessories	$15,000	$17,000	$22,000	$25,000

1. What is the purpose of the report?

   (A) To raise money for a business
   (B) To negotiate a merger
   (C) To identify locations for a business
   (D) To recommend revisions to a budget

2. What kind of business does Costa Gusta plan to open?

   (A) A coffee shop
   (B) A kitchen goods store
   (C) An import-export service
   (D) A beverage manufacturing and bottling company

3. When does Costa Gusta expect to sell $22,000 worth of products decorated with the company logo?

   (A) Year 1
   (B) Year 2
   (C) Year 3
   (D) Year 4

Questions 4-7 refer to the following e-mail.

From:	jrobins@rayaxo.com
To:	rmajewski@rayaxo.com
Subject:	Accuracy of specifications
Date:	November 19
Attachment:	🔗 CF-4500

Dear Mr. Majewski,

We just received the Polish edition of the CF-4500 production specifications from Julia Kaminska. Could you please look over the attachment and make sure it matches the English original in our files? Although we have always been satisfied with the quality of Ms. Kaminska's work, the CF-4500 is especially important. As you know, we've contracted with a manufacturer in Poland to produce the lighting fixtures and controls, and the process will undergo a test run next Friday. Therefore, it is important that you double-check all the figures referring to the sizes. Any inaccuracies could lead to cost overruns and potentially delay production.

Please complete your review by tomorrow afternoon at the latest and let me know if you find any errors in the Polish version. We must forward the specifications to the production engineer on Monday so that their equipment can be ready for Friday's test run. Representatives from the client will be on hand to watch it.

Thank you.

Jessica Robins

4. What services does Ms. Kaminska provide?

(A) Design
(B) Printing
(C) Translation
(D) Accounting

5. What is Mr. Majewski asked to do?

(A) Investigate reports of delays
(B) Compare two documents
(C) Repair faulty equipment
(D) Travel to Poland

6. What is one piece of information contained in the attachment?

(A) The schedule of tests
(B) The quality of materials
(C) The layout of a building
(D) The dimensions of parts

7. What will happen on Monday?

(A) A document will be sent.
(B) An agreement will be finalized.
(C) Production equipment will be cleaned.
(D) A manufacturing process will be tested.

1. 지문 내용 중 사실인 것, 혹은 사실이 아닌 것을 찾는 문제로 정답 근거가 지문 곳곳에 흩어져 있다.
2. 보기는 지문 내용과 사실 관계가 상이한 정보, 혹은 지문을 통해 알 수 없는 정보가 섞여 있다.

문제 유형
- What is NOT stated in the return policy? 반품 정책에 명시되지 않은 것은?
- What is mentioned about the service? 서비스에 대해 언급된 것은?

ETS 예제 광고 · · · · · · · · · · · · · · · · 번역 p.186 · · · · · · **풀이 전략**

Q. What is indicated about Jones Tree Professionals? •----------

(A) It specializes in only certain types of trees.
(B) It provides free service estimates.
(C) It is offering a discount to new customers. •----------
(D) It was founded last winter.

Take advantage of the fall season to take care of your trees. Winter snowstorms can cause branches to break and fall on your property. Jones Tree Professionals is here to help! Call us for any tree services, ranging from pruning to removal. First-time customers will receive a 20 percent discount on all services. •----------

STEP 1 질문을 파악한다.

특정 회사(고유명사)에 대해 명시된 사실 관계를 파악하는 문제이다.

STEP 2 지문을 읽는다.

지문에서 제시된 사실들을 요약하며 읽는다.

신규 고객은 모든 서비스에 대해 **20퍼센트 할인**을 받을 수 있습니다.

STEP 3 보기를 읽고 정답을 구한다.

(C) 신규 고객에게 할인을 제공하고 있다.

정답으로 가는 PARAPHRASING

지문 속 사실 관계가 드러나는 정답의 단서	패러프레이징된 정답
The **€5 registration fee required of all race entrants** will be donated to the Crennon Animal Care Society.	**Q** 경기 참여자에 대해 **사실인** 것은? → They **must pay an entry fee.**
Our services are **individually tailored to meet your financial situation**.	**Q** 서비스에 대해 **명시된** 것은? → Pricing **options are available for all budgets.**
We are dedicated to meeting the workplace safety needs as well as **training your employees in a wide variety of safety issues**.	**Q** 서비스의 종류로 **언급된** 것은? → **Training staff in on-the-job safety practices**
This full-time position requires a person with at least **four years of experience** in the tourism industry. **Computer literacy** and **knowledge of at least one foreign language** also required.	**Q** 자격 요건이 **아닌** 것은? → (A) **Skill in using computers** (B) **Work experience** in a similar job (C) **Proficiency in languages** (D) A degree in marketing

Questions 1-4 refer to the following article.

HOUSTON (July 11) – Retexo, Inc., a leader in global product analytics, announced today an assistance program to provide startup companies with access to its world-class services for a reduced price. — [1] —.

Retexo aggregates data on users' interactions with programs or applications on computers, smartphones, or handheld devices. — [2] —. The results ensure that updates to clients' programs and applications are based on actual customers' needs.

Retexo helps companies of all sizes retain customers by improving end-user engagement and overall satisfaction. — [3] —. Recent Retexo projects include Io's Rumist, an interior design program for desktop computers, and Zoida's Relay 4, an exercise monitoring application for smartphones.

With this new pricing option, Retexo is offering startup companies access to its full suite of services at 10 to 20 percent off the regular price. — [4] —. Accepted clients will be able to access weekly analyses of user interactions at the reduced rate for a period of twelve months. Details and application forms are available on the company's Web site (www.retexo.net). Applications will be accepted for the next month.

1. What products can Retexo help improve?

(A) Computer software
(B) Sporting goods
(C) Household furnishings
(D) Stereo equipment

2. What is stated as a benefit companies get from Retexo's service?

(A) An increase in customers
(B) A reduction in production costs
(C) More effective opinions
(D) Greater customer loyalty

3. How long can clients access Retexo's services at a reduced price?

(A) For one week
(B) For twenty weeks
(C) For ten months
(D) For one year

4. In which of the positions marked [1], [2], [3], and [4] does the following sentence best belong?

"Analyses of the data are then posted online for review by the client's development team."

(A) [1]
(B) [2]
(C) [3]
(D) [4]

Questions 1-4 refer to the following job advertisement.

Noorah's Market is Hiring

Noorah's Market is proud to be a long-time pillar of the Clendenin community. For more than five decades we have stocked our store with healthy products, including produce and meat from local farmers. We are currently hiring for the following positions.

Store Manager: Responsibilities include overseeing daily operations, developing promotional materials, maintaining face-to-face communication with customers to resolve issues, motivating sales teams, and training staff. Full-time, Monday–Friday.

Stocking Associate: Responsibilities include assisting in receiving products, loading and unpacking, refilling displays, monitoring inventory, and mopping and sweeping floors. Part-time, weekends required.

Floral Designer: Responsibilities include creating and displaying floral arrangements and ordering products for the department. Prior experience in a floral department is necessary. Physical requirements: Must be able to lift and carry up to 25 kilograms. Work schedule includes weekends and holidays.

Sales Associate: Responsibilities include performing cashier duties, greeting customers, helping customers locate products, and providing customers with information about daily deals and discounts. Part-time, Monday–Thursday.

We offer competitive compensation and paid vacation time. Applicants should send a résumé and cover letter to Jessica Le Havre at jlehavre@noorahs.com.

---

1. What does the advertisement mention about Noorah's Market?

   (A) It plans to open a new location in Clendenin.
   (B) It recently expanded the produce department.
   (C) It was established by local farmers.
   (D) It has been in business for over 50 years.

2. What is NOT listed as a responsibility of a store manager?

   (A) Providing training
   (B) Motivating staff members
   (C) Setting up displays in the store
   (D) Dealing with customer concerns

3. What is suggested about floral designers at Noorah's Market?

   (A) They may have to lift heavy objects.
   (B) They teach customers how to make flower arrangements.
   (C) They often receive tips on holidays.
   (D) They deliver flowers to homes and offices.

4. What is indicated about all the advertised positions?

   (A) They include work shifts on Saturdays.
   (B) They are full-time.
   (C) They require candidates to apply in person.
   (D) They entitle employees to paid time off.

Questions 5-8 refer to the following letter.

Marcus Schmidt • 4 Gaffney Street • South Melbourne VIC 3205

8 February

Kylie Garimara
Anywhere Deliveries Ltd.
60 Parkes Road
Melbourne VIC 3000

Dear Ms. Garimara,

I am writing to apply for the position of truck driver at Anywhere Deliveries Ltd. My colleague Byung-Hun Hahn recommended that I send you my CV, which is enclosed. Mr. Hahn and I have known each other since we attended truck-driving school together, and he mentioned how much he enjoys transporting goods for Anywhere Deliveries.

As a dedicated and hardworking individual, I offer twelve years of experience transporting and delivering goods from warehouses to retail stores and businesses. I started off delivering fresh produce for Anerap Company and now deliver construction machinery for Simpson Trucking. I take great pride in always doing my work in a safe and timely manner.

As a driver for Simpson Trucking, I travel across the country, often driving hundreds or thousands of kilometres in a single round trip. I was commended by my manager for my 91 percent efficiency rating and for my ability to effectively communicate with mechanics, engineers, customers, and other drivers. Additionally, I was honoured to be selected as the Employee of the Year at Simpson Trucking two years ago.

I look forward to an opportunity to hear back from you about my application.

Sincerely,

Marcus Schmidt
Marcus Schmidt

Enclosure

---

5. Who most likely is Mr. Hahn?

(A) A hiring manager
(B) A driving instructor
(C) A store owner
(D) A truck driver

6. What does Mr. Schmidt indicate about his current position?

(A) It started twelve years ago.
(B) It required him to relocate to Melbourne.
(C) It involves transporting machinery.
(D) It is at the Anerap Company.

7. The word "manner" in paragraph 2, line 5, is closest in meaning to

(A) way
(B) appearance
(C) class
(D) appointment

8. What is indicated about Mr. Schmidt?

(A) He prefers longer trips to shorter ones.
(B) He received an award from his employer.
(C) He was given high ratings by his peers.
(D) He has taken classes in communication.

출제 공식

1. 지문에 제시된 근거 문장을 바탕으로 유추할 수 있는 2차 정보를 고르는 문제 유형이다.
2. 글쓴이의 직업, 수신자와의 관계, 글이 게시될 만한 장소 등을 묻는 전체 정보 추론 문제와, 특정 제품 혹은 특정 인물 등에 대해 묻는 세부 정보 추론 문제로 구분된다.

문제 유형

■ For whom is the information most likely intended? 누구를 대상으로 하는 정보이겠는가?
■ What is suggested about Ms. Wilson? 윌슨 씨에 대해 알 수 있는 것은?

ETS 예제 광고   번역 p.189   **풀이 전략**

Q. What is suggested about the bus tickets? ⋯⋯⋯⋯   **STEP 1** 질문을 파악한다.

(A) They may be exchanged.   버스 티켓에 대해 추론하는 세부 정보 추론 문제이다.
(B) They are discounted for round trips.
(C) They may be bought in advance. ⋯⋯   **STEP 2** 지문을 읽는다.
(D) They are sold at stores in Coltonville.
                                                        지문에서 티켓과 관련된 내용을 정독한다.

Mercury Coaches: Official travel partner of the   티켓은 버스에서 혹은 **웹사이트를 통해 구매 가능**합니다.
Oceanwaves Music Festival

Our comfortable buses help transport concertgoers to the   **STEP 3** 보기를 읽고 정답을 구한다.
Oceanwaves Music Festival each day from June 17 to June
21. One-way tickets are $10.00 each. Round-trip tickets   (C) 미리 구입할 수 있다.
are available for $20.00. Buses depart from Coltonville   → 웹사이트를 통해 구매할 수 있다는 것은 버스를 타기
at 10:30 A.M. and return from the festival main gate at   전에 표를 미리 구매할 수 있다는 것을 의미하므로
8:00 P.M. Tickets can be purchased on the bus or through   올바른 추론 범주에 속한다.
our Web site. For more information, visit https://www.
mercurycoaches.com.

정답으로 가는 PARAPHRASING

지문 속 추론/암시가 드러나는 정답의 단서   패러프레이징된 정답

The community is to be constructed **on the former site of the Crestwood Motel**. 이전에 크레스트우드 모텔이 있던 곳이다.	**Q** 크레스트우드 모텔에 대해 알 수 있는 것은? → It **no longer exists**. 추론: 현재는 존재하지 않는 건물이다.
In an effort to limit congestion in Morristown, the city council is planning changes in parking regulations. 모리스타운의 도로 혼잡을 통제하고자 한다.	**Q** 모리스타운에 대해 알 수 있는 것은? → It has a **traffic problem**. 추론: 모리스타운에는 교통 문제가 있다.
Bellam Pharmaceutical has an immediate opening for a laboratory manager at our South City location. 벨람 제약에서 매니저를 급구한다.	**Q** 벨람 제약에 대해 알 수 있는 것은? → It **hopes to quickly fill the position**. 추론: 공석을 빨리 채우고자 한다.
EDLP customers are given one month's notice if the current rate is expected to **rise by over 10 percent**. 10% 이상 요금 인상 시 고객은 고지를 받는다.	**Q** EDLP사에 대해 알 수 있는 것은? → It can increase rates **without notice**. 추론: 고지 없이 요금을 인상할 수도 있다. (10% 미만 인상 시)

Questions 1-4 refer to the following e-mail.

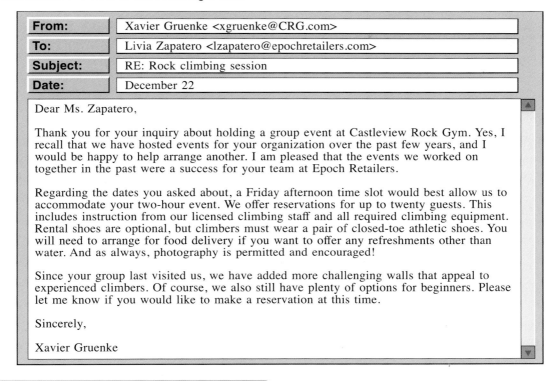

From:	Xavier Gruenke <xgruenke@CRG.com>
To:	Livia Zapatero <lzapatero@epochretailers.com>
Subject:	RE: Rock climbing session
Date:	December 22

Dear Ms. Zapatero,

Thank you for your inquiry about holding a group event at Castleview Rock Gym. Yes, I recall that we have hosted events for your organization over the past few years, and I would be happy to help arrange another. I am pleased that the events we worked on together in the past were a success for your team at Epoch Retailers.

Regarding the dates you asked about, a Friday afternoon time slot would best allow us to accommodate your two-hour event. We offer reservations for up to twenty guests. This includes instruction from our licensed climbing staff and all required climbing equipment. Rental shoes are optional, but climbers must wear a pair of closed-toe athletic shoes. You will need to arrange for food delivery if you want to offer any refreshments other than water. And as always, photography is permitted and encouraged!

Since your group last visited us, we have added more challenging walls that appeal to experienced climbers. Of course, we also still have plenty of options for beginners. Please let me know if you would like to make a reservation at this time.

Sincerely,

Xavier Gruenke

1. What is suggested about Ms. Zapatero?

(A) She has visited Castleview Rock Gym in the past.
(B) She was recently promoted to a new position.
(C) She is usually available for meetings on Friday afternoons.
(D) She is a retail sales manager for a recreational equipment company.

2. What does Castleview Rock Gym offer during group events?

(A) Rock-climbing instruction
(B) Discounts on climbing gear
(C) A group photograph
(D) A variety of refreshments

3. What is indicated about Castleview Rock Gym?

(A) It is open every day of the week.
(B) It employs a staff of twenty people.
(C) It can accommodate climbers with varying levels of ability.
(D) It will soon be closing temporarily for renovation work.

4. The phrase "appeal to" in paragraph 3, line 1, is closest in meaning to

(A) request
(B) attract
(C) provide
(D) organize

ETS 고득점 실전 문제

Questions 1-4 refer to the following article.

How Gunther Weinman Got Started

Thirty-five years ago, Gunther Weinman was the guitar player in a band, traveling around Europe in a bus. — [1] —. The band performed in small venues and never drew much of a following. Today Mr. Weinman is the head of Guwemus GmbH, a multimillion-dollar company that sells new and vintage recording equipment online.

— [2] —. When his band broke up, Mr. Weinman bought a house near Freiburg and moved in. Over time, he renovated the house and turned it into a recording studio where he recorded local musicians. — [3] —.

One day he received an emergency call from the famous jazz singer Gina Scotto, who needed a microphone for a local concert. "That was unexpected," recalled Mr. Weinman. "I was just the owner of a small studio." After visiting the studio, Ms. Scotto decided to record there. — [4] —. One album they made, *Whispers*, sold well and brought widespread recognition to Mr. Weinman's studio. Over time, Mr. Weinman recruited staff, set up a Web site, and became more involved in selling equipment online.

"Today we are the go-to source for many musicians and recording engineers," said Mr. Weinman.

1. What is suggested about Mr. Weinman?

   (A) He was a well-known guitar player.
   (B) He started playing music in his thirties.
   (C) He founded a company with his band members.
   (D) He started a business in his home.

2. What is NOT mentioned as a reason for Mr. Weinman's success?

   (A) Magazine advertising
   (B) The Internet
   (C) A remodeling project
   (D) A lucky encounter

3. What is implied about Ms. Scotto?

   (A) She sang with Mr. Weinman's first band.
   (B) She was successful before she met Mr. Weinman.
   (C) She expected Mr. Weinman's studio to be larger.
   (D) She recommended that Mr. Weinman sell items online.

4. In which of the positions marked [1], [2], [3], and [4] does the following sentence best belong?

   "He also became an expert at restoring vintage equipment."

   (A) [1]
   (B) [2]
   (C) [3]
   (D) [4]

Questions 5-8 refer to the following press release.

For Immediate Release | Contact: Mary Hannagan, 020 913 3000

KILLARNEY (8 August)—Killarney Property Ltd., a premier lodging development company headquartered in southwest Ireland, is pleased to announce the acquisition of ten currently vacant homes for future development.

The houses are located in various towns around the Ring of Kerry, a scenic drive in County Kerry. Each home will be renovated to create a small boutique hotel. The hotels will range in size from five to fifteen rooms and will open over the course of the next three years. When complete, the new hotels will employ over 100 local townspeople.

The Ring of Kerry's beautiful physical setting and charming small towns continue to draw an increasing number of tourists from around the world. Tourist traffic to the area continues to increase at a rate of approximately 7 percent per year.

By choosing to renovate smaller properties instead of building large hotels to accommodate the increased demand for lodging, Killarney Property Ltd. continues its tradition of developing accommodations that conform to the uniqueness of southwest Ireland without adversely affecting the area's charm.

For more information, contact Mary Hannagan, Director of Communications for Killarney Property Ltd., at 020 913 3000.

---

5. What is the press release about?

(A) The completion of a hotel
(B) The purchase of some properties
(C) The challenges of local vehicular traffic
(D) The increase of tourism to Irish cities

6. What is indicated about the new hotels?

(A) They will open at the same time.
(B) They will be built on vacant land.
(C) They will be completed over a period of three years.
(D) They will each have fifteen rooms.

7. The word "draw" in paragraph 3, line 2, is closest in meaning to

(A) attract
(B) design
(C) express
(D) prepare

8. What is suggested about Killarney Property Ltd.?

(A) It manages hotels in all regions of Ireland.
(B) It partners with local tourism agencies.
(C) It is looking to fill positions at its headquarters.
(D) It builds hotels that fit into the surroundings.

UNIT 20 동의어 문제

출제비율 1~5문제 / 54문항

출제 공식

1. 지문 내에 쓰인 단어가 문맥상 지니는 특정 뜻이 무엇인지 동의어로 고르는 문제 유형이다.
2. 동의어는 해당 단어를 의미상 대체할 수 있어야 하며, 구조상으로도 동일한 쓰임을 지녀야 한다.

문제 유형

■ The word "address" in paragraph 4, line 3, is closest in meaning to
네 번째 단락 3행의 'address'와 의미상 가장 가까운 단어는?

ETS 예제 **이메일**　　　　　　　　번역 p.192　　**풀이 전략**

Q. The word "due" in paragraph 1, line 8 is closest in meaning to

(A) billed
(B) considered
(C) owed
(D) scheduled

Dear Mr. Okamoto,

Congratulations on choosing a new residence in Cardiff. Your lease signing is scheduled for tomorrow, 29 March, at 9 A.M. It is a two-year lease starting in April. Please bring proof of employment (such as a pay stub), two forms of personal identification, and your current landlord's contact information. At the lease signing, be prepared to pay the real estate agent's fee to us and the security deposit to the landlord. Your first month's rent will be due on 1 April.

Please contact us with any questions.

Best,

Effix Homes

STEP 1 질문을 파악한다.

"due"의 동의어를 찾는 문제이다.

STEP 2 지문을 읽는다.

"due"가 포함된 문장 전체를 해석한다.

귀하의 첫 달 임대료는 4월 1일까지 **지불되어야 합니다.**

지문에서 "due"의 뜻: (돈을) 지불해야 하는

STEP 3 보기를 읽고 정답을 구한다.

Your first month's rent will be ------- on 1 April.

(A) billed 청구되는
(B) considered 고려되는
(C) owed 지불될 의무가 있는
(D) scheduled (for) ~로 예정된

(C) 귀하의 첫 달 임대료는 4월 1일까지 지불되어야 합니다.
→ 의미상, 구조상 due를 대체할 수 있는 owed를 정답으로 고른다.

빈출 동의어 리스트

address ❶ 다루다 ❷ 보내다
❶ deal with ❶ handle
❷ refer ❷ direct

cover ❶ 다루다 ❷ 대신하다 ❸ 충당하다
❶ address ❷ take over
❸ pay for

serve ❶ 제공하다 ❷ 일[기능]하다
❶ offer ❶ distribute
❷ work ❷ function

term ❶ 기간 ❷ 용어 ❸ 조건(-s)
❶ period ❶ duration
❷ word ❸ conditions

recognize ❶ 알아보다 ❷ 인정하다
❶ identify ❶ remember
❷ honor ❷ acknowledge

mark ❶ 표시하다 ❷ 기념하다
❶ write ❶ indicate
❷ celebrate

keep ❶ 보관하다 ❷ 계속[유지]하다
❶ retain ❶ store
❷ continue ❷ maintain

measure ❶ 조치 ❷ 척도
❶ action ❶ step
❷ standard ❷ criteria

hold ❶ 갖다 ❷ 개최하다 ❸ 간주하다
❶ keep ❷ possess
❷ host ❸ consider

ETS 유형 연습

Questions 1-4 refer to the following e-mail.

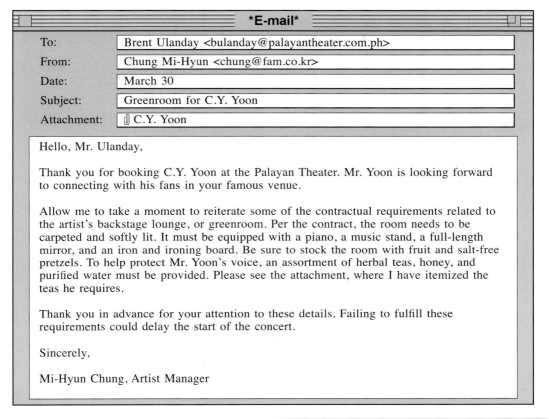

To:	Brent Ulanday <bulanday@palayantheater.com.ph>
From:	Chung Mi-Hyun <chung@fam.co.kr>
Date:	March 30
Subject:	Greenroom for C.Y. Yoon
Attachment:	🖉 C.Y. Yoon

E-mail

Hello, Mr. Ulanday,

Thank you for booking C.Y. Yoon at the Palayan Theater. Mr. Yoon is looking forward to connecting with his fans in your famous venue.

Allow me to take a moment to reiterate some of the contractual requirements related to the artist's backstage lounge, or greenroom. Per the contract, the room needs to be carpeted and softly lit. It must be equipped with a piano, a music stand, a full-length mirror, and an iron and ironing board. Be sure to stock the room with fruit and salt-free pretzels. To help protect Mr. Yoon's voice, an assortment of herbal teas, honey, and purified water must be provided. Please see the attachment, where I have itemized the teas he requires.

Thank you in advance for your attention to these details. Failing to fulfill these requirements could delay the start of the concert.

Sincerely,

Mi-Hyun Chung, Artist Manager

---

1. Why did Ms. Chung send Mr. Ulanday the e-mail?

(A) To request tickets for an upcoming event
(B) To inquire about a change in venue
(C) To remind him of the terms of an agreement
(D) To praise him for his management skills

2. Who most likely is Mr. Yoon?

(A) A singer
(B) A comedian
(C) A dancer
(D) A violinist

3. The word "softly" in paragraph 2, line 3, is closest in meaning to

(A) patiently
(B) gently
(C) easily
(D) smoothly

4. What did Ms. Chung send along with the e-mail?

(A) A list
(B) A contract
(C) A schedule
(D) A résumé

Questions 1-3 refer to the following Web page.

http://www.wellesbeachwear.com.au/shippingpolicy

Our Shipping Policy

Welles Beachwear offers express overnight shipping to some cities in Australia and New Zealand. In these areas, orders that are placed on our Web site before 10:00 P.M. will be delivered the next business day. Express shipping is not available for other destinations in Australia and New Zealand, as Welles Beachwear cannot guarantee delivery speed. International shipping is available for orders bound for Southeast Asia. Please see the table below for details.

Destination	Express/Delivery Time	Standard/Delivery Time
Australia (Adelaide, Brisbane, Melbourne, Perth, Sydney)	$9.95/Next day	FREE/3 business days
New Zealand (Auckland, Christchurch, Wellington)	$10.95/Next day	FREE/3 business days
Australia and New Zealand (other areas)	Not available	$7.95/5 business days
Southeast Asia	Not available	$15.95 and up/ 7–10 business days

1. What is NOT indicated about Welles Beachwear?

   (A) It is recruiting delivery drivers.
   (B) It ships to some areas at no cost.
   (C) It offers overnight shipping to some locations.
   (D) Its standard delivery time varies by region.

2. The word "placed" in paragraph 1, line 2, is closest in meaning to

   (A) ranked
   (B) submitted
   (C) mentioned
   (D) positioned

3. What is the minimum cost to send an order to Southeast Asia?

   (A) $7.95
   (B) $9.95
   (C) $10.95
   (D) $15.95

Questions 4-7 refer to the following e-mail.

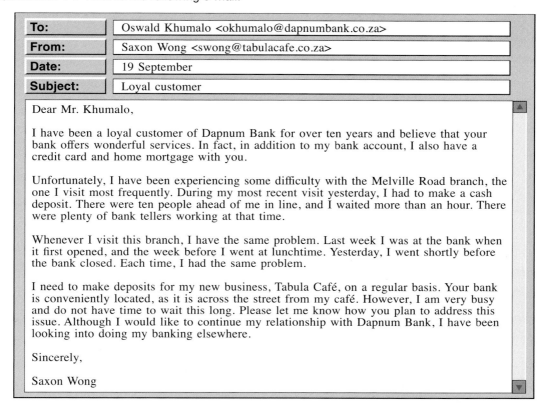

To:	Oswald Khumalo <okhumalo@dapnumbank.co.za>
From:	Saxon Wong <swong@tabulacafe.co.za>
Date:	19 September
Subject:	Loyal customer

Dear Mr. Khumalo,

I have been a loyal customer of Dapnum Bank for over ten years and believe that your bank offers wonderful services. In fact, in addition to my bank account, I also have a credit card and home mortgage with you.

Unfortunately, I have been experiencing some difficulty with the Melville Road branch, the one I visit most frequently. During my most recent visit yesterday, I had to make a cash deposit. There were ten people ahead of me in line, and I waited more than an hour. There were plenty of bank tellers working at that time.

Whenever I visit this branch, I have the same problem. Last week I was at the bank when it first opened, and the week before I went at lunchtime. Yesterday, I went shortly before the bank closed. Each time, I had the same problem.

I need to make deposits for my new business, Tabula Café, on a regular basis. Your bank is conveniently located, as it is across the street from my café. However, I am very busy and do not have time to wait this long. Please let me know how you plan to address this issue. Although I would like to continue my relationship with Dapnum Bank, I have been looking into doing my banking elsewhere.

Sincerely,

Saxon Wong

4. What does Mr. Wong find disappointing about Dapnum Bank?

(A) The inadequate number of employees
(B) The long wait times
(C) The rates on his credit card
(D) The limited hours of operation

5. When did Mr. Wong visit the Melville Road branch on September 18 ?

(A) Right after it opened
(B) At lunchtime
(C) In the middle of the afternoon
(D) Just before it closed

6. What is suggested about Tabula Café?

(A) It has been in business for ten years.
(B) It is owned by Mr. Wong.
(C) It is popular with Dapnum Bank customers.
(D) It is next door to Dapnum Bank.

7. The word "address" in paragraph 4, line 3, is closest in meaning to

(A) send
(B) label
(C) deal with
(D) talk about

UNIT 21 의도 파악 문제

● 출제비율 2문제/54문항

출제 공식

1. 문자 메시지와 온라인 채팅 지문에서 각 1문항씩 출제된다.
2. 특정 인물이 특정 문장을 어떤 의도로 썼는지 파악하는 문제로, 대화자들 간의 관계 및 주어진 상황에 대한 종합적 이해를 바탕으로 문제 풀이에 접근해야 한다.

문제 유형

■ At 9:40 A.M., what does Mr. Valerio most likely mean when he writes, "I can't tell"?
오전 9시 40분에 발레리오 씨가 "말씀드릴 수 없어요"라고 쓴 의도는?

ETS 예제 **문자 메시지**   번역 p.194   **풀이 전략**

Q. At 11:40 A.M., what does Ms. Ng most likely mean when she writes, "You can't miss it"?

(A) She does not want Mr. Hovakimyan to leave.
(B) She wants Mr. Hovakimyan to join her for lunch.
(C) The balloon is very easy to find.
(D) A presentation will be interesting

Armen Hovakimyan [11:38 A.M.]
Hi Jun. I just got into the convention center. It's huge! So many vehicles! Reggie asked me to bring over some more brochures. Where's our booth?

Jun Ng [11:40 A.M.]
I'm glad you're here. We're getting a lot of interest in the new electric sedan. The booth is in Aisle M. From the front doors, turn left, go straight ahead, then turn right at the giant balloon that looks like a Virit oil bottle. You can't miss it. I'm all the way in the back toward the food stalls.

Armen Hovakimyan [11:42 A.M.]
Thanks. Be right there.

STEP 1 질문을 파악한다.

문자 메시지에서 "You can't miss it"이라고 쓴 의도를 파악하는 문제이다.

STEP 2 지문을 읽는다.

인물 관계와 상황을 고려하여 해당 문장을 해석한다.

> 왼쪽으로 돌아서 직진한 후 대형 풍선이 있는 곳에서 우측으로 돌아요. **찾기 쉬워요.**

STEP 3 해석과 일치하는 보기를 고른다.

(C) 풍선을 찾기 아주 쉽다.
→ 동료에게 특정 장소로 찾아오는 길을 안내하면서 건넨 말이므로, 길을 찾는 것이 어렵지 않다는 의도로 한 말임을 알 수 있다.

빈출 구어체 표현

That works. 그거 괜찮네요.	**No need.** 그럴 필요 없어요.	**That will do.** 그거면 돼요.
Got it. 알겠습니다.	**I doubt it.** 그렇지 않을 걸요.	**That's a relief.** 다행이네요.
Will do. 그렇게 하겠습니다.	**Not necessarily.** 꼭 그렇진 않아요.	**Good to know.** 다행이네요.
Sure thing. 물론입니다.	**Don't bother.** 안 그래도 돼요.	**Keep me posted.** 소식 주세요.
No question about it. 당연하죠.	**Not really.** 그다지요.	**It can't be helped.** 어쩔 수 없어요.
That makes sense. 일리 있네요.	**I can't make it.** 못 해[가]요.	**Same here.** 저도 마찬가지예요.

Questions 1-4 refer to the following online chat discussion.

> **Florence Clark, 10:30 A.M.** I'm sorry I had to change our usual chat time. I'm leaving for a conference in Paris in two hours. Jae-Ho, can you give us an update on our advertising campaign?
>
> **Jae-Ho Kong, 10:33 A.M.** Yes. As you know, we've expanded our advertising presence on several platforms—print, social media, and Internet. It seems to be working nicely. Our pool of listeners is growing.
>
> **Florence Clark, 10:34 A.M.** Well, that's good news. Anna, can you tell the others about some of the new shows that are in development?
>
> **Anna Goswami, 10:36 A.M.** Sure. We have a new show that will debut on Saturday morning. It features news, followed by a listener call-in segment. Also, do you remember Trina Thompson, who hosted the short-lived *Everything Under the Sun* show? She's doing a new program now, *Thompson, Take Two*. We've also expanded our Sunday folk music afternoons to two hours. Esmond might be able to tell you more about that.
>
> **Esmond Seco, 10:40 A.M.** Yes, definitely. I'm actually writing up some notes now with all the details about what the extra hour will involve: production costs, schedules, and so on. I'll e-mail it out to all of you later today.
>
> **Florence Clark, 10:42 A.M.** OK. Well, I'm going to wrap up the meeting then, so I can head out to the airport and catch my plane. I'll talk to all of you in two weeks.

1. For what type of business do the chat participants most likely work?

(A) A travel agency
(B) A theater company
(C) A radio station
(D) An advertising firm

2. What does Mr. Kong indicate to the others about their business?

(A) It is in the process of revising its Web page.
(B) It is becoming more popular.
(C) It has corrected a computer problem.
(D) It is expanding to other countries.

3. Who most likely is Ms. Thompson?

(A) The host of a new show
(B) A call center employee
(C) A folk musician
(D) A writer for a newspaper

4. At 10:40 A.M., what does Mr. Seco most likely mean when he writes, "Yes, definitely"?

(A) He is sure that Ms. Goswami's information is correct.
(B) He believes that he can have his work completed on time.
(C) He is willing to do one of Ms. Clark's tasks while she is away.
(D) He is confident that he can provide information to the others.

PART 7

UNIT 21

Questions 1-4 refer to the following text-message chain.

> **Thea Gibb (2:31 P.M.)** Hi, Desmond and Clerio. The Auto Renters' Association conference is coming up in two weeks. We'd better get moving and order the promotional fliers we'll be handing out.
>
> **Desmond Brower (2:33 P.M.)** Hi, Thea. That's right, we didn't finish discussing it during our Monday call. Which flier would you like to use this year?
>
> **Clerio Cardoso (2:34 P.M.)** Do we know how many fliers we'll need?
>
> **Desmond Brower (2:36 P.M.)** Not yet. When I get back to the office tomorrow, I'll call the association's conference planner to see how many people have registered. Then I'll add another 5 percent for latecomers.
>
> **Thea Gibb (2:38 P.M.)** For this year's conference, let's use the brochures with the foldout map showing all six of our car rental locations. Once you determine how many fliers we'll need, could one of you reach out to Orson's again for an estimate? Also, let's see if we can get a better price from them than we got last year.
>
> **Clerio Cardoso (2:40 P.M.)** Sure, I'll do that. And I'll get estimates from at least two other printing firms as well.
>
> **Thea Gibb (2:44 P.M.)** That makes sense. Please also see if the fliers can be shipped directly to the conference center by March 3. Otherwise one of you will have to pick them up and bring them to the conference on your own.

1. Where do the writers most likely work?

(A) At a public-relations firm

(B) At a car-rental company

(C) At a printing shop

(D) At a conference center

2. What is probably true about Mr. Brower?

(A) He intends to register for a conference.

(B) He is currently out of the office.

(C) He is Ms. Gibb's supervisor.

(D) He designed a brochure.

3. What is indicated about Orson's?

(A) It will be closed for inventory on March 3.

(B) It is planning to host a conference.

(C) It printed items for the writers last year.

(D) It offers a free delivery service.

4. At 2:44 P.M., what does Ms. Gibb most likely mean when she writes, "That makes sense"?

(A) She supports a decision that was made on Monday.

(B) She likes the idea of enlarging the foldout map.

(C) She wants Mr. Cardoso and Mr. Brower to visit Orson's together.

(D) She approves of Mr. Cardoso's plan to compare prices.

Questions 5-8 refer to the following online chat discussion.

   — □ X

Carissa Wright [8:55 A.M.]
Hello, Jarren. Did you get the file I sent? It's a photo I took of the new city hall. Mayor Diforio would like it printed as large as possible. It's for the lobby of her office.

Jarren Smith [8:57 A.M.]
Hi, Carissa. Yes, I did. I noticed that the image file is small, with a resolution that would be best at 8 by 10 inches. But I should be able to make the image bigger without losing too much quality.

Carissa Wright [8:58 A.M.]
Thanks. What do you propose?

Jarren Smith [9:00 A.M.]
I'll see what I can do, but I think that I can enlarge it to 16 by 20 inches without making the print blurry. I also think that using matte photographic paper would be best so that there will be no glare. I could have that ready by tomorrow afternoon.

Carissa Wright [9:02 A.M.]
What about a frame? We'd like to have it framed.

Jarren Smith [9:03 A.M.]
Framing will take a little longer. I would choose a black, two-inch-wide wood frame, something simple so as not to distract from the photo itself. I'll let you know when it's finished.

Carissa Wright [9:04 A.M.]
Thanks. I'll pick it up when you let me know that it's ready.

5. What most likely is Mr. Smith's job?
(A) Architectural photographer
(B) Professional printer
(C) Property manager
(D) Commercial builder

6. At 8:58 A.M., what does Ms. Wright most likely want to know when she writes, "What do you propose?"
(A) How large Mr. Smith can make the photo
(B) Where in the lobby to hang the photo
(C) How she should send a file
(D) If she should put something else in the lobby

7. Why does Mr. Smith want to use matte photographic paper?
(A) It enhances contrast.
(B) It has a pearl-like texture.
(C) It does not cause glare.
(D) It does not require special handling.

8. What does Mr. Smith suggest about framing?
(A) It will not take extra time.
(B) It would not be a good idea.
(C) A basic frame would be best.
(D) An extra-large frame will cost more.

문장 삽입 문제

🍀 출제비율 2문제/54문항

출제 공식
1. 3문제 또는 4문제가 딸린 지문에서 마지막 문제로 등장한다.
2. 제시문을 주고 지문에서 문맥상 제시문이 들어가기에 적합한 위치를 찾는 문제 유형이다.

문제 유형
- In which of the positions marked [1], [2], [3], and [4] does the following sentence best belong?
  "The package was perfect for our needs."
  [1], [2], [3], [4]로 표시된 곳 중에서 다음 문장이 들어가기에 가장 적합한 위치는?
  "해당 패키지는 우리의 요구 조건에 완벽히 맞았습니다."

ETS 예제 **이메일**
번역 p.197
풀이 전략

Q. In which of the positions marked [1], [2], [3], and [4]
does the following sentence best belong?

"Your merchandise is now estimated to arrive on Friday,
October 28."

(A) [1]   (B) [2]   (C) [3]   (D) [4]

Dear Ms. Crispin,

Thank you for your bulk order of computer parts, reference
number 88426. We had originally promised delivery
on Friday, October 14. We regret to inform you that
this shipment has been delayed. —[1]—. We sincerely
apologize for the inconvenience.

We understand how important on-time delivery is to your
business and we have refunded your shipping fee for this
order. —[2]—. We would also like to offer you a discount of
25 percent off your next purchase. —[3]—.

Thank you for choosing Raymer as your computer
hardware supplier. —[4]—.

STEP 1 질문에서 주어진 제시문을 해석한다.
"귀하의 상품은 10월 28일 금요일에 도착할 것으로 현재 예상됩니다."

STEP 2 지문을 읽으면서 제시문과 관련된 내용을 찾는다.
배송일을 언급하는 부분을 정독한다.

원래는 **10월 14일** 배송을 약속 드렸으나, 유감스럽게도 **해당 배송이 지연**되었음을 알려드립니다.

STEP 3 제시문을 삽입하여 앞뒤 해석을 검토한다.
[1] 앞에서 원래의 배송일과 배송 지연에 대해 언급했으므로, 제시문을 [1]에 삽입하면 뒤따르는 사과 문장과 자연스럽게 연결된다.

제시문 속 빈출 단서

also "Vacationers will **also** benefit."	피서객들 **또한** 이득입니다. → 이득을 누리는 다른 집단 뒤에 위치
인칭 대명사 "**It** must be replaced."	**그것은** 교체되어야 합니다. → 교체할 단수 사물 명사 뒤에 위치
정관사, 지시어 "We e-mailed you in May about **this** increase."	5월에 **이** 인상에 대해 이메일을 보냈습니다. → 인상을 언급하는 문장 뒤에 위치
접속부사 "**To that end**, the company has invested $100,000."	**이를 위해**, 회사는 10만 달러를 투자했습니다. → 투자의 목적을 기술한 문장 뒤에 위치

ETS 유형 연습

Questions 1-4 refer to the following letter.

8 February

Denise Darrel
Highland Mills Associates
Route 41
Crawford Bay, BC V0B 1B0

Dear Ms. Darrel,

Thank you for meeting with me about the commercial cleaning needs at Highland Mills Associates. It was a pleasure to learn more about your firm. — [1] —.

During our meeting, you expressed concerns about your current cleaning service. — [2] —. I have taken careful note of these matters, which we would address.

We pride ourselves on providing excellent service at a fair price. That is why we offer the Clean Ways guarantee: if you are not satisfied with our work, we will make it right at no extra cost to you. — [3] —.

• We use the safest and highest-quality detergents and other cleaning supplies.

• We will send the same cleaning crew on each visit.

• We will regularly follow up with you by phone or in person.

I am happy to provide you with recommendations from current Clean Ways clients. — [4] —. To make any changes to the enclosed proposal, please contact me. You can reach me at my office number at 565-555-0175.

Sincerely,
Tristen Corey

Enclosure

1. What is the purpose of the letter?

   (A) To confirm a new project
   (B) To announce a job opening
   (C) To describe a service
   (D) To request a meeting

2. What is suggested about Ms. Darrel?

   (A) She is managing a new building.
   (B) She is considering changing a service provider.
   (C) She has just received a promotion.
   (D) She is opening a new company in Crawford Bay.

3. What is indicated about Clean Ways?

   (A) It maintains the same team assignment at client locations.
   (B) It provides 24-hour customer support.
   (C) It charges extra for the use of special cleaning supplies.
   (D) It cleans homes and apartments.

4. In which of the positions marked [1], [2], [3], and [4] does the following sentence best belong?

   "Several are long-term customers with high-profile businesses in the area."

   (A) [1]
   (B) [2]
   (C) [3]
   (D) [4]

ETS 고득점 실전 문제

Questions 1-4 refer to the following contract.

Contract between Meuleman Construction, Inc., and the Southeast Regional Association of Builders (SRAB)

I. This is a binding contract between Meuleman Construction, Inc., and the Southeast Regional Association of Builders (SRAB), by which Meuleman Construction enrolls in the SRAB with all commensurate rights and responsibilities. —[1]—. The terms of this contract shall apply to all building projects undertaken by Meuleman Construction in the Southeast region.

II. In all applicable projects, Meuleman Construction agrees to use only those materials authorized by the SRAB. —[2]—. Complete lists of authorized materials for residential and commercial projects are listed in Appendices A and B, respectively. —[3]—. The purpose of these restricted lists is to promote a high level of quality in all building projects, thereby reducing the number and frequency of repair and maintenance issues.

III. Meuleman Construction and the SRAB agree that revisions to either list of authorized materials may be necessary or desirable in the future. Changes in materials technology and safety developments may be cited by either party for this purpose. —[4]—. The process for proposing and negotiating a revision to this contract is outlined in Appendix C.

---

1. What is the relationship between Meuleman Construction and the SRAB?

   (A) The SRAB is a client of Meuleman Construction.
   (B) The SRAB and Meuleman Construction recently merged.
   (C) Meuleman Construction is a supplier for the SRAB.
   (D) Meuleman Construction is a member of the SRAB.

2. According to the contract, what does Meuleman Construction agree to do for each of its projects?

   (A) Use only certain types or brands of materials
   (B) Offer a guarantee on the quality of the work done
   (C) Give a discount to businesses in the Southeast region
   (D) Cover the costs of all repair or maintenance issues

3. What might lead to a change to the contract?

   (A) If the price of building materials rises dramatically
   (B) If a new technology in building materials is developed
   (C) If a project is not completed by a stated deadline
   (D) If the region is affected by adverse weather conditions

4. In which of the positions marked [1], [2], [3], and [4] does the following sentence best belong?

   "New government regulations may also be a valid reason."

   (A) [1]
   (B) [2]
   (C) [3]
   (D) [4]

276

Questions 5-8 refer to the following article.

Easing Commutes

A recent survey by Keats Research revealed that the average daily round-trip commute in Holden now tops an hour and a half. Many workers arrive at their job exhausted from their journey and irritated about the cost of commuting. These long commutes lead to lower employee productivity, decreased job satisfaction, and a high turnover rate. — [1] —. Consequently, many companies are looking for ways to ease employees' rough commutes.

Telecommuting is one possible solution. An increasing number of businesses have been allowing employees to work from home a few days a week. — [2] —. This is worthwhile for everyone. Eliminating long, stressful commutes leads to employees starting the workday relaxed. This results in increased productivity and a reduction in absenteeism.

Another solution is carpools. By reducing the number of vehicles on the road, carpools can reduce overall traffic, resulting in shorter commute times for all. Employees can also decrease their personal commuting costs and arrive at work feeling less stressed. Companies can also choose to organize low-cost carpools for employees who need to work on-site. — [3] —.

One more way to ease commutes is allowing employees to work on-site during nontraditional hours. This option can significantly cut commuting times by getting workers off the road during rush hour.

Not all companies are able to implement changes that will help reduce commuting times. — [4] —. However, for those that can, the recent survey results may provide additional incentives to make adjustments sooner rather than later.

5. What is one purpose of the article?

(A) To promote new technology
(B) To discuss the results of a study
(C) To highlight changes in traffic patterns
(D) To report an increase in worker productivity

6. What does the article suggest about many workers in Holden?

(A) They often report late to work.
(B) They disagree with the results of a survey.
(C) They are buying more economical vehicles.
(D) They arrive at work already feeling tired.

7. What is NOT mentioned in the article as a way to improve commutes?

(A) Offering discounted tickets for public transportation
(B) Allowing employees to work from home
(C) Scheduling different work hours
(D) Arranging carpools

8. In which of the positions marked [1], [2], [3], and [4] does the following sentence best belong?

"To make this arrangement succeed, employees need a good Internet connection at home."

(A) [1]
(B) [2]
(C) [3]
(D) [4]

PART 7

UNIT 22

UNIT 23 연계 문제

🕐 출제비율 8~10문제/54문항

출제 공식

1. 이중지문과 삼중지문에서 출제되며, 두 지문의 정보를 조합하여 하나의 정보를 도출해 내는 유형이다.
   이중지문에서는 세트당 총 1~2문제, 삼중지문에서는 세트당 2문제가 연계로 출제된다.
2. 추론 유형의 문제와 단답형 보기로 이루어진 문제는 연계 문제일 가능성이 높다.

문제 유형

■ What position requirement might Ms. Nora NOT meet?
노라 씨가 충족하지 못하는 업무 자격 요건은?

지문 1: 노라 씨는 3년 경력이 있다.⌐
지문 2: 5년 이상 경력자 지원 가능 ⌐ → **정답: 경력**

ETS 예제 **공지 + 이메일**   번역 p.200   **풀이 전략**

Q. Which event is Mr. Durbin most likely attending? •-------

(A) Sibley Springs Orchestra
(B) Lorenz Choral Ensemble
(C) Midland Jazz Trio •
(D) Ada Youth Symphony

Upcoming Events at Hartford Hall
Sibley Springs Orchestra – Friday, 14 February, 7:30 P.M.
Lorenz Choral Ensemble – Sunday, 23 February, 6:00 P.M.
Midland Jazz Trio – Thursday, 12 March, 8:00 P.M. •
Ada Youth Symphony – Saturday, 28 March, 2:00 P.M.
Vehicle parking for Hartford Hall events is now
available at a new parking garage.
– 후략 –

To: parking@hartfordhall.au
From: michaeld@netserve.au
Date: Wednesday, 11 March •
Subject: Request
Dear Mr. Jamison,
I am attending an event at Hartford Hall tomorrow night. •
I would like to request a special permit to park behind the
building. – 중략 –
Thank you for your assistance,
Michael Durbin

STEP 1 질문에서 주어진 제시문을 해석한다.

더빈 씨가 참석할 것 같은 행사를 묻는 문제이다.

STEP 2 지문을 읽는다.

첫 번째 지문에는 행사 일정이 나열되어 있다.

> 2월 14일 – 시블리 스프링스 오케스트라
> 2월 23일 – 로렌츠 합창 앙상블
> **3월 12일 – 미들랜드 재즈 트리오**
> 3월 28일 – 에이더 청소년 심포니

→ 해당 지문의 정보만으로는 질문에 답을 할 수 없으므로
   두 번째 지문으로 넘어간다.

> 날짜: **3월 11일 수요일**
> 저는 내일 밤 하트퍼드 강당에서 열리는 행사에 참석할
> 예정입니다.

STEP 3 두 정보를 조합해서 정답을 구한다.

이메일을 쓴 날이 3월 11일이고, 내일 있을 행사에
참석한다고 했으므로 3월 12일자 행사인 (C) 미들랜드
재즈 트리오가 정답이다.

ETS 연계 문제 출제 패턴

◆ 이중 지문 연계

> 서비스 센터는 주말에 오전 9시에서 오후 1시까지 정상 영업합니다.

+

> 저는 서비스 센터가 문을 여는 시간에 도착했습니다.

질문 데이브 씨가 서비스 센터에 도착한 시간은? → 오전 9시

> 회사 차량 이용 시 주유비는 따로 지급되지 않습니다.

+

> 숙박: 100달러   식비: 80달러
> 교통비(주유): 45달러

질문 앤더슨 씨가 환급받지 못하는 금액은? → 45달러

◆ 삼중 지문 연계

> 색상 및 모델명:
> 골드(TP21)
> 실버(TP22)
> 블랙(TP23)

+

> 조립에 필요한 부품:
> 상판: 1개 서랍: 2개
> 지지대: 4개
> 조립용 나사: 14개

+

> 블랙, 골드가 품절이라 아쉬웠다. 15개들이 나사 케이스가 자석이라 나사 분실 염려가 덜했다.

질문 1 후기 작성자는 어떤 모델을 구매했겠는가? → TP22
질문 2 조립 후 남았을 것 같은 부품은? → 나사

> 신제품 '프로팅'은 식약청의 승인 심사를 앞두고 있다.

+

> 다음 달 출시 예정인 '프로팅' 홍보를 위한 야간 임시직 모집

+

> 임시직 지원자: 조던
> 오전, 주말 근무 가능

질문 1 '프로팅'에 대해 알 수 있는 것은? → 식약청의 승인을 받았다.
질문 2 지원자의 결격 사유는? → 야간 근무가 불가능하다.

> 강좌명 / 강사
> 〈자산관리〉 J. 에밀리
> 〈부동산〉 M. 미아
> 〈아웃소싱〉 K. 브라운

+

> 제나 씨께,
> 미아 씨의 강좌가 연기되었습니다. 변경된 주차권을 동봉합니다.

+

> 일일 주차권
> 구역: B4
> 일시: 5월 21일
> 오전 10시~오후 12시

질문 1 제나 씨는 어떤 강좌를 신청했는가? → 부동산
질문 2 변경된 강의일은 언제이겠는가? → 5월 21일

Questions 1-5 refer to the following advertisement and contract.

Image Bonanza

Do you need attention-grabbing photographs to use on your Web site? Do you want to stop dealing with copyright restrictions and high fees? Come to Image Bonanza! We let you bypass the hassle and instantly liven up your online blogs, ads, and articles with top-quality stock photos.

We offer a variety of fixed-term, low-cost licenses that accommodate a wide range of project needs without breaking your budget. All photos on our site are ready for immediate download and can be purchased individually or as part of a package.

Customers who purchase an annual subscription receive special offers and benefits, including unlimited licenses that never expire. And first-time customers receive FIVE free photos with a minimum purchase of ten photos. Details are available on our Web order form.

Browse our inventory. You'll be dazzled by our selection.

LICENSE AGREEMENT

The following license terms are hereby granted by **Image Bonanza LLC** to **Caspar Oudsten** ("Buyer") for the use of images marketed by Image Bonanza. All uses of these images must comply with these terms.

1. Grant of Rights. Upon full payment of the license fee, Image Bonanza grants the Buyer the right to use the images listed in the attached invoice. The images may be used in non-commercial and commercial contexts, including digital advertisements. Use in television or film is not granted by this license. The Buyer is granted the right to edit the image, including cropping, adapting color, and adding text.

2. Term of License (check one).

_____ The above rights are granted for a period of _____ year(s), starting from the date that full payment is received.

___✓___ The above rights are granted permanently, starting from the date that full payment is received and with no end date.

1. Who would most likely be a customer of Image Bonanza?

   (A) A professional photographer
   (B) A copyright lawyer
   (C) A Web site developer
   (D) A video streaming service

2. What is NOT mentioned as a reason to purchase items from Image Bonanza?

   (A) They can be used right away.
   (B) They are affordably priced.
   (C) They can be purchased as part of a package.
   (D) They feature people from around the world.

3. In the advertisement, the word "accommodate" in paragraph 2, line 1, is closest in meaning to

   (A) have room for
   (B) are appropriate for
   (C) are necessary to
   (D) become accustomed to

4. According to the contract, what can the buyer do with the images?

   (A) Make changes to them
   (B) Sell them to a third party
   (C) Display them on television
   (D) Transfer them to film

5. What can be inferred about Mr. Oudsten's relationship with Image Bonanza?

   (A) He is a first-time customer.
   (B) He is an annual subscriber.
   (C) He is a full-time employee.
   (D) He is a freelance photographer.

IBI Sets Sights on Lewis City

LEWIS CITY (April 22)—Invarta Bicycles, Inc. (IBI), based in Smithville, will be opening its first location in Lewis City. Like its Smithville location, the new store will offer several popular brands of bicycles and bicycle accessories. Its grand opening is scheduled for August 15.

"Our market research has shown that residents in and around Lewis City are avid bicyclists, so opening a location here made perfect sense," noted Audra Laflaye, the CEO of IBI, following a meeting with local city officials.

It is, therefore, by design rather than by accident that the new IBI facility will be located right next to the Parales Greenway. The area boasts an extensive cycling path that connects several suburban areas with the city's business district.

While IBI will be moving its headquarters from Smithville to Lewis, the Smithville location will remain in business.

Lewis City
Tracts Zoned for Retail Use
Note: each tract is 300 meters x 600 meters (three standard city blocks)

Waterfront Street

| Public Rail Station | Tract A | Tract B | Tract C | Tract D | Parales Greenway |

Maple Street

Invarta Bicycles, Inc.
Invitation

Join us for the grand opening of our new location on September 15 from 12:00 noon to 5:00 P.M. at 28 Maple Street.

Mayor Osman Yusuf, IBI's CEO Audra Laflaye, and Mr. Kwame Alcindor, president of IBI's employees association, will be addressing the audience.

Complimentary coffee, tea, juice, and snacks will be served throughout the event. The first 100 guests will receive a free water bottle.

Guests will also have the opportunity to take part in our three-kilometer bike challenge on the nearby bike paths, with challenges being held every thirty minutes. The participant posting the fastest time in any given challenge will receive a premium bicycle backpack.

6. According to the article, what does IBI specialize in?

   (A) Bicycle tours
   (B) Bicycle manufacturing
   (C) The sale of bicycles
   (D) The construction of bicycle pathways

7. What is indicated in the article about IBI's Smithville location?

   (A) It will soon be closing permanently.
   (B) It is located near a popular park.
   (C) It is currently the company's headquarters.
   (D) It is the most profitable store.

8. In what tract will the new IBI facility be located?

   (A) Tract A
   (B) Tract B
   (C) Tract C
   (D) Tract D

9. What is indicated on the map?

   (A) All of the tracts have access to Waterfront Street.
   (B) Some tracts are larger than others.
   (C) The rail station is located next to the Parales Greenway.
   (D) An apartment complex will be built on Maple Street.

10. What will happen at the grand opening of the new store?

   (A) Live entertainment will be provided.
   (B) Some guests will ride bicycles on the Parales Greenway.
   (C) Refreshments and snacks will be sold.
   (D) A lottery drawing will be held every hour.

Questions 1-5 refer to the following e-mails.

To:	pkoutrakis@kic.com
From:	bghosh@rhonesystems.com
Subject:	Meeting Follow-Up
Date:	May 4, 6:49 P.M.

Dear Mr. Koutrakis,

It was a pleasure to meet you this morning to discuss your interest in retaining Rhone Systems to provide computer support services to Koutrakis Insurance Company.

You expressed interest in our Silver Service Plan, which comes with automatic updates for your software programs. Additionally, it allows for on-site biannual cleaning of your equipment and on-site as well as remote support service. The subscription fee for this plan is $45 per month, or $540 annually. As we currently have a special promotion going on, we are pleased to offer you a one-year contract instead of our typical contract term of 18 months. Moreover, accept this offer by May 6 and you will receive a $10 discount on your monthly subscription fee for the duration of the contract. Should you opt for an annual subscription, you will receive a one-time reduction of $120.

Sincerely,

Bishnupada Ghosh
Senior Sales Representative, Rhone Systems

E-mail

To:	bghosh@rhonesystems.com
From:	pkoutrakis@kic.com
Re:	Meeting Follow-Up
Date:	May 8, 8:31 A.M.

Dear Mr. Ghosh,

My apologies for my delayed response. Shortly after meeting with you, I was unexpectedly called away for an urgent matter. Unfortunately, during that time I had no access to the Internet.

I have decided on an annual subscription of the Silver Plan. Please accept my gratitude for extending the promotion deadline. In our meeting you had also mentioned that you could cover an additional location within 20 miles of our main office for free. Since our satellite office is 21 miles from our main office, we were wondering if it could be included in the agreement. Finally, we'd like to increase the cloud storage by 50 gigabytes per month. I understand that doing so would not result in any additional costs. Please let me know your position on these matters.

Sincerely,

Peter Koutrakis
President, Koutrakis Insurance Company

1. What does the first e-mail indicate about Mr. Ghosh?

   (A) He spoke to Mr. Koutrakis over the phone.
   (B) He has been a Rhone Systems employee for 18 years.
   (C) He manages the help desk at Rhone Systems.
   (D) He is making Mr. Koutrakis a special offer.

2. According to the first e-mail, what is NOT included in the Silver Service Plan?

   (A) Software upgrades
   (B) Data recovery
   (C) Equipment cleaning
   (D) Remote assistance

3. What is a reason why Mr. Koutrakis wrote to Mr. Ghosh?

   (A) To update contact information
   (B) To request a contract extension
   (C) To continue negotiations
   (D) To confirm a meeting

4. In the second e-mail, the word "cover" in paragraph 2, line 3, is closest in meaning to

   (A) pay for
   (B) report on
   (C) take the place of
   (D) provide services to

5. What is suggested about Mr. Koutrakis?

   (A) He missed a deadline.
   (B) He opted for a different plan.
   (C) He generally prefers annual subscriptions.
   (D) He had declined the cloud storage feature at first.

Questions 6-10 refer to the following e-mail and testimonial.

To:	sdurance@caffeystudio.net
From:	customerrelations@orbdesignsoftware.com
Date:	October 5
Subject:	Orb Graphic Design Tool

Dear Ms. Durance:

I received your online form requesting more information about the Orb graphic design tool. This tool makes it easy to create professional-looking documents, presentations, and marketing materials. One of the best things about the tool is that no graphic design experience is required. Our layout templates and drag-and-drop editing feature allow anyone to create attractive documents with very little effort.

Here is an overview of the account types we offer.

Basic, $0. For individual use only. Account holders receive one folder for organizing designs, access to hundreds of design templates, and a database of free stock images.

Business Lite, $14/month. Includes account access for up to five of your team members. Account holders receive all Basic account benefits plus additional design templates and stock images and priority technical support.

Business Elite, $30/month. Unlimited account access for your entire team. Account holders receive all Business Lite account benefits with the added ability to save custom color palettes and branding information.

Please let me know if I can help you further.

Patricia Fenoglio, Orb Customer Relations

Customer Testimonial

As the owner of a small start-up company with just ten employees, I know that everyone who works for me has to be able to do a little bit of everything. What I really like about the Orb graphic design tool is that, even though not a single one of my employees is a design or marketing professional, the software allows any of us to easily transform an idea into a nice-looking design in just a few minutes. A feature I especially appreciate is the ability to import branding information such as logos, fonts, and color schemes, so that these can be accessed by everyone on my team when creating new materials.

The only issue I have had is that the Orb tool seems to act sluggish while I am working with photos. Once, when I dragged an image into the content area of a flyer I was creating, the screen froze, and I had to restart my computer. It might have been an issue with my computer's performance. Fortunately, I got the image and template to work after a few attempts.

All in all, I think the Orb graphic design tool is excellent for both businesses and individuals! I put it to use on nearly a daily basis.

—Sally Durance

6. What benefit of the Orb graphic design tool does the e-mail emphasize?

(A) Ease of use
(B) Affordable pricing
(C) Compatibility with other programs
(D) Extensive sorting capabilities

7. What does the testimonial indicate about the staff members at Ms. Durance's company?

(A) They have extensive experience in the design field.
(B) They are currently working on a new logo.
(C) They are often hired on a temporary basis.
(D) They have multiple roles in the business.

8. What is implied about Ms. Durance?

(A) She took advantage of a seasonal discount.
(B) She purchased a Business Elite account.
(C) She often needs assistance with editing images.
(D) She meets regularly with the Orb marketing team.

9. In the testimonial, what does Ms. Durance state about a flyer?

(A) It was created with her favorite template.
(B) It was designed by a famous artist.
(C) She had a technical problem while creating it.
(D) She uses it as a sample for potential clients.

10. In the testimonial, the word "performance" in paragraph 2, line 4, is closest in meaning to

(A) operation
(B) exhibition
(C) portrayal
(D) accomplishment

Survey Cosmos
The #1-ranked application in *Entrepreneur Notes*!

Do you need up-to-date information about customer preferences and product demand? Survey Cosmos is an application that can help you gather the most essential information for making decisions throughout all stages of product development, from initial design to advertising.

Features
- Notifications: Reminders to complete surveys are sent to customers (boosting response rates by an average of 50 percent).
- Reporting: Several filtering options allow you to isolate specific market trends and preferences.
- Question Library: Over 400 available questions in various categories can be used to customize your surveys.
- Data Storage: Retain a complete record of survey results in one place (with a new no-expiration-date policy).

MEMO

From: Seira Katou, Vice-President of Product Development
To: Product Development Staff
Date: February 8
Subject: New application

This is to inform you that we have purchased a license for Survey Cosmos, which we will be using for our market research surveys next month. As you know, understanding customer preferences is essential for the production and sale of our cereals, waffles, and energy bars. The management believes that Survey Cosmos, in spite of its cost, is a sound investment in that it has the potential to increase the reliability of our survey data. I am particularly pleased that the application has a notifications feature.

Technology Support Services will be installing the software on department computers between February 21 and February 25. In addition, training sessions on the use of the software will be held on March 4, 11, and 18. Participation in one of these sessions is mandatory, since you are expected to know how to use the application before March 19, which is the date we will begin using the application. On April 1, we will collect feedback from you on the use of the application.

11. What is a purpose of the application mentioned in the advertisement?

(A) To improve market research
(B) To attract more users to a Web site
(C) To keep accurate records of product orders
(D) To protect confidential information

12. What feature was most recently added to the application?

(A) Automatic installation of updated versions of the application
(B) Automatic reminders for users to back up information
(C) The ability to generate a variety of reports
(D) The ability to store information for a longer period of time

13. In what industry does Ms. Katou work?

(A) Software development
(B) Food
(C) Corporate training
(D) Advertising

14. What aspect of the company surveys does Ms. Katou especially hope to improve?

(A) The quality of the survey questions
(B) The cost of implementing surveys
(C) The number of people who respond to surveys
(D) The amount of time it takes to complete a survey

15. Before what date must all employees have learned how to use the application?

(A) February 21
(B) February 25
(C) March 19
(D) April 1

ACCRA, GHANA (17 February)—Sankofa Manufacturing, maker of clothing and accessories, has entered into a partnership with fashion house Akofena. Known for its clothing and handmade jewelry inspired by Yoruba culture, Akofena markets its products in Africa, Europe, and the Americas. The collaboration between the companies, both based here in Accra, means that Sankofa's products will be infused with the designs and bright colors that Akofena's products are known for. The new line will be marketed under the brand name Uwezo.

Work on the Uwezo line has already begun, with planning underway for a private fashion show for industry professionals in late May. Members of the public will be able to view photographs of the show online. The complete line is expected to be available in stores in July.

E-mail

To:	omotola_dauda@akofena.com.gh
From:	rudi.amoako@sankofa.com.gh
Date:	27 June
Subject:	The Uwezo line
Attachment:	🔗 Report

Dear Omotola,

Attached to this e-mail is the report on the initial reviews of Uwezo's product line from the 6 June fashion show. It includes results from the surveys of fashion show attendees, reviews from top fashion critics, and commentary from several major fashion sites.

While people were quite pleased with the clothes overall, they were less enthusiastic about the accessories, describing them as plain. Several critics felt that the Uwezo jewelry and scarves should capture aspects of African culture so that the products are inseparably linked with Africa.

Based on this feedback, we would like your team to come up with some new accessory designs. Please submit these to me by 4 July. As you know, our goal was to have the new line ready by the second week of July so that we could begin selling it at the expo of the African Organization for Commerce and Industry (AOCI) the week after. We have decided to make the clothes available, but we will wait until we are confident in the accessories before offering them to the public.

I appreciate your efforts.

Sincerely,

Rudi Amoako
Chief Marketing Officer, Sankofa Manufacturing

16. What is NOT mentioned in the article about Akofena's products?

    (A) They are influenced by a particular culture.
    (B) They are sold internationally.
    (C) They are reasonably priced.
    (D) They are brightly colored.

17. What does the article suggest about the Uwezo product line?

    (A) It will be produced in Accra.
    (B) It will be sold by Akofena.
    (C) It will have only handmade products.
    (D) It will be available in stores in May.

18. What is the main purpose of the e-mail?

    (A) To apologize for some delays
    (B) To approve a survey
    (C) To request new designs
    (D) To explain a cancellation

19. What is indicated about the fashion show?

    (A) It took place at Akofena's headquarters.
    (B) It was attended by members of the public.
    (C) It had to be moved to a larger location.
    (D) It was held later than planned.

20. What is indicated about the AOCI expo?

    (A) It promotes business partnerships.
    (B) It will take place in July.
    (C) Its sponsors include Akofena and Sankofa Manufacturing.
    (D) Its significance has grown over the years.

Excellent Opportunity!

Imagine having your next office address at the distinguished Brinkley Building in downtown Toronto. This late-nineteenth-century gem was designed by renowned architect Jacob Clements. It was originally the headquarters of the Gable Publishing Company, which occupied the building for 75 years. The building has been largely renovated and modernized, though some of its classic features have been retained. It also offers a full-service, street-level restaurant, Lowry's on the Avenue. On-site parking for the Brinkley Building's commercial tenants is available at reasonable monthly rates, and public transportation is nearby.

Contact Liz Seeley at lseeley@brinkleyleasing.ca for more information.

---

https://www.ardenmedicalassociates.ca

Arden Medical Associates is pleased to announce the opening of its second clinic location on 26 October. The clinic will be in the Brinkley Building at 94 Blake Avenue, Suite 200. Our team of health care professionals is ready to provide the highest standard of care to patients in the heart of downtown Toronto. Walk-ins are welcome, and same-day appointments will be available. Call 416-555-0109 to arrange an appointment during our regular Monday through Saturday hours.

We also extend a warm welcome to the newest member of our team, Dr. Yuri Sharov, who specializes in family medicine and will join our staff on 1 November.

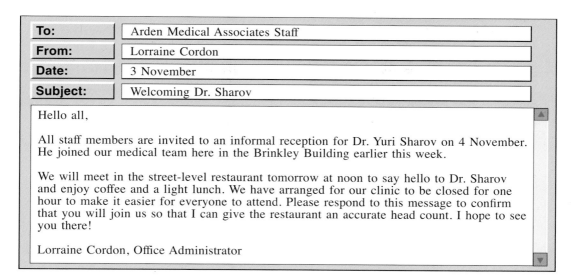

To:	Arden Medical Associates Staff
From:	Lorraine Cordon
Date:	3 November
Subject:	Welcoming Dr. Sharov

Hello all,

All staff members are invited to an informal reception for Dr. Yuri Sharov on 4 November. He joined our medical team here in the Brinkley Building earlier this week.

We will meet in the street-level restaurant tomorrow at noon to say hello to Dr. Sharov and enjoy coffee and a light lunch. We have arranged for our clinic to be closed for one hour to make it easier for everyone to attend. Please respond to this message to confirm that you will join us so that I can give the restaurant an accurate head count. I hope to see you there!

Lorraine Cordon, Office Administrator

21. What is a purpose of the advertisement?

(A) To promote tourism in downtown Toronto

(B) To attract tenants for commercial office space

(C) To recruit architects for a renovation project

(D) To find a buyer for an old property

22. What is indicated about the Gable Publishing Company?

(A) It was founded by Mr. Clements.

(B) It no longer occupies the Brinkley Building.

(C) It used to be the largest employer in Toronto.

(D) It is managed by Ms. Seeley.

23. What is suggested about Arden Medical Associates' new clinic?

(A) It is interviewing professionals for administrative positions.

(B) It does not accept patients without appointments.

(C) It is close to public transportation.

(D) It welcomes patients seven days a week.

24. What will most likely occur on November 4 ?

(A) A gathering at Lowry's on the Avenue

(B) The first day of appointments at a clinic in the Brinkley Building

(C) The promotion of a new clinic director

(D) A monthly meeting for administrative staff

25. What does Ms. Cordon ask staff members to do?

(A) Call to reserve seats

(B) Prepare a short presentation

(C) Update a staff directory

(D) Reply by e-mail

To:	HR Professionals Distribution List
From:	Caden Everett <ceverett@steubenweiss.com>
Date:	July 15
Subject:	Excellence in Human Resources
Attachment:	📎 Nomination form

The Steuben and Weiss Excellence in Human Resources Awards recognize our industry's most valuable players. This year our celebration will take place in the stunning Fitzgraff Towers. The night will include a sit-down dinner catered by the restaurant Dulce, jazz music by the Clemence Octet, and a celebration of those who have excelled in our industry this year. We would like to invite you to attend.

Date: September 14
Time: 6 P.M.–11:30 P.M.
Location: Fitzgraff Towers, 2108 East Markley Street, Chicago
Respond by: August 31

If you would like to nominate someone for an award, please fill out the attached form and e-mail it to nominees@steubenweiss.com by July 31.

Best regards,

Caden Everett
Board Chair, Steuben and Weiss

Steuben and Weiss Excellence in Human Resources Awards Nomination Form

Name of nominee	Amaya Nonaka
Name of nominator	Gavin Dreyling
Relationship to nominee	Coworker
Nominee's company	Anderson and Woods Consulting (A&WC)
Nominee's years at company	16
Years nominee has been working in field	23

Reasons for nomination

Ms. Nonaka has consistently brought in new employees who are ideally suited for their roles and has provided support for them throughout their tenure at A&WC.

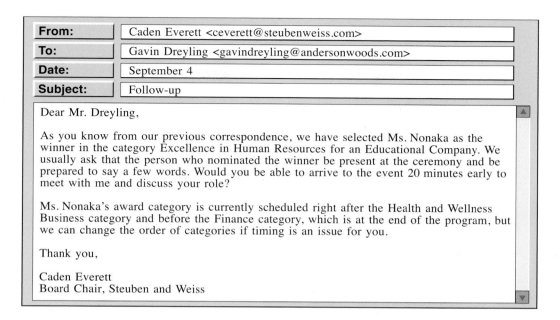

From:	Caden Everett <ceverett@steubenweiss.com>
To:	Gavin Dreyling <gavindreyling@andersonwoods.com>
Date:	September 4
Subject:	Follow-up

Dear Mr. Dreyling,

As you know from our previous correspondence, we have selected Ms. Nonaka as the winner in the category Excellence in Human Resources for an Educational Company. We usually ask that the person who nominated the winner be present at the ceremony and be prepared to say a few words. Would you be able to arrive to the event 20 minutes early to meet with me and discuss your role?

Ms. Nonaka's award category is currently scheduled right after the Health and Wellness Business category and before the Finance category, which is at the end of the program, but we can change the order of categories if timing is an issue for you.

Thank you,

Caden Everett
Board Chair, Steuben and Weiss

26. According to the first e-mail, what will the awards ceremony include?

(A) A lifetime achievement award
(B) A raffle for prizes
(C) A live band
(D) A speech by the president of Steuben and Weiss

27. According to the form, what most likely is one of Ms. Nonaka's primary job duties?

(A) Recruiting employees
(B) Advising on salary packages
(C) Managing employees' benefits
(D) Mentoring supervisors

28. What type of business most likely is Anderson and Woods Consulting?

(A) Event management
(B) Education
(C) Finance
(D) Health and wellness

29. What is the purpose of the second e-mail?

(A) To announce a group of winners
(B) To request Ms. Nonaka's contact information
(C) To ask Mr. Dreyling to speak at an event
(D) To describe awards categories

30. Where does Mr. Everett want to meet Mr. Dreyling?

(A) At Dulce
(B) At Fitzgraff Towers
(C) At Steuben and Weiss
(D) At Anderson and Woods Consulting

Questions 31-35 refer to the following review, Web page, and e-mail.

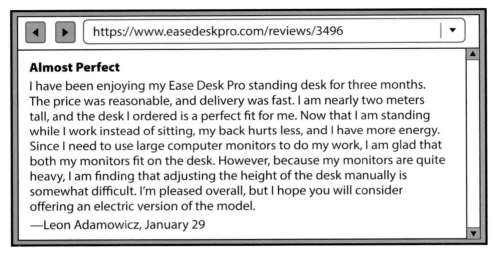

https://www.easedeskpro.com/reviews/3496

Almost Perfect

I have been enjoying my Ease Desk Pro standing desk for three months. The price was reasonable, and delivery was fast. I am nearly two meters tall, and the desk I ordered is a perfect fit for me. Now that I am standing while I work instead of sitting, my back hurts less, and I have more energy. Since I need to use large computer monitors to do my work, I am glad that both my monitors fit on the desk. However, because my monitors are quite heavy, I am finding that adjusting the height of the desk manually is somewhat difficult. I'm pleased overall, but I hope you will consider offering an electric version of the model.

—Leon Adamowicz, January 29

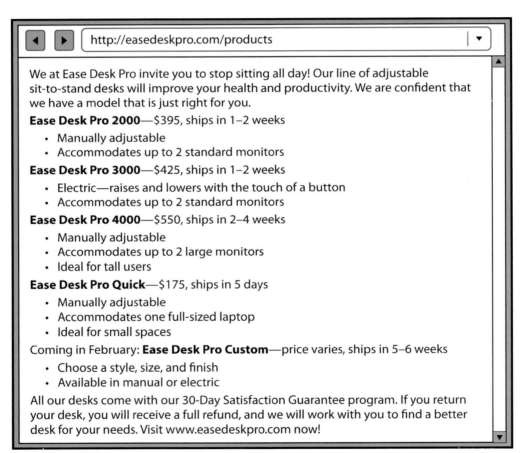

http://easedeskpro.com/products

We at Ease Desk Pro invite you to stop sitting all day! Our line of adjustable sit-to-stand desks will improve your health and productivity. We are confident that we have a model that is just right for you.

Ease Desk Pro 2000—$395, ships in 1–2 weeks
- Manually adjustable
- Accommodates up to 2 standard monitors

Ease Desk Pro 3000—$425, ships in 1–2 weeks
- Electric—raises and lowers with the touch of a button
- Accommodates up to 2 standard monitors

Ease Desk Pro 4000—$550, ships in 2–4 weeks
- Manually adjustable
- Accommodates up to 2 large monitors
- Ideal for tall users

Ease Desk Pro Quick—$175, ships in 5 days
- Manually adjustable
- Accommodates one full-sized laptop
- Ideal for small spaces

Coming in February: **Ease Desk Pro Custom**—price varies, ships in 5–6 weeks
- Choose a style, size, and finish
- Available in manual or electric

All our desks come with our 30-Day Satisfaction Guarantee program. If you return your desk, you will receive a full refund, and we will work with you to find a better desk for your needs. Visit www.easedeskpro.com now!

From:	ayala.drachman@easedeskpro.com
To:	ladamowicz@siftermail.com
Date:	February 7
Subject:	Your Ease Desk Pro review

Dear Mr. Adamowicz,

Thank you for your online review and for your helpful suggestion. We have heard from many customers who would like the chance to mix and match features from different Ease Desk Pro models, and I am happy to announce a new product option that we are introducing this month—Ease Desk Pro Custom. With Ease Desk Pro Custom, you can design your own desk to fit your specific height and space needs in both manual and electric versions. If you choose to order an Ease Desk Pro Custom, we will allow you to return your current desk for a full refund. To take advantage of this offer, simply reply to this e-mail, and an Ease Desk Pro representative will contact you to begin designing the desk of your dreams.

Sincerely,

Ayala Drachman, Customer Care Specialist
Ease Desk Pro

31. In the review, what does Mr. Adamowicz mention about his desk?

(A) It was damaged during delivery.
(B) It blends in nicely with his other furniture.
(C) Assembling it was difficult.
(D) Using it has reduced his back pain.

32. What feature of his desk does Mr. Adamowicz think can be improved?

(A) The color
(B) The adjustability
(C) The weight
(D) The quality of materials

33. What desk model does Mr. Adamowicz most likely have?

(A) Ease Desk Pro 2000
(B) Ease Desk Pro 3000
(C) Ease Desk Pro 4000
(D) Ease Desk Pro Quick

34. What does the Web page indicate about all Ease Desk Pro models?

(A) They can be returned within a specific time period.
(B) They are designed to be transported easily.
(C) They fit well into small office spaces.
(D) They can accommodate two computer monitors.

35. What can be concluded about the desk that Ms. Drachman recommends?

(A) It costs less than $550.
(B) It will be delivered free of charge.
(C) It is available in one size only.
(D) It will take more than one month to be shipped.

To:	Farhan Suryani
From:	Julia Sands
Date:	March 1
Subject:	Your proposal

Dear Mr. Suryani,

Thank you for your contribution to the Business Expansion Initiative of Calzano Enterprises. We were pleased that our request for proposals has met with such an overwhelming response from employees.

The Business Expansion Committee has carefully studied your proposal to open a store in the Fernwood Shopping Plaza (FSP). A few issues of concern became apparent in the process. First, in recent years the area has seen a decline in the number of retail businesses, itself the result of population relocation. We anticipate, therefore, that sales would be weak at best. Additionally, it has come to our attention that Hilltop, one of our main competitors, will be opening a location at FSP in July. If we were to open a store there as well, there would be significant product overlap between their business and ours, which would impact sales as well. The committee has, therefore, concluded that implementation of your proposal is not practical at this time.

I hope you can appreciate our decision. We thank you again for your input and welcome any other suggestion you may have regarding the initiative.

Sincerely,

Julia Sands, Chair, Business Expansion Initiative
Calzano Enterprises

FERNWOOD (June 20)—Next month, Hilltop, the company that markets ice cream, frozen yogurt, and various other milk products under the brand name Lunamiel, will open a location in the Fernwood Shopping Plaza (FSP). The store will be located across from The Gadget Hut. With such remarkable ice cream and frozen yogurt varieties as "Chili Peanut Butter" and "Rosewater Pistachio," Hilltop is sure to attract lovers of frozen treats. And because the company buys its ingredients locally, other area businesses may well benefit from its presence.

Business insiders have expressed surprise over the company's move, pointing out that in the last nine months four businesses have closed their FSP locations due to lack of consumer interest. Still, there has been speculation that other companies might follow Hilltop's example, among which, in theory, would be Calzano Enterprises. However, a company spokesperson has denied those speculations. She said that while a proposal to open a store at the shopping center had been submitted to company management, top officials had expressed no support for it.

Information about other stores at FSP is available at www.fernshops.com.

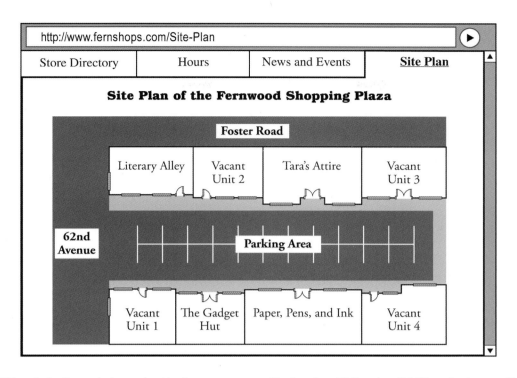

http://www.fernshops.com/Site-Plan

| Store Directory | Hours | News and Events | **Site Plan** |

Site Plan of the Fernwood Shopping Plaza

Foster Road

| Literary Alley | Vacant Unit 2 | Tara's Attire | Vacant Unit 3 |

62nd Avenue

Parking Area

| Vacant Unit 1 | The Gadget Hut | Paper, Pens, and Ink | Vacant Unit 4 |

36. What is indicated about the Business Expansion Initiative?

(A) It generated much interest from employees.

(B) It aims to attract younger customers.

(C) It was developed by Mr. Suryani.

(D) It will end in July.

37. What is a purpose of the e-mail?

(A) To announce the results of an employee survey

(B) To explain the reasons for rejecting an idea

(C) To gather information about a competitor

(D) To highlight a company's strengths

38. In what industry is Calzano Enterprises?

(A) Staffing

(B) Entertainment

(C) Food manufacturing

(D) Property management

39. In what FSP unit will Hilltop be located?

(A) In Unit 1

(B) In Unit 2

(C) In Unit 3

(D) In Unit 4

40. What aspect of Hilltop's frozen products does the article emphasize?

(A) Their healthy ingredients

(B) Their interesting colors

(C) Their high quality

(D) Their unique flavors

Questions 41-45 refer to the following invoice and e-mails.

Wellness Outlook Clinic

May 28

Customer ID: 3076
Due date: June 30

Sonia Addo
4052 Hancock Street
Corvallis, OR 97330

Service Date	Description	Reference Code	Amount
5/15	60-minute deep stretch session	0029	$80
5/15	30-minute deep tissue massage	0018	$40
5/15	Hot stones application	0074	$15
		TOTAL	$135

Thank you for visiting our newest clinic location! We hope you feel much better after your visit. For questions about your invoice, contact our billing department at pay@wellnessoutlookclinic.com.

To:	<pay@wellnessoutlookclinic.com>
From:	Sonia Addo <saddo74@rapidonet.com>
Date:	May 31
Subject:	A couple of questions

Dear Wellness Outlook Clinic,

I was referred to your massage therapist by my family doctor. The service I received from Jenna Wiseman was professional and thorough. She was courteous and responsive to my needs. I would like to book an additional session with her next month. Is she available on June 21?

I also have a question about the invoice I received. At the beginning of my appointment, Ms. Wiseman presented various options of treatment that she could provide in our session. I opted for some deep tissue massage during my stretch session. It was my understanding that this service was to be included as part of the deep stretch session. Why am I being charged for a 30-minute massage session in addition to my appointment, when I was only seen for 60 minutes?

Sincerely,

Sonia Addo

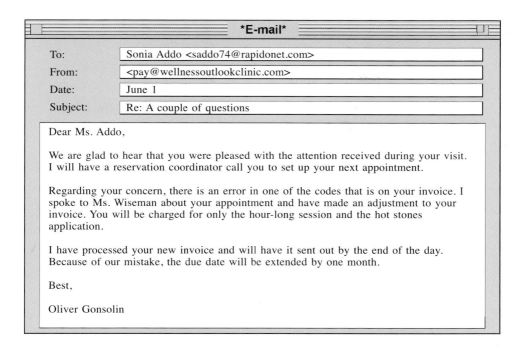

E-mail

To:	Sonia Addo <saddo74@rapidonet.com>
From:	<pay@wellnessoutlookclinic.com>
Date:	June 1
Subject:	Re: A couple of questions

Dear Ms. Addo,

We are glad to hear that you were pleased with the attention received during your visit. I will have a reservation coordinator call you to set up your next appointment.

Regarding your concern, there is an error in one of the codes that is on your invoice. I spoke to Ms. Wiseman about your appointment and have made an adjustment to your invoice. You will be charged for only the hour-long session and the hot stones application.

I have processed your new invoice and will have it sent out by the end of the day. Because of our mistake, the due date will be extended by one month.

Best,

Oliver Gonsolin

41. What does the invoice imply about Wellness Outlook Clinic?

(A) It has multiple clinic locations.
(B) It provides fitness classes.
(C) It has a new Web site.
(D) It provides discounts for frequent visits.

42. According to the first e-mail, what would Ms. Addo like to do?

(A) See a different massage provider
(B) Write a review about the service
(C) Have an update sent to her doctor
(D) Schedule another appointment

43. What code is Ms. Addo concerned about?

(A) 3076
(B) 0029
(C) 0018
(D) 0074

44. Who most likely is Mr. Gonsolin?

(A) A reservation coordinator
(B) A billing specialist
(C) A massage therapist
(D) A family doctor

45. What is the due date on Ms. Addo's revised invoice?

(A) May 15
(B) May 31
(C) June 30
(D) July 30

*toeic.

토익 단기공략

850+

LC RC

정답과 해설

LC PART 1

UNIT 1 인물 중심 사진

ETS 유형 연습
본책 p.20

1 (C) **2** (B) **3** (B)

1 M-Cn

(A) A man is oiling some equipment.
(B) A man is turning a steering wheel.
(C) A man is operating a sewing machine.
(D) A man is unwinding a roll of cloth.

(A) 남자가 장비에 윤활유를 치고 있다.
(B) 남자가 핸들을 돌리고 있다.
(C) **남자가 재봉틀을 작동시키고 있다.**
(D) 남자가 감긴 옷감을 풀고 있다.

해설 | 1인 등장 사진 – 작업실
(A) **동작 묘사 오답:** 남자가 장비에 윤활유를 치고 있는(is oiling) 모습이 아니다.
(B) **동작 묘사 오답:** 남자가 핸들을 돌리고 있는(is turning) 모습이 아니다.
(C) **정답:** 남자가 재봉틀을 작동시키고 있는(is operating) 모습을 잘 묘사했으므로 정답이다.
(D) **사진에 없는 명사 언급 오답:** 사진 속에 감긴 옷감(a roll of cloth)이 보이지 않는다.

어휘 | equipment 장비 steering wheel 핸들 sewing machine 재봉틀 unwind 풀다

2 W-Am

(A) He's setting a pan on a stove.
(B) He's holding a serving utensil in one hand.
(C) He's leading some guests to a patio.
(D) He's turning on lights in a dining room.

(A) 남자가 레인지 위에 팬을 얹고 있다.
(B) **남자가 한 손에 서빙용 식기를 들고 있다.**
(C) 남자가 손님들을 테라스로 데려가고 있다.
(D) 남자가 식당에 불을 켜고 있다.

해설 | 1인 등장 사진 – 식당
(A) **사진에 없는 명사 언급 오답:** 사진 속에 레인지(stove)가 보이지 않는다.
(B) **정답:** 남자가 한 손에 서빙용 식기를 들고 있는(is holding) 모습을 잘 묘사했으므로 정답이다.
(C) **사진에 없는 명사 언급 오답:** 사진 속에 손님들(guests)과 테라스(patio)가 보이지 않는다.
(D) **동작 묘사 오답:** 남자가 불을 켜고 있는(is turning on lights) 모습이 아니다.

어휘 | utensil 기구

3 M-Cn

(A) She's bending over to tie her shoe.
(B) She's removing an item from a shelf.
(C) She's adjusting the belt on her jacket.
(D) She's fixing a wheel on a cart.

(A) 여자가 신발끈을 묶으려고 구부리고 있다.
(B) **여자가 선반에서 물건을 꺼내고 있다.**
(C) 여자가 재킷 벨트를 조절하고 있다.
(D) 여자가 카트 바퀴를 고치고 있다.

해설 | 1인 등장 사진 – 상점
(A) **동작 묘사 오답:** 여자가 신발끈을 묶으려고(to tie her shoe) 구부리고 있는 모습이 아니다.
(B) **정답:** 여자가 선반에서 물건을 꺼내고 있는(is removing an item) 모습을 잘 묘사했으므로 정답이다.
(C) **동작 묘사 오답:** 여자가 재킷 벨트를 조절하고 있는(is adjusting) 모습이 아니다.
(D) **동작 묘사 오답:** 여자가 카트 바퀴를 고치고 있는(is fixing) 모습이 아니다.

어휘 | bend over 몸을 숙이다, 굽히다 adjust 조절하다, 조정하다 fix 수리하다

ETS 유형 연습
본책 p.21

1 (A) **2** (D) **3** (D)

1 W-Br

(A) They're selecting some food in a cafeteria.
(B) The woman is putting an item in a bag.
(C) The man is standing in a doorway.
(D) The man is wiping off a refrigerator handle.

(A) 사람들이 구내식당에서 음식을 고르고 있다.
(B) 여자가 물건을 가방에 넣고 있다.
(C) 남자가 출입구에 서 있다.
(D) 남자가 냉장고 손잡이를 닦고 있다.

해설 | 2인 이상 등장 사진 – 식당
(A) **정답:** 사람들이 구내식당에서 음식을 고르고 있는(are selecting some food) 모습을 잘 묘사했으므로 정답이다.
(B) **동작 묘사 오답:** 여자가 가방에 물건을 넣고 있는(is putting an item) 모습이 아니다.
(C) **사진에 없는 명사 언급 오답:** 사진 속에 출입구(doorway)가 보이지 않는다.
(D) **사진에 없는 명사 언급 오답:** 사진 속에 냉장고 (refrigerator)가 보이지 않는다.

어휘 | doorway 출입구 **wipe off** 닦아 내다

2 M-Cn

(A) One of the men is gripping the rails of a fence.
(B) One of the men is emptying a bucket.
(C) One of the men is repairing a broken wheel.
(D) One of the men is loading a bale of hay onto a cart.

(A) 남자들 중 한 명이 울타리 난간을 꽉 잡고 있다.
(B) 남자들 중 한 명이 양동이를 비우고 있다.
(C) 남자들 중 한 명이 고장 난 바퀴를 수리하고 있다.
(D) **남자들 중 한 명이 건초 한 더미를 카트에 싣고 있다.**

해설 | 2인 이상 등장 사진 – 실외
(A) **동작 묘사 오답:** 남자가 울타리 난간을 꽉 잡고 있는(is gripping) 모습이 아니다.
(B) **동작 묘사 오답:** 남자가 양동이를 비우고 있는(is emptying) 모습이 아니다.
(C) **동작 묘사 오답:** 남자가 고장 난 바퀴를 수리하고 있는(is repairing) 모습이 아니다.
(D) **정답:** 남자가 건초 한 더미를 카트에 싣고 있는(is loading) 모습을 잘 묘사했으므로 정답이다.

어휘 | grip 꽉 쥐다 **rail** 난간 **empty** 비우다 **load** 싣다 **bale** 더미, 뭉치

3 M-Cn

(A) One of the men is repairing a wheelbarrow.
(B) One of the men is changing a tire.
(C) A truck is waiting at a stoplight.
(D) The men are unloading materials from a vehicle.

(A) 남자 한 명이 손수레를 수리하고 있다.
(B) 남자 한 명이 타이어를 교체하고 있다.
(C) 트럭이 정지 신호등에서 기다리고 있다.
(D) **남자들이 차량에서 자재를 내리고 있다.**

해설 | 2인 이상 등장 사진 – 실외
(A) **동작 묘사 오답:** 남자가 손수레를 수리하고 있는(is repairing a wheelbarrow) 모습이 아니다.
(B) **동작 묘사 오답:** 남자가 타이어를 교체하고 있는(is changing a tire) 모습이 아니다.
(C) **위치 묘사 오답:** 트럭이 정지 신호등(at a stoplight)에 있지 않다.
(D) **정답:** 남자들이 차량에서 자재를 내리고 있는(are unloading materials) 모습을 잘 묘사했으므로 정답이다.

어휘 | wheelbarrow 외바퀴 손수레 **tire** 타이어(= tyre) **stoplight** 정지 신호등, 빨간불 **unload** 내리다 **vehicle** 차량

ETS 고득점 실전 문제   본책 p.22

| **1** (A) | **2** (C) | **3** (C) | **4** (C) | **5** (A) | **6** (C) |
| **7** (B) | **8** (C) | **9** (D) | **10** (D) | **11** (B) | **12** (A) |

1 M-Cn

(A) He's sawing off a branch.
(B) He's turning on a machine.
(C) He's cutting some rope off a tree.
(D) He's carrying a piece of wood.

(A) 남자가 나뭇가지를 톱으로 잘라 내고 있다.
(B) 남자가 기계를 켜고 있다.
(C) 남자가 나무에서 밧줄을 잘라내고 있다.
(D) 남자가 나무를 나르고 있다.

해설 | 1인 등장 사진 – 실외
(A) **정답:** 남자가 나뭇가지를 톱으로 잘라 내고 있는(is sawing off) 모습을 잘 묘사했으므로 정답이다.
(B) **동작 묘사 오답:** 남자가 기계의 전원을 켜고 있는(is turning on) 모습이 아니다.
(C) **사진에 없는 명사 언급 오답:** 사진 속에 밧줄(rope)이 보이지 않는다.
(D) **동작 묘사 오답:** 남자가 나무를 나르고 있는(is carrying) 모습이 아니다.

어휘 | saw off 톱으로 잘라 내다 **branch** 나뭇가지

2 M-Au

(A) She's looking at a clock on the wall.
(B) She's reading a book on a sofa.
(C) She's on a stool at a counter.
(D) She's selecting a book from a shelf.

(A) 여자가 벽에 있는 시계를 보고 있다.
(B) 여자가 소파에서 책을 읽고 있다.
(C) 여자가 카운터에서 스툴에 앉아 있다.
(D) 여자가 책장에서 책을 고르고 있다.

해설 | 1인 등장 사진 – 실내
(A) **동작 묘사 오답:** 여자가 벽에 있는 시계를 보고 있는(is looking at a clock) 모습이 아니다.
(B) **위치 묘사 오답:** 여자가 소파에서(on a sofa) 책을 읽고 있는 모습이 아니다.
(C) **정답:** 여자가 카운터에서 스툴에 앉아 있는(is on a stool) 모습을 잘 묘사했으므로 정답이다.
(D) **사진에 없는 명사 언급·동작 묘사 오답:** 사진 속에 책장(shelf)이 보이지 않으며, 책을 고르고 있는(is selecting) 모습이 아니다.

어휘 | stool (등받이와 팔걸이가 없는) 의자, 스툴

3 W-Am

(A) One of the women is handing over a credit card.
(B) One of the women is holding some bottles.
(C) The women are on opposite sides of a counter.
(D) The women are making a bouquet.

(A) 여자 한 명이 신용카드를 건네고 있다.
(B) 여자 한 명이 병을 몇 개 들고 있다.
(C) 여자들이 서로 카운터 반대편에 있다.
(D) 여자들이 꽃다발을 만들고 있다.

해설 | 2인 이상 등장 사진 – 상점
(A) **사진에 없는 명사 언급·동작 묘사 오답:** 사진 속에 신용카드(credit card)가 보이지 않으며, 건네고 있는(is handing over) 모습이 아니다.
(B) **동작 묘사 오답:** 여자가 병을 들고 있는(is holding) 모습이 아니다.
(C) **정답:** 여자들이 서로 카운터 반대편에(on opposite sides of a counter) 있는 모습을 잘 묘사했으므로 정답이다.
(D) **동작 묘사 오답:** 여자들이 꽃다발을 만들고 있는(is making a bouquet) 모습이 아니다.

어휘 | hand over 넘겨주다 **opposite** 반대의

4 W-Br

(A) Some leaves are being swept off a street.
(B) Some tree branches are being trimmed.
(C) The people are seated near the water.
(D) The people are swimming in the water.

(A) 거리에서 나뭇잎들이 쓸리고 있다.
(B) 나뭇가지가 다듬어지고 있다.
(C) 사람들이 물가에 앉아 있다.
(D) 사람들이 물에서 수영을 하고 있다.

해설 | 사람·사물 혼합 사진 – 물가
(A) **진행 상황 묘사 오답:** 나뭇잎들이 쓸리고 있는(are being swept off) 상황이 아니다.
(B) **진행 상황 묘사 오답:** 나뭇가지가 다듬어지고 있는(are being trimmed) 상황이 아니다.
(C) **정답:** 사람들이 물가에 앉아 있는(are seated near the water) 모습을 잘 묘사했으므로 정답이다.
(D) **동작 묘사 오답:** 사람들이 물에서 수영을 하고 있는(are swimming) 모습이 아니다.

어휘 | sweep off 쓸어내다 **trim** 손질하다, 다듬다

5 M-Cn

(A) The woman is putting on protective work gear.
(B) The man is locking up some personal belongings.
(C) The man is adjusting a helmet on his head.
(D) The woman is trying on a pair of sunglasses.

(A) 여자가 작업용 보호장비를 착용하고 있다.
(B) 남자가 개인 소지품을 보관소에 넣고 있다.
(C) 남자가 머리에 쓴 헬멧을 바로잡고 있다.
(D) 여자가 선글라스를 써 보고 있다.

해설 | 2인 이상 등장 사진 – 탈의실
(A) **정답:** 여자가 작업용 보호장비를 착용하고 있는(is putting on) 동작을 잘 묘사했으므로 정답이다.
(B) **동작 묘사 오답:** 남자가 소지품을 보관소에 넣고 있는(is locking up) 모습이 아니다.
(C) **상태 묘사·동작 묘사 오답:** 남자가 헬멧을 머리에 쓴 상태(on his head)가 아니며, 바로잡고 있는(is adjusting) 모습도 아니다.
(D) **동작 묘사 오답:** 여자가 선글라스를 써 보고 있는(is trying on) 모습이 아니다.

어휘 | protective 보호하는, 보호용의 **lock up** 안전한 곳에 넣어두다 **personal belongings** 개인 소지품 **adjust** 바로잡다, 조절하다

6 M-Cn

(A) A walkway is being cleaned.
(B) A man's arranging potted plants.
(C) A man's approaching some steps.
(D) A pile of stones is being moved.

(A) 통로가 청소되고 있다.
(B) 남자가 화분에 심은 식물을 정리하고 있다.
(C) 남자가 계단에 다가가고 있다.
(D) 돌무더기가 옮겨지고 있다.

해설 | 사람·사물 혼합 사진
(A) **진행 상황 묘사 오답:** 통로가 청소되고 있는(is being cleaned) 상황이 아니다.
(B) **동작 묘사 오답:** 남자가 화분에 심은 식물을 정리하고 있는(is arranging) 모습이 아니다.
(C) **정답:** 남자가 계단에 다가가고 있는(is approaching some steps) 모습을 잘 묘사했으므로 정답이다.
(D) **사진에 없는 명사 언급·진행 상황 묘사 오답:** 사진 속에 돌무더기(A pile of stones)가 보이지 않으며, 옮겨지고 있는(is being moved) 상황도 아니다.

어휘 | walkway 통로   arrange 정리하다, 배열하다
approach 다가가다

7 W-Am

(A) The women are inserting pictures into metal frames.
(B) The women are touching a page in a binder.
(C) One of the women is pointing to the ceiling.
(D) One of the women is reading a bulletin board.

(A) 여자들이 금속 액자에 사진을 끼우고 있다.
(B) 여자들이 바인더의 한 페이지를 만지고 있다.
(C) 여자 한 명이 천장을 가리키고 있다.
(D) 여자 한 명이 게시판을 읽고 있다.

해설 | 2인 이상 등장 사진 – 사무실
(A) **동작 묘사 오답:** 여자들이 금속 액자에 사진을 끼우고 있는(are inserting pictures) 모습이 아니다.
(B) **정답:** 여자들이 바인더의 한 페이지를 만지고 있는(are touching a page) 모습을 잘 묘사했으므로 정답이다.
(C) **사진에 없는 명사 언급 오답:** 사진 속에 천장(ceiling)이 보이지 않는다.
(D) **사진에 없는 명사 언급 오답:** 사진 속에 게시판(bulletin board)이 보이지 않는다.

어휘 | insert 삽입하다, 끼우다   bulletin board 게시판

8 M-Cn

(A) The woman is putting on her sunglasses.
(B) Some flowers are being watered.
(C) The woman is choosing a plant.
(D) Some leaves are being raked in a pile.

(A) 여자가 선글라스를 쓰고 있다.
(B) 꽃에 물이 주어지고 있다.
(C) 여자가 식물을 고르고 있다.
(D) 나뭇잎들이 갈퀴로 모아 쌓이고 있다.

해설 | 사람·사물 혼합 사진 – 화분 선반 앞
(A) **동작 묘사 오답:** 여자가 선글라스를 쓰려는 동작을 하고 있는(is putting on) 모습이 아니다.
(B) **진행 상황 묘사 오답:** 꽃에 물을 주고 있는(are being watered) 상황이 아니다.
(C) **정답:** 여자가 식물을 고르고 있는(is choosing) 모습을 잘 묘사했으므로 정답이다.
(D) **진행 상황 묘사 오답:** 나뭇잎들을 갈퀴로 모아 쌓이고 있는(are being raked in a pile) 상황이 아니다.

어휘 | rake 갈퀴로 모으다

9 W-Br

(A) She's hanging some clothes on a clothesline.
(B) She's climbing a fence.
(C) Some shrubs are being trimmed.
(D) Some rope is lying on the ground.

(A) 여자가 빨랫줄에 옷을 널고 있다.
(B) 여자가 울타리를 오르고 있다.
(C) 관목이 다듬어지고 있다.
(D) 밧줄이 땅에 놓여 있다.

해설 | 사람·사물 혼합 사진 – 실외
(A) **사진에 없는 명사 언급·동작 묘사 오답:** 사진 속에 옷(clothes)이 보이지 않으며, 빨랫줄에 널고 있는(is hanging) 모습도 아니다.
(B) **동작 묘사 오답:** 여자가 울타리를 오르고 있는(is climbing) 모습이 아니다.
(C) **진행 상황 묘사 오답:** 관목이 다듬어지고 있는(are being trimmed) 상황이 아니다.
(D) **정답:** 밧줄이 땅에 놓여 있는(is lying on the ground) 모습을 잘 묘사했으므로 정답이다.

어휘 | clothesline 빨랫줄   shrub 관목   trim 손질하다, 다듬다

10 M-Cn

(A) A car is being repaired in a garage.
(B) An attendant is washing a car.
(C) A man is exiting a parking area.
(D) A car is being filled up at a fuel station.

(A) 자동차가 정비소에서 수리되고 있다.
(B) 종업원이 세차하고 있다.
(C) 남자가 주차장에서 나가고 있다.
(D) 자동차가 주유소에서 주유되고 있다.

해설 | 사람·사물 혼합 사진 – 주유소
(A) **사진에 없는 명사 언급·진행 상황 묘사 오답:** 사진 속에 정비소(garage)가 보이지 않으며, 차가 수리되고 있는(is being repaired) 상황이 아니다.
(B) **사진에 없는 명사 언급·동작 묘사 오답:** 사진 속에 종업원(attendant)이 보이지 않으며, 세차하고 있는(is washing a car) 모습이 아니다.
(C) **동작 묘사 오답:** 남자가 주차장에서 나가고 있는(is exiting a parking area)는 모습이 아니다.
(D) **정답:** 차가 주유소에서 주유되고 있는(is being filled up) 모습을 잘 묘사했으므로 정답이다.

어휘 | garage 차고, 차량 정비소   attendant 종업원, 안내원

11 W-Br

(A) Some people are walking through a garden.
(B) Some people are sitting under a canopy.
(C) Benches are being carried across the grass.
(D) Fruit is being displayed in a market.

(A) 사람들이 정원을 거닐고 있다.
(B) 사람들이 캐노피 아래에 앉아 있다.
(C) 벤치가 잔디밭을 가로질러 운반되고 있다.
(D) 과일이 시장에 진열되어 있다.

해설 | 사람·사물 혼합 사진 – 실외
(A) **동작 묘사 오답:** 사람들이 정원을 거닐고 있는(are walking) 모습이 아니다.
(B) **정답:** 사람들이 캐노피 아래에 앉아 있는(are sitting under a canopy) 모습을 잘 묘사했으므로 정답이다.
(C) **진행 상황 묘사 오답:** 벤치가 잔디밭을 가로질러 운반되고 있는(are being carried) 상황이 아니다.
(D) **사진에 없는 명사 언급 오답:** 사진 속에 과일(Fruit)과 시장(market)이 보이지 않는다.

어휘 | canopy 캐노피, 덮개

12 W-Br

(A) A toolbox has been set on the ground.
(B) A brick wall is being demolished.
(C) One of the men is pointing at a ceiling.
(D) They're crouching to lift some wood.

(A) 연장통이 바닥에 놓여 있다.
(B) 벽돌로 된 벽이 철거되고 있다.
(C) 남자 한 명이 천장을 가리키고 있다.
(D) 사람들이 나무를 들어올리기 위해 쭈그려 앉아 있다.

해설 | 사람·사물 혼합 사진 – 공사장
(A) **정답:** 연장통(toolbox)이 바닥에 놓여 있는(has been set on the ground) 모습을 잘 묘사했으므로 정답이다.
(B) **진행 상황 묘사 오답:** 벽돌로 된 벽이 철거되고 있는(is being demolished) 상황이 아니다.
(C) **사진에 없는 명사 언급 오답:** 사진 속에 천장(ceiling)이 보이지 않는다.
(D) **동작 묘사 오답:** 사람들이 나무를 들어올리기 위해(to lift some wood) 쭈그려 앉아 있는 모습이 아니다.

어휘 | toolbox 연장통   demolish 철거하다   crouch 쭈그리다, 쭈그려 앉다

UNIT 2 사물·풍경 중심 사진

ETS 유형 연습   본책 p.24

1 (B)   **2** (D)   **3** (C)

1 M-Au

(A) Wood has been loaded onto a trailer.
(B) Equipment is parked alongside some trees.
(C) Vehicles are stopped at an intersection.
(D) A hole has been dug near a building.

(A) 목재가 트레일러에 실려 있다.
(B) 장비가 나무들 옆에 나란히 주차되어 있다.
(C) 차량이 교차로에 정지해 있다.
(D) 건물 근처에 구멍이 파여 있다.

해설 | 사물·풍경 사진 – 마당/공터
(A) **상태 묘사 오답:** 목재가 트레일러에 실려 있는(has been loaded) 상태가 아니다.

(B) **정답:** 장비가 나무 옆에 나란히 주차되어 있는(is parked alongside some trees) 모습을 잘 묘사했으므로 정답이다.

(C) **사진에 없는 명사 언급 오답:** 사진 속에 교차로 (intersection)는 보이지 않는다.

(D) **사진에 없는 명사 언급 오답:** 사진 속에 구멍(hole)과 건물(building)이 보이지 않는다.

어휘 | equipment 장비 alongside ~옆에, 나란히 intersection 교차로

2 W-Br

(A) Dishes are being handed to customers.
(B) Some fruit is being washed.
(C) A coffee pot is sitting in the sink.
(D) A power cord has been plugged into an outlet.

(A) 요리가 손님들에게 건네지고 있다.
(B) 과일이 씻겨지고 있다.
(C) 커피포트가 개수대에 놓여 있다.
(D) 전선이 콘센트에 꽂혀 있다.

해설 | 사물 사진 – 주방

(A) **사진에 없는 명사 언급·진행 상황 묘사 오답:** 사진 속에 손님들(customers)은 보이지 않으며, 요리가 건네지고 있는(are being handed) 상황도 아니다.

(B) **진행 상황 묘사 오답:** 과일을 씻고 있는(is being washed) 상황은 아니다.

(C) **사진에 없는 명사 언급 오답:** 사진 속에 커피포트(coffee pot)는 보이지 않는다.

(D) **정답:** 전선이 콘센트에 꽂혀 있는(has been plugged into an outlet) 모습을 잘 묘사했으므로 정답이다.

어휘 | hand 건네주다, 넘겨주다 outlet 콘센트

3 M-Au

(A) A pathway leads to a parking area.
(B) Some hedges are being trimmed.
(C) Tools are propped against a wall.
(D) Some equipment has been left on a step.

(A) 길이 주차장으로 이어져 있다.
(B) 울타리가 손질되고 있다.
(C) **연장이 벽에 받쳐져 있다.**
(D) 몇몇 장비가 계단에 남겨져 있다.

해설 | 사물·풍경 사진 – 건물 앞

(A) **사진에 없는 명사 언급 오답:** 사진 속에 주차장(parking area)은 보이지 않는다.

(B) **진행 상황 묘사 오답:** 울타리가 손질되고 있는(are being trimmed) 상황은 아니다.

(C) **정답:** 연장이 벽에 받쳐져 있는(are propped against a wall) 모습을 잘 묘사했으므로 정답이다.

(D) **사진에 없는 명사 언급 오답:** 사진 속에 계단(step)은 보이지 않는다.

어휘 | pathway 좁은 길, 오솔길 hedge (관목으로 이어진) 울타리 trim 다듬다, 손질하다 prop against ~에 받쳐 놓다, 괴어 놓다 equipment 장비 step 계단

ETS 유형 연습

본책 p.25

1 (D) **2** (C) **3** (A)

1 M-Cn

(A) People are ascending a staircase.
(B) Banners have been suspended from some lampposts.
(C) Shoppers are browsing in a stall.
(D) A railing separates two walkways.

(A) 사람들이 계단을 오르고 있다.
(B) 가로등 기둥에 현수막이 걸려 있다.
(C) 쇼핑객들이 가판대를 둘러보고 있다.
(D) 난간이 두 통로 사이를 가르고 있다.

해설 | 사람·사물 혼합 사진 – 실외

(A) **동작 묘사 오답:** 사람들이 계단을 오르고 있는(are ascending) 모습이 아니다.

(B) **사진에 없는 명사 언급 오답:** 사진 속에 현수막(Banners)은 보이지 않는다.

(C) **사진에 없는 명사 언급 오답:** 사진 속에 가판대(stall)는 보이지 않는다.

(D) **정답:** 난간이 두 통로 사이를 가르고 있는(separates two walkways) 모습을 잘 묘사했으므로 정답이다.

어휘 | ascend 오르다 banner 현수막 suspend 걸다, 매달다 browse 둘러보다 stall 가판대, 좌판 separate (둘 사이를) 가르다

2 M-Au

(A) A worker is handing some cash to a woman.
(B) Some plates are stacked next to a cash register.
(C) A box is on the counter between two people.
(D) A customer is leaning against a display case.

(A) 종업원이 여자에게 현금을 건네고 있다.
(B) 접시들이 금전 등록기 옆에 쌓여 있다.
(C) 상자가 두 사람 사이의 카운터 위에 있다.
(D) 고객이 진열 선반에 기대고 있다.

해설 | 사람·사물 혼합 사진 – 카운터
(A) **사진에 없는 명사 언급 오답:** 사진 속에 현금(cash)은 보이지 않는다.
(B) **위치 묘사 오답:** 접시들이 금전 등록기 옆에(next to a cash register) 쌓여 있는 모습이 아니다.
(C) **정답:** 상자가 두 사람 사이의 카운터 위에 있는(is on the counter) 모습을 잘 묘사했으므로 정답이다.
(D) **동작 묘사 오답:** 고객이 진열 선반에 기대고 있는(is leaning against) 모습이 아니다.

어휘 | stack 쌓다 **cash register** 금전 등록기 **lean against** 기대다

3 M-Cn

(A) Some merchandise is being displayed for sale.
(B) Shoppers are lining up to make a purchase.
(C) Shoe boxes have been stacked in a corner.
(D) A vendor is standing outside of a shop.

(A) 상품이 판매를 위해 진열되어 있다.
(B) 쇼핑객들이 구입하기 위해 줄 서 있다.
(C) 신발 상자들이 구석에 쌓여 있다.
(D) 상인이 상점 바깥에 서 있다.

해설 | 사람·사물 혼합 사진 – 상점
(A) **정답:** 상품이 판매를 위해 진열되어 있는(is being displayed for sale) 모습을 잘 묘사했으므로 정답이다.
(B) **사진에 없는 명사 언급 오답:** 사진 속에 쇼핑객들(Shoppers)은 보이지 않는다.
(C) **사진에 없는 명사 언급 오답:** 사진 속에 신발 상자들(Shoe boxes)은 보이지 않는다.
(D) **위치 묘사 오답:** 상인이 상점 바깥(outside of a shop)이 아니라 안에 있다.

어휘 | merchandise 상품 **make a purchase** 구입하다 **stack** 쌓다

ETS 고득점 실전 문제
본책 p.27

| 1 (A) | 2 (D) | 3 (D) | 4 (B) | 5 (C) | 6 (A) |
| 7 (B) | 8 (C) | 9 (D) | 10 (B) | 11 (D) | 12 (B) |

1 M-Au

(A) Some lamps are switched on.
(B) A blanket has been rolled up.
(C) Some clothing has been folded on the bed.
(D) Some pillows are scattered on the carpet.

(A) 몇 개 램프에 불이 켜져 있다.
(B) 이불이 말려 있다.
(C) 옷이 침대 위에 개어져 있다.
(D) 베개들이 카펫 위에 흩어져 있다.

해설 | 사물 사진 – 침실
(A) **정답:** 램프에 불이 켜져 있는(are switched on) 모습을 잘 묘사했으므로 정답이다.
(B) **상태 묘사 오답:** 이불이 말려 있는(has been rolled up) 상태가 아니다.
(C) **사진에 없는 명사 언급 오답:** 사진 속에 옷(clothing)은 보이지 않는다.
(D) **위치 묘사 오답:** 베개들이 침대 위에는 있지만 카펫 위에는 (on the carpet) 없다.

어휘 | scatter 흩뿌리다

2 W-Br

(A) A market is full of shoppers.
(B) Some signs have been posted on a bulletin board.
(C) There are some cooking utensils on the ground.
(D) Fruit and vegetables have been put on display.

(A) 시장이 쇼핑객들로 가득하다.
(B) 표지판들이 게시판에 게시되어 있다.
(C) 바닥에 조리기구들이 놓여 있다.
(D) 과일과 채소가 진열되어 있다.

해설 | 사물 사진 – 시장
(A) **사진에 없는 명사 언급 오답:** 사진 속에 쇼핑객들 (shoppers)이 보이지 않는다.
(B) **사진에 없는 명사 언급 오답:** 사진 속에 게시판(bulletin board)은 보이지 않는다.
(C) **사진에 없는 명사 언급 오답:** 사진 속에 조리기구(cooking utensils)가 보이지 않는다.
(D) **정답:** 과일과 채소가 진열되어 있는(have been put on display) 모습을 잘 묘사했으므로 정답이다.

어휘 | be full of ~으로 가득 차다 **bulletin board** 게시판 **utensil** 기구 **put on display** 진열하다, 전시하다

3 M-Cn

(A) She's taking some food items from a display case.
(B) She's holding a cafeteria menu.
(C) A handbag has been set on a counter.
(D) A touch screen monitor has been placed on a stand.

(A) 여자가 진열대에서 음식을 꺼내고 있다.
(B) 여자가 구내식당 메뉴를 들고 있다.
(C) 핸드백이 카운터에 놓여 있다.
(D) 터치스크린 모니터가 스탠드에 놓여 있다.

해설 | 사람·사물 혼합 사진 – 실내
(A) **사진에 없는 명사 언급 오답:** 사진 속에 음식(food items)과 진열대(display case)가 보이지 않는다.
(B) **동작 묘사 오답:** 여자가 구내식당 메뉴를 들고 있는(is holding) 모습이 아니다.
(C) **위치 묘사 오답:** 핸드백은 여자가 메고 있으며 카운터에 놓여(has been set on a counter) 있지 않다.
(D) **정답:** 터치스크린 모니터가 스탠드에 놓여 있는(has been placed on a stand) 모습을 잘 묘사했으므로 정답이다.

어휘 | place 놓다, 두다

4 W-Am

(A) A backpack has been left against a wall.
(B) A jacket has been hung up on the back of a chair.
(C) One of the women is painting a picture.
(D) One of the women is removing a lid from a plastic cup.

(A) 배낭이 벽에 기대어져 있다.
(B) **재킷이 의자 등받이에 걸려 있다.**
(C) 여자 한 명이 그림을 그리고 있다.
(D) 여자 한 명이 플라스틱 컵의 뚜껑을 열고 있다.

해설 | 사람·사물 혼합 사진 – 실내
(A) **위치 묘사 오답:** 배낭이 벽에(against a wall) 기대어 있지 않고 의자에 기대어 있다.
(B) **정답:** 의자 등받이에(on the back of a chair) 겉옷이 걸려 있는(has been hung up) 모습을 잘 묘사했으므로 정답이다.
(C) **동작 묘사 오답:** 누구도 그림을 그리고 있는(is painting a picture) 모습이 아니다.
(D) **동작 묘사 오답:** 누구도 플라스틱 컵의 뚜껑을 열고 있는(is removing a lid from a plastic cup) 모습이 아니다.

어휘 | lid 뚜껑

5 M-Cn

(A) Some windows are being installed.
(B) Some cars are exiting a garage.
(C) Some lines have been painted in a parking area.
(D) Some plants have been lined up along a walkway.

(A) 창문이 설치되고 있다.
(B) 차들이 차고에서 나가고 있다.
(C) **주차장에 선이 그려져 있다.**
(D) 통로를 따라 식물들이 줄지어 있다.

해설 | 사물·풍경 사진 – 건물 앞 주차장
(A) **진행 상황 묘사 오답:** 창문이 설치되고 있는(are being installed) 모습이 아니다.
(B) **사진에 없는 명사 언급·상태 묘사 오답:** 사진 속에 차고(garage)가 보이지 않으며, 차들이 나가고(are exiting) 있지 않고 주차되어 있다.
(C) **정답:** 주차장에 선이 그려져 있는(have been painted) 모습을 잘 묘사했으므로 정답이다.
(D) **사진에 없는 명사 언급 오답:** 통로에 식물들이(Some plants) 보이지 않는다.

어휘 | install 설치하다   line up 줄을 서다

6 M-Au

(A) Some light fixtures are mounted on a building.
(B) Some plants are displayed on a window ledge.
(C) Some roof tiles are being installed.
(D) A ladder is leaning against a bench.

(A) **건물에 조명 기구들이 고정되어 있다.**
(B) 창턱에 식물들이 진열되어 있다.
(C) 지붕 타일이 설치되고 있다.
(D) 사다리가 벤치에 기대어 있다.

해설 | 사물·풍경 사진 – 건물 밖
(A) **정답:** 건물에 조명 기구들이 고정되어 있는(are mounted) 모습을 잘 묘사했으므로 정답이다.
(B) **위치 묘사 오답:** 식물들이 창턱이(on a window ledge) 아니라 바닥에 있다.
(C) **진행 상황 묘사 오답:** 지붕 타일이 설치되고 있는(are being installed) 상황이 아니다.
(D) **사진에 없는 명사 언급·위치 묘사 오답:** 사진에 벤치(bench)가 보이지 않으며, 사다리는 벽에 기대어 있는 모습이다.

어휘 | light fixture 조명 기구   mount 고정시키다   window ledge 창턱   install 설치하다

7 W-Br

(A) A flag is flying from a roof.
(B) Some clothes are hanging on a patio.
(C) Umbrellas are shading a balcony.
(D) Lights are strung between two columns.

(A) 지붕에서 깃발이 펄럭이고 있다.
(B) 테라스에 옷들이 걸려 있다.
(C) 파라솔들이 발코니에 그늘을 드리우고 있다.
(D) 두 개의 기둥 사이로 조명이 매달려 있다.

해설 | 사물·풍경 사진 – 발코니
(A) **사진에 없는 명사 언급 오답:** 사진 속에 깃발(flag)이 보이지 않는다.
(B) **정답:** 테라스에 옷들이 걸려 있는(are hanging) 모습을 잘 묘사했으므로 정답이다.
(C) **사진에 없는 명사 언급 오답:** 사진 속에 파라솔 (Umbrellas)이 보이지 않는다.
(D) **상태 묘사 오답:** 두 개의 기둥 사이로 조명 같이 보이는 것이 천장에 있지만, 매달려 있는(are strung) 상태는 아니다.

어휘 | shade 그늘지게 하다   string 묶다, 매달다   column 기둥

8 M-Au

(A) The man is moving some documents on a cart.
(B) The man is putting a poster in a frame.
(C) Stacks of paper have been piled on the floor.
(D) Some shelves are being installed in a storage room.

(A) 남자가 서류를 카트로 옮기고 있다.
(B) 남자가 포스터를 액자에 넣고 있다.
(C) 종이더미가 바닥에 쌓여 있다.
(D) 창고에 선반들이 설치되고 있다.

해설 | 사람·사물 혼합 사진 – 창고
(A) **사진에 없는 명사 언급 오답:** 사진 속에 카트(cart)가 보이지 않는다.
(B) **사진에 없는 명사 언급·동작 묘사 오답:** 사진 속에 포스터(poster)가 보이지 않으며, 남자가 액자에 넣고 있는(is putting a poster in a frame) 모습이 아니다.
(C) **정답:** 종이더미(Stacks of paper)가 바닥에 쌓여 있는(have been piled on the floor) 상태를 잘 묘사했으므로 정답이다.
(D) **진행 상황 묘사 오답:** 창고에 선반들이 설치되고 있는(are being installed) 상황이 아니다.

어휘 | a stack of 한 무더기의   pile 쌓다   storage 저장, 보관

9 M-Cn

(A) Some pots are suspended from the ceiling.
(B) Some drinking glasses are stacked on a tray.
(C) Meals are waiting to be delivered to some tables.
(D) There is a vent over a cooking area.

(A) 냄비들이 천장에 매달려 있다.
(B) 음료 잔들이 쟁반에 쌓여 있다.
(C) 식사가 테이블로 전달되기 위해 대기 중이다.
(D) 조리 구역 위쪽으로 환기구가 있다.

해설 | 사물 사진 – 주방
(A) **위치 묘사 오답:** 냄비들이 조리대와 벽 선반 위에 놓여 있으며, 천장에 매달려(are suspended) 있지 않다.
(B) **사진에 없는 명사 언급·상태 묘사 오답:** 사진 속에 쟁반(tray)이 보이지 않으며, 음료 잔이 쌓여 있는(are stacked) 모습도 보이지 않는다.
(C) **사진에 없는 명사 언급 오답:** 사진 속에 음식(Meals)이 보이지 않는다.
(D) **정답:** 조리 구역 위쪽(over a cooking area)으로 환기구(vent)가 있는 모습을 잘 묘사했으므로 정답이다.

어휘 | suspend 걸다, 매달다   stack 쌓다   vent 환기구, 통풍구

10 W-Br

(A) There are umbrellas shading each of the balconies.
(B) There are cars parked on the ground level of a building.
(C) There are some windows on the second floor being replaced.
(D) There is heavy traffic on the street.

(A) 발코니마다 그늘을 만들어 주는 파라솔이 있다.
(B) 건물 1층에 주차된 차들이 있다.
(C) 2층의 유리창들이 교체되고 있다.
(D) 거리에 교통체증이 심하다.

해설 | 사물·풍경 사진 – 건물 차고
(A) **사진에 없는 명사 언급 오답:** 사진 속에 파라솔 (umbrellas)이 보이지 않는다.
(B) **정답:** 건물 1층에 주차된 차들이 있는(There are cars parked) 상태를 잘 묘사했으므로 정답이다.
(C) **진행 상황 묘사 오답:** 2층의 유리창들이 교체되고 있는(being replaced) 상황이 아니다.
(D) **상태 묘사 오답:** 거리가 비어 있으며, 교통체증이 심한(heavy traffic) 상태가 아니다.

어휘 | shade 그늘지게 하다   replace 교체하다

11 W-Br

(A) A bus is parked in a parking area.
(B) The women are exercising on the grass.
(C) There's a picnic area next to a storefront.
(D) A walkway separates a parking area from a lawn.

(A) 버스가 주차장에 주차되어 있다.
(B) 여자들이 잔디밭에서 운동하고 있다.
(C) 상점 앞 공간 옆에 피크닉 장소가 있다.
(D) 통로가 주차장과 잔디밭을 가르고 있다.

해설 | 사람·사물 혼합 사진 – 실외
(A) **사진에 없는 명사 언급 오답:** 사진 속에 버스(bus)가 보이지 않는다.
(B) **동작 묘사 오답:** 여자들이 잔디밭에서 운동하고 있는(are exercising) 모습이 아니다.
(C) **사진에 없는 명사 언급 오답:** 사진 속에 상점(store)이 보이지 않는다.
(D) **정답:** 통로가 주차장과 잔디밭을 가르는(separates a parking area from a lawn) 상태를 잘 묘사했으므로 정답이다.

어휘 | storefront 가게 앞 공간   separate (둘 사이를) 가르다

12 M-Au

(A) Some place mats are stacked on a table.
(B) Some glasses have been filled with beverages.
(C) Eating utensils are piled on a plate.
(D) Vegetables have been collected in a basket.

(A) 식탁 깔개가 탁자 위에 쌓여 있다.
(B) 유리잔에 음료가 채워져 있다.
(C) 수저와 포크가 접시 위에 쌓여 있다.
(D) 채소가 바구니 안에 모아져 있다.

해설 | 사물 사진 – 식탁
(A) **상태 묘사 오답:** 식탁 깔개가 놓여 있지만, 탁자 위에 쌓여 있는(are stacked) 상태가 아니다.
(B) **정답:** 유리잔에 음료가 채워져 있는(have been filled with beverages) 상태를 잘 묘사했으므로 정답이다.
(C) **상태 묘사 오답:** 수저와 포크가 보이지만 접시 위에 쌓여 있는(are piled) 상태가 아니다.
(D) **사진에 없는 명사 언급 오답:** 사진 속에 바구니(basket)가 보이지 않는다.

어휘 | stack 쌓다   beverage 음료   utensil 기구   collect 모으다, 쌓이다

LC | PART 2

UNIT 3 Who / What·Which 의문문

ETS 유형 연습   본책 p.36

1 (A) **2** (A) **3** (A) **4** (A) **5** (B) **6** (A)

1 W-Am / W-Br

Who made the slide show for the presentation?
(A) Paul, from the marketing department.
(B) On the second slide.
(C) I went to the show.

발표 자료 슬라이드쇼를 누가 만들었죠?
(A) 마케팅 부서의 폴이요.
(B) 두 번째 슬라이드에서요.
(C) 저는 그 공연을 보러 갔어요.

해설 | 담당자를 묻는 Who 의문문
(A) **정답:** 슬라이드쇼를 만든 사람을 묻는 질문에 구체적인 이름(Paul)을 제시했으므로 정답이다.
(B) **관련 없는 오답:** Where 의문문에 적합한 응답이다.
(C) **다의어 오답:** 질문에 나오는 show는 '슬라이드쇼'에서의 '쇼'이고, 보기의 show는 '공연'이라는 뜻이다.

어휘 | presentation 발표   department 부서

2 W-Am / W-Br

Who's got this month's budget report?
(A) I have it right here.
(B) For him, I think.
(C) On the radio.

이번 달 예산보고서는 누가 갖고 있나요?
(A) 제가 여기 갖고 있습니다.
(B) 그를 위해서라고 생각해요.
(C) 라디오에서요.

해설 | 보고서 소지자를 묻는 Who 의문문
(A) **정답:** 내가 여기에 갖고 있다(I have it right here)며 구체적으로 제시했으므로 정답이다.
(B) **인칭 오류 오답:** 대명사 him이 가리키는 대상이 질문에 없다.
(C) **관련 없는 오답:** Where 의문문에 적합한 응답이다.

3 M-Au / M-Cn

Who's responsible for authorizing credit card purchases?
(A) Isn't it the manager?
(B) Not if you use cash.
(C) Only for office supplies.

신용카드 구매 승인 담당자가 누구인가요?
(A) 부장님 아닌가요?
(B) 현금을 사용하면 그렇지 않아요.
(C) 사무용품을 구입할 때만요.

해설 | 담당자를 묻는 Who 의문문
(A) **정답:** 담당자가 부장이 아닌지 되묻고(Isn't it the manager?) 있으므로 가장 적절한 응답이다.
(B) **연상 작용 오답:** 질문의 credit card purchases에서 연상 가능한 cash를 이용한 오답이다.
(C) **연상 작용 오답:** 질문의 credit card purchases에서 연상 가능한 office supplies를 이용한 오답이다.

어휘 | be responsible for ~을 담당하다 **authorize** 허가하다 **purchase** 구매; 구매하다 **office supplies** 사무용품

4 W-Am / M-Cn

Who's looking into the problems with the printer?
(A) No one's had a chance yet.
(B) It looks that way.
(C) I'll print it out right away.

프린터에 생긴 문제들은 누가 살펴보고 있어요?
(A) 아직 아무도 그럴 기회가 없었어요.
(B) 그래 보여요.
(C) 제가 지금 바로 출력할게요.

해설 | 담당자를 묻는 Who 의문문
(A) **정답:** 아무도 그런 사람이 없다(No one)고 상황 설명을 하고 있으므로 가장 적절한 응답이다.
(B) **단어 반복 오답:** 질문의 look을 반복 이용한 오답이다.
(C) **파생어 오답:** 질문의 printer와 파생어 관계인 print를 이용한 오답이다.

어휘 | look into 조사하다, 살펴보다

5 W-Br / M-Cn

Who gave the presentation on current market trends?
(A) No, not recently.
(B) I can't remember the person's name.
(C) Sales are up by twenty percent.

현재 시장 동향에 관한 발표는 누가 했어요?
(A) 아니요, 최근은 아닙니다.
(B) 이름이 기억나지 않네요.
(C) 매출이 20퍼센트 상승했습니다.

해설 | 발표자를 묻는 Who 의문문
(A) **Yes/No 대답 불가 오답:** 의문사 의문문에는 Yes/No로 대답할 수 없다.
(B) **정답:** 발표자 이름이 기억나지 않는다(I can't remember the person's name)며 모른다는 말을 우회적으로 드러낸 적절한 응답이다.
(C) **연상 작용 오답:** 질문의 market trends에서 연상 가능한 Sales를 이용한 오답이다.

어휘 | presentation 발표 **current** 현재의 **recently** 최근에

6 W-Am / M-Cn

Who can help me set up my computer monitor?
(A) I always ask William my technical questions.
(B) They're monitoring customer satisfaction.
(C) That's a great deal.

누가 제 컴퓨터 모니터 설치를 도와줄 수 있나요?
(A) 저는 기술 문제는 항상 윌리엄에게 요청해요.
(B) 그들은 고객 만족도를 모니터링하고 있어요.
(C) 저렴하네요.

해설 | 도움 제공자를 묻는 Who 의문문
(A) **정답:** 기술 문제는 항상 윌리엄(William)에게 요청한다며 구체적인 이름을 제시했으므로 정답이다.
(B) **인칭 오류 및 다의어 오답:** 대명사 They가 가리키는 대상이 질문에 없으며, 다의어 monitor(모니터-모니터하다, 추적 관찰하다)를 이용한 오답이다.
(C) **관련 없는 오답:** 질문과 상관없는 답변을 제시한 오답이다.

어휘 | set up 설치하다 **technical** 기술적인 **satisfaction** 만족

ETS 유형 연습

본책 p.37

| 1 (B) | 2 (A) | 3 (A) | 4 (A) | 5 (B) | 6 (A) |

1 W-Am / M-Cn

What's the log-on password?
(A) The file cabinet is full.
(B) The instructions are on your desk.
(C) We passed by the bank.

로그인 패스워드가 어떻게 되죠?
(A) 문서 보관함이 꽉 찼어요.
(B) 설명서가 책상 위에 있어요.
(C) 우리는 은행을 지나쳤어요.

해설 | 패스워드를 묻는 What 의문문
(A) **관련 없는 오답:** 질문과 상관없는 답변을 제시한 오답이다.
(B) **정답:** 설명서가 책상 위에 있다(The instructions are on your desk)며 설명서를 참고하라는 것을 우회적으로 드러낸 적절한 응답이다.
(C) **유사 발음 오답:** 질문의 password와 부분적으로 발음이 동일한 pass를 이용한 오답이다.

어휘 | instructions 설명, 지시 **pass by** 지나가다

2 M-Cn / M-Au

What other companies were at the job fair?
(A) I have the complete list in my briefcase.
(B) He did get a job offer.
(C) It'll be nice to have company at lunch.

채용 박람회에 어떤 다른 회사들이 있었나요?
(A) 제 서류가방에 전체 명단이 있어요.
(B) 그가 정말 일자리를 제안 받았어요.
(C) 점심 때 일행이 있으면 좋을 거예요.

해설 | 참가 회사를 묻는 **What 의문문**

(A) **정답:** 자신의 서류가방에 전체 명단이 있다(have the complete list in my briefcase)면서 곧 정보를 알려줄 수 있음을 우회적으로 말한 정답이다.

(B) **단어 반복 및 인칭 오류 오답:** 질문에 나온 job을 반복 이용했고, 질문에 He가 가리키는 대상이 없으므로 오답이다.

(C) **다의어 오답:** 질문의 company는 '회사'라는 뜻으로, 보기의 company는 '일행'이라는 뜻으로 썼다.

어휘 | company 회사; 일행 complete 완전한 briefcase 서류가방 have company 동행[일행]이 있다

3 W-Br / M-Cn

Which contract are we discussing at today's board meeting?

(A) The one for Dagwood Incorporated.
(B) The bulletin board by the kitchen.
(C) Just a couple of days ago.

오늘 이사회에서 어떤 계약 건에 대해 논의하나요?

(A) 대그우드 사 계약이요.
(B) 부엌 옆에 있는 게시판이요.
(C) 불과 며칠 전에요.

해설 | 논의할 계약 건을 묻는 **Which 의문문**

(A) **정답:** 대명사 the one(the contract)을 사용하여 대그우드 사와의 계약 건(The one for Dagwood Incorporated)이라고 답하고 있으므로 정답이다.

(B) **다의어 오답:** 질문의 board는 '이사회'라는 뜻으로, 보기의 board는 '게시판'이라는 뜻으로 썼다.

(C) **관련 없는 오답:** When 의문문에 적합한 응답이다.

어휘 | contract 계약(서) incorporated 주식회사 bulletin board 게시판 a couple of 두서너 개의, 몇 개의

4 M-Cn / W-Am

What construction project are you involved in?

(A) We're building a recreation center.
(B) I didn't read the instructions.
(C) The projected budget is seven million dollars.

어떤 공사 프로젝트에 관여하고 있나요?

(A) 저희는 레크리에이션 센터를 짓고 있어요.
(B) 설명서를 읽지 않았어요.
(C) 추정 예산은 7백만 달러입니다.

해설 | 공사 프로젝트를 묻는 **What 의문문**

(A) **정답:** 레크리에이션 센터(a recreation center)를 짓고 있다고 답했으므로 정답이다.

(B) **유사 발음 오답:** 질문의 construction과 발음이 유사한 instructions를 이용한 오답이다.

(C) **다의어 오답:** 질문의 project는 '프로젝트, 사업'이라는 뜻으로 보기의 project는 '예상하다, 추정하다'라는 의미로 썼다.

어휘 | construction 건설, 공사 be involved in ~에 관여하다 instructions 설명, 지시 project 프로젝트, 사업; 예상하다, 추정하다

5 M-Au / W-Br

What's the policy for taking vacation time?

(A) I prefer the mountains.
(B) It requires management approval.
(C) A nine A.M. start time.

휴가 사용 정책이 뭐죠?

(A) 저는 산이 더 좋아요.
(B) 관리자 승인이 필요해요.
(C) 오전 9시에 시작해요.

해설 | 휴가 사용 정책에 대해 묻는 **What 의문문**

(A) **연상 작용 오답:** 질문의 vacation에서 연상 가능한 mountains를 언급한 오답이다.

(B) **정답:** 관리자의 승인이 필요하다(It requires management approval)며 휴가를 가려면 관리자의 허락이 필요하다고 말하고 있으므로 정답이다.

(C) **단어 반복 오답:** 질문의 time을 반복 이용한 오답이다.

어휘 | require 요구하다, 필요로 하다 management 관리, 경영진 approval 승인

6 M-Au / M-Cn

Which tourist attractions do you recommend?

(A) Helen will show you around.
(B) The expressway is faster.
(C) No, they're from Guangzhou.

어떤 관광 명소를 추천하시나요?

(A) 헬렌이 안내해 드릴 겁니다.
(B) 고속도로가 더 빨라요.
(C) 아니요, 그들은 광저우 출신이에요.

해설 | 관광 명소 추천을 묻는 **Which 의문문**

(A) **정답:** 헬렌이 안내해 줄 것(Helen will show you around)이라며 본인은 잘 모른다는 사실을 우회적으로 드러낸 적절한 응답이다.

(B) **연상 작용 오답:** 질문의 do you recommend에서 연상 가능한 faster를 언급한 오답이다.

(C) **Yes/No 대답 불가 오답:** 의문사 의문문에는 Yes/No로 대답할 수 없다.

어휘 | tourist attraction 관광 명소 recommend 추천하다

ETS 고득점 실전 문제   본책 p.38

1 (A) **2** (A) **3** (C) **4** (B) **5** (A) **6** (B)
7 (A) **8** (C) **9** (B) **10** (C) **11** (C) **12** (B)
13 (B) **14** (C) **15** (B) **16** (B) **17** (B) **18** (A)
19 (A) **20** (A)

1 M-Au / W-Am

Who's in charge of sending out the event invitations?

(A) Hyun-Soo Choi is handling it.
(B) Cash or credit card?
(C) That makes sense.

행사 초청장 발송은 누가 담당해요?
(A) 현수 최가 처리하고 있어요.
(B) 현금이에요, 아니면 신용카드예요?
(C) 일리가 있네요.

해설 | 담당자를 묻는 Who 의문문
(A) **정답:** 담당자 이름을 Hyun-Soo Choi라고 구체적으로
　　제시했으므로 정답이다.
(B) **연상 작용 오답:** 질문의 charge를 '요금'이라는 뜻으로 잘못
　　이해했을 경우 연상 가능한 Cash, credit card를 이용한
　　오답이다.
(C) **유사 발음 오답:** 질문의 sending과 발음이 유사한 sense로
　　혼동을 준 오답이다.

어휘 | in charge of ~을 맡아서, 담당해서 **invitation** 초대,
초청 **make sense** 말이 되다, 타당하다

2　M-Au / W-Am
What should I provide to complete my travel
request?
(A) Your passport will be fine.
(B) To see my family.
(C) The end of the week.

출장 요청을 완료하려면 무엇을 드려야 하나요?
(A) 여권이면 됩니다.
(B) 가족을 만나려고요.
(C) 이번 주말이요.

해설 | 제출 서류를 묻는 What 의문문
(A) **정답:** 제출 서류를 구체적으로 여권(Your passport)이라고
　　제시했으므로 정답이다.
(B) **연상 작용 오답:** 질문의 travel에서 연상 가능한 To see my
　　family를 이용한 오답이다.
(C) **관련 없는 오답:** When 의문문에 적합한 응답이다.

어휘 | provide 제공하다 **complete** 완료하다 **request**
요청(서)

3　W-Br / M-Au
Who do I talk to about changing my seat?
(A) A three-hour direct flight.
(B) No, I don't know my seat number.
(C) The agent at the airline counter.

좌석 변경에 관해 누구에게 이야기하죠?
(A) 3시간 직항편이요.
(B) 아니요, 제 좌석 번호를 몰라요.
(C) 항공사 카운터 직원이요.

해설 | 담당자를 묻는 Who 의문문
(A) **연상 작용 오답:** 질문의 seat에서 연상 가능한 flight를
　　언급한 오답이다.
(B) **Yes/No 대답 불가 및 단어 반복 오답:** 의문사 의문문에는
　　Yes/No로 대답할 수 없으며, 질문의 seat을 반복 사용한
　　오답이다.
(C) **정답:** 담당자를 구체적으로 항공사 카운터 직원(The agent
　　at the airline counter)이라고 제시했으므로 정답이다.

어휘 | agent 대리인

4　M-Au / W-Am
What should I prepare for the sales workshop?
(A) A group of us went.
(B) Didn't Elizabeth take care of everything?
(C) That should be fine.

영업 워크숍을 위해서 저는 무엇을 준비해야 할까요?
(A) 우리 팀이 갔어요.
(B) 엘리자베스가 모든 일을 처리하지 않았나요?
(C) 괜찮을 것 같아요.

해설 | 준비 사항을 묻는 What 의문문
(A) **관련 없는 오답:** Who 의문문에 적합한 응답이다.
(B) **정답:** 엘리자베스가 모든 일을 처리하지 않았냐(Didn't
　　Elizabeth take care of everything?)고 되물으며
　　준비할 것이 없다고 우회적으로 말하는 적절한 응답이다.
(C) **관련 없는 오답:** 질문과 상관없는 답변을 제시한 오답이다.

어휘 | prepare for ~을 준비하다 **take care of** ~을 처리하다

5　M-Au / M-Cn
What vendors will be at the trade show?
(A) The list isn't available yet.
(B) The exhibit space on the fourth floor.
(C) No, for the latest automobiles.

무역 박람회에 어떤 업체들이 참가할까요?
(A) 목록이 아직 안 나왔어요.
(B) 4층에 있는 전시 공간이요.
(C) 아니요, 최신 자동차를 위한 거예요.

해설 | 참여 업체를 묻는 What 의문문
(A) **정답:** 목록이 아직 안 나왔다(The list isn't available
　　yet)며 알려줄 수 없음을 우회적으로 드러내고 있으므로 가장
　　적절한 응답이다.
(B) **연상 작용 오답:** 질문의 trade show에서 연상 가능한
　　exhibit space를 이용한 오답이다.
(C) **Yes/No 대답 불가 오답:** 의문사 의문문에는 Yes/No로
　　대답할 수 없다.

어휘 | vendor 판매 회사 **available** 이용 가능한, 구할 수 있는
exhibit 전시 **latest** 최신의

6　W-Am / M-Cn
Who's the new department supervisor?
(A) I bought it at the department store.
(B) The position is still open.
(C) On Forty-Second Avenue.

신임 부서장은 누구죠?
(A) 백화점에서 샀어요.
(B) 그 자리는 아직 공석이에요.
(C) 42번 가에서요.

해설 | 특정 인물을 묻는 Who 의문문
(A) **단어 반복 오답:** 질문의 department를 반복 이용한
　　오답이다.

(B) **정답:** 그 자리는 아직 공석(The position is still open)이라며 제3의 답변을 한 가장 적절한 응답이다.

(C) **관련 없는 오답:** Where 의문문에 적합한 응답이다.

어휘 | supervisor 감독관, 관리자 position 직책

7 M-Cn / W-Am

Who's organizing the reunion for our graduating class?

(A) That's been delayed until February.

(B) No, I don't qualify for that discount.

(C) I did well in that course.

우리 졸업반 동창회는 누가 준비하고 있죠?

(A) 2월로 연기됐어요.

(B) 아니요, 저는 할인 받을 자격이 안 돼요.

(C) 저는 그 과목을 잘 했어요.

해설 | 담당자를 묻는 Who 의문문

(A) **정답:** 동창회가 2월로 연기됐다(That's been delayed until February)며 아직 누군지 알 수 없음을 우회적으로 드러내고 있으므로 가장 적절한 응답이다.

(B) **Yes/No 대답 불가 오답:** 의문사 의문문에는 Yes/No로 대답할 수 없다.

(C) **연상 작용 오답:** 질문의 class에서 연상 가능한 course를 언급한 오답이다.

어휘 | organize 준비하다, 조직하다 reunion 동창회, 모임 delay 미루다, 연기하다 qualify for ~의 자격이 되다

8 W-Am / M-Cn

What do you think of Dr. Smith?

(A) I thought so, too.

(B) No, on Milton Avenue.

(C) She's been Ravi's doctor for ten years.

스미스 의사 선생님을 어떻게 생각하세요?

(A) 저도 그렇게 생각했어요.

(B) 아니요, 밀튼 가에서요.

(C) 10년간 라비의 주치의였어요.

해설 | 의견을 묻는 What 의문문

(A) **단어 반복 오답:** 질문의 think를 과거형 thought로 반복 이용한 오답이다.

(B) **Yes/No 대답 불가 오답:** 의문사 의문문에는 Yes/No로 대답할 수 없다.

(C) **정답:** 10년간 라비의 주치의였다(She's been Ravi's doctor for ten years)고 말함으로써 스미스 씨가 괜찮은 의사라는 의미를 내포한 우회적인 응답이다.

9 M-Au / W-Am

What's your opinion of the new accountant?

(A) A college degree in finance.

(B) She seems really competent.

(C) I've read the company's safety policy.

새 회계사에 대해 어떻게 생각해요?

(A) 재무학 학사 학위요.

(B) 아주 유능해 보여요.

(C) 회사 안전 정책을 읽어 봤어요.

해설 | 의견을 묻는 What 의문문

(A) **연상 작용 오답:** 질문의 accountant에서 연상 가능한 finance를 언급한 오답이다.

(B) **정답:** 새 회계사에 대해 아주 유능해 보인다(She seems really competent)는 의견을 제시했으므로 정답이다.

(C) **관련 없는 오답:** 질문과 상관없는 답변을 제시한 오답이다.

어휘 | accountant 회계사 degree 학위 finance 재무 competent 유능한, 적임의 policy 정책

10 W-Br / M-Cn

Which management seminar do you want to attend?

(A) Henry was recently promoted.

(B) Thanks, but I already have one.

(C) I prefer the one on leadership skills.

어떤 경영 세미나에 참석하고 싶으세요?

(A) 헨리는 최근에 승진했어요.

(B) 고맙지만 이미 갖고 있어요.

(C) 리더십 역량에 관한 것이 좋아요.

해설 | 참석 희망 세미나를 묻는 Which 의문문

(A) **관련 없는 오답:** 질문과 상관없는 답변을 제시한 오답이다.

(B) **연상 작용 오답:** Which 의문문에서 연상 가능한 대명사 one을 언급한 오답이다.

(C) **정답:** 리더십 역량에 관한 것(the one on leadership skills)이라고 구체적으로 제시했으므로 정답이다.

어휘 | management 관리, 경영 attend 참석하다 be promoted 승진하다

11 W-Br / M-Cn

Who's involved in organizing the town festival?

(A) Admission and activities are free.

(B) It's on Saturday morning.

(C) Oh, are you interested in helping out?

마을 축제 준비와 관련된 사람이 누구죠?

(A) 입장료와 행사비가 무료입니다.

(B) 토요일 아침이에요.

(C) 아, 도와주려고요?

해설 | 행사 관계자를 묻는 Who 의문문

(A) **연상 작용 오답:** 질문의 festival에서 연상 가능한 admission과 activities를 이용한 오답이다.

(B) **관련 없는 오답:** When 의문문에 적합한 응답이다.

(C) **정답:** 마을 축제 준비 관련 질문에 도와줄 의향이 있는지(are you interested in helping out?) 되물어 질문자의 협조를 구하고 있으므로 적절한 응답이다.

어휘 | be involved in ~에 관여하다 admission 입장(료) activity 행사, 활동 be interested in ~에 관심이 있다

12 M-Cn / W-Br

What are the qualifications for the job?
(A) Yes, the fabric is high quality.
(B) The company hasn't posted any details yet.
(C) It's stored under the sink.

그 일자리에 필요한 자격은 어떻게 되나요?
(A) 네, 직물이 고급이에요.
(B) 회사에서 아직 세부 사항을 게시하지 않았어요.
(C) 개수대 아래 보관되어 있어요.

해설 | 구직 자격을 묻는 What 의문문
(A) Yes/No 대답 불가 및 유사 발음 오답: 의문사 의문문에는 Yes/No로 대답할 수 없으며, 질문의 qualifications와 부분적으로 발음이 유사한 quality를 이용한 오답이다.
(B) 정답: 회사에서 세부 사항을 게시하지 않아서(The company hasn't posted any details yet) 아직 모른다는 사실을 우회적으로 답한 적절한 응답이다.
(C) 관련 없는 오답: 질문과 상관없는 답변을 제시한 오답이다.

어휘 | qualification 자격, 자질   post 게시하다   store 보관하다

13 W-Br / M-Cn

What are you going to include in the report?
(A) Thanks, it's very helpful.
(B) That's the committee's decision.
(C) We found them behind the desk.

보고서에 무엇을 포함시킬 예정인가요?
(A) 고맙습니다. 도움이 많이 됐어요.
(B) 그건 위원회에서 결정해요.
(C) 책상 뒤에서 찾았어요.

해설 | 보고서 포함 내용을 묻는 What 의문문
(A) 관련 없는 오답: 요청·제안문에 적합한 응답이다.
(B) 정답: 그건 위원회에서 결정한다(That's the committee's decision)며 자신은 알 수 없음을 우회적으로 표현한 적절한 응답이다.
(C) 관련 없는 오답: Where 의문문에 적합한 응답이다.

어휘 | committee 위원회   decision 결정

14 M-Au / W-Am

Who's the target audience for the ad campaign?
(A) That's a lot of résumés.
(B) You just bought new audio equipment.
(C) For print or social media?

그 광고 캠페인의 목표 대상은 누구죠?
(A) 이력서가 많네요.
(B) 새 음향 장비를 샀군요.
(C) 인쇄 광고요, 아니면 소셜미디어요?

해설 | 광고 대상을 묻는 Who 의문문
(A) 관련 없는 오답: 질문과 상관없는 답변을 제시한 오답이다.
(B) 유사 발음 오답: 유사 발음 audience와 audio를 이용한 오답이다.
(C) 정답: 광고 대상을 밝히기에 앞서 인쇄 광고인지 소셜미디어인지(For print or social media?) 되묻고 있으므로 가장 적절한 응답이다.

어휘 | audience 청중, 관객   ad 광고   equipment 장비

15 W-Am / M-Au

Who do you think should be in charge of the new project?
(A) The receptionist has one.
(B) Noriko has great leadership skills.
(C) You can borrow my phone charger.

새 프로젝트를 누가 맡아야 한다고 생각하세요?
(A) 접수 직원이 하나 갖고 있어요.
(B) 노리코가 훌륭한 리더십 역량을 갖췄죠.
(C) 제 전화 충전기를 빌려 드릴 수 있어요.

해설 | 담당자를 묻는 Who 의문문
(A) 연상 작용 오답: 질문의 Who에서 연상 가능한 receptionist를 언급한 오답이다.
(B) 정답: 노리코가 훌륭한 리더십 역량을 갖췄다(Noriko has great leadership skills)며 Noriko가 적임자라는 말을 우회적으로 말하고 있으므로 정답이다.
(C) 파생어 오답: 질문의 charge와 파생어 관계인 charger를 이용한 오답이다.

어휘 | in charge of ~을 맡아서, 담당해서

16 M-Cn / W-Am

What information did our director of sales and marketing request?
(A) I'm sorry, that house sold yesterday.
(B) Our recent sales report.
(C) At the farmers market.

영업 마케팅 이사가 어떤 정보를 요청했나요?
(A) 죄송하지만, 그 집은 어제 팔렸어요.
(B) 최근 영업보고서요.
(C) 농산물 직판장에서요.

해설 | 요청 정보를 묻는 What 의문문
(A) 연상 작용 오답: 질문의 sales에서 연상 가능한 sold를 이용한 오답이다.
(B) 정답: 최근 영업보고서(Our recent sales report)라고 구체적으로 제시했으므로 정답이다.
(C) 파생어 오답: 질문의 marketing과 파생어 관계인 market을 이용한 오답이다.

어휘 | request 요청하다

17 M-Au / W-Am

Which image should we use on our home page for our Web site?
(A) No, we already tried the search function.
(B) Doesn't Maria have some good photographs?
(C) It saves as soon as changes are made.

웹사이트를 위한 홈페이지에 어떤 사진을 사용해야 할까요?
(A) 아니요, 검색 기능은 이미 써 봤어요.
(B) 마리아에게 멋진 사진들이 있지 않아요?
(C) 변경이 이뤄지면 바로 저장돼요.

해설 | 홈페이지 사진을 묻는 **Which 의문문**
(A) **Yes/No 대답 불가 오답:** 의문사 의문문에는 Yes/No로 대답할 수 없다.
(B) **정답:** 마리아에게 멋진 사진들이 있지 않냐(Doesn't Maria have some good photographs?)고 되묻고 있으므로 가장 적절한 응답이다.
(C) **관련 없는 오답:** 질문과 상관없는 답변을 제시한 오답이다.

어휘 | function 기능 as soon as ~하자마자

18 W-Br / M-Cn

Who can I call about a maintenance issue in my apartment?
(A) Repair requests must be submitted online.
(B) No, it's tomorrow.
(C) On the corner of Main Street.

아파트 유지 보수 관련해서 누구에게 전화하면 되나요?
(A) 보수 요청은 온라인으로 제출해야 해요.
(B) 아니요, 내일이에요.
(C) 메인 가 모퉁이에요.

해설 | 담당자를 묻는 **Who 의문문**
(A) **정답:** 보수 요청은 온라인으로 제출해야 한다(Repair requests must be submitted online)며 구체적으로 'online'을 제시했으므로 정답이다.
(B) **Yes/No 대답 불가 오답:** 의문사 의문문에는 Yes/No로 대답할 수 없다.
(C) **유사 발음 오답:** 질문의 maintenance와 부분적으로 발음이 유사한 Main을 이용한 오답이다.

어휘 | maintenance 유지 보수 submit 제출하다

19 M-Au / W-Am

Who's attending the company picnic from your department?
(A) I have a mandatory training that day.
(B) Yes, the catering is confirmed.
(C) A nearby park.

당신 부서에서는 회사 야유회에 누가 참석해요?
(A) 저는 그날 의무 교육이 있어요.
(B) 네, 케이터링 서비스가 확정됐어요.
(C) 인근 공원이요.

해설 | 회사 야유회 참석자를 묻는 **Who 의문문**
(A) **정답:** 자신은 야유회 날 의무 교육이 있다(I have a mandatory training that day)며 참석하지 못한다는 것을 우회적으로 말한 적절한 응답이다.
(B) **Yes/No 대답 불가 및 연상 작용 오답:** 의문사 의문문에는 Yes/No로 대답할 수 없으며, 질문의 company picnic에서 연상 가능한 catering을 이용한 오답이다.
(C) **연상 작용 오답:** 질문의 company picnic에서 연상 가능한 park를 언급한 오답이다.

어휘 | attend 참석하다 mandatory 의무적인 nearby 인근의

20 M-Cn / M-Au

What's your availability on Tuesday morning?
(A) That's when Mr. Yang arrives.
(B) Yes, they saw the show last Friday.
(C) Well, it's a lot of responsibility.

화요일 아침에 시간이 되세요?
(A) 양 씨가 그때 도착해요.
(B) 네, 그들은 지난 금요일에 공연을 봤어요.
(C) 음, 책임이 많네요.

해설 | 특정 시점의 가능 여부를 묻는 **What 의문문**
(A) **정답:** 양 씨가 그때 도착한다(That's when Mr. Yang arrives)며 시간이 안 된다는 것을 우회적으로 말한 적절한 응답이다.
(B) **Yes/No 대답 불가 오답:** 의문사 의문문에는 Yes/No로 대답할 수 없다.
(C) **유사 발음 오답:** 질문의 availability와 부분적으로 발음이 유사한 responsibility를 이용한 오답이다.

어휘 | availability 가용성, 유효성 responsibility 책임

UNIT 4 When / Where 의문문

ETS 유형 연습
본책 p.40

1 (A)	2 (A)	3 (C)	4 (B)	5 (A)	6 (B)

1 W-Br / M-Cn

When does the performance start tonight?
(A) There's a show at 8:30.
(B) He just started working there.
(C) Is this seat taken?

오늘 밤 공연이 언제 시작되죠?
(A) 8시 30분에 공연이 있어요.
(B) 그는 거기서 막 일하기 시작했어요.
(C) 여기 자리 있나요?

해설 | 공연 시작 시점을 묻는 **When 의문문**
(A) **정답:** 구체적인 공연 시작 시점(at 8:30)을 제시했으므로 정답이다.
(B) **단어 반복 오답:** 질문의 start를 반복 이용한 오답이다.
(C) **연상 작용 오답:** 질문의 performance에서 연상 가능한 seat를 이용한 오답이다.

어휘 | performance 공연

2 M-Cn / W-Br

When does the computer update go into effect?
(A) Mr. Yang might know.
(B) A new laptop computer.
(C) I'm upstairs on the left.

컴퓨터 업데이트는 언제 실행되나요?
(A) 양 씨가 알 겁니다.
(B) 새 노트북 컴퓨터요.
(C) 저는 위층 왼편에 있어요.

해설 | 컴퓨터 업데이트 시점을 묻는 When 의문문
(A) **정답:** 양 씨가 알 것(Mr. Yang might know)이라며 본인은 모른다는 사실을 우회적으로 답한 적절한 응답이다.
(B) **단어 반복 오답:** 질문의 computer를 반복 이용한 오답이다.
(C) **관련 없는 오답:** Where 의문문에 적합한 응답이다.

어휘 | go into effect 효력이 발생하다, 실시되다

3 M-Au / W-Br
When will the hiring decision be made?
(A) I think so too.
(B) The other job candidate.
(C) By Monday at the latest.

언제 채용 결정이 나요?
(A) 제 생각도 그렇습니다.
(B) 다른 입사 지원자예요.
(C) 늦어도 월요일까지는 날 거예요.

해설 | 결정 시기를 묻는 When 의문문
(A) **관련 없는 오답:** 의견을 전달하는 평서문에 적합한 응답이다.
(B) **연상 작용 오답:** 질문의 hiring에서 연상 가능한 job candidate를 이용한 오답이다.
(C) **정답:** 늦어도 월요일까지(By Monday at the latest)라고 구체적 시점으로 대답하고 있으므로 정답이다.

어휘 | hiring 채용 **decision** 결정 **job candidate** 입사 지원자 **at the latest** 늦어도

4 M-Cn / W-Br
When is the employee picnic?
(A) Just sandwiches and salad.
(B) It's on the corporate calendar.
(C) Thanks, Cindy helped me pick it out.

직원 야유회가 언제인가요?
(A) 샌드위치와 샐러드만요.
(B) 회사 달력에 있어요.
(C) 고마워요, 신디가 고르는 것을 도와주었어요.

해설 | 야유회 시기를 묻는 When 의문문
(A) **연상 작용 오답:** 질문의 picnic에서 연상 가능한 sandwiches and salad를 이용한 오답이다.
(B) **정답:** 회사 달력에 써 있다(It's on the corporate calendar)고 우회적으로 표현한 적절한 응답이다.
(C) **유사 발음 오답:** 질문의 picnic과 부분적으로 발음이 유사한 pick을 이용한 오답이다.

어휘 | employee 직원 **corporate** 기업의 **pick out** 선택하다

5 M-Au / W-Br
When did you want me to install your computer software?
(A) How about at three o'clock?
(B) No, it's downstairs.
(C) The electronics store has one.

컴퓨터 소프트웨어를 언제 설치해 드렸으면 하셨죠?
(A) 3시 어때요?
(B) 아니요, 아래층입니다.
(C) 그 전자제품 매장에 하나 있어요.

해설 | 설치 시점을 묻는 When 의문문
(A) **정답:** 3시(at three o'clock)라고 구체적인 설치 시점을 제시했으므로 정답이다.
(B) **Yes/No 대답 불가 오답:** 의문사 의문문에는 Yes/No로 대답할 수 없다.
(C) **연상 작용 오답:** 질문의 computer에서 연상 가능한 electronics store를 언급한 오답이다.

어휘 | install 설치하다 **electronics** 전자 기기

6 W-Am / W-Br
When will the copy machine be installed?
(A) Sure, I can make the copies.
(B) Judy called the technician about that.
(C) Several thousand dollars.

복사기는 언제 설치될까요?
(A) 물론이죠, 제가 복사할 수 있어요.
(B) 주디가 그것에 대해 기술자에게 전화했어요.
(C) 수천 달러요.

해설 | 설치 시점을 묻는 When 의문문
(A) **Yes/No 대답 불가 및 단어 반복 오답:** 의문사 의문문에 대답할 수 없는 Yes의 대체 표현인 Sure를 사용했으며, 질문에 나온 copy의 복수형인 copies를 이용한 오답이다.
(B) **정답:** 주디가 기술자에게 전화했다(Judy called the technician about that)고 하며 원하는 답을 곧 듣게 되리라는 것을 우회적으로 말한 적절한 답변이다.
(C) **관련 없는 오답:** 가격을 묻는 How much 의문문에 적합한 응답이다.

어휘 | copy machine 복사기 **install** 설치하다 **technician** 기술자 **several** 몇몇의

ETS 유형 연습
본책 p.41

| 1 (C) | 2 (A) | 3 (A) | 4 (B) | 5 (C) | 6 (A) |

1 W-Am / M-Au
Where did the coordinator say she was going to post the contact list?
(A) At ten o'clock.
(B) To the post office.
(C) In the break room.

진행자가 연락처 목록을 어디에 게시할 거라고 했나요?
(A) 10시에요.
(B) 우체국으로요.
(C) 휴게실에요.

해설 | 연락처 게시 위치를 묻는 Where 의문문
(A) **관련 없는 오답:** When 의문문에 적합한 응답이다.
(B) **다의어 오답:** 질문에 나오는 post는 '게시하다'라는 뜻의 동사이고, 보기의 post는 '우편(물)'이라는 뜻의 명사이다.
(C) **정답:** 휴게실(In the break room)이라고 구체적인 위치를 제시했으므로 정답이다.

어휘 | post 게시하다; 우편(물)   **contact list** 연락처 목록

---

2   M-Au / W-Am

Where can I go to get a spare office key?
(A) Try the maintenance office.
(B) When you went through training.
(C) They're free on Wednesday.

어디로 가면 사무실 보조 열쇠를 받을 수 있나요?
(A) 관리사무실에 알아보세요.
(B) 당신이 교육 받을 때요.
(C) 수요일은 무료예요.

해설 | 열쇠 받을 장소를 묻는 Where 의문문
(A) **정답:** 관리사무실에 가보라(Try the maintenance office)고 구체적인 장소를 제시해 주고 있으므로 정답이다.
(B) **관련 없는 오답:** When 의문문에 적합한 응답이다.
(C) **관련 없는 오답 및 인칭 오류 오답:** When 의문문에 적합한 응답이고, 질문에 They가 가리키는 대상이 없으므로 오답이다.

어휘 | spare 예비의   **go through** ~을 겪다   **training** 교육

---

3   W-Am / M-Am

Where will you be staying while you're in London?
(A) With an old friend.
(B) Not at this time of year.
(C) It was a dinner invitation.

런던에 있는 동안 어디서 묵을 거예요?
(A) 옛 친구네요.
(B) 연중 이맘때는 아니에요.
(C) 그건 저녁 초대였어요.

해설 | 머물 장소를 묻는 Where 의문문
(A) **정답:** 옛 친구와(With an old friend) 지낼 것이라고 하므로 가장 적절한 응답이다.
(B) **관련 없는 오답:** When 의문문에 적합한 응답이다.
(C) **관련 없는 오답:** 질문과 상관없는 답변을 제시한 오답이다.

어휘 | stay 묵다, 체류하다   **invitation** 초대

---

4   W-Br / W-Am

Where should we hold the press conference?
(A) Newspapers and magazines.
(B) We'll need a large space.
(C) Ten-thirty.

기자회견을 어디에서 열어야 할까요?
(A) 신문과 잡지예요.
(B) 넓은 공간이 필요할 거예요.
(C) 10시 30분이요.

해설 | 기자회견 장소를 묻는 Where 의문문
(A) **연상 작용 오답:** press conference에서 연상 가능한 Newspapers와 magazines를 이용한 오답이다.
(B) **정답:** 기자회견을 열려면 넓은 공간(a large space)이어야 한다는 조건을 제시한 가장 적절한 응답이다.
(C) **관련 없는 오답:** When 의문문에 적합한 응답이다.

어휘 | press conference 기자회견   **magazine** 잡지

---

5   W-Br / M-Cn

Where can I buy a machine to clean my carpet?
(A) Yes, I vacuum it every day.
(B) You can just use it anywhere.
(C) At either of the appliance stores in town.

카펫을 청소할 기계는 어디서 살 수 있죠?
(A) 네, 저는 매일 진공청소기로 청소해요.
(B) 어디서든 사용하실 수 있어요.
(C) 시내 가전제품 매장 중 한 곳에서요.

해설 | 구매 가능 장소를 묻는 Where 의문문
(A) **Yes/No 대답 불가 오답:** 의문사 의문문에는 Yes/No로 대답할 수 없다.
(B) **연상 작용 오답:** 질문의 Where에서 연상 가능한 anywhere를 언급한 오답이다.
(C) **정답:** 시내 가전제품 매장 중 한 곳(At either of the appliance stores in town)이라고 대략적인 장소를 제시했으므로 정답이다.

어휘 | vacuum 진공청소기로 청소하다   **appliance** (가정용) 기기, 가전제품

---

6   W-Br / M-Au

Where's the local farmer's market?
(A) I just moved to this neighborhood.
(B) I have your office supplies.
(C) Table for three, please.

지역 농산물 직판장이 어디죠?
(A) 이 근처로 막 이사 왔어요.
(B) 제가 당신의 사무용품을 갖고 있어요.
(C) 3인 테이블 부탁해요.

해설 | 위치를 묻는 Where 의문문
(A) **정답:** 이 근처로 막 이사 와서(I just moved to this neighborhood) 모른다는 사실을 우회적으로 드러낸 적절한 응답이다.
(B) **관련 없는 오답:** 질문과 상관없는 답변을 제시한 오답이다.
(C) **관련 없는 오답:** 질문과 상관없는 답변을 제시한 오답이다.

어휘 | farmer's market 농산물 직판장   **neighborhood** 근처, 이웃

1 (B)	2 (C)	3 (B)	4 (B)	5 (C)	6 (B)
7 (B)	8 (A)	9 (C)	10 (A)	11 (B)	12 (C)
13 (C)	14 (C)	15 (B)	16 (B)	17 (B)	18 (B)
19 (A)	20 (A)				

1 W-Am / M-Cn

When can you take a look at the summer festival schedule?
(A) In Winslow Park.
(B) I'll do it now.
(C) You should take a jacket with you.

여름 축제 일정을 언제 보실 수 있어요?
(A) 윈스로우 공원에서요.
(B) 지금 할게요.
(C) 재킷을 가져가셔야 해요.

해설 | 시점을 묻는 When 의문문
(A) **관련 없는 오답:** Where 의문문에 적합한 응답이다.
(B) **정답:** 일정을 지금(now) 보겠다며 구체적인 시점으로 대답했으므로 정답이다.
(C) **단어 반복 오답:** 질문의 take를 반복 이용한 오답이다.

2 W-Am / M-Au

Where is the packing slip for the shipment to Tokyo?
(A) Some carry-on luggage.
(B) At ten o'clock.
(C) Check on Justine's desk.

도쿄행 선적물의 운송 전표가 어디에 있나요?
(A) 기내 휴대 수하물이 몇 개 있어요.
(B) 10시예요.
(C) 저스틴의 책상을 확인해 보세요.

해설 | 위치를 묻는 Where 의문문
(A) **연상 작용 오답:** 질문의 shipment에서 연상 가능한 luggage를 이용한 오답이다.
(B) **관련 없는 오답:** When 의문문에 적합한 응답이다.
(C) **정답:** 저스틴의 책상을 확인해 보라(Check on Justine's desk)며 구체적인 위치로 대답하고 있으므로 정답이다.

어휘 | packing slip 운송 전표　shipment 선적물　carry-on luggage 기내 휴대 수하물　check on ~을 확인하다

3 W-Am / W-Br

Where can I heat my food?
(A) Thanks, I already ate.
(B) There's a microwave in the break room.
(C) Isn't it hot in here?

음식을 어디서 데울 수 있죠?
(A) 감사합니다만, 저는 이미 먹었어요.
(B) 휴게실에 전자레인지가 있어요.
(C) 여기 덥지 않나요?

해설 | 장소를 묻는 Where 의문문
(A) **연상 작용 오답:** 질문의 food에서 연상 가능한 ate을 이용한 오답이다.
(B) **정답:** 휴게실(in the break room)에 전자레인지가 있다며 구체적인 장소를 제시했으므로 정답이다.
(C) **연상 작용 오답:** 질문의 heat에서 연상 가능한 hot을 이용한 오답이다.

어휘 | microwave 전자레인지　break room 휴게실

4 W-Br / M-Au

When can I make my presentation to the board?
(A) She should be present to receive the award.
(B) There will be time at the next meeting.
(C) Yes, he was very bored.

제가 이사회에서 언제 발표를 할 수 있을까요?
(A) 그녀는 상을 받기 위해 참석해야 해요.
(B) 다음 회의 때 시간이 있을 거예요.
(C) 예, 그는 매우 지루해 했어요.

해설 | 발표 가능 시점을 묻는 When 의문문
(A) **파생어 오답:** 질문에 언급된 presentation과 파생어 관계인 present를 이용한 오답이다.
(B) **정답:** 다음 회의 때 시간이 있다(There will be time at the next meeting)고 우회적으로 말한 적절한 응답이다.
(C) **Yes/No 대답 불가 및 유사 발음 오답:** 의문사 의문문에는 Yes/No로 대답할 수 없고, 질문의 board와 발음이 동일한 bored를 이용한 오답이다.

어휘 | make a presentation 발표하다　board 이사회　present 출석한　receive 받다　award 상

5 W-Am / M-Au

When does the IT Department hold its workshops?
(A) No, it's not working.
(B) The apartment is above the shop.
(C) On the first Tuesday of every month.

IT 부서는 언제 워크숍을 여나요?
(A) 아니요, 작동하지 않아요.
(B) 아파트는 상점 위에 있어요.
(C) 매월 첫 번째 화요일이에요.

해설 | 워크숍 일정을 묻는 When 의문문
(A) **Yes/No 대답 불가 오답:** 의문사 의문문에는 Yes/No로 대답할 수 없다.
(B) **유사 발음 오답:** 유사 발음 Department/apartment, workshops/shop을 이용한 오답이다.
(C) **정답:** 매월 첫 번째 화요일(On the first Tuesday of every month)이라는 구체적인 시간을 제시했으므로 정답이다.

6 W-Br / M-Cn

When will construction on the south museum wing be completed?
(A) Yes, the modern art exhibit.
(B) Probably in late April.
(C) Admission is fifteen dollars.

박물관 남쪽 건물 공사는 언제 완료될 예정이죠?
(A) 네, 현대미술 전시회요.
(B) 아마 4월 말일 거예요.
(C) 입장료는 15달러입니다.

해설 | 공사 완료 시점을 묻는 When 의문문
(A) **Yes/No 대답 불가 오답:** 의문사 의문문에는 Yes/No로
대답할 수 없다.
(B) **정답:** 4월 말(in late April)이라는 날짜를 제시했으므로
정답이다.
(C) **연상 작용 오답:** 질문의 museum에서 연상 가능한
Admission을 이용한 오답이다.

어휘 | construction 건설, 공사 wing 부속 건물
complete 완료하다 admission 입장, 입장료

7 M-Au / W-Br

Where can I take an online Italian class?
(A) He usually takes his time.
(B) Newton University offers one.
(C) I like that kind of pizza.

이탈리아어 온라인 강의는 어디서 들을 수 있죠?
(A) 그는 보통 늑장을 부려요.
(B) 뉴턴 대학교에서 제공해요.
(C) 저는 그런 피자를 좋아해요.

해설 | 강의 제공처를 묻는 Where 의문문
(A) **단어 반복 오답:** 질문의 take를 반복 이용한 오답이다.
(B) **정답:** Newton University에서 제공한다고 구체적인 곳을
답했으므로 정답이다.
(C) **연상 작용 오답:** 질문의 Italian에서 연상 가능한 pizza를
이용한 오답이다.

어휘 | take a class 수업을 듣다 take one's time 천천히
하다

8 M-Cn / W-Am

When are you taking a vacation?
(A) I need to finish a big project first.
(B) Three days of vacation in total.
(C) It's just to the left.

휴가는 언제 가세요?
(A) 큰 프로젝트를 먼저 끝내야 해요.
(B) 총 3일간의 휴가예요.
(C) 왼쪽이에요.

해설 | 휴가 시점을 묻는 When 의문문
(A) **정답:** 큰 프로젝트를 먼저 끝내야 한다(I need to finish a
big project first)며 아직 예정이 없다는 것을 우회적으로
말한 적절한 응답이다.
(B) **단어 반복 오답:** 질문의 vacation을 반복 이용한 오답이다.
(C) **관련 없는 오답:** Where 의문문에 적합한 응답이다.

어휘 | take a vacation 휴가를 가다 in total 총, 통틀어

9 W-Am / M-Cn

Where can we unload all these crates?
(A) That's what I've been told.
(B) Don't forget your umbrella.
(C) At the back of the building.

이 상자들을 전부 어디에 내려놓으면 되나요?
(A) 그렇게 들었어요.
(B) 우산 잊지 마세요.
(C) 건물 뒤편에요.

해설 | 장소를 묻는 Where 의문문
(A) **관련 없는 오답:** 질문과 상관없는 답변을 제시한 오답이다.
(B) **관련 없는 오답:** 질문과 상관없는 답변을 제시한 오답이다.
(C) **정답:** 건물 뒤편(At the back of the building)이라고
구체적인 장소를 제시했으므로 정답이다.

어휘 | unload (짐을) 내리다 crate 상자

10 W-Am / M-Au

Where's our catering order?
(A) The delivery truck is running a little late.
(B) Actually, we had a very nice trip.
(C) A few dollars extra.

주문한 출장 요리는 어디 있죠?
(A) 배달 트럭이 약간 늦어지고 있어요.
(B) 사실 즐거운 여행이었어요.
(C) 몇 달러 추가로 들어요.

해설 | 음식이 있는 곳을 묻는 Where 의문문
(A) **정답:** 배달 트럭이 약간 늦어지고 있다(The delivery truck
is running a little late)며 아직 음식이 도착하지 않았다는
것을 우회적으로 말한 적절한 응답이다.
(B) **관련 없는 오답:** 질문과 상관없는 답변을 제시한 오답이다.
(C) **연상 작용 오답:** 질문의 order에서 연상 가능한 dollars를
이용한 오답이다.

11 M-Cn / W-Am

When did you visit the new office location?
(A) Only about ten minutes away.
(B) I just got back from there.
(C) She's on vacation this week.

새 사무실은 언제 방문하셨어요?
(A) 10분 거리밖에 안 돼요.
(B) 지금 막 거기서 돌아왔어요.
(C) 그녀는 이번 주에 휴가예요.

해설 | 방문 시점을 묻는 When 의문문
(A) **연상 작용 오답:** 질문의 office location에서 연상 가능한
ten minutes away를 이용한 오답이다.
(B) **정답:** 막 거기서(새 사무실) 돌아왔다(I just got back from
there)고 답변했으므로 정답이다.
(C) **인칭 오류 오답:** 대명사 She가 가리키는 대상이 질문에 없다.

어휘 | on vacation 휴가로

12 M-Au / W-Am

When should we set up the display of the new toaster ovens?
(A) From the East Coast.
(B) No, the oven wasn't expensive.
(C) Our priority today is coffee makers.

신제품 토스터기 진열은 언제 해야 할까요?
(A) 동해안으로부터요.
(B) 아니요. 오븐은 비싸지 않아요.
(C) 오늘 우선순위는 커피메이커예요.

해설 | 진열 시점을 묻는 When 의문문
(A) **유사 발음 오답:** 질문의 toaster와 발음이 유사한 Coast를 이용한 오답이다.
(B) **Yes/No 대답 불가 및 단어 반복 오답:** 의문사 의문문에는 Yes/No로 대답할 수 없고, 질문의 oven을 반복 이용한 오답이다.
(C) **정답:** 우선순위는 커피메이커(Our priority today is coffee makers)라며 토스터기 진열 시점은 나중이라는 것을 우회적으로 말한 적절한 응답이다.

어휘 | priority 우선 사항

13 W-Am / W-Br

Where can I go for an eye exam?
(A) On Wednesday morning.
(B) It's a good offer.
(C) I like the clinic on Third Street.

시력 검사를 받으러 어디로 가야 할까요?
(A) 수요일 오전에요.
(B) 괜찮은 제안이네요.
(C) 3번 가에 있는 병원이 좋아요.

해설 | 검사 장소를 묻는 Where 의문문
(A) **관련 없는 오답:** When 의문문에 적합한 응답이다.
(B) **유사 발음 오답:** 질문의 go for와 발음이 유사한 good offer를 이용한 오답이다.
(C) **정답:** 3번 가에 있는 병원(the clinic on Third Street)이 좋다고 구체적인 장소를 제시했으므로 정답이다.

14 M-Au / W-Br

Where's the product prototype we've been working on?
(A) He's the type of employee we need.
(B) Online product reviews.
(C) Oh, it's locked in the lab.

우리가 작업하고 있는 제품 원형이 어디 있죠?
(A) 그는 우리가 필요로 하는 스타일의 직원입니다.
(B) 온라인 제품 후기요.
(C) 아, 실험실 안에 잠가 뒀어요.

해설 | 보관 장소를 묻는 Where 의문문
(A) **유사 발음 오답:** 질문의 prototype과 발음이 부분적으로 유사한 type을 이용한 오답이다.
(B) **단어 반복 오답:** 질문의 product를 반복 이용한 오답이다.
(C) **정답:** 실험실 안에(in the lab) 잠가 뒀다고 구체적인 위치를 제시했으므로 정답이다.

어휘 | prototype 원형 employee 고용인, 직원 lab 실험실

15 M-Au / W-Am

When can we expect more inventory to arrive?
(A) That's a good idea.
(B) The truck's on its way.
(C) Departures and arrivals.

재고가 언제 더 도착할 걸로 예상하세요?
(A) 좋은 생각입니다.
(B) 트럭이 오고 있어요.
(C) 출발과 도착이요.

해설 | 도착 예상 시점을 묻는 When 의문문
(A) **관련 없는 오답:** 질문과 상관없는 답변을 제시한 오답이다.
(B) **정답:** 트럭이 오고 있다(The truck's on its way)며 곧 도착 예정이라는 것을 우회적으로 말한 적절한 응답이다.
(C) **파생어 오답:** 질문의 arrive와 파생어 관계인 arrival을 이용한 오답이다.

어휘 | inventory 재고, 물품 목록 departure 출발 arrival 도착

16 W-Am / M-Cn

Where can I find your discounted tablet computers?
(A) Yes, I downloaded it.
(B) The sale starts next week.
(C) Mostly to record video games.

할인되는 태블릿 컴퓨터는 어디에 있나요?
(A) 네, 제가 다운로드했어요.
(B) 세일은 다음 주에 시작돼요.
(C) 주로 비디오 게임을 녹화하려고요.

해설 | 할인 상품의 위치를 묻는 Where 의문문
(A) **Yes/No 대답 불가 오답:** 의문사 의문문에는 Yes/No로 대답할 수 없다.
(B) **정답:** 세일은 다음 주에 시작된다(The sale starts next week)며 아직 할인되는 상품이 없음을 우회적으로 말한 적절한 응답이다.
(C) **연상 작용 오답:** 질문의 computers에서 연상 가능한 games를 이용한 오답이다.

17 M-Cn / W-Br

Where do we keep our notepads?
(A) About 200 words.
(B) Rita just went to buy office supplies.
(C) Sure, you can keep it.

메모지를 어디에 보관하죠?
(A) 200단어 정도요.
(B) 리타가 방금 사무용품을 사러 갔어요.
(C) 물론이죠, 가지세요.

해설 | 보관 장소를 묻는 Where 의문문
(A) **연상 작용 오답:** 질문의 notepads에서 연상 가능한 words를 이용한 오답이다.
(B) **정답:** 리타가 사무용품을 사러 갔다(Rita just went to buy office supplies)며 메모지가 현재 다 떨어졌음을 우회적으로 말한 적절한 응답이다.

(C) **Yes/No 대답 불가 및 단어 반복 오답:** 의문사 의문문에
Yes의 대체 표현인 Sure로 대답할 수 없으며, 질문의
keep을 반복 사용한 오답이다.

어휘 | office supply 사무용품

18 W-Br / M-Cn

When does the television advertisement need to
be ready?
(A) A well-known movie actor, apparently.
(B) The clients are always changing the schedule.
(C) Yes, I like that too.

TV 광고는 언제 준비되어야 합니까?
(A) 보아하니 유명한 영화배우예요.
(B) 고객들이 항상 일정을 변경해요.
(C) 네, 저도 좋아요.

해설 | 광고 준비 시점을 묻는 When 의문문
(A) **연상 작용 오답:** 질문의 television에서 연상 가능한 movie
actor를 이용한 오답이다.
(B) **정답:** 고객들이 항상 일정을 변경한다(The clients are
always changing the schedule)며 고객에 따라 일정이
달라질 수 있음을 우회적으로 말한 적절한 응답이다.
(C) **Yes/No 대답 불가 오답:** 의문사 의문문에는 Yes/No로
대답할 수 없다.

어휘 | advertisement 광고 **apparently** 듣자 하니,
보아하니

19 M-Cn / W-Am

When will the next container ship set sail from the
port?
(A) Haven't you seen the schedule?
(B) No, they belong in the other container.
(C) He's in the parking lot.

다음 컨테이너선은 항구에서 언제 출발할 예정인가요?
(A) 시간표를 보지 않으셨나요?
(B) 아니요. 그것들은 다른 컨테이너에 있어요.
(C) 그는 주차장에 있어요.

해설 | 출발 시간을 묻는 When 의문문
(A) **정답:** 시간표를 보지 않으셨냐(Haven't you seen
the schedule?)고 되물으면서 시간표에 나와 있음을
우회적으로 말한 적절한 응답이다.
(B) **Yes/No 대답 불가 및 단어 반복 오답:** 의문사 의문문에는
Yes/No로 대답할 수 없으며, 질문의 container를 그대로
반복 이용한 오답이다.
(C) **인칭 오류 오답:** 대명사 He가 가리키는 대상이 질문에 없다.

어휘 | set sail 출발하다 **port** 항구 **belong** 속하다

20 M-Au / M-Cn

Where can I buy a new oven for my kitchen?
(A) Isn't yours only a year old?
(B) Cook it for ten minutes.
(C) Sure, it's really easy.

주방에 놓을 새 오븐을 어디서 사면 될까요?
(A) 당신 오븐은 1년밖에 안 되지 않았어요?
(B) 10분간 조리하세요.
(C) 물론이죠. 정말 쉬워요.

해설 | 구매 장소를 묻는 Where 의문문
(A) **정답:** 당신 오븐은 1년밖에 안 되지 않았느냐(Isn't yours
only a year old?)고 하면서 왜 또 사는지 우회적으로
되묻고 있으므로 가장 적절한 응답이다.
(B) **연상 작용 오답:** 질문의 oven과 kitchen에서 연상 가능한
Cook을 언급한 오답이다.
(C) **Yes/No 대답 불가 오답:** 의문사 의문문에 Yes의 대체
표현인 Sure로 대답할 수 없다.

UNIT 5 Why / How 의문문

ETS 유형 연습

본책 p.44

1 (A) **2** (C) **3** (C) **4** (C) **5** (C) **6** (B)

1 M-Au / W-Br

Why will the bakery be closed tomorrow morning?
(A) Because the oven's being replaced.
(B) I'll take a dozen chocolate cookies.
(C) No, it's on Mulberry Street.

내일 오전에 제과점이 왜 문을 닫나요?
(A) 오븐이 교체될 거라서요.
(B) 초콜릿 쿠키 한 다스를 살게요.
(C) 아니요. 멀버리 가에 있어요.

해설 | 문을 닫는 이유를 묻는 Why 의문문
(A) **정답:** 오븐이 교체될 것(Because the oven's being
replaced)이기 때문이라는 구체적인 이유를 제시했으므로
정답이다.
(B) **연상 작용 오답:** 질문의 bakery에서 연상 가능한
cookies를 이용한 오답이다.
(C) **Yes/No 대답 불가 오답:** 의문사 의문문에는 Yes/No로
대답할 수 없다.

어휘 | replace 교체하다

2 W-Am / W-Br

Why hasn't the "For Sale" sign been put up yet?
(A) Near the intersection.
(B) A very nice apartment.
(C) I haven't made one yet.

"판매 중" 표지판을 왜 아직 내걸지 않았죠?
(A) 교차로 근처요.
(B) 아주 훌륭한 아파트예요.
(C) 아직 만들지 않았어요.

해설 | **표지판을 걸지 않은 이유를 묻는 Why 의문문**
(A) **관련 없는 오답:** Where 의문문에 적합한 응답이다.
(B) **연상 작용 오답:** 질문의 For Sale에서 연상 가능한 apartment를 이용한 오답이다.
(C) **정답:** 아직 표지판을 만들지 않았다(I haven't made one yet)는 구체적인 이유를 제시한 정답이다.

어휘 | put up a sign 간판을 내걸다   intersection 교차로

3 W-Br / M-Cn
Why does the copy machine keep overheating?
(A) Yes, she can.
(B) I usually take my bike.
(C) Is the internal fan on?

복사기가 왜 계속 과열되나요?
(A) 네, 그녀가 할 수 있어요.
(B) 저는 보통 자전거를 타요.
(C) 내부 팬이 켜져 있나요?

해설 | **복사기 과열 이유를 묻는 Why 의문문**
(A) **Yes/No 대답 불가 오답:** 의문사 의문문에는 Yes/No로 대답할 수 없다.
(B) **관련 없는 오답:** 교통수단을 묻는 How 의문문에 적합한 응답이다.
(C) **정답:** 내부 팬이 켜져 있는지(Is the internal fan on?) 되물으며 확인하고 있으므로 가장 적절한 응답이다.

어휘 | internal 내부의

4 W-Br / M-Au
Why did Mr. Arlington return these documents to me?
(A) Yes—please download them.
(B) Actually, I'm not leaving until next week.
(C) He wants you to revise them before he signs them.

알링턴 씨는 왜 이 서류들을 저에게 되돌려 보냈죠?
(A) 네, 다운로드해 주세요.
(B) 사실 저는 다음 주까지 여기 있어요.
(C) 서명하기 전에 당신이 수정했으면 하던데요.

해설 | **서류 반송 이유를 묻는 Why 의문문**
(A) **Yes/No 대답 불가 오답:** 의문사 의문문에는 Yes/No로 대답할 수 없다.
(B) **연상 작용 오답:** 질문의 return을 '되돌아가다'로 잘못 이해했을 때 연상 가능한 leaving을 이용한 오답이다.
(C) **정답:** 서명하기 전에 수정하길 원한다(He wants you to revise them before he signs them)고 구체적인 이유를 제시한 정답이다.

어휘 | revise 수정하다, 변경하다

5 M-Au / M-Cn
Why hasn't Jason been in the office all week?
(A) No, I haven't seen him.
(B) Typically until six o'clock or so.
(C) You'll have to ask his manager.

제이슨은 왜 일주일 내내 사무실에 없는 거죠?
(A) 아뇨, 못 봤어요.
(B) 보통 6시쯤까지입니다.
(C) 그의 매니저에게 물어봐야 할 거예요.

해설 | **사무실에 없는 이유를 묻는 Why 의문문**
(A) **Yes/No 대답 불가 오답:** 의문사 의문문에는 Yes/No로 대답할 수 없다.
(B) **연상 작용 오답:** office에서 연상 가능한 until six o'clock을 이용한 오답이다.
(C) **정답:** 매니저에게 물어봐야 한다(have to ask his manager)는 말로 자신은 모른다는 것을 우회적으로 표현한 적절한 응답이다.

어휘 | typically 보통, 대체로

6 W-Am / W-Br
Why didn't Beverly submit her expense report yesterday?
(A) Yes, it's more expensive than I thought.
(B) It's possible that she forgot.
(C) I'll enter those figures in the spreadsheet.

비벌리는 왜 어제 지출품의서를 제출하지 않았죠?
(A) 네, 제가 생각했던 것보다 더 비싸요.
(B) 잊어버렸을 수도 있어요.
(C) 제가 스프레드시트에 수치를 입력할게요.

해설 | **서류 미제출 이유를 묻는 Why 의문문**
(A) **Yes/No 대답 불가 및 파생어 오답:** 의문사 의문문에는 Yes/No로 대답할 수 없고, 질문의 expense와 파생어 관계인 expensive를 이용한 오답이다.
(B) **정답:** 그녀가 잊어버렸을 수도 있다(It's possible that she forgot)며 가능한 이유를 제시했으므로 정답이다.
(C) **연상 작용 오답:** 질문의 expense report에서 연상 가능한 figures를 이용한 오답이다.

어휘 | submit 제출하다   expense report 지출품의서   figure 숫자, 수치

ETS 유형 연습 본책 p.45

1 (A)	**2** (B)	**3** (A)	**4** (A)	**5** (C)	**6** (A)

1 M-Cn / W-Br
How has the building design been modified?
(A) Just as you suggested.
(B) She's an excellent designer.
(C) I will notify them on Tuesday.

건물 설계는 어떻게 변경됐나요?
(A) 제안하신 그대로요.
(B) 그녀는 훌륭한 디자이너예요.
(C) 제가 화요일에 그들에게 알릴게요.

해설 | **설계 변경 상황을 묻는 How 의문문**
(A) **정답:** 제안한 그대로(Just as you suggested)라면서 별도의 변경은 없다는 의미로 말하고 있으므로 적절한 응답이다.

(B) **인칭 오류 및 파생어 오답:** 보기의 She가 가리키는
　　대상이 질문에 없으며, 질문의 design과 파생어 관계인
　　designer를 이용한 오답이다.
(C) **인칭 오류 및 유사 발음 오답:** 보기의 them이 가리키는
　　대상이 질문에 없으며, 질문의 modified와 발음이 유사한
　　notify them으로 혼동을 준 오답이다.

어휘 | modify 수정하다, 변경하다　notify 통지하다, 통보하다

2 M-Au / M-Cn

How far away is the dance studio?
(A) Twenty dollars per class.
(B) Three or four miles.
(C) Mostly modern dance.

댄스 스튜디오는 얼마나 멀죠?
(A) 강좌당 20달러예요.
(B) **3, 4마일요.**
(C) 주로 현대무용이요.

해설 | 거리를 묻는 How 의문문
(A) **관련 없는 오답:** 가격을 묻는 How much 의문문에 적합한
　　응답이다.
(B) **정답:** 3, 4마일(Three or four miles)이라고 대략적인
　　거리를 알려 주었으므로 정답이다.
(C) **단어 반복 오답:** 질문의 dance를 반복 이용한 오답이다.

3 M-Cn / W-Am

How should I store these photographs?
(A) Mateo is responsible for that.
(B) From the company picnic.
(C) Yes, the staff is very helpful.

이 사진들을 어떻게 보관해야 할까요?
(A) **마테오가 담당이에요.**
(B) 회사 야유회에서요.
(C) 네, 직원들이 잘 도와줍니다.

해설 | 사진 보관 방법을 묻는 How 의문문
(A) **정답:** 담당자(Mateo)를 언급하며 자신은 모른다는 것을
　　우회적으로 표현하고 있으므로 정답이다.
(B) **연상 작용 오답:** 질문의 photographs에서 연상 가능한
　　company picnic을 이용한 오답이다.
(C) **Yes/No 대답 불가 오답:** 의문사 의문문에는 Yes/ No로
　　대답할 수 없다.

어휘 | store 저장하다　be responsible for ~을 담당하다

4 M-Au / W-Am

How long until we have to change the air
conditioner filter?
(A) We just put in a new one.
(B) That model isn't for sale.
(C) Yes, there's plenty of storage space.

에어컨 필터를 바꾸려면 얼마나 남았죠?
(A) **막 새 걸 넣었어요.**
(B) 그 모델은 판매하지 않아요.
(C) 네, 저장 공간이 많아요.

해설 | 남은 기간을 묻는 How 의문문
(A) **정답:** 막 새 걸 넣었다(We just put in a new one)며 남은
　　기간이 많다는 것을 우회적으로 말한 적절한 응답이다.
(B) **연상 작용 오답:** 질문의 air conditioner에서 연상 가능한
　　That model을 이용한 오답이다.
(C) **Yes/No 대답 불가 오답:** 의문사 의문문에는 Yes/No로
　　대답할 수 없다.

어휘 | plenty of 많은　storage 저장, 보관

5 M-Cn / W-Am

How many projects does this team work on?
(A) Probably one week.
(B) Scientific experiments.
(C) It varies from month to month.

이 팀은 몇 개의 프로젝트를 진행하고 있죠?
(A) 아마 1주일이요.
(B) 과학 실험이요.
(C) **달마다 달라요.**

해설 | 수량을 묻는 How 의문문
(A) **관련 없는 오답:** 기간을 묻는 How long 의문문에 적합한
　　응답이다.
(B) **연상 작용 오답:** 질문의 projects에서 연상 가능한
　　experiments를 이용한 오답이다.
(C) **정답:** 달마다 다르다(It varies from month to month)며
　　정확한 개수는 알 수 없음을 나타내는 적절한 응답이다.

어휘 | experiment 실험　vary 달라지다, 달리 하다

6 M-Cn / M-Au

How do we know who's on the fund-raising
committee?
(A) The list was in an e-mail.
(B) Yes, I'd be glad to.
(C) In meeting room C.

누가 모금 위원회 소속인지 어떻게 알 수 있나요?
(A) **이메일에 목록이 있어요.**
(B) 네, 그럴게요.
(C) C 회의실에서요.

해설 | 명단을 알 수 있는 방법을 묻는 How 의문문
(A) **정답:** 이메일에 목록이 있다(The list was in an e-mail)고
　　말함으로써 알 수 있는 방법을 우회적으로 표현한 적절한
　　응답이다.
(B) **Yes/No 대답 불가 오답:** 의문사 의문문에는 Yes/No로
　　대답할 수 없다.
(C) **연상 작용 오답:** 질문의 committee에서 연상 가능한
　　meeting room을 이용한 오답이다.

어휘 | fund-raising 모금

LC

PART 2

ETS 고득점 실전 문제

본책 p.46

1 (B)	2 (B)	3 (B)	4 (B)	5 (B)	6 (A)
7 (A)	8 (B)	9 (C)	10 (B)	11 (C)	12 (B)
13 (B)	14 (B)	15 (A)	16 (B)	17 (C)	18 (A)
19 (A)	20 (C)				

1 W-Am / M-Au

Why is Helen late this morning?
(A) From seven to ten thirty.
(B) There's a construction project on Route 23.
(C) Next in line, please.

헬렌은 오늘 아침에 왜 늦죠?
(A) 7시에서 10시 30분까지요.
(B) 23번 길에서 공사를 하고 있어요.
(C) 다음 분 오세요.

해설 | 늦는 이유를 묻는 Why 의문문
(A) 관련 없는 오답: When 의문문에 적합한 응답이다.
(B) 정답: 23번 길에서 공사를 하고 있다(There's a construction project on Route 23)며 늦는 이유를 구체적으로 제시했으므로 정답이다.
(C) 관련 없는 오답: 질문과 상관없는 답변을 제시한 오답이다.

어휘 | next in line 다음 차례인, 두 번째로

2 M-Au / W-Am

How should we change our logo design?
(A) No, I didn't go yesterday.
(B) We should make the font smaller.
(C) Your change is three dollars.

로고 디자인을 어떻게 변경해야 할까요?
(A) 아니요, 저는 어제 안 갔어요.
(B) 폰트를 더 작게 해야 해요.
(C) 거스름돈은 3달러입니다.

해설 | 디자인 변경 방법을 묻는 How 의문문
(A) Yes/No 대답 불가 오답: 의문사 의문문에는 Yes/No로 대답할 수 없다.
(B) 정답: 폰트를 더 작게 해야 한다(We should make the font smaller)며 디자인 변경에 대한 구체적인 방법을 제시했으므로 정답이다.
(C) 다의어 오답: 질문에 나오는 change는 '바꾸다'라는 뜻의 동사이고, 보기의 change는 '거스름돈'이라는 뜻의 명사이다.

어휘 | font 글꼴, 서체

3 M-Cn / W-Br

How often are the factory floors waxed?
(A) That's an interesting fact.
(B) Every three months.
(C) The mail room is on the second floor.

공장 바닥은 얼마나 자주 왁스 작업을 하나요?
(A) 흥미로운 사실이군요.
(B) 3개월마다요.
(C) 우편물실은 2층에 있어요.

해설 | 빈도를 묻는 How 의문문
(A) 유사 발음 오답: 질문의 factory와 부분적으로 발음이 유사한 fact로 혼동을 준 오답이다.
(B) 정답: 3개월마다(Every three months)라고 빈도로 응답했으므로 정답이다.
(C) 단어 반복 오답: 질문의 floor를 반복 이용한 오답이다.

어휘 | wax 왁스를 입히다, 왁스로 광을 내다

4 M-Au / M-Cn

Why do you think you'd make a good addition to our company?
(A) It was printed in last week's newspaper.
(B) I have a decade of experience in the industry.
(C) They're looking forward to meeting you.

왜 저희 회사에 좋은 보탬이 되는 인재가 될 거라고 생각하시나요?
(A) 지난주 신문에 게재됐어요.
(B) 저는 그 업계에서 10년의 경력을 갖고 있습니다.
(C) 그들은 당신을 만나기를 고대하고 있어요.

해설 | 이유를 묻는 Why 의문문
(A) 관련 없는 오답: 질문과 상관없는 답변을 제시한 오답이다.
(B) 정답: 그 업계에서 10년의 경력을 갖고 있다(I have a decade of experience in the industry)고 구체적인 이유를 제시했으므로 정답이다.
(C) 인칭 오류 오답: 보기의 They가 가리키는 대상이 질문에 없다.

어휘 | decade 10년 look forward to ~을 고대하다

5 M-Au / W-Br

Why hasn't the sales team met their monthly targets?
(A) Seven in the morning, I think.
(B) Because team members have been out on vacation.
(C) That's our target demographic.

영업팀은 왜 월간 목표량을 맞추지 못했죠?
(A) 아침 7시인 것 같은데요.
(B) 팀원들이 휴가를 가서 없었거든요.
(C) 그것이 저희 목표 대상입니다.

해설 | 목표량 미달 이유를 묻는 Why 의문문
(A) 관련 없는 오답: When 의문문에 적합한 응답이다.
(B) 정답: 팀원들이 휴가를 가서(Because team members have been out on vacation) 인력이 부족했던 것이 이유라고 제시했으므로 정답이다.
(C) 단어 반복 오답: 질문의 target을 반복 이용한 오답이다.

어휘 | demographic 인구 집단

6 M-Cn / W-Am

How many chairs need to be set up for the reception?

(A) Claudine should know.

(B) Until eight o'clock tonight.

(C) No, I wasn't invited!

환영 연회에 의자를 몇 개나 준비해야 할까요?

(A) 클로딘이 알 거예요.

(B) 오늘 밤 8시까지요.

(C) 아니요, 저는 초대받지 못했어요!

해설 | 수량을 묻는 How 의문문

(A) **정답:** 클로딘이 알 것(Claudine should know)이라며 자신은 모른다는 것을 우회적으로 드러낸 적절한 응답이다.

(B) **연상 작용 오답:** 질문의 set up for the reception에서 연상 가능한 Until eight o'clock tonight을 이용한 오답이다.

(C) **Yes/No 대답 불가 및 연상 작용 오답:** 의문사 의문문에는 Yes/No로 대답할 수 없으며, 질문의 reception에서 연상 가능한 invited를 이용한 오답이다.

어휘 | set up 설치하다, 준비하다   reception 환영 연회

7 M-Cn / W-Br

How did you like the movie?

(A) I'm surprised it received so many awards.

(B) The old theater on Twenty-Second Street.

(C) That sounds great, thanks.

그 영화 어땠어요?

(A) 그렇게 많은 상을 받았다니 놀라워요.

(B) 22번 가의 오래된 극장이요.

(C) 그거 좋네요, 고마워요.

해설 | 의견을 묻는 How 의문문

(A) **정답:** 그렇게 많은 상을 받았다니 놀랍다(I'm surprised it received so many awards)며 긍정적인 의견을 제시했으므로 정답이다.

(B) **연상 작용 오답:** 질문의 the movie에서 연상 가능한 theater를 이용한 오답이다.

(C) **시제 오류 오답:** 과거에 어땠는지를 묻는 질문에 현재(sounds)로 답하는 것은 어색하다.

8 M-Au / M-Cn

Why did they decide to move their factory?

(A) That's definitely a factor.

(B) Because they need more production space.

(C) Let's move to the other room.

그들은 왜 공장을 이전하기로 결정했나요?

(A) 분명 그것이 요인이죠.

(B) 생산 공간이 더 필요해서요.

(C) 다른 방으로 옮깁시다.

해설 | 공장 이전 이유를 묻는 Why 의문문

(A) **유사 발음 오답:** 질문의 factory와 발음이 유사한 factor를 이용한 오답이다.

(B) **정답:** 생산 공간이 더 필요해서(Because they need more production space)라며 구체적인 이유를 제시했으므로 정답이다.

(C) **단어 반복 오답:** 질문의 move를 반복 이용한 오답이다.

어휘 | definitely 분명히, 절대   production 생산

9 M-Au / M-Cn

How does Soo-Hee like the company she works for?

(A) No, they haven't used that product.

(B) We will open at nine A.M.

(C) Well, she's been there twenty years.

수희는 본인이 일하는 회사를 마음에 들어 하나요?

(A) 아니요, 그들은 그 제품을 사용하지 않았어요.

(B) 저희는 오전 9시에 문을 엽니다.

(C) 음, 그녀는 거기서 20년간 일했습니다.

해설 | 의견을 묻는 How 의문문

(A) **Yes/No 대답 불가 오답:** 의문사 의문문에는 Yes/No로 대답할 수 없다.

(B) **관련 없는 오답:** When 의문문에 적합한 응답이다.

(C) **정답:** 그녀가 거기서 20년간 일했다(Well, she's been there twenty years)며 긍정적인 생각을 우회적으로 드러낸 적절한 응답이다.

10 M-Cn / W-Br

Why didn't the director send us the project timeline?

(A) About fifteen more employees.

(B) It's in the folder on the shared network.

(C) I'll need a projector.

이사님은 왜 우리에게 프로젝트 일정표를 보내지 않은 거죠?

(A) 직원 약 15명 더요.

(B) 공유 네트워크에 폴더가 있어요.

(C) 저는 프로젝터가 필요할 거예요.

해설 | 이유를 묻는 Why 의문문

(A) **관련 없는 오답:** 수량을 묻는 How many 의문문에 적합한 응답이다.

(B) **정답:** 공유 네트워크 폴더(It's in the folder on the shared network)를 언급하여 해당 정보를 알 수 있는 방법을 알려 주고 있으므로 가장 적절한 응답이다.

(C) **파생어 오답:** 질문의 project와 파생어 관계인 projector를 이용한 오답이다.

11 W-Am / M-Au

How much is the train fare to Eastwood Station?

(A) Turn left at the corner.

(B) The job fair starts tomorrow.

(C) I've never gone to that stop.

이스트우드역까지 기차 요금이 얼마예요?

(A) 모퉁이에서 좌회전하세요.

(B) 취업 박람회가 내일 시작돼요.

(C) 저는 그 역에 가 본 적이 없는데요.

해설 | 가격·요금을 묻는 How 의문문
(A) **연상 작용 오답:** 질문의 How 의문사와 장소 Eastwood Station만 듣고 길을 묻는 상황으로 잘못 이해하면 연상 가능한 Turn left at the corner를 이용한 오답이다.
(B) **유사 발음 오답:** 질문의 fare와 발음이 동일한 fair로 혼동을 준 오답이다.
(C) **정답:** 그 역에 가 본 적이 없다(I've never gone to that stop)며 아는 바가 없음을 우회적으로 드러낸 적절한 응답이다.

어휘 | job fair 취업 박람회

12 W-Am / M-Cn

How will we get to the theater?
(A) No, we won't need any.
(B) My car seats five people.
(C) Only ten dollars.

극장에 어떻게 갈까요?
(A) 아니요, 아무것도 필요 없어요.
(B) **제 차에 다섯 명을 태울 수 있어요.**
(C) 겨우 10달러예요.

해설 | 교통수단을 묻는 How 의문문
(A) **Yes/No 대답 불가 오답:** 의문사 의문문에는 Yes/No로 대답할 수 없다.
(B) **정답:** 차에 다섯 명을 태울 수 있다(My car seats five people)며 차를 언급하고 있으므로 가장 적절한 응답이다.
(C) **관련 없는 오답:** 가격을 묻는 How much 의문문에 적합한 응답이다.

어휘 | seat ~을 수용하다

13 M-Au / W-Am

Why is our company relocating the factory to Melbourne?
(A) Sure, I'll prepare the inventory checklist.
(B) Managers will be sharing information at today's meeting.
(C) Men's formal attire is upstairs.

우리 회사는 왜 멜버른으로 공장을 이전하는 거죠?
(A) 물론이죠, 제가 재고 점검표를 준비할게요.
(B) **관리자들이 오늘 회의에서 정보를 공유할 겁니다.**
(C) 남성 정장은 위층에 있습니다.

해설 | 공장 이전 이유를 묻는 Why 의문문
(A) **Yes/No 대답 불가 오답:** 의문사 의문문에 Yes의 대체 표현인 Sure로 대답할 수 없다.
(B) **정답:** 관리자들이 오늘 회의에서 정보를 공유할 것(Managers will be sharing information at today's meeting)이라며 곧 그 이유를 알게 될 것임을 우회적으로 드러낸 적절한 응답이다.
(C) **연상 작용 오답:** 질문의 relocating the factory에서 연상 가능한 upstairs를 이용한 오답이다.

어휘 | relocate 이전하다 inventory 재고, 물품 목록
formal attire 정장

14 W-Br / M-Cn

Why wasn't Mr. Jenkins' package delivered on Wednesday?
(A) From that furniture store in West Ingram.
(B) He wasn't home to sign for it.
(C) Sometime between one and four P.M.

젠킨스 씨의 소포는 왜 수요일에 배송되지 않았죠?
(A) 웨스트 잉그램에 있는 그 가구점에서요.
(B) **집에 없어서 수령 확인 서명을 못했어요.**
(C) 오후 1시에서 4시 사이요.

해설 | 소포 미배송 이유를 묻는 Why 의문문
(A) **관련 없는 오답:** Where 의문문에 적합한 응답이다.
(B) **정답:** 그가 집에 없어서 수령 확인 서명을 못했다(He wasn't home to sign for it)는 구체적인 이유를 제시했으므로 정답이다.
(C) **관련 없는 오답:** When 의문문에 어울리는 응답이다.

어휘 | sign for ~을 수령했다고 서명하다

15 M-Cn / W-Br

How long will it take to process my payment?
(A) The computer system is down.
(B) The maps are in the top drawer.
(C) No, a new financial advisor.

제 급여를 처리하는 데 시간이 얼마나 걸릴까요?
(A) **컴퓨터 시스템이 다운됐어요.**
(B) 지도가 맨 위 서랍에 있어요.
(C) 아니요, 새 재정 고문이에요.

해설 | 기간을 묻는 How 의문문
(A) **정답:** 컴퓨터 시스템이 다운됐다(The computer system is down)며 시간이 걸릴 것임을 우회적으로 드러낸 적절한 응답이다.
(B) **관련 없는 오답:** 질문과 상관없는 답변을 제시한 오답이다.
(C) **Yes/No 대답 불가 오답:** 의문사 의문문에는 Yes/No로 대답할 수 없다.

어휘 | financial 금융의, 재무의 advisor 고문, 자문가

16 M-Cn / W-Br

Why isn't this Web page loading for me?
(A) Thanks for the suggestion.
(B) I'm good with computers.
(C) That was a heavy load to carry.

이 웹페이지는 왜 로딩이 안 되는 걸까요?
(A) 제안해 주셔서 감사합니다.
(B) **제가 컴퓨터를 잘 다뤄요.**
(C) 나르기엔 무거운 짐이었어요.

해설 | 이유를 묻는 Why 의문문
(A) **관련 없는 오답:** 질문과 상관없는 답변을 제시한 오답이다.
(B) **정답:** 내가 컴퓨터를 잘 다룬다(I'm good with computers)며 관련 상황 해결 방법을 우회적으로 드러낸 적절한 응답이다.
(C) **다의어 오답:** 질문의 load는 '로딩되다, 로딩하다'라는 의미의 동사, 보기의 load는 '짐'이라는 의미의 명사이다.

어휘 | load 짐; 로딩하다, 로딩되다

17 M-Au / W-Am

Why aren't you going to tonight's dinner party?
(A) I wish I'd been there.
(B) Thanks, I'd love to!
(C) I've already made plans.

오늘 저녁 파티에 왜 안 가세요?
(A) 갔으면 좋았을 텐데요.
(B) 감사합니다, 그러고 싶어요!
(C) 이미 약속이 있어서요.

해설 | 이유를 묻는 Why 의문문
(A) **시제 오류 오답:** 미래(오늘 저녁)에 대해 묻는 질문에 가정법 과거완료 I'd been으로 응답하는 것은 어색하다.
(B) **연상 작용 오답:** 질문의 Why aren't you를 제안의 의미로 잘못 들었을 경우 연상 가능한 제안 수락의 응답인 Thanks, I'd love to를 언급한 오답이다.
(C) **정답:** 이미 약속이 있다(I've already made plans)는 구체적인 이유를 제시했으므로 정답이다.

18 M-Au / W-Am

How many more deliveries need to be made?
(A) My shift just started.
(B) Yes, every once in a while.
(C) About 50 kilometers per hour.

배송을 몇 건 더 해야 하죠?
(A) 제 교대근무가 이제 막 시작됐어요.
(B) 네, 가끔요.
(C) 시속 약 50km요.

해설 | 수량을 묻는 How 의문문
(A) **정답:** 교대근무가 이제 막 시작됐다(My shift just started)며 아직 확실한 것을 모른다는 말을 우회적으로 표현한 적절한 답변이다.
(B) **Yes/No 대답 불가 오답:** 의문사 의문문에는 Yes/No로 대답할 수 없다.
(C) **관련 없는 오답:** 질문과 상관없는 답변을 제시한 오답이다.

어휘 | every once in a while 이따금, 가끔

19 W-Am / M-Au

How's the accounting firm that we hired working out?
(A) They've identified several ways to increase our profits!
(B) That machine is out of order.
(C) Thanks, but I just worked out at the gym.

우리가 고용한 회계사무소는 어떻게 되어 가나요?
(A) 저희 수익을 늘릴 몇 가지 방법을 찾아냈어요!
(B) 그 기계는 고장났어요.
(C) 감사하지만, 저는 헬스클럽에서 막 운동을 했어요.

해설 | 진행 상황을 묻는 How 의문문
(A) **정답:** 그들이 수익을 늘릴 몇 가지 방법을 찾아냈다(They've identified several ways to increase our profits)며 구체적인 진행 상황을 언급했으므로 정답이다.
(B) **연상 작용 오답:** 질문의 working에서 연상 가능한 out of order를 이용한 오답이다.

(C) **다의어 오답:** 질문의 working out은 '잘 풀리다'라는 뜻이지만, 보기의 work out은 '운동하다'라는 의미이다.

어휘 | accounting 회계 **firm** 회사 **identify** 발견하다, 찾다 **profit** 수익, 수입 **out of order** 고장난

20 M-Au / W-Am

Why is Helen out of the office today?
(A) Yes, I would prefer to sit outside.
(B) Check the supply cabinet.
(C) Everyone deserves a day off, don't they?

헬렌은 왜 오늘 사무실에 없나요?
(A) 네, 저는 밖에 앉는 것이 좋아요.
(B) 물품함을 확인해 보세요.
(C) 누구나 하루 쉴 수 있잖아요, 그렇지 않나요?

해설 | 이유를 묻는 Why 의문문
(A) **Yes/No 대답 불가 오답:** 의문사 의문문에는 Yes/No로 대답할 수 없다.
(B) **연상 작용 오답:** 질문의 office에서 연상 가능한 the supply cabinet을 이용한 오답이다.
(C) **정답:** 누구나 하루 쉴 수 있지 않냐(Everyone deserves a day off, don't they?)고 되물으며 휴가 갔음을 우회적으로 드러낸 적절한 응답이다.

어휘 | supply cabinet 소모품 캐비닛, 물품함 **deserve** ~을 받을 만하다, 누릴 자격이 있다

UNIT 6 일반 / 선택 의문문

ETS 유형 연습
본책 p.48

1 (C) **2** (C) **3** (A) **4** (C) **5** (C) **6** (B)

1 M-Cn / W-Br

Did you have a chance to read that article on recent business trends?
(A) Check their business hours.
(B) He started working here recently.
(C) I was just about to look at it.

최근 비즈니스 동향에 관한 그 기사를 읽을 기회가 있었나요?
(A) 그들의 운영시간을 확인해 보세요.
(B) 그는 최근에 여기서 일하기 시작했어요.
(C) 막 보려던 참이었어요.

해설 | 기사를 읽었는지 묻는 일반 의문문
(A) **단어 반복 오답:** 질문의 business를 반복 이용한 오답이다.
(B) **인칭 오류 및 파생어 오답:** 보기의 He가 가리키는 대상이 질문에 없으며, 질문의 recent와 파생어 관계인 recently를 이용한 오답이다.
(C) **정답:** 기사를 막 보려던 참(I was just about to look at it)이었다고 말함으로써 아직 보지 않았음을 우회적으로 표현한 정답이다.

어휘 | article 기사 **be about to** 막 ~하려고 하다

29

2 W-Am / M-Cn

Have the interns been trained to use the teleconference system?
(A) The conference starts at ten thirty.
(B) The train doesn't stop at this station.
(C) I don't think they'll need to use it.

인턴들은 화상 회의 시스템을 사용하는 교육을 받았나요?
(A) 회의는 10시 30분에 시작해요.
(B) 열차는 이 역에 정차하지 않습니다.
(C) 그들은 그것을 사용할 필요가 없을 것 같아요.

해설 | 완료 여부를 확인하는 일반 의문문
(A) **파생어 오답:** 질문의 teleconference와 파생어 관계인 conference를 이용한 오답이다.
(B) **다의어 오답:** 질문의 train은 '교육하다'라는 의미의 동사이고, 보기의 train은 '열차'라는 의미의 명사이다.
(C) **정답:** 인턴들이 그것을 사용할 필요가 없을 것 같다(I don't think they'll need to use it)며 교육을 받지 않았음을 우회적으로 말한 정답이다.

어휘 | teleconference 화상 회의

3 W-Am / M-Au

Excuse me, do you have this sweater in blue?
(A) That color's only sold online.
(B) A discounted price.
(C) The weather should be perfect.

실례지만, 이 스웨터 파란색 있나요?
(A) 그 색상은 온라인으로만 판매해요.
(B) 할인된 가격입니다.
(C) 날씨가 무척 좋을 거예요.

해설 | 재고 여부를 묻는 일반 의문문
(A) **정답:** 그 색상(파란색)은 온라인으로만 판매한다(That color's only sold online)며 없다는 말을 우회적으로 표현한 적절한 응답이다.
(B) **연상 작용 오답:** 질문의 sweater에서 연상 가능한 price를 이용한 오답이다.
(C) **유사 발음 오답:** 질문의 sweater와 발음이 유사한 weather로 혼동을 준 오답이다.

4 M-Au / W-Am

Are you going to rent that apartment you looked at last night?
(A) I've ordered the part online.
(B) No, the first time.
(C) Well, it is quite expensive.

어젯밤에 본 그 아파트를 빌릴 건가요?
(A) 그 부품을 온라인으로 주문했어요.
(B) 아뇨, 처음이에요.
(C) 글쎄요, 꽤 비싸서 말이죠.

해설 | 계획을 확인하는 일반 의문문
(A) **유사 발음 오답:** 질문의 apartment와 일부 발음이 유사한 part를 이용한 오답이다.
(B) **연상 작용 오답:** 질문의 last에서 연상 가능한 first를 이용한 오답이다.

(C) **정답:** 아파트 임대료가 꽤 비싸다(it is quite expensive)며 우회적으로 부정적인 의견을 제시한 적절한 응답이다.

어휘 | rent 빌리다, 임대하다 part 부품

5 M-Cn / M-Au

Do you know where the convention center is?
(A) The annual marketing conference.
(B) Did you bring your lunch?
(C) Yes, I've been there several times.

컨벤션 센터가 어디에 있는지 아세요?
(A) 연례 마케팅 회의요.
(B) 점심을 가져오셨나요?
(C) 네, 몇 번 가 봤어요.

해설 | 위치를 묻는 간접 의문문
(A) **연상 작용 오답:** 질문의 convention center에서 연상 가능한 conference를 이용한 오답이다.
(B) **관련 없는 오답:** 질문과 상관없는 답변을 제시한 오답이다.
(C) **정답:** Yes라고 응답한 후, 몇 번 가 봤다(I've been there several times)고 덧붙였으므로 정답이다.

어휘 | annual 연례의, 연간의

6 W-Br / M-Cn

Does your catering company offer a variety of meal options?
(A) Don't forget your apron.
(B) Let me show you the menu.
(C) A table for two, please.

당신네 케이터링 업체는 다양한 식사를 제공하나요?
(A) 앞치마를 잊지 마세요.
(B) 메뉴를 보여드릴게요.
(C) 두 명 앉을 자리 주세요.

해설 | 제공 여부를 묻는 일반 의문문
(A) **연상 작용 오답:** 질문의 meal에서 연상 가능한 apron을 이용한 오답이다.
(B) **정답:** 메뉴를 보여드리겠다(Let me show you the menu)며 식사 메뉴가 다양함을 우회적으로 표현한 적절한 응답이다.
(C) **연상 작용 오답:** 질문의 meal에서 연상 가능한 A table for two, please를 이용한 오답이다.

어휘 | a variety of 다양한 apron 앞치마

ETS 유형 연습

1 (A)	**2** (A)	**3** (C)	**4** (B)	**5** (C)	**6** (A)

1 W-Am / M-Cn

Do you want your invoice to be mailed to you or sent electronically?
(A) Please send me a paper copy.
(B) Sure, let me spell it.
(C) Yes, I already sent it.

청구서를 우편으로 보내드릴까요, 아니면 이메일로 보내드릴까요?
(A) 종이 서류로 보내주세요.
(B) 그럼요. 제가 철자를 써 볼게요.
(C) 네, 이미 보냈어요.

해설 | 발송 방법을 묻는 선택 의문문
(A) **정답:** 종이 서류로 보내 달라(send me a paper copy)는 것은 우편으로 보내 달라는 의미이므로, 둘 중 전자를 선택한 적절한 응답이다.
(B) **관련 없는 오답:** 질문과 상관없는 답변을 제시한 오답이다.
(C) **단어 반복 오답:** 질문의 sent를 반복 이용한 오답이다.

어휘 | invoice 청구서, 송장 electronically 이메일로, 전자식으로

2 W-Br / M-Cn

Would you like your business cards single- or double-sided?
(A) How much does each kind cost?
(B) They printed too many copies.
(C) Double the original price.

명함을 단면으로 인쇄하시겠어요, 아니면 양면으로 하시겠어요?
(A) 각각 비용이 얼마입니까?
(B) 그들은 인쇄를 너무 많이 했어요.
(C) 원래 가격의 두 배로 하세요.

해설 | 인쇄 면을 묻는 선택 의문문
(A) **정답:** 각각 가격이 얼마인지(How much does each kind cost?) 되묻고 있으므로 가장 적절한 응답이다.
(B) **연상 어휘 오답:** 질문의 single- or double-sided에서 연상 가능한 print를 이용한 오답이다.
(C) **단어 반복 오답:** 질문의 double을 반복 이용한 오답이다.

어휘 | cost 비용이 들다 original price 정가

3 M-Cn / M-Au

Is it cheaper to buy a car or to lease one?
(A) Around five hundred dollars.
(B) A two-year warranty.
(C) Lease payments are generally lower.

차를 사는 것과 리스하는 것 중 어느 쪽이 더 싼가요?
(A) 약 500달러요.
(B) 2년간의 품질 보증서요.
(C) 대개 리스가 더 저렴해요.

해설 | 더 저렴한 것을 묻는 선택 의문문
(A) **연상 작용 오답:** 질문의 buy a car에서 연상 가능한 five hundred dollars를 이용한 오답이다.
(B) **연상 작용 오답:** 질문의 lease에서 연상 가능한 warranty를 언급한 오답이다.
(C) **정답:** 대개 리스가 더 저렴하다(Lease payments are generally lower)며 후자를 선택하여 답했으므로 정답이다.

어휘 | lease 임대하다; 임대차 계약 warranty 품질 보증서 generally 보통, 대개

4 M-Au / W-Br

Are you ready to leave, or are you still packing?
(A) The package arrived this morning.
(B) Our flight isn't until eight.
(C) Is Carlos leaving some for us?

떠날 준비가 됐나요, 아니면 아직 짐을 싸고 있나요?
(A) 소포가 오늘 아침에 도착했어요.
(B) 우리 비행기는 8시는 되어야 떠요.
(C) 칼로스가 우리 것도 좀 남길까요?

해설 | 사실을 묻는 선택 의문문
(A) **파생어 오답:** 질문의 packing과 파생어 관계인 package를 이용한 오답이다.
(B) **정답:** 비행기 시간이 8시(flight isn't until eight)라며 아직 여유가 있음을 나타내고 있으므로 가장 적절한 응답이다.
(C) **다의어 오답:** 질문의 leave는 '떠나다'는 의미이고, 보기의 leave는 '남기다'라는 뜻이다.

어휘 | pack 짐을 꾸리다 package 소포 flight 항공편

5 W-Br / M-Cn

Should we take a group photo now or in the afternoon?
(A) On the stairs by the entrance is best.
(B) The picture turned out really well!
(C) Some people are leaving before noon.

단체 사진을 지금 찍어야 하나요, 오후에 찍어야 하나요?
(A) 입구 옆 계단이 가장 좋아요.
(B) 사진이 정말 잘 나왔어요!
(C) 정오 전에 몇 명이 떠날 거예요.

해설 | 사진 찍을 시점을 묻는 선택 의문문
(A) **관련 없는 오답:** Where 의문문에 적합한 응답이다.
(B) **연상 어휘 오답:** 질문의 photo에서 연상 가능한 picture를 이용한 오답이다.
(C) **정답:** 정오 전에 몇 명이 떠날 거라고(Some people are leaving before noon) 대답함으로써 우회적으로 전자(now)를 선택한 적절한 응답이다.

어휘 | take a group photo 단체사진을 찍다 stairs 계단 entrance 입구 turn out well 잘 나오다

6 W-Br / M-Au

Should we work on this project, or hire a consultant to do it for us?
(A) We don't have time to do it ourselves.
(B) Yes, it's been remodeled.
(C) Not for a while.

우리가 이 프로젝트를 수행해야 할까요, 아니면 대신해 줄 자문 위원을 고용해야 할까요?
(A) 우리가 할 시간이 없어요.
(B) 네, 리모델링됐어요.
(C) 당분간은 아니에요.

해설 | 프로젝트 수행자를 묻는 선택 의문문
(A) **정답:** 우리가 할 시간이 없다(We don't have time to do it ourselves)면서 우회적으로 후자를 선택한 적절한 응답이다.
(B) **연상 작용 오답:** 질문의 work on this project에서 연상 가능한 remodeled를 이용한 오답이다.
(C) **연상 작용 오답:** 질문의 Should we work on this project에서 연상 가능한 대답 Not for a while를 이용한 오답이다.

어휘 | for a while 얼마 동안, 당분간

ETS 고득점 실전 문제

본책 p.50

1 (C)	**2** (A)	**3** (B)	**4** (C)	**5** (C)	**6** (B)
7 (C)	**8** (A)	**9** (A)	**10** (C)	**11** (C)	**12** (C)
13 (C)	**14** (A)	**15** (B)	**16** (B)	**17** (B)	**18** (C)
19 (C)	**20** (A)				

1 W-Am / M-Au

Did you read the newspaper this morning?
(A) Two dollars and fifty cents per issue.
(B) She's the new publisher.
(C) Only the front page.

오늘 아침에 신문 읽었어요?
(A) 한 호당 2달러 50센트예요.
(B) 그녀가 새 발행인입니다.
(C) 1면만요.

해설 | 신문을 읽었는지 묻는 일반 의문문
(A) **연상 작용 오답:** 질문의 newspaper에서 연상 가능한 issue를 언급한 오답이다.
(B) **연상 작용 오답:** 질문의 newspaper에서 연상 가능한 publisher를 언급한 오답이다.
(C) **정답:** 1면만(Only the front page)이라고 구체적으로 답변했으므로 정답이다.

어휘 | issue (정기 간행물의) 호   publisher 출판사, 발행인

2 W-Br / W-Am

Would you like to purchase a ticket for the seven o'clock flight or the nine o'clock flight?
(A) For the earlier one, please.
(B) Of course he does.
(C) Here's my credit card.

7시 항공권을 구입하시겠어요, 아니면 9시 항공권을 구입하시겠어요?
(A) **빠른 것으로 주세요.**
(B) 그는 물론 그렇게 하죠.
(C) 제 신용카드 여기 있습니다.

해설 | 항공권 시간 선택을 묻는 선택 의문문
(A) **정답:** 빠른 것(the earlier one)으로 답했으므로 전자를 선택한 정답이다.
(B) **인칭 오류 오답:** 보기의 he가 가리키는 대상이 질문에 없다.
(C) **연상 작용 오답:** 질문의 purchase에서 연상 가능한 지불 수단 credit card를 이용한 오답이다.

어휘 | purchase 구입하다

3 M-Au / W-Br

Should I order the supplies now, or wait until next week?
(A) A total of seventy-five dollars.
(B) Actually, I already sent the order.
(C) It's in the supply closet.

물품을 지금 주문해야 할까요, 아니면 다음 주까지 기다릴까요?
(A) 전부 75달러예요.
(B) **사실, 벌써 주문서를 보냈는데요.**
(C) 물품 보관실에 있어요.

해설 | 주문 시점을 묻는 선택 의문문
(A) **연상 어휘 오답:** 질문의 order the supplies에서 연상 가능한 가격 표현 A total of seventy-five dollars를 이용한 오답이다.
(B) **정답:** 벌써 주문서를 보냈다(I already sent the order)며 새로 주문할 필요가 없음을 우회적으로 말한 적절한 응답이다.
(C) **단어 반복 오답:** 질문에 언급된 supplies의 단수형인 supply를 이용한 오답이다.

어휘 | supplies 물품   supply closet 물품 보관실

4 W-Br / M-Au

Have you called tech support for help?
(A) Until next Monday.
(B) That table is made of wood.
(C) Rita knows how to fix this.

기술 지원팀에 전화해 도움을 요청하셨나요?
(A) 다음 주 월요일까지요.
(B) 그 탁자는 나무로 만들었어요.
(C) **리타가 고치는 방법을 알아요.**

해설 | 요청 여부를 묻는 일반 의문문
(A) **관련 없는 오답:** When 의문문에 적합한 응답이다.
(B) **관련 없는 오답:** 질문과 상관없는 답변을 제시한 오답이다.
(C) **정답:** 리타가 고치는 방법을 안다(Rita knows how to fix this)며 기술 지원팀에 요청하지 않았음을 우회적으로 표현한 적절한 응답이다.

어휘 | fix 고치다

5 M-Au / W-Am

Do you have this shirt in a larger size?
(A) Two skirts and a jacket.
(B) We only accept cash payments.
(C) A new shipment comes in tomorrow.

이 셔츠 더 큰 사이즈가 있나요?
(A) 치마 두 개와 재킷 하나요.
(B) 저희는 현금 결제만 받습니다.
(C) 새 물품이 내일 들어옵니다.

해설 | 재고 여부를 묻는 일반 의문문
(A) 연상 작용 오답: 질문의 shirt에서 연상 가능한 skirts와 jacket을 이용한 오답이다.
(B) 연상 작용 오답: 질문의 shirt에서 연상 가능한 cash payments를 언급한 오답이다.
(C) 정답: 새 물품이 내일 들어온다(A new shipment comes in tomorrow)며 지금은 없지만 내일 오면 있을 것이라는 말을 우회적으로 한 적절한 응답이다.

어휘 | accept 수락하다   shipment 선적, 수송품

6 W-Br / M-Cn
Would you like to pay cash or use a credit card?
(A) Yes, I play soccer.
(B) I never carry cash with me.
(C) Fifteen dollars.

현금으로 지불하시겠어요, 아니면 신용카드를 사용하시겠어요?
(A) 네, 저는 축구를 합니다.
(B) 저는 현금을 안 가지고 다녀요.
(C) 15달러입니다.

해설 | 지불 수단을 묻는 선택 의문문
(A) 유사 발음 오답: 질문의 pay와 발음이 유사한 play로 혼동을 준 오답이다.
(B) 정답: 현금을 가지고 다니지 않는다(I never carry cash with me)고 말함으로써 후자(신용카드)를 선택한 적절한 응답이다.
(C) 연상 작용 및 관련 없는 오답: 질문의 pay cash에서 연상 가능한 Fifteen dollars를 언급한 오답이며, 가격을 묻는 How much 의문문에 적합한 응답이다.

7 W-Br / M-Au
Do you want to schedule the inspection for the morning or the afternoon?
(A) Safety gloves and goggles.
(B) The parking lot in the back.
(C) The afternoon would be best.

점검 일정을 오전으로 잡고 싶으세요, 아니면 오후로 잡고 싶으세요?
(A) 안전 장갑과 고글이요.
(B) 뒤편 주차장이요.
(C) 오후가 가장 좋겠어요.

해설 | 일정을 묻는 선택 의문문
(A) 연상 작용 오답: 질문의 inspection에서 연상 가능한 Safety를 언급한 오답이다.
(B) 관련 없는 오답: 질문과 상관없는 답변을 제시한 오답이다.
(C) 정답: 오후가 가장 좋겠다(The afternoon would be best)고 후자를 선택하여 답했으므로 정답이다.

어휘 | schedule 일정을 잡다, 예정하다   inspection 점검
safety gloves 안전 장갑

8 M-Au / W-Br
Can you tell me where booth 219 is located?
(A) Of course, third row on your right.
(B) Some local musicians.
(C) Unfortunately, it isn't.

219번 부스가 어디 있는지 알려 주실 수 있나요?
(A) 물론이죠, 오른쪽 세 번째 열에 있어요.
(B) 지역 음악가들이요.
(C) 유감스럽지만 아니에요.

해설 | 부스 위치를 묻는 간접 의문문
(A) 정답: 오른쪽 세 번째 열에 있다(third row on your right)고 구체적인 위치 설명을 덧붙였으므로 정답이다.
(B) 유사 발음 오답: 질문의 located와 부분적으로 발음이 유사한 local로 혼동을 준 오답이다.
(C) 관련 없는 오답: 질문과 상관없는 답변을 제시한 오답이다.

어휘 | be located 위치하다   unfortunately 유감스럽게도

9 M-Au / W-Br
Will the fliers be ready today, or do you need more time to finish them?
(A) I'll start work on them now.
(B) I don't know who's going.
(C) Her flight's late.

전단이 오늘 준비될까요, 아니면 마무리할 시간이 더 필요한가요?
(A) 지금 일을 시작할 거예요.
(B) 누가 가는지 모르겠어요.
(C) 그녀의 비행기가 연착했어요.

해설 | 전단 준비 시점을 묻는 선택 의문문
(A) 정답: 지금 일을 시작할 것(I'll start work on them now)이라고 우회적으로 말함으로써 시간이 더 필요하다는 후자(need more time)를 선택한 정답이다.
(B) 연상 어휘 오답: 질문의 flier를 '전단'이 아니라 '여객기 승객'으로 오해한 경우 연상 가능한 who's going을 이용한 오답이다.
(C) 유사 발음 오답: 질문의 fliers와 발음이 일부 유사한 flight를 이용한 오답이다.

어휘 | flier 전단, 여객기 승객   flight 비행기

10 W-Br / W-Am
Would you rather troubleshoot your software issues by phone or in person?
(A) Yes, once the trouble's been sorted out.
(B) They issued me a new password.
(C) I'd like to talk to someone face-to-face.

소프트웨어 문제를 전화로 해결하시겠어요, 아니면 직접 해결하시겠어요?
(A) 네, 문제가 해결되면요.
(B) 그들이 새 비밀번호를 발급해 줬어요.
(C) 직접 보고 이야기하고 싶어요.

(A) 유사 발음 오답: 질문의 troubleshoot과 부분적으로 발음이
    동일한 trouble을 이용한 오답이다.
(B) 다의어 오답: 질문에 나오는 issues는 '문제'라는 뜻의
    명사이고, 보기의 issue는 '발급해 주다'라는 뜻의 동사이다.
(C) 정답: 직접 보고 이야기하고 싶다(I'd like to talk to
    someone face-to-face)며 후자를 우회적으로 선택한
    적절한 응답이다.

어휘 | troubleshoot 문제를 해결하다 in person 직접 sort
out 문제를 해결하다

11 W-Am / M-Cn

Will our proposal get to the city council on time?
(A) In the central square.
(B) A ten percent increase.
(C) I sent it by overnight mail.

우리의 제안서가 시의회에 제때 도착할까요?
(A) 중앙광장에서요.
(B) 10퍼센트 증가했어요.
(C) 제가 빠른 우편으로 보냈어요.

해설 | 미래 사실을 확인하는 일반 의문문
(A) 관련 없는 오답: Where 의문문에 적합한 응답이다.
(B) 관련 없는 오답: 질문과 상관없는 답변을 제시한 오답이다.
(C) 정답: 빠른 우편으로 보냈기(sent it by overnight mail)
    때문에 제때 도착할 거라고 우회적으로 대답하고 있으므로
    정답이다.

어휘 | proposal 제안(서) get to ~에 도착하다 city
council 시의회 on time 정각에, 제때 central square
중앙광장 increase 증가 by overnight mail 익일[빠른]
우편으로

12 W-Br / M-Cn

Will you be leading the budgeting workshop or the
database training?
(A) On the desk by the window, thanks.
(B) By commuter train every morning.
(C) I still have to complete these monthly reports.

예산 책정 워크숍을 진행하시나요, 아니면 데이터베이스 교육을 진행
하시나요?
(A) 창문 옆에 있는 책상 위에요, 감사합니다.
(B) 매일 아침 통근 열차로요.
(C) 전 아직 이번 달 월간 보고서를 완료해야 해요.

해설 | 진행 내용을 묻는 선택 의문문
(A) 관련 없는 오답: Where 의문문에 적합한 응답이다.
(B) 유사 발음 오답: 질문의 training과 부분적으로 발음이
    동일한 train을 이용한 오답이다.
(C) 정답: 이번 달 월간 보고서를 완료해야 한다(I still have to
    complete these monthly reports)면서 둘 다 진행할
    수 없음을 우회적으로 드러낸 적절한 응답이다.

어휘 | budget 예산을 세우다 commuter 통근자
complete 완료하다

13 M-Cn / W-Br

Will there be a fee if I have to cancel my hotel
reservation?
(A) You can make a reservation on our Web site.
(B) Did you enjoy your stay?
(C) Not if you give 24 hours' notice.

제가 호텔 예약을 취소해야 한다면 요금이 발생하나요?
(A) 저희 웹사이트에서 예약하시면 됩니다.
(B) 즐겁게 머무르셨나요?
(C) 24시간 전에 통보하시면 그렇지 않습니다.

해설 | 요금 발생 여부를 묻는 일반 의문문
(A) 단어 반복 오답: 질문의 reservation을 반복 이용한
    오답이다.
(B) 연상 작용 오답: 질문의 hotel에서 연상 가능한 stay를
    이용한 오답이다.
(C) 정답: 24시간 전에 통보하면 그렇지 않다(Not if you give
    24 hours' notice)고 구체적으로 알려 주고 있으므로
    정답이다.

어휘 | make a reservation 예약하다

14 M-Am / W-Br

Do you know who was hired as the new program
director?
(A) It hasn't been decided yet.
(B) No, he didn't direct the show.
(C) I think Ms. Shin likes that program.

새 프로그램 책임자로 누가 고용되었는지 아세요?
(A) 아직 결정되지 않았어요.
(B) 아니요, 그는 그 공연을 감독하지 않았어요.
(C) 신 씨가 그 프로그램을 좋아하는 것 같아요.

해설 | 인물을 묻는 간접 의문문
(A) 정답: 아직 결정되지 않았다(It hasn't been decided
    yet)며 모른다는 사실을 우회적으로 표현한 적절한 응답이다.
(B) 파생어 오답: 질문에 언급된 director와 파생어 관계인
    direct를 이용한 오답이다.
(C) 단어 반복 오답: 질문의 program을 반복 이용한 오답이다.

어휘 | director 책임자, 관리자 direct 감독하다, 연출하다

15 W-Am / M-Cn

Are we producing these parts ourselves, or are we
getting them from a supplier?
(A) To calculate the shipping costs.
(B) We're buying them from a vendor.
(C) I need a different part.

우리는 이 부품들을 스스로 생산하나요, 아니면 공급업체로부터 받나요?
(A) 수송비를 계산하려고요.
(B) 판매업체에서 구입해요.
(C) 저는 다른 부품이 필요해요.

34

해설 | 부품 생산 여부를 묻는 선택 의문문
(A) **관련 없는 오답:** 목적을 묻는 Why 의문문에 적합한 응답이다.
(B) **정답:** 판매업체에서 구입한다(We're buying them from a vendor)고 답함으로써 후자(supplier)를 선택한 정답이다.
(C) **단어 반복 오답:** 질문의 part를 반복 이용한 오답이다.

어휘 | part 부품   **calculate** 계산하다   **vendor** 판매업체, 판매상

16 W-Br / M-Cn

Did they have the opening ceremony for the new bridge?
(A) The start button.
(B) There was a thunderstorm that day.
(C) The office is on the tenth floor.

그들은 새 교량을 위한 개통식을 했나요?
(A) 시작 버튼이요.
(B) 그날 폭풍우가 쳤어요.
(C) 사무실은 10층에 있습니다.

해설 | 진행 여부를 묻는 일반 의문문
(A) **연상 작용 오답:** 질문의 opening, new에서 연상 가능한 start를 이용한 오답이다.
(B) **정답:** 그날 폭풍우가 쳤다(There was a thunderstorm that day)고 말함으로써 개통식을 하지 못했다고 우회적으로 말한 적절한 응답이다.
(C) **관련 없는 오답:** 질문과 상관없는 답변을 제시한 오답이다.

어휘 | ceremony 의식, 식   **thunderstorm** 폭풍우

17 W-Am / M-Cn

Is Ms. Choi attending the product launch tomorrow?
(A) The stairs on your right.
(B) Diego has the guest list.
(C) Because it was too crowded.

최 씨는 내일 제품 출시 행사에 참석하나요?
(A) 오른쪽 계단이요.
(B) 디에고가 방문객 목록을 갖고 있어요.
(C) 너무 붐벼서요.

해설 | 행사 참석을 묻는 일반 의문문
(A) **관련 없는 오답:** 질문과 상관없는 답변을 제시한 오답이다.
(B) **정답:** 디에고가 방문객 목록을 갖고 있다(Diego has the guest list)며 자신은 모른다는 사실을 우회적으로 표현한 적절한 응답이다.
(C) **관련 없는 오답:** Why 의문문에 적합한 응답이다.

18 W-Am / M-Cn

Did the bank offer you the position verbally or in writing?
(A) Please deposit this in my savings account.
(B) I'll have some herbal tea.
(C) I accepted an offer in Tokyo, actually.

은행에서 해당 직책을 구두로 제안했나요, 아니면 서면으로 했나요?
(A) 이걸 제 저축 예금 계좌에 예금해 주세요.
(B) 저는 허브차를 마실게요.
(C) 사실 도쿄에서 제안을 수락했어요.

해설 | 제안 형태를 묻는 선택 의문문
(A) **연상 작용 오답:** 질문의 bank에서 연상 가능한 deposit, savings account를 언급한 오답이다.
(B) **유사 발음 오답:** 질문의 verbally와 부분적으로 발음이 유사한 herbal로 혼동을 준 오답이다.
(C) **정답:** 사실 도쿄에서 제안을 수락했다(I accepted an offer in Tokyo, actually)며 제3의 대답을 제시한 정답이다.

어휘 | verbally 구두로   **in writing** 서면으로   **deposit** 예금하다, 예치하다   **savings account** 저축 예금

19 M-Au / W-Br

Have you been to the medical clinic's new location?
(A) You're right about that!
(B) A health certificate.
(C) My appointment isn't until tomorrow.

새로 이전한 병원에 가 보셨어요?
(A) 당신이 맞아요!
(B) 건강 진단서요.
(C) 제 예약은 내일이나 되어야 해요.

해설 | 방문 여부를 묻는 일반 의문문
(A) **관련 없는 오답:** 질문과 상관없는 답변을 제시한 오답이다.
(B) **연상 작용 오답:** 질문의 medical clinic에서 연상 가능한 A health certificate를 언급한 오답이다.
(C) **정답:** 내 예약은 내일(My appointment isn't until tomorrow)이라며 아직 못 가봤다는 말을 우회적으로 한 적절한 응답이다.

어휘 | health certificate 건강 진단서

20 M-Au / M-Cn

Would you rather meet in person or by video conference?
(A) I'd prefer to be in the same room.
(B) No, we haven't met yet.
(C) Yes, I liked that movie.

직접 만나고 싶으세요, 아니면 화상 회의가 좋으세요?
(A) 같은 회의실에서 했으면 해요.
(B) 아니요, 우리는 아직 만난 적이 없어요.
(C) 네, 그 영화 좋았어요.

해설 | 회의 방식을 묻는 선택 의문문
(A) **정답:** 같은 회의실에서 했으면 한다(I'd prefer to be in the same room)고 전자를 선택해 우회적으로 응답했으므로 정답이다.
(B) **단어 반복 오답:** 질문의 meet를 과거분사형인 met로 반복 이용한 오답이다.
(C) **연상 작용 오답:** 질문의 video에서 연상 가능한 movie를 언급한 오답이다.

어휘 | in person 직접   **video conference** 화상 회의

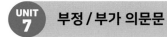

UNIT 7 부정 / 부가 의문문

ETS 유형 연습
본책 p.52

1 (C) **2** (A) **3** (B) **4** (C) **5** (B) **6** (A)

1 W-Br / M-Au

Don't we need to discuss the budget report?
(A) The bottom drawer.
(B) Do you accept credit cards?
(C) Yes, let's do that now.

예산 보고서에 대해 논의해야 하지 않나요?
(A) 맨 아래 서랍이요.
(B) 신용카드 받나요?
(C) 네, 지금 하시죠.

해설 | 논의 필요 여부를 확인하는 부정 의문문
(A) **관련 없는 오답:** 질문과 상관없는 답변을 제시한 오답이다.
(B) **연상 작용 오답:** 질문의 budget에서 연상 가능한 credit cards를 이용한 오답이다.
(C) **정답:** Yes라고 응답한 후, 지금 하자(let's do that now)고 덧붙였으므로 정답이다.

어휘 | budget 예산 bottom drawer 맨 아래 서랍

2 W-Br / M-Cn

Didn't Daniel accept the job offer?
(A) He'll let us know tomorrow.
(B) We expect a large crowd.
(C) Yes, I will.

대니얼이 그 일자리 제안을 수락하지 않았나요?
(A) 그가 내일 알려줄 거예요.
(B) 많은 사람들이 올 거라고 생각해요.
(C) 네, 그럴게요.

해설 | 사실을 확인하는 부정 의문문
(A) **정답:** 대니얼이 내일 알려줄 것(He'll let us know tomorrow)이라며 자신은 아직 모른다는 것을 우회적으로 표현한 적절한 응답이다.
(B) **유사 발음 오답:** 질문의 accept와 발음이 유사한 expect를 이용한 오답이다.
(C) **인칭 오류 오답:** Daniel(He)이 아니라 화자 본인(I)의 의견을 제시하고 있으므로 오답이다.

어휘 | accept 수락하다 expect 기대하다 crowd 군중

3 W-Br / M-Au

Isn't the security software updated regularly?
(A) They weren't produced locally.
(B) Yes, and this is the newest version.
(C) My calendar's up to date.

보안 소프트웨어는 정기적으로 업데이트되지 않나요?
(A) 그것들은 지역에서 생산되지 않았어요.
(B) 네, 이것이 최신 버전이에요.
(C) 제 일정표는 최근 거예요.

해설 | 업데이트 여부를 확인하는 부정 의문문
(A) **인칭 오류 오답:** 보기의 They가 가리키는 대상이 질문에 없다.
(B) **정답:** Yes라고 응답한 후, 이것이 최신 버전(this is the newest version)이라고 하며 업데이트가 되고 있음을 우회적으로 말한 적절한 응답이다.
(C) **유사 발음 오답:** 질문의 updated와 발음이 유사한 up to date로 혼동을 준 오답이다.

어휘 | regularly 정기적으로 up to date 최근의, 최신의

4 M-Cn / W-Am

Don't you want to attend the workshop?
(A) Leadership skills for junior managers.
(B) That's my favorite shop in town.
(C) No, I already did the training online.

워크숍 참석을 원하지 않으세요?
(A) 하급 관리자를 위한 리더십 역량이요.
(B) 제가 시내에서 가장 좋아하는 상점이에요.
(C) 아니요. 이미 온라인으로 교육을 받았어요.

해설 | 참석 희망 여부를 확인하는 부정 의문문
(A) **연상 작용 오답:** 질문의 workshop에서 연상 가능한 Leadership skills를 언급한 오답이다.
(B) **유사 발음 오답:** 질문의 workshop과 부분적으로 발음이 동일한 shop을 이용한 오답이다.
(C) **정답:** No라고 응답한 후, 이미 온라인으로 교육을 받았다(I already did the training online)고 덧붙였으므로 정답이다.

어휘 | junior manager 하급 관리자

5 M-Cn / W-Am

Can't we use the phone application to track our order?
(A) Train track number four.
(B) I'll get my phone.
(C) The sales results were good.

주문을 추적하기 위해 전화기 어플을 이용할 수 있지 않아요?
(A) 4번 선로요.
(B) 제 전화기를 가져올게요.
(C) 판매 결과가 좋았어요.

해설 | 사용 가능 여부를 확인하는 부정 의문문
(A) **다의어 오답:** 질문에 나오는 track은 '추적하다'라는 뜻의 동사이고, 보기의 track은 '선로'라는 뜻의 명사이다.
(B) **정답:** 내 전화기를 가져오겠다(I'll get my phone)며 우회적으로 긍정의 응답을 드러내고 있으므로 정답이다.
(C) **연상 작용 오답:** 질문의 order에서 연상 가능한 sales를 언급한 오답이다.

어휘 | track 추적하다; 선로

6 M-Au / W-Am

Aren't we meeting this afternoon to discuss the TV ad?

(A) There's a leadership seminar from one to four.

(B) It was nice to meet you, too.

(C) Which brand of television do you recommend?

오늘 오후에 TV 광고에 대해 논의하기 위해 만나지 않나요?

(A) 1시부터 4시까지 리더십 세미나가 있어요.

(B) 저도 만나서 반가웠습니다.

(C) 어떤 브랜드의 TV를 추천하세요?

해설 | 미팅 여부를 확인하는 부정 의문문

(A) **정답:** 1시부터 4시까지 리더십 세미나가 있다(There's a leadership seminar from one to four)며 오후에 만날 수 없음을 우회적으로 표현한 적절한 응답이다.

(B) **파생어 오답:** 질문의 meeting과 파생어 관계인 meet를 이용한 오답이다.

(C) **단어 반복 오답:** 질문의 TV를 보기의 television으로 반복 이용한 오답이다.

어휘 | recommend 추천하다, 권장하다

ETS 유형 연습
본책 p.53

1 (A)	**2** (C)	**3** (C)	**4** (B)	**5** (B)	**6** (C)

1 M-Cn / W-Br

This cabinet comes preassembled, doesn't it?

(A) No, but the directions are easy to follow.

(B) He's working late at the factory.

(C) They should be in the top drawer.

이 캐비닛은 조립되어서 오는 거죠, 그렇지 않나요?

(A) 아니요, 하지만 설명이 따라하기 쉬워요.

(B) 그는 공장에서 늦게까지 일하고 있어요.

(C) 그것들은 맨 위 서랍에 있을 거예요.

해설 | 조립 여부를 확인하는 부가 의문문

(A) **정답:** No라고 응답한 후, 설명이 따라하기 쉽다(the directions are easy to follow)고 덧붙였으므로 정답이다.

(B) **인칭 오류 및 연상 작용 오답:** 보기의 He가 가리키는 대상이 질문에 없으며, 질문의 preassembled에서 연상 가능한 factory를 이용한 오답이다.

(C) **인칭 오류 및 연상 작용 오답:** 보기의 They가 가리키는 대상이 질문에 없고, 질문의 cabinet에서 연상 가능한 맨 위 서랍(top drawer)을 언급한 오답이다.

어휘 | preassemble 사전 조립하다

2 W-Am / M-Cn

The guests in room 343 requested a late checkout time, didn't they?

(A) The shuttle to the airport.

(B) No, the account was paid by credit card.

(C) Yes, they'd like to leave after lunch.

343호 투숙객들이 늦은 체크아웃을 요청했죠, 그렇지 않나요?

(A) 공항으로 가는 셔틀이요.

(B) 아니요, 그 거래 건은 신용카드로 결제됐어요.

(C) 네, 그들은 점심 식사 후에 출발하고 싶어 해요.

해설 | 사실을 확인하는 부가 의문문

(A) **연상 작용 오답:** 질문의 The guests in room 343에서 호텔을 연상하게 되며 호텔에서 연상 가능한 shuttle을 이용한 오답이다.

(B) **연상 작용 오답:** 질문의 checkout에서 연상 가능한 paid by credit card를 언급한 오답이다.

(C) **정답:** Yes라고 응답한 후, 점심 식사 후에 출발하고 싶어 한다(they'd like to leave after lunch)고 덧붙였으므로 정답이다.

어휘 | account 신용 거래, 계정

3 W-Br / M-Au

The bookshelf included instructions for assembly, didn't it?

(A) I returned the books to the library yesterday.

(B) Yes, it was closed for construction.

(C) I'm not sure about that.

책장에 조립 설명서가 들어있었죠, 그렇지 않나요?

(A) 저는 어제 도서관에 책을 반납했어요.

(B) 네, 공사 때문에 닫았어요.

(C) 잘 모르겠네요.

해설 | 사실을 확인하는 부가 의문문

(A) **유사 발음·연상 작용 오답:** 질문의 bookshelf와 부분적으로 발음이 동일한 books를 이용했으며, bookshelf에서 연상 가능한 library를 이용한 오답이다.

(B) **유사 발음 오답:** 질문의 instructions와 발음이 부분적으로 유사한 construction으로 혼동을 준 오답이다.

(C) **정답:** 책장에 조립 설명서가 들어있었는지 잘 모르겠다(I'm not sure about that)고 답했으므로 가장 적절한 답변이다.

어휘 | instructions 설명, 지시   assembly 조립

4 W-Br / M-Au

You aren't going to be at the art gallery opening, are you?

(A) That painting needs a new frame.

(B) No, I'll be out of town.

(C) Please close the door.

미술관 개관식에 안 갈 거죠, 그렇죠?

(A) 그 그림은 새 액자가 필요해요.

(B) 못 가요, 저는 여기 없을 거예요.

(C) 문 좀 닫아주세요.

해설 | 확인을 구하는 부가 의문문

(A) **연상 작용 오답:** 질문의 art gallery에서 연상 가능한 painting을 언급한 오답이다.

(B) **정답:** No라고 응답한 후, 여기 없을 것(I'll be out of town)이라고 덧붙였으므로 정답이다.

(C) **연상 작용 오답:** 질문의 opening에서 연상 가능한 close를 언급한 오답이다.

어휘 | out of town 시내에 없는, 출장 중인

5 M-Cn / W-Br

The dinner reservation is for six o'clock, right?

(A) Including the service fee?

(B) The meeting doesn't end till seven.

(C) The catering menu has been updated.

저녁 예약이 6시로 되어 있죠, 그렇죠?

(A) 서비스 요금을 포함해서요?

(B) 회의가 7시나 되어야 끝나요.

(C) 출장 요리 메뉴가 새로워졌어요.

해설 | 예약 시간을 확인하는 부가 의문문

(A) 연상 작용 오답: 질문의 dinner reservation에서 연상 가능한 service fee를 언급한 오답이다.

(B) 정답: 회의가 7시나 되어야 끝난다(The meeting doesn't end till seven)며 예약 시간 변경이 필요하다는 것을 우회적으로 드러내고 있으므로 정답이다.

(C) 연상 작용 오답: 질문의 dinner reservation에서 연상 가능한 catering menu를 언급한 오답이다.

6 M-Au / M-Cn

This prototype looks good, doesn't it?

(A) He can't type very well.

(B) No, I don't need anything right now.

(C) The 3D printer was a great investment.

이 시제품은 멋지네요, 그렇지 않나요?

(A) 그는 타자를 아주 잘 치지는 못해요.

(B) 아니요, 지금은 아무 것도 필요 없어요.

(C) 3D 프린터는 훌륭한 투자였어요.

해설 | 의견을 확인하는 부가 의문문

(A) 인칭 오류 및 유사 발음 오답: 보기의 He가 가리키는 대상이 질문에 없고, 질문의 prototype과 부분적으로 발음이 동일한 type을 이용한 오답이다.

(B) 관련 없는 오답: 질문과 상관없는 답변을 제시한 오답이다.

(C) 정답: 3D 프린터는 훌륭한 투자였다(The 3D printer was a great investment)며 동의의 표현을 우회적으로 드러낸 적절한 응답이다.

어휘 | prototype 원형, 시제품   investment 투자

ETS 고득점 실전 문제

본책 p.54

1 (A)	**2** (A)	**3** (A)	**4** (A)	**5** (A)	**6** (A)
7 (C)	**8** (A)	**9** (A)	**10** (A)	**11** (C)	**12** (A)
13 (B)	**14** (A)	**15** (C)	**16** (A)	**17** (B)	**18** (B)
19 (C)	**20** (B)				

1 M-Cn / W-Am

Aren't there any front row seats left?

(A) These are the closest, I'm afraid.

(B) I'll bring it back.

(C) No, they haven't left yet.

앞줄에 남은 자리가 없나요?

(A) 이게 가장 가까운 자리 같은데요.

(B) 다시 가져올게요.

(C) 아니요, 그들은 아직 안 떠났어요.

해설 | 좌석을 확인하는 부정 의문문

(A) 정답: 여기가 가장 가까운 자리(These are the closest, I'm afraid)라는 말로 앞줄에는 남은 좌석이 없음을 우회적으로 표현한 적절한 응답이다.

(B) 연상 어휘 오답: 질문의 front에 대해 반의어로 연상 가능한 back을 이용한 오답이다.

(C) 단어 반복 오답: 질문의 left를 반복 이용한 오답이다.

어휘 | row 열, 줄

2 M-Au / W-Am

The concert tickets are for reserved seats, aren't they?

(A) Yes, our seats are next to each other.

(B) An international tour.

(C) No, they're still here.

음악회 표는 지정석이죠, 그렇지 않나요?

(A) 네, 우리는 나란히 붙은 좌석이에요.

(B) 해외 여행이요.

(C) 아니요, 그들은 아직 여기 있어요.

해설 | 사실을 확인하는 부가 의문문

(A) 정답: Yes라고 응답한 후, 우리는 나란히 붙은 좌석(our seats are next to each other)이라고 덧붙였으므로 정답이다.

(B) 연상 작용 오답: 질문의 reserved seats에서 연상 가능한 tour를 언급한 오답이다.

(C) 단어 반복 오답: 질문의 they를 반복 이용한 오답이다.

어휘 | reserved seat 지정석, 예약석   next to each other 나란히

3 W-Br / M-Au

Don't you have any available doctor appointments next week?

(A) No, unfortunately the doctor doesn't have any openings.

(B) Over there in the corner.

(C) Yes, it's closed.

다음 주에 가능한 진료 예약 시간이 있나요?

(A) 아니요. 아쉽게도 의사선생님이 비는 시간이 없네요.

(B) 저쪽 모퉁이요.

(C) 네, 닫았어요.

해설 | 예약 시간을 확인하는 부정 의문문

(A) 정답: No라고 응답한 후, 의사선생님이 비는 시간이 없다(the doctor doesn't have any openings)고 덧붙였으므로 정답이다.

(B) 연상 작용 오답: 질문의 Don't you have any available에서 상품을 찾는 질문으로 잘못 이해하고 연상 가능한 위치를 나타내는 표현 Over there in the corner를 언급한 오답이다.

(C) 관련 없는 오답: 질문과 상관없는 답변을 제시한 오답이다.

어휘 | available 이용 가능한, 구할 수 있는   opening 빈 자리, 공석

4 M-Au / W-Br

We have one more job candidate to interview today, right?
(A) There aren't any more résumés.
(B) It's actually on the right.
(C) An interesting experience.

오늘 면접을 볼 지원자가 한 명 더 있죠, 그렇죠?
(A) 더 이상 이력서가 없어요.
(B) 그건 사실 오른쪽에 있어요.
(C) 흥미로운 경험이에요.

해설 | 사실을 확인하는 부가 의문문
(A) **정답:** 더 이상 이력서가 없다(There aren't any more résumés)며 면접자가 더 이상 없다는 말을 우회적으로 표현한 적절한 응답이다.
(B) **다의어 오답:** 질문에 나오는 right는 '옳은'이라는 뜻의 형용사이고, 보기의 right는 '오른쪽'이라는 뜻의 명사이다.
(C) **연상 작용 오답:** 질문의 interview에서 연상 가능한 experience를 언급한 오답이다.

어휘 | job candidate 구직자, 입사 지원자

5 M-Cn / W-Br

You reserved the audiovisual equipment for the meeting, didn't you?
(A) No, I forgot to do that.
(B) Your hotel reservation is confirmed.
(C) I'll ask the server to bring us some menus.

회의에 쓸 시청각 장비를 예약하셨죠, 그렇지 않나요?
(A) 아니요, 하는 걸 잊어버렸어요.
(B) 귀하의 호텔 예약이 확정됐습니다.
(C) 서빙 직원에게 메뉴를 가져다 달라고 요청할게요.

해설 | 예약 여부를 확인하는 부가 의문문
(A) **정답:** No라고 응답한 후, 예약하는 걸 잊었다(I forgot to do that)고 덧붙였으므로 정답이다.
(B) **파생어 오답:** 질문의 reserved와 파생어 관계인 reservation을 이용한 오답이다.
(C) **연상 작용 오답:** 질문의 reserved에서 연상 가능한 menus를 언급한 오답이다.

어휘 | reserve 예약하다   equipment 장비

6 M-Au / M-Cn

Weren't our dinner reservations originally for six people?
(A) Michelle won't be able to come.
(B) With the corporate group discount.
(C) A larger table than we thought.

원래 6명으로 저녁 식사를 예약하지 않았나요?
(A) 미셸은 못 올 거예요.
(B) 기업 단체 할인으로요.
(C) 우리가 생각했던 것보다 더 큰 테이블이요.

해설 | 사실을 확인하는 부정 의문문
(A) **정답:** 예약 인원수를 확인하는 질문에, 미셸은 못 올 것(Michelle won't be able to come)이라는 말로 한 명이 줄어든다는 점을 우회적으로 표현한 정답이다.
(B) **연상 어휘 오답:** 질문의 reservations originally for six people에서 연상 가능한 group discount를 이용한 오답이다.
(C) **연상 어휘 오답:** 질문의 dinner reservations에서 연상 가능한 table을 이용한 오답이다.

어휘 | originally 당초, 처음에   corporate 회사의

7 W-Br / W-Am

Didn't we spend over a thousand dollars on advertising?
(A) Sure, I'll buy a few more of them.
(B) Well, you'll have to submit a request.
(C) Yes, but it was a necessary expense.

우리가 광고에 천 달러 넘게 쓰지 않았나요?
(A) 그럼요, 제가 몇 개 더 살게요.
(B) 음, 요청서를 제출해야 할 겁니다.
(C) 네, 하지만 필요한 비용이었어요.

해설 | 사실을 확인하는 부정 의문문
(A) **연상 작용 오답:** 질문의 spend over a thousand dollars에서 연상 가능한 buy를 언급한 오답이다.
(B) **관련 없는 오답:** 질문과 상관없는 답변을 제시한 오답이다.
(C) **정답:** Yes라고 응답한 후, 필요한 비용이었다(it was a necessary expense)고 덧붙였으므로 정답이다.

어휘 | advertising 광고   submit 제출하다   expense 비용, 경비

8 M-Cn / W-Am

I don't owe a library fine, do I?
(A) Not unless your book is overdue.
(B) Yes, I'm planning to read it.
(C) The library's closed on Sundays.

제가 내야 할 도서관 연체료가 없죠, 그렇죠?
(A) 책 반납 기한을 넘기지 않는 한 없어요.
(B) 네, 읽을 계획이에요.
(C) 도서관은 매주 일요일에 휴관입니다.

해설 | 연체료 유무를 확인하는 부가 의문문
(A) **정답:** 책 반납 기한을 넘기지 않는 한 없다(Not unless your book is overdue)고 동의하는 답변을 우회적으로 표현한 정답이다.
(B) **연상 작용 오답:** 질문의 library에서 연상 가능한 read를 언급한 오답이다.
(C) **단어 반복 오답:** 질문의 library를 반복 이용한 오답이다.

어휘 | owe 빚지고 있다   fine 벌금   overdue 기한이 지난

9 M-Cn / W-Br

The grand opening for the store is tomorrow, isn't it?

(A) No, it's been postponed until next month.

(B) A lot of great promotions and sales.

(C) I closed the filing cabinet.

이 상점 개업식이 내일이죠, 그렇지 않나요?

(A) 아니요, 다음 달로 연기됐어요.

(B) 좋은 판촉행사와 세일이 많아요.

(C) 제가 문서 보관함을 닫았어요.

해설 | 정보를 확인하는 부가 의문문

(A) **정답:** No라고 응답한 후, 다음 달로 연기됐다(it's been postponed until next month)고 덧붙였으므로 정답이다.

(B) **연상 작용 오답:** 질문의 grand opening에서 연상 가능한 promotions and sales를 언급한 오답이다.

(C) **연상 작용 오답:** 질문의 opening에서 연상 가능한 closed를 언급한 오답이다.

어휘 | postpone 미루다, 연기하다 **promotion** 판촉, 홍보

10 W-Br / W-Am

Won't you be attending our morning business meeting?

(A) I'll be conducting a building inspection.

(B) It was a very informative meeting.

(C) Three flight attendants on duty.

오전 비즈니스 회의에 참석하지 않으실 거죠?

(A) 저는 건물 점검을 할 겁니다.

(B) 굉장히 유익한 회의였어요.

(C) 근무 중인 세 명의 승무원이요.

해설 | 참석 의사를 묻는 부정 의문문

(A) **정답:** 건물 점검을 할 것(I'll be conducting a building inspection)이라며 참석이 어렵다는 대답을 우회적으로 표현한 적절한 응답이다.

(B) **단어 반복 오답:** 질문의 meeting을 반복 이용한 오답이다.

(C) **파생어 오답:** 질문의 attending과 파생어 관계인 attendants를 이용한 오답이다.

어휘 | conduct (특정한 활동을) 하다 **informative** 유용한 정보를 주는, 유익한 **on duty** 근무 중

11 M-Cn / W-Br

You've been notified about the shipping delay, haven't you?

(A) An additional charge.

(B) Let's update our billing information.

(C) No, when is the estimated delivery date?

수송 지연에 대해 통보를 받으셨죠, 그렇지 않나요?

(A) 추가 요금이요.

(B) 우리 요금 정보를 업데이트합시다.

(C) 아니요, 예상 배송일자가 언제죠?

해설 | 사실을 확인하는 부가 의문문

(A) **연상 작용 오답:** 질문의 shipping delay에서 연상 가능한 additional charge를 언급한 오답이다.

(B) **연상 작용 오답:** 질문의 shipping에서 연상 가능한 billing information을 언급한 오답이다.

(C) **정답:** No라고 응답한 후, 예상 배송일자가 언제인지(when is the estimated delivery date) 관련 상황에 대해 되묻고 있으므로 정답이다.

어휘 | additional charge 추가 요금 **estimated** 예상되는

12 M-Au / M-Cn

You can help me upload this photograph to the Web site, can't you?

(A) I'm not sure I know how.

(B) Yes, he's the senior editor.

(C) It's been very helpful.

웹사이트에 이 사진 업로드하는 걸 도와주실 수 있죠, 그렇지 않나요?

(A) 제가 방법을 아는지 잘 모르겠어요.

(B) 네, 그는 선임 편집자예요.

(C) 큰 도움이 됐어요.

해설 | 도움 요청을 확인하는 부가 의문문

(A) **정답:** 방법을 아는지 잘 모르겠다(I'm not sure I know how)고 우회적으로 거절하고 있으므로 적절한 응답이다.

(B) **인칭 오류 오답:** 보기의 he가 가리키는 대상이 질문에 없다.

(C) **파생어 오답:** 질문의 help와 파생어 관계인 helpful을 이용한 오답이다.

어휘 | senior editor 선임 편집자

13 M-Au / W-Am

Wouldn't it be nice if today's meeting ended early?

(A) They go there every year.

(B) There's not much on the agenda.

(C) Nice to meet you.

오늘 회의가 일찍 끝나면 좋지 않을까요?

(A) 그들은 매년 거기에 가요.

(B) 회의 안건이 그리 많지 않아요.

(C) 만나서 반갑습니다.

해설 | 의견을 확인하는 부정 의문문

(A) **인칭 오류 오답:** 보기의 대명사 They가 가리키는 대상이 질문에 없다.

(B) **정답:** 회의 안건이 그리 많지 않다(There's not much on the agenda)며 일찍 끝날 것이라고 우회적으로 표현한 적절한 응답이다.

(C) **단어 반복 및 파생어 오답:** 질문의 nice를 반복 이용하고, 질문의 meeting과 파생어 관계인 meet를 이용한 오답이다.

어휘 | agenda 회의 안건

14 M-Au / W-Am

The bank isn't still looking for tellers, is it?

(A) I believe the positions have all been filled.

(B) More than three years of experience.

(C) We offer competitive employee benefits.

그 은행이 여전히 창구 직원을 구하고 있지는 않죠, 그렇죠?

(A) 모두 충원된 걸로 아는데요.

(B) 3년 이상의 경력이요.

(C) 저희는 경쟁력 있는 직원 복지를 제공합니다.

해설 | 사실을 확인하는 부가 의문문

(A) **정답:** 모두 충원된 걸로 안다(I believe the positions have all been filled)며 직원 모집은 끝났다는 것을 우회적으로 드러낸 적절한 응답이다.

(B) **연상 작용 오답:** 질문의 looking for tellers에서 연상 가능한 three years of experience를 언급한 오답이다.

(C) **연상 작용 오답:** 질문의 looking for tellers에서 연상 가능한 employee benefits를 언급한 오답이다.

어휘 | teller 출납계 직원, 창구 직원 competitive 경쟁력 있는 employee benefits 직원 복지

15 W-Br / M-Au

Haven't you been certified to conduct inspections?

(A) She wasn't asked to stay later than usual.

(B) I've already shipped the package.

(C) Yes, but certifications expire every two years.

검사 시행 자격증이 있지 않으세요?

(A) 그녀는 평소보다 늦게까지 있으라는 요청을 받지 않았어요.

(B) 이미 소포를 보냈어요.

(C) 네, 하지만 자격증이 2년마다 만료되거든요.

해설 | 사실 여부를 확인하는 부정 의문문

(A) **인칭 오류 오답:** 보기의 She가 가리키는 대상이 질문에 없다.

(B) **관련 없는 오답:** 질문과 상관없는 답변을 제시한 오답이다.

(C) **정답:** Yes라고 응답한 후, 자격증이 2년마다 만료된다(certifications expire every two years)고 덧붙였으므로 정답이다.

어휘 | be certified 공인되다, 인증받다 certification 증명, 자격증 expire 만료되다

16 W-Br / M-Au

Isn't today your day off?

(A) Alex wasn't able to cover his shift.

(B) Next to the filing cabinet.

(C) The light can stay on.

오늘 휴무 아니세요?

(A) 알렉스가 교대 근무를 못 했어요.

(B) 문서 보관함 옆이요.

(C) 조명은 계속 켜 둘 수 있어요.

해설 | 휴가 일정을 확인하는 부정 의문문

(A) **정답:** 알렉스가 교대 근무를 못 했다(Alex wasn't able to cover his shift)고 말함으로써 본인이 휴무임에도 출근한 사실을 우회적으로 표현한 적절한 응답이다.

(B) **관련 없는 오답:** 질문과 상관없는 답변을 제시한 오답이다.

(C) **연상 작용 오답:** 질문의 off에서 연상 가능한 on을 언급한 오답이다.

어휘 | day off (근무) 쉬는 날

17 M-Cn / W-Br

Felipe knows how to fix this computer problem, right?

(A) Just six pages, please.

(B) He's going to a training session this afternoon.

(C) Oh, I know that book.

펠리페가 이 컴퓨터 문제 해결책을 알죠, 그렇죠?

(A) 여섯 페이지만요.

(B) 그는 오늘 오후 교육 들으러 갈 거예요.

(C) 아, 그 책 알아요.

해설 | 사실 여부를 확인하는 부가 의문문

(A) **유사 발음 오답:** 질문의 fix와 발음이 부분적으로 유사한 six로 혼동을 준 오답이다.

(B) **정답:** 그는 오늘 오후 교육 들으러 갈 것(He's going to a training session this afternoon)이라며 그가 오늘은 도와줄 수 없음을 우회적으로 말하고 있으므로 가장 적절한 응답이다.

(C) **단어 반복 오답:** 질문의 know를 반복 이용한 오답이다.

어휘 | training session 교육 과정

18 M-Cn / W-Br

Didn't Trevor say he was going to turn in those reports today?

(A) On the evening news report.

(B) He said he had a lot of work to finish.

(C) But you drove last time.

트레버가 그 보고서들을 오늘 제출할 거라고 하지 않았나요?

(A) 저녁 뉴스 보도에서요.

(B) 끝내야 할 일이 많다고 하더군요.

(C) 하지만 지난번에는 당신이 운전했잖아요.

해설 | 사실을 확인하는 부정 의문문

(A) **단어 반복 오답:** 질문의 reports를 반복 이용한 오답이다.

(B) **정답:** 그가 끝낼 일이 많다(he had a lot of work to finish)고 했다며 오늘 보고서를 제출하지 못한다는 것을 우회적으로 표현한 정답이다.

(C) **연상 어휘 오답:** 질문의 turn에서 연상 가능한 drove를 이용한 오답이다.

어휘 | turn in 제출하다

19 W-Br / M-Au

Aren't you going to apply for more research funding?

(A) The research assistant.

(B) I thought the party was really fun.

(C) This year's deadline's already passed.

연구 기금을 더 신청하지 않으실 건가요?

(A) 연구 보조요.

(B) 파티가 정말 재미있었던 것 같아요.

(C) 올해 기한은 이미 지났어요.

해설 | **신청 계획을 확인하는 부정 의문문**
(A) **단어 반복 오답:** 질문의 research를 반복 이용한 오답이다.
(B) **유사 발음 오답:** 질문의 funding과 부분적으로 발음이 유사한 fun으로 혼동을 준 오답이다.
(C) **정답:** 올해 기한은 이미 지났다(This year's deadline's already passed)며 기금을 신청할 수 없다는 것을 우회적으로 드러낸 적절한 응답이다.

어휘 | apply for ~을 신청하다 funding 자금, 기금

20 W-Am / M-Cn
All the employees have received orientation packets, haven't they?
(A) Sure, I can work at the career fair next week.
(B) Some new hires don't start until tomorrow.
(C) The next stop on the tour is the Shipping Department.

전 직원이 오리엔테이션 물품을 받았죠, 그렇지 않나요?
(A) 물론이죠, 다음 주 취업 박람회에서 일할 수 있습니다.
(B) **일부 신입사원들은 내일 되어야 시작해요.**
(C) 다음 견학 장소는 운송 부서입니다.

해설 | **수령 여부를 확인하는 부가 의문문**
(A) **연상 작용 오답:** 질문의 employees와 orientation에서 연상 가능한 career fair를 언급한 오답이다.
(B) **정답:** 일부 신입사원들은 내일 시작한다(Some new hires don't start until tomorrow)며 아직 물품을 받지 못한 직원도 있다는 것을 우회적으로 드러낸 적절한 응답이다.
(C) **연상 작용 오답:** 질문의 employees와 orientation에서 연상 가능한 부서명 Shipping Department를 언급한 오답이다.

어휘 | career fair 취업 박람회 new hire 신입사원

UNIT 8 요청·제안문 / 평서문

ETS 유형 연습
본책 p.56

| 1 (A) | 2 (B) | 3 (A) | 4 (C) | 5 (C) | 6 (C) |

1 W-Am / M-Cn
Would you like a slice of pie?
(A) I had a big lunch.
(B) A kitchen renovation.
(C) By the oven.

파이 한 조각 드실래요?
(A) **점심을 많이 먹었어요.**
(B) 주방 보수요.
(C) 오븐 옆이요.

해설 | **제안·권유의 의문문**
(A) **정답:** 점심을 많이 먹었다(I had a big lunch)며 우회적으로 거절의 의사를 밝혔으므로 정답이다.

(B) **연상 작용 오답:** 질문의 pie에서 연상 가능한 kitchen을 언급한 오답이다.
(C) **연상 작용 오답:** 질문의 pie에서 연상 가능한 oven을 언급한 오답이다.

어휘 | renovation 보수, 개조

2 W-Br / M-Au
Can we end the meeting in ten minutes?
(A) I met Rosa last week.
(B) No, we have a lot more to discuss.
(C) It's a five-minute walk.

10분 후에 회의를 마칠 수 있을까요?
(A) 지난주에 로사를 만났어요.
(B) **아니요, 논의할 사항이 더 많이 있어요.**
(C) 걸어서 5분 거리예요.

해설 | **부탁·요청의 의문문**
(A) **파생어 오답:** 질문의 meeting과 파생어 관계인 동사 meet의 과거형 met를 이용한 오답이다.
(B) **정답:** No라고 응답한 후, 논의할 사항이 더 많이 있다(we have a lot more to discuss)고 덧붙임으로써 10분 후에 회의를 마칠 수 없다고 우회적으로 말한 정답이다.
(C) **단어 반복 오답:** 질문의 minute를 반복 이용한 오답이다.

3 W-Am / M-Cn
Could you lend me your stapler?
(A) Jin-Ho is using it.
(B) How much do we need to borrow?
(C) Sure, I could review the report.

스테이플러 좀 빌려주실 수 있나요?
(A) **진호가 쓰고 있어요.**
(B) 얼마나 많이 빌려야 해요?
(C) 그럼요, 제가 보고서를 검토할 수 있어요.

해설 | **부탁·요청의 의문문**
(A) **정답:** 진호가 쓰고 있다(Jin-Ho is using it)며 빌려줄 수 없음을 우회적으로 표현한 적절한 응답이다.
(B) **연상 작용 오답:** 질문의 lend에서 연상 가능한 borrow를 언급한 오답이다.
(C) **단어 반복 오답:** 질문의 Could를 반복 이용한 오답이다.

4 W-Am / M-Cn
Would you like to join our group for coffee?
(A) Thanks, I'll send you a copy now.
(B) A discounted membership fee.
(C) Sorry, I'm on my way to a meeting.

저희와 함께 커피 드실래요?
(A) 감사합니다, 지금 사본을 보낼게요.
(B) 할인된 회비요.
(C) **죄송하지만 회의에 가는 길이에요.**

해설 | **제안·권유의 의문문**
(A) **유사 발음 오답:** 질문의 coffee와 발음이 유사한 copy를 이용한 오답이다.
(B) **유사 발음 오답:** 질문의 coffee와 부분적으로 발음이 유사한 fee로 혼동을 준 오답이다.

(C) **정답:** 회의에 가는 길(I'm on my way to a meeting)이라며 우회적으로 거절의 의사를 밝혔으므로 정답이다.

어휘 | on one's way ~ 가는 길에

5 W-Am / M-Cn

Please put price tags on all of the shoes we received this morning.
(A) By express mail.
(B) I'll check the receipt.
(C) Harumi already took care of that.

오늘 아침에 받은 모든 신발에 가격표를 붙여 주세요.
(A) 특급 우편으로요.
(B) 제가 영수증을 확인할게요.
(C) 하루미가 이미 처리했어요.

해설 | 행동을 요청하는 명령문
(A) **연상 작용 오답:** 질문의 received에서 연상 가능한 express mail을 이용한 오답이다.
(B) **파생어 오답:** 질문의 received와 파생어 관계인 receipt를 이용한 오답이다.
(C) **정답:** 하루미가 이미 처리했다(Harumi already took care of that)고 말함으로써 그 일을 할 필요가 없음을 우회적으로 말한 정답이다.

어휘 | express mail 특급 우편 receipt 영수증, 수령 take care of ~을 돌보다, 처리하다

6 M-Au / W-Br

Why don't you use local ingredients at the restaurant?
(A) Forks and knives are in the drawer.
(B) Tuesdays at noon.
(C) Sorenson Foods is a local supplier.

식당에서 지역 재료를 이용하는 게 어때요?
(A) 포크와 나이프는 서랍에 있어요.
(B) 매주 화요일 정오에요.
(C) 소렌슨 푸드가 지역 공급업체예요.

해설 | 제안·권유의 의문문
(A) **연상 작용 오답:** 질문의 restaurant에서 연상 가능한 Forks and knives를 언급한 오답이다.
(B) **관련 없는 오답:** When 의문문에 적합한 응답이다.
(C) **정답:** 소렌슨 푸드가 지역 공급업체(Sorenson Foods is a local supplier)라며 이미 지역 재료를 사용하고 있음을 우회적으로 답변한 정답이다.

어휘 | ingredient 재료, 성분 supplier 공급업체

ETS 유형 연습

본책 p.57

1 (B) **2** (A) **3** (B) **4** (B) **5** (A) **6** (B)

1 W-Am / M-Cn

I'll try to find a photographer within your budget.
(A) The photographs are on the wall.
(B) That would be great—thank you!
(C) Both cash and credit cards.

당신의 예산 내에서 사진작가를 찾아볼게요.
(A) 사진들은 벽에 걸려 있어요.
(B) 그럼 좋겠네요, 감사합니다!
(C) 현금과 신용카드 둘 다요.

해설 | 제안을 하는 평서문
(A) **파생어 오답:** 질문의 photographer와 파생어 관계인 photographs를 이용한 오답이다.
(B) **정답:** 그럼 좋겠다(That would be great)고 하며 감사의 인사를 덧붙였으므로 가장 적절한 응답이다.
(C) **연상 작용 오답:** 질문의 budget에서 연상 가능한 cash, credit cards를 언급한 오답이다.

어휘 | photographer 사진작가 budget 예산

2 W-Am / M-Au

It's cold in this room.
(A) Oh, the windows are open.
(B) Put these boxes in the storage room.
(C) A coat and scarf.

이 방은 춥네요.
(A) 아, 창문이 열려 있어요.
(B) 이 상자들을 보관실에 두세요.
(C) 코트와 목도리요.

해설 | 문제 상황을 언급하는 평서문
(A) **정답:** 방이 춥다는 말에 대해, 창문이 열려 있다(the windows are open)며 추운 이유를 설명한 가장 적절한 응답이다.
(B) **단어 반복 오답:** 질문의 room을 반복 이용한 오답이다.
(C) **유사 발음 및 연상 작용 오답:** 질문의 cold와 발음이 유사한 coat and로 혼동을 주고 있으며, 질문의 cold에서 연상 가능한 A coat and scarf를 이용한 오답이다.

어휘 | storage room 보관실

3 M-Au / W-Br

You should present your research data at the next department meeting.
(A) No, I didn't.
(B) I'd be happy to.
(C) In the database.

당신이 다음 부서 회의 때 연구 데이터를 발표해야 해요.
(A) 아니요, 저는 안 했어요.
(B) 기꺼이 할게요.
(C) 데이터베이스에요.

해설 | 제안을 하는 평서문
(A) **시제 오류 오답:** 미래의 행동을 제안하는 말에 과거동사 didn't로 답하는 것은 어색하다.
(B) **정답:** 발표 제안에 기꺼이 하겠다(I'd be happy to)고 수락의 의사를 밝혔으므로 정답이다.

(C) **유사 발음 오답:** 질문의 data와 부분적으로 발음이 동일한 database를 이용한 오답이다.

어휘 | present 발표하다

4 W-Am / M-Au

The rent on this apartment is really high.
(A) I work in that department.
(B) All utilities are included.
(C) Next to the post office.

이 아파트 임대료 정말 비싸네요.
(A) 저는 그 부서에서 일해요.
(B) 모든 공과금이 포함된 겁니다.
(C) 우체국 옆이요.

해설 | 의견을 제시하는 평서문
(A) **유사 발음 오답:** 질문의 apartment와 부분적으로 발음이 유사한 department로 혼동을 준 오답이다.
(B) **정답:** 모든 공과금이 포함된 것(All utilities are included)이라며 추가 설명을 하고 있으므로 가장 적절한 응답이다.
(C) **관련 없는 오답:** Where 의문문에 적합한 응답이다.

어휘 | utilities (수도, 전기, 가스 등) 공과금

5 M-Cn / W-Br

We've decided to recruit more participants for the research study.
(A) How many more people do you need?
(B) A seventy-three percent response rate.
(C) Those are the extra lab coats from storage.

연구에 더 많은 참가자를 모집하기로 결정했어요.
(A) 사람이 얼마나 더 많이 필요해요?
(B) 응답률 78퍼센트요.
(C) 저것들은 보관실에서 가져온 여분의 실험실 가운이에요.

해설 | 사실을 전달하는 평서문
(A) **정답:** 더 많은 참가자를 모집하기로 결정했다는 말에 대해, 사람이 얼마나 더 많이 필요한지(How many more people do you need?) 관련 상황을 되묻고 있으므로 가장 적절한 응답이다.
(B) **연상 작용 오답:** 질문의 participants에서 연상 가능한 response rate를 언급한 오답이다.
(C) **연상 작용 오답:** 질문의 research에서 연상 가능한 lab coats를 언급한 오답이다.

어휘 | response rate 응답률, 회답률

6 W-Br / M-Au

I forgot my phone charger!
(A) He was in charge until the store closed.
(B) I have one in my backpack.
(C) She'll explain during the call.

전화기 충전기를 깜빡했어요!
(A) 상점을 닫을 때까지 그가 책임자였어요.
(B) 제 배낭에 하나 있어요.
(C) 그녀가 통화하면서 설명할 겁니다.

해설 | 문제 상황을 언급하는 평서문
(A) **파생어 오답:** 질문의 charger와 파생어 관계인 charge를 이용한 오답이다.
(B) **정답:** 배낭에 하나 있다(I have one in my backpack)며 충전기를 빌려줄 수 있음을 우회적으로 나타낸 적절한 응답이다.
(C) **인칭 오류 및 연상 작용 오답:** 보기의 She가 가리키는 대상이 질문에 없고, 질문의 phone에서 연상 가능한 call을 언급한 오답이다.

어휘 | in charge ~을 맡아서, 책임지는

ETS 고득점 실전 문제 본책 p.58

1 (B)	**2** (B)	**3** (A)	**4** (A)	**5** (B)	**6** (A)
7 (C)	**8** (B)	**9** (B)	**10** (C)	**11** (B)	**12** (C)
13 (C)	**14** (A)	**15** (A)	**16** (B)	**17** (C)	**18** (C)
19 (A)	**20** (A)				

1 M-Au / W-Br

I'd like you to fill this order by tomorrow.
(A) Kurt says he likes it too.
(B) That shouldn't be a problem.
(C) We feel it's very new.

내일까지 이 주문서를 작성해 주셨으면 합니다.
(A) 커트도 그게 맘에 든다고 하네요.
(B) 문제 될 건 없을 거예요.
(C) 굉장히 새롭다고 생각해요.

해설 | 행동을 요청하는 평서문
(A) **단어 반복 오답:** 질문의 like를 반복 이용한 오답이다.
(B) **정답:** 문제 될 건 없을 것(That shouldn't be a problem)이라면서 수락의 의사를 밝혔으므로 정답이다.
(C) **유사 발음 오답:** 질문의 fill과 발음이 유사한 feel로 혼동을 준 오답이다.

2 W-Am / M-Au

Can you make the dinner reservations?
(A) He stayed at the new hotel.
(B) Sure, I don't mind doing that.
(C) Two weeks of vacation time.

저녁 식사 예약을 해 주실 수 있나요?
(A) 그는 새 호텔에 묵었어요.
(B) 물론이죠, 해 드릴 수 있어요.
(C) 2주간의 휴가요.

해설 | 부탁·요청의 의문문
(A) **인칭 오류 오답:** 보기의 He가 가리키는 대상이 질문에 없다.
(B) **정답:** 예약을 부탁하는 요청에 Sure라고 수락의 표현을 한 후, 해 줄 수 있다(I don't mind doing that)고 덧붙였으므로 정답이다.
(C) **연상 작용 오답:** 질문의 reservations에서 연상 가능한 vacation을 이용한 오답이다.

어휘 | make a reservation 예약하다

3 W-Br / M-Cn

We're planning on hiring a salesperson.
(A) Where can I find an application?
(B) The building for sale.
(C) No, thanks—I called a car service.

저희는 판매원을 채용할 계획입니다.
(A) 신청서를 어디서 찾을 수 있나요?
(B) 매매로 나온 건물입니다.
(C) 아니요, 괜찮아요. 차량 서비스를 불렀어요.

해설 | 정보를 전달하는 평서문
(A) **정답:** 채용 계획을 알리는 말에 신청서를 어디서 찾을 수 있는지(Where can I find an application?) 관련된 상황을 되묻고 있으므로 가장 적절한 응답이다.
(B) **파생어 오답:** 질문의 salesperson과 파생어 관계인 sale을 이용한 오답이다.
(C) **연상 작용 오답:** 질문의 salesperson에서 연상 가능한 service를 이용한 오답이다.

어휘 | application 신청, 신청서

4 W-Am / M-Au

We should consider expanding our warehouse space.
(A) Our production has been increasing steadily.
(B) Actually, I usually wear business attire.
(C) A ten-kilometer race.

우리 창고 공간 확장을 고려해야 해요.
(A) 생산이 꾸준히 증가했어요.
(B) 사실 저는 보통 정장을 입어요.
(C) 10km 경주예요.

해설 | 의견을 제시하는 평서문
(A) **정답:** 생산이 꾸준히 증가했다(Our production has been increasing steadily)며 우회적으로 동조하는 의견을 제시했으므로 정답이다.
(B) **유사 발음 오답:** 질문의 warehouse와 부분적으로 발음이 동일한 wear로 혼동을 준 오답이다.
(C) **유사 발음 오답:** 질문의 space와 부분적으로 발음이 유사한 race로 혼동을 준 오답이다.

어휘 | expand 확장하다, 확대하다   warehouse 창고
business attire 정장

5 M-Cn / W-Am

Could I discuss the budget proposal with you later today?
(A) Twenty copies, please.
(B) I'll be leaving early.
(C) That can't be right.

오늘 이따가 예산 제안서에 대해 논의할 수 있을까요?
(A) 20부 부탁해요.
(B) 저는 일찍 나갈 예정이에요.
(C) 설마 그럴 리가요.

해설 | 부탁·요청의 의문문
(A) **연상 작용 오답:** 질문의 budget proposal에서 연상 가능한 Twenty copies를 언급한 오답이다.
(B) **정답:** 일찍 나갈 예정(I'll be leaving early)이라며 우회적으로 거절의 의사를 밝혔으므로 정답이다
(C) **관련 없는 오답:** 질문과 상관없는 답변을 제시한 오답이다.

6 W-Br / M-Cn

I can't figure out how to assemble this bicycle.
(A) It didn't come with instructions?
(B) Several business cycles.
(C) An employee discount, I think.

이 자전거 조립 방법을 모르겠어요.
(A) 설명서가 같이 안 왔어요?
(B) 여러 번의 경기 변동이요.
(C) 직원 할인인 것 같아요.

해설 | 상황을 설명하는 평서문
(A) **정답:** 자전거 조립 방법을 모르겠다는 말에 설명서가 같이 안 왔는지(It didn't come with instructions?) 관련 상황을 되묻고 있으므로 정답이다.
(B) **유사 발음 오답:** 질문의 bicycle과 부분적으로 발음이 유사한 cycles로 혼동을 준 오답이다.
(C) **관련 없는 오답:** 질문과 상관없는 답변을 제시한 오답이다.

어휘 | figure out 알아내다, 생각해 내다   assemble 조립하다
come with ~이 딸려 있다   instructions 설명, 지시

7 M-Au / W-Br

Would you mind e-mailing me that attachment again?
(A) The post office closes at three.
(B) I read that, too.
(C) I'll resend it after my next meeting.

저한테 첨부 파일을 이메일로 다시 보내주실 수 있나요?
(A) 우체국은 3시에 문을 닫아요.
(B) 저도 읽었어요.
(C) 다음 회의 끝나고 다시 보낼게요.

해설 | 부탁·요청의 의문문
(A) **연상 작용 오답:** 질문의 e-mail을 mail(우편)로 잘못 이해하고 연상 가능한 post office를 언급한 오답이다.
(B) **연상 작용 오답:** 질문의 attachment에서 연상 가능한 read that을 언급한 오답이다.
(C) **정답:** 다음 회의 끝나고 다시 보내겠다(I'll resend it after my next meeting)며 수락의 의사를 밝혔으므로 정답이다.

어휘 | attachment 첨부 파일

8 M-Cn / W-Br

Would you like to take a short break?
(A) We threw the broken ones away.
(B) Richard asked for this report by noon.
(C) Check the higher shelf.

잠시 휴식을 취하실래요?
(A) 고장난 것들을 버렸어요.
(B) 리처드가 이 보고서를 정오까지 요청했어요.
(C) 더 위에 있는 선반을 확인하세요.

해설 | 제안·권유의 의문문
(A) **다의어 오답:** 질문의 break는 '휴식'이라는 뜻의 명사이고, 보기의 broken은 '고장 나다'라는 의미의 동사 break의 과거분사이다.
(B) **정답:** 휴식을 권유하는 말에 리처드가 이 보고서를 정오까지 요청했다(Richard asked for this report by noon)며 우회적으로 거절의 의사를 밝혔으므로 정답이다.
(C) **관련 없는 오답:** 질문과 상관없는 답변을 제시한 오답이다.

어휘 | take a break 휴식을 취하다

9 M-Au / W-Br

That company's new smartphone was launched today!
(A) No, I can't make it on time.
(B) The previous model is just as good.
(C) He's on the phone right now.

그 회사의 새 스마트폰이 오늘 출시됐어요!
(A) 아니요, 저는 제시간에 못 가요.
(B) 이전 모델도 그만큼 좋았어요.
(C) 그는 지금 통화 중이에요.

해설 | 정보를 전달하는 평서문
(A) **연상 작용 오답:** 질문의 launch을 lunch(점심)로 잘못 이해하고 연상 가능한 make it on time을 언급한 오답이다.
(B) **정답:** 이전 모델도 그만큼 좋았다(The previous model is just as good)고 덧붙여 의견을 말하고 있으므로 적절한 응답이다.
(C) **인칭 오류 및 유사 발음 오답:** 보기의 He가 가리키는 대상이 질문에 없고, 질문의 smartphone과 부분적으로 발음이 동일한 phone을 이용한 오답이다.

어휘 | make it 시간 맞춰 가다 **previous** 이전의

10 W-Br / M-Au

Why don't you offer an internship program?
(A) I already have a membership card.
(B) Thanks for the offer.
(C) That's still being discussed.

인턴십 프로그램을 제공하는 게 어때요?
(A) 이미 회원 카드가 있어요.
(B) 제안에 감사드립니다.
(C) 아직 논의 중입니다.

해설 | 제안·권유의 의문문
(A) **유사 발음 오답:** 질문의 internship과 부분적으로 발음이 동일한 membership으로 혼동을 준 오답이다.
(B) **다의어 오답:** 질문의 offer는 '제공하다'라는 뜻의 동사이고, 보기의 offer는 '제안'이라는 의미의 명사이다.
(C) **정답:** 인턴십 프로그램이 아직 논의 중(That's still being discussed)이라며 아직 결정되지 않았음을 우회적으로 표현한 적절한 응답이다.

11 M-Cn / W-Am

There's a pottery workshop at our art studio.
(A) She doesn't enjoy shopping.
(B) A lot of people have asked about that.
(C) A box of paints.

저희 화실에서 도예 워크숍이 열립니다.
(A) 그녀는 쇼핑을 즐기지 않아요.
(B) 많은 분들이 그것에 관해 물어보셨어요.
(C) 물감 한 상자요.

해설 | 정보를 전달하는 평서문
(A) **인칭 오류 및 유사 발음 오답:** 보기의 She가 가리키는 대상이 질문에 없고, 질문의 workshop과 부분적으로 발음이 동일한 shopping을 이용한 오답이다.
(B) **정답:** 많은 분들이 그것(워크숍)에 관해 물어보셨다(A lot of people have asked about that)며 관련 상황을 부연 설명하고 있으므로 가장 적절한 응답이다.
(C) **연상 작용 오답:** 질문의 art studio에서 연상 가능한 paints를 언급한 오답이다.

어휘 | pottery 도자기, 도예

12 W-Br / W-Am

Please tell Sunita to park near the Weber Building.
(A) There's some on the fifth floor.
(B) Yes, the rent is high.
(C) She's taking the train.

수니타에게 웨버 빌딩 근처에 주차하라고 말해주세요.
(A) 5층에 좀 있어요.
(B) 네, 임대료가 비싸요.
(C) 그녀는 기차를 탈 거예요.

해설 | 행동을 요청하는 명령문
(A) **연상 작용 오답:** 질문의 Building에서 연상 가능한 fifth floor를 언급한 오답이다.
(B) **연상 작용 오답:** 질문의 Building에서 연상 가능한 rent를 언급한 오답이다.
(C) **정답:** 그녀는 기차를 탈 것(She's taking the train)이라며 차를 갖고 오지 않을 것임을 우회적으로 밝힌 적절한 응답이다.

13 M-Cn / M-Au

Would you be willing to pick up the food order for the party?
(A) The break room is downstairs.
(B) A table for two, please.
(C) I have a client call in ten minutes.

파티를 위해 주문한 음식을 찾아와 주실 수 있을까요?
(A) 휴게실은 아래층에 있어요.
(B) 두 명 자리 주세요.
(C) 저는 10분 뒤에 고객 통화가 있어요.

해설 | 부탁·요청의 의문문
(A) **연상 작용 오답:** 질문의 party에서 연상 가능한 break room을 이용한 오답이다.

(B) **연상 작용 오답:** 질문의 food order에서 연상 가능한 A table for two를 언급한 오답이다.

(C) **정답:** 10분 뒤에 고객 통화가 있다(I have a client call in ten minutes)며 지금 음식을 찾으러 갈 수 없음을 우회적으로 밝힌 적절한 응답이다.

14 W-Am / W-Br

There isn't enough light in this office.
(A) There's a sale at the lamp store this weekend.
(B) The second office on the left.
(C) No, the box isn't light enough to carry.

이 사무실은 조명이 충분치 않네요.
(A) 이번 주말에 램프 매장에서 세일이 있어요.
(B) 왼쪽 두 번째 사무실이요.
(C) 아니요, 상자가 들고 갈 만큼 가볍지 않아요.

해설 | 상황을 설명하는 평서문
(A) **정답:** 이번 주말에 램프 매장에서 세일이 있다(There's a sale at the lamp store this weekend)며 매장에 가서 사올 것을 우회적으로 제안한 적절한 응답이다.
(B) **단어 반복 및 연상 작용 오답:** 질문의 office를 반복 이용했으며, 질문의 light를 right(오른쪽)로 잘못 이해하고 연상 가능한 left를 언급한 오답이다.
(C) **다의어 오답:** 질문의 light는 '조명'이라는 뜻의 명사이고, 보기의 light는 '가벼운'이라는 의미의 형용사이다.

15 W-Am / M-Cn

Can you give me the new employee's contact information?
(A) It should be in her file.
(B) The contract will expire in November.
(C) Are these discounted?

그 신입사원 연락처 좀 알려 주실 수 있나요?
(A) 그녀의 파일에 있을 겁니다.
(B) 계약은 11월에 만료될 겁니다.
(C) 이것들은 할인되나요?

해설 | 부탁·요청의 의문문
(A) **정답:** 연락처를 요청하는 질문에 그녀의 파일에 있을 것(It should be in her file)이라고 알 수 있는 방법을 우회적으로 알려 준 적절한 응답이다.
(B) **유사 발음 오답:** 질문의 contact와 발음이 유사한 contract로 혼동을 준 오답이다.
(C) **관련 없는 오답:** 질문과 상관없는 답변을 제시한 오답이다.

어휘 | contract 계약 **expire** 만료되다

16 M-Au / W-Br

The new menu needs to be sent to the print shop this morning.
(A) That tastes delicious.
(B) We haven't chosen a layout yet.
(C) I usually eat at home.

오늘 아침 인쇄소로 새 메뉴를 보내야 합니다.
(A) 맛있네요.
(B) 아직 레이아웃을 고르지 못했는데요.
(C) 저는 주로 집에서 식사해요.

해설 | 문의·요청을 전달하는 평서문
(A) **연상 작용 오답:** 질문의 menu에서 연상 가능한 tastes delicious를 언급한 오답이다.
(B) **정답:** 아직 레이아웃을 고르지 못했다(We haven't chosen a layout yet)며 아직 보내면 안 된다는 말을 우회적으로 표현한 적절한 응답이다.
(C) **연상 작용 오답:** 질문의 menu에서 연상 가능한 eat at home을 언급한 오답이다.

어휘 | layout 레이아웃, 지면 배치

17 M-Au / W-Br

We could conduct your next appointment over the phone.
(A) I can point you in the right direction.
(B) An application for a smartphone.
(C) It doesn't take me much time to come to your office.

다음 예약은 전화로 할 수 있어요.
(A) 올바른 방향을 알려드릴 수 있어요.
(B) 스마트폰 앱입니다.
(C) 제가 당신 사무실까지 가는 데 시간이 오래 걸리지 않아요.

해설 | 의견을 제시하는 평서문
(A) **유사 발음 오답:** 질문의 appointment와 부분적으로 발음이 유사한 point로 혼동을 준 오답이다.
(B) **파생어 오답:** 질문의 phone과 파생어 관계인 smartphone을 이용한 오답이다.
(C) **정답:** 당신 사무실까지 가는 데 시간이 오래 걸리지 않는다(It doesn't take me much time to come to your office)며 전화로 예약하지 않아도 된다는 말을 우회적으로 한 적절한 응답이다.

어휘 | conduct (특정한 활동을) 하다

18 W-Br / W-Am

Why don't we drive to the train station together?
(A) At the end of the platform.
(B) Yesterday's training seminar.
(C) Let's see if Antonio wants to join us.

기차역까지 함께 차를 타고 가면 어때요?
(A) 승강장 끝에요.
(B) 어제 있었던 교육 세미나요.
(C) 안토니오가 함께 가고 싶어 하는지 알아보죠.

해설 | 제안·권유의 의문문
(A) **연상 작용 오답:** 질문의 train station에서 연상 가능한 platform을 이용한 오답이다.
(B) **다의어 오답:** 질문의 train은 '기차'라는 의미이며, 보기의 training은 '교육, 훈련'이라는 의미로, '훈련하다, 교육시키다'라는 의미의 동사 train의 명사형이다.
(C) **정답:** 안토니오가 함께 가고 싶어 하는지 알아보자(Let's see if Antonio wants to join us)고 우회적으로 수락의 의사를 밝혔으므로 정답이다.

19 W-Am / M-Cn

The system updates are taking a long time to install.
(A) I have something you can work on in the meantime.
(B) I thought the buses were on time today.
(C) No, they're loading packages.

시스템 업데이트 설치하는 데 오래 걸리네요.
(A) 그동안 할 수 있는 일이 있어요.
(B) 오늘은 버스들이 제시간에 온 것 같아요.
(C) 아니요, 그들은 소포를 싣고 있어요.

해설 | 상황을 설명하는 평서문
(A) **정답:** 그동안 할 수 있는 일이 있다(I have something you can work on in the meantime)며 시스템 업데이트가 설치되는 동안 할 일을 제안하는 적절한 응답이다.
(B) **단어 반복 오답:** 질문의 time을 반복 이용한 오답이다.
(C) **연상 작용 오답:** 질문의 system updates에서 연상 가능한 loading을 언급한 오답이다.

어휘 | install 설치하다 in the meantime 그동안

20 W-Am / M-Au

Would you be willing to give the keynote speech at the trade fair?
(A) I'll be hosting our board members on that day.
(B) Do you have the key to the supply cabinet?
(C) Yes, I gave them their gifts.

무역 박람회에서 기조 연설을 해 주실 수 있을까요?
(A) 저는 그날 이사회 회원들을 모실 겁니다.
(B) 소모품 캐비닛 열쇠를 갖고 계세요?
(C) 네, 제가 그들에게 선물을 줬어요.

해설 | 부탁·요청의 의문문
(A) **정답:** 그날 이사회 회원들을 모실 것(I'll be hosting our board members on that day)이라고 우회적으로 거절의 의사를 밝혔으므로 정답이다.
(B) **유사 발음 오답:** 질문의 keynote와 부분적으로 발음이 동일한 key로 혼동을 준 오답이다.
(C) **단어 반복 오답:** 질문의 give를 과거형 gave로 반복 사용한 오답이다.

어휘 | keynote speech 기조 연설 board 이사회 supply cabinet 소모품 캐비닛

LC PART 3

UNIT 9 주제·목적 / 화자·장소 문제

❶ 주제·목적 문제

고득점 전략 단서 포착하기   본책 p.68

여	안녕하세요, 와타루. 경영진을 위한 분기 보고서를 준비 중인데요.
남	그래서 고객 만족에 대해 알고 싶으신 거죠?
여	맞아요. 고객 서비스 부서장으로서, 사람들이 지속적으로 칭찬하는 우리 컴퓨터의 기능을 파악하셨나요?

어휘 | quarterly 분기의 management 경영진, 경영 identify 확인하다, 찾다 consistently 지속적으로, 일관되게

문제 | 여자가 방문한 목적은?
(A) 동료를 축하하려고
(B) 새 절차를 설명하려고
(C) 정보를 수집하려고
(D) 고소장을 제출하려고

어휘 | colleague 동료 procedure 절차 complaint 불평, 고소장

ETS 유형 연습   본책 p.69

1 (A) **2** (C) **3** (C) **4** (A) **5** (C) **6** (C)
7 (D) **8** (C) **9** (B)

[1-3] W-Am / M-Au

W **1**Gordon, I was looking at the floor plan for this year's toy industry trade show. The deadline is coming up to reserve an exhibit space at the conference center, so we need to decide which exhibit space will work best to show our products.

M **2**Well, I definitely think we should get a larger space than last year. We're showing more toys this year, so if we want to display all of them, we'll need plenty of room.

W I see your point. **3**Here's a list of the pricing for all of the available exhibit spaces—would you mind looking it over and seeing if any of the larger spaces are within our price range?

여 **1**고든, 올해 완구업계 무역 박람회 도면을 보고 있었는데요. 컨퍼런스센터 전시 공간 예약 기한이 다가와요. 그러니 어떤 전시 공간이 우리 제품을 보여주기에 가장 좋은지 결정해야 해요.

남 　²음, 작년보다 더 넓은 공간을 잡아야 한다고 확신해요. 올해는 더 많은 장난감을 보여줄 예정이니 모두 전시하려면 충분한 공간이 필요할 거예요.

여 　알겠어요. ³이용 가능한 전시 공간 전체의 가격표예요. 살펴보시고 우리 가격대 안에서 더 큰 공간이 있는지 확인해 주시겠어요?

어휘 | floor plan 평면도, 도면　trade show 무역 박람회　deadline 기한　exhibit 전시　definitely 분명히, 확실히　plenty of 많은　available 이용 가능한　price range 가격대

---

1 화자들은 무엇에 대해 이야기하는가?
(A) 무역 박람회　　　(B) 미술 전시회
(C) 전 매장 할인　　　(D) 건물 개조

해설 | 대화의 주제
여자가 첫 대사에서 올해 완구업계 무역 박람회 도면(the floor plan for this year's toy industry trade show)을 보고 있었다고 하므로 (A)가 정답이다.

어휘 | storewide 점포 전체의　renovation 개조, 보수

2 남자는 무엇을 권하는가?
(A) 시간을 더 많이 잡기　(B) 예산 증액하기
(C) 더 넓은 공간 예약하기　(D) 제품 품질 개선하기

해설 | 남자의 제안 사항
남자가 작년보다 더 넓은 공간을 잡아야 한다(I definitely think we should get a larger space than last year)고 하므로 (C)가 정답이다.

어휘 | budget 예산

Paraphrasing 대화의 get a larger space
→ 정답의 Reserving a larger space

3 여자는 남자에게 무엇을 주는가?
(A) 신청서　　　(B) 주문증
(C) 가격표　　　(D) 제품 설명

해설 | 여자가 남자에게 주는 것
대화 마지막에 여자가 가격표가 여기에 있다(Here's a list of the pricing)고 하므로 (C)가 정답이다.

어휘 | application form 신청서　description 설명

Paraphrasing 대화의 a list of the pricing
→ 정답의 A price list

[4-6] M-Cn / W-Br

M 　Hi, Michelle. ⁴This is Mario Baxter from the Sloan Clinic. We reviewed your résumé for the dental assistant position, and we're very impressed.

W 　Oh, that's great. Thank you!

M 　⁵I'd like to schedule an interview with you. Could you let me know when you're available next week?

W 　Well, Tuesday would work best for me. I can come in any time that day.

M 　Let's plan for Tuesday at ten A.M., then. The interview will last about an hour. ⁶Please bring your dental certification with you. I'll just need to see that before we move forward.

남 　안녕하세요, 미셸. ⁴슬로안 클리닉의 마리오 박스터입니다. 치위생사 자리에 내 주신 이력서를 검토했는데, 매우 인상적이었습니다.

여 　아, 잘됐네요. 감사합니다!

남 　⁵면접 일정을 잡고 싶은데요. 다음 주 언제 시간이 되는지 알려 주시겠어요?

여 　음, 화요일이 가장 좋을 것 같아요. 그날은 언제든지 갈 수 있어요.

남 　그럼 화요일 오전 10시로 계획을 잡죠. 면접은 한 시간 정도 진행될 겁니다. ⁶치과 자격증을 가져오세요. 일을 진행하기에 앞서 봐야 할 테니까요.

어휘 | résumé 이력서　dental assistant 치위생사　impressed 인상 깊게 생각하는, 감명받은　available 시간이 되는　certification 증명서, 증명　move forward 추진하다

---

4 남자는 어떤 종류의 업체에 근무하는가?
(A) 치과　　　(B) 식당
(C) 은행　　　(D) 피트니스 센터

해설 | 남자의 근무 장소
남자가 첫 대사에서 클리닉(from the Sloan Clinic)이라고 자기소개를 했으며, 치위생사 자리(the dental assistant position)에 제출한 이력서를 검토했다고 하므로 치과임을 알 수 있다. 따라서 (A)가 정답이다.

5 남자가 여자에게 전화한 목적은?
(A) 회의에 등록하려고
(B) 투자 계획을 논의하려고
(C) 면접을 잡으려고
(D) 영업시간을 확인하려고

해설 | 전화의 목적
남자가 두 번째 대사에서 면접 일정을 잡고 싶다(I'd like to schedule an interview with you)고 하므로 (C)가 정답이다.

어휘 | register for ~에 등록하다, 신청하다　investment 투자　arrange 마련하다, 주선하다

Paraphrasing 대화의 schedule an interview
→ 정답의 arrange a job interview

6 남자는 어떤 서류를 언급하는가?
(A) 청구서　　　(B) 설문지
(C) 전문 자격증　(D) 거래 내역서

해설 | 남자가 언급한 서류
대화 마지막에 남자가 치과 자격증(your dental certification)을 가져오라고 하므로 (C)가 정답이다.

어휘 | invoice 청구서, 송장　bank statement 은행 거래 내역서

Paraphrasing 대화의 dental certification
→ 정답의 A professional certificate

W Thank you for taking my call, Mr. Pham. **7, 8**I wanted some advice about the legal implications of my company's plan to expand business internationally next year.

M **8**I'm glad you reached out to my firm, Ms. Silva. Yes, there are a lot of regulations that you'll have to navigate, **depending on the countries you want to sell your products in.**

W Well, to simplify the plan, **9**I thought we'd start by introducing our latest model of smartphone to the Middle Eastern region and then introduce our other products, especially our tablets and headphones, at a later date.

여 전화 받아 주셔서 감사합니다, 팸 씨. **7, 8**내년에 해외로 사업을 확대하려는 저희 회사 계획의 법률적 영향에 대해 조언을 구하고 싶어요.

남 **8**저희 회사에 연락해 주셔서 감사합니다, 실바 씨. 네, 제품을 판매하고자 하는 국가에 따라 **처리하셔야 할 규정이 많아요.**

여 계획을 간단히 설명하자면 **9**중동 지역에 저희 최신형 스마트폰을 소개하는 것으로 출발하고, 나중에는 다른 제품, 특히 태블릿과 헤드폰을 소개할 것으로 생각했어요.

어휘 | legal 법률과 관련된 implication 영향, 결과 regulation 규정, 규제 navigate 다루다, 처리하다 depending on ~에 따라 simplify 간소화하다 at a later date 나중에

7 대화는 주로 무엇에 관한 것인가?
(A) 소매점 임대 (B) 새 제조업체와의 계약
(C) 해외 여행 (D) 신규 시장 진입

해설 | **대화의 주제**
여자가 첫 대사에서 내년에 해외로 사업을 확대하려는 회사 계획(my company's plan to expand business internationally next year)을 언급하고 있으므로 (D)가 정답이다.

어휘 | lease 임대하다 retail space 소매점 contract 계약하다

Paraphrasing 대화의 expand business internationally → 정답의 Entering new markets

8 남자는 누구이겠는가?
(A) 부동산 중개인 (B) 투자자
(C) 변호사 (D) 마케팅 전문가

해설 | **남자의 신분**
여자가 첫 대사에서 회사 계획의 법률적 영향에 대해 조언을 구하고 싶다(I wanted some advice about the legal implications of my company's plan)고 했으며, 남자가 그의 회사에 연락해 줘서 감사하다(I'm glad you reached out to my firm)고 답변한 후 규정(regulations)에 대해 언급하므로 남자가 변호사임을 추측할 수 있다. 따라서 (C)가 정답이다.

어휘 | real estate agent 부동산 중개인 investor 투자자 specialist 전문가

---

9 여자의 회사는 무엇을 판매하는가?
(A) 건설 장비 (B) 전자 기기
(C) 자동차 부품 (D) 스포츠 용품

해설 | **여자의 회사가 판매하는 것**
대화 마지막에 여자가 최신형 스마트폰(our latest model of smartphone), 태블릿과 헤드폰(our tablets and headphones)을 소개해야 한다고 하므로 (B)가 정답이다.

어휘 | construction 건설 equipment 장비 automotive 자동차의

Paraphrasing 대화의 smartphone, tablets, headphones → 정답의 Electronic devices

❷ 화자·장소 문제

고득점 전략 **단서 포착하기** 본책 p.70

남1 오늘 시간을 내어 만나 주셔서 감사합니다, 이사벨. TV 프로그램 리허설을 하시느라 꽤 바쁘신 걸로 알고 있어요.

여 다행히 오늘은 제 대사 연습이 일찍 끝났어요. 이번 에피소드에서는 많은 장면에 나오진 않거든요. 어쨌든 귀사의 브랜드를 대표하는 일을 논의하게 되어 기뻐요.

남2 저희 제품을 홍보해 주시면 큰 도움이 될 겁니다.

어휘 | particular 특정한 represent 대표하다 endorsement (유명인에 의한) 상품의 보증, 홍보

문제 | 여자는 누구이겠는가?
(A) 배우 (B) 출장요리 업자
(C) 메이크업 아티스트 (D) 의상 디자이너

ETS 유형 연습 본책 p.71

1 (C)	**2** (A)	**3** (D)	**4** (C)	**5** (D)	**6** (B)
7 (A)	**8** (C)	**9** (B)			

M Rosa, I met with an official from the Organic Food Commission yesterday. **1**He said there are things we should be doing now in order to become a certified organic farm.

W Right. **2**One thing I want to do right away is start rotating our crops during the growing season. That way we can enrich the soil without using fertilizers.

M I agree. And it's never too early to start looking for new markets for our vegetables. **3**Today, I'm going to put together a list of stores and restaurants in the area that we may be able to work with.

남 로사, 제가 어제 유기농 식품 위원회의 관리자를 만났는데요. **1**저희가 공인 유기농 농장이 되려면 지금 해야 할 일들이 있다고 해요.

10 남자가 전화를 건 목적은?

(A) 결제 방식에 대해 문의하려고
(B) 오배송에 관해 불만을 제기하려고
(C) 카탈로그를 요청하려고
(D) 상품을 찾아갈 수 있도록 처리하려고

해설 | **전화의 목적**
남자가 첫 대사에서 집으로 갈색 가죽 소파를 배송하는 주문 건을 받았는데 가죽 말고 갈색 천 소파를 주문했다(He has an order to deliver a brown leather sofa to my home, but I ordered the sofa in a brown fabric, not in leather)고 하므로 (B)가 정답이다.

어휘 | payment plan 결제 방식 arrange 일을 처리하다 merchandise 상품

11 여자는 무엇이 잘못 입력됐다고 말하는가?

(A) 물품 코드   (B) 이메일 주소
(C) 아파트 호수   (D) 배송일자

해설 | **잘못 입력된 것**
여자의 첫 대사에서 덮개 종류 코드가 잘못 입력됐다(The code for the type of upholstery was entered incorrectly)고 하므로 (A)가 정답이다.

Paraphrasing | 대화의 The code for the type of upholstery → 정답의 An item code

12 여자는 무엇을 하겠다고 말하는가?

(A) 환불해 주기   (B) 직원에게 이야기하기
(C) 배송 긴급 처리하기   (D) 확정서 보내기

해설 | **여자가 할 일**
대화 마지막에 여자가 내일 배송될 수 있게 주문을 "긴급"으로 표시하겠다(I'll mark the order "rush" to get it delivered tomorrow)고 하므로 (C)가 정답이다.

어휘 | issue a refund 환불해 주다 confirmation 확인

Paraphrasing | 대화의 mark the order "rush" to get it delivered tomorrow → 정답의 Rush a delivery

---

[13-15] W-Br / M-Cn

W Hi, Charles. **13**Can we chat about the upcoming Clear Glen jazz performance?

M Yeah, I'm looking forward to the assignment. **14**I just spoke to the editor in chief of the newspaper, and she confirmed that all the press photographers will be right in front of the stage. We'll be able to get some great photos from that location.

W Um, so there's one problem to mention— **15**I just discovered that one of our low-light camera lenses is cracked.

M Hm. We should order a new one then, before the event.

여 안녕하세요, 찰스. **13**다가오는 클리어글렌 재즈 공연에 대해 얘기 좀 나눌 수 있을까요?

남 네, 그 업무를 무척 고대하고 있어요. **14**방금 신문 편집장님께 말씀드렸는데 모든 언론사 사진기자들이 무대 바로 앞에 위치할 거라고 확인해 주셨어요. 그 자리에서는 멋진 사진들을 찍을 수 있을 거예요.

여 저, 그래서 얘기해야 할 문제가 하나 있어요. **15**우리 저조도 카메라 렌즈 중 하나에 금이 간 걸 방금 발견했어요.

남 음. 그럼 행사 전에 새 렌즈를 주문해야겠네요.

어휘 | upcoming 다가오는, 곧 있을 look forward to 고대하다 assignment 과제, 임무 editor in chief 편집장 confirm 확인하다 press 언론 low-light 저조도 cracked 금이 간

13 화자들은 어떤 종류의 행사에 대해 이야기하는가?

(A) 워크숍   (B) 공예전
(C) 선거   (D) 음악회

해설 | **화자들이 논의하는 행사**
대화의 첫 대사에서 여자가 다가오는 클리어글렌 재즈 공연(the upcoming Clear Glen jazz performance)에 대해 언급하고 있으므로 (D)가 정답이다.

어휘 | election 선거

Paraphrasing | 대화의 jazz performance → 정답의 A concert

14 화자들은 어떤 업계에서 일하겠는가?

(A) 서비스   (B) 언론
(C) 음악   (D) 패션

해설 | **화자들이 종사하는 업계**
남자가 첫 대사에서 신문 편집장(the editor in chief of the newspaper)과 모든 언론사 사진기자들(all the press photographers)을 언급했으므로 언론계에서 일할 것이라고 추측할 수 있다. 따라서 (B)가 정답이다.

어휘 | hospitality 서비스업, 환대 journalism 언론

15 여자는 어떤 문제를 언급하는가?

(A) 주문 물품이 도착하지 않았다.
(B) 좌석이 더 필요하다.
(C) 발표자를 구할 수 없다.
(D) 장비가 고장 났다.

해설 | **여자가 언급한 문제점**
여자가 마지막 대사에서 저조도 카메라 렌즈 중 하나에 금이 간 걸 방금 발견했다(I just discovered that one of our low-light camera lenses is cracked)고 하므로 (D)가 정답이다.

어휘 | presenter 발표자 unavailable 구할 수 없는

Paraphrasing | 대화의 one of our low-light camera lenses is cracked → 정답의 Some equipment is broken.

W1 Priyanka and Carlos, as you know, ¹⁶our next company workshop on skills development is in a month. What if we formed teams to help with the planning?

M That's a great idea. ¹⁷There are a lot of details to take care of, so it'll be a lot faster if we divide up the work. My team can oversee the training content.

W1 Perfect. And Priyanka, what about your team?

W2 My team can manage promotion and attendance. ¹⁸We'll start by creating some flyers to publicize the event.

여1 프리얀카, 칼로스. 아시다시피 ¹⁶다음 사내 역량 개발 워크숍이 한 달 뒤에 있습니다. 기획을 도울 팀을 구성하면 어떨까요?

남 좋은 생각이네요. ¹⁷처리해야 할 세부 사항이 많으니 업무를 분담하면 훨씬 빨라질 겁니다. 저희 팀은 교육 내용을 감독할 수 있어요.

여1 좋습니다. 프리얀카 씨 팀은 어때요?

여2 저희 팀은 홍보와 참석률을 관리할 수 있어요. ¹⁸행사를 홍보하는 전단을 만드는 것부터 시작할게요.

어휘 | development 개발   divide up 분담하다   oversee 감독하다   promotion 홍보   attendance 참석, 참석률   flyer 전단   publicize 홍보하다

16 화자들은 주로 무엇에 대해 이야기하는가?
(A) 사무실 이전 관리   (B) 신제품 홍보
(C) 예산 기획   (D) 워크숍 준비

해설 | 대화의 주제
여자 1이 첫 대사에서 다음 사내 역량 개발 워크숍이 한 달 뒤에 있다(our next company workshop on skills development is in a month)고 하며, 기획을 도울 팀을 구성하면 어떠냐(What if we formed teams to help with the planning?)고 하므로 (D)가 정답이다.

어휘 | budget 예산

17 남자는 제안한 내용의 어떤 점을 마음에 들어 하는가?
(A) 신규 고객을 유치할 것이다.
(B) 시간이 절약될 것이다.
(C) 직원들에게 동기 부여가 될 것이다.
(D) 비용을 줄여줄 것이다.

해설 | 남자가 마음에 들어 하는 제안 사항
남자의 첫 대사에서 업무를 분담하면 훨씬 빨라질 것(it'll be a lot faster if we divide up the work)이라고 하므로 (B)가 정답이다.

어휘 | motivate 동기를 부여하다

Paraphrasing   대화의 be a lot faster → 정답의 save time

18 프리얀카는 자신의 팀이 무엇을 먼저 하겠다고 말하는가?
(A) 웹사이트 구축하기   (B) 피드백 수집하기
(C) 홍보 자료 만들기   (D) 물품 구입하기

해설 | 프리얀카 팀이 시작할 일
대화 마지막에 여자 2가 행사를 홍보하는 전단을 만드는 것부터 시작하겠다(We'll start by creating some flyers to publicize the event)고 하므로 (C)가 정답이다.

어휘 | material 자료

Paraphrasing   대화의 flyers → 정답의 publicity materials

M Tomoko, ¹⁹we've had to stop the automobile assembly line. Some hinges on the passenger doors have been welded on in the wrong place. Do you know what the problem could be?

W ²⁰One of the robotic welding machines might be in the wrong position. I think Hassan calibrated one of them this morning. ²⁰Maybe it was adjusted incorrectly.

M Maybe. Do you know which machine it was?

W I think B-5?

M OK. ²¹I'll check Hassan's repair report for robot B-5 to see what he did.

남 토모코, ¹⁹자동차 조립 라인을 중단시켜야만 했어요. 조수석 문 경첩을 엉뚱한 곳에 용접했더라고요. 무슨 문제인지 아세요?

여 ²⁰자동 용접 기계 중 하나가 잘못된 위치에 있었을 겁니다. 오늘 아침에 핫산이 한 대를 조정한 것 같아요. ²⁰아마 잘못 조정된 모양입니다.

남 그렇겠네요. 어떤 기계인지 아세요?

여 B-5인 것 같은데요?

남 네. ²¹핫산이 뭘 했는지 확인하려면 그의 로봇 B-5 수리 보고서를 봐야겠어요.

어휘 | assembly 조립   hinge 경첩   weld 용접하다   calibrate 조정하다, 눈금을 맞추다   adjust 조정하다   incorrectly 부정확하게

19 화자들은 어디서 일하겠는가?
(A) 여행사   (B) 자동차 공장
(C) 운송업체   (D) 전자제품 매장

해설 | 화자들의 근무 장소
남자가 첫 대사에서 자동차 조립 라인을 중단시켜야만 했다(we've had to stop the automobile assembly line)고 하므로 화자들이 자동차 공장에서 일한다는 것을 추론할 수 있다. 따라서 (B)가 정답이다.

어휘 | travel agency 여행사   shipping (해상)운송   electronics 전자 기기

20 여자에 따르면, 무엇이 문제를 발생시켰겠는가?
(A) 근로자가 오늘 결근이어서
(B) 설명이 불확실해서
(C) 기계가 잘못 조정되어서
(D) 장비가 없어져서

해설 | **문제의 발생 요인**

여자가 첫 대사에서 자동 용접 기계 중 하나가 잘못된 위치에 있었을 것(One of the robotic welding machines might be in the wrong position)이고, 아마 잘못 조정된 것 같다(Maybe it was adjusted incorrectly)고 하므로 (C)가 정답이다.

어휘 | instructions 설명, 지시

21 남자는 무엇을 하겠다고 말하는가?
(A) 일부 업무 재배정하기
(B) 프로젝트 재시작하기
(C) 문서 확인하기
(D) 연장 찾기

해설 | **남자가 할 일**

대화 마지막에 남자가 핫산의 로봇 B-5 수리 보고서를 봐야겠다(I'll check Hassan's repair report for robot B-5)고 하므로 (C)가 정답이다.

어휘 | reallocate 재배정하다

Paraphrasing 대화의 check Hassan's repair report → 정답의 Check a document

[22-24] M-Cn / W-Am

> M ²²Joining us on our radio program today is Amal Rashad, director of the city's Department of Transportation. Great to have you on the show!
> W Glad to be here, Richard!
> M ²³Our first question is about the new funding allocated for your department. How will the resources be used?
> W Well, the plan is to construct two additional train stations on the blue line.
> M That'll really allow you to expand service.
> W Absolutely. ²⁴And we'll be having local artists paint murals on the walls. I'm really excited about that!
>
> 남 ²²오늘 저희 라디오 프로그램에 시 교통부서장 아말 라샤드 씨가 나와 주셨습니다. 모시게 되어 반갑습니다!
> 여 나오게 되어 기쁩니다, 리처드!
> 남 ²³첫 번째 질문은 부서에 할당된 신규 자금에 관한 것인데요. 해당 재원은 어떻게 사용될까요?
> 여 파란색 노선에 기차역 두 곳을 추가로 건설할 계획입니다.
> 남 서비스를 크게 확장할 수 있겠군요.
> 여 물론입니다. ²⁴또한 지역 화가들에게 벽화를 그리게 할 예정입니다. 굉장히 기대가 큽니다!
>
> 어휘 | transportation 교통, 운송 funding 자금 allocate 할당하다 expand 확장하다 mural 벽화

22 여자는 누구인가?
(A) 시 공무원   (B) 회계사
(C) 건축가   (D) 영업부장

해설 | **여자의 신분**

남자가 첫 대사에서 시 교통부서장 아말 라샤드 씨(Amal Rashad, director of the city's Department of Transportation)를 소개하고 있으므로 (A)가 정답이다.

어휘 | accountant 회계사 architect 건축가

Paraphrasing 대화의 director of the city's Department of Transportation → 정답의 A city official

23 남자는 무엇에 대해 물어보는가?
(A) 서비스 계약   (B) 채용 계획
(C) 자금   (D) 정책 변경 사항

해설 | **남자의 문의 사항**

남자가 두 번째 대사에서 첫 번째 질문은 부서에 할당된 신규 자금에 관한 것(Our first question is about the new funding allocated for your department)이라고 하므로 (C)가 정답이다.

어휘 | agreement 계약, 협정 policy 정책

24 여자는 무엇이 기대된다고 말하는가?
(A) 경비 절감   (B) 신문 기사
(C) 지역 축제   (D) 미술품

해설 | **여자의 기대 사항**

대화 마지막에 여자가 지역 화가들에게 벽화를 그리게 할 예정이라 굉장히 기대가 크다(we'll be having local artists paint murals on the walls. I'm really excited about that!)고 하므로 (D)가 정답이다.

어휘 | cost saving 경비 절감

Paraphrasing 대화의 murals → 정답의 Some artwork

UNIT 10 세부 사항 / 문제점·걱정거리 문제

① 세부 사항 문제

고득점 전략 단서 포착하기   본책 p.74

> 여 지난주는 이곳 신규 사무실로 이전하느라 패 혼란스러웠죠.
> 남 맞아요. 혹시 제 책상 달력을 보셨나요? 유럽 도시 사진이 있는 달력이요. 확실히 챙겼다고 생각했는데 배송된 상자 어느 곳에도 없어요.
> 여 못 봤어요. 그런데 사실 저도 몇 가지 물건이 없어졌어요.
>
> 어휘 | chaotic 혼란스러운 by any chance 혹시라도 actually 사실

문제 | 화자들의 회사는 지난주에 무엇을 했는가?
(A) 부국장을 채용했다.
(B) 새 사무 공간으로 이전했다.
(C) 추가 고객을 영입했다.
(D) 로고 디자인을 바꿨다.

어휘 | acquire 얻다, 획득하다 additional 추가의

ETS 유형 연습

본책 p.75

1 (C) **2** (D) **3** (A) **4** (D) **5** (C) **6** (B)
7 (A) **8** (B) **9** (C)

[1-3] M-Cn / W-Am

M Hi, Karima. ¹I remember that you helped with the company health fair last year, **and it was great— the fitness activities were very popular.** ¹So, I'm putting you in charge of organizing activities for this year's health fair.

W Sounds good. I know everyone really loved the yoga class. ²I'll see if that instructor can come back this year.

M Good idea. I think we should also have at least one cardio exercise class. ³Maybe a modern dance class would be something new to try.

남 안녕하세요, 카리마. ¹**작년에 회사 건강 박람회에 도움을 주신 것으로 기억해요.** 정말 훌륭했죠. 피트니스 활동의 인기가 무척 많았잖아요. ¹**그래서 당신에게 올해 건강 박람회의 활동 준비를 맡기려고 합니다.**

여 좋아요. 모두가 요가 강습을 정말 좋아했어요. ²**그 강사가 올해도 다시 올 수 있는지 알아볼게요.**

남 좋은 생각이네요. 최소 한 가지 유산소 운동 강습도 있어야 할 것 같아요. ³**현대 무용 강습이 새로운 시도가 될 것 같군요.**

어휘 | in charge of ~을 맡아서, 담당해서 instructor 강사 at least 최소한 cardio exercise 유산소 운동

---

1 남자가 해당 업무를 위해 여자를 선택한 이유는?
(A) 이번 주에 업무량이 적다.
(B) 동료가 추천했다.
(C) 관련 경험이 있다.
(D) 피트니스에 관심을 표했다.

해설 | **남자가 업무를 위해 여자를 선택한 이유**
남자가 첫 대사에서 여자가 작년에 회사 건강 박람회에 도움을 준 것을 기억한다(I remember that you helped with the company health fair last year)고 하면서 올해 건강 박람회의 활동 준비를 맡기려고 한다(So, I'm putting you in charge of organizing activities for this year's health fair)고 하므로 (C)가 정답이다.

어휘 | assignment 임무, 과제 relevant 관련 있는

2 여자는 무엇을 할 것이라고 말하는가?
(A) 기획 위원회 조성
(B) 판매업체 면담
(C) 행사 공간 조사
(D) 강사가 시간이 되는지 확인

해설 | **여자가 할 일**
여자가 첫 대사에서 그 강사가 올해도 다시 올 수 있는지 알아보겠다(I'll see if that instructor can come back this year)고 하므로 (D)가 정답이다.

어휘 | committee 위원회 vendor 판매업체 availability 시간을 낼 수 있음

Paraphrasing 대화의 see if that instructor can come back → 정답의 Check an instructor's availability

3 남자는 어떤 종류의 활동을 제안하는가?
(A) 무용 강습
(B) 자전거 경주
(C) 배구 대회
(D) 수영 강습

해설 | **남자가 제안하는 활동의 종류**
대화 마지막에 남자가 현대 무용 강습이 새로운 시도가 될 것(Maybe a modern dance class would be something new to try)이라고 하므로 (A)가 정답이다.

[4-6] M-Cn / W-Br

M Marcela, were you able to hear that announcement? ⁴Why is the train slowing down?

W ⁴I believe the conductor said there's a lot of snow on the tracks. They want to be cautious during the snowstorm.

M That makes sense. ⁵I'm worried we might be late for our client meeting. I'm going to call our office so the receptionist can notify the clients.

W Good idea. ⁶And suggest that the clients go to the company cafeteria and have coffee. We should arrive in about 30 minutes.

남 마르셀라, 안내방송 들으셨나요? ⁴**열차가 왜 느려지는 거죠?**

여 ⁴**승무원 말로는 트랙에 눈이 많이 쌓였다고 했어요. 눈보라가 치는 동안엔 조심하죠.**

남 이해가 되네요. ⁵**고객 회의에 늦을까 봐 걱정이지만요.** 제가 사무실에 전화할게요. 그러면 안내 직원이 고객들에게 알릴 수 있을 겁니다.

여 좋은 생각이에요. ⁶**고객들에게 회사 카페테리아로 가서 커피를 마시라고 제안해 보세요.** 우린 약 30분 후에 도착할 겁니다.

어휘 | announcement 발표, 안내방송 conductor 승무원 cautious 조심스러운 make sense 말이 되다, 이해가 되다 notify 알리다

---

4 여자는 무엇 때문에 문제가 생긴다고 말하는가?
(A) 직원 부족
(B) 일정 오류
(C) 도로 건설
(D) 악천후

해설 | **여자가 언급한 문제의 원인**
남자가 첫 대사에서 열차가 느려지는 원인을 물었고(Why is the train slowing down?), 여자가 트랙에 눈이 많이 쌓여서 조심한다(I believe the conductor said there's a lot of snow on the tracks. They want to be cautious during the snowstorm)고 하므로 (D)가 정답이다.

어휘 | staffing 직원 채용 shortage 부족 construction 건설

Paraphrasing 대화의 there's a lot of snow, the snowstorm → 정답의 Poor weather conditions

5 남자는 무엇에 대해 우려하는가?

(A) 예산 초과   (B) 프로젝트 기한 초과

(C) 회의 지각   (D) 검사 통과

해설 | **남자의 우려 사항**

남자가 두 번째 대사에서 고객 회의에 늦을까 봐 걱정이다(I'm worried we might be late for our client meeting)라고 하므로 (C)가 정답이다.

어휘 | go over budget 예산을 초과하다   miss a deadline 기한을 놓치다   inspection 검사, 점검

6 여자는 고객들이 무엇을 해야 한다고 제안하는가?

(A) 여행 취소하기   (B) 카페테리아 방문하기

(C) 감독관에게 말하기   (D) 문서 검토하기

해설 | **여자의 제안 사항**

대화 마지막에 여자가 고객들에게 회사 카페테리아에 가서 커피를 마시라고 제안하라(And suggest that the clients go to the company cafeteria and have coffee)고 하므로 (B)가 정답이다.

어휘 | supervisor 감독관

[7-9] W-Br / M-Au

> **W** Thanks for agreeing to meet with me, Mr. Jenson. [7]I'm writing a magazine article on the latest trends in women's business clothes. As director of PHR Fashions, can you give me a preview of what customers can expect to see in the coming year?
>
> **M** Yes, I'd be happy to. The latest fashion trend right now is using color in women's business wear. [8]We are redesigning our traditional business suits in a variety of colors. We expect that this will be especially popular with women aged 25 to 35.
>
> **W** Interesting. I see you have samples of these new suits in your showroom. [9]Could I take some photographs to include with the article I'm writing?
>
> 여 만나기로 해 주셔서 감사합니다, 젠슨 씨. **[7]제가 여성 정장 최신 트렌드에 관한 잡지 기사를 쓰고 있는데요.** PHR 패션 임원으로서 고객들이 새해에 기대하는 바를 미리 알려 주실 수 있을까요?
>
> 남 네, 그럼요. 최근 패션 트렌드는 여성의 정장에 색상을 활용하는 겁니다. **[8]저희의 전통적인 정장을 다양한 색상으로 재디자인하고 있어요.** 25~35세 여성에게 특히 인기가 많을 것으로 예상합니다.
>
> 여 흥미롭군요. 전시실에서 이런 신상품 견본을 봤습니다. **[9]제가 쓰는 기사에 포함시킬 사진을 좀 찍어도 될까요?**
>
> 어휘 | latest 최신의, 최근의

7 여자는 누구이겠는가?

(A) 기자   (B) 판매원

(C) 화가   (D) 재단사

해설 | **여자의 신분**

여자가 첫 대사에서 여성 정장 최신 트렌드에 관한 잡지 기사를 쓰고 있다(I'm writing a magazine article on the latest trends in women's business clothes)고 하므로, 여자가 기자임을 추측할 수 있다. 따라서 (A)가 정답이다.

8 남자에 따르면, 어떤 변화가 예상되는가?

(A) 제조 비용이 감소할 것이다.

(B) 의상 디자인에 더 많은 색상이 활용될 것이다.

(C) 상품은 온라인으로만 구매 가능할 것이다.

(D) 직원들은 직장에서 평상복을 입기 시작할 것이다.

해설 | **남자가 예상하는 변화**

남자가 전통적인 정장을 다양한 색상으로 재디자인하고 있다(We are redesigning our traditional business suits in a variety of colors)고 하므로 (B)가 정답이다.

어휘 | manufacturing cost 제조 비용   available 구할 수 있는, 이용 가능한

Paraphrasing   대화의 redesigning our traditional business suits in a variety of colors

→ 정답의 More colors will be used in clothing designs.

9 여자는 무엇을 하겠다고 요청하는가?

(A) 개인적으로 견학하기   (B) 회장 면담하기

(C) 사진 촬영하기   (D) 창고 방문하기

해설 | **여자의 요청 사항**

여자가 마지막 대사에서 기사에 포함시킬 사진을 찍어도 되는지(Could I take some photographs to include with the article I'm writing?)를 묻고 있으므로 (C)가 정답이다.

어휘 | warehouse 창고

❷ 문제점·걱정거리 문제

고득점 전략   **단서 포착하기**   본책 p.76

> 여 알렉시, 월요일에 자비에르 솔라 에너지에서 태양 전지판 때문에 우리 사무실 건물을 평가하러 이곳에 왔다고 들었는데요. 어떻게 됐나요?
>
> 남1 건물 대부분이 후보지로 이상적이긴 한데요. 동쪽 몇 군데는 태양 전지판을 생산적으로 운영하기엔 근처 나무들 때문에 그늘이 너무 많이 져요.
>
> 남2 알겠어요. 나무를 좀 베어야겠군요. 어떻게 생각하세요, 카렌?
>
> 어휘 | evaluate 평가하다   solar panel 태양 전지판   ideal 이상적인   candidate 후보   productive 생산성 있는, 생산적인

문제 | 알렉시는 어떤 문제를 언급하는가?

(A) 건물 일부에 그늘이 너무 많이 진다.

(B) 발전기 일부가 전력을 너무 많이 소모한다.

(C) 평가 보고서가 도착하지 않았다.

(D) 프로젝트가 예산을 초과했다.

어휘 | generator 발전기

ETS 유형 연습

본책 p.77

1 (D)	2 (C)	3 (B)	4 (B)	5 (C)	6 (A)
7 (D)	8 (D)	9 (A)			

[1-3] M-Au / W-Br

M Welcome to Premiere Signmakers.

W [1]I manage an apartment complex, and I want to replace the signs on our buildings.

M You mean the signs that tell you which units are in the buildings?

W Yes. [2]And our tenants say that delivery people complain that the signs are too small and hard to read.

M Sure. [3]I need you to send me some photos of your apartment complex before I can start on a design.

남 프리미어 사인메이커스입니다.

여 [1]저는 아파트 단지를 관리하는데요, 저희 건물 표지판을 교체하고 싶어서요.

남 건물 내 호수를 안내하는 표지판 말씀이신가요?

여 네. [2]저희 임차인들 말로는 배송 기사들이 표지판이 너무 작고 읽기가 어렵다고 불평한대요.

남 알겠습니다. [3]제가 디자인을 시작하기 전에 아파트 단지 사진을 보내 주셔야 합니다.

어휘 | tenant 임차인

---

1 여자는 어디서 일하는가?

(A) 관공서   (B) 페인트 매장
(C) 주차장   (D) 아파트 단지

해설 | 여자의 근무 장소
여자가 첫 대사에서 아파트 단지를 관리한다(I manage an apartment complex)고 하므로 (D)가 정답이다.

어휘 | government office 관공서

2 여자는 어떤 문제를 논의하는가?

(A) 가격이 올랐다.   (B) 입구가 봉쇄됐다.
(C) 간판을 읽기가 어렵다.   (D) 조명이 작동되지 않는다.

해설 | 여자가 언급한 문제점
여자가 두 번째 대사에서 배송 기사들이 표지판이 너무 작고 읽기가 어렵다고 불평한다(the signs are too small and hard to read)고 하므로 (C)가 정답이다.

어휘 | entrance 입구

Paraphrasing 대화의 hard to read
→ 정답의 difficult to read

3 남자는 여자에게 무엇을 해 달라고 요청하는가?

(A) 예약 일정 변경하기   (B) 사진 보내기
(C) 서류 제출하기   (D) 건물 방문하기

해설 | 남자의 요청 사항
대화 마지막에 남자가 여자에게 아파트 단지 사진을 보내 줘야 한다(I need you to send me some photos of your apartment complex)고 하므로 (B)가 정답이다.

어휘 | reschedule 일정을 변경하다

[4-6] 3인 대화 M-Au / W-Br / W-Am

M We've made impressive progress [4]since we came together as a professional dance company. Today, I'd like to hear your ideas for the future.

W1 [5]Actually, Heidi and I talked about registering us for a series of tournaments to compete against other high-ranking teams. [6]But, there's a logistical concern. The tournament we were looking at… they allow a maximum of three dancers per team.

W2 [6]Right—and since we have eight members, we're worried that we won't all be able to participate.

M No problem. We can easily split our team into subgroups, and all of us can enter the tournament at various levels. That way everyone can compete. But we'll need several new routines.

남 [4]우리는 전문 무용단으로 합친 후 눈부신 진전을 이뤘어요. 오늘 여러분의 향후 계획을 들어보고 싶네요.

여1 [5]사실 하이디와 저는 일련의 대회에 등록해 다른 상위 팀과 겨루는 것에 대해 이야기 나눴어요. [6]하지만 팀 조직에 관한 우려가 있어요. 우리가 생각하는 대회는 팀당 최대 3명의 무용수만을 허용해요.

여2 [6]맞아요. 우리 팀원은 8명이니 참가하지 못할까 걱정이 됩니다.

남 괜찮아요. 우리 팀을 간단히 소집단으로 나누면 모두 다양한 수준으로 대회에 참가할 수 있습니다. 그렇게 하면 모두가 참가할 수 있죠. 하지만 몇 가지 새로운 동작이 필요할 거예요.

어휘 | register for ~에 등록하다   compete 경쟁하다, 참가하다 high-ranking 중요한   logistical 업무 조직에 관한, 물류에 관한 subgroup 소집단   enter 참가하다

4 화자들은 무엇을 전문적으로 하는가?

(A) 요리   (B) 춤
(C) 의상 디자인   (D) 행사 기획

해설 | 화자들의 전문 분야
남자가 첫 대사에서 우리가 전문 무용단으로 합친 후(since we came together as a professional dance company)라고 하므로 (B)가 정답이다.

5 무엇이 논의되고 있는가?

(A) 전문성 개발 워크숍   (B) 새로운 마케팅 전략
(C) 일련의 대회   (D) 회사 연회

해설 | **논의 사항**
여자 1이 대회에 등록해 다른 상위 팀과 겨루는 것에 대해
하이디와 이야기 나눴다(Heidi and I talked about
registering us for a series of tournaments to compete
against other high-ranking teams)고 하므로 (C)가
정답이다.

어휘 | strategy 전략   competition 대회, 경쟁   banquet
연회

Paraphrasing   대화의 a series of tournaments
→ 정답의 A series of competitions

6 여자들은 무엇을 우려하는가?
(A) 모두가 참가할 수 있도록 하는 것
(B) 정책 변경을 시행하는 것
(C) 자선 행사를 위해 모금하는 것
(D) 징계 처분을 내리는 것

해설 | **여자들의 우려 사항**
여자 1이 대회는 팀당 최대 3명의 무용수만을 허용한다고
우려(But, there's a logistical concern. The tournament
we were looking at… they allow a maximum of three
dancers per team)하자 여자 2는 팀원이 8명이니 참가하지
못할까 걱정이 된다(Right—and since we have eight
members, we're worried that we won't all be able to
participate)고 하므로 (A)가 정답이다.

어휘 | implement 시행하다   policy 정책   raise funds
모금하다   charity 자선   disciplinary action 징계 처분, 처벌

[7-9] W-Br / M-Cn

> W Hi, Antonio. **7** Are you ready to teach tonight?
> M I think so! **7** The kitchen stations are prepped
>   and ready with mixing bowls and cooking
>   utensils. **8** But I was expecting our food
>   shipment earlier this afternoon. I really need
>   those ingredients for the class tonight.
> W All right. Not to worry. Write me a list of the
>   ingredients you need, and **9** I'll hurry over to the
>   grocery store right now to get everything.
>
> 여 안녕하세요, 안토니오. **7** 오늘 저녁 수업 준비가 되셨나요?
> 남 그런 것 같아요! **7** 주방은 믹싱볼과 조리 기구가 준비됐습니다.
>   **8** 하지만 식품 배송이 오늘 오후에 일찍 올 걸로 기대했어요.
>   오늘 저녁 수업을 위해 그 재료들이 꼭 필요하거든요.
> 여 알겠어요. 염려 마세요. 저한테 필요한 재료 목록을 적어 주시면
>   **9** 지금 식료품점에 빨리 가서 전부 사 올게요.
>
> 어휘 | prep 준비하다   utensil 기구   ingredient 재료

7 화자들은 어떤 행사를 준비하겠는가?
(A) 지역사회 축제   (B) 식당 개업식
(C) 회사 야유회   (D) 요리 강좌

해설 | **화자들이 준비하는 행사**
여자가 첫 대사에서 오늘 저녁 수업 준비가 되었는지(Are you
ready to teach tonight?)를 묻고, 남자가 주방은 믹싱볼과

조리 기구가 준비됐다(The kitchen stations are prepped
and ready with mixing bowls and cooking utensils)고
하므로 (D)가 정답이다.

8 남자는 어떤 문제를 언급하는가?
(A) 날씨가 안 좋을 것으로 예상된다.
(B) 가전제품이 고장 났다.
(C) 손님 명단이 승인되지 않았다.
(D) 배송 물품이 도착하지 않았다.

해설 | **남자가 언급한 문제점**
남자가 대사에서 식품 배송이 오늘 오후에 일찍 올 걸로
기대했다(But I was expecting our food shipment
earlier this afternoon)고 하므로 (D)가 정답이다.

어휘 | appliance 가전제품   approve 승인하다

9 여자는 어떻게 돕겠다고 말하는가?
(A) 물품을 가져와서
(B) 판매업체를 알아봐서
(C) 직원을 추가로 채용해서
(D) 행사 시간을 변경해서

해설 | **여자가 도움을 주는 방법**
대화 마지막에 여자가 지금 식료품점에 빨리 가서 전부 사
오겠다(I'll hurry over to the grocery store right now to
get everything)고 하므로 (A)가 정답이다.

어휘 | vendor 판매업체

Paraphrasing   대화의 hurry over to the grocery store
right now to get everything → 정답의 picking up some
items

ETS 고득점 실전 문제   본책 p.78

1 (A)	2 (B)	3 (A)	4 (C)	5 (A)	6 (D)
7 (C)	8 (B)	9 (D)	10 (C)	11 (B)	12 (A)
13 (C)	14 (D)	15 (B)	16 (B)	17 (C)	18 (D)
19 (D)	20 (D)	21 (B)	22 (A)	23 (C)	24 (A)

[1-3] M-Au / W-Br

> M Good news, Ji-Min. I have a second interview
>   with GRQ Industries this week!
> W That's great! Interesting that they do two
>   interviews.
> M Yeah, **1** the first one focused on technical
>   things, like my knowledge of algorithms and
>   various computer-coding languages. The
>   second one will be more about me and the
>   actual job.
> W I see.
> M Yeah, **2** I'm a little worried about talking about
>   my management experience—I don't have

much, and the role requires managing a small team that designs new software products.

W You'll be fine! You're a great leader. ³Will you have to relocate, or can you work from home?

남 좋은 소식이 있어요, 지민. 이번 주에 GRQ 인더스트리즈와 2차 면접을 보게 됐어요!

여 잘됐네요! 면접을 2차까지 치른다는 게 흥미로워요.

남 네, ¹1차는 알고리즘과 다양한 컴퓨터 코딩 언어에 관한 지식처럼 기술적인 사항에 중점을 뒀어요. 2차는 저 자신과 실질적인 업무에 관한 것이 될 거예요.

여 그렇군요.

남 네, ²제 관리 경력에 대해 얘기하는 부분이 좀 걱정스러워요. 경력이 많지 않은데, 해당 직책은 신규 소프트웨어 제품을 설계하는 소규모 팀을 관리해야 하거든요.

여 잘하실 거예요! 훌륭한 리더이시잖아요. ³이동하셔야 해요, 아니면 재택근무를 할 수 있어요?

어휘 | technical 기술적인 knowledge 지식 various 다양한 management 관리, 경영 relocate 이전하다, 이동하다 work from home 재택근무하다

---

1 남자의 전문 분야는 무엇이겠는가?
(A) 컴퓨터 프로그래밍 (B) 회계
(C) 인사 (D) 건축

해설 | **남자의 전문 분야**
남자가 두 번째 대사에서 1차 인터뷰는 알고리즘과 다양한 컴퓨터 코딩 언어에 관한 지식처럼 기술적인 사항에 중점을 뒀다(the first one focused on technical things, like my knowledge of algorithms and various computer-coding languages)고 하므로 (A)가 정답이다.

어휘 | accounting 회계 architecture 건축

2 남자가 걱정하는 이유는?
(A) 무엇을 입어야 할지 몰라서
(B) 경력이 충분치 않을 수 있어서
(C) 절차가 비효율적이라고 생각해서
(D) 자격증을 갱신해야 할지도 몰라서

해설 | **남자의 걱정 이유**
남자가 마지막 대사에서 관리 경력에 대해 얘기하는 부분이 경력이 많지 않아서 좀 걱정스럽다(I'm a little worried about talking about my management experience — I don't have much)고 하므로 (B)가 정답이다.

어휘 | inefficient 비효율적인 renew 갱신하다, 재개하다 certification 증명, 자격증

Paraphrasing 대화의 my management experience — I don't have much → 정답의 not have enough experience

3 여자는 남자에게 무엇에 대해 물어보는가?
(A) 업무 지역이 바뀔지 여부
(B) 추천서가 필요한지 여부
(C) 면접을 녹화하는지 여부
(D) 회사에 구인하는 다른 자리가 있는지 여부

해설 | **여자의 문의 사항**
대화 마지막에 여자가 남자에게 이동해야 하는지 아니면 재택근무를 할 수 있는지(Will you have to relocate, or can you work from home?)를 묻고 있으므로 (A)가 정답이다.

어휘 | recommendation letter 추천서 job opening 일자리

Paraphrasing 대화의 have to relocate
→ 정답의 work location will change

[4-6] 3인 대화 W-Am / M-Au / M-Cn

W Nice to meet you, Charles and Jin-Ho. ⁴Thanks for hiring me to help prepare you both for next spring's city marathon. It's a difficult race, but we're starting early.

M1 ⁵You were recommended by our coworker, Anjali Krishnan. ⁴You trained her for this same marathon several years ago.

M2 Yes, and she credited you for her success. ⁵This year she came in first place in her age group.

W I remember. Now you know, in addition to running, diet and sleep play an important role.

M1 What would you recommend as a sleep regimen?

W I recommend eight hours a night. ⁶Try to go to sleep and wake up at the same time every day.

여 만나서 반가워요, 찰스, 진호. ⁴내년 봄에 있을 시 마라톤 준비를 돕도록 저를 채용해 주셔서 감사합니다. 힘든 경주지만 우리는 시작을 일찍 하는 거예요.

남1 ⁵저희 동료 안잘리 크리슈난이 당신을 추천했어요. ⁴몇 년 전 같은 마라톤 대회를 위해 그녀를 훈련시켜 주셨다고요.

남2 맞아요, 그녀는 자신의 성공을 당신의 공으로 돌렸어요. ⁵올해 그녀의 나이대에서 1등을 했죠.

여 기억해요. 아시겠지만 달리기 이외에 식단과 수면도 중요한 역할을 합니다.

남1 수면 요법으로 무엇을 권장하시나요?

여 8시간 수면을 권장해요. ⁶매일 같은 시간에 잠자리에 들고 일어나도록 하세요.

어휘 | credit A for B B를 A의 공으로 돌리다 come in first place 1등을 차지하다 in addition to ~에 더해 play an important role 중요한 역할을 하다 regimen 요법

---

4 여자는 누구이겠는가?
(A) 스포츠 담당 기자 (B) 내과 의사
(C) 피트니스 트레이너 (D) 행사 기획자

해설 | **여자의 신분**
여자가 첫 대사에서 내년 봄에 있을 마라톤 준비를 돕도록 채용해 줘서 고맙다(Thanks for hiring me to help prepare you both for next spring's city marathon)고 하자 남자 1이 몇 년 전 같은 마라톤 대회를 위해 그의 동료를 훈련시켜 주었다(You trained her for this same marathon several years

ago)고 상기시켜 주므로 여자의 직업이 피트니스 트레이너임을 추론할 수 있다. 따라서 (C)가 정답이다.

어휘 | physician 내과 의사

5 안잘리 크리슈난은 올해 무엇을 했는가?
(A) 경주에 참가했다.
(B) 새로운 일자리에 지원했다.
(C) 장학금을 받았다.
(D) 사업을 성공적으로 개시했다.

해설 | **안잘리 크리슈난이 올해 한 일**
남자 1이 첫 대사에서 동료 안잘리 크리슈난이 추천했다(You were recommended by our coworker, Anjali Krishnan)고 했으며, 남자 2가 올해 그녀의 나이대에서 1등을 했다(This year she came in first place in her age group)고 하므로 (A)가 정답이다.

어휘 | apply for 지원하다, 신청하다　scholarship 장학금

6 여자는 남자들에게 무엇을 하라고 권하는가?
(A) 매일 기록하기
(B) 팀 규모 늘리기
(C) 추가로 더 많은 전문가들에게 이야기하기
(D) 일관된 일정 유지하기

해설 | **여자의 권고 사항**
대화 마지막에 여자가 매일 같은 시간에 잠자리에 들고 일어나도록 하라(Try to go to sleep and wake up at the same time every day)고 하므로 (D)가 정답이다.

어휘 | keep a record 기록하다　maintain 유지하다
consistent 한결 같은, 일관된

Paraphrasing 대화의 sleep and wake up at the same time every day → 정답의 Maintain a consistent schedule

[7-9] M-Au / W-Br

> M　Hello, can I help you with something?
> W　Yes, [7]I saw your ad in the paper for this brand of carpet. [8]I like the pale blue color, but I'm concerned it will stain easily.
> M　[8]Oh, you shouldn't worry about that. It's made out of a treated material that makes the fibers extremely resistant to stains.
> W　Thanks, that's good to know. [9]Do you also install the carpets you sell?
> M　[9]Yes. As a matter of fact, that cost is included in the price.
>
> 남　안녕하세요, 도와드릴 일이 있나요?
> 여　네, [7]신문에 실린 귀사의 카펫 광고를 봤는데요. [8]연한 파란색이 마음에 드는데 쉽게 얼룩질까 봐 걱정되네요.
> 남　[8]아, 그건 걱정하지 않으셔도 됩니다. 섬유가 얼룩에 매우 강하도록 처리된 소재로 만들어졌거든요.
> 여　감사합니다, 좋은 정보네요. [9]판매하는 카펫을 깔아 주기도 하시나요?
> 남　[9]네. 사실 설치 비용이 가격에 포함되어 있습니다.

어휘 | concerned 걱정하는　stain 얼룩지다, 더러워지다
resistant to ~에 저항하는, 내성이 있는　as a matter of fact 사실

7 여자가 특별히 해당 매장을 방문한 이유는?
(A) 이웃이 추천했다.
(B) 진열창에서 물품을 보았다.
(C) 신문 광고를 봤다.
(D) 할인 쿠폰을 갖고 있다.

해설 | **여자가 매장을 방문한 이유**
여자가 첫 대사에서 신문에 실린 귀사의 카펫 광고를 봤다(I saw your ad in the paper for this brand of carpet)고 하므로 (C)가 정답이다.

Paraphrasing 대화의 I saw your ad in the paper
→ 정답의 She saw a newspaper advertisement.

8 남자는 제품에 대해 무엇이라고 말하는가?
(A) 손바느질했다.　　(B) 쉽게 얼룩지지 않는다.
(C) 한정판의 일부이다.　(D) 다양한 색상이 있다.

해설 | **남자가 제품에 대해 언급한 것**
여자가 첫 대사에서 연한 파란색이 마음에 드는데 쉽게 얼룩질까 봐 걱정된다(I like the pale blue color, but I'm concerned it will stain easily)고 하자 남자가 그건 걱정하지 않아도 되며 섬유가 얼룩에 매우 강하도록 처리된 소재로 만들어졌다(It's made out of a treated material that makes the fibers extremely resistant to stains)고 하므로 (B)가 정답이다.

어휘 | stitch 바느질하다　limited edition 한정판

9 남자는 가격에 무엇이 포함되어 있다고 말하는가?
(A) 할인　　　　　(B) 품질 보증서
(C) 특급 배송　　　(D) 설치

해설 | **가격에 포함된 것**
여자가 마지막 대사에서 남자가 판매하는 카펫을 깔아 주는지(Do you also install the carpets you sell?) 묻자, 남자는 그(설치) 비용이 가격에 포함되어 있다(Yes. As a matter of fact, that cost is included in the price)고 답하므로 (D)가 정답이다.

어휘 | warranty 품질 보증서

[10-12] M-Au / W-Am

> M　Hello. You've reached Greenway Apartments. How can I help you?
> W　Hi, my name's Maria Fontana. [10]I moved into one of your rental units yesterday. Suite 3B on Oak Street. [11]I tried to use the stove, but it won't turn on.
> M　I'm sorry to hear that. We'll have our repair technician take a look and fix it if necessary. Will you be home this afternoon?
> W　Yes, I'll be here all day, unpacking.

M OK, **12**let me check with the technician, but he should be able to stop by soon.

W Thanks, I appreciate the help!

남 여보세요. 그린웨이 아파트입니다. 어떻게 도와드릴까요?

여 안녕하세요, 저는 마리아 폰타나라고 해요. **10**임대하시는 **아파트에 어제 입주했어요.** 오크 가 3B실인데요. **11 가스레인지를 사용하려고 했는데 켜지지 않아서요.**

남 죄송합니다. 저희 수리 기술자가 한 번 보고 필요하면 수리할 수 있도록 할게요. 오늘 오후에 집에 계세요?

여 네, 하루 종일 짐을 풀면서 집에 있을 거예요.

남 네, **12**그럼 기술자에게 확인해 보겠지만 곧 들을 수 있을 겁니다.

여 도와주셔서 감사합니다!

어휘 | unpack 짐을 풀다 stop by 잠깐 들르다

10 남자는 누구이겠는가?
(A) 건설 도급업자   (B) 건축가
(C) 부동산 관리인   (D) 인테리어 디자이너

해설 | **남자의 신분**
여자가 첫 대사에서 남자가 임대하는 아파트에 어제 입주했다(I moved into one of your rental units yesterday)고 하므로 남자는 부동산 관리인임을 추론할 수 있다. 따라서 (C)가 정답이다.

어휘 | contractor 계약인, 도급업체

11 여자는 어떤 문제를 보고하는가?
(A) 주소가 잘못되었다.
(B) 가전제품이 작동하지 않는다.
(C) 배달 트럭이 늦게 왔다.
(D) 약속을 놓쳤다.

해설 | **여자가 언급한 문제점**
여자가 첫 대사에서 가스레인지를 사용하려고 했는데 켜지지 않는다(I tried to use the stove, but it won't turn on)고 하므로 (B)가 정답이다.

어휘 | appliance 가전제품, 기기

Paraphrasing 대화의 the stove → 정답의 An appliance
대화의 won't turn on → 정답의 is not working

12 남자는 무엇을 할 것이라고 말하는가?
(A) 직원에게 연락   (B) 지불 처리
(C) 마감일 연장   (D) 계약서 검토

해설 | **남자가 할 일**
대화 마지막에 남자가 기술자에게 확인해 보겠다(let me check with the technician)고 하므로 (A)가 정답이다.

Paraphrasing 대화의 check with the technician
→ 정답의 Contact a worker

[13-15] W-Br / M-Cn

W Can I help you?

M Yes—**13**I have a nine-thirty appointment with Dr. Umaru for a physical examination. My last name is Sanchez.

W OK, let's see… It looks like this is your first visit, **14**so here's some new-patient paperwork you need to fill out.

M Sure. Should I give you the completed forms?

W No, please turn them in to Dr. Umaru—she'll need to see them.

M OK, thanks.

W One other thing… **15**I'd recommend getting our mobile application. You can use the app to schedule upcoming appointments and pay your bills.

여 제가 도와드릴까요?

남 네, **13**9시 30분에 우마루 박사님께 건강 검진 예약이 되어 있는데요. 제 성은 산체스입니다.

여 네, 한번 볼게요. 첫 방문이신 것 같네요. **14**여기 작성하셔야 할 신규 환자 서류가 있습니다.

남 알겠습니다. 작성한 서류를 드려야 하나요?

여 아니요, 우마루 박사님께 드리세요. 보셔야 할 겁니다.

남 네, 감사합니다.

여 한 가지 더요… **15**저희 모바일 앱을 쓰시는 것을 권장합니다. 앱을 이용해서 앞으로 있을 예약 일정을 잡고 비용을 지불할 수 있거든요.

어휘 | appointment 약속, 예약 physical examination 건강 검진 fill out 작성하다, 기입하다 turn in 제출하다 pay the bill 비용을 지불하다

13 화자들은 어디에 있겠는가?
(A) 미용실   (B) 피트니스 센터
(C) 병원   (D) 자동차 수리점

해설 | **대화 장소**
남자가 첫 대사에서 9시 30분에 우마루 박사님께 건강 검진 예약이 되어 있다(I have a nine-thirty appointment with Dr. Umaru for a physical examination)고 한 것으로 보아 (C)가 정답이다.

14 남자는 약속 전 무엇을 해야 하는가?
(A) 옷 갈아입기   (B) 차 옮기기
(C) 결제하기   (D) 서류 작성하기

해설 | **남자가 약속 전 해야 할 것**
여자가 두 번째 대사에서 여기 작성하셔야 할 신규 환자 서류가 있다(so here's some new-patient paperwork you need to fill out)고 하므로 정답은 (D)이다.

어휘 | make a payment 결제하다 complete a form 서류를 작성하다

Paraphrasing 대화의 some new-patient paperwork you need to fill out → 정답의 Complete some forms

15 여자는 무엇을 하라고 제안하는가?
(A) 버스 시간표 확인하기   (B) 모바일 앱 다운로드하기
(C) 기사 읽기   (D) 로비에서 기다리기

해설 | 여자의 제안 사항

대화 마지막에 여자가 모바일 앱을 쓸 것을 권장(I'd recommend getting our mobile application)하므로 (B)가 정답이다.

Paraphrasing 대화의 getting our mobile application
→ 정답의 Downloading a mobile application

[16-18] M-Au / W-Am

M Simone, many employees have been complaining that they don't know what's going on in the company.

W ¹⁶Well, we've nearly doubled our staff this year, so it's been hard to keep everyone up to date.

M ¹⁷I was thinking we should have weekly staff meetings—maybe just 30 minutes to give everyone an update on company news.

W I like the idea. ¹⁷My only concern is that it'll be difficult to find a time when everyone can go.

M Most people are here on Wednesday mornings. I'll set something up.

W ¹⁸Could you also arrange catering? I think if we offer coffee and bagels, it could turn out to be quite successful.

남 시몬, 많은 직원들이 회사에 일어나는 일들에 대해 모른다고 불평하고 있어요.

여 ¹⁶음, 올해 직원이 거의 두 배로 늘었죠. 그래서 모두에게 최신 정보를 알려 주기가 어려워요.

남 ¹⁷주간 직원회의를 해야 한다고 생각하고 있었어요. 30분 정도만 해서, 모두에게 회사 최신 소식을 알려주는 거죠.

여 좋네요. ¹⁷단 한 가지 우려되는 건 모두가 참여할 수 있는 시간을 잡기가 어려울 거라는 점이에요.

남 대부분 수요일 오전에 여기 있어요. 제가 준비해 볼게요.

여 ¹⁸음식도 마련해 주실 수 있나요? 커피와 베이글을 제공하면 꽤 성공적일 것 같은데요.

어휘 | nearly 거의   **keep ~ up to date** ~에게 최신 정보를 제공하다

---

16 화자들은 무엇에 대해 이야기하는가?

(A) 주간 매출 목표 달성하기
(B) 직원들에게 정보 알리기
(C) 직원들에게 재택 근무 허용하기
(D) 다른 지점 열기

해설 | 대화의 주제

여자가 첫 대사에서 올해 직원이 거의 두 배로 늘어서 모두에게 최신 정보를 알려 주기가 어렵다(it's been hard to keep everyone up to date)고 하므로 (B)가 정답이다.

어휘 | meet a goal 목표를 달성하다   **keep informed** 정보를 알리다, 통보하다   **work from home** 재택 근무하다

Paraphrasing 대화의 keep everyone up to date
→ 정답의 Keeping employees informed

17 여자는 무엇에 대해 우려하는가?

(A) 부정적인 고객 피드백   (B) 부동산 가격 상승
(C) 회의 시간 잡기   (D) 생산성 감소

해설 | 여자의 우려 사항

남자가 두 번째 대사에서 주간 직원회의를 해야 한다고 생각한다(I was thinking we should have weekly staff meetings)고 하자 여자는 모두가 참여할 수 있는 시간을 잡기가 어려울 것이 우려된다(My only concern is that it'll be difficult to find a time when everyone can go)고 하므로 (C)가 정답이다.

어휘 | decrease 하락, 감소   **productivity** 생산성

18 여자는 남자에게 무엇을 해 달라고 요청하는가?

(A) 안건 출력하기
(B) 회의실 열기
(C) 점검에 대비하기
(D) 행사를 위한 음식 주문하기

해설 | 여자의 요청 사항

대화 마지막에 여자가 음식도 마련해 줄 수 있는지(Could you also arrange catering?)를 묻고 있으므로 (D)가 정답이다.

어휘 | conference room 회의실   **inspection** 점검, 검열

Paraphrasing 대화의 arrange catering
→ 정답의 Order food for an event

[19-21] M-Au / W-Br

M Nancy, since you're the shift supervisor I wanted to speak with you right away.

W Why? ¹⁹Are we going to make our production deadline? Is there an issue on the assembly line?

M Well, ²⁰a shipment of metal casings didn't arrive today as expected, and that's a problem. Without them, we'll have to halt production of our solar panels in a few hours.

W Does Yuri know? He's the supply coordinator.

M Yes, he's already on the phone with the shipper.

W OK, thanks for letting me know. ²¹I'll see if I can participate in the call.

남 낸시, 교대근무 관리자이시니 지금 이야기를 나누고 싶어요.

여 왜요? ¹⁹생산 마감 기한을 맞출 수 있겠어요? 조립 라인에 문제가 있나요?

남 음, ²⁰금속 케이싱 배송이 오늘 예상대로 도착하지 않아서 문제입니다. 그게 없으면 몇 시간 후 태양 전지판 생산을 중단해야 할 거예요.

여 유리가 알아요? 공급 담당자잖아요.

남 네, 이미 배송업체와 통화 중입니다.

여 네, 알려 줘서 고마워요. ²¹통화에 참여할 수 있는지 확인해 봐야겠어요.

어휘 | supervisor 감독관   **deadline** 기한   **assembly** 조립   **casing** 케이싱(기계의 내부를 밀폐하기 위해 피복 역할을 하는 부분)   **halt** 중단시키다

19 화자들은 어디서 일하겠는가?

(A) 수리점   (B) 백화점
(C) 체육 시설   (D) 공장

해설 | 화자들의 근무 장소
여자가 첫 대사에서 생산 마감 기한과 조립 라인(Are we going to make our production deadline? Is there an issue on the assembly line?)에 대해 언급하고 있으므로 공장에서 근무하고 있을 거라고 추론할 수 있다. 따라서 (D)가 정답이다.

어휘 | facility 시설

20 남자는 어떤 문제를 언급하는가?

(A) 기계가 고장 났다.   (B) 주문이 취소됐다.
(C) 직원이 도착하지 않았다. (D) 배송이 지연됐다.

해설 | 남자가 언급한 문제점
남자가 두 번째 대사에서 금속 케이싱 배송이 오늘 예상대로 도착하지 않아서 문제(a shipment of metal casings didn't arrive today as expected, and that's a problem)라고 하므로 (D)가 정답이다.

어휘 | break down 고장 나다

Paraphrasing 대화의 a shipment of metal casings didn't arrive today as expected
→ 정답의 A shipment was delayed.

21 여자는 다음으로 무엇을 하겠는가?

(A) 공급 목록 업데이트하기 (B) 통화 참여하기
(C) 이메일 쓰기   (D) 설명서 확인하기

해설 | 여자가 다음에 할 일
대화 마지막에 여자가 통화에 참여할 수 있는지 확인해 봐야겠다(I'll see if I can participate in the call)고 하므로 (B)가 정답이다.

어휘 | manual 설명서

Paraphrasing 대화의 participate in the call
→ 정답의 Join a telephone call

[22-24] W-Am / M-Au

W Good morning, Hiroshi. **22**What's the status on the grant that we're submitting to the Department of Transportation?
M The one that provides funds for traffic signal maintenance?
W Yes, **23**I was thinking about revising one of the details on the application.
M Oh. **22**I submitted it right before the deadline.
W I understand. I hope we're approved anyway. This would be a great opportunity—our traffic signals are really outdated.
M I agree! **24**It will be more energy efficient if we're able to attach solar panels to the posts.

여 안녕하세요, 히로시. **22**교통부에 제출할 보조금은 상황이 어떤가요?
남 신호등 유지 보수를 위한 기금 제공 보조금이요?
여 네, **23**신청 관련 세부 사항 중 하나를 변경할까 생각 중이라서요.
남 아. **22**마감 직전에 제출했어요.
여 그래요. 어쨌든 승인이 됐으면 좋겠네요. 정말 좋은 기회가 될 겁니다. 신호등이 무척 낡았으니까요.
남 맞아요! **24**기둥에 태양 전지판을 부착할 수 있다면 에너지 효율이 훨씬 높을 겁니다.

어휘 | status 상황 **grant** 보조금 **fund** 기금 **maintenance** 유지 보수 **revise** 변경하다, 수정하다 **application** 신청 **outdated** 구식의, 매우 낡은 **energy efficient** 에너지 효율성이 좋은 **solar panel** 태양 전지판

22 화자들은 무엇을 신청했는가?

(A) 보조금   (B) 대출
(C) 계약   (D) 허가증

해설 | 화자들이 신청한 것
여자가 첫 대사에서 교통부에 제출할 보조금 상황에 대해 묻자(What's the status on the grant that we're submitting to the Department of Transportation?) 남자는 두 번째 대사에서 마감 직전에 제출했다(I submitted it right before the deadline)고 답하므로 (A)가 정답이다.

어휘 | loan 대출 **permit** 허가증

23 남자가 "마감 직전에 제출했어요"라고 말할 때, 그 의도는 무엇인가?

(A) 절차를 개선해야 한다. (B) 동료가 시간이 안 된다.
(C) 바꿀 수가 없다.   (D) 연체료가 부과되지 않았다.

해설 | 화자의 의도
여자가 두 번째 대사에서 신청 관련 세부 사항 중 하나를 변경할까 생각 중이었다(I was thinking about revising one of the details on the application)고 말하자 남자는 마감 직전에 이미 제출했다고 응답하는 것을 보아 세부 사항을 변경할 수 없다고 볼 수 있다. 따라서 (C)가 정답이다.

어휘 | late fee 연체료

Paraphrasing 대화의 revising → 정답의 change

24 화자들은 어떤 기술을 사용하고 싶어 하는가?

(A) 태양 전지판
(B) 전기차
(C) 비접촉 결제 시스템
(D) 대량 수송 전철

해설 | 사용하고 싶어하는 기술
대화 마지막에 남자가 기둥에 태양 전지판을 부착할 수 있다면 에너지 효율이 훨씬 높을 것(It will be more energy efficient if we're able to attach solar panels to the posts)이라고 하므로 (A)가 정답이다.

어휘 | contactless 비접촉식의 **payment** 결제 **high-capacity** 대용량의, 고성능의

요청·제안 / 다음에 할 일 문제

1 요청·제안 문제

고득점 전략 **단서 포착하기** 본책 p.80

남	안녕하세요, 마리, 니콜라이. 역사지구에 정류장 몇 개를 더 만들어서 버스 노선을 추가하는 프로젝트가 어떻게 되어가는지 알고 싶었어요. 알다시피 시에서는 여름 관광 시즌까지 운영되기를 원해요.
여	네. 새 노선에 있는 정류장 표지판 다는 일을 처리하라고 요청하셨는데요. 이미 그 내용을 작업 지시서에 넣어 두었어요.
남	좋아요. 해당 노선을 맡을 기사를 더 채용하는 일은 어떻게 됐나요? 니콜라이, 지금까지 받은 지원서를 검토해 보셨어요?

어휘 | **historic district** 역사지구 **in operation** 가동 중인, 운영 중인 **application** 지원서, 신청서 **so far** 지금까지

문제 | 여자는 무엇을 하라고 요청 받았는가?
(A) 허가증 신청 (B) 웹사이트 업데이트
(C) 표지판 요청 (D) 다과 주문

어휘 | **permit** 허가증 **refreshments** 다과

ETS 유형 연습 본책 p.81

1 (D)	**2** (B)	**3** (A)	**4** (B)	**5** (D)	**6** (A)
7 (D)	**8** (A)	**9** (B)			

[1-3] W-Br / M-Au

W Hi Sanjay. You have experience editing digital photographs, right? ¹I'm calling to ask a favor. I have a picture that I'd really like to use for my Web site, but there's a hotel billboard in the background. How hard would it be for you to remove it?

M Well, it doesn't sound too difficult, ²but it really depends on the picture. Can you send it to me so I can see what it looks like?

W Oh, great—I really appreciate it! I'll e-mail it to you right now. Please let me know if it's too much trouble though. ³I usually ask my coworker Tomas to help me with things like this. But he's working on another project and he doesn't have any time.

여 안녕하세요, 산제이. 디지털 사진 편집 경력이 있으시죠, 그렇죠? ¹부탁드리려고 전화했어요. 제 웹사이트에 정말 쓰고 싶은 사진이 있는데 배경에 호텔 광고판이 나와 있어서요. 없애 주시기 어려울까요?

남 음, 그리 어렵지 않을 것 같은데요. ²하지만 사진에 따라 무척 달라요. 어떤지 볼 수 있도록 사진을 저에게 보내 주시겠어요?

여 아, 좋아요. 정말 감사합니다! 지금 바로 이메일로 보낼게요. 하지만 너무 어렵다면 말씀해 주세요. ³보통 이런 일은 동료 토마스에게 도와 달라고 요청하는데요. 그가 다른 프로젝트를 맡고 있어서 시간이 없어요.

어휘 | **edit** 편집하다 **ask a favor** 부탁하다 **billboard** 광고판 **depend on** ~에 달려 있다 **coworker** 동료

1 여자가 전화를 건 목적은?
(A) 제안하려고 (B) 제품을 주문하려고
(C) 배송을 확인하려고 (D) 도움을 청하려고

해설 | **전화의 목적**
여자가 첫 번째 대사에서 부탁하려고 전화했다(I'm calling to ask a favor)고 하므로 (D)가 정답이다.

어휘 | **make a suggestion** 제안하다 **confirm** 확인하다

Paraphrasing 대화의 ask a favor
→ 정답의 ask for assistance

2 남자는 여자에게 무엇을 해 달라고 요청하는가?
(A) 사진 촬영 준비하기 (B) 사진 보내기
(C) 청구서 제출하기 (D) 연락처 제공하기

해설 | **남자의 요청 사항**
남자가 첫 대사에서 사진에 따라 편집 가능 여부가 달라지므로 (but it really depends on the picture), 어떤지 볼 수 있도록 그것(사진)을 보내 달라고 요청(Can you send it to me so I can see what it looks like?)하므로 (B)가 정답이다.

어휘 | **arrange** 준비하다, 마련하다 **invoice** 청구서, 송장

Paraphrasing 대화의 the picture → 정답의 a photograph

3 여자는 자신의 부서에 있는 동료에 대해 무엇이라고 말하는가?
(A) 매우 바쁘다. (B) 승진했다.
(C) 예술가를 추천했다. (D) 메시지를 삭제했다.

해설 | **여자가 부서 동료에 대해 언급한 것**
대화 마지막에 여자가 보통 이런 일은 동료 토마스에게 도와 달라고 요청하는데 그가 다른 프로젝트를 맡고 있어서 시간이 없다(I usually ask my coworker Tomas to help me ~ he's working on another project and he doesn't have any time)고 하므로 (A)가 정답이다.

어휘 | **department** 부서 **promote** 승진시키다 **delete** 삭제하다

Paraphrasing 대화의 he doesn't have any time
→ 정답의 He is very busy.

[4-6] W-Am / M-Cn

W ⁴I'm calling to find out if I can take my bicycle on the intercity train and if there are any restrictions.

M Yes, you can take your bicycle on the train. However, it gets really crowded in the morning and at night during rush hour, so ⁵I suggest you travel between the hours of 10:00 A.M. and 4:00 P.M.

W Oh, OK. Is there any way I can reserve a place now for the bike?

M ⁶I'm sorry, but storage racks for bicycles are available on a first-come, first-served basis… however, trains run pretty often, so if space is not available on one, you'll have plenty of chances to get on another.

여 ⁴도시 간 열차에 자전거를 가지고 탈 수 있는지, 제한이 있는지 알아보려고 전화했어요.

남 네, 가지고 타실 수 있습니다. 하지만 혼잡 시간대인 아침과 밤에는 무척 붐벼요. 그래서 ⁵오전 10시와 오후 4시 사이 시간대에 이동하시는 것을 추천합니다.

여 아, 알겠습니다. 지금 자전거 자리를 예약할 방법이 있을까요?

남 ⁶죄송하지만 자전거 보관대는 선착순으로 이용 가능합니다. 하지만 열차가 꽤 자주 운행되니 자리가 없다면 다른 열차를 탈 수 있는 기회가 아주 많습니다.

어휘 | intercity 도시 간의 restriction 제한 storage rack 보관대, 보관 선반 available 이용 가능한 on a first-come, first served basis 선착순으로 plenty of 많은

4 여자는 무엇을 하고 싶어 하는가?
 (A) 반려동물 데리고 이동하기
 (B) 자전거 실어 나르기
 (C) 단체 여행 준비하기
 (D) 특급 노선 이용하기

해설 | 여자가 하고 싶은 것
여자가 첫 번째 대사에서 도시 간 열차에 자전거를 가지고 탈 수 있는지를 알아보려고 전화했다(I'm calling to find out if I can take my bicycle on the intercity train)고 하므로 (B)가 정답이다.

어휘 | transport 수송하다, 실어 나르다 arrange 주선하다, 마련하다

Paraphrasing 대화의 take my bicycle on the intercity train → 정답의 Transport a bicycle

5 남자는 여자에게 무엇을 하라고 제안하는가?
 (A) 버스로 환승 (B) 신용카드로 결제
 (C) 특수 캐리어 구입 (D) 특정 시간대에 이동

해설 | 남자의 제안 사항
남자의 첫 번째 대사에서 오전 10시와 오후 4시 사이 시간대에 이동할 것을 추천한다(I suggest you travel between the hours of 10:00 A.M. and 4:00 P.M.)고 하므로 (D)가 정답이다.

어휘 | transfer 갈아타다 specific 특정한

Paraphrasing 대화의 between the hours of 10:00 A.M. and 4:00 P.M. → 정답의 during a specific time

6 남자가 사과하는 이유는?
 (A) 보관대를 예약할 수 없어서
 (B) 일부 열차가 연착되어서
 (C) 탑승권을 교환할 수 없어서
 (D) 역이 공사 중이어서

해설 | 남자의 사과 이유
대화 마지막에 남자가 죄송하지만 자전거 보관대는 선착순으로 이용 가능하다(I'm sorry, but storage racks for bicycles are available on a first-come, first-served basis)고 하므로 (A)가 정답이다.

어휘 | under construction 공사 중인

Paraphrasing 대화의 storage racks for bicycles are available on a first-come, first-served basis → 정답의 A storage space cannot be reserved.

[7-9] 3인 대화 W-Am / M-Au / W-Br

W1 Thanks for meeting with me, Diego and Mei Na. ⁷I'd like your ideas on how our interior-design firm can use marketing to increase our client base.

M Well, we already do a lot of advertising online, so I was thinking we could take a different approach: we could design a brochure. What do you think, Mei Na?

W2 Good idea, ⁸but mailing brochures would be expensive. Why not collaborate with real estate agents? They can give our brochures to their clients. That'll eliminate postage fees.

M Good point, Mei Na. If we go that route, ⁹I'm happy to e-mail local agents and see if they'd want to partner with us.

여1 만나 주셔서 감사합니다, 디에고, 메이 나. ⁷저희 인테리어 디자인 회사의 고객층 확대를 위해 마케팅을 어떻게 활용해야 하는지 의견 주신 내용이 좋았어요.

남 음, 저희는 이미 온라인 광고를 많이 하고 있어서 다른 접근법을 취할 수 있을 거라고 생각했습니다. 안내 책자를 디자인하는 거죠. 어떻게 생각하세요, 메이 나?

여2 좋은 생각이네요, ⁸그런데 안내 책자 발송에 돈이 많이 들 거예요. 부동산 중개업체와 협력하면 어때요? 그들이 우리 안내 책자를 고객들에게 줄 수 있을 겁니다. 그럼 우편 요금이 안 드니까요.

남 좋은 지적입니다, 메이 나. 그렇게 할 거라면 ⁹제가 지역 중개업체에 이메일을 써서 제휴를 원하는지 알아볼게요.

어휘 | client base 고객층 approach 접근법, 처리 방법 collaborate with ~와 협력하다 real estate 부동산 eliminate 없애다 postage fee 우편 요금 local 지역의

7 회의를 한 목적은?
 (A) 모금 행사를 계획하려고
 (B) 설문조사 결과를 검토하려고
 (C) 새로운 고객을 소개하려고
 (D) 마케팅 아이디어에 관해 논의하려고

PART 3

해설 | 회의의 목적

여자 1이 첫 번째 대사에서 인테리어 디자인 회사의 고객층 확대를 위해 마케팅을 어떻게 활용해야 하는지 의견을 준 내용이 좋았다(I'd like your ideas on how our interior-design firm can use marketing to increase our client base)고 하므로 (D)가 정답이다.

어휘 | fund-raising event 모금 행사

---

8 메이 나는 무엇을 걱정하는가?

(A) 비용   (B) 직원 채용
(C) 기한   (D) 교통편

해설 | 메이 나의 우려 사항

여자 2의 대사에서 안내 책자 발송에 돈이 많이 들 거라(mailing brochures would be expensive)고 하므로 (A)가 정답이다.

어휘 | staffing 직원 채용   **deadline** 기한

Paraphrasing 대화의 expensive → 정답의 Costs

---

9 남자는 무엇을 하겠다고 제안하는가?

(A) 디자인 트렌드 조사   (B) 이메일 발송
(C) 장소 확인   (D) 계약서 초안 작성

해설 | 남자의 제안 사항

대화 마지막에 남자가 지역 중개업체에 이메일을 쓰겠다(I'm happy to e-mail local agents)고 하므로 (B)가 정답이다.

어휘 | draft 초안을 작성하다   **contract** 계약, 계약서

Paraphrasing 대화의 e-mail local agents
→ 정답의 Send some e-mails

---

❷ 다음에 할 일 문제

고득점 전략 단서 포착하기   본책 p.82

> 여   안녕하세요, 사토 재활용센터입니다.
> 남   안녕하세요, 귀사에서 자재를 구입하고 싶은데요. 밀크 저그와 주스 병에서 재활용된 플라스틱이요.
> 여   아쉽게도 저희는 플라스틱 가공을 중단했습니다. 음, 필요하신 물건을 갖고 있을 것 같은 다른 재활용 업체를 알고 있어요. 분명히 제 책상에 전화번호가 있을 거예요. 잠시만요.
>
> **어휘 | milk jug** 밀크 저그(홍차용 우유 주전자)   **material** 재료, 자재

문제 | 여자는 다음으로 무엇을 하겠는가?

(A) 관리자가 시간이 되는지 확인하기
(B) 생산 일정 확인하기
(C) 연락처 찾기
(D) 배송비 계산하기

어휘 | production 생산   **calculate** 계산하다

ETS 유형 연습   본책 p.83

1 (D)	2 (A)	3 (D)	4 (B)	5 (D)	6 (A)
7 (B)	8 (D)	9 (A)			

[1-3] M-Cn / W-Am

> M   Hi, Ji-Min. At our last town council meeting, we talked about bringing more tourists to the area. I had an idea. ¹We could repair historic Seaview Manor so that it could be open to visitors.
> W   You know, we've considered that, ²but the main problem is that we don't have money in the budget to make the necessary repairs. Some are quite expensive.
> M   I've heard of an organization that provides funding for these types of projects. ³They're having a workshop to explain how to apply for a grant—I'll attend so that we can see if it's something we should do.
>
> 남   안녕하세요, 지민. 지난번 마을 의회 회의에서 지역 내 관광객들을 더 많이 유치하는 일에 관해 이야기했잖아요. 저에게 좋은 생각이 있어요. ¹역사적인 씨뷰 매너를 보수해 관광객들에게 개방할 수 있도록 하는 겁니다.
> 여   음, 저희도 고려했던 사항인데요. ²하지만 가장 큰 문제는 필요한 보수를 하기 위한 예산이 없다는 거예요. 일부는 돈이 꽤 들더군요.
> 남   이런 유형의 프로젝트에 자금을 대는 단체에 대해 들은 적이 있어요. ³거기서 보조금 신청 방법을 설명해 주는 워크숍을 열 겁니다. 제가 참석해서 이것을 우리가 하면 좋을지 알아보도록 하죠.
>
> **어휘 | town council** 마을 의회   **historic** 역사적으로 중요한, 역사적인   **budget** 예산   **organization** 단체, 조직   **funding** 자금   **apply for** 신청하다   **grant** 보조금

1 대화는 주로 무엇에 관한 것인가?

(A) 주차장 포장   (B) 교량 건설
(C) 기차역 재개장   (D) 건물 보수

해설 | 대화의 주제

남자가 첫 번째 대사에서 역사적인 씨뷰 매너를 보수할 수 있다(We could repair historic Seaview Manor)고 하므로 (D)가 정답이다.

어휘 | pave 포장하다   **construct** 건설하다

Paraphrasing 대화의 repair historic Seaview Manor
→ 정답의 Renovating a building

2 여자는 어떤 문제에 관해 언급하는가?

(A) 프로젝트 비용이 너무 비쌀 것이다.
(B) 기한을 맞추지 못할 것이다.
(C) 일부 직원들이 시간을 낼 수 없다.
(D) 자재 일부가 도착하지 못했다.

해설 | 여자가 언급한 문제점

여자의 대사에서 가장 큰 문제는 필요한 보수를 하기 위한 예산이 없고 일부는 돈이 꽤 든다(the main problem is that we don't have money ~ Some are quite expensive)고 하므로 (A)가 정답이다.

어휘 | unavailable 구할 수 없는, 시간이 없는

3 남자는 무엇을 할 것이라고 말하는가?
(A) 교육 시간 마련 　　　(B) 관리자에게 연락
(C) 입사 지원서 검토 　　 (D) 워크숍 참석

해설 | 남자가 할 일
대화 마지막에 남자가 워크숍에 참석해서 해야 할 일이 있는지 알아보겠다(They're having a workshop to explain how to apply for a grant—I'll attend so that we can see if it's something we should do)고 하므로 (D)가 정답이다.

어휘 | organize 준비하다 　**job application** 입사 지원서

[4-6] M-Au / W-Br

M You've reached Events Management. David Bryant speaking.
W Morning, David. This is Anna Chung calling. ⁴Thanks for inviting me and my band to play at your music festival.
M Well, hello, Anna. We're looking forward to having you perform. I hope everything's OK with the contract we sent.
W ⁵I noticed that there's no provision for our travel expenses in this contract.
M Since this particular event is a charitable fund-raiser, many of the participants are paying their own way. However, since you're the only ones traveling all the way from the West Coast, ⁶let me speak with my manager to see if we can make an exception. Her office is only two doors down.

남 이벤트 매니지먼트의 데이비드 브라이언트입니다.
여 안녕하세요, 데이비드. 저는 애나 청입니다. **⁴음악 축제에 저희 악단을 초청해 주셔서 감사해요.**
남 아, 안녕하세요, 애나. 공연해 주시기를 고대하고 있어요. 저희가 보내 드린 계약서가 괜찮았으면 좋겠네요.
여 **⁵이 계약서에 저희 여비에 관련된 조항이 없던데요.**
남 이번 행사는 자선 모금 행사라서 참가자들 다수가 직접 여비를 지불하십니다. 하지만 유일하게 웨스트 코스트에서부터 오시니 **⁶저희 관리자에게 이야기해서 예외를 둘 수 있는지 확인할게요.** 관리자 사무실이 옆옆방이거든요.

어휘 | reach (전화로) 연락하다 　**look forward to** 고대하다 **perform** 연주하다, 공연하다 　**contract** 계약, 계약서 **provision** 조항 　**particular** 특정한 　**charitable** 자선의 **fund-raiser** 모금 행사 　**make an exception** 예외를 두다

4 여자는 누구이겠는가?
(A) 출장요리 업자 　　　(B) 음악가
(C) 여행사 직원 　　　　(D) 변호사

해설 | 여자의 신분
여자가 첫 번째 대사에서 저희 악단(my band)이라고 하므로 음악인이라는 것을 추론할 수 있다. 따라서 (B)가 정답이다.

Paraphrasing 대화의 band → 정답의 musician

5 여자는 어떤 문제를 언급하는가?
(A) 항공편이 연착됐다.
(B) 행사가 취소되어야 한다.
(C) 계약서가 전달되지 않았다.
(D) 일부 비용이 처리되지 않는다.

해설 | 여자가 언급한 문제점
여자가 두 번째 대사에서 계약서에 여비 조항이 없다(I noticed that there's no provision for our travel expenses in this contract)고 하므로 (D)가 정답이다.

어휘 | cover 돈을 대다

Paraphrasing 대화의 no provision for our travel expenses → 정답의 Some expenses are not covered.

6 남자는 다음으로 무엇을 하겠는가?
(A) 관리자와 상의 　　　(B) 호텔 객실 예약
(C) 영수증 요청 　　　　(D) 직원 추가 채용

해설 | 남자가 다음에 할 일
대화의 마지막에 남자가 관리자와 이야기하겠다(let me speak with my manager to see)고 하므로 (A)가 정답이다.

어휘 | consult 상의하다 　**additional** 추가의

Paraphrasing 대화의 speak with my manager → 정답의 Consult with a manager

[7-9] W-Am / M-Au

W Hi, Silas. It's Helen. The box of rubber safety gloves in the laboratory has run out. ⁷Could you put more in our supply cabinet?
M ⁸Unfortunately, I can't right now. There aren't any left. I ordered more from our supplier, but the shipment is behind schedule. The supplier assured me, though, that the gloves will be here by noon at the latest.
W Well, I really hope the gloves get here by then. ⁹My partners are coming in at 1:30 to work on an experiment.

여 안녕하세요, 사일러스. 헬렌입니다. 실험실 고무 안전장갑이 다 떨어졌어요. **⁷저희 물품함에 더 채워 주실 수 있나요?**
남 **⁸죄송하지만 지금은 안 돼요. 남은 게 없어요. 공급업체에 더 주문했는데 배송이 일정보다 늦어지고 있어요.** 하지만 공급업체에서 늦어도 정오까지 도착할 거라고 확실히 얘기했어요.
여 음, 그때까지 오면 정말 좋겠네요. **⁹동료들이 실험하러 1시 30분에 오거든요.**

어휘 | laboratory 실험실 　**run out** 다 떨어지다 　**behind schedule** 예정보다 늦게 　**assure** 확언하다, 장담하다 　**at the latest** 늦어도

7 여자는 남자에게 무엇을 해 달라고 요청하는가?
(A) 절차 업데이트하기 　　(B) 물품 채워넣기
(C) 신제품 시식하기 　　　(D) 물품함 재배치하기

해설 | 여자의 요청 사항

여자가 첫 번째 대사에서 물품함에 더 채워 줄 것을 요청(Could you put more in our supply cabinet?)하므로 (B)가 정답이다.

어휘 | procedure 절차 **restock** 다시 채우다 **sample** 시식하다, 시음하다 **rearrange** 재배치하다

Paraphrasing 대화의 put more in our supply cabinet → 정답의 Restock some supplies

8 남자가 도움을 주지 못하는 이유는?
(A) 정보가 충분히 수집되지 않아서
(B) 장비가 고장 나서
(C) 연구원이 현재 시간이 되지 않아서
(D) 배송이 늦어져서

해설 | 남자가 도와주지 못하는 이유

남자의 대사에서 지금은 남은 게 없고 공급업체에 더 주문했는데 배송이 일정보다 늦어지고 있다(the shipment is behind schedule)고 하므로 (D)가 정답이다.

어휘 | out of order 고장 난 **currently** 현재

Paraphrasing 대화의 behind schedule → 정답의 late

9 1시 30분에 무슨 일이 있을 것인가?
(A) 여자의 동료들이 도착할 것이다.
(B) 남자가 상점에 갈 것이다.
(C) 실험실이 문을 닫을 것이다.
(D) 유지 보수팀이 수리를 할 것이다.

해설 | 1시 30분에 일어날 일

대화 마지막에 여자가 동료들이 실험하러 1시 30분에 올 것(My partners are coming in at 1:30 to work on an experiment)이라고 하므로 (A)가 정답이다.

어휘 | colleague 동료 **maintenance** 유지 보수

Paraphrasing 대화의 My partners are coming in → 정답의 The woman's colleagues will arrive.

ETS 고득점 실전 문제
본책 p.84

1 (C)	**2** (D)	**3** (A)	**4** (C)	**5** (D)	**6** (B)
7 (A)	**8** (C)	**9** (D)	**10** (A)	**11** (C)	**12** (D)
13 (B)	**14** (D)	**15** (A)	**16** (A)	**17** (B)	**18** (B)
19 (A)	**20** (A)	**21** (D)	**22** (D)	**23** (B)	**24** (C)

[1-3] W-Br / M-Cn

W Abdullah, **1**air traffic control just radioed us. They said our flight's not cleared for takeoff yet, and we'll have to wait here on the runway.

M Well, our passengers won't be happy about that. Most of them have an overseas connecting flight to make. What's the problem?

W **2**The controller told me there's a fast-moving thunderstorm headed toward the area. We won't be able to start takeoff procedures until that passes.

M OK. **3**I'll get on the intercom system and tell our passengers about it. Can you go ask the flight attendants to pass around some refreshments?

여 압둘라, **1**항공 교통 관제소에서 방금 무전이 왔어요. 우리 항공편이 아직 이륙 허가를 못 받아서 이곳 활주로에서 대기해야 한다고 해요.

남 음, 승객들이 불만이겠네요. 대다수가 해외로 가는 연결 항공편을 타니까요. 문제가 뭔가요?

여 **2**관제사 말로는 이 지역을 향해서 빠르게 움직이는 뇌우가 있다고 합니다. 뇌우가 지나갈 때까지는 이륙 절차를 개시할 수 없을 거예요.

남 알겠습니다. **3**기내 방송을 해서 승객들에게 알릴게요. 승무원들에게 다과를 나눠 주라고 요청해 주시겠어요?

어휘 | air traffic control 항공 교통 관제소 **clear for** ~을 허가하다 **takeoff** 이륙 **runway** 활주로 **connecting flight** 연결 항공편 **thunderstorm** 뇌우 **head toward** ~을 향해서 가다 **procedure** 절차, 수순 **passenger** 승객 **refreshments** 다과

1 화자들은 누구이겠는가?
(A) 공항 안전요원 (B) 세관원
(C) 항공기 조종사 (D) 매표원

해설 | 화자들의 신분

여자가 첫 번째 대사에서 항공 교통 관제소에서 방금 무전이 왔는데(air traffic control just radioed us), 항공편이 아직 이륙 허가를 못 받아서 이곳 활주로에서 대기해야 한다(They said our flight's not cleared for takeoff yet, and we'll have to wait here on the runway)고 하므로 (C)가 정답이다.

어휘 | security guard 안전요원 **customs officer** 세관원

2 연착이 발생한 이유는?
(A) 직원 부족 (B) 유지 보수 문제
(C) 교통 혼잡 (D) 악천후

해설 | 연착 이유

여자가 두 번째 대사에서 관제사 말로는 이 지역을 향해서 빠르게 움직이는 뇌우가 있다(The controller told me there's a fast-moving thunderstorm headed toward the area)고 하므로 (D)가 정답이다.

어휘 | shortage 부족 **maintenance** 유지 보수 **congestion** 혼잡

Paraphrasing 대화의 a fast-moving thunderstorm → 정답의 Poor weather conditions

3 남자는 다음에 무엇을 할 것인가?
(A) 공지하기 (B) 공항 직원에게 연락하기
(C) 신분증 확인하기 (D) 설명서 찾아보기

해설 | **남자가 다음에 할 일**
대화 마지막에 남자가 기내 방송을 해서 승객들에게 알릴 것(I'll get on the intercom system and tell our passengers about it)이라고 하므로 (A)가 정답이다.

어휘 | identification 신분 확인, 신분증

Paraphrasing 대화의 tell our passengers about it
→ 정답의 Make an announcement

[4-6] 3인 대화 W-Am / W-Br / M-Cn

> W1 Oh no... ⁴I think we just missed our train stop.
> W2 Wait, aren't we getting off at Spring Street?
> W1 No, the client's office is on Third Avenue.
> W2 Excuse me, sir, did we pass the stop for Third Avenue?
> M Yes, that was the last station. ⁵But the next stop is coming up soon. You could get off there and walk back a block. It's not far.
> W2 OK, thank you.
> W1 Well, let's do that, Nadia. ⁶Can you ask the client to go straight to the restaurant?
> W2 Yes, I'll send him a message now.
>
> 여1 저런... ⁴우리가 내릴 기차역을 막 지나친 것 같아요.
> 여2 잠시만요, 스프링 가에서 내리지 않나요?
> 여1 아니요, 고객 사무실은 3번 가에 있어요.
> 여2 죄송하지만 3번 가로 가는 역을 지났나요?
> 남 네, 이전 정거장이었어요. ⁵하지만 곧 다음 역입니다. 거기서 내리셔서 한 블록 다시 걸어가세요. 멀지 않거든요.
> 여2 네, 감사합니다.
> 여1 그렇게 하죠, 나디아. ⁶고객에게 식당으로 바로 오시라고 요청해 주시겠어요?
> 여2 네, 지금 메시지를 보낼게요.
>
> 어휘 | go straight to ~으로 곧장 가다

4 대화는 어디서 이뤄지겠는가?
(A) 공원   (B) 택시
(C) 기차   (D) 비행기

해설 | **대화의 장소**
여자 1이 첫 번째 대사에서 내릴 기차역을 막 지나친 것 같다(I think we just missed our train stop)고 하므로 (C)가 정답이다.

5 남자는 여자들에게 무엇을 하자고 제안하는가?
(A) 운전기사에게 돌아가 달라고 요청하기
(B) 회의 취소하기
(C) 환불 요청하기
(D) 다른 역에서 하차하기

해설 | **남자의 제안 사항**
남자가 곧 다음 역이니 거기서 내려서 한 블록 다시 걸어가라(But the next stop is coming up soon. You could get off there and walk back a block.)고 하므로 (D)가 정답이다.

어휘 | refund 환불

Paraphrasing 대화의 the next stop
→ 정답의 a different stop

6 나디아는 고객에게 무엇을 해 달라고 요청할 것인가?
(A) 온라인 결제하기   (B) 식당에서 만나기
(C) 강의실 좌석 맡기   (D) 제품 시식하기

해설 | **나디아의 요청 사항**
여자 1이 마지막 대사에서 고객에게 식당으로 바로 오시라고 요청해 달라(Can you ask the client to go straight to the restaurant?)고 하므로 (B)가 정답이다.

어휘 | make a payment 결제하다   lecture 강의

Paraphrasing 대화의 go straight to the restaurant
→ 정답의 Meet at a restaurant

[7-9] M-Cn / W-Br

> M ⁷Thanks for coming out today to inspect the hotel's pipes. As you saw, the hotel still has the original pipes from when it was built. We want to replace them before we have any problems.
> W Are you thinking, only the pipes? Or do you want us to replace the fixtures too, like the faucets?
> M Just the pipes. ⁸And because we'll remain open during the renovation, the work'll have to be done room by room.
> W That's possible, but it'll increase the cost.
> M How much are we looking at here?
> W ⁹I can put together an estimate of the total amount.
>
> 남 ⁷오늘 호텔 배관 점검을 위해 나와 주셔서 감사합니다. 보다시피 호텔이 건축될 때 있던 원래의 배관이 아직 있어요. 문제가 생기기 전에 교체하고 싶어요.
> 여 배관만 생각하시는 건가요? 아니면 수도꼭지 같은 설비도 교체하길 원하시나요?
> 남 배관만요. ⁸그리고 보수 공사 중에 계속 문을 열 거라서 방마다 차례로 공사를 해야 합니다.
> 여 가능합니다만 비용이 올라갈 겁니다.
> 남 얼마나 될까요?
> 여 ⁹총 금액 견적서를 준비해 드릴 수 있어요.
>
> 어휘 | inspect 점검하다   fixture (천장·벽 등의) 고정물, 설비
> faucet 수도꼭지, 수전   renovation 개조, 보수   estimate
> 견적서

7 여자의 직업은 무엇이겠는가?
(A) 배관공   (B) 안전 감독관
(C) 정원사   (D) 사무실 관리자

해설 | **여자의 신분**
남자가 첫 번째 대사에서 오늘 호텔 배관 점검을 위해 나와 줘서 감사하다(Thanks for coming out today to inspect the hotel's pipes)고 하므로 여자의 직업이 배관공임을 추론할 수 있다. 따라서 (A)가 정답이다.

어휘 | plumber 배관공 safety inspector 안전 감독관
landscaper 정원사, 조경사

8 남자는 보수 기간 동안의 호텔에 대해 무엇이라고 말하는가?
(A) 매일 청소가 이뤄질 것이다.
(B) 가격을 낮출 것이다.
(C) 계속 문을 열 것이다.
(D) 신입사원 채용을 중단할 것이다.

해설 | **남자가 호텔에 대해 말한 것**
남자가 두 번째 대사에서 보수 공사 중에 계속 문을 열 거라(we'll remain open during the renovation)고 하므로 (C)가 정답이다.

9 여자는 무엇을 하겠다고 제안하는가?
(A) 예약   (B) 객실 확인
(C) 물품 구입   (D) 비용 계산

해설 | **여자의 제안 사항**
대화 마지막에 여자가 총 금액 견적서를 준비해 주겠다(I can put together an estimate of the total amount)고 하므로 (D)가 정답이다.

어휘 | make an appointment 약속을 잡다

Paraphrasing 대화의 put together an estimate
→ 정답의 Calculate a cost

[10-12] W-Am / M-Au

> **W** Umesh, **10**remember we talked about a new mobile application for our customers?
>
> **M** I do—the app to track their clothing orders, right? It'll definitely improve the customer experience.
>
> **W** I agree. **11**I think we'll need to hire two full-time programmers for that project.
>
> **M** Have you seen the budget for this year?
>
> **W** Oh, right. Maybe we can make do with only one new hire.
>
> **M** Or maybe hiring a firm to develop the app for us is a better option. **12**I could look into some firms that offer that service this afternoon.
>
> 여 우메쉬, **10**우리가 고객들을 위한 새 모바일 앱에 대해 얘기 나눈 거 기억해요?
>
> 남 네. 의류 주문을 추적하는 앱 말이죠, 맞죠? 분명 고객 경험을 향상시킬 겁니다.
>
> 여 맞아요. **11**그 프로젝트를 위해 정규직 프로그래머를 두 명 더 채용해야 할 것 같아요.
>
> 남 올해 예산 보셨나요?
>
> 여 아, 맞아요. 아마 신입 사원 한 명만 고용할 수 있겠네요.
>
> 남 아니면 앱을 개발해 줄 업체를 고용하는 것이 더 나아요. **12**오늘 오후에 해당 서비스를 제공하는 업체들을 알아볼게요.

어휘 | definitely 분명, 확실히 customer experience 고객 경험

10 화자들은 무엇에 대해 주로 이야기하는가?
(A) 소프트웨어 개발   (B) 신입사원 교육
(C) 장비 주문   (D) 불만 사항 응대

해설 | **대화의 주제**
여자가 첫 번째 대사에서 고객들을 위한 새 모바일 앱에 대해 얘기 나눈 것을 기억하는지(remember we talked about a new mobile application for our customers?)를 묻고 있으므로 (A)가 정답이다.

어휘 | respond to ~에 대응하다 complaint 불평, 항의

Paraphrasing 대화의 a new mobile application
→ 정답의 Developing some software

11 남자가 "올해 예산 보셨나요?"라고 말할 때, 그 의도는 무엇인가?
(A) 결정을 내려야 한다고 생각한다.
(B) 자료 일부가 없다.
(C) 제안에 대해 의구심이 든다.
(D) 작업이 언제 끝날지 알고 싶다.

해설 | **화자의 의도**
여자가 두 번째 대사에서 그 프로젝트를 위해 정규직 프로그래머를 두 명 더 채용해야 할 것 같다(I think we'll need to hire two full-time programmers for that project)고 했고, 이에 대해 남자가 '올해 예산 보셨나요?(Have you seen the budget for this year?)'라고 묻는데 이는 여자의 제안이 올해 예산을 초과하게 되므로 적절하지 않다는 의미이므로 (C)가 정답이다.

어휘 | have doubt about ~에 대해 의심을 품다

12 남자는 오늘 오후에 무엇을 할 것인가?
(A) 설문지 발송
(B) 새 컴퓨터 구입
(C) 업무 일정 변경
(D) 업체 조사

해설 | **남자가 오늘 오후에 할 일**
대화 마지막에 남자가 오늘 오후에 해당 서비스를 제공하는 업체들을 알아보겠다(I could look into some firms that offer that service this afternoon)고 하므로 (D)가 정답이다.

어휘 | research 조사하다, 연구하다

Paraphrasing 대화의 look into some firms
→ 정답의 Research some companies

[13-15] W-Br / M-Cn

> **W** Thanks for meeting with me, Alberto. **13**I'm excited we'll be launching the summer line of women's casual wear soon.
>
> **M** Yes, the designs are great. There is one issue, though. **14**The linen supplier we were hoping to use won't be able to provide all of the fabric we'll need.
>
> **W** I see. **14**We'll need to look into using other sources, then. Can you do some research this week?

M Absolutely. ¹⁵I'll e-mail you my findings on Wednesday.

W Great, thank you. It may take me some time to get back to you ¹⁵because I'll be out that afternoon for a medical checkup.

여 만나주셔서 감사합니다, 알베르토. ¹³여성 여름 캐주얼 의류를 곧 출시하게 되어 기뻐요.

남 네, 디자인이 훌륭합니다. 그런데 한 가지 문제가 있어요. ¹⁴우리가 이용하고 싶은 리넨 공급업체가 우리에게 필요한 옷감을 전부 공급하지는 못할 것 같아요.

여 알겠어요. ¹⁴그럼 다른 공급업체를 알아봐야겠네요. 이번 주에 조사해 주실 수 있나요?

남 그럼요. ¹⁵수요일에 조사 결과를 이메일로 보내드리겠습니다.

여 좋아요, 고맙습니다. ¹⁵제가 그날 오후엔 건강검진 때문에 자리에 없어서 답장하는 데 시간이 좀 걸릴 거예요.

어휘 | launch 출시하다 absolutely 틀림없이 findings 조사 결과 medical checkup 건강검진

13 화자들의 회사는 무엇을 생산하는가?
(A) 커튼   (B) 의류
(C) 가구   (D) 여행 가방

해설 | 회사가 생산하는 것
여자가 첫 번째 대사에서 여성 여름 캐주얼 의류를 곧 출시하게 되어 기쁘다(I'm excited we'll be launching the summer line of women's casual wear soon)고 하므로 (B)가 정답이다.

어휘 | luggage 여행 가방, 수화물

Paraphrasing 대화의 casual wear → 정답의 Clothing

14 여자는 남자에게 무엇을 해 달라고 요청하는가?
(A) 제조시설 방문
(B) 재고 조사 보고서 완료
(C) 유지보수 요청서 제출
(D) 직물 공급업체 조사

해설 | 여자의 요청 사항
남자가 첫 번째 대사에서 리넨 공급업체가 옷감을 전부 공급하지는 못할 것 같다(The linen supplier ~ won't be able to provide all of the fabric)고 하자, 여자가 다른 공급업체를 알아봐야겠다고 하면서 남자에게 이번 주에 조사해 줄 수 있는지(We'll need to look into using other sources, then. Can you do some research this week?)를 요청하므로 (D)가 정답이다.

어휘 | manufacturing 제조 facility 시설 inventory 재고, 물품 목록

Paraphrasing 대화의 The linen → 정답의 fabric

15 여자가 수요일 오후에 자리를 비우는 이유는?
(A) 진료 예약에 갈 예정이라서
(B) 회계사를 만날 예정이라서
(C) 새 사무실로 이사할 예정이라서
(D) 가족 행사에 참석할 예정이라서

해설 | 여자가 자리를 비우는 이유
대화 마지막에 여자가 그날 오후엔 건강검진 때문에 자리에 없다(because I'll be out that afternoon for a medical checkup)고 하므로 (A)가 정답이다.

어휘 | accountant 회계사

Paraphrasing 대화의 be out ~ for a medical checkup → 정답의 be at a medical appointment

[16-18] 3인 대화 W-Am / W-Br / M-Cn

W1 Hi, Mr. Sanchez. Thanks for meeting us here at our warehouse.

W2 Yes, Geeta and I are excited to discuss our vision for transforming it into an art gallery.

M ¹⁶I like transforming older interiors into modern spaces. ¹⁷When do you plan on opening?

W2 On June sixth.

M That could work. ¹⁸I'd like to do a concept study—spend time here at different times of the day to see how the space interacts with the natural light.

여1 안녕하세요, 산체스 씨. 저희 창고에 와 주셔서 감사합니다.

여2 네, 기타와 저는 창고를 화랑으로 바꾸려는 저희 생각을 논의하게 되어 기뻐요.

남 ¹⁶오래된 인테리어를 현대적인 공간으로 변모시키는 작업을 좋아합니다. ¹⁷언제 문을 열 계획이세요?

여2 6월 6일이요.

남 괜찮겠네요. ¹⁸콘셉트 연구를 하고 싶은데요. 다양한 시간대에 이곳에서 시간을 보내며 공간이 자연광과 어떻게 상호작용하는지 보고 싶습니다.

어휘 | warehouse 창고 transform 완전히 바꾸다, 변형시키다 interact with ~와 상호작용하다, 교류하다

16 남자의 직업은 무엇이겠는가?
(A) 인테리어 디자이너   (B) 전기 기사
(C) 식당 요리사   (D) 연구원

해설 | 남자의 신분
남자가 첫 번째 대사에서 오래된 인테리어를 현대적인 공간으로 변모시키는 작업을 좋아한다(I like transforming older interiors into modern spaces)고 하므로 (A)가 정답이다.

어휘 | electrician 전기 기사

17 남자는 여자들에게 어떤 정보를 물어보는가?
(A) 우편 주소   (B) 개관일
(C) 주문번호   (D) 생산 비용

해설 | 남자가 묻는 정보
남자가 첫 번째 대사에서 언제 문을 열 계획인지(When do you plan on opening?)를 묻고 있으므로 (B)가 정답이다.

어휘 | mailing address 우편 주소

18 남자는 무엇을 할 계획이라고 말하는가?
(A) 도서관 방문　　　　　(B) 연구 진행
(C) 전문가 인터뷰　　　　(D) 온라인 조사

해설 | 남자가 계획하는 일
대화 마지막에 남자가 콘셉트 연구를 하고 싶다(I'd like to do a concept study)고 하므로 (B)가 정답이다.

어휘 | conduct 실시하다, 수행하다

Paraphrasing 대화의 do a concept study
→ 정답의 Conduct a study

[19-21] W-Br / M-Au

> W　George, **19**I was thinking about the new guided bus tour to Hampton National Park we're going to operate. We really should decide what route we're going to take.
>
> M　I was thinking about that, too. In fact, I marked some possible routes on the map. There's a direct route that'd give us more time in the park. Or we could take the longer scenic route with more stops along the way.
>
> W　OK, **20**let's look at your map. Hmm. I like the longer route. It looks more interesting.
>
> M　Yes, I agree. But before we decide, **21**let's drive the two routes to see which we like better. Then I'll start working on the tour material.
>
> 여　조지, 햄튼 국립공원에서 운영할 **19**새로운 버스 가이드 투어에 대해 생각해 보고 있었는데요. 어떤 노선으로 갈지 꼭 결정해야 해요.
>
> 남　저도 그 생각을 하고 있었어요. 사실 가능한 노선들을 지도에 표시해 봤는데요. 공원에서 시간을 더 보낼 수 있는 직선로가 있어요. 아니면 노선에 더 많은 정류장을 배치한 더 길고 경치 좋은 노선으로 갈 수도 있고요.
>
> 여　좋아요, **20**지도를 한번 보죠. 음. 저는 긴 노선이 좋은데요. 더 흥미로워 보여요.
>
> 남　네, 맞아요. 하지만 결정하기 전에 **21**두 노선을 달려 봐서 어느 쪽이 더 좋은지 확인해 보죠. 그러고 나서 투어 자료 작업을 시작할게요.
>
> **어휘 | direct route** 직선로　**scenic** 경치가 좋은

19 화자들의 업체는 어떤 서비스를 제공하는가?
(A) 가이드 투어　　　　(B) 촬영
(C) 행사 기획　　　　　(D) 자전거 대여

해설 | 화자들의 업체가 제공하는 서비스
여자가 첫 번째 대사에서 새로운 버스 가이드 투어에 대해 생각해 보고 있었다(I was thinking about the new guided bus tour)고 하므로 (A)가 정답이다.

20 화자들은 어떤 자료를 찾아보는가?
(A) 도로 지도　　　　　(B) 달력
(C) 회사 웹사이트　　　(D) 훈련 교재

해설 | 화자들이 찾아보는 자료
여자가 두 번째 대사에서 지도를 보자고 하면서 긴 노선이 좋다(let's look at your map)고 하므로 (A)가 정답이다.

어휘 | consult 찾아보다

21 남자는 무엇을 하자고 제안하는가?
(A) 특별 할인 제공　　　(B) 고객에게 피드백 요청
(C) 사진 촬영　　　　　(D) 선택지 확인

해설 | 남자의 제안 사항
대화 마지막에 남자가 두 노선을 달려 봐서 어느 쪽이 더 좋은지 확인해 보자(let's drive the two routes to see which we like better)고 하므로 (D)가 정답이다.

Paraphrasing 대화의 see which we like better
→ 정답의 Testing some options

[22-24] W-Br / M-Cn

> W　Mustafa! **22**I heard that the building plans your team designed for the new science museum were approved. Congratulations!
>
> M　Thanks! It took us over a year to complete the blueprints.
>
> W　So, is your team doing anything to celebrate?
>
> M　**23**I just made a reservation at Noriko's Restaurant for next Friday.
>
> W　**23**There's an architectural design convention in New York next Friday. Almost everybody from our office is going.
>
> M　Oh, right, I forgot. In that case, **24**I'd better call Noriko's Restaurant to explain the situation.
>
> 여　무스타파! **22**당신의 팀이 신규 과학 박물관을 위해 디자인한 건축 설계가 승인됐다고 들었어요. 축하해요!
>
> 남　고마워요! 청사진을 완성하는 데 일 년이 넘게 걸렸어요.
>
> 여　팀에서 축하하기 위해 뭐라도 하나요?
>
> 남　**23**다음 주 금요일 노리코 레스토랑에 예약했어요.
>
> 여　**23**다음 주 금요일엔 뉴욕에서 건축 설계 대회가 있는데요. 우리 사무실 대다수가 가잖아요.
>
> 남　아, 맞아요. 깜빡했네요. 그러면 **24**노리코 레스토랑에 전화해서 상황 설명을 하는 편이 낫겠네요.
>
> **어휘 | approve** 승인하다　**complete** 완료하다　**blueprint** 청사진, 계획　**make a reservation** 예약하다　**architectural** 건축학의

22 화자들은 어디서 일하겠는가?
(A) 소프트웨어 회사　　(B) 광고대행사
(C) 연구소　　　　　　(D) 건축사무소

해설 | 화자들의 근무 장소
여자가 첫 번째 대사에서 당신의 팀이 신규 과학 박물관을 위해 디자인한 건축 설계가 승인됐다고 들었다(the building plans your team designed)고 하므로 화자들이 건축사무소에 근무한다고 추론할 수 있다. 따라서 (D)가 정답이다.

어휘 | research laboratory 연구소

23 여자가 "우리 사무실 대다수가 가잖아요"라고 말할 때, 그 의도는 무엇인가?

(A) 남자가 대형 버스를 예약했으면 한다.

(B) 남자가 일정을 변경해야 한다고 생각한다.

(C) 예산 초과를 우려한다.

(D) 회의가 매우 인기 있었다는 것을 깨닫지 못했다.

해설 | 화자의 의도

남자가 두 번째 대사에서 다음 주 금요일 노리코 레스토랑에 예약했다(I just made a reservation at Noriko's Restaurant for next Friday)고 말하자 여자가 다음 주 금요일엔 뉴욕에서 건축 설계 대회가 있으며(There's an architectural design convention in New York next Friday) 우리 사무실 대다수가 간다(Almost everybody from our office is going)고 말하는 것은 레스토랑 예약 일정 변경이 필요할 거라는 의도이므로 (B)가 정답이다.

어휘 | be concerned about ~을 걱정하다, 우려하다 **exceed** 초과하다 **budget** 예산

24 남자는 무엇을 하겠다고 말하는가?

(A) 이메일 인쇄하기　　　(B) 카드에 서명하기

(C) 전화하기　　　　　　(D) 발표 준비하기

해설 | 남자가 할 일

대화 마지막에 남자가 노리코 레스토랑에 전화해서 상황 설명을 하는 편이 낫겠다(I'd better call Noriko's Restaurant to explain the situation)고 하므로 (C)가 정답이다.

Paraphrasing 대화의 call

→ 정답의 Make a telephone call

 UNIT 12 의도 파악 / 시각 정보 연계 문제

① 의도 파악 문제

고득점 전략 **단서 포착하기**　　　본책 p.86

남　시몬, 복사기에 대해 아는 거 있어요? 오늘 오후 회의를 위해 인쇄물을 복사하려고 하는데, 백지만 인쇄되네요.

여　아. 어떻게 고치는지 모르겠어요. 우리 기술지원팀이 아주 잘하는데요.

남　네. 하지만 우선 작동되는지 한 번 더 해 봐야겠어요.

어휘 | handout 인쇄물, 유인물

문제 | 여자가 "우리 기술지원팀이 아주 잘하는데요"라고 말한 이유는?

(A) 결정에 대해 불만을 제기하려고

(B) 놀라움을 표하려고

(C) 제안을 거절하려고

(D) 추천하려고

어휘 | refuse 거절하다

ETS 유형 연습　　　　　　　본책 p.87

| **1** (D) | **2** (A) | **3** (C) | **4** (B) | **5** (C) | **6** (D) |
| **7** (D) | **8** (B) | **9** (A) |

[1-3] M-Cn / W-Am

M　Welcome to Zepo's! I see you already have a menu. Are you ready to order?

W　Not just yet. **1**I'm waiting for a friend… she should arrive soon.

M　Great! While you're waiting, **2**I want to let you know that we're offering a special four-course meal today. It comes with an appetizer, a salad, a main course, and a dessert.

W　That's a lot of food.

M　Well, for something lighter, the menu options are also wonderful. The chef here is excellent.

W　Yes, everything looks interesting. Oh, I should probably ask—**3**do you accept credit cards?

M　Unfortunately, no. But there's a bank directly across the street.

남　제포스에 오신 것을 환영합니다! 이미 메뉴를 받으셨군요. 주문하실 준비가 되셨나요?

여　아직이요. **1**친구를 기다리고 있는데, 곧 도착할 거예요.

남　알겠습니다! 기다리시는 동안 **2**오늘 저희가 4코스 특별 요리를 제공하고 있음을 알려드려요. 전채요리, 샐러드, 정식, 후식이 나옵니다.

여　음식이 많네요.

남　음, 더 가볍게 드시려면 메뉴에 나온 음식들도 훌륭합니다. 요리사가 뛰어나시거든요.

여　네, 다 좋아 보이네요. 아, **3**신용카드를 받으시는지 여쭤봐야겠군요.

남　죄송하지만 안 됩니다. 하지만 길 바로 건너편에 은행이 있어요.

어휘 | appetizer 전채요리 **accept** 받아 주다, 수락하다

1 여자가 무엇을 기다리고 있는가?

(A) 메뉴　　　　　　　　(B) 전화

(C) 서빙 직원　　　　　　(D) 친구

해설 | 여자가 기다리는 것

여자가 첫 번째 대사에서 친구를 기다리고 있다(I'm waiting for a friend)고 하므로 (D)가 정답이다.

2 여자가 "음식이 많네요"라고 말한 이유는?

(A) 제안을 거절하려고

(B) 오해를 바로잡으려고

(C) 정책에 대해 불만을 제기하려고

(D) 도움을 청하려고

해설 | 화자의 의도

남자가 두 번째 대사에서 4코스 특별 요리를 제안하자(I want to let you know that we're offering a special four-course meal today. It comes with an appetizer, a

---

salad, a main course, and a dessert.) 여자가 음식이
많다(That's a lot of food)고 응답한 것으로 보아 여자가
남자의 제안을 거부한 것임을 알 수 있다. 따라서 (A)가
정답이다.

어휘 | decline 거절하다   correct 바로잡다, 정정하다   policy
정책   assistance 도움

3 여자는 무엇에 대해 물어보는가?
(A) 요리사 이름   (B) 조리법
(C) 결제 방식   (D) 폐점 시간

해설 | 여자의 문의 사항
여자가 마지막 대사에서 신용카드를 받는지(do you accept
credit cards?)를 묻고 있으므로 (C)가 정답이다.

어휘 | payment 결제

[4-6] W-Br / M-Cn

W	Good morning. How may I help you?
M	Hi, I'm supposed to be boarding a flight to Hong Kong in fifteen minutes, but I have a problem. ^{4, 5}I don't know what gate.
W	I can check. Oh, ⁵I'm sorry, my computer's down, but the airline has a mobile phone application.
M	Oh right, I forgot. Let me take a look. I see, my gate's in Terminal Two.
W	That's on the other side of the airport.
M	Oh! Will I be able to make it there on time?
W	It's a twenty-minute walk, but ⁶if you take the airport shuttle you can make it there in ten.
M	Thank you so much!

여   안녕하세요. 어떻게 도와드릴까요?
남   안녕하세요, 15분 후에 홍콩행 비행기를 타야 하는데 문제가
     생겼어요. ^{4, 5}어떤 게이트인지 모르겠네요.
여   제가 확인해 드릴 수 있습니다. 아, ⁵죄송하지만 제 컴퓨터가
     작동하지 않아요. 하지만 항공사의 휴대전화 앱이 있어요.
남   아, 네. 깜빡했어요. 한번 볼게요. 아, 제 게이트는 2번 터미널에
     있네요.
여   거긴 공항 반대편입니다.
남   아! 제시간에 도착할 수 있을까요?
여   걸어서 20분 걸리지만 ⁶공항 셔틀을 타시면 10분 만에 도착할 수
     있어요.
남   감사합니다!

어휘 | be supposed to ~하기로 되어 있다, ~할 예정이다
make it 시간 맞춰 가다

4 남자에게 어떤 문제가 있는가?
(A) 항공편을 놓쳤다.   (B) 게이트 번호를 모른다.
(C) 탑승권을 잃어버렸다.   (D) 좌석을 바꾸고 싶어 한다.

해설 | 남자의 문제
남자가 첫 번째 대사에서 어떤 게이트인지 모르겠다(I don't
know what gate)고 하므로 (B)가 정답이다

어휘 | boarding pass 탑승권

Paraphrasing 대화의 I don't know what gate
→ 정답의 He does not know his gate number.

5 여자가 "항공사의 휴대전화 앱이 있어요"라고 말한 이유는?
(A) 고객 의견을 요청하려고
(B) 연착에 대해 설명하려고
(C) 제안하려고
(D) 오류를 정정하려고

해설 | 화자의 의도
남자가 첫 번째 대사에서 어떤 게이트인지 모르겠다(I don't
know what gate)고 하자 여자가 컴퓨터가 작동하지
않는다(I'm sorry, my computer's down)고 하면서 대신에
항공사의 휴대전화 앱이 있다(the airline has a mobile
phone application)고 응답했다. 여자가 휴대전화 앱을 사용할
것을 제안하므로 (C)가 정답이다

어휘 | correct 바로잡다, 정정하다

6 남자는 다음으로 무엇을 하겠는가?
(A) 정식 항의   (B) 항공편 일정 변경
(C) 게이트 직원에게 전화   (D) 셔틀 탑승

해설 | 남자가 다음에 할 일
여자가 마지막 대사에서 공항 셔틀을 타면 10분 만에 도착할 수
있다(if you take the airport shuttle you can make it
there in ten)고 하므로 (D)가 정답이다.

어휘 | file a complaint 항의를 제기하다   official 공식의

[7-9] M-Au / W-Br

M	Summerville Garden Landscapers. How can I help you?
W	Hi. ⁷I got your phone number from my neighbor. Your company just built some flower beds in her garden. I need help with a project for my yard as well.
M	OK. What did you have in mind?
W	Well, ⁸I'm looking for someone with expertise in native plants. I'd like to use plants that don't require much watering.
M	Oh, I've done three projects like that this month.
W	Perfect.
M	If you'd like to see what I've done, ⁹I have some pictures I can forward to you.
W	Thanks, that'd be great.

남   서머빌 가든 랜스케이퍼입니다. 어떻게 도와드릴까요?
여   안녕하세요. ⁷이웃에게서 전화번호를 받았어요. 이웃 정원에
     화단을 만들어 주셨더라고요. 저희 마당을 위한 프로젝트에도
     도움이 필요해서요.
남   네. 어떤 걸 염두에 두고 계세요?
여   음, ⁸자생 식물을 전문으로 하는 분을 찾고 있어요. 물을 많이
     주지 않아도 되는 식물을 이용하고 싶어요.
남   아, 이번 달에 그런 프로젝트를 세 건 완료했어요.
여   좋네요.

남　제가 한 작업을 보고 싶으시면 **9사진을 보내드릴 수 있습니다.**
여　감사합니다, 잘됐군요.

어휘 | have in mind 염두에 두다　expertise 전문성
forward 전달하다, 보내 주다

---

7 여자는 어디서 업체에 대해 들었는가?
(A) 동료　　　　　　　(B) 웹사이트
(C) 라디오 광고　　　　(D) 이웃

해설 | 여자가 업체를 알게 된 계기
여자가 첫 번째 대사에서 이웃에게서 전화번호를 받았다(I got
your phone number from my neighbor)고 하므로 (D)가
정답이다.

어휘 | coworker 동료

8 남자가 "이번 달에 그런 프로젝트를 세 건 완료했어요"라고 말할
때, 그 의도는 무엇인가?
(A) 일정이 꽉 차 있다.
(B) 경력이 많다.
(C) 새로운 스타일이 인기 있다.
(D) 일부 작업은 오래 걸리지 않을 것이다.

해설 | 화자의 의도
여자가 두 번째 대사에서 자생 식물을 전문으로 하는 분을 찾고
있으며 물을 많이 주지 않아도 되는 식물을 이용하고 싶다(I'm
looking for someone with expertise in native
plants. I'd like to use plants that don't require much
watering.)고 말하자 남자가 이번 달에 그런 프로젝트를 세
건 완료했다(I've done three projects like that this
month)고 응답하는 것은 본인에게 경험이 많다는 의미이므로
(B)가 정답이다.

9 남자는 무엇을 보내겠다고 제안하는가?
(A) 사진　　　　　　　(B) 참고 문헌
(C) 씨앗　　　　　　　(D) 설명서

해설 | 남자가 보내 줄 것
남자가 마지막 대사에서 사진을 보내드릴 수 있다(I have some
pictures I can forward to you)고 하므로 (A)가 정답이다.

어휘 | reference 참고 문헌, 추천서　instructions 설명, 지시

❷ 시각 정보 연계 문제

고득점 **전략** **단서 포착하기**　　　　　본책 p.88

여　안녕하세요, 랜스턴 미술관에 오신 것을 환영합니다. 입장권을
구입하시겠어요?
남　아니요. 저는 아닐 프라사드라고 하는데요. 오늘 사진 촬영
차 왔습니다. 미술관 2월 잡지에 특집 예술가편으로 실릴
예정입니다.
여　아, 알겠습니다. 홍보 담당자에게 전화해서 오셨다고
알리겠습니다.
남　좋습니다. 감사합니다. 사실 커피를 마시고 싶은데요. 담당자께
준비되시면 카페에서 뵙는 것으로 요청해 주실 수 있을까요?

어휘 | feature 특별히 포함하다　publicity 홍보

┌─────────────────┐
│ 1층: 상설 전시회 │
│ **2층: 카페** │
│ 3층: 기념품점 │
│ 4층: 특별 전시 │
└─────────────────┘

어휘 | permanent 영구적인, 상설의

문제 | 시각 정보에 따르면, 남자는 다음으로 몇 층에 갈 것인가?
(A) 1층　　　　　　　(B) 2층
(C) 3층　　　　　　　(D) 4층

ETS 유형 연습　　　　　　　　본책 p.89

1 (B)　**2** (A)　**3** (D)　**4** (B)　**5** (D)　**6** (A)

[1-3] W-Am / M-Au

W　Hello, welcome to RKE Consulting.
M　Hi, my name's Yan Chen. I have a two
o'clock appointment with Julie Farooq—**¹I'm
interviewing for a marketing position.**
W　OK, I see your appointment here. Ms. Farooq's
on the third floor, office number 307. If you take
the elevators, **²don't use the elevator closest
to the windows.** It's been running slowly today.
M　Good to know.
W　I'll notify Ms. Farooq that you're here. But
before you head up, I have to make you a
visitor's badge. **³I'll just need to see an ID.**

여　안녕하세요, RKE 컨설팅에 오신 것을 환영합니다.
남　안녕하세요, 저는 얀 첸이라고 해요. 줄리 파루크와 2시 정각에
약속이 잡혀 있어요. **¹마케팅 직책 면접을 볼 겁니다.**
여　네, 여기 약속이 되어 있네요. 파루크 씨는 3층 307호실에
계십니다. 엘리베이터를 타시게 되면 **²창문과 가장 가까운
엘리베이터는 이용하지 마세요.** 오늘 느리거든요.
남　좋은 정보네요.
여　파루크 씨께 오셨다고 알릴게요. 하지만 가시기 전에 방문객
명찰을 만들어 드려야 해요. **³신분증을 확인해야 합니다.**

어휘 | notify 알리다, 통보하다

어휘 | entrance 입구

---

1 남자가 RKE 컨설팅을 찾은 이유는?
(A) 마케팅 발표를 하려고   (B) 면접을 보려고
(C) 신규 고객을 만나려고   (D) 기계를 점검하려고

해설 | 남자가 특정 업체를 찾은 이유
남자가 첫 번째 대사에서 마케팅 직책 면접을 볼 것(I'm interviewing for a marketing position)이라고 하므로 (B)가 정답이다.

어휘 | inspect 조사하다, 점검하다

Paraphrasing 대화의 for a marketing position
→ 정답의 for a job

2 시각 정보에 따르면, 남자는 어떤 엘리베이터를 타면 안 되는가?
(A) 1번 엘리베이터   (B) 2번 엘리베이터
(C) 3번 엘리베이터   (D) 4번 엘리베이터

해설 | 시각 정보 연계
여자가 두 번째 대사에서 창문과 가장 가까운 엘리베이터는 이용하지 말라(don't use the elevator closest to the windows)고 하는데 평면도를 보면 창문 가장 가까이에 1번 엘리베이터가 위치해 있으므로 (A)가 정답이다.

3 남자는 다음으로 무엇을 하겠는가?
(A) 자신의 차로 돌아가기   (B) 이메일 주소 제공하기
(C) 지원서 제출하기   (D) 신분증 보여주기

해설 | 남자가 다음에 할 일
대화 마지막에 여자가 신분증을 확인해야 한다(I'll just need to see an ID)고 하므로 (D)가 정답이다.

어휘 | application 신청서, 지원서   **identification** 신분증

Paraphrasing 대화의 see an ID
→ 정답의 Show his identification

[4-6] M-Cn / W-Am

M Theresa, **4**can we talk about our diner in Elmdale?

W Sure. That restaurant opened just over a year ago. Is everything OK?

M It's just, I've been reviewing our numbers from last year. **5**We didn't get as many lunch customers at the Elmdale location during the winter as we had expected. The summer figure was actually the lowest, but we anticipated that since the university is closed then.

W Well—**6**our estimates were based on revenue from our other diners in the city center, where there's more foot traffic during the winter than in Elmdale.

M That's a good point.

남 테레사, **4**엘름데일에 있는 우리 식당에 대해 얘기 나눌 수 있나요?

여 그럼요. 그 식당은 1년여 전에 개업했어요. 별일 없죠?

남 작년 수치를 검토했는데요. **5**겨울 동안 엘름데일 매장에 점심 고객들이 예상했던 것만큼 많이 오지 않았어요. 여름 수치가 사실상 가장 낮지만 그때는 대학교가 문을 닫았기 때문에 그렇게 예상했죠.

여 음, **6**저희 추정치는 도심에 있는 저희 다른 식당의 수익을 토대로 한 거예요. 겨울철엔 엘름데일보다 유동인구가 많죠.

남 좋은 지적이네요.

어휘 | diner 식당, 식사 손님   **expect** 예상하다, 기대하다
figure 수치   **anticipate** 예상하다   **estimate** 추정, 추산
be based on ~을 근거로 하다, 토대로 하다   **revenue** 수입
foot traffic 유동인구

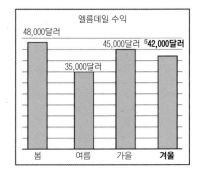

4 화자들은 어떤 업계에 종사하겠는가?
(A) 제조업   (B) 요식업
(C) 출판업   (D) 소매업

해설 | 화자들이 종사하는 업계
남자가 첫 번째 대사에서 엘름데일에 있는 우리 식당에 대해 얘기 나눌 수 있는지(can we talk about our diner in Elmdale?)를 묻고 있으므로 화자들이 요식업에 종사하고 있음을 추론할 수 있다. 따라서 (B)가 정답이다.

어휘 | publishing 출판   **retail** 소매

5 시각 정보에 따르면, 예상 밖의 수치는 어느 것인가?
(A) 48,000달러   (B) 35,000달러
(C) 45,000달러   (D) 42,000달러

해설 | 시각 정보 연계
남자가 두 번째 대사에서 겨울 동안 엘름데일 매장에 예상했던 것만큼 점심 고객들이 오지 않았다(We didn't get as many lunch customers at the Elmdale location during the winter as we had expected)고 하므로 겨울 동안의 수치가 예상 밖이라는 것을 알 수 있다. 그래프를 보면 겨울철에 $42,000로 나와 있으므로 (D)가 정답이다.

어휘 | unexpected 예상 밖의

6 여자에 따르면, 추정치는 어떻게 냈는가?
(A) 다른 매장의 매출을 고려해서
(B) 업계 인맥과 이야기를 나눠서
(C) 웹사이트의 통계를 이용해서
(D) 외부 자문위원을 채용해서

해설 | **추정치를 내는 방법**

여자가 마지막 대사에서 추정치는 도심에 있는 다른 식당의 수익을 토대로 한 것(our estimates were based on revenue from our other diners in the city center)이라고 하므로 (A)가 정답이다.

어휘 | contact 연줄, 인맥   statistics 통계

Paraphrasing   대화의 revenue from our other diners
→ 정답의 sales from other locations

ETS 고득점 실전 문제
본책 p.90

1 (C)	**2** (D)	**3** (C)	**4** (D)	**5** (D)	**6** (C)
7 (D)	**8** (B)	**9** (A)	**10** (D)	**11** (C)	**12** (C)
13 (D)	**14** (A)	**15** (A)	**16** (D)	**17** (C)	**18** (A)
19 (B)	**20** (A)	**21** (D)	**22** (A)	**23** (B)	**24** (C)

[1-3] M-Cn / W-Br

> **M** Thanks for letting me visit, Dr. Sanchez. **1**Our company has just released some new equipment that could be very useful for your dentistry practice.
>
> **W** Sure. Are you talking about your new machine for cleaning dental instruments?
>
> **M** Yes. **2**It's our patented Lockbox Machine, an ultrasonic cleaner designed specifically for dental offices. And best of all, our research shows that it saves time!
>
> **M** Well, we're not as busy here as you would think.
>
> **M** **3**I'd still like to leave the demo machine here with you. Try it out for a week and then let me know what you think.

> **남** 방문하게 해 주셔서 감사합니다, 산체스 박사님. **1**저희가 귀하의 치과에서 아주 유용하게 쓰일 새 장비를 출시했습니다.
>
> **여** 네. 치과 의료 기구를 세척하는 새 기계 말씀이세요?
>
> **남** 네. **2**특허 등록된 락박스 머신입니다. 특별히 치과를 위해 설계된 초음파 세척기예요. 무엇보다도 저희 연구 결과에 따르면 시간이 절감됩니다!
>
> **여** 음, 저희는 생각하시는 것만큼 바쁘지 않아서요.
>
> **남** **3**그래도 시연 기계를 두고 갔으면 합니다. 1주일 동안 써 보시고 어떻게 생각하시는지 알려 주세요.

어휘 | release 출시하다   equipment 장비   dentistry 치과학   practice (의사, 변호사 등의) 사무실   dental instrument 치과 의료 기구   patented 특허 등록된, 특허를 받은   ultrasonic 초음파의   specifically 특별히

1 대화는 어디서 이루어지겠는가?
(A) 피트니스 센터 　　(B) 대학교 강의실
(C) 치과 　　(D) 약국

해설 | **대화 장소**

남자가 첫 번째 대사에서 귀하의 치과에서 아주 유용하게 쓰일 새 장비를 출시했다(Our company has just released some new equipment that could be very useful for your dentistry practice)고 하므로 치과에서 이루어지는 대화임을 추론할 수 있다. 따라서 (C)가 정답이다.

어휘 | pharmacy 약국

Paraphrasing   대화의 dentistry practice
→ 정답의 dental clinic

---

2 여자가 "저희는 생각하시는 것만큼 바쁘지 않아서요"라고 말할 때, 그 의도는 무엇인가?
(A) 다른 곳으로 이전하고 싶다.
(B) 신규 고객과 협력할 수 있다.
(C) 자신의 업체에 대해 염려스럽다.
(D) 제품에 관심이 없다.

해설 | **화자의 의도**

남자가 두 번째 대사에서 특허 등록된 락박스 머신은 특별히 치과를 위해 설계된 초음파 세척기로 시간이 절감된다(It's our patented Lockbox Machine, an ultrasonic cleaner designed specifically for dental offices. And best of all, our research shows that it saves time!)고 말하자 여자가 생각하시는 것만큼 바쁘지 않다(we're not as busy here as you would think)고 응답했다. 즉, 바쁘지 않아서 시간이 절감되는 세척기가 필요하지 않다는 의미이므로 (D)가 정답이다.

3 남자는 무엇을 하겠다고 말하는가?
(A) 동영상 보여주기 　　(B) 이메일로 가격표 보내기
(C) 장비 두고 가기 　　(D) 정보 패킷 제공하기

해설 | **남자가 할 일**

대화 마지막에 남자가 시연 기계를 두고 갔으면 한다(I'd still like to leave the demo machine here with you)고 하므로 (C)가 정답이다.

어휘 | information packet 정보 패킷

Paraphrasing   대화의 the demo machine
→ 정답의 some equipment

[4-6] W-Am / M-Au

> **W** Your presentation was very informative. **4**You made a good case for purchasing the YIELD soil monitoring system for my farm.
>
> **M** Thanks. **4**If you're looking to improve the nutrient levels in your soil, the YIELD system is the best way to do that. As you know, **5**farmers must frequently test soil, and with the YIELD system, there's a device that takes care of it automatically throughout the year.
>
> **W** Yes, **5**but it's just a lot to consider. I've been doing it the same way for years.

M [6]I also offer consulting if you want me to come out and help you plan a system that works for your farm.

여 발표가 매우 유익했어요. [4]저희 농장에 쓸 YIELD 토양 모니터링 시스템 구입의 좋은 사례가 됐어요.

남 감사합니다. [4]토양의 양분 수준을 개선하고자 하신다면 YIELD 시스템이 최선의 방법입니다. 알다시피 [5]농부들은 토양을 자주 테스트해야 해요. YIELD 시스템을 사용하면 일 년 내내 자동으로 토양을 관리하는 장치가 있어요.

여 네, [5]하지만 고려할 사항이 많아요. 몇 년 동안 같은 방식으로 해 왔거든요.

남 제가 나가서 귀하의 농장에 적합한 시스템을 계획하는 걸 도와주길 바라신다면 [6]자문도 해 드리고 있습니다.

- -

어휘 | informative 유익한 nutrient 영양분 frequently 자주 device 장치 automatically 자동으로 throughout the year 일 년 내내 consulting 자문

4 화자들은 무엇에 대해 이야기하는가?
(A) 영농 규정 준수　　(B) 새로운 수확 기구 사용
(C) 다른 농부들과의 협력　(D) 토양 양분 수준 모니터링

해설 | 대화의 주제
여자가 첫 번째 대사에서 YIELD 토양 모니터링 시스템 구입의 좋은 사례가 됐다(You made a good case for purchasing the YIELD soil monitoring system for my farm)고 하자 남자가 토양의 양분 수준을 개선하자 한다면 YIELD 시스템이 최선의 방법(If you're looking to improve the nutrient levels in your soil, the YIELD system is the best way to do that)이라고 응답하므로 (D)가 정답이다.

어휘 | regulation 규정 collaborate 협력하다

5 여자가 "몇 년 동안 같은 방식으로 해 왔거든요"라고 말할 때, 그 의도는 무엇인가?
(A) 자신의 분야에서 전문가이다.
(B) 절차가 불만스럽다.
(C) 농업이 보람 있다고 생각한다.
(D) 변화가 망설여진다.

해설 | 화자의 의도
남자가 첫 번째 대사에서 농부들은 토양을 자주 테스트해야 하는데 YIELD 시스템을 사용하면 일 년 내내 자동으로 토양을 관리하는 장치가 있다(farmers must frequently test soil, ~ takes care of it automatically throughout the year)고 말하자 여자는 고려할 사항이 많으며 몇 년 동안 같은 방식으로 해 왔다(but it's just a lot to consider. I've been doing it the same way for years)고 응답했다. 여자가 몇 년간 해온 같은 방식을 바꾸는 것을 주저한다는 의미이므로 (D)가 정답이다.

어휘 | expert 전문가 frustrated 좌절한, 불만스러운 rewarding 보람 있는 hesitant 망설이는, 주저하는

6 남자는 무엇을 하겠다고 제안하는가?
(A) 요금 인하　　　(B) 사진 발송
(C) 자문 제공　　　(D) 단체 설립

해설 | 남자의 제안 사항
대화 마지막에 남자가 자문도 해 드리고 있다(I also offer consulting)고 하므로 (C)가 정답이다.

어휘 | form an organization 단체를 만들다

────────

Paraphrasing 대화의 offer consulting
→ 정답의 Provide a consultation

[7-9] M-Cn / W-Br

M Irina, so [7]what did you think about the project manager's announcement?

W I wasn't at yesterday's meeting.

M Oh! Well, [8]apparently our client wants their videoconferencing software delivered earlier than planned.

W We do have a working prototype right now. [9]But what concerns me is that there are still a lot of flaws and bugs in the software to fix. We haven't been able to get it working consistently when more than five people join the conference at the same time.

남 이리나, [7]프로젝트 관리자의 발표에 대해 어떻게 생각하세요?
여 저는 어제 회의에 참석하지 않았어요.
남 아! [8]고객이 화상회의 소프트웨어가 계획보다 빨리 납품됐으면 한대요.
여 지금 구동 시제품이 나와 있어요. [9]하지만 소프트웨어에 아직 고쳐야 할 결함과 오류가 많이 있다는 점이 걱정되네요. 다섯 명 이상이 동시에 회의에 들어올 때 계속 잘 구동하도록 만들지 못했거든요.

- -

어휘 | announcement 발표 apparently 듣자 하니 videoconferencing 화상회의 prototype 원형, 시제품 flaw 결함 consistently 일관되게

7 여자가 "저는 어제 회의에 참석하지 않았어요"라고 말할 때, 그 의도는 무엇인가?
(A) 자신은 프로젝트 팀원이 아니다.
(B) 자신은 결정에 대해 책임이 없다.
(C) 현재 업무량을 관리하는 데 도움이 필요하다.
(D) 정보를 알지 못한다.

해설 | 화자의 의도
남자가 첫 번째 대사에서 프로젝트 관리자의 발표에 대해 어떻게 생각하는지(what did you think about the project manager's announcement?)를 묻자 여자가 어제 회의에 참석하지 않았다(I wasn't at yesterday's meeting)고 응답하므로 여자는 발표에 대해 알지 못한다는 것을 의미한다. 따라서 (D)가 정답이다.

어휘 | current 현재의 be unaware of ~을 알지 못하다

8 화자들은 어디서 일하겠는가?
(A) 법률사무소　　　(B) 소프트웨어 회사
(C) 컴퓨터 수리점　　(D) 영화 제작사

해설 | **화자들의 근무 장소**
남자가 두 번째 대사에서 고객이 화상회의 소프트웨어가 계획보다 빨리 납품됐으면 한다(apparently our client wants their videoconferencing software delivered earlier than planned)고 하므로 소프트웨어 회사에서 근무한다는 것을 추론할 수 있다. 따라서 (B)가 정답이다.

어휘 | law office 법률사무소

9 여자는 무엇이 걱정된다고 말하는가?
(A) 제품 결함을 바로잡는 것
(B) 주요 고객을 잃는 것
(C) 예산을 초과하는 것
(D) 숙련된 직원을 채용하는 것

해설 | **여자의 우려 사항**
대화 마지막에 여자가 소프트웨어에 아직 고쳐야 할 결함과 오류가 많이 있다는 점이 걱정된다(But what concerns me is that there are still a lot of flaws and bugs in the software to fix)고 하므로 (A)가 정답이다.

어휘 | exceed 초과하다 recruit 모집하다 skilled 숙련된

Paraphrasing 대화의 a lot of flaws and bugs in the software → 정답의 a flawed product

[10-12] W-Br / M-Au

W Hi, Hassan. **10**I'd like to follow up about the meetings you had in Toronto last week. Did the company representatives you met with sign contracts with us?

M Yes. **11**The soap company has hired us to design their packaging, and the express shipping company wants a new logo and banners for their Web site.

W Great! It's always a good idea to travel to meet prospective clients in person. These projects should help us attract even more business. By the way, **12**be sure to file an expense report for your trip.

M OK, but I've never filed a travel expense report.

W **12**Ms. Ito in the accounting office can show you how.

여 안녕하세요, 핫산. **10**지난주 토론토에서 참석하신 회의에 대해 더 알고 싶은데요. 만나보신 회사 대표들이 우리와 계약을 체결했나요?
남 네. **11**비누업체가 포장 디자인에 저희를 고용했고요. 특급 배송업체에서 웹사이트를 위한 새 로고와 배너를 작업해 달라고 합니다.
여 훌륭합니다! 가서 잠재 고객을 직접 만나는 것이 항상 좋아요. 이 프로젝트들은 우리가 훨씬 더 많은 업체들을 유치하는 데 도움이 될 겁니다. 그나저나 **12**출장 지출 품의서를 정리하도록 하세요.
남 네, 그런데 출장 지출 품의서를 정리해 본 적이 없어서요.
여 **12**경리부서 이토 씨가 방법을 알려드릴 겁니다.

어휘 | follow up 더 알아보다 representative 대표
sign a contract 계약을 맺다, 계약서에 서명하다
prospective 장래의, 유망한 in person 직접
file a report 보고서를 정리하다 expense report 지출 품의서
accounting office 회계 사무소, 경리부서

10 남자는 지난주에 무엇을 했는가?
(A) 전당대회에 참석했다.
(B) 대규모 수송 건을 처리했다.
(C) 직원 수련회에 참석했다.
(D) 잠재 고객들을 만났다.

해설 | **남자가 지난주에 한 일**
여자가 첫 번째 대사에서 지난주 토론토에서 참석한 회의에 대해 더 알고 싶다고 하면서 만났던 회사 대표들과 계약을 체결했는지(I'd like to follow up about the meetings you had in Toronto last week. Did the company representatives you met with sign contracts with us?)를 묻고 있으므로 (D)가 정답이다.

어휘 | national convention 전당 대회 process 처리하다
participate in ~에 참석하다 staff retreat 직원 수련회
potential client 잠재 고객

11 화자들은 어떤 업체에서 일하겠는가?
(A) 건축회사   (B) 법률사무소
(C) 그래픽 디자인 업체   (D) 보험 영업점

해설 | **화자들의 근무 장소**
남자가 첫 번째 대사에서 비누업체에서 포장 디자인을 요청했다(The soap company has hired us to design their packaging)고 하므로 디자인 업체에서 근무한다는 것을 추론할 수 있다. 따라서 (C)가 정답이다.

어휘 | architecture 건축 insurance 보험

12 남자가 "출장 지출 품의서를 정리해 본 적이 없어요"라고 말한 이유는?
(A) 정책에 동의하지 않는다고 말하려고
(B) 실수에 대해 설명하려고
(C) 도움을 요청하려고
(D) 프로젝트에 대해 불만을 제기하려고

해설 | **화자의 의도**
여자가 두 번째 대사에서 출장 지출 품의서를 정리하라고 요청하자(be sure to file an expense report for your trip) 남자는 출장 지출 품의서를 정리해 본 적이 없다(I've never filed a travel expense report)고 응답했다. 이어서 여자가 경리부서 이토 씨가 방법을 알려줄 것(Ms. Ito in the accounting office can show you how)이라고 하므로 남자가 도움을 요청하려는 것임을 알 수 있다. 따라서 (C)가 정답이다.

어휘 | policy 정책 assistance 도움

[13-15] W-Br / M-Cn

W **13**Welcome to our Springvale department store location, Mr. Farooq!

M Thank you, Maryam. Ever since I started as district manager, I've been incredibly busy. I finally found time to visit.

W My team is also happy to meet you. **¹⁴We've prepared a reception in the break room.**

M Great, but let's take a quick walk around the store first. Do you have any questions about the new display plans we've designed for all stores in the district?

W Well, yes… about the housewares display plan. **¹⁵At this location, we sell a lot of dessert plates, so I'd like to move them to a higher shelf—where they'll be more visible.**

M That's fine. **¹⁵You could swap them with the drinking glasses.**

여 **¹³저희 스프링베일 백화점에 와 주셔서 감사합니다,** 파루크 씨!

남 감사합니다, 마리암. 제가 구역 관리자 일을 시작한 이후로 엄청나게 바빠서요. 드디어 방문할 시간이 났어요.

여 저희 팀도 만나뵙게 되어 반갑습니다. **¹⁴휴게실에 연회를 준비해 뒀습니다.**

남 좋아요, 그런데 먼저 매장을 빨리 둘러봅시다. 저희가 구역 내 모든 매장을 위해 만든 새 진열 계획에 대해 질문이 있으신가요?

여 음… 네… 가정용품 진열 계획에 대해서요. **¹⁵저희 지점에서는 디저트 접시를 많이 판매해요. 그래서 더 잘 보이는 높은 선반으로 옮기고 싶습니다.**

남 좋아요. **¹⁵유리컵과 바꾸시면 됩니다.**

어휘 | district 구역　incredibly 엄청나게, 믿을 수 없을 정도로
break room 휴게실　houseware 가정용품　visible 보이는
swap 바꾸다

¹⁵선반 1: 유리컵
선반 2: 정찬용 접시
선반 3: 정찬용 냅킨
선반 4: 디저트 접시

13 대화는 어디서 이루어지는가?
(A) 제조 공장　(B) 연회장
(C) 커피숍　(D) 백화점

해설 | 대화 장소
여자가 첫 번째 대사에서 스프링베일 백화점에 와 주셔서 감사하다(Welcome to our Springvale department store location)고 하므로 (D)가 정답이다.

어휘 | manufacturing plant 제조 공장　banquet 연회

14 여자에 따르면, 여자의 팀은 무엇을 했는가?
(A) 연회 준비　(B) 새 유니폼 구입
(C) 점검 완료　(D) 강의 신청

해설 | 여자의 팀이 한 일
여자가 두 번째 대사에서 휴게실에 연회를 준비해 뒀다(We've prepared a reception in the break room)고 하므로 (A)가 정답이다.

어휘 | inspection 조사, 점검　sign up for 신청하다

15 시각 정보에 따르면, 디저트 접시는 어디로 옮겨질 것인가?
(A) 선반 1　(B) 선반 2
(C) 선반 3　(D) 선반 4

해설 | 시각 정보 연계
여자가 마지막 대사에서 디저트 접시를 많이 판매하는데 더 잘 보이는 높은 선반으로 옮기고 싶다(At this location, we sell a lot of dessert plates, so I'd like to move them to a higher shelf—where they'll be more visible)고 하자, 남자가 유리컵과 바꾸면 된다고(You could swap them with the drinking glasses)고 응답했다. 표를 보면 유리컵은 선반 1에 위치해 있으므로 (A)가 정답이다

[16-18] M-Cn / W-Am

M Hi, this is Pierre, who's been renting your apartment for the past week. **¹⁶The automotive trade show I was here for ended earlier today, and I'm leaving for the airport right now.**

W Thanks for letting me know, Pierre!

M **¹⁷We agreed that I'd put the apartment key in your mailbox. But the name labels are really hard to read. ¹⁷Which one is yours?**

W **¹⁷It's the one on the bottom right.** So, did you like your stay?

M Yes, **¹⁸and I especially liked that I could see the skyline of the entire city from the apartment. It was a gorgeous sight every evening.**

남 안녕하세요, 지난주 당신의 아파트를 빌렸던 피에르입니다. **¹⁶제가 참석한 자동차 박람회가 오늘 예정보다 일찍 끝났어요.** 그래서 지금 공항으로 떠납니다.

여 알려주셔서 감사합니다, 피에르!

남 **¹⁷우편함에 아파트 열쇠를 두기로 했잖아요. 그런데 이름표를 읽기가 너무 어려워요. ¹⁷어떤 것이 당신 우편함이죠?**

여 **¹⁷오른쪽 아래 거예요.** 즐겁게 지내셨나요?

남 네, **¹⁸아파트에서 도시 전체의 스카이라인을 볼 수 있는 점이 특히 맘에 들었어요.** 매일 저녁 멋진 풍경이었죠.

어휘 | rent 임대하다　trade show 무역 박람회

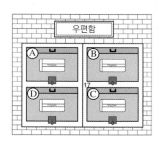

우편함

16 남자가 도시를 방문한 목적은?
(A) 가족을 만나려고
(B) 관광하려고
(C) 면접에 참석하려고
(D) 박람회에 참가하려고

해설 | 도시 방문 목적
남자가 첫 번째 대사에서 참석한 자동차 박람회가 오늘 예정보다 일찍 끝났다(The automotive trade show I was here for ended earlier today)고 하므로 (D)가 정답이다.

어휘 | sightseeing 관광

17 시각 정보에 따르면, 남자는 열쇠를 어디에 둘 것인가?
(A) 우편함 A
(B) 우편함 B
(C) 우편함 C
(D) 우편함 D

해설 | 시각 정보 연계
남자가 두 번째 대사에서 우편함에 아파트 열쇠를 두기로 했는데 어떤 것이 여자의 우편함인지(We agreed that I'd put the apartment key in your mailbox ~ Which one is yours?)를 묻자 여자가 오른쪽 아래의 것(It's the one on the bottom right)이라고 응답했다. 시각 정보를 보면 오른쪽 아래 우편함은 ⓒ이므로 (C)가 정답이다.

18 남자는 아파트의 어떤 점을 마음에 들어했는가?
(A) 도시 경관
(B) 방 크기
(C) 장식
(D) 조명

해설 | 아파트가 마음에 든 점
대화 마지막에 남자가 아파트에서 도시 전체의 스카이라인을 볼 수 있는 점이 특히 맘에 들었다(I especially liked that I could see the skyline of the entire city from the apartment)고 하므로 (A)가 정답이다.

Paraphrasing 대화의 the skyline of the entire city
→ 정답의 The view of the city

[19-21] M-Au / W-Am

M　You know, **19**I'm happy how our research team handled this latest project.
W　Yes, we worked well together.
M　**20**I'd like to hold a meeting to gather everyone's thoughts about how things went and what we can improve going forward with our next project. Let's try to do that on Wednesday afternoon.
W　Sure. Hold on, I'll pull up everyone's schedule. OK, here it is. Hmm. Looks like Ibrahim's time is limited. He's preparing for a conference right now.

M　OK, **21**please go ahead and schedule the meeting at the time Ibrahim is available. I know you and I were planning to chat about the internship program then, Marisol, but we could easily move that to another day.

남　**19**우리 연구팀이 최근 프로젝트를 처리한 방식이 맘에 들어요.
여　네, 모두 잘 협력했어요.
남　일이 어떻게 진행되었고 다음 프로젝트를 진행하면서 무엇을 개선할 수 있을지에 관해 **20**회의를 열어서 모두의 생각을 모으고 싶은데요. 수요일 오후로 해 봅시다.
여　좋아요. 잠시만요, 제가 모두의 일정을 끌어올게요. 네, 여기 있어요. 음. 이브라힘은 시간이 충분치 않은 것 같네요. 지금 회의 준비 중이라서요.
남　네, **21**이브라힘이 시간이 될 때로 회의 일정을 잡아주세요. 마리솔, 우린 이제 인턴십 프로그램에 관해 얘기 나눌 계획이었잖아요. 그런데 다른 날로 그냥 옮겨도 되겠어요.

어휘 | handle 다루다, 처리하다　**go forward with** 진행시키다

	수요일			
	오후 1시	오후 2시	오후 3시	**21**오후 4시
애나	✕			✕
데이비드			✕	✕
이브라힘	✕	✕	✕	
마리솔				✕

19 화자들은 어떤 팀에서 일하는가?
(A) 마케팅
(B) 연구
(C) 회계
(D) 법률

해설 | 화자들이 근무하는 팀
남자가 첫 번째 대사에서 우리 연구팀(our research team)이라고 했으므로 (B)가 정답이다.

어휘 | accounting 회계　**legal** 법률과 관련된

20 남자가 팀 회의를 열고 싶어하는 이유는?
(A) 의견을 모으려고
(B) 정책을 명시하려고
(C) 새로운 팀원을 소개하려고
(D) 업무 공간 재편성에 대해 논의하려고

해설 | 팀 회의 개최 이유
남자가 두 번째 대사에서 회의를 열어서 모두의 생각을 모으고 싶다(I'd like to hold a meeting to gather everyone's thoughts)고 하므로 (A)가 정답이다.

어휘 | clarify 분명히 말하다　**reorganization** 재편성, 개편

Paraphrasing 대화의 gather everyone's thoughts
→ 정답의 collect feedback

21 시각 정보에 따르면, 화자들은 몇 시에 팀 회의를 열겠는가?
(A) 오후 1시
(B) 오후 2시
(C) 오후 3시
(D) 오후 4시

해설 | 시각 정보 연계
대화 마지막에 남자가 이브라힘이 시간이 될 때로 회의 일정을 잡아줄 것(please go ahead and schedule the meeting at the time Ibrahim is available)을 요청했는데 표를 보면 이브라힘이 비어 있는 시간대는 오후 4시이므로 (D)가 정답이다.

[22-24] W-Br / M-Cn

> W Charles, ²²what did you think about the mayor's suggestion at the end of our city council meeting yesterday? That a separate department should be established to promote arts and cultural affairs.
>
> M Well, it makes sense. ²³We're the second fastest-growing city in the region. And with the new university opening here…
>
> W Right. ²⁴I'm just worried we don't have the financial resources for what he's suggesting. At least not without redirecting funds from other areas.
>
> 여 찰스, ²²어제 시 의회 회의 말미에 시장님이 하신 제안을 어떻게 생각하세요? 별도의 부서가 설립되어 예술 문화 관련 업무를 촉진해야 한다는 거요.
>
> 남 음, 맞는 말씀이에요. ²³우리가 지역 내에서는 두 번째로 빠르게 성장하는 도시잖아요. 대학교도 새로 개교하고요…
>
> 여 맞아요. ²⁴시장님이 제안하는 사항에 쓸 재정 자원이 없는 것이 걱정이죠. 적어도 다른 영역에서 자금을 끌어오지 않는 한 없죠.

어휘 | mayor 시장 **city council** 시 의회 **separate** 별개의 **promote** 촉진하다, 홍보하다 **financial** 재정적인, 금융의 **resource** 자원 **at least** 최소한 **redirect** 돌려쓰다, 전용하다

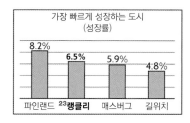

가장 빠르게 성장하는 도시
(성장률)

8.2% / 6.5% / 5.9% / 4.8%

파인랜드 ²³랭클리 매스버그 길위치

어휘 | growth rate 성장률

22 시장은 시 의회 회의에서 무엇을 제안했는가?
(A) 신규 부서 창설
(B) 여가시설 건립
(C) 시 공원 개선
(D) 대학생 채용

해설 | 시장의 제안 사항
여자가 첫 번째 대사에서 어제 시 의회 회의 말미에 시장님이 하신 제안에 대한 의견을 물으면서 별도의 부서가 설립되어 예술 문화 관련 업무를 촉진해야 한다(what did you think about the mayor's suggestion at the end of our city council meeting yesterday? That a separate department should be established to promote arts and cultural affairs.)는 내용이었다고 하므로 (A)가 정답이다.

어휘 | facility 시설

Paraphrasing 대화의 a separate department should be established → 정답의 Creating a new department

23 시각 정보에 따르면, 화자들은 어떤 도시에 대해 이야기하는가?
(A) 파인랜드
(B) 랭클리
(C) 매스버그
(D) 길위치

해설 | 시각 정보 연계
남자가 지역 내에서 두 번째로 빠르게 성장하는 도시(We're the second fastest-growing city in the region)라고 했고, 그래프에서 두 번째로 빠른 성장을 보인 도시는 랭클리이므로 (B)가 정답이다.

24 여자는 무엇에 대해 우려하는가?
(A) 안전
(B) 직원 교육
(C) 자금
(D) 주민 불만 사항

해설 | 여자의 우려 사항
대화 마지막에 여자가 시장님이 제안하는 사항에 쓸 재정 자원이 없는 것이 걱정(I'm just worried we don't have the financial resources for what he's suggesting)이라고 하므로 (C)가 정답이다.

어휘 | resident 거주자, 주민

Paraphrasing 대화의 the financial resources → 정답의 Funding

LC PART 4

UNIT 13 전화 메시지

고득점 전략 담화 흐름 파악하기   본책 p.100

W-Am 안녕하세요, 윌리스. 스턴튼 모바일 고객 서비스팀의 줄리 오스본이라고 합니다. 곧 있을 파슨스 통신회사와의 합병에 대한 귀하의 우려가 담긴 메시지를 봤습니다. 다음 달 파슨스와 합병한 후에도 귀하의 국제전화 요금제는 그대로 유지된다는 점을 확실히 말씀드리고 싶습니다. 한편 저희는 이번 주에 자주 묻는 질문들에 대한 답변을 웹사이트에 게시할 예정입니다. 한번 보실 기회가 있었으면 합니다. 전화 주시고 이용해 주셔서 감사합니다.

어휘 | concern 우려, 걱정   merger 합병   assure 확언하다, 장담하다   consolidate 통합하다   in the meantime 한편, 그 동안에   frequently asked questions 자주 묻는 질문(= FAQ)

1 메시지의 목적은?
    (A) 결제를 요청하려고   (B) 고객의 우려를 해결해 주려고
    어휘 | payment 결제, 지불   address (문제 등을) 다루다, 처리하다

2 스턴튼은 어떤 종류의 업체인가?
    (A) 시장조사 업체   (B) 통신업체
    어휘 | market research 시장 조사

3 화자에 따르면, 스턴튼 사는 이번 주에 무엇을 할 것인가?
    (A) 웹사이트에 정보 게시   (B) 기자 회견 개최
    어휘 | hold 열다, 개최하다   press conference 기자 회견

ETS 유형 연습   본책 p.101

1 (C)   **2** (D)   **3** (C)   **4** (C)   **5** (C)   **6** (A)
7 (B)   **8** (B)   **9** (A)

[1-3] 전화 메시지

M-Au Hi, Satomi. This is John. [1] I'm calling about our upcoming conference—the one where we're presenting on cybersecurity techniques. [1,2] I just changed my flight, so I will leave a day after our conference ends. [3] I'm planning to attend a free local music festival Saturday in the city's central park and fly home on Sunday. I know you've been to outdoor festivals before— [3] why don't you come with me? Flights on Sunday were filling up, so if you want to do this, you'd better change your flight quickly. Hope you can make it!

안녕하세요, 사토미. 존입니다. [1] 곧 있을 회의 관련해서 전화 드려요. 사이버 보안 기술에 관해 발표하는 회의요. [1,2] 저는 항공편을 변경해서 회의 끝나고 하루 뒤에 출발할 겁니다. [3] 토요일에 시 중앙 공원에서 열리는 무료 지역 음악 축제에 참석하고 일요일에 돌아올 계획이에요. 전에 야외 축제에 가셨던 걸로 아는데요. [3] 저랑 함께 가면 어때요? 일요일엔 비행기가 꽉 차서 그렇게 하시려면 항공편을 빨리 변경하시는 편이 나아요. 갈 수 있었으면 좋겠네요!

어휘 | cybersecurity technique 사이버 보안 기술   attend 참석하다   fill up 가득 차다   make it 가다, 참석하다

1 화자가 이동하는 이유는?
    (A) 지점을 시찰하려고   (B) 고객을 만나려고
    (C) 회의에 참석하려고   (D) 가족을 만나려고
    해설 | 화자의 이동 이유
    초반부에서 곧 있을 회의 관련해서 전화를 한다(I'm calling about our upcoming conference)고 한 후, 항공편을 변경했다(I just changed my flight)고 했으므로, 회의 참석을 위해서 비행기를 탄다는 것을 알 수 있다. 따라서 (C)가 정답이다.
    어휘 | inspect 검사하다, 시찰하다   branch office 지점

2 화자는 최근에 무엇을 했는가?
    (A) 법인 신용카드를 신청했다.
    (B) 보안 정책을 변경했다.
    (C) 추가 교육을 요청했다.
    (D) 항공편 예약을 변경했다.
    해설 | 화자가 최근에 한 일
    초반부에서 항공편을 변경했다(I just changed my flight)고 했으므로 (D)가 정답이다.
    어휘 | register for ~에 등록하다, ~을 신청하다   revise 변경하다, 개정하다   policy 정책   reservation 예약
    Paraphrasing 담화의 just → 질문의 recently
    담화의 changed my flight → 정답의 changed a flight reservation

3 화자는 청자가 어디에 참석하도록 초대하는가?
    (A) 환영회   (B) 역사 탐방
    (C) 음악 축제   (D) 워크숍
    해설 | 화자가 초대한 행사
    중반부에서 토요일에 시 중앙 공원에서 열리는 무료 지역 음악 축제에 참석하겠다(I'm planning to attend a free local music festival Saturday in the city's central park)고 한 후, 함께 갈 것(why don't you come with me?)을 제안하므로 (C)가 정답이다.
    어휘 | reception 환영회, 접수처

[4-6] 전화 메시지

W-Br [4] I'm calling from Crescent Furniture Gallery about the living-room furniture you recently purchased. [5] I'd like to confirm your delivery time for tomorrow. Currently, your sofa and end tables are scheduled to arrive between noon and three o'clock. If that's not a convenient time, please call us back so we can make other arrangements. In a few days, [6]you'll also receive an e-mail from us. That e-mail contains a customer service survey. It's a brief survey, but we'd appreciate your feedback about your purchasing experience.

[4]크레센트 가구 갤러리인데요. 최근 구입하신 거실용 가구에 관해 전화 드립니다. [5]내일 배송 시간을 확인하고 싶어서요. 현재로서는 소파와 작은 탁자가 정오에서 3시 사이에 도착할 예정입니다. 그 시간대가 편하지 않으시다면 다시 전화 주세요. 다른 일정을 잡을 수 있습니다. 며칠 후에는 [6]저희가 보내 드리는 이메일을 받으실 텐데요. 이메일에는 고객 서비스 설문 조사가 들어 있어요. 간단한 설문입니다만 구입 경험에 대한 의견을 주시면 감사하겠습니다.

어휘 | confirm 확인하다 currently 현재 be scheduled to ~할 예정이다 arrangements 준비, 계획

4 화자는 어디서 일하는가?
(A) 전자제품 매장　　　　(B) 우체국
(C) 가구 매장　　　　　　(D) 렌터카 업체

해설 | 화자의 근무 장소
초반부에 크레센트 가구 갤러리인데 최근 구입하신 거실용 가구에 관해 전화를 했다(I'm calling from Crescent Furniture Gallery about the living-room furniture you recently purchased)고 했으므로 (C)가 정답이다.

어휘 | electronics 전자 기기

5 전화를 건 목적은?
(A) 주문을 취소하려고　　(B) 결제에 관해 물어보려고
(C) 배송 시간을 확인하려고 (D) 고객 불만을 해결하려고

해설 | 전화의 목적
초반부에서 내일 배송 시간을 확인하고 싶다(I'd like to confirm your delivery time for tomorrow)고 했으므로 (C)가 정답이다.

어휘 | payment 결제, 지불 resolve 해결하다

6 청자는 이메일로 무엇을 받을 것인가?
(A) 설문 조사　　　　　　(B) 영수증
(C) 전액 환불　　　　　　(D) 할인 코드

해설 | 청자가 받을 이메일 자료
후반부에서 이메일을 받으실 텐데 이메일에는 고객 서비스 설문 조사가 들어 있다(That e-mail contains a customer service survey)고 했으므로 (A)가 정답이다.

어휘 | receipt 영수증 full refund 전액 환불

[7-9] 전화 메시지

M-Cn Hi, Seema. This is Hao Nan from the travel office. [7]I wanted to let you know that I'm currently looking at different hotels near the client's office for your business trip next month. [8]I'm going to send

you a list of all the possible options to choose from so [7]I can book it for you. [8]But please keep in mind, I've talked to the Finance Department, and they're trying to cut costs. Oh, and one last thing—[9]I've been having some problems with my computer, so I can't access my e-mail. Please call me back when you get the chance.

안녕하세요, 시마. 출장팀의 하오 난입니다. [7]다음 달에 가실 출장 건으로, 제가 지금 고객 사무실 근처의 다른 호텔들을 살펴보고 있어요. [8]선택 가능한 전체 목록을 보내 드리고, [7]제가 예약해 드릴 수 있도록 할게요. [8]제가 재무부서에 얘기해 봤는데 그쪽에서 비용을 줄이려 한다는 사실을 유념해 주세요. 아, 마지막으로 [9]제 컴퓨터에 문제가 생겨서 이메일에 접속할 수가 없습니다. 기회 되실 때 전화 주세요.

어휘 | keep in mind 기억하다, 명심하다 finance 재무, 재정 cut costs 비용을 줄이다

7 화자는 청자가 무엇을 하는 것을 돕는가?
(A) 화상 회의 일정 잡기　(B) 호텔 예약하기
(C) 저녁식사 예약하기　　(D) 연설문 작성하기

해설 | 청자를 돕는 일
초반부에서 다음 달에 가실 출장 건으로, 지금 고객 사무실 근처의 다른 호텔들을 살펴보고 있다(I wanted to let you know that I'm currently looking at different hotels near the client's office for your business trip next month)고 한 후, 예약해 드릴 수 있도록 하겠다(I can book it for you)고 했으므로 (B)가 정답이다.

어휘 | conference call 화상 회의 speech 연설, 연설문

8 화자가 "그쪽에서 비용을 줄이려 한다"라고 말할 때, 그 의도는 무엇인가?
(A) 청자는 신용카드로 결제해야 한다.
(B) 청자는 비싼 선택지를 고르면 안 된다.
(C) 계산 오류가 있었다.
(D) 행사 일정을 변경해야 한다.

해설 | 화자의 의도
중반부에서 선택 가능한 전체 목록을 보내 드린다(I'm going to send you a list of all the possible options to choose from)고 한 후, 재무부서에 얘기해 봤는데 그쪽에서 비용을 줄이려 한다는 사실을 유념해 달라(But please keep in mind, I've talked to the Finance Department, and they're trying to cut costs)고 했다. 이 말은 비용을 줄이려면 비싼 것은 선택할 수 없다는 뜻으로 (B)가 정답이다.

어휘 | calculation 계산 reschedule 일정을 변경하다

9 화자가 전화로 연락해 달라고 요청한 이유는?
(A) 컴퓨터가 작동하지 않는다.
(B) 자리를 비울 것이다.
(C) 즉시 답변을 들어야 한다.
(D) 정보가 기밀이다.

해설 | 화자의 전화 연락 요청 이유
후반부에서 컴퓨터에 문제가 생겨서 이메일에 접속할 수가
없다(I've been having some problems with my
computer, so I can't access my e-mail)고 한 후. 기회
되실 때 전화 달라(Please call me back when you get the
chance)고 했으므로 (A)가 정답이다.

어휘 | immediately 즉시 **confidential** 기밀의, 비밀의

─────────────────
Paraphrasing 담화의 having some problems with my
computer → 정답의 His computer is not working.

ETS 고득점 실전 문제
본책 p.102

1 (D)	**2** (D)	**3** (A)	**4** (C)	**5** (B)	**6** (A)
7 (D)	**8** (C)	**9** (D)	**10** (A)	**11** (D)	**12** (C)
13 (A)	**14** (D)	**15** (A)	**16** (A)	**17** (C)	**18** (D)
19 (A)	**20** (D)	**21** (B)			

[1-3] 전화 메시지

W-Am Doctor Alaoui, this is Aisha Samir with the
Southwest Medical Foundation. [1, 2]I'm calling to let
you know that your project's been awarded one of
our medical research grants. Congratulations! Our
selection committee was very impressed with your
proposal to study sleep disorders. [3]We'd like to
invite you to a reception we're hosting for all of the
grant award winners. It'll be held at the Rosedale
Restaurant next month. A formal invitation will be
mailed to you soon.

알라우이 박사님, 사우스웨스트 의료재단의 아이샤 사미르입니다.
[1, 2]박사님의 프로젝트에 저희 의학 연구 보조금 중 하나가 수여됐다고
알려드리려 전화했습니다. 축하합니다! 저희 선정위원회는
수면장애를 연구하겠다는 박사님의 제안서에 깊은 감명을 받았어요.
보조금 수여자 전원을 위해 개최하는 [3]축하 연회에 박사님을
초청하고 싶은데요. 다음 달 로즈데일 레스토랑에서 열릴 예정입니다.
정식 초청장이 곧 우편으로 발송될 겁니다.

어휘 | foundation 재단 **award** 수여하다 **grant** 보조금
selection committee 선정 위원회 **sleep disorder**
수면장애 **formal** 정식의

1 청자는 어떤 분야에서 일하는가?
(A) 금융 (B) 언론
(C) 공학 (D) 의학

해설 | 청자가 종사하는 분야
초반부에서 프로젝트에 저희 의학 연구 보조금 중 하나가
수여됐다(your project's been awarded one of our
medical research grants)고 했으므로 (D)가 정답이다.

어휘 | finance 금융, 재무

2 전화를 건 주목적은?
(A) 기사를 위해 정보를 요청하려고
(B) 채용 공고에 관해 문의하려고
(C) 출장 세부 사항을 확인하려고
(D) 청자에게 프로젝트 승인 사실을 알리려고

해설 | 전화의 목적
초반부에서 프로젝트에 의학 연구 보조금 중 하나가 수여됐다고
알려 주려고 전화를 했다(I'm calling to let you know that
your project's been awarded one of our medical
research grants)고 했으므로 (D)가 정답이다.

어휘 | inquire 문의하다, 물어보다 **job opening** 일자리
approve 승인하다

3 청자는 무엇을 하도록 요청받았는가?
(A) 축하 연회 참석 (B) 시설 견학
(C) 위원회 합류 (D) 기부

해설 | 청자가 요청 받은 일
후반부에서 축하 연회에 박사님을 초청하고 싶다(We'd like to
invite you to a reception)고 했으므로 (A)가 정답이다.

어휘 | facility 시설 **donation** 기부

[4-6] 전화 메시지

M-Au This is Chan-Ho Lee from Oakmont
Furnishings. [4]Thank you for sending us a draft
of your review of our Executive Style office chair.
We appreciate the preview of your article, and
we're excited that it will be published in such a
prestigious trade magazine. [5]We were pleased
to see that you gave the chair five stars for being
easy to assemble. But, we were surprised by one
thing. [6]You wrote that you wished the chair had
an adjustable back support. The Executive Style
has that feature. [6]If I can refer you to page four
of the assembly instructions, I think you'll find the
information. Anyway, please give me a call at your
earliest convenience. Thanks.

오크몬트 퍼니싱의 찬호 리입니다. [4]저희 이그제큐티브 스타일 사무용
의자에 관한 후기 초안을 보내 주셔서 감사합니다. 기사 선공개에
감사드리고 그렇게 명망 있는 업계지에 게재된다니 기대가 큽니다.
[5]조립이 쉽다는 이유로 별점 5점을 주셔서 기뻤습니다. 그런데 한
가지 놀란 점이 있는데요. [6]조절 가능한 등받이가 있었으면 좋겠다고
하셨습니다만, 이그제큐티브 스타일에 해당 기능이 있습니다. [6]조립
설명서 4쪽을 참조하시면 해당 정보를 찾으실 수 있을 겁니다. 아무튼
가능한 한 빨리 전화 부탁드립니다. 감사합니다.

어휘 | draft 초안 **publish** 출판하다, 게재하다 **prestigious**
명망 있는, 일류의 **assemble** 조립하다 **adjustable** 조절
가능한 **feature** 기능 **refer** 참조하게 하다 **instructions**
설명, 지시 **at your earliest convenience** 가급적 빨리

4 화자는 청자에게 무엇을 받았다고 말하는가?
(A) 영수증　　　　　　　(B) 무선 송금
(C) 기사 초안　　　　　　(D) 주문서

해설 | **화자가 받은 것**
초반부에서 이그제큐티브 스타일 사무용 의자에 관한 후기 초안을 보내 주셔서 감사하다(Thank you for sending us a draft of your review of our Executive Style office chair)고 한 후, 기사 선공개에 감사드린다(We appreciate the preview of your article)고 했으므로 (C)가 정답이다.

어휘 | money transfer 현금 이체, 송금　order form 주문서

5 제품의 어떤 점이 청자에게 깊은 인상을 주었는가?
(A) 편안하다.　　　　　　(B) 조립하기에 쉽다.
(C) 가격이 적당하다.　　　(D) 가볍다.

해설 | **청자에게 깊은 인상을 준 제품의 특징**
중반부에서 조립이 쉽다는 이유로 별점 5점을 주셔서 기뻤다(We were pleased to see that you gave the chair five stars for being easy to assemble)고 했으므로 (B)가 정답이다.

어휘 | affordable (가격이) 알맞은　lightweight 가벼운

6 화자가 "이그제큐티브 스타일에 해당 기능이 있습니다"라고 말한 이유는?
(A) 오해를 바로잡으려고　　(B) 제품을 추천하려고
(C) 제안을 거절하려고　　　(D) 칭찬하려고

해설 | **화자의 의도**
중반부에서 조절 가능한 등받이가 있었으면 좋겠다고 하셨는데(You wrote that you wished the chair had an adjustable back support), 이그제큐티브 스타일에 해당 기능이 있다고 하면서 조립 설명서 4쪽을 참조하면 해당 정보를 찾으실 수 있을 것(If I can refer you to page four of the assembly instructions, I think you'll find the information)이라고 했다. 이 말은 조절 가능한 등받이가 없다는 오해를 바로잡는 것이므로 (A)가 정답이다.

어휘 | correct 바로잡다, 정정하다　misunderstanding 오해
refuse 거절하다, 거부하다　compliment 칭찬

[7-9] 녹음 메시지

W-Am ⁷Thank you for calling Adept Television Cable Services. We are aware that some customers are having problems accessing their channels, and ⁸we apologize for the interruption to the service. We believe the problem has been corrected for most of our customers, but if you're still unable to access any of your channels, please stay on the line. A representative will guide you with step-by-step instructions on how to reset your system. And ⁹to find out about all our latest offers and discounts, be sure to visit our Web site at www. adeptcable.com.

⁷어뎁트 텔레비전 케이블 서비스에 전화 주셔서 감사합니다. 일부 고객께서 채널 접속 문제를 겪고 계신 것을 잘 알고 있습니다.

⁸서비스 중단에 대해 사과의 말씀을 드립니다. 대다수 고객은 문제가 해결되었지만 아직도 채널 접속이 안 된다면 전화를 끊지 말고 기다려 주십시오. 상담원이 시스템 재설정 방법을 단계별로 설명해 드립니다. ⁹최근 혜택 및 할인에 대해 알고 싶으시다면 저희 웹사이트 www.adeptcable.com을 방문하세요.

어휘 | aware 알고 있는　access 접속하다, 이용하다
apologize 사과하다　interruption 중단　stay on the line 수화기를 들고 기다리다　representative 대표, 직원　step-by-step 단계적인, 점진적인　latest 최근의

7 어떤 종류의 업체에 전화를 걸었는가?
(A) 은행　　　　　　　　(B) 전자제품 매장
(C) 배송 서비스 업체　　　(D) 케이블 텔레비전 회사

해설 | **전화 수신 업체의 종류**
초반부에서 어뎁트 텔레비전 케이블 서비스에 전화 주셔서 감사하다(Thank you for calling Adept Television Cable Services)고 했으므로 (D)가 정답이다.

8 화자는 무엇에 대해 사과하는가?
(A) 부정확한 설명서　　　(B) 훼손된 제품
(C) 중단된 서비스　　　　(D) 사무실 폐쇄

해설 | **화자가 사과하는 것**
초반부에서 서비스 중단에 대해 사과의 말씀을 드린다(we apologize for the interruption to the service)고 했으므로 (C)가 정답이다.

어휘 | incorrect 부정확한, 맞지 않는　damaged 훼손된, 손상된　closure 폐쇄, 종료

9 화자에 따르면, 청자들은 왜 웹사이트를 방문해야 하는가?
(A) 계정 정보를 확인하려고
(B) 새 부품을 주문하려고
(C) 최신 일정 소식을 받으려고
(D) 신규 혜택에 대해 알아보려고

해설 | **청자들이 웹사이트에 방문해야 하는 이유**
후반부에 최근 혜택 및 할인에 대해 알고 싶으시다면 웹사이트를 방문하라(to find out about all our latest offers and discounts, be sure to visit our Web site at www.adeptcable.com)고 했으므로 (D)가 정답이다.

어휘 | account 계정

Paraphrasing　담화의 to find out about all our latest offers → 정답의 To learn about new offers

[10-12] 전화 메시지

M-Cn Hi. ¹⁰This is Carlos from Kennedy Housing Rentals calling about your application for a first-floor studio apartment in the city center. We currently have two suitable listings for you. They're both decent size and near public transportation, so I think you'll like them. ¹¹Keep in mind that to secure either lease will require a down payment of first and last months' rent. ¹²If you'd like to see these apartments, please call me back so we can set up a time. Just so you know, we have other people interested.

안녕하세요. ¹⁰케네디 하우징 렌털의 카를로스입니다. 도심 원룸형 아파트 1층을 신청하셔서 전화 드립니다. 현재 적합한 두 곳이 있어요. 둘 다 크기가 괜찮고 대중교통과 가까워서 마음에 드실 것 같아요. ¹¹두 곳 중 하나를 임대하시려면 첫 달과 마지막 달 임대료를 계약금으로 내야 하는 점을 기억해 주세요. ¹²아파트를 보고 싶으시면 시간을 잡을 수 있도록 전화 주세요. 아시다시피, 관심 있는 분들이 더 계십니다.

> **어휘** | application 신청 studio apartment 원룸형 아파트 suitable 적절한, 알맞은 decent 괜찮은 public transportation 대중교통 lease 임대차 계약 down payment 계약금, 착수금

10 화자는 누구이겠는가?
- (A) 부동산 중개인
- (B) 녹음 스튜디오 기사
- (C) 건축가
- (D) 청소부

해설 | 화자의 신분
초반부에서 케네디 하우징 렌털의 카를로스라고 자신을 소개하면서 도심 원룸형 아파트 1층을 신청해주셔서 전화를 한다(This is Carlos from Kennedy Housing Rentals calling about your application for a first-floor studio apartment in the city center)고 했으므로 (A)가 정답이다.

> **어휘** | real estate 부동산 architect 건축가

11 어떤 요건이 언급되는가?
- (A) 허가증
- (B) 시작 일자
- (C) 자재 유형
- (D) 비용 지불

해설 | 언급된 요건 사항
중반부에서 두 곳 중 하나를 임대하시려면 첫 달과 마지막 달 임대료를 계약금으로 내야 하는 점을 기억하라(require a down payment of first and last months' rent)고 했으므로 (D)가 정답이다.

> **어휘** | requirement 요구 사항, 요건 permit 허가증 material 자재, 재료

12 화자가 "관심 있는 분들이 더 계십니다"라고 말할 때, 그 의도는 무엇인가?
- (A) 메시지가 잘못됐다.
- (B) 요청을 들어줄 수 없다.
- (C) 청자는 빠르게 행동해야 한다.
- (D) 청자는 더 많은 도움을 제공해야 한다.

해설 | 화자의 의도
후반부에서 아파트를 보고 싶으시면 시간을 잡을 수 있도록 전화를 해달라(If you'd like to see these apartments, please call me back so we can set up a time)고 한 후, 관심 있는 분들이 더 있다(we have other people interested)고 하는 것은 서둘러야 한다는 의미이므로 (C)가 정답이다.

> **어휘** | fulfill a request 부탁을 들어주다

[13-15] 전화 메시지

W-Am Tommaso, it's Li Chen. After our conversation about budgeting, ¹³I looked over our expenses to see where we could reduce operating costs at our restaurant. Our electricity bill is very high. ¹⁴Most of our kitchen appliances are older, so they require a lot of energy to run. There are newer models that are much more efficient. It would be an investment, of course, but in the long run, upgrading would lower our monthly electricity bill. ¹⁵I've even found a foundation that offers grants to help small businesses become more energy efficient. I'm going to reach out to them to find out more about their program. Let me know what you think.

토마소, 리 첸입니다. 예산 수립에 관해 대화를 나누고 나서 ¹³우리 식당 운영비용을 줄일 수 있는 곳을 찾기 위해 경비 지출을 검토했어요. 우리 전기요금이 아주 높더군요. ¹⁴주방 기기 대부분이 오래되어 작동하는 데 전력이 많이 듭니다. 훨씬 더 효율적인 신형 모델들이 있어요. 물론 투자를 해야 하지만 업그레이드하면 결국 월 전기요금을 줄여 줄 겁니다. ¹⁵소규모 업체들이 에너지 효율성을 더 높일 수 있도록 보조금을 제공하는 재단을 찾았어요. 연락해서 프로그램에 대해 더 알아볼게요. 어떻게 생각하는지 알려주세요.

> **어휘** | budgeting 예산 수립 expenses 소요 경비 operating cost 운영비 electricity bill 전기요금 appliance 가전제품 energy efficient 에너지 효율이 좋은 investment 투자 in the long run 결국에는 foundation 재단 grant 보조금 reach out 연락하다

13 화자가 전화를 건 목적은?
- (A) 비용 절감 방법을 제안하려고
- (B) 최근 고지서 관련 세부 사항에 대해 물어보려고
- (C) 직원 급여 인상을 권하려고
- (D) 구입이 이뤄진 사실을 확인하려고

해설 | 전화 이유
초반부에서 식당 운영비용을 줄일 수 있는 곳을 찾기 위해 경비 지출을 검토했다(I looked over our expenses to see where we could reduce operating costs at our restaurant)고 했으므로 (A)가 정답이다.

Paraphrasing 담화의 reduce operating costs → 정답의 saving money

14 화자는 기계에 관해 어떤 문제점을 언급하는가?
- (A) 올바른 위치에 놓여 있지 않다.
- (B) 작동이 어렵다.
- (C) 수리해야 한다.
- (D) 에너지 효율이 나쁘다.

해설 | 언급한 기계의 문제점
중반부에서 주방 기기 대부분이 오래되어 동작하는 데 전력이 많이 든다(Most of our kitchen appliances are older, so they require a lot of energy to run)고 했으므로 (D)가 정답이다.

Paraphrasing 담화의 our kitchen appliances
→ 질문의 some machines
담화의 require a lot of energy to run
→ 정답의 not energy efficient

15 화자가 단체에 연락하려는 이유는?
(A) 보조금 프로그램에 관해 알아보려고
(B) 구직자들에 대해 알아보려고
(C) 사업 서비스를 제공하려고
(D) 요금에 관해 항의하려고

해설 | 단체에 연락하려는 이유
후반부에서 보조금을 제공하는 재단을 찾았다(I've even found a foundation that offers grants)고 한 후, 연락해서 프로그램에 대해 더 알아보겠다(I'm going to reach out to them to find out more about their program)고 했으므로 (A)가 정답이다.

어휘 | identify (신원 등을) 알아보다, 확인하다 job candidate 구직자

Paraphrasing 담화의 reach out to → 질문의 contact
담화의 a foundation → 질문의 an organization
담화의 find out → 정답의 learn about

[16-18] 전화 메시지

M-Cn Hello. We're calling because you completed our online survey. In the survey, **16**you indicated that you'd be willing to have your dog test out a new play toy that our company is designing for pets! The session we're organizing will be held on October second, and all selected participants will receive a gift certificate to a local pet store upon completion. **17**To confirm your interest, please call 555-0168. We will choose only ten for this session. And, keep in mind, the list of interested participants is growing. **18**Selected participants will be sent detailed driving directions.

안녕하세요. 저희 온라인 설문 조사에 응해 주셔서 전화 드립니다. 설문 조사에서 **16**저희 회사가 반려동물을 위해 디자인한 새 놀이 장난감을 귀하의 개에게 시험해 보겠다고 하셨는데요! 저희가 준비하고 있는 세션이 10월 2일에 열릴 예정이고, 완료 시 선발된 모든 참가자는 지역 반려동물 상점에서 쓸 수 있는 상품권을 받게 됩니다. **17**관심이 있다고 알려주시려면 555-0168로 전화 주세요. 이번 세션에서는 열 분만 선발할 예정입니다. 아울러 관심 있는 참가자 수가 늘어나고 있다는 점을 기억해 주세요. **18**선발된 참가자들에게는 상세한 운전 경로가 발송됩니다.

어휘 | complete a survey 설문 조사에 응답하다 indicate 알리다, 표시하다 be willing to 기꺼이 ~하다 organize 준비하다, 조직하다 participant 참가자 gift certificate 상품권

16 메시지의 주제는?
(A) 제품 테스트 세션   (B) 반려동물 훈련 강좌
(C) 면접   (D) 직원 워크숍

해설 | 메시지의 주제
초반부에서 반려동물을 위해 디자인한 새 놀이 장난감을 개에게 시험해 보겠다고 했다(you indicated that you'd be willing to have your dog test out a new play toy that our company is designing for pets)고 한 후, 준비하고 있는 세션이 10월 2일에 열릴 예정(The session we're organizing will be held on October second)이라고 했으므로 (A)가 정답이다.

Paraphrasing 담화의 test out a new play toy
→ 정답의 A product test session

17 화자가 "관심 있는 참가자 수가 늘어나고 있다"라고 말할 때, 그 의도는 무엇인가?
(A) 행사가 며칠간 이어질 것이다.
(B) 직원이 지시를 따르지 않았다.
(C) 답을 빨리 줘야 한다.
(D) 등록 절차가 개선됐다.

해설 | 화자의 의도
중반부에서 관심이 있다고 알려주시려면 555-0168로 전화를 달라(To confirm your interest, please call 555-0168)고 요청하면서 이번 세션에서는 열 분만 선발할 예정(We will choose only ten for this session)이라고 한 후, 관심 있는 참가자 수가 늘어나고 있다(the list of interested participants is growing)고 덧붙였다. 이는 참여 여부를 빨리 알려 달라는 의도라고 볼 수 있으므로 (C)가 정답이다.

어휘 | instructions 지시, 설명 registration 등록

18 화자는 참가자들에게 무엇을 보낼 것이라고 말하는가?
(A) 견본   (B) 청구서
(C) 설문지   (D) 길 안내

해설 | 참가자들에게 보내 줄 것
후반부에서 선발된 참가자들에게는 상세한 운전 경로가 발송된다(Selected participants will be sent detailed driving directions)고 했으므로 (D)가 정답이다.

어휘 | invoice 청구서, 송장 questionnaire 설문지

[19-21] 전화 메시지 + 배치도

M-Cn Rita, this is Diego. I'm calling to discuss the plan for this year's growing season. I sent you a map of how the fields were laid out last year. **19**I was thinking we could replace the soybeans with spinach this year. Remember, the harsh winter weather caused a lot of crop damage, especially for our soybeans. We can't afford to lose any profits from another bad harvest season. And **20**we'll need that money if we hope to purchase new farming equipment next year. **21**I'd also like to talk about expanding our farm stand at the city farmers market. The stall next to ours just became vacant. Call me back so that we can discuss.

리타, 디에고예요. 올해 재배 시기 계획을 논의하려고 전화했어요. 작년에 밭이 어떻게 배치됐는지 표시한 지도를 보냈습니다. **¹⁹올해는 콩을 시금치로 교체할 수 있을 거라고 생각했어요.** 혹독한 겨울 날씨로 많은 작물, 특히 우리 콩이 피해를 입었잖아요. 우리에겐 또다시 흉작 기간의 수익을 잃어도 될 만한 여유가 없어요. 그리고 **²⁰내년에 새 농기구를 구입하고자 한다면 돈이 필요할 테고요. ²¹그리고 시 농산물 직판장의 농산물 가판대를 확장하는 문제도 얘기하고 싶어요. 우리 옆 가판대가 비었거든요.** 얘기 나눌 수 있게 전화 주세요.

어휘 | be laid out 배치되다 **harsh** 혹독한 **crop damage** 작물 피해 **can't afford to** ~할 여유가 없다 **profit** 수익, 수입 **expand** 확장하다, 확대하다 **stand** 가판대, 좌판 **stall** 가판대 **vacant** 비어 있는

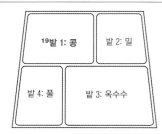

19 시각 정보에 따르면, 새 작물은 어디에 심어질 것인가?
  (A) 밭 1   (B) 밭 2
  (C) 밭 3   (D) 밭 4

해설 | 시각 정보 연계
초반부에서 올해는 콩을 시금치로 교체할 수 있을 거라고 생각한다(I was thinking we could replace the soybeans with spinach this year)고 했다. 밭 배치도를 보면 콩은 밭 1에 배치되어 있으므로 (A)가 정답이다.

20 화자는 내년에 무엇을 하고 싶다고 말하는가?
  (A) 서비스 계약 갱신   (B) 직원 추가 채용
  (C) 자격증 과정 완료   (D) 새 장비 구입

해설 | 화자가 내년에 하고 싶은 일
중반부에서 내년에 새 농기구를 구입하고자 한다면 돈이 필요할 것(we'll need that money if we hope to purchase new farming equipment next year)이라고 했으므로 (D)가 정답이다.

어휘 | renew a contract 계약을 갱신하다 **complete a course** 과정을 마치다, 수료하다 **certification** 증명, 증명서

21 화자는 시 농산물 직판장에 대해 무엇이라고 말하는가?
  (A) 가판대 비용이 올랐다.
  (B) 추가로 공간을 이용할 수 있다.
  (C) 시간대가 연장됐다.
  (D) 주차가 한정되어 있다.

해설 | 시 농산물 직판장에 대해 언급된 내용
후반부에서 시 농산물 직판장의 농산물 가판대를 확장하는 문제도 얘기하고 싶다(I'd also like to talk about expanding our farm stand at the city farmers market)고 한 후, 옆 가판대가 비었다(The stall next to ours just became vacant)고 했으므로 (B)가 정답이다.

어휘 | additional 추가의 **limited** 제한된, 한정된

UNIT 14 공지 / 회의

고득점 전략 **담화 흐름 파악하기** 본책 p.104

W-Am 5분밖에 남지 않았지만 안건 마지막 사항을 짚고 싶습니다. 우리 창고를 더 효율적으로 정리하자는 제안서로, 서머빌 매장에서 제출해 주셨어요. 제안서 사본을 만들었으니 한 부 가져가세요. 연장과 교체 부품을 찾느라 소요되는 자동차 정비 시간을 줄이고자 하는 계획인데요. 흥미로운 아이디어들이 있는데 모든 지점에 적용될지 잘 모르겠어요. 여러분 중 몇몇은 다른 지점 세 곳을 잘 아시죠. 전반적으로 변경 사항을 실행하는 것에 관한 여러분의 생각을 이메일로 보내 주시겠어요? 고맙습니다!

어휘 | touch on 언급하다 **agenda** 안건, 의제 **storage** 저장, 보관 **auto mechanic** 자동차 정비소 **replacement** 교체 **apply to** ~에 적용되다 **implement** 실행하다 **across the board** 전반에 걸쳐

1 화자는 무엇을 논의하고 싶어하는가?
  (A) 보관 장소 재정리 계획   (B) 서머빌 직원 급여 인상

2 화자들은 어떤 유형의 업체에서 일하겠는가?
  (A) 자동차 수리 서비스   (B) 전자제품 매장

3 화자는 청자들에게 무엇을 해 달라고 요청하는가?
  (A) 계약서 변경하기   (B) 이메일로 의견 보내기

어휘 | revise 변경하다, 개정하다

ETS 유형 연습

본책 p.105

1 (D) **2** (A) **3** (C) **4** (B) **5** (A) **6** (D)
7 (C) **8** (B) **9** (D)

[1-3] 매장 안내 방송

W-Am Attention, customers. **¹**We're committed to offering the lowest prices on all our products, from clothing and jewelry to electronics and furniture. **²**We encourage everyone to sign up for our frequent-shopper membership card. You'll earn reward points with each purchase to use for discounts in the future. Members also receive early notifications by e-mail about concerts and other special events at the store—**³**like the bakers' showcase currently taking place on the second floor, where local pastry bakers are giving out samples of their creative creations.

고객 여러분께 알려드립니다. **¹저희는 의류, 장신구부터 전자제품 및 가구에 이르기까지 전 제품을 최저 가격으로 제공하고자 노력하고 있습니다. ²모두 저희 단골 고객 회원 카드를 신청하실 것을 권합니다.** 구매 시마다 향후 할인을 받을 수 있는 보상 포인트를 받습니다. 또한 회원은 매장에서 열리는 음악회 및 기타 특별

행사에 관해 이메일로 미리 알림 메시지를 받을 수 있습니다. **³현재 2층에서 열리고 있는 제빵업체 공개 행사도 마찬가지인데요.** 지역 내 페이스트리 업체들이 창의적으로 만든 시식용 제품을 나눠 드리고 있습니다.

1 안내는 어디에서 이뤄지겠는가?
(A) 식당 (B) 극장
(C) 자동차 대리점 (D) 백화점

해설 | **안내 장소**
초반부에서 의류, 장신구부터 전자제품 및 가구에 이르기까지 전 제품을 최저 가격으로 제공하고자 노력하고 있다(We're committed to offering the lowest prices on all our products, from clothing and jewelry to electronics and furniture)고 했으므로 (D)가 정답이다.

어휘 | car dealership 자동차 대리점

2 청자들에게 무엇을 신청하라고 권하는가?
(A) 보상 프로그램 (B) 대회
(C) 워크숍 (D) 포커스 그룹

해설 | **청자들에게 권장한 신청**
초반부에서 모두 단골 고객 회원 카드를 신청하실 것을 권한다(We encourage everyone to sign up for our frequent-shopper membership card)고 했으므로 (A)가 정답이다.

어휘 | reward 보상 focus group 포커스 그룹(상품시장이나 선거동향의 조사를 위해 뽑힌 소수의 샘플 그룹)

Paraphrasing 담화의 our frequent-shopper membership card → 정답의 A rewards program

3 청자들은 2층에서 무엇을 할 수 있는가?
(A) 음악 감상 (B) 유명 인사와의 만남
(C) 시식 (D) 사진 촬영

해설 | **청자들이 2층에서 할 수 있는 것**
후반부에서 현재 2층에서 지역 내 페이스트리 업체들이 창의적으로 만든 시식용 제품을 나눠주고 있다(like the bakers' showcase currently taking place on the second floor, where local pastry bakers are giving out samples of their creative creations)고 했으므로 (C)가 정답이다.

어휘 | celebrity 유명 인사 sample 시식하다, 시음하다

Paraphrasing 담화의 local pastry bakers are giving out samples of their creative creations → 정답의 Sample some food

[4-6] 회의 발췌

M-Cn **⁴Before you begin your shifts, I have some good news. ⁴, ⁵A new fabric-cutting machine will be installed on the assembly line this week.** This machine will speed up clothing production, but it operates differently than the previous one. Everyone is required to be trained on using this piece of equipment. **⁶Several training sessions will be held throughout the week. Please sign up for one before you leave today.** The sign-up sheet is in the break room.

⁴교대 근무를 시작하시기 전에 좋은 소식을 전합니다. ⁴, ⁵이번 주에 새 직물 재단 기계가 조립 라인에 설치될 예정입니다. 이 기계는 의류 생산 속도를 높여 주겠지만 이전 기계와는 다르게 작동합니다. 모두 해당 장비 사용 교육을 받아야 해요. **⁶한 주에 걸쳐 교육이 몇 회 있을 겁니다. 오늘 퇴근하기 전에 하나 신청해 주세요.** 신청서는 휴게실에 있습니다.

4 청자들은 누구이겠는가?
(A) 수리 기술자 (B) 공장 근로자
(C) 가구 판매원 (D) 공사 인부

해설 | **청자들의 신분**
초반부에서 교대 근무를 시작하시기 전에 좋은 소식을 전한다(Before you begin your shifts, I have some good news)고 한 후, 이번 주에 새 직물 재단 기계가 조립 라인에 설치될 예정(A new fabric-cutting machine will be installed on the assembly line this week)이라고 했으므로 (B)가 정답이다.

어휘 | construction 건설, 공사

5 화자는 어떤 변화를 알리는가?
(A) 새 장비가 설치될 예정이다.
(B) 일부 교대 근무 시간이 일찍 종료될 것이다.
(C) 시설이 확장될 것이다.
(D) 새 계약서에 서명할 것이다.

해설 | **화자가 알린 변화**
초반부에서 이번 주에 새 직물 재단 기계가 조립 라인에 설치될 예정(A new fabric-cutting machine will be installed on the assembly line this week)이라고 했으므로 (A)가 정답이다.

어휘 | enlarge 확장하다, 확대하다 contract 계약

Paraphrasing 담화의 A new fabric-cutting machine → 정답의 Some new equipment

6 청자들은 무엇을 하라고 요청을 받았는가?
(A) 설명서 읽기 (B) 설문지 작성하기
(C) 견본 가져가기 (D) 교육 신청하기

해설 | **청자들에게 요청한 일**
후반부에서 한 주에 걸쳐 교육이 몇 회 있을 건데 오늘 퇴근 전에 하나 신청해 달라(Several training sessions ~ sign up for one before you leave today)고 했으므로 (D)가 정답이다.

어휘 | fill out a questionnaire 설문지를 작성하다

Paraphrasing 담화의 sign up for → 정답의 Register for

W-Am At our last team meeting, ⁷I asked everyone to write a detailed description of their work responsibilities, and those are due today. The reason I wanted everyone to do this is because each of you will be assigned a backup. That person will take over your responsibilities on the days you're not available. ⁸After this meeting, I'll e-mail you a staff list that includes the name of each person's backup. ⁹Please share the draft of your job description with your backup so that any needed clarifications can be made. The final version isn't due until the end of the month, but several staff members are taking vacations this month.

지난 팀 회의에서 ⁷모든 분께 직무를 상세 기술해 달라고 요청했는데요. 오늘까지입니다. 모든 분이 해 주셨으면 했던 이유는 각자 지원 인력을 배정받을 것이기 때문입니다. 해당 인력은 여러분의 시간이 되지 않을 때 여러분의 직무를 인계 받을 겁니다. ⁸이 회의가 끝나면 각자의 지원 인력 이름이 담긴 직원 목록을 이메일로 보내겠습니다. ⁹직무 기술 초안을 지원 인력과 공유해서 필요한 부분은 설명이 이뤄질 수 있도록 하세요. 최종 버전은 월말까지 하지 않아도 되지만 몇몇 직원이 이번 달에 휴가를 가니까요.

어휘 | detailed 상세한 description 묘사, 서술 responsibility 책무 due 하기로 되어 있는 assign 임무를 배정하다 backup 지원 take over 인계 받다 job description 직무기술서 clarification 설명

7 청자들은 오늘까지 무엇의 초안을 작성하도록 요청을 받았는가?
(A) 제품 후기 　　　　　(B) 예산 제안서
(C) 직무 기술서 　　　　(D) 사용자 설명서

해설 | 청자들이 작성 요청을 받은 것
초반부에서 모든 분께 직무를 상세 기술해 달라고 요청했고, 오늘까지(I asked everyone to write a detailed description of their work responsibilities, and those are due today)라고 했으므로 (C)가 정답이다.

어휘 | budget 예산

Paraphrasing 담화의 due today → 질문의 by today
담화의 a detailed description of their work responsibilities → 정답의 Job descriptions

8 화자는 회의 후 무엇을 하겠다고 말하는가?
(A) 이력서 검토 　　　　(B) 명단 전송
(C) 참가 신청서 게시 　　(D) 프로젝트 일정표 생성

해설 | 회의 후 할 일
중반부에서 이 회의가 끝나면 각자의 지원 인력 이름이 담긴 직원 목록을 이메일로 보내겠다(After this meeting, I'll e-mail you a staff list that includes the name of each person's backup)고 했으므로 (B)가 정답이다.

어휘 | résumé 이력서 sign-up sheet 참가 신청서

Paraphrasing 담화의 e-mail you a staff list that includes the name of each person's backup → 정답의 Send a list of names

9 화자가 "몇몇 직원이 이번 달에 휴가를 가니까요"라고 말한 이유는?
(A) 직장 혜택 예시를 제공하려고
(B) 추가 자원을 요청하려고
(C) 지연 이유를 제공하려고
(D) 청자들이 일을 빨리 완료할 수 있도록 독려하려고

해설 | 화자의 의도
후반부에서 직무 기술 초안을 지원 인력과 공유해서 필요한 부분은 설명이 이뤄질 수 있도록 하라(Please share the draft of your job description with your backup so that any needed clarifications can be made)고 한 후, 최종 버전은 월말까지 하지 않아도 된다(The final version isn't due until the end of the month)고 했다. 이어서 몇몇 직원이 이번 달에 휴가를 간다(several staff members are taking vacations this month)고 말하는 것은 휴가 가는 직원들이 있으니 미리 해두라는 의미이므로 (D)가 정답이다.

어휘 | benefit 혜택 additional 추가의 resource 자원

ETS 고득점 실전 문제　　　　본책 p.106

1 (C)	2 (B)	3 (D)	4 (C)	5 (D)	6 (B)
7 (D)	8 (C)	9 (A)	10 (A)	11 (C)	12 (D)
13 (B)	14 (C)	15 (C)	16 (C)	17 (A)	18 (D)
19 (B)	20 (C)	21 (B)			

[1-3] 회의 발췌

W-Am Good morning, staff. ¹Please be aware that, next week, the main parking area in front of our office building will be closed for repaving. Parking will be very limited because of the trucks and machines and the work that'll be going on. So ²I ask employees to carpool as much as possible. Or you could consider taking a taxi or public transit. ³I want to emphasize that the date will be the same for our annual five-kilometer race. The asphalt will have settled by then, so our parking area will be ready to accommodate cars.

안녕하세요, 직원 여러분. ¹다음 주에 사무실 건물 앞 주요 주차 공간이 재포장 때문에 폐쇄된다는 것을 알아 두세요. 트럭과 기계, 진행 중인 작업 때문에 주차 공간이 매우 한정될 겁니다. 그래서 ²가능한 한 카풀을 하시라고 요청 드립니다. 아니면 택시나 대중교통을 이용하는 것도 고려해 보실 수 있죠. ³우리 연례 5km 경주는 날짜가 그대로라는 걸 강조하고 싶네요. 그때까지 아스팔트는 완료될 테니 우리 주차 공간은 차를 수용할 준비가 갖춰질 겁니다.

1 화자는 주로 무엇에 대해 이야기하는가?
(A) 회사 합병   (B) 이전 기회
(C) 공사 프로젝트   (D) 곧 있을 워크숍

해설 | 이야기 주제
초반부에서 사무실 건물 앞 주요 주차 공간이 재포장 때문에 폐쇄된다(the main parking area in front of our office building will be closed for repaving)고 했으므로 (C)가 정답이다.

어휘 | merger 합병   relocation 이동, 이전

2 화자는 청자들에게 무엇을 하라고 요청하는가?
(A) 방으로 여분의 의자 가져오기
(B) 대체 교통 수단 고려하기
(C) 회의가 끝날 때까지 질문하지 않고 기다리기
(D) 추가로 업무하기

해설 | 화자의 요청 사항
중반부에서 가능한 한 카풀을 요청하고 아니면 택시나 대중교통을 이용하는 것도 고려해 보실 수 있다(I ask employees to carpool ~ Or you could consider taking a taxi or public transit)고 했으므로 (B)가 정답이다.

어휘 | alternate 대안의   transportation 수송, 운송

3 화자는 곧 있을 경주에 대해 무엇을 강조하는가?
(A) 홍보가 더 필요하다.
(B) 올해 다른 경로로 갈 것이다.
(C) 예산이 증액되지 않을 것이다.
(D) 행사 일자는 변경되지 않을 것이다.

해설 | 곧 있을 경주에 대한 강조 사항
후반부에서 연례 5km 경주는 같은 날짜라는 걸 강조하고 싶다(I want to emphasize that the date will be the same for our annual five-kilometer race)고 했으므로 (D)가 정답이다.

어휘 | publicity 홍보

Paraphrasing 담화의 be the same → 정답의 not change

[4-6] 회의 발췌

W-Am [4]As the president of the company, I've reviewed the proposals submitted by Dr. Bora's team and Mr. Gupta's team. [5]Each group of developers refined their designs for our next motorcycle model, with the understanding that only one proposal would be funded. As you know, we were looking for several key attributes: wireless technology, adjustable padding in the seat, and, of course, superior road handling. [6]Today I am pleased to announce that both proposals will

advance to the next stage of development. I see a lot of surprised faces in the audience! Well, we received some last-minute funding in the budget!

[4]저는 사장으로서 보라 박사님의 팀과 굽타 씨의 팀이 제출한 제안서들을 검토했습니다. [5]각 개발자 팀들이 단 하나의 제안서만 기금을 받을 수 있다는 조건 하에 우리 다음 오토바이 모델 디자인을 개선해 주셨는데요. 알다시피 우리는 무선 기술, 조절 가능한 좌석 안장 충전재, 그리고 당연히 우수한 도로 주행 등 몇 가지 주요 특징을 추구하고 있죠. [6]오늘 두 개의 제안서 모두 다음 개발 단계로 진행된다는 사실을 알리게 되어 기쁩니다. 청중석에서 놀란 표정이 많이 보이네요. 네, 막바지에 예산 기금을 받았습니다!

4 화자는 누구인가?
(A) 품질 관리 감독관   (B) 부품 납품업자
(C) 사장   (D) 채용 관리자

해설 | 화자의 신분
초반부에서 사장으로서 보라 박사님의 팀과 굽타 씨의 팀이 제출한 제안서들을 검토했다(As the president of the company, I've reviewed the proposals submitted by Dr. Bora's team and Mr. Gupta's team)고 했으므로 (C)가 정답이다.

어휘 | inspector 감독관, 조사관   supplier 납품업자, 제공업체

5 어떤 종류의 제품이 언급되는가?
(A) 사무용 가구   (B) 컴퓨터 소프트웨어
(C) 헤드폰   (D) 오토바이

해설 | 언급된 제품의 종류
초반부에서 각 개발자 팀들이 다음 오토바이 모델 디자인을 개선해 주었다(Each group of developers refined their designs for our next motorcycle model)고 했으므로 (D)가 정답이다.

6 화자가 "막바지에 예산 기금을 받았습니다"라고 말한 이유는?
(A) 일정표에 관해 불만을 제기하려고
(B) 결정을 내리게 된 이유를 설명하려고
(C) 동료들에게 프로젝트에 자원하도록 요청하려고
(D) 장비 업그레이드를 제안하려고

해설 | 화자의 의도
후반부에서 오늘 두 개의 제안서 모두 다음 개발 단계로 진행된다는 사실을 알리게 되어 기쁘다(Today I am pleased to announce that both proposals will advance to the next stage of development)고 한 후, 막바지에 예산 기금을 받았다(we received some last-minute funding in the budget)고 했다. 이는 예산 기금 덕분에 일을 진행할 수 있게 결정되었다는 의미이므로 (B)가 정답이다.

어휘 | timeline 일정표   decision 결정   colleague 동료

M-Cn [7]Before you begin your factory shifts today, I want to mention an issue that's come to my attention. [7, 8]The buttons on a number of men's shirts aren't lining up with the buttonholes. I'm guessing this defect was caused when the measurements were taken to create the pattern. I plan to investigate this, but I'm sorry…[9]I'm going to have to give you new assignments for the next few days. You're going to be moved to the fabric cutting room. Please let me know if you have any questions.

[7]오늘 공장 교대 근무를 시작하기 전에, 제가 알게 된 문제에 관해 언급하고 싶습니다. [7, 8]많은 남성 셔츠의 단추가 단춧구멍과 줄이 맞지 않아요. 옷본을 만들기 위해 치수를 잴 때 해당 결함이 생긴 걸로 짐작합니다. 이 문제를 조사할 계획인데요. 죄송하지만 [9]여러분께 앞으로 며칠간 새 업무를 드려야 할 것 같습니다. 여러분은 직물 재단실로 이동하실 겁니다. 질문이 있으면 알려주세요.

어휘 | come to one's attention 알게 되다 line up with ~와 일렬로 세우다 defect 결함 measurements 치수 investigate 조사하다 assignment 과제, 임무

7 화자는 어디에 있겠는가?
(A) 공예작품점   (B) 드라이클리닝 업체
(C) 백화점   (D) 의류 제조 공장

해설 | **화자가 있는 장소**
초반부에서 오늘 공장 교대 근무를 시작하기 전(Before you begin your factory shifts today)이라고 했고, 다량의 남성 셔츠 단추가 단춧구멍과 줄이 맞지 않는다(The buttons on a number of men's shirts aren't lining up with the buttonholes)고 했으므로 (D)가 정답이다.

어휘 | craft 공예 manufacturing plant 제조 공장
Paraphrasing 담화의 factory → 정답의 manufacturing plant
담화의 shirts → 정답의 clothing

8 화자는 어떤 문제를 언급하는가?
(A) 판매량이 감소했다.
(B) 배송이 지연됐다.
(C) 일부 제품에 결함이 있다.
(D) 경쟁이 늘어났다.

해설 | **화자가 언급하는 문제점**
초반부에서 많은 남성 셔츠의 단추가 단춧구멍과 줄이 맞지 않는다(The buttons on a number of men's shirts aren't lining up with the buttonholes)고 했으므로 (C)가 정답이다.

어휘 | decline 줄어들다, 감소하다 defective 결함이 있는
Paraphrasing 담화의 The buttons ~ aren't lining up with the buttonholes
→ 정답의 Some products are defective.

9 청자들은 무엇을 해야 하는가?
(A) 다른 구역에서 근무하기   (B) 교육 강좌 듣기
(C) 관리자와 면담하기   (D) 일찍 출근하기

해설 | **청자들이 해야 할 일**
후반부에서 여러분께 앞으로 며칠간 새 업무를 드려야 할 것 같다(I'm going to have to give you new assignments for the next few days)고 한 후, 직물 재단실로 이동할 것(You're going to be moved to the fabric cutting room)이라고 했으므로 (A)가 정답이다.

어휘 | supervisor 감독관, 관리자

W-Br I'd like to announce that our company has decided to franchise five locations in California by year's end. Our business will start selling the right for entrepreneurs to operate their own restaurants under our name. [10]I was initially hesitant because it would mean that certain store-specific choices would no longer be up to us. But now I feel confident that this is the right next step to take. [11]I spent time over the past week with a consulting firm, and we agreed that this will help us invest in our brand. And [12]California was an obvious choice for franchising, as the new restaurants will be close to many of the farmers who grow our food.

우리 회사는 올해 말까지 캘리포니아에 5개 지점에 가맹점 영업권을 주기로 결정했음을 알려드립니다. 기업가들에게 저희 이름을 걸고 자신의 식당을 운영할 권한을 판매하기 시작하는 겁니다. [10]특정 매장별 선택이 더 이상 우리가 결정할 수 있는 사안이 아니라는 점 때문에 처음에는 망설였어요. 하지만 이것이 올바른 다음 조치라고 확신합니다. [11]지난주에 컨설팅 업체와 시간을 보냈는데요. 이것이 우리 브랜드에 투자하도록 돕는다는 사실에 동의했어요. [12]캘리포니아는 가맹점 영업권을 판매하기에 확실한 선택지입니다. 새 식당들이 우리 식량을 재배하는 다수의 농부들과 가까울 테니까요.

어휘 | franchise 가맹점 영업권을 주다 entrepreneur 기업가 operate 운영하다 initially 처음에 hesitant 망설이는, 주저하는 no longer 더 이상 ~아닌 be up to ~에 달렸다 obvious 분명한, 확실한

10 화자가 처음에 결정에 대해 자신 없었던 이유는?
(A) 회사가 통제권을 포기해야 해서
(B) 회사가 대규모 초기 투자를 해야 해서
(C) 회사가 신규 시장 조사를 해야 해서
(D) 회사가 직원을 더 채용해야 해서

해설 | **화자가 처음에 자신 없었던 이유**
중반부에서 특정 매장별 선택이 더 이상 화자의 회사가 결정할 수 있는 사안이 아니라는 점 때문에 처음에는 망설였다(I was initially hesitant ~ certain store-specific choices would no longer be up to us)고 했으므로 (A)가 정답이다.

Paraphrasing 담화의 initially hesitant → 질문의 unsure about a decision at first
담화의 certain store-specific choices would no longer be up to us → 정답의 giving up some control

11 화자는 지난주에 무엇을 했다고 말하는가?
(A) 투자자들에게 콘셉트를 발표했다.
(B) 휴가 정책을 재평가했다.
(C) 컨설턴트들을 만났다.
(D) 새 장비를 구입했다.

해설 | 화자가 지난주에 한 일
중반부에서 지난주에 컨설팅 업체와 시간을 보냈다(I spent time over the past week with a consulting firm)고 했으므로 (C)가 정답이다.

어휘 | reevaluate 재평가하다 policy 정책

Paraphrasing 담화의 spent time with a consulting firm → 정답의 met with consultants

12 회사가 캘리포니아를 선택한 이유는?
(A) 본사와 가까워서
(B) 많은 잠재 고객이 있어서
(C) 다양한 부동산 선택지를 제공해서
(D) 많은 납품업체들이 기반을 둔 곳이라서

해설 | 캘리포니아를 선택한 이유
후반부에서 캘리포니아는 가맹점 영업권을 판매하기에 확실한 선택지(California was an obvious choice for franchising)인데, 그 이유로 새 식당들이 우리 식품을 재배하는 다수의 농부들과 가까울 것(as the new restaurants will be close to many of the farmers who grow our food)이라고 했으므로 (D)가 정답이다.

어휘 | headquarters 본사 potential customer 잠재 고객 real estate 부동산 supplier 공급업체, 납품업체

Paraphrasing 담화의 many of the farmers who grow our food → 정답의 many suppliers

[13-15] 영화관 안내 방송

W-Am Attention Cinema Oldies patrons. **13**The eight o'clock showing of the classic movie *Adventures in the Forest* is sold out, but there are plenty of tickets available for tomorrow's shows. And remember, **14**tickets are half price for the first show tomorrow at one P.M. To view our full movie schedule, please visit our Web site. **15**If you purchase your movie tickets online, you'll be entered in a contest to win some fabulous prizes. Thank you for visiting Cinema Oldies.

시네마 올디스 고객 여러분께 알려드립니다. **13**고전 영화 〈숲속의 모험〉 8시 상영은 매진되었습니다만, 내일 영화표는 많이 있습니다. **14**내일 오후 1시 첫 상영은 표가 반값이라는 사실을 기억해 주세요. 전체 상영 시간표를 보시려면 저희 웹사이트를 방문하세요. **15**저희 영화표를 온라인으로 구입하시면 멋진 경품을 받을 수 있도록 응모가 이뤄집니다. 시네마 올디스를 찾아 주셔서 감사합니다.

어휘 | attention (안내방송에서) 알립니다 patron 후원자, 고객 plenty of 많은 available 구할 수 있는, 이용 가능한 enter 참가하게 하다 fabulous 엄청난, 굉장한

13 안내 방송의 주목적은?
(A) 표 가격 인상에 대해 설명하려고
(B) 극장 상영 관련 정보를 제공하려고
(C) 스낵바의 특별 음식에 관해 설명하려고
(D) 청자들에게 휴대전화를 무음으로 해 달라고 요청하려고

해설 | 안내 방송의 목적
초반부에서 고전 영화 8시 상영은 매진되었지만, 내일 영화표는 많이 있다(The eight o'clock showing of the classic movie *Adventures in the Forest* is sold out, but there are plenty of tickets available for tomorrow's shows)고 했으므로 (B)가 정답이다.

어휘 | increase 인상, 증가 silence 조용하게 만들다

14 화자는 내일 오후 1시 상영에 관해 무엇이라고 말하는가?
(A) 영화 개봉작이다.
(B) 영화제의 일부이다.
(C) 표 가격이 인하된다.
(D) 유명 인사가 사인을 해 줄 것이다.

해설 | 화자가 내일 오후 1시 상영에 관해 언급한 것
중반부에서 내일 오후 1시 첫 상영은 표가 반값(tickets are half price for the first show tomorrow at one P.M.)이라고 했으므로 (C)가 정답이다.

어휘 | premiere 개봉, 초연 celebrity 유명 인사 sign an autograph 사인을 하다

Paraphrasing 담화의 show → 질문의 movie
담화의 tickets are half price → 정답의 Ticket prices are reduced.

15 청자들은 온라인으로 티켓 구입 시 무엇을 받게 되는가?
(A) 무료 간식　　　　　　(B) 영화 기념품
(C) 경품 응모　　　　　　(D) 고객 포인트 적립 카드

해설 | 청자들이 온라인 티켓 구입시 받는 것
후반부에서 영화표를 온라인으로 구입하시면 멋진 경품을 받을 수 있도록 응모가 이뤄진다(If you purchase your movie tickets online, you'll be entered in a contest to win some fabulous prizes)고 했으므로 (C)가 정답이다.

어휘 | complimentary 무료의 souvenir 기념품 loyalty card 포인트 적립 카드

Paraphrasing 담화의 be entered in a contest → 정답의 A contest entry

[16-18] 진료실 안내 방송

W-Br Attention, please. **16**For those of you who have come in for a doctor's appointment, please know that our self-check-in kiosks are not functioning properly—our technical support team is working on the machines now. **17**The issue will be resolved soon, but in the meantime, we need to stay on schedule with your appointments. There are two associates at the front desk. I'll make another announcement when the self-check-in kiosks are ready to use again. **18**If you haven't yet completed the required medical forms, please use your smartphone to go online and fill them out while you're waiting. Thank you.

알립니다. **16**진료 예약 건으로 오신 분들께 저희 셀프 체크인 단말기가 제대로 작동하지 않음을 알려드립니다. 기술 지원팀이 지금 기계를 손보고 있습니다. **17**문제가 곧 해결될 예정입니다만 그동안 여러분의 예약을 일정대로 진행해야 합니다. 안내데스크에 두 명의 직원이 있습니다. 셀프 체크인 단말기를 사용할 준비가 되면 다시 공지를 드리겠습니다. **18**필요한 진료 서식을 아직 작성하지 않으셨다면 대기하시는 동안 스마트폰으로 온라인에 접속하셔서 작성해 주세요. 감사합니다.

어휘 | appointment 약속, 예약 function (제대로) 기능하다, 작용하다 properly 제대로 resolve 해결하다 in the meantime 그동안, 당분간 associate 동료 make an announcement 공표하다, 발표하다 fill out 기입하다

16 안내 방송은 어디서 이뤄지겠는가?
(A) 호텔 　　　　　　(B) 미용실
(C) 병원 　　　　　　(D) 회의장

해설 | 안내 방송 장소
초반부에서 진료 예약 건으로 오신 분들(For those of you who have come in for a doctor's appointment)이라고 했으므로 (C)가 정답이다.

어휘 | take place 개최되다, 일어나다

17 화자가 "안내데스크에 두 명의 직원이 있습니다"라고 말한 이유는?
(A) 청자들에게 안내해 주려고
(B) 추가로 직원을 요청하려고
(C) 절차가 느리다고 항의하려고
(D) 직원 추가 채용 제안에 동의하려고

해설 | 화자의 의도
중반부에서 문제가 곧 해결될 예정입니다만 그동안 예약을 일정대로 진행해야 한다(The issue will be resolved soon, but in the meantime, we need to stay on schedule with your appointments)고 한 후 안내데스크에 두 명의 직원이 있다(There are two associates at the front desk)고 했다. 이는 두 명의 직원이 도와줄 거라는 의미이므로 (A)가 정답이다.

어휘 | instructions 설명, 지시 process 절차

18 화자는 일부 청자에게 온라인에서 무엇을 하라고 안내하는가?
(A) 동영상 시청 　　　　(B) 소식지 신청
(C) 의견 전달 　　　　　(D) 서류 작성

해설 | 청자가 온라인에서 할 일
후반부에서 필요한 진료 서식을 아직 작성하지 않았다면 대기하는 동안 스마트폰으로 온라인에 접속해서 작성해 달라(If you haven't yet completed the required medical forms, please use your smartphone to go online and fill them out while you're waiting)고 했으므로 (D)가 정답이다.

어휘 | sign up for ~을 신청하다

Paraphrasing 담화의 completed the required medical forms / fill them out → 정답의 Complete some forms

[19-21] 회의 발췌 + 목록

W-Br Before we wrap up this marketing team meeting, let's go over our project list. **19**The clients called to say how pleased they were with the radio advertisement we created, so congratulations! Since that's done, what's our highest priority now? Well, even though the deadline is further out, **20**we need to focus on the promotional contest this week. The preparations for it will be complicated. In fact, **21**Adriana—I'd like you to work on that. Please sketch out a plan and get it to me tomorrow.

오늘 마케팅팀 회의를 마무리하기 전에 프로젝트 목록을 검토해 봅시다. **19**고객들이 전화해서 우리가 만든 라디오 광고가 아주 만족스러웠다고 얘기했어요. 축하합니다! 그건 완료됐으니 이제 우리의 최우선 사항은 뭐죠? 음, 기한이 더 남긴 했지만 **20**이번 주에는 경품 행사에 집중해야 합니다. 준비가 복잡할 거예요. 사실,**21**아드리아나가 준비를 맡아 줬으면 해요. 대략적인 계획을 세워서 내일 저에게 주세요.

어휘 | wrap up 마무리 짓다 priority 우선 사항 deadline 마감, 기한 promotional 홍보의, 판촉의 preparation 준비 complicated 복잡한 sketch out ~의 개략을 쓰다

프로젝트 목록	기한
1. 라디오 광고	3월 3일
2. 웹사이트	3월 10일
203. 경품 행사	3월 26일
4. 고객 설문 조사	4월 5일

19 화자가 팀에게 축하를 건넨 이유는?
(A) 업무 공간이 정리되어 있다.
(B) 고객들이 만족하고 있다.
(C) 수익이 예상보다 크다.
(D) 광고가 상을 받았다.

해설 | 팀 축하 이유
초반부에서 고객들이 전화해서 팀에서 만든 라디오 광고가 아주 만족스러웠다고 말했다며 축하한다(The clients called to say how pleased they were with the radio advertisement we created, so congratulations)고 했으므로 (B)가 정답이다.

어휘 | organized 정리된, 체계 있는 profit 수익, 수입 win an award 상을 받다, 수상하다

20 시각 정보에 따르면, 이번 주에 팀은 어떤 프로젝트에 집중할 것인가?
(A) 프로젝트 1　　　　(B) 프로젝트 2
(C) 프로젝트 3　　　　(D) 프로젝트 4

해설 | 시각 정보 연계
중반부에서 이번 주에는 경품 행사에 집중해야 한다(we need to focus on the promotional contest this week)고 했다. 목록을 보면 경품 행사는 프로젝트 3에 있으므로 (C)가 정답이다.

21 화자는 아드리아나에게 내일까지 무엇을 해 달라고 요청하는가?
(A) 로고 디자인 그리기　　(B) 프로젝트 계획 초안 잡기
(C) 질문 목록 준비하기　　(D) 계약서 보내기

해설 | 화자의 요청 사항
후반부에서 아드리아나가 준비를 맡아 줬으면 한다(Adriana—I'd like you to work on that)고 한 후, 대략적인 계획을 세워서 내일 달라(Please sketch out a plan and get it to me tomorrow)고 했으므로 (B)가 정답이다.

어휘 | draft 초안을 작성하다　contract 계약서

Paraphrasing 담화의 sketch out a plan
→ 정답의 Draft a project plan

UNIT 15 설명 / 소개

고득점 전략 담화 흐름 파악하기　　본책 p.108

M-Au 반갑습니다, 여러분. 서로 인사 나누고 요리 경력에 대해 얘기할 기회가 있었기를 바랍니다. 여러분 모두 프레시 카페 팀에서 요리를 시작하게 된 것을 기뻐하고 계시죠. 앞으로 몇 주간 이 프로그램에서 여러분은 혁신적인 요리 준비 방법, 고객 특별 요청 및 식이 관련 사항 처리 방법 등 저희 매장에서 일을 시작하며 알아야 할 것들을 배울 것입니다. 마지막 날에는 지역 농장으로 갑니다. 저희가 제철 채소를 공급받는 곳이죠. 늘 알찬 하루 보내세요!

어휘 | innovative 혁신적인　handle 다루다, 처리하다
dietary 음식의, 식이 요법의

1 청자들은 누구이겠는가?
(A) 지역사회 정원사들　　(B) 전문 요리사들

2 프로그램의 주목적은?
(A) 신입사원 교육　　　　(B) 고객층 확대

어휘 | customer base 고객층

3 화자는 청자들이 마지막 날 무엇을 할 것이라고 말하는가?
(A) 시연 보기　　　　　　(B) 지역 공급업체 방문하기

어휘 | demonstration 시범 설명, 입증

ETS 유형 연습　　本책 p.109

| **1** (C) | **2** (D) | **3** (D) | **4** (B) | **5** (A) | **6** (D) |
| **7** (B) | **8** (C) | **9** (D) | | | |

[1-3] 연설

W-Am [1]I'd like to thank the Lintown Chamber of Commerce for honoring us with their Strategic Growth Excellence award. When we started this company ten years ago, [2]all we had was a small farm and a dream. We never imagined we'd become the main supplier of fruits and vegetables to restaurants and grocery stores across the region. To celebrate our success, [3]I'm proud to announce that my company is making a pledge to the Lintown Community Center to fund summer educational programs about healthy eating.

[1]전략적 성장 우수상을 저희에게 주신 린타운 상공회의소에 감사드리고 싶습니다. 10년 전 회사를 처음 시작했을 때, [2]가진 거라고는 작은 농장과 꿈밖에 없었습니다. 지역 전체 식당과 상점에 과일과 채소를 납품하는 주요 업체가 되리라는 것은 상상도 못 했어요. 저희 회사는 성공을 기념하기 위해 [3]건강한 식생활에 관한 하계 교육 프로그램 기금을 린타운 커뮤니티 센터에 제공하겠다고 자랑스럽게 약속합니다.

어휘 | chamber of commerce 상공회의소　honor ~에게 영예를 주다　strategic 전략적인　make a pledge 서약하다
fund ~에 자금을 제공하다

1 연설은 어디서 이뤄지겠는가?
(A) 주주회의　　　　　(B) 은퇴 기념식
(C) 시상식　　　　　　(D) 영업 발표

해설 | 연설 장소
초반부에서 전략적 성장 우수상을 주신 린타운 상공회의소에 감사드리고 싶다(I'd like to thank the Lintown Chamber of Commerce for honoring us with their Strategic Growth Excellence award)고 했으므로 (C)가 정답이다.

어휘 | shareholder 주주　retirement 은퇴, 퇴직　awards ceremony 시상식

2 화자는 어떤 업계에서 일하겠는가?
(A) 부동산　　　　　　(B) 금융
(C) 의료　　　　　　　(D) 농업

해설 | 화자가 종사하는 업계
중반부에서 가진 거라고는 작은 농장과 꿈밖에 없었는데(a small farm) 지역 전체 식당과 상점에 과일과 채소를 납품하는 주요 업체가 되리라는 것은 상상도 못 했다(we'd become the main supplier of fruits and vegetables)고 했으므로 (D)가 정답이다.

어휘 | real estate 부동산　agriculture 농업

3 화자의 업체는 무엇을 하겠다고 약속하는가?
(A) 하계 축제에 음식 기부
(B) 지역에 취업 프로그램 설립
(C) 새 커뮤니티 센터 건립
(D) 교육 프로그램 기금 제공

해설 | **화자의 업체가 약속한 일**
후반부에서 건강한 식생활에 관한 하계 교육 프로그램 기금을 린타운 커뮤니티 센터에 제공하겠다고 자랑스럽게 약속한다(my company is making a pledge to the Lintown Community Center to fund summer educational programs)고 했으므로 (D)가 정답이다.

어휘 | donate 기부하다

Paraphrasing 담화의 fund summer educational programs → 정답의 Provide funding for educational programs

[4-6] 설명

M-Au Thanks for attending this seminar. [4]Today I'll be talking about the benefits of small-batch production. As you know, this type of manufacturing is about producing small quantities at a time. [5]It's a great strategy when you're just starting out, because it's not as costly as launching large-scale production. I'd say this is one of the greatest benefits to it. [6]If you're interested in reading case studies about small-batch production, I'd recommend Marisol Garcia's latest book.

세미나에 참석해 주셔서 감사합니다. **[4]오늘 저는 소량 생산의 이점에 대해 이야기하려고 합니다.** 알다시피 이런 제조 유형은 한 번에 소량을 생산하는 것입니다. **[5]이제 막 시작한 업체라면 훌륭한 전략이죠. 대규모 생산을 시작하는 것만큼 비용이 많이 들지 않기 때문입니다.** 가장 좋은 이점 중 하나라고 말할 수 있겠네요. **[6]소량 생산에 관한 사례 연구를 읽어 보고 싶으시다면 마리솔 가르시아의 최신 도서를 추천합니다.**

어휘 | small-batch production 소량 생산   manufacturing 제조   strategy 전략   costly 값이 비싼   large-scale production 대규모 생산   case study 사례 연구   latest 최근의, 최신의

4 담화는 주로 무엇에 관한 것인가?
(A) 소셜 미디어 광고   (B) 소량 제조
(C) 제품 해외 수송   (D) 프랜차이즈 투자

해설 | **담화의 주제**
초반부에서 오늘 소량 생산의 이점에 대해 이야기하려고 한다(Today I'll be talking about the benefits of small-batch production)고 한 후, 이런 제조 유형은 한 번에 소량을 생산하는 것(this type of manufacturing is about producing small quantities at a time)이라고 했으므로 (B)가 정답이다.

Paraphrasing 담화의 producing small quantities → 정답의 Manufacturing in small quantities

5 화자는 사업 전략에 대해 어떤 이점을 언급하는가?
(A) 비용이 덜 든다.
(B) 품질 관리가 더 쉽다.
(C) 피드백을 더 빨리 제공할 수 있다.
(D) 더 많은 청중에게 도달할 수 있다.

해설 | **화자가 언급한 사업 전략의 이점**
중반부에서 이제 막 시작한 업체라면 훌륭한 전략이라며 대규모 생산을 시작하는 것만큼 비용이 많이 들지 않기 때문(It's a great strategy ~ because it's not as costly as launching large-scale production)이라고 했으므로 (A)가 정답이다.

어휘 | regulate 관리하다, 조절하다   audience 청중, 관중

Paraphrasing 담화의 not as costly as → 정답의 less expensive

6 화자에 따르면, 청자들은 더 많은 정보를 어떻게 찾을 수 있는가?
(A) 공장을 견학해서   (B) 웹사이트를 방문해서
(C) 강좌에 참석해서   (D) 책을 읽어서

해설 | **청자들이 추가 정보를 찾는 방법**
후반부에서 소량 생산에 관한 사례 연구를 읽어보고 싶으시다면 마리솔 가르시아의 최신 도서를 추천한다(If you're interested in reading case studies about small-batch production, I'd recommend Marisol Garcia's latest book)고 했으므로 (D)가 정답이다.

[7-9] 여행 정보

W-Br Welcome to the one o'clock tour of the historic Bremington Estate. [7]I'm handing out headsets so you'll all be able to hear me during the tour. This beautiful home and the surrounding gardens date back to the eighteenth century. [8]The Bremington Estate is famous for being the filming location of the movie *The Elliot Sisters*. Throughout the tour, I'll point out the rooms used in some memorable scenes. Now, [9]the property is very large, but don't worry, we are open until five o'clock.

역사적인 브레밍턴 에스테이트 1시 투어 프로그램에 오신 것을 환영합니다. 투어 중 제 말을 들으실 수 있도록 [7]헤드셋을 나눠드리겠습니다. 이 아름다운 주택과 주위 정원은 18세기로 거슬러 올라갑니다. [8]브레밍턴 에스테이트는 영화 〈엘리엇 시스터즈〉의 촬영지로 유명하죠. 투어를 하는 동안, 기억할 만한 장면들에 나온 방들을 알려드리겠습니다. 자, [9]구내가 매우 넓지만 걱정 마세요. 5시까지 문을 여니까요.

어휘 | hand out 나눠주다   surrounding 주위의   date back to ~으로 거슬러 올라가다   point out 언급하다   property 건물, 구내, 부동산

7 화자는 청자들에게 무엇을 주는가?
(A) 방문자 명찰   (B) 오디오 헤드셋
(C) 건물 안내도   (D) 투어 티켓

해설 | **화자가 준 것**
초반부에서 헤드셋을 나눠드리겠다(I'm handing out headsets)고 했으므로 (B)가 정답이다.

8 화자에 따르면, 브레밍턴 에스테이트는 무엇으로 알려져 있는가?
(A) 조경상 수상   (B) 광범위한 예술 소장품
(C) 영화 촬영지   (D) 유명 건축가의 설계

해설 | 브레밍턴 에스테이트가 알려진 것
중반부에서 브레밍턴 에스테이트는 영화 〈엘리엇 시스터즈〉의 촬영지로 유명하다(The Bremington Estate is famous for being the filming location of the movie *The Elliot Sisters*)고 했으므로 (C)가 정답이다.

어휘 | landscaping 조경 **extensive** 폭넓은, 광범위한 **architect** 건축가

Paraphrasing 담화의 famous for → 질문의 known for

9 화자가 "5시까지 문을 여니까요"라고 말할 때, 그 의도는 무엇인가?
(A) 직원들이 잘못된 일정표를 받았다.
(B) 안내 책자를 수정해야 한다.
(C) 청자들은 도움을 기다려야 한다.
(D) 청자들이 모든 것을 볼 만한 시간이 있을 것이다.

해설 | 화자의 의도
후반부에서 구내가 매우 넓지만 걱정 말라(the property is very large, but don't worry)고 한 후, 5시까지 문을 연다(we are open until five o'clock)고 덧붙였다. 이 말은 구내가 넓지만 볼 시간이 충분하다는 의도라고 볼 수 있으므로 (D)가 정답이다.

어휘 | revise 수정하다, 변경하다

ETS 고득점 실전 문제　　　本책 p.110

1 (D)　**2** (B)　**3** (D)　**4** (D)　**5** (A)　**6** (C)
7 (B)　**8** (C)　**9** (C)　**10** (D)　**11** (C)　**12** (A)
13 (A)　**14** (C)　**15** (D)　**16** (D)　**17** (B)　**18** (D)
19 (A)　**20** (D)　**21** (B)

[1-3] 인물 소개

M-Au Welcome, everyone. [1]We have over 200 small-business owners here at today's workshop who are all interested in reaching more international customers through the Internet. Our guest speaker is Ming Yang—an expert with over ten years of experience using online marketing tools. [2]He recently published a book on the topic, which has become an international best seller. Before I let Ming take the floor, [3]I'd like to remind you that we've prepared handouts for you. If you didn't pick them up by the entrance when you came in, please do that now.

반갑습니다, 여러분. [1]오늘 이곳 워크숍에는 인터넷을 통해 더 많은 해외 고객에게 다가가는 데 관심이 있는 소규모 업체 소유주 200분 이상이 오셨습니다. 객원 연설자는 밍 양입니다. 온라인 마케팅 도구 활용 경력이 10년이 넘는 전문가이시죠. [2]최근 해당 주제에 관한 책을 출판하셨는데 국제적인 베스트셀러가 됐습니다. 밍 씨를 무대로 모시기에 앞서, [3]여러분을 위한 유인물을 준비했음을 알려드립니다. 들어오실 때 입구 옆에서 가져오지 않으셨다면 지금 가져오십시오.

어휘 | guest speaker 객원 연설자　**handout** 인쇄물, 유인물

1 워크숍의 주제는?
(A) 재무 계획
(B) 책 집필
(C) 리더십 역량
(D) 디지털 마케팅

해설 | 워크숍의 주제
초반부에서 오늘 이곳 워크숍에는 인터넷을 통해 더 많은 해외 고객에게 다가가는 데 관심이 있는 소규모 업체 소유주 200분 이상이 오셨다(We have over 200 small-business owners here at today's workshop who are all interested in reaching more international customers through the Internet)고 했으므로 (D)가 정답이다.

어휘 | financial 금융의, 재무의

Paraphrasing 담화의 through the Internet
→ 정답의 Digital
담화의 reaching more international customers
→ 정답의 marketing

2 밍 양은 최근에 무엇을 했는가?
(A) 상을 받았다.
(B) 책을 출간했다.
(C) TV에 출연했다.
(D) 해외여행을 했다.

해설 | 밍 양이 최근에 한 일
중반부에서 최근 해당 주제에 관한 책을 출판하셨다(He recently published a book on the topic)고 했으므로 (B)가 정답이다.

어휘 | win an award 수상하다　**appear** 나오다, 출연하다

3 화자는 청자들에게 무엇을 하라고 상기시키는가?
(A) 축하연 참석
(B) 다른 워크숍 신청
(C) 피드백 남기기
(D) 유인물 가져오기

해설 | 청자들에게 상기시키는 사항
후반부에서 유인물을 준비했음을 알려드린다(I'd like to remind you that we've prepared handouts for you)고 한 후, 들어올 때 입구 옆에서 가져오지 않았다면 지금 가져오라(If you didn't pick them up by the entrance when you came in, please do that now)고 했으므로 (D)가 정답이다.

어휘 | reception 환영회, 접수처　**sign up for** ~을 신청하다

[4-6] 연설

M-Cn Good morning. [4]As president of RTS Auto Service Centers, I welcome all of you to this shareholders' meeting. I'll begin by talking about our newest service center, which is unique in that it only services electric vehicles. [5]Electric vehicles are still an emerging market, so we were taking a risk by opening a service center with such a narrow focus. But, just last week, a national magazine published an article about us! We've also applied for a grant from a government agency, which I hope will be approved. If it is, ⁶we can use the funds to send our staff to more training programs that specialize in electric vehicles.

안녕하세요. ⁴RTS 오토 서비스 센터 회장으로서, 주주회의에 오신 여러분 모두 환영합니다. 먼저 저희 최신 서비스 센터에 대해 이야기하겠습니다. 전기차만을 정비하는 점이 독특한데요. ⁵전기차는 여전히 부상 중인 시장이기 때문에 그렇게 초점을 좁혀서 서비스 센터를 열며 모험을 하고 있었습니다. 하지만 지난주에 국내 잡지에서 우리에 관한 기사를 게재했어요! 또한 정부기관 보조금을 신청했는데 승인되길 바랍니다. 그렇게 된다면 ⁶전기차에 특화된 교육 프로그램에 직원들을 더 많이 보내는 데 자금을 사용할 수 있습니다.

어휘 | shareholder 주주 emerging 신흥의, 부상하는 take a risk 모험을 하다 apply for ~을 신청하다 grant 보조금 specialize in ~을 전문으로 하다

4 화자는 누구인가?
(A) 정비공   (B) 판매원
(C) 기자   (D) 업체 회장

해설 | 화자의 신분
초반부에서 RTS 오토 서비스 센터 회장으로서, 주주회의에 오신 여러분 모두 환영한다(As president of RTS Auto Service Centers, I welcome all of you to this shareholders' meeting)고 했으므로 (D)가 정답이다.

Paraphrasing 담화의 president of RTS Auto Service Centers → 정답의 A company president

5 화자가 "국내 잡지에서 우리에 관한 기사를 게재했어요"라고 말할 때, 그 의도는 무엇인가?
(A) 사업 계획이 유망해 보인다.
(B) 마케팅 캠페인이 불필요하다.
(C) 문제가 빨리 해결돼야 한다.
(D) 결정이 이미 내려졌다.

해설 | 화자의 의도
중반부에서 전기차는 여전히 부상 중인 시장이기 때문에 그렇게 초점을 좁혀서 서비스 센터를 열며 모험을 하고 있었다(Electric vehicles are still an emerging market ~ by opening a service center with such a narrow focus)고 한 후, 국내 잡지에서 우리에 관한 기사를 게재했다(a national magazine published an article about us)고 덧붙였다. 이는 전기차 서비스 사업이 유망해 보인다는 의도라고 볼 수 있으므로 (A)가 정답이다.

어휘 | promising 유망한, 촉망되는

6 화자는 보조금이 어디에 쓰일 수 있다고 말하는가?
(A) 더 많은 제품 구입   (B) 대출 상환
(C) 교육 기회 제공   (D) 환경 조사 실시

해설 | 보조금을 사용할 곳
후반부에서 전기차에 특화된 교육 프로그램에 직원들을 더 많이 보내는 데 자금을 사용할 수 있다(we can use the funds to send our staff to more training programs that specialize in electric vehicles)고 했으므로 (C)가 정답이다.

어휘 | acquire 획득하다, 습득하다 pay off a loan 대출을 다 갚다 conduct (특정 활동을) 하다

Paraphrasing 담화의 send our staff to more training programs → 정답의 Providing training opportunities

[7-9] 설명

> **M-Cn** OK, I think everyone's here… let's get started. As you know, I'm committed to running an environmentally friendly establishment. ⁷I've had that aim in mind since opening the restaurant. Until now, though, we've been throwing away a lot of food, which isn't good for the environment. So, ⁸starting next month, we'll be changing our waste-disposal practices. Specifically, we'll begin using a composting system for all uneaten or spoiled food. Staff will collect and transport food waste to the composter beside the building. ⁹Let me take you there now to show you how the composter works. It's simple to operate, but it'll be helpful to see it in action.

좋습니다, 모두 모인 것 같네요. 시작하죠. 알다시피 저는 환경 친화적인 시설을 운영하는 데 전념하고 있습니다. ⁷식당 개업 이후 그 목표를 계속 염두에 뒀어요. 하지만 지금까지 우리는 많은 양의 음식을 버렸고 이는 환경에 좋지 않습니다. 따라서 ⁸다음 달부터 쓰레기 처리 관례를 바꿀 예정입니다. 구체적으로 말하면, 먹지 않거나 상한 모든 음식에 대해 비료화 처리 시스템을 사용하기 시작할 겁니다. 직원들은 음식물 쓰레기를 모아 건물 옆 비료 처리기로 가져갈 겁니다. ⁹지금 그곳으로 가서 비료 처리기가 어떻게 작동하는지 보여드리죠. 작동은 간단하지만 작동하는 모습을 보시면 도움이 될 겁니다.

어휘 | be committed to ~에 전념하다, 헌신하다 environmentally friendly 환경 친화적인 establishment 기관, 시설 waste-disposal 폐기물 처리, 쓰레기 처리 practice 관행, 관례 specifically 특별히, 구체적으로 말하면 composting 비료화 처리 in action 작동하는

7 화자는 누구이겠는가?
(A) 환경 과학자   (B) 식당 주인
(C) 건물 조사관   (D) 청소부

해설 | 화자의 신분
초반부에서 식당 개업 이후 그 목표를 계속 염두에 뒀다(I've had that aim in mind since opening the restaurant)고 했으므로 (B)가 정답이다.

어휘 | sanitation 공중 위생; 위생 설비, 하수 처리

8 다음 달에 무엇이 변경될 것인가?
(A) 대중교통 체계   (B) 토지이용 제한법
(C) 쓰레기 처리 절차   (D) 공과금

해설 | 다음 달 변경 사항
중반부에서 다음 달부터 쓰레기 처리 관례를 바꿀 예정(starting next month, we'll be changing our waste-disposal practices)이라고 했으므로 (C)가 정답이다.

어휘 | zoning law 토지이용 제한법 utility fee 공과금

Paraphrasing 담화의 waste-disposal practices
→ 정답의 A waste-disposal process

9 화자는 다음으로 무엇을 할 것인가?
(A) 실천 계획 작성하기　(B) 공고문 게시하기
(C) 시범 보여주기　　　(D) 점심 먹으러 가기

해설 | **화자가 다음에 할 일**
후반부에서 지금 그곳으로 가서 비료 처리기가 어떻게 작동하는지 보여드리겠다(Let me take you there now to show you how the composter works)고 했으므로 (C)가 정답이다.

어휘 | notice 공고문, 안내문 demonstration 시범 설명

Paraphrasing 담화의 show you how the composter works → 정답의 Give a demonstration

[10-12] 여행 정보

W-Br As you walk around the Sorrentino Museum today, **10** you'll learn about the entire history of human flight, from the very first airplanes all the way to space travel. We have twelve rooms with permanent exhibits, along with a planetarium that screens films every thirty minutes. **11** Our collection is expanding, so you might notice some labels missing from the wall next to a few of the artifacts, but there are museum employees in every room. **12** You're welcome to take as many photographs as you'd like, and we invite you to post them on the visitor's page of our Web site.

오늘 소렌티노 박물관 주변을 걸으며 **10** 최초의 비행기부터 우주 여행까지 인류 비행의 전 역사에 대해 배우실 겁니다. 30분마다 영화를 상영하는 천체 투영관과 더불어 상설 전시회가 있는 12개의 전시실이 있습니다. **11** 저희 소장품이 늘어나고 있어 몇몇 전시품은 벽에 라벨이 없는 것이 눈에 띄지만, 전시실마다 박물관 직원이 있습니다. **12** 원하시는 만큼 사진을 찍으셔도 좋습니다. 저희 웹사이트의 방문자 페이지에 사진을 올려 주세요.

어휘 | permanent 영구적인, 상설의 planetarium 천체 투영관 expand 확대되다, 확장되다 artifact 인공 유물, 공예품

10 청자들은 박물관에서 무엇에 대해 알게 될 것인가?
(A) 미술사　　　　　(B) 영화사
(C) 과학사　　　　　(D) 항공 역사

해설 | **청자들이 박물관에서 알게 될 사항**
초반부에서 최초의 비행기부터 우주 여행까지 인류 비행의 전 역사에 대해 배울 것(you'll learn about the entire history of human flight, from the very first airplanes all the way to space travel)이라고 했으므로 (D)가 정답이다.

Paraphrasing 담화의 the entire history of human flight → 정답의 The history of flight

11 화자가 "전시실마다 박물관 직원이 있습니다"라고 말할 때, 그 의도는 무엇인가?
(A) 박물관은 재정 지원이 충분하다.
(B) 인공 유물은 잘 보존되고 있다.
(C) 청자들은 질문을 할 수 있다.
(D) 박물관은 오늘 매우 붐빌 것이다.

해설 | **화자의 의도**
중반부에서 소장품이 늘어나고 있어 인공 유물 몇 점 옆에 있는 벽에 라벨이 없다(Our collection is expanding, so you might notice some labels missing from the wall next to a few of the artifacts)고 한 후, 전시실마다 박물관 직원이 있다(there are museum employees in every room)고 덧붙였다. 이는 직원으로부터 도움을 받을 수 있다는 의도라고 볼 수 있으므로 (C)가 정답이다.

어휘 | well funded 투자를 많이 받은, 충분한 재원이 마련된

12 화자는 청자들에게 무엇을 하라고 청하는가?
(A) 웹사이트에 사진 게시　(B) 특별 전시 방문
(C) 기념품 구입　　　　　(D) 박물관 회원 가입

해설 | **화자의 요청 사항**
후반부에서 원하시는 만큼 사진을 찍으셔도 좋다(You're welcome to take as many photographs as you'd like)고 한 후, 웹사이트의 방문자 페이지에 사진을 올려 달라(we invite you to post them on the visitor's page of our Web site)고 했으므로 (A)가 정답이다.

어휘 | souvenir 기념품

[13-15] 설명

M-Au Hello, and welcome to my online channel, *Outdoor Inspirations*. In today's video, **13** I'm going to give you a step-by-step guide for designing your home garden. **14** The first thing you need to do is take measurements of the space. This will ensure that the plants you choose will fit nicely in your available space. Now, **15** some of my viewers have sent me questions asking how to attract or incorporate animals into their outdoor spaces. Thank you for those! I'll discuss a couple of options today, such as planting native shrubs and trees that will attract beneficial insects and songbirds.

안녕하세요, 제 온라인 채널 〈아웃도어 인스퍼레이션〉에 오신 것을 환영합니다. 오늘 영상에서는 **13** 여러분께 집 정원 디자인에 관해 단계별 지침을 알려드리려고 합니다. **14** 첫 번째로 하셔야 할 것은 공간 측정입니다. 이렇게 하면 선택하시는 식물들이 이용 가능한 공간에 잘 맞을 수 있습니다. 자, **15** 시청자들 중 자신의 야외 공간에 동물을 오게 하거나 통합하는 방법을 물어보는 분들이 있는데요. 감사합니다! 오늘 토종 관목이나 나무를 심어 유익한 곤충과 새를 불러들이는 몇 가지 방법을 얘기해 보려고 해요.

어휘 | step-by-step 단계적인, 점진적인 take measurements 치수를 재다 incorporate 포함시키다 beneficial 유익한

13 화자의 직업은 무엇이겠는가?

(A) 조경 디자이너 　　　(B) 플로리스트
(C) 행사 기획자 　　　　(D) 공원 관리원

해설 | 화자의 직업
초반부에서 집 정원 디자인에 관해 단계별 지침을 알려
주겠다(I'm going to give you a step-by-step guide for
designing your home garden)고 했으므로 (A)가 정답이다.

어휘 | landscape 풍경, 조경　**ranger** 공원 관리원

14 화자는 처음으로 무엇을 하라고 제안하는가?

(A) 목록 준비하기 　　　(B) 테이블 공간 치우기
(C) 치수 재기 　　　　　(D) 판매업체 찾기

해설 | 화자의 첫 제안 사항
중반부에서 첫 번째로 하셔야 할 것은 공간 측정(The first
thing you need to do is take measurements of the
space)이라고 했으므로 (C)가 정답이다.

어휘 | vendor 판매자, 판매업체

15 화자는 시청자에게 무엇을 해줘서 감사하다고 하는가?

(A) 조리법 공유 　　　　(B) 사진 전송
(C) 노래 추천 　　　　　(D) 질문

해설 | 화자가 시청자에게 감사해하는 것
중반부에서 시청자들 중 자신의 야외 공간에 동물을 오게
하거나 포함시키는 방법을 물어보는 분들이 있다(some of
my viewers have sent me questions asking how to
attract or incorporate animals into their outdoor
spaces)고 한 후, 감사하다(Thank you for those)고
했으므로 (D)가 정답이다.

[16-18] 연설

W-Am We're halfway through our initiative to
improve the office environment. **16**I've gathered
results from surveys about how satisfied employees
are with their work spaces, and the data shows
that the addition of shared work and relaxation
areas with comfortable couches has made a huge
difference. **17**Making room for those took a lot of
rearranging, so thanks to the Facilities Department
for their efforts. Next, several people mentioned
that the light from their computer screens bothers
them. **18**We'll be providing blue-light-blocking
glasses to everyone. You don't have to wear them,
but an eye doctor did make this recommendation,
and we all spend a lot of time staring at screens.

우리는 사무실 환경 개선 계획의 중간쯤에 있습니다. **16**직원들이
업무 공간에 얼마나 만족하는지에 관한 설문 조사 결과를
취합했는데요. 자료에 따르면 안락한 소파를 갖춘 작업 및 휴식용
공유 공간 추가가 큰 변화를 가져왔다고 합니다. **17**이러한 공간을
만드는 데는 많은 재배치가 필요했기에, 시설 부서의 노고에
감사드립니다. 다음으로, 컴퓨터 화면 불빛이 신경 쓰인다고 여러

명이 언급했는데요. **18**모두에게 블루라이트 차단 안경을 제공할
예정입니다. 꼭 착용하실 필요는 없지만, 안과 의사가 권장하는
사항입니다. 우리 모두 화면을 보며 많은 시간을 보내니까요.

어휘 | initiative 계획　**addition** 추가　**make a difference**
변화를 가져오다, 차이를 낳다　**rearrange** 재배치하다, 재조정하다

16 화자는 어떤 종류의 자료에 대해 이야기하는가?

(A) 업무시간 기록 　　　(B) 연간 영업보고서
(C) 고객 서비스 전화 기록 　(D) 직원 설문 조사 결과

해설 | 화자가 논의하는 자료
초반부에서 직원들이 업무 공간에 얼마나 만족하는지에 관한 설문
조사 결과를 취합했다(I've gathered results from surveys
about how satisfied employees are with their work
spaces)고 했으므로 (D)가 정답이다.

어휘 | record 기록　**annual** 매년의, 연간의　**log** 기록, 일지

Paraphrasing　담화의 results from surveys about how
satisfied employees are with their work spaces
→ 정답의 Employee survey results

17 화자가 시설 부서 직원들에게 감사하는 이유는?

(A) 더 빠른 서버를 설치해서
(B) 업무 공간을 재배치해서
(C) 페인트칠 프로젝트를 완료해서
(D) 가구를 수리해서

해설 | 시설 부서 직원들에게 감사하는 이유
중반부에서 이러한 공간을 만드는 데는 많은 재배치가
필요했기에(Making room for those took a lot of
rearranging) 시설 부서의 노고에 감사드린다고 했으므로
(B)가 정답이다.

Paraphrasing　담화의 Making room for those took a
lot of rearranging → 정답의 rearranged some work
spaces

18 화자가 "우리 모두 화면을 보며 많은 시간을 보내니까요"라고
말한 이유는?

(A) 업무 시간이 변경된 이유를 설명하려고
(B) 일부 직원들의 노고를 인정하려고
(C) 정책이 지켜지지 않은 것에 대해 불만을 제기하려고
(D) 전문가의 권장 사항을 강조하려고

해설 | 화자의 의도
후반부에서 모두에게 블루라이트 차단 안경을 제공할 예정(We'll
be providing blue-light-blocking glasses to
everyone)이라고 하면서 꼭 착용하실 필요는 없지만 안과
의사가 권장하는 사항(You don't have to wear them, but
an eye doctor did make this recommendation)이라고
한 후, 우리 모두 화면을 보며 많은 시간을 보낸다(we all spend
a lot of time staring at screens)고 덧붙였다. 이 말은
안과의사의 권장 사항을 강조하려는 의도라고 볼 수 있으므로
(D)가 정답이다.

어휘 | recognize 공인하다, 인정하다　**policy** 정책
emphasize 강조하다

W-Br I'm excited to talk with you today about investment opportunities with Outdoor Wanders. ¹⁹Your investment in this company will help us expand and grow. At Outdoor Wanders, we design and make outdoor clothing, and ²⁰when I founded this company two years ago, I made protecting the environment a priority. That's why our products are all made from recycled materials. But using recycled materials isn't the cheapest way to manufacture clothing. ²¹For example, take a look at this item. One hundred and eighty-five dollars is a lot, right? But we promise high quality and environmentally friendly products. That's a promise you can't put a price tag on.

오늘 아웃도어 원더스 투자 기회에 대해 말씀드리게 되어 기쁩니다. ¹⁹**이 회사에 투자하시면 저희의 확장 및 성장에 도움이 될 겁니다.** 아웃도어 원더스는 아웃도어 의류를 디자인하고 생산합니다. ²⁰**제가 2년 전 이 회사를 설립할 때** 환경 보호를 최우선 사항으로 삼았는데요. 저희 제품이 모두 재활용 소재로 만들어지는 이유입니다. 하지만 재활용 소재를 사용하는 것은 의류를 제조하는 가장 저렴한 방법은 아닙니다. ²¹**일례로 이 제품을 한번 보세요. 185달러면 비싸죠, 그렇죠?** 하지만 저희는 고품질의 환경친화적인 제품을 약속합니다. 가격표를 매길 수 없는 약속이죠.

어휘 | expand 확장하다, 확대하다 priority 우선 사항

83달러	100달러	129달러
트레킹 장갑		
185달러	멀티 포켓 바지	전천후 자켓
²¹**트레일블레이저 신발**		

어휘 | all-weather 전천후의

19 화자가 청자들을 만난 이유는?
(A) 자금 지원을 요청하려고   (B) 회장을 소개하려고
(C) 소재를 구입하려고   (D) 제조 규정을 개정하려고

해설 | **화자가 청자들을 만난 이유**
초반부에서 이 회사에 투자하면 회사의 확장 및 성장에 도움이 될 것(Your investment in this company will help us expand and grow)이라고 했으므로 (A)가 정답이다.

어휘 | revise 변경하다, 수정하다 regulation 규정, 규제

Paraphrasing 담화의 investment → 정답의 funding

20 화자는 누구이겠는가?
(A) 제품 검사관   (B) 재무 컨설턴트
(C) 시 공무원   (D) 회사 소유주

해설 | **화자의 신분**
중반부에서 2년 전 이 회사를 설립할 때(when I founded this company two years ago)라고 했으므로 (D)가 정답이다.

어휘 | financial 재정의, 금융의

21 시각 정보에 따르면, 화자는 어떤 제품을 예로 들었는가?
(A) 트레킹 장갑   (B) 트레일블레이저 신발
(C) 멀티 포켓 바지   (D) 전천후 자켓

해설 | **시각 정보 연계**
후반부에서 일례로 이 제품을 한번 보라(For example, take a look at this item)고 한 후, 185달러면 비싸지 않은지(One hundred and eighty-five dollars is a lot, right?)를 묻고 있다. 가격표를 보면 트레일블레이저 신발이 185달러이므로 (B)가 정답이다.

UNIT 16 광고 / 방송

고득점 전략 **담화 흐름 파악하기**   본책 p.112

M-Au 오늘 경제 뉴스에서는 〈랭커스터 모닝 타임즈〉가 구독자 수가 계속 늘고 있다고 보도했습니다. 해당 신문이 1년 전 발행을 시작했을 때, 많은 사람들이 재정적 위험이 있다고 여겼습니다. 요즘 대부분 뉴스를 컴퓨터와 모바일 기기로 보니까요. 〈모닝 타임즈〉 편집장 마크 암스트롱은 신문의 성공을 지역 뉴스 및 행사에 초점을 둔 덕분이라고 보고 있습니다. 〈모닝 타임즈〉는 지역 사회에 더 깊이 관여할 계획입니다. 암스트롱 씨는 2월에 랭커스터 지역 고등학생들이 쓰는 주간 섹션을 시작할 것이라고 밝혔습니다.

어휘 | subscription 구독, 가입 publication 출판, 게재 venture (사업상의) 모험 attribute A to B A를 B의 덕분으로(결과로) 보다 be involved in ~에 관련되다, 개입되다

1 〈랭커스터 모닝 타임즈〉는 최근 무엇이 바뀌었는가?
(A) 웹사이트를 재디자인했다.
(B) 구독자 수가 증가했다.

2 마크 암스트롱에 따르면, 어떤 점이 신문의 성공에 도움이 되었는가?
(A) 상세 재무 계획 실행
(B) 지역 뉴스에 초점

어휘 | implement 실행하다

3 마크 암스트롱은 2월에 신문에서 무엇을 할 것이라고 말하는가?
(A) 새 주간 섹션 게재
(B) 가정 배달 제공

ETS 유형 연습

본책 p.113

1 (B) **2** (B) **3** (C) **4** (D) **5** (B) **6** (C)
7 (A) **8** (D) **9** (D)

[1-3] 뉴스 보도

M-Au And in today's business news, **¹**fragrance manufacturer Spellman Incorporated has announced a growth in profits of four percent over the past year. **²**Spellman recently launched a very successful line of perfumes that use only organic ingredients. **³**In an interview, chief executive officer Maria Ortiz indicated that she has the firm's marketing department to thank for the sales boom. In her opinion, the campaign they developed was key to the recent success.

오늘 경제 뉴스에서는 **¹**향수 제조업체 스펠만 주식회사가 작년 4%의 수익 상승이 있었다고 발표했습니다. **²**스펠만은 최근 유기농 성분만을 사용한 향수 제품을 성공리에 출시했는데요. **³**최고 경영자 마리아 오티즈는 인터뷰에서 매출 급증에 대해 회사 마케팅 부서에 감사한다는 뜻을 내비쳤습니다. 마케팅 부서에서 개발한 캠페인이 최근 성공의 비결이었다는 의견입니다.

어휘 | fragrance 향수 launch 출시하다 organic 유기농의 ingredient 성분, 재료 chief executive officer 최고 경영자 indicate 내비치다, 시사하다 sales boom 매출 급증

1 스펠만 주식회사는 무엇을 발표했는가?
(A) 임원진 변경   (B) 수익 증가
(C) 가격 인하   (D) 공장 이전

해설 | 스펠만 주식회사의 발표 내용
초반부에서 스펠만 주식회사가 작년 4%의 수익 상승이 있었다고 발표했다(fragrance manufacturer Spellman Incorporated has announced a growth in profits of four percent over the past year)고 했으므로 (B)가 정답이다.

어휘 | reduction 감소, 인하 relocation 이전
Paraphrasing 담화의 a growth in profits
→ 정답의 An increase in profits

2 신제품은 어떤 점이 특별한가?
(A) 생산비가 비싸지 않다.   (B) 유기농 재료를 사용한다.
(C) 유명인이 광고한다.   (D) 해외에서 수입한다.

해설 | 신제품의 특별한 점
중반부에서 스펠만은 최근 유기농 성분만을 사용한 향수 제품을 성공리에 출시했다(Spellman recently launched a very successful line of perfumes that use only organic ingredients)고 했으므로 (B)가 정답이다.

어휘 | inexpensive 비싸지 않은 celebrity 유명 인사 import 수입하다

Paraphrasing 담화의 launched a very successful line of perfumes → 질문의 new products

3 마리아 오티즈는 인터뷰에서 누구를 언급했는가?
(A) 오랜 고객들
(B) 소매업체 소유주들
(C) 스펠만 주식회사의 마케팅 직원들
(D) 스펠만 주식회사의 영업 부서

해설 | 마리아 오티즈가 인터뷰에서 언급한 사람
중반부에서 최고경영자 마리아 오티즈는 인터뷰에서 매출 급증에 대해 회사 마케팅 부서에 감사한다는 뜻을 내비쳤다(In an interview, chief executive officer Maria Ortiz indicated that she has the firm's marketing department to thank for the sales boom)고 했으므로 (C)가 정답이다.

어휘 | retail 소매

Paraphrasing 담화의 the firm's marketing department → 정답의 Spellman Incorporated's marketing staff

[4-6] 광고

M-Au **⁴**Does your washing machine take up too much space in your home? **⁴, ⁵**Then you should check out the 500X, Cleaning Pro's newest washing machine. It has the same great quality you expect from all Cleaning Pro appliances, but **⁵**it's smaller than any other model on the market! That's right—it's the perfect size for your tiny apartment. **⁶**Stop by your local appliance store to buy one today. Inventory is limited.

⁴세탁기가 집 공간을 너무 많이 차지하나요? **⁴, ⁵**그렇다면 클리닝 프로의 최신 세탁기 500X를 확인해 보셔야 합니다. 클리닝 프로의 모든 제품에서 기대하시는 것과 동일하게 뛰어난 품질을 갖췄으면서도, **⁵**시중의 다른 어떤 모델보다도 작습니다! 네, 여러분의 작은 아파트에 완벽한 크기입니다. **⁶**오늘 여러분이 사는 지역의 가전제품 매장에 들러 한 대 구입하세요. 재고가 한정되어 있습니다.

어휘 | take up space 공간을 차지하다 expect 기대하다, 예상하다 appliance 가전제품 inventory 재고 limited 한정된

4 무엇을 광고하고 있는가?
(A) 토스터기   (B) 냉장고
(C) 진공청소기   (D) 세탁기

해설 | 광고하는 것
초반부에서 세탁기가 집 공간을 너무 많이 차지하나요(Does your washing machine take up too much space in your home?)라고 물은 후, 그렇다면 클리닝 프로의 최신 세탁기 500X를 확인해 보셔야 한다(Then you should check out the 500X, Cleaning Pro's newest washing machine)고 했으므로 (D)가 정답이다.

어휘 | vacuum cleaner 진공청소기

5 500X 모델의 특별한 점은 무엇인가?
(A) 빠르다.　　　　　　　(B) 작다.
(C) 조용하다.　　　　　　(D) 에너지 효율이 좋다.

해설 | 500X 모델의 특별한 사항
중반부에서 클리닝 프로의 최신 세탁기 500X를 확인해 봐야 한다(you should check out the 500X, Cleaning Pro's newest washing machine)고 한 후, 시중의 다른 어떤 모델보다도 작다(it's smaller than any other model on the market)고 했으므로 (B)가 정답이다.

어휘 | energy efficient 에너지 효율이 좋은

6 화자가 "재고가 한정되어 있습니다"라고 말할 때, 그 의도는 무엇인가?
(A) 추가 품목들이 곧 도착할 예정이다.
(B) 매장이 붐빌 것이다.
(C) 청자들은 빠르게 행동을 취해야 한다.
(D) 청자들은 한 가지 품목만 구입할 수 있다.

해설 | 화자의 의도
후반부에서 오늘 여러분이 사는 지역의 가전제품 매장에 들러 한 대 구입하라(Stop by your local appliance store to buy one today)고 한 후, 재고가 한정되어 있다(Inventory is limited)고 덧붙였다. 이는 재고가 한정되어 있으므로 오늘 구매를 서둘러 달라는 의도라고 볼 수 있으므로 (C)가 정답이다.

어휘 | additional 추가의　**crowded** 붐비는, 복잡한

[7-9] 방송

> **W-Br** Welcome to *Eating Out in Glendale*, the show about the local food scene. [7]Today we're going to discuss one of the fastest growing trends—food trucks. A recent report stated there are over twenty food trucks operating in the city. [8]Their popularity is due largely to the variety of food they sell. [9]Today we invited Jerome Weber here for an interview. He is the owner of Jerome's Tasty Food. He'll talk about the challenges that his workers have preparing food inside a vehicle.
>
> 지역 음식에 관한 프로그램 〈이팅 아웃 인 글렌데일〉을 시청해 주셔서 감사합니다. [7]오늘은 가장 빠르게 성장하는 트렌드 중 하나인 푸드 트럭에 대해 이야기할 예정입니다. 최근 보고서에서는 시에서 운영하는 푸드 트럭이 스무 대가 넘는다고 말합니다. [8]푸드 트럭의 인기는 주로 판매하는 음식의 다양성 때문인데요. [9]오늘 인터뷰를 위해 제롬 웨버를 초대했습니다. 제롬 테이스티 푸드의 주인이시죠. 그의 직원들이 차량 안에서 음식을 준비하는 어려움에 대해 이야기할 예정입니다.
>
> ⋯⋯⋯⋯⋯⋯⋯⋯⋯⋯⋯⋯⋯⋯⋯⋯⋯⋯
>
> **어휘 | state** 말하다, 명시하다　**due to** ~때문에

7 오늘 방송의 주제는?
(A) 푸드 트럭　　　　　(B) 온라인 식사 주문
(C) 농산물 직판장의 확대　(D) 카페 개점

해설 | 오늘 방송의 주제
초반부에서 오늘은 가장 빠르게 성장하는 트렌드 중 하나인 푸드 트럭에 대해 이야기할 예정(Today we're going to discuss one of the fastest growing trends—food trucks)이라고 했으므로 (A)가 정답이다.

어휘 | expansion 확장, 확대

8 화자에 따르면, 이런 종류의 업체는 왜 인기가 많은가?
(A) 재료가 지역에서 생산된다. (B) 가격이 적당하다.
(C) 무료 배송을 해 준다.　(D) 선택의 폭이 넓다.

해설 | 특정 업체가 인기가 많은 이유
중반부에서 푸드 트럭의 인기는 주로 판매하는 음식의 다양성 때문(Their popularity is due largely to the variety of food they sell)이라고 했으므로 (D)가 정답이다.

어휘 | ingredient 성분, 재료　**affordable** (가격이) 알맞은

Paraphrasing　담화의 the variety of food
→ 정답의 a wide selection

9 제롬 웨버는 누구인가?
(A) 농부　　　　　　　(B) 기자
(C) 시 공무원　　　　　(D) 업체 소유주

해설 | 제롬 웨버의 신분
후반부에서 오늘 인터뷰를 위해 제롬 웨버를 초대했다(Today we invited Jerome Weber here for an interview)고 한 후, 제롬 테이스티 푸드의 주인(He is the owner of Jerome's Tasty Food)이라고 했으므로 (D)가 정답이다.

어휘 | official 관료, 공무원

Paraphrasing　담화의 the owner of Jerome's Tasty Food → 정답의 A business owner

---

ETS 고득점 실전 문제　　본책 p.114

1 (A)	**2** (D)	**3** (B)	**4** (D)	**5** (A)	**6** (B)
7 (B)	**8** (A)	**9** (C)	**10** (A)	**11** (B)	**12** (D)
13 (A)	**14** (C)	**15** (B)	**16** (A)	**17** (B)	**18** (A)
19 (C)	**20** (B)	**21** (A)			

[1-3] 방송

> **W-Br** Hello, everyone, and thank you for coming to this press conference. [1]I'm Claudine Kim, the city's mayor. Today, [2]we're announcing a request for proposals to design and build a new port for the offshore wind industry. This port facility will be used as a staging area for assembling wind farm components such as turbines and blades, [3]creating many well-paying jobs. The city is pleased that these job opportunities will be available right here in our region.

안녕하세요, 여러분. 오늘 기자회견에 와 주셔서 감사합니다. **¹저는 시장 클로딘 김입니다.** 오늘 **²해상 풍력 발전 업계를 위해 새 항구를 설계하고 건설하기 위한 입찰제안서 모집을 발표합니다.** 항만 시설은 터빈, 블레이드와 같은 풍력 발전 구성품을 조립하기 위한 집결지로 활용되며 **³많은 고임금 일자리를 창출할 것입니다. 우리 시에서는 지역 내에 이러한 구직 기회가 있다는 점이 흡족합니다.**

어휘 | press conference 기자회견 **offshore wind** 해상 풍력 발전 **staging area** 집결지 **component** 구성품 **assemble** 조립하다 **well-paying** 보수가 좋은

---

1 화자는 누구인가?
(A) 공무원 　　　　　　 (B) 기자
(C) 건축가 　　　　　　 (D) 종합 건설업자

해설 | 화자의 신분
초반부에서 자신이 시장 클로딘 김(I'm Claudine Kim, the city's mayor)이라고 했으므로 (A)가 정답이다.

어휘 | architect 건축가 **general contractor** 종합 건설업자

Paraphrasing 담화의 the city's mayor
→ 정답의 A government official

2 화자는 어떤 공사 프로젝트에 대해 이야기하는가?
(A) 사무실 단지 　　　 (B) 고속도로
(C) 기차역 　　　　　　 (D) 항만 시설

해설 | 화자가 이야기하는 공사 프로젝트
중반부에서 해상 풍력 발전 업계를 위해 새 항구를 설계하고 건설하기 위한 입찰제안서 모집을 발표한다(we're announcing ~ to design and build a new port for the offshore wind industry)고 했으므로 (D)가 정답이다.

Paraphrasing 담화의 a new port → 정답의 A port facility

3 화자가 흡족해하는 이유는?
(A) 예산이 초과되지 않았다.
(B) 새 일자리가 창출될 것이다.
(C) 수익이 증가할 것이다.
(D) 지연이 해결됐다.

해설 | 화자가 흡족해하는 이유
후반부에서 많은 고임금 일자리를 창출할 것(creating many well-paying jobs)이라고 한 후, 우리 시에서는 지역 내에 이러한 구직 기회가 있다는 점이 흡족하다(The city is pleased that these job opportunities will be available right here in our region)고 했으므로 (B)가 정답이다.

어휘 | budget 예산 **resolve** 해결하다

Paraphrasing 담화의 creating many well-paying jobs
→ 정답의 New jobs will be created.

[4-6] 광고

W-Br **⁴Every year, consumers waste thousands of dollars using air conditioning systems that need maintenance. Why not make sure your system is working at its best? ⁵Call Trident Repair Services at 555-0152, and arrange for a free energy audit.**

One of our air conditioning specialists will inspect your system and let you know exactly what has to be done. And **⁶until the end of this month, there's a thirty percent discount on any parts you purchase from us**—so call today!

⁴고객들은 매년 유지 보수가 필요한 냉방 시스템 이용에 수천 달러를 낭비합니다. 귀하의 시스템이 최적의 상태에서 작동하도록 하면 어떨까요? **⁵트리덴트 수리 서비스에 555-0152로 전화해 무료 에너지 진단 계획을 잡아 보세요.** 저희 냉방 전문가가 귀하의 시스템을 점검하고 정확히 무엇을 해야 하는지 알려드립니다. **⁶이번 달 말까지는 저희로부터 구입하시는 모든 부품이 30퍼센트 할인됩니다.** 오늘 바로 전화하세요!

어휘 | maintenance 유지 보수 **energy audit** (에너지 절감을 위한) 에너지 진단 **specialist** 전문가

---

4 무엇을 광고하는가?
(A) 장비 재활용 　　　 (B) 상업 부동산
(C) 기술 학교 　　　　 (D) 냉방 유지 보수

해설 | 광고하는 것
초반부에서 고객들은 매년 유지 보수가 필요한 냉방 시스템 이용에 수천 달러를 낭비한다(Every year, consumers waste thousands of dollars using air conditioning systems that need maintenance)고 했으므로 (D)가 정답이다.

어휘 | commercial 상업의 **real estate** 부동산

5 청자들에게 전화하라고 요청하는 이유는?
(A) 점검을 준비하려고 　　 (B) 픽업을 준비하려고
(C) 시연 동영상을 받으려고 (D) 워크숍을 신청하려고

해설 | 전화하라고 요청하는 이유
중반부에서 트리덴트 수리 서비스에 555-0152로 전화해 무료 에너지 진단 계획을 잡아보라(Call Trident Repair Services at 555-0152, and arrange for a free energy audit)고 한 후, 냉방 전문가가 귀하의 시스템을 점검하고 정확히 무엇을 해야 하는지 알려드린다(One of our air conditioning specialists will inspect your system and let you know exactly what has to be done)고 했으므로 (A)가 정답이다.

어휘 | inspection 점검 **demonstration** 시범 설명, 입증

Paraphrasing 담화의 arrange for a free energy audit → 정답의 set up an inspection

6 월말에 무슨 일이 있을 것인가?
(A) 지불 기한이 될 것이다.
(B) 특별 할인이 종료될 것이다.
(C) 건물 공사가 시작될 것이다.
(D) 보고서가 발표될 것이다.

해설 | 월말에 있을 일
후반부에서 이번 달 말까지는 저희로부터 구입하시는 모든 부품이 30퍼센트 할인된다(until the end of this month, there's a thirty percent discount on any parts you purchase from us)고 했으므로 (B)가 정답이다.

어휘 | due (돈을) 지불해야 하는

Paraphrasing 담화의 a thirty percent discount
→ 정답의 A special discount

[7-9] 방송

M-Cn ⁷Welcome viewers to our televised cooking contest. Today's chefs are on stage behind me, busy arranging their kitchen stations, as they prepare to impress our panel of judges. ⁸Now many people think that the judges base their decisions only on how the food tastes. Always remember though, they do see the dish before they taste it. Our head judge tonight is Anya Wilson. ⁹Anya has worked in food service for more than two decades and just this year opened her own culinary school where the next generation of chefs is being trained.

⁷저희 TV 요리 대회 시청자 여러분, 반갑습니다. 오늘 요리사들이 제 뒤 무대에 나와 있는데요. 심사위원단에게 좋은 인상을 줄 준비를 하며 자신의 조리 구역을 정리하느라 바쁩니다. ⁸많은 분들이 **심사위원들은 음식 맛에만 기반해서 결정을 내린다고 생각하시죠.** 하지만 항상 기억하세요. 맛을 보기 전에 요리를 살펴본답니다. 오늘 밤 심사위원장은 안야 윌슨입니다. ⁹안야는 20년 이상 요리업에 종사했고, **올해, 차세대 요리사를 교육하는 자신의 요리 학교를 열었습니다.**

어휘 | arrange 정리하다, 배열하다   impress 깊은 인상을 주다   culinary 요리의   generation 세대

7 무엇에 관한 TV 프로그램인가?
(A) 저녁식사 파티 주최에 관한 조언
(B) 요리 대회
(C) 전 세계의 조리법
(D) 요식업계 동향

해설 | TV 프로그램의 내용
초반부에서 TV 요리 대회 시청자들에게 반갑다(Welcome viewers to our televised cooking contest)고 했으므로 (B)가 정답이다.

어휘 | competition 대회, 시합, 경쟁

Paraphrasing 담화의 cooking contest
→ 정답의 A cooking competition

8 화자가 "맛을 보기 전에 요리를 살펴본답니다"라고 말한 이유는?
(A) 오해를 바로잡으려고
(B) 지연에 대해 설명하려고
(C) 요리사를 칭찬하려고
(D) 다른 접시를 사용하라고 제안하려고

해설 | 화자의 의도
중반부에서 많은 분들이 심사위원들은 음식 맛에만 기반해서 결정을 내린다고 생각한다(Now many people think that the judges base their decisions only on how the food tastes)고 한 후, 맛을 보기 전에 요리를 살펴본다(they do see the dish before they taste it)고 덧붙였다. 이 말은 많은 사람들의 오해를 바로잡으려는 의도라고 볼 수 있으므로 (A)가 정답이다.

어휘 | misconception 오해   compliment 칭찬하다

9 안야 윌슨은 최근에 무엇을 했는가?
(A) 식당을 개업했다.
(B) 해외 여행을 했다.
(C) 요리 학교를 열었다.
(D) 조리도구 제품을 디자인했다.

해설 | 안야 윌슨이 최근에 한 일
후반부에서 안야는 20년 이상 요식업에 종사했고, 올해 차세대 요리사를 교육하는 자신의 요리 학교를 열었다(Anya has worked ~ and just this year opened her own culinary school)고 했으므로 (C)가 정답이다.

어휘 | cookware 취사 도구, 조리 기구

Paraphrasing 담화의 just this year → 질문의 recently
담화의 opened her own culinary school
→ 정답의 She started a culinary school.

[10-12] 광고

W-Am Planning a trip to Chicago? Looking for somewhere stylish to stay during your visit? Consider Robinson Suites, ¹⁰a hotel designed by Stefan Samir, a world-renowned architect. Don't let the historic appearance fool you. ¹¹On the second floor, we have a full business center, which has all the modern amenities you'll need. And as an added perk, ¹²if you are in town for business, we'll take ten dollars off your nightly rate! Just show us your company ID card at check-in.

시카고 여행을 계획하시나요? 방문 중 머물 세련된 장소를 찾으십니까? ¹⁰**세계적으로 이름난 건축가 스테판 사미르가 설계한 호텔,** 로빈슨 스위트를 고려해 보세요. 역사가 느껴지는 외관에 속지 마세요. ¹¹**2층에는 완벽한 비즈니스 센터가 있어,** 필요한 현대식 소모품이 모두 갖춰져 있습니다. 추가 혜택으로, ¹²**출장 차 방문하셨다면 숙박 요금을 10달러 할인해 드립니다!** 체크인하실 때 사원증만 제시해 주세요.

어휘 | world-renowned 세계적으로 유명한   architect 건축가   appearance 외관   amenity 소모품, 편의 시설   perk 특전

10 화자는 스테판 사미르에 관해 무엇이라고 말하는가?
(A) 유명 건축가이다.
(B) 호텔을 소유하고 있다.
(C) 기념식에서 연설할 예정이다.
(D) 건물을 매각했다.

해설 | 스테판 사미르에 관해 언급한 것
초반부에서 세계적으로 이름난 건축가 스테판 사미르가 설계한 호텔(a hotel designed by Stefan Samir, a world-renowned architect)이라고 했으므로 (A)가 정답이다.

어휘 | property 재산, 부동산, 건물

Paraphrasing 담화의 a world-renowned architect
→ 정답의 a famous architect

11 호텔의 2층에는 무엇이 있는가?
(A) 피트니스 룸　　　　　(B) 비즈니스 센터
(C) 수영장　　　　　　　(D) 식당

해설 | 호텔 2층에 있는 시설
중반부에서 2층에는 완벽한 비즈니스 센터가 있다(On the second floor, we have a full business center)고 했으므로 (B)가 정답이다.

12 어떤 호텔 투숙객이 할인을 받을 수 있는가?
(A) 퇴직자　　　　　　　(B) 아이가 있는 가족
(C) 재방문 고객　　　　　(D) 직장인

해설 | 할인을 받을 수 있는 호텔 투숙객
후반부에서 출장 차 방문하셨다면 숙박 요금을 10달러 할인해 드린다(if you are in town for business, we'll take ten dollars off your nightly rate)라고 했으므로 (D)가 정답이다.

어휘 | retiree 퇴직자, 은퇴자

Paraphrasing 담화의 take ten dollars off
→ 질문의 receive a discount
담화의 you are in town for business
→ 정답의 Businesspeople

[13-15] 뉴스 보도

W-Br In local news, ¹³, ¹⁴city officials have been receiving complaints about traffic around the construction zone near the new shopping center. Many streets will remain closed until construction is completed in June. But residents will be happy to hear that a city council member has put forth a proposal that would require the owners to make half of the shopping center's parking garage available to the public. ¹⁵The proposal will only pass, however, if enough local residents voice their support. In fact, the city council has scheduled a special forum on Wednesday night.

본 지역 뉴스에서는 ¹³, ¹⁴시 공무원들이 새 쇼핑센터 근처 공사 구역 인근의 교통 문제에 관한 항의를 받고 있음을 전해드립니다. 6월 공사가 완료될 때까지 많은 도로들이 계속 폐쇄될 예정인데요. 하지만 주민들은 시의회 의원들이 소유주들에게 쇼핑센터 주차장 절반을 대중이 이용할 수 있도록 의무화하는 제안서를 제출한 사실을 알게 되면 만족할 것 같습니다. ¹⁵그러나 이 제안서는 충분한 수의 지역 주민들이 지지의 목소리를 낼 경우에만 통과될 것입니다. 사실 시의회는 수요일 밤에 특별 포럼 일정을 잡은 상태입니다.

어휘 | resident 주민 city council 시의회 put forth 제시하다, 제안하다 available 이용 가능한

13 일부 주민들은 시 공무원들에게 무엇에 대해 항의했는가?
(A) 교통　　　　　　　　(B) 임대료
(C) 소음　　　　　　　　(D) 대중교통 부족

해설 | 주민들이 시 공무원에게 항의한 것
초반부에서 시 공무원들이 새 쇼핑센터 근처 공사 구역 인근의 교통 문제에 관한 항의를 받고 있음을 전해드린다(city officials

have been receiving complaints about traffic)고 했으므로 (A)가 정답이다.

어휘 | public transportation 대중교통

14 어떤 종류의 공사 프로젝트에 관해 논의하는가?
(A) 교량 보수　　　　　　(B) 도로 재포장
(C) 쇼핑센터 건립　　　　(D) 역사적 건물 복원

해설 | 논의되는 공사 프로젝트의 내용
초반부에서 새 쇼핑센터 근처 공사구역(the construction zone near the new shopping center)이라고 했으므로 (C)가 정답이다.

어휘 | repave 재포장하다 restore 복원하다, 복구하다

15 화자가 "시의회는 수요일 밤에 특별 포럼 일정을 잡은 상태입니다"라고 말할 때, 그 의도는 무엇인가?
(A) 출력된 일정표에 오류가 있다.
(B) 의견을 제공할 기회가 있을 것이다.
(C) 기한 연장이 수락됐다.
(D) 인부들이 추가로 필요할 것이다.

해설 | 화자의 의도
후반부에서 제안서는 충분한 수의 지역 주민들이 지지의 목소리를 낼 경우에만 통과될 것(The proposal will only pass, however, if enough local residents voice their support)이라고 한 후, 시의회는 수요일 밤에 특별 포럼 일정을 잡은 상태(the city council has scheduled a special forum on Wednesday night)라고 덧붙였다. 이 말은 지역 주민들의 지지를 얻고자 특별 포럼 일정을 잡은 것이라는 의도로 볼 수 있으므로 (B)가 정답이다.

어휘 | extension 연장

Paraphrasing 담화의 voice their support
→ 정답의 provide feedback

[16-18] 광고

M-Au If you're looking for a weekend activity, ¹⁶visit the Riverdale Art Museum to see our upcoming exhibit… *Beijing Landscapes*. It opens next Friday and features paintings by a young generation of artists from China. If you're interested in seeing the exhibit on the opening day, ¹⁷you must reserve your place on our Web site. ¹⁸Your reservation will include entry to a reception where we'll show a video of the artists at work.

주말 활동을 찾고 계신다면 ¹⁶리버데일 미술관에 오셔서 곧 있을 전시회 〈베이징 풍경〉을 구경하세요. 다음 주 금요일에 시작하며 중국의 신세대 화가들이 그린 그림을 전시합니다. 개막일에 전시회를 관람하고 싶으시다면 ¹⁷저희 웹사이트에서 자리를 예약하셔야 합니다. ¹⁸예약하시면 작업 중인 화가들의 동영상을 상영하는 축하 연회 입장도 포함됩니다.

어휘 | upcoming 다가오는, 곧 있을 feature 특별히 포함하다 reserve 예약하다 reception 환영회, 접수처

16 무엇을 광고하는가?

(A) 미술 전시회　　　　(B) 스포츠 행사
(C) 음악 공연　　　　　(D) 지역사회 축제

해설 | 광고하는 것
초반부에서 리버데일 미술관에 와서 곧 있을 전시회 〈베이징 풍경〉을 구경하라(visit the Riverdale Art Museum to see our upcoming exhibit… *Beijing Landscapes*)고 했으므로 (A)가 정답이다.

Paraphrasing 담화의 exhibit → 정답의 An art exhibition

17 화자는 청자들이 웹사이트에서 무엇을 할 수 있다고 말하는가?

(A) 전기 읽기　　　　　(B) 예약하기
(C) 안내도 다운로드하기　(D) 후기 제출하기

해설 | 청자들이 웹사이트에서 할 일
중반부에서 저희 웹사이트에서 자리를 예약해야 한다(you must reserve your place on our Web site)고 했으므로 (B)가 정답이다.

어휘 | biography 전기

Paraphrasing 담화의 reserve your place
→ 정답의 Make a reservation

18 축하 연회에서 어떤 일이 있을 것인가?

(A) 동영상이 상영될 것이다.
(B) 유명 인사가 사인을 해 줄 것이다.
(C) 식사가 제공될 것이다.
(D) 시상이 있을 것이다.

해설 | 축하 연회에서 있을 일
후반부에서 예약하시면 작업 중인 화가들의 동영상을 상영하는 축하 연회 입장도 포함된다(Your reservation will include entry to a reception where we'll show a video of the artists at work)고 했으므로 (A)가 정답이다.

어휘 | celebrity 유명 인사

Paraphrasing 담화의 we'll show a video of the artists
→ 정답의 A video will be shown.

[19-21] 라디오 방송 + 일정표

> **W-Br** Hello, I'm your host, Anna Moreau. This is the *Sports Sunday Radio Show*. If you're like me, [19]the only thing on your mind today is—basketball! That's right—there are a lot of basketball games scheduled for this afternoon, but [20]the one you really won't want to miss is the matchup between the Rovers and the Turtles. This rivalry has been building all season, ever since the Rovers had a surprise win back in November. Today, [21]I'll talk with special guest Alexi Solokov. He writes for a popular online sports blog, and he'll join us after the commercial break to discuss this eagerly anticipated game.

> 안녕하세요, 저는 진행자 애나 모로이고요. 〈스포츠 선데이 라디오 쇼〉입니다. 여러분도 저와 마찬가지라면, [19]오늘 마음속에 유일하게 떠오르는 건 농구밖에 없으실 텐데요! 맞습니다. 오늘 오후로 예정된 농구 경기가 많은데요. 단연 [20]놓치고 싶지 않은 경기는 로버스와 터틀스의 대결이겠죠. 로버스가 11월에 다시 깜짝 승리를 거둔 후, 시즌 내내 경쟁 구도가 이뤄졌습니다. 오늘 [21]특별 게스트 알렉시 솔로코프와 얘기 나눌 텐데요. 유명 온라인 스포츠 블로그에 글을 쓰고 계시죠. 잠시 광고 듣고 모셔서 대망의 경기에 대해 이야기해 보겠습니다.

어휘 | host 진행자　**matchup** 대결　**rivalry** 경쟁
commercial break 광고 방송 시간　**eagerly-anticipated** 대망의

일요일 일정표	
오전 11시 30분	리젠트 대 맬러드
[20]오후 1시 45분	로버스 대 터틀스
오후 4시	다이아몬드 대 세일러스
오후 6시 45분	스타즈 대 라이트닝

19 화자는 어떤 스포츠에 대해 이야기하는가?

(A) 소프트볼　　　　　(B) 축구
(C) 농구　　　　　　　(D) 배구

해설 | 화자가 논의하는 스포츠
초반부에서 오늘 마음속에 유일하게 떠오르는 건 농구밖에 없을 것(the only thing on your mind today is—basketball)이라고 했으므로 (C)가 정답이다.

20 시각 정보에 따르면, 추천한 경기는 몇 시에 시작하는가?

(A) 오전 11시 30분　　(B) 오후 1시 45분
(C) 오후 4시　　　　　(D) 오후 6시 45분

해설 | 시각 정보 연계
중반부에서 놓치고 싶지 않은 경기는 로버스와 터틀스의 대결(the one you really won't want to miss is the matchup between the Rovers and the Turtles)이라고 했다.
일정표를 보면 로버스와 터틀스의 대결은 오후 1시 45분으로 표기되어 있으므로 (B)가 정답이다.

21 알렉시 솔로코프는 누구인가?

(A) 작가　　　　　　　(B) 운동선수
(C) 개인 트레이너　　　(D) TV 프로듀서

해설 | 알렉시 솔로코프의 신분
후반부에서 오늘 특별 게스트 알렉시 솔로코프와 얘기 나눌 것(I'll talk with special guest Alexi Solokov)이라고 한 후, 그는 유명 온라인 스포츠 블로그에 글을 쓴다(He writes for a popular online sports blog)고 했으므로 (A)가 정답이다.

RC PART 5

UNIT 1 명사

전략포인트 1   본책 p.124

1 (B)   **2** (D)   **3** (C)

1 (B)

번역 | 매 분기마다 열리는 검토 및 교육 시간에 직원들의 역량이 테스트된다.

해설 | 빈칸은 동사 is와 연결되는 주어를 만드는 자리이며, 앞에 정관사 the가 있고 뒤에 전치사구가 이어지므로 명사가 필요하다. 따라서 단수명사인 (B) competence와 복수명사인 (D) competences 중에 골라야 하는데, 단수동사인 is tested와 수가 일치하는 (B) competence가 정답이다.

어휘 | competence 역량 session (수업) 시간 hold 열다, 개최하다 quarter 분기

2 (D)

번역 | 뚜렷한 매출 신장으로 인해 갤럭시 툴즈는 확장 계획을 추진할 수 있게 되었다.

해설 | 빈칸은 전치사 for의 목적어 자리이므로 명사인 (D) expansion이 정답이다.

어휘 | marked 뚜렷한 enable 가능하게 하다 move forward with ~을 추진하다 expansion 확장

3 (C)

번역 | 그랜드 오프닝 세일이 크게 성공하여 어스라이즈 쥬얼러스는 세일 기간을 월말까지 연장했다.

해설 | 빈칸은 동사 was의 보어 자리로, 부정관사 a와 형용사 huge의 수식을 받으므로 명사가 들어가야 한다. 따라서 (C) success가 정답이다.

어휘 | huge 큰 extend 연장하다

전략포인트 2   본책 p.124

1 (A)   **2** (C)   **3** (B)

1 (A)

번역 | 그 의뢰인의 컴퓨터에서는 그 전자문서를 열 수 없으므로 다른 형식으로 보내야 할 것이다.

해설 | 빈칸은 전치사 in의 목적어 역할을 하며 부정관사 a와 형용사 different의 수식을 받는 명사 자리이므로 단수명사인 (A) format이 정답이다.

어휘 | electronic 전자의

2 (C)

번역 | 기계는 필요한 유지보수가 완료되어 작동이 원활하다.

해설 | 빈칸은 정관사 the와 형용사 necessary의 수식을 받는 명사 자리로 빈칸 뒤 has와 수 일치되어야 한다. 따라서 (C) maintenance가 정답이다.

어휘 | function 기능하다 smoothly 순조롭게 now that ~이기 때문에 maintenance 유지, 보수

3 (B)

번역 | 평소 공급 업체 중 일부는 잔지바르 메탈스의 지불 절차 변경에 대해 불만이다.

해설 | 빈칸은 소유격 its와 형용사 usual의 수식을 받는 명사 자리로 '불만이다(are unhappy)'의 주체가 되어야 하므로 사람명사인 (B) suppliers가 정답이다.

어휘 | supplier 공급업체 payment process 지불 절차

전략포인트 3   본책 p.125

1 (B)   **2** (A)   **3** (A)

1 (B)

번역 | 예기치 못한 사정으로 인하여 본 미용실은 다음 달까지 예약을 받지 않고 있습니다.

해설 | 빈칸은 동사 is scheduling의 목적어 자리이므로 명사가 들어가야 한다. appointment는 가산명사인데 빈칸 앞에 관사나 소유격이 없으므로 복수형인 (B) appointments가 정답이다.

어휘 | unforeseen 예측하지 못한 circumstances 상황, 사정 appointment 약속, 예약

2 (A)

번역 | 회사 웹 사이트의 각 주문은 12시간 이내에 처리되고 한 번에 발송됩니다.

해설 | 빈칸 뒤에 단수명사인 order가 왔으므로 (A) Each가 정답이다. (B) Some과 (D) All은 단수명사와 쓸 수 없고, (C) Another는 문맥상 어울리지 않으므로 답이 될 수 없다.

어휘 | fill an order 주문을 처리하다 at once 한번에, 동시에

3 (A)

번역 | 고객 서비스 개선과 관련하여 고객의 어떠한 조언도 환영합니다.

해설 | any는 가산 단·복수명사 그리고 불가산명사와 함께 쓸 수 있지만 '어떠한 조언도 환영합니다'가 문맥상 가장 어울리므로 불가산명사 (A) advice가 정답이다. 가산명사의 단수형인 (B) estimate, (C) alternative, (D) permit도 any와 쓸 수 있지만 의미가 어색하므로 오답이다.

어휘 | regarding ~에 관하여 improvement 개선, 향상

전략포인트 4   본책 p.126

1 (A)   **2** (D)   **3** (A)

1 (A)

번역 | 우리 잡지의 구독자분들께 편리한 온라인 청구 시스템을 이용하시기를 권해 드립니다.

해설 | 빈칸은 동사 advise의 목적어인 명사 자리로 문맥상 '온라인 청구 시스템을 이용하는 주체'가 되어야 하므로 '구독자'를 뜻하는 (A) subscribers가 정답이다.

어휘 | subscriber 구독자　take advantage of ~을 이용하다　convenient 편리한　billing 청구서 발부

2 **(D)**

번역 | 무인 가판대 이용 중 문제가 발생하면 계산대의 저희 직원들 중 한 명에게 문의하세요.

해설 | 빈칸은 ask의 목적어로, 앞의 명사 sales와 함께 복합명사를 만들 수 있는 명사 자리이다. 문맥상 '영업 직원 중 한 명에게 문의하다'라는 내용이 자연스러우므로 복수명사인 (D) associates가 정답이다.

어휘 | encounter 맞닥뜨리다　kiosk 가판대　associate 직원, 동료　checkout 계산대　association 협회

3 **(A)**

번역 | 태양열 발전에 대한 연구는 주로 태양전지를 더 효율적으로 만드는 데 초점을 두고 있다.

해설 | 빈칸은 전치사구 on solar power의 수식을 받아 문장의 주어가 될 수 있는 명사 자리이다. 따라서, '연구'라는 의미의 불가산명사인 (A) Research가 정답이다. 사람명사인 (B) Researcher는 가산명사로 관사나 한정사 없이 단독으로 주어 자리에 올 수 없다.

어휘 | solar power 태양열 발전　focus on ~에 초점을 맞추다　mostly 주로　solar cell 태양전지　efficient 효율적인

전략포인트 5
본책 p.126

1 (B)　**2** (D)　**3** (A)

1 **(B)**

번역 | 프렌지 성은 북부 호수 지역에서 가장 방문객이 많이 찾는 관광 명소이다.

해설 | 빈칸은 동사 is의 보어로 최상급 형용사 most visited의 수식을 받으면서 명사 tourist와 함께 복합명사를 이루는 명사 자리이다. 따라서 명사 (B) attraction이 정답이다. '관광 명소'라는 뜻의 복합명사 tourist attraction은 자주 출제되므로 암기해 두자.

어휘 | castle 성　tourist attraction 관광 명소　lake 호수　region 지역

2 **(D)**

번역 | 하이드레인지어 호텔 예약에 대한 이메일 확인을 받지 못한 경우 고객 서비스 부서에 연락 주세요.

해설 | 빈칸은 receive의 목적어로 e-mail과 함께 복합명사를 이루는 자리이다. 문맥상, '호텔 예약에 대한 이메일 확인'이라는 의미가 되어야 자연스러우므로 '확인'이라는 뜻의 (D) confirmation이 정답이다.

어휘 | confirmation 확인　booking 예약　contribution 기여　guidance 안내　admission 입장

3 **(A)**

번역 | 모든 직원들은 매달 판매 할당량을 채워야 한다는 지시를 받았다.

해설 | 빈칸에는 동사 meet의 목적어 역할을 하며 quota와 함께 복합명사를 이루는 명사가 와야 한다. 문맥상 '판매 할당량'이라는 의미가 적절하므로 '판매량, 매출액'을 뜻하는 (A) sales가 정답이다.

어휘 | instruct 지시하다　meet 채우다　sales quota 판매 할당량

ETS 고득점 실전 문제
본책 p.128

1 (D)　**2** (D)　**3** (B)　**4** (C)　**5** (D)　**6** (C)
7 (D)　**8** (C)　**9** (B)　**10** (D)　**11** (D)　**12** (A)
13 (D)　**14** (B)　**15** (B)　**16** (C)　**17** (A)　**18** (C)
19 (C)　**20** (B)

1 **(D)**

번역 | 획기적인 표본 추출 방법에 대한 추 씨의 발표는 아주 뜨거운 박수를 받았다.

해설 | 빈칸은 동사 received의 목적어로 형용사 warm의 수식을 받는 명사 자리이다. 따라서 명사인 (D) applause가 정답이다. (A) applaud는 동사이므로 답이 될 수 없다.

어휘 | innovative 획기적인　sampling 표본 추출　method 방법　applause 박수

2 **(D)**

번역 | 저희 웹사이트의 채팅 기능은 고객이 재무 담당자와 직접 대화할 수 있게 해 줍니다.

해설 | 빈칸 앞에 부정관사 a가 있으므로 빈칸은 가산 단수명사 자리이다. 문맥상 '재무 담당자와 직접 대화할 수 있다'는 내용이 되어야 자연스러우므로 '대리인, 직원'을 뜻하는 가산 단수명사인 (D) representative가 정답이다.

어휘 | chat 대화　feature 기능　directly 직접적으로　financial 재무의　representative 대표, 대변인

3 **(B)**

번역 | 새로운 회의 공간을 갖춘 스텔웨이 호텔은 현재 브룩웰 컨벤션 센터와 직접적인 경쟁을 벌이고 있다.

해설 | 빈칸은 전치사 in의 목적어로 온 명사 competition을 수식하는 형용사 자리이다. 따라서 '직접적인'이라는 의미의 형용사인 (B) direct가 정답이다.

어휘 | space 공간　direct 직접적인　competition 경쟁　direction 방향

4 **(C)**

번역 | 챔버스 브라더스사는 좋은 직원 복리 후생을 제공하는 것으로 유명하다.

해설 | 빈칸 앞 형용사 good부터 빈칸 뒤 복수명사 benefits까지가 offering의 목적어이다. 형용사 good의 수식을 받으면서 benefits와 복합명사를 만들 수 있는 (C) employee가 정답이다. 사람명사가 복수형이 아니거나 한정사와 같이 쓰이지 않았다면 대체로 다른 명사를 수식하는 명사이다. 참고로 employee benefits는 대표적인 복합명사로 '직원 복리 후생'이라는 뜻이다.

어휘 | be known for ~으로 유명하다   offer 제공하다
benefits (회사의) 복리 후생

5 **(D)**

번역 | 팽 씨는 창고 직원들의 도움으로 새로운 재고 관리 시스템을 시행할 수 있었다.

해설 | 앞에 정관사 the가 있고 뒤에 전치사 of가 있으므로 빈칸은 명사 자리이다. 문맥상 '창고 직원들의 도움으로'라는 내용이 되어야 적절하므로 '도움'이라는 뜻의 추상명사 (D) assistance가 정답이다. (C) assistant는 '조수'라는 뜻의 가산명사이다.

어휘 | implement 시행하다   inventory 재고
management 관리   warehouse 창고

6 **(C)**

번역 | 컨퍼런스 참석자 명단은 일정표 뒷면에서 찾을 수 있다.

해설 | 빈칸은 명사 conference와 함께 복합명사를 이루는 명사 자리이고, 문맥상 '컨퍼런스 참석자'라는 의미가 되어야 자연스러우므로 '참석자'라는 뜻의 명사 (C) attendees가 정답이다.

어휘 | program 일정표, 계획표   attendance 참석

7 **(D)**

번역 | 프로그램에 대한 관심 부족은 1주일 후에 감독에 의해 그것이 취소되는 결과를 초래했다.

해설 | 빈칸은 동사 resulted의 주어로, 전치사구 of interest in the program의 수식을 받는 명사 자리이다. 따라서 '부족'이라는 뜻의 명사인 (D) Lack이 정답이다.

어휘 | lack 부족   result in ~을 초래하다   cancel 취소하다

8 **(C)**

번역 | RGMA는 고객의 인터넷 보안 요구에 효과적인 해결책을 제공하는 것에 자부심을 가지고 있다.

해설 | 빈칸은 전치사 for의 목적어 자리이자 소유격 clients'의 뒤에 오는 명사 자리이다. 문맥상 앞의 복합명사 Internet security와 함께 쓰여 '인터넷 보안 요구'라는 뜻의 복합명사를 만들 수 있는 명사 (C) needs가 정답이다.

어휘 | take pride in ~을 자랑하다   effective 효과적인
solution 해결책   security 보안

9 **(B)**

번역 | 잦은 쇼핑은 한 개인이 개인 물품에 너무 많은 돈을 쓰는 결과를 초래할 수 있다.

해설 | 빈칸은 형용사 Frequent의 수식을 받으면서 문장의 주어 역할을 하는 명사 자리이다. 문맥상 '잦은 쇼핑은 ~한 결과를 초래할 수 있다'라는 의미가 되어야 하므로, (B) shopping이 정답이다.

어휘 | frequent 잦은, 빈번한   result in ~을 초래하다
individual 개인, 사람   personal 개인의, 개인적인

10 **(D)**

번역 | 보서스 여과 시스템은 자사 제품 사용에 대한 온라인 안내를 제공한다.

해설 | 빈칸은 provide의 목적어로 형용사 online의 수식을 받는 명사 자리이다. '제품 사용에 대한 온라인 안내'라는 의미가 되어야 하므로 '안내'를 뜻하는 (D) guidance가 정답이다.

어휘 | filtration 여과   guidance 안내   variety 다양성
assembly 조립   judgment 판단

11 **(D)**

번역 | 물류 관리 직원은 상품을 배송하기 전에 트리랜드 토이즈가 계약서에 서명하고 돌려주기를 기다리고 있다.

해설 | 빈칸은 '배송하다'라는 뜻의 동사 ship의 동명사인 shipping의 목적어 자리로, 문맥상 물류 관리 직원이 배송하는 대상이 될 수 있는 명사가 와야 한다. 따라서 '상품'이라는 뜻의 (D) merchandise가 정답이다. 참고로 merchandise는 대표 불가산명사인 점도 기억하자.

어휘 | logistics 물류 관리   clerk 직원   contract
계약서   ship 배송하다   merchandise 상품   trade 거래
transportation 운송, 수송

12 **(A)**

번역 | 젤라빌 상공회의소는 역사적인 해안가를 성공적인 관광지로 개발하려는 계획에 착수했다.

해설 | 빈칸은 전치사 into의 목적어로 형용사 viable의 수식을 받으면서 명사 tourist와 복합명사를 이루는 명사 자리이다. 문맥상 '성공적인 관광지로'라는 의미가 되어야 자연스러우므로 '목적지'를 뜻하는 (A) destination이 정답이다. '관광지'를 뜻하는 복합명사 'tourist destination'과 '관광 명소'를 뜻하는 'tourist attraction'을 암기해 두자.

어휘 | chamber of commerce 상공회의소   initiate
착수시키다   develop 개발하다   historic 역사적인
waterfront 해안가   viable 성공할 수 있는   destination
목적지   population 인구   method 방법   stage 무대, 단계

13 **(D)**

번역 | 주민센터의 수영장은 매주 청소가 예정되어 있습니다.

해설 | 빈칸은 전치사 for의 목적어 역할을 하는 명사 자리이다. 문맥상 '매주 청소가 예정되어 있다'가 자연스러우므로, 청소라는 뜻의 불가산명사 (D) cleaning이 정답이다. (B) cleaner는 가산명사로 앞에 관사도 없고 복수형도 아니므로 단독으로 명사 자리에 올 수 없다.

어휘 | community center 주민센터   scheduled 예정된
cleaning 청소

14 (B)

번역 | 몇 주 내로 시스네로스 씨는 프로젝트의 컨설턴트에서 관리자가 되었다.

해설 | 빈칸은 전치사 to의 목적어 역할을 하는 명사 자리로 뒤에 오는 대명사 it을 목적어로 취할 수 있어야 하므로 동명사인 (B) managing이 정답이다

어휘 | consultant 자문 위원

15 (B)

번역 | 몇몇 연구는 너무 많은 휴가가 노동 생산성을 떨어뜨릴 수 있다는 것을 보여준다.

해설 | 빈칸은 reduce의 목적어로, 앞의 명사 worker와 복합명사를 이루는 명사 자리이다. 문맥상 '노동 생산성을 떨어뜨리다'라는 의미가 되어야 하므로 '생산성'이라는 뜻의 (B) productivity가 정답이다. worker productivity는 대표적인 복합명사로 '노동 생산성'을 의미한다.

어휘 | reduce 줄이다 productivity 생산성 production 생산

16 (C)

번역 | 마르콘 시장이 제안한 최근의 계획은 대부분의 지역 주민들에게 긍정적으로 인식되었다.

해설 | 빈칸은 최상급 형용사 latest와 과거분사 proposed의 수식을 받는 명사 자리이다. 문맥상 '제안된 최근의 계획'이라는 의미가 되어야 자연스러우므로 '계획'이라는 뜻의 명사인 (C) initiative가 정답이다. (A) initiator와 (B) initiation도 명사이기는 하나 각각 '발기인'과 '시작'이라는 의미로 문맥에 어울리지 않는다.

어휘 | initiative 계획, 프로젝트 perceive 인지[인식]하다 local 지역의, 현지의 resident 주민

17 (A)

번역 | 많은 인터뷰 대상자들은 펠턴 섬유의 근무 환경이 가장 큰 매력이라고 평했다.

해설 | 전치사 on의 목적어로 앞의 명사 work과 함께 문맥상 '근무 환경'이라는 뜻의 복합명사를 만들 수 있는 명사 (A) environment가 정답이다.

어휘 | comment 논평하다 work environment 근무 환경 primary 주요한 attraction 매력 environmentalist 환경운동가

18 (C)

번역 | J.D. 쿠퍼는 자기 레스토랑의 메뉴에 이전보다 훨씬 더 다양한 선택 범위의 요리가 포함될 것이라고 말했다.

해설 | 빈칸은 동사 feature의 목적어로 비교급 형용사 larger의 수식을 받는 명사 자리이다. 문맥상 '훨씬 더 다양한 종류의 요리를 포함하다'라는 의미가 되는 것이 자연스러우므로, '선택'이라는 뜻의 (C) selection이 정답이다. '선택 범위가 다양한'이라는 뜻으로 흔히 쓰이는 'a large selection of'에서 large를 비교급으로 바꾸고 그 앞에 비교급 강조를 위한 even이 추가된 형태이다.

어휘 | feature (특별히) 포함하다 a selection of 다양한 length 길이 source 원천 dimension 크기

19 (C)

번역 | 햄프턴 로지스틱스는 자사의 여러 창고에 고객을 위한 장기 보관 상품을 제공합니다.

해설 | provide의 목적어로 형용사 long-term의 수식을 받는 명사 자리이다. 따라서 '보관'이라는 뜻의 명사인 (C) storage가 정답이다. (B) store도 명사이기는 하지만 '상점'이라는 의미로 문맥에 어울리지 않고, 가산명사이므로 복수형이거나 한정사가 동반되어야 한다. 장소명사가 일반적으로 가산명사라는 점을 알아두면 유용하다.

어휘 | provide 제공하다 long-term 장기적인 storage 보관, 저장

20 (B)

번역 | 관광 시즌 기간 동안의 높은 수요로 여행비자 처리가 예상보다 오래 걸릴 것이다.

해설 | 빈칸은 동사 will take의 주어 자리로, 전치사구인 of travel visas의 수식을 받는 명사 자리이다. 문맥상 '여행비자의 처리'라는 의미가 자연스러우므로 '처리'라는 뜻의 (B) Processing이 정답이다. (A) Process는 '과정'이라는 뜻의 가산명사로 앞에 관사도 없고 복수형도 아니므로 단독으로 명사 자리에 올 수 없다.

어휘 | processing 처리 due to ~ 때문에 demand 수요 procedure 절차 proceed 나아가다 process 과정

UNIT 2 대명사

전략포인트 1 본책 p.130

1 (C) **2** (B) **3** (A)

1 (C)

번역 | 우리의 광고 컨설턴트인 박 씨는 금요일에 그의 첫 보고서를 제출할 것이다.

해설 | 빈칸 뒤에 형용사 first와 명사 report가 왔으므로 이 명사구를 수식할 수 있는 소유격 인칭대명사가 들어가야 한다. 따라서 정답은 (C) his이다.

어휘 | advertising 광고 submit 제출하다

2 (B)

번역 | 앤더슨 씨는 피블스 씨와 이야기를 나누었고 그녀에게 보이시에서 열리는 무역 박람회에 참석해 달라고 요청했다.

해설 | ask는 목적어와 목적격 보어를 취하는 5형식 동사이다. 'ask + 목적어 + to부정사' 구조에서 빈칸은 목적어 자리이므로 Ms. Peebles를 대신하는 목적격 인칭대명사가 들어가야 한다. 따라서 (B) her가 정답이다.

어휘 | attend ~에 참석하다 trade fair 무역 박람회

3 (A)

번역 | 린트 전자의 연구원들은 그들이 수 년간 연구해온 웨어러블 기기에 대해 논의할 것이다.

해설 | 빈칸 앞에 목적격 관계대명사 that이 있고, 빈칸 뒤에 동사 have been developing이 있으므로 동사 앞에서 주어 역할을 하는 주격 인칭대명사가 들어가야 한다. 문맥상 Researchers가 주어이므로 이를 대신하는 (A) they가 정답이다.

어휘 | wearable devices 웨어러블 기기 (입거나 몸에 붙여 휴대할 수 있는 정보통신 기기)

전략포인트 2
본책 p.130

1 (B) **2** (D) **3** (C)

1 (B)

번역 | 렌터카를 찾아가는 여자들에게 그들의 것이 파란색 미니밴이라고 알려주어야 한다.

해설 | 명사절 that절에서 동사 is의 주어가 와야 하는 자리이므로, 빈칸에는 주격이면서 단수 취급되는 대명사가 들어가야 한다. 따라서 정답은 소유대명사인 (B) theirs이다. 이때 theirs는 their rental vehicle을 의미한다.

어휘 | rental 대여 vehicle 차량 minivan 미니밴

2 (D)

번역 | 매니토바주는 전자제품에 7%의 판매세를 부과하고 있지만, 이쪽 우리 것은 10%이다.

해설 | 접속사 but절에서 동사 is의 주어가 와야 하는 자리이므로, 빈칸에는 주격이면서 단수 취급되는 대명사가 들어가야 한다. 따라서 정답은 소유대명사인 (D) ours이다. 이때 ours는 our sales tax를 의미한다.

어휘 | province 주, 도 sales tax 판매세 electronic 전자 기기[제품]

3 (C)

번역 | 이글슨 씨는 언젠가 미래에 자기 자신의 사업을 시작하기를 바라기 때문에 경영학 프로그램에 등록했다.

해설 | 문맥상 '자기 자신의 사업을 시작하기를 바란다'라는 의미가 되는 것이 가장 자연스러우므로, 빈칸에는 전치사 of와 함께 쓰여 '자기 소유의'의 의미를 강조하는 (C) his own이 들어가야 한다. 이때 a business of his own은 his own business로도 쓸 수 있다.

어휘 | enroll in ~에 등록하다 business management 경영(학)

전략포인트 3
본책 p.131

1 (D) **2** (C) **3** (A)

1 (D)

번역 | 지난주에 사라판 씨는 배정된 모든 업무를 직접 완수했다.

해설 | 빈칸이 없어도 완전한 문장이므로 빈칸은 부사 자리이다. 따라서 강조적 용법의 재귀대명사가 들어가야 하므로 (D) himself 가 정답이다

어휘 | assigned 배정된

2 (C)

번역 | 헨더슨 씨는 지원자들에게 다가올 취업 박람회에서의 면접에 대비하라고 조언했다.

해설 | to prepare의 의미상의 주어가 the applicants이므로 빈칸에는 '지원자들 자신(applicants)'을 뜻하는 재귀대명사가 와야 한다. 따라서 (C) themselves가 정답이다. 참고로 'prepare oneself for'는 '~에 대비하다'라는 표현이다.

어휘 | applicant 지원자 prepare oneself for ~에 대비하다 upcoming 다가오는 job fair 취업 박람회

3 (A)

번역 | 이번 분기 동안 각 팀의 멤버들은 저희들끼리 아이디어를 공유하고 오토바이 시제품을 개발해야 한다.

해설 | 전치사 among 뒤에는 복수 형태의 목적어가 와야 하므로 보기 중 단수인 (B) himself는 제외된다. 재귀대명사는 주어와 일치해야 하고 문장의 주어인 The members가 3인칭 복수이므로 (A) themselves가 정답이다. among themselves는 '저희들끼리'라는 의미의 관용 표현이다.

어휘 | prototype 시제품, 시작품

전략포인트 4
본책 p.132

1 (B) **2** (B) **3** (D)

1 (B)

번역 | 네틀스 씨는 오늘밤 야근하기를 원하는 사람들에게 오후 4시까지 알려 달라고 부탁했다.

해설 | 주격 관계대명사 who 앞에서 '사람들'이라는 뜻으로 쓸 수 있는 대명사인 (B) those가 정답이다. (C) them도 asked 뒤에 목적어로 가능해 보이지만 인칭대명사는 뒤에 수식어구를 동반할 수 없으므로 오답이다.

2 (B)

번역 | 생물 의학 분야에서의 경력을 고려하는 모든 사람들은 홀스턴 박사가 이끄는 세미나에 참석해야 한다.

해설 | '~한 사람들'이라는 의미를 나타내는 'those + who + be동사 + 현재분사 / 과거분사' 구조에서 주격 관계대명사 who와 be동사가 생략된 형태이다. 과거분사인 (A) considered와 현재분사인 (B) considering 중에서 빈칸 뒤의 목적어 a career를 이끌 수 있는 것은 현재분사이므로 (B) considering이 정답이다.

어휘 | consider 고려하다 career 경력 field 분야 biomedicine 생물 의학

3 (D)

번역 | 스미스 씨는 그 프로젝트를 원래 담당하는 사람들보다 무엇을 해야 하는지 더 잘 알고 있다.

해설 | 문맥상 '원래 담당하는 사람들보다 더 잘 알고 있다'가 자연스러우므로 '사람들'의 의미인 (D) those가 정답이다. (A) who는 접속사이며 (C) those who는 접속사 who를 지니고 있으므로 뒤에 본동사가 따라야 하며, 인칭대명사 (B) them은 전치사구의 수식을 받을 수 없기 때문에 오답이다.

어휘 | in charge of ~을 맡아서, 담당해서

전략포인트 5
본책 p.132

1 (A) **2** (A) **3** (D)

1 **(A)**

번역 | 이번 휴일에 상점에 쇼핑하러 온 사람의 수는 이전 휴일의 그것과[수와] 비슷하다.

해설 | 빈칸은 전치사 to의 목적어로 앞서 언급된 단수명사 number를 대신 받는 대명사 자리이다. 따라서 (A) that이 정답이다. (B) those는 복수명사를 받아야 하므로 오답이다.

어휘 | similar 비슷한 previous 이전의

2 **(A)**

번역 | 실제 색상이 카탈로그 설명에 나온 것과 달랐기 때문에 에트왈 가운은 레이스 2상자를 공급업체로 반송했다.

해설 | 빈칸은 전치사 from의 목적어 자리이고, 앞서 언급된 단수명사 color를 대신 받는 대명사 자리이다. 따라서 정답은 (A) that이다.

어휘 | actual 실제의 differ 다르다 description 묘사 lace 레이스 supplier 공급업체

3 **(D)**

번역 | 단종된 피부관리 제품들과 달리 올해에 출시된 제품들은 공기가 들어가지 않는 펌프 병으로 되어 있습니다.

해설 | 빈칸 뒤 과거분사 released의 수식을 받아 주어가 될 수 있는 대명사는 (C) that와 (D) those이다. 문맥상 빈칸은 복수명사 products를 대신해야 하므로 대명사 (D) those가 정답이다. 반복되는 명사를 대신할 때 쓰는 지시대명사는 비교상황에서 주로 쓰이는데 지문에서는 전치사 unlike가 비교 관련 어휘이다.

어휘 | discontinued 단종된 release 출시하다 airless 공기가 통하지 않는

전략포인트 6
본책 p.133

1 (A) **2** (B) **3** (A)

1 **(A)**

번역 | 우리의 고객 서비스 설문 조사는 1,000명에게 발송되었지만, 많은 사람들이 응답하지 않았다.

해설 | but절의 주어 역할을 하면서 앞의 명사 one thousand people을 받는 부정대명사가 필요하므로 '많은 사람들'을 나타내는 (A) many가 정답이다. much는 불가산명사를 대신하므로 답이 될 수 없다.

어휘 | respond 응답하다

2 **(B)**

번역 | 직원들이 생산성을 높이기 위해 서로 동기부여를 하는 것이 이상적이다.

해설 | 빈칸은 동사 motivate의 목적어 자리이고, 문맥상 '생산성 향상을 위해 서로 동기부여를 한다'라는 것이 자연스러우므로 '서로'를 의미하는 부정대명사인 (B) each other가 정답이다.

어휘 | ideal 이상적인 productivity 생산성

3 **(A)**

번역 | 청중들은 강연을 즐겼으나, 연설이 끝났을 때 아무도 연설자에게 질문을 하지 않았다.

해설 | 빈칸은 주절의 주어 자리이므로 주어 역할을 할 수 있는 명사나 대명사가 와야 한다. 문맥상 '강연은 즐겼으나, 아무도 질문을 하지 않았다'라는 의미가 되어야 하므로 부정대명사 (A) none이 정답이다.

어휘 | conclude 끝나다, 마치다

전략포인트 7
본책 p.134

1 (D) **2** (C) **3** (A)

1 **(D)**

번역 | 데니스 칸토르는 오늘밤 이번 주 업무의 대부분이 끝날 때까지 계속 일할 것이다.

해설 | 빈칸 뒤의 명사구 her assignments를 수식할 수 있는 것은 보기 중 (D) most of 밖에 없으며, 문맥상으로도 '그녀의 업무 중 대부분이 끝날 때까지'가 자연스러우므로 정답은 (D) most of이다. (A) mostly와 (C) almost는 부사이기 때문에 her assignments를 수식할 수 없고, (B) most는 어순이 her와 assignments 사이에 들어가야 한다.

어휘 | assignment 할당 업무, 임무

2 **(C)**

번역 | 창고에 도착한 상자의 일부는 운송 중에 파손되었다.

해설 | 빈칸은 이 문장의 주어 자리로 'of + 복수명사'의 수식을 받을 수 있는 대명사가 들어가야 한다. 따라서 정답은 (C) Some이다. (A) That은 대신 받는 명사가 언급되어 있지 않고, (B) Anything과 (D) Much는 'of + 복수명사'와 함께 쓸 수 없다.

어휘 | crate (운송용) 상자 warehouse 창고 damage 손상을 주다 in transit 운송 중에

3 **(A)**

번역 | 팀원 다섯 명 중 한 명도 8월 판매 할당량을 채우지 못했다.

해설 | 빈칸은 주어 자리로 'of+복수명사'의 수식을 받을 수 있는 명사나 대명사가 들어가야 한다. 따라서 '하나도 ~않다'를 뜻하는 (A) None이 정답이다. (B) No, (C) Nothing, (D) Nobody는 'of+복수명사'와 함께 쓸 수 없다.

어휘 | fulfill 채우다 sales quota 판매 할당

ETS 고득점 실전 문제
본책 p.136

1 (C) **2** (D) **3** (B) **4** (A) **5** (C) **6** (A)
7 (B) **8** (A) **9** (C) **10** (D) **11** (A) **12** (D)
13 (C) **14** (C) **15** (B) **16** (A) **17** (A) **18** (D)
19 (B) **20** (C)

1 **(C)**

번역 | 레이놀즈 씨와 그녀의 팀은 내일 회의에서 발표를 할 예정이다.

해설 | 빈칸에는 명사 team을 수식할 수 있는 소유격이 들어가야 한다. 따라서 정답은 (C) her이다.

2 **(D)**

번역 | 관리자는 에반스 씨와 클락 씨에게 취업 박람회에서 발표를 해달라고 요청했고 그들에게 아주 구체적인 방식으로 자료를 준비하라고 지시했다.

해설 | 빈칸은 and절에서 동사 instructed의 목적어가 와야 하는 자리이며, 준비하도록 지시를 받은 대상은 Mr. Evans and Mr. Clark임을 알 수 있으므로, 정답은 (D) them이다.

어휘 | job fair 취업 박람회 instruct 지시하다 specific 구체적인

3 **(B)**

번역 | 이사회에서 제시된 두 안건 중 어느 것도 승인되지 않았다.

해설 | 빈칸은 동사 were의 주어 자리로 빈칸 뒤 'of+복수명사'의 수식을 받을 수 있고 단수/복수동사와 같이 쓸 수 있는 부정대명사가 들어가야 한다. 따라서 (B) Neither가 정답이다. 복수동사와 수 일치가 되지 않는 (A) Another와 접속사 역할을 하는 복합관계대명사 (C) Whatever는 답이 될 수 없다. (D) Those는 앞서 언급된 명사를 대신하거나 '사람들'을 뜻하므로 오답이다.

어휘 | proposal 제안 present 제시하다 approve 승인하다

4 **(A)**

번역 | 모든 사람들이 발표자를 분명히 볼 수 있도록 무대 위에 대형 비디오 스크린을 설치할 것이다.

해설 | 빈칸은 부사절 접속사 so that절의 주어 자리이다. '~하기 위해서'의 의미인 so that은 조동사 can과 주로 사용되며 that을 생략한 'so (that) 주어 can ~'의 구조로 쓰이기도 한다. 문맥상 '모든 사람들이 발표자를 분명히 볼 수 있게 하기 위해서'가 자연스러우므로 (A) everyone이 정답이다.

어휘 | set up 설치하다 so that ~하도록 presenter 발표자

5 **(C)**

번역 | 안젤라 머서는 위원회에 의해 그녀의 제안 하나가 선정되어 영광스러웠다.

해설 | 문맥상 '그녀의 제안 하나'라는 의미가 되어야 하고, 'of+빈칸'이 a proposal을 수식하고 있으므로 '명사+of+ 소유대명사' 구조임을 알 수 있다. 따라서 빈칸에는 (C) hers가 들어가야 한다.

어휘 | honor 명예[영예]를 주다 proposal 제안 select 선택하다 committee 위원회

6 **(A)**

번역 | 최근 고객만족 설문조사에서 불만사항의 반 이상이 서비스의 신속함에 관한 것이었다.

해설 | 빈칸은 주어 More than half of the complaints의 동사 자리이다. 부분을 나타내는 부정대명사 half가 단수주어처럼 보여도, 복수명사인 complaints의 반을 나타내므로 주어는 복수이며 동사는 복수주어와 수 일치되어야 한다. 따라서, (A) were가 정답이다.

어휘 | more than ~이상 speed 신속

7 **(B)**

번역 | 교육이 꽤 어려웠지만, 컴퓨터 프로그램 자체는 사용 경험을 거의 요구하지 않았다.

해설 | 빈칸이 없어도 문장이 성립하므로 빈칸은 주어인 the computer program 뒤에서 주어를 강조하는 부사 자리이다. 따라서 재귀대명사 (B) itself가 정답이다.

어휘 | training session 교육, 연수 require 요구하다

8 **(A)**

번역 | 관리자는 마크 워커에게 그가 지원한 자리가 내부 지원자에 의해 채워졌다는 것을 알려줄 것이다.

해설 | '명사구+빈칸+타동사' 구조로 빈칸은 주격 인칭대명사 자리이다. 따라서 (A) he가 정답이다. 빈칸 앞 the job이 선행사로 목적격 관계대명사가 생략되어 바로 관계절의 주어로 연결되고 있다.

어휘 | inform 알리다 apply 지원하다 fill 채우다 internal 내부의 candidate 지원자

9 **(C)**

번역 | 마크 켄트는 모든 문서를 스스로 번역할 수 있다고 주장했다.

해설 | 문맥상 '스스로, 혼자서'라는 의미가 되는 것이 가장 자연스러우므로, 전치사 on과 함께 쓰여 '혼자서, 스스로'의 의미를 강조하는 (C) his own이 정답이다.

어휘 | insist 주장하다 translate 번역하다 document 서류, 문서

10 **(D)**

번역 | 마케팅 팀원들과 마찬가지로 회계 팀의 그들[팀원들]도 대부분 석사 이상의 학위를 가지고 있다.

해설 | 빈칸은 앞서 언급된 복수명사 members를 반복해서 사용하는 것을 피하기 위해 쓰는 지시대명사 자리이다. 따라서 정답은 (D) those이다. 마케팅 팀원들과 회계 팀원들은 각각 다른 대상이므로, 정확히 동일한 대상을 지칭할 때 쓰는 인칭대명사 (A) them은 오답이다.

어휘 | accounting 회계 advanced degree (석사 이상의) 고급 학위

11 **(A)**

번역 | 300명의 고객에게 특별 할인 소식이 갔지만, 거의 모든 사람들이 온라인 상점에서 어떤 것도 주문하지 않았다.

해설 | 빈칸은 주절의 주어 자리이며, while 부사절의 customers를 가리키는 대명사로 '거의 모든 고객들이 주문하지 않았다'라는 의미가 적절한 (A) few가 정답이다. (B) little과 (C) much는 불가산명사로 취급하므로 답이 될 수 없다.

어휘 | special offer 특별 할인

12 (D)
번역 | 수리 작업은 공장 내 4개의 조립 라인 각각에서 동시에 실시되어야 한다.

해설 | 빈칸은 전치사 on의 목적어 자리로 'of + 복수명사'의 수식을 받을 수 있는 명사가 들어가야 한다. 따라서 정답은 (D) each이다. (A) which, (B) other, (C) every는 'of + 복수명사'와 함께 쓸 수 없다.

어휘 | at once 한번에, 동시에   assembly line 조립 라인

13 (C)
번역 | 대부분의 근로자들은 모든 복지 혜택을 받지만, 파트타임으로 일하는 근로자들은 유급 휴가를 받지 못할 수도 있다.

해설 | 빈칸은 but절의 주어로 working part time의 수식을 받는 자리이다. 따라서 분사구의 수식을 받을 수 있는 (C) those가 정답이다.

어휘 | benefits (회사의) 복리 후생   time off 휴가

14 (C)
번역 | 듀몬트 씨는 최고 경영자에게 그의 신규 사업이 1년간 자금 지원을 받은 후에도 지속될 수 있는지 물었다.

해설 | 빈칸은 타동사 sustain 뒤의 목적어 자리이며, 이에 맞는 재귀대명사를 고르는 문제이다. sustain의 주어는 his startup이고, 재귀대명사는 주어와 동일해야 하므로 (C) itself가 정답이다.

어휘 | startup 신규 사업   sustain 지속시키다   funding 자금 지원

15 (B)
번역 | 최근에 많은 직원들이 신분증을 새로 요청해 왔기 때문에 보안 책임자는 직원들과 이야기를 나누었다.

해설 | 빈칸은 since절에서 주어 역할을 하면서 복수동사인 have와 쓸 수 있는 명사나 대명사 자리이다. 따라서 앞에 언급된 the workers(직원들)을 나타내는 (B) many가 정답이다.

어휘 | security 보안   ID card 신분증

16 (A)
번역 | 모든 서빙 직원들은, 심지어 선임이라도, 주방의 요리사들보다 더 중요하지 않다.

해설 | 빈칸에는 뒤에 오는 명사구 those with seniority의 의미를 강조하면서 수식할 수 있는 부사가 들어가야 한다. 문맥상 '심지어 선임이라도'라는 의미가 적절하므로 정답은 (A) even이 된다.

어휘 | wait staff 서빙 직원들   seniority 선임

17 (A)
번역 | 다른 상품으로 교환하기를 원하는 써니 셔츠 고객에게는 차액이 청구된다.

해설 | 관계사절의 동사 wish의 목적어 역할을 하는 to부정사에 들어갈 동사 어휘를 고르는 문제이다. '~한 고객에게 차액이 청구된다'고 하였으므로 문맥상 '교환하다'는 의미의 (A) exchange가 정답이다. 참고로 another는 '같은 종류의 다른 제품으로 교환해주다'라는 문맥으로 exchange 동사와 자주 출제되니 익혀 두자.

어휘 | charge 청구하다

18 (D)
번역 | 아직 어떤 설문지도 돌아오지 않았기 때문에 경영진은 직원들이 근무 조건에 대해 어떻게 생각하는지 확신하지 못하고 있다.

해설 | 빈칸은 because절의 주어 자리로 'of + 복수명사'의 수식을 받을 수 있는 대명사가 들어가야 한다. 따라서 정답은 (D) none이다. (A) no, (B) no one, (C) nothing은 모두 'of + 복수명사' 구조와 함께 쓸 수 없다.

어휘 | management 경영진   work conditions 근무 조건

19 (B)
번역 | 위원회는 다음 달에 모든 직무기술서를 검토하고 변경이 필요한 사항은 수정할 예정이다.

해설 | 빈칸은 동사 revise의 목적어 자리이자 관계사 that절의 수식을 받고 있으므로, 접속사인 (A) what과 (C) which는 답이 될 수 없다. 또한 빈칸에 들어갈 부정대명사는 job descriptions를 대신하므로 사람을 뜻하는 (D) somebody는 부적절하다. 따라서 (B) any가 정답이다.

어휘 | committee 위원회   review 검토하다   description 설명서   revise 수정하다

20 (C)
번역 | 오페라 무료 입장권을 먼저 신청하는 사람들은 접수원에게 입장권을 받게 될 것입니다.

해설 | will be given의 주어 역할을 하며, first request ~ the opera까지를 문장의 주어로 만드는 접속사가 필요하므로, '~하는 사람들'을 의미하는 (C) Those who가 정답이다. those who와 거의 같은 문맥에서 쓰이는 복합관계대명사인 (B) Whoever는 단수 취급하므로 복수동사인 request와 쓰일 수 없다. (D) Someone은 접속사 역할을 할 수 없으므로 오답이다.

어휘 | request 요청[신청]하다   complimentary 무료의   receptionist 접수원

UNIT 3 형용사 & 부사

전략포인트 1	본책 p.138

1 (D)   2 (B)   3 (C)

1 (D)
번역 | 직원들의 넉넉한 기부로 타나카 씨의 승진을 축하하기 위한 꽃을 구입했다.

해설 | 빈칸은 전치사 with의 목적어 역할을 하는 명사 contributions를 수식하는 형용사 자리이다. 따라서 정답은 (D) generous이다.

어휘 | generous 넉넉한 contribution 기부 celebrate 축하하다 promotion 승진

2 (B)

번역 | 맥키니 씨는 허버트 씨의 연설에 참석하는 것에 대해 유일하게 열성적인 사람이었다.

해설 | 빈칸이 포함된 문장은 주격 관계대명사 who와 동사 is가 생략된 관계사절이다. 따라서 빈칸에는 be동사 is의 보어이자 전치사 about과 어울려 쓰이는 형용사가 들어가야 한다. 문맥상 '연설에 참석하는 것에 열성적이다'라는 내용이 되어야 자연스러우므로 be enthusiastic about의 형태로 자주 쓰이는 '~에 열성적이다'라는 뜻의 (B) enthusiastic이 정답이다.

어휘 | individual 개인, 사람 enthusiastic 열성적인

3 (C)

번역 | 시연에 적합한 시제품은 댈러스의 창고에 있는 것으로 확인되었습니다.

해설 | 빈칸이 포함된 문장은 주격 관계대명사 which와 동사 are가 생략된 관계사절이다. 따라서 빈칸에는 be동사 are의 보어이자 전치사 for와 어울려 쓰이는 형용사가 들어가야 한다. 문맥상 '시연에 적합한 시제품'이라는 내용이 되어야 자연스러우므로 be suitable for의 형태로 자주 쓰이는 '~에 적합하다'라는 뜻의 (C) suitable이 정답이다.

어휘 | determine 결정하다, 알아내다 prototype 시제품 demonstration 시연 warehouse 창고

전략포인트 **2**   본책 p.138

1 (C) 2 (A) 3 (D)

1 (C)

번역 | 와이먼 자동차는 브레이크 시스템에 필수적인 소프트웨어를 하나를 출시했다.

해설 | 빈칸은 관계사절의 be동사 is 뒤에 오는 보어 자리로 선행사인 a piece of software를 수식하는 형용사가 필요하다. 따라서 형용사인 (C) essential이 정답이다.

어휘 | release 출시[발표]하다 essential 필수적인

2 (A)

번역 | 지역 경제에 도움이 되는 건설 프로젝트가 있을 것이라는 것은 조짐이 좋다.

해설 | 2형식 동사 sound 뒤에는 주격 보어가 와야 하므로, 형용사인 (A) promising이 정답이다.

어휘 | promising 촉망되는, 조짐이 좋은 construction 건설 local 지역의, 현지의 economy 경제

3 (D)

번역 | 앨리스 스틸은 최근에 설치된 회계 프로그램으로 일하는 것을 매우 즐겁게 느낀다.

해설 | 빈칸은 동사 finds의 목적격 보어 역할을 하는 형용사 pleasant를 수식해 주는 부사 자리이므로, '즐겁게'를 의미하는 부사인 (D) delightfully이 정답이다.

어휘 | find 느끼다 accounting 회계 recently 최근에 install 설치하다 delightfully 즐겁게 pleasant 기분 좋은

전략포인트 **3**   본책 p.139

1 (A) 2 (D) 3 (A)

1 (A)

번역 | 반죽을 밀어서 크러스트를 만들기 전에 표면에 약간의 밀가루를 펴 바르는 것이 중요하다.

해설 | 빈칸은 불가산명사 flour를 수식할 수 있는 수량 형용사 자리이다. 문맥상 '반죽을 밀기 전에 표면에 약간의 밀가루를 펴 바르다'라는 의미가 되어야 하므로, 정답은 (A) some이다. (B) many와 (C) few는 복수명사와 함께 써야 하며, (D) any는 의미상 적절하지 않다.

어휘 | spread 펴다, 펴 바르다 surface 표면 roll out (반죽을) 밀어서 펴다 dough 밀가루 반죽 crust 크러스트

2 (D)

번역 | 지난해 개보수 이후 담당자들은 주차 관련해서 더 적은 불만을 처리했다.

해설 | 빈칸은 동사 have dealt with의 목적어인 명사 자리로, 빈칸 앞에 수량 형용사 fewer가 왔으므로 가산 복수명사인 (D) complaints가 정답이다.

어휘 | renovation 수리 representative 대리인, 담당자 deal with 처리하다 complaint 불만 regarding ~에 관하여

3 (A)

번역 | 얼터랩닷컴에서 제공받는 모든 통계 분석은 분야 전문가들에 의해 전개되고 해석됩니다.

해설 | 빈칸은 문장의 주어 Every statistical analysis에 수 일치되는 be동사 자리이다. 수량 형용사인 every는 단수명사만 취하므로 analysis는 단수이며 이에 어울리는 (A) is가 정답이다. 참고로 analysis는 끝이 '-s'로 끝나지만 단수명사이므로 주의해야 한다. 복수형은 '-is'의 어미가 '-es'로 변형된 analyses이다.

어휘 | statistical 통계적인 analysis 분석 interpret 해석하다, 설명하다 industry 분야, 산업

전략포인트 **4**   본책 p.139

1 (D) 2 (A) 3 (B)

1 (D)

번역 | 품질관리는 제품에 대한 철저한 검토를 필요로 한다.

해설 | 빈칸은 뒤에 온 명사 reviews를 수식하는 형용사 자리이고, '철저한 검토'라는 의미가 되어야 자연스러우므로 (D) exhaustive가 정답이다.

어휘 | quality control 품질관리 exhaustive 철저한 exhaust 고갈시키다, 지치게 하다 exhausted 고갈된, 지친

2 **(A)**

번역 | 우리의 거의 모든 수습생들이 정보처리 기사 자격증을 위한 자격 시험에 합격했다.

해설 | 빈칸은 뒤에 온 명사 exam을 수식하는 형용사 자리이고, '자격 시험'이라는 의미가 되어야 자연스러우므로 '자격을 주는'이라는 뜻의 형용사인 (A) qualifying이 정답이다.

어휘 | virtually 거의, 사실상 apprentice 수습생 data processing engineer 정보처리기사

3 **(B)**

번역 | 천안 시내에 있는 어시장의 활기찬 분위기가 여행객들을 끌어들인다.

해설 | 빈칸은 명사 atmosphere와 어울리는 형용사 자리이므로 '활기찬 분위기'의 (B) lively가 정답이다.

어휘 | atmosphere 분위기 be appealing to 관심을 끌다 live 생방송의

전략포인트 5   본책 p.140

1 (B)   **2** (B)   **3** (C)

1 **(B)**

번역 | 아넬리 자동차는 영업 부서를 운영할 경험 많고 지략 있는 지도자를 찾고 있다.

해설 | 빈칸은 and 앞에 있는 형용사 experienced와 함께 명사 leader를 수식하는 형용사 자리이다. 따라서 '지략 있는'이라는 의미의 형용사인 (B) resourceful이 정답이다.

어휘 | seek 찾다 experienced 경험이 풍부한 resourceful 지략 있는 resourced 자원 제공을 받은 division 부서

2 **(B)**

번역 | 대부분의 주민들은 제인 토머스가 다가오는 시장 선거의 유력한 승자가 될 것이라고 믿고 있다.

해설 | 빈칸은 뒤에 온 명사 winner를 수식하는 형용사 자리이다. 따라서 '유력한'이라는 의미의 형용사인 (B) likely가 정답이다.

어휘 | resident 거주민 likely 가망 있는, 유력한 upcoming 다가오는 election 선거 mayor 시장 liken ~에 비유하다

3 **(C)**

번역 | 그 비영리단체(NGO)의 주요 관심사는 기업들이 오염물질 배출을 확실히 안 하는지를 감시하는 것이다.

해설 | 빈칸은 형용사 primary와 전치사구 of the NGO의 수식을 받아 문장의 주어가 될 수 있는 명사 자리이다. 문맥상 '비영리단체의 주요 관심사'라는 의미가 적절하므로 '관심사, 우려'라는 의미의 (C) concern이 정답이다. '주요 관심사, 가장 중요시 여기는 것'의 의미인 primary concern은 하나의 표현으로 자주 쓰이므로 같이 익혀 두는 것이 좋다.

어휘 | primary 주요한 concern 관심사, 우려 monitor 감시하다 release 방출하다

전략포인트 6   본책 p.140

1 (C)   **2** (D)   **3** (A)

1 **(C)**

번역 | 실리 씨는 확실한 연구 요소가 결여된 보고서에 대해 비판적이다.

해설 | 빈칸은 주어인 Ms. Sealey를 설명하는 주격 보어 자리이므로 형용사가 들어가야 한다. 따라서 '비판적인'을 뜻하는 형용사 (C) critical이 정답이다. 'be critical of'는 '~에 대해 비판적이다'라는 표현이므로 외워 두도록 한다. (A) critic은 '비평가'를 뜻하는 명사이므로 주의하자.

어휘 | critical 비판적인 lack 부족하다 component 요소 critic 비평가

2 **(D)**

번역 | 상근 직원은 휴대전화 수당을 받을 자격이 된다.

해설 | 빈칸은 보어 자리로 'be＋형용사＋to부정사'의 구조이다. 문맥상 '휴대전화 수당을 받을 수 있다'는 내용이 되어야 자연스러우므로 to부정사와 함께 쓰여 '~할 자격이 있다'는 의미를 나타내는 (D) eligible이 정답이다.

어휘 | eligible 자격이 되는 allowance 수당 profitable 이익이 되는 accurate 정확한

3 **(A)**

번역 | 로스 씨는 홍보직에 가장 적합한 후보입니다.

해설 | 뒤에서 명사를 수식하는 suited는 전치사 for나 to와 함께 '~에 적합한'이라는 뜻으로 쓰인다. 따라서 정답은 (A) for이다.

어휘 | candidate 후보자 suited 적합한 public relations 홍보

전략포인트 7   본책 p.141

1 (A)   **2** (B)   **3** (D)

1 **(A)**

번역 | 핼리팩스 데일리는 다음 달부터 더 이상 무료 구독을 제공하지 않는다.

해설 | 빈칸 앞에 조동사 will 이 있고 빈칸 뒤에 목적어 free subscriptions가 있으므로 빈칸은 동사 자리이다. 따라서 동사 (A) provide가 정답이다. 참고로 no longer는 '더 이상 ~이 아닌'의 의미인 부사이며 조동사 will과 동사원형 사이에서 동사를 수식한다.

어휘 | no longer 더 이상 ~이 아닌 subscription 구독

2 **(B)**

번역 | 서비스 품질 향상을 위해 레이나 액티비티 센터는 고객에게 정기적으로 의견을 요청한다.

해설 | 완전한 문장에서 동사 requests를 수식하는 부사 자리이다. 따라서 정답은 (B) regularly이다.

어휘 | improve 향상시키다 quality 품질 regularly 정기적으로

3 (D)

번역 | 최근 우리 웹사이트의 방문객 수 증가는 주로 소셜 미디어 캠페인의 결과이다.

해설 | 빈칸이 없어도 완전한 문장을 이루고 있으므로 빈칸에는 부사가 들어가야 한다. 따라서 '주로'라는 뜻의 부사 (D) largely가 정답이다. 부사는 일반적으로 명사를 수식하지 않지만 '관사+명사' 앞에 놓일 때는 강조하는 역할을 한다.

어휘 | recent 최근의 increase 증가 traffic 이동량 largely 주로 result 결과

전략포인트 8   본책 p.141

1 (C) **2** (B) **3** (C)

1 (C)

번역 | 주말 축구 경기의 하이라이트는 일요일 저녁 10시 직후 온라인에 게시된다.

해설 | 빈칸이 없어도 완전한 문장을 이루고 있으므로 빈칸은 부사 자리이다. 따라서 전치사 after 앞에 쓰여 '~직후에'라는 의미를 나타낼 수 있는 부사인 (C) shortly가 정답이다.

어휘 | post 게시하다 shortly 곧

2 (B)

번역 | 신입사원들과 함께 등록 절차를 끈기 있게 검토해 주셔서 감사합니다.

해설 | 앞에 전치사 for가 있고 뒤에 전치사의 목적어로 온 동명사가 있으므로 빈칸은 부사 자리이다. 따라서 동명사를 수식하는 부사 (B) patiently가 정답이다.

어휘 | patiently 끈기 있게 enrollment 등록 procedure 절차 patient 참을성 있는 patience 인내심

3 (C)

번역 | 유감스럽게도, 토마스 씨는 너무 늦게 공항에 도착해서 피렌체 행 비행기를 타지 못했다.

해설 | 완전한 문장이므로 빈칸에는 문장 전체를 수식하는 부사가 들어가야 한다. 따라서 정답은 '유감스럽게도'라는 의미의 부사인 (C) Regrettably이다.

어휘 | regrettably 유감스럽게도, 아쉽게도 catch a flight 비행기를 타다

전략포인트 9   본책 p.142

1 (B) **2** (A) **3** (C)

1 (B)

번역 | 사무실에 펜이 항상 너무 빨리 소진되어서 우리는 펜을 대량 구입한다.

해설 | 빈칸은 뒤의 부사 quickly를 수식하는 강조부사 자리이며 문장 뒤쪽에 있는 that절이 문제 풀이의 단서이다. 부사나 형용사의 원급을 수식하는 강조부사들 중 so가 that절과 연결되어 '너무 ~해서 …하다'의 의미가 되므로 (B) so가 정답이다. (A) very와 (C) quite은 that절과 어울리지 않고, (D) too는 to부정사와 써야 하므로 오답이다.

어휘 | run out of ~이 소진되다 in bulk 대량으로

2 (A)

번역 | 블레어 씨는 그녀가 도심에서 일하는 것보다 교외에서 일하는 것이 훨씬 더 행복하다고 주장했다.

해설 | 빈칸 뒤에 비교급 형용사 happier가 왔으므로 빈칸에는 이를 수식하는 부사가 들어가야 한다. 따라서 정답은 '훨씬'이라는 뜻으로 비교급을 수식하는 (A) much이다. '훨씬'이라고 해석하는 비교급 강조 부사에는 much, even, still, far, a lot 등이 있다.

어휘 | claim 주장하다 suburb 교외 urban 도시의

3 (C)

번역 | 재스민 슈퍼마켓은 공급자들로부터 얻을 수 있는 가장 큰 딸기만을 판매한다.

해설 | 빈칸은 정관사 the와 최상급 largest 사이에서 최상급을 수식하는 부사 자리이므로, 최상급을 강조하는 (C) very가 정답이다.

어휘 | acquire 얻다, 획득하다 supplier 공급자, 공급 업체

전략포인트 10   본책 p.143

1 (D) **2** (D) **3** (B)

1 (D)

번역 | 메인스트리트 북스는 소프트웨어 회사와의 합병을 발표했고, 주식은 극적으로 올랐다.

해설 | 빈칸은 have와 p.p. 사이에 있으므로 동사를 수식하는 부사 자리이다. (C) highly는 일반동사를 수식할 수 없고 (A) exactly와 (B) alternately는 문맥상 적절하지 않으므로 오답이다. '극적으로'라는 뜻으로 증감동사를 수식하는 부사인 (D) dramatically가 정답이다.

어휘 | announce 발표하다 merger 합병 share 주식 dramatically 극적으로 alternately 번갈아 가며

2 (D)

번역 | 예상 밖의 유지 관리 요청으로 인해 시스템 서버를 일시적으로 이용할 수 없습니다.

해설 | 빈칸은 be 동사와 형용사 unavailable 사이의 부사 자리이다. 따라서 '일시적으로'라는 뜻의 (D) temporarily가 정답이다. (A) previously는 '이전에'라는 뜻으로 과거 시제와 잘 어울려 쓰인다.

어휘 | temporarily 일시적으로 unavailable 이용할 수 없는 maintenance 유지 관리 previously 이전에 individually 개별적으로

3 (B)

번역 | 강당에서 그녀의 연설이 끝난 후 곧 기조 연설자를 위한 환영회가 있을 것이다.

해설 | 빈칸은 뒤에 오는 전치사구 following her talk의 의미를 강조하면서 수식할 수 있는 부사 자리이다. 따라서 전치사구 앞에 놓여 '끝난 후 바로, 곧'이라는 의미로 전치사구를 강조하는 부사 (B) shortly가 정답이다.

어휘 | reception 환영회   keynote speaker 기조 연설자
following ~후에

전략포인트 11

본책 p.144

1 (D)   **2** (D)   **3** (B)

1 (D)

번역 | 공연이 시작되기로 한 5분 전에 극장 안에는 여전히
아무도 없었다.

해설 | 빈칸에 적절한 부사를 선택하는 문제로, There was
nobody와 함께 '여전히 아무도 없었다'라는 뜻을 이루는 부사
(D) still이 가장 적절하다.

어휘 | performance 공연   be scheduled to부정사 ~할
예정이다.

2 (D)

번역 | 회의실은 월요일에 대략 오전 10시부터 이용 가능하다.

해설 | 빈칸 뒤에 숫자가 있으므로, 주로 숫자 앞에서 '대략,
거의'라는 의미를 나타내는 부사 (D) approximately가
정답이다.

어휘 | available 이용 가능한   approximately 대략
extremely 극히   variously 다양하게   exceptionally
특별히

3 (B)

번역 | 그 식당은 전에 받았었던 고객 수의 두 배를 수용하기 위해
현재 보수 공사 중이다.

해설 | 빈칸은 be동사 is와 진행 수동태의 being p.p. 사이에
위치해 있으므로 부사 자리이며, 보기 중 현재 진행시제와
어울리는 부사인 (B) currently가 정답이다. (A) extremely는
주로 형용사, 부사를 수식하므로 동사와 어울리지 않고,
(C) once는 과거 시제와 어울리며, (D) yet은 부정문이나
의문문에서 부사 역할을 한다.

어휘 | currently 현재   accommodate 수용하다

ETS 고득점 실전 문제

본책 p.146

1 (A)   **2** (C)   **3** (B)   **4** (C)   **5** (B)   **6** (D)
7 (B)   **8** (C)   **9** (B)   **10** (D)   **11** (C)   **12** (B)
13 (A)   **14** (C)   **15** (A)   **16** (B)   **17** (C)   **18** (A)
19 (B)   **20** (D)

1 (A)

번역 | 쿠니시 주식회사의 소프트웨어 교육을 받으면 금전적으로
보상이 되는 직업으로 이어질 것입니다.

해설 | 빈칸 뒤의 형용사 rewarding을 수식하는 자리이므로
'재정적으로'를 의미하는 부사 (A) financially가 정답이다.

어휘 | pursue 따르다, 추구하다   training 교육   lead to
~으로 이어지다   rewarding 돈을 많이 버는

2 (C)

번역 | 근무 시간 기록표 제출에 대한 지침은 첨부된 도움말
문서를 참조하십시오.

해설 | 빈칸은 정관사 the와 명사 document 사이에서
명사를 수식하는 형용사 자리이다. 문맥상 '도움이 되는 문서를
참조하라'는 의미가 되어야 자연스러우므로 '도움이 되는'을
뜻하는 형용사 (C) helpful이 정답이다. (B) helped는 '도움을
받은'이라는 뜻으로 document를 수식하는 말로 적절하지 않다.

어휘 | instructions 지침   submit 제출하다   time sheet
근무 시간 기록표   attached 첨부된

3 (B)

번역 | 대부분의 기업들에게는 신규 고객을 유치하는 것보다 단골
고객을 유지하는 것이 더 이득이다.

해설 | keeping loyal customers가 문장의 주어이고 동사는
is이므로 빈칸에는 보어 역할을 할 수 있는 형용사가 와서
비교급을 완성해야 한다. 따라서 정답은 (B) profitable이다.

어휘 | loyal customer 단골 고객   attract 끌어들이다.

4 (C)

번역 | 최고 품질이라는 것을 확실히 하기 위해 전문가들이 모든
원료를 검사한다.

해설 | 빈칸 앞 of the와 뒤의 quality를 단서로 '최고급의,
극상의'를 뜻하는 관용 표현 'of the highest quality'를 떠올릴
수 있다. 따라서 (C) highest가 정답이다.

어휘 | examine 검사하다   .raw material 원료   make sure
확실하게 하다

5 (B)

번역 | 관찰력이 뛰어나지만 경험이 부족한 직원은 주로 교육을 더
받기 위해 본사로 보내진다.

해설 | 빈칸 뒤의 등위접속사 yet과 형용사 inexperienced가
문제 해결의 단서로, 등위접속사는 같은 품사를 연결하므로 보기
중에서 형용사인 (B) observant가 정답이다.

어휘 | observant 관찰력이 좋은, (법, 규정 등을) 준수하는
inexperienced 경험이 부족한   headquarters 본사
undergo 겪다[받다]

6 (D)

번역 | 파워스 씨는 아주 자신 있게 프레젠테이션을 해서 몇 명의
새로운 고객을 확보할 수 있었다.

해설 | '너무 ~해서 …하다'라고 표현할 때는 'so + 형용사/
부사 + that절'의 형태를 쓴다. so 앞의 문장이 완전하므로 부사인
(D) confidently가 정답이다. 참고로 주어가 보어를 요하는
2형식 동사일 때는 so 뒤에 형용사가 온다.

어휘 | confidently 자신 있게   acquire 얻다, 획득하다
confide 신임하다

7 (B)

번역 | 니아 리는 그녀의 데뷔 소설을 향한 찬사를 고려해 볼 때 곧
널리 명성을 얻을 것으로 기대된다.

해설 | 빈칸에는 미래에 대한 일을 예상할 때 쓰이는 is expected to와 어울려 쓸 수 있는 부사가 들어가야 한다. '곧 명성을 얻을 것으로'라는 내용이 되어야 자연스러우므로 미래 시제와 어울리는 시간 부사 (B) soon이 정답이다.

어휘 | given ~을 고려해 볼 때, ~을 감안하면 praise 찬사 widespread 널리 퍼진 fame 명성

8 (C)
번역 | 픽 티셔츠도 면 혼방이지만 우리가 주문한 다른 브랜드보다 눈에 띄게 부드럽다.

해설 | be동사 are 뒤에 보어로 비교급 형용사 softer가 왔으므로 빈칸에는 형용사를 수식하는 부사가 와야 한다. 따라서 정답은 (C) noticeably이다. noticeably는 '상당히'를 뜻하는 considerably, significantly와 함께 비교급을 강조하는 부사로 자주 출제된다.

어휘 | blend 혼합 noticeably 눈에 띄게

9 (B)
번역 | 박물관 보수 공사는 6주 이내에 완료될 예정이다.

해설 | 문맥상 '6주 이내에'라는 내용이 되어야 자연스럽다. 따라서 숫자 앞에 쓰여 '(양 · 수치 등이) ~미만의'를 뜻하는 전치사 (B) under가 정답이다.

어휘 | renovation 보수 complete 완료하다

10 (D)
번역 | 프로젝트 접근 방법에 대한 서로 다른 많은 의견에도 불구하고 회의는 놀라울 정도로 '잘' 진행되었다.

해설 | 빈칸이 없어도 완전한 문장이고 뒤에 온 부사 well을 수식하는 자리이므로 '놀라울 정도로'를 뜻하는 부사 (D) surprisingly가 정답이다. go는 '진행하다'의 의미이며 부사 well과 함께 쓰여 '잘 진행되다'라는 뜻이다.

어휘 | despite ~에도 불구하고 differing 상이한 approach 접근하다

11 (C)
번역 | 모스 씨는 자사의 오트밀 마케팅 캠페인에 회의적이었으나, 팀은 그 잠재력에 대해 그녀를 납득시켰다.

해설 | 쉼표 뒤의 절에 '하지만 팀은 마케팅 캠페인의 잠재력에 대해 그녀를 납득시켰다'고 했으므로, 빈칸이 들어 있는 절은 '모스 씨가 마케팅 캠페인에 대해 확신하지 못한다'는 내용이 되어야 연결이 자연스럽다. 따라서 '회의적인'이라는 의미의 (C) skeptical이 정답이다.

어휘 | skeptical 회의적인 oatmeal 오트밀 convince 납득시키다 potential 잠재력 aware 알고 있는

12 (B)
번역 | 멜라니는 열심히 연습하고 그녀가 공연 오디션을 볼 때 뽑힐 것으로 종종 기대한다.

해설 | 빈칸은 접속사 and가 이끄는 절에서 동사 expects를 수식하는 부사 자리이다. 동사의 시제가 현재이므로 빈도부사인 often이 잘 어울리며, '종종 뽑힐 것으로 기대한다'라는 의미도 적절하므로 (B) often이 정답이다.

어휘 | audition 오디션을 보다 performance 공연

13 (A)
번역 | 멜린스키 호텔의 웹사이트는 언제 어디서나 모바일 기기를 통해 접속할 수 있다.

해설 | 빈칸은 '항상'의 뜻인 전치사구 at all times와 함께 동사 can be accessed를 수식하는 부사가 들어갈 자리이다. 따라서 '어디서나'를 뜻하는 부사 (A) anywhere가 정답이다.

어휘 | access 접속하다 at all times 항상 device 장치

14 (C)
번역 | 라자르 씨는 지난달에야 채용되었지만 그럼에도 불구하고 이미 회사에 상당한 금액을 절약해 주었다.

해설 | 문맥을 적절하게 연결할 수 있는 부사 어휘를 고르는 문제이다. 빈칸 앞에서 '라자르 씨가 지난달에 채용되었다'고 했고, 뒤에서는 '벌써 회사에 상당한 금액을 아껴주었다'고 했으므로 반대되는 내용을 연결해주는 접속부사가 필요하다. 따라서 '그럼에도 불구하고'라는 뜻의 (C) nevertheless가 정답이다.

어휘 | nevertheless 그럼에도 불구하고 significant 상당한 moreover 게다가 namely 즉 similarly 비슷하게

15 (A)
번역 | 목록에 있는 업무를 다음 한 시간 안에 할 수 있게 빨리 볼 일을 보고 오세요.

해설 | 문맥상 '업무를 한 시간 안에 할 수 있을 만큼 충분히 빨리'라는 의미가 되어야 하므로, '~하기에 충분히…하다'라는 뜻의 'enough+to부정사'가 적절하다. 따라서 정답은 (A) enough가 된다. 참고로 enough는 형용사나 부사를 뒤에서 수식하므로 부사인 fast를 후치 수식하고 있다.

어휘 | run an errand 심부름을 하다, 볼 일을 보다 enough to부정사 ~할 만큼 (충분히) assignment 과제, 임무

16 (B)
번역 | 집주인은 크게 소리를 지르거나 주민들을 괴롭히는 다른 소음을 내는 세입자들에게 벌금을 부과할 것이다.

해설 | 빈칸은 주격 관계대명사 who가 이끄는 절에서 동사 shout를 수식하는 부사 자리이다. 따라서 '큰소리로'를 뜻하는 부사 (B) loudly가 정답이다.

어휘 | landlord 집주인 fine 벌금을 부과하다 tenant 세입자 bother 괴롭히다 resident (입)주민

17 (C)
번역 | 고객 추천 글은 우리 소프트웨어를 사용하는 것이 정말 얼마나 강력하고 쉬운지 보여준다.

해설 | 빈칸은 show의 목적어인 명사절 how powerful and easy it is를 강조하는 부사 자리이다. 따라서 '정말, 완전히'라는 의미로 명사구나 명사절을 강조하는 부사 (C) just가 정답이다.

어휘 | testimonial 추천 글, 사용 후기

18 (A)

번역 | 왓슨 로지스틱스는 도시의 산업단지에 위치한 거의 모든 공장에 배달을 합니다.

해설 | 빈칸은 virtually와 어울려 명사구인 the factories를 수식하는 자리이다. '거의 모든 공장에 배달을 한다'라는 의미가 가장 자연스러우므로 '모든'을 뜻하는 (A) all이 정답이다. '거의'의 의미를 지닌 부사 'virtually'는 '모든'의 'every'나 'all'과 어울리는 어휘이므로 함께 익혀 두도록 한다. 참고로 한정사 (B) every는 다른 한정사(the)와 같이 쓸 수 없으므로 'every the 명사'는 불가능하다.

어휘 | virtually 사실상, 거의   located ~에 위치한   park (특정 목적을 위한) 지역[단지]

19 (B)

번역 | 모든 사람들은 데이브 아놀드가 분명히 우승자이고 심사위원들에 의해 선발되어야 한다고 믿었다.

해설 | 빈칸은 동사 was와 명사구 사이의 부사 자리이다. 문맥상 '데이브 아놀드가 분명히 우승자이다'라는 의미가 적절하므로 '분명히'라는 뜻의 부사인 (B) clearly가 정답이다. clearly는 명사구 the winner를 강조한다.

어휘 | clearly 분명히   judge 심사위원   overly 몹시

20 (D)

번역 | 라이퍼 테크놀로지는 최신형의 휴대폰에 상당한 업데이트를 실시했다.

해설 | 빈칸은 has made의 목적어 역할을 하는 명사 updates를 수식하는 형용사 자리이다. 변화, 향상의 의미를 지닌 update는 '상당한'이라는 뜻의 (D) substantial과 어울린다.

어휘 | substantial 상당한   latest 최신의   generation (제품 등의) 세대, 형

UNIT 4 전치사

전략포인트 1   본책 p.148

1 (A)   **2** (A)   **3** (B)

1 (A)

번역 | 포멀 의류 제품은 구매일로부터 30일 이내에 전액 환불 받을 수 있다.

해설 | 빈칸은 완전한 절 뒤에 명사구 30 days (of purchase)를 절과 연결하는 전치사 자리이다. 기간의 표현인 30days를 단서로 이와 어울리는 전치사를 골라야 한다. 따라서 '~이내에'의 의미인 (A) within이 정답이다. 참고로 (D) by는 '~까지'의 의미로 시점의 표현과 써야 하므로 오답이다.

어휘 | return 반환하다   full refund 전액 환불

2 (A)

번역 | 베스티노 은행의 라우 씨는 사업 대출 절차 전반에 걸쳐 많은 도움을 주었다.

해설 | 빈칸은 완전한 절에 명사구를 연결하는 자리이므로 전치사가 필요하다. 문맥상 '전반적인 사업 대출 절차 내내 도움을 주었다'라는 내용이 되어야 자연스럽다. 따라서 '~내내, ~의 전체에 걸쳐서'라는 뜻의 (A) throughout이 정답이다.

어휘 | entire 전체의   loan 대출

3 (B)

번역 | 사르디스 인더스트리얼의 관리자들은 목요일 오후 1시까지 분기 보고서를 완료해야 한다.

해설 | 동사 complete와 함께 쓰여 '목요일 오후 1시까지'라는 완료의 의미를 나타내는 전치사인 (B) by가 정답이다. (C) until은 계속의 의미를 나타내므로 정답이 될 수 없다.

어휘 | complete 완료하다   quarterly 분기별의

전략포인트 2   본책 p.148

1 (D)   **2** (A)   **3** (B)

1 (D)

번역 | 버드 슈퍼마켓은 북서부 지역에 걸쳐 50개 이상의 지점을 가지고 있다.

해설 | 문맥상 '북서부 지역에 걸쳐'라는 내용이 되어야 자연스러우므로, '~전역에 걸쳐, ~을 가로질러'라는 뜻으로 장소를 나타내는 전치사인 (D) across가 정답이다.

어휘 | location 장소, 지점   region 지역

2 (A)

번역 | 헤이스팅스 호텔에서 걸어갈 수 있는 거리 내에 몇 군데 인기 있는 식당이 있다.

해설 | 문맥상 '걸어갈 수 있는 거리 내에'라는 의미가 되어야 자연스러우므로 범위를 나타내는 전치사인 (A) within이 정답이다.

어휘 | several 몇몇의   popular 인기 있는   distance 거리

3 (B)

번역 | 하워드 건설은 그 건설 프로젝트에 고려되고 있는 회사들 중 하나이다.

해설 | 문맥상 '건설 프로젝트에 고려되고 있는 회사들 중의 하나'라는 의미가 되어야 하므로 '~중에서, ~중의 하나'의 뜻을 지닌 전치사 (B) among이 정답이다.

어휘 | construction 건설   firm 회사   consider 고려하다

전략포인트 3   본책 p.149

1 (C)   **2** (A)   **3** (C)

1 (C)

번역 | 악천후 때문에 675 항공편의 출발이 지연되었다.

해설 | 빈칸은 쉼표 뒤 완전한 절에 명사구 inclement weather를 연결하는 자리이므로 전치사가 들어가야 한다. 따라서 부사인 (A) Nevertheless와 접속사인 (D) Whenever는 답이 될 수 없다. 문맥상 '악천후 때문에'가 되어야 적절하므로 '~때문에'를 뜻하는 전치사구 (C) Because of가 정답이다.

어휘 | inclement weather 악천후   departure 출발
delay 지연시키다

2 (A)
번역 | 교육 연수는 행정부를 제외한 모든 부서에서 의무적으로
참석해야 한다.

해설 | 문맥상 '행정부를 제외한 모든 부서'라는 의미가 되어야
자연스러우므로 제외를 나타내는 전치사 (A) except가
정답이다. 참고로 except는 all, every, always나 no 뒤에서
자주 사용되며, '~을 제외하고 모두(항상)', 또는 '~만 제외하고
~하지 못하다'라는 의미를 이룬다.

어휘 | session 수업 (시간)   mandatory 의무적인
department 부서   administration 행정

3 (C)
번역 | 광범위한 마케팅 캠페인에도 불구하고, 연례 영화제의
참석자 수는 저조했다.

해설 | 빈칸은 콤마 뒤의 완전한 절과 명사구 the extensive
marketing campaign을 연결하는 전치사 자리이다. 콤마
앞에서 광범위한 마케팅 캠페인을 언급했으나, 뒤따르는 절에서
참석자 수는 저조했다고 했으므로, '~에도 불구하고'라는 뜻의
대조를 나타내는 전치사 (C) Despite가 정답이다.

어휘 | extensive 광범위한   attendance 출석, 참석자 수
annual 연례의

전략포인트 4   본책 p.149

1 (C)   2 (A)   3 (D)

1 (C)
번역 | 내일 경주의 주자들은 비와 안개를 포함한 악천후를
예상해야 한다.

해설 | 빈칸은 완전한 절에 명사구 rain and fog를 연결하는
자리이므로 전치사가 들어가야 한다. 문맥상 '비와 안개를 포함한
악천후'가 되어야 자연스러우므로 '~을 포함하여'를 뜻하는
전치사 (C) including이 정답이다. including은 such as(~와
같은)처럼 예시를 통해 종류를 나타낼 때 자주 쓰이는 전치사이다.

어휘 | race 경주   including ~을 포함하여   according to
~에 따르면   meanwhile 그동안에   provided that ~이라면

2 (A)
번역 | 채용 위원회 위원들은 얀센 씨를 그 자리에 가장 적합한
후보로 인정했다.

해설 | 보기가 모두 전치사이므로 문맥상 가장 적합한 단어를
골라야 한다. '가장 적합한 후보로서'라는 자격의 의미를 나타내는
(A) as가 정답이다.

어휘 | hiring 고용   committee 위원회   identify
확인[인정]하다   candidate 후보자

3 (D)
번역 | 역사학자들은 원본 원고가 1800년 경에 쓰여졌다고
믿는다.

해설 | 빈칸 뒤에 나온 숫자 표현 1800이 문제 해결의 단서로,
숫자 앞에서 '약 ~, ~쯤'을 뜻하는 전치사 around가 들어가면
'1800년 경에'라는 의미가 되어 문맥이 자연스럽다. 따라서 (D)
around가 정답이다.

어휘 | historian 역사학자   original 원래의   manuscript
원고

전략포인트 5   본책 p.150

1 (A)   2 (C)   3 (C)

1 (A)
번역 | 가을마다 겨울에 대비하여 장작을 모은다.

해설 | 문맥상 '겨울에 대비하여'라는 의미가 되어야 하므로, '~에
대비하여'라는 뜻의 전치사구 in preparation for를 완성하는
(A) for가 정답이다.

어휘 | fall 가을   firewood 장작   gather 모으다   in
preparation for ~에 대비하여

2 (C)
번역 | 서면 조항은 합의된 일정에 따라 완료되어야 한다.

해설 | 빈칸은 완전한 절 뒤에 명사구 the agreed-upon
schedule을 연결하는 자리이므로 전치사가 들어가야 한다.
따라서 접속사인 (D) so that은 답이 될 수 없다. 문맥상 '합의된
일정에 따라'가 되어야 적절하므로 '~에 따라'를 뜻하는 전치사구
(C) according to가 정답이다.

어휘 | article (계약서의) 조항   complete 완료하다
agreed-upon 합의된

3 (C)
번역 | 가급적 빨리 학술회 참여 가능 여부를 알려주세요.

해설 | at your earliest convenience는 '가급적 빨리'라는
뜻의 관용 표현이므로 정답은 (C) at이다.

어휘 | notify 알려주다   availability (참여) 가능성

전략포인트 6   본책 p.150

1 (B)   2 (A)   3 (D)

1 (B)
번역 | 밴스 이삿짐 센터는 운행 차량으로 하이브리드 승합차에
투자할 것이라고 확인했다.

해설 | 빈칸 앞의 자동사 invest는 전치사 in과 결합하여 '~에
투자하다'라는 의미로 쓰인다. 따라서 (B) in이 정답이다.

어휘 | moving company 이삿짐 운송 업체   confirm
확인하다   invest 투자하다   fleet (한 기관이 소유한 전체
비행기/버스/택시 등의) 무리

2 (A)
번역 | 기사는 문제가 무엇인지를 알아내기 위해 컴퓨터를
분해해야 할 것이다.

해설 | 빈칸은 will have to 다음에 이어지는 동사원형 자리이며, 빈칸 뒤 your computer와 문맥상 잘 어울리는 '분해하다'라는 뜻의 구동사 (A) take apart가 정답이다.

어휘 | technician 기술자, 기사 determine 밝혀내다 take place (행사 등이) 열리다 take up (공간을) 차지하다

3 (D)
번역 | 회사 설문 조사는 대다수의 직원들이 관리자를 신뢰하고 있는 것을 보여주었다.

해설 | 문맥상 '직원들이 관리자에 신뢰를 가진다'라는 의미가 되어야 적절하므로 전치사 in과 함께 쓰여 '~에 대한 신뢰'를 의미하는 (D) confidence가 정답이다.

어휘 | reveal 드러내다 the majority of ~대다수의 confidence 신뢰 strength 힘 motivation 동기 부여

ETS 고득점 실전 문제
본책 p.152

1 (B)	**2** (C)	**3** (D)	**4** (C)	**5** (A)	**6** (A)
7 (D)	**8** (D)	**9** (B)	**10** (B)	**11** (A)	**12** (B)
13 (A)	**14** (C)	**15** (A)	**16** (C)	**17** (A)	**18** (B)
19 (C)	**20** (D)				

1 (B)
번역 | 보수공사 기간 동안 1층 사무실 직원들은 3층 회의실에서 근무할 예정이다.

해설 | 빈칸은 쉼표 뒤 완전한 절에 명사구 the renovations를 연결하는 자리이므로 전치사가 들어가야 한다. 따라서 '~동안'이라는 의미의 전치사 (B) During이 정답이다.

어휘 | renovation 보수 temporary 임시의

2 (C)
번역 | 버드브랜치 극장에서 현재 상영 중인 〈백조 분수〉는 2주 뒤 막을 내릴 것이다.

해설 | 빈칸 뒤의 명사구를 연결하는 자리이므로 전치사가 필요하다. 빈칸 뒤 명사구(two weeks)가 기간 표현이고 문맥상 '2주 뒤에'라는 의미가 되어야 자연스러우므로 (C) in이 정답이다.

어휘 | swan 백조 fountain 분수 current 현재의 production (영화·연극 등의) 상연, 연극 작품

3 (D)
번역 | 이번 달 수입 목재의 판매 수익은 6월에 비해 2% 높다.

해설 | 문맥상 '수입 목재의 판매로부터 나온 수익'이라는 내용이 되어야 자연스러우므로, 출처를 나타내는 전치사 (D) from이 정답이다.

어휘 | revenue 수익 imported 수입된 lumber 목재

4 (C)
번역 | 조사 결과에 따르면, 우리는 작업 흐름 용량을 늘릴 필요가 있다.

해설 | 빈칸은 콤마 뒤 완전한 절에 명사구 the survey results를 연결하는 자리이므로 전치사가 들어가야 한다. 문맥상 '~에 따르면'이라는 의미의 전치사구인 (C) According to가 정답이다.

어휘 | result 결과 increase 늘리다 workflow 작업 흐름 capacity 용량

5 (A)
번역 | 무료 체험 기간 후, 대부분의 사람들은 노커크의 소프트웨어를 구매하기로 결정한다.

해설 | 빈칸은 콤마 뒤의 완전한 절에 명사구 a free trial period를 연결하는 자리이므로 전치사가 들어가야 한다. 문맥상 '무료 체험 기간 후'가 되어야 자연스러우므로 '~ 후에'를 뜻하는 전치사 (A) After가 정답이다.

어휘 | trial period 체험 기간

6 (A)
번역 | 작업자는 품질관리 부서에 제품을 보내기 전에 반드시 필수로 정해진 경고 라벨을 부착해야 한다.

해설 | 빈칸에는 뒤에 나온 동명사구를 목적어로 취해 빈칸 앞의 완전한 절에 연결해 줄 수 있는 전치사가 필요하다. 문맥상 동명사 sending과 함께 쓰여 '보내기 전에'라는 의미를 나타내는 전치사인 (A) prior to가 정답이다.

어휘 | affix 부착하다 required 필수의 warning 경고 quality 품질 department 부서

7 (D)
번역 | 시의 웹사이트에 나온 정보와 달리, 수영장은 현재 저녁 9시까지 운영한다.

해설 | 빈칸은 콤마 뒤 완전한 절에 명사구 the information ~을 연결하는 자리이므로 전치사가 들어가야 한다. 따라서 '~와 반대로'라는 의미의 전치사 (D) Contrary to가 정답이다. 나머지는 모두 '주어+동사'가 뒤따르는 접속사구이다.

어휘 | contrary to ~와 반대로 provided that ~이라면 as long as ~하는 한

8 (D)
번역 | 여러분은 저희의 새로운 은행 앱으로 스마트폰을 이용해 수표를 입금할 수 있습니다.

해설 | 빈칸은 명사구 our new banking app을 연결하는 전치사 자리이며, '새로운 은행 앱을 통해'라는 의미가 적절하므로 '~을 통해'라는 뜻의 수단을 나타내는 (D) through가 정답이다.

어휘 | deposit 예금하다 check 수표

9 (B)
번역 | 입사지원자와 면접 후 매번 채용팀원들은 각자의 소감을 공유하는 시간을 가져야 한다.

해설 | 빈칸은 콤마 뒤 완전한 절에 명사구를 연결하는 전치사 자리이다. 빈칸 뒤에 시간 표현 명사구 each session이 있고, 문맥상 '각각의 세션 이후'라는 의미가 적절하므로 '~ 후에'라는 뜻의 전치사인 (B) Following이 정답이다.

어휘 | session (특정 활동) 시간 candidate 후보자
recruitment 채용 impression 인상

10 (B)

번역 | 여행이 시작될 때 약간의 기계적인 문제로 어려움을 겪었음에도 불구하고, 기차는 제시간에 도착했다.

해설 | 빈칸은 콤마 뒤 완전한 절에 동명사구 suffering some mechanical issues ~를 연결하는 전치사 자리이다. 콤마 앞에서 기계적인 문제를 언급했으나, 뒤따르는 절에서 제시간에 도착했다고 했으므로, '~임에도 불구하고'라는 뜻의 전치사 (B) Despite가 정답이 된다.

어휘 | suffer 겪다 mechanical 기계적인 on time 정시에

11 (A)

번역 | 전문성 개발 워크숍에 대한 관심이 부족한 점을 감안하면, 그것을 취소한 것은 옳은 결정이었다.

해설 | 콤마 뒤에서 워크숍을 취소한 것이 옳은 결정이라고 했으므로 문맥상 '전문성 개발 워크숍에 대한 관심이 부족한 점을 감안하면'이라는 내용이 되어야 자연스럽다. 따라서 '~을 고려해 볼 때'라는 뜻의 전치사인 (A) Given이 정답이다.

어휘 | lack 부족, 결핍 professional 직업적인, 전문가의 development 개발 decision 결정 cancel 취소하다

12 (B)

번역 | 직원 수련회에는 현지에 머물 안내원을 제외한 전 직원이 참여할 예정이다.

해설 | 빈칸은 콤마 뒤 완전한 절에 명사구를 연결하는 전치사 자리이다. 문맥상 '안내원을 제외하고'라는 의미가 되어야 자연스러우므로 (B) Except for가 정답이다. 참고로 all, every, always나 the entire는 except와 자주 사용되며, '~을 제외하고 모두[항상]'이라는 뜻이다.

어휘 | on-site 현장의 entire 전체의 participate in ~에 참가하다 retreat 수련회 likewise 마찬가지로 prior to ~전에

13 (A)

번역 | 권위 있는 소프트웨어 산업 상의 후보들 중에는 케이더블유 테크라고 불리는 스타트업 회사가 있다.

해설 | 보어 역할을 하는 전치사구(Among the nominees for the prestigious software industry award)가 문장 앞으로 나가서 주어(a startup firm called KW Tech)와 동사(is)가 도치된 문장으로, 빈칸 뒤 명사 the nominees와 어울려 가장 자연스러운 의미를 만드는 전치사를 택해야 한다. '소프트웨어 산업 상의 후보들 중에'라는 범주의 의미가 되어야 하므로 (A) Among이 정답이다.

어휘 | nominee 후보, 지명된 사람 prestigious 명망 있는 firm 회사

14 (C)

번역 | 퀸시 난방 고객은 제품 설치비뿐 아니라 배송비도 지불해야 합니다.

해설 | 빈칸 앞뒤에 '배송비'와 '설치비'라는 두 가지 비용이 언급되고 있으므로 문맥상 '설치비뿐 아니라'라는 의미가 적절하다. 따라서 '뿐만 아니라, ~외에'라는 뜻을 지닌 전치사구 (C) on top of가 가장 적절하다.

어휘 | delivery charge 배송비 installation 설치
appliance (가정용) 기기 in exchange 답례로

15 (A)

번역 | 추운 기온과 상관없이, 그 도시의 연례 퍼레이드는 예정대로 10월 9일에 열릴 것입니다.

해설 | 빈칸에는 뒤에 나온 명사구와 완전한 절인 주절을 연결하는 전치사가 들어가야 한다. 따라서 유일한 전치사구로 '~와 관계없이'라는 뜻의 (A) Regardless of가 정답이다.

어휘 | regardless of ~에 상관없이 annual 연례의 예정대로 assuming that ~이라고 가정하면 consequently 따라서

16 (C)

번역 | 안전 점검 실패 때문에 추후 통지가 있을 때까지 엘리베이터는 출입이 금지됩니다.

해설 | 빈칸 뒤에 온 명사구 further notice가 문제 해결의 단서로, further notice는 전치사 until과 함께 쓰여 '다음 통지가 있을 때까지'라는 의미를 나타낸다. 따라서 (C) until이 정답이다.

어휘 | owing to ~때문에 inspection 검사 off limits 출입금지(의)

17 (A)

번역 | 월간 스포츠월드는 잡지업계가 겪고 있는 전반적인 감소에도 불구하고 꾸준한 구독자의 증가를 경험했다.

해설 | 빈칸은 뒤에 온 명사구 the general decline을 목적어로 취하는 전치사 자리이다. 빈칸 뒤에서 전반적인 감소를 언급했으나, 콤마 앞에서 '꾸준한 구독자의 증가를 경험했'고 했으므로, '~에도 불구하고'라는 뜻의 대조를 나타내는 전치사 (A) notwithstanding이 정답이 된다.

어휘 | steady 꾸준한 subscriber 구독자 decline 감소 go through 겪다 furthermore 게다가 eventually 결국

18 (B)

번역 | 인사팀은 한 명의 전임 경리를 고용할지 아니면 두 명의 시간제 경리를 고용할지에 대해 아직 확신하지 못하고 있다.

해설 | 빈칸은 whether가 이끄는 명사절을 목적어로 취하는 전치사 자리이며, 빈칸 앞 '~에 관한'의 전치사와 함께 자주 쓰이는 unsure를 단서로 '~인지 아닌지에 관해 확신하지 못한다'라는 의미를 이루는 전치사 (B) as to가 정답이다.

어휘 | HR (human resources) 인사부 bookkeeper 회계 담당자, 경리 ahead of ~보다 앞서

19 (C)

번역 | 계약 조건에 따라 고객은 서비스를 취소하려면 30일 전에 통보해야 합니다.

해설 | 문맥상 '계약 조건에 따라'라는 의미가 자연스러우므로 '~에 따라서'라는 뜻의 구전치사 (C) In accordance with가 정답이다.

어휘 | in accordance with ~에 따라서 terms 조건, 조항 agreement 계약 notice 알림, 통지 as a consequence ~의 결과로서 on behalf of ~을 대표하여 in case of ~의 경우를 대비하여

20 (D)

번역 | 온라인 설문 조사를 완료하는 즉시 고객은 다음 구매 시 15%를 할인 받는 코드를 전송 받습니다.

해설 | 빈칸 뒤에 나온 동명사구 completing the online survey가 문제 해결의 단서로, 동명사와 함께 쓰여 '~하자마자, ~할 때'라는 의미를 이루는 (D) Upon이 정답이다. 참고로 (A) Over와 (C) During이 '~동안'의 의미로 '설문조사를 끝내는 동안'이라고 해석이 되는 듯하지만 이 전치사들은 동명사를 목적어로 취하지 않는다는 점에 주의해야 한다.

어휘 | complete 완료하다 survey 설문 조사 discount code 할인 코드 purchase 구매

UNIT 5 자·타동사 / 수 일치 / 태 / 시제

전략포인트 1 본책 p.154

1 (D) **2** (C) **3** (B)

1 (D)

번역 | 티나 네스가 최고 경영자로 선임된 후 다링가 어패럴의 주가는 급격히 올랐다.

해설 | 문맥상 '주가가 급격히 올랐다'는 내용이 되어야 자연스러우므로 '오르다'는 뜻의 자동사 (D) rose가 정답이다. 'rise, increase, fall, decrease'와 같이 증감을 나타내는 동사들은 'sharply(급격히), significantly(상당히), dramatically(극적으로)'와 같은 변화의 정도를 나타내는 부사들과 잘 어울리므로 암기해 두자.

어휘 | apparel 의류 stock price 주가 rise (과거형 rose) 오르다 sharply 급격히 land 착륙하다

2 (C)

번역 | 스미스 씨의 노고 덕분에 결함이 있는 파이프를 교체하는 것이 생각보다 쉬운 것으로 밝혀지고 있다.

해설 | 빈칸 뒤에 목적어가 없으므로 수동태라고 생각하기 쉽지만, 보기는 모두 능동형의 현재분사로 현재진행형임을 알 수 있다. 문맥상 '파이프 교체가 생각보다 쉬운 것으로 밝혀지고 있다'라는 의미가 자연스럽다. 따라서 형용사를 보어로 취하는 '~임이 판명되다, 밝혀지다'라는 뜻의 자동사 (C) proving이 정답이다.

어휘 | replace 교체하다 faulty 흠이 있는 prove ~임이 판명되다, 밝혀지다

3 (B)

번역 | 논쟁을 불러일으킬 만한 사항들이 해결되었기 때문에, 합병이 순조롭게 진행되었다.

해설 | 빈칸 앞 동사 went는 1형식 자동사 go의 과거동사이므로 뒤에 부사만이 올 수 있다. 따라서 (B) smoothly가 정답이다.

어휘 | merger 합병 go 진행되다 smoothly 순조롭게 contentious 논쟁을 불러일으키는 resolve 해결하다

전략포인트 2 본책 p.154

1 (A) **2** (C) **3** (D)

1 (A)

번역 | 스프링필드 도서관은 대여하고 기한까지 반납되지 않은 자료들에 대해 이용자들에게 연체료를 부과한다.

해설 | 문맥상 '이용자들에게 연체료를 부과한다'라는 의미가 적절하므로 '~에게 …을 하다'라는 구조를 취할 수 있는 4형식 동사 (A) charges가 정답이다. 참고로 (B) informs도 '이용자들에게 연체료에 대해 알려주다'로 해석이 되는 것 같아도 사람 목적어 다음에 전치사 of나 about이 와야 하기 때문에 답이 될 수 없다.

어휘 | charge 부과하다 patron 고객 late fee 연체료 material 자료 borrow 빌리다 due date 기한일

2 (C)

번역 | 관리자는 직원들에게 이번 달 마감일을 상기시켰다.

해설 | 빈칸 뒤 사람 목적어 'her employees'와 그 뒤의 전치사 of를 함께 취하는 동사를 골라야 한다. '문맥상 직원들에게 이번 달 마감일을 상기시켰다'라는 의미가 자연스러우므로 (C) reminded가 정답이다.

어휘 | observe 관찰하다, 준수하다 intend 의도하다

3 (D)

번역 | 홀리데이 씨는 회의 중에 그의 비서가 중요한 전화는 어떤 것이라도 알려주기를 원한다.

해설 | 문맥상 '어떠한 중요한 전화라도 알려주기를 원한다'라는 의미가 적절하다. 빈칸 뒤에 있는 전치사 of와 함께 '~에게 …을 알리다'라는 의미를 만드는 (D) inform이 정답이다.

어휘 | secretary 비서 inform A of B A에게 B를 알려주다

전략포인트 3 본책 p.155

1 (D) **2** (B) **3** (C)

1 (D)

번역 | 거래처에서 전화가 왔고 라미레즈 씨와 입고되는 선적에 관련하여 이야기할 것을 요청했다.

해설 | 빈칸 뒤 with와 함께 '~와 이야기하다'라는 의미를 만드는 자동사 (D) speak가 정답이다. 참고로 (A) discuss와 (B) contact는 타동사이며 (C) say는 that절을 목적어로 취하거나 'say to+사람'의 형식을 취한다.

어휘 | regarding ~에 관하여 shipment 선적, 출하

2 (B)

번역 | 카리 제이 컵케이크 가게는 도시의 대로에 위치해 있기 때문에 많은 고객 유입량으로부터 이득을 본다.

해설 | 빈칸 뒤에 온 전치사 from이 핵심 단서로, '고객 유입량이 많아서 이득을 본다'는 의미를 만드는 (B) benefits가 정답이다. 나머지 동사들은 타동사이므로 전치사 from과 함께 쓸 수 없다.

어휘 | situated 위치한 benefit 이득을 보다 volume 양 promote 홍보하다 extend 연장하다 explore 탐험하다

3 (C)

번역 | 수익성 있게 운영되려면 디버스 인터내셔널은 하루 14시간씩 조립 라인을 가동해야 한다.

해설 | '운영되다'라는 뜻의 자동사 operate를 수식하는 부사 자리이다. 따라서 '수익성 있게'라는 뜻의 부사인 (C) profitably가 정답이다. 참고로 operate는 완전자동사와 타동사 모두 가능한 동사이며 문맥에 따라 부사와 목적어를 고르는 문제가 자주 출제된다.

어휘 | operate 운영하다 profitably 수익성 있게 run 가동하다 assembly line 조립 라인

전략포인트 4
본책 p.156

1 (B) **2** (A) **3** (C)

1 (B)

번역 | 온라인 상점에서 판매되는 많은 상품들은 4시간 이내에 배송될 준비가 되어 있다.

해설 | Many of the items (sold at the online store)가 문장의 주어이고, 빈칸은 동사자리이다. many는 복수를 나타내므로 복수동사인 (B) are가 정답이다.

어휘 | ship 수송[운송]하다

2 (A)

번역 | 새로운 연구과제를 승인하는 것은 관련 서류가 검토되어야 하기 때문에 시간이 걸립니다.

해설 | 빈칸은 동사 자리로 주어가 동명사인 Approving이므로 단수동사를 써야 한다. 또한 빈칸 뒤에 목적어 time이 있으므로 능동태가 와야 한다. 따라서 단수동사이면서 능동태인 (A) takes가 정답이다.

어휘 | approve 승인하다 relevant 관련된 document 서류

3 (C)

번역 | 오늘 오후까지 햄튼 씨가 서명해야 할 서류를 가지고 택배 기사가 올 거예요.

해설 | Mr. Hampton은 목적격 관계대명사절의 주어이고 빈칸은 동사 자리이다. 따라서 정답은 3인칭 단수주어와 수 일치되는 단수동사 (C) needs이다. the documents와 Mr. Hampton 사이에 목적격 관계대명사가 생략된 형태이다.

어휘 | courier 배달원, 택배 기사 document 서류

전략포인트 5
본책 p.156

1 (A) **2** (A) **3** (B)

1 (A)

번역 | 웨스트 햄튼 쇼핑 센터에서 열린 겨울 세일은 하루에 2만 5천 명 이상의 고객을 끌 것으로 예상된다.

해설 | 주어가 The winter sale (at the West Hampton Shopping Center)이고 빈칸은 동사 자리로, 단수명사와 수 일치가 되어 뒤의 to부정사와 연결되는 (A) is expected가 정답이다.

어휘 | attract 끌다, 유치하다

2 (A)

번역 | 직장 안전 문제를 다루는 정부 규정은 직원들에 의해 항상 준수되어야 한다.

해설 | 빈칸 뒤의 by employees가 문제 해결의 단서로, 'by+행위자'는 수동태에 뒤따르는 전치사구이며, 3인칭 복수명사 주어인 Government regulations와 수 일치를 따져보면 (A) must be followed가 정답이다. 참고로 조동사는 주어의 수에 영향을 받지 않는다.

어휘 | regulations 규정 cover 다루다

3 (B)

번역 | 근무를 시작하기 전에 직원들이 받아야 하는 교육은 완료하는 데 3주까지 필요하다.

해설 | The training은 목적격 관계대명사가 생략되어 있는 관계사절인 'the staffers ~ employment'의 수식을 받고 있으며, 문장의 주어 역할을 하고 있다. 단수주어이므로 (B) requires와 (C) is required가 답이 될 수 있는데, 교육(The training)은 3주를 필요로 하는 주체이므로 능동태인 (B) requires가 정답이다.

어휘 | staffer 직원 undergo 겪다, 받다 employment 고용 complete 끝내다, 완료하다

전략포인트 6
본책 p.157

1 (D) **2** (A) **3** (C)

1 (D)

번역 | 회계부에 있는 모든 프린터는 12월에 교체되었다.

해설 | All printers ~가 주어, 빈칸이 동사인 문장으로 빈칸 뒤에 목적어가 아닌 전치사 수식구 in December가 왔으므로 정답은 수동태인 (D) were replaced이다.

어휘 | accounting 회계 replace 교체하다

2 (A)

번역 | 의사의 서명이 필요한 서류들은 바로 사무실로 보내져야 한다.

해설 | Forms ~가 주어, should be sent가 동사인 완전한 문장이다. 빈칸에는 수동태인 should be sent를 수식할 부사가 들어가야 하므로 (A) directly가 정답이다.

어휘 | form 서류, 양식 directly 바로

3 (C)

번역 | 매러타임 해운과의 합병 제안을 받아들일지에 대한 의견은 크게 차이가 났다.

해설 | 빈칸은 전치사구인 regarding부터 Shipping까지의 수식을 받는 주어 Opinions와 연결되는 동사자리이다. 완전자동사 differ는 능동태만 가능하고 주어가 복수이므로 (C) differed가 정답이다. (A) will be differed와 (D) have been differed는 수동태이므로 답이 될 수 없고, (B) has differed는 주어 opinions와 수 일치가 안 되므로 오답이다.

어휘 | regarding ~에 관하여 proposal 제안 merge 합병하다 differ (의견이) 다르다

전략포인트 7   본책 p.157

1 (A)   **2** (A)   **3** (D)

1 **(A)**

번역 | 앤더슨 씨는 지난 주말 대회에서 자신이 낸 성과로 메달을 받았다.

해설 | 빈칸에는 수동태가 되어도 뒤에 명사가 올 수 있는 4형식이나 5형식 동사가 와야 한다. '메달을 받았다'라는 의미가 적절하므로 4형식 동사 (A) given이 정답이다.

어휘 | performance 성과, 실적

2 **(A)**

번역 | 몬트리올에서 유럽으로 가는 누구에게나 다음 항공권을 위한 바우처가 제공될 것이다.

해설 | 빈칸 앞에는 will be, 뒤에는 전치사가 to가 있으므로 빈칸에는 offer 동사의 과거분사가 들어가 수동태를 만들어야 한다. 따라서 (A) offered가 정답이다.

어휘 | voucher 상품권, 할인권 offer 주다, 제공하다

3 **(D)**

번역 | 마르티네즈 씨는 봉사활동 프로그램의 진행자로 임명되었다.

해설 | 빈칸 앞 동사가 수동태로 되어 있어서 빈칸에 명사가 못 온다고 생각하기 쉽다. 그러나 appoint는 '~을 ~으로 임명하다'라는 뜻의 5형식 동사로 수동태가 되어도 목적격 보어인 명사가 뒤이어 올 수 있다. 따라서 '진행자'라는 의미의 명사 (D) facilitator가 정답이다.

어휘 | appoint 임명하다 facilitator 진행자, 조력자 outreach 봉사 활동

전략포인트 8   본책 p.158

1 (C)   **2** (A)   **3** (A)

1 **(C)**

번역 | 냉장 트럭은 운송 과정에서 과일과 채소가 상하는 것을 막을 수 있다.

해설 | 빈칸 앞의 동사 keep과 빈칸 뒤 spoiling이 문제 해결의 단서로, 문맥상 '과일과 채소가 상하는 것을 막다'라는 의미가 적절하다. 'keep + 명사 + from + V + ing'은 '~이 …하지 못하게 하다'라는 뜻이므로 (C) from이 정답이다.

어휘 | refrigerated 냉장 장치가 된 spoil 상하다 transportation 운송, 수송

2 **(A)**

번역 | 모금행사에서 각 자원 봉사자들은 특정 임무에 배정될 것이다.

해설 | 문맥상 적절한 동사를 선택하는 문제로 '각 자원 봉사자는 특정 임무에 배정될 것이다'라는 내용이 되어야 자연스러우므로 be 뒤에서 수동태로 '배정되다'라는 의미를 만드는 (A) assigned가 정답이다. 'be assigned'는 전치사 to와 쓰이므로 'be assigned to 명사'를 외워 두도록 한다.

어휘 | fund-raising gala 모금행사 be assign to ~에 배치하다, 배정하다 influence 영향을 미치다 acquire 습득하다 correspond 일치하다

3 **(A)**

번역 | 손님용 입장권을 소지한 모든 방문객은 지도에서 녹색으로 음영처리 된 모든 지역에 출입이 허용됩니다.

해설 | Visitors (with guest passes)가 주어이고, 빈칸 뒤에 목적어가 없으므로 수동태가 되어야 한다. 따라서 수동의 의미를 지닌 과거분사가 들어가야 한다. 문맥상 '방문객은 출입이 허용된다'라는 의미가 되어야 하므로 정답은 (A) permitted이다.

어휘 | pass 출입 허가증 permit 허용하다 shaded 음영처리된

전략포인트 9   본책 p.159

1 (D)   **2** (C)   **3** (D)

1 **(D)**

번역 | 니트로 헬스장이 정기적으로 다양한 단체 수업을 제공하기 때문에 주민들은 헬스장 회원권을 구입한다.

해설 | 빈칸은 because절의 동사 자리이며 빈도부사 regularly와 어울리고 단수주어 it과 수 일치되는 현재 시제 (D) offers가 정답이다. 준동사 (A) to offer와 (C) offering은 동사 자리에 올 수 없다.

어휘 | resident (입)주민 purchase 구매하다 offer 제공하다 range 범위

2 **(C)**

번역 | 콜 센터의 신임 관리자인 카산드라 베라스는 이전에 20명의 고객 서비스 직원으로 구성된 팀을 관리했다.

해설 | 빈칸은 과거동사를 수식하는 부사 자리이다. 문맥상 '신임 감독관은 이전에 20명의 고객 서비스 직원으로 구성된 팀을 관리했다'라는 의미가 가장 자연스러우므로 정답은 '이전에'라는 뜻의 부사 (C) previously이다.

어휘 | supervisor 관리자, 책임자 previously 이전에 agent 대리인, 직원

3 **(D)**

번역 | 디트리히 씨는 냉방 시스템이 곧 수리에 들어가게 될지 여부를 결정하지 않았다.

해설 | 문장 끝에 soon이라는 미래 표현의 부사가 있으므로 미래 시제인 (D) will undergo가 정답이다. 참고로 이 문장의 if절은 부사절이 아닌 '~인지'의 의미인 명사절이므로 조동사 will이 쓰일 수 있다.

어휘 | undergo 겪다, 받다 repair 수리

전략포인트 10   본책 p.159

1 (B)   **2** (B)   **3** (C)

1 (B)

번역 | 카드웰 씨는 치과 조무사 자리에 대한 이력서를 받는 대로 심사하고 있다.

해설 | Mr. Cardwell이 주어, 빈칸이 동사, the résumés가 목적어인 문장으로, 빈칸에는 목적어를 취할 수 있는 능동태 동사가 와야 한다. 또한 맥락상 '이력서를 받는 대로 심사하고 있다'라는 현재진행의 의미가 되어야 하므로, 능동태이면서 현재진행 시제인 (B) is screening이 정답이다.

어휘 | screen (지원자를) 가려내다, 심사하다 résumé 이력서 dental assistant 치과 조무사

2 (B)

번역 | 크레이머 씨는 회의실의 불이 꺼졌을 때 이사진들에게 연설을 하고 있었다.

해설 | 접속사 when으로 연결된 부사절에 과거의 한 시점이 언급되고 있으므로 주절의 시제도 이에 상응하는 시제가 와야 한다. 따라서 과거진행 시제인 (B) was delivering이 정답이다.

어휘 | deliver a speech 연설하다 board members 이사진 conference 회의 go out (전기가) 나가다

3 (C)

번역 | 사무실이 보수 공사를 위해 문을 닫는 동안 팀원들은 집에서 정규 업무를 수행할 것입니다.

해설 | 빈칸은 주절의 동사가 들어갈 자리로 '사무실이 문을 닫는(is closed) 특정 기간 동안(while), 진행될 일이므로, 미래의 일이 되어야 자연스럽다. 따라서 (C) will be carrying이 정답이다. (B) carries도 시제 상으로는 맞을 수 있지만, 주어인 team members와 수가 일치하지 않는다.

어휘 | renovation 보수, 개조 carry out 수행하다 regular 통상의, 보통의 duty 직무, 의무

전략포인트 11   본책 p.160

1 (B)   **2** (C)   **3** (D)

1 (B)

번역 | 지난 몇 주 동안, 도서관 이용자들은 평소보다 훨씬 더 높은 비율로 책을 대출해 갔다.

해설 | library patrons가 주어이고 빈칸은 동사 자리로 빈칸 뒤 out과 함께 목적어 books를 취하고 있으므로 능동태가 와야 한다. 또한, 현재완료 시제와 어울리는 During the past few weeks가 있으므로, 능동태이면서 현재완료인 (B) have been checking이 정답이다.

어휘 | patron 고객 check out 대출하다

2 (C)

번역 | FC 하우스홀드의 신제품 진공청소기가 매장에 도착할 즈음에는 그 팀은 매뉴얼의 사용 설명을 명확히 해 놓을 것이다.

해설 | 새 진공청소기가 들어오는 것은 미래이고, 매뉴얼 설명이 그 시점 즈음에는(By the time) 완료되어야 한다고 했으므로 빈칸에는 미래완료 시제가 와야 한다. 따라서 (C) will have clarified가 정답이다.

어휘 | clarify 명확하게 설명하다 instruction 사용 설명(서)

3 (D)

번역 | 건설 회사가 건물의 보수 공사를 완료했을 즈음에는, 소유주는 예상보다 20퍼센트나 더 많은 돈을 썼다.

해설 | 예상보다 20퍼센트나 더 많은 돈을 쓴 것은 건물의 보수 공사를 완료했을 때보다 더 먼저 일어난 일이므로 과거완료 시제인 (D) had spent가 정답이다.

어휘 | construction 건설 complete 끝마치다, 완료하다 renovation 보수, 개조

전략포인트 12   본책 p.160

1 (C)   **2** (C)   **3** (B)

1 (C)

번역 | 다음 주 아무 때나 비즈니스 강좌에 등록하시면, 학원에서 10% 할인을 제공해 드릴 것입니다.

해설 | if는 '~한다면'이라는 뜻으로 조건 부사절을 이끄는 접속사이다. 조건 부사절에서는 현재 시제가 미래 시제를 대신하며, 또한 주어 you와 어울려야 하므로 (C) enroll이 정답이다.

어휘 | enroll 등록하다 institute 학원, 기관

2 (C)

번역 | 항공사 직원들은 탑승객들이 체크인 전에 가방이 충분히 작은 것을 확실히 해 두기 위해 재 보아야 한다고 조언한다.

해설 | '조언하다'라는 뜻의 동사 advise에 뒤따르는 that절에서는 '(should)+동사원형'을 써야 하므로, (C) measure가 정답이다.

어휘 | official 공무원[관리], 직원 measure 재다[측정하다] prior to ~에 앞서 ensure 확실하게 하다

3 (B)

번역 | 사용 전에 조리 기구에서 상표를 제거해야 합니다.

해설 | 가주어 It으로 시작하는 구문에서 be동사 뒤에 당위성을 나타내는 형용사 necessary가 나오므로 that절에 '(should)+동사원형'이 와야 한다. 따라서 (B) be가 정답이다.

어휘 | remove 제거하다 cookware 취사 도구

전략포인트 13
본책 p.161

1 (B) **2** (B) **3** (D)

1 (B)

번역 | 직원들은 올해의 직원상 수상자로 자격이 있는 동료들을 지명하도록 알림을 받는다.

해설 | 주어인 Staff members가 '알림을 받는다'라는 의미가 되어야 하므로 수동태인 'be reminded to 동사원형'의 구조를 이루며 주어와 수가 일치하는 (B) are reminded가 정답이다. 'remind + 목적어 + to부정사 (목적격 보어)'는 '~에게 …하라고 상기시키다'라는 뜻의 능동태 구조로 목적어를 주어로 보내면 'be reminded to부정사'의 수동태 구조가 된다.

어휘 | nominate 지명하다 deserving 자격이 있는, 받을 만한 award 상

2 (B)

번역 | 최근 몇 년 동안 기술 발전으로 인해 자동차 디자이너의 수가 증가했다.

해설 | 빈칸은 동사 자리이며 주어인 The number of automobile designers와 수가 일치하고 과거 또는 현재완료와 쓰이는 시간 표현인 in recent years와 어울리는 (B) has increased 가 정답이다. 참고로 'the number of 복수명사'는 '~의 수'라는 뜻으로 단수동사와 수 일치한다.

어휘 | increase 증가하다 due to ~ 때문에 development 발전

3 (D)

번역 | 척박한 기후 조건의 영향 아래 그 프로젝트의 실행가능성을 조사하는 것은 한 달 정도 후에는 끝날 것이다.

해설 | 주어는 The investigation이므로 단수동사와 수가 일치해야 하고 빈칸 뒤에 목적어가 없이 전치사구가 나오기 때문에 타동사인 complete의 수동태가 와야 한다. 미래 시제와 어울리는 'in a month(한 달 후에)'가 있으므로 (D) will be completed가 정답이다.

어휘 | viability 실행가능성 hostile 척박한, 적대적인

전략포인트 14
본책 p.161

1 (C) **2** (B) **3** (C)

1 (C)

번역 | 인터넷이 된다면, 직원은 고객의 납부 기록에 대해 알아볼 수 있을 텐데.

해설 | 주절의 동사 시제 관련 문제이다. If절의 주어는 단수이지만 동사가 were인 점을 보아 가정법 시제임을 알 수 있다. 따라서 현재를 가정하는 가정법 과거인 (C) could find out이 정답이다. 참고로 조동사 would나 could는 가정법에 많이 쓰이므로 if절의 시제를 함께 확인해야 한다.

어휘 | representative 직원 payment 납부, 지불

2 (B)

번역 | 제임슨 씨가 전화를 받았더라면, 계약을 할 수 있었을 텐데.

해설 | If절 동사의 시제 관련 문제이다. 주절의 시제는 'would have p.p.'이며, 이는 과거의 일을 가정하는 가정법 과거완료 시제이다. 따라서 If절의 시제는 'had p.p.'의 구조를 취하는 (B) had answered가 정답이다.

어휘 | sign a contract 계약서에 서명하다

3 (C)

번역 | 직장 안전 규정에 대한 위반사항을 보고하시려면 내선번호 100번을 이용해 주세요.

해설 | 빈칸 뒤에 주어와 동사가 나오므로 빈칸이 포함된 절은 종속절이다. 종속절의 경우 접속사가 맨 앞에 나오는 것이 일반적인데, 보기에 모두 조동사만 제시되었으므로 종속절의 접속사가 생략된 도치 구조라는 것을 알 수 있다. 문맥상 '위반사항을 보고해야(have to report any violations) 한다면'이라는 가정이 나와야 자연스러우므로 (C) Should가 정답이다. 'if+주어+should+동사원형(~이라면)'에서 if가 생략되면 'Should+주어+동사원형'이 된다.

어휘 | report 보고하다 violation 위반 extension 내선번호

ETS 고득점 실전 문제
본책 p.163

1 (B)	**2** (B)	**3** (B)	**4** (B)	**5** (C)	**6** (C)
7 (D)	**8** (C)	**9** (C)	**10** (C)	**11** (D)	**12** (A)
13 (D)	**14** (A)	**15** (A)	**16** (A)	**17** (C)	**18** (C)
19 (D)	**20** (A)	**21** (D)	**22** (A)	**23** (A)	**24** (B)
25 (D)	**26** (A)	**27** (D)	**28** (D)	**29** (A)	**30** (B)

1 (B)

번역 | 페더비의 마케팅 팀원들은 모든 광고 캠페인 작업에 협력해야 한다.

해설 | Members (of the Featherbee's marketing team)가 주어이고 work가 동사인 완전한 절로 빈칸에는 동사 work를 수식하는 부사가 들어가면 된다. 따라서 '협력하여'라는 의미의 부사인 (B) collaboratively가 정답이다.

어휘 | collaboratively 협력하여 advertising 광고

2 (B)

번역 | 가끔 버크 씨는 직원들이 어울릴 수 있도록 팀 회식을 마련한다.

해설 | 주어가 3인칭 단수인 Ms. Burke이고, 현재 시제와 자주 쓰이는 빈도 부사인 Every once in a while이 있으므로 단수동사이면서 현재 시제인 (B) organizes가 정답이 된다. 준동사인 (A) to organize와 (C) organizing은 동사 자리에 올 수 없다.

어휘 | every once in a while 가끔 organize 준비[마련]하다 so that ~ ~하도록 socialize 어울리다

3 (B)

번역 | 그린빌 시는 시내버스 요금을 인하한 이래로 승객의 증가를 목격했다.

해설 | 빈칸은 종속절의 동사 자리로, 주절의 시제가 현재완료일 때, since절의 시제는 단순과거이다. 시내버스 요금을 인하한 것은 승객의 증가보다 더 먼저 일어난 일이므로 과거 시제인 (B) lowered가 정답이다.

어휘 | lower 낮추다   local 현지의, 지역의   observe 관찰하다, 목격하다   increase 증가   passenger 승객

4 (B)

번역 | Q3 무선 헤드폰 제품 설명서가 회사 웹사이트에 게시되었다.

해설 | 먼저 주어가 The Q3 wireless headphone product manual로 단수이므로 단수동사가 필요하다. post는 타동사인데 빈칸 뒤에 목적어가 없으므로 수동태가 되어야 한다. 따라서 (B) has been posted가 정답이다.

어휘 | manual 설명서   post 게시하다

5 (C)

번역 | 그녀 부서의 소비 습관을 검토하자, 매든 씨는 새로운 복사기를 살 만하다고 확신했다.

해설 | review는 타동사인데 빈칸 뒤에 목적어가 있으므로 빈칸에는 목적어를 취할 수 있는 능동태가 와야 한다. 또한 시간상으로 볼 때, 매든 씨가 소비 습관을 검토한 후에 새 복사기를 살 만하다고 확신한 것이므로 소비 습관을 검토한 것이 주절 시제인 과거보다 먼저 일어난 일이 된다. 따라서 정답은 능동태이면서 과거완료 시제인 (C) had reviewed가 정답이다.

어휘 | confident 확신하는   affordable (가격 등이) 감당할 수 있는

6 (C)

번역 | 돕슨사의 CEO 마틴 바트는 내일 그의 강연에서 아시아 시장 진출 방법에 대해 논의할 것이다.

해설 | 문장 끝에 tomorrow라는 미래 표현과 목적어인 'how to부정사'가 있으므로, 미래 시제이면서 능동태인 (C) will discuss가 정답이다.

어휘 | discuss 논의하다

7 (D)

번역 | 오늘 워크숍은 더 나은 경영 결정을 내리기 위한 재무 데이터 활용에 중점을 둔다.

해설 | 문맥상 적절한 동사를 선택하는 문제이다. 빈칸 뒤에 목적어가 없으므로 자동사이면서 전치사 on과 어울리는 동사가 들어가야 한다. '재무 데이터 활용에 중점을 둔다'는 내용이 되어야 자연스러우므로 전치사 on과 함께 '~에 중점을 두다'라는 의미를 만드는 (D) focuses가 정답이다.

어휘 | financial 재무의   belong 제자리에 있다   cooperate 협력하다

8 (C)

번역 | 상사가 그 파일을 승인했을 때 즈음에 프리츠 씨가 설문 조사에서 몇 문항을 변경해 놨다.

해설 | 빈칸은 동사 자리이며 뒤에 목적어 some이 있으므로 능동태가 필요하다. 종속절 'by the time + 주어 + 과거동사'와 연결되는 주절의 시제는 과거완료이며 '~했을 때 즈음에 …이 되어 있었다'라고 해석된다. 따라서 (C) had changed가 정답이다.

어휘 | supervisor 감독관, 관리자   approve 승인[인정]하다

9 (C)

번역 | 포스 씨는 검수 받기 위해 그 자재의 새로운 견본을 주문했다.

해설 | 목적어 new samples 뒤에 of가 있어 (B) reminded와 (D) notified를 고를 수 있지만, 이 동사들은 '~에게'로 연결되는 사람명사만 취하는 점을 꼭 기억해야 한다. 사물명사 new samples를 목적어로 취해 '새로운 견본을 주문했다'라고 해야 자연스러우므로, '주문하다'의 (C) ordered가 정답이다.

어휘 | material 원료, 자재   imply 시사하다   notify 알리다

10 (C)

번역 | 대출 신청서가 제출되는 즉시 은행 직원은 그것을 해당 부서에 전달할 것이다.

해설 | as soon as는 '~하자마자'라는 뜻으로 시간 부사절을 이끄는 접속사이다. 주절의 동사가 will forward로 미래를 나타내고 있지만, 시간 부사절에서는 현재 시제가 미래를 대신하므로 (C) has been이 정답이다.

어휘 | loan 대출   forward 전달하다   appropriate 적절한

11 (D)

번역 | 맛이 독특하기 때문에 음식 평론가들은 해물 파스타의 맛의 조합을 즐긴다.

해설 | 빈칸은 주절의 동사 자리이며 since절의 현재 시제가 단서가 된다. 현재 시제를 지닌 since절은 '~때문에'의 의미이며, 주절에도 현재 시제가 와야 하므로 (D) enjoy가 정답이다. 참고로 since가 '~이래로'의 의미일 때 since절의 시제는 과거이어야 하고 주절에는 현재완료가 온다.

어휘 | critic 비평가   combination 결합, 조합   flavor 맛, 풍미   unique 독특한

12 (A)

번역 | 방문객들은 박물관 내에서 항상 전시물의 사진 촬영이 금지된다.

해설 | 빈칸은 are의 주격 보어 자리이다. 문맥상 '방문객들은 박물관 내에서 사진 촬영이 금지된다'라는 의미가 적절하므로 '금지된'이라는 뜻의 분사형 형용사 (A) prohibited가 정답이다. '~하는 것이 금지되다'라는 뜻의 'be prohibited from ~ ing' 표현을 암기해 둔다.

어휘 | exhibit 전시물   prohibit 금지하다   at all times 항상   veto 기각하다, (제안·의안 등을) 거부하다

13 (D)

번역 | 작년의 모델과 달리, 올해 생산된 모델들은 5,000달러 미만으로 팔린다.

해설 | 동사가 필요한 자리이며, 주어가 those manufactured this year이므로 복수주어에 수 일치하여 복수동사를 써야 한다. retail은 자·타동사 모두 가능하며, '팔리다'의 의미일 때는 자동사 또는 수동태 'be+retailed'가 쓰인다. (A) is retailed는 수동태이지만 주어와 수가 일치하지 않아 오답이다. 따라서 (D) retail이 정답이다.

어휘 | manufacture 제조하다   retail (특정 가격에) 팔리다

14 (A)

번역 | 수아레스 씨가 운전 중에 네비게이션을 사용했었다면 그 건물을 쉽게 찾을 수 있었을 텐데.

해설 | 주절의 동사가 '조동사의 과거형+have+p.p.'이므로, if절의 동사 자리에는 과거완료 시제가 들어가야 하는 가정법 과거완료이다. 따라서 (A) had used가 정답이다.

어휘 | navigation system (자동차의) 운행 유도 시스템

15 (A)

번역 | 마지막 사람이 방을 나갈 때는 실험실을 치워두는 것이 권장된다.

해설 | leave는 5형식 동사로 'leave+목적어+목적격 보어'의 구조로 쓰인다. 목적어 laboratory가 주어로 와서 수동태 구조가 되었으므로 빈칸에는 목적격 보어가 와야 한다. 따라서 정답은 '실험실이 깨끗한 채로 남겨져 있어야 한다'라는 의미를 이루는 형용사 (A) clean이다.

어휘 | recommend 권장하다   laboratory 실험실

16 (A)

번역 | 임대료를 납부하지 않은 경우 세입자는 12월 5일에 추가요금을 물게 된다는 점을 다시 한번 알려드립니다.

해설 | that이 이끄는 명사절에서 tenants가 주어, 빈칸이 동사, an additional charge가 목적어인 문장이므로, 빈칸에는 목적어를 취할 수 있는 능동태 동사가 와야 한다. 또한 'This is a reminder'는 공지사항을 나타내는 표현이므로 미래 시제와 잘 어울린다. '임대료를 납부하지 않은 경우 추가요금을 낼 것이다'라는 의미가 적절하므로 능동태이면서 미래 시제인 (A) will incur가 정답이다.

어휘 | reminder 상기시키는 것, 독촉장   tenant 세입자, 임차인 incur (비용을) 물게 되다   additional 추가의   charge 요금 rent 임대료

17 (C)

번역 | 음식은 반드시 최소 행사 1주일 전에 요리업자와 마무리되어야 한다.

해설 | 빈칸 뒤 that절의 동사 be finalized가 문제 해결의 단서이다. 가주어 It으로 시작하는 구문에서 be동사 뒤에 당위성을 나타내는 형용사가 오면 that절에 '(should)+동사원형'이 온다. 따라서 '반드시 해야 하는'이라는 당위성을 나타내는 형용사 (C) imperative가 정답이다.

어휘 | imperative 반드시 해야 하는, 필수적인   finalize 마무리 짓다   caterer (행사의) 음식 공급자[사]   at least 적어도

18 (C)

번역 | 존 헤인즈 칼리지는 경영대학원으로 높이 평가받고 있다.

해설 | 빈칸 앞에 부사 highly가 있고 뒤에 동사 is가 있으므로 빈칸에는 형용사/분사가 들어가야 한다. 존 헤인즈 칼리지는 '높이 평가되는'이라는 의미가 적절하므로 과거분사인 (C) regarded가 정답이다. 보어가 도치되어 문장 앞에 쓰이는 경우에는 '보어+동사+주어'의 어순이 된다.

어휘 | regard ~으로 여기다[평가하다]

19 (D)

번역 | 세미나에 일찍 등록한 사람은 킹맨 박사를 직접 만날 수 있는 기회를 얻을 것이다.

해설 | 주어는 Individuals ~이고 빈칸은 will be와 함께 쓰일 준동사 자리이다. 들어갈 동사가 4형식 동사인 offer이므로 문맥을 따져야 한다. 주어로 온 '사람들'이 기회를 주는 것이 아니라 기회를 얻는 것이므로 수동의 의미를 이루는 과거분사 (D) offered가 정답이다.

어휘 | individual 개인, 사람   register 등록하다 be offered+명사 ~을 얻다, 받다   in person 직접

20 (A)

번역 | 케빈 파커는 R&D 부서에서 일하는 가장 유능한 사람으로 여겨진다.

해설 | 주어는 Kevin Parker이고 is와 어울리는 형태의 동사가 빈칸에 들어가야 한다. 문맥상 '캐빈 파커는 가장 유능한 사람으로 여겨진다'라는 의미가 되어야 하고 빈칸 뒤에 명사(the most competent person)가 나오므로 수동태 일 때도 목적격 보어를 취할 수 있는 5형식 동사 (A) considered가 정답이다. (C) regarded는 as와 함께 '~으로 여겨지다'라는 의미를 만들 수 있으므로 오답이다.

어휘 | consider 여기다, 간주하다   competent 유능한

21 (D)

번역 | 에퀴덴셜의 최고 경영자인 일라이 프라이가 초보 투자자들을 위한 투자 전략 세미나를 진행할 예정이다.

해설 | a seminar를 목적어로 받아 '세미나를 진행할 예정이다'라는 문맥이 되어야 자연스러우므로 '인도하다, 이끌다'라는 의미의 (D) lead가 정답이다. 참고로 'conduct a seminar(세미나를 하다)'처럼 conduct와 의미가 비슷한 behave는 대개 자동사로 쓰이기 때문에 목적어를 취할 수 없다.

어휘 | investment 투자   strategy 전략   novice 초보자 investor 투자자   behave (예의 바르게) 행동하다   charge 청구하다

22 (A)

번역 | 올해 카마인 제조사의 기록적인 수익은 영업 직원들의 노고 덕분입니다.

해설 | 문맥상 '기록적인 수익은 영업 직원들의 노고 덕분이다'라는 의미가 되어야 하므로 'be attributed to (~ 덕분이다)'라는 수동태 관용 표현을 이루는 (A) attributed가 정답이다.

어휘 | record profit 기록적인 수익   attribute 덕분으로 보다
sales force 판매 인력, 영업 직원

23 (A)

번역 | 논의된 채용 방법에는 계약 보너스를 지급하고, 신규
직원들에게 이사비를 지급하는 방안이 포함된다.

해설 | 주어는 Debated recruiting methods이고 뒤에 두
개의 동명사 목적어(offering/paying)가 나오므로 빈칸에는
타동사가 들어가야 한다. 따라서 타동사이면서 복수주어와 수
일치되는 (A) include가 정답이다.

어휘 | recruiting 채용활동   method 방법   include
포함하다   signing bonus 계약 보너스 (계약 체결 시 선지급하는
보너스) relocation 이사, 이전

24 (B)

번역 | 사흘 전 발표된 자유무역협정이 일시적으로 중단됐다.

해설 | 단수명사인 The free-trade agreement가 문장의
주어이고, that ~ ago는 주어를 수식하는 관계사절이며,
빈칸은 관계사절의 동사 자리이다. 주격 관계대명사 뒤의 동사는
선행사와 수가 일치되어야 하고 빈칸 뒤에 목적어가 아닌 부사구
three days ago(사흘 전)가 나오기 때문에 수동태인 (B) was
announced가 정답이다.

어휘 | free-trade 자유 무역   agreement 협정   announce
발표하다   temporarily 일시적으로

25 (D)

번역 | 가공된 냉동식품은 식품 산업에서 수익성이 높은 품목이
되어왔다.

해설 | 빈칸 뒤에 있는 형용사 frozen과 함께 명사 meals를
수식하는 형용사 자리이므로 문맥상 '가공된'이라는 의미의
분사형 형용사 (D) Processed가 정답이 된다. 두 개의
형용사는 연달아서 하나의 명사를 수식할 수 있다. 참고로
(C) Processing을 동명사로 본다면 '냉동식품을 가공하는
것은'이라고 해석이 되는 듯하지만 이 문장의 본동사는 'have
been'이므로 단수주어 취급을 하는 동명사 주어와 동사의 수가
일치하지 않는다.

어휘 | process 가공시키다   profitable 수익성이 있는

26 (A)

번역 | 공급자는 상품의 재고가 있다는 것을 확인했지만, 특정
품목들이 재고 기록에서 누락된 것을 발견했다.

해설 | 시간상으로 볼 때, 상품의 재고를 확인한 후에 재고
기록에서 누락된 품목을 발견한 것이므로 상품의 재고를 확인한
것이 but이 이끄는 절의 시제인 과거보다 먼저 일어난 일이다.
따라서 정답은 (A) had confirmed이다.

어휘 | supplier 공급자, 공급 업체   confirm 확인하다   stock
재고   inventory 재고

27 (D)

번역 | 새라 스튜어트는 새 프로젝트를 수행하는 팀의 책임자로
임명되었다.

해설 | 문맥상 '새라 스튜어트는 팀의 책임자로 임명되었다'라는
의미가 되어야 하므로 '감독관'이라는 뜻의 (D) supervisor가
정답이다. 관직, 신분, 직함이 한 사람인 경우 관사는 생략
가능하므로 supervisor는 가산명사이지만 관사 없이
단수형으로 쓴다.

어휘 | appoint 임명하다   supervisor 책임자, 관리자

28 (D)

번역 | 크랜슨 밸리 종합병원은 친구나 가족들의 각 방문 시간을
30분으로 제한하도록 요구한다.

해설 | '요구하다'라는 뜻의 동사 requires 뒤 that절에서는
'(should)+동사원형'을 써야 한다. 또한 '30분으로
제한된다'라는 의미가 되어야 하므로 전치사 to와 함께 '~으로
제한되다'라는 의미를 이루는 (D) be limited가 정답이다.

어휘 | require 요구하다   limit 제한하다

29 (A)

번역 | 면접위원회는 지원자들이 브리즈번을 방문할 수 있도록
교통비를 제공할 것이다.

해설 | 빈칸 뒤의 전치사 with가 문제 해결의 단서로 with는
동사 provide와 함께 '~에게 …을 제공하다'라는 의미를 이룬다.
따라서 (A) provide가 정답이다. 참고로 give나 offer와 같은
일반적인 4형식 동사는 '간접목적어(~에게)+직접목적어(~을)'의
순으로 쓰는 반면, provide는 목적어를 하나만 취하는 3형식
동사이므로 'provide+'간접목적어'(~에게)+with (~을/~을
가지고)'의 구조로 쓰인다.

어휘 | committee 위원회   transportation fee 교통비

30 (B)

번역 | 주방장 크리스티나 페드리치가 식당의 메뉴를 바꾼 이후로
손님들은 개선된 다양한 선택의 기회에 대해 언급해 왔다.

해설 | 주절의 주어 diners는 복수명사로 언급을 하는
주체이므로 동사는 복수동사의 능동태가 와야 한다. 종속절인
Since(~이후로)절에서 과거 시제(changed)가 사용되었으므로,
주절에는 현재완료(진행) 시제가 와야 한다. 따라서 능동태이면서
현재완료진행 시제인 (B) have been commenting이
정답이다. comment는 수동태를 만들 수 없는 자동사이며
전치사 on과 함께 쓰인다는 점도 기억하자.

어휘 | diner 식사하는 사람[손님]   improve 개선하다
variety 다양성, 종류   option 선택(권)

UNIT 6 to부정사 & 동명사

전략포인트 1   본책 p.166

1 (A)   **2** (B)   **3** (D)

1 (A)

번역 | 이 행사의 목적은 주민들에게 무료 건강검진을 제공하는
것이다.

해설 | 주어가 objective, aim, purpose 등과 같은 '목표, 목적'이라는 뜻의 명사일 때 주격 보어로는 '~하는 것'이라는 뜻의 명사 역할의 to부정사가 온다. 따라서 정답은 (A) to offer이다.

어휘 | objective 목적, 목표 offer 제공하다 health screening 건강 검진 resident (입)주민

2 (B)

번역 | 오래된 공장을 주거용 아파트로 개조하려면 건물주가 시 공무원의 허가를 받아야 한다.

해설 | 문맥상 '오래된 공장을 주거용 아파트로 개조하기 위해'라는 능동의 의미가 자연스러우므로 to부정사의 부사적 용법으로 '목적'을 나타내는 (B) To convert가 정답이다.

어휘 | convert 전환시키다, 개조하다 residential 주거의 permission 허가 official 공무원

3 (D)

번역 | 벨미드의 모든 전동 공구에 대한 사용설명서는 따라하기에 간단하고 쉽다.

해설 | 빈칸은 주어 The instructions ~를 수식하는 보어 자리로, 등위접속사 and 뒤의 easy와 어울려 주어를 수식하는 알맞은 형용사를 골라야 한다. '형용사+to부정사'는 '~하기에 …하다'라고 해석되기도 하는데, 여기에서도 'to follow'와 결합하여 '설명서가 따라 하기에 간단하고 쉽다'는 의미가 되어야 적절하므로 '간단한'을 뜻하는 (D) simple이 정답이다.

어휘 | instructions 설명서 tool 도구 smooth 매끄러운

전략포인트 **2**　　　　　　　　　　본책 p.166

1 (A)　**2** (A)　**3** (C)

1 (A)

번역 | 회장은 규제의 차이에도 불구하고 유럽으로 사업을 추진하기로 결정했다.

해설 | 문장의 동사는 decided인데, decide는 to부정사를 목적어로 취하는 동사이므로 (A) to promote가 정답이다.

어휘 | promote 추진하다, 촉진하다 regulations 규정, 규제

2 (A)

번역 | 시의회는 시청 광장을 재즈 페스티벌에 사용할 수 있도록 하는 것에 동의했다.

해설 | 빈칸은 본동사 자리로, 빈칸 뒤 to부정사를 목적어로 취하여 '시청 광장을 사용할 수 있도록 하는 데 동의했다'라는 의미를 만드는 (A) agreed가 정답이다.

어휘 | make ~ available ~을 사용할 수 있도록 하다

3 (C)

번역 | 퍼킨 푸드는 인력 확충을 목표로 하여 125명의 신규 조립 라인 근로자를 모집하기를 바란다.

해설 | 'Aiming ~ its work force'는 주어 Perquin Foods를 수식하는 분사구문으로, 분사 aiming은 동사 aim의 성질을 그대로 유지한다. aim은 to부정사를 목적어로 취하여

'~하는 것을 목표로 하다'라는 의미로 쓰이므로 정답은 (C) to expand이다.

어휘 | aim 목표하다 expand 확대하다 work force 인력 recruit 모집하다 assembly-line 조립 라인의

전략포인트 **3**　　　　　　　　　　본책 p.167

1 (D)　**2** (B)　**3** (C)

1 (D)

번역 | 차량 통행량의 증가는 그 지역의 도로 개선에 투자해야 하는 또 다른 이유다.

해설 | An increase in vehicle traffic이 주어, is가 동사, another reason이 주격 보어인 완전한 문장에서, 빈칸은 명사 reason을 뒤에서 꾸미는 준동사 자리이다. 보기 중 (B) investing과 (D) to invest가 가능한데, 명사 reason은 to부정사와 어울리므로 (D) to invest가 정답이다.

어휘 | increase 증가 vehicle 차량 traffic 교통량 invest in ~에 투자하다 improve 개선하다 region 지역

2 (B)

번역 | 라이셋 씨는 참을성 있고 쉽게 복잡한 아이디어를 고객에게 전달할 수 있는 능력으로 찬사를 받았다.

해설 | 빈칸 앞에 완전한 문장이 나오므로 빈칸은 앞에 온 명사 ability를 수식할 수식어가 들어갈 자리이다. 따라서 (B) to communicate가 정답이다. 문장에 본동사인 was praised for가 있으므로 동사 형태인 나머지 보기들은 답이 될 수 없다.

어휘 | praise 칭찬하다 complex 복잡한 patiently 참을성 있게

3 (C)

번역 | 마무리가 안 된 목재 표면은 적절히 처리되지 않으면 색상이 변하는 경향이 있다.

해설 | 문맥상 '색상이 변하는 경향이 있다'는 내용이 되어야 자연스러우므로 '경향'이라는 의미의 (C) tendency가 정답이다. tendency는 to부정사와 어울리는 명사이므로 '~하는 경향'의 의미인 'tendency to부정사'를 암기한다.

어휘 | surface 표면 tendency 경향 treat 처리하다 properly 적절히 routine 순서 trend 동향

전략포인트 **4**　　　　　　　　　　본책 p.167

1 (B)　**2** (B)　**3** (C)

1 (B)

번역 | 업그레이드된 데이터베이스는 연구자들이 이전 연구들을 더 쉽게 검색할 수 있게 해줄 것이다.

해설 | 빈칸은 동사 enable과 연결되는 목적격 보어 자리이다. enable은 목적어 뒤에 to부정사를 목적격 보어로 취하는 대표 5형식 동사이므로 (B) to search가 정답이다.

어휘 | enable ~하게 해주다

2 (B)

번역 | 주민센터는 방문객들에게 정비 작업으로 북쪽 끝에 있는 엘리베이터를 이용하지 말 것을 권고했다.

해설 | 주어진 문장은 '주어＋동사＋목적어＋to부정사' 구조로 빈칸에는 to부정사를 목적격 보어로 취하는 5형식 동사가 들어가야 한다. 문맥상 '방문객들에게 엘리베이터를 이용하지 말 것을 권고했다'라는 의미를 나타내는 (B) advised가 정답이다.

어휘 | community center 주민센터 advise 권고하다, 조언하다 due to ~때문에 maintenance 유지보수, 점검

3 (C)

번역 | 델코놈의 전 직원은 내일 새로운 이메일 시스템 교육에 참석해야 한다.

해설 | 빈칸 뒤에 온 to부정사(to attend)와 함께 쓰여 '교육에 참석해야 한다'는 의미가 되어야 자연스럽다. 따라서 정답은 수동태로 '요구된다'라는 의미를 만드는 (C) required이다. 'be required to부정사(~해야 한다/~하도록 요구되다)'로 암기해 두자.

어휘 | require 요구하다 consider 고려하다 indicate 나타내다 insist 주장하다

전략포인트 5   본책 p.168

1 (A)   **2** (B)   **3** (C)

1 (A)

번역 | 벤슨 항공은 예약을 한 승객이 다른 사람에게 티켓을 양도하는 것을 허용하지 않습니다.

해설 | 빈칸은 사역동사 let의 목적격 보어 자리로, 원형부정사가 와야 한다. 따라서 동사원형인 (A) transfer가 정답이다.

어휘 | passenger 승객 booking 예약 transfer 양도하다

2 (B)

번역 | 부동산 관리인은 냉방 장치를 설치하게 했다.

해설 | 빈칸은 사역동사 had의 목적격 보어 자리로, 목적어와의 관계가 능동이면 원형부정사를 쓰고 수동이면 과거분사를 써야 한다. 여기서는 목적어가 the air-conditioning units라는 사물로 '설치되는 대상'이므로, 수동 관계를 나타내는 과거분사인 (B) installed가 정답이다.

어휘 | property 부동산 unit 장치, 설비 install 설치하다

3 (C)

번역 | 바쁜 납세 기간에 시간제 직원을 고용하는 것은 간부 직원들의 부담을 덜어주는 데 도움이 될 것이다.

해설 | 조동사 will과 동사 alleviate 사이에는 부사, 또는 동사원형을 보어로 취할 수 있는 동사가 들어갈 수 있다. 따라서 정답은 동사원형을 보어로 취할 수 있는 동사인 (C) help이다. 동사 help는 준동사를 목적격 보어로 취할 때 목적어를 생략할 수 있기 때문에 동사원형이 마치 목적어처럼 help 바로 뒤에 올 수 있다.

어휘 | hire 고용하다 tax 세금 alleviate 경감[완화]하다 pressure 압박, 부담 senior 고위의, 상급의 assure 확언하다 advise 권고하다

전략포인트 6   본책 p.168

1 (C)   **2** (C)   **3** (B)

1 (C)

번역 | 직원들에게 필요한 항공편을 준비하는 것은 총무부의 책임이다.

해설 | 빈칸은 뒤에 오는 명사구 any necessary flights for employees를 목적어로 취하면서, 동사 is의 주어 역할을 하는 자리이므로 동명사인 (C) Arranging이 정답이다.

어휘 | arrange 준비[마련]하다 responsibility 책임 the administrative department 총무부, 관리부서

2 (C)

번역 | 비용을 줄이기 위해, 넬슨 씨는 그의 사업을 다른 지역으로 이전하는 것을 고려했다.

해설 | 빈칸 앞에 온 considered가 문제 해결의 단서로, consider는 동명사를 목적어로 취하는 동사이다. 따라서 동명사인 (C) relocating이 정답이다.

어휘 | reduce 줄이다 consider 고려하다 relocate 이전[이동]시키다

3 (B)

번역 | 테오스 은행의 스마트폰 애플리케이션은 이동 중에 계좌 활동 내역을 확인하는 편리한 방법입니다.

해설 | 빈칸은 전치사 of의 목적어 자리이자 빈칸 뒤의 명사구 account activity를 목적어로 취할 수 있는 능동형의 동명사 자리이다. 따라서 (B) checking이 정답이다. (D) being checked는 수동으로 목적어를 취할 수 없다. 참고로 'a way of 동사+ing'는 '~하는 방법'이라는 의미로 외워 두도록 한다.

어휘 | application 응용프로그램 convenient 편리한 account 계좌 on the go 이동하면서 이용하는

전략포인트 7   본책 p.169

1 (A)   **2** (D)   **3** (D)

1 (A)

번역 | 경량 케이스는 노트북이 운반되는 동안 노트북의 파손되기 쉬운 전자 장치를 보호하도록 설계되었다.

해설 | 빈칸에는 전치사 for의 목적어 역할을 하며, 빈칸 뒤에 오는 명사구 the delicate electronics of the laptop을 목적어로 취할 수 있는 동명사가 들어가야 한다. 따라서 정답은 (A) protecting이다.

어휘 | protect 보호하다 delicate 깨지기 쉬운 electronics 전자 장치 in transit 운송 중인

2 (D)

번역 | 이사진은 퇴임하는 현 CEO의 후임자를 아직 선정하지 못했다.

해설 | 빈칸은 준동사 to select의 목적어 자리이며 앞에 부정관사 a가 있고 뒤에는 전치사 for가 있으므로 명사 (D) replacement가 정답이다.

어휘 | board member 이사(회), 임원 replacement 후임자 current 현재의 step down 퇴진[사직]하다 have yet to부정사 아직 ~하지 않다

3 (D)

번역 | 설문 조사는 지역 내 중간 규모의 기업 관리자들과 직접 접촉하여 실시되었다.

해설 | 빈칸 앞에 전치사 by가 있고, 빈칸 뒤에는 전치사의 목적어가 되는 동명사 contacting이 있다. 동명사는 동사의 성질이 있기 때문에 형용사가 아닌 부사의 수식을 받는다. 따라서 정답은 동명사를 수식하는 부사 (D) directly이다.

어휘 | conduct 실행[실시]하다 directly 직접

전략포인트 8 본책 p.169

1 (C) **2** (B) **3** (D)

1 (C)

번역 | 공장 근로자는 장비를 조작하는 동안 부상을 피할 수 있게 도와주는 보호 장비를 착용해야 한다.

해설 | 빈칸 앞에 온 avoid가 문제 해결의 단서로, avoid는 동명사를 목적어로 취하는 동사이다. 따라서 동명사인 (C) injuring이 정답이다.

어휘 | protective gear 보호 장비 avoid 피하다 injure 부상을 입히다 operate 가동시키다 equipment 장비

2 (B)

번역 | 시장의 경쟁이 더 치열해지기 때문에, 게일 씨는 대체 수익원을 찾을 것을 권했다.

해설 | 빈칸 뒤에 온 seeking이 문제 해결의 단서이다. 빈칸은 주절의 동사 자리로 동명사를 목적어로 취하는 동사가 와야 한다. 따라서 (B) recommended가 정답이다.

어휘 | competitive 경쟁이 치열한 recommend 권고하다 alternative 대체의 revenue stream 수익원, 매출원

3 (D)

번역 | 국제 여행객은 목적지로 출발하기 전에 올바른 비자를 확보해야 한다.

해설 | 빈칸 뒤에 동명사 departing이 있으므로 빈칸에는 동명사를 목적어로 취할 수 있는 전치사가 와야 한다. 문맥상 '출발하기 전에 올바른 비자를 확보하다'라는 의미가 자연스러우므로 '~에 앞서'라는 뜻의 전치사구 (D) prior to가 정답이다.

어휘 | secure 확보하다 prior to ~에 앞서 depart 출발하다 destination 목적지

전략포인트 9 본책 p.170

1 (B) **2** (C) **3** (A)

---

1 (B)

번역 | 그린웨이 슈퍼마켓은 플라스틱 쓰레기를 30퍼센트까지 줄이겠다는 목표에 도달했다는 소식을 전하게 되어 기쁩니다.

해설 | 빈칸 앞의 is delighted가 문제 해결의 단서로, '~하게 되어 기쁘다'라는 의미의 to부정사 관용 표현인 'be delighted to부정사'를 완성하는 (B) to report가 정답이다.

어휘 | delighted 기쁜, 기뻐하는 reach 도달하다 goal 목표

2 (C)

번역 | 계약서가 엉망으로 쓰여져서 일부 조항은 해석을 필요로 한다.

해설 | 빈칸은 전치사 to의 목적어 자리이므로 명사나 동명사가 들어갈 수 있는데, 빈칸 뒤에 목적어가 없으므로 명사인 (C) interpretation이 정답이다. 'be subject to (동)명사'는 '~될 수 있다. ~에 달려 있다'라는 뜻의 빈출 표현이므로 암기해 둔다.

어휘 | poorly worded 엉망으로 쓰여진 terms 조항 be subject to ~될 수 있다 interpretation 해석

3 (A)

번역 | 업무 분배는 업무량을 최소화하는 데에 기여한다.

해설 | 빈칸 앞의 contribute가 문제 해결의 단서로, '~에 기여하다'라는 의미의 동사 관용 표현인 'contribute to 동명사'를 완성하는 (A) to minimizing이 정답이다.

어휘 | delegation of task 일의 위임, 업무의 분배 contribute to ~에 기여하다 minimize 최소화하다 workload 업무량

ETS 고득점 실전 문제 본책 p.172

1 (A) **2** (D) **3** (B) **4** (B) **5** (B) **6** (A)
7 (D) **8** (B) **9** (A) **10** (C) **11** (B) **12** (B)
13 (D) **14** (B) **15** (D) **16** (C) **17** (D) **18** (A)
19 (B) **20** (D)

1 (A)

번역 | 프로젝트의 마감 기한을 연장하는 것이 작업의 고품질을 보장하는 가장 좋은 방법이다.

해설 | 빈칸은 뒤에 오는 명사구 the deadline for the project를 목적어로 취하면서, 동사 is의 주어 역할을 하는 자리이므로 동명사인 (A) Extending이 정답이다.

어휘 | extend 연장하다 ensure 보장하다

2 (D)

번역 | 기자 회견 동안, 장 인더스트리얼의 대변인은 베이징 현장에서의 향후 계획에 대해 논의하는 것을 거절했다.

해설 | 빈칸은 본동사 자리로 빈칸 뒤의 to discuss를 목적어로 취하는 동사가 들어가야 한다. 따라서 to부정사를 목적어로 취해 '~하기를 거절하다'라는 의미를 나타내는 동사 (D) declined가 정답이다.

어휘 | press conference 기자 회견 spokesperson 대변인 decline 거절하다 site 현장, 장소

3 (B)

번역 | 커크랜드 씨는 카펫을 얼마나 사야 할지 결정할 수 있도록 설비업체가 거실의 크기를 측정하도록 했다.

해설 | 빈칸은 사역동사 had의 목적격 보어 자리로, 목적어와의 관계가 능동이면 원형부정사를 쓰고 수동이면 과거분사를 써야 한다. 여기서는 목적어가 her living room이라는 사물로 '측정되는 대상'이므로, 수동 관계를 나타내는 과거분사인 (B) measured가 정답이다.

어휘 | measure 측정하다 contractor 건축업자, 설비업체 determine 결정하다 purchase 구매하다

4 (B)

번역 | 교육생들이 그 과정을 이수하기 위해서는 회사의 정책과 관련된 시험을 통과해야 한다.

해설 | 문맥상 '교육생들이 과정을 이수하기 위해'라는 의미가 자연스러우므로 to부정사의 부사적 용법으로 '목적'을 나타내는 (B) to complete가 정답이다. 참고로 빈칸 앞 for trainees는 to부정사의 의미상의 주어이며, 'in order to부정사' 구문에도 의미상의 주어인 'for+목적격'이 들어갈 수 있다.

어휘 | trainee 교육생 complete 마치다, 완료하다 related 관련된 policy 정책

5 (B)

번역 | 새로운 회계 소프트웨어는 직원들이 경비 내역서를 매우 쉽게 제출할 수 있도록 해주었다.

해설 | 빈칸은 본동사 자리로 빈칸 뒤의 employees를 목적어로, to submit을 목적격 보어로 취하는 5형식 동사가 들어가야 한다. 따라서 (B) allows가 정답이다. 참고로 (A) lets는 사역동사이므로 목적격 보어에 동사원형이나 과거분사를 취한다.

어휘 | accounting 회계 allow A to부정사 A가 ~하게 하다 submit 제출하다 expense 비용, 경비

6 (A)

번역 | 네비스 호텔에서 뛰어난 고객 서비스를 받는 고객은 그 호텔 체인을 다시 선택할 가능성이 더 높다.

해설 | 빈칸 앞에 be 동사와 비교급을 나타내는 more가 있고 빈칸 뒤에는 to부정사가 이어지므로 빈칸에는 형용사가 들어가야 한다. 문맥상 '호텔 체인을 다시 선택할 가능성이 높다'라는 의미가 되어야 하므로, '~할 가능성이 있다'라는 의미를 이루는 'be likely to부정사'가 적절하다. 따라서 (A) likely가 정답이다.

어휘 | outstanding 훌륭한 be likely to-v ~할 가능성이 높다 chain (상점·호텔 등의) 체인 likelihood 있음직함

7 (D)

번역 | 만지 비스킷 회사는 지난 이사회에서 식품 안전 정책을 갱신하는 데 전념했다.

해설 | 빈칸 앞 be devoted는 전치사 to와 함께 '~하는 데 전념[헌신]하다'의 의미로 쓰인다. 빈칸 뒤에 명사구가 있으므로 전치사 to 다음에는 동명사가 필요하다는 것을 알 수 있다. 따라서

(D) to updating이 정답이다. 'be devoted to 동명사/명사'는 빈출 표현이므로 암기해 두자.

어휘 | board 이사회 policy 정책

8 (B)

번역 | 검사관들이 해결되어야 할 시설 내 잠재적인 안전 문제를 파악할 것으로 예상된다.

해설 | expect는 목적격 보어로 to부정사를 취하는 동사로, 주어진 문장은 'expect+목적어+to부정사'를 수동태로 쓴 문장이다. 따라서 정답은 (B) to identify이다. 'be expected to부정사'는 '~할 것으로 예상되다'라는 의미로 자주 쓰이는 표현이니 익혀 두자.

어휘 | inspector 검사관 identify 파악하다 potential 잠재적인 facility 시설 resolve 해결하다

9 (A)

번역 | BC 홈 퍼니싱의 새 크리스탈 꽃병은 너무 깨지기 쉬워서 표준 포장으로 배송할 수 없습니다.

해설 | 빈칸 뒤 형용사 fragile을 강조하며 뒤의 to부정사인 to ship과 연결되어 '너무 깨지기 쉬워 표준 포장으로 배송할 수 없다'의 의미를 이루는 부사 (A) too가 정답이다. '너무 ~해서 …할 수 없다'의 'too 형/부 …to부정사'는 자주 쓰이는 표현이니 익혀두자.

어휘 | fragile 깨지기 쉬운 ship 수송[운송]하다

10 (C)

번역 | 발표자의 말을 자주 끊은 후, 청중들은 강의가 끝날 때까지 질문을 아낄 것을 요청 받았다.

해설 | 빈칸은 전치사 After 뒤의 자리로 얼핏 봐서는 명사나 동명사가 와야 할 것 같지만, 빈칸 뒤에 interrupting이라는 동명사가 있다. 따라서 빈칸에는 동명사 interrupting을 수식할 수 있는 부사가 와야 하므로 (C) frequently가 정답이다.

어휘 | frequently 자주, 빈번히 interrupt 중단하다, 끼어들다

11 (B)

번역 | 직원들은 2층에 있는 실험실에 출입하기 위해 신분증을 스캔해야 한다.

해설 | 빈칸 앞에 전치사 for가 있고 빈칸 뒤에 전치사 to가 있으므로 '~으로의 접근'이라는 의미의 'access to'를 완성하는 (B) access가 정답이다. 참고로 (D) accessing은 타동사 access의 동명사이므로 바로 뒤에 목적어를 취해야 하기 때문에 답이 될 수 없다.

어휘 | access 접근, 입장 laboratory 실험실

12 (B)

번역 | 경영진은 모든 직원들이 그것에 대해 알 때까지 새로운 보안 조치를 연기하는 것을 고려 중이다.

해설 | 빈칸 앞에 온 considering이 문제 해결의 단서로, consider는 동명사를 목적어로 취하는 동사이다. 따라서 동명사인 (B) postponing이 정답이다. (D) having been postponed도 동명사가 될 수 있지만 수동태이기 때문에 뒤에 오는 the new security measures와 연결이 되지 않는다.

어휘 | security 보안 measures 조치, 방안 brief 알려주다, 보고하다

13 (D)
번역 | 슬레턴 엔터프라이즈는 수익을 회사의 홍보에 더욱 재투자함으로써 탄탄한 고객 기반을 구축하기를 희망한다.

해설 | 빈칸에는 뒤에 있는 동명사 reinvesting을 목적어로 취하면서 '수익을 회사의 홍보에 더욱 재투자함으로써'라는 의미를 나타내는 (D) By가 들어가야 한다. 'by+동명사'는 '~함으로써'의 의미로 자주 쓰이는 표현이므로 익혀 두어야 한다.

어휘 | reinvest 재투자하다 profit 이익, 수익 promote 홍보하다 solid 튼튼한, 견고한

14 (B)
번역 | HG 파이낸셜의 강점과 약점을 비판적으로 평가하기 위해 사업 자문가가 고용되었다.

해설 | 빈칸은 완전한 문장 뒤에 오는 부사 자리이기 때문에, to evaluate를 수식하는 부사 (B) critically이 정답이다. to부정사는 동사의 성질이 있기 때문에 형용사가 아닌 부사의 수식을 받는다는 점을 유의하자.

어휘 | hire 고용하다 evaluate 평가하다 critically 비판적으로

15 (D)
번역 | 박물관의 설립자는 그 지역에 중요한 역사적 유물들을 보존하는 데 헌신해 왔다.

해설 | 문맥상 '역사적 유물들을 보존하는 데 헌신했다'라는 의미가 되어야 하므로, '헌신하다'라는 의미를 이루는 'dedicate oneself+to 동명사'가 적절하다. 따라서 정답은 (D) to preserving이다.

어휘 | founder 설립자 dedicate 헌신하다 preserve 보존하다 artifact 유물 significant 중요한 region 지역

16 (C)
번역 | 엄청난 인기 덕분에, 앨런 마리노 감독의 최신 영화는 흥행 기록을 깰 가능성이 있다.

해설 | 빈칸 앞에 정관사 the가 있고 뒤에 to break box office records가 있으므로, 명사를 수식하는 to부정사 구조임을 알 수 있다. 문맥상 '기록을 깰 가능성'이라는 뜻이 자연스러우므로 정답은 (C) potential이다.

어휘 | enormous 막대한, 엄청난 popularity 인기 potential 가능성

17 (D)
번역 | 예비 배터리는 냉장고나 다른 주요 주방 기기들을 작동시킬 수 있을 정도로 강력합니다.

해설 | 문맥상 '작동시킬 수 있을 정도로 충분히 강력하다'라는 의미가 되어야 하므로, '~하기에 충분히 …하다'라는 의미를 이루는 'enough+to부정사'가 적절하다. 따라서 (D) enough가 정답이다. 참고로 enough는 형용사나 부사를 뒤에서 수식하므로 형용사인 powerful 뒤에 왔다는 것도 알아 두자.

어휘 | run 가동시키다 appliance (전자)기기

18 (A)
번역 | 화재 경보기가 울리면 건물 전 객실이 직원들에 의해 비워져야 한다.

해설 | 빈칸 앞에 동사 need가 있고 빈칸 뒤에 by employees가 있으므로, 빈칸에는 need의 목적어 역할을 하는 to부정사의 수동태 구조가 들어가야 한다. 따라서 (A) to be vacated가 정답이다. 동사 need는 to부정사를 목적어로 취하는 대표 동사이다.

어휘 | vacate 비우다, 떠나다

19 (B)
번역 | 맞춤형 제품과 서비스를 제공함으로써, 그 회사는 불경기 동안 고객 기반을 확보할 수 있었다.

해설 | 빈칸 앞의 전치사 By 뒤에는 명사나 명사구가 목적어로 올 수 있는데, 뒤에 목적어인 customized products and services가 왔으므로 목적어를 취할 수 있는 동명사 (B) providing이 정답이다. 참고로 (A) provided도 '분사+명사'의 구조로 가능한 듯하지만 '제공된 맞춤형 제품과 서비스에 의해 고객을 확보했다'라는 문맥이 부자연스럽다. 'by+V-ing'는 '~함으로써'라는 의미로 사용 빈도가 높은 표현이니 암기해 두자.

어휘 | provide 제공하다 customized 맞춤형의 secure 확보하다 base 기반 recession 불경기

20 (D)
번역 | 새 피트니스 앱은 사용자들이 다양한 범주에서 진행 상황을 추적하는 데 도움을 줄 수 있다.

해설 | 빈칸은 목적어로 users를, 목적격 보어로 원형부정사인 track을 취할 수 있는 동사 자리이므로 (D) help가 정답이다. help는 목적격 보어로 원형부정사와 to부정사를 둘 다 취할 수 있지만, 보기의 나머지 동사들은 목적격 보어 자리에 to부정사만 취한다.

어휘 | fitness 신체 단련 app 앱(=application) track 추적하다 a variety of 다양한 category 범주

UNIT 7 분사 & 분사구문

전략포인트 1   본책 p.174
1 (C)   **2** (C)   **3** (A)

1 (C)
번역 | 이번이 회사의 첫 번째 주요 수상 후보가 된 것인 것만큼, 직원들은 상당히 흥분된 상태입니다.

해설 | 주절에서 be동사는 보어가 필요한 동사로, 빈칸에는 명사 또는 형용사가 들어가야 하는데 빈칸 앞에 부사 quite가 있으므로 '흥분된'이라는 의미의 분사형 형용사인 (C) excited가 정답이다.

어휘 | award 상 nomination 지명, (수상) 후보

2 (C)

번역 | 수아레즈 시장은 제안된 도시 공원이 도심 지역의 상업을 활성화할 것이라고 생각하는 이유를 설명했다.

해설 | 빈칸 앞에 정관사 the, 빈칸 뒤에 명사구 city park가 있으므로 빈칸은 명사를 수식하는 형용사 자리이다. 따라서 (C) proposed가 정답이다.

어휘 | mayor 시장   commerce 상업   proposal 제안, 청혼

3 (A)

번역 | 많은 청중들은 이 박사의 강의가 매우 흥미롭다고 전했다.

해설 | fascinate는 '마음을 사로잡다'라는 감정 타동사이며, 빈칸에는 동사 find의 목적격 보어 역할을 하는 형용사가 와야 한다. 목적격 보어의 의미상의 주어는 목적어이므로 Dr. Lee's lecture가 '매우 흥미롭다'라는 능동의 의미를 만드는 현재분사 (A) fascinating이 정답이다. (B) fascinated는 '(사람이) 매료된'이라는 뜻이므로 어울리지 않는다.

어휘 | audience 청중   fascinating 매우 흥미로운

전략포인트 2　　　　　　본책 p.174

1 (D)　2 (D)　3 (C)

1 (D)

번역 | 이곳은 고객을 위해 따로 마련된 곳이므로 직원들은 지정된 장소에 주차하지 않도록 주의를 받는다.

해설 | 빈칸은 명사 spots를 수식하는 형용사 자리이다. 보기 중 현재분사인 (B) designating과 과거분사인 (D) designated가 형용사 역할을 할 수 있는데, spots는 지정이 되는 대상이므로 수동의 의미를 나타내는 (D) designated가 정답이 된다.

어휘 | remind 다시 알려주다   designated 지정된   spot 장소   reserved 지정된, 예약된

2 (D)

번역 | 자원봉사자들은 기부된 옷들을 크기별로 분류하여 지역 전역의 자선단체로 보낼 수 있도록 할 것이다.

해설 | 빈칸 앞에 정관사 the가 있고 뒤에 clothes라는 명사가 나오므로 빈칸은 형용사 자리이다. 보기 중 현재분사인 (C) donating과 과거분사인 (D) donated가 형용사 역할을 할 수 있는데, clothes는 기부가 되는 대상이므로 수동의 의미를 나타내는 (D) donated가 정답이 된다.

어휘 | volunteer 자원봉사자   sort 분류하다   donate 기부하다   charity 자선단체   region 지역

3 (C)

번역 | 대부분의 방문객들은 호텔 로비에 있는 예술작품이 흡족한 방식으로 배치되어 있다는 것에 동의한다.

해설 | 빈칸 뒤의 사물명사인 way를 수식하는 자리이므로 형용사 역할을 할 수 있는 분사가 빈칸에 들어가야 한다. 문맥상 '흡족한 방식'이라는 의미가 되어야 하며, way가 감정을 유발하고 있으므로 능동의 의미를 나타내는 현재분사인 (C) pleasing이 정답이 된다.

어휘 | agree 동의하다   artwork 예술작품   arrange 배열하다   pleasing 즐거운, 만족스러운   pleasure 기쁨

전략포인트 3　　　　　　본책 p.175

1 (A)　2 (C)　3 (D)

1 (A)

번역 | 컨테이너를 트럭에 고정하는 어떤 끈이든 출발 전에 다시 확인되어야 한다.

해설 | should 앞까지가 주어이므로 빈칸에는 앞의 명사 straps를 수식하는 동시에 뒤의 the containers를 목적어로 취하는 분사가 들어가야 한다. Any straps는 '고정시키는' 주체이므로 능동의 의미를 갖는 현재분사 (A) securing이 정답이다.

어휘 | strap 끈, 줄   secure 고정시키다   container (화물 수송용) 컨테이너   double-check 재확인하다   departure 출발

2 (C)

번역 | 금속 울타리로 분리된 두 개의 부동산은 같은 회사의 것이지만, 하나는 팔릴 것이다.

해설 | 문장에 본동사 belong to가 있으므로 빈칸에는 주어인 명사 properties를 수식하는 분사가 들어가야 한다. 빈칸 뒤 전치사 by가 있으므로 과거분사인 (C) separated가 정답이다. 현재분사인 (A) separating과 명사를 뒤에서 수식할 수 있는 to부정사 (B) to separate는 목적어를 수반해야 하므로 정답이 될 수 없다.

어휘 | property 부동산   separated 분리된   belong to ~의 소유이다

3 (D)

번역 | 안 좋은 날씨 때문에 사우스엔드에서 출발하는 휴블리 행 버스가 운영이 중단되었습니다.

해설 | 문장에 본동사 is가 있으므로 빈칸은 주어인 the bus를 수식하는 분사 자리이다. depart는 현재분사만 만들 수 있는 완전 자동사이므로 (D) departing이 정답이다.

어휘 | due to ~때문에   inclement weather 악천후   out of service 운행하지 않는

전략포인트 4　　　　　　본책 p.175

1 (D)　2 (B)　3 (B)

1 (D)

번역 | 최고의 판매 전략을 파악하기 위해 각 신흥 시장에 연구자 한 팀이 배정되었다.

해설 | 빈칸 앞에 한정사 each가 있고 뒤에 market이라는 명사가 나오므로 빈칸은 형용사가 들어갈 자리이다. 따라서 '신흥의'라는 뜻의 현재분사 (D) emerging이 정답이다.

어휘 | be assigned to ~에 배정되다, 배치되다   emerging 신흥의   identify 파악하다   strategy 전략   emerge 부상하다

2 (B)

번역 | 시민 게시판에 올라오는 압도적인 수의 민원은 시의 대중교통 체계에 관한 것이다.

해설 | 빈칸 뒤의 사물명사 number를 수식하는 자리이므로 형용사 역할을 할 수 있는 분사가 빈칸에 들어가야 한다. 문맥상 수가 '압도하는' 것이므로 능동의 의미를 나타내는 현재분사인 (B) overwhelming이 정답이다.

어휘 | complaint 불만, 민원 overwhelm 압도하다 citizen 시민 public transit 대중교통

3 (B)

번역 | 관리자는 세무 회계 업무를 수행하기 위해 중견 기업을 고용하는 것을 선호합니다.

해설 | 빈칸은 부정관사인 an과 명사 company 사이에서 명사를 수식하는 자리이므로 분사가 들어갈 수 있다. company는 입증이 되는 대상이므로 수동의 의미를 나타내는 과거분사 (B) established가 정답이다. 참고로 established company는 '중견 기업'의 의미로 자주 사용되니 익혀 두는 것이 좋다.

어휘 | prefer to부정사 ~하기를 선호하다 established 입증된, 중견의 carry out 수행하다 tax accounting 세금 회계 duty 직무, 업무

전략포인트 5   본책 p.176

1 (D) **2** (B) **3** (C)

1 (D)

번역 | 투자자들은 그 건설 프로젝트가 예정보다 3주 앞당겨진 것을 알고 기뻐했다.

해설 | 주어 The investors와 호응하는 보어가 필요한 자리인데, 문맥상 사람이 느끼는 감정을 나타내는 형용사가 와야 하므로, 과거분사인 (D) pleased가 정답이 된다.

어휘 | investor 투자자 please 기쁘게 하다 discover 알다, 깨닫다 construction 건설 ahead of ~보다 먼저

2 (B)

번역 | 데본 씨는 회사의 우수한 실적에 대한 다른 고무적인 소식과 함께 높은 매출을 발표했다.

해설 | 빈칸 앞에 형용사 other가 있고 뒤에 news라는 명사가 나오므로 빈칸은 형용사가 들어갈 자리이다. 뉴스(news)는 고무되는 것이 아니라 '고무적인' 것이므로 현재분사 (B) encouraging이 정답이다.

어휘 | announce 발표하다 sales 매출, 판매액 encouraging 고무적인 performance 실적, 성과

3 (C)

번역 | 마감일을 맞추자마자, 매니저는 지친 제작진들에게 절실히 필요한 휴식을 주었다.

해설 | 빈칸 앞에 정관사 the가 있고 뒤에 명사가 나오므로 빈칸은 형용사가 들어갈 자리이다. 형용사 (B) exhaustive와 형용사 역할을 하는 과거분사 (C) exhausted 중에 선택해야 하는데, 제작진은 지치는 대상이므로, 수동의 의미를 나타내는 과거분사인 (C) exhausted가 정답이 된다. '철저한'이라는 뜻의 형용사 (B) exhaustive는 의미상 적절하지 않다.

어휘 | deadline 마감 일자 exhausted 지친 much-needed 몹시 필요한 exhaustive 철저한

전략포인트 6   본책 p.176

1 (B) **2** (C) **3** (D)

1 (B)

번역 | 지난해 2분기에 완공되었지만 데번포트 쇼핑센터는 관광객들이 많이 찾는 곳이다.

해설 | 주어가 the Davenport Shopping Center이고, 동사가 is인 주절 앞에 있는 콤마 앞은 부사 자리이며 보기는 모두 준동사이다. 부사적 용법의 준동사는 분사구문이나 to부정사가 가능하며 목적어의 유무에 따라 능동, 수동으로 나뉜다. 빈칸 뒤에 목적어가 없으므로 수동태 모습의 준동사가 들어가야 한다. 따라서 정답은 (B) Completed이다.

어휘 | complete 완성[완료]하다 quarter 분기 destination 목적지

2 (C)

번역 | 교육 협회의 리더이기 때문에 데이비스 씨는 신입 교사들에게 강의를 해달라고 초대받았다.

해설 | 주절 앞에 있는 콤마 앞은 부사적 용법의 준동사 자리이다. 보기 중 (A) To be와 (C) Being이 부사적 용법의 준동사이지만 문맥상 이유의 의미를 지닌 분사구문이 더 자연스럽기 때문에 (C) Being이 정답이다. 참고로 (A) To be는 '리더가 되기 위해, 강의해 달라고 초대받았다'고 해석이 되는데 문맥이 어색하다. 이처럼 to부정사와 분사구문은 해석을 통해 구분할 수 있으며, '~하기 위해서'라는 의미인 to부정사부터 접근하는 것이 효율적이다. 부사절을 축약해 놓은 분사구문은 전체 내용을 파악하기 전엔 해석이 쉽지 않다.

어휘 | association 협회

3 (D)

번역 | 이전에 경유로 인한 문제를 겪은 적이 있었기 때문에 슬론 씨는 출장을 위해 도쿄로 가는 직항편을 예약했다.

해설 | 주어가 Mr. Sloan이고, 동사가 booked인 문장으로, 보기 중에서 동사 형태인 (A) Experiences는 제외시킨다. 빈칸 뒤에 목적어 issues가 있으므로 능동태 분사구문인 (D) Having experienced가 정답이다. (B) Being experienced와 (C) Experienced는 수동형 분사로 목적어를 취할 수 없으므로 오답이다. 참고로 having p.p.는 주절에 쓰인 시제보다 앞서 일어난 일을 표현할 때 쓸 수 있다.

어휘 | experience 겪다 layover 경유 previously 이전에 book 예약하다 direct flight 직항

전략포인트 7   본책 p.177

1 (A) **2** (D) **3** (B)

1 (A)

번역 | 이번 시즌에 순조롭게 진행되었기 때문에, 그 춤 페스티벌은 더 의미 있는 행사가 될 가능성을 갖고 있다.

해설 | 주절 앞에 있는 콤마 앞은 부사적 용법의 준동사 자리이므로 (C) Go와 (D) Be gone은 답이 될 수 없다. 완전자동사 go는 능동태만 가능하므로, 능동이면서 주절보다 앞선 시제를 보여주는 분사구문인 (A) Having gone이 정답이다.

어휘 | smoothly 순조롭게, 무리 없이 potential 가능성, 잠재력

2 (D)

번역 | 그 슈퍼마켓은 플라스틱 사용 안 하기 정책을 채택했고, 그래서 지역 사회로부터 긍정적인 호응을 얻었다.

해설 | 빈칸 앞에는 완전한 문장과 콤마, 빈칸 뒤에는 목적어 positive responses가 있는 점을 보아 능동태의 분사구문을 만드는 준동사 자리임을 알 수 있다. 따라서 (D) receiving이 정답이다. 참고로 분사구문이 완전한 문장을 후치 수식할 때는 '그래서 ~하다'라는 의미로 해석되기도 한다.

어휘 | adopt 채택하다 policy 정책 positive 긍정적인 community 지역사회

3 (B)

번역 | 그레이스톤사의 관리자는 4월의 모든 출장을 취소했고, 대신 회의에 원격 회의 소프트웨어를 사용하기로 결정했다.

해설 | 빈칸 앞에 완전한 절이 왔고 접속사가 없는 문장이므로, 콤마 뒤는 분사구문이 되어야 한다. 빈칸 뒤에 명사 형태의 목적어가 없으므로 자칫 과거분사가 들어간다고 생각하기 쉽지만, decide는 to부정사를 목적어로 취하는 동사이며, 빈칸 뒤에 오는 to부정사가 목적어이다. 또한 주어와의 관계를 따져볼 때, 주어인 그레이스톤사의 관리자는 동사 '결정하다(decide)'의 능동적인 주체이다. 따라서 정답은 현재분사인 (B) deciding이다.

어휘 | corporation 기업 teleconference (원격) 화상회의

전략포인트 8   본책 p.177

1 (D) 2 (C) 3 (D)

1 (D)

번역 | 신입 사원과 소통할 때는 지시를 명확히 하고 질문에 답할 시간을 내십시오.

해설 | 주절 앞은 부사절 접속사인 when을 생략하지 않은 분사구문의 구조이다. 주절이 ensure로 시작하는 명령문이므로 생략된 주어는 you이다. 따라서 '(당신이) 신입 사원과 소통할 때'라는 능동의 의미가 되어야 하므로 (D) interacting이 정답이다. 참고로 자동사인 interact는 with와 함께 쓰인다.

어휘 | interact 소통하다 ensure 확실하게 하다 instructions 지시, 설명

2 (C)

번역 | 웹사이트에 나와 있는 것처럼, 주문 제작 상품의 반품은 일반적으로 받지 않습니다.

해설 | 문맥상 '웹사이트에 나와 있는 것처럼'이라는 수동의 의미가 되어야 하므로, 과거분사인 (C) indicated가 정답이다. 'as+p.p.'는 '~되어 있듯이, ~된 대로'라는 뜻으로 자주 쓰이는 구조이니 암기해 두자.

어휘 | indicate 나타내다 return 반납, 반품 custommade 주문 제작한 accept 받아주다, 수락하다

3 (D)

번역 | 일단 창고에서 성공적으로 발송되면 상품이 도착하는 데 약 5일이 걸립니다.

해설 | 빈칸 앞엔 부사절 접속사 Once가 있고 빈칸 뒤에는 과거분사가 있다. 접속사 once 뒤에 '주어+동사'를 갖춘 절의 형태가 아니라면 분사구문을 떠올려야 하며, 접속사와 분사인 dispatched 사이에는 준동사를 수식하는 부사가 올 수 있다. 따라서 (D) successfully가 정답이다.

어휘 | once 일단 ~하면 dispatch 발송하다 warehouse 창고 merchandise 상품 approximately 대략

ETS 고득점 실전 문제   본책 p.178

1 (B) **2** (C) **3** (A) **4** (C) **5** (D) **6** (A)
7 (A) **8** (B) **9** (C) **10** (A) **11** (D) **12** (A)
13 (C) **14** (B) **15** (C) **16** (D) **17** (A) **18** (A)
19 (B) **20** (A)

1 (B)

번역 | 피셔맨즈 코브는 아름다운 해변가와 바다가재 양식장 때문에 캐나다 동북부 지역에서 방문객이 가장 많이 찾는 관광 명소이다.

해설 | 빈칸에는 the most와 연결되어 tourist attraction을 수식하는 형용사가 필요하다. 관광 명소는 '방문되는' 것이므로 수동의 과거분사인 (B) visited가 정답이다. '관광 명소'라는 뜻의 복합명사 tourist attraction도 자주 출제되므로 암기해 두자.

어휘 | tourist attraction 관광 명소 farm 양식장

2 (C)

번역 | 메타 씨의 실험실에서 행해진 두 개의 유사 연구는 상반된 결과를 낳았다.

해설 | 빈칸은 동사 yielded의 목적어로 온 명사 results를 수식하는 형용사 자리이다. 따라서 '상반되는'이라는 의미의 형용사 (C) conflicting이 정답이다.

어휘 | similar 유사한 conduct (특정 활동을) 하다 laboratory 실험실 yield 산출하다 conflicting 상반되는

3 (A)

번역 | 브로셔에 설명된 대로, 메이컨 리조트의 모든 객실은 오션뷰와 개인 수영장 이용과 그 밖의 많은 시설을 갖추고 있다.

해설 | 문맥상 '브로셔에 설명된 대로'라는 수동의 의미가 되어야 하므로, 과거분사인 (A) described가 정답이다. 'as+p.p.'는 '~되어 있듯이, ~된 대로'라는 뜻으로 자주 쓰이는 구조이니 암기해 두자.

어휘 | describe 설명하다 access 출입, 이용 amenities 편의 용품

4 (C)

번역 | 회의 등록비에 포함된 식사와 간식은 채식주의자들에게 적합하다.

해설 | 문장에 본동사 are가 있으므로 빈칸에는 앞의 명사 The meals and snacks를 수식하는 분사가 들어가야 한다. 빈칸 뒤에 목적어가 없고, 전치사 in이 있으므로 수동 형태인 과거분사 (C) included가 정답이다.

어휘 | include 포함하다   registration 등록   suitable 적합한   vegetarian 채식주의자

5 (D)

번역 | 정부 보조금은 신흥 기술이 그들의 최대 잠재력에 도달하도록 돕는다.

해설 | 빈칸은 뒤따라오는 명사 technologies를 수식하는 형용사 자리로, '최근 생겨난, 신흥의'라는 뜻의 분사형 형용사인 (D) emerging이 정답이다.

어휘 | grant 보조금   emerging 신흥의   reach 도달하다 potential 잠재력

6 (A)

번역 | 그래픽 디자인 부서는 새로운 시각적인 캠페인을 준비하면서 엄청난 헌신을 보여주었다.

해설 | 빈칸 앞에 접속사 while이 있으므로 '주어＋동사'의 구조가 있어야 하지만 주어진 보기들과 빈칸 뒤에 명사구가 절을 이루지 못한다. 부사절 접속사와 분사가 결합하여 분사구문을 만들 수 있고, 뒤에 목적어가 있는 경우 능동의 형태인 현재분사가 쓰인다. 따라서 (A) preparing이 정답이다.

어휘 | tremendous 엄청난   dedication 헌신, 전념 visual 시각의

7 (A)

번역 | 브라이언트 씨는 관리 경험이 있지만, 여러 지점에 걸쳐 팀을 다루는 것은 어려운 일이었다.

해설 | 주절의 be동사는 주격 보어가 필요하므로, 빈칸에는 명사 또는 형용사가 들어가야 한다. 따라서 '도전적인, 어려운'이라는 의미의 분사형 형용사인 (A) challenging이 정답이다. 명사인 (B) challenges는 주어인 handling ~과 동격 관계가 아니고, '장애가 있는'이라는 뜻의 (C) challenged는 의미상 자연스럽지 않으므로 정답이 될 수 없다.

어휘 | management 관리   handle 다루다   branch 지점 challenging 어려운

8 (B)

번역 | 브라이언 루비오 감독의 새 영화를 본 대다수의 사람들은 해변의 장면이 재미있다고 생각했다.

해설 | 5형식 동사 found의 목적어 beach scene과 호응하는 목적격 보어가 필요한 자리이다. 문맥상 '해변의 장면이 재미있다'라는 의미가 되어야 하며, the beach scene이 감정을 유발하고 있으므로 현재분사 (B) amusing이 정답이다. 명사인 (A) amusement는 목적어인 the beach scene과 동격이 아니므로 오답이다.

어휘 | the majority of 대다수의   amusement 재미, 오락 amuse 즐겁게 하다

9 (C)

번역 | 법률 사무직에 지원하려면 인사부로 이력서와 작성된 지원서를 이메일로 보내십시오.

해설 | 빈칸은 복합명사 job application을 수식하는 형용사 자리이다. '작성된 지원서'라는 의미가 되어야 자연스러우므로 '작성된'을 의미하는 (C) completed가 정답이다. (A) terminated는 '(계약기간, 상황 등이) 종료된'이라는 뜻으로 서류를 나타내는 job application과 어울리지 않는다. '양식이나 서류를 작성하다'라는 의미의 동사 complete의 과거분사인 completed가 적절한 표현이다.

어휘 | apply for 지원하다   paralegal 준법률가, 법률 사무원   completed 작성된, 완성된   application 지원서 terminated 종료된   proficient 능숙한   immediate 즉각적인

10 (A)

번역 | 스타크빌 트리뷴지의 독자들은 서밋 인베스트먼트의 인사이동을 강조하기 위해 게재된 신문기사를 즐겼다.

해설 | 문장에 본동사 enjoyed가 있으므로 빈칸에는 앞의 명사 article을 수식하는 준동사인 분사가 들어가야 한다. 빈칸 뒤에 목적어가 나오지 않고, to부정사의 부사적 용법이 있으므로 수동태 형태인 과거분사 (A) published가 정답이다.

어휘 | article 기사   publish (기사 등을) 게재하다   highlight 강조하다   personnel 직원의, 인사의

11 (D)

번역 | 그 조경회사는 모든 미지급금이 정산될 때까지 그 부동산을 다시 방문하지 않을 것이다.

해설 | 빈칸 뒤 명사 payment를 수식하는 형용사 자리이다. 문맥상 '미지급이 정산되다'라는 의미가 가장 자연스러우므로 모두 형용사인 보기 중에서 '미지불된, 미해결된'이라는 뜻의 분사형 형용사인 (D) outstanding이 정답이다.

어휘 | landscaping 조경   property 부동산, 소유지 outstanding 미지불된   settle 지불[정산]하다   responsive 즉각 대응하는   timely 시기 적절한   dependable 믿을만한

12 (A)

번역 | 애쉬빌 시는 관대한 세금 감면과 그 밖의 다른 우대책을 제공한다. 그래서 많은 소규모 사업체들을 끌어들인다.

해설 | 빈칸 앞에 완전한 절이 왔고 접속사가 없는 문장이므로, 분사구문으로 연결되어야 한다. 빈칸 뒤에 목적어 many small businesses가 있으므로 능동의 의미를 나타내는 현재분사 (A) attracting이 정답이다. (B) attracted와 (C) being attracted는 수동형 분사로 목적어를 취할 수 없으므로 오답이다.

어휘 | offer 제공하다   generous 관대한   tax break 세금 감면   incentive 장려[우대]책   attract 끌다, 유인하다

13 (C)

번역 | 차량 손상에 대한 보험 청구를 하는 것은 고객에게 불만스러운 경험이 될 수 있습니다.

해설 | 빈칸 뒤에 있는 명사 experience를 수식하는 자리이므로 형용사 역할을 할 수 있는 분사가 빈칸에 들어가야 한다. 문맥상 '불만을 느끼게 하는 경험'이라는 의미가 되어야 하며, experience가 감정을 유발하는 것이므로 현재분사인 (C) frustrating이 정답이 된다.

어휘 | file 제출하다 insurance claim 보험 청구 damage 손상 frustrating 좌절감[불만]을 느끼게 하는

14 (B)

번역 | 지역 공원에서의 안전을 논의하는 중에 주민들은 공원에 보안 카메라를 설치하는 것에 동의했다.

해설 | 주절 앞에 있는 콤마 앞은 부사 자리이고, 빈칸부터 콤마 앞까지인 discussing safety in the community park는 분사구문이다. 분사구문은 부사절을 축약해 놓은 것으로 정확한 의미 전달을 위해 접속사는 생략하지 않고 놔두기도 한다. '안전을 논의하는 중에'라는 의미가 자연스러운 접속사 (B) While이 정답이다. (A) Despite와 (D) In은 전치사이므로 '동사원형+ing'를 취할 수는 있으나 문맥에 맞지 않고, 등위접속사 (C) So는 문장 맨 앞에 올 수 없으므로 오답이다.

어휘 | resident 주민 install 설치하다

15 (C)

번역 | 계약에 명확히 명시되지 않으면, 공급자의 책임과 관련하여 약간의 혼란이 있을 수 있습니다.

해설 | 분사는 동사의 성질을 지니므로 부사의 수식을 받는다. 빈칸은 과거분사 stated를 수식하는 자리이므로 정답은 부사인 (C) clearly이다.

어휘 | state 진술하다 agreement 계약, 협정 confusion 혼란 regarding ~에 관하여 supplier 공급자

16 (D)

번역 | 1주일 동안 비어 있으면, 호텔 객실은 청결함을 유지하기 위해 다시 청소됩니다.

해설 | 부사절 접속사 If 이하 콤마 앞까지는 분사구문이다. leave는 5형식 동사로 'leave + 목적어 + 목적격 보어'로 쓰이는데, 목적어 the hotel room이 주어로 와서 수동태 구조가 되었고 be동사와 같이 생략되었으므로 빈칸에는 목적격 보어가 와야 한다. 따라서 정답은 '비어 있는 채로 남겨져 있다면'이라는 의미를 이루는 형용사 (D) vacant이다. 명사인 (A) vacancy는 주어인 the hotel room과 동격이 아니므로 오답이다.

어휘 | vacant 비어 있는 maintain 유지하다 vacancy 공석

17 (A)

번역 | 각 당사자를 대표하는 협상가들은 그들의 계약 변경 제안을 논의하기 위해 다시 만날 필요가 있다.

해설 | 문장의 본동사 need가 있고 빈칸 뒤에 each party라는 목적어가 있으므로 빈칸은 The negotiators를 수식하는 현재분사 자리이다. 따라서 '~을 대표하는'이라는 뜻인 (A) representing이 정답이다.

어휘 | negotiator 협상자 represent 대표하다 party (계약, 소송 등의) 당사자 proposed 제안된

18 (A)

번역 | 제약회사에서 근무하기를 희망했기 때문에 그 연구원은 출판 목록과 함께 이력서를 제출했다.

해설 | 빈칸은 부사적 용법의 준동사 자리이며 hope 동사는 to부정사를 목적어로 취하기 때문에 능동형인 현재분사 (A) Hoping과 to부정사 (C) To hope가 가능하다. '근무를 희망하기 때문에' 또는 '근무를 희망하면서'로 해석되는 분사구문이 자연스러우므로 (A) Hoping이 정답이다. (C) To hope은 '근무를 희망하기 위해'라는 뜻으로 문맥상 어색하다.

어휘 | pharmaceutical 제약의 publication 출판물

19 (B)

번역 | 오염 수준에 대한 최근의 보고서는 공무원들에게 더 엄격한 환경 규제의 필요성을 알려 주었다.

해설 | 문장에서 동사 kept는 목적격 보어가 필요한 5형식 동사로, 빈칸에는 명사 또는 형용사가 들어가야 한다. 과거분사인 (B) informed와 현재분사인 (C) informing이 형용사 역할을 할 수 있는데, 문장의 목적어인 명사 officials는 알려지는 대상이므로 수동의 의미를 갖는 과거분사인 (B) informed가 정답이다. 참고로 'keep + 목적어 + informed of(~에게 …에 대해 알려주다)'도 자주 쓰이는 표현이므로 외워 두도록 한다.

어휘 | official 공무원[관리] regulation 규제

20 (A)

번역 | 적어도 20년 이상 지속될 것이 개인적으로 보장되기 때문에, 조 개리슨에 의해 설치된 지붕들은 품질이 좋다.

해설 | 주절 앞에 있는 콤마 앞의 분사는 분사구문이며, 분사는 부사의 수식을 받는다. 따라서 빈칸은 과거분사 guaranteed를 수식하는 부사 자리이므로 (A) Personally가 정답이다.

어휘 | guarantee 보장하다 last 지속되다 install 설치하다

UNIT 8 부사절 접속사 & 등위·상관접속사

전략포인트 1 본책 p.180

1 (A) **2** (B) **3** (C)

1 (A)

번역 | 일단 이사회 안건이 확정되면 메모가 발송될 예정이다.

해설 | 빈칸 뒤에 주어와 동사를 갖춘 완전한 절이 왔으므로 접속사가 들어가야 한다. 따라서 '일단 ~하면'이라는 의미의 부사절 접속사 (A) once가 정답이다.

어휘 | agenda 안건 board meeting 이사회 finalize 마무리짓다

2 (B)

번역 | 리히터 부사장의 일정이 변경되면 전략 세션을 차후로 옮길 예정이다.

해설 | 빈칸은 완전한 두 절을 연결하는 자리이므로 접속사가 들어가야 한다. 문맥상 '일정이 변경되면'이라는 내용이 되어야 하므로 조건을 나타내는 접속사 (B) If가 정답이다. 등위접속사 (D) So는 절과 절 사이에서 내용을 연결하는 접속사이므로 문장 맨 앞에 들어갈 수 없다.

어휘 | vice president 부사장   strategy 전략   session (특정 활동) 시간

3 (C)

번역 | 에반스 카펫 담당자는 모든 측정이 완료되는 즉시 견적 계산을 시작할 것입니다.

해설 | 빈칸 앞뒤로 주어와 동사를 갖춘 완전한 절이 나오므로 빈칸에는 접속사가 들어가야 한다. 따라서 '~하자마자'라는 뜻의 시간의 부사절 접속사인 (C) as soon as가 정답이다. (D) so는 문장과 문장을 연결할 수 있어 문법적으로는 가능하지만 문맥상 시간의 흐름이 맞지 않다. 나머지 보기들은 모두 전치사로 문장과 문장을 연결시키지 못하므로 오답이다.

어휘 | representative 대표, 대리인   calculate 계산하다   estimate 견적   measurement 측정

전략포인트 2   본책 p.180

1 (A)   **2** (A)   **3** (A)

1 (A)

번역 | 일부 회사들은 온라인 상의 인지도를 높여 준다는 이유로 소셜 미디어에서 자사에 "좋아요"를 누르는 고객에게 할인을 제공한다.

해설 | 빈칸 앞뒤로 주어와 동사를 갖춘 절이 왔으므로 빈칸에는 접속사가 필요하다. 따라서 '~때문에'라는 뜻의 접속사인 (A) because가 정답이다. (B) instead(대신에)와 (D) moreover(게다가)는 부사, (C) despite(~에도 불구하고)는 전치사이므로 답이 될 수 없다.

어휘 | enhance 높이다   presence 존재감

2 (A)

번역 | 고 씨는 국가훈장을 받았음에도 불구하고 자신의 공헌을 사소한 것으로 여긴다.

해설 | 빈칸 뒤에 주어와 동사를 갖춘 완전한 두 절이 왔으므로 빈칸에는 접속사가 필요하다. 따라서 부사절 접속사인 (A) Even though가 정답이다. (B) Given that은 '~을 감안하면'이라는 뜻의 부사절 접속사지만 문맥상 부자연스럽다.

어휘 | Medal of Merit 공로훈장   contribution 공헌[기여]   trivial 사소한

3 (A)

번역 | 우달 씨가 3년 간의 고객 서비스 경험을 가지고 있다는 것을 감안하면, 제안된 시간당 요금은 합리적이다.

해설 | 빈칸 뒤에 주어와 동사를 갖춘 완전한 두 절이 나오므로 빈칸에는 접속사가 들어가야 한다. 문맥상 '우달 씨가 3년 간의 고객 서비스 경험을 가지고 있다는 것을 감안하면'이라는 내용이 되어야 자연스러우므로 빈칸 뒤의 that과 함께 쓰여 '~을 감안하면, 고려하면'이라는 의미의 접속사인 (A) Considering이 정답이다.

어휘 | considering that ~을 감안하면   hourly rate 시간당 요금   reasonable 합리적인   rather than ~보다는

전략포인트 3   본책 p.181

1 (C)   **2** (B)   **3** (B)

1 (C)

번역 | 각 향수의 샘플은 고객이 구매하기 전에 써 볼 수 있도록 이용 가능합니다.

해설 | 빈칸 앞뒤로 주어와 동사를 갖춘 완전한 문장이 나오므로 빈칸에는 절을 이끄는 접속사가 와야 한다. 문맥상 '고객이 구매하기 전에 써 볼 수 있도록'이라고 하는 것이 자연스러우므로 정답은 (C) in order that이다. 부사인 (B) anyhow와 구전치사인 (D) across from은 절을 연결할 수 없으므로 오답이다.

어휘 | available 이용 가능한   in order that ~하도록   whereas 반면에   across from 바로 맞은편에

2 (B)

번역 | 귀하가 신규 고객이든 재가입 구매자이든지에 상관없이, 블라우벨트 은행은 귀하에게 담보 대출을 해 줄 수 있습니다.

해설 | 빈칸 뒤로 주어와 동사를 갖춘 완전한 두 절이 나오므로 빈칸에는 접속사가 들어가야 한다. 뒤에 오는 or가 문제 해결의 단서로, 'A이든 B이든지에 상관없이'라는 양보의 뜻을 나타내는 접속사 (B) Whether가 정답이다. (A) As well as는 상관접속사, (C) According to와 (D) Throughout는 전치사이므로 오답이다.

어휘 | mortgage 담보 대출, 융자

3 (B)

번역 | 이번 주 스페셜에서는 어떤 것이든 고객들이 원하는 세 가지 메뉴를 시식할 기회를 드립니다.

해설 | 빈칸 앞에 완전한 절이 나오고, 빈칸 뒤에 주어와 동사가 있으므로 빈칸에는 접속사가 들어가야 한다. 따라서 부사절을 이끄는 복합관계대명사 (B) whichever가 정답이다. 나머지 보기는 모두 접속사 역할을 하지 못하므로 오답이다.

어휘 | opportunity 기회   sample 시식하다   prefer 선호하다

전략포인트 4   본책 p.181

1 (B)   **2** (B)   **3** (A)

1 (B)

번역 | 직원들은 저자에 의해 제출된 원고를 편집할 때 지침들을 주의 깊게 따르도록 당부를 받는다.

해설 | '원고를 편집할 때 지침을 따르다'라는 의미가 적합하므로 when they are editing을 축약한 when editing이 되어야 한다. 따라서 정답은 '~할 때'라는 의미의 접속사 (B) when이다. 전치사 뒤에 동명사가 올 수 있어 자칫 (D) onto을 고르기 쉽지만 문맥상 맞지 않는다. 부사절 접속사 뒤에도 현재분사인 '동사원형＋ing'가 올 수 있다는 점을 유의하자.

어휘 | edit 편집하다 manuscript 원고 author 작가

2 (B)

번역 | 일찍 발송되었지만 구입하신 제품이 아직 통관 중입니다.

해설 | 부사절 접속사 Although 이후에는 '주어+동사'의 절이 와야 하지만, 그렇지 않은 경우 '주어+동사'가 생략되고 분사가 바로 오는 분사구문을 만들 수 있다. 빈칸 뒤에 전치사 out이 있으므로 과거분사 (B) sent가 정답이다.

어휘 | purchase 구입한 물건 customs 세관 go through (절차를) 거치다

3 (A)

번역 | 박물관에 있는 동안에는 음식물 및 음료가 허용되지 않기 때문에 쓰레기통이 밖에 놓여 있습니다.

해설 | 빈칸 앞에 완전한 문장이 오고 빈칸 뒤에 수식어구인 전치사구가 나오므로 주어와 be동사가 생략된 분사구문의 형태이다. '박물관에 있는 동안'이라는 의미가 적합하므로 while you are in the museum에서 you are를 생략한 while in the museum이 되어야 한다. 따라서 정답은 '~동안'이라는 의미의 접속사 (A) while이다. 부사절 접속사 while과 when은 장소의 전치사구와 자주 쓰이므로 함께 익혀 두는 것이 좋다.

어휘 | receptacle 그릇, 용기 position 두다, 배치하다 beverage 음료 permit 허용하다

1 (C) 2 (C) 3 (B)

1 (C)

번역 | 근무 시간 기록표를 살펴보고 변경하려면 회사 웹사이트의 직원 포털 섹션으로 로그인하세요.

해설 | 빈칸 앞에 등위접속사 and가 있으므로, 빈칸에는 and 앞의 to부정사구와 대등하게 연결될 수 있는 to부정사구나 to가 생략된 원형부정사가 들어가야 한다. 따라서 정답은 (C) make이다.

어휘 | view (세심히) 보다 time sheet 근무 시간 기록표

2 (C)

번역 | 이무라 씨는 사무실에 없지만 구나디 씨는 고객을 만날 수 있다.

해설 | 빈칸 앞뒤의 두 절을 연결할 수 있는 접속사가 필요하다. 문맥상 '이무라 씨는 사무실에 없지만 구다니 씨는 만날 수 있다'는 내용이 되어야 하므로, 상반되는 의미를 연결할 때 쓰이는 (C) but이 정답이다.

어휘 | available 시간이 있는, 이용 가능한

3 (B)

번역 | 음악제의 좌석은 선착순이라서 참석자들은 일찍 도착해야 한다.

해설 | 문맥상 '좌석이 선착순이라서 일찍 도착해야 한다'라는 내용이 되어야 하므로 '따라서'라는 의미의 등위접속사 (B) so가 정답이다. 참고로 (C) yet도 but과 같은 의미의 등위접속사로 쓸 수 있지만 문맥이 맞지 않아 오답이다.

어휘 | first-come, first-served basis 선착순

1 (B) 2 (A) 3 (C)

1 (B)

번역 | 기내 휴대용 가방은 머리 위 선반이나 앞 좌석 아래에 보관해야 합니다.

해설 | either가 문제 해결의 단서로, 문맥상 '머리 위 선반이나 앞 좌석 아래 중 하나'라는 의미가 되어야 한다. 따라서 either와 함께 'either A or B(A나 B 둘 중 하나)'를 이루는 (B) or가 정답이 된다.

어휘 | carry-on 기내 휴대용의 stow 집어넣다 overhead bin (기내의) 머리 위 선반

2 (A)

번역 | 노트북 유지관리 서비스에는 바이러스 활동에 대한 장비 점검과 내부 케이스의 먼지 제거가 모두 포함됩니다.

해설 | and가 문제 해결의 단서로, 문맥상 '바이러스 활동에 대한 장비 점검과 먼지 제거를 둘 다 포함한다'라는 의미가 되어야 한다. 따라서 and와 함께 'both A and B, 'A와 B 둘 다'라는 의미를 이루는 (A) both가 정답이다.

어휘 | laptop 휴대용 컴퓨터 maintenance 유지, 보수 include 포함하다 device 기기, 장치 remove 제거하다 dust 먼지

3 (C)

번역 | 시작 시간이 늦어서 수채화 수업도 유화 수업도 정원이 다 차지 않았다.

해설 | 빈칸 앞의 neither가 문제 해결의 단서로, neither와 함께 'neither A nor B'의 형태로 'A도 아니고 B도 아닌'이라는 의미를 나타내는 (C) nor가 정답이다.

어휘 | due to ~ 때문에 watercolor 수채화 oil painting 유화 at capacity 정원이 꽉 찬

ETS 고득점 실전 문제

1 (B) 2 (D) 3 (A) 4 (C) 5 (C) 6 (A)
7 (B) 8 (D) 9 (A) 10 (C) 11 (D) 12 (C)
13 (D) 14 (C) 15 (D) 16 (B) 17 (B) 18 (C)
19 (D) 20 (A)

1 (B)

번역 | 에너지 효율이 좋은 에어컨이 새로 설치되어서 현장의 전기 사용이 상당히 줄었다.

해설 | 빈칸 뒤에 주어와 동사가 나오므로 빈칸에는 절을 이끄는 접속사가 와야 한다. 문맥상 '에너지 효율이 좋은 에어컨이 새로 설치되어서'라고 하는 것이 자연스러우므로 '~이므로, ~이기 때문에'라는 뜻의 부사절 접속사 (B) Now that이 정답이다.

어휘 | energy-efficient 에너지 효율이 좋은   install 설치하다
electricity 전기   significantly 상당히

2 (D)

번역 | 해리시 데이럴의 추리 소설이 우수 도서 상을 수상한 뒤, 그는 빠르게 속편을 썼다.

해설 | 빈칸은 쉼표 앞으로 주어와 동사를 갖춘 완전한 절을 연결하는 자리이므로 접속사가 들어가야 한다. 따라서 '~한 뒤'라는 시간의 의미를 나타내는 부사절 접속사인 (D) After가 정답이다. 참고로 (A) However도 '얼마나 ~하든지에 상관없이'라는 뜻의 부사절 접속사지만 문맥상 어색하다. (B) Furthermore와 (C) Naturally는 모두 부사이므로 문장을 연결할 수 없다.

어휘 | exceptional 특출한   sequel (영화 · 책 등의) 속편

3 (A)

번역 | 스트라우드 예배당은 이 마을에서 가장 오래되고 관광객들이 방문할 수 있는 가장 인기 있는 건축물이다.

해설 | 빈칸 앞의 최상급 oldest와 등위접속사 and가 문제 해결의 단서다. 등위접속사 and는 같은 품사를 연결하므로, 보기 중 최상급인 (A) most가 정답이 된다.

어휘 | structure 구조(물), 건축물

4 (C)

번역 | 직원들은 상관에게 미리 알리기만 하면 오후 4시 세미나에 참석할 수 있다.

해설 | 빈칸 뒤에 주어와 동사를 갖춘 절이 왔으므로 빈칸에는 접속사가 필요하다. 문맥상 '상관에게 미리 알리기만 하면'이라는 내용이 되어야 연결이 자연스러우므로 '~하기만 하면'이라는 뜻의 접속사인 (C) as long as가 정답이다. (B) at least는 부사구이므로 오답이고 (A) in case는 '~할 경우에 대비해서', (D) except that은 '~이라는 것 외에는'이라는 뜻으로 문맥상 적절하지 않다.

어휘 | notify 알리다   supervisor 감독관   in advance 미리

5 (C)

번역 | 자원봉사자들은 국립공원 방문객들이 쉽게 알아볼 수 있도록 신분증을 착용해야 한다.

해설 | 빈칸 뒤에 주어 visitors ~와 동사 can easily identify가 나오므로, 빈칸에는 절을 이끄는 접속사가 와야 한다. 따라서 '~할 수 있도록'이라는 목적을 나타내는 접속사인 (C) so that이 정답이다. 참고로, 조동사 can/may/could/would가 so that 뒤에 자주 쓰인다는 것을 알아 두면 문제 해결의 단서로 이용할 수 있다.

어휘 | volunteer 자원봉사자   ID badge 신분증   identify 식별하다

6 (A)

번역 | 일부 참가자들의 웹사이트 접속이 끊겼음에도 불구하고 온라인 교육은 계속되었다.

해설 | 빈칸 뒤에 주어와 동사를 갖춘 완전한 절이 왔으므로 빈칸에는 접속사가 들어가야 한다. 따라서 '~에도 불구하고'의 뜻인 부사절 접속사 (A) even though가 정답이다.

어휘 | training session 교육 (과정)   participant 참가자
connection 연결, 접속

7 (B)

번역 | 극장 객석에 있는 동안에는 다른 사람에게 방해가 되지 않도록 전화기를 꺼둡니다.

해설 | 부사절의 주어와 be동사가 생략된 분사구문의 형태로 빈칸 뒤에 주어와 동사를 갖춘 완전한 절이 나오므로 빈칸에는 접속사가 들어가야 한다. 문맥상 '극장 객석에 있는 동안에'라는 의미가 되어야 하므로 '~하는 동안'이라는 시간을 나타내는 부사절 접속사인 (B) While이 정답이다.

어휘 | auditorium 관람석, 객석   turn off 끄다   disturb 방해하다

8 (D)

번역 | 전시회 입장권은 안내 데스크에서 구입할 수 있지만, 박물관 회원들은 온라인으로도 주문할 수 있다.

해설 | 빈칸은 콤마 양쪽에 있는 두 개의 완전한 절을 연결하는 접속사 자리이다. 문맥상 '안내 데스크에서 살 수 있지만 온라인으로도 살 수 있다'는 내용이 되어야 하므로, 상반되는 내용을 연결할 때 쓰이는 등위접속사 (D) but이 정답이다. 부사절 접속사인 (C) unless도 두 개의 완전한 문장을 앞뒤로 연결할 수 있지만 문맥상 맞지 않아 오답이다.

어휘 | exhibit 전시회   purchase 구입하다   order 주문하다

9 (A)

번역 | 단열재가 올바르게 설치된다면, 건물의 난방비는 약 20% 절감될 것입니다.

해설 | 빈칸 뒤에 주어와 동사를 갖춘 절이 왔으므로, 빈칸에는 접속사가 들어가야 한다. 따라서 '~ 이라면'이라는 조건을 나타내는 (A) Provided that이 정답이다.

어휘 | provided that ~이라면   insulation 단열   install 설치하다   approximately 대략

10 (C)

번역 | 헨더슨 씨는 예산 심사 기한을 연장하는 대신, 그녀의 부서에 초과 근무를 하라고 촉구했다.

해설 | 빈칸 앞에 완전한 절이 오고 빈칸 뒤에 동사원형 extend가 나오므로, 주어를 생략하고 같은 품사나 구조끼리 대등하게 연결할 수 있는 등위접속사나 상관접속사가 빈칸에 올 수 있다. 따라서 '~하기보다/~대신'이라는 뜻의 상관접속사 (C) rather than이 정답이다. 이때 extend는 주절의 to work와 병렬 구조를 이루며, to부정사끼리 병렬 구조를 이룰 때는 주로 to를 생략한다. 참고로 (D) in regard to는 '~에 관한'이라는 전치사이므로 뒤에 동사원형이 올 수 없다.

어휘 | urge A to부정사 A가 ~하도록 촉구하다   extend 연장하다   budget 예산

11 (D)

번역 | 대표단이 모국어로 회담을 들을 수 있게 하기 위해서 정상회담에 통역사가 고용되었다.

해설 | 빈칸 앞뒤에 완전한 절이 나오므로 빈칸에는 접속사가 와야 한다. 빈칸 뒤 조동사 can을 단서로 '~하기 위해서'의 'so that+주어+(can)'을 떠올릴 수 있고 '대표단이 모국어로 회담을 들을 수 있게 하기 위해서'의 문맥이 자연스러우므로 (D) so가 정답이다. '~하기 위해서'인 부사절 접속사 so that은 that을 생략할 수 있기 때문에 'so+주어+can'의 구문도 가능하다.

어휘 | interpreter 통역사 summit 정상 회담 delegate 대표, 사절 talks 회담

12 (C)

번역 | 가장 예상치 못한 언제든지 문제가 발생할 수 있기 때문에 여행 보험에 가입하는 것은 좋은 생각이다.

해설 | 빈칸 앞 arise는 자동사이므로 빈칸 뒤에 완전한 절과 연결되는 부사절 접속사가 필요하다. 문맥상 '가장 예상치 못한 언제라도'라는 의미가 되어야 자연스러우므로 복합관계부사인 (C) whenever가 정답이다. (A) whichever 또한 부사절을 이끄는 복합관계대명사이지만 뒤에 주어나 목적어를 필요로 하는 불완전한 문장이 오기 때문에 답이 될 수 없다.

어휘 | travel insurance 여행 보험 arise 일어나다, 발생하다

13 (D)

번역 | 투숙객이 온라인으로 방을 예약하든 전화로 예약하든지 상관없이 15분 이내에 이메일 확인을 받게 됩니다.

해설 | 빈칸 뒤로 주어와 동사를 갖춘 완전한 두 절이 나오므로 빈칸에는 접속사가 들어가야 한다. 뒤에 오는 or가 문제 해결의 단서로, 'A이든 B이든지에 상관없이'라는 양보의 뜻을 이루는 접속사 (D) Whether가 정답이다. (A) Although는 문맥상 맞지 않고 (B) Thus는 부사이므로 오답이다. (C) Either는 or와 함께 상관접속사로 사용되기도 하지만 either 자체가 접속사 역할을 할 수는 없다.

어휘 | reserve 예약하다 confirmation 확인

14 (C)

번역 | 6피트를 초과하는 사다리는 다른 직원이 아래쪽을 잡고 있을 때만 사용해야 한다.

해설 | 빈칸 앞뒤로 주어와 동사를 갖춘 완전한 절이 나오므로 빈칸에는 접속사가 들어가야 한다. 따라서 '~할 때'라는 시간의 의미를 나타내는 부사절 접속사인 (C) when이 정답이다. (A) should와 (B) than은 절을 연결할 수 없고, 접속사 (D) that은 명사절을 이끌 때는 앞에 불완전한 문장, 형용사절을 이끌 땐 선행사가 있어야 하므로 오답이다.

어휘 | exceed 넘다, 초과하다 at the bottom 아래쪽에

15 (D)

번역 | 금요일에는 퇴근 시간 전에 임무를 마친 직원들은 일찍 퇴근할 수 있다.

해설 | 관계사절에 동사와 목적어가 있으므로 빈칸에는 명사구 the closing time과 함께 수식어구를 이루는 전치사가 와야 한다. 문맥상 '퇴근 시간 전에 임무를 마친 직원들'이라는 의미가 되어야 하므로 '~전에'라는 뜻의 전치사인 (D) before가 정답이다. 이때 전치사 by가 before를 대신할 수 있다는 점도 기억하자. 참고로 (C) until도 '퇴근 시간까지 임무를 마친 직원들'이라고 해석이 되는 듯하여도 완료를 나타내는 동사 'finish'와 연결될 수 없다. until은 'valid until(~까지

유효한)'이나 'wait until(~까지 기다리다)'와 같이 계속적인 상태나 진행을 나타내는 표현들과 함께 쓰인다.

어휘 | assignment 임무 be permitted to ~하도록 허용되다

16 (B)

번역 | 청소용품의 포장이 이전에는 버려져야 했지만, 이제는 완전히 재활용될 수 있다.

해설 | 빈칸 뒤에 주어와 동사를 갖춘 완전한 절이 두 개가 나오므로 빈칸에는 접속사가 들어가야 한다. 'previously'와 'now'를 대조하는 내용이므로 '~인 반면에'를 의미하는 (B) Whereas가 정답이다.

어휘 | previously 이전에 discard 버리다, 폐기하다 fully 완전히

17 (B)

번역 | 위원회에 의해 제시된 창의적이지만 실용적인 제안은 회사가 돈을 절약하는 것을 도울 것이다.

해설 | 빈칸 뒤의 등위접속사 yet과 형용사 practical이 문제 해결의 단서로, 등위접속사는 같은 품사를 연결하므로 보기 중에서 형용사인 (B) creative가 정답이다.

어휘 | creative 창의적인 practical 실용적인 suggestion 제안 put forth 제시하다 committee 위원회

18 (C)

번역 | 소프트웨어에 여전히 결함이 있는 것을 감안하면, 예정된 날짜에 시장에 출시되지는 않을 것이다.

해설 | 빈칸 뒤로 주어와 동사를 갖춘 완전한 절 두 개가 나오므로 빈칸에는 접속사가 들어가야 한다. '소프트웨어에 여전히 결함이 있는 것을 감안하면'이라는 내용이 되어야 자연스러우므로 '~을 감안하면/고려하면'이라는 뜻의 접속사인 (C) Given that이 정답이다. (A) Despite는 전치사, (D) Moreover 부사이며 (B) As if는 가정법 시제와 쓰이는 부사절 접속사이므로 오답이다.

어휘 | given that ~을 고려하면, 감안하면 defect 결함

19 (D)

번역 | 일반 페인트에 완전히 섞일 때 그 가루는 도장의 내구성을 3배까지 높일 것이다.

해설 | '일반 페인트에 완전히 섞일 때'라는 의미가 적합하므로 When the powder is thoroughly mixed into regular paint를 분사구문으로 축약한 When thoroughly mixed가 되어야 한다. 따라서 정답은 '~할 때'라는 의미인 접속사 (D) When이다. 부사절 접속사 뒤에 '주어+동사'를 갖춘 절이 오지 않는다면, 분사구문일 확률이 높다. 목적어의 유무에 따라 현재분사, 과거분사를 구분하는 유형이나 분사를 수식하는 부사를 묻는 유형들도 자주 출제되므로 '부사절 접속사+부사+분사'의 구조에 유의한다.

어휘 | thoroughly 완전히 coat 칠, 도장 up to ~까지 durable 내구성 있는

20 (A)

번역 | 호텔의 메인 로비는 눈에 거슬리지만 다른 로비보다 더 넓다.

해설 | 부사절에서 '눈에 거슬린다'라고 했지만, 주절에서 '로비는 다른 로비보다 더 넓다'라고 했으므로, '비록 ~이긴 하지만'이라는 양보의 의미를 나타내는 접속사 (A) though가 정답이다. 빈칸은 주절에 삽입된 형태로 부사절에서 주어와 be동사가 생략된 분사구문의 형태이다.

어휘 | unpleasant 불쾌한, 불편한 spacious 널찍한, 넓은

본책 p.186

UNIT 9 관계사

전략포인트 1
본책 p.186

1 (D) **2** (B) **3** (C)

1 (D)

번역 | 25년간 그린포드 테크놀로지스에서 근무하다 은퇴하는 저우 씨를 위한 송별회가 금요일에 열릴 예정이다.

해설 | 빈칸 이하는 선행사 Ms. Zhou를 수식하는 관계사절로, 빈칸 뒤에 동사가 나오므로 주격 관계대명사가 필요하다. 관계사 that은 콤마 뒤에는 쓰지 않으므로 (D) who가 정답이다.

어휘 | farewell party 송별회 retire 은퇴하다

2 (B)

번역 | 렌웨이 극장은 이전에는 계단으로만 이용 가능했던 정문에 경사로를 설치했다.

해설 | 빈칸을 포함한 절이 its front entrance를 수식하고 있으므로 빈칸에는 관계대명사가 들어가야 한다. 따라서 (B) which가 정답이다. (C) and는 문장의 주어 The Renway Theater와 동사 was를 연결시키므로 문맥상 적절하지 않고 (A) since와 (D) unless는 부사절 접속사로, 앞뒤 모두 완전한 문장이 와야 하므로 오답이다.

어휘 | install 설치하다 ramp 경사로 previously 이전에 accessible 접근[이용] 가능한

3 (C)

번역 | 다양한 기능이 전문 화가처럼 그림을 그릴 수 있게 도와주는 우리의 그림 도구를 사용해 보세요.

해설 | 빈칸 이하는 선행사 our drawing tool을 수식하는 관계사절로, 빈칸 뒤에 명사구 various functions가 나오므로 명사구를 수식할 수 있는 소유격 관계대명사 (C) whose가 정답이다.

어휘 | tool 도구 function 기능 create 창조[창작]하다

전략포인트 2
본책 p.186

1 (B) **2** (D) **3** (C)

1 (B)

번역 | 행사장에 늦게 도착하는 회의 참석자들은 강당 뒤쪽에 앉으셔야 합니다.

해설 | 문맥상 '행사장에 늦게 도착하는 회의 참석자들'이라는 의미로 빈칸 앞에 나오는 명사 Those convention attendees를 수식하는 것이 적절하므로, who are가 생략되어 현재분사만 남은 (B) arriving이 정답이다.

어휘 | convention 회의 venue (경기, 회담 등의) 장소 auditorium 강당

2 (D)

번역 | 보안 문제에 대해 공지를 받은 직원들은 정비관리 전에 중요한 자료들을 백업해야 한다.

해설 | 주어는 Employees이고 should back up이 본동사이므로 빈칸은 앞의 명사 Employees를 후치 수식하는 분사 자리이다. 빈칸 뒤에 목적어 없이 바로 of가 있는 점을 보아 수동의 과거분사가 필요하므로 (D) informed가 정답이다. 참고로 후치 수식하는 분사는 주로 주격 관계대명사와 be동사가 생략된 구조이다.

어휘 | informed of ~에 대해 공지 받은 security 보안 maintenance 정비, 유지, 관리

3 (C)

번역 | 우리가 제공하는 맛있는 음식들 때문에 고객들은 종종 소셜 미디어를 통해 식당을 칭찬합니다.

해설 | 빈칸 이하는 the delicious dishes를 수식하는 관계사절로 빈칸 앞에는 목적격 관계대명사인 that이 생략되어 있다. 빈칸 뒤에 동사 offer가 왔으므로, 빈칸은 주어 자리임을 알 수 있다. 따라서 주격 인칭대명사인 (C) we가 정답이다.

어휘 | frequently 종종 praise 칭찬하다

전략포인트 3
본책 p.187

1 (C) **2** (A) **3** (C)

1 (C)

번역 | 보조금이 수여된 연구자는 재생에너지에 대한 그의 연구를 진행하고 있다.

해설 | 빈칸에는 전치사 to와 함께 쓰일 수 있는 관계대명사가 들어가야 한다. 선행사가 The researcher이며 전치사 to의 목적어가 들어갈 자리이므로, 목적격 관계대명사인 (C) whom이 정답이다. 참고로 전치사의 목적어으로 명사절 접속사 what도 쓰일 수 있는데, '전치사+what' 뒤에는 불완전한 문장이 오기 때문에 (A) what은 오답이다. '전치사+관계대명사' 뒤에는 완전한 문장이 온다.

어휘 | grant 보조금, 장학기금 renewable energy 재생에너지

2 (A)

번역 | 이 투어는 안에서 어린이들이 놀이를 즐길 수 있는 마술의 집 방문을 포함합니다.

해설 | 빈칸에는 전치사 inside와 함께 쓰일 수 있는 관계대명사가 들어가야 한다. 선행사가 a magic house이며 전치사 inside의 목적어가 들어갈 자리이므로, 목적격 관계대명사인 (A) which가 정답이다.

어휘 | amusements 놀이, 즐길 거리

3 (C)

번역 | 신입 사원들이 회사에 대해 배우는 오리엔테이션 세션은 약 4시간 동안 진행될 것입니다.

해설 | 관계대명사 앞에 쓰일 전치사를 선택하는 문제로, 선행사가 The orientation session이므로 '오리엔테이션 세션 중에'라는 의미를 이루는 (C) during이 정답이다.

어휘 | last 계속[지속]하다 approximately 대략

전략포인트 **4**
본책 p.187

1 (D) **2** (A) **3** (D)

1 (D)

번역 | 맷슨 호텔은 북서부 지역에 10개 지점을 운영하고 있으며, 그 중 3개는 해변에 위치해 있다.

해설 | 문장에서 operates와 are located가 동사이며, 동사가 두 개인 문장에서 접속사가 없으므로 접속사 역할을 할 수 있는 관계대명사가 들어가야 한다. 빈칸은 전치사 of 뒤 목적격 자리이며, 선행사가 ten sites이므로 정답은 목적격 관계대명사 (D) which이다.

어휘 | operate 운영하다 site 위치, 장소 region 지역 located 위치한

2 (A)

번역 | 올리비에 디자인의 직원은 8명의 건축가를 포함하며, 그들 중 대부분은 명문 대학을 졸업했다.

해설 | 문장에서 includes와 graduated가 동사이며, 동사가 두 개인 문장에서 접속사가 없으므로 접속사 역할을 할 수 있는 것을 선택해야 한다. 따라서 eight architects를 선행사로 하여 관계대명사로 연결되는 (A) most of whom이 정답이다. (B) some of whose는 뒤에 명사가 와야 하므로 오답이다.

어휘 | include 포함하다 architect 건축가 prestigious 명망 있는, 일류의

3 (D)

번역 | 그 수리점은 오래된 시계를 취급하는 것으로 잘 알려져 있는데, 그 시계들 중 일부는 단종되었다.

해설 | 문장에서 is와 have been discontinued가 동사이며, 동사가 두 개인 문장에서 접속사가 없으므로 접속사 역할을 할 수 있는 것을 선택해야 한다. 따라서 old watches를 선행사로 취하고 some of와 연결될 수 있는 접속사 (D) which가 정답이다.

어휘 | repair 수선 known for ~으로 유명한 discontinue (생산을) 중단하다

전략포인트 **5**
본책 p.188

1 (A) **2** (A) **3** (D)

1 (A)

번역 | 여름은 그 지역의 동식물상의 풍경이 관광객들을 끄는 계절이다.

해설 | 빈칸 이하는 시간 선행사인 the season을 부연 설명하는 관계사절로, 빈칸 뒤에 완전한 절이 왔으므로 관계부사 (A) when이 정답이다.

어휘 | flora and fauna 동식물상

2 (A)

번역 | 운전자들은 면허증을 시청에서 직접 갱신해야 하며, 거기서 직원이 사진을 새로 찍어 줄 것이다.

해설 | 빈칸 이하는 장소 선행사인 City Hall을 부연 설명하는 관계사절로, 빈칸 뒤에 완전한 절이 왔으므로 관계부사 (A) where가 정답이다.

어휘 | renew 갱신하다 license 면허증 in person 직접

3 (D)

번역 | 제안서 승인을 받으시려면 본인의 프로젝트가 왜 필요한지에 대한 정당한 이유를 제시하세요.

해설 | 빈칸 앞에는 이유의 의미를 지닌 justification이 있고 빈칸 뒤에 완전한 문장 구조가 있으므로 관계부사 (D) why가 정답이다.

어휘 | proposal 제안서 justification 정당한 이유

전략포인트 **6**
본책 p.188

1 (C) **2** (D) **3** (B)

1 (C)

번역 | 올해 무역 박람회는 댈러스에서 열릴 것이며, 거기에서 참석자들은 풍부한 숙박 선택의 기회를 찾을 수 있다.

해설 | 빈칸 이하는 장소 선행사인 Dallas를 부연 설명하는 관계사절로, 빈칸 뒤에 완전한 절이 왔으므로 관계부사 (C) where가 정답이다.

어휘 | take place 개최되다 plenty of 많은, 풍부한 option 선택(권) accommodation 숙박

2 (D)

번역 | 노란색 태그가 있는 상품은 30% 추가 할인됩니다.

해설 | 빈칸 이하는 선행사 The items를 수식하는 관계사절로, 빈칸 뒤에 동사가 나오므로, 주격 관계대명사 (D) that이 정답이다. (B) how는 관계부사로 완전한 절을 이끌므로 오답이다.

어휘 | tag 꼬리표, 태그 additional 추가의

3 (B)

번역 | 관광객들은 통근자들이 출근하는 아침 시간 동안에는 대중교통을 피해야 한다.

해설 | 빈칸 이하는 시간 선행사인 morning hours를 부연 설명하는 관계사절로, 빈칸 뒤에 완전한 절이 왔으므로 관계부사 (B) when이 정답이다. 참고로 등위접속사 (A) or는 앞뒤로 완전한 절을 취할 수 있지만, 문맥상 맞지 않아 오답이다.

어휘 | urge 촉구하다 avoid 피하다 public transportation 대중교통 commuter 통근자

ETS 고득점 실전 문제

본책 p.190

1 (B) **2** (C) **3** (A) **4** (D) **5** (C) **6** (B)
7 (C) **8** (C) **9** (B) **10** (B) **11** (D) **12** (B)
13 (C) **14** (B) **15** (A) **16** (D) **17** (B) **18** (B)
19 (C) **20** (B)

1 (B)

번역 | 피트 맥키언은 수많은 주민들의 배관 공사를 도운 경험 많은 건축업자이다.

해설 | 빈칸에는 부정관사 an과 형용사 experienced의 수식을 받는 명사가 들어가야 한다. 빈칸은 또한 관계사절의 수식을 받고 있으며 관계대명사 who 앞에는 사람 선행사가 와야 하므로 '건축업자'를 뜻하는 명사 (B) contractor가 정답이다.

어휘 | experienced 경험이 많은 countless 수많은
resident 주민 plumbing 배관 contractor 건축업자

2 (C)

번역 | 약사는 때때로 약물에 수반되는 부작용을 명확하게 설명했다.

해설 | 빈칸은 주격 관계대명사 that절에서 동사 accompany를 앞에서 수식하는 부사 자리이므로 '때때로'라는 의미의 부사 (C) sometimes가 정답이다.

어휘 | pharmacist 약사 side effect 부작용
accompany 동반[수반]하다 medication 약물

3 (A)

번역 | 통화 후 바로 도착한 택시는 승객들을 공항까지 데려다 주었다.

해설 | 빈칸은 which가 이끄는 관계사절에서 부사 promptly의 수식을 받는 동사가 들어갈 자리이다. 전체 문장의 동사가 took인 과거이므로 관계사절에도 과거형 동사가 쓰여야 한다. 따라서 (A) arrived가 정답이다.

어휘 | promptly 즉시, 신속하게 passenger 승객

4 (D)

번역 | 올해 매출 수익에서 아마도 빌텍스튜어를 능가할 수 있는 유일한 회사는 레몬트 패브릭스이다.

해설 | be동사 is의 주어 역할을 하는 동시에 빈칸 앞 The only와 빈칸 뒤 관계사절의 수식을 받아 '빌텍스튜어를 능가할 수 있는 유일한 ~은'이라는 의미를 만들 수 있어야 한다. 따라서 부정대명사 (D) one이 정답이다.

어휘 | conceivably 아마도 surpass 능가하다 revenue 수익

5 (C)

번역 | 그 상에 지명된 기자는 아주 흥미로운 이야깃거리를 조사하는 것으로 유명하다.

해설 | 빈칸에는 전치사와 함께 쓰일 수 있는 관계대명사가 들어가야 한다. 선행사가 The journalist이며 전치사

for의 목적어가 들어갈 자리이므로, 목적격 관계대명사인 (C) whom이 정답이다. (B) that은 전치사 뒤에 쓰일 수 없고, (D) whoever는 선행사를 지닐 수 없으므로 오답이다.

어휘 | name 지명[임명]하다 known for ~으로 유명한
investigate 조사하다 intriguing 아주 흥미로운

6 (B)

번역 | 매니저는 최근 호텔에 추가된 운동시설이 매일 이용 가능하다고 설명했다.

해설 | 빈칸은 주격 관계대명사 which의 선행사 자리로 exercise와 결합하여 복합명사를 이루어야 한다. 주격 관계대명사 뒤의 동사 have been은 복수명사와 수가 일치해야 하므로 (B) facilities가 정답이다.

어휘 | facility 시설 recently 최근에 add 추가하다
available 이용 가능한 facilitate 용이하게 하다

7 (C)

번역 | 시의회에서 일하기를 원하는 사람에게는 글렌빌에 거주가 필수이다.

해설 | 빈칸 이하는 '사람들'을 뜻하는 선행사 those를 수식하는 관계사절이다. 빈칸 뒤에 동사가 나오므로 빈칸에는 주격 관계대명사가 필요하다. 따라서 정답은 (C) who이다. 참고로 'those who'는 '~하는 사람들'이라는 뜻으로 뒤에 복수동사가 따라온다.

어휘 | residency 거주 be required 필수이다 serve 일[봉사]하다 city council 시의회

8 (C)

번역 | ㅣ월드 여행사는 이 분야에 대한 그들의 진정한 관심이 회사의 자산인 여행사 직원을 고용한다.

해설 | 빈칸 이하는 선행사 travel agents를 수식하는 관계사절로, 빈칸 뒤에 명사구(genuine interest in the field)가 나오므로 명사구를 수식할 수 있는 소유격 관계대명사 (C) whose가 정답이다.

어휘 | travel agent 여행사 직원 genuine 진심인 field 분야 asset 자산

9 (B)

번역 | 본 설명서는 브렘리 슈퍼마켓에서 계산원이 의무적으로 받는 교육을 위한 것이다.

해설 | 빈칸은 목적격 관계대명사가 생략된 관계사절에서 동사가 들어갈 자리이다. 주어가 the cashiers로 복수명사이므로 이에 어울리는 복수동사 (B) undergo가 정답이다. 참고로 목적격 관계대명사가 생략된 관계사절은 선행사 뒤 주어와 목적어가 없는 타동사로 이루어져 있다. the cashiers 뒤의 undergo도 타동사이며 뒤에 목적어가 없는 것을 알 수 있다.

어휘 | mandatory 법에 정해진, 의무의 cashier 계산원
undergo 겪다[받다]

10 (B)

번역 | 초콜릿 바가 만들어지는 그 공장은 다양한 아침식사용 시리얼도 생산한다.

해설 | 빈칸부터 made까지는 장소 선행사인 The factory를 수식하는 관계사절로, 빈칸 뒤에 완전한 절이 왔으므로 관계부사 (B) where가 정답이다.

어휘 | candy bar 초콜릿 바 produce 생산하다 a variety of 다양한 cereal 곡물, 시리얼

11 (D)

번역 | 피트니스 강사는 운동선수들이 근육통을 예방할 수 있는 두 가지 방법을 보여주었다.

해설 | 빈칸 이하는 방법을 나타내는 선행사인 two ways를 부연 설명하는 관계사절로, 빈칸 뒤에 완전한 절이 왔으므로 관계부사 how를 대신할 수 있는 '전치사＋관계대명사'가 들어가면 된다. 따라서 (D) in which가 정답이다. 부사절 접속사 (A) in that은 '~이라는 점에서'라는 의미로 문맥에 어울리지 않고, 복합관계부사인 (B) however 또한 '얼마나 ~이든지에 상관없이'로 문맥에 맞지 않다. 관계대명사 (C) what은 선행사 없이 쓰이고 불완전한 절을 이끌어야 하므로 오답이다.

어휘 | instructor 강사 demonstrate 보여주다 athlete 운동선수 prevent 막다, 예방하다 sore muscle 근육통

12 (B)

번역 | 약을 투여한 후 계절성 알레르기가 있는 사람들에게서 증상이 거의 발견되지 않았다.

해설 | 빈칸 앞의 전치사 in의 목적어 역할을 하면서 빈칸 뒤 전치사구 'with seasonal allergies'의 수식을 받을 수 있는 '사람들'을 의미하는 대명사 (B) those가 정답이다. (A) whoever, (C) those who, (D) anyone who 모두 접속사를 지니고 있으므로 뒤에 동사가 와야 한다.

어휘 | medication 약, 약물 symptom 증상 seasonal allergy 계절성 알레르기

13 (C)

번역 | 잡지 기사는 실크 같은 섬세한 직물이 보통 필요로 하는 관리 목록을 보여준다.

해설 | 선행사가 사물인 'a list of care'이며, 관계사절에는 주어 delicate fabric such as silk와 동사 requires가 있지만 동사의 목적어가 없다. 따라서 선행사가 목적어 역할을 하는 것이므로 목적격 관계대명사 (C) which가 정답이다.

어휘 | article 기사 delicate 섬세한 fabric 직물, 천 require 요구하다

14 (B)

번역 | 고객은 소포가 도착할 때까지 2주 동안 기다려야 하며, 그 후에는 분실 신고를 할 수 있습니다.

해설 | 빈칸에는 전치사와 함께 쓰일 수 있는 관계대명사가 들어가야 한다. 선행사가 two weeks이며 전치사 after의 목적어가 들어갈 자리이므로, 목적격 관계대명사인 (B) which가 정답이다.

어휘 | missing 실종된, 분실된

15 (A)

번역 | 컨퍼런스의 기술자들은 강연 중에 슬라이드를 보여줄 예정인 어떤 발표자와든 대화하기를 원한다.

해설 | 빈칸 이하는 선행사 any presenters를 수식하는 관계사절로, 빈칸 뒤에 동사가 나오므로, 주격 관계대명사 (A) who가 정답이다. plan을 '계획'이라는 명사로 잘못 이해한 경우 (C) whose를 정답으로 잘못 고를 수 있으니 유의하자. (D) whoever는 주격 자리에 올 수 있지만 선행사를 포함하는 복합관계대명사이므로 선행사 뒤에 올 수 없다.

어휘 | technician 기술자 slide 슬라이드 talks 회담, 회의

16 (D)

번역 | 출판사에 의해 거절된 원고들 중 대부분은 여전히 2년 동안 파일로 보관되어 있다.

해설 | 문장에 본동사 are still kept가 있으므로 빈칸에는 앞의 명사 the manuscripts를 수식하는 분사가 들어가야 한다. 빈칸 뒤에 목적어가 나오지 않았으므로 수동의 의미를 갖는 과거분사 (D) rejected가 정답이다.

어휘 | manuscript 원고 reject 거절하다 publisher 출판사 keep ~ on file ~을 파일로 보관하다

17 (B)

번역 | 레예스 씨가 지원한 상근 영업직은 많은 출장을 요구한다.

해설 | 관계사절에 수반되는 전치사는 관계대명사 앞으로 끌어와서 쓸 수 있는데, applied와 함께 '~에 지원하다'라는 의미를 나타내는 (B) for가 정답이다.

어휘 | sales position 영업직, 판매직 apply for ~에 지원하다 require 요구하다

18 (B)

번역 | 스토어 씨는 몇몇 사무실 건물을 둘러보았는데, 그 건물들 중 어느 것도 그녀의 법률 업무에 적합하지 않아 보였다.

해설 | 문장에서 toured와 seem이 동사이며, 동사가 두 개인 문장에 접속사가 없으므로 접속사 역할을 할 수 있는 관계대명사가 들어가야 한다. 빈칸은 none of 뒤의 목적격 자리이며, 선행사가 office buildings이므로 정답은 목적격 관계대명사 (B) which이다.

어휘 | tour 순회하다, 둘러보다 suitable 적합한, 알맞은 legal practice 법률 업무[사무]

19 (C)

번역 | 직원들이 가장 높게 평가하는 워크숍은 다음 분기에 다시 제공될 것이다.

해설 | 문장에 동사가 rate와 will be offered 두 개이므로 접속사가 필요하다. 빈칸 앞 명사구(The workshops)와 빈칸 뒤 타동사 rate가 있고 목적어가 없는 점을 보아 목적격 관계대명사가 생략되어 있는 것을 알 수 있다. 관계사절의 주어가 필요하므로 (C) employees가 정답이다. 참고로 the highest가 rate의 목적어처럼 보이지만 '가장 높이'라는 부사의 최상급이다.

어휘 | rate 평가하다 offer 제공하다 employment 고용

20 (B)

번역 | 예산 때문에 실내 장식가는 고객이 요청한 모든 것을 진행할 수 없었다.

해설 | 빈칸은 전치사 with의 목적어이자, 목적격 관계대명사가 생략되어 있는 관계사절의 선행사 자리이다. 보기 모두 관계사의 수식을 받을 수 있는 대명사이지만, 문맥상 '고객이 요청한 모든 것을 진행할 수 없다'라는 의미가 가장 적절하므로 (B) everything이 정답이다.

어휘 | due to ~ 때문에   budget 예산   proceed with ~을 진행하다   client 고객   request 요청하다

UNIT 10 명사절 접속사

본책 p.192

전략포인트 1

1 (A)   **2** (C)   **3** (B)

1 (A)

번역 | 기사는 인터넷 연결을 개선하기 위해 새 라우터를 구입할 것을 제안했다.

해설 | 빈칸은 동사 suggested의 목적어 역할을 하는 명사절을 이끄는 접속사 자리로 '~할 것을 제안했다'라는 의미가 되어야 하므로 정답은 (A) that이다.

어휘 | technician 기사, 기술자   router 라우터(네트워크 공유기)   improve 개선하다   connectivity 연결

2 (C)

번역 | 웨슬 360 공기청정기의 한 가지 특징은 사용자가 그것이 자동으로 꺼지도록 설정할 수 있다는 것이다.

해설 | 빈칸 이하는 동사 is의 보어 역할을 하는 명사절을 이끄는 접속사 자리로, '공기청정기의 한 가지 특징은 ~이라는 것이다'라는 의미가 되어야 하므로 (C) that이 정답이다. '~인지 아닌지'를 의미하는 접속사 (D) whether도 보어 역할을 하는 명사절을 이끌 수 있지만 미확정 상황에서 쓰기 때문에 문맥상 어울리지 않는다.

어휘 | feature 특징   air purifier 공기청정기

3 (B)

번역 | 그 기사는 인정이 직원들이 의욕을 느끼도록 돕는 비결이라고 말한다.

해설 | 빈칸 앞 동사 states는 타동사로 목적어를 필요로 하며 빈칸 뒤에는 완전한 절이 이어지므로 빈칸에는 목적절을 이끄는 명사절 접속사가 와야 한다. 따라서 (B) that이 정답이다. that은 형용사절과 명사절을 모두 이끄는 접속사이며 이 둘의 구분은 that 앞의 선행사(명사구)의 유무로 판단한다. 명사절을 이끄는 that은 완전한 문장이 뒤따라오지만 관계대명사로 쓰일 때는 뒤에 불완전한 구조가 온다. 참고로 (A) unless와 (C) if는 부사절 접속사이며 앞뒤 모두 완전한 구조를 취한다.

어휘 | article 기사   state 진술하다   recognition 인정   motivated 동기가 부여된, 의욕이 넘치는

전략포인트 2

본책 p.192

1 (A)   **2** (B)   **3** (D)

1 (A)

번역 | 페레이라 씨는 회사의 브랜드 이미지를 쇄신하려는 노력이 성공할 것이라고 확신한다.

해설 | 빈칸은 be동사의 보어 자리로, 빈칸 뒤에 온 that절과 함께 쓸 수 있는 형용사가 와야 한다. 따라서 'that 이하의 내용을 확신한다'라는 뜻을 이루는 (A) confident가 정답이다.

어휘 | confident 확신하는   rebrand 브랜드 이미지를 쇄신하다   effort 노력   strategic 전략적인

2 (B)

번역 | 극장 방문객들은 공연 중에 휴대폰 전원이 꺼져 있어야 한다는 것을 인지해야 한다.

해설 | 빈칸은 be동사의 보어 자리로, 빈칸 뒤에 온 that절과 함께 쓸 수 있는 형용사가 와야 한다. 문맥상 '휴대폰 전원이 꺼져 있어야 한다는 것을 인지하다'라는 의미가 자연스러우므로 '인지하는'이라는 뜻의 형용사 (B) aware가 정답이다.

어휘 | aware 알고 있는, 인지하는   performance 공연

3 (D)

번역 | 박물관 자원봉사자들은 근무 중에 신분증을 착용해야 한다는 점을 다시 한번 알려드립니다.

해설 | 빈칸 뒤의 완전한 절을 이끌 수 있는 명사절 접속사 (D) that이 정답이다. 참고로 '~이라고 상기시키다'라는 의미로 'be동사+reminded+that+주어+동사'의 구조가 자주 쓰인다는 것을 알아 두자.

어휘 | ID badge 신분증   on duty 근무 중인

전략포인트 3

본책 p.193

1 (B)   **2** (B)   **3** (A)

1 (B)

번역 | 세율 변경이 승인될지 여부는 대중의 지지에 달려 있다.

해설 | 빈칸부터 approved까지가 문장의 주어이므로 빈칸에는 명사절을 이끄는 접속사가 필요한데, 문맥상 '~인지 아닌지'라는 의미가 되어야 하므로 (B) Whether가 정답이다. (A) If도 whether와 같은 역할을 할 수 있지만 주어 자리에는 올 수 없으므로 오답이다.

어휘 | tax rate 세율   approve 승인하다   depend on ~에 달려 있다

2 (B)

번역 | 그 새 책장은 충분한 무게를 견딜 수 있는지 확인하기 위해 몇 가지 시험을 거쳤다.

해설 | 빈칸 이하는 determine의 목적어 역할을 하는 명사절로, 문맥상 '충분한 무게를 견딜 수 있는지 확인하기 위해'라는 의미가 되어야 한다. 따라서 '~인지 아닌지'라는 의미의 명사절 접속사 (B) if가 정답이다. (A) unless와 (D) while은 부사절 접속사이기 때문에 앞뒤로 완전한 절이 와야 하고, (C) than은 비교급 표현과 써야 하므로 오답이다.

어휘 | put through ~을 거치다   determine 확인하다, 측정하다   withstand 견디다

3 (A)

번역 | 지원자의 이력서가 인상적인지에 상관없이 마감일이 지나면 받지 않습니다.

해설 | 빈칸 이하는 전치사 Regardless of의 목적어절로, 문맥상 '~인지 아닌지에 상관없이'라는 의미가 되어야 한다. 따라서 '~인지 아닌지'라는 뜻의 명사절 접속사 (A) whether가 정답이다. (B) concerning은 '~에 관한'이라는 전치사이므로 답이 될 수 없고, 접속사인 (C) that은 전치사의 목적어가 되질 못하므로, 또한 (D) when은 전치사의 목적어가 가능한 명사절 접속사이지만 문맥이 맞질 않아 오답이다.

어휘 | regardless of ~에 상관없이   applicant 지원자 impressive 인상적인

전략포인트 4   본책 p.193

1 (A)   **2** (D)   **3** (C)

1 (A)

번역 | 가이드는 참가자들에게 등산에 무엇이 권장되는 지를 설명할 것이다.

해설 | 빈칸에는 explain의 목적어 역할을 할 수 있는 명사절을 이끄는 접속사가 필요한데, 빈칸 뒤에 주어가 빠진 불완전한 문장이 있고 문맥상, '무엇이 하이킹에 권장되는지'라는 의미가 되어야 하므로 (A) what이 정답이다. (B) how와 (C) where는 완전한 절을 이끄므로 오답이다.

어휘 | recommend 추천[권장]하다   hike 등산, 도보 여행

2 (D)

번역 | 그 정보 제공 동영상은 박물관 직원들이 전시를 위해 예술 작품들을 어떻게 준비하는지 간략하게 보여준다.

해설 | 빈칸은 동사 outlines의 목적어 역할을 하는 명사절을 이끄는 접속사 자리이다. 완전한 형태의 명사절을 이끌 수 있는 의문사가 들어가야 하므로 정답은 (D) how이다.

어휘 | outline (개요를) 간략히 설명하다   artifact 예술작품으로 사용되는 물건   display 전시

3 (C)

번역 | 수상 후보 신청서에 그 사람이 회사에 어떤 기여를 했는지 정확히 기재해 주세요.

해설 | 빈칸은 동사 describe의 목적어인 명사절을 이끄는 접속사 자리이다. 빈칸 뒤에 가산명사인 contribution이 관사 없이 단독으로 왔으므로, 빈칸에는 contribution을 수식할 수 있는 의문형용사가 필요하다. 따라서 (C) what이 정답이다.

어휘 | nomination 지명, 임명   form 양식   describe 기술하다   exactly 정확하게   contribution 기여, 공헌

전략포인트 5   본책 p.194

1 (D)   **2** (D)   **3** (B)

1 (D)

번역 | 밀러 씨는 부기 업무를 아웃소싱할 것인지, 아니면 그녀의 사업을 위한 전임 회계사를 고용할 것인지를 고려하고 있다.

해설 | 빈칸은 바로 뒤에 온 to부정사구와 결합하여 동사 is considering의 목적어 역할을 할 수 있어야 한다. 따라서 to부정사와 결합하여 '~할지 안 할지'라는 명사구를 이룰 수 있는 명사절 접속사 (D) whether가 정답이다.

어휘 | consider 고려하다   outsource 아웃소싱하다, 외부에 위탁하다   bookkeeping 부기   accountant 회계사

2 (D)

번역 | 온라인 사용자 설명서는 전화기의 공장 설정을 복구하는 방법을 보여준다.

해설 | 빈칸은 바로 뒤에 온 to부정사구와 결합하여 동사 shows의 목적어 역할을 할 수 있어야 한다. 따라서 정답은 to부정사와 결합하여 '~하는 방법'의 의미를 이루는 명사절 접속사 (D) how이다. 참고로 (A) what도 to부정사와 결합하여 목적어 역할을 할 수 있지만, what to+타동사 (목적어 없음)'의 구조가 와야 하므로 오답이다.

어휘 | restore 복구[복원]하다   setting 설정

3 (B)

번역 | 직원 명부 내의 메모는 다양한 상황에서 누구에게 연락해야 하는지를 설명합니다.

해설 | 빈칸은 바로 뒤에 온 to부정사구와 결합하여 동사 explain의 목적어 역할을 할 수 있는 명사절 접속사이어야 한다. 빈칸 뒤 타동사인 to contact 다음에 목적어가 없는 것을 보아 접속사와 목적어 역할을 하는 (B) whom과 (D) what이 가능하다. 문맥상 '누구에게 연락해야 하는지'라는 의미가 자연스러우므로 정답은 (B) whom이다. (A) where와 (C) whether도 명사절을 이끌고 to부정사와 연결될 수 있지만 to부정사의 동사가 목적어를 필요치 않는 완전한 구조를 갖추고 있어야 한다.

전략포인트 6   본책 p.194

1 (A)   **2** (D)   **3** (A)

1 (A)

번역 | 무역 박람회의 다양한 부스는 참석자들이 그들의 관심을 끄는 어떤 것이든지 탐색할 수 있도록 한다.

해설 | 빈칸은 to부정사 to explore의 목적어인 명사절을 이끄는 접속사 자리이다. 따라서 명사절 접속사인 복합관계대명사 (A) whatever가 정답이다. (C) whenever는 부사절을 이끄는 복합관계부사이고 (D) anything은 anything that으로 써야 빈칸 뒤 동사(catches)와 연결될 수 있다.

어휘 | trade fair 무역 박람회   explore 탐색하다

2 (D)

번역 | 우리 회사를 대표할 사람으로 선발된 사람은 누구나 홍보 대변인 역할을 하게 될 것이다.

해설 | 문장에 동사가 is selected와 will serve로 두 개이므로 빈칸에는 접속사가 들어가야 한다. 빈칸은 명사절에서 동사 is selected의 주어 자리이므로, 주어와 명사절 접속사 역할을 동시에 할 수 있는 복합관계대명사가 필요하다. 따라서 보기 중에 이와 같은 역할을 할 수 있는 (D) Whoever가 정답이다.

참고로 (A) Who도 명사절을 이끌고 뒤에 불완전한 구조가 오기 때문에 문법적으로 가능해 보여도 '누가 선택되는지는 역할을 할 것이다'라고 해석이 되기 때문에 문맥상 맞지 않다.

어휘 | represent 대표[대신]하다   serve as ~의 역할을 하다
public relations 홍보   spokesperson 대변인

3 (A)

번역 | 그 건축가는 설계도를 보내기 위해 브롱크스 택배든 하트필드 해운이든 덜 비싼 쪽을 이용할 것이다.

해설 | 빈칸 앞의 완전한 절과 연결되고 뒤에 본동사 is가 있으므로 빈칸은 접속사 자리이다. 빈칸 앞에서 선택 범위(브롱크스 택배든 하트필드 해운이든)가 언급되었으므로 '둘 중 어느 쪽이든 덜 비싼'을 의미하여 부사절을 이끌 수 있는 복합관계대명사 (A) whichever가 정답이다. (B) when과 (D) however도 부사절을 이끌지만 뒤에 완전한 문장이 와야 한다.

어휘 | architect 건축가   blueprint 청사진, 설계도

ETS 고득점 실전 문제
본책 p.196

1 (C)	**2** (B)	**3** (D)	**4** (A)	**5** (A)	**6** (B)
7 (C)	**8** (B)	**9** (C)	**10** (D)	**11** (D)	**12** (B)
13 (C)	**14** (B)	**15** (B)	**16** (C)	**17** (D)	**18** (A)
19 (A)	**20** (B)				

1 (C)

번역 | 시 위원회는 시내버스가 더 필요한지 여부를 결정하기 위해 대중교통 이용 패턴을 분석하고 있다.

해설 | 빈칸은 determine의 목적어 역할을 하는 명사 자리이고 빈칸 뒤에 절이 왔으므로 명사절을 이끄는 접속사가 필요하다. 따라서 '~인지'라는 뜻의 명사절 접속사 (C) whether가 정답이다.

어휘 | commission 위원회   analyze 분석하다   mass transit 대중교통   determine 결정하다

2 (B)

번역 | 일주일에 40시간 이상 일하는 사람은 누구나 초과 근무 수당을 받을 수 있는 자격이 있다.

해설 | 문장에 동사가 works와 will be entitled to로 두 개이므로 빈칸에는 접속사가 들어가야 한다. 따라서 접속사 역할을 할 수 있는 복합관계대명사 (B) Whoever가 정답이다. (A) Those who에는 단수동사 works가 쓰일 수 없고, (C) Anybody와 (D) Everyone은 Anybody who와 같이 접속사 역할을 하는 관계대명사를 함께 써야 복합관계대명사와 같은 역할을 할 수 있다.

어휘 | be entitled to ~에 대한 자격이[권리가] 있다
overtime pay 초과 근무 수당

3 (D)

번역 | 그 웹사이트는 성장을 촉진하기 위해 식물들이 어떻게 다루어져야 하는지를 사용자에게 알려준다.

해설 | 빈칸에는 informs의 목적어 역할을 할 수 있는 명사절을 이끄는 접속사가 필요한데, 뒤에 주어와 동사가 있는 완전한 문장을 이끌면서, 문맥상 '성장을 촉진하기 위해 식물들이 어떻게 다루어져야 하는지'라는 의미가 되어야 하므로 '어떻게'라는 뜻의 의문사인 (D) how가 정답이다. 참고로 동사 inform은 'inform+사람 목적어+명사절'의 구조일 때 4형식 동사로 쓰여 '~에게(간접목적어) …을(직접목적어) 알려주다'라고 해석된다.

어휘 | inform 알리다   treat 다루다   promote 촉진하다

4 (A)

번역 | 경연의 심사위원단은 어떤 작품이 요구 조건을 가장 잘 충족시키는지를 정할 것이다.

해설 | 빈칸은 동사 decide의 목적어인 명사절을 이끄는 접속사 자리이다. 또한 뒤에 온 명사 artwork을 수식하는 역할을 해야 하므로 '어떤 작품'이라는 의미를 이루는 의문형용사 (A) which가 정답이다.

어휘 | judging panel 심사 위원(단)   meet 충족시키다
requirement 요구 조건

5 (A)

번역 | 회사가 대중에게 영향을 미칠 수 있는 안전상의 위험을 알게 되면 제품은 회수될 것입니다.

해설 | 문장의 동사가 will be recalled와 learns이므로 이들을 연결하는 접속사가 필요하다. 빈칸 앞은 문장 구조가 완전하기 때문에 부사절 접속사가 와야 하고 (A) if 와 (D) whether가 가능하다. 주절의 시제가 미래(will be recalled)인 반면 종속절의 시제는 현재(learns)인 점을 보아 조건의 부사절 접속사 (A) if가 정답임을 알 수 있다. 참고로 if명사절은 타동사 뒤에 오므로 완전한 절이 앞뒤로 와야 하는 if부사절과 구분이 된다.

어휘 | recall 회수하다   hazard 위험   affect 영향을 주다

6 (B)

번역 | 밤에 보안 경보를 설정한 사람은 누구나 다른 사람들이 모두 건물 밖으로 나갔는지를 확인해야 한다.

해설 | 빈칸 앞에는 목적어를 필요로 하는 동사 make sure가 있고 빈칸 뒤에는 완전한 문장이 있으므로 명사절 접속사가 필요하다. 따라서 명사절 접속사인 (B) that이 정답이다. (A) once는 부사절을 이끌기 때문에 앞뒤 모두 완전한 문장이 나와야 하며, 명사절 접속사인 (C) who와 (D) what은 뒤에 불완전한 문장이 오기 때문에 오답이다.

어휘 | security 보안, 안보   alarm 경보(기)

7 (C)

번역 | 관리자들은 은행 직원들이 더 전문적인 이미지를 보여주기 위해 유니폼을 입어야 하는지 여부를 고려 중이다.

해설 | 빈칸 이하는 동사 are considering의 목적절로, 문맥상 '~인지 아닌지 여부를 고려 중이다'라는 의미가 되어야 한다. 따라서 동사 consider와 함께 쓰여 '~인지 아닌지'라는 의미를 나타내는 명사절 접속사인 (C) whether가 정답이다. 참고로 (A) who와 (D) whoever도 명사절을 이끌지만 뒤에 불완전한 문장이 오므로 오답이다.

어휘 | project 보여주다   professional 전문적인

8 (B)

번역 | 메이슨 마케팅의 낮은 이직률은 회사가 후한 급여 보수를 제공하고 있다는 사실에 기인한다.

해설 | 빈칸은 동사 is attributed to의 목적어 자리로, that 뒤에 완전한 문장이 왔으므로 동격의 접속사 that과 함께 쓰는 추상명사 자리임을 알 수 있다. 문맥상 '회사가 후한 급여 보수를 제공하고 있다는 사실'이 자연스러우므로 정답은 (B) fact이다.

어휘 | turnover rate 이직률   be attributed to ~에 기인하다, ~ 덕택이다   generous 후한, 관대한
compensation package (급여와 복리 후생을 포함한) 보수

9 (C)

번역 | 시의원들은 지역 공원 예산을 삭감할지 여부에 대해 투표할 것이다.

해설 | 빈칸 뒤에 온 to cut이 문제 해결의 단서이다. 명사절 접속사 whether와 의문사는 to부정사와 결합할 수 있는 특징이 있다. 문맥상 '예산을 삭감할지 여부에 대해 투표하다'라는 의미가 적절하므로 (C) whether가 정답이다. (B) if는 명사절 접속사로 쓰일 때 whether와 같은 뜻이지만 to부정사와 결합할 수 없으므로 오답이다. (A) who와 (D) what은 to부정사의 목적어 역할을 하는데, 지문에는 to cut 뒤 the budget이라는 목적어가 이미 있기 때문에 답이 될 수 없다.

어휘 | city council 시의회   vote 투표하다   cut 삭감하다
budget 예산   local 지역의, 현지의

10 (D)

번역 | 배관공은 무엇이 누수의 원인이 되었는지 구체적으로 알아내지 못했다.

해설 | 빈칸에는 동사 determine의 목적어 역할을 할 수 있는 명사절을 이끄는 접속사가 필요한데, 빈칸 뒤에 주어가 빠진 불완전한 문장이 나오므로 (D) what이 정답이다. (A) when과 (C) that은 완전한 문장을 이끄는 명사절 접속사이므로 오답이다.

어휘 | plumber 배관공   determine 알아내다, 밝히다
specifically 구체적으로   contribute 기여하다, ~의 원인이 되다

11 (D)

번역 | 성공한 기업가들은 위험을 감수하지 않으면 사업을 확장할 수 없다는 것을 알고 있다.

해설 | 빈칸 뒤로 주어와 동사를 갖춘 완전한 두 절이 나오므로 빈칸에는 접속사가 들어가야 한다. 따라서 '~하지 않는 한'이라는 조건의 의미를 나타내는 부사절 접속사인 (D) unless가 정답이다. 대명사 (A) these는 문장을 연결할 수 없고, 접속사로도 쓰이는 (B) which와 (C) what은 완전한 절과 쓰이지 않으므로 오답이다.

어휘 | entrepreneur 사업가[기업가]   realize 알다, 깨닫다
take a risk 위험을 감수하다   expand 확장하다

12 (B)

번역 | 10명의 회계사 중 가장 먼저 일을 끝낸 사람은 누구든지 집에 일찍 가는 것이 허락된다.

해설 | 빈칸부터 first까지가 전부 will be allowed의 주어이므로 빈칸에는 명사절 접속사가 들어가야 한다. '10명의 회계사 중에서(of the ten accountants)'라는 선택 범위가 주어지므로 '~중 어느 쪽이든'이라는 뜻의 (B) Whichever가 정답이다. 참고로, whichever는 사물과 사람을 모두 지칭할 수 있다.

어휘 | accountant 회계사   be allowed to 부정사 ~하는 것이 허락되다

13 (C)

번역 | 병원의 의료진은 어떤 일이 닥쳐와도 처리할 수 있어야 한다.

해설 | 빈칸 이하가 동사 handle의 목적어이므로 명사절을 이끄는 접속사가 필요하다. 따라서 정답은 복합관계대명사인 (C) whatever이다. (D) however는 복합관계부사로 부사절을 이끈다. 복합관계대명사는 명사절과 부사절을 이끌 수 있고, 복합관계부사는 부사절을 이끈다는 점을 알아 두자.

어휘 | medical 의학[의료]의   personnel 직원, 인원
handle 처리하다   come one's way (일, 기회 등이) 닥치다

14 (B)

번역 | 호평 받는 많은 학자들이 모여 대체 에너지원을 개발하는 것이 왜 중요한지 논의할 것이다.

해설 | 빈칸 뒤에 주어와 동사를 갖춘 절이 나오므로 빈칸은 접속사 자리이다. 빈칸 앞 동사 discuss의 목적어 역할을 하는 명사절을 이끄는 접속사가 필요하며 뒤에 완전한 문장이 있으므로 의문부사인 (B) why가 정답이다. 참고로 (D) in that은 '~하다는 점에 있어서'라는 뜻의 부사절 접속사이며, 앞뒤에 모두 완전한 절이 와야 한다.

어휘 | a number of 많은   acclaimed 호평 받는   gather 모이다   alternative energy 대체 에너지   source 원천, 근원

15 (B)

번역 | 기획 위원회는 올해 열리는 학회가 어떤 주제들을 다뤄야 할지 여전히 결정해야 한다.

해설 | 빈칸은 choose의 목적어인 명사절을 이끄는 접속사 자리이다. 빈칸 뒤에 명사 topics를 수식하고 뒤의 문장과 연결되어, '어떤 주제를 다뤄야 할지 여전히 결정해야 한다'의 의미가 자연스러운 의문형용사 (B) which가 정답이다.

어휘 | planning committee 기획 위원회   cover 다루다

16 (C)

번역 | 이 씨는 문서들을 검토하여 어떤 것들이 활성 고객 파일에 추가되어야 할지 결정할 것이다.

해설 | 빈칸은 decide의 목적어 역할을 하는 명사절을 이끄는 접속사 자리이다. 빈칸 뒤 명사절에 주어가 없고 동사 need만 있으므로 빈칸에는 명사절 접속사와 주어 역할을 동시에 할 수 있는 보기가 들어가야 한다. 따라서 명사절을 이끄는 의문형용사 which와 주어 역할을 하는 부정대명사 ones가 결합되어 '어떤 것들'이라는 의미를 이루는 (C) which ones가 정답이다.

어휘 | document 서류   active file 활동 파일(사용중인 데이터 파일)

17 (D)
번역 | 앞으로 어떤 수준의 서비스가 우리 조직에 가장 적합한지를 결정해야 한다.

해설 | 빈칸은 의문형용사 which가 이끄는 명사절의 동사 자리이다. 주절의 동사가 need(현재)이며, '어떤 수준의 서비스가 우리 조직에 적합한지를 결정해야 한다'며 현재 해야 할 일에 대해 설명하고 있으므로 과거 시제 (C) fitted는 어울리지 않는다. 따라서 (D) fits가 정답이다.

어휘 | fit 적합하다   organization 조직   going forward 앞으로

18 (A)
번역 | 그 휴대폰 서비스 공급업체는 다음 분기에는 새로운 시장으로 확장할 것이라고 확신한다.

해설 | 빈칸은 be 동사와 어울려 that절을 뒤에 취하는 형용사 자리이다. that절을 목적어로 취하며 '~이라는 것을 확신하다'라는 의미를 이루는 (A) positive가 정답이다.

어휘 | be positive that ~이라는 것을 확신하다   expand into ~으로 확장하다   responsive 반응을 보이는   representative 대표하는   comprehensive 종합적인

19 (A)
번역 | 기술자가 얼마를 청구하든지 간에 컴퓨터를 다시 작동시키는 것은 가치가 있을 것이다.

해설 | 빈칸 뒤의 'much+주어+동사' 구조가 문제 해결의 단서로, 빈칸에는 해당 구조를 이끌 수 있는 부사절 접속사가 와야 한다. 따라서 (A) However가 정답이다. 일반적으로 복합관계부사 however는 형용사나 부사 바로 앞에 놓여 '얼마나 ~하든지'라는 뜻으로 쓰이는데, 여기에서는 수량을 나타내는 부정대명사 much와 연결이 되어 '얼마를 청구하는지 간에'의 의미로 연결된다.

어휘 | technician 기술자   charge 청구하다   be worth it to-v ~할 가치가 있다   operate 가동시키다

20 (B)
번역 | 고객들은 보통 어떤 차를 살지 결정하기 전에 여러 대의 차를 시승해야 한다고 주장한다.

해설 | 빈칸 앞의 접속사 which one은 deciding의 목적어 역할을 하는 명사절을 이끈다. '의문접속사+주어+should 동사원형'은 '의문접속사+to부정사'로 축약될 수 있다. 따라서 '어떤 것을 사야 할지'의 의미로 연결되는 (B) to buy가 정답이다.

어휘 | typically 보통   insist on ~을 주장하다

UNIT 11 ETS 기출 어휘

ETS 고득점 실전 문제 1   본책 p.208

1 (B)   **2** (B)   **3** (B)   **4** (C)   **5** (D)   **6** (B)
7 (B)   **8** (C)   **9** (D)   **10** (D)

1 (B)
번역 | 직원 안내서는 고용주와 직원 간 관계의 기본 요소에 대해 개략적으로 설명한다.

해설 | 빈칸에 들어갈 명사는 앞의 형용사 basic(기본적인)과 뒤의 전치사구 of the employer-employee relationship (고용주와 직원 간 관계의) 수식을 받으면서 직원 안내서에 다뤄지는 것을 나타낼 수 있어야 한다. '고용주와 직원 간 관계의 기본 요소'라는 의미가 되면 자연스러우므로 '요소'라는 뜻의 (B) elements가 정답이다.

어휘 | outline 개요를 서술하다   similarity 유사점

2 (B)
번역 | 외부 감사는 자선 재단을 전문으로 하는 독립 회계 법인에 의해 실시되고 있다.

해설 | 동사 is being conducted의 주어 자리로 '실시되다'와 호응하는 명사를 고르면 된다. 따라서 '감사'를 뜻하는 (B) audit이 정답이다.

어휘 | independent 독립적인   specialize in ~을 전문으로 하다   charitable 자선의   foundation 재단

3 (B)
번역 | 왕실 부부의 국립 박물관 방문은 이 지역 교통에 크게 영향을 미칠 것으로 보인다.

해설 | to affect를 수식하여 적절한 문맥을 완성하는 부사를 고르는 문제이다. '교통에 크게 영향을 미친다'는 의미가 되어야 자연스러우므로 '극적으로'라는 뜻의 (B) dramatically가 정답이다.

어휘 | royal 왕실의   previously 이전에   punctually 시간을 엄수하여   sternly 엄격하게

4 (C)
번역 | 노 씨는 압둘라히 씨가 회의에 늦는 일은 거의 없다고 말했다.

해설 | 빈칸 뒤 형용사 late를 수식하는 자리이므로 부사가 필요하다. 보기 모두 부사가 될 수 있는데 문맥상 '좀처럼 늦지 않는다'가 적절하므로 부정의 빈도 부사인 (C) seldom이 정답이다.

어휘 | note 언급하다   little (a little(bit)으로 쓰여) 약간   far 멀리

5 (D)
번역 | 기능이 추가된 나덱스 N10은 시장에서 거의 틀림없이 가장 진보한 스마트폰이다.

해설 | 명사구 the most advanced smartphone을 수식하기에 적절한 부사를 고르는 문제이다. 문맥상 가장 진보한 스마트폰이라는 최상급 표현을 강조하는 말이 들어가야 자연스러우므로 '거의 틀림없이'라는 의미의 (D) arguably가 정답이다.

어휘 | feature 기능 advanced 선진의 negatively 부정적으로 doubtfully 미심쩍게 sincerely 진심으로

6 (B)

번역 | 고객 만족은 고객층 확대를 목표로 하는 회사에 가장 중요한 것이다.

해설 | 'of+추상명사'는 형용사 역할을 하며, 따라서 'of importance'는 be 동사의 보어로서 important(중요한)와 같은 기능을 한다. '최고로 중요한'이라는 의미가 되어야 적절하므로 '최고의'라는 뜻의 (B) utmost가 정답이다. 참고로 'of help'는 helpful(도움이 되는), 'of use'는 useful(쓸모 있는), 'of no use'는 useless(쓸모 없는)라는 것도 알아 두자.

어휘 | aim 목표하다 client base 고객층 diminished 감소된 conditional 조건부의 farthest 가장 먼

7 (B)

번역 | 유명하고 유능한 금융인이 투자 전략에 관한 세미나 시리즈에서 기조 연설을 했다.

해설 | 빈칸 앞의 형용사 well-known과 함께 명사 financier를 수식하여 '유명하고 유능한 금융인'이라는 의미가 되어야 적절하므로 '유능한'을 뜻하는 (B) accomplished가 정답이다.

어휘 | financier 금융인 keynote speech 기조 연설 investment 투자 strategy 전략 predicted 예상되는 categorized 분류된 apparent 명백한

8 (C)

번역 | 공사장 주변은 교통이 혼잡하여 운전자들은 아예 그 지역을 피하도록 권고받고 있다.

해설 | 교통이 혼잡하니 그 지역을 '아예 피하라'는 내용이 되어야 자연스럽다. 따라서 '아예, 완전히'를 뜻하는 (C) altogether가 정답이다. (B) absolutely는 사실이나 의사 표현을 강조할 때, (D) overall은 전체 혹은 종합적인 사항을 고려할 때 쓰는 말로 문맥에 어울리지 않는다.

어휘 | absolutely 틀림없이 overall 종합적으로

9 (D)

번역 | 비용을 낮추기 위해 마투니스 패션은 스포츠웨어 라인의 생산을 외부에 위탁할 것이다.

해설 | 동사 outsource의 목적어 자리이자 전치사구 of its sportswear line의 수식을 받아 '스포츠웨어 라인의 생산을 외부에 위탁한다'는 의미를 만드는 (D) production이 정답이다.

어휘 | cost 비용 outsource 외부에 위탁하다 objective 목표

10 (D)

번역 | 임시 관리자는 너무 바빠서 추가적인 업무를 떠맡을 수 없을지도 모른다.

해설 | 문맥상 바빠서 일을 더 할 수 없다는 내용이 되어야 한다. 따라서 목적어 responsibilities와 함께 쓰여 '(권력·책임을) 떠맡다'라는 뜻을 이루는 (D) assume이 정답이다.

어휘 | interim 임시의 responsibility 책무, 책임 locate (~의 위치를) 찾다 deny 부정하다 criticize 비판하다

ETS 고득점 실전 문제 2
본책 p.209

1 (D) **2** (D) **3** (D) **4** (A) **5** (A) **6** (A)
7 (D) **8** (B) **9** (B) **10** (C)

1 (D)

번역 | 이 회사는 첫해 성장 기록을 모두 갈아치우면서 명성을 얻었다.

해설 | 빈칸 앞에 rose to가 있고 문맥상 '회사가 명성을 얻었다'는 내용이 되면 자연스러우므로 '유명해지다'를 의미하는 관용표현 'rise to fame'을 만드는 명사 (D) fame이 정답이다.

어휘 | rose (rise의 과거) 오르다 neglect 방치 fame 명성

2 (D)

번역 | 무링 회계는 정직함과 진실함이라는 핵심 가치로 지역 사회에 기여하는 것에 대해 높이 평가받고 있다.

해설 | '가치(values)'를 수식하여 '정직함과 진실함이라는 핵심 가치'라는 의미가 되어야 적절하므로 '핵심적인'이라는 의미의 (D) core가 정답이다.

어휘 | regard 평가하다 serve 기여하다 value 가치 honesty 정직 integrity 진실성 prompt 즉각적인

3 (D)

번역 | 데플드 퍼펙션은 목표로 하는 사업 확장의 일환으로 12개의 새로운 지역 매장을 열 예정이다.

해설 | '사업 확장의 일환'이라는 내용으로 보아 빈칸 앞의 형용사 twelve new와 함께 명사 '매장(stores)'를 수식하여 '12개의 새로운 지역 매장'이라는 의미가 되어야 적절하므로 '지역의'라는 의미의 (D) regional이 정답이다.

어휘 | targeted 목표로 하는 expansion 확장 adverse 부정적인 incidental 부수적인 consequential 중대한

4 (A)

번역 | 모든 사용자가 이용할 수 있도록 지정된 폴더에 데이터를 저장해 주세요.

해설 | '데이터가 모든 사용자에 의해 이용될 수 있도록'이라는 의미가 되어야 적절하므로 '이용[접근]하다'는 의미의 (A) accessed가 정답이다.

어휘 | designated 지정된 tolerate 참다 simplify 단순화하다 contribute 기여하다

5 (A)

번역 | 분실된 파일을 찾아 사방을 둘러보았으나 결국 찾지 못한 팀은 파일을 실수로 버린 것으로 믿었다.

해설 | 분실된 파일을 '찾아본다(looking for)'를 수식하기에 적절한 부사를 골라야 한다. '사방으로 찾아봤는데 못 찾았다'라는 내용이 되어야 자연스러우므로 '사방으로, 곳곳마다'라는 뜻의 (A) everywhere가 정답이다.

어휘 | missing 분실된 accidentally 실수로 discard 버리다

6 (A)

번역 | 개조된 시립 미술관의 재개관은 매년 열리는 예술 축제와 동시에 하기로 예정되어 있다.

해설 | '동시에 하다'는 의미가 되어야 자연스러우므로 전치사 with와 함께 쓰여 '~와 동시에 일어나다'라는 뜻이 되는 (A) coincide가 정답이다.

어휘 | advance 진전되다

7 (D)

번역 | 회사는 최근 환경 규제 준수를 확실히 하기 위해 사내 재활용 프로그램을 확대했다.

해설 | 환경 규제 준수를 확실히 한다는 내용이 되어야 적절하고, compliance는 'with + 법[규정]' 등과 함께 쓰여 '법[규정]의 준수'를 뜻하므로 (D) compliance가 정답이다.

어휘 | in-house 내부의 ensure 확실히 하다 regulation 규제 settlement 합의, 해결 relaxation 완화 approval 찬성

8 (B)

번역 | 회계 소프트웨어 구입 시 갖고 있는 컴퓨터와 호환이 되는지 확인하는 것이 중요하다.

해설 | 빈칸 뒤의 전치사 with와 함께 쓰여 '~와 호환이 되는'이라는 뜻을 이루는 (B) compatible이 정답이다.

어휘 | confident 확신하는 determined 단호한 specialized 전문적인

9 (B)

번역 | 실습 교육 과정은 교실 수업이 끝난 뒤 시작될 예정이다.

해설 | 교육 일정을 안내하는 문장으로 교실 수업이 끝난 뒤 '실습 교육이 시작된다'는 내용이 되어야 자연스럽다. 따라서 '시작하다'는 뜻의 (B) commence가 정답이다.

어휘 | hands-on 직접 해 보는 instruction 가르침 conclude 끝나다 withdraw 철수하다 anticipate 예상하다 reveal 드러내다

10 (C)

번역 | 판매업자는 개인 맞춤 티셔츠의 주문을 이행하는 데 영업일로 연속 10일 미만이 걸릴 것이라고 보장한다.

해설 | '연속 10일 미만이 걸린다'는 의미가 적절하므로 '연속적인, 연이은'이라는 뜻의 (C) consecutive가 정답이다. 참고로 '서수(the tenth) + consecutive day' 혹은 '기수(ten) + consecutive days'로 표현한다.

어휘 | vendor 판매자 guarantee 보장하다 personalized 개인 맞춤형의 fulfill (약속 등을) 이행하다

selective 선택적인 calculated 계산된 accumulated 축적된

ETS 고득점 실전 문제 3

본책 p.210

1 (D)	2 (A)	3 (D)	4 (A)	5 (D)	6 (B)
7 (C)	8 (B)	9 (D)	10 (B)		

1 (D)

번역 | 소토 씨와 그의 팀이 이번 주 중으로 사무실을 방문할 예정이다.

해설 | 빈칸에 적절한 부사를 선택하는 문제이다. 조동사 will이 쓰여 미래에 대한 일을 이야기하고 있으므로 '이번 주 중으로'라는 의미가 되어야 자연스럽다. '나중에'를 뜻하는 시간 부사 later는 시간 표현과 함께 쓰여 해당 주[달, 년도] 중에 일어날 일을 언급할 때 쓰인다. 따라서 (D) later가 정답이다.

2 (A)

번역 | 몬빌 타운 의회는 화이트크레스트 역이 다음 달부터 정기 정비를 받을 예정이라고 발표했다.

해설 | 어떤 일 등을 겪다[받다]의 뜻을 가진 동사 will undergo의 목적어 자리로 routine의 수식을 받아 '정기 정비를 받을 것이다'라는 내용이 되어야 문맥상 자연스럽다. 따라서 건물이나 기계 등을 정기적으로 점검 및 보수하는 '유지'라는 의미의 (A) maintenance가 정답이다.

어휘 | undergo 받다[겪다] reassurance 안심 resignation 사퇴

3 (D)

번역 | 이 게임의 인기는 EMJJ 게이밍이 업계 선두주자로서 입지를 확고히 하는 데 도움이 되었다.

해설 | '업계 선두주자로서 입지를 굳히다'는 내용이 되어야 하므로 '굳히다, 확고히 하다'는 뜻의 (D) solidify가 정답이다.

어휘 | revise 수정하다 organize 준비하다 insure 보험에 들다

4 (A)

번역 | 구내식당은 오후 1시에 문을 닫으므로 직원들은 점심 시간을 그에 따라 계획해야 한다.

해설 | '계획해야 한다(should plan)'를 수식하는 부사로, '식당이 1시에 문을 닫으므로 그에 맞게 계획해야 한다'는 내용이 되어야 자연스럽다. 따라서 '그에 따라'를 뜻하는 (A) accordingly가 정답이다.

어휘 | primarily 주로 definitely 분명히 subsequently 그 뒤에

5 (D)

번역 | 시장실에서 매년 열리는 축제 때 안내데스크에서 일할 자원봉사자를 모집하고 있다.

해설 | to부정사에 들어갈 동사 어휘를 고르는 문제로, 목적어인 '안내데스크'를 자연스럽게 연결할 수 있어야 한다. 문맥상 '안내데스크에서 직원으로 일할'이라는 내용이 되어야 적절하므로 '~의 직원으로 근무하다'를 뜻하는 (D) staff가 정답이다.

어휘 | mayor 시장   employ 고용하다   load (짐 등을) 싣다

6 (B)

번역 | 윤구 박사는 필수 건강 검진에 대한 인식을 높인 데 대해 현지에서 공로를 인정받았다.

해설 | 문맥상 '필수 건강 검진에 대한 인식을 높이다'라는 내용이 되어야 자연스러우므로 raise(높이다)의 목적어로 '인식'을 뜻하는 명사 (B) awareness가 정답이다.

어휘 | recognize 인정하다   health screening 건강 검진   output 생산량   resource 자원   space 공간

7 (C)

번역 | 협상팀은 이번 합병 계약이 양사에 바람직한 결과를 가져다 줄 것이라고 확신한다.

해설 | 명사 outcome을 수식하여 '양사에 바람직한 결과'라는 의미가 되어야 적절하므로 (C) desirable이 정답이다.

어휘 | negotiating 협상   merger 합병   deal 합의   outcome 결과   comprehensive 포괄적인   pessimistic 비관적인

8 (B)

번역 | 환경에 대한 관심이 높아지면서 지역 기업 대표들이 친환경 제품을 지지하게 되었다.

해설 | 지도자들이 '친환경 제품을 지지한다'는 내용이 되어야 적절하므로 '(공개적으로) 지지하다, (유명인이 특정 상품을) 홍보하다'는 뜻을 가진 (B) endorse가 정답이다.

어휘 | increased 증가한   concern 관심   eco-friendly 친환경의   disregard 무시하다   project 추정하다

9 (D)

번역 | 늦게 제출한 출품작은 심사 위원단에 의해 받아들여지거나 검토되지 않을 것이다.

해설 | 빈칸에 들어갈 명사는 심사 위원이 받아 주거나 검토하는 대상이 될 수 있는 것이어야 한다. 따라서 '출품작'을 뜻하는 (D) entries가 정답이다.

어휘 | panel 패널(조언을 제공하는 전문가 집단)   judge 심사 위원   interviewer 면접관

10 (B)

번역 | 이 직책은 경영학 석사 학위 또는 4년의 동등한 직장 경력을 필요로 한다.

해설 | 직책에 대한 지원 자격으로 경영학 석사 학위에 상응하는 대체 요건을 나타낼 수 있어야 한다. 따라서 명사 experience를 수식하는 '동등한'이라는 의미의 (B) equivalent가 정답이다.

어휘 | Master's Degree 석사 학위   business administration 경영학   obligated 의무가 있는   substitute 대용의; 대체하다

ETS 고득점 실전 문제 4

본책 p.211

1 (D)   **2** (C)   **3** (B)   **4** (B)   **5** (B)   **6** (A)
7 (D)   **8** (D)   **9** (C)   **10** (D)

1 (D)

번역 | 컴퓨터 시스템을 업그레이드함으로써 발생되는 비용 절감액은 초기 투자금을 훨씬 넘어선다.

해설 | 전치사구 of cost savings(비용 절감의)의 수식을 받은 것으로 보아 빈칸에는 돈과 관련된 명사가 적합하다는 것을 알 수 있으며, '초기 투자금을 넘어선다'고 했으므로 '비용 절감액이 투자금을 넘어선다'라는 의미가 되어야 문맥이 자연스럽다. 따라서 '액수'를 뜻하는 (D) amount가 정답이다.

어휘 | cost savings 비용 절감   generate 발생시키다   far 훨씬   exceed 넘다   initial 초기의   investment 투자(료)   statistic 통계

2 (C)

번역 | 웬달 바닥재는 고객 불만에 즉시 대응할 것을 약속합니다.

해설 | '고객 불만에 즉시 대응할 것이다'라는 내용이 되어야 적절하므로 '즉시'를 의미하는 (C) promptly가 정답이다.

어휘 | flooring 바닥재   complaint 불만   abruptly 뜻밖에   lively 생기 있게   hardly 거의 ~ 아니다

3 (B)

번역 | 웨인타운 스토어는 새로운 치위생용품 라인인 덴탈라이즈의 공식 출시 행사를 개최할 예정이다.

해설 | 문맥상 적절한 동사를 선택하는 문제이다. '공식 출시 행사를 개최할 예정이다'라는 내용이 되어야 자연스러우므로 '개최하다'는 의미의 (B) host가 정답이다.

어휘 | official 공식의   launch 출시 (행사)   dental hygiene 치위생   sample 시식[시음]하다   charge 청구하다

4 (B)

번역 | 우리는 버컴 시 규제 당국에 토지 이용법을 개정할 것을 촉구한다.

해설 | 목적어 뒤 목적격 보어 자리에 to부정사가 있으며, 문맥상 '시 당국에 법을 개정할 것을 촉구한다'는 내용이 되어야 적절하다. 따라서 'urge + 목적어 + to부정사'의 형태로 쓰여 '~가 …하도록 촉구[충고]하다'를 뜻하는 (B) urge가 정답이다.

어휘 | regulator 규제 기관   arise 발생하다   opt 선택하다   recite 암송하다

5 (B)

번역 | 우리는 사무용품을 필요할 때만 주문함으로써 낭비를 줄인다는 방침을 갖고 있다.

해설 | 빈칸 앞에 완전한 절이 있으므로 빈칸에는 뒤에 있는 분사구를 수식하는 부사가 들어가야 하고, 필요할 때만 주문하는 방침이 있다는 빈칸 앞 절의 내용과 낭비를 줄인다는 분사구를 자연스럽게 연결할 수 있는 접속부사가 필요하다. '필요할 때만

주문해서 낭비를 줄인다'는 인과 관계로 연결되어야 적절하므로 '그렇게 함으로써'를 뜻하는 (B) thereby가 정답이다.

어휘 | office supplies 사무용품 otherwise 그렇지 않으면

6 (A)

번역 | 미국에 있는 사무실로 전근 가는 직원은 그곳의 이사 담당 팀에 팁을 주는 것이 관례라는 점을 알고 있어야 한다.

해설 | 팁을 주는 것이 관례라는 내용이 되어야 적절하므로 '관례적인'이라는 뜻의 (A) customary가 정답이다.

어휘 | transfer 전근 가다 -based ~에 기반을 둔 tip ~에게 팁을 주다 crew 작업반 optimistic 낙관적인 accustomed 익숙한

7 (D)

번역 | 시립 도서관은 젊은이들의 독서 흥미를 유발하기 위해 독서클럽을 후원한다.

해설 | '독서에 대한 흥미를 발생시키다'는 의미가 되어야 자연스러우므로 '발생시키다, 만들어 내다'는 뜻의 (D) generate가 정답이다.

어휘 | sponsor 후원하다 limit 제한하다 replace 대신하다

8 (D)

번역 | 마르셀사의 연간 수익은 더 큰 경쟁사들의 연간 수익과 맞먹는다.

해설 | 빈칸 뒤의 전치사 to와 함께 쓰여 '~와 맞먹는'이라는 뜻을 이루는 (D) equivalent가 정답이다.

어휘 | revenue 수익 competitor 경쟁사 considerable 상당한 promoted 홍보된 potential 잠재적인

9 (C)

번역 | 해변 리조트 지역의 방문자 감소는 주로 평소와 달리 비가 많이 오는 날씨 때문이었다.

해설 | 방문자가 감소한 이유를 수식하는 부사로 '주로 ~ 때문이다'라는 의미를 이루는 (C) primarily가 정답이다. 참고로 primarily 대신 largely를 쓸 수 있고, '부분적으로 ~ 때문이다'라고 할 때는 partly를 쓸 수 있다.

어휘 | unusually 평소와 달리 favorably 유리하게 conditionally 조건부로

10 (D)

번역 | 우리 매장은 공급업체로부터 할인된 가격에 남는 재고품을 구입하여 절약한 금액이 고객에게 가도록 합니다.

해설 | 문맥상 할인가에 남는 재고를 사들인다는 내용이 되어야 적절하므로 '잉여의'라는 뜻의 (D) excess가 정답이다.

어휘 | inventory 재고(품) pass 넘겨주다 savings 절약된 금액 compliant 순응하는 diminished 감소된

ETS 고득점 실전 문제 5   본책 p.212

1 (D)	2 (A)	3 (C)	4 (A)	5 (A)	6 (D)
7 (B)	8 (A)	9 (C)	10 (C)		

1 (D)

번역 | 영화 제작자는 인근 사업체에 주는 지장을 최소화하기 위해 교통 통제 직원을 고용해야 한다.

해설 | 빈칸 뒤의 명사 business를 수식하여 '인근의 사업체'라는 의미가 되어야 적절하므로 '인근의'라는 뜻의 형용사 (D) nearby가 정답이다.

어휘 | minimize 최소화하다 disruption 지장, 중단 convenient 편리한 pleasant 즐거운

2 (A)

번역 | 의학 연구소에 대한 잠재적 투자자들의 관심을 끌기 위해 칼리냐 박사는 설명회를 준비 중이다.

해설 | '~의 관심을 끌다'는 의미의 동사 interest의 목적어 자리이므로 사람명사가 들어가야 한다. 또한 문맥상 '잠재적 투자자들의 관심을 끌기 위해'라는 의미가 되어야 적절하므로 '투자자'를 의미하는 (A) investors가 정답이다.

어휘 | potential 잠재적인 laboratory 연구소, 실험실 informational 정보를 제공하는 session (특정 활동) 시간 supplies 물품

3 (C)

번역 | 통근 열차의 지정된 조용한 구역에서는 전화 통화가 금지된다.

해설 | 문맥상 적절한 동사를 선택하는 문제이다. '전화 통화가 금지된다'는 내용이 되어야 자연스러우므로 be 뒤에서 수동태로 '금지되다'는 의미를 만드는 (C) forbidden이 정답이다.

어휘 | conversation 대화 designated 지정된 commuter train 통근 열차 resume 다시 시작하다

4 (A)

번역 | 그레이슨 구즈의 제품은 우수한 품질을 보장하기 위해 한정된 수량으로 생산된다.

해설 | 문맥상 '우수한 품질을 보장하기 위해'라는 의미가 되어야 자연스러우므로 '보장하다'는 의미의 (A) ensure가 정답이다.

어휘 | exceptional 우수한 goods 상품 apply 적용하다 arrange 배열하다

5 (A)

번역 | 당사의 모든 컨설턴트는 사무실 밖에서 주기적으로 이메일 내역을 확인하고 긴급한 문의에 답변할 수 있습니다.

해설 | 빈칸은 monitor를 수식하는 자리로, '이메일을 주기적으로 확인한다'는 내용이 되어야 하므로 '주기적으로'를 뜻하는 (A) periodically가 정답이다.

어휘 | monitor 확인[점검]하다 respond 응답하다 urgent 긴급한 inquiry 문의 principally 주로 progressively (꾸준히) 계속해서 suitably 알맞게

6 (D)

번역 | 라일리 슈퍼마켓에 제품을 판매하고자 하는 모든 공급업체는 품질 및 신뢰성에 대한 엄격한 기준을 충족해야 한다.

해설 | 명사 criteria를 수식하여 '엄격한 기준'을 충족해야 한다는 의미가 되어야 적합하므로 '엄격한'을 뜻하는 (D) rigorous가 정답이다.

어휘 | criteria 기준 reliability 신뢰성 transformed 변형된 probationary 수습의 nominated 지명된

7 (B)

번역 | 데이터를 보호하기 위해 원격 작업자는 자신의 랩톱 장치에 안티바이러스 소프트웨어를 반드시 설치해야 한다.

해설 | 데이터 보호를 위해 꼭 해야 할 일에 대해 언급하는 내용이므로 '반드시 소프트웨어를 설치해야 한다'는 의미가 되어야 한다. 따라서 '반드시 해야 하는'이라는 뜻의 (B) imperative가 정답이다.

어휘 | remote 원격의 device 장치 expanded 확장된

8 (A)

번역 | 온라인 구인 사이트로 귀사를 위한 새로운 직원 채용 과정이 매우 쉬워질 수 있습니다.

해설 | '채용 과정을 쉽게 할 수 있다'는 내용이 되어야 자연스러우므로 '쉽게 하다, 용이하게 하다'는 뜻의 (A) facilitate가 정답이다.

어휘 | recruiting 채용 greatly 크게 process 과정 hiring 고용 obligate 강요하다 approach 접근하다 impress 감명을 주다

9 (C)

번역 | 사용하고자 하는 건축 자재에 대한 세부 사항은 작업 계약서에 명확하게 쓰여 있어야 한다.

해설 | 계약서에 '명확하게' 쓰여 있어야 한다는 의미가 되어야 적절하므로 (C) expressly가 정답이다.

어휘 | detail 세부 사항 material 자재 controllably 조종 가능하게 arguably 거의 틀림없이 seriously 진지하게

10 (C)

번역 | 우리에게는 통계 데이터를 해석하고 그 결과를 이해할 수 있는 용어로 제시할 수 있는 전문가 팀이 있습니다.

해설 | 문맥상 데이터의 의미를 해석하고 그 결과를 이해하기 쉽게 제시한다는 내용이 되어야 하므로 '데이터를 해석한다'는 의미를 이루는 '(의미를) 해석[이해]하다'는 뜻의 (C) interpret이 정답이다. (A) know는 단순한 인식 및 인지의 의미로서 '알다'를 뜻하므로 이 문맥에는 어울리지 않는다.

어휘 | statistical 통계상의 present 제시하다 understandable 이해할 수 있는 term 용어 express 표현하다

ETS 고득점 실전 문제 6

본책 p.213

1 (B) 2 (A) 3 (A) 4 (D) 5 (A) 6 (B)
7 (A) 8 (C) 9 (D) 10 (C)

1 (B)

번역 | 이번 달 경매에 나온 골동품 대부분이 상태가 훌륭했다.

해설 | 문맥상 '골동품이 훌륭한 상태였다'는 의미가 되어야 자연스러우므로 '상태'라는 의미의 (B) condition이 정답이다.

어휘 | antique 골동품 auction 경매 value 가치

2 (A)

번역 | 노무라 씨는 회계연도 말에 급여 인상을 받을 자격이 될 것이다.

해설 | 빈칸에 적절한 형용사 어휘를 고르는 문제이다. 'be+형용사+for'의 형태로 쓸 수 있어야 하며, 문맥상 '급여 인상을 받을 자격이 될 것이다'는 내용이 되어야 자연스럽다. 따라서 전치사 for와 함께 쓰여 '~할 자격이 되는'을 뜻하는 (A) eligible이 정답이다.

어휘 | raise 인상 fiscal year 회계연도 capable of ~할 수 있는 likely to부정사 ~할 것 같은 beneficial 유익한

3 (A)

번역 | 재무부가 연례 야유회를 위한 예산 증액 요청을 승인했다.

해설 | 빈칸 뒤 to부정사가 핵심 단서이다. request는 to부정사와 함께 쓰여 '~해 달라는 요청'을 의미하며, 문맥상 '예산을 올려 달라는 요청'이라는 내용이 자연스러우므로 '요청'을 뜻하는 명사 (A) request가 정답이다.

4 (D)

번역 | 디지털 피아노 앱의 최종 디자인은 원래 아이디어와는 상당히 다른 것으로 나타났다.

해설 | 빈칸 뒤의 명사 idea를 수식하여 '원래 아이디어'라는 의미가 되어야 최종 디자인과 많이 다르다는 문맥이 자연스럽게 완성되므로 '원래의, 기존의'라는 뜻의 (D) original이 정답이다.

어휘 | turn out 나타나다 quite 상당히 frequent 자주

5 (A)

번역 | 모긴슨 아트 엠포리움은 신진 및 기성 예술가들의 엄선된 희귀 화보들을 제공한다.

해설 | 문맥상 희귀 화보들을 엄선하여 손님들에게 제공한다는 의미가 적절하다. 따라서 '엄선된'이라는 뜻의 'a selection of'를 완성하는 (A) selection이 정답이다.

어휘 | emerging 최근 생겨난 established 인정받는 commitment 헌신 extension 확대

6 (B)

번역 | 직원들은 월요일에 열리는 건강한 생활 워크숍에 참석하도록 권장된다.

해설 | 빈칸은 선행사 our Healthy Living Workshop을 수식하는 관계사절의 동사 자리로, 문맥상 '월요일에 열리는 워크숍에'라는 내용이 되어야 자연스러우므로 '열리다, 개최되다'를 의미하는 (B) takes place가 정답이다.

어휘 | encourage 장려하다

7 (A)

번역 | 사업가는 사업 계획의 세부 사항을 은행원과 논의할 준비가 되어 있어야 한다.

해설 | 사업가가 은행원과 논의하는 사안이므로 '사업 계획의 세부 사항'이 되어야 적합하다. 따라서 '세부 사항'을 뜻하는 (A) particulars가 정답이다. specifics와 마찬가지로 particulars도 '자세한 사항'을 뜻하는 명사로 쓰일 때는 복수로 쓴다.

어휘 | entrepreneur 사업가 climate 분위기 closure 폐쇄

8 (C)

번역 | 그 식당의 수석 요리사는 "최고의 페이스트리 요리사"를 포함하여 여러 명망 높은 요리상을 수상했다.

해설 | 뒤의 명사구 culinary awards를 수식하여 '명망 높은 요리상'이라는 의미가 되어야 적절하므로 '명망 있는'을 뜻하는 (C) prestigious가 정답이다.

어휘 | culinary 요리의 imaginative 상상력이 풍부한 disposable 일회용의 attractive 매력적인

9 (D)

번역 | 시끄러운 소리에 장기적으로 노출되면 위험할 수 있으므로 생산직 근로자들은 반드시 보호용 헤드셋을 착용해야 한다.

해설 | 명사 exposure를 수식하여 '장기적인 노출'이라는 의미가 되어야 자연스러우므로 (D) Prolonged가 정답이다.

어휘 | exposure 노출 production 생산 protective 보호용의 keen 예리한 competitive 경쟁을 하는

10 (C)

번역 | 시내의 대형 사무실 건물들과 인접해 있어서 그 호텔은 출장 여행자들에게 인기가 있다.

해설 | 호텔이 출장자들에게 인기 있는 이유로 사무실 건물과의 근접성을 드는 것이 적절하므로, 전치사 to와 함께 쓰여 '~와의 근접성'을 나타내는 (C) proximity가 정답이다. (D) position은 전치사 to와 함께 쓰지 않으므로 답이 될 수 없다.

어휘 | locale 현장 appearance 외관 position 자리

ETS 고득점 실전 문제 7   본책 p.214

1 (B) **2** (C) **3** (C) **4** (A) **5** (A) **6** (D)
7 (B) **8** (C) **9** (A) **10** (C)

1 (B)

번역 | 주민센터 건설은 새로운 주택 사업의 마지막 단계이다.

해설 | 명사 '단계(phase)'를 수식하는 말로는 순서를 나타내는 형용사가 적절하다. 문맥상 '새로운 주택 사업의 마지막 단계'라는 의미가 되어야 자연스러우므로 '마지막의'라는 의미의 (B) final이 정답이다.

어휘 | community center 주민센터 housing 주택

2 (C)

번역 | 웹사이트는 최신 일기 예보를 보여줄 수 있도록 자주 업데이트 된다.

해설 | 빈칸은 동사 is updated를 수식하여 최신 정보 제공을 위한 웹사이트의 업데이트 빈도를 설명하는 내용의 문장을 완성해야 하므로, '자주'를 뜻하는 빈도 부사 (C) frequently가 정답이다. 특히 현재 시제로 설명하는 내용의 문장에서는 빈도 부사가 자주 답이 된다는 점을 알아 두자.

어휘 | eagerly 열심히 severely 심하게 indefinitely 무기한으로

3 (C)

번역 | 명절 장식은 이번 달에 전시될 수 있지만, 다음 달에는 철거해야 한다.

해설 | 등위접속사 but으로 연결되어 '이번 달에는 전시될 수 있지만'이라는 앞 절의 내용과는 반대되는 내용이 들어가야 하므로, be 뒤에서 수동태로 '철거되다'를 의미하는 (C) taken down이 정답이다.

4 (A)

번역 | 기사는 충분한 검토 시간을 남겨 주기 위해 발행일 2주 전에 제출되어야 한다.

해설 | 빈칸 뒤 명사 time을 수식해 '검토를 위한 충분한 시간'이라는 의미를 만들어야 자연스러우므로 '충분한'을 뜻하는 형용사 (A) adequate가 정답이다.

어휘 | perpetual 빈번한 impulsive 충동적인 deficient 부족한

5 (A)

번역 | 홍콩 대표단이 화요일에 도착하면 하트 씨가 그들에게 실험실 견학을 시켜 줄 예정이다.

해설 | 동사 arrive(도착하다)의 주체가 되면서, members를 수식하여 '대표단의 구성원들이 도착하다'라는 의미가 되어야 자연스러우므로 '대표단'을 뜻하는 (A) delegation이 정답이다.

어휘 | precision 정확성 intention 의도 translation 번역

6 (D)

번역 | 시 관계자들은 공원 개선 사업의 범위를 넓힐 것이라고 말했다.

해설 | 동사 broaden의 목적어이므로 넓히거나 확대하는 대상이 될 수 있어야 하고, 문맥상 '사업의 범위를 넓힌다'는 의미가 되어야 적절하므로 '범위'를 뜻하는 (D) scope가 정답이다.

어휘 | city official 시 관계자　broaden 넓히다
improvement 개선　variety 다양성, 품종　decision 결정

7　(B)

번역 | 자동차 회사의 경영진은 신형 전기 승합차 개발을
진행하기를 망설이고 있다.

해설 | 뒤에 나온 to부정사와 함께 쓰여 '~하기를 망설이는'이라는
의미를 만드는 (B) reluctant가 정답이다.

어휘 | automaker 자동차 회사　proceed with ~을 진행하다
electric van 전기 승합차　obvious 명백한　denied 거부된

8　(C)

번역 | 이 회사는 소문에 의하면 팩스가 여전히 많이 사용되는
유일한 곳이다.

해설 | '유일한 곳'이라는 것이 소문에 의한 정보라는 문맥이
자연스러우므로 '소문에 의하면'이라는 의미의 (C) reportedly가
정답이다.

어휘 | heavily 아주 많이　revealingly 드러나게　sincerely
진심으로　comparably 동등하게

9　(A)

번역 | 모든 관객은 음악 공연 동안 사진 촬영을 자제하도록
요구된다.

해설 | '사진 촬영을 자제하다'는 내용이 되어야 적절하므로
from과 함께 쓰여 '삼가다'라는 뜻을 이루는 (A) refrain이
정답이다. '단념시키다'라는 뜻의 (C) deter와 '막다'는 뜻의
(D) stop은 타동사로, 'deter[stop] A from –ing'의 형태로
쓰이므로 답이 될 수 없다.

어휘 | attempt 시도하다　deter 단념시키다

10　(C)

번역 | "100% 천연"이라는 라벨이 붙으려면 그 제품은 유기농
성분으로만 구성되어야 한다.

해설 | '~로 구성되다'는 뜻의 동사구 consist of를 수식하여
'오로지 ~로만 구성된다'는 의미를 이루는 (C) solely가
정답이다.

어휘 | label 라벨을 붙이다　consist of ~로 구성되다
ingredient 성분　severely 엄하게　apparently 듣자 하니
variously 여러 가지로

ETS 고득점 실전 문제 8　　본책 p.215

1 (A)　**2** (B)　**3** (C)　**4** (D)　**5** (D)　**6** (A)
7 (D)　**8** (C)　**9** (A)　**10** (D)

1　(A)

번역 | 다가오는 회의 주제에 대한 제안을 놓고 현재 고려
중입니다.

해설 | 빈칸의 수식을 받는 동사가 are being considered
이므로 현재진행 시제와 어울려 쓰이는 시간 부사가 들어가면
된다. 문맥상 '현재 고려되고 있다'는 내용이 되면 자연스러우므로
'현재'를 뜻하는 (A) currently가 정답이다.

어휘 | suggestion 제안　theme 주제　upcoming 다가오는

2　(B)

번역 | 스프링필드 병원은 예약 없이 내원한 환자를 환영합니다.

해설 | 빈칸은 주어 Walk-in patients를 수식하는 보어 자리로,
문맥상 '예약 없이 그냥 온 환자를 환영한다'는 의미가 되어야
적절하므로 '환영 받는'을 뜻하는 (B) welcome이 정답이다.

어휘 | walk-in 예약이 안 된　patient 환자　relative 상대적인

3　(C)

번역 | 고객들에게 희소식인데, 블링고는 휴대 전화 서비스 지역을
빠르게 확장하고 있다.

해설 | 동사 is expanding을 수식하여 '빠르게 확장하고 있다'는
의미가 되어야 자연스러우므로 '빠르게'를 뜻하는 (C) rapidly가
정답이다.

어휘 | to the delight of ~에게 희소식인데　expand 확장하다
coverage 서비스 지역　strangely 이상하게　formerly
이전에

4　(D)

번역 | 내부 문의는 감사부로 보내야 한다.

해설 | 명사 inquiries(문의)를 수식하여 '내부 문의'라는 의미가
되어야 자연스러우므로 '내부의'를 뜻하는 (D) Internal이
정답이다.

어휘 | Compliance Department 감사부(규정 준수를
체크하는 부서)　preferable 선호하는

5　(D)

번역 | 송장 발부를 위한 새 소프트웨어 프로그램은 청구 부서의
업무 흐름을 간소화할 것으로 기대된다.

해설 | 빈칸 뒤 목적어인 workflow(업무 흐름)와 의미가 가장
자연스럽게 어울리는 동사를 선택해야 한다. 따라서 '업무 흐름을
간소화하다'라는 의미를 이루는 (D) streamline이 정답이다.

어휘 | invoicing 송장 발부　billing 청구서 발부　occupy
차지하다　recall 회상하다

6　(A)

번역 | 박물관 안내 가이드는 교육을 받기는 하지만 예술에 대한
전반적인 지식이 있어야 한다.

해설 | to be 뒤에 들어가 주어인 Museum tour guides를
수식하기에 적절한 형용사를 고르는 문제이다. 문맥상 '교육은
받지만 전반적으로 지식을 갖추고 있어야 한다'는 내용이 되어야
자연스러우므로 '지식이 있는'을 뜻하는 (A) knowledgeable이
정답이다.

어휘 | training 교육　generally 전반적으로　predictable
예측 가능한　distinctive 독특한

7 (D)

번역 | 기차가 연착되고 있어서 일부 직원들은 오전 9시 이후에나 출근할 수 있다.

해설 | 빈칸 뒤 the office를 목적어로 받아 '사무실에 도착하지 못할 수도 있다'는 의미가 되어야 하므로 '도착하다'는 의미의 타동사 (D) reach가 정답이다.

8 (C)

번역 | 그린빌 도심 순환선의 지하철은 각 역에 20분 간격으로 도착한다.

해설 | 빈칸 앞의 시간 표현 twenty-minute과 자연스럽게 어울리는 명사를 고르면 된다. '20분 간격으로'라는 의미가 되어야 하므로 '간격'을 뜻하는 (C) intervals가 정답이다.

어휘 | inner-city 도심   loop 고리   division 분배   priority 우선 사항   intersection 교차로

9 (A)

번역 | 새 직물 절단기는 공장 면적의 상당히 큰 부분을 차지할 것이다.

해설 | 명사 portion을 수식하여 '상당히 큰 부분'이라는 의미를 이루는 '꽤 큰'이라는 뜻의 (A) sizable이 정답이다. (B) plenty는 수량이 풍부하다는 뜻이므로 답이 될 수 없다.

어휘 | portion 부분   consecutive 연속의   considerate 사려 깊은

10 (D)

번역 | 이 공사장은 엄격한 안전 기준을 준수하므로 근로자들은 보호복을 항상 착용해야 한다.

해설 | 복합명사인 safety standards를 수식하여 '엄격한 안전 기준'이라는 의미가 되어야 적합하므로 '엄격한'을 뜻하는 (D) stringent가 정답이다.

어휘 | adhere to ~을 준수하다   protective 보호용의   relaxed 느긋한   differential 차별하는   maintained 유지된

ETS 고득점 실전 문제 9

본책 p.216

1 (A) **2** (D) **3** (B) **4** (A) **5** (B) **6** (B)
7 (C) **8** (A) **9** (B) **10** (D)

1 (A)

번역 | 벤츄라 은행은 전 담보 대출 회사 부사장인 빈 싱이 대출 부서를 감독하게 된 것을 환영한다.

해설 | 복합명사 mortgage company vice president를 수식해 '전 담보 대출 회사 부사장'이라는 의미가 되어야 자연스러우므로 '이전의'라는 뜻의 (A) former가 정답이다.

어휘 | mortgage (담보) 대출   oversee 감독하다   loan 대출

2 (D)

번역 | 모든 연구 실험실에서 식음료는 엄격히 금지된다.

해설 | 동사 are prohibited를 수식해 '엄격히 금지된다'는 내용이 되어야 자연스러우므로 '엄격하게'라는 의미의 (D) strictly가 정답이다.

어휘 | scientifically 과학적으로   importantly 중요하게   accurately 정확하게

3 (B)

번역 | 케이프타운에 본사를 둔 마이릭 시빌즈는 도로 건설 업계에서 가장 존경받는 회사 중 하나이다.

해설 | 최상급을 나타내는 부사 most의 수식을 받아 뒤의 명사 companies를 자연스럽게 꾸며주는 형용사를 고르는 문제이다. '가장 존경받는 회사 중 하나'라는 내용이 되어야 적절하므로 '존경받는'을 뜻하는 (B) admired가 정답이다.

어휘 | based in ~에 기반을 둔   operational 운영의

4 (A)

번역 | 비록 1분기에는 매출이 부진했지만 오카루스사는 다시 한 번 경쟁사를 제쳤다.

해설 | 빈칸 뒤의 명사 the competition을 목적어로 받아 '1분기 매출은 부진했지만 경쟁사를 제쳤다'는 내용이 되어야 자연스러우므로, 정답은 '능가하다'는 의미의 (A) outperformed이다.

어휘 | sluggish 부진한   competition 경쟁사   display 전시하다   relocate 이전하다   delegate 위임하다

5 (B)

번역 | 여름 인턴들은 주로 경영학을 전공하는 학생들이다.

해설 | 문맥상 '여름 인턴들은 주로 경영 전공 학생들이다'는 내용이 되어야 하므로 '주로'를 뜻하는 (B) primarily가 정답이다. 부사는 일반적으로 명사를 수식하지 않지만 'largely'와 'primarily'는 '주로 ~이다'로 명사를 강조하는 역할로 쓰일 수 있다.

어휘 | major in ~을 전공하다   business administration 경영학   closely 면밀히

6 (B)

번역 | 회의실이 우리 직원들에 의해 거의 사용되지 않기 때문에 다른 부서로 배정되어야 할 것 같다.

해설 | 문맥상 '사무실이 다른 부서로 배정되어야 할 것 같다'는 내용과 부합하려면 '사용이 거의 되지 않는다'는 이유가 오는 것이 적절하므로 '거의 ~하지 않는'을 뜻하는 부정 부사 (B) rarely가 정답이다.

어휘 | assign 배정하다   wisely 현명하게   readily 손쉽게   publicly 공공연히

7 (C)

번역 | 엘름우드 인쇄는 지방 공급업체에서 유명한 지역 유통업체로 발돋움했다.

해설 | 빈칸 뒤 'from A to B(A에서 B로)'가 핵심 단서로, '지방 공급업체에서 유명한 지역 유통업체로 발전했다'라는 의미를 이루는 '진화하다, 발전하다'라는 뜻의 (C) evolved가 정답이다.

어휘 | supplier 공급업체 distributor 유통업체 determine 결정하다 focus 집중하다 permit 허용하다

8 (A)

번역 | 노섬은 바람이 강한 지역이라서 재생 가능한 풍력 에너지가 주민을 위한 전력 공급원으로 대체될 수 있다.

해설 | 풍력 에너지가 전력 공급원으로 대신 쓰일 수 있다는 내용이 되어야 적합하므로 '대체[대신]하다'라는 뜻의 (A) substitute가 정답이다.

어휘 | renewable 재생 가능한 source 원천 electricity 전력 manufacture 제조하다 represent 대표하다 apply 적용하다

9 (B)

번역 | 비계를 세우기 전에 공사 관리자의 점검을 이미 받았는지 확인하세요.

해설 | 빈칸이 있는 문장은 '비계를 세우기 전에' 완료할 일에 대해 당부하는 내용이므로 '점검을 이미[전에] 받았는지 확인하라'는 의미가 되어야 한다. 따라서 (B) already가 정답이다.

어휘 | erect 세우다 scaffolding 비계 inspect 점검하다

10 (D)

번역 | 총회 동안 각 연사는 연달아 이전 강연에서 언급된 요점을 보강했다.

해설 | 빈칸 앞의 한정사 each와 함께 명사 speaker를 수식하여 '각각의 연달아 나온 연사'라는 의미가 되어야 적절하므로 '연이은, 연속적인'을 뜻하는 (D) successive가 정답이다.

어휘 | reinforce 강화하다 selective 선택적인

ETS 고득점 실전 문제 10　　　본책 p.217

1 (A)	2 (C)	3 (B)	4 (A)	5 (C)	6 (C)
7 (B)	8 (A)	9 (C)	10 (A)		

1 (A)

번역 | 기술자가 영업소를 방문하여 컴퓨터의 작동 속도가 느린 원인을 파악할 것이다.

해설 | 컴퓨터의 작동 속도가 느린 원인을 '파악하다' 또는 '밝혀내다'는 의미가 되어야 적합하므로 (A) determine이 정답이다.

어휘 | operating 조작상의 anticipate 예상하다 exchange 교환하다

2 (C)

번역 | 센트럴 시티의 건강 엑스포는 최근 몇 년간 전례 없는 수준의 참석률을 경험했다.

해설 | '(참석률) 수준'이라는 명사를 수식하기에 적절한 형용사로 '전례 없는'이라는 뜻의 (C) unprecedented가 정답이다.

어휘 | attendance 참석(률) impressed 감명받은 absolute 절대적인

3 (B)

번역 | 배더슨사는 가구 제품을 제작하는 데 최고 품질의 재료만을 사용하는 것을 자랑스러워한다.

해설 | 가구를 제작하는 데 있어 '최고 품질의 재료만 사용한다'는 의미가 되어야 적합하므로 '활용[사용]하다'는 의미의 (B) utilize가 정답이다.

어휘 | material 자재 standardize 표준화하다 merge 합병하다

4 (A)

번역 | 이 스마트폰은 단단한 표면까지 최대 2미터의 낙하 거리를 견딜 수 있다고 증명되었다.

해설 | 빈칸 뒤의 목적어 drop(낙하 거리)과 잘 어울리는 동사를 골라야 한다. '최대 2미터의 낙하 거리를 견딘다'는 의미가 되어야 적절하므로 '견디다'를 뜻하는 (A) withstand가 정답이다.

어휘 | prove 증명하다 surface 표면 involve 수반하다 last 지속되다 affect 영향을 주다

5 (C)

번역 | 연구는 한 가지 주제에만 초점을 둔 짧은 회의가 의미 있는 결과를 낼 수 있다는 것을 보여 주었다.

해설 | 문맥상 '짧은 회의가 의미 있는 결과를 낸다'는 내용이 되어야 적합하므로 '(결과 등을) 내다, 산출하다'는 의미의 (C) yield가 정답이다.

어휘 | significant 의미 있는 appeal 호소하다 predict 예측하다

6 (C)

번역 | 소셜 미디어 광고는 젊은 소비자들 사이에 새로운 브랜드에 대한 인지도를 높이도록 돕는다.

해설 | 문맥상 '브랜드의 인지도를 높인다'는 의미가 되어야 적합하므로 '인지도'라는 뜻의 (C) recognition이 정답이다. 참고로, '브랜드 인지도'를 뜻하는 brand awareness와 brand recognition을 알아 두자.

어휘 | replacement 교체 motivation 동기 부여

7 (B)

번역 | 은행 직원들은 처리 시간을 확보하기 위해 오후 4시 이전에 고객과의 모든 거래를 완료해야 한다.

해설 | 문맥상 고객을 상대로 하는 은행 업무를 지칭하는 명사가 와야 하므로 '거래'를 뜻하는 (B) transactions가 정답이다.

어휘 | processing 처리 currency 통화

8 **(A)**

번역 | 보고서는 레저 여행객의 호텔 및 활동 선호도에 관한 철저한 연구 결과를 요약하고 있다.

해설 | 보고서에 연구 결과가 요약되어 있다는 내용의 문장이므로 명사 study를 수식하여 '철저한 연구'라는 의미가 되어야 자연스럽다. 따라서 '철저한'이라는 뜻의 (A) exhaustive가 정답이다.

어휘 | summarize 요약하다 preference 선호(도) upcoming 다가오는 influenced 영향을 받은 invested 투자된

9 **(C)**

번역 | 주자를 위한 훈련 프로그램은 단거리 달리기부터 시작한 다음 점차적으로 거리를 늘려야 한다.

해설 | 증감 동사인 increase(늘리다)를 수식하는 부사 자리이므로 '점차적으로'를 의미하는 (C) incrementally가 정답이다.

어휘 | distance 거리 downwardly 아래쪽으로 economically 경제적으로 invaluably 귀중하게

10 **(A)**

번역 | 학습 센터의 요리 워크숍 시리즈의 과거 참가자들은 이 프로그램을 높이 평가한다.

해설 | speak을 수식하여 '높이 평가한다'라는 의미가 되어야 적합하므로 정답은 (A) highly이다. 참고로, '높이 평가되는'을 뜻하는 'highly regarded'도 자주 출제된다.

어휘 | expectedly 예상대로 softly 부드럽게 carelessly 무심코

RC PART 6

UNIT 12 문법 문제

ETS 예제   본책 p.222

모금 위원회는 우리 단체에 대한 기부금을 추적하기 위한 다양한 소프트웨어 옵션을 조사해 오고 있습니다. 목표는 기부의 동향을 더 잘 이해하는 것입니다. 지난 3개월 동안 위원회는 몇 가지 옵션을 테스트해 왔습니다. 이제 3월 23일로 예정된 이사회 회의에서 선택안에 대해 논의할 준비가 되었습니다. 꼭 참석하도록 애써 주세요.

어휘 | fundraising 모금 committee 위원회 track 추적하다 gain 얻다 trend 동향, 추세 alternative 대안

ETS 유형 연습   본책 p.223

1 (B)   **2** (C)   **3** (D)   **4** (D)

[1-4] 보도

긴급 보도

연락처: 제프 베인스, 504-555-0162

반도, 추진력을 얻다.

뉴올리언스 (6월 1일)—비셋 재생에너지는 반도 연안 풍력 발전 프로젝트의 30% 지분을 **¹**인수했다. 이는 일본에서 가장 큰 연안 풍력 발전소가 될 반도의 자금 조달에 있어 핵심적인 도약이었다. 프로젝트의 시험 단계에서 두 개의 터빈이 건설되었다. **²**프로젝트의 다음 단계에는 50개가 더 설치될 것이다. 반도 프로젝트의 총 터빈 수는 소규모 도시에 전력을 공급하기에 충분할 것이다.

"우리는 이런 중요한 프로젝트의 핵심 참여자들을 지원하게 되어 기쁩니다. 반도는 아시아에서 강력한 풍력 발전소가 될 **³**뿐 아니라, 해외 후원사들의 참여로 이러한 유형의 프로젝트에 새로운 선례 또한 남기게 될 것입니다. 우리는 이로 인해 이 지역에 대한 향후 **⁴**투자가 장려되기를 바랍니다."라고 비셋 재생에너지의 최고 경영자인 마사 와이즈먼은 말했다.

어휘 | immediate 즉각적인 release 보도 boost (신장시키는) 힘 renewables 재생 가능 에너지 interest 지분 offshore 연안의 wind farm 풍력 발전소 financing 자금 조달 trial phase 시험 단계 turbine 터빈 stage 단계 power 전력을 공급하다 delighted 즐거운 involvement 관여 precedent 선례

1 **(B)**

해설 | 빈칸 뒤에 목적어 a 30 percent interest가 있으므로 수동태인 (A) was acquired는 답이 될 수 없다. 빈칸이 있는 문장에서 언급된 사건을 뒤 문장에서 This로 받아 '이는 핵심적인 도약이었다(This was a key step)'고 과거 시제로

표현한 것으로 보아 비셋 재생에너지가 30% 지분을 인수한 일은 이미 일어난 사건임을 알 수 있다. 따라서 정답은 (B) has acquired이다.

2 (C)

번역 | (A) 비셋 재생에너지는 다른 나라 발전소의 터빈에도 자금을 댄다.
(B) 풍력 발전소는 가까운 미래에 몇 가지 도전에 직면할 것이다.
(C) 프로젝트의 다음 단계에는 50개가 더 설치될 것이다.
(D) 몇몇 회사는 추가적인 터빈에 자금을 조달하지 않기로 결정했다.

해설 | 빈칸 앞 문장에서 프로젝트의 시험 단계에서 두 개의 터빈(two turbines)이 건설되었다고 했고, 뒤 문장에서 반도 프로젝트의 총 터빈 수(The total number of turbines)는 소규모 도시에 전력을 공급하기에 충분할 것이라고 했다. 따라서 글의 흐름상 빈칸에도 터빈의 수에 대한 내용이 언급되어야 적절하므로 앞으로 50개의 터빈이 더 설치될 것이라는 내용의 (C)가 정답이다.

어휘 | fund 자금을 대다 challenge 도전 finance 자금을 대다

3 (D)

해설 | 빈칸 앞의 Not only가 문제 해결의 단서로, not only와 함께 'not only A but (also) B'의 형태로 'A뿐만 아니라 B도'라는 의미를 나타내는 (D) but이 정답이다.

4 (D)

해설 | 앞에서 중요한 프로젝트의 핵심 참여자들을 지원 (support)하게 되어 기쁘다고 했고 해외 후원사들의 참여(the involvement of foreign sponsors)로 이러한 프로젝트에 새로운 선례를 남기게 될 것이라고 했다. 빈칸이 있는 문장은 앞서 언급된 프로젝트 자금 지원 사례들로 인한 효과에 대한 내용이므로 '지역에 대한 투자가 활성화되기를 바란다'는 내용이 되어야 적합하다. 따라서 '투자'를 뜻하는 (D) investment가 정답이다.

ETS 고득점 실전 문제

1 (B) **2** (C) **3** (A) **4** (D) **5** (A) **6** (B)
7 (A) **8** (A) **9** (A) **10** (C) **11** (B) **12** (A)
13 (B) **14** (C) **15** (D) **16** (A)

[1-4] 기사

커치, 노틀리 리즈 최고 경영자로 임명되다.

전국 치과 공급업체 연맹인 노틀리 리즈 파트너스는 업계 경영인 페데리코 커치가 차기 최고 경영자가 될 것이라고 발표했다. "커치 회장은 우수함과 성장에 대한 우리의 ¹헌신을 공유하고 있으며, 그가 우리를 앞으로 이끌고 나가게 되어 정말 기쁩니다."라고 앨런 파울 이사회 임원은 말했다.

커치 씨는 25년 동안 의료업체를 성장시켜 온 경험을 갖고 있다.

그는 이전에 랜들 진료 센터에서 최고 경영자직을 맡으며 30개 주로 확장하는 것을 감독했다. ²그가 거기에 있는 동안 수익은 10% 증가했다. "저는 노틀리 리즈를 새로운 시장으로 진출시키고 조직을 성장시키게 되어 매우 ³흥분됩니다."라고 커치 씨는 말했다.

엘패소에 본사를 둔 노틀리 리즈는 국내 ⁴곳곳의 치과의사들과 제휴하여 관리 및 지원 서비스를 제공하고 있다.

어휘 | appoint 임명하다 provider 공급업체 executive 경영진 board 이사회 medical practice 의료업 previously 이전에 surgery 진료 oversee 감독하다 expansion 확장 thrilled 신이 난 organization 조직 based in ~에 본사를 둔

1 (B)

해설 | 동사 shares의 목적어 역할로 소유격 뒤 명사가 와야 하므로, 빈칸은 명사 자리이다. 문맥상 '우수함과 성장에 대한 우리의 헌신을 공유하고 있다'는 내용이 되어야 하므로 '약속, 헌신'이라는 의미의 추상명사인 (B) commitment가 정답이다.

2 (C)

번역 | (A) 스미스-콕스 채용은 그대로 유지되어 구인을 담당한다.
(B) 노틀리 리즈 경영진 전원은 이 경험을 활용할 수 있었다.
(C) 그가 거기에 있는 동안 수익은 10% 증가했다.
(D) 합병은 많은 업계 전문가들에게 놀라운 일이었다.

해설 | 앞 문장에서 커치 씨가 25년간 의료업체를 성장시킨 경험이 있고 랜들 진료 센터에서 최고 경영자직을 맡으며 30개 주로 확장하는 것을 감독했다고 했다. 커치 씨가 이전 업체에서 거둔 업적 및 성과에 대해 소개하는 문맥이므로 이전 업체의 CEO로서 사업 확장을 주도하며 일궈낸 성과가 뒤따르는 것이 자연스럽다. 따라서 정답은 (C)이다.

어휘 | retain 유지하다 merger 합병 expert 전문가

3 (A)

해설 | 기사의 첫 문장에서 노틀리 리즈 파트너스에서 업계 경영인인 페데리코 커치가 차기 최고 경영자가 될 것이라고 발표했다고 했다. 따라서 커치 씨는 앞으로 최고 경영자로서 노틀리 리즈를 새로운 시장에 진출시키고 조직을 성장시킬 수 있게 된 일에 대해 현재 흥분되고 들뜬 기분을 느낀다는 것이므로 정답은 현재 시제인 (A) am이다.

4 (D)

해설 | 빈칸 뒤의 장소 명사 the country를 목적어로 취해 '전국 도처에 있는 치과의사들'이라는 의미가 되어야 하므로 '~ 도처에, ~ 곳곳의'를 뜻하는 (D) throughout이 정답이다.

[5-8] 이메일

수신: ⟨martin90@rapidonet.co.uk⟩
발신: ⟨careers@attacomma.co.uk⟩
날짜: 4월 16일
제목: 취업 기회

마틴 씨께,

아타코마사는 현재 셰필드에서 직원 모집 중입니다. 정규직, 시간제, 계절직 자리에 지원 가능합니다. www.attacomma.co.uk/jobs를

방문하여 여러분5에게 맞는 자리를 확인하세요. 창고 근로자의
초봉은 시간당 18파운드입니다. 6하지만 입사 6개월 뒤 성과급 급여
인상에 대한 자격이 부여됩니다. 높은 노동 수요를 7충족시키기
위해 연말까지 합격한 지원자들에게 추가적으로 100파운드의
등록 보너스가 제공될 것입니다. 8이력서나 이전 경력은 필요하지
않습니다. 온라인 신청서를 작성하기만 하면 됩니다.

제나 로빈슨, 인재 채용 전담

어휘 | eligible ~을 할 수 있는 merit-based 성과 기반
raise 급여 인상 demand 수요 labor 노동 sign-up 등록
applicant 지원자 fill out 작성하다 application 지원서

5 (A)
해설 | 문맥상 '여러분을 위한', '여러분에게 맞는'이라는 의미가
되어야 하므로 '~을 위한, ~에 적합한'을 뜻하는 (A) for가
정답이다.

6 (B)
해설 | 빈칸 앞 문장에서 창고 근로자의 초봉은 시간당
18파운드(£18 an hour)라고 했는데 뒤 문장에서 입사 6개월
뒤 성과급 급여 인상에 대한 자격이 부여된다(become eligible
for merit-based raises)며 일정 시간이 지나면 급여가
달라질 수 있음을 암시하고 있다. 앞 문장(시간당 18파운드)과 뒤
문장(급여 인상 가능)이 서로 대조되는 내용이므로 역접 관계를
나타내는 (B) However가 정답이다.

어휘 | regardless 상관없이 consequently 그 결과

7 (A)
해설 | 빈칸 뒤의 명사구를 쉼표 뒤 완전한 절에 수식구로
연결하는 자리이므로 동사 (B) Meet은 들어갈 수 없다. 문맥상
'높은 노동 수요를 충족시키기 위해'라는 의미가 되어야 하므로
'~을 위해, ~할 수 있도록'이라는 목적의 의미를 나타내는
to부정사 표현이 와야 한다. 따라서 정답은 (A) To meet이다.

8 (A)
번역 | (A) 이력서나 이전 경력은 필요하지 않습니다.
　　　(B) 아타코마사는 사업을 확장 중입니다.
　　　(C) 이 할인권은 5월 11일까지 상품으로 교환되어야
　　　　 합니다.
　　　(D) 셰필드는 이 지역에서 가장 인구가 많은 도시입니다.

해설 | 빈칸 뒤 문장에서 그냥(Simply) 온라인 신청서만
작성하면 된다고 했으므로 온라인 신청서 외에 이력서나 경력
같은 다른 것은 필요 없다는 내용이 와야 한다. 따라서 정답은
(A)이다.

어휘 | redeem 상품으로 교환하다 populous 인구가 많은

[9-12] 공지

켈윈 신발 공장에서 견학 또는 설명회를 신청하시려면 KelwinShoes.
com을 방문하십시오. 견학은 금방 자리가 찬다는 점에 유의해
주십시오. 9따라서 사전 계획이 권장됩니다. 귀하에게 적합한 날짜가
현재 목록에 없는 경우, 주기적으로 일정 페이지를 확인해 보시기를
권합니다. 새로운 견학 날짜가 10정기적으로 게시됩니다. 귀하의 학급
또는 단체를 위한 특별 단체 견학을 예약하시려면 특별 견학 신청서

제출하시면 됩니다. 11저희 웹사이트에서 해당 양식의 전자 사본
파일을 찾으실 수 있습니다. 특별 견학은 단체만 이용 가능하다는
점을 주의해 주십시오. 12관심 있는 단체는 희망일 최소 2주 전에
신청하셔야 합니다.

어휘 | register for ~에 등록하다 fill up 가득 차다 routinely
주기적으로 arrange 주선하다 organization 단체 party
단체 desired 바라는

9 (A)
번역 | (A) 따라서 사전 계획이 권장됩니다.
　　　(B) 아쉽게도 그것들은 취소되었습니다.
　　　(C) 운전자들은 저희의 많은 주차장 중 한 곳에 주차하실
　　　　 수 있습니다.
　　　(D) 저희 웹사이트에서는 제품을 쉽게 비교할 수 있습니다.

해설 | 앞에서 공장에서의 견학 또는 설명회 신청 방법을 알려
주면서 견학은 금방 자리가 찬다(tours fill up quickly)고
했으므로, 견학을 원한다면 미리 계획하고 신청해야 한다는
권고가 뒤따르는 것이 자연스럽다. 따라서 정답은 (A)이다.

어휘 | advanced 사전의 lot (특정 용도용) 부지
comparison 비교

10 (C)
해설 | 앞 문장에서 적당한 날짜가 목록에 없는 경우
'주기적으로(routinely)' 일정 페이지를 확인하라고 권하는
것으로 보아, 새로운 견학 날짜가 '정기적으로' 게시된다는
내용이 되어야 자연스럽다. 따라서 '정기적으로'를 뜻하는 (C)
regularly가 정답이다.

어휘 | separately 별도로 internally 내부적으로
favorably 유리하게

11 (B)
해설 | 빈칸에는 뒤의 명사 Web site를 수식하는 말이 필요하다.
글의 첫 문장에서 켈윈 신발 공장에서 견학 또는 설명회를
신청하려면 KelwinShoes.com으로 우리를 방문하라(visit
us)고 웹사이트 주소를 알려 준 것으로 보아, 신청서 양식의 전자
사본 파일 또한 앞서 알려준 웹사이트에서 찾아보라는 것임을
알 수 있다. 웹사이트 주소를 알려 주며 우리(us)라고 했으므로
빈칸에는 '우리'의 소유격이 들어가야 한다. 따라서 (B) our가
정답이다.

12 (A)
해설 | 빈칸은 뒤의 명사 parties(단체)를 수식하는 형용사
자리이다. 문맥상 사람이 느끼는 감정을 나타내는 형용사가
와야 하므로, '관심 있는'을 뜻하는 과거분사 (A) Interested가
정답이다.

[13-16] 이메일

수신: 크리스 피쿨라 〈cpikula@lmnmail.com〉
발신: 조니 칼린 〈jcarlin@brighting.com〉
날짜: 4월 18일
제목: 자판기 재고

안녕하세요, 크리스,

¹³우리 자판기에 들어가는 상품 선정에 약간의 변화를 요청하고 싶습니다. 가능하다면 다음번 목요일 재고 보충 방문 시 이 변경 사항이 ¹⁴적용되면 좋겠습니다.

직원들 사이에서 프레첼, 크래커, 캔디바가 빠르게 소진됩니다. 기계 내에 이 제품들의 수량을 두 배로 늘릴 수 있을까요? 충분한 공간을 만들려면, 아마도 덜 인기 있는 제품 중 일부를 빼면 될 것 같습니다. 지난번 방문 때 보셨듯이 특정 과자 종류는 거의 구매되지 않고 있습니다. ¹⁵그러니 이것들을 한꺼번에 없애는 것도 가능합니다. ¹⁶나머지 재고 품목은 변함없이 유지하면 됩니다.

정말 감사합니다!

조니

어휘 | vending machine 자판기 stock 재고 take effect 적용되다 restocking 재고 보충 quantity 양 eliminate 제거하다 rarely 드물게 get rid of 없애다

13 (B)

해설 | 빈칸 앞에 its(그것의)나 such(그러한)로 받을 수 있는 명사가 언급되지 않았으므로 (A) its와 (C) such는 답이 될 수 없다. 빈칸 뒤에 나오는 내용의 문맥상 이메일의 발신인(Joanie)과 수신인(Chris)이 함께 관리 중인 자판기에 들어가는 상품 선정에 변화를 주고 싶다는 것이므로 '우리 자판기'가 되어야 적절하다. 따라서 정답은 (B) our이다.

14 (C)

해설 | would like는 to부정사를 목적격 보어로 취하여 'would like + 목적어 + to부정사'의 형태로 쓰인다. 빈칸은 would like의 목적격 보어 자리이므로 정답은 (C) to take이다.

15 (D)

해설 | 앞 문장에서 특정 과자 종류는 거의 구매되지 않고 있다(certain snack types are rarely purchased)고 했고 뒤 문장에는 이것들을 싹 없애도(get rid of them all together) 되겠다고 했다. 두 문장이 잘 팔리지 않으니 치워도 된다는 인과관계를 나타내고 있으므로, '그러므로'를 뜻하는 (D) Therefore가 정답이 된다.

16 (A)

번역 | (A) 나머지 재고 품목은 변함없이 유지하면 됩니다.
(B) 자판기는 편리한 위치에 있습니다.
(C) 우리 직원들은 구내식당에 들르는 것을 즐깁니다.
(D) 새로운 기계를 기대합니다.

해설 | 빈칸 앞에서 잘 팔리는 제품은 수량을 두 배로 늘릴 것(double the quantity), 인기 낮은 제품은 제거할 것(could be eliminated), 구매율 낮은 과자는 모두 치울 것(get rid of them)이라며 자판기의 재고 관리, 특히 잘 팔리지 않는 제품에 대해 집중적으로 언급하고 있으므로 뒤에는 그 외에 나머지 제품들에 대해서는 어떻게 할지에 대한 내용이 나오면 자연스럽다. 따라서 정답은 (A)이다.

어휘 | rest 나머지 inventory 재고 목록 conveniently 편리하게

ETS 예제   본책 p.228

제목: 사무실 폐쇄

12월 20일 토요일 연말 직원 연회를 준비하기 위해 12월 19일 금요일 오후 3시에 사무실 문을 닫을 예정입니다. – 중략 – 토요일 일과 관련해 이번 주에 제가 이메일 초대장을 보내 드릴 예정입니다. 파티에 몇 명이 올 계획인지 알 수 있도록 즉시 답변 부탁드립니다.

어휘 | affair 일 promptly 신속하게

ETS 유형 연습   본책 p.229

1 (B) **2** (D) **3** (C) **4** (A)

[1-4] 제품 후기

분유는 일반 우유와 맛이 다를 것 같아 먹어 보기가 ¹망설여 졌습니다. 하지만 지난주 우리 동네 식료품점에 일반 우유가 품절되어 주미 밀크를 시도해 보기로 결심했습니다. 저는 ²기분 좋은 놀라움을 느꼈습니다.

³처음에는 적정 농도를 맞추는 것이 어려웠습니다. 그래서 고속 믹서기를 사용해 더 많은 양을 섞어봤습니다. 이 방법은 시간이 더 걸리기는 하지만 우유가 부드럽고 맛있습니다. 더 수고롭기는 하지만 ⁴이 방법을 적극 추천하고 싶습니다.

다음에 쇼핑할 때 일반 우유를 사겠지만 주미 밀크도 계속 보관해 두고 먹을 생각입니다. 일반 우유와 달리 몇 년이고 선반에 보관할 수 있으니까요.

–신시아 시스네로스

어휘 | powdered milk 분유 grocery store 식료품점 blender 믹서기 quantity 양 method 방법 smooth 부드러운 tasty 맛있는 definitely 분명히 on hand 준비된

1 (B)

해설 | hesitant는 'be hesitant to부정사'의 형태로 쓰여 '~하는 것을 망설이다'를 의미한다. '분유를 먹어 보기가 망설여 졌다'는 내용이 되어야 하므로 (B) hesitant가 정답이다. 자동사 hesitate는 수동태로 쓰이지 않으므로 (A) hesitated는 답이 될 수 없다.

2 (D)

해설 | 문맥상 적절하게 형용사 surprised를 수식하는 부사를 고르는 문제이다. 앞 문장에서 우유가 품절되어 주미 밀크를 시도하게 되었다고 했는데, 뒤에서 고속 믹서기로 많은 양을 섞어 먹었더니 우유가 부드럽고 맛있었다(smooth and tasty)고 좋은 평가를 내렸으므로 '기분 좋게 놀랐다'는 내용이 되어야 자연스럽다. 따라서 '즐겁게, 유쾌하게'를 뜻하는 (D) pleasantly가 정답이다.

어휘 | rarely 좀처럼 ~하지 않는 remotely 멀리서

3 (C)

번역 | (A) 다시는 그런 실수를 하지 않겠습니다.
(B) 더 큰 슈퍼마켓에는 더 많은 선택권이 있었을 것입니다.
(C) 처음에는 적정 농도를 맞추는 것이 어려웠습니다.
(D) 주미 밀크는 대부분의 조리법에서 대체로 사용될 수 있습니다.

해설 | 빈칸 뒤에서 그래서(Then) 고속 믹서기를 사용해 더 많은 양을 섞어봤다고 한 것으로 보아, 앞서 시도했을 때는 우유 농도 조절에 실패했음을 알 수 있다. 따라서 처음에는 적정 농도를 맞추는 게 어려웠다는 내용의 (C)가 정답이다.

어휘 | consistency 농도 challenge 도전 substitute 대체물

4 (A)

해설 | 앞 문장에서 고속 믹서기를 사용해 더 많은 양을 섞어봤는데 이 방법(This method)은 더 오래 걸리지만 우유가 부드럽고 맛있다고 했으므로, 앞서 언급된 방법(this method)을 추천하고 있음을 알 수 있다. 빈칸에는 this method를 대신할 수 있는 대명사가 필요하므로 (A) it이 정답이다.

ETS 고득점 실전 문제 본책 p.230

1 (C)	2 (B)	3 (A)	4 (D)	5 (B)	6 (B)
7 (A)	8 (C)	9 (C)	10 (A)	11 (A)	12 (C)
13 (B)	14 (A)	15 (D)	16 (C)		

[1-4] 회람

수신: 전 직원
발신: 반다나 틸락다아리, 제노빅 연구소 CEO
제목: SWD와의 합병
날짜: 8월 23일

오늘 일자 자사 온라인 일간 소식지 〈비즈노트〉를 보셨다면 당사와 스코샤 도매 유통업체 간 합병 협상이 마무리 단계에 있다는 것을 이미 알고 계실 것입니다. 이번 **1**제휴는 우리에게 제약산업에서 경쟁력을 더 높일 수 있는 수단을 제공해 줄 것입니다.

여러분 중 많은 분들이 이번 합병이 여러분의 현재 직위에 **2**미칠 수 있는 영향에 대해 궁금해하고 계시다는 점을 잘 알고 있습니다. 저는 전 직원이 일자리를 유지할 것이라고 장담합니다. **3**사실, 곧 직원을 추가로 채용할 계획입니다. 따라서 이 점에 있어서는 우려하실 이유가 전혀 없습니다.

목요일 전 직원 회의에서 여러분의 질문이나 우려 사항에 대해 기꺼이 답변을 드릴 예정입니다. 지난 6개월 **4**동안 경영진에 보여주신 인내심에 감사드립니다.

어휘 | edition 호 merger 합병 negotiation 협상 wholesale 도매의 distributor 유통업체 means 수단 competitive 경쟁력 있는 pharmaceutical 제약의 impact 영향 assure 보장하다 retain 유지하다 in this respect 이 점에 있어 whatsoever 전혀 concerned 걱정하는 address (문제 등에 대해) 다루다 patience 인내심

1 (C)

해설 | 앞 문장에서 당사와 스코샤 도매 유통업체 간 합병 협상이 마무리 단계에 있다고 했고, 빈칸 뒤로는 협상이 가져다 줄 이점(provide us with the means to be more competitive)에 대한 설명이 이어지고 있으므로 빈칸에는 '제휴'가 들어가야 적절하다. 따라서 정답은 (C) partnership이다.

어휘 | study 연구 measure 조치 partnership 제휴

2 (B)

해설 | 빈칸은 선행사 the impact를 수식하며 목적격 관계사가 생략된 관계사절의 주어 the merger 뒤 동사 자리이다. 앞뒤 문맥에서 앞으로 예정된 합병으로 인한 효과 및 영향에 대해 설명하고 있으므로, 가능성을 나타내는 may가 들어가 '현재 직위에 미칠 수 있는 영향'이라는 내용이 되어야 자연스럽다. 따라서 정답은 (B) may have이다.

3 (A)

번역 | (A) 사실, 곧 직원을 추가로 채용할 계획입니다.
(B) 그 결과, 직원 회의가 취소되었습니다.
(C) 게다가 우리 물류 센터는 주문품을 신속하게 배송합니다.
(D) 물론, 우리는 경쟁사를 과소평가하지 않습니다.

해설 | 앞 문장에는 전 직원이 일자리를 유지할 것(all employees will retain their jobs)이라고 장담한다고 했고 뒤 문장에는 따라서 이 점에 있어서는 우려할 이유가 전혀 없다(no reason whatsoever to be concerned)고 했으므로, 빈칸에는 직원들의 고용 불안이 해소될 만한 내용이 들어가야 적절하다. 따라서 직원 추가 채용에 대한 계획을 밝히고 있는 (A)가 정답이다.

어휘 | consequently 그 결과 underestimate 과소평가하다

4 (D)

해설 | 빈칸 뒤의 기간 표현 the last six months와 어울려 쓸 수 있어야 하며, 문맥상 '지난 6개월간'이라는 내용이 되어야 자연스럽다. 따라서 기간 앞에서 '~ 동안'을 뜻하는 (D) over가 정답이다.

[5-8] 이메일

수신: 전 회원들께
발신: 라자트 싱할
날짜: 4월 8일, 월요일
제목: 신규 총회 장소

친애하는 HNA 회원 여러분,

우리의 통제를 벗어난 상황으로 인해, 올해 하리아나 간호사 협회(HNA)의 연례 총회 장소를 옮겨야만 했습니다. 이제 총회는 시민 회의 센터 대신 하리아나 관리공단에서 **5**열릴 예정입니다. 워크숍과 프레젠테이션에 많은 시간이 소요되겠지만, 행사장을 **6**둘러보실 기회 또한 이용하시기 바랍니다. **7**정말 숨이 막힐 정도로 아름답습니다. 나무가 우거진 길을 따라 산책하시거나 장엄한 전망에서 조류 관찰을

즐기실 수 있습니다. 그리고 부지 내에 위치한 호수는 이른 아침이나 늦은 오후 수영에 ⁸안성맞춤입니다. 그러니 편안한 옷과 신발, 수영복, 그리고 조류를 관찰하실 분들은 쌍안경을 구비해 오시기를 권합니다.

6월에 만나 뵙기를 기대합니다.

라자트 싱할, 회의 진행자

하리아나 간호사 협회

어휘 | circumstance 상황 association 협회 relocate 이전하다 conservancy 관리소 municipal 시의 undoubtedly 의심할 여지없이 consume 소모하다 venue 장소 stroll 산책하다 lush 우거진 majestic 장엄한 overlook 전망 on the premises 부지 내에서 binoculars 쌍안경

5 (B)

해설 | 빈칸은 주어 it의 동사 자리이므로 (D) taking은 답이 될 수 없다. 빈칸의 앞 문장에는 올해 총회 장소를 옮겨야만 했다(had to be relocated)며 총회에 대한 변경 사항을 전달했고, 빈칸 뒤 문장에는 워크숍과 프레젠테이션에 많은 시간이 소요되겠지만(will consume) 기회를 이용하기 바란다(we hope you will also use the opportunity)고 한 것으로 보아 총회는 미래에 일어날 일임을 알 수 있다. 빈칸이 있는 문장은 앞으로 열릴 총회의 변경된 장소에 대해 안내하는 내용이므로 정답은 미래 시제인 (B) will take이다.

6 (B)

해설 | 명사 opportunity를 수식하는 to부정사에 들어갈 적절한 동사 어휘를 고르는 문제이다. 회의 참석자들을 대상으로 하는 글이고, 뒤 문장에서 산책을 하거나 조류 관찰을 즐길 수 있다며 회의 장소를 돌아다니며 할 수 있는 일에 대해 언급하고 있으므로 '행사장을 둘러볼 기회'라는 내용이 되어야 연결이 자연스럽다. 따라서 '둘러보다, 답사하다'는 의미의 (B) explore가 정답이다.

7 (A)

번역 | (A) 정말 숨이 막힐 정도로 아름답습니다.
(B) 많은 경제 활동을 수반합니다.
(C) 많은 바다 생물의 서식지입니다.
(D) 회의 참가자에게만 판매됩니다.

해설 | 빈칸 앞에서 행사장을 둘러볼 기회를 가지라고 권하고 있고, 빈칸 뒤에서 나무가 우거진 길을 산책하거나 장엄한 전망에서 조류 관찰을 즐길 수 있다며 행사 장소에서 누릴 수 있는 것들에 대해 소개하고 있으므로 행사장의 경관에 대해 언급하는 내용이 들어가야 연결이 자연스럽다. 따라서 행사장의 아름다움에 대해 언급하고 있는 (A)가 정답이다.

어휘 | breathtaking (너무 아름답거나 놀라) 숨이 막히는 economic 경제의 creature 생물 goer ~에 다니는 사람

8 (C)

해설 | 주어 the lake를 수식하는 보어 자리에 적절한 형용사 어휘를 고르는 문제이다. '호수가 이른 아침이나 늦은 오후 수영을 하기에 안성맞춤이다'라는 내용이 되어야 자연스러우므로 전치사 for와 함께 'be perfect for'의 형태로 '~에 완벽한'을 뜻하는 (C) perfect가 정답이다.

[9-12] 공지

10월 2일 교통 정보: 도로 폐쇄 예정

오늘 이스턴 테라스에 도로 폐쇄가 있을 예정입니다. 홈스테드 가와 레이크 플레이스 사이 거리는 도로 재포장을 ⁹위해 오전 8시부터 오후 5시까지 폐쇄될 예정입니다.

웨스트 5번가와 웨스트 6번가 사이에 있는 홈스테드 초등학교 앞에 있는 홈스테드 가에 추가적인 폐쇄가 있을 것입니다. 잠시 동안의 이 폐쇄는 오후 1시에서 2시 30분 사이 학교 ¹⁰특별 행사를 위한 공간을 제공할 것입니다.

설리반 웨이와 스프루스 가 사이의 웨스트 엘름 가는 가을 축제 퍼레이드를 준비하기 위해 10월 4일 금요일에 폐쇄될 예정입니다. 폐쇄는 오후 2시에 시작됩니다. 또한 이 지역은 10월 5일 토요일에는 실제 퍼레이드를 ¹¹위해 하루 종일 폐쇄됩니다. ¹²이 거리는 10월 5일 토요일 저녁 8시에 재개통될 예정입니다.

어휘 | advisory 상황 보고 upcoming 다가오는 closure 폐쇄 resurfacing 재포장 occur 발생하다 elementary school 초등학교 brief 짧은 accommodate 수용하다

9 (C)

해설 | 빈칸 앞에 완전한 절이 있고, 빈칸 뒤의 전치사구 for street resurfacing을 연결해 '도로 재포장을 할 수 있도록'이라는 내용이 되어야 하므로 '~하기 위해서'라는 목적의 의미를 지니는 (C) to allow가 정답이다.

10 (A)

해설 | 빈칸 뒤의 명사인 행사(event)를 수식하기에 적절한 형용사를 골라야 한다. 학교에서 열리는 '특별한 행사'라는 내용이 되어야 자연스러우므로 정답은 (A) special이다. (B) numerous는 '많은'을 뜻하므로 하나를 뜻하는 부정관사 a와 함께 쓸 수 없다.

11 (A)

해설 | 문맥상 '실제 퍼레이드를 위해'라는 의미가 되어야 하므로, 목적을 나타내는 전치사 (A) for가 정답이다.

12 (C)

번역 | (A) 거리 봉쇄 장벽을 공급해 주셔서 감사합니다.
(B) 학교 행사에 참여하시기를 바랍니다.
(C) 이 거리는 10월 5일 토요일 저녁 8시에 재개통될 예정입니다.
(D) 귀하의 지속적인 기여에 감사드립니다.

해설 | 앞에서 엘름 가의 폐쇄 일정을 열거하며 10월 5일 토요일에는 하루 종일 폐쇄된다고 했으므로 빈칸에는 이 지역에서 다시 통행이 허용되는 시점을 안내하는 내용이 들어가야 자연스럽다. 따라서 정답은 (C)이다.

어휘 | barrier 장벽 contribution 기여

[13-16] 회람

수신: 베흐람 가 주민 및 사업주
발신: 코타이 유니버설 그룹
날짜: 9월 3일

제목: 일정표 업데이트

코타이 유니버설 그룹은 공사 일정표에 다음과 같은 업데이트를 발표합니다.

베흐람 로에 위치한 20층짜리 건물의 공사가 계획대로 진행 중입니다. 주로 뭄바이 법인 사무실 역할을 하겠지만, 새 건물에는 텔레비전 스튜디오와 기타 미디어 공간 ¹³또한 입주할 예정입니다. 기존 건축물의 철거는 지난 여름에 시작되었으나 우리가 기대했던 것보다 더 오래 걸리고 있습니다. ¹⁴그것은 두 달 뒤에 완료될 것으로 예상됩니다. ¹⁵인근 주민들은 적정 수준의 소음을 계속해서 듣게 될 것입니다. 전체 프로젝트는 대략 2년 안에 완공될 것입니다. 여러분의 ¹⁶인내에 감사드립니다. 장기간의 공사로 인해 불편하시겠지만 완공된 건물은 이 지역에 환영받고 가치 있는 자산이 될 것이라고 확신합니다.

어휘 | release 발표하다   story (건물의) 층   proceed 진행하다   serve as ~의 역할을 하다   corporate 기업의   house 수용하다   demolition 철거   existing 기존의   structure 건축물   lengthy 긴   inconvenience 불편   worthwhile 가치 있는   asset 자산   neighborhood 지역

13 (B)

해설 | 빈칸 앞 문장에서 신축 건물이 주로 뭄바이 법인 사무실 역할을 할 것이라고 했는데 뒤 문장에서 이 건물에 텔레비전 스튜디오와 기타 미디어 공간이 입주할 것이라고 안내하고 있다. 사무실 이외에도 스튜디오와 미디어 공간으로서 건물의 추가적인 역할에 대해 언급하는 문장을 연결해야 하므로 '또한'이라는 의미의 부사가 들어가야 자연스럽다. 따라서 정답은 (B) also이다.

14 (A)

해설 | 두 달 뒤에 완료될 것으로 예상되는 것은 기존 건축물의 철거(Demolition of the existing structures)이므로 이를 지칭하는 It이 주어로 와야 한다. 따라서 (A) It is가 정답이다.

15 (D)

번역 | (A) 공사 규정이 최근 몇 년 동안 갱신되었습니다.
(B) 코타이 직원들은 소셜 미디어를 통해 회사 소식을 공유할 수 있습니다.
(C) 다른 두 방송사가 인근에 있습니다.
(D) 인근 주민들은 적정 수준의 소음을 계속해서 듣게 될 것입니다.

해설 | 빈칸 앞에서 건축물의 철거가 예상보다 오래 걸리고 있다며 두 달 뒤 완료될 예정이라고 했고, 빈칸 뒤에서는 전체 프로젝트가 2년 내 완료될 것이라며 인내에 감사한다고 했다. 빈칸 앞뒤로 공사가 계속 진행되고 있음을 언급하며 양해를 구하고 있으므로 그 사이에는 문맥의 흐름상 이 공사로 발생되는 영향에 대한 내용이 들어가면 자연스럽다. 따라서 주민들이 계속 소음을 듣게 될 것이라는 내용의 (D)가 정답이다.

어휘 | code 규정   broadcasting 방송   exist 존재하다   in the vicinity 인근에   moderate 적정한

16 (C)

해설 | 앞 문장에서 전체 프로젝트는 대략 2년 안에 완공될 것이라고 했고, 뒤 문장에서 장기간 공사로 불편할 수 있다는 점(lengthy construction can be inconvenience)을 알고 있다며 양해를 구하고 있으므로 빈칸이 있는 문장은 장기 공사로 인한 불편함을 참고 이해해 주어 감사하다는 내용이 되면 적절하다. 따라서 정답은 '인내'를 뜻하는 (C) patience이다.

UNIT 14   접속부사 문제

ETS 예제 — 본책 p.234

농업 심의 이사회가 곧 발표할 보고서는 내년에 25년 만에 처음으로 콩 생산량이 감소할 것으로 내다본다. 이와는 대조적으로 곡물 생산량은 증가할 것으로 보인다. – 중략 – 곡물 공급으로 밀, 옥수수, 쌀 가격은 낮게 유지되는 반면, 콩의 가격은 급등할 수 있다.

어휘 | soy 콩   grain 곡물   skyrocket 급등하다   wheat 밀

ETS 유형 연습

본책 p.235

1 (D)   **2** (A)   **3** (D)   **4** (C)

[1-4] 이메일

수신: 실로마크 직원
발신: 다비트 사분지안
제목: 직원 설문 조사
날짜: 3월 3일

안녕하세요, 여러분,

직원 만족도 설문 조사를 ¹완료하는 데 할애해주신 여러분의 시간, 배려, 사려 깊음에 감사드립니다. 이제 관리자급 직원들이 모든 답변을 검토할 기회를 가졌고, 경영진은 여러분의 우려 사항을 가장 잘 해결하기 위한 방법을 인사부와 상의했습니다. ²그 결과, 우리는 이미 일부 직원 복리 후생 확대를 위한 조치를 취할 수 있었습니다. ³이 변경 사항에 대한 정보는 다음 주에 여러분께 보내 드리겠습니다. 조만간 추가적으로 긍정적인 ⁴발전 사항에 대해 말씀드릴 예정입니다. 우선은 실로마크를 위해 헌신해 주신 모든 여러분께 다시 한 번 감사드립니다.

다비트 사분지안

기업 발전 부사장

어휘 | thoughtfulness 사려 깊음   determine 결정하다   address 다루다   take steps 조치를 취하다   expand 확대시키다   benefits 복지후생   dedication 헌신

1 (D)

해설 | 빈칸은 전치사 in의 목적어 자리이므로 명사나 동명사가 들어갈 수 있는데, 빈칸 뒤에 the employee satisfaction survey라는 목적어가 있으므로 정답은 동명사인 (D) completing이다.

2 (A)

해설 | 빈칸 앞에서는 관리자급 직원들이 설문 조사 답변을 모두 검토했으며 경영진이 직원들의 우려를 해결하기 위한 방안을 인사부와 상의했다고 했고, 빈칸 뒤에서는 이미 복지 확대를 위한 일부 조치를 취했다고 했다. 두 문장이 서로 인과관계를 나타내고 있으므로 '그 결과'를 뜻하는 (A) As a result가 정답이다.

3 (D)

번역 | (A) 반드시 이 서류에 서명하고 신속히 반납해 주십시오.
(B) 그 문제들을 해결하기 위해 우리 웹사이트를 업데이트하는 중입니다.
(C) 다음 달에 직장 설문 조사 수행에 관한 설명회가 제공될 예정입니다.
(D) 이 변경 사항에 대한 정보는 다음 주에 여러분께 보내 드리겠습니다.

해설 | 앞 문장에서 이미 일부 직원 복리 후생 확대를 위한 조치(steps toward expanding some of our employee benefits)를 취했다고 했으므로, 앞서 언급된 조치를 '이 변경 사항(these changes)'이라고 받아 관련 정보를 보내 주겠다는 내용이 뒤따라야 문맥이 자연스럽다. 따라서 정답은 (D)이다.

어휘 | promptly 신속히   in the process of ~의 진행 중에

4 (C)

해설 | 앞 문장에서 직원 복지 확대를 위해 일부 조치를 취했다고 했고, 빈칸 앞에 '추가적인(additional)'이라는 수식어가 붙은 것으로 보아 빈칸에 들어갈 명사는 직원 복지 증대를 위해 추가적으로 '개선되는 것'들을 일컫는 것임을 알 수 있다. 따라서 '발전, 개발'을 의미하는 (C) developments가 정답이다.

어휘 | performance 성과   regulation 규정

ETS 고득점 실전 문제

본책 p.236

1 (D)	2 (C)	3 (A)	4 (A)	5 (C)	6 (A)
7 (B)	8 (D)	9 (B)	10 (D)	11 (A)	12 (D)
13 (B)	14 (A)	15 (A)	16 (D)		

[1-4] 공지

헌터 클래식 극장은 극장 조명이 ¹어두워지면 스마트폰과 태블릿과 같은 모든 휴대 기기의 전원을 끄고 치워 줄 것을 요청합니다. 단지 기기를 무음으로 설정하는 것만으로는 영화 상영 중 기기를 사용하는 것과 관련된 다른 문제를 해결할 수 없습니다. 이 기기들을 사용함으로써 근처의 ²관람객들에게 방해가 될 수 있습니다. ³예를 들어, 작은 화면에서 나오는 빛은 다른 사람들이 큰 화면 속 영화에 집중하는 것을 매우 어렵게 만듭니다.

때때로, 전화를 걸거나 문자 메시지를 확인해야 할 경우도 있습니다. ⁴이 경우에는 상영관을 나가서 로비로 가 주십시오. 자리로 돌아올 때는 근처에 앉아 있는 사람들에게 방해가 되지 않도록 해 주십시오.

어휘 | merely 단지   silent 묵음인   address 해결하다   distract 방해하다   concentrate 집중하다   on occasion 때때로   disturb 방해하다

---

1 (D)

해설 | 빈칸은 once 이하 절에서 복수명사 주어 the theater lights의 동사 자리이다. 따라서 복수동사가 와야 하므로 (D) have dimmed가 정답이다.

2 (C)

해설 | 빈칸의 뒤 문장에서 화면에서 나오는 빛은 다른 사람들이 영화에 집중하는 것을 어렵게 만든다고 부연 설명을 하고 있으므로, 주변 관람객들에게 방해가 될 수 있는 상황에 대해 언급하는 것임을 알 수 있다. 따라서 '관람객'을 뜻하는 (C) viewers가 정답이다.

3 (A)

해설 | 빈칸 앞에는 기기를 사용함으로써 근처 관람객들에게 방해가 될 수 있다고 했고, 빈칸 뒤에는 화면에서 나오는 빛 때문에 다른 사람들이 영화에 집중하는 것이 어려워진다며 구체적인 사례를 제시하고 있다. 따라서 '예를 들어'라는 의미의 접속부사인 (A) for example이 정답이다.

4 (A)

번역 | (A) 이 경우에는 상영관을 나가서 로비로 가 주십시오.
(B) 문제가 있으면 극장 직원에게 알려 주십시오.
(C) 공연이 즐거우셨기를 바랍니다.
(D) 유감스럽게도, 환불은 불가합니다.

해설 | 앞 문장에서 전화를 걸거나 문자 메시지를 확인해야 할 경우도 있다며, 뒤 문장에서 자리로 돌아올 때 근처의 사람들에게 방해가 되지 않도록 해 달라는 당부를 했다. 통화하거나 문자 메시지를 확인해야 할 경우를 '이 경우(In this case)'로 받아 자리에서 나가 다른 곳으로 이동해 달라는 문장이 들어가면 연결이 자연스러우므로 (A)가 정답이다.

어휘 | regrettably 유감스럽게도   issue 지급하다

[5-8] 이메일

발신: 레베카 이프라
날짜: 10월 29일
수신: 파르한 알몬테이저
제목: 특별 감사

안녕하세요, 파르한 씨

우리 고객 웰컴 키트의 평가에 참여해 주신 모든 분들께 감사 말씀 전해주세요. 특히, 간사 씨께요. 그녀가 두 가지 중요한 문제를 저에게 알려 주셨어요. 먼저, 그녀는 평가 과정 초기에 몇 가지 ⁵승인이 누락된 점을 알려 주셨어요. 어째서인지 제가 그 허가 받는 일에 대해 완전히 놓치고 있었더라고요. ⁶또한 그녀는 제품 세부 사항과 관련된 불일치를 발견해 저에게 알려 주시고는 솔선해서 수정해 주셨어요.

간사 씨는 우리 마케팅 일정을 세심하게 챙기시고 웰컴 키트가 완성될 수 있도록 ⁷돕기 위해 열심히 일해 주셨습니다. 그녀의 적극적인 노력과 유연함, 대응력은 우리가 마감일보다 일찍 프로젝트를 끝내는 데 도움이 되었습니다. ⁸그녀와 다시 일하기를 기대합니다. 다시 한 번, 모두에게 감사드립니다.

레베카 이프라 부장, 고객 관리 전문가

브라잇나이트 마케팅

어휘 | convey 전달하다 in particular 특히 attention 관심 process 과정 missing 빠진 somehow 왜 그런지 obtain 얻다 authorization 허가 escape 기억나지 않다 discrepancy 차이 involve 관련시키다 take the initiative 솔선해서 하다 sensitivity 세심함 timeline 일정 diligently 열심히 proactive 적극적인 flexibility 유연성 responsiveness 대응성

5 (C)

해설 | 빈칸에는 평가 과정 초기에 누락된 어떤 것이 들어가야 하는데, 뒤 문장에서 빈칸에 들어갈 명사를 받아 '그 허가'를 받는 일(obtaining those authorizations)에 대해 완전히 놓치고 있었다고 언급하고 있으므로 빈칸에는 '허가'와 바꿔 쓸 수 있는 단어가 들어가야 한다. 따라서 정답은 '승인'을 뜻하는 (C) approvals이다.

6 (A)

해설 | 앞 내용에서 간사 씨가 두 가지 문제(two important matters)를 알려 주었다면서 먼저(First) 몇 가지 승인이 누락된 점을 알려 주었다고 했고, 뒤 문장에서는 제품 세부 사항과 관련된 불일치를 발견해 알려 주었다며 간사 씨가 알려 준 두 문제 중 나머지에 대해 추가적으로 언급하고 있다. 따라서 빈칸에는 정보를 추가로 언급할 때 쓰는 '게다가, 또한'이라는 표현이 어울리므로 (A) In addition이 정답이다.

7 (B)

해설 | 빈칸 앞에 완전한 절이 있고 빈칸 뒤 us를 목적어로 취할 수 있어야 하므로 to부정사가 와야 한다. 문맥상 '우리를 돕기 위해 열심히 일했다'는 내용이 되면 자연스러우므로 '~하기 위해서'라는 목적의 의미를 지니는 (B) to assist가 정답이다.

8 (D)

번역 | (A) 그러므로 그것은 수정되어야 합니다.
(B) 키트는 모든 신규 고객에게 발송됩니다.
(C) 그녀의 평가서를 첨부했습니다.
(D) 그녀와 다시 일하기를 기대합니다.

해설 | 앞 내용에서 간사 씨가 업무에 기여한 점들에 대해 언급하고 있고 앞 문장에서 간사 씨 덕분에 마감일보다 일찍 프로젝트를 끝내는 데 도움이 되었다(Her ~ helped us to finish our project ahead of the deadline)고 했으므로 빈칸에는 그녀와 다시 일하기를 원한다는 내용이 들어가야 문맥이 자연스럽다. 따라서 정답은 (D)이다.

[9-12] 기사

웰링턴 (4월 3일)—봉제 기계 제조업체인 랩시디는 이번 주 새로운 그린 스티치(GS) 사업을 시작한다고 발표했다. GS 사업은 랩시디의 전 세계 고객들 사이에서 자재의 재활용을 ⁹장려하고자 한다. 새로운 웹사이트에서 ¹⁰사용자들은 기부를 원하는 직물 조각의 목록을 올릴 수 있다. 전 세계의 의류 생산자들은 이 사이트에서 그들이 원하는 직물을 검색할 수 있다. GS 사업 커뮤니티의 회원들에게는 모든 물품이 무료로 제공될 것이다. ¹¹그러나 배송비는 각자 부담해야 한다. ¹²요금은 주문한 물품의 무게에 따라 달라진다.

어휘 | sewing-machine 재봉틀 initiative 사업 계획 material 자재 scrap 조각 browse 검색하다 free of charge 무료인 cover (돈을) 대다

9 (B)

해설 | seeks는 to부정사를 목적어로 취하여 '~하려고 하다'는 의미로 쓰인다. 따라서 정답은 (B) to encourage이다.

10 (D)

해설 | 동사 allow는 'allow + 목적어 + to부정사'의 형태로 자주 쓰인다. 빈칸은 동사 allow와 목적격 보어 to부정사 사이의 목적어 자리이므로 명사가 들어가야 한다. 따라서 정답은 (D) users이다.

11 (A)

해설 | 빈칸 앞 문장에서 회원들에게는 모든 물품이 무료로(free of charge) 제공될 것이라고 했는데 빈칸 뒤 문장에서 배송비는 각자 부담해야 한다(cover shipping costs)며 서로 상반된 내용이 이어지고 있다. 따라서 역접 관계를 나타내는 (A) However가 정답이다.

12 (D)

번역 | (A) 랩시디의 수익은 지난 분기 동안 꾸준히 성장했다.
(B) 어떤 자재는 상당히 비쌀 수 있다.
(C) 직물의 용도 변경은 새로운 아이디어가 아니다.
(D) 요금은 주문한 물품의 무게에 따라 달라진다.

해설 | 앞 내용에서 GS 사업 커뮤니티의 회원들에게는 모든 물품이 무료로 제공될 것이지만 배송비는 각자 부담해야 한다며 배송비에 대해 언급하고 있으므로 배송에 대한 세부 사항을 설명하는 내용이 연결되면 자연스럽다. 따라서 배송비가 책정되는 기준을 설명한 (D)가 정답이다.

어휘 | earning 수익 steadily 꾸준히 quite 상당히 repurposing 용도 변경 vary 달라진다

[13-16] 이메일

수신: 드미트리 라다스, 계약 담당자
발신: 레노어 벨리스
날짜: 7월 7일
제목: 새로운 유통업체 필요

라다스 씨께,

현재 우리 공급업체인 토카탄 유통 시스템이 결국 내년에 미국 시장에 진출하지 않을 것임을 방금 알게 되었습니다. ¹³따라서 저는 올리브 오일을 위한 새로운 유통업체를 구할 예정입니다. 아시다시피, 당사의 3개년 확장 계획은 이것을 핵심 목표로 꼽고 있습니다. ¹⁴우리는 8월 1일까지 계약을 맺고 싶습니다.

당신은 작년에 우리 수입 치즈를 위해 새로운 유통업체를 찾아 주셨습니다. 당시 물색 중에 다양한 올리브 오일을 제공하는 유통업체들 중 우연히 알게 된 곳이 있을까요? ¹⁵구체적으로 저는 그리스에서 생산되는 올리브 오일을 찾기를 희망합니다. 혹시 단서가 있다면 저에게 연락처를 보내주실 수 있나요?

수요일까지 당신이 갖고 있는 정보를 보내주시면 ¹⁶감사하겠습니다.

감사합니다.

레노어 벨리스

13 (B)

해설 | 앞 문장에서 기존 공급업체가 내년에 미국 시장에 진출하지 않을 것임을 방금 알게 되었다고 했고 뒤 문장에서 올리브 오일을 위한 새 유통업체를 구할 것이라고 했다. 두 문장이 서로 인과관계를 나타내고 있으므로 '따라서, 그러므로'를 뜻하는 (B) Therefore가 정답이다.

14 (A)

번역 | (A) 우리는 8월 1일까지 계약을 맺고 싶습니다.
(B) 우리의 이전 유통업체는 폐업했습니다.
(C) 당사의 유통 비용 사본을 제출해 주세요.
(D) 9월까지 재고 조사를 완료할 예정입니다.

해설 | 앞에서 새로운 올리브 오일 유통업체를 구해야 하고 3개년 확장 계획에서 이를 핵심 목표로 꼽고 있다며 새 유통업체와의 계약에 대한 중요성을 언급하고 있다. 따라서 8월 1일이라는 시한을 제시하며 계약을 체결하기를 원한다는 내용이 들어가야 문맥상 가장 자연스러우므로 (A)가 정답이다.

어휘 | out of business 폐업한 inventory 재고 조사

15 (A)

해설 | 앞 문장에서 올리브 오일을 제공하는 유통업체들 중 우연히 알게 된 곳이 있는지를 물었고 빈칸 뒤에서 그리스에서 생산되는 올리브 오일을 찾기를 바란다고 했다. 뒤 문장에서 앞의 질문에 대해 좀 더 구체적이고 명확한 기준을 제시하고 있으므로 빈칸에는 이를 표현해 줄 수 있는 부사가 들어가야 한다. 따라서 '구체적으로'라는 의미의 (A) Specifically가 정답이다.

16 (D)

해설 | 조동사 would 뒤에는 동사원형이 와야 하므로, (D) appreciate가 정답이다.

UNIT 15 문장 고르기 문제

ETS 예제   본책 p.240

필 테리픽 피트니스 앱

흠뻑 땀 흘리고 싶으신가요? 필 테리픽 피트니스 앱을 사용해 보세요. – 중략 – 우리는 다양한 수준의 능력을 가진 사람들을 위한 선택 사항을 제공합니다. 초보자부터 상급자까지 선택하실 수 있습니다. 각 운동 일과 옆에 표시된 난이도를 확인하실 수 있습니다. 90일 동안 무료로 앱을 사용해 보세요. 무료 체험 기간이 끝나면 매월 단 14.99달러에 필 테리픽 피트니스 앱을 계속 사용하실 수 있습니다.

번역 | (A) 계정은 언제든지 취소하실 수 있습니다.
(B) 운동 전에 스트레칭을 하는 것은 중요합니다.
(C) 운동 매트 구입을 추천 드립니다.
(D) 초보자부터 상급자까지 선택하실 수 있습니다.

ETS 유형 연습   본책 p.241

1 (B) **2** (C) **3** (D) **4** (D)

[1-4] 이메일

수신: srafid@rafidfitness.co.uk
발신: hlloyed@mugpro.co.uk
날짜: 2월 12일
제목: 피트니스 장비

라피드 씨께,

맨체스터에서 가장 큰 피트니스 센터 중 한 곳의 주인으로서, 귀하께서는 고품질의 운동 기계가 얼마나 [1]비싼지 잘 알고 계십니다. 그 기계들은 특히 기능성과 신뢰성 때문에 가격이 높습니다. [2]그럼에도 불구하고 아무리 좋은 장비라도 결국 고장 나게 마련입니다. 피트니스 센터를 운영하는 데에 드는 가장 큰 경비 중 하나는 장비 교체에 지출되는 돈입니다. 기계를 구입하실 계획이지만 비용 문제로 [3]고충을 겪는다면, 마리노 중고 체육관 제품에 유명 브랜드의 중고 기계들이 있습니다. [4]무엇보다도 우리는 그것들을 원래 판매가의 일부 금액에 제공합니다.

자세한 정보 및 풍부한 경험을 가진 저희 영업 사원의 무료 견적을 원하시면 0160 496 0063으로 전화 주십시오.

헤이든 로이드

1 (B)

해설 | 빈칸 뒤 문장에서 그 기계들은 특히 기능성과 신뢰성 때문에 가격이 높다(valued)고 했으므로 빈칸에는 비싼 가격을 나타내는 형용사가 들어가야 문맥상 자연스럽다. 따라서 '비싼'을 뜻하는 (B) expensive가 정답이다.

어휘 | committed 헌신적인 fragile 깨지기 쉬운 elevated 높은

2 (C)

해설 | 앞 문장에는 고품질 운동 기계들은 특히 기능성과 신뢰성 때문에 가격이 높다고 했는데, 뒤 문장에는 아무리 좋은 장비라도 결국 고장 나게 마련이라며 상반된 내용을 언급하고 있다. 따라서 '고품질 기계들은 가격이 높은데도 불구하고 결국 고장 난다'고 양보의 의미로 연결되어야 자연스러우므로 '그럼에도 불구하고'를 뜻하는 (C) Nevertheless가 정답이다.

3 (D)

해설 | 등위접속사 but 뒤에 주어 you가 생략되어 있고, 앞의 동사 are shopping과 대등하게 연결될 수 있는 보기를 골라야 한다. 빈칸 뒤에 목적어가 없어 수동태가 되어야 하므로 능동태를 이루는 다른 보기들은 모두 답이 될 수 없고 (D) are challenged가 정답이다.

4 (D)

번역 | (A) 저희 서비스 부서에 지원해 주셔서 감사합니다.
(B) 뿐만 아니라 여기에 선수권 대회 무료 입장권을 같이 드립니다.
(C) 늘 그랬듯이 저희 회사에 대한 귀하의 공공 지원에 대단히 감사드립니다.
(D) 무엇보다도 우리는 그것들을 원래 판매가의 일부 금액에 제공합니다.

해설 | 앞 문장에서 기계를 구입할 계획이지만 비용 문제로 고충이 있다면 마리노 중고 체육관 제품에 유명 브랜드의 중고 기계들(the brand-name used machines)이 있다고 했으므로, 앞서 언급한 중고 기계들을 them으로 받아 이것들을 원래 판매가의 일부 금액에 제공한다며 비용 절감 측면에 있어서 추가적인 이점을 언급하는 내용이 이어져야 자연스럽다. 따라서 정답은 (D)이다.

어휘 | best of all 무엇보다도 fraction 부분

ETS 고득점 실전 문제
본책 p.242

1 (C) **2** (B) **3** (A) **4** (A) **5** (C) **6** (A)
7 (D) **8** (C) **9** (A) **10** (D) **11** (A) **12** (C)
13 (C) **14** (D) **15** (C) **16** (B)

[1-4] 이메일

발신: 매튜 팔체티
날짜: 5월 17일
수신: 도서관 직원
제목: 2층 와이파이 신호

직원 여러분께:

최근 도서관 2층에 새로운 무선 인터넷 연결 지점이 설치되었습니다. [1]현재 그곳의 공공 열람 구역에 무선 신호가 잡힙니다. 과거에는 신호가 그다지 강하지 않아서 그 구역에서 이용객들이 인터넷에 접속하는 [2]것을 권장하지 않았습니다. [3]더 이상은 그러지 않아도 됩니다.

이것은 우리가 설치할 세 곳의 연결 지점 중 첫 번째입니다. 곧 미술관과 로비에서도 신호 [4]강도가 개선될 것으로 기대합니다.

매튜 팔체티

정보 서비스 책임자

어휘 | discourage 좌절시키다 patron 이용객

---

1 (C)

해설 | 앞 문장에서 최근 도서관 2층에 새로운 무선 인터넷 연결 지점이 설치되었다고 했으므로 '현재' 그곳에서 무선 신호가 잡힌다는 내용이 되어야 자연스럽다. 따라서 '지금, 현재'라는 뜻의 부사 (C) now가 정답이다.

2 (B)

해설 | 빈칸 앞 동사 discouraged가 핵심 단서이다. discourage는 전치사 from과 함께 'discourage A from -ing'의 형태로 쓰여 'A가 -ing하는 것을 막다'를 뜻하는데, 문맥상 '이용객들이 인터넷에 접속하는 것을 권하지 않았다'는 내용이 되면 자연스러우므로 (B) from이 정답이다.

3 (A)

번역 | (A) 더 이상은 그러지 않아도 됩니다.
(B) 이 구역은 유아 출입이 제한됩니다.
(C) 이 소식은 금요일자 신문에 실릴 예정입니다.
(D) 많은 이용객들이 자신의 컴퓨터를 가져옵니다.

해설 | 바로 앞 문장에서 과거에는 신호가 강하지 않아 인터넷 접속을 권장하지 않았다고 했지만 그 앞 내용에서 최근 도서관 2층에 새 무선 인터넷 연결 지점을 설치하여 현재는 무선 신호가 잡힌다고 했으므로, 더 이상은 인터넷 이용을 막을 필요가 없을 것이라는 문장이 연결되면 자연스럽다. 따라서 정답은 (A)이다.

어휘 | off-limits 출입금지의 feature 특별히 포함하다

4 (A)

해설 | to부정사 to improve의 목적어 역할로 정관사 뒤에서 signal과 함께 복합명사를 이루는 명사가 와야 하므로 정답은 (A) strength이다.

[5-8] 초대장

관계자 분들께:

저희 라이브 그린 서밋은 히긴스턴 공원에서 매년 열리는 그린 클린업 데이에 귀사를 초대하고 싶습니다. 매년, 저희는 이 행사의 성공을 돕기 위해 지역 기업들에 [5]직원 파견을 요청 드리고 있습니다. 자원봉사자는 우리 공동체가 가장 아끼는 녹지 중 한 곳을 청소하는 활동에 하루 동안 참여하게 됩니다. 모든 참가자들이 공원에서 최소 3시간 이상 [6]일해 주실 것을 부탁드립니다. [7]그러면 하루만에 청소를 끝낼 수 있습니다.

6월 30일까지 답변 부탁드립니다. 모든 참가 업체들로부터 답변을 듣는 즉시 좀 더 자세한 내용과 함께 연락 드리겠습니다. 청소 일정은 7월 20일 또는 그 [8]전에 발송될 예정입니다. 언제나처럼, 귀사 직원분들께서 할애해 주시는 시간에 감사드립니다.

마리아 쿠오모, 라이브 그린 서밋 팀 운영자

어휘 | effort (특정 성과를 위한 집단의) 활동 be in touch with ~와 연락하다 detail 세부 사항 grateful 감사하는

5 (C)

해설 | 뒤 문장에서 이 자원봉사자들(those volunteers)은 청소 활동에 참여하게 된다고 한 것으로 보아, 지역 기업들에게 '직원'을 보내 달라고 요청했고 이 직원들이 자원봉사자로 참여하게 되는 것임을 알 수 있다. 따라서 (C) representatives가 정답이다.

6 (A)

해설 | 앞 문장에서 자원봉사자는 녹지 중 한 곳을 청소하는 활동에 하루 동안 참여하게 된다고 안내했으므로, 참가자들이 공원에서 3시간 동안 해 달라고 부탁받은 일은 청소임을 알 수 있다. 보기 중 청소 활동을 대신할 수 있는 동사는 '일하다'이므로 (A) work가 정답이다.

7 (D)

번역 | (A) 프리 레인지 푸드는 참가 업체 중 하나입니다.
(B) 우리 공동체에는 공원이 여섯 곳 있습니다.
(C) 히긴스턴 공원은 다니엘 히긴스턴 경의 이름을 따서 지은 것입니다.
(D) 그러면 하루만에 청소를 끝낼 수 있습니다.

해설 | 앞에서 자원봉사자는 하루 동안 청소 활동에 참여하게 된다는 안내를 하며 공원에서 최소 3시간 이상 일해 달라고 부탁하고 있으므로, 빈칸에는 3시간 이상 일해 달라고 요청한 이유가 뒤따르면 연결이 자연스럽다. 따라서 '그러면(then)'이라는 접속부사와 함께 하루만에 청소를 끝낼 수 있다며 이유를 설명한 (D)가 정답이다.

8 (C)

해설 | 전치사 on과 함께 등위접속사 or로 대등하게 연결됨과 동시에 빈칸 뒤 July 20을 목적어로 취하기에 적절한 전치사가 들어가야 한다. July 20은 특정 날짜로 시점을 나타내고, 문맥상 '7월 20일 또는 그 전에'라는 내용이 되어야 자연스럽다. 따라서 '~전에'를 뜻하는 시점 전치사 (C) before가 정답이다.

[9-12] 이메일

수신: 마크 쿠트만
발신: 바체바 아바디
날짜: 4월 23일
제목: 연회

우리 현악 4중주단은 다음 달에 있을 당신의 야외 연회에서 연주하기를 고대하고 있습니다. 우리는 야외 공연을 할 때 몇 가지 특정 요구 사항이 있다는 점에 유의해 주시기 바랍니다. 햇빛과 습기로부터 보호되는 그늘진 곳에 **⁹악기**를 설치해야 합니다. 바이올린과 비올라, 첼로는 좋지 않은 기상 환경으로 인해 손상될 수 있기 때문에 이는 필수적입니다. **¹⁰또한** 밖에 바람이 심할 경우 다른 장소로 이동해야 할 수도 있습니다. **¹¹악보대가 날아가는 상황을 원치 않습니다.** 마지막으로, 만약 공연일에 날씨가 너무 덥거나 추울 경우 실내로 장소를 옮겨야 할 것입니다. **¹²극한** 온도에서는 차갑거나 땀에 젖은 손가락으로 연주하기가 어렵습니다. 궁금한 점이나 걱정되는 점이 있으시면 언제든지 저에게 연락주세요.

바체바 아바디

어휘 | string quartet 현악 4중주단   shady 그늘진   moisture 습기   adverse 부정적인   alternate 대안의   indoors 실내로   sweaty 땀에 젖은

9 (A)

해설 | 빈칸이 있는 문장만으로는 정답을 고르기 어려우며, 빈칸 주변의 내용을 확인해야 하는 문제이다. 글의 첫 문장에서 현악 4중주단이 야외 연회에서 연주하는 일에 대해 언급하였으므로, 악기를 설치하는 것에 대해 말하고 있음을 알 수 있다. 따라서 '악기'를 뜻하는 (A) instruments가 정답이다.

어휘 | experiment 실험

10 (D)

해설 | 빈칸 앞에서 햇빛과 습기로부터 보호되는 그늘진 곳에 악기를 설치해야 한다고 했고 빈칸 뒤에는 밖에 바람이 심할 경우 다른 장소로 이동해야 할 수도 있다고 했다. 빈칸 양쪽 모두 악기 설치에 필요한 기상 요건에 대해 언급하고 있으므로 빈칸에는 비슷한 내용을 추가할 때 쓰는 접속부사가 필요하다. 따라서 정답은 '또한, 게다가'라는 의미의 (D) In addition이다.

11 (A)

번역 | (A) 악보대가 날아가는 상황을 원치 않습니다.
(B) 행사가 늦게 시작할 경우 추가 요금이 부과됩니다.
(C) 작은 행사에서는 보통 실내 연주를 선호합니다.
(D) 우리 웹사이트에서 적합한 장소를 쉽게 찾을 수 있습니다.

해설 | 앞 문장에서 밖에 바람이 심할 경우 다른 장소로 이동해야 할 수도 있다고 했으므로, 바람이 부는 상황으로 인한 장소 변경 필요성에 대해 부연 설명하는 문장이 뒤따르면 자연스럽다. 따라서 악보대가 날아가는 상황을 원하지 않는다는 내용의 (A)가 정답이다.

어휘 | music stand 악보대   blow 바람에 날리다   suitable 적합한

12 (C)

해설 | 빈칸은 전치사 in의 목적어 역할을 하는 명사 temperatures 앞에서 명사를 수식하는 형용사 자리이다. 따라서 정답은 '극단적인'을 뜻하는 형용사 (C) extreme이다.

[13-16] 회람

수신: 모든 관리 직원
발신: 남혜진 인사 과장
날짜: 5월 15일
제목: 근무 시간 기록표 제출에 대한 새 규정

6월 15일자로, 모든 관리 직원은 새로운 근무 시간 기록표 제출 절차 두 가지를 **¹³준수해야** 합니다. 첫째, 모든 휴가 신청은 새로운 온라인 포털인 알파 타임을 통해 이루어져야 합니다. **¹⁴현재 사용 중인 소프트웨어는 폐기할 예정입니다.** 새로운 온라인 시스템은 훨씬 더 효율적일 것입니다. 둘째, 시간외 근무는 이제 OH 코드 아래에 기입해야 합니다. OT 코드는 시스템에서 더 이상 **¹⁵유효하지** 않습니다. 마지막으로, 근무 시간 기록표에 관한 **¹⁶질문은** 칼 피가로에게 보내 주시기 바랍니다.

13 (C)

해설 | 글의 제목이 근무 시간 기록표 제출에 대한 새 규정이고 직원들이 지켜야 할 사항에 대해 안내하는 글이므로 '새로운 절차 두 가지를 준수해야 한다'는 내용이 되어야 한다. 따라서 '준수하다'를 뜻하는 (C) comply with가 정답이다.

어휘 | provide for ~을 대비하다 measure 측정하다

14 (D)

번역 | (A) 이 방침들은 이해하기 어려울 수 있습니다.
(B) 월요일은 전 직원이 휴가입니다.
(C) 예를 들어, 그것은 복잡한 기능을 수행할 수 있습니다.
(D) 현재 사용 중인 소프트웨어는 폐기할 예정입니다.

해설 | 앞 문장에서 새 시스템만을 사용해야 한다고 했고 뒤 문장에서는 새 시스템이 더 효율적이라고 장점을 언급하며 안심시키고 있으므로 그 사이에는 그간 사용해 오던 시스템은 더 이상 쓰지 않을 것이라는 내용이 들어가면 자연스럽다. 따라서 정답은 현 시스템은 폐기할 것이라는 내용의 (D)이다.

어휘 | policy 방침 complicated 복잡한 vacation 휴가 for instance 예를 들어 function 기능 retire (기계 등을) 폐기하다

15 (C)

해설 | 앞 문장에서 시간외 근무는 이제 OH 코드 아래에 기입해야 한다고 했으므로 OT 코드는 더 이상 유효하지 않다는 내용이 되어야 한다. 따라서 '유효한'을 의미하는 (C) valid가 정답이다.

어휘 | actual 실제의 restricted 제한된 confident 확신하는

16 (B)

해설 | 빈칸은 that절의 주어 자리이므로 명사가 들어가야 한다. question은 가산명사이므로 한정사가 없을 경우는 복수 형태가 되어야 한다. 따라서 정답은 (B) questions이다.

RC PART 7

INTRO

ETS 예제 | 본책 p.248

고객님께,

9월 1일에 디바인 초콜릿이 새로운 도시로 이전한다는 것을 알려 드리기 위해 이 글을 씁니다. 새 주소는 매사추세츠 01602, 우스터, 포레스트 로드 2165번지입니다. 기록해 두시기 바랍니다. 우리의 주요 연락처는 그대로 (508) 555-0120입니다.

우리 회사는 10년 전 설립된 이래 고객의 변함없는 지원을 통해 수년간 건실하게 성장할 수 있었습니다. **164이러한 성장의 결과 현재 시설은 보관 및 작업 공간에 대한 수요와 요건을 더 이상 충족할 수 없게 되었습니다. 그리하여 우리는 좀 더 넓은 장소로 옮길 수 있도록 준비를 했습니다.** 고객에 대한 우리의 약속에는 변함이 없으니 안심하십시오. **166,167고객분들께 세계 각지에서 온 최고의 초콜릿을 제공하기 위해 계속해서 165최선을 다할 것입니다.** 새로운 장소와 관련하여 궁금한 점이 있으시면 언제든지 문의해 주십시오.

로베르타 보그트, 관리자

어휘 | relocate 이전하다 make a note of ~을 적다 found 설립하다 loyal 충실한 enable 가능하게 하다 steadily 꾸준히 facility 시설 storage 보관 arrangement 준비 spacious 넓은 be assured that ~이니 안심하다 commitment 약속 devote (노력·시간 등을) 바치다 concerning ~에 관한

UNIT 16 주제 / 목적 문제

ETS 예제 | 본책 p.250

날짜: 2월 23일
제목: 후속 조치

제나 씨께,

3월 15일부터 4월 10일까지 크레인을 대여하기로 합의했던 이번 주 초 전화 통화에 대한 후속 조치를 위해 글을 씁니다. – 중략 – 실제로 일주일 뒤인 3월 22일부터 4월 17일까지 크레인이 필요합니다. 이 날짜에 크레인을 사용할 수 있을까요? 날짜 변경과 관련하여 추가 요금이 발생되는지요? 가능하실 때 연락 주십시오.

감사합니다.

데이비드 콴

어휘 | follow-up 후속 조치; 더 알아보다 crane 크레인

Q 콴 씨는 왜 이메일을 썼는가?
(A) 서비스 요금의 오류를 지적하려고
(B) 합의 사항 변경을 요청하려고
(C) 파바트 렌탈의 서비스에 대한 의견을 제공하려고
(D) 카론 씨에게 건설 현장에 방문해 달라고 부탁하려고

어휘 | point out 지적하다 adjustment 조정 agreement 합의, 계약

ETS 유형 연습

본책 p.251

1 (A) **2** (B) **3** (D)

[1-3] 보고서

기술 지원 센터 상황 보고서	
문제:	[1]현재 웨스트우드와 제이타운에 있는 우리 사무소에서 전화 연결 장애가 발생 중입니다. 어제부터 많은 직원들이 전화 수신 및 발신을 하지 못하고 있다고 보고하고 있습니다. 어젯밤에 이 문제를 해결해 달라는 불편 사항이 접수되었습니다.
영향을 받는 직원:	웨스트우드와 제이타운 사무소에 근무 중인 모든 피어스 사의 직원
[2]기술 지원 센터 불편 사항 접수 시간:	[2]7월 5일, 오후 6시 30분
예상 해결 시간:	7월 7일, 오전 9시
피어스사에 미치는 영향:	[3]웨스트우드와 제이타운 직원은 외부 기관으로부터 걸려오는 전화를 받을 수 없습니다. 웨스트우드와 제이타운 외부에 있는 피어스사 직원들은 이 두 사무소로 전화를 걸 수 없습니다.
권고 사항:	[3]내일 연결 장애가 해결될 때까지 이메일을 이용하십시오.

어휘 | status 상황 outage 정전, 정지 incoming 들어오는 outgoing 나가는 address (문제 등을) 다루다 affected 영향을 받은 file 제기[제출]하다 estimated 추측의 resolution 해결 impact 영향 organization 기관

1 이 보고서의 목적은 무엇인가?
(A) 전화 연결 장애를 설명하는 것
(B) 사용자에게 소프트웨어 업데이트를 알리는 것
(C) 사용자에게 인터넷 중단을 알리는 것
(D) 임시 사무소 이전을 발표하는 것

해설 | 주제 / 목적
보고서 문제(Issue)의 첫 문장에서 현재 웨스트우드와 제이타운에 있는 우리 사무소에서 전화 연결 장애가 발생 중(We are currently experiencing a phone outage in our offices in Westwood and Jaytown)이라고 했으므로 (A)가 정답이다.

어휘 | notify 알리다 alert 알리다 disruption 중단 temporary 임시의 relocation 이전

2 기술 지원 센터는 언제 불편 사항을 접수 받았는가?
(A) 7월 4일   (B) 7월 5일
(C) 7월 6일   (D) 7월 7일

해설 | 세부 사항
기술 지원 센터 불편 사항 접수 시간(Ticket filed with Technology Assistance Center) 항목에 7월 5일(July 5)이라고 나와 있으므로 (B)가 정답이다.

3 기술 지원 센터는 직원들에게 무엇을 하라고 권하는가?
(A) 인스턴트 메시지를 통한 통신
(B) 개인 휴대 전화 사용
(C) 곧 있을 전화회의 취소
(D) 웨스트우드와 제이타운 직원과 이메일 연락

해설 | 세부 사항
피어스사에 미치는 영향(Impact on Pearce Corporation)의 첫 문장에서 웨스트우드와 제이타운 직원은 외부 기관으로부터 걸려오는 전화를 받을 수 없다(Westwood and Jaytown employees will be unable to receive calls from outside organizations)고 했고, 권고 사항(Recommendations)에서 내일 연결 장애가 해결될 때까지 이메일을 이용하라(Please use e-mail until the outage is resolved tomorrow)고 했으므로 (D)가 정답이다.

Paraphrasing 지문의 use e-mail
→ 보기의 contact ~ by e-mail

ETS 고득점 실전 문제

본책 p.252

1 (D) **2** (C) **3** (A) **4** (B) **5** (A) **6** (C)
7 (D)

[1-3] 이메일

수신: d.marusik@seltermanhospital.org
발신: y.shaw@seltermanhospital.org
[1]제목: 지원 요청
날짜: 10월 15일

마루식 씨께:

저는 현재 스틸워터 대학교에서 병원 관리를 가르치고 있습니다. 제 목표 중 하나는 학생들에게 우리 병원 같은 곳이 어떻게 운영되는지에 대해 내부자의 관점을 제공하는 것입니다. 이러한 목적으로 [2]11월 5일에 [1]저는 학생들을 데리고 우리 병원 내에서 가장 필수적인 부서들을 둘러볼 예정입니다. 각 분과별로 20분간 설명회를 진행하며, [2(A), 2(B)]이 시간 동안 각 분과별 직원이 간략하게 일상적인 업무에 대해 설명하고 학생들의 질문에 답변을 하게 될 것입니다. [2]견학은 오전 10시에 시작해 오후 3시 즈음 끝날 것으로 예상합니다. [2(D)]점심 식사는 정오부터 오후 1시까지 쉬는 시간에 제공됩니다.

[1,3]의료 기록 부서의 당신의 직원들에게 이 활동에 참여해 줄 수 있는 사람이 있는지 물어봐 주십시오. 그리고 최대한 빠른 시일 내에, 단, 늦어도 10월 31일까지 그 사람의 이름을 저에게 알려 주십시오.

이 문제에 대한 당신의 도움에 감사드립니다.

유야 쇼 박사
셀터맨 병원 행정 서비스 총괄 보조

어휘 | insider 내부자 perspective 관점 run 운영하다 to this end 이를 위해 vital 필수의 briefly 간단히

1 쇼 박사는 왜 이메일을 보냈는가?
(A) 병원 관리 강좌를 홍보하려고
(B) 변경된 방 배정에 대해 공지하려고
(C) 일련의 면접 일정을 잡으려고
(D) 자원봉사자를 모집하려고

해설 | **주제/목적**
이메일의 제목이 지원 요청(Subject: Request for assistance)이고, 첫 단락 세 번째 문장에서 저는 학생들을 데리고 우리 병원 내에서 가장 필수적인 부서들을 둘러볼 예정(I will be taking ~ within our hospital)이라고 했고, 두 번째 단락 첫 문장에서 의료 기록 부서 직원들에게 이 활동에 참여해 줄 수 있는 사람이 있는지 물어봐 달라(Please ask your staff ~ participate in this activity)고 했다. 따라서 쇼 박사는 학생들의 병원 견학에 자원해서 도움을 줄 직원을 구하고 있으므로 정답은 (D)이다.

어휘 | assignment 배정 recruit 모집하다

2 11월 5일 행사에 대해 명시된 것이 아닌 것은?
(A) 다양한 직무 책임에 대한 설명이 포함된다.
(B) 여러 부서의 직원이 참여한다.
(C) 두 시간 동안 지속될 예정이다.
(D) 식사가 포함된다.

해설 | **Not/True**
첫 단락의 세 번째 문장에서 11월 5일에 학생들을 데리고 병원 내 필수 부서들을 둘러볼 예정(on November 5 ~ within our hospital)이라고 했고, 다섯 번째 문장에서 견학은 오전 10시에 시작해 오후 3시 즈음 끝날 것으로 예상한다(The tour will begin ~ end by 3:00 P.M.)고 했으므로 11월 5일에 있을 견학은 다섯 시간이 걸린다는 것을 알 수 있다. 따라서 (C)가 정답이다. 각 분과별로 설명회를 진행하며 이 시간 동안 각 분과별 직원이 일상적인 업무에 대해 설명하고 학생들의 질문에 답하게 될 것이라고 했으므로 (A)와 (B)가 언급되었고, 여섯 번째 문장에서 점심 식사가 제공된다고 했으므로 (D)도 언급되었다.

어휘 | description 설명 involve 참여시키다 last 지속하다

3 마루식 씨에 대해 알 수 있는 것은?
(A) 의료 기록 부서에 근무한다.
(B) 병원 직원에게 정기적으로 프레젠테이션을 한다.
(C) 스틸워터 대학에서 강의를 했었다.
(D) 쇼 박사의 보조원이다.

해설 | **추론/암시**
두 번째 단락의 첫 문장에서 의료 기록 부서의 당신의 직원들에게 이 활동에 참여해 줄 수 있는 사람이 있는지 물어봐 달라(Please ask your staff ~ participate in this activity)고 한 것으로 보아 마루식 씨는 의료 기록 부서의 담당자임을 알 수 있다. 따라서 (A)가 정답이다.

[4-7] 기사

뉴볼드 (8월 7일)—온라인 상점의 인기로 인해 많은 만화 가게들이 문을 닫는 시대에 **⁴카일의 코믹 라이프가 뉴볼드에 문을 열었다.** **⁴남녀노소 모두를 위한 인기 있는 모임 장소가 될 ⁶⁽ᴬ⁾카일의 코믹 라이프는 액션 피규어와 장난감 외에도 방대한 빈티지 및 신작 만화책 소장 목록을 뽐낸다.** 게다가 오락과 휴식을 위한 라운지도 있으며, 방문객들이 직접 다과를 가져와 즐길 수 있도록 권장한다. **⁵라운지의 독특한 실내 장식은 인기 공상 과학 만화책의 배경을 닮아 있다.**

라운지에서는 매월 시인, 음악가, 코미디언과 기타 예술가들이 자신의 작품을 선보이는 오픈 마이크 나이트가 열릴 것이다. **⁶⁽ᴮ⁾토요일 오후는 가족 활동을 위한 날이고,** **⁶⁽ᴰ⁾일요일 저녁에는 보드 게임광을 위한 모임이 있다.** 뿐만 아니라 **⁷이 가게는 다양한 테마 행사를 제공할 계획이다.** 첫 번째는 9월 18일과 19일로 예정된 슈퍼히어로 위켄드이다.

카일의 코믹 라이프는 뉴볼드 사우스 가 2204번지에 위치해 있다.

어휘 | era 시대 in favor of ~을 지지하여 destined ~할 운명인 gathering 모임 spot 장소 boast 뽐내다 collection 소장품 figure 모형 장난감(피규어) relaxation 휴식 refreshments 다과 décor 실내 장식 resemble 닮다 setting 배경 poet 시인 showcase 전시하다 enthusiast 애호가 themed 테마가 있는

4 기사의 목적은 무엇인가?
(A) 만화책 시리즈 논평 (B) 새로운 사업체 소개
(C) 매장 이전 발표 (D) 웹사이트 홍보

해설 | **주제/목적**
첫 단락의 첫 문장에서 카일의 코믹 라이프가 뉴볼드에 문을 열었다(Kyle's Comic Life just opened its doors in Newbold)며 남녀노소 모두를 위한 인기 있는 모임 장소가 될 카일의 코믹 라이프는 액션 피규어와 장난감 외에도 방대한 빈티지 및 신작 만화책 소장 목록을 뽐낸다(Destined to become ~ action figures and toys)고 새로 매장을 여는 업체에 대해 소개하고 있으므로 (B)가 정답이다.

5 라운지에 대해 언급된 것은?
(A) 책의 배경처럼 장식되어 있다.
(B) 행사 일정이 온라인에 게시되어 있다.
(C) 스낵을 구매할 수 있다.
(D) 지역 예술가들의 소유이다.

해설 | **Not/True**
첫 단락의 마지막 문장에서 라운지의 독특한 실내 장식은 인기 공상 과학 만화책의 배경을 닮아 있다(The unique décor in the lounge ~ comic book)고 했으므로 (A)가 정답이다.

6 카일의 코믹 라이프에 대해 언급된 것이 아닌 것은?
(A) 장난감을 판매한다.
(B) 가족 행사를 주최한다.
(C) 동네에서 가장 인기 있는 가게이다.
(D) 보드 게임을 할 수 있는 곳이다.

해설 | **Not/True**
첫 단락의 두 번째 문장에서 카일의 코믹 라이프는 액션 피규어와 장난감 외에도 방대한 빈티지 및 신작 만화책 소장 목록을 뽐낸다(Kyle's Comic Life boasts ~ action figures and toys)고 했으므로 (A)는 사실, 두 번째 단락 두 번째 문장에서

토요일 오후는 가족 활동을 위한 날이고 일요일 저녁에는 보드 게임광을 위한 모임이 있다(Saturday afternoons are ~ board game enthusiasts)고 했으므로 (B)와 (D)도 사실이다. 동네에서 가장 인기 있는 가게라는 언급은 없으므로 (C)가 정답이다.

7 [1], [2], [3], [4]로 표시된 곳 중에서 다음 문장이 들어가기에 가장 적합한 위치는?

"첫 번째는 9월 18일과 19일로 예정된 슈퍼히어로 위켄드이다."

(A) [1]   (B) [2]
(C) [3]   (D) [4]

해설 | 문장 삽입
제시된 문장은 '첫 번째는 9월 18일과 19일로 예정된 슈퍼히어로 위켄드이다'라며 가장 먼저 열리게 될 테마 행사의 일정에 대한 정보를 제공하고 있다. 따라서 가게에서 주최할 테마 행사(the store plans to offer a variety of themed events)에 대해 언급하는 문장 뒤에 들어가는 것이 글의 흐름상 자연스러우므로 (D)가 정답이다.

UNIT 17 세부 사항 문제

ETS 예제
본책 p.254

임시 폐쇄

사우스뱅크의 더럼 로에 있는 아서의 유럽 요리(ACC)에 오늘 저희와 함께 해 주셔서 감사합니다. 저희를 또 찾아주시고 식사해 주시기를 바라지만 **본 지점은 2월 8일 화요일 오후 4시부터 마감 시간까지 비공개 파티를 위해 문을 닫을 예정입니다.** 저희의 다른 지점들은 그 날짜에 일반 고객분들을 위해 운영됩니다. 예약을 하시려면 원하시는 지점에 전화하시거나 저희 웹사이트 www.arthurscc.com.au를 방문해 주십시오.

어휘 | temporary 임시의 **closure** 폐쇄 **continental** 유럽 대륙의 **cuisine** 요리 **dine** 식사하다 **private** 비공개의

Q 2월 8일에 무슨 일이 있을 예정인가?
(A) 칼튼 지점은 평소보다 늦게까지 운영한다.
(B) ACC 직원들을 위해 깜짝 파티가 열릴 예정이다.
(C) ACC의 사우스뱅크 지점에서 비공개 행사가 열릴 예정이다.
(D) 더럼 로가 임시 폐쇄될 예정이다.

ETS 유형 연습
본책 p.255

1 (A)   **2** (C)   **3** (C)   **4** (D)

[1-4] 보도

긴급 보도   연락처: 펠릭스 월터, fwalter@rbcorp.net
¹래번사 2분기 재무 성과 발표

오리건 주 파크데일 (7월 20일)—**¹에너지 솔루션 분야의 글로벌**

리더인 래번사는 2분기 재무 보고서를 8월 1일 태평양 표준 오후 1시(미국 동부 표준 오후 4시) 전화 회의에서 공개한다고 오늘 발표했다. 이 행사는 래번의 최근 재무 성과 및 전망을 논의할 **³기회**를 제공할 것이다. 5월 19일에 열린 1분기 전화 회의 및 웹캐스트에는 200여 명이 참여했으며 좋은 반응을 얻었다. **⁴최근 에네랄 라인 서비스의 성공으로 이번 전화 회의에는 더 많은 관심이 기대된다.** 투자자 및 업계 분석가들은 다음과 같이 전화 회의 또는 웹캐스트에 참여하기 바란다.

²래번사 2분기 전화 회의
²날짜: 8월 1일
시간: 태평양 표준 오후 1시 (미국 동부 표준 오후 4시)
미국 전화 회의 번호: 1-888-555-0181
국제 전화 회의 번호: 1-206-555-0181
회의 ID: 3885650
웹캐스트: http://www.rbcorp.net/investor-relations

웹캐스트는 관찰 및 정보 제공의 목적으로만 제공된다. 토론에 참여하려면 전화 회의에 라이브로 참여해야 한다. 웹캐스트와 전화 회의의 녹화 버전은 방송 후 30일 동안 회사 웹사이트에서 이용 가능하다.

어휘 | corporation 기업 **quarter** 분기, 4분의 1 **pacific** 태평양 **outlook** 전망 **upcoming** 다가오는 **investor** 투자자 **analyst** 분석가 **observational** 관찰의 **informational** 정보를 제공하는

---

1 보도의 목적은 무엇인가?
(A) 재무 보고서에 대한 정보 제공
(B) 래번사의 신제품 소개
(C) 에너지 시장에 대한 토론에 기자 초청
(D) 새로운 에네랄 서비스 사용법 설명

해설 | 주제/목적
글의 제목이 래번사 2분기 재무 성과 발표(Raeburne Corporation to Announce Second-Quarter Financial Results)이고 첫 문장에서 에너지 솔루션 분야의 글로벌 리더인 래번사는 2분기 재무 보고서를 8월 1일 태평양 표준 오후 1시(미국 동부 표준 오후 4시) 전화 회의에서 공개한다고 오늘 발표했다(Raeburne Corporation, a global leader ~ Pacific Time (4:00 P.M. Eastern Time))고 했으므로 정답은 (A)이다.

2 참가자는 언제 전화 회의를 할 수 있는가?
(A) 5월 19일   (B) 7월 20일
(C) 8월 1일   (D) 9월 30일

해설 | 세부 사항
두 번째 단락의 첫 줄에 래번사 2분기 전화 회의(Raeburne Corporation Second-Quarter Conference Call)의 날짜가 8월 1일(Date: August 1)이라고 나와 있으므로 정답은 (C)이다.

3 첫 번째 단락 4행의 "chance"와 의미가 가장 가까운 단어는?
(A) 입장권   (B) 위험
(C) 기회   (D) 확률

해설 | 동의어
의미상 행사가 논의 '기회'를 제공할 것이라는 뜻으로 쓰인 것이므로 정답은 (C) opportunity이다.

4 다가오는 행사에 대해 알 수 있는 것은?
(A) 기업의 리더십 변화에 대해 설명한다.
(B) 법적 요건 충족을 위해 기록될 것이다.
(C) 서면 보고서로 요약된다.
(D) 이전 행사보다 참석률이 더 좋을 것 같다.

해설 | 추론/암시
첫 단락의 네 번째 문장에서 최근 에네랄 라인 서비스의 성공으로 이번 전화 회의에는 더 많은 관심이 기대된다(More interest is expected ~ Eneral line of services)고 했으므로 더 많은 인원이 참석할 것으로 예상할 수 있다. 따라서 정답은 (D)이다.

어휘 | meet 충족시키다   legal 법적인   summarize 요약하다

Paraphrasing 지문의 More interest is expected ~ → 보기의 will likely be better attended

---

ETS 고득점 실전 문제
본책 p.256

1 (A)   **2** (A)   **3** (C)   **4** (C)   **5** (B)   **6** (D)
7 (A)

[1-3] 보고서

경영 보고서

개요
[1]코스타 구스타사는 수입 및 도매 활동을 늘릴 매장 사업 개발을 위한 자금 확보를 추진 중이다. 추가 대출 신청 정보는 10쪽부터 확인할 수 있다.

상품 및 서비스
[2]코스타 구스타사가 개발할 사업은 자사의 유명 수입 원두로 생산한 음료 판매를 통해 수익을 창출시킬 것이다. [3]신규 사업에서는 또한 브랜드 커피 머그잔과 회사 로고가 새겨진 다른 부대 용품뿐 아니라 페이스트리와 같은 보완 제품을 판매할 예정이다.

판매 예측
업계에서 인정받은 명성 덕분에 코스타 구스타는 사업 시작 이후 높은 성장률을 예측한다. 향후 4년간의 예상 매출액은 아래 표에 나와 있다

제품 유형	1년차	2년차	3년차	4년차
음료	81,000달러	122,000달러	134,000달러	140,000달러
식품	22,000달러	36,000달러	41,000달러	50,000달러
[3]브랜드 부대 용품	15,000달러	17,000달러	[3]22,000달러	25,000달러

어휘 | executive summary 경영 보고서   overview 개요   seek 구하다   storefront 상점   augment 늘리다   import 수입; 수입하다   wholesale 도매의   further 추가의   loan 대출   generate 발생시키다   revenue 수익   complementary 보완의   established 인정받는   reputation 명성   trade 업계   rate 비율   operation 사업   projection 예상

1 보고서의 목적은 무엇인가?
(A) 사업 자금 조성   (B) 합병 협상
(C) 사업체를 위한 장소 물색   (D) 예산 수정 권고

해설 | 주제/목적
개요(Overview)에서 코스타 구스타사는 수입 및 도매 활동을 늘릴 매장 사업 개발을 위한 자금 확보를 추진 중(Costa Gusta, Inc., is seeking to obtain funds ~ wholesale activities)이라고 했으므로 사업을 위한 자금 조달을 위한 보고서임을 알 수 있다. 따라서 (A)가 정답이다.

어휘 | raise (자금 등을) 모으다   negotiate 협상하다   merger 합병   identify 찾다   revision 수정

Paraphrasing 지문의 obtain funds → 보기의 raise money

2 코스타 구스타는 어떤 종류의 사업체를 열 계획인가?
(A) 커피숍   (B) 주방용품점
(C) 수출입 서비스   (D) 음료 제조 및 병음료 회사

해설 | 세부 사항
상품 및 서비스(Products and Services) 항목의 첫 문장에서 코스타 구스타사가 개발할 사업은 자사의 유명 수입 원두로 생산한 음료 판매를 통해 수익을 창출시킬 것(The business to be developed by Costa Gusta ~ imported coffee beans)이라고 했으므로 커피를 팔 계획임을 알 수 있다. 따라서 (A)가 정답이다.

어휘 | goods 제품   export 수출   bottling 병에 든 음료

3 코스타 구스타는 언제 22,000달러 상당의 회사 로고가 장식된 제품을 판매할 예정인가?
(A) 1년차   (B) 2년차
(C) 3년차   (D) 4년차

해설 | 세부 사항
상품 및 서비스(Products and Services) 항목의 두 번째 문장에서 신규 사업에서는 브랜드 커피 머그잔과 회사 로고가 새겨진 다른 부대 용품 등의 보완 제품을 팔 것(The new business will also sell ~ accessories with the company logo)이라고 했고 판매 예측 표에 따르면 22,000달러 상당의 제품 판매 중 브랜드 부대 용품은 3년차로 예정되어 있으므로 (C)가 정답이다.

[4-7] 이메일

발신: jrobins@rayaxo.com
수신: rmajewski@rayaxo.com
제목: 사양의 정확성
날짜: 11월 19일
첨부: CF-4500

마예브스키 씨께,

[4]방금 줄리아 카민스카로부터 CF-4500 생산 사양의 폴란드어 버전을 받았습니다. [4, 5, 6]첨부 파일을 검토하셔서 우리 파일의 영문 원본과 일치하는지 확인해 주시겠습니까? 카민스카 씨의 작업 수준에 항상 만족해 왔지만, CF-4500은 특히 중요합니다. 아시다시피, 폴란드의 제조업체 한 곳과 조명 기구와 제어 장치를 생산하기로 계약을 맺었고 다음 주 금요일에 시험 가동에 들어갈 예정입니다. 그래서 [6]마예브스키 씨께서 크기에 관한 모든 수치를 재확인해 주시는 것이 중요합니다. 부정확한 수치로 인해 경비 초과가 발생하고 잠재적으로 생산이 지연될 수 있습니다.

늦어도 내일 오후까지는 검토를 완료해 주시고 폴란드어 버전에 오류가 있을 경우 알려 주시기 바랍니다. ⁷**월요일에 생산 엔지니어에게 사양을 보내야 금요일 시험 가동에 맞춰 그쪽 장비를 준비할 수 있습니다.** 고객사 대표들이 참석해 관람할 예정입니다.

감사합니다.

제시카 로빈스

어휘 | accuracy 정확성 specification 사양 Polish 폴란드의; 폴란드어 edition 판 attachment 첨부(물) lighting fixture 조명 기구 process 절차 undergo 겪다[받다] test run 시운전[시험 운행] figure 수치 referring to ~에 관하여 inaccuracy 부정확 lead to ~로 이어지다 cost overrun 경비 초과 potentially 잠재적으로 at the latest 늦어도 forward 보내다 on hand 참석한

---

4 카민스카 씨가 제공하는 서비스는 무엇인가?

(A) 설계 (B) 인쇄
(C) 번역 (D) 회계

해설 | 세부 사항
첫 문장에서 방금 줄리아 카민스카로부터 CF-4500 생산 사양의 폴란드어 버전을 받았다(We just received the Polish edition ~ from Julia Kaminska)며 첨부 파일을 검토해 우리 파일의 영문 원본과 일치하는지 확인해 줄 수 있는지(Could you please look over ~ English original in our files?)를 묻고 있는 것으로 보아 카민스카 씨는 영문을 폴란드어로 번역했음을 알 수 있다. 따라서 정답은 (C)이다.

5 마예브스키 씨가 요청받은 일은 무엇인가?

(A) 지연 보고 조사 (B) 두 문서 비교
(C) 장비 결함 수리 (D) 폴란드 출장

해설 | 세부 사항
첫 단락 두 번째 문장에서 마예브스키 씨에게 첨부 파일을 검토해 우리 파일의 영문 원본과 일치하는지 확인해 줄 수 있는지(Could you please look over ~ English original in our files?)를 묻고 있으므로 (B)가 정답이다.

어휘 | investigate 조사하다 faulty 결함이 있는

6 첨부 파일에 포함된 정보는 무엇인가?

(A) 테스트 일정 (B) 재료의 품질
(C) 건물 배치도 (D) 부품의 치수

해설 | 세부 사항
첫 단락 두 번째 문장에서 첨부 파일을 검토해 줄 수 있는지 (Could you please look over ~ English original in our files?)를 물었고, 크기에 관한 모든 수치를 재확인하는 것이 중요하다(it is important that you double-check all the figures referring to the sizes)고 했으므로 첨부 파일에 제품 크기의 치수가 포함되어 있음을 알 수 있다. 따라서 (D)가 정답이다.

어휘 | material 재료 layout 배치 dimension 치수, 크기

Paraphrasing 지문의 figures referring to the sizes → 보기의 dimensions

---

7 월요일에 무슨 일이 있을 예정인가?

(A) 문서가 발송된다.
(B) 합의가 마무리된다.
(C) 생산 장비가 청소된다.
(D) 제조 과정이 테스트된다.

해설 | 세부 사항
두 번째 단락 두 번째 문장에서 월요일에 생산 엔지니어에게 사양을 보내야 금요일 시험 가동에 맞춰 그쪽 장비를 준비할 수 있다(We must forward the specifications ~ Friday's test run)고 했으므로 월요일에 제품 사양서를 보낼 것임을 알 수 있다. 따라서 정답은 (A)이다.

Paraphrasing 지문의 specifications → 보기의 document

UNIT 18 Not/True 문제

ETS 예제   본책 p.258

가을을 활용해 나무를 돌보세요. 겨울 눈보라로 인해 나뭇가지들이 부러지고 건물에 떨어질 수 있습니다. 존스 트리 프로페셔널즈가 도와드리겠습니다! 가지치기부터 제거에 이르는 각종 나무 관련 서비스가 필요하시면 저희에게 전화하세요. **신규 고객은 모든 서비스에 20% 할인을 받으실 수 있습니다.**

어휘 | take advantage of ~을 이용하다 cause ~을 야기하다 branch 나뭇가지 property 건물 (구내) range (범위가 ~에서 …에) 이르다 pruning 가지치기 removal 제거

Q 존스 트리 프로페셔널즈에 대해 명시된 것은?

(A) 특정 종류의 나무만을 전문으로 한다.
(B) 무료 서비스 견적을 제공한다.
(C) 신규 고객에게 할인을 제공하고 있다.
(D) 지난 겨울에 설립되었다.

어휘 | specialize in ~을 전문으로 하다 estimate 견적서 found 설립하다

ETS 유형 연습   본책 p.259

1 (A) **2** (D) **3** (D) **4** (B)

[1-4] 기사

휴스턴 (7월 11일)—글로벌 제품 분석 분야의 선두 주자인 레텍소사는 오늘 신생 기업에 할인된 가격으로 세계적 수준의 서비스 이용권을 제공하는 지원 프로그램을 발표했다. ^{1,4}**레텍소는 컴퓨터, 스마트폰, 손에 들고 쓰는 장치의 프로그램 또는 앱과 사용자의 상호 작용에 대한 데이터를 집계한다.** 그런 다음 고객사의 개발팀이 검토할 수 있도록 데이터 분석 자료를 온라인에 게시한다. ¹결과는 고객사의 프로그램 및 앱에 대한 업데이트가 실제 고객의 요구를 기반으로 하도록 보장한다.
    ²레텍소는 각종 규모의 회사들이 최종 사용자의 참여와 전반적인 만족도를 개선함으로써 고객을 유지할 수 있도록 돕는다. 최근 레텍소

프로젝트에는 데스크톱 컴퓨터용 인테리어 디자인 프로그램인 이오의 루미스트와 스마트폰용 운동 관리 앱인 조이다의 릴레이 4가 있다.

이 새로운 가격 옵션으로 렉텍소는 신생 기업들에 정가에서 10%에서 20%까지 할인된 가격에 모든 서비스에 대한 이용권을 제공하고 있다. ³인증 고객은 12개월 동안 할인된 요금으로 사용자 상호 작용에 대한 주간 분석 자료를 이용할 수 있다. 세부 사항과 신청서는 회사 웹사이트(www.retexo.net)에서 확인할 수 있다. 신청서는 다음달까지 접수될 예정이다.

어휘 | analytics 분석 정보 aggregate 종합하다 interaction 상호 작용 handheld 손에 들고 쓰는 device 장치 retain 유지하다 end-user 최종 사용자 engagement 참여 overall 전반적인 pricing 가격 책정 suite 세트 analyses (analysis의 복수) 분석 rate 요금 application form 신청서

1 렉텍소가 개선에 도움을 줄 수 있는 제품은 무엇인가?
(A) 컴퓨터 소프트웨어　　(B) 스포츠 용품
(C) 가정용 가구　　(D) 스테레오 장비

해설 | 세부 사항
두 번째 단락의 첫 문장에서 렉텍소는 컴퓨터, 스마트폰, 손에 들고 쓰는 장치의 프로그램 또는 앱과 사용자의 상호 작용에 대한 데이터를 집계한다(Retexo aggregates data on users' interactions ~ handheld devices)고 했고, 이어서 결과는 고객사의 프로그램 및 앱에 대한 업데이트가 실제 고객의 요구를 기반으로 하도록 보장한다(The results ensure that updates ~ actual customers' needs)고 했으므로 정답은 (A)이다.

어휘 | household 가정 equipment 장비

Paraphrasing 지문의 programs or applications
→ 보기의 software

2 렉텍소의 서비스로부터 기업들이 얻는 혜택으로 언급된 것은?
(A) 고객 증가　　(B) 생산 비용 절감
(C) 더 효과적인 의견　　(D) 고객 충성도 향상

해설 | Not/True
세 번째 단락의 첫 문장에서 렉텍소는 각종 규모의 회사들이 최종 사용자의 참여와 전반적인 만족도를 개선함으로써 고객을 유지할 수 있도록 돕는다(Retexo helps companies of all sizes retain customers ~ overall satisfaction)고 했으므로 (D)가 정답이다.

어휘 | reduction 감소 effective 효과적인 loyalty 충성도

Paraphrasing 지문의 retain customers
→ 보기의 greater customer loyalty

3 고객은 얼마나 오래 렉텍소의 서비스를 할인된 가격에 이용할 수 있는가?
(A) 일주일　　(B) 20주
(C) 10개월　　(D) 1년

해설 | 세부 사항
네 번째 단락의 두 번째 문장에서 인증 고객은 12개월 동안 할인된 요금으로 사용자 상호 작용에 대한 주간 분석 자료를 이용할 수 있다(Accepted clients will be able to access ~ reduced rate for a period of twelve months)고 했으므로 정답은 (D)이다.

Paraphrasing 지문의 twelve months → 보기의 one year

4 [1], [2], [3], [4]로 표시된 곳 중에서 다음 문장이 들어가기에 가장 적합한 위치는?
"그런 다음 고객사의 개발팀이 검토할 수 있도록 데이터 분석 자료를 온라인에 게시한다."
(A) [1]　　(B) [2]
(C) [3]　　(D) [4]

해설 | 문장 삽입
제시된 문장의 Analyses of the data are then posted가 문제 해결의 단서이다. then(그런 다음)으로 미루어 보아 주어진 문장 앞에는 데이터 분석 자료를 게시하기 전에 필요한 일 즉, 데이터 수집 및 분석과 같은 내용이 언급되어야 한다. 따라서 렉텍소는 컴퓨터, 스마트폰, 손에 들고 쓰는 장치의 프로그램 또는 앱과 사용자의 상호 작용에 대한 데이터를 집계한다(Retexo aggregates data on users' interactions ~ handheld devices)는 내용 뒤인 (B)가 정답이다.

ETS 고득점 실전 문제　　본책 p.260

1 (D)　**2** (C)　**3** (A)　**4** (D)　**5** (D)　**6** (C)
7 (A)　**8** (B)

[1-4] 구인 광고

누라스 마켓 직원 모집 중

누라스 마켓은 클레데닌 지역사회의 오랜 기둥임을 자랑스럽게 생각합니다. ¹50년 이상 우리 매장은 지역 농부들의 농산물과 육류를 포함한 건강 식품을 취급해 왔습니다. 우리는 현재 다음과 같은 직책에 직원을 모집 중입니다.

²매장 관리자: 업무에는 일상 운영 감독, 홍보 자료 개발, 문제 해결을 위한 고객과의 대면 의사소통 유지, 판매팀 동기 부여, 직원 교육이 포함됩니다. 월요일부터 금요일까지 상근직입니다.

재고 담당자: 업무에는 제품 수령, 적재 및 포장 해체, 진열품 채워 넣기, 재고 추적 관찰, 걸레질 및 바닥 쓸기 보조 업무가 포함됩니다. 시간제 근무이며 주말 근무가 요구됩니다.

꽃 디자이너: 업무에는 꽃꽂이 제작 및 전시, 부서를 위한 제품 주문이 포함됩니다. 화훼 부서에서의 사전 경험이 필수 사항입니다. ³신체 조건: 최대 25kg까지 들어올리고 운반할 수 있어야 합니다. 근무 시간표에는 주말과 휴일이 포함됩니다.

판매 사원: 업무에는 출납원 업무 수행, 고객맞이, 고객이 제품을 찾도록 지원하는 일, 고객에게 일일 판매 행사 및 할인 정보 제공이 포함됩니다. 월요일부터 목요일까지 시간제 근무입니다.

⁴당사는 경쟁력 있는 보상과 유급 휴가를 제공합니다. 지원자들은 이력서와 자기소개서를 제시카 르 아브르에게 jlehavre@noorahs.com으로 보내야 합니다.

어휘 | pillar 기둥 decade 10년 stock 채우다 produce 농산물 oversee 감독하다 maintain 유지하다 resolve 해결하다 motivate 동기를 부여하다 load 적재하다 unpack (짐을) 풀다 monitor 추적 관찰하다 inventory 재고 mop 걸레질하다 sweep (빗자루로) 쓸다 arrangement 배치

locate 위치를 찾다 competitive 경쟁력 있는
compensation 보상 paid 유급의 cover letter 자기소개서

1 광고에서 누라스 마켓에 대해 언급한 것은?
(A) 클렌데닌에 새 지점을 열 계획이다.
(B) 최근에 농산물 부서를 확장했다.
(C) 지역 농부들이 설립했다.
(D) 50년 이상 사업을 해 왔다.

해설 | **Not / True**
첫 단락의 두 번째 문장에서 50년 이상 우리 매장은 지역
농부들의 농산물과 육류를 포함한 건강 식품을 취급해 왔다(For
more than five decades ~ from local farmers)고
했으므로 누라스 마켓은 50년 이상 매장을 운영해 왔음을 알 수
있다. 따라서 (D)가 정답이다.

Paraphrasing 지문의 more than five decades
→ 보기의 over 50 years

2 매장 관리자의 직무로 기재되지 않은 것은?
(A) 교육 제공
(B) 직원 동기 부여
(C) 매장 내 디스플레이 설치
(D) 고객 불만 처리

해설 | **Not / True**
두 번째 단락의 매장 관리자(Store Manager)에 대한 직무
안내에서 업무에는 일상 운영 감독, 홍보 자료 개발, 문제 해결을
위한 고객과의 대면 의사소통 유지, 판매팀 동기 부여, 직원
교육이 포함된다(Responsibilities include ~ and training
staff)고 했고, 디스플레이 설치에 대해서는 언급되지 않았으므로
(C)가 정답이다.

Paraphrasing 지문의 resolve issues
→ 보기의 Dealing with ~ concerns

3 누라스 마켓의 꽃 디자이너에 대해 알 수 있는 것은?
(A) 무거운 물건을 들어야 할 수도 있다.
(B) 고객들에게 꽃꽂이하는 방법을 가르친다.
(C) 휴일에는 종종 봉사료를 받는다.
(D) 집과 사무실로 꽃을 배달한다.

해설 | **추론 / 암시**
네 번째 단락에서 꽃 디자이너는 신체 조건으로 최대 25kg까지
들어올리고 운반할 수 있어야 한다(Physical requirements:
Must be ~ 25 kilograms)고 한 것으로 보아 (A)가 정답이다.

어휘 | object 물건 tip 봉사료

4 광고된 직책들에 대해 명시된 것은?
(A) 토요일 교대 근무를 포함한다.
(B) 상근직이다.
(C) 지원자들이 직접 지원할 것을 요구한다.
(D) 직원들에게 유급 휴가를 준다.

해설 | **Not / True**
마지막 단락의 첫 문장에서 당사는 경쟁력 있는 보상과 유급
휴가를 제공한다(We offer competitive compensation
and paid vacation time)고 했으므로 (D)가 정답이다.

어휘 | shift 교대 근무 in person 직접 entitle 권리를 주다
Paraphrasing 지문의 vacation time → 보기의 time off

[5-8] 편지

마커스 슈미트 • 개프니 가 4번지 • 사우스 멜버른 VIC 3205

2월 8일

카일리 가리마라
애니웨어 딜리버리 주식회사
파크스 로 60번지
멜버른 VIC 3000

가리마라 씨께,

애니웨어 딜리버리사의 트럭 운전기사 자리에 지원하고자 이 글을
씁니다. 제 동료인 한병훈 씨가 당신에게 동봉된 이력서를 보내라고
추천했습니다. **[5]한 씨와 저는 트럭 운전 교습소를 함께 다녔을 때부터
서로 알고 지냈는데, 그가 애니웨어 딜리버리에서 물품을 운송하는
일이 얼마나 즐거운지에 대해 이야기했습니다.**

저는 헌신적이고 근면한 사람으로서, 12년 동안 창고에서 소매 점포
및 사업체로 상품을 운송하고 배달한 경력을 제공합니다. 애너랩사를
위해 신선한 농산물을 배송하는 일로 시작해 **[6]현재는 심슨 트럭킹을
위해 건설 장비를 운송하는 일을 하고 있습니다.** 저는 항상 안전하고
시간을 엄수하는 **[7]방식**으로 업무를 수행하는 것에 큰 자부심을 갖고
있습니다.

심슨 트럭킹의 운전기사로서, 저는 전국을 누비며 한 번의 왕복 주행에
종종 수백 혹은 수천 킬로미터를 운전합니다. 저는 91%의 능률 점수와
정비사, 엔지니어, 고객 및 기타 운전기사들과의 효과적인 소통
능력에 대해 관리자로부터 칭찬을 받았습니다. 또한 **[8]2년 전에는 심슨
트럭킹에서 올해의 직원으로 선정되는 영광도 누렸습니다.**

저의 지원과 관련하여 회신을 받을 수 있는 기회를 갖기를
기대합니다.

마커스 슈미트

동봉물

어휘 | CV 이력서 enclose 동봉하다 transport 운송하다
goods 제품 dedicated 헌신적인 individual 개인
warehouse 창고 produce 농산물 take pride in ~을
자랑하다 timely 때맞춘 round trip 왕복 여행 commend
칭찬하다 efficiency 능률 rating 점수 mechanic 정비공
enclosure 동봉물

5 한 씨는 누구일 것 같은가?
(A) 채용 담당자   (B) 운전 강사
(C) 가게 주인   (D) 트럭 운전사

해설 | **추론 / 암시**
첫 단락의 세 번째 문장에서 한 씨와 저는 트럭 운전 교습소를
함께 다녔을 때부터 서로 알고 지냈는데 그가 애니웨어
딜리버리에서 물품을 운송하는 일이 얼마나 즐거운지에 대해
이야기했다(Mr. Hahn and I have known ~ for Anywhere
Deliveries)고 했으므로 한 씨가 운송 일을 하는 트럭 운전사임을
알 수 있다. 따라서 (D)가 정답이다.

6 슈미트 씨가 자신의 현재 직업에 대해 언급한 것은?

(A) 12년 전에 시작했다.
(B) 멜버른으로 이사해야 했다.
(C) 기기 운반 작업을 수반한다.
(D) 애너랩 사에 있다.

해설 | Not/True

두 번째 단락의 두 번째 문장에서 현재는 심슨 트럭킹을 위해 건설 장비를 운송하는 일을 하고 있다(now deliver construction machinery for Simpson Trucking)고 했으므로 (C)가 정답이다.

Paraphrasing 지문의 deliver → 보기의 transporting

7 두 번째 단락 5행의 "manner"와 의미가 가장 가까운 단어는?

(A) 방법   (B) 외관
(C) 등급   (D) 약속

해설 | 동의어

의미상 안전하고 시간을 엄수하는 '방식'으로 업무를 수행한다는 뜻으로 쓰인 것이므로 정답은 (A) way이다.

8 슈미트 씨에 대해 명시된 것은?

(A) 짧은 여행보다 긴 여행을 선호한다.
(B) 고용주로부터 상을 받았다.
(C) 동료들로부터 높은 평가를 받았다.
(D) 의사소통 관련 강좌를 들었다.

해설 | Not/True

세 번째 단락의 마지막 문장에서 2년 전에 심슨 트럭킹에서 올해의 직원으로 선정되는 영광을 누렸다(I was honoured to be selected as the Employee of the Year at Simpson Trucking two years ago)고 했으므로 (B)가 정답이다. 장거리 선호에 대한 언급은 없으므로 (A)는 알 수 없고, 91%의 높은 능률 점수는 받았으나 동료들로부터 받은 것이 아니므로 (C)는 오답, 효과적인 소통 능력에 대해 관리자로부터 칭찬을 받았으나 강좌를 들었다는 언급은 없으므로 (D)도 오답이다.

어휘 | employer 고용주   peer 동료

Paraphrasing 지문의 be selected as the Employee of the Year → 보기의 received an award from his employer

UNIT 19 추론/암시 문제

[ETS 예제]   본책 p.262

머큐리 버스: 오션웨이브즈 음악 축제의 공식 여행 파트너

저희 편안한 버스는 6월 17일부터 6월 21일까지 매일 오션웨이브즈 음악 축제에 가는 사람들의 이동을 돕습니다. 편도 승차권은 각 10달러입니다. 왕복 승차권은 20달러에 구입할 수 있습니다. 버스는 콜튼빌에서 오전 10시 30분에 출발해 축제 정문에서 오후 8시에 돌아옵니다. **승차권은 버스에서 또는 웹사이트를 통해 구입할 수 있습니다.** 자세한 정보를 원하시면 https://www.mercurycoaches. com을 방문하세요.

어휘 | coach 버스   transport 수송하다   concertgoer 콘서트에 가는 사람   round-trip 왕복 여행의

Q 버스 승차권에 대해 알 수 있는 것은?

(A) 교환 가능하다.
(B) 왕복 승차는 할인이 된다.
(C) 미리 구입할 수 있다.
(D) 콜튼빌에 있는 가게에서 판다.

ETS 유형 연습   본책 p.263

1 (A)   **2** (A)   **3** (C)   **4** (B)

[1-4] 이메일

발신: 자비에 그룬케 〈xgruenke@CRG.com〉
수신: 리비아 자파테로 〈lzapatero@epochretailers.com〉
제목: 회신: 암벽 등반 과정
날짜: 12월 22일

자파테로 씨께,

[1]**캐슬뷰 록 체육관에서 단체 행사를 개최하는 일에 대해 문의해 주셔서 감사합니다. 네,** 지난 몇 년간 귀사를 위해 행사를 주최해 온 것을 기억하며, 이번 새 행사 준비도 기꺼이 돕겠습니다. 과거에 우리가 함께 작업했던 행사가 이포크 리테일러즈의 고객님들 팀에게 성공작이었다는 것에 대해 기쁘게 생각합니다.

문의하신 날짜에 관해서는 금요일 오후 시간대가 2시간짜리 행사를 진행하기에 가장 좋을 것 같습니다. [2]**최대 20명까지 예약해 드릴 수 있습니다. 여기에는 저희 공인 등반 담당 직원의 안내와 모든 필수 등반 장비가 포함됩니다.** 대여 신발은 선택 사항이지만 등반가들은 반드시 발가락을 감싸는 운동화를 착용해야 합니다. 물 외에 다른 다과를 제공하시려면 음식 배달을 따로 준비하셔야 합니다. 언제나처럼 사진 촬영이 허용되며 권장됩니다!

귀사에서 지난번 방문하신 이후, [3]**우리는 숙련된 등반가들에게** [4]**어필하는 더 어려운 암벽을 추가했습니다.** 물론 입문자들을 위한 옵션도 여전히 많이 있습니다. 이 시간에 예약하기를 원하시는지 알려 주시기 바랍니다.

자비에 그룬케

어휘 | inquiry 문의   recall 기억하다   arrange 준비하다   time slot 시간대   accommodate 수용하다   instruction 안내   licensed 자격증을 소지한   athletic shoes 운동화   refreshments 다과   permit 허용하다   challenging 까다로운   appeal 관심을 끌다   plenty of 많은

1 자파테로 씨에 대해 알 수 있는 것은?

(A) 과거에 캐슬뷰 록 체육관을 방문한 적이 있다.
(B) 최근에 새로운 직책으로 승진했다.
(C) 보통 금요일 오후에 회의를 할 수 있는 시간이 된다.
(D) 레저 장비 회사의 소매 판매 담당자이다.

해설 | 추론/암시

첫 문장에서 자파테로 씨에게 캐슬뷰 록 체육관에서 단체 행사를 개최하는 일에 대해 문의 주셔서 감사하다(Thank you for your inquiry ~ Castleview Rock Gym)고 했고, 지난 몇 년간 귀사를 위해 행사를 주최해 온 것을 기억한다(I recall that we have hosted ~ over the past few years)고 했으므로 자파테로 씨는 수년간 캐슬뷰 록 체육관에서 단체 행사를 진행해 왔음을 알 수 있다. 따라서 (A)가 정답이다.

2 캐슬뷰 록 체육관은 단체 행사 시 무엇을 제공하는가?
(A) 암벽 등반 안내　　　(B) 등반 장비 할인
(C) 단체 사진　　　　　(D) 다양한 다과

해설 | 세부 사항
두 번째 단락의 두 번째 문장에서 최대 20명까지 예약해 드릴 수 있다(We offer reservations for up to twenty guests)고 했고 여기에는 저희 공인 등반 담당 직원의 안내와 모든 필수 등반 장비가 포함된다(This includes instruction ~ climbing equipment)고 했으므로 (A)가 정답이다.

3 캐슬뷰 록 체육관에 대해 알 수 있는 것은?
(A) 일주일 내내 문을 연다.
(B) 20명의 직원을 고용하고 있다.
(C) 다양한 수준의 능력을 가진 등반가들을 수용할 수 있다.
(D) 보수 공사를 위해 곧 임시 휴업할 예정이다.

해설 | 추론/암시
세 번째 단락의 첫 문장에서 우리는 숙련된 등반가들에게 어필하는 더 어려운 암벽을 추가했다(we have added more ~ experienced climbers)고 했고 물론 입문자들을 위한 옵션도 여전히 많이 있다(Of course, we also still have plenty of options for beginners)고 했다. 따라서 캐슬뷰 록 체육관에는 입문자부터 상급자에 이르는 다양한 등반가를 위한 암벽 코스가 있음을 알 수 있으므로 정답은 (C)이다.

어휘 | varying 다양한　**temporarily** 임시로

4 세 번째 단락 1행의 "appeal to"와 의미가 가장 가까운 단어는?
(A) 요청하다　　　　　(B) 마음을 끌다
(C) 제공하다　　　　　(D) 조직하다

해설 | 동의어
의미상 숙련된 등반가들에게 '어필하다'라는 뜻으로 쓰인 것이므로 정답은 (B) attract이다.

ETS 고득점 실전 문제
본책 p.264

1 (D)　**2** (A)　**3** (B)　**4** (C)　**5** (B)　**6** (C)
7 (A)　**8** (D)

[1-4] 기사

> **건터 와인먼은 어떻게 시작했나**
>
> 35년 전, 건터 와인먼은 버스를 타고 유럽을 여행하는 밴드의 기타 연주자였다. 이 밴드는 작은 행사장에서 공연을 했고 많은 추종자를 끌어모은 적이 없었다. 오늘날 와인먼 씨는 온라인으로 신제품 및 빈티지 녹음 장비를 판매하는 수백만 달러 규모 회사인 구어무스사의 대표이다.

밴드가 해체되었을 때 와인먼 씨는 프라이부르크 인근에 집을 사서 이사했다. **1, 2(C), 4**시간이 지나면서 그는 집을 개조해 녹음 스튜디오로 바꾸었고 현지 음악인들을 위해 녹음을 했다. 그는 또한 빈티지 장비를 복원하는 전문가가 되었다.

3어느 날 그는 유명한 재즈 가수 지나 스코토로부터 긴급 전화를 받았고, 그녀는 현지 콘서트를 위해 마이크가 필요했다. "예상치 못한 일이었어요. 저는 작은 스튜디오의 주인일 뿐이었어요."라고 와인먼 씨는 회상했다. **2(D)**스코토 씨는 스튜디오를 방문한 뒤, 그곳에서 녹음하기로 결심했다. 그들이 만든 앨범 〈휘스퍼스〉는 잘 팔렸고 와인먼 씨의 스튜디오는 널리 알려졌다. 시간이 흐르면서 와인먼 씨는 직원을 모집했고 **2(B)**웹사이트를 개설했으며 온라인으로 장비를 판매하는 일에 더욱 열중하게 되었다.

"이제 우리는 많은 음악가들과 녹음 기사들이 즐겨 찾는 공급자가 되었습니다."라고 와인먼 씨는 말했다.

어휘 | venue 행사장　**draw** 끌어모으다　**following** 추종자들　**emergency call** 긴급 전화　**unexpected** 예상치 못한　**recall** 회상하다　**widespread** 널리 퍼진　**recognition** 인식　**recruit** 모집하다　**involve** 관련시키다　**go-to** (정보 등을 얻기 위해) 찾는 곳　**source** 공급자

1 와인먼 씨에 대해 알 수 있는 것은?
(A) 유명한 기타 연주자였다.
(B) 30대에 음악을 연주하기 시작했다.
(C) 밴드 멤버들과 함께 회사를 세웠다.
(D) 집에서 사업을 시작했다.

해설 | 추론/암시
두 번째 단락의 두 번째 문장에서 시간이 지나면서 그는 집을 개조해 녹음 스튜디오로 바꾸었고 현지 음악인들을 위해 녹음을 했다(Over time, he renovated ~ local musicians)고 했으므로 와인먼 씨는 자신의 집에서 사업을 시작했음을 알 수 있다. 따라서 (D)가 정답이다.

어휘 | well-known 유명한　**found** 설립하다

Paraphrasing 지문의 the house → 보기의 his home

2 와인먼 씨가 성공한 이유로 언급된 것이 아닌 것은?
(A) 잡지 광고　　　　　(B) 인터넷
(C) 주택 개조 프로젝트　(D) 행운의 만남

해설 | Not/True
두 번째 단락의 두 번째 문장에서 집을 개조해 녹음 스튜디오로 바꾸었다(he renovated the house and turned it into a recording studio)고 했으므로 (C), 세 번째 단락의 네 번째 문장에서 유명한 재즈 가수인 스코토 씨가 스튜디오를 방문한 뒤 그곳에서 녹음하기로 결심했다(After visiting the studio, Ms. Scotto decided to record there)고 했으므로 (D), 세 번째 단락의 마지막 문장에서 웹사이트를 개설해 온라인으로 장비를 판매하는 일에 더욱 열중하게 되었다(set up a Web site ~ selling equipment online)고 했으므로 (B)가 와인먼 씨의 성공 이유로 언급되었다. 잡지 광고에 대한 언급은 없으므로 (A)가 정답이다.

어휘 | encounter 만남[조우]

Paraphrasing 지문의 renovated → 보기의 remodeling
지문의 a Web site, online → 보기의 The Internet

3 스코토 씨에 대해 암시된 것은?

(A) 와인먼 씨의 첫 밴드에서 노래를 불렀다.

(B) 와인먼 씨를 만나기 전에 성공했다.

(C) 와인먼 씨의 스튜디오가 더 클 것이라고 예상했다.

(D) 와인먼 씨에게 온라인으로 물건을 판매하라고 권했다.

해설 | **추론/암시**

세 번째 단락의 첫 문장에서 어느 날 와인먼 씨는 유명한 재즈 가수 지나 스코토로부터 긴급 전화를 받았고 그녀는 현지 콘서트를 위해 마이크가 필요했다(One day he received ~ for a local concert)고 한 것으로 보아 스코토 씨는 와인먼 씨를 만나기 전에 이미 성공한 유명 가수였음을 알 수 있다. 따라서 (B)가 정답이다.

4 [1], [2], [3], [4]로 표시된 곳 중에서 다음 문장이 들어가기에 가장 적합한 위치는?

"그는 또한 빈티지 장비를 복원하는 전문가가 되었다."

(A) [1]　　　　　　　(B) [2]

(C) [3]　　　　　　　(D) [4]

해설 | **문장 삽입**

제시된 문장의 He also became an expert가 문제 해결의 단서이다. 와인먼 씨가 직업적으로 어떤 일을 했는지에 대해 언급하며 also를 사용했으므로 주어진 문장 앞에서도 와인먼 씨가 업무상 한 일에 대해 소개하는 내용이 와야 한다. 따라서 집을 개조해 녹음 스튜디오로 바꾸고 음악인들을 위해 녹음을 했다(he renovated the house and turned it into a recording studio where he recorded local musicians)는 문장 뒤인 (C)가 정답이다.

[5-8] 보도

> **긴급 보도 | 연락처: 메리 해너건, 020 913 3000**
>
> 킬라니 (8월 8일)—⁵**아일랜드 남서부에 본사를 둔 최고의 숙박시설 개발 회사인 킬라니 프로퍼티사는 향후 개발을 위해 현재 비어 있는 주택 10채를 인수한다고 발표하게 되어 기쁩니다.**
>
> 이 주택들은 케리 카운티의 경치 좋은 도로인 링 오브 케리 주변의 여러 마을에 위치해 있습니다. 각 주택은 소규모의 부티크 호텔을 만들기 위해 개조될 예정입니다. ⁶**호텔의 규모는 객실 5개에서 15개까지 다양하며 향후 3년에 걸쳐 개관할 예정입니다.** 완공되면 새로운 호텔들은 100명 이상의 현지인을 고용하게 될 것입니다.
>
> 링 오브 케리의 아름다운 물리적 환경과 매력적인 작은 마을들은 계속해서 전 세계로부터 점점 더 많은 수의 관광객들을 ⁷**끌어들이고** 있습니다. 이 지역으로 오는 관광객은 매년 약 7% 비율로 증가하고 있습니다.
>
> 숙박에 대한 늘어나는 수요를 수용하기 위해 대형 호텔을 짓는 대신 소규모의 건물을 개조하는 방식을 택함으로써 ⁸**킬라니 프로퍼티사는 아일랜드 남서부의 매력에 악영향을 끼치지 않으면서도 이 지역의 독특함에 부합하는 숙박시설을 개발하는 전통을 지속하고 있습니다.**
>
> 자세한 내용은 020 913 3000으로 킬라니 프로퍼티사의 대외 관계 담당 이사인 메리 해너건에게 문의하십시오.

어휘 | **property** 부동산　**premier** 최고의　**lodging** 숙소　**headquartered in** ~에 본사를 둔　**acquisition** 인수　**vacant** 비어 있는　**scenic drive** 경치가 좋은 도로　**range** (범위가) ~에 이르다　**course** 경과　**physical** 물리적인

setting 환경　**charming** 매력적인　**draw** 끌어들이다　**rate** 비율　**accommodate** 수용하다　**demand** 수요　**tradition** 전통　**accommodation** 숙소　**conform to** ~에 부합하다　**uniqueness** 독특함　**adversely** 부정적으로

5 보도는 무엇에 관한 것인가?

(A) 호텔의 완공

(B) 일부 부동산의 구입

(C) 지역 차량 교통의 문제점

(D) 아일랜드 도시 관광의 증가

해설 | **주제/목적**

첫 단락에서 아일랜드 남서부에 본사를 둔 최고의 숙박시설 개발 회사인 킬라니 프로퍼티사는 향후 개발을 위해 현재 비어 있는 주택 10채를 인수한다고 발표하게 되어 기쁘다(Killarney Property Ltd., ~ vacant homes for future development)고 했으므로 (B)가 정답이다.

어휘 | **challenge** 문제　**vehicular** 차량과 관련된　**Irish** 아일랜드의

Paraphrasing　지문의 the acquisition of ~ homes → 보기의 The purchase of some properties

6 새 호텔에 대해 명시된 것은?

(A) 동시에 개관한다.

(B) 공터에 건축된다.

(C) 3년에 걸쳐 완공된다.

(D) 각각 객실 15개를 갖춘다.

해설 | **Not/True**

두 번째 단락의 세 번째 문장에서 호텔의 규모는 객실 5개에서 15개까지 다양하며 향후 3년에 걸쳐 개관할 예정(The hotels will range ~ over the course of the next three years)이라고 했으므로 (C)가 정답이다.

Paraphrasing　지문의 over the course of the next three years → 보기의 over a period of three years

7 세 번째 단락 2행의 "draw"와 의미가 가장 가까운 단어는?

(A) 끌어들이다　　　　(B) 설계하다

(C) 표현하다　　　　　(D) 준비하다

해설 | **동의어**

의미상 점점 더 많은 관광객을 '끌어들인다'는 뜻으로 쓰인 것이므로 정답은 (A) attract이다.

8 킬라니 프로퍼티사에 대해 알 수 있는 것은?

(A) 아일랜드 모든 지역의 호텔을 관리한다.

(B) 현지 관광사와 제휴하고 있다.

(C) 본사 일자리를 충원하는 방안을 모색하고 있다.

(D) 주위 환경에 적합한 호텔을 짓는다.

해설 | **추론/암시**

네 번째 단락에서 킬라니 프로퍼티사는 아일랜드 남서부의 매력에 악영향을 끼치지 않으면서도 이 지역의 독특함에 부합하는 숙박시설을 개발하는 전통을 지속하고 있다(Killarney Property Ltd. continues its ~ without adversely affecting the area's charm)고 했으므로 (D)가 정답이다.

어휘 | **partner with** ~와 제휴하다 **fill** 채우다 **fit** 적합하다

Paraphrasing 지문의 conform to the uniqueness of southwest Ireland → 보기의 fit into the surroundings

UNIT 20 동의어 문제

ETS 예제   본책 p.266

오카모토 씨께,

카디프에 새 거주지를 선택하신 것을 축하드립니다. 내일 3월 29일 오전 9시에 임대차 계약이 예정되어 있습니다. 4월부터 시작하는 2년짜리 임대입니다. 고용 증명서(예: 급여 명세서), 신분증 두 가지, 현재 집주인의 연락처를 가져오십시오. 임대차 계약 시, 저희에게는 부동산 중개료를, 집주인에게는 보증금을 지불할 준비를 해 주세요. 귀하의 첫 달 임대료는 4월 1일**까지 지불되어야 합니다.**

문의 사항이 있으면 저희에게 연락 주세요.

에픽스 홈즈

어휘 | **congratulation** 축하 **residence** 거주지 **lease** 임대차 계약 **signing** 계약 **proof** 증거 **employment** 고용 **pay stub** 급여 명세서 **form** 형태 **identification** 신분증 **landlord** (집)주인 **real estate agent** 부동산 중개인 **fee** 수수료 **security deposit** 임대 보증금 **rent** 임대료

Q 첫 번째 단락 8행의 "due"와 의미가 가장 가까운 단어는?
(A) 청구되는   (B) 고려되는
(C) 지불될 의무가 있는 (D) 예정된

ETS 유형 연습   본책 p.267

1 (C) **2** (A) **3** (B) **4** (A)

[1-4] 이메일

수신: 브렌트 울란데이 〈bulanday@palayantheater.com.ph〉
발신: 정미현 〈chung@fam.co.kr〉
날짜: 3월 30일
제목: C.Y. 윤을 위한 그린룸
첨부: ◍C.Y. 윤

안녕하세요, 울란데이 씨,

팔라얀 극장에 C.Y. 윤을 예약해 주셔서 감사합니다. 윤 씨는 귀하의 유명한 장소에서 팬들과 소통하기를 고대하고 있습니다. **¹잠시 짬을 내어 아티스트의 백스테이지 라운지, 즉 출연자 대기실과 관련된 계약 조건을 다시 한 번 말씀드리겠습니다.** 계약서에 따르면, 룸은 카펫이 깔리고 **³은은하게 조명되어야 합니다. ²피아노, 악보대, 전신 거울, 다리미와 다리미판이 갖춰져야 합니다.** 과일과 무염 프레첼을 방에 비치해 주세요. **²윤 씨의 목소리를 보호하기 위해 각종 허브차 모음과 꿀, 정제수가 제공되어야 합니다. ⁴첨부 파일에 그가 요구하는 차를 항목별로 적어 두었으니 확인해 주세요.**

이러한 세부 사항에 관심을 기울여 주셔서 미리 감사드립니다. 이 요건이 충족되지 못할 경우 공연 시작이 지연될 수 있습니다.

아티스트 매니저 정미현

어휘 | **venue** 장소 **reiterate** 반복하다 **contractual** 계약상의 **lit** (light의 과거분사) 비추다 **equipped** 장비를 갖춘 **iron** 다리미 **ironing board** 다리미판 **stock** 갖추다 **assortment** 모음 **purified** 정제된 **attachment** 첨부한 것 **itemize** 항목별로 적다 **attention** 주의 **fulfill** 이행하다

1 정 씨는 왜 울란데이 씨에게 이메일을 보냈는가?
(A) 다가오는 행사의 입장권을 요청하려고
(B) 장소 변경에 대해 문의하려고
(C) 계약 조건을 상기시켜주려고
(D) 그의 관리 능력을 칭찬하려고

해설 | **주제 / 목적**
두 번째 단락의 첫 문장에서 잠시 짬을 내어 아티스트의 백스테이지 라운지, 즉 출연자 대기실과 관련된 계약 조건을 다시 한 번 말씀드리겠다(Allow me to take ~ backstage lounge, or greenroom)고 했으므로 정답은 (C)이다.

어휘 | **inquire** 문의하다 **terms** 조건 **praise** 칭찬하다

Paraphrasing 지문의 the contractual requirements → 보기의 the terms of an agreement

2 윤 씨는 누구일 것 같은가?
(A) 가수   (B) 코미디언
(C) 댄서   (D) 바이올리니스트

해설 | **추론 / 암시**
두 번째 단락의 세 번째 문장에서 피아노, 악보대 등이 갖춰져야 한다(It must be equipped with a piano, a music stand ~)고 했고, 다섯 번째 문장에서 윤 씨의 목소리를 보호하기 위해 각종 허브차 모음과 꿀, 정제수가 제공되어야 한다(To help protect ~ purified water must be provided)고 한 것으로 보아 윤 씨는 음악을 하고 목을 쓰는 사람이므로 (A)가 정답이다.

3 두 번째 단락 3행의 "softly"와 의미가 가장 가까운 단어는?
(A) 끈기 있게   (B) 은은하게
(C) 쉽게   (D) 매끄럽게

해설 | **동의어**
의미상 '은은하게' 조명되어야 한다는 뜻으로 쓰인 것이므로 정답은 (B) gently이다.

4 정 씨는 이메일과 함께 무엇을 보냈는가?
(A) 목록   (B) 계약서
(C) 일정표   (D) 이력서

해설 | **세부 사항**
두 번째 단락의 마지막 문장에서 첨부 파일에 그가 요구하는 차를 항목별로 적어 두었으니 확인하라(Please see the attachment, where I have itemized the teas he requires)고 했으므로 (A)가 정답이다.

ETS 고득점 실전 문제

본책 p.268

1 (A) **2** (B) **3** (D) **4** (B) **5** (D) **6** (B)
7 (C)

[1-3] 웹페이지

http://www.wellesbeachwear.com.au/shippingpolicy

당사의 배송 정책

¹⁽ᶜ⁾**웰레스 비치웨어는 호주와 뉴질랜드의 일부 도시로 특급 익일 배송을 제공합니다.** 이 지역에서 오후 10시 이전에 당사 웹사이트에 ²접수된 주문들은 다음 영업일에 배달될 것입니다. 웰레스 비치웨어는 배송 속도를 보장할 수 없기 때문에 호주 및 뉴질랜드의 기타 지역에는 특급 배송이 가능하지 않습니다. 동남아시아로 가는 주문은 국제 배송이 가능합니다. 자세한 내용은 아래 표를 참고하십시오.

목적지	특급 / 배송 시간	표준 / 배송 시간
호주(애들레이드, 브리즈번, 멜버른, 퍼스, 시드니)	9.95달러 / 익일	¹⁽ᴮ⁾무료 / ¹⁽ᴰ⁾영업일 3일
뉴질랜드(오클랜드, 크라이스트처치, 웰링턴)	10.95달러 / 익일	¹⁽ᴮ⁾무료 / ¹⁽ᴰ⁾영업일 3일
호주 및 뉴질랜드(기타 지역)	불가	7.95달러 / ¹⁽ᴰ⁾영업일 5일
³동남아시아	불가	³15.95달러 이상 / ¹⁽ᴰ⁾영업일 7-10일

어휘 | express 신속한 overnight 익일 배송의 bound for ~행의 table 표

1 웰레스 비치웨어에 대해 명시된 것이 아닌 것은?
(A) 배달 기사를 모집하고 있다.
(B) 일부 지역에는 무료로 배송한다.
(C) 일부 지역에는 익일 배송을 제공한다.
(D) 표준 배송 시간은 지역에 따라 다르다.

해설 | Not / True
첫 문장에서 웰레스 비치웨어는 호주와 뉴질랜드의 일부 도시로 특급 익일 배송을 제공한다(Welles Beachwear offers ~ Australia and New Zealand)고 했으므로 (C), 표의 표준 배송에서 일부 지역에는 무료(Free)라고 나와 있으므로 (B), 표의 표준 배송 시간이 지역에 따라 3일, 5일, 7-10일로 다르므로 (D)는 사실이고, 배달 기사를 모집 중이라는 언급은 없으므로 (A)가 정답이다.

어휘 | recruit 모집하다 at no cost 무료로 vary 다르다

Paraphrasing 지문의 free → 보기의 at no cost

2 첫 번째 단락 2행의 "placed"와 의미가 가장 가까운 단어는?
(A) 순위가 매겨진   (B) 제출된
(C) 언급된   (D) 배치된

해설 | 동의어
의미상 웹사이트에 '접수된' 주문들이라는 뜻으로 쓰인 것이므로 정답은 (B) submitted이다.

3 동남아시아로 주문품을 보내는 데 드는 최소 비용은 얼마인가?
(A) 7.95달러   (B) 9.95달러
(C) 10.95달러   (D) 15.95달러

해설 | 세부 사항
표의 맨 마지막 행에서 목적지가 동남아시아일 경우 배송비가 15.95달러 이상이라고 나와 있으므로 (D)가 정답이다.

[4-7] 이메일

수신: 오스왈드 쿠말로 〈okhumalo@dapnumbank.co.za〉
발신: 색슨 웡 〈swong@tabulacafe.co.za〉
⁵날짜: 9월 19일
제목: 충실한 고객

쿠말로 씨께,

저는 10년 넘게 다프넘 은행의 충실한 고객이었고 귀사가 훌륭한 서비스를 제공한다고 믿고 있습니다. 사실 제 은행 계좌 외에도 저는 귀사의 신용카드와 주택 담보 대출도 이용하고 있습니다.

⁴안타깝게도 저는 제가 가장 자주 방문하는 멜빌 가 지점에서 어려움을 겪고 있습니다. 어제 가장 최근에 방문했을 때, 저는 현금 예금을 해야 했습니다. 제 앞에 열 명이 줄을 서 있었고 ⁴저는 한 시간이 넘게 기다렸습니다. 그 당시 많은 은행 창구 직원들이 근무 중이었습니다.

⁴이 지점을 방문할 때마다 같은 문제를 겪습니다. 지난주에는 은행이 막 문을 열었을 때, 그리고 그 일주일 전에는 점심시간에 은행에 갔습니다. ⁵어제는 은행이 문을 닫기 직전에 갔습니다. 그때마다 저는 똑같은 문제를 겪었습니다.

⁶저는 저의 새로운 사업체인 타불라 카페로 인해 정기적으로 예금을 해야 합니다. 귀사의 은행은 제 카페의 길 건너편에 있어 위치가 편리합니다. 하지만 저는 무척 바쁘고 이렇게 오래 기다릴 시간이 없습니다. 이 문제를 어떻게 ⁷해결할 계획인지 알려 주시기 바랍니다. 다프넘 은행과 거래를 지속하고 싶지만 다른 곳에서 은행 업무를 보려고 알아보고 있습니다.

색슨 웡

어휘 | loyal 충실한 home mortgage 주택 담보 대출 deposit 예금 bank teller 은행원 basis 기준 address 다루다 elsewhere 다른 곳에서

4 웡 씨는 다프넘 은행의 어떤 점에 대해 실망스럽다고 생각하는가?
(A) 불충분한 직원 수   (B) 긴 대기 시간
(C) 신용 카드 이자율   (D) 한정된 운영 시간

해설 | 세부 사항
두 번째 단락의 첫 문장에서 웡 씨가 안타깝게도 가장 자주 방문하는 멜빌 가 지점에서 어려움을 겪고 있다(Unfortunately, I have been ~ the one I visit most frequently)며 한 시간이 넘게 기다렸다(I waited more than an hour)고 했고 세 번째 단락의 첫 문장에서 이 지점을 방문할 때마다 같은 문제를 겪는다(I had the same problem)고 했다. 따라서 웡 씨는 다프넘 은행에서의 대기 시간이 매번 긴 점에 대해 실망했음을 알 수 있다. 따라서 정답은 (B)이다.

어휘 | inadequate 불충분한 rate 요율 limited 한정된

5 웡 씨는 9월 18일에 언제 멜빌 가 지점을 방문했는가?
(A) 개점 직후 　　　　　 (B) 점심시간
(C) 한낮 시간대 　　　　 (D) 폐점 직전

해설 | 세부 사항
이메일이 작성된 날짜는 9월 19일이고, 세 번째 단락의 세 번째 문장에서 어제는 은행이 문을 닫기 직전에 갔다(Yesterday, I went shortly before the bank closed)고 했으므로 (D)가 정답이다.

6 타불라 카페에 대해 알 수 있는 것은?
(A) 10년 동안 영업을 해 왔다.
(B) 웡 씨가 소유자이다.
(C) 다프넘 은행 고객들에게 인기가 있다.
(D) 다프넘 은행 바로 옆이다.

해설 | 추론 / 암시
네 번째 단락의 첫 문장에서 웡 씨가 저의 새로운 사업체인 타불라 카페로 인해 정기적으로 예금을 해야 한다(I need to make deposits for my new business, Tabula Café, on a regular basis)고 했으므로 웡 씨는 타불라 카페의 소유주임을 알 수 있다. 따라서 (B)가 정답이다.

Paraphrasing 지문의 my ~ business
→ 보기의 owned by Mr. Wong

7 네 번째 단락 3행의 "address"와 의미가 가장 가까운 단어는?
(A) 보내다 　　　　　　 (B) 상표를 붙이다
(C) 처리하다 　　　　　 (D) 이야기하다

해설 | 동의어
의미상 문제를 어떻게 '해결할'지 라는 뜻으로 쓰인 것이므로 정답은 (C) deal with이다.

UNIT 21 의도 파악 문제

ETS 예제 　　　　　　　　　　　　 본책 p.270

아르멘 호바키미안 [오전 11시 38분]
안녕하세요, 준. 저 방금 컨벤션 센터로 들어왔어요. 거대하네요! 차도 정말 많아요! 레지가 안내 책자를 좀 더 가져와 달라고 부탁했는데, 우리 전시장은 어디 있죠?

준 응 [오전 11시 40분]
여기 와줘서 기뻐요. 우리는 신형 전기 세단에 많은 관심을 받고 있어요. 전시장은 M 통로에 있어요. 정문에서 **왼쪽으로 꺾어서 앞으로 쭉 가다가 비릿 기름병처럼 생긴 거대한 풍선에서 오른쪽으로 꺾으세요. 찾기 쉬워요.** 저는 음식 매대쪽 저 뒤편에 있어요.

아르멘 호바키미안 [오전 11시 42분]
고마워요. 바로 그리로 갈게요.

어휘 | booth 전시장 **sedan** 승용차 **aisle** 통로 **ahead** 앞으로 **miss** 지나치다 **stall** 가판대

Q 오전 11시 40분에 응 씨가 "찾기 쉬워요"라고 쓴 의도는 무엇인가?
(A) 호바키미안 씨가 떠나는 것을 원하지 않는다.
(B) 호바키미안 씨랑 같이 점심을 먹고 싶어한다.
(C) 풍선을 찾기 아주 쉽다.
(D) 발표가 흥미로울 것이다.

ETS 유형 연습 　　　　　　　 본책 p.271

1 (C) 　 **2** (B) 　 **3** (A) 　 **4** (D)

[1-4] 온라인 채팅

플로렌스 클라크 (오전 10시 30분) 평소 채팅 시간을 바꿔서 미안해요. 제가 2시간 뒤에 파리에서 열리는 회의에 참석하러 떠나거든요. 재호, 우리 광고 캠페인에 대한 최신 정보를 알려 주실 수 있나요?
공재호 (오전 10시 33분) 네, 아시다시피 [2]우리는 인쇄물, 소셜 미디어, 인터넷 등 여러 플랫폼에서 광고 입지를 확대했는데 잘되고 있는 것 같습니다. [1, 2]우리 청취자수가 증가하고 있습니다.
플로렌스 클라크 (오전 10시 34분) 그거 좋은 소식이네요. 안나, 다른 사람들에게 개발 중인 새로운 쇼에 대해 말씀 좀 해 주시겠어요?
안나 고스와미 (오전 10시 36분) 물론입니다. [1]토요일 오전에 새로운 쇼를 선보일 예정이에요. 뉴스를 다루고 청취자 참여 전화 코너가 뒤따르는 점이 특징이죠. [3]그리고 짧게 방송했던 쇼 〈태양 아래 모든 것〉을 진행했던 트리나 톰슨을 기억하세요? 그녀가 현재 〈톰슨, 테이크 투〉라는 새로운 프로그램을 하고 있어요. [4]또 일요일 오후 포크 음악 시간을 2시간으로 늘렸습니다. 에스몬드가 이것에 대해 더 많은 것을 말해 줄 수 있을 겁니다.
에스몬드 세코 (오전 10시 40분) 네, 맞아요. [4]사실 제작비, 일정 등 추가 시간에 수반될 것들에 대한 모든 세부 내용이 담긴 메모를 작성 중입니다. 오늘 중으로 여러분 모두에게 이메일로 보내 드리겠습니다.
플로렌스 클라크 (오전 10시 42분) 알겠습니다. 그럼 이만 제가 공항으로 가서 비행기를 탈 수 있도록 회의를 끝내겠습니다. 2주 후에 얘기 나누도록 하지요.

어휘 | presence 입지 **pool** 이용 가능 인력 **debut** 데뷔하다 **feature** 특징으로 하다 **segment** 부문 **short-lived** 오래가지 못하는 **definitely** 확실히 **involve** 수반하다 **wrap up** 끝내다 **head** 향하다

1 채팅 참여자들은 어떤 종류의 업체에서 일할 것 같은가?
(A) 여행사 　　　　　　 (B) 극단
(C) 라디오 방송국 　　　 (D) 광고 회사

해설 | 추론 / 암시
10시 33분에 공 씨가 우리 청취자수가 증가하고 있다(Our pool of listeners is growing)고 했고, 10시 36분에 고스와미 씨가 토요일 오전에 새로운 쇼를 선보일 예정(We have a new show ~ Saturday morning)이며 뉴스를 다루고 청취자 참여

전화 코너가 뒤따르는 점이 특징(It features news ~ listener call-in segment)이라고 했으므로 채팅 참여자는 라디오 방송국에서 일하고 있음을 알 수 있다. 따라서 정답은 (C)이다.

2 공 씨가 그들의 사업에 대해 다른 사람들에게 암시하는 것은?
(A) 웹페이지를 수정하는 과정에 있다.
(B) 점점 인기를 얻고 있다.
(C) 컴퓨터 문제를 바로잡았다.
(D) 다른 나라로 확장하고 있다.

해설 | 추론 / 암시
10시 33분에 공 씨가 인쇄물, 소셜 미디어, 인터넷 등 여러 플랫폼에서 광고 입지를 확대했는데(we've expanded our advertising presence ~ and Internet) 잘되고 있는 것 같다(It seems to be working nicely)고 했고 청취자수가 증가하고 있다(Our pool of listeners is growing)고 한 것으로 보아 (B)가 정답이다.

3 톰슨 씨는 누구일 것 같은가?
(A) 새로운 쇼의 진행자   (B) 콜센터 직원
(C) 포크 음악가   (D) 신문기자

해설 | 추론 / 암시
10시 36분에 고스와미 씨가 짧게 방송했던 쇼 〈태양 아래 모든 것〉을 진행했던 트리나 톰슨을 기억하는지(do you remember Trina Thompson ~ *Everything Under the Sun* show?) 물으며 그녀가 현재 〈톰슨, 테이크 투〉라는 새로운 프로그램을 하고 있다(She's doing a new program now, *Thompson, Take Two*)고 했으므로 톰슨 씨는 새 쇼의 진행자임을 알 수 있다. 따라서 정답은 (A)이다.

4 오전 10시 40분에 세코 씨가 "네, 맞아요"라고 쓴 의도는 무엇인가?
(A) 고스와미 씨의 정보가 맞다고 확신한다.
(B) 제시간에 일을 마칠 수 있다고 믿는다.
(C) 클라크 씨가 없는 동안 그녀의 업무 중 하나를 기꺼이 해 줄 것이다.
(D) 다른 사람들에게 정보를 제공할 수 있다고 확신한다.

해설 | 의도 파악
10시 36분에 고스와미 씨가 일요일 오후 포크 음악 시간을 2시간으로 늘렸다(We've also expanded our Sunday folk music afternoons to two hours)고 했고 에스몬드가 이것에 대해 더 많은 것을 말해 줄 수 있을 것(Esmond might be able to tell you more about that)이라고 하자, 10시 40분에 에스몬드 세코 씨가 맞다(Yes, definitely)면서 제작비, 일정 등 추가 시간에 수반될 것들에 대한 모든 세부 내용이 담긴 메모를 작성 중(I'm actually writing up ~ schedules, and so on)이라고 했다. 따라서 세코 씨가 자신이 포크 음악 쇼에 대해 더 자세한 정보를 알려 줄 수 있다는 의도로 한 말이므로 (D)가 정답이다.

ETS 고득점 실전 문제
본책 p.272

1 (B) **2** (B) **3** (C) **4** (D) **5** (B) **6** (A)
7 (C) **8** (C)

[1-4] 문자 메시지

> **테아 킴 (오후 2시 31분)**
> 안녕하세요, 데스몬드 그리고 클레리오. 자동차 임대업자 협회 총회가 2주 뒤로 다가오고 있어요. 배포용 홍보 전단도 주문하고 일을 좀 진행시키는 게 좋겠어요.

> **데스몬드 브라우어 (오후 2시 33분)**
> 안녕하세요, 테아. 맞아요. 월요일에 통화했을 때 논의를 마무리하지 못했네요. 올해에는 어떤 전단지를 사용하고 싶으세요?

> **클레리오 카르도소 (오후 2시 34분)**
> 전단지가 얼마나 많이 필요할지 아시나요?

> **데스몬드 브라우어 (오후 2시 36분)**
> 아직요. ²내일 사무실로 돌아가면 협회 총회 기획자에게 전화해 얼마나 많은 인원이 등록했는지 알아볼게요. 그리고 나서 후발 등록자를 감안해 5%를 추가하겠습니다.

> **테아 킴 (오후 2시 38분)**
> ¹올해 총회에서는 당사의 자동차 대여 지점 6곳을 모두 보여주는 접이식 지도가 딸린 안내 책자를 사용해 봅시다. ³·⁴필요한 전단지 수를 확인하는 대로 오슨스에 연락해 견적서를 받아 주시겠어요? 그리고 우리가 작년에 했던 가격보다 더 좋은 가격으로 할 수 있는지도 봅시다.

> **클레리오 카르도소 (오후 2시 40분)**
> 물론이죠. 그렇게 하겠습니다. ⁴최소한 다른 인쇄소 두 곳에서도 견적서를 받아 보겠습니다.

> **테아 킴 (오후 2시 44분)**
> 그러면 좋겠네요. 3월 3일까지 회의 센터로 곧장 전단지를 배송해 줄 수 있는지도 확인하세요. 그렇지 않으면 두 분 중 한 분이 직접 총회로 전단지를 가져 오셔야 할 겁니다.

어휘 | association 협회 **flier** 전단지 **hand out** 배포하다 **register** 등록하다 **latecomer** 늦게 오는 사람 **foldout** 접는 방식의 **determine** 결정하다 **reach** 연락하다 **estimate** 견적서 **make sense** 타당하다 **directly** 바로 **otherwise** 그렇지 않으면

1 메시지 작성자들은 어디서 일할 것 같은가?
(A) 홍보 회사   (B) 렌터카 회사
(C) 인쇄소   (D) 회의 센터

해설 | 추론 / 암시
2시 38분에 킴 씨가 올해 총회에서는 당사의 자동차 대여 지점 6곳을 모두 보여주는 접이식 지도가 딸린 안내 책자를 사용해 보자(For this year's conference ~ our car rental locations)고 한 것으로 보아 메시지 작성자들은 자동차 대여 업체에서 근무하고 있음을 알 수 있다. 따라서 (B)가 정답이다.

2 브라우어 씨에 대해 사실일 것 같은 것은?
(A) 협회에 등록할 생각이다.
(B) 현재 사무실에 있지 않다.
(C) 킴 씨의 상사이다.
(D) 안내 책자를 디자인했다.

해설 | Not / True
2시 36분에 브라우어 씨가 내일 사무실로 돌아가면 협회 총회 기획자에게 전화해 얼마나 많은 인원이 등록했는지 알아 보겠다(When I get back to the office ~ people have

registered)고 했으므로 브라우어 씨는 현재 사무실에서 근무하고 있지 않다는 것을 알 수 있다. 따라서 (B)가 정답이다.

어휘 | intend (~하려고) 생각하다 **supervisor** 관리자

Paraphrasing 지문의 get back to the office tomorrow → 보기의 is currently out of the office

3 오슨스에 대해 알 수 있는 것은 무엇인가?
(A) 3월 3일에 재고 조사를 위해 문을 닫을 예정이다.
(B) 총회를 개최할 계획이다.
(C) 작년에 메시지 작성자들을 위해 인쇄 작업을 했다.
(D) 무료 배송 서비스를 제공한다.

해설 | 추론 / 암시
2시 38분에 김 씨가 필요한 전단지 수를 확인하는 대로 오슨스에 연락해 견적서를 받아 줄 수 있는지(Once you determine ~ for an estimate?)를 물으며 우리가 작년에 했던 가격보다 더 좋은 가격으로 할 수 있는지 보자(Also, let's see ~ we got last year)고 한 것으로 보아 메시지 작성자들은 작년에 오슨스에서 전단 작업을 했음을 짐작할 수 있다. 따라서 (C)가 정답이다.

어휘 | inventory 재고 조사

4 오후 2시 44분에 김 씨가 "그러면 좋겠네요"라고 쓴 의도는 무엇인가?
(A) 월요일에 내려진 결정을 지지한다.
(B) 접이식 지도를 확대하자는 아이디어를 좋아한다.
(C) 카르도소 씨와 브라우어 씨가 오슨스에 함께 방문하기를 원한다.
(D) 가격을 비교하자는 카르도소 씨의 계획에 찬성한다.

해설 | 의도 파악
2시 38분에 김 씨가 오슨스에 연락해 견적서를 받아 줄 수 있는지(Once you determine ~ for an estimate?)를 물으며 작년에 했던 가격보다 더 좋은 가격으로 할 수 있는지 보자(Also, let's see ~ we got last year)고 하자, 2시 40분에 카르도소 씨가 최소한 다른 인쇄소 두 곳에서도 견적서를 받아 보겠다(I'll get estimates ~ printing firms as well)고 제안했고 2시 44분에 김 씨가 그러면 좋겠다(That makes sense)고 대답한 것이므로 가격을 비교해 보자는 카르도소 씨의 생각에 동의하려는 의도로 한 말임을 알 수 있다. 따라서 (D)가 정답이다.

어휘 | enlarge 확대하다 approve 찬성하다

[5-8] 온라인 채팅

캐리사 라이트 [오전 8시 55분]
안녕하세요, 재런. **5제가 보낸 파일은 받으셨나요?** 새로운 시청 청사를 찍은 사진이에요. **5디포리오 시장님이 그 사진을 가능한 한 크게 출력하기를 원하세요.** 시장님 집무실 로비용이에요.

재런 스미스 [오전 8시 57분]
안녕하세요, 캐리사. 네, 받았습니다. **5이미지 파일이 작아서 최적 해상도가 8x10인치쯤 되겠네요.** 그래도 **6제가 화질에 영향 없이 이미지를 더 크게 만들 수 있을 겁니다.**

캐리사 라이트 [오전 8시 58분]
고맙습니다. 어떻게 하시려고요?

재런 스미스 [오전 9시]
제가 뭘 할 수 있는지 알아보겠지만, 사진이 흐릿하지 않게 16x20인치로 확대할 수 있을 것 같아요. **7번쩍거리지 않도록 무광택 사진 용지를 사용하는 게 가장 좋을 것 같고요.** 내일 오후까지 준비해 놓을 수 있을 것 같습니다.

캐리사 라이트 [오전 9시 2분]
액자는 어떤가요? 사진을 액자에 넣고 싶은데요.

재런 스미스 [오전 9시 3분]
액자에 끼우는 작업은 좀 더 걸릴 거에요. **8저라면 검정색 2인치 폭의 나무 액자를 선택할 겁니다.** 단순해서 사진 자체에 방해가 되지 않도록 말이죠. 완료되면 알려 드리겠습니다.

캐리사 라이트 [오전 9시 4분]
고맙습니다. 준비됐다고 알려 주시면 가지러 가겠습니다.

어휘 | resolution 해상도 propose 제안하다 enlarge 확대하다 blurry 흐릿한 matte 무광의 glare 번쩍이는 빛 frame 액자; 액자에 넣다 framing 액자에 넣기 distract (주의를) 딴 데로 돌리다

5 스미스 씨의 직업은 무엇일 것 같은가?
(A) 건축 사진작가   (B) 전문 인쇄업자
(C) 부동산 관리자   (D) 상업용 건축업자

해설 | 추론 / 암시
8시 55분에 라이트 씨가 제가 보낸 파일은 받으셨냐(Did you get the file I sent?)고 물으며 디포리오 시장님이 그 사진을 가능한 한 크게 출력하기를 원한다(Mayor Diforio would like ~ as possible)고 했고, 8시 57분에 스미스 씨가 이미지 파일이 작아서 최적 해상도가 8x10인치쯤 되겠다(I noticed that ~ 8 by 10 inches)고 설명하는 것으로 보아 스미스 씨는 인쇄 업무를 전문적으로 하는 사람임을 알 수 있다. 따라서 (B)가 정답이다.

어휘 | architectural 건축의 property 부동산 commercial 상업의

6 오전 8시 58분에 라이트 씨가 "어떻게 하시려고요?"라고 쓸 때, 무엇을 알고 싶어하는 것 같은가?
(A) 스미스 씨가 사진을 얼마나 크게 만들 수 있는지
(B) 로비의 어디에 사진을 걸지
(C) 파일을 어떻게 보내야 할지
(D) 로비에 다른 무언가를 놓아야 할지

해설 | 의도 파악
8시 57분에 스미스 씨가 제가 화질에 영향 없이 이미지를 더 크게 만들 수 있을 것(I should be able to ~ too much quality)이라고 하자 8시 58분에 라이트 씨가 어떻게 하시려고요(What do you propose?)라고 물은 것이므로, 라이트 씨는 이미지 크기와 관련해 스미스 씨가 어떻게 얼마나 크게 만들 수 있다는 것인지에 대한 추가 정보를 구하려는 의도로 질문한 것임을 알 수 있다. 따라서 (A)가 정답이다.

7 스미스 씨는 왜 무광택 사진 용지를 사용하기를 원하는가?
(A) 명암을 높여준다.
(B) 진주 같은 질감을 가진다.
(C) 번쩍거림을 일으키지 않는다.
(D) 특별한 취급이 필요하지 않다.

해설 | 세부 사항

9시에 스미스 씨가 번쩍거리지 않도록 무광택 사진 용지를 사용하는 게 가장 좋을 것 같다(I also think that ~ so that there will be no glare)고 했으므로 정답은 (C)이다.

어휘 | enhance 높이다 contrast 명암 pearl 진주 texture 질감 cause 일으키다 handling 취급

8 스미스 씨는 사진을 액자에 넣는 일에 대해 무엇을 제안하는가?
(A) 시간이 추가로 소요되지 않을 것이다.
(B) 좋은 생각이 아닌 것 같다.
(C) 기본 액자가 가장 좋을 것 같다.
(D) 초대형 액자는 더 비쌀 것이다.

해설 | 세부 사항

9시 3분에 스미스 씨가 본인이라면 단순해서 사진 자체에 방해가 되지 않도록 검정색 2인치 폭의 나무 액자를 선택할 것(I would choose a black ~ distract from the photo itself)이라고 했으므로 (C)가 정답이다.

Paraphrasing 지문의 simple → 보기의 basic

UNIT 22 문장 삽입 문제

ETS 예제   본책 p.274

크리스핀 씨께,

참조 번호 88426 컴퓨터 부품의 대량 주문에 감사드립니다. **저희는 원래 10월 14일 금요일에 배송을 약속했습니다. 이 배송이 지체되었음을 알려 드리게 되어 유감스럽게 생각합니다. 귀하의 상품은 10월 28일 금요일에 도착할 것으로 현재 예상됩니다. 불편을 끼쳐드려 진심으로 사죄드립니다.**

저희는 귀사의 사업에 정시 배송이 얼마나 중요한지 잘 알고 있으며 이번 주문에 대한 배송비를 환불해 드렸습니다. 또한 다음 구매 시 25%를 할인해 드리고자 합니다.

레이머를 귀하의 컴퓨터 하드웨어 공급업체로 선택해 주셔서 감사드립니다.

어휘 | bulk 대량 part 부품 regret 유감이다 inconvenience 불편 on-time 정시의

Q [1], [2], [3], [4]로 표시된 곳 중에서 다음 문장이 들어가기에 가장 적합한 위치는?
"귀하의 상품은 10월 28일 금요일에 도착할 것으로 현재 예상됩니다."
(A) [1]   (B) [2]
(C) [3]   (D) [4]

ETS 유형 연습   본책 p.275

1 (C)   **2** (B)   **3** (A)   **4** (D)

[1-4] 편지

2월 8일

데니스 대럴
하이랜드 밀스 어소시에이츠
41번 로
크로포드 베이, BC VOB 1B0

대럴 씨께,

²하이랜드 밀스 어소시에이츠의 상업 시설 청소 대행이 필요하신 일로 저를 만나 주셔서 감사합니다. 귀사에 대해 자세히 알게 되어 기뻤습니다.

²회의 중에 고객님께서는 현재 청소 대행 서비스에 대해 우려를 표하셨습니다. 저희가 다루게 될 그 문제들에 대해 저는 꼼꼼하게 주의를 기울였습니다.

¹저희는 합당한 가격에 우수한 서비스를 제공하는 것에 자부심을 느낍니다. 그것이 저희가 클린 웨이즈 보증을 제공하는 이유입니다. 만약 저희 작업에 만족하지 못하실 경우 추가 비용 없이 다시 제대로 처리해 드립니다.

• **¹가장 안전하며 최상 품질의 세제 및 기타 세척 용품을 사용합니다.**
• **³매 방문 시 동일한 청소 작업팀을 보냅니다.**
• 정기적으로 전화하거나 직접 방문하여 사후 관리합니다.

⁴현재 클린 웨이즈 고객들의 추천서를 즐거운 마음으로 제공해 드립니다. 일부 고객은 이 지역에서 유명한 사업을 하시는 장기 고객입니다. 동봉된 제안서에 변경 사항이 있으시면 저에게 연락 주십시오. 제 사무실 전화번호 565-555-0175로 연락하시면 됩니다.

트리스텐 코리

동봉물

어휘 | commercial 상업의 express 표현하다 address 다루다 fair 타당한 guarantee 보증 detergent 세제 supplies 용품 crew 작업반 high-profile 세간의 이목을 끄는 enclosed 동봉된

1 편지의 목적은 무엇인가?
(A) 새 프로젝트 확정   (B) 구인 공고
(C) 서비스 설명   (D) 회의 요청

해설 | 주제 / 목적

세 번째 단락의 첫 문장에서 저희는 합당한 가격에 우수한 서비스를 제공하는 것에 자부심을 느낀다(We pride ourselves ~ at a fair price)고 했고, 네 번째 단락의 첫 문장에서 가장 안전하며 최상 품질의 세제 및 기타 세척 용품을 사용한다(We use the safest ~ cleaning supplies)는 내용을 비롯해 코리 씨가 자신의 업체에서 제공하는 서비스 및 장점에 대해 설명하는 내용이 주를 이루므로 (C)가 정답이다.

2 대럴 씨에 대해 무엇을 알 수 있는가?
(A) 새 건물을 관리하고 있다.
(B) 서비스 업체를 바꾸는 것을 고려 중이다.
(C) 최근에 승진했다.
(D) 크로포드 베이에 신생 회사를 차린다.

해설 | 추론 / 암시

첫 문장에서 대럴 씨에게 하이랜드 밀스 어소시에이츠의 상업 시설 청소 대행이 필요하신 일로 저를 만나 주셔서 감사하다(Thank you for meeting ~ Mills Associates)고 했고, 두 번째 단락의 첫 문장에서 회의 중에 고객님께서는

현재 청소 대행 서비스에 대해 우려를 표하셨다(During our meeting ~ current cleaning service)고 했다. 따라서 대럴 씨는 현재 청소 대행 업체에 만족하지 못해 업체를 바꾸려고 알아보는 중임을 알 수 있으므로 (B)가 정답이다.

3 클린 웨이즈에 대해 무엇이 명시되는가?
(A) 고객이 있는 곳에 동일한 팀 배정을 유지한다.
(B) 24시간 고객 지원을 제공한다.
(C) 특수 청소 용품 이용료는 추가로 부과된다.
(D) 집과 아파트를 청소한다.

해설 | **Not / True**
네 번째 단락의 두 번째 문장에서 매 방문 시 동일한 청소 작업팀을 보낸다(We will send the same cleaning crew on each visit)고 했으므로 (A)가 정답이다.

어휘 | assignment 배정   charge 부과하다

Paraphrasing   지문의 send the same cleaning crew → 보기의 maintains the same team assignment

4 [1], [2], [3], [4]로 표시된 곳 중에서 다음 문장이 들어가기에 가장 적합한 위치는?
"일부 고객은 이 지역에서 유명한 사업을 하시는 장기 고객입니다."
(A) [1]   (B) [2]
(C) [3]   (D) [4]

해설 | **문장 삽입**
제시된 문장의 Several are long-term customers가 문제 해결의 단서이다. 몇몇(several)이 장기 고객이라고 했으므로 several이 대신한 명사는 '고객들'임을 알 수 있다. 따라서 주어진 문장 앞에 '고객들'이 언급되어야 하므로, 현재 고객들로부터 받은 추천서를 제공한다며 '고객들'을 언급한 문장 뒤인 (D)가 정답이다.

어휘 | high-profile 세간의 이목을 끄는, 유명한

ETS 고득점 실전 문제

1 (D) **2** (A) **3** (B) **4** (D) **5** (B) **6** (D)
7 (A) **8** (B)

[1-4] 계약서

물먼 건설사와 남동부 지역 건설 협회 (SRAB) 간의 계약

I. **¹본 계약은 물먼 건설사와 남동부 지역 건설 협회(SRAB)가 맺은 법적 구속력을 가진 계약으로, 물먼 건설은 이에 상응하는 모든 권리 및 책임을 갖고 SRAB에 가입한다.** 본 계약의 조건은 남동부 지역에서 물먼 건설이 수행하는 모든 건축 프로젝트에 적용된다.

II. **²모든 해당 프로젝트에서, 물먼 건설은 SRAB가 승인한 자재만을 사용하는 데 동의한다. 주거 및 상업용 프로젝트에 대한 승인 자재의 전체 목록은 부록 A와 B에 각각 열거되어 있다.** 이 같은 목록 제한의 목적은 모든 건축 프로젝트에서 높은 수준의 품질을 촉진하여 보수 및 유지 관리 문제의 횟수 및 빈도를 줄이고자 함이다.

III. **³물먼 건설과 SRAB는 향후 승인 자재 목록의 수정이 필요하다거나 바람직할 수 있다는 데 동의한다.** ³, ⁴양 당사자는 이러한 목적으로

자재 기술 및 안전 개발상의 변경을 언급할 수 있다. 새로운 정부 규제 또한 타당한 이유가 될 수 있다. 본 계약에 대한 수정안의 제안 및 협상 절차는 부록 C에 요약되어 있다.

어휘 | association 협회   binding 법적 구속력이 있는   enroll 등록하다   commensurate 상응하는   right 권리   term 조건   apply 적용하다   undertake 착수하다   applicable 해당하는   authorized 인증된   residential 거주의   commercial 상업의   appendices (appendix의 복수) 부록   respectively 각각   restricted 제한된   promote 촉진시키다   thereby 그렇게 함으로써   frequency 빈도   maintenance 유지관리   revision 수정   desirable 바람직한   cite 언급[인용]하다   party 당사자   process 절차   negotiate 협상하다   outline 개요를 서술하다

1 물먼 건설과 SRAB는 어떤 관계인가?
(A) SRAB는 물먼 건설의 고객이다.
(B) SRAB와 물먼 건설은 최근에 합병했다.
(C) 물먼 건설은 SRAB의 공급 업체이다.
(D) 물먼 건설은 SRAB의 회원이다.

해설 | **세부 사항**
1번 조항의 첫 문장에서 본 계약은 물먼 건설사와 남동부 지역 건설 협회(SRAB)가 맺은 법적 구속력을 가진 계약으로, 물먼 건설사는 이에 상응하는 모든 권리 및 책임을 갖고 SRAB에 가입한다(This is a binding contract ~ rights and responsibilities)고 했으므로 정답은 (D)이다.

Paraphrasing   지문의 enrolls in the SRAB
→ 보기의 a member of the SRAB

2 계약서에 따르면, 물먼 건설은 각 프로젝트에 대해 무엇을 하기로 동의하는가?
(A) 특정 종류 또는 상표의 자재만 사용한다.
(B) 완료된 공사의 품질에 대한 보증을 제공한다.
(C) 동남 지역 사업체에 할인을 제공한다.
(D) 모든 수리 또는 유지 관리 문제에 대한 비용을 부담한다.

해설 | **세부 사항**
2번 조항의 첫 문장에서 모든 해당 프로젝트에서 물먼 건설은 SRAB가 승인한 자재만을 사용하는 데 동의한다(In all applicable projects ~ authorized by the SRAB)고 했고, 주거 및 상업용 프로젝트에 대한 승인 자재의 전체 목록은 부록 A와 B에 각각 열거되어 있다(Complete lists of ~ A and B, respectively)고 했으므로 (A)가 정답이다.

3 계약 변경으로 이어질 수 있는 사항은 무엇인가?
(A) 건축 자재의 가격이 급격히 상승할 경우
(B) 건축 자재에 신기술이 개발될 경우
(C) 정해진 기한까지 프로젝트를 완료하지 못한 경우
(D) 해당 지역이 악천후로 인해 영향을 받은 경우

해설 | **세부 사항**
3번 조항의 첫 문장에서 물먼 건설과 SRAB는 향후 승인 자재 목록의 수정이 필요하다거나 바람직할 수 있다는 데 동의한다(Meuleman Construction ~ desirable in the future)고 했고, 양 당사자는 이러한 목적으로 자재 기술 및 안전 개발상의 변경을 언급할 수 있다(Changes in materials ~ for this purpose)고 했으므로 (B)가 정답이다.

어휘 | dramatically 급격히 stated 정해진 adverse 불리한

Paraphrasing 지문의 Changes in materials technology → 보기의 a new technology in building materials

4 [1], [2], [3], [4]로 표시된 곳 중에서 다음 문장이 들어가기에 가장 적합한 위치는?

"새로운 정부 규제 또한 타당한 이유가 될 수 있다."

(A) [1] (B) [2]
(C) [3] (D) [4]

해설 | 문장 삽입
제시된 문장의 may also be a valid reason이 문제 해결의 단서이다. 이유가 될 수 있는 사항에 대해 언급하며 also를 사용했으므로 주어진 문장 앞에서도 어떤 일의 이유나 목적으로 들 수 있는 사항에 관해 제시하는 내용이 와야 한다. 따라서 자재 기술 및 안전 개발상의 변경을 자재 목록 수정의 목적으로 언급할 수 있다(~ may be cited ~ for this purpose)는 내용 뒤인 (D)가 정답이다.

[5-8] 기사

> **통근 부담 완화**
>
> ⁵키츠 리서치의 최근 조사에 따르면 홀든의 하루 평균 왕복 통근 시간은 현재 1시간 30분 이상이라고 한다. ⁵, ⁶많은 직장인들이 출근근 여정에 지치고 그 비용 때문에 짜증난 채로 직장에 도착한다. 이러한 오랜 출퇴근 시간은 직원 생산성 저하, 직업 만족도 저하, 높은 이직률로 이어진다. ⁵그 결과, 많은 기업들이 직원들의 힘든 통근 부담을 완화할 수 있는 방안을 모색 중이다.
>
> ⁷⁽ᴮ⁾가능한 해결책 중 하나로 재택근무가 있다. ⁸점점 더 많은 기업들이 일주일에 며칠 동안 직원들이 집에서 근무할 수 있도록 허용하고 있다. 이 방식이 성공하려면 직원들 집에서의 인터넷 연결 상태가 좋아야 한다. 이는 모두에게 가치 있는 일이다. 길고 스트레스로 가득한 출퇴근을 없애면 직원들은 편안하게 근무를 시작하게 된다. 이로 인해 생산성이 향상되고 잦은 결근이 줄어들게 된다.
>
> ⁷⁽ᴰ⁾또 다른 해결책은 카풀이다. 카풀은 도로 위 차량의 수를 줄임으로써 전체적인 교통량을 줄일 수 있고, 결과적으로 모두의 통근 시간을 단축시킬 수 있다. 직원들은 또한 개인적인 출퇴근 비용을 줄일 수 있고 스트레스를 덜 받으며 직장에 도착할 수 있다. 기업들은 현장에서 근무해야 하는 직원들을 위해 저렴한 카풀을 편성하는 것을 선택할 수 있다.
>
> ⁷⁽ᶜ⁾통근 부담을 완화할 수 있는 또 하나의 방법은 직원들이 통상적이지 않은 시간에 현장에서 일할 수 있도록 허용하는 것이다. 이 옵션은 출퇴근 시간 동안 직장인들을 도로에서 벗어나게 함으로써 통근 시간을 상당히 단축시킬 수 있다.
>
> 모든 기업이 통근 시간 단축에 도움이 되는 변화를 시행할 수 있는 것은 아니다. 그러나 그럴 수 있는 기업들에게는 최근의 조사 결과가 일찌감치 조정을 할 수 있는 추가적인 동기로 작용할 수도 있다.

어휘 | ease 수월하게 하다 commute 통근; 통근하다 reveal 드러내다 top (~보다) 더 높다 exhausted 지친 journey 여행 irritated 짜증난 productivity 생산성 decreased 감소된 turnover rate 이직률 consequently 그 결과 rough 힘든 telecommuting 재택근무 worthwhile 가치 있는 eliminate 없애다 reduction 감소 absenteeism 잦은 결근 on-site 현장에서 nontraditional 예전과는 다른

---

significant 상당히 implement 시행하다 incentive 동기 adjustment 조정 sooner rather than later 차라리 일찌감치

5 기사의 목적은 무엇인가?

(A) 신기술 홍보 (B) 조사 결과 논의
(C) 교통 패턴의 변화 강조 (D) 직원 생산성 향상 보고

해설 | 주제 / 목적
첫 단락의 첫 문장에서 키츠 리서치의 최근 조사에 따르면 홀든의 하루 평균 왕복 통근 시간은 현재 1시간 30분 이상이라고 한다(A recent survey ~ an hour and a half)고 했고, 많은 직장인들이 출퇴근 여정에 지치고 그 비용 때문에 짜증난 채로 직장에 도착한다(Many workers arrive ~ cost of commuting)며 조사 결과를 설명하고 있다. 그리고 같은 단락의 마지막 문장에서 그 결과, 많은 기업들이 직원들의 통근 부담 완화 방안을 모색 중(Consequently, many companies ~ rough commutes)이라고 언급했고, 이어서 모색 방안들에 대해 논하고 있으므로 기사는 조사 결과 및 그에 따른 방안 모색을 논의하기 위한 것임을 알 수 있다. 따라서 정답은 (B)이다.

6 기사가 홀든의 많은 직장인들에 대해 암시하는 것은?

(A) 종종 늦게 출근한다.
(B) 조사 결과에 동의하지 않는다.
(C) 더 경제적인 차를 구입하고 있다.
(D) 이미 피곤한 상태로 직장에 도착한다.

해설 | 추론 / 암시
첫 단락의 두 번째 문장에서 많은 직장인들이 출퇴근 여정에 지치고 그 비용 때문에 짜증난 채로 직장에 도착한다(Many workers arrive ~ irritated about the cost of commuting)고 했으므로 (D)가 정답이다.

Paraphrasing 지문의 exhausted → 보기의 tired

7 통근을 개선하기 위한 방법으로 기사에 언급된 것이 아닌 것은?

(A) 대중교통 할인권 제공 (B) 직원의 재택근무 허용
(C) 다른 시간대의 근무 일정 (D) 카풀 주선

해설 | Not / True
두 번째 단락 첫 문장에서 가능한 해결책 중 하나로 재택근무가 있다(Telecommuting is one possible solution)고 했으므로 (B), 세 번째 단락 첫 문장에서 또 다른 해결책은 카풀(Another solution is carpools)이라고 했으므로 (D), 네 번째 단락 첫 문장에서 통근 부담을 완화할 수 있는 또 하나의 방법은 직원들이 통상적이지 않은 시간에 현장에서 일할 수 있도록 허용하는 것(One more way to ~ during nontraditional hours)이라고 했으므로 (C)는 모두 기사에 언급되었고, 대중교통 할인권에 대한 내용은 없으므로 정답은 (A)이다.

8 [1], [2], [3], [4]로 표시된 곳 중에서 다음 문장이 들어가기에 가장 적합한 위치는?

"이 방식이 성공하려면 직원들 집에서의 인터넷 연결 상태가 좋아야 한다."

(A) [1] (B) [2]
(C) [3] (D) [4]

RC

PART 7

해설 | 문장 삽입

제시된 문장에서 '이 방식이 성공하려면 직원들 집에서의 인터넷 연결 상태가 좋아야 한다'며 직원들이 집에서 근무할 수 있는 요건에 대해 언급하고 있다. 따라서 제시된 문장 앞에는 재택 근무 방식에 대한 설명이 와야 자연스러우므로 (B)가 정답이다.

UNIT 23 연계 문제

ETS 예제
본책 p.278

하트퍼드 강당의 다가오는 행사들	
시블리 스프링스 오케스트라	2월 14일 금요일 오후 7시 30분
로렌츠 합창 앙상블	2월 23일 일요일 오후 6시

미들랜드 재즈 트리오	**3월 12일 목요일 오후 8시**
에이더 청소년 심포니	3월 28일 토요일 오후 2시

하트퍼드 강당 행사를 위한 차량 주차는 이제 새 주차장을 이용하실 수 있습니다. – 후략 –

어휘 | upcoming 다가오는 **youth** 청년 **vehicle** 차량 **garage** 주차장

수신: parking@hartfordhall.au
발신: michaeld@netserve.au
날짜: 3월 11일 수요일
제목: 요청

재미슨 씨께,

내일 밤 하트퍼드 강당에서 열리는 행사에 참석할 예정입니다. 건물 뒤편에 주차할 수 있도록 특별 주차권을 신청하고자 합니다. – 중략 –

도와 주셔서 감사합니다.

마이클 더빈

어휘 | permit 허가증 **assistance** 도움, 지원

Q 더빈 씨는 어떤 행사에 참석할 것 같은가?
(A) 시블리 스프링스 오케스트라
(B) 로렌츠 합창 앙상블
(C) 미들랜드 재즈 트리오
(D) 에이더 청소년 심포니

ETS 유형 연습
본책 p.280

1 (C)	**2** (D)	**3** (B)	**4** (A)	**5** (B)	**6** (C)
7 (C)	**8** (D)	**9** (A)	**10** (B)		

[1-5] 광고+계약서

이미지 보난자

¹**웹사이트에서 사용하기 위해 눈길을 사로잡는 사진이 필요하십니까?**

저작권 제약과 높은 수수료를 다루는 일을 그만두고 싶으십니까? ¹**이미지 보난자로 오세요! 번거로움 없이 최상 품질의 보유 사진으로 온라인 블로그, 광고 및 기사에 즉각 활기를 불어넣어 드립니다.**

²(B)**저희는 예산을 초과하는 일 없이 매우 다양한 프로젝트 요구 사항을 ³수용할 수 있는 여러 정기 저가 사용권을 제공합니다.** ²(A)**저희 사이트의 모든 사진들은 즉시 다운로드할 수 있으며** ²(C)**개별적으로 또는 패키지의 일부로 구입할 수 있습니다.**

⁵**연간 이용권을 구입하시는 고객은 만기가 없는 무제한 사용권을 포함해 특별 가격 및 혜택을 제공받습니다.** 처음 구매하시는 고객께서는 최소 10장의 사진 구매 시 5장의 사진을 무료로 받으시게 됩니다. 자세한 내용은 웹 주문서에서 확인하실 수 있습니다.

저희가 보유한 사진들을 둘러보십시오. 저희의 선택 목록에 빠져드실 겁니다.

어휘 | attention-grabbing 주목을 끄는 **restriction** 제약 **bypass** 건너뛰다 **hassle** 귀찮은 일 **instantly** 즉시 **liven up** 활기를 불어넣다 **stock** 재고 **fixed-term** 기간이 고정된 **license** 허가(증) **accommodate** 수용하다 **a wide range of** 다양한 **individually** 개별적으로 **subscription** 구독, (서비스) 사용 **unlimited** 무제한의 **expire** 만료되다 **order form** 주문서 **browse** 둘러보다 **inventory** 재고 목록 **dazzle** 황홀하게 하다 **selection** 선택 가능한 것들

사용권 계약

다음 사용권 약정은 **이미지 보난자사**가 **캐스퍼 우드스텐**("구매자")에게 이미지 보난자가 판매하는 이미지의 사용에 대해 승인하는 것이다. 이미지의 모든 사용은 다음 약정을 준수해야 한다.

1. 권리 승인. 사용권 수수료를 전액 지불하는 즉시 이미지 보난자는 구매자에게 첨부된 청구서에 기재된 이미지를 사용할 권리를 승인한다. 이미지는 디지털 광고를 포함한 비상업적 및 상업적 환경에서 사용될 수 있다. 본 사용권은 텔레비전이나 영화에서의 사용을 승인하지 않는다. ⁴**구매자에게는 이미지 잘라 내기, 색상 조정, 문구 추가를 포함한 이미지 편집 권리가 부여된다.**

2. 사용권 기간(택 1).

____ 상기 권리는 전액 지급을 수령한 날부터 ____년 동안 부여된다.

⁵ ✓ **상기 권리는 전액 지급을 수령한 날부터 종료일 없이 영구적으로 부여된다.**

어휘 | terms 조건, 기간 **hereby** 이로써 **grant** 승인하다 **market** (상품을) 내놓다 **comply with** ~을 준수하다 **right** 권리 **commercial** 상업의 **context** 맥락, 환경 **crop** 잘라 내다 **adapt** 조정하다 **permanently** 영구적으로

---

1 이미지 보난자의 고객은 누구일 것 같은가?
(A) 전문 사진작가
(B) 저작권 변호사
(C) 웹사이트 개발자
(D) 동영상 스트리밍 서비스 업체

해설 | 추론/암시

광고의 첫 문장에서 웹사이트에서 사용하기 위해 눈길을 사로잡는 사진이 필요하십니까(Do you need attention-grabbing photographs ~ Web site?)라고 물으며 이미지 보난자로 오시라(Come to Image Bonanza!)고 했고, 번거로움 없이 최상 품질의 보유 사진으로 온라인 블로그, 광고 및 기사에 즉각

활기를 불어넣어 드린다(We let you bypass ~ with top-quality stock photos)고 했다. 따라서 이미지 보난자는 웹사이트 개발자 및 운영자들을 대상으로 사진이나 이미지를 제공하는 업체임을 알 수 있으므로 (C)가 정답이다.

2 이미지 보난자에서 상품을 구매하는 이유로 언급된 것이 아닌 것은?
(A) 바로 사용 가능하다.
(B) 가격이 적당하다.
(C) 패키지의 일부로 구매할 수 있다.
(D) 전 세계 사람들이 등장한다.

해설 | Not/True
광고의 두 번째 단락에서 저희는 예산을 초과하는 일 없이 다양한 프로젝트 요구 사항을 수용할 수 있는 여러 정기 저가 사용권을 제공한다(We offer a variety of ~ without breaking your budget)고 했으므로 (B), 저희 사이트의 모든 사진들은 즉시 다운로드 할 수 있다(All photos on our site are ready for immediate download)고 했으므로 (A), 개별적으로 또는 패키지의 일부로 구입할 수 있다(can be purchased individually or as part of a package)고 했으므로 (C)는 이미지 보난자를 이용해야 하는 이유로 언급되었으나 사진에 쓰이는 인물에 대한 언급은 없으므로 (D)가 정답이다.

어휘 | affordably 적당히 **feature** 특별히 포함하다

Paraphrasing 지문의 low-cost
→ 보기의 affordably priced
지문의 immediate → 보기의 right away

3 광고에서 두 번째 단락 1행의 "accommodate"와 의미가 가장 가까운 단어는?
(A) 공간이 있다   (B) 적합하다
(C) 필수적이다   (D) 익숙해지다

해설 | 동의어
의미상 다양한 프로젝트 요구 사항을 '수용할' 수 있는 사용권이라는 뜻으로 쓰인 것이므로 정답은 (B) are appropriate for이다.

4 계약서에 따르면, 구매자는 이미지로 무엇을 할 수 있는가?
(A) 이미지 변경   (B) 제3자에 판매
(C) 텔레비전 방영   (D) 영화로 전환

해설 | 세부 사항
계약서의 두 번째 단락 마지막 문장에서 구매자에게는 이미지 잘라 내기, 색상 조정, 문구 추가를 포함한 이미지 편집 권리가 부여된다(The Buyer is granted ~ and adding text)고 했으므로 (A)가 정답이다.

어휘 | transfer 전환하다

Paraphrasing 지문의 edit → 보기의 Make changes

5 우드스텐 씨와 이미지 보난자의 관계에 대해 추론할 수 있는 것은?
(A) 처음 구매하는 손님이다.
(B) 연간 구독자이다.
(C) 정규직 직원이다.
(D) 프리랜서 사진작가이다.

해설 | 연계
광고의 세 번째 단락 첫 문장에서 연간 이용권을 구입하는 고객은 만기가 없는 무제한 사용권을 포함해 특별 가격 및 혜택을 제공받는다(Customers who purchase ~ that never expire)고 했고, 계약서의 2번 사용권 기간(2. Term of License) 조항에서 우드스텐 씨는 상기 권리는 전액 지급을 수령한 날부터 종료일 없이 영구적으로 부여된다(The above rights are ~ with no end date)고 설명된 항목을 택하였다. 따라서 우드스텐 씨는 사용권을 영구적으로 쓸 수 있는 혜택이 포함된 연간 이용권을 구입한 것이므로 (B)가 정답이다.

[6-10] 기사+지도+초대장

IBI, 루이스 시티를 겨냥하다

루이스 시티 (4월 22일)—**⁶스미스빌에 본사를 둔 인바르타 자전거사(IBI)가 루이스 시티에 첫 지점을 열 예정이다.** 스미스빌 지점과 마찬가지로 새로운 매장은 여러 유명 브랜드의 자전거와 자전거 부속품을 제공할 것이다. 개점일은 8월 15일로 예정되어 있다.

오드라 라플라예 IBI 최고 경영자는 현지 시 관계자들과 만남을 가진 후 "당사의 시장 조사에 따르면 루이스 시티 내부 및 인근 주민들은 열렬한 자전거 이용자이므로, 이곳에 지점을 여는 것은 매우 당연한 일입니다."라고 말했다.

⁸, ¹⁰따라서 새로운 IBI 시설이 파랄레스 그린웨이 바로 옆에 위치하는 것은 우연이 아니라 의도된 것이다. 이곳은 여러 교외 지역과 도시의 상업 지구를 연결하는 광범위한 자전거 도로를 뽐낸다.

⁷IBI가 스미스빌에서 루이스로 본사를 이전하는 동안 스미스빌 지점은 계속 운영될 예정이다.

어휘 | sight 광경 **based in** ~에 본사가 있는 **accessories** 부속품 **avid** 열렬한 **make sense** 합당하다 **city official** 시 공무원 **by design** 계획적으로 **by accident** 우연히 **facility** 시설 **boast** 자랑하다 **extensive** 광범위한 **suburban** 교외의 **district** 구역

루이스 시티
소매업용 지정 구역
참고: 각 구역은 300m x 600m(표준 도시 블록 3개)입니다.

⁹워터프론트 가			
기차역	⁹구역 A	⁹구역 B	⁹구역 C	**⁸,⁹구역 D**	파랄레스 그린웨이
메이플 가			

어휘 | tract 구역 **retail** 소매 **standard** 표준

인바르타 자전거
초대장

9월 15일 낮 12시부터 오후 5시까지 메이플 가 28번지에서 열리는 **¹⁰새 지점의 개점식에 참석해 주십시오.**

오스만 유수프 시장, 오드라 라플라예 IBI 최고 경영자, 콰메 알신도르 IBI 직원협회장 등이 청중들을 상대로 연설을 할 예정입니다.

무료 커피, 차, 주스, 간식이 행사 내내 제공됩니다. 선착순 100명에게는 무료 물병을 증정합니다.

¹⁰**손님에게는 인근 자전거 도로에서 매 30분마다 열리는 3km 자전거 경주에 참여할 기회도 주어집니다.** 경주에서 가장 빠른 시간을 기록하는 참가자에게는 고급 자전거 백팩을 증정합니다.

> **어휘 |** mayor 시장 association 협회 address 연설하다
> complimentary 무료의 serve 제공하다

6 기사에 따르면, IBI는 무엇을 전문으로 하는가?
(A) 자전거 여행　　　(B) 자전거 제조
(C) 자전거 판매　　　(D) 자전거 도로 건설

> **해설 | 세부 사항**
> 기사의 첫 단락 첫 문장에서 스미스빌에 본사를 둔 인바르타 자전거사(IBI)가 루이스 시티에 첫 지점을 열 예정(Invarta Bicycles, Inc. ~ in Lewis City)이라며, 스미스빌 지점과 마찬가지로 새로운 매장은 여러 유명 브랜드의 자전거와 자전거 부속품을 제공할 것(Like its Smithville location ~ bicycle accessories)이라고 했으므로 정답은 (C)이다.

7 IBI의 스미스빌 지점에 대해 기사에 명시된 것은?
(A) 곧 영구적으로 문을 닫을 예정이다.
(B) 인기 있는 공원 옆에 있다.
(C) 현재 이 회사의 본사이다.
(D) 가장 수익이 좋은 매장이다.

> **해설 | Not / True**
> 기사의 마지막 단락에서 IBI가 스미스빌에서 루이스로 본사를 이전하는 동안 스미스빌 지점은 계속 운영될 예정(While IBI will be ~ remain in business)이라고 했다. 따라서 스미스빌 지점이 현재 인바르타 자전거의 본점이므로 (C)가 정답이다.

> **어휘 |** permanently 영구적으로 profitable 수익이 나는

8 새로운 IBI 시설은 어느 구역에 위치할 예정인가?
(A) 구역 A　　　(B) 구역 B
(C) 구역 C　　　(D) 구역 D

> **해설 | 연계**
> 기사의 세 번째 단락 첫 문장에서 새로운 IBI 시설이 파랄레스 그린웨이 바로 옆에 위치하는 것이 우연이 아니라 의도된 것(It is, therefore, ~ the Parales Greenway)이라고 했고, 지도에 따르면 파랄레스 그린웨이 바로 옆은 D 구역이므로 (D)가 정답이다.

9 지도에 명시된 것은 무엇인가?
(A) 모든 구역은 워터프론트 가로 연결된다.
(B) 일부 구역은 다른 구역보다 크다.
(C) 기차역은 파랄레스 그린웨이 옆에 있다.
(D) 메이플 거리에 아파트 단지가 들어설 예정이다.

> **해설 | Not / True**
> 지도에 따르면 모든 구역이 워터프론트 가(Waterfront Street)와 맞닿아 있으므로 (A)가 정답이다. 참고 사항에서 각 구역은 300m× 600m(Note: each tract is 300 meters×600 meters)라고 나와 있으므로 (B)는 오답, 기차역(Public Rail Station)은 파랄레스 그린웨이에서 가장 멀리 떨어진 구역 A 옆에 있으므로 (C)도 오답, 아파트 단지에 대한 내용은 보이지 않으므로 (D)도 오답이다.

10 새 매장의 개점식에 무슨 일이 있을 예정인가?
(A) 라이브 공연이 제공될 것이다.
(B) 일부 손님들은 파랄레스 그린웨이에서 자전거를 탈 것이다.
(C) 다과 및 간식이 판매될 것이다.
(D) 매시간 복권 추첨 행사가 열릴 것이다.

> **해설 | 연계**
> 기사의 세 번째 단락에서 새로운 IBI 시설이 파랄레스 그린웨이 바로 옆에 위치하는 것은 우연이 아니라 의도된 것(It is, therefore, ~ Parales Greenway)이고 이곳은 여러 교외 지역과 도시의 상업 지구를 연결하는 광범위한 자전거 도로를 뽐낸다(The area boasts ~ the city's business district)고 했으므로 파랄레스 그린웨이는 자전거 도로임을 알 수 있다. 또한 초대장의 첫 문장에서 새 지점의 개점식에 참석해 달라(Join us for the grand opening of our new location)며 마지막 단락 첫 문장에서 손님에게는 인근 자전거 도로에서 매 30분마다 열리는 3km 자전거 경주에 참여할 기회가 주어진다(Guests will also have ~ held every thirty minutes)고 했다.
> 따라서 새 지점의 개점 행사에서 일부 손님들은 자전거 도로인 파랄레스 그린웨이에서 자전거 경주에 참여할 것임을 알 수 있으므로 (B)가 정답이다.

> **어휘 |** refreshments 다과 lottery 복권 drawing 추첨

ETS 고득점 실전 문제　　　본책 p.284

1 (D)	**2** (B)	**3** (C)	**4** (D)	**5** (A)	**6** (A)
7 (D)	**8** (B)	**9** (C)	**10** (A)	**11** (A)	**12** (D)
13 (B)	**14** (C)	**15** (C)	**16** (C)	**17** (A)	**18** (C)
19 (D)	**20** (B)	**21** (B)	**22** (B)	**23** (C)	**24** (A)
25 (D)	**26** (C)	**27** (A)	**28** (B)	**29** (C)	**30** (B)
31 (D)	**32** (B)	**33** (C)	**34** (A)	**35** (D)	**36** (A)
37 (B)	**38** (C)	**39** (B)	**40** (D)	**41** (A)	**42** (D)
43 (C)	**44** (B)	**45** (D)			

[1-5] 이메일+이메일

> 수신: pkoutrakis@kic.com
> 발신: bghosh@rhonesystems.com
> 제목: 회의 후속 조치
> 날짜: 5월 4일 오후 6시 49분
>
> 쿠트라키스 씨께,
>
> 오늘 아침에 만나 뵙고 쿠트라키스 보험사에 컴퓨터 지원 서비스를 제공하기 위해 론 시스템을 유지하는 것에 관한 귀하의 관심에 대해 논의하게 되어 즐거웠습니다.
>
> ²⁽ᴬ⁾**실버 서비스 플랜에 관심을 표하셨고, 해당 플랜에는 귀사의 소프트웨어 프로그램에 대한 자동 업데이트가 제공됩니다.** ²⁽ᶜ⁾, ²⁽ᴰ⁾**추가로, 연 2회 장비의 현장 청소와 현장 및 원격 지원 서비스를 제공합니다.** 이 플랜의 이용료는 월 45달러, 즉 540달러입니다. ¹**현재 특별 판촉을 진행 중이므로 통상적인 계약 기간인 18개월 대신**

1년 계약을 제안해 드릴 수 있어 기쁩니다. 게다가 ⁵5월 6일까지 이 제안을 수락하시면 계약 기간 동안 월간 이용료를 10달러 할인해 드립니다. 연간 구독을 선택하시면 120달러를 1회 할인받으실 수 있습니다.

비슈누파다 고시
론 시스템 수석 판매 담당자

어휘 | retain 유지하다 insurance 보험 on-site 현장의 biannual 연 2회의 remote 원격의 subscription 구독[이용] typical 보통의 term 기간 accept 수락하다 duration 기간 opt for ~을 선택하다 reduction 할인

수신: bghosh@rhonesystems.com
발신: pkoutrakis@kic.com
답장: 회의 후속 조치
⁵날짜: 5월 8일 오전 8시 31분

고시 씨께,

답변이 늦어 죄송합니다. 당신을 만난 직후 갑자기 급한 일로 불려가게 되었습니다. 안타깝게도 그 시간 동안 인터넷에 접속할 수 없었습니다.

저는 실버 플랜을 연간 구독하기로 결정했습니다. ⁵판촉 기한을 연장해 주셔서 감사합니다. ³우리가 만났을 때 우리 본사에서 20마일 이내에 있는 추가 지점을 무료로 ⁴포함시켜 주시겠다고 언급하셨습니다. 우리 지사가 본사로부터 21마일 떨어져 있어서 여기가 계약에 포함될 수 있는지 궁금합니다. 마지막으로 클라우드 저장 용량을 매월 50 기가바이트 늘리고 싶습니다. 이로 인한 추가 비용은 발생하지 않는 것으로 알고 있습니다. 이 문제들에 대한 당신의 입장을 알려 주세요.

피터 쿠트라키스
쿠트라키스 보험사 사장

어휘 | response 회신 shortly 곧 unexpectedly 뜻밖에 urgent 긴급한 gratitude 감사 extend 연장하다 cover 포함시키다 satellite office 지사 storage 저장

1 첫 번째 이메일에서 고시 씨에 대해 명시된 것은?
(A) 쿠트라키스 씨와 전화로 통화했다.
(B) 18년 동안 론 시스템 직원으로 일했다.
(C) 론 시스템에서 업무 지원 센터를 관리하고 있다.
(D) 쿠트라키스 씨에게 특별 제안을 하고 있다.

해설 | Not / True
첫 이메일의 두 번째 단락 네 번째 문장에서 현재 특별 판촉을 진행 중이므로 통상적인 계약 기간인 18개월 대신 1년 계약을 제안할 수 있어 기쁘다(As we currently have a special ~ contract term of 18 months)고 했고, 게다가 5월 6일까지 이 제안을 수락하면 계약 기간 동안 월간 이용료를 10달러 할인해 준다(Moreover, accept this offer ~ duration of the contract)고 했으므로 (D)가 정답이다.

2 첫 번째 이메일에 따르면, 실버 서비스 플랜에 포함된 것이 아닌 것은?
(A) 소프트웨어 업그레이드   (B) 데이터 복구
(C) 장비 청소   (D) 원격 지원

해설 | Not / True
첫 이메일의 두 번째 단락 첫 문장에서 실버 서비스 플랜에 관심을 표하셨고 해당 플랜에는 귀사의 소프트웨어 프로그램에 대한 자동 업데이트가 제공된다(You expressed interest ~ software programs)고 했으므로 (A), 추가로 연 2회 장비의 현장 청소와 현장 및 원격 지원 서비스를 제공한다(Additionally, it allows for ~ remote support service)고 했으므로 (C)와 (D)가 실버 서비스에 포함된다는 것을 알 수 있다. 데이터에 대한 언급은 없으므로 (B)가 정답이다.

어휘 | recovery 복구 assistance 지원

Paraphrasing 지문의 support → 보기의 assistance

3 쿠트라키스 씨가 고시 씨에게 이메일을 쓴 이유는 무엇인가?
(A) 연락처 정보를 수정하려고 (B) 계약 연장을 요청하려고
(C) 협상을 계속하려고   (D) 회의를 확정하려고

해설 | 주제 / 목적
두 번째 이메일의 두 번째 단락 세 번째 문장에서 우리가 만났을 때 우리 본사에서 20마일 이내에 있는 추가 지점을 무료로 포함시켜 주시겠다고 언급하셨다(In our meeting ~ within 20 miles of our main office for free)고 했고, 이어서 지사가 본사에서 21마일 떨어져 있음(our satellite office is 21 miles from our main office)을 언급하며 계약에 포함시켜 줄 수 있는지(we were wondering if it could be included in the agreement) 문의하고 있으므로 정답은 (C)이다.

어휘 | extension 연장 continue 계속하다 negotiation 협상

4 두 번째 이메일에서 두 번째 단락 3행의 "cover"와 의미가 가장 가까운 단어는?
(A) 지불하다   (B) 보고하다
(C) 대신하다   (D) 서비스를 제공하다

해설 | 동의어
추가 지점을 무료로 서비스에 '포함'시켜 준다는 뜻으로 쓰인 것이므로 추가 지점에 무료로 '서비스를 제공해 준다'는 의미라고 볼 수 있다. 따라서 정답은 (D) provide services to이다.

5 쿠트라키스 씨에 대해 알 수 있는 것은?
(A) 마감기한을 놓쳤다.
(B) 다른 플랜을 선택했다.
(C) 보통 연간 이용을 선호한다.
(D) 처음에 클라우드 저장 기능을 거절했다.

해설 | 연계
첫 이메일의 두 번째 단락 다섯 번째 문장에서 5월 6일까지 이 제안을 수락하면 계약 기간 동안 월간 이용료를 10달러 할인해 준다(accept this offer by May 6 ~ of the contract)고 했는데, 두 번째 이메일의 작성 날짜가 5월 8일(Date: May 8)이고 두 번째 단락 두 번째 문장에서 쿠트라키스 씨가 판촉 기한을 연장해 주셔서 감사하다(Please accept ~ promotion deadline)고 했다. 따라서 쿠트라키스 씨는 5월 6일이었던 판촉 기한을 놓쳤다는 것을 알 수 있으므로 정답은 (A)이다.

어휘 | generally 보통 decline 거절하다 feature 특징, 기능

수신: sdurance@caffeystudio.net
발신: customerrelations@orbdesignsoftware.com
날짜: 10월 5일
제목: Orb 그래픽 디자인 도구

듀런스 씨께:

Orb 그래픽 디자인 도구에 대해 더 많은 정보를 요청하는 귀하의 온라인 양식을 받았습니다. ⁶이 도구를 사용하면 전문적으로 보이는 문서, 프레젠테이션 및 마케팅 자료를 쉽게 만들 수 있습니다. 이 도구의 가장 좋은 점 중 하나는 그래픽 디자인 경험이 필요하지 않다는 것입니다. 저희의 레이아웃 견본과 끌어 놓기 편집 기능으로 누구나 아주 적은 노력만으로 매력적인 문서를 만들 수 있습니다.

여기 저희가 제공하는 계정 유형에 대한 개요가 있습니다.

기본, 0달러. 개인 전용. 계정 소유자는 디자인 정리를 위한 폴더 하나, 수백 개의 디자인 견본 사용권, 무료 이미지 재고 데이터베이스를 받습니다.

비즈니스 라이트, 14달러/월. 최대 5명의 팀 구성원이 계정을 이용할 수 있습니다. 계정 소유자는 모든 기본 계정 혜택에 더불어 추가 디자인 견본, 이미지 재고, 우선 기술 지원을 받습니다.

⁸비즈니스 엘리트, 30달러/월. 팀 전원이 무제한으로 계정을 이용할 수 있습니다. 계정 소유자는 모든 비즈니스 라이트 계정 혜택과 함께 추가적으로 맞춤 컬러 팔레트 및 브랜드 정보를 저장할 수 있는 기능을 제공받습니다.

제가 더 도와드릴 일이 있으면 알려 주세요.

패트리샤 페놀리오, Orb 고객 관리부

어휘 | layout 배치 template 견본 feature 기능
overview 개요 account 계정 individual 개인의
organize 체계화하다 stock 재고 priority 우선순위
unlimited 무제한의 custom 맞춤 further 추가로

고객 추천 글

⁷직원이 10명밖에 안 되는 작은 신생 회사의 사주로서, 저를 위해 일하는 모두가 모든 일을 조금씩은 다 할 수 있어야 한다는 것을 알고 있습니다. Orb 그래픽 디자인 도구에 관해 정말 좋았던 점은 저희 직원 중 디자이너나 마케팅 전문가가 단 한 명도 없는데도 불구하고 이 소프트웨어로 우리 중 누구라도 단 몇 분 만에 아이디어를 근사해 보이는 디자인으로 쉽게 바꿀 수 있다는 것입니다. ⁸제가 특히 인정하는 기능은 로고, 폰트, 색채 조합 등의 브랜드 정보를 불러와서 모든 팀원이 새로운 자료를 만들 때 이 정보들을 이용할 수 있다는 점입니다.

제가 겪었던 유일한 문제는 사진 작업을 하는 동안 Orb 도구가 느리게 작동하는 것 같다는 점입니다. ⁹한번은 제가 만들고 있는 전단지의 내용 영역에 이미지를 끌어다 놓았는데 화면이 멈춰서 컴퓨터를 다시 시작해야 했습니다. 컴퓨터 ¹⁰성능상의 문제였을 수도 있습니다. 다행스럽게도 몇 번의 시도 끝에 이미지와 견본을 작동시킬 수 있었습니다.

전반적으로 저는 Orb 그래픽 디자인 도구가 기업과 개인 모두에게 훌륭하다고 생각합니다! 저는 거의 매일 이것을 사용합니다.

—샐리 듀런스

어휘 | testimonial 추천서 transform 변형시키다 import (데이터를) 불러오다 color scheme 색채 조합 sluggish 느릿느릿한 drag 끌어오다 flyer 전단지 froze (freeze의 과거) (컴퓨터 화면이) 멈추다 performance 실행 attempt 시도

6 이메일은 Orb 그래픽 디자인 도구의 어떤 이점을 강조하는가?
(A) 사용 편의성
(B) 적당한 가격
(C) 다른 프로그램과의 호환성
(D) 광범위한 분류 기능

해설 | 세부 사항
이메일의 첫 단락 두 번째 문장에서 Orb 그래픽 디자인 도구를 사용하면 전문적으로 보이는 문서, 프레젠테이션 및 마케팅 자료를 쉽게 만들 수 있다(This tool makes it easy ~ marketing materials)고 했고 이 도구의 가장 좋은 점 중 하나는 그래픽 디자인 경험이 필요하지 않다는 것(One of the best things ~ experience is required)이라며 사용하기 쉬운 장점에 대해 강조하고 있으므로 (A)가 정답이다.

어휘 | ease 편의성 affordable (가격이) 적당한 compatibility 호환성 extensive 광범위한 sorting 분류 capability 능력

7 추천서에서 듀런스 씨의 회사 직원들에 대해 알 수 있는 것은?
(A) 디자인 분야에서 폭넓은 경험을 갖고 있다.
(B) 현재 새로운 로고를 만들고 있다.
(C) 종종 임시직으로 고용된다.
(D) 사업에서 여러 역할을 수행한다.

해설 | 추론/암시
추천서의 첫 문장에서 듀런스 씨가 직원이 10명밖에 안 되는 작은 신생 회사의 사주로서 저를 위해 일하는 모두가 모든 일을 조금씩은 다 할 수 있어야 한다는 것을 알고 있다(As the owner of ~ a little bit of everything)고 한 것으로 보아 직원들이 다양한 업무를 수행하고 있다는 점을 알 수 있다. 따라서 (D)가 정답이다.

어휘 | extensive 광범위한 field 분야 basis 기준

Paraphrasing 지문의 do a little bit of everything
→ 보기의 have multiple roles

8 듀런스 씨에 대해 암시되는 것은?
(A) 계절 할인을 이용했다.
(B) 비즈니스 엘리트 계정을 구입했다.
(C) 종종 이미지 편집에 도움이 필요하다.
(D) Orb 마케팅 팀과 정기적으로 만난다.

해설 | 연계
이메일에서 비즈니스 엘리트(Business Elite)는 팀 전원이 무제한으로 계정을 이용할 수 있고(Unlimited account access for your entire team) 계정 소유자는 모든 비즈니스 라이트 계정 혜택과 함께 추가적으로 맞춤 컬러 팔레트 및 브랜드 정보를 저장할 수 있는 기능을 제공받는다(Account holders receive ~ save custom color palettes and branding information)고 했고, 추천서에서 듀런스 씨는 자신이 특히 인정하는 기능은 로고, 폰트, 색채 조합 등의 브랜드 정보를

불러와서 모든 팀원이 새로운 자료를 만들 때 이 정보들을 이용할 수 있다는 점(A feature I especially appreciate ~ when creating new materials)이라고 했다. 따라서 듀런스 씨는 비즈니스 엘리트 계정의 맞춤 컬러 팔레트 및 브랜드 정보의 저장 기능을 사용하고 있는 것이므로 정답은 (B)이다.

어휘 | take advantage of ~을 이용하다 seasonal 계절에 따른

9 추천서에서 듀런스 씨가 전단지에 대해 언급한 것은?
(A) 그녀가 가장 좋아하는 견본으로 만들었다.
(B) 유명한 예술가가 디자인했다.
(C) 만드는 동안 기술적인 문제가 있었다.
(D) 잠재 고객을 위한 견본으로 이용했다.

해설 | Not/True
추천서의 두 번째 단락 두 번째 문장에서 듀런스 씨가 한번은 제가 만들고 있는 전단지의 내용 영역에 이미지를 끌어다 놓았는데 화면이 멈춰서 컴퓨터를 다시 시작해야 했다(Once, when I dragged an image ~ restart my computer)고 한 것으로 보아 (C)가 정답이다.

───────
Paraphrasing 지문의 the screen froze → 보기의 had a technical problem

10 추천서에서 두 번째 단락 4행의 "performance"와 의미가 가장 가까운 단어는?
(A) 실행   (B) 전시
(C) 묘사   (D) 업적

해설 | 동의어
의미상 컴퓨터의 '성능' 또는 '실행' 문제라는 뜻으로 쓰인 것이므로 정답은 (A) operation이다.

[11-15] 광고+회람

┌─────────────────────────────────────┐
│ **서베이 코스모스**
│ 〈사업가 노트〉에서 1위를 차지한 애플리케이션
│
│ **11고객 선호도 및 제품 수요에 대한 최신 정보가 필요하십니까?**
│ 서베이 코스모스는 초기 디자인부터 광고까지 제품 개발 전 단계에
│ 걸쳐 의사 결정에 필요한 가장 필수적인 정보를 수집할 수 있도록
│ 도와주는 애플리케이션입니다.
│
│ **특징**
│ • **14알림:** 설문 조사를 작성하라는 알림 메시지가 고객에게
│   발송됩니다(응답률 평균 50% 향상).
│ • 보고: 몇 가지 필터링 옵션으로 특정 시장 동향 및 선호도를 식별할
│   수 있습니다.
│ • 질문 라이브러리: 다양한 범주의 400개가 넘는 질문을 사용해 설문
│   조사를 맞춤 제작할 수 있습니다.
│ • **12데이터 저장:** 설문 조사 결과에 대한 전체 기록을 한곳에
│   보관합니다**12(새로운 무기한 정책 적용).**
└─────────────────────────────────────┘

어휘 | ranked (등급을) 차지한 entrepreneur 사업가
up-to-date 최신의 preference 선호(도) initial 초기의
feature 특징 notification 알림 reminder 상기시켜 주는
메모 boost 높이다 response rate 응답률 filter 거르다
isolate 분리하다 specific 특정한 customize 주문 제작하다
storage 저장 retain 보유하다 expiration 만기

───────

회람

발신: 세이라 카토우, 제품 개발 담당 부사장
수신: 제품 개발 직원
날짜: 2월 8일
제목: 새로운 애플리케이션

우리가 다음 달 시장 조사 설문지에 사용할 서베이 코스모스 이용권을 구입했음을 알려 드립니다. 아시다시피 **13당사의 시리얼과 와플, 에너지 바의 생산 및 판매를 위해서는 고객 선호도를 이해하는 것이 필수적입니다.** 경영진은 서베이 코스모스가 그 비용에도 불구하고 우리 설문 조사 데이터의 신뢰도를 높여줄 잠재성이 있다는 점에 있어 건전한 투자라고 믿고 있습니다. **14저는 이 애플리케이션에 알림 기능이 있어 특히 만족합니다.**

기술 지원 서비스 부서에서 2월 21에서 25일 사이에 부서 컴퓨터에 소프트웨어를 설치할 예정입니다. 또한 3월 4일, 11일, 18일에는 소프트웨어 사용에 대한 교육이 진행될 것입니다. 애플리케이션 사용 시작일인 **153월 19일 이전에 애플리케이션 사용법을 숙지해야 하므로** 이 교육 시간 중 하나에 의무적으로 참여해야 합니다. 4월 1일에는 애플리케이션 사용에 대한 여러분의 피드백을 수집할 예정입니다.

───────
어휘 | license 인가 sound 견실한 investment 투자
reliability 신뢰도 mandatory 의무적인

11 광고에 언급된 애플리케이션의 목적은 무엇인가?
(A) 시장 조사 개선
(B) 웹사이트로 더 많은 사용자 유치
(C) 정확한 제품 주문 기록 유지
(D) 기밀 정보 보호

해설 | 세부 사항
광고의 첫 단락에서 고객 선호도 및 제품 수요에 대한 최신 정보가 필요한지(Do you need ~ product demand?) 물으며 서베이 코스모스는 초기 디자인부터 광고까지 제품 개발 전 단계에 걸쳐 의사 결정에 필요한 가장 필수적인 정보를 수집할 수 있도록 도와주는 애플리케이션(Survey Cosmos is ~ from initial design to advertising)이라고 했다. 따라서 서베이 코스모스는 시장 조사용 정보 수집을 돕는 앱이므로 (A)가 정답이다.

어휘 | accurate 정확한 confidential 기밀의

12 애플리케이션에 최근 추가된 특징은 무엇인가?
(A) 애플리케이션의 업데이트 버전 자동 설치
(B) 사용자에게 정보 백업 요청 자동 알림
(C) 다양한 보고서 생성 기능
(D) 정보 저장 기간 연장 기능

해설 | 세부 사항
광고의 특징 중 마지막 항목에서 데이터 저장(Data Storage) 기능을 설명하며 새로운 무기한 정책이 적용된다(with a new no-expiration-date policy)고 덧붙인 것으로 보아 데이터 저장 기간을 무기한으로 늘릴 수 있는 특징이 새롭게 추가되었음을 알 수 있다. 따라서 정답은 (D)이다.

어휘 | generate 만들어내다 store 저장하다 period 기간

───────
Paraphrasing 지문의 no-expiration-date → 보기의 a longer period of time

13 카토우 씨는 어떤 업종에서 일하는가?

(A) 소프트웨어 개발　　(B) 식품
(C) 기업 교육　　　　　(D) 광고

해설 | 세부 사항
회람의 첫 단락 두 번째 문장에서 카토우 씨가 당사의 시리얼과 와플, 에너지 바의 생산 및 판매를 위해서는 고객 선호도를 이해하는 것이 필수적(understanding customer preferences ~ and energy bars)이라고 했으므로 정답은 (B)이다.

――――――――――
Paraphrasing 지문의 cereals, waffles, and energy bars → 보기의 food

14 카토우 씨는 회사 설문 조사의 어떤 점을 개선하기를 특히 바라는가?

(A) 설문 조사 질문의 수준
(B) 설문 조사 시행 비용
(C) 설문 조사의 응답자 수
(D) 설문 조사 완료에 걸리는 시간

해설 | 연계
광고의 특징 중 첫 항목에서 알림(Notifications) 기능을 설명하며 설문 조사를 작성하라는 알림 메시지가 고객에게 발송되어(Reminders to complete surveys are sent to customers) 응답률을 평균 50% 향상시킨다(boosting response rates by an average of 50 percent)고 했고, 회람의 첫 단락 마지막 문장에서 카토우 씨가 이 애플리케이션에 알림 기능이 있어 특히 만족한다(I am particularly pleased that the application has a notifications feature)고 했다. 따라서 카토우 씨는 앱의 알림 기능으로 설문 조사 응답률을 높일 수 있기를 기대하는 것이므로 (C)가 정답이다.

어휘 | quality 품질 **implement** 실행하다
――――――――――
Paraphrasing 지문의 response rates → 보기의 The number of people who respond to surveys

15 전 직원은 며칠까지 애플리케이션 사용법을 익혀야 하는가?

(A) 2월 21일　　(B) 2월 25일
(C) 3월 19일　　(D) 4월 1일

해설 | 세부 사항
회람의 두 번째 단락 세 번째 문장에서 3월 19일 이전에 애플리케이션 사용법을 숙지해야 한다(you are expected to know how to use the application before March 19)고 했으므로 (C)가 정답이다.

[16-20] 기사+이메일

아크라, 가나 (2월 17일)—의류 및 액세서리 제조업체인 산코파 제조가 패션 회사인 아코페나와 파트너십을 체결했다. **16(A), 16(B)**요루바 문화에 영감을 받은 의류 및 수제 보석으로 잘 알려진 아코페나는 아프리카, 유럽, 아메리카 대륙에서 제품을 판매하고 있다. **16(D),** **17**이곳 아크라에 본사를 둔 두 회사간 협업은 아코페나 제품의 유명한 디자인과 밝은 색상이 산코파 제품에 스며들 것임을 의미한다. **17**이 새로운 제품 라인은 우베조라는 브랜드명으로 시장에 선보일 예정이다.

19우베조 라인의 작업은 이미 시작되었으며, 5월 말 업계 전문가를 대상으로 하는 비공개 패션쇼를 계획하고 있다. 일반 회원들은 온라인으로 이 쇼의 사진을 볼 수 있을 예정이다. 완전한 제품 라인은 7월에 매장에서 구입할 수 있을 것으로 예상된다.

어휘 | jewelry 보석류 **inspired** 영감을 받은 **market** (상품을) 내놓다 **collaboration** 협업 **based** 본사를 둔 **be infused with** ~이 배어 있다 **private** 비공개의

――――――――――――――――――――

수신: omotola_dauda@akofena.com.gh
발신: rudi.amoako@sankofa.com.gh
날짜: 6월 27일
제목: 우베조 제품 라인
첨부: ⬆️보고서

오모톨라 씨께,

19이 이메일에 첨부된 파일은 6월 6일 패션쇼에 선보인 우베조 제품 라인에 대한 첫 평가 보고서입니다. 패션쇼 참석자들을 대상으로 한 설문 조사 결과와 최고 패션 평론가들의 평가, 몇몇 주요 패션 사이트들의 논평이 담겨 있습니다.

사람들이 전반적으로 옷에 만족하는 반면, 액세서리에 대해서는 밋밋하다고 평하며 호응이 덜했습니다. 몇몇 평론가들은 우베조 보석과 스카프에 아프리카 문화의 특징을 담아내 제품들이 아프리카와 뗄 수 없는 관계가 되도록 해야 한다는 의견입니다.

18이 피드백을 바탕으로, 귀사의 팀에서 새로운 액세서리 디자인을 제안해 주셨으면 합니다. 7월 4일까지 저에게 이것들을 보내 주십시오. 아시다시피, **20**우리 목표는 7월 둘째 주까지 신상 라인을 준비해서 그 다음 주에 있을 아프리카 상공협회(AOCI) 엑스포에서 판매를 시작할 수 있도록 하는 것이었습니다. 의류는 생산하기로 결정하였으나, 액세서리는 시장에 내놓기 전에 확신이 들 때까지 기다리고자 합니다.

노고에 감사드립니다.

루디 아모아코
수석 마케팅 담당자, 산코파 제조

어휘 | initial 처음의 **critic** 평론가 **commentary** 논평 **enthusiastic** 열광적인 **plain** 밋밋한 **capture** 담아내다 **aspect** 면 **inseparably** 불가분하게 **commerce** 상업

16 아코페나의 제품에 대해 기사에 언급된 것이 아닌 것은?

(A) 특정 문화의 영향을 받았다.
(B) 국제적으로 판매되고 있다.
(C) 가격이 합리적이다.
(D) 색상이 밝다.

해설 | Not/True
기사의 첫 단락 두 번째 문장에서 요루바 문화에 영감을 받은 의류 및 수제 보석으로 잘 알려진 아코페나는 아프리카, 유럽, 아메리카 대륙에서 제품을 판매하고 있다(Known for its clothing ~ Europe, and the Americas)고 했으므로 (A)와 (B)는 사실이다. 또한 아크라에 본사를 둔 두 회사간 협업은 아코페나 제품의 유명한 디자인과 밝은 색상이 산코파 제품에 스며들 것을 의미한다(The collaboration between ~ bright colors that Akofena's products are known for)고 했으므로 (D)도 사실이다. 가격에 대한 사항은 언급되지 않았으므로 (C)가 정답이다.

어휘 | influence 영향을 주다 particular 특정한
reasonably 합리적으로

17 기사는 우베조 제품 라인에 대해 무엇을 암시하는가?
(A) 아크라에서 생산될 것이다.
(B) 아코페나에 의해 판매될 것이다.
(C) 수제품만 있을 예정이다.
(D) 5월에 매장에서 판매될 것이다.

해설 | 추론 / 암시
기사의 첫 단락 세 번째 문장에서 이곳 아크라에 본사를 둔 두 회사간 협업은 아코페나 제품의 유명한 디자인과 밝은 색상이 산코파 제품에 스며들 것임을 의미한다(The collaboration between ~ Akofena's products are known for)고 했고, 이 새로운 제품 라인은 우베조라는 브랜드명으로 시장에 선보일 예정(The new line ~ brand name Uwezo)이라고 했다. 따라서 우베조 제품은 두 회사가 기반을 두고 있는 아크라에서 생산될 것임을 알 수 있으므로 정답은 (A)이다.

18 이메일의 주된 목적은 무엇인가?
(A) 일부 지연에 대한 사과
(B) 설문 조사 승인
(C) 새로운 디자인 요청
(D) 취소에 대한 설명

해설 | 주제 / 목적
이메일의 첫 두 단락에서 우베조 라인의 피드백에 대해 설명한 뒤, 세 번째 단락 첫 문장에서 이 피드백을 바탕으로 귀사의 팀에서 새로운 액세서리 디자인을 제안해 주셨으면 한다(Based on this feedback ~ new accessory designs)면서 7월 4일까지 이것들을 보내 달라(Please submit these to me by 4 July)고 요청하고 있으므로 (C)가 정답이다.

19 패션쇼에 대해 알 수 있는 것은?
(A) 아코페나의 본사에서 열렸다.
(B) 일반 회원들이 참석했다.
(C) 더 큰 장소로 옮겨야 했다.
(D) 계획보다 늦게 열렸다.

해설 | 연계
기사의 두 번째 단락 첫 문장에서 우베조 라인의 작업은 이미 시작되었으며 5월 말 업계 전문가를 대상으로 하는 비공개 패션쇼를 계획하고 있다(Work on the Uwezo line ~ in late May)고 했고, 이메일의 첫 문장에서 이 이메일에 첨부된 파일은 6월 6일 패션쇼에 선보인 우베조 제품 라인에 대한 첫 평가 보고서(Attached to this e-mail ~ 6 June fashion show)라고 했다. 따라서 패션쇼가 원래 계획했던 5월 말보다 늦은 6월 6일에 열린 것이므로 (D)가 정답이다.

20 AOCI 엑스포에 대해 암시된 것은?
(A) 비즈니스 파트너십을 촉진한다.
(B) 7월에 열릴 예정이다.
(C) 아코페나와 산코파 제조가 후원사에 속한다.
(D) 지난 수년간 행사의 중요성이 증대했다.

해설 | 추론 / 암시
이메일의 세 번째 단락 세 번째 문장에서 우리 목표는 7월 둘째 주까지 신상 라인을 준비해서 그 다음 주에 있을 아프리카 상공협회(AOCI) 엑스포에서 판매를 시작할 수 있도록 하는 것(our goal was to have the new line ready ~ African Organization for Commerce and Industry (AOCI) the week after)이라고 했으므로 AOCI는 7월에 열린다는 것을 알 수 있다. 따라서 정답은 (B)이다.

어휘 | promote 촉진[고취]하다 **significance** 중요성, 의미

[21-25] 광고+웹페이지+이메일

절호의 기회!

²¹당신의 다음 사무실 주소가 토론토 시내에 있는 저명한 브링클리 빌딩이라고 상상해 보세요. 이 19세기 후반의 보석은 유명한 건축가 제이콥 클레멘츠가 설계했습니다. ²²원래는 게이블 출판사의 본사로, 이 빌딩에 75년 동안 입주해 있었습니다. 빌딩은 일부 고전적인 특징은 보존되었지만 대대적으로 개조되고 현대화되었습니다. ²⁴또한 풀서비스를 제공하는 1층 식당 로우리스 온 디 애비뉴도 있습니다. 브링클리 빌딩의 상업 세입자를 위한 현장 주차는 합리적인 월간 요금으로 이용할 수 있으며 ²³대중교통이 가까이 있습니다. 자세한 정보를 원하시면 lseeley@brinkleyleasing.ca로 리즈 실리에게 연락하세요.

어휘 | distinguished 유명한 **gem** 보석 **renowned** 유명한
occupy 사용하다 **modernize** 현대화하다 **feature** 특징
retain 유지하다 **full-service** 포괄적인 서비스를 제공하는
on-site 현장의 **commercial** 상업의 **tenant** 세입자
reasonable 합리적인 **rate** 요금

---

https://www.ardenmedicalassociates.ca

²³아덴 메디컬 어소시에이츠는 10월 26일 두 번째 진료소 개업을 발표하게 되어 기쁩니다. 병원은 블레이크 가 94번지에 있는 브링클리 빌딩 스위트 200입니다. 저희 의료진은 토론토 시내 중심부에서 환자들에게 최고 수준의 치료를 제공할 준비가 되어 있습니다. 예약 없이 방문하는 환자를 환영하며 당일 예약도 가능합니다. 월요일부터 토요일까지 정규 시간에 진료 예약을 잡으시려면 416-555-0109로 전화 주십시오.

또한 가정의학 전공의 유리 샤로프 박사님이 저희 팀의 새로운 구성원으로 오시게 된 것을 환영하며 그는 11월 1일에 합류할 예정입니다.

어휘 | associate 동료 **patient** 환자 **walk-ins** 외래 환자
extend (환영 등을) 나타내다 **specialize in** ~을 전문으로 하다
family medicine 가정 의학

수신: 아덴 메디컬 어소시에이츠 직원
발신: 로레인 코든
날짜: 11월 3일
제목: 샤로프 박사님 환영

모두 안녕하십니까,

²⁴11월 4일에 유리 샤로프 박사님을 위한 비공식 환영회에 직원 여러분 모두를 초대합니다. 그는 이번 주 초에 이곳 브링클리 빌딩에 있는 우리 의료진에 합류했습니다.

²⁴내일 정오에 1층 식당에서 만나 샤로프 박사님과 인사를 나누고 커피와 가벼운 점심 식사를 할 예정입니다. 모두 쉽게 참석할 수 있도록 1시간 동안 병원 문을 닫도록 조정했습니다. ²⁵식당에 정확한 인원수를 알려줄 수 있도록 이 메시지에 참석 여부 확인을 위한 답장을 해주시기 바랍니다. 거기서 뵙기를 기대합니다!

로레인 코튼, 사무실 관리자

어휘 | informal 비공식의 arrange for 준비하다 accurate 정확한 head count 인원수 administrator 관리자

21 광고의 목적은 무엇인가?
(A) 토론토 시내 관광 홍보
(B) 상업용 사무 공간 입주자 유치
(C) 보수 공사를 위한 건축가 모집
(D) 오래된 건물의 구매자 찾기

해설 | **주제/목적**
광고의 첫 문장에서 당신의 다음 사무실 주소가 토론토 시내에 있는 저명한 브링클리 빌딩이라고 상상해 보라(Imagine having ~ downtown Toronto)고 한 것으로 보아 브링클리 빌딩에 사무실을 임대할 세입자를 모집하고 있음을 알 수 있다. 따라서 (B)가 정답이다.

어휘 | promote 홍보하다 tourism 관광 attract 끌어들이다 space 공간 recruit 모집하다 renovation 개조[보수] property 건물, 부동산

22 게이블 출판사에 대해 명시된 것은?
(A) 클레멘츠 씨가 창립했다.
(B) 더 이상 브링클리 빌딩에 입주해 있지 않다.
(C) 토론토에서 가장 큰 고용주였다.
(D) 실리 씨가 관리하고 있다.

해설 | **Not/True**
광고의 세 번째 문장에서 원래는 게이블 출판사의 본사로 브링클리 빌딩에 75년 동안 입주해 있었다(It was originally ~ for 75 years)고 한 것으로 보아 게이블 출판사는 브링클리 빌딩의 과거 입주자였음을 알 수 있다. 따라서 정답은 (B)이다. 브링클리 빌딩을 클레멘츠 씨가 설계했다고 했으므로 (A)는 오답, 빌딩 입주를 위한 정보가 필요할 경우 리즈 실리에게 연락하라고 했으므로 (D)도 오답, 게이블 출판사가 토론토에서 가장 큰 고용주였는지에 대한 언급은 나와 있지 않으므로 (C)도 답이 될 수 없다.

어휘 | found 창립하다 employer 고용주 manage 관리하다

23 아덴 메디컬 어소시에이츠의 새 진료소에 대해 암시된 것은?
(A) 행정직을 위한 전문가를 면접 중이다.
(B) 예약하지 않은 환자는 받지 않는다.
(C) 대중교통과 가깝다.
(D) 일주일에 7일 동안 환자를 받는다.

해설 | **연계**
광고의 여섯 번째 문장에서 브링클리 빌딩이 대중교통이 가까이 있다(public transportation is nearby)고 했고 웹페이지의 첫 문장에서 아덴 메디컬 어소시에이츠는 10월 26일 두 번째 진료소 개업을 발표하게 되어 기쁘다(Arden Medical Associates ~ on 26 October)며 병원은 블레이크 가

94번지에 있는 브링클리 빌딩 스위트 200(The clinic will be ~ Suite 200)이라고 했다. 아덴 메디컬 어소시에이츠의 새 진료소는 브링클리 빌딩에 있으므로 대중교통과 가깝다는 것을 알 수 있다. 따라서 (C)가 정답이다.

어휘 | administrative 행정의 accept 받아 주다

24 11월 4일에 무슨 일이 일어날 것 같은가?
(A) 로우리스 온 디 애비뉴에서의 모임
(B) 브링클리 빌딩 진료소의 첫 진료
(C) 새로운 진료소장의 승진
(D) 관리직원 월례 회의

해설 | **연계**
광고의 다섯 번째 문장에서 브링클리 빌딩에 풀서비스를 제공하는 1층 식당 로우리스 온 디 애비뉴도 있다(It also offers ~ Lowry's on the Avenue)고 했고, 이메일의 첫 문장에서 11월 4일에 유리 샤로프 박사님을 위한 비공식 환영회에 직원 여러분 모두를 초대한다(All staff members ~ on 4 November)고 했고 그는 이번 주 초에 이곳 브링클리 빌딩에 있는 우리 의료진에 합류했다(He joined our medical ~ earlier this week)면서 내일 정오에 1층 식당에서 만나 샤로프 박사님과 인사를 나누고 커피와 가벼운 점심 식사를 할 예정(We will meet in ~ a light lunch)이라고 했다. 따라서 11월 4일 샤로프 박사를 위한 비공식 환영회는 브링클리 빌딩의 1층 식당 로우리스 온 디 애비뉴에서 열리는 것이므로 (A)가 정답이다.

Paraphrasing 지문의 informal reception
→ 보기의 gathering

25 코튼 씨는 직원들에게 무엇을 요청하는가?
(A) 좌석 예약 전화 (B) 간단한 발표 준비
(C) 직원 명부 업데이트 (D) 이메일 답장

해설 | **세부 사항**
이메일의 두 번째 단락 세 번째 문장에서 식당에 정확한 인원수를 알려줄 수 있도록 이 메시지에 참석 여부 확인을 위한 답장을 해주시기 바란다(Please respond to this message ~ accurate head count)고 했으므로 (D)가 정답이다.

Paraphrasing 지문의 respond → 보기의 Reply

[26-30] 이메일+양식+이메일

수신: 인사 전문가 발송 명단
발신: 케이든 에버렛〈ceverett@steubenweiss.com〉
날짜: 7월 15일
제목: 우수 인적 자원
첨부: 추천서

²⁶스투벤과 바이스 우수 인적자원상은 우리 업계에서 가장 소중한 인재에게 표창하는 상입니다. ^{26, 30}올해 기념 행사는 멋진 피츠그래프 타워에서 열릴 예정입니다. 이날 밤 행사에는 레스토랑 둘세에서 마련하는 정찬좌담회, 클레망스 옥텟의 재즈 음악, 올해 우리 업계에서 탁월했던 이들을 위한 축하 등이 포함됩니다. 귀하께 참석을 권합니다.

날짜: 9월 14일
시간: 저녁 6시 – 11시 30분
장소: 시카고 동 마크리 대로 2108번지 피츠그래프 타워
회신 기한: 8월 31일

수상자를 추천하시고 싶으시면 첨부된 양식을 작성하여 7월 31일까지 nominees@steubenweiss.com으로 이메일을 보내주시기 바랍니다.

케이든 에버렛
스투벤과 바이스 이사회 의장

어휘 | recognize (공로를) 인정[표창]하다 valuable 소중한 stunning 멋진 cater 음식을 공급하다 excel 탁월하다 nominate 추천하다 board 이사회 chair 의장

스투벤과 바이스 우수 인적자원상 추천서

²⁸후보자 이름   아마야 노나카
지명자 이름   개빈 드레일링
후보자와의 관계   동료
²⁸후보자의 회사   앤더슨 앤 우즈 컨설팅 (A&WC)
후보자의 재직 기간   16년
후보자의 업계 근무 기간 23년
²⁷추천 사유
노나카 씨는 지속적으로 자신의 역할에 아주 적합한 신입 사원들을 영입하고 그들이 A&WC 재직하는 기간 내내 지원을 제공해 왔습니다.

어휘 | nominee 후보 nominator 지명자 consistently 지속적으로 suit (~에게) 적합하다 tenure 임기

발신: 케이든 에버렛 〈ceverett@steubenweiss.com〉
수신: 개빈 드레일링 〈gavindreyling@andersonwoods.com〉
날짜: 9월 4일
제목: 후속 조치

드레일링 씨께,

이전 서신을 통해 아시다시피, ²⁸저희는 노나카 씨를 교육 기업 부문 우수 인적자원상 수상자로 선정했습니다. ²⁹저희는 보통 수상자를 추천한 사람에게 시상식에 참석하여 몇 마디 할 준비를 해 달라고 요청합니다. ²⁹, ³⁰행사에 20분 일찍 도착하셔서 저와 만나 당신의 역할에 대해 논의할 수 있을까요?

노나카 씨의 수상 부문은 현재 건강 사업 부문 직후, 프로그램 종료 시점인 재무 부문 이전으로 예정되어 있지만 시간대가 문제가 될 경우 부문 순서를 변경할 수 있습니다.

케이든 에버렛
스투벤과 바이스 이사회 의장

어휘 | correspondence 서신 present 참석한

---

26 첫 번째 이메일에 따르면, 시상식에는 무엇이 포함될 예정인가?
(A) 공로상
(B) 경품 추첨
(C) 라이브 밴드
(D) 스투벤과 바이스 사장 연설

해설 | **세부 사항**
첫 이메일의 첫 문장에서 스투벤과 바이스 우수 인적자원상(The Steuben and Weiss Excellence in Human Resources Awards)에 대해 소개하며 올해 기념 행사는 멋진 피츠그래프 타워에서 열릴 예정(This year our celebration ~ Fitzgraff Towers)이고 이날 밤 행사에는 레스토랑 둘세에서 마련하는 정찬좌담회, 클레망스 옥텟의 재즈 음악, 올해 우리 업계에서 탁월했던 이들을 위한 축하 등이 포함된다(The night will include ~ our industry this year)고 했다. 따라서 정답은 (C)이다.

어휘 | achievement 업적 raffle 추첨 prize 경품

Paraphrasing 지문의 jazz music by the Clemence Octet → 보기의 A live band

27 양식에 따르면, 노나카 씨의 주된 업무 중 하나는 무엇일 것 같은가?
(A) 직원 모집
(B) 급여 패키지에 대한 조언
(C) 직원 복지 관리
(D) 관리자 지도

해설 | **추론 / 암시**
양식 하단의 추천 사유(Reasons for nomination)에서 노나카 씨는 지속적으로 자신의 역할에 이상적인 신입 사원들을 영입하고 그들이 A&WC 재직하는 기간 내내 지원을 제공해 왔다(Ms. Nonaka has consistently brought in ~ tenure at A&WC)고 했으므로 직원 채용 및 관리 업무를 담당하고 있음을 짐작할 수 있다. 따라서 (A)가 정답이다.

어휘 | recruit 모집하다 benefits 복리 후생 mentor 지도하다 supervisor 관리자

Paraphrasing 지문의 brought in new employees → 보기의 Recruiting employees

28 앤더슨 앤 우즈 컨설팅은 어떤 종류의 사업체일 것 같은가?
(A) 행사 관리
(B) 교육
(C) 금융
(D) 건강과 웰니스

해설 | **연계**
양식에서 후보자 이름(Name of nominee)에 아마야 노나카 씨(Amaya Nonaka), 후보자의 회사(Nominee's company)에 앤더슨 앤 우즈 컨설팅 (A&WC)(Anderson and Woods Consulting)이라고 나와 있고 두 번째 이메일의 첫 문장에서 노나카 씨를 교육 기업 부문 우수 인적자원상 수상자로 선정했다(we have selected Ms. Nonaka as the winner in the category Excellence in Human Resources for an Educational Company)고 했으므로, 노나카 씨가 근무하는 A&WC는 교육 기업임을 알 수 있다. 따라서 (B)가 정답이다.

29 두 번째 이메일의 목적은 무엇인가?
(A) 수상자 그룹 발표
(B) 노나카 씨의 연락처 요청
(C) 드레일링 씨에게 행사에서의 연설 부탁
(D) 수상 부문 설명

해설 | **주제 / 목적**
두 번째 이메일의 첫 단락 두 번째 문장에서 저희는 보통 수상자를 추천한 사람에게 시상식에 참석하여 몇 마디 할 준비를 해 달라고 요청한다(We usually ask ~ to say a few words)고 설명했고, 행사에 20분 일찍 도착하셔서 저와 만나 당신의 역할에 대해 논의할 수 있을지(Would you be able to ~ discuss your role?)를 문의하고 있으므로 드레일링 씨에게 행사에서 발언을 해달라는 부탁을 하기 위해 이메일을 썼음을 알 수 있다. 따라서 정답은 (C)이다.

Paraphrasing 지문의 say a few words → 보기의 speak

30 에버렛 씨는 어디서 드레일링 씨를 만나고 싶어하는가?
(A) 둘세
(B) 피츠그래프 타워
(C) 스투벤과 바이스
(D) 앤더슨 앤 우즈 컨설팅

해설 | 연계

첫 이메일의 두 번째 문장에서 올해 기념 행사는 멋진 피츠그래프 타워에서 열릴 예정(This year our celebration ~ Fitzgraff Towers)이라고 했고, 두 번째 이메일의 첫 단락 마지막 문장에서 에버렛 씨는 드레일링 씨에게 행사에 20분 일찍 도착하셔서 저와 만나 당신의 역할에 대해 논의할 수 있을지(Would you be able to ~ discuss your role?)를 묻고 있다. 따라서 에버렛 씨는 드레일링 씨에게 행사 장소인 피츠그래프 타워에서 만나자고 제안하는 것이므로 (B)가 정답이다.

[31-35] 후기+웹페이지+이메일

---

https://www.easedeskpro.com/reviews/3496

거의 완벽합니다.

나는 3개월 동안 이즈 데스크 프로 스탠딩 데스크를 즐겨 사용하고 있습니다. 가격은 적당하고 배송은 빨랐습니다. **33저는 키가 2미터 가까이 되는데, 제가 주문한 책상은 저에게 안성맞춤이었습니다.** **31앉는 대신 서서 일을 하니까 허리 통증이 줄고 활력이 더욱 넘칩니다. 33저는 일을 하려면 대형 컴퓨터 모니터를 사용해야 하기 때문에 모니터 두 대가 모두 책상에 들어가서 다행입니다.** 하지만 **32저의 모니터가 꽤 무거워서 책상 높이를 수동으로 조정하는 것이 다소 어렵게 느껴집니다. 전반적으로 만족하지만 전자동 모델을 제공하는 것을 고려해 주셨으면 좋겠습니다.**

—레온 아다모비치, 1월 29일

어휘 | reasonable 합리적인　**fit** 맞는 것　**now that** ~이므로　**adjust** 조정하다　**height** 높이　**manually** 수동으로　**somewhat** 다소　**overall** 전반적으로

---

http://easedeskpro.com/products

이즈 데스크 프로로 하루 종일 앉아 있는 것은 이제 그만 멈추세요! 저희 좌입식 조절 가능 책상이 여러분의 건강과 생산성을 향상시켜 드릴 것입니다. 여러분에게 꼭 맞는 모델이 저희에게 있다고 확신합니다.

이즈 데스크 프로 2000—395달러, 1~2주 후 배송
- 수동 조절 가능
- 표준 모니터 최대 2대 탑재 가능

이즈 데스크 프로 3000—425달러, 1~2주 후 배송
- 전자동—버튼 터치로 올림/내림 기능
- 표준 모니터 최대 2대 탑재 가능

33이즈 데스크 프로 4000—550달러, 2~4주 후 배송
- 수동 조절 가능
- **33대형 모니터 최대 2대 탑재 가능**
- **33키 큰 사용자에게 적합**

이즈 데스크 프로 퀵—175달러, 5일 후 배송
- 수동 조절 가능
- 일반 크기의 노트북 1대 탑재 가능
- 좁은 공간에 적합

2월 출시: **35이즈 데스크 프로 커스텀**—다양한 가격, 5~6주 후 배송
- 스타일, 크기, 마감 선택
- 수동 또는 전동식 구매 가능

34모든 책상에는 30일 만족 보장 프로그램이 제공됩니다. 책상을 반품하실 경우 전액 환불해 드리며 고객님의 요구 사항에 적합한 더 좋은 책상을 찾으실 수 있도록 도와드립니다. 지금 바로 www.easedeskpro.com을 방문하세요!

어휘 | adjustable 조정할 수 있는　**productivity** 생산성　**accommodate** 수용하다　**raise** 올리다　**lower** 낮추다　**ideal** 이상적인　**full-sized** 일반 크기의　**vary** 각기 다르다　**finish** 마감재　**manual** 수동의　**guarantee** 보증

발신: ayala.drachman@easedeskpro.com
수신: ladamowicz@siftermail.com
날짜: 2월 7일
제목: 귀하의 이즈 데스크 프로 후기

아다모비치 씨께,

고객님의 온라인 후기와 도움이 되는 제안에 감사드립니다. 다양한 이즈 데스크 프로 모델의 서로 다른 기능을 혼합해 쓰고자 하는 많은 고객들의 의견을 들어 왔고 이번 달에 선보이는 신제품 옵션인 이즈 데스크 프로 커스텀을 발표하게 되어 기쁩니다. 이즈 데스크 프로 커스텀을 사용해 수동과 전동 버전 모두 고객님께 필요한 특정 높이와 공간에 맞춰 자신만의 책상을 설계할 수 있습니다. **35이즈 데스크 프로 커스텀을 주문하기로 선택하시면 현재 갖고 계신 책상을 전액 환불로 반품하실 수 있도록 해 드리겠습니다.** 이 제안을 이용하시려면 이 이메일에 답장해 주세요. 이즈 데스크 프로 직원이 고객님께서 꿈꾸시던 책상의 설계를 시작하기 위해 연락드릴 것입니다.

아얄라 드라크만, 고객 관리 전문가
이즈 데스크 프로

어휘 | mix and match 짜 맞추다　**feature** 기능　**specific** 특정한　**take advantage of** ~을 이용하다　**representative** 직원

---

31 후기에서, 아다모비치 씨가 자신의 책상에 대해 언급한 것은?
(A) 배송 중에 파손되었다.
(B) 그의 다른 가구들과 잘 어울린다.
(C) 조립이 어려웠다.
(D) 책상을 사용하고 요통이 줄었다.

해설 | Not/True

후기의 네 번째 문장에서 앉는 대신 서서 일을 하니까 허리 통증이 줄고 활력이 더욱 넘친다(Now that I am standing ~ I have more energy)고 했으므로 (D)가 정답이다.

어휘 | blend 섞이다　**assemble** 조립하다　**back pain** 요통

Paraphrasing　지문의 my back hurts less
→ 보기의 reduced his back pain

32 아다모비치 씨는 책상의 어떤 특징이 개선될 수 있다고 생각하는가?
(A) 색상　　　　　　　(B) 조절 기능
(C) 무게　　　　　　　(D) 재료의 품질

해설 | 세부 사항

후기의 여섯 번째 문장에서 아다모비치 씨가 저의 모니터가 꽤 무거워서 책상 높이를 수동으로 조정하는 것이 다소 어렵게 느껴진다(because my monitors ~ manually is somewhat difficult)며 전반적으로 만족하지만 전자동 모델을 제공하는 것을 고려해 주면 좋겠다(I'm pleased overall ~ electric version of the model)고 했으므로 정답은 (B)이다.

33 아다모비치 씨는 어떤 책상 모델을 갖고 있을 것 같은가?

(A) 이즈 데스크 프로 2000　　(B) 이즈 데스크 프로 3000

(C) 이즈 데스크 프로 4000　　(D) 이즈 데스크 프로 퀵

해설 | **연계**

후기의 세 번째 문장에서 아다모비치 씨가 저는 키가 2미터
가까이 된다(I am nearly two meters tall)고 했고 다섯 번째
문장에서 일을 하려면 대형 컴퓨터 모니터를 사용해야 하기
때문에 모니터 두 대가 모두 책상에 들어가서 다행(Since I
need to use large ~ my monitors fit on the desk)이라고
했다. 웹페이지의 이즈 데스크 프로 4000 모델 설명에 대형
모니터 최대 2대 탑재 가능(Accommodates up to 2 large
monitors), 키 큰 사용자에게 적합(Ideal for tall users)이라고
나와 있으므로 정답은 (C)이다.

34 웹페이지에서 모든 이즈 데스크 프로 모델에 대해 명시한 것은?

(A) 특정 기간 내에 반환될 수 있다.

(B) 쉽게 운반될 수 있도록 설계되었다.

(C) 작은 사무실 공간에 잘 맞는다.

(D) 두 대의 컴퓨터 모니터를 놓을 수 있다.

해설 | **Not/True**

웹페이지의 마지막 단락 첫 문장에서 모든 책상에는 30일 만족
보장 프로그램이 제공된다(All our desks come with ~
Guarantee program)며 책상을 반품할 경우 전액 환불해
준다(If you return your desk, you will receive a full
refund)고 했으므로 정답은 (A)이다.

어휘 | period 기간　transport 운반하다

35 드라크만 씨가 추천하는 책상에 대해 어떤 결론을 내릴 수 있는가?

(A) 가격이 550달러 미만이다.

(B) 무료로 배송된다.

(C) 한 가지 크기로만 구매 가능하다.

(D) 배송되는 데 한 달 이상 걸릴 것이다.

해설 | **연계**

이메일의 네 번째 문장에서 드라크만 씨가 이즈 데스크 프로
커스텀을 주문하기로 선택하시면 현재 갖고 계신 책상을 전액
환불로 반품하실 수 있도록 해 드리겠다(If you choose to
order ~ for a full refund)며 이즈 데스크 프로 커스텀을
추천했고, 웹페이지에 따르면 이즈 데스크 프로 커스텀은 다양한
가격에 5~6주 후 배송된다(price varies, ships in 5-6
weeks)고 나와 있으므로 정답은 (D)이다.

Paraphrasing　지문의 ships in 5-6 weeks
→ 보기의 more than one month to be shipped

[36-40] 이메일+기사+지도

수신: 파르한 수리야니

발신: 줄리아 샌즈

날짜: 3월 1일

제목: 당신의 제안

수리야니 씨께,

**36칼자노 엔터프라이즈의 사업 확장 계획에 기여해 주셔서
감사합니다.** 제안을 요청했던 일이 직원들로부터 압도적인 반응을
얻어 무척 기뻤습니다.

**37사업 확장 위원회는 펀우드 쇼핑 플라자(FSP)에 매장을 열자는
당신의 제안을 신중하게 검토했습니다.** 그 과정에서 몇 가지 우려
사항이 분명해졌습니다. 첫째, 최근 몇 년간 이 지역에서는 인구
이동의 결과로 소매업체의 수가 감소했습니다. 따라서 우리는 판매가
잘해 봐야 약세를 보일 것으로 예상합니다. 게다가, **38우리의 주요
경쟁 업체 중 한 곳인 힐탑이 7월에 FSP에 지점을 열 것이라는
것을 알게 되었습니다.** 만일 우리도 그곳에 매장을 낸다면, 그들과
우리의 사업에 상당한 제품 중복이 있을 것이고 판매에도 영향을
미칠 것입니다. **37그래서 위원회는 당신의 제안을 실행하는 것이 현
시점에서는 실효성이 없다고 결론 내렸습니다.**

우리의 결정을 이해해 주시기 바랍니다. 당신의 의견에 다시 한 번
감사드리며 본 계획과 관련하여 다른 제안이 있으시면 환영하는
바입니다.

줄리아 샌즈, 사업 확장 계획 의장

칼자노 엔터프라이즈

어휘 | contribution 기여　expansion 확장　initiative
계획　overwhelming 압도적인　response 반응　apparent
분명한　decline 감소　relocation 이동　anticipate 예상하다
at best 기껏　competitor 경쟁자　significant 상당한
overlap 중복　impact 영향을 주다　conclude 결론을 내리다
implementation 실행　practical 실현 가능한　appreciate
인정하다　input 의견

펀우드 (6월 20일) —**38다음 달, 루나미엘이라는 브랜드명으로
아이스크림과 냉동 요거트 및 다양한 유제품을 취급하는 기업인
힐탑이 펀우드 쇼핑 플라자(FSP)에 지점을 연다. 39매장은 가젯 헛의
맞은 편에 위치할 예정이다. 40힐탑은 '칠리 땅콩버터'와 '로즈워터
피스타치오'와 같은 놀라운 아이스크림과 냉동 요거트 품목으로 냉동
디저트 애호가들을 사로잡을 것이 분명하다.** 그리고 이 기업은 재료를
현지에서 구입하기 때문에 이 지역의 다른 업체들도 힐탑 매장이
있음으로 인해 이익을 얻을 수 있을 것이다.

업계 관계자들은 지난 9개월 동안 네 군데 업체가 소비자의 관심
부족으로 FSP 지점을 닫았다고 지적하며 힐탑의 움직임에 놀라움을
표했다. 그럼에도 불구하고 여타 기업들이 힐탑의 예를 따를 것이라는
추측이 있으며, 이론상 칼자노 엔터프라이즈가 그중 하나로 여겨지고
있다. 그러나 회사 대변인은 이러한 추측을 부인했다. 그녀는 쇼핑
센터에 매장을 열자는 제안서가 회사 경영진에 제출되었으나, 고급급
임원들은 이에 대해 지지를 표명하지 않았다고 말했다.

FSP의 기타 매장에 대한 정보는 www.fernshops.com에서 확인할 수
있다.

어휘 | market (상품을) 내놓다　remarkable 놀라운　treat
간식　ingredient 재료　presence 존재　insider 관계자
point out 지적하다　lack 부족　consumer interest
소비자 관심　speculation 추측　in theory 이론상으로는
spokesperson 대변인　deny 부인하다　official 임원

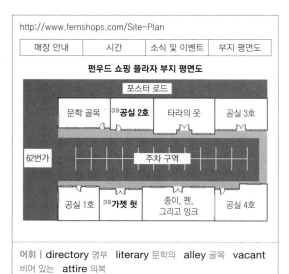

http://www.fernshops.com/Site-Plan

| 매장 안내 | 시간 | 소식 및 이벤트 | 부지 평면도 |

펀우드 쇼핑 플라자 부지 평면도

포스터 로드

| 문학 골목 | ³⁹공실 2호 | 타라의 옷 | 공실 3호 |

62번가 | 주차 구역 |

| 공실 1호 | ³⁹가젯 헛 | 종이, 펜, 그리고 잉크 | 공실 4호 |

어휘 | directory 명부 literary 문학의 alley 골목 vacant 비어 있는 attire 의복

36 사업 확장 계획에 대해 명시된 것은?
(A) 직원들로부터 많은 관심을 불러일으켰다.
(B) 젊은 고객 유치를 목표로 한다.
(C) 수리야니 씨가 개발했다.
(D) 7월에 끝날 예정이다.

해설 | Not/True
이메일의 첫 문장에서 칼자노 엔터프라이즈의 사업 확장 계획에 기여해 주셔서 감사하다(Thank you for your contribution ~ Calzano Enterprises)며 제안을 요청했던 일이 직원들로부터 압도적인 반응을 얻어 무척 기뻤다(We were pleased ~ overwhelming response from employees)고 했으므로 (A)가 정답이다.

Paraphrasing 지문의 met with such an overwhelming response → 보기의 generated much interest

어휘 | generate 발생시키다

37 이메일의 목적은 무엇인가?
(A) 직원 설문 조사 결과 발표
(B) 아이디어에 대한 거부 이유 설명
(C) 경쟁사에 대한 정보 수집
(D) 회사의 장점 강조

해설 | 주제/목적
이메일의 두 번째 단락 첫 문장에서 사업 확장 위원회는 펀우드 쇼핑 플라자(FSP)에 매장을 열자는 당신의 제안을 신중히 검토했다(The Business Expansion Committee ~ Fernwood Shopping Plaza (FSP))고 했고 뒤이어 여러 이유에 대해 설명한 뒤 같은 단락 마지막 문장에서 그래서 위원회는 당신의 제안을 실행하는 것이 현 시점에서는 실효성이 없다고 결론 내렸다(The committee has ~ not practical at this time)고 했다. 따라서 이 이메일은 직원의 매장 오픈 제안을 고사하게 된 이유를 설명하기 위한 것이므로 (B)가 정답이다.

어휘 | reject 거부하다 gather 모으다 highlight 강조하다 strength 장점

38 칼자노 엔터프라이즈는 어떤 산업군에 속하는가?
(A) 인력 채용   (B) 엔터테인먼트
(C) 식품 제조   (D) 자산 관리

해설 | 연계
이메일의 두 번째 단락 다섯 번째 문장에서 칼자노 엔터프라이즈의 주요 경쟁업체 중 한 곳인 힐탑이 7월에 FSP에 지점을 열 것이라는 것을 알게 되었다(it has come to our attention ~ FSP in July)고 했고, 기사의 첫 문장에서 다음 달에 루나미엘이라는 브랜드명으로 아이스크림과 냉동 요거트 및 다양한 유제품을 취급하는 기업인 힐탑이 펀우드 쇼핑 플라자(FSP)에 지점을 연다(Next month, Hilltop, the company ~ Fernwood Shopping Plaza (FSP))고 했으므로 칼자노 엔터프라이즈는 힐탑과 같은 유제품 업체임을 알 수 있다. 따라서 정답은 (C)이다.

Paraphrasing 지문의 ice cream, frozen yogurt, and various other milk products → 보기의 food

39 힐탑은 FSP에서 몇 호실에 위치할 예정인가?
(A) 1호실   (B) 2호실
(C) 3호실   (D) 4호실

해설 | 연계
기사의 첫 단락 두 번째 문장에서 힐탑 매장은 가젯 헛의 맞은 편에 위치할 예정(The store will be located across from The Gadget Hut)이라고 했고, 지도에 따르면 가젯 헛의 맞은 편에는 공실 2호가 있으므로 정답은 (B)이다.

40 기사는 힐탑의 냉동 제품의 어떤 특성에 대해 강조하는가?
(A) 건강한 재료   (B) 흥미로운 색상
(C) 높은 품질   (D) 독특한 맛

해설 | 세부 사항
기사의 첫 단락 세 번째 문장에서 힐탑은 '칠리 땅콩버터'와 '로즈워터 피스타치오'와 같은 놀라운 아이스크림과 냉동 요거트 품목으로 냉동 디저트 애호가들을 사로잡을 것이 분명하다(With such remarkable ice cream ~ attract lovers of frozen treats)고 한 것으로 보아 독특한 맛이 제품의 특징임을 알 수 있다. 따라서 (D)가 정답이다.

Paraphrasing 지문의 remarkable varieties → 보기의 unique flavors

[41-45] 청구서+이메일+이메일

웰니스 아웃룩 클리닉

5월 28일   고객 ID: 3076
                                    ⁴⁵만기일: 6월 30일

소니아 아도
4052 행콕 가
코르발리스, 오리건 주 97330

서비스 날짜	설명	참조 코드	금액
5/15	60분 딥 스트레치 치료	0029	80달러
5/15	⁴³30분 딥 티슈 마사지	⁴³0018	40달러
5/15	핫스톤 적용	0074	15달러
	총액		135달러

⁴¹저희의 가장 최신식 클리닉 지점을 방문해 주셔서 감사합니다! 방문하시고 난 후 훨씬 좋아지셨기를 바랍니다. 청구서 관련 문의 사항에 대해서는 pay@wellnessoutlookclinic.com으로 저희 청구서 발급 부서에 연락 주세요.

어휘 | due date 만기일 description 설명 reference 참조 application 적용 invoice 청구서 billing 청구서 발부

수신: 〈pay@wellnessoutlookclinic.com〉
발신: 소니아 아도 〈saddo74@rapidonet.com〉
날짜: 5월 31일
제목: 몇 가지 문의 사항

웰니스 아웃룩 클리닉 여러분께,

저는 주치의로부터 귀사의 마사지 치료사를 소개받았습니다. 제나 와이즈먼으로부터 받은 서비스는 전문적이고 꼼꼼했습니다. 그녀는 예의 바르고 제 요구에 바로 응해 주었습니다. **⁴²다음 달에 그녀에게 추가로 치료를 예약하고 싶습니다. 6월 21일에 가능할까요?**

제가 받은 청구서에 대해서도 질문이 있습니다. 치료를 시작할 때 와이즈먼 씨는 치료에서 제공하는 다양한 치료 옵션을 보여주셨습니다. **⁴³저는 스트레치 치료 동안 딥 티슈 마사지를 받기로 선택했습니다. 저는 이 서비스가 딥 스트레치 치료의 일부로 포함되어 있다고 이해하고 있습니다. 저는 60분만 치료를 받았는데, 어째서 제 치료 시간에 마사지 시간 30분이 추가 청구되어 있나요?**

소니아 아도

어휘 | refer 소개하다 thorough 꼼꼼한 courteous 정중한 responsive 즉각 대응하는 present 제시하다 treatment 치료 opt for ~을 선택하다

수신: 소니아 아도 〈saddo74@rapidonet.com〉
발신: 〈pay@wellnessoutlookclinic.com〉
날짜: 6월 1일
제목: 답장: 몇 가지 문의 사항

아도 씨께,

방문하셨을 때 받으신 치료가 만족스러우셨다고 듣게 되어 기쁩니다. 다음 약속을 잡기 위해 예약 담당자가 전화 드리도록 하겠습니다.

고객님께서 걱정하신 부분에 관해서는, 청구서에 기재된 코드 중 하나에 오류가 있었습니다. **⁴⁴와이즈먼 씨와 고객님의 치료에 관해 확인하고 청구서를 수정했습니다.** 1시간짜리 치료 시간과 핫스톤 적용 서비스만 요금이 부과될 것입니다.

⁴⁴, ⁴⁵고객님의 새 청구서를 처리하였고 오늘 저녁까지 발송해 드리겠습니다. 저희 측 실수로 인한 일이니, **⁴⁵만기일이 한 달 연장될 예정입니다.**

올리버 곤솔린

어휘 | attention 치료, 처리 coordinator 조정자 adjustment 수정 process 처리하다 extend 연장하다

41 청구서가 웰니스 아웃룩 클리닉에 대해 암시하는 것은?
(A) 진료소가 여러 곳 있다.
(B) 피트니스 강좌를 제공한다.
(C) 새 웹사이트를 갖고 있다.
(D) 자주 방문하는 사람들을 위해 할인을 제공한다.

해설 | **추론/암시**
청구서 하단에 저희의 가장 최신식 클리닉 지점을 방문해 주셔서 감사하다(Thank you for visiting our newest clinic location!)고 한 것으로 보아 웰니스 아웃룩 클리닉은 아도 씨가 방문한 지점 외에 여러 지점이 있음을 짐작할 수 있다. 따라서 (A)가 정답이다.

어휘 | multiple 다수의 frequent 빈번한

42 첫 번째 이메일에 따르면, 아도 씨는 무엇을 하고 싶어 하는가?
(A) 다른 마사지 제공자에게 치료받기
(B) 서비스에 대한 후기 작성하기
(C) 주치의에게 변경 사항 알려 주기
(D) 추가 진료 예약 잡기

해설 | **세부 사항**
첫 이메일의 첫 단락 네 번째 문장에서 아도 씨가 다음 달에 제나 와이즈먼 씨에게 추가로 치료를 예약하고 싶다(I would like to book an additional session with her next month)며 6월 21일에 가능한지(Is she available on June 21?)를 묻고 있으므로 (D)가 정답이다.

Paraphrasing 지문의 book an additional session
→ 보기의 Schedule another appointment

43 아도 씨는 어떤 코드 때문에 걱정하는가?
(A) 3076   (B) 0029
(C) 0018   (D) 0074

해설 | **연계**
첫 이메일의 두 번째 단락 세 번째 문장에서 아도 씨는 스트레치 치료 동안 딥 티슈 마사지를 받기로 선택(I opted for ~ stretch session)했으며 이 서비스가 딥 스트레치 치료의 일부로 포함되어 있다고 이해하고 있다(It was my understanding ~ deep stretch session)고 했고, 60분만 치료를 받았는데 어째서 치료 시간에 마사지 시간 30분이 추가 청구되어 있는지(Why am I being charged ~ only seen for 60 minutes?)에 대해 문의하고 있다. 송장의 표에 따르면 아도 씨가 문제로 삼은 30분짜리 딥 티슈 마사지(30-minute deep tissue massage)는 0018 코드이므로 (C)가 정답이다.

44 곤솔린 씨는 누구일 것 같은가?
(A) 예약 담당자   (B) 청구서 발부 담당자
(C) 마사지 치료사   (D) 주치의

해설 | **추론/암시**
두 번째 이메일의 두 번째 단락 두 번째 문장에서 곤솔린 씨가 자신이 와이즈먼 씨와 고객님의 치료에 관해 확인하고 청구서를 수정했다(I spoke to Ms. Wiseman ~ adjustment to your invoice)고 했고, 세 번째 단락 첫 문장에서 고객님의 새 청구서를 처리하였고 오늘 저녁까지 보내 드리겠다(I have processed ~ by the end of the day)고 한 것으로 보아 청구서 발부를 담당하고 있음을 알 수 있다. 따라서 정답은 (B)이다.

45 아도 씨의 수정된 청구서의 납기일은 언제인가?

(A) 5월 15일
(B) 5월 31일
(C) 6월 30일
(D) 7월 30일

해설 | **연계**

청구서의 상단에 만기일(Due date)이 6월 30일(June 30)이라고 나와 있고, 두 번째 이메일의 세 번째 단락 첫 문장에서 아도 씨에게 고객님의 새 청구서를 처리하였고 오늘 저녁까지 보내 드리겠다(I have processed ~ by the end of the day)며 만기일이 한 달 연장될 예정(the due date will be extended by one month)이라고 했다. 따라서 새 청구서의 납기일은 원래의 6월 30일에서 한 달 뒤인 7월 30일임을 알 수 있으므로 (D)가 정답이다.

YBM

토익 단기공략 850⁺

실전 모의고사

YBM

LISTENING TEST

In the Listening test, you will be asked to demonstrate how well you understand spoken English. The entire Listening test will last approximately 45 minutes. There are four parts, and directions are given for each part. You must mark your answers on the separate answer sheet. Do not write your answers in your test book.

PART 1

Directions: For each question in this part, you will hear four statements about a picture in your test book. When you hear the statements, you must select the one statement that best describes what you see in the picture. Then find the number of the question on your answer sheet and mark your answer. The statements will not be printed in your test book and will be spoken only one time.

Statement (C), "They're sitting at a table," is the best description of the picture, so you should select answer (C) and mark it on your answer sheet.

1.

2.

GO ON TO THE NEXT PAGE ➤

3.

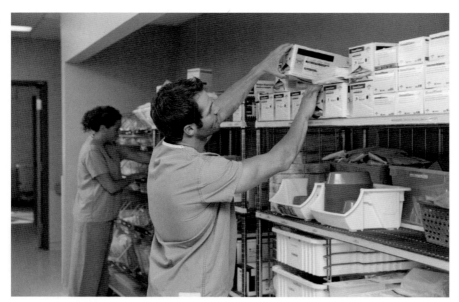

4.

5.

6.

GO ON TO THE NEXT PAGE

PART 2

Directions: You will hear a question or statement and three responses spoken in English. They will not be printed in your test book and will be spoken only one time. Select the best response to the question or statement and mark the letter (A), (B), or (C) on your answer sheet.

7. Mark your answer on your answer sheet.

8. Mark your answer on your answer sheet.

9. Mark your answer on your answer sheet.

10. Mark your answer on your answer sheet.

11. Mark your answer on your answer sheet.

12. Mark your answer on your answer sheet.

13. Mark your answer on your answer sheet.

14. Mark your answer on your answer sheet.

15. Mark your answer on your answer sheet.

16. Mark your answer on your answer sheet.

17. Mark your answer on your answer sheet.

18. Mark your answer on your answer sheet.

19. Mark your answer on your answer sheet.

20. Mark your answer on your answer sheet.

21. Mark your answer on your answer sheet.

22. Mark your answer on your answer sheet.

23. Mark your answer on your answer sheet.

24. Mark your answer on your answer sheet.

25. Mark your answer on your answer sheet.

26. Mark your answer on your answer sheet.

27. Mark your answer on your answer sheet.

28. Mark your answer on your answer sheet.

29. Mark your answer on your answer sheet.

30. Mark your answer on your answer sheet.

31. Mark your answer on your answer sheet.

PART 3

Directions: You will hear some conversations between two or more people. You will be asked to answer three questions about what the speakers say in each conversation. Select the best response to each question and mark the letter (A), (B), (C), or (D) on your answer sheet. The conversations will not be printed in your test book and will be spoken only one time.

32. What is the purpose of the call?

(A) To cancel a service
(B) To apply for a job
(C) To pay a bill
(D) To report a problem

33. According to the woman, what has the business changed?

(A) A software program
(B) A branch location
(C) Its monthly prices
(D) Its business hours

34. What does the woman say she will do?

(A) Upgrade a package
(B) Issue a refund
(C) Update an address
(D) Send a new document

35. What is the conversation mainly about?

(A) Finance
(B) Healthcare
(C) Education
(D) Recycling

36. According to the woman, what was the cause of the problem?

(A) A business closure
(B) A staffing shortage
(C) An error on a calendar
(D) A broken vehicle

37. What will the listeners most likely hear next?

(A) A product review
(B) A traffic update
(C) Some advertisements
(D) Some interviews

38. What does the man tell the woman about?

(A) He will visit a client next week.
(B) He has to postpone a demonstration.
(C) He would like to hire temporary workers.
(D) He needs to cancel a business trip.

39. What does the man say about an order form?

(A) It was not received by the supplier.
(B) It was filled out incorrectly.
(C) It has not been approved by a manager.
(D) It can be downloaded from a Web site.

40. What will the woman probably do next?

(A) Schedule an interview
(B) Adjust a budget
(C) Update an agenda
(D) Register for an event

41. Why does the woman visit the business?

(A) To register for a tournament
(B) To buy some tickets
(C) To book a stadium tour
(D) To cancel a reservation

42. What should the woman select?

(A) What to drink
(B) When to begin
(C) Where to sit
(D) How to receive details

43. What does the man recommend doing?

(A) Joining a mailing list
(B) Bringing rain gear
(C) Keeping a receipt
(D) Using a shuttle service

GO ON TO THE NEXT PAGE

44. What does the woman need help with?

(A) Organizing some files
(B) Moving some furniture
(C) Painting a room
(D) Selecting some carpet

45. What does the woman say happened this morning?

(A) A delivery of supplies arrived.
(B) A water pipe broke.
(C) An employee was out sick.
(D) A computer malfunctioned.

46. Why does the woman say, "It separates into three pieces"?

(A) To agree with the man
(B) To give a warning
(C) To complain about an item
(D) To reassure the man

47. What is the topic of the conversation?

(A) Jewelry
(B) Appliances
(C) Footwear
(D) Automobiles

48. What does Ryan want to do?

(A) Purchase production equipment
(B) Increase a budget
(C) Change a supplier
(D) Conduct further testing

49. What does the woman suggest doing?

(A) Adding people to a team
(B) Changing a deadline
(C) Holding a meeting
(D) Researching a business

50. What most likely is the woman's job?

(A) Architect
(B) Lawyer
(C) Financial consultant
(D) University professor

51. What does the man ask the woman to do?

(A) Meet with board members
(B) Provide some feedback
(C) Recommend an employee
(D) Take on more work

52. What will be given to the woman?

(A) Bonus pay
(B) Extra vacation time
(C) A job promotion
(D) New equipment

53. What are the speakers discussing?

(A) A home appliance
(B) A security alarm
(C) A power tool
(D) A mobile phone

54. According to the woman, what feature do customers like about a product?

(A) Its compact size
(B) Its energy efficiency
(C) Its clear instructions
(D) Its quiet operation

55. Why does the woman say, "The French restaurant is always busy"?

(A) To explain a delay
(B) To make a suggestion
(C) To express disappointment
(D) To reject an invitation

56. What kind of event is being planned?

(A) A product launch party
(B) A music festival
(C) A sports match
(D) A company retreat

57. What is the woman concerned about?

(A) An arrival time
(B) A limited menu
(C) A lack of parking
(D) A safety issue

58. What is offered to the site's customers?

(A) A loyalty program
(B) Complimentary snacks
(C) Help with setup
(D) Video recording equipment

---

59. Where are the speakers?

(A) At a car dealership
(B) At a print shop
(C) At a fitness center
(D) At a restaurant

60. What problem does the man tell the woman about?

(A) A special offer has ended.
(B) A coupon contained a misprint.
(C) A form of payment cannot be used.
(D) A business will close soon.

61. What does the woman thank the man for?

(A) Recommending a business
(B) Saving a space
(C) Waiving a fee
(D) Calling another branch

Description	Code
Internet Connection Issues	101
New Operating System	102
Virus Removal	103
Memory Upgrade	104

62. What is the woman preparing to do?

(A) Place an order
(B) Purchase a computer
(C) Pay a bill
(D) Contact a client

63. Look at the graphic. Which code are the speakers looking at?

(A) 101
(B) 102
(C) 103
(D) 104

64. What does the man say will happen next month?

(A) A Web site will be launched.
(B) A task will be automated.
(C) A product will be discontinued.
(D) A fee will be changed.

GO ON TO THE NEXT PAGE

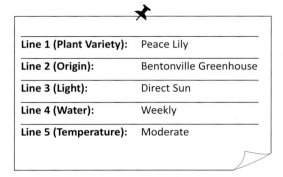

Line 1 (Plant Variety):	Peace Lily
Line 2 (Origin):	Bentonville Greenhouse
Line 3 (Light):	Direct Sun
Line 4 (Water):	Weekly
Line 5 (Temperature):	Moderate

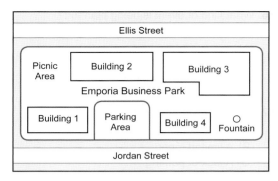

65. What does the man think is necessary?

(A) Hiring more workers
(B) Expanding delivery options
(C) Attending a festival
(D) Increasing prices

66. What does the woman say she would like to do?

(A) Change the business hours
(B) Use a different supplier
(C) Consult an expert
(D) Rent a vehicle

67. Look at the graphic. Which line of the label has an error?

(A) Line 2
(B) Line 3
(C) Line 4
(D) Line 5

68. Why will the man visit the woman?

(A) To give a sales presentation
(B) To drop off some samples
(C) To take some photographs
(D) To conduct an interview

69. Look at the graphic. In which building does the woman work?

(A) Building 1
(B) Building 2
(C) Building 3
(D) Building 4

70. What does the woman warn the man about?

(A) A phone service is having problems.
(B) There is a fee for parking.
(C) Traffic in the area is heavy.
(D) An entrance cannot be used.

Directions: You will hear some talks given by a single speaker. You will be asked to answer three questions about what the speaker says in each talk. Select the best response to each question and mark the letter (A), (B), (C), or (D) on your answer sheet. The talks will not be printed in your test book and will be spoken only one time.

71. What kind of business is being advertised?

(A) A cleaning company
(B) An accounting firm
(C) A hair salon
(D) A dental clinic

72. What will be available from June 1?

(A) Free consultations
(B) A walk-in service
(C) Startup discounts
(D) A second branch location

73. Why are the listeners encouraged to visit a Web site?

(A) To create an account
(B) To read customer reviews
(C) To download a coupon
(D) To see a list of fees

74. What does the speaker express appreciation about?

(A) An employee completed a task early.
(B) A manager approved a request.
(C) The listeners worked on the weekend.
(D) The listeners made useful suggestions.

75. What will take place on March 7?

(A) A building tour
(B) An awards ceremony
(C) A grand opening
(D) A trade fair

76. What does the speaker imply when he says, "there are quite a few rooms"?

(A) More time is needed for a task.
(B) More guests can be invited.
(C) A lot of employees will be needed.
(D) A payment may be changed.

77. What does the speaker say about the café?

(A) It mainly caters to vegetarians.
(B) It uses locally grown ingredients.
(C) It can be booked for private events.
(D) It has customers' ideas on its menu.

78. Who is Carmen?

(A) A cooking instructor
(B) An event planner
(C) A manager
(D) An investor

79. Why most likely does the speaker say, "I'm having it again tomorrow"?

(A) To explain a problem
(B) To recommend an item
(C) To emphasize a size
(D) To confirm her expertise

80. Where are the listeners?

(A) On an airplane
(B) On a train
(C) At a bus station
(D) At an airport

81. According to the speaker, what has caused a problem?

(A) Some equipment is broken.
(B) Severe weather was reported.
(C) Some tickets contained a misprint.
(D) A computer has malfunctioned.

82. Why should the listeners speak to an employee?

(A) To receive a snack
(B) To get an upgrade
(C) To request a refund
(D) To complete a form

83. Who most likely is the speaker?

(A) A truck mechanic
(B) An apartment manager
(C) A delivery person
(D) A sales representative

84. What kind of business does the speaker most likely work for?

(A) A mattress store
(B) A paper distributor
(C) An appliance manufacturer
(D) A utility company

85. What does the speaker mean when he says, "that section is empty"?

(A) He needs some contact information.
(B) He recommends a service.
(C) A product has not been selected.
(D) An address has not been confirmed.

---

86. What is the speaker mainly discussing?

(A) A building relocation
(B) An accounting program
(C) Security procedures
(D) Survey results

87. Why did the speaker hire BT Inc.?

(A) It was under a suggested budget.
(B) It was recommended by a colleague.
(C) It recently added new services.
(D) It is locally owned.

88. According to the speaker, what can the listeners get from Darlene?

(A) An access code
(B) A list of rules
(C) A temporary pass
(D) A business card

---

89. According to the speaker, what did the city do?

(A) Build a new public park
(B) Receive additional funding
(C) Sponsor some music lessons
(D) Make improvements to a school

90. Why are some people opposed to a project?

(A) Because of environmental damage
(B) Because of budget problems
(C) Because of noise disturbances
(D) Because of job shortages

91. What will the speaker most likely do next?

(A) Explain a policy
(B) Speak with listeners
(C) Interview an expert
(D) Introduce a product

---

92. What does the speaker apologize for?

(A) Some payments were made late.
(B) Some instructions were confusing.
(C) A machine is not working.
(D) A meeting ran longer than expected.

93. Where do the listeners work?

(A) In a fitness center
(B) In a library
(C) In a call center
(D) In a warehouse

94. What will be given to the listeners?

(A) Protective gear
(B) A new password
(C) Schedule updates
(D) Meal vouchers

Thursday	Friday	Saturday	Sunday
Rainy	Rainy	Partly Cloudy	Sunny

Regional Conference Schedule	
9:00	William Kline, Improving Teamwork
11:00	Zheng Lang, How to Find New Customers
Noon	Lunch
1:00	Rafael Alves, Time Management Skills
3:00	Chelsea Deacon, Social Media Advantages

95. What event is the news report about?

(A) A cooking demonstration
(B) A music competition
(C) A film festival
(D) A sports tournament

96. According to the speaker, what is available on a Web site?

(A) A map of the park
(B) A list of sponsors
(C) Parking passes
(D) Admission tickets

97. Look at the graphic. When will the event be held?

(A) On Thursday
(B) On Friday
(C) On Saturday
(D) On Sunday

98. What is the speaker calling the listener about?

(A) The directions to an office
(B) The number of participants
(C) A new product
(D) A change in a schedule

99. Look at the graphic. Who most likely is the listener?

(A) William Kline
(B) Zheng Lang
(C) Rafael Alves
(D) Chelsea Deacon

100. What is the listener asked to do by Thursday?

(A) Provide a mailing address
(B) Make travel arrangements
(C) Sign a contract
(D) Send presentation materials

This is the end of the Listening test. Turn to Part 5 in your test book.

GO ON TO THE NEXT PAGE

READING TEST

In the Reading test, you will read a variety of texts and answer several different types of reading comprehension questions. The entire Reading test will last 75 minutes. There are three parts, and directions are given for each part. You are encouraged to answer as many questions as possible within the time allowed.

You must mark your answers on the separate answer sheet. Do not write your answers in your test book.

PART 5

Directions: A word or phrase is missing in each of the sentences below. Four answer choices are given below each sentence. Select the best answer to complete the sentence. Then mark the letter (A), (B), (C), or (D) on your answer sheet.

101. Mr. Quimby needs several staff members to assist ------- with the booth at the trade fair.
(A) his
(B) he
(C) him
(D) himself

102. The department store's loyalty club members receive advanced ------- of sales promotions.
(A) notify
(B) notification
(C) noticed
(D) noticeably

103. ------- a month, the maintenance team checks the air filters in the air conditioning system.
(A) Since
(B) Directly
(C) Exactly
(D) Twice

104. Mr. Carlyle was not allowed to enter the building ------- presenting a valid ID.
(A) because
(B) regarding
(C) despite
(D) which

105. Promotional events for Petunia Footwear's new sneakers will be held ------- the country.
(A) aboard
(B) upon
(C) toward
(D) across

106. Lab technicians should ------- open the sealed containers to avoid spillage.
(A) more cautious
(B) caution
(C) cautious
(D) cautiously

107. BV Financial is dedicated to keeping customers' personal information ------- at all times.
(A) protective
(B) affordable
(C) confidential
(D) generated

108. Ms. Simmons ------- the instructions several times so there would be no confusion among the loading crew.
(A) repetition
(B) repeated
(C) repetitive
(D) repeating

109. The new woodworking machines will -------
a considerable portion of the room.
(A) take up
(B) apply to
(C) stand by
(D) set up

110. ------- any visitors to the trade fair decided
to hire Renner Carpeting for a project.
(A) Finely
(B) Very
(C) Hardly
(D) Only

111. Following the awards ceremony, Ms. Sievert
------- her colleagues on their various
notable achievements.
(A) supervised
(B) congratulated
(C) acquainted
(D) reflected

112. The owner of the historic building explained
that costs had become ------- due to a need
for ongoing repairs.
(A) considerably
(B) considerable
(C) consideration
(D) consider

113. One aim of Hamada Inc.'s employee retreat
is to build cooperation ------- each
department.
(A) until
(B) within
(C) over
(D) during

114. Depending on the specified amount, the
bank ------- you to send the funds in two
separate transactions.
(A) is required
(B) must be required
(C) may require
(D) to be requiring

115. ------- Crane Housewares builds its
distribution center, the local economy will
benefit greatly.
(A) Rather
(B) Next to
(C) Wherever
(D) In order that

116. The battery-operated camping lantern emits
light up to 30 feet in any -------.
(A) direction
(B) directs
(C) directive
(D) director

117. The Westler Clinic's Health Festival was
created to teach residents about the
importance ------- preventative health
measures.
(A) with
(B) by
(C) at
(D) of

118. The Write-Way staff puts up ------- historical
manuscripts on its Web site for the general
public to enjoy.
(A) simply
(B) simplification
(C) simplifies
(D) simplified

119. ------- the application documents are
received, the paperwork will be sent to the
Loan Approval Committee.
(A) Apart from
(B) Even though
(C) As soon as
(D) Not only

120. CT Enterprises carries out regular audits of
its investment portfolio to make sure the
funds ------- responsibly.
(A) had been reinvested
(B) are being reinvested
(C) to be reinvested
(D) would have reinvested

GO ON TO THE NEXT PAGE

121. After visiting the headquarters, it will be easier to navigate the building on ------- trips.

(A) subsequent
(B) former
(C) suitable
(D) overdue

122. Indigo Insurance issued new ------- and reporting procedures for employees who take business trips.

(A) reimburse
(B) reimburses
(C) reimbursement
(D) reimbursed

123. One of Mr. Thornton's admirable ------- reported in his evaluation was his positive attitude.

(A) disciplines
(B) requirements
(C) qualities
(D) rewards

124. Analysts believe the increase in sales is ------- the result of Tye Software's advertising campaign.

(A) cleared
(B) clearly
(C) clearing
(D) clear

125. The theater's stage manager must be prepared for ------- the director requests.

(A) another
(B) anything
(C) every
(D) that

126. In the past quarter, the Rinehart branch finished fifth ------- in new account acquisitions.

(A) readily
(B) favorably
(C) overall
(D) elsewhere

127. ------- the expansion of the spa is completed, there is enough space for a steam room and on-site café.

(A) Similarly
(B) Now that
(C) Whether
(D) On top of

128. Branson Industrial is currently seeking an architect ------- specializes in urban design for residential properties.

(A) however
(B) who
(C) what
(D) whose

129. ------- flavoring is added to some of the juice drinks from Gelato Beverages to enhance the taste.

(A) Perishable
(B) Artificial
(C) Unforeseen
(D) Indicative

130. The manager was hesitant to approve the proposal for flexible working hours but eventually she -------.

(A) paid back
(B) used up
(C) gave in
(D) handed down

PART 6

Directions: Read the texts that follow. A word, phrase, or sentence is missing in parts of each text. Four answer choices for each question are given below the text. Select the best answer to complete the text. Then mark the letter (A), (B), (C), or (D) on your answer sheet.

Questions 131-134 refer to the following advertisement.

Special deal for first-time GetGo Car Rentals customers!

GetGo Car Rentals is offering discounts to new customers. -------
131.
. That's why we're giving you

significant savings on your first rental. Depending on the size of the vehicle you choose, you

could be paying ------- $10 per day, including insurance, to rent a vehicle. To take advantage of
132.

this special offer, ------- visit our Web site and create an account. There you can browse the
133.

vehicle you would like to ------- and input the rental dates. At checkout, use the code
134.

NEWGETGO.

---

131. (A) You must be at least eighteen years
old to use the service.
(B) Fuel-efficient cars have been added
to our fleet recently.
(C) We're confident you'll love our
excellent rental service.
(D) Dropping off the car at a different
location is allowed.

132. (A) otherwise
(B) nearby
(C) less than
(D) instead of

133. (A) even
(B) just
(C) soon
(D) ever

134. (A) cancel
(B) reserve
(C) maintain
(D) proceed

GO ON TO THE NEXT PAGE

Questions 135-138 refer to the following instructions.

Letz Inc. pays for all expenses related to travel for business purposes. Company credit cards

------- to certain senior members of staff. These can be used while on business trips. However,
135.

even employees without a company card can receive ------ for business-related expenses. You
136.

should keep your receipts for purchases and complete a request form. ------ must include
137.

information about the date of and reason for each purchase. ------ . Send an e-mail to one of
138.

our members, and we will get back to you with a response as quickly as possible.

135. (A) are issuing
(B) are issued
(C) issue
(D) issued

136. (A) benefit
(B) reimbursement
(C) contribution
(D) information

137. (A) They
(B) Those
(C) It
(D) We

138. (A) Please select the travel time that is
most convenient for you.
(B) Our finance team is happy to answer
any questions you may have.
(C) Meeting customers in person is a
good way to build relationships.
(D) You must then return the card after
you return.

To: sylviaherrington@brammail.com
From: zapata_d@locklearco.com
Date: April 10
Subject: Senior Analyst Position
Attachment: contract_sample.docx

Dear Ms. Herrington,

After ------- the various job candidates, our hiring committee has decided to offer you the
         139.

position of Senior Analyst. Please find attached a contract with our proposed terms. You can see

in the contract that you ------- a $500 bonus upon signing the contract. The start date for this
                      140.

position is April 28. On the first day of work, all employees attend an orientation session. -------
                                                                                        141.

learning about the company's policies, employees complete the necessary HR paperwork.

If you have any questions, please feel free to contact me at this address. ------- .
                                                                      142.

Sincerely,

Darren Zapata
HR Manager, Locklear Co.

---

139. (A) achieving
     (B) obtaining
     (C) discussing
     (D) accepting

140. (A) did receive
     (B) will receive
     (C) receives
     (D) receiving

141. (A) As soon as
     (B) In addition to
     (C) Both
     (D) Only

142. (A) These duties may change over
         time.
     (B) The building should not be difficult
         to find.
     (C) It is checked regularly throughout
         business hours.
     (D) Please select an interview time in
         advance.

GO ON TO THE NEXT PAGE

(September 8)—Odessa, which produces tires for a variety of automotive companies, has announced plans to research an innovative recycling idea. The company aims to turn rubber tires ------- pellets that would then be used to cast new tires. Car sales are projected to increase
143.
by eighteen percent over the next three years, resulting in an accompanying increase in tires sales. ------- . Odessa officials hope to ease this problem.
144.

The ------- is being partially funded by a government grant. Public funding will be used to hire
145.
researchers and carry out tests. If Odessa can provide a new solution for ------- , it would be a
146.
great benefit to not only the industry and consumers but also the environment.

143. (A) as
   (B) into
   (C) against
   (D) at

144. (A) Nevertheless, Odessa has become a market leader.
   (B) The high content of rubber makes the tires flexible.
   (C) Furthermore, hybrid vehicles are gaining more popularity.
   (D) This sort of demand can put pressure on raw materials.

145. (A) errand
   (B) forecast
   (C) initiative
   (D) favor

146. (A) manufactures
   (B) manufacturing
   (C) manufactured
   (D) manufacturer

PART 7

Directions: In this part you will read a selection of texts, such as magazine and newspaper articles, e-mails, and instant messages. Each text or set of texts is followed by several questions. Select the best answer for each question and mark the letter (A), (B), (C), or (D) on your answer sheet.

Questions 147-148 refer to the following text message.

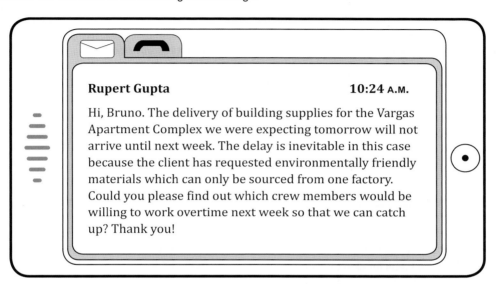

Rupert Gupta   10:24 A.M.

Hi, Bruno. The delivery of building supplies for the Vargas Apartment Complex we were expecting tomorrow will not arrive until next week. The delay is inevitable in this case because the client has requested environmentally friendly materials which can only be sourced from one factory. Could you please find out which crew members would be willing to work overtime next week so that we can catch up? Thank you!

147. Where most likely does Mr. Gupta work?

(A) At an accounting firm
(B) At a construction company
(C) At a delivery firm
(D) At a real estate agency

148. What does Mr. Gupta want Bruno to do?

(A) Research environmental regulations
(B) Speak to some employees
(C) Work additional hours
(D) Inspect a factory

GO ON TO THE NEXT PAGE

≡ E-Mail message ≡

To:	Paradise Sporting Goods Employees
From:	Kenny Hoyt
Date:	October 6
Subject:	Annual Clearance Sale

Our Annual Clearance Sale will begin on October 10 and run for two weeks. I want to make sure that you remember that we do not allow returns on clearance items. We will put up signs about this in the display areas to keep customers informed.

Should you encounter a customer who is upset about not being able to make a return, please direct them to the shift manager, who will handle all of these cases. I appreciate your cooperation.

Sincerely,

Kenny Hoyt
Store Manager, Paradise Sporting Goods

---

149. What is the purpose of the e-mail?

(A) To ask for ideas for sign designs
(B) To request help in setting up displays
(C) To remind staff about a policy
(D) To announce changes to a sales period

150. According to Mr. Hoyt, what will the shift manager do?

(A) Deal with customer complaints
(B) Check the level of stock
(C) Issue refunds on returns
(D) Determine the discount level

http://www.sullivanpublishing.com	▼

Home	Publications List	Careers	**About**	Contact

Sullivan Publishing was founded twelve years ago with the goal of sharing unique stories and perspectives with the world. We work with both seasoned and amateur writers, helping them through every step of the editing process and providing marketing support.

Our staff benefits from our recently launched Strive Program, which pairs junior staff members with senior ones. Through the program, junior staff members can improve their skills and advance along their career paths in the field.

For information about in-house job opportunities at Sullivan Publishing, click here.

151. What is suggested about Sullivan Publishing's staff?

(A) They are allowed to work remotely.
(B) They sometimes deal with first-time authors.
(C) They take ongoing marketing classes.
(D) They have impressive educational backgrounds.

152. Why was the Strive Program launched?

(A) To support career development
(B) To promote healthy work habits
(C) To improve the company's reputation
(D) To identify experts in the field

GO ON TO THE NEXT PAGE

Ella Alvarez	9:19 A.M.
Todd, will you be here soon? The representatives from Nubia Enterprises have just arrived for the building tour.	

Todd Broderick	9:20 A.M.
There was an accident on Highway 17, so traffic congestion is heavy. Could you handle it yourself?	

Ella Alvarez	9:21 A.M.
Sure. I've done that kind of task before.	

Todd Broderick	9:22 A.M.
Thank you so much. I'll be there in half an hour or less, definitely before the scheduled time for the presentation.	

Ella Alvarez	9:23 A.M.
That's a relief. This is one of our largest accounts. We've got to make a good impression.	

Todd Broderick	9:25 A.M.
Exactly. I'm doing my best, and I'll be there shortly.	

153. What does Ms. Alvarez agree to do?

(A) Deliver a presentation
(B) Give a tour
(C) Reschedule a visit
(D) Give Mr. Broderick a ride

154. At 9:25 A.M., what does Mr. Broderick mean when he writes, "Exactly"?

(A) He will take a different route next time.
(B) He thinks the company made a good impression.
(C) He will create an account for Ms. Alvarez.
(D) He understands that a client is important.

Spotlight on Charlotte Francis

As part of our monthly Spotlight series, we would like to recognize Charlotte Francis from the Quality Control Team. —[1]—. We are impressed with Charlotte's attention to detail, especially when assessing prototypes before we begin mass production. —[2]—. Recently, Charlotte discovered a fault in our new Progon space heater which could have caused dangerous overheating, resulting in a costly product recall. —[3]—.

Because of this incident, Charlotte has drafted a plan to make the quality control checks more comprehensive. —[4]—. We appreciate all of the contributions Charlotte is making to the company.

---

155. Why was the article written?

(A) To introduce a new employee
(B) To announce a product recall
(C) To praise an employee's efforts
(D) To explain a monthly article

156. How did Ms. Francis contribute to the Progon project?

(A) She organized some feedback comments.
(B) She recommended a product designer.
(C) She repaired some overheating equipment.
(D) She noticed a potential safety issue.

157. In which of the positions marked [1], [2], [3], and [4] does the following sentence best belong?

"The additional steps will help to prevent future issues."

(A) [1]
(B) [2]
(C) [3]
(D) [4]

GO ON TO THE NEXT PAGE

Questions 158-160 refer to the following information.

Thank you for purchasing a Filbert Co. Digital Kitchen Scale! Regular maintenance of this scale will ensure that it will last far beyond the two-year warranty. We recommend wiping down the outside of the scale after each use and performing a deep clean every six months. When the red light turns on, this signifies that the batteries need to be replaced.

To take a measurement, turn the scale on, place your container (if used) on the scale and press the Zero button. If the red light is flashing, it means the scale is on an uneven surface. Please note that the scale is designed to operate only at room temperature. The accuracy of the scale may be compromised if this is not the case.

158. Where would this information most likely be printed?

(A) In a newspaper advertisement
(B) On a leaflet inside a product's box
(C) In a product catalog
(D) On a store's sign

159. According to the information, when should a battery be replaced?

(A) Every six months
(B) Every two years
(C) When the red light turns on
(D) When the red light starts blinking

160. What is indicated about the scale's accuracy?

(A) It is guaranteed under the warranty.
(B) It can be affected by the temperature.
(C) It should be tested regularly.
(D) It may decline over time.

▶ ◀   http://www.pompanoaquarium.com

Pompano Aquarium and Research Center

The Pompano Aquarium is dedicated to not only teaching the public about the diversity of marine life but also helping endangered species. A portion of our proceeds from admission fees and events goes directly toward our rehabilitation facility. This facility helps injured animals, such as sea turtles, to recover and eventually be released back into the wild.

To learn more about this process, we invite the public to a lecture by Dr. Tammy Seda, who is currently studying the effects of commercial fishing on the Acosta Bay area. Dr. Seda will talk about her team's most recent efforts, developments in this field, and opportunities for volunteerism. The lecture will take place at 4 P.M. on Saturday, April 4, in the aquarium's auditorium. Tickets are $8 per person, but those with Pompano Aquarium membership can get 10% off as usual. Seating is on a first-come, first-served basis.

For more information about this or other upcoming activities taking place at the aquarium, visit the Events page. To book a private tour, call 555-7979.

161. What is true about the Pompano Aquarium?

(A) It will raise its admission fees.
(B) It depends heavily on private donations.
(C) It changes its marine exhibits regularly.
(D) It rehabilitates injured animals.

162. Who is Tammy Seda?

(A) A well-known author
(B) A tour guide
(C) A research scientist
(D) A local reporter

163. What benefit to members is suggested in the Web page?

(A) Cheaper lecture tickets
(B) Free private tours
(C) Priority seating at events
(D) Gift shop discounts

GO ON TO THE NEXT PAGE

Questions 164-167 refer to the following online chat discussion.

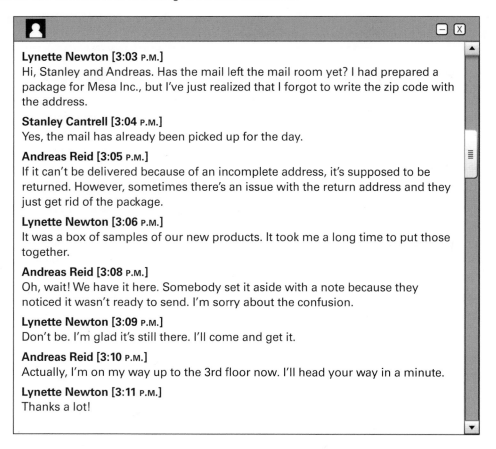

Lynette Newton [3:03 P.M.]
Hi, Stanley and Andreas. Has the mail left the mail room yet? I had prepared a package for Mesa Inc., but I've just realized that I forgot to write the zip code with the address.

Stanley Cantrell [3:04 P.M.]
Yes, the mail has already been picked up for the day.

Andreas Reid [3:05 P.M.]
If it can't be delivered because of an incomplete address, it's supposed to be returned. However, sometimes there's an issue with the return address and they just get rid of the package.

Lynette Newton [3:06 P.M.]
It was a box of samples of our new products. It took me a long time to put those together.

Andreas Reid [3:08 P.M.]
Oh, wait! We have it here. Somebody set it aside with a note because they noticed it wasn't ready to send. I'm sorry about the confusion.

Lynette Newton [3:09 P.M.]
Don't be. I'm glad it's still there. I'll come and get it.

Andreas Reid [3:10 P.M.]
Actually, I'm on my way up to the 3rd floor now. I'll head your way in a minute.

Lynette Newton [3:11 P.M.]
Thanks a lot!

---

164. Why did Ms. Newton contact Mr. Cantrell and Mr. Reid?

(A) She wants to know the cost of sending a package.
(B) She forgot to add some information to an address.
(C) She is expecting an important delivery today.
(D) She discovered that an item was damaged in transit.

165. What does Mr. Reid explain?

(A) An item has been insured.
(B) A schedule has recently changed.
(C) A package may be discarded.
(D) A delivery can be tracked.

166. At 3:09 P.M., what does Ms. Newton mean when she writes, "Don't be"?

(A) She has already completed a task.
(B) She wants Mr. Reid to be more careful.
(C) She does not need Mr. Reid's help.
(D) She is not upset about a situation.

167. What will Ms. Newton probably do next?

(A) Prepare more samples
(B) Call a package recipient
(C) Go to the mail room
(D) Stay at her workstation

```
╔═══════════════════════ E-Mail message ═══════════════════════╗
║  ┌─────────┐  ┌──────────────────────────────────────────┐   ║
║  │   To:   │  │ All Hartway Co. Staff                    │   ║
║  └─────────┘  └──────────────────────────────────────────┘   ║
║  ┌─────────┐  ┌──────────────────────────────────────────┐   ║
║  │  From:  │  │ Ramone Trahan                            │   ║
║  └─────────┘  └──────────────────────────────────────────┘   ║
║  ┌─────────┐  ┌──────────────────────────────────────────┐   ║
║  │  Date:  │  │ February 2                               │   ║
║  └─────────┘  └──────────────────────────────────────────┘   ║
║  ┌─────────┐  ┌──────────────────────────────────────────┐   ║
║  │Subject: │  │ Professional development                 │   ║
║  └─────────┘  └──────────────────────────────────────────┘   ║
```

Dear Staff,

At Hartway Co., we do our best to support our staff in any way possible. Professional development workshops are an important part of career advancement. —[1]—. Previously, training sessions were led by our management team, but we would like to try working with an outside trainer this time. We are wondering whether you would rather attend training sessions here at the office or at another site. An off-site location would help to eliminate distractions because the setting would be entirely dedicated to the purpose of training. —[2]—. On the other hand, training off site would involve some amount of traveling. —[3]—. Please e-mail me back with your opinions.

For those of you interested in why we will hire a separate firm for our training, studies have shown that this is more effective than having in-house managers train staff. This is because professional trainers specialize in teaching, so the way the training is presented would be much better. With our CEO confirming the opening of our second location next quarter, there will be many opportunities for new leadership roles. —[4]—. Therefore, this training is more important than ever.

We look forward to hearing from you, and we appreciate your cooperation in this matter.

Ramone Trahan
Human Resources Director, Hartway Co.

---

168. What is the purpose of the e-mail?

(A) To announce a job opening
(B) To recruit volunteers for a workshop
(C) To schedule a training session
(D) To ask about employee preferences

169. What benefit of a third-party instructor does Mr. Trahan mention?

(A) Saving time for managers
(B) Higher quality of instruction
(C) Cutting the company's expenses
(D) Fair treatment of participants

170. What will Hartway Co. do next quarter?

(A) Assess employee performance
(B) Open a new branch
(C) Hire a different CEO
(D) Launch a product line

171. In which of the positions marked [1], [2], [3], and [4] does the following sentence best belong?

"But rest assured that we would do our best to minimize this."

(A) [1]
(B) [2]
(C) [3]
(D) [4]

GO ON TO THE NEXT PAGE

The Orlando Interior Design Fair

May 3–5 • Kemper Hotel and Conference Center • Orlando, Florida

Schedule for May 3

"Assessing a Client's Style"	10:00 A.M.–11:30 A.M. Rose Room

A presentation by Sean McGrath based on his popular book by the same name. Mr. McGrath will talk about the right questions to ask to uncover the right style choices for your client.

"Styling Interiors for Photo Shoots"	12:30 P.M.–1:45 P.M. Main Hall

This workshop led by Viola Gomez will teach you how to make a room look its best in photos. Feel free to bring some examples of your work and the workshop leader will assess them after the talk.

"Functional Furniture"	2:00 P.M.–3:15 P.M. Assembly Hall

A workshop by Michelle Whitte of Witty Designs. Learn about furniture pieces that are beautiful as well as useful. Ms. Whitte will set up the room with examples of the merchandise she discusses. Participants can order goods at a discount.

"The Future of Open-Plan Layouts"	3:30 P.M.–4:30 P.M. Lily Room

Attend this workshop to find out the predicted outcome of the open-plan trend and how you can adapt your plans accordingly. Taught by Glen Rhodes.

- Please turn your phone to silent mode when you arrive so as not to disturb any of the events.
- During the lunch break, participants may visit any of the numerous restaurants in the neighborhood.
- Early registration is encouraged, and a 15% discount on fees will be offered until March 5.

172. What is true about the opening day of the Orlando Interior Design Fair?

(A) The sessions are for practicing interior designers only.
(B) A presentation will be given by a business owner.
(C) All of the events will last for ninety minutes.
(D) All of the workshops take place in the afternoon.

173. What is suggested about Ms. Gomez?

(A) She will distribute handouts after the workshop.
(B) She will evaluate participants' previous work.
(C) She will bring camera equipment for participants.
(D) She will focus on decorating open-plan layouts.

174. According to the schedule, where can attendees view some products?

(A) In the Rose Room
(B) In the Main Hall
(C) In the Assembly Hall
(D) In the Lily Room

175. What are the design fair attendees instructed to do?

(A) Park in a designated area
(B) Stay on-site for lunch
(C) Use a certain phone setting
(D) Arrive early to find a seat

GO ON TO THE NEXT PAGE

http://www.keyfitness.com/shipping ▶

| Home | Catalog | Clearance | **Shipping** | Contact |

Key Fitness
Quality workout equipment to help you meet your fitness goals!

We offer a variety of shipping options to suit our customers' schedules and budgets. All items are shipped from our distribution center in Vancouver. At Key Fitness, customer service counts, so if you have any issues with your order, please let our team know as soon as possible. Our helpline is available 24 hours a day, 7 days a week at 1-833-985-8021.

Destination	Overnight Shipping (order by 2 P.M.)	Premium Shipping (2–4 days)	Standard Shipping (5–9 days)
Within Canada	$15	$8	$3
Within the U.S.	$20	$10	$6
All other countries	Please call our customer service line for a price quote.	$35	$22

To:	contact@keyfitness.com
From:	eichnera@hankinson.com
Date:	April 30
Subject:	Order #06467

To Whom It May Concern:

I placed an order for an exercise ball yesterday and paid for overnight shipping to my address in Canada because I was in a hurry. I just received the delivery, but there was no air pump in the box. That means I cannot inflate it. I downloaded the suggested workout routine from your Web site this morning because I was excited about getting started using the ball. Unfortunately, that won't be possible until this issue is resolved. Please let me know how you plan to deal with my situation.

Sincerely,

Adrian Eichner

176. What does the Web page indicate about Key Fitness?

(A) It offers in-person classes in Vancouver.
(B) U.S. customers must wait at least four days for delivery.
(C) Its shortest standard delivery is five days.
(D) Overnight shipping is not available for some countries.

177. In the Web page, the word "counts" in paragraph 1, line 3, is closest in meaning to

(A) records
(B) estimates
(C) includes
(D) matters

178. Why did Mr. Eichner write the e-mail?

(A) To ask how to use some equipment
(B) To request a refund on a purchase
(C) To report a missing item
(D) To check the status of a delivery

179. How much did Mr. Eichner pay for his order?

(A) $3
(B) $8
(C) $15
(D) $20

180. Why did Mr. Eichner visit a Web site?

(A) To watch some instructional videos
(B) To download some exercise examples
(C) To check a user account
(D) To report the problem he describes

GO ON TO THE NEXT PAGE

National Healthcare Conference Dalmeny Conference Centre, Manchester, England, 8–10 February	
Day 3 Proposed Schedule	
8:00 A.M.–9:00 A.M.	Networking Breakfast Take the opportunity to chat with your fellow conference attendees while enjoying fruit, pastries, and coffee.
9:00 A.M.–10:30 A.M.	Presentation: "Advances in Diagnostic Imaging" Evie Robinson, Bulbeck Hospital, Liverpool
10:30 A.M.–11:30 A.M.	Presentation: "Digital Technology for Improving Care" Louise Hurst, Grenoble Medical Centre, Sheffield
11:30 A.M.–12:30 P.M.	Presentation: "Security in Electronic Record-Keeping" Jude Chambers, Guildford Hospital, Leeds
12:30 P.M.–1:30 P.M.	Lunch Buffet lunch served in Room 104. Show your conference pass for entry.
1:30 P.M.–3:00 P.M.	Various Workshops: See registration packet
3:00 P.M.–4:00 P.M.	Presentation: "Tips for Organizing Clinical Trials" Ethan Schofield, Welton Research Lab, London
4:00 P.M.–5:00 P.M.	Presentation: "Treating Chronic Disease" Francesca Hammond, Finborough Medical Clinic, York

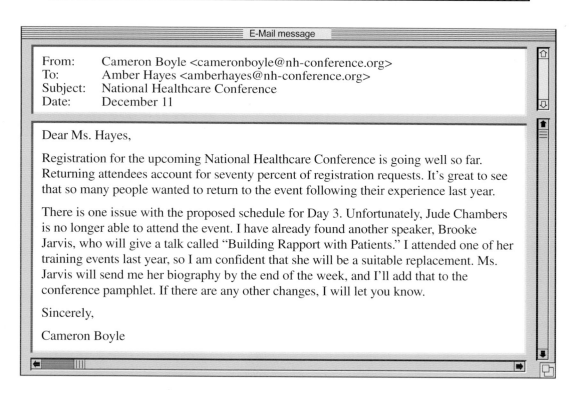

E-Mail message

From: Cameron Boyle <cameronboyle@nh-conference.org>
To: Amber Hayes <amberhayes@nh-conference.org>
Subject: National Healthcare Conference
Date: December 11

Dear Ms. Hayes,

Registration for the upcoming National Healthcare Conference is going well so far. Returning attendees account for seventy percent of registration requests. It's great to see that so many people wanted to return to the event following their experience last year.

There is one issue with the proposed schedule for Day 3. Unfortunately, Jude Chambers is no longer able to attend the event. I have already found another speaker, Brooke Jarvis, who will give a talk called "Building Rapport with Patients." I attended one of her training events last year, so I am confident that she will be a suitable replacement. Ms. Jarvis will send me her biography by the end of the week, and I'll add that to the conference pamphlet. If there are any other changes, I will let you know.

Sincerely,

Cameron Boyle

181. What is true about Ms. Robinson's presentation?

(A) It will be swapped with another speaker's time slot.
(B) It will last for approximately one hour.
(C) It will be on the last day of the conference.
(D) It will take place in the afternoon.

182. Who will give a talk about setting up trials?

(A) Louise Hurst
(B) Jude Chambers
(C) Ethan Schofield
(D) Francesca Hammond

183. In the e-mail, the phrase "account for" in paragraph 1, line 2, is closest in meaning to

(A) take place
(B) make up
(C) calculate
(D) explain

184. Which presentation will be replaced with "Building Rapport with Patients"?

(A) Advances in Diagnostic Imaging
(B) Digital Technology for Improving Care
(C) Security in Electronic Record-Keeping
(D) Treating Chronic Disease

185. What will Ms. Jarvis send to Mr. Boyle this week?

(A) Some company brochures
(B) Information on her background
(C) Her final presentation slides
(D) A signed contract

GO ON TO THE NEXT PAGE

E-Mail message	
To	Jason Dunn <jdunn@ambermail.net>
From	Lucille Madigan <madigan_l@natureworksclub.org>
Date	April 12
Subject	Environmental Education Day
Attachment	📎 voucher

Dear Mr. Dunn,

The Nature Works Club is hosting an Environmental Education Day on Saturday, May 7. This event will be an opportunity to teach the public about using resources responsibly. We would like to invite you to an exclusive workshop at the event, which is only available to our club members. You can register by replying to this e-mail. Just like the other parts of the event, this workshop is also offered at no cost. In addition, since you have volunteered at our recent park cleanup project, I am sending you a voucher for a surprise gift at the event.

Warmest regards,

Lucille Madigan
President, Nature Works Club

Nature Works Club Environmental Education Day, May 7

Assigned Tasks

- Event Promotion: Gemma Spencer
- Supply Coordinator: Ravi Adwani
- Workshops: Cathy Torbett (Locally sourced food),
                           Ian Ross (Non-toxic cleaning products)
- Kids' Corner: Lucille Madigan (Making crafts from reused objects)
- Presentations: Mike Gibbs, George Lanning, Bella Embry, Soomin Hwang

First-Ever Environmental Education Day

by Toby Meekin

MAY 9—The Nature Works Club held an Environmental Education Day for the public on Saturday at the Bridgeport Community Center. In addition to various activities, the group set up a collection point for e-waste, such as old computers.

Admission to the event was free, but donations were collected at the entrance. These will go toward purchasing solar panels for the roof of the community center. Complimentary refreshments, donated by local businesses, were served. In addition, those with a special voucher were given a tote bag with the Nature Works Club's logo.

Many attendees praised the event for its educational value. "I was initially interested in the talks on recycling household waste and the importance of bees, but I was surprised by how interesting Soomin Hwang's talk on electric cars was," said Ashley Cecil, who attended the event with her family.

The most popular activity, which was enjoyed by audience members of all ages, was Bella Embry's presentation about planting a vegetable garden. She showed a short clip and gave out packets of seeds at the end to make it easy for people to start that project right away.

Mayor Holly Steward attended the event and was impressed with the turnout. She said that she is in full support of similar events in the future. Indeed, it seems she will get her wish, as the group's event promoter hinted in her closing remarks that planning for another education day has already begun.

---

186. What does Ms. Madigan encourage Mr. Dunn to do?

(A) Sign up for a special session
(B) Submit presentation ideas
(C) Join the Nature Works Club
(D) Host an event activity

187. Why did some attendees receive a free tote bag?

(A) They registered for the event early.
(B) They volunteered at a previous event.
(C) They won a prize drawing.
(D) They made a financial donation.

188. What most likely is Ms. Hwang's specialty?

(A) Recycling
(B) Gardening
(C) Insects
(D) Vehicles

189. What is indicated about the presentation on gardening?

(A) It was short.
(B) It included a video.
(C) Its original presenter was changed.
(D) It was for club members only.

190. Who most likely gave a closing talk?

(A) Mr. Lanning
(B) Ms. Madigan
(C) Ms. Steward
(D) Ms. Spencer

GO ON TO THE NEXT PAGE

Planning for a BRIGHT FUTURE

Invest in your future!

The Louisville Business Development Center (LBDC) can provide you with the right tools to take your career to the next level. By completing our certification in designing Web sites, your skills will be more attractive to business owners and job recruiters. Some of our graduates have gone on to work at multinational corporations such as Lyndon International and Cabell. We offer daytime, evening, and weekend classes, so you can complete your certification even if you work full time. And you can spread out the course fees over the term to make them more manageable. Our distinguished faculty members, including Dylan Selleck of Vista Inc., and Phoebe Kendall of Mineola, are currently working in the field and have a deep understanding of the industry.

To enroll in our next term, visit www.lbdc.edu.

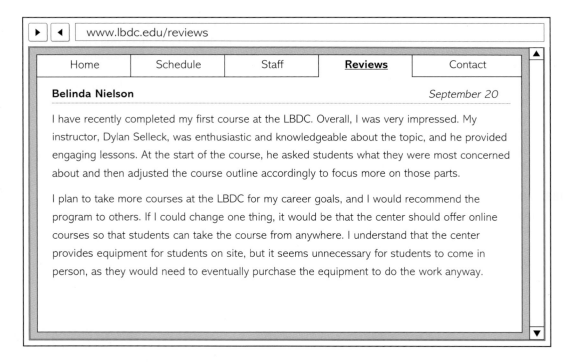

www.lbdc.edu/reviews

| Home | Schedule | Staff | **Reviews** | Contact |

Belinda Nielson   *September 20*

I have recently completed my first course at the LBDC. Overall, I was very impressed. My instructor, Dylan Selleck, was enthusiastic and knowledgeable about the topic, and he provided engaging lessons. At the start of the course, he asked students what they were most concerned about and then adjusted the course outline accordingly to focus more on those parts.

I plan to take more courses at the LBDC for my career goals, and I would recommend the program to others. If I could change one thing, it would be that the center should offer online courses so that students can take the course from anywhere. I understand that the center provides equipment for students on site, but it seems unnecessary for students to come in person, as they would need to eventually purchase the equipment to do the work anyway.

```
╔══════════════════════════════════════════════════════════════╗
║                        E-Mail message                        ║
╠═══════════╦══════════════════════════════════════════════════╣
║ From:     ║ Lance Tyler <ltyler@lbdc.edu>                     ║
╠═══════════╬══════════════════════════════════════════════════╣
║ To:       ║ Belinda Nielson <belinda5@bastinmail.com>         ║
╠═══════════╬══════════════════════════════════════════════════╣
║ Date:     ║ October 1                                         ║
╠═══════════╬══════════════════════════════════════════════════╣
║ Subject:  ║ LBDC Review                                       ║
╚═══════════╩══════════════════════════════════════════════════╝
```

Dear Ms. Nielson,

Thank you for posting a review about your experience with the LBDC. We are especially interested in your negative feedback, as this helps us to make improvements to our service. Your concern has been shared by quite a few students, and we are, therefore, planning to address it promptly. You'll see the relevant change starting in December. Please feel free to share more feedback with me directly.

Warmest regards,

Lance Tyler

191. Who would probably be most interested in this brochure?

(A) Prospective business investors
(B) Job recruiters
(C) Web site designers
(D) Company owners

192. What is true about the LBDC?

(A) It guarantees job placement after graduation.
(B) It is located in downtown Louisville.
(C) It only operates classes on weekdays.
(D) It allows people to pay in installments.

193. What does Ms. Nielson indicate about her course?

(A) It used a new software program.
(B) It encouraged interaction between students.
(C) It included more work than she expected.
(D) It was adjusted to suit students' needs.

194. Where does Ms. Nielson's instructor work in addition to the LBDC?

(A) At Lyndon International
(B) At Cabell
(C) At Vista Inc.
(D) At Mineola

195. How does the LBDC plan to respond to some complaints?

(A) By reviewing course topics
(B) By changing class times
(C) By offering online courses
(D) By upgrading some equipment

GO ON TO THE NEXT PAGE

Bastin Garage Seeks
FULL-TIME Auto Mechanic

Bastin Garage has an immediate opening for a full-time auto mechanic. We are looking for someone who can perform basic mechanic tasks, such as repairing timing belts, rotating tires, etc. Your manager will instruct you on more complex tasks until you are comfortable doing them on your own. You must have at least one year of professional hands-on experience. The successful applicant will have good communication skills. The hours are Monday to Friday, 8 A.M. to 5 P.M. Overtime work is available, if desired.

To apply for this position, visit www.bastingarage.com/apply.

▶ ◀ | www.bastingarage.com/apply

Please complete all fields before submitting the application.

Name: Russell McKinsey   **Application Date:** March 5

Phone Number: 782-555-3251   **E-mail Address:** r.mckinsey@torrington.com

Related Experience/Education (most recent first):
Company, Duration, Job Title, Description

1. DX Auto Body Shop, 1 year, Junior Mechanic, performed basic maintenance and repair work
2. Rivas Garage, 4 months, Apprentice, introduction to all parts of the role
3. Oil Masters, 2 years, carried out oil changes on a wide variety of car models

[+Line]

Comments: I am currently getting my Auto Technician Safety Certification, which will be completed next month. At DX Auto Body Shop, I was the head of my team. That meant I was always the one to speak to customers, which helped me improve my communication skills greatly. Joel Gallo, who owns DX Auto Body Shop, said he received many comments from customers about my professionalism.

Attachments: McKinseyR_résumé, McKinseyR-references

[**Click to Submit**]

Shannon Dermott
Bastin Garage
342 Caswell Road
Boise, ID 83716

Dear Ms. Dermott,

I am writing on behalf of Russell McKinsey, who has applied for the mechanic position at your garage. I can confidently recommend Mr. McKinsey for this role. I had the opportunity to work with him toward the end of his apprenticeship with us. He was always reliable and on time, and he was well-liked by other team members thanks to his teamwork and positive attitude. Should you wish to discuss Mr. McKinsey's employment further, please feel free to contact me at 555-9090.

Please find attached a brochure outlining our business's services, of which Mr. McKinsey worked with all of them.

Warmest regards,

Terry Sullivan

196. What is true about the auto mechanic position?

(A) It may require work at different branches.
(B) It involves managing other staff members.
(C) It includes some on-the-job training.
(D) It is for a one-year contract term.

197. What is indicated about Mr. McKinsey?

(A) He has held his most recent job for two years.
(B) He has completed a safety course.
(C) He is able to work overtime.
(D) He has the necessary hands-on experience.

198. Who is Joel Gallo?

(A) A technical instructor
(B) A business owner
(C) A trainee technician
(D) A job recruiter

199. What is implied about DX Auto Body Shop?

(A) It will be Mr. McKinsey's employer until next month.
(B) It primarily offers an oil change service.
(C) Some of its managers started their own business.
(D) Only its team leaders interact with customers.

200. Where most likely does Mr. Sullivan work?

(A) At Bastin Garage
(B) At DX Auto Body Shop
(C) At Rivas Garage
(D) At Oil Masters

Stop! This is the end of the test. If you finish before time is called, you may go back to Parts 5, 6, and 7 and check your work.

Answer Keys

1 (C)   2 (A)   3 (D)   4 (D)   5 (C)   6 (A)   7 (C)   8 (B)   9 (C)   10 (A)

11 (C)   12 (C)   13 (B)   14 (C)   15 (B)   16 (C)   17 (B)   18 (B)   19 (C)   20 (A)

21 (C)   22 (A)   23 (A)   24 (B)   25 (C)   26 (C)   27 (B)   28 (C)   29 (C)   30 (B)

31 (B)   32 (D)   33 (A)   34 (D)   35 (D)   36 (C)   37 (C)   38 (B)   39 (B)   40 (C)

41 (B)   42 (C)   43 (B)   44 (B)   45 (B)   46 (D)   47 (C)   48 (D)   49 (A)   50 (A)

51 (D)   52 (A)   53 (A)   54 (D)   55 (B)   56 (A)   57 (C)   58 (C)   59 (D)   60 (C)

61 (B)   62 (C)   63 (B)   64 (B)   65 (C)   66 (D)   67 (B)   68 (D)   69 (B)   70 (D)

71 (A)   72 (B)   73 (C)   74 (C)   75 (C)   76 (C)   77 (D)   78 (C)   79 (B)   80 (B)

81 (A)   82 (B)   83 (C)   84 (A)   85 (A)   86 (C)   87 (B)   88 (B)   89 (B)   90 (C)

91 (B)   92 (B)   93 (D)   94 (A)   95 (C)   96 (B)   97 (C)   98 (B)   99 (B)   100 (D)

101 (C)   102 (B)   103 (D)   104 (C)   105 (D)   106 (D)   107 (C)   108 (B)   109 (A)   110 (C)

111 (B)   112 (B)   113 (B)   114 (C)   115 (C)   116 (A)   117 (D)   118 (D)   119 (C)   120 (B)

121 (A)   122 (C)   123 (C)   124 (B)   125 (B)   126 (C)   127 (B)   128 (B)   129 (B)   130 (C)

131 (C)   132 (C)   133 (B)   134 (B)   135 (B)   136 (B)   137 (C)   138 (B)   139 (C)   140 (B)

141 (B)   142 (C)   143 (B)   144 (D)   145 (C)   146 (B)   147 (B)   148 (B)   149 (C)   150 (A)

151 (B)   152 (A)   153 (B)   154 (D)   155 (C)   156 (D)   157 (D)   158 (B)   159 (C)   160 (B)

161 (D)   162 (C)   163 (A)   164 (B)   165 (C)   166 (D)   167 (D)   168 (D)   169 (B)   170 (B)

171 (C)   172 (D)   173 (B)   174 (C)   175 (C)   176 (C)   177 (D)   178 (C)   179 (C)   180 (B)

181 (C)   182 (C)   183 (B)   184 (C)   185 (B)   186 (A)   187 (B)   188 (D)   189 (B)   190 (D)

191 (C)   192 (D)   193 (D)   194 (C)   195 (C)   196 (C)   197 (D)   198 (B)   199 (D)   200 (C)

ANSWER SHEET

실전 모의고사

수험번호

응시일자 : 20   년   월   일

성명	한글	
	한자	
	영자	

LISTENING (Part I ~ IV)

#				#				#				#			
1	ⓐⓑⓒⓓ			21	ⓐⓑⓒⓓ			41	ⓐⓑⓒⓓ			61	ⓐⓑⓒⓓ			81	ⓐⓑⓒⓓ
2	ⓐⓑⓒⓓ			22	ⓐⓑⓒⓓ			42	ⓐⓑⓒⓓ			62	ⓐⓑⓒⓓ			82	ⓐⓑⓒⓓ
3	ⓐⓑⓒⓓ			23	ⓐⓑⓒⓓ			43	ⓐⓑⓒⓓ			63	ⓐⓑⓒⓓ			83	ⓐⓑⓒⓓ
4	ⓐⓑⓒⓓ			24	ⓐⓑⓒⓓ			44	ⓐⓑⓒⓓ			64	ⓐⓑⓒⓓ			84	ⓐⓑⓒⓓ
5	ⓐⓑⓒⓓ			25	ⓐⓑⓒⓓ			45	ⓐⓑⓒⓓ			65	ⓐⓑⓒⓓ			85	ⓐⓑⓒⓓ
6	ⓐⓑⓒⓓ			26	ⓐⓑⓒⓓ			46	ⓐⓑⓒⓓ			66	ⓐⓑⓒⓓ			86	ⓐⓑⓒⓓ
7	ⓐⓑⓒ			27	ⓐⓑⓒⓓ			47	ⓐⓑⓒⓓ			67	ⓐⓑⓒⓓ			87	ⓐⓑⓒⓓ
8	ⓐⓑⓒ			28	ⓐⓑⓒⓓ			48	ⓐⓑⓒⓓ			68	ⓐⓑⓒⓓ			88	ⓐⓑⓒⓓ
9	ⓐⓑⓒ			29	ⓐⓑⓒⓓ			49	ⓐⓑⓒⓓ			69	ⓐⓑⓒⓓ			89	ⓐⓑⓒⓓ
10	ⓐⓑⓒ			30	ⓐⓑⓒⓓ			50	ⓐⓑⓒⓓ			70	ⓐⓑⓒⓓ			90	ⓐⓑⓒⓓ
11	ⓐⓑⓒ			31	ⓐⓑⓒⓓ			51	ⓐⓑⓒⓓ			71	ⓐⓑⓒⓓ			91	ⓐⓑⓒⓓ
12	ⓐⓑⓒ			32	ⓐⓑⓒⓓ			52	ⓐⓑⓒⓓ			72	ⓐⓑⓒⓓ			92	ⓐⓑⓒⓓ
13	ⓐⓑⓒ			33	ⓐⓑⓒⓓ			53	ⓐⓑⓒⓓ			73	ⓐⓑⓒⓓ			93	ⓐⓑⓒⓓ
14	ⓐⓑⓒ			34	ⓐⓑⓒⓓ			54	ⓐⓑⓒⓓ			74	ⓐⓑⓒⓓ			94	ⓐⓑⓒⓓ
15	ⓐⓑⓒ			35	ⓐⓑⓒⓓ			55	ⓐⓑⓒⓓ			75	ⓐⓑⓒⓓ			95	ⓐⓑⓒⓓ
16	ⓐⓑⓒ			36	ⓐⓑⓒⓓ			56	ⓐⓑⓒⓓ			76	ⓐⓑⓒⓓ			96	ⓐⓑⓒⓓ
17	ⓐⓑⓒ			37	ⓐⓑⓒⓓ			57	ⓐⓑⓒⓓ			77	ⓐⓑⓒⓓ			97	ⓐⓑⓒⓓ
18	ⓐⓑⓒ			38	ⓐⓑⓒⓓ			58	ⓐⓑⓒⓓ			78	ⓐⓑⓒⓓ			98	ⓐⓑⓒⓓ
19	ⓐⓑⓒ			39	ⓐⓑⓒⓓ			59	ⓐⓑⓒⓓ			79	ⓐⓑⓒⓓ			99	ⓐⓑⓒⓓ
20	ⓐⓑⓒ			40	ⓐⓑⓒⓓ			60	ⓐⓑⓒⓓ			80	ⓐⓑⓒⓓ			100	ⓐⓑⓒⓓ

READING (Part V ~ VII)

#				#				#				#			
101	ⓐⓑⓒⓓ			121	ⓐⓑⓒⓓ			141	ⓐⓑⓒⓓ			161	ⓐⓑⓒⓓ			181	ⓐⓑⓒⓓ
102	ⓐⓑⓒⓓ			122	ⓐⓑⓒⓓ			142	ⓐⓑⓒⓓ			162	ⓐⓑⓒⓓ			182	ⓐⓑⓒⓓ
103	ⓐⓑⓒⓓ			123	ⓐⓑⓒⓓ			143	ⓐⓑⓒⓓ			163	ⓐⓑⓒⓓ			183	ⓐⓑⓒⓓ
104	ⓐⓑⓒⓓ			124	ⓐⓑⓒⓓ			144	ⓐⓑⓒⓓ			164	ⓐⓑⓒⓓ			184	ⓐⓑⓒⓓ
105	ⓐⓑⓒⓓ			125	ⓐⓑⓒⓓ			145	ⓐⓑⓒⓓ			165	ⓐⓑⓒⓓ			185	ⓐⓑⓒⓓ
106	ⓐⓑⓒⓓ			126	ⓐⓑⓒⓓ			146	ⓐⓑⓒⓓ			166	ⓐⓑⓒⓓ			186	ⓐⓑⓒⓓ
107	ⓐⓑⓒⓓ			127	ⓐⓑⓒⓓ			147	ⓐⓑⓒⓓ			167	ⓐⓑⓒⓓ			187	ⓐⓑⓒⓓ
108	ⓐⓑⓒⓓ			128	ⓐⓑⓒⓓ			148	ⓐⓑⓒⓓ			168	ⓐⓑⓒⓓ			188	ⓐⓑⓒⓓ
109	ⓐⓑⓒⓓ			129	ⓐⓑⓒⓓ			149	ⓐⓑⓒⓓ			169	ⓐⓑⓒⓓ			189	ⓐⓑⓒⓓ
110	ⓐⓑⓒⓓ			130	ⓐⓑⓒⓓ			150	ⓐⓑⓒⓓ			170	ⓐⓑⓒⓓ			190	ⓐⓑⓒⓓ
111	ⓐⓑⓒⓓ			131	ⓐⓑⓒⓓ			151	ⓐⓑⓒⓓ			171	ⓐⓑⓒⓓ			191	ⓐⓑⓒⓓ
112	ⓐⓑⓒⓓ			132	ⓐⓑⓒⓓ			152	ⓐⓑⓒⓓ			172	ⓐⓑⓒⓓ			192	ⓐⓑⓒⓓ
113	ⓐⓑⓒⓓ			133	ⓐⓑⓒⓓ			153	ⓐⓑⓒⓓ			173	ⓐⓑⓒⓓ			193	ⓐⓑⓒⓓ
114	ⓐⓑⓒⓓ			134	ⓐⓑⓒⓓ			154	ⓐⓑⓒⓓ			174	ⓐⓑⓒⓓ			194	ⓐⓑⓒⓓ
115	ⓐⓑⓒⓓ			135	ⓐⓑⓒⓓ			155	ⓐⓑⓒⓓ			175	ⓐⓑⓒⓓ			195	ⓐⓑⓒⓓ
116	ⓐⓑⓒⓓ			136	ⓐⓑⓒⓓ			156	ⓐⓑⓒⓓ			176	ⓐⓑⓒⓓ			196	ⓐⓑⓒⓓ
117	ⓐⓑⓒⓓ			137	ⓐⓑⓒⓓ			157	ⓐⓑⓒⓓ			177	ⓐⓑⓒⓓ			197	ⓐⓑⓒⓓ
118	ⓐⓑⓒⓓ			138	ⓐⓑⓒⓓ			158	ⓐⓑⓒⓓ			178	ⓐⓑⓒⓓ			198	ⓐⓑⓒⓓ
119	ⓐⓑⓒⓓ			139	ⓐⓑⓒⓓ			159	ⓐⓑⓒⓓ			179	ⓐⓑⓒⓓ			199	ⓐⓑⓒⓓ
120	ⓐⓑⓒⓓ			140	ⓐⓑⓒⓓ			160	ⓐⓑⓒⓓ			180	ⓐⓑⓒⓓ			200	ⓐⓑⓒⓓ

ANSWER SHEET

실전 모의고사

수험번호

응시일자 : 20   년   월   일

성명 / 한글 / 영자

| 한글 |
| 성명 |
| 영자 |
| 수험자 |

LISTENING (Part I ~ IV)

1 2 3 4 5 6 7 8 9 10 11 12 13 14 15 16 17 18 19 20
21 22 23 24 25 26 27 28 29 30 31 32 33 34 35 36 37 38 39 40
41 42 43 44 45 46 47 48 49 50 51 52 53 54 55 56 57 58 59 60
61 62 63 64 65 66 67 68 69 70 71 72 73 74 75 76 77 78 79 80
81 82 83 84 85 86 87 88 89 90 91 92 93 94 95 96 97 98 99 100

READING (Part V ~ VII)

101 102 103 104 105 106 107 108 109 110 111 112 113 114 115 116 117 118 119 120
121 122 123 124 125 126 127 128 129 130 131 132 133 134 135 136 137 138 139 140
141 142 143 144 145 146 147 148 149 150 151 152 153 154 155 156 157 158 159 160
161 162 163 164 165 166 167 168 169 170 171 172 173 174 175 176 177 178 179 180
181 182 183 184 185 186 187 188 189 190 191 192 193 194 195 196 197 198 199 200

ANSWER SHEET

실전 모의고사

수험번호

응시일자 : 20   년   월   일

성 명

	한 글
	한 자
	영 자

LISTENING (Part I ~ IV)

READING (Part V ~ VII)

ANSWER SHEET

실전 모의고사

수험번호

응시일자 : 20   년   월   일

LISTENING (Part I ~ IV)

1	ⓐ ⓑ ⓒ ⓓ
2	ⓐ ⓑ ⓒ ⓓ
3	ⓐ ⓑ ⓒ ⓓ
4	ⓐ ⓑ ⓒ ⓓ
5	ⓐ ⓑ ⓒ ⓓ
6	ⓐ ⓑ ⓒ ⓓ
7	ⓐ ⓑ ⓒ ⓓ
8	ⓐ ⓑ ⓒ ⓓ
9	ⓐ ⓑ ⓒ ⓓ
10	ⓐ ⓑ ⓒ ⓓ
11	ⓐ ⓑ ⓒ ⓓ
12	ⓐ ⓑ ⓒ ⓓ
13	ⓐ ⓑ ⓒ ⓓ
14	ⓐ ⓑ ⓒ ⓓ
15	ⓐ ⓑ ⓒ ⓓ
16	ⓐ ⓑ ⓒ ⓓ
17	ⓐ ⓑ ⓒ ⓓ
18	ⓐ ⓑ ⓒ ⓓ
19	ⓐ ⓑ ⓒ ⓓ
20	ⓐ ⓑ ⓒ ⓓ

(Questions 21–40, 41–60, 61–80, 81–100 each with answer bubbles ⓐ ⓑ ⓒ ⓓ)

READING (Part V ~ VII)

(Questions 101–120, 121–140, 141–160, 161–180, 181–200 each with answer bubbles ⓐ ⓑ ⓒ ⓓ)

성명

학원   응시자

영묘   학원   영자

MEMO

MEMO